# WILEY CPA EXAM REVIEW 2007

## Auditing and Attestation

O. Ray Whittington, CPA, PhD

Patrick R. Delaney, CPA, PhD

JOHN WILEY & SONS, INC.

ISBN 0-471-79756-1

ISBN 13: 978-0471-79756-2

Printed in the United States of America

10 9 8 7 6 5 4 3 2 1

# CONTENTS

---

[1] *As explained in Chapter 1, this book is organized into 6 modules (manageable study units).*

# PREFACE

**Passing the CPA exam upon your first attempt is possible!** The *Wiley CPA Examination Review* preparation materials provide you with the necessary materials (visit our Web site at www.wiley.com/cpa for more information). It's up to you to add the hard work and commitment. Together we can beat the pass rate on each section of about 40%. All Wiley CPA products are continuously updated to provide you with the most comprehensive and complete knowledge base. Choose your products from the Wiley preparation materials and you can proceed confidently. You can select support materials that are exam-based and user-friendly. You can select products that will help you pass!

**Remaining current is one of the keys to examination success. Here is a list of what's new in this edition of the** *Wiley CPA Examination Review Auditing and Attestation* **text.**

- The new AICPA Content Specification Outline on Auditing and Attestation for the Computerized CPA Examination
- AICPA questions released in 2006
- The new simulation interface
- Coverage of new auditing and attestation standards, especially:

  - AICPA Statement on Auditing Standard 103, *Audit Documentation*
  - AICPA Statement on Auditing Standard 112, *Communicating Internal Control Related Matters Identified in an Audit*

The objective of this work is to provide you with the knowledge to pass the Auditing and Attestation portion of the Uniform Certified Public Accounting (CPA) Exam. The text is divided up into six areas of study called modules. Each module contains written text with discussion, examples, and demonstrations of the key exam concepts. Following each text area, actual American Institute of Certified Public Accountants (AICPA) unofficial questions and answers are presented to test your knowledge. We are indebted to the AICPA for permission to reproduce and adapt examination materials from past examinations. Author constructed questions and simulations are provided for new areas or areas that require updating. All author constructed questions and simulations are modeled after AICPA question formats. The multiple-choice questions are grouped into topical areas, giving candidates a chance to assess their areas of strength and weakness. Selection and inclusion of topical content is based upon current AICPA Content Specification Outlines. Only testable topics are presented. If the CPA exam does not test it, this text does not present it.

The CPA exam is one of the toughest exams you will ever take. It will not be easy. But if you follow our guidelines and focus on your goal, you will be thrilled with what you can accomplish.

Ray Whittington
November 2006

**Don't forget to visit our Web site at www.wiley.com/cpa
for supplements and updates.**

# ABOUT THE AUTHORS

**Ray Whittington**, PhD, CPA, CMA, CIA, is the dean of the College of Commerce at DePaul University. Prior to joining the faculty at DePaul, Professor Whittington was the Director of Accountancy at San Diego State University. From 1989 through 1991, he was the Director of Auditing Research for the American Institute of Certified Public Accountants (AICPA), and he previously was on the audit staff of KPMG. He previously served as a member of the Auditing Standards Board of the AICPA and as a member of the Accounting and Review Services Committee and the Board of Regents of the Institute of Internal Auditors. Professor Whittington has published numerous textbooks, articles, monographs, and continuing education courses.

**Patrick R. Delaney** was the Arthur Andersen LLP Alumni Professor of Accountancy and Department Chair at Northern Illinois University. He received his PhD in Accountancy from the University of Illinois. He had public accounting experience with Arthur Andersen LLP and was coauthor of *GAAP: Interpretation and Application*, also published by John Wiley & Sons, Inc. He served as Vice President and a member of the Illinois CPA Society's Board of Directors, and was Chairman of its Accounting Principles Committee; was a past president of the Rockford Chapter, Institute of Management Accountants; and had served on numerous other professional committees. He was a member of the American Accounting Association, American Institute of Certified Public Accountants, and Institute of Management Accountants. Professor Delaney was published in *The Accounting Review* and was a recipient of the Illinois CPA Society's Outstanding Educator Award, NIU's Excellence in Teaching Award, and Lewis University's Distinguished Alumnus Award. He was involved in NIU's CPA Review Course as director and instructor.

# ABOUT THE CONTRIBUTORS

**Kurt Pany**, PhD, CPA, is a Professor of Accounting at Arizona State University. Prior to entering academe, he worked as a staff auditor for Deloitte and Touche. He is a former member of the AICPA's Auditing Standards Board and has taught in the Arizona CPA Review course.

# 1 BEGINNING YOUR CPA REVIEW PROGRAM

To maximize the efficiency of your review program, begin by studying (not merely reading) this chapter and the next three chapters of this volume. They have been carefully organized and written to provide you with important information to assist you in successfully completing the Auditing and Attestation section of the CPA exam. Beyond providing a comprehensive outline to help you organize the material tested on the Auditing and Attestation exam, Chapter 1 will assist you in organizing a study program to prepare for the exam. Self-discipline is essential.

## GENERAL COMMENTS ON THE EXAMINATION

The Uniform CPA Examination is now delivered using computer-based testing (CBT). The final paper-based version of the CPA exam was given in November 2003. Computer-based testing has several advantages. You may take the exam one section at a time. As a result, your studies can be focused on that one section, improving your chances for success. In addition, the exam is no longer offered twice a year. During eight months of every year, you may take the exam on your schedule, six days a week and in the morning or in the afternoon.

Successful completion of the Auditing and Attestation section is an attainable goal. Keep this point foremost in your mind as you study the first four chapters in this volume and develop your study plan.

### Purpose of the Examination[1]

The Uniform CPA Examination is designed to test the entry-level knowledge and skills necessary to protect the public interest. These knowledge and skills were identified through a Practice Analysis performed in 2000, which served as a basis for the development of the content specifications for the new exam. The skills identified as necessary for the protection of the public interest include

- Analysis—the ability to organize, process, and interpret data to develop options for decision making.
- Judgment—the ability to evaluate options for decision-making and provide an appropriate conclusion.
- Communication—the ability to effectively elicit and/or express information through written or oral means.
- Research—the ability to locate and extract relevant information from available resource materials.
- Understanding—the ability to recognize and comprehend the meaning and application of a particular matter.

---

[1] *More information may be obtained from the AICPA's **Uniform CPA Examination Candidate Bulletin**, which you can find on the AICPA's Web site at www.cpa-exam.org.*

For the Auditing and Attestation section the Board of Examiners have provided the following matrix to illustrate the interaction of content and skills.

| Content Specification Outline Areas | Skill Categories | | | | | Content Weights |
|---|---|---|---|---|---|---|
| | Communication | Research | Analysis | Judgment | Understanding | |
| I. Planning the engagement | | | | | | 22-28% |
| II. Internal controls | | | | | | 12-18% |
| III. Obtain and document information | | | | | | 32-38% |
| IV. Review engagement and evaluate information | | | | | | 8-12% |
| V. Prepare communications | | | | | | 12-18% |
| **Skills Weights** | 10-20% | 6-16% | 12-22% | 12-22% | 35-45% | |

You should keep these skills foremost in your mind as your prepare and sit for the Auditing and Attestation Section.

The CPA examination is one of many screening devices to assure the competence of those licensed to perform the attest function and to render professional accounting services. Other screening devices include educational requirements, ethics examinations, and work experience.

The CPA examination appears to test the material covered in accounting programs of the better business schools. It also appears to be based upon the body of knowledge essential for the practice of public accounting and the audit of a medium-sized client. Since the examination is primarily a textbook or academic examination, you should plan on taking it as soon as possible after completing your required education.

### Examination Content

Guidance concerning topical content of the new computer-based exam in Auditing and Attestation can be found in a document prepared by the Board of Examiners of the AICPA entitled *Uniform CPA Examination—Examination Content Specifications*. We have included the content outline for Auditing and Attestation at the beginning of Chapter 5. The outline should be used as an indication of the topics' relative emphasis on the exam.

The Board's objective in preparing this detailed listing of topics tested on the exam is to help "in assuring the continuing validity and reliability of the Uniform CPA Examination." These outlines are an excellent source of guidance concerning the areas and emphasis to be given each area on future exams.

They are provided to each candidate in *CPA Candidate Bulletin*, which may be downloaded at the AICPA's exam Web site, www.cpa-exam.org.

New accounting and auditing pronouncements, including those in the governmental and not-for-profit areas, are tested in the testing window starting six months after the pronouncement's *effective* date. If early application is permitted, a pronouncement is tested six months after the *issuance* date; candidates are responsible for the old pronouncement also until it is superseded. Federal laws are tested six months following their *effective date*. The AICPA posts content changes regularly on its Internet site at www.cpa-exam.org.

### Nondisclosure and Computerization of Examination

Beginning May 1996, the Uniform CPA Examination became nondisclosed. For each exam section, candidates are required to agree to a *Statement of Confidentiality*, which states that they will not divulge the nature and content of any exam question. In April of 2004, the CPA exam became computer-based. After that date, candidates take the exam at Prometric sites in the 54 jurisdictions in which the CPA exam is offered. From April 5, 2004, going forward the CPA exam is offered continually during the testing windows shown below.

| Testing Window (Exam Available) | January through February | April through May | July through August | October through November |
|---|---|---|---|---|
| AICPA Review & Update (Exam Unavailable) | March | June | September | December |

One or more exam sections may be taken during any exam window, and the sections may be taken in any desired order. **However, no candidate will be allowed to sit for the same section more than once during any given testing window.** In addition, a candidate must pass all four sections of the CPA exam within a "rolling" eighteen-month period, which begins on the date he or she passes a section. In other words, you must pass the other three sections of the exam within eighteen months of when you pass the first section. If you do not pass all sections within the eighteen-month period, credit for any section(s) passed outside the eighteen-month period will expire and the section(s) must be retaken.

The following table compares the sections of the prior pencil-and-paper exam with the new computer-based exam. If you have earned conditional credit on the pencil-and-paper exam, the table also shows the section of the computer-based exam for which you will be given credit.

| *Pencil-and-Paper Examination up to November 2003 (15.5 hours in 2 days)* | *Computer-Based Examination commencing April 5, 2004 (14 hours over flexible period of time)* |
| --- | --- |
| Auditing (4.5 hours) | Auditing & Attestation (4.5 hours) |
| Financial Accounting & Reporting (4.5 hours) | Financial Accounting & Reporting (4 hours) |
| Accounting & Reporting (3.5 hours) | Regulation (3 hours) |
| Business Law & Professional Responsibilities (3 hours) | Business Environment & Concepts (2.5 hours) |

Candidates should keep abreast of the latest developments regarding transition rules and requirements from their state boards of accountancy. We will post more detailed information as it becomes available on the CPA Examination Review Wiley Web site at www.wiley.com/cpa.

### *Types of Questions*

The computer-based Uniform CPA Examination consists of two basic question formats.

1.  Multiple-Choice—questions requiring the selection of one of four responses to a short scenario.
2.  Simulations—case studies that are used to assess knowledge and skills in a context approximating that found on the job through the use of realistic scenarios and tasks, and access to normally available and familiar resources.

The multiple-choice questions are much like the ones that have constituted a majority of the CPA examination for years. **And the good news is that these types of questions constitute about 65% of the Auditing and Attestation section.** The simulations are new and information about this type of question is somewhat limited. However, we have attempted in this manual to use the latest available information to design study materials that will make you successful in answering simulation problems. You should refer to the AICPA Web site (www.cpa-exam.org) for the latest information about the format and content of this new type of question.

### *Process for Sitting for the Examination*

While there are some variations in the process from state to state, the basic process for sitting for the CPA examination may be described as follows:

1.  Apply to take the examination (request, complete, and submit an application)
2.  Receive your Notice to Schedule (NTS)
3.  Schedule your examination(s)
4.  Take your examination(s)
5.  Receive you score report(s)

### *Applying to Take the Examination*

The right to practice public accounting as a CPA is governed by individual state statutes. While some rules regarding the practice of public accounting vary from state to state, all State Boards of Accountancy use the Uniform CPA Examination and AICPA advisory grading service as one of the requirements to practice public accounting. Every candidate should contact the applicable State Board of Accountancy to determine the requirements to sit for the exam (e.g., education requirements). For comparisons of requirements for various state boards and those policies that are uniform across jurisdictions you should refer to the Web site of the National Association of State Boards of Accountancy (NASBA) at www.nasba.org.

A frequent problem candidates encounter is failure to apply by the deadline. **Apply to sit for the examination early. Also, you should use extreme care in filling out the application and mailing required materials to your State Board of Accountancy.** If possible, have a friend review your completed application before mailing with check and other documentation. The name on your application must appear exactly the same as it appears on the identification you plan to use at the testing center. Candidates may miss a particular

CPA examination window simply because of minor technical details that were overlooked (check not signed, items not enclosed, question not answered on application, etc.). **Because of the very high volume of applications received in the more populous states, the administrative staff does not have time to call or write to correct minor details and will simply reject your application.**

The various state boards, their Web sites, and telephone numbers are listed on the following page. Be sure to inquire of your state board for specific and current requirements.

It is possible for candidates to sit for the examination at a Prometric site in any state or territory. Candidates desiring to do so should contact the State Board of Accountancy in their home state.

### Exam Scheduling

Once you have been cleared to take the exam by the applicable state board, you will receive by mail a Notice to Schedule (NTS) and may then schedule to sit for one or more sections of the exam.

You have the following three options for scheduling your examination:

1. **Visit www.prometric.com/cpa on the Internet**
   This is the easiest and quickest way to schedule an examination appointment (or cancel and reschedule an appointment, if necessary). Simply go to the Web site, select SCHEDULE APPOINTMENT, and follow the directions. It is advised that you print and keep for your records the confirmation number for your appointment.
2. **Call 800-580-9648 (Candidate Services Call Center)**
   Before you call, you must have your NTS in front of you, and have in mind several times, dates, and locations that would work for you. You will not receive written confirmation of your appointment. Be sure to write down the date, time, location, and confirmation number for each of your appointments.
3. **Call your local test center**
   While this method is not recommended, you may call your local test center and schedule appointments. Again, be sure to have your NTS in front of you and write down the date, time, location, and confirmation number for each of your appointments.

You should also be aware that if you have to cancel or reschedule your appointment, you may be subject to a cancellation/rescheduling fee. The AICPA's *Uniform CPA Examination Candidate Bulletin* lists the rescheduling and cancellation fees.

**To assure that you get your desired location and time period it is imperative that you schedule early. To get your first choice of dates, you are advised to schedule at least 45 days in advance. You will not be scheduled for an exam fewer than 5 days before testing.**

## ATTRIBUTES OF EXAMINATION SUCCESS

Your primary objective in preparing for the Auditing and Attestation section is to pass. Other objectives such as learning new and reviewing old material should be considered secondary. The six attributes of examination success discussed below are **essential**. You should study the attributes and work toward achieving/developing each of them **before** taking the examination.

1. **Knowledge of Material**
   Two points are relevant to "knowledge of material" as an attribute of examination success. **First,** there is a distinct difference between being familiar with material and knowing the material. Frequently candidates confuse familiarity with knowledge. Can you remember when you just could not answer an examination question or did poorly on an examination, but maintained to yourself or your instructor that you knew the material? You probably were only familiar with the material. On the CPA examination, familiarity is insufficient; you must know the material. Remember, the exam will test your ability to analyze data, make judgments, communicate, perform research, and demonstrate understanding of the material. Knowledgeable discussion of the material is required on the CPA examination. This text contains outlines of the topical areas in auditing including outlines of professional pronouncements, etc. Return to the original material (e.g., SAS, your auditing textbook, etc.) only if the outlines do not reinforce material you already know. **Second,** the Auditing and Attestation exam tests a literally overwhelming amount of material at a rigorous level. **Furthermore,** as noted earlier, the CPA exam will test new material, sometimes as early as six months after issuance. In other words, you are not only responsible for material you learned in your auditing and attestation course(s), but also for all new developments in auditing and attestation.

| | STATE BOARD WEB ADDRESS | TELEPHONE # |
|---|---|---|
| **AK** | www.commerce.state.ak.us/occ/pcpa.htm | (907) 465-3811 |
| **AL** | www.asbpa.alabama.gov | (334) 242-5700 |
| **AR** | www.state.ar.us/asbpa | (501) 682-1520 |
| **AZ** | www.azaccountancy.gov | (602) 364-0804 |
| **CA** | www.dca.ca.gov/cba | (916) 263-3680 |
| **CO** | www.dora.state.co.us/accountants | (303) 894-7800 |
| **CT** | www.ct.gov/sboa | (860) 509-6179 |
| **DC** | dcra.dc.gov/dcra | (202) 442-4320 |
| **DE** | www.dpr.delaware.gov | (302) 744-4500 |
| **FL** | www.myflorida.com | (850) 487-1395 |
| **GA** | www.sos.state.ga.us/plb/accountancy/ | (478) 207-1400 |
| **GU** | www.guamboa.org | (671) 647-0813 |
| **HI** | www.hawaii.gov/dcca/areas/pvl/boards/accountancy | (808) 586-2696 |
| **IA** | www.state.ia.us/iacc | (515) 281-5910 |
| **ID** | www.isba.idaho.gov | (208) 334-2490 |
| **IL** | www.ilboa.org | (217) 531-0950 |
| **IN** | www.in.gov/pla/bandc/accountancy/ | (317) 234-3040 |
| **KS** | www.ksboa.org | (785) 296-2162 |
| **KY** | cpa.ky.gov | (502) 595-3037 |
| **LA** | www.cpaboard.state.la.us | (504) 566-1244 |
| **MA** | www.mass.gov/reg/boards/pa | (617) 727-1806 |
| **MD** | www.dllr.state.md.us/license/occprof/account.html | (410) 230-6322 |
| **ME** | www.maineprofessionalreg.org | (207) 624-8603 |
| **MI** | www.michigan.gov/accountancy | (517) 241-9249 |
| **MN** | www.boa.state.mn.us | (651) 296-7938 |
| **MO** | pr.mo.gov/accountancy.asp | (573) 751-0012 |
| **MS** | www.msbpa.state.ms.us | (601) 354-7320 |
| **MT** | www.publicaccountant.mt.gov | (406) 841-2389 |
| **NC** | www.nccpaboard.gov | (919) 733-4222 |
| **ND** | www.state.nd.us/ndsba | (800) 532-5904 |
| **NE** | www.nol.org/home/BPA | (402) 471-3595 |
| **NH** | www.nh.gov/accountancy | (603) 271-3286 |
| **NJ** | www.state.nj.us/lps/ca/nonmed.htm | (973) 504-6380 |
| **NM** | www.rld.state.nm.us/b&c/accountancy/index.htm | (505) 841-9108 |
| **NV** | www.nvaccountancy.com/ | (775) 786-0231 |
| **NY** | www.op.nysed.gov/cpa.htm | (518) 474-3817 |
| **OH** | www.acc.ohio.gov/ | (614) 466-4135 |
| **OK** | www.oab.state.ok.us | (405) 521-2397 |
| **OR** | egov.oregon.gov/BOA/ | (503) 378-4181 |
| **PA** | www.dos.state.pa.us/account | (717) 783-1404 |
| **PR** | www.estado.gobierno.pr/contador.htm | (787) 722-4816 |
| **RI** | www.dbr.state.ri.us | (401) 222-3185 |
| **SC** | www.llr.state.sc.us/POL/Accountancy | (803) 896-4770 |
| **SD** | www.state.sd.us/dcr/acountancy | (605) 367-5770 |
| **TN** | www.state.tn.us/commerce/boards/tnsba/index.html | (615) 741-2550 |
| **TX** | www.tsbpa.state.tx.us | (512) 305-7800 |
| **UT** | www.dopl.utah.gov | (801) 530-6396 |
| **VA** | www.boa.virginia.gov | (804) 367-8505 |
| **VI** | www.dlca.gov.vi | (340) 773-4305 |
| **VT** | vtprofessionals.org/opr1/accountants | (802) 828-2837 |
| **WA** | www.cpaboard.wa.gov | (360) 753-2585 |
| **WI** | www.drl.wi.gov/index.htm | (608) 266-5511 |
| **WV** | www.wvboacc.org | (304) 558-3557 |
| **WY** | cpaboard.state.wy.us | (307) 777-7551 |

*NOTE: The publisher does not assume responsibility for errors in the above information. You should request information concerning requirements in your state at least six months in advance of the exam dates.*

2.  **Commitment to Exam Preparation**

    Your preparation for the CPA exam should begin at least two months prior to the date you plan to schedule your seating for an exam part. If you plan to take more than one part, you should start earlier. Over the course of your preparation, you will experience many peaks and valleys. There will be days when you feel completely prepared and there will also be days when you feel totally overwhelmed. This is not unusual and, in fact, should be expected.

    The CPA exam is a very difficult and challenging exam. How many times in your college career did you study months for an exam? Probably not too many. Therefore, candidates need to remain focused on the objective—succeeding on the CPA exam.

    Develop a personal study plan so that you are reviewing material daily. Of course, you should schedule an occasional study break to help you relax, but don't schedule too many breaks. Candidates who dedicate themselves to studying have a much greater chance of going through this process one time. On the other hand, a lack of focus and piecemeal preparation will only extend the process over a number of exam sittings.

3.  **Solutions Approach**

    The solutions approach is a systematic approach to solving the questions and simulations found on the CPA examination. Many candidates know the material fairly well when they sit for the CPA exam, but they do not know how to take the examination. Candidates generally neither work nor answer questions efficiently in terms of time or grades. The solutions approach permits you to avoid drawing "blanks" on CPA exam questions; using the solutions approach coupled with grading insights (see below) allows you to pick up a sizable number of points on test material with which you are not familiar. Chapter 3 outlines the solutions approach for multiple-choice questions and simulations.

4.  **Grading Insights**

    Your score on each section of the exam is determined by the sum of points assigned to individual questions and simulation parts. Thus, you must attempt to maximize your points on each individual item.

    The number of points assigned to a multiple-choice question varies depending upon its difficulty level, easy, medium, or hard. **In other words, you receive more points for correctly answering a hard question than correctly answering an easy question.** Multiple-choice questions are organized in 30-question testlets, and each testlet includes questions from all of the content areas of the Auditing & Attestation section.

    With respect to the multiple-choice testlets, the CPA exam uses a form of adaptive testing known as multistage testing. Using this technique the average difficulty of subsequent testlet(s) is determined by how the candidate has performed on the previous testlet(s). Therefore, if you get a testlet with a preponderance of very difficult questions, do not become discouraged. It may mean that you performed very well on the previous testlet(s). In addition, since the number of points assigned to hard or medium questions will be greater than the number of points for easy questions, you have an opportunity to accumulate a large number of total points on that testlet.

    Each multiple-choice testlet contains "operational" and "pretest" questions. The operational questions are the only ones that are used to determine your score. Pretest questions are not scored; they are being tested for future use as operational questions. However, you have no way of knowing which questions are operational and which questions are pretest questions. Therefore, you must approach each question as if it will be used to determine your grade.

    Simulations include more extensive scenarios and a number of requirements. For example, the requirements may involve calculations, form completion, research, and written communication. The points assigned to the requirements will vary according to their difficulty. Most of the requirements are graded by the computer. Only those that involve written communication are graded manually. The simulations make use of a number of commonly used tools such as spreadsheets and electronic research databases. Therefore, you need to become proficient in the use of these tools to maximize your score on the simulations.

    CPA Exam scores are reported on a scale from 0 to 99. The total score is not a percent correct score. It is a combination of scores from the multiple-choice and simulation portions of the exam considering the relative difficulty of the items. A total score of 75 is required to pass each section.

    The AICPA includes sample examination questions on its Web site that allow you to get experience with the use of the actual computer tools used on the CPA exam. Also, more experience with computer testing can be obtained by using *Wiley CPA Review Practice Software.*

5. **Examination Strategy**

   Prior to sitting for the examination, it is important to develop an examination strategy (i.e., an approach to working efficiently throughout the exam). Your ability to cope successfully with 4 1/2 hours of examination can be improved by

   a. Recognizing the importance and usefulness of an examination strategy
   b. Using Chapter 4, Taking the Examination, and previous examination experience to develop a "personal strategy" for the exam
   c. Testing your "personal strategy" on example examinations under conditions similar to those at the testing centers (using similar tools and databases and with a time limit)

6. **Examination Confidence**

   You need confidence to endure the physical and mental demands of 4 1/2 hours of test-taking under tremendous pressure. Examination confidence results from proper preparation for the exam which includes mastering the first five attributes of examination success. Examination confidence is necessary to enable you to overcome the initial frustration with questions for which you may not be specifically prepared.

   This study manual, when properly used, contributes to your examination confidence. Build confidence by completing the questions contained herein.

*Common Candidate Mistakes*

The CPA Exam is a formidable hurdle in your accounting career. With a pass rate of about 40% on each section, the level of difficulty is obvious. The good news, though, is that about 75% of all candidates (first-time and re-exam) sitting for each examination eventually pass. The authors believe that the first-time pass rate could be higher if candidates would be more careful. Eight common mistakes that many candidates make are

1. Failure to understand the exam question requirements
2. Misunderstanding the supporting text of the problem
3. Lack of knowledge of material tested, especially recently issued pronouncements
4. Failure to develop proficiency with computer-based testing and practice tools such as electronic research databases and spreadsheets
5. Inability to apply the solutions approach
6. Lack of an exam strategy (e.g., allocation of time)
7. Sloppiness and logical errors
8. Failure to proofread and edit

These mistakes are not mutually exclusive. Candidates may commit one or more of the above items. Remind yourself that when you decrease the number of common mistakes, you increase your chances of successfully becoming a CPA. Take the time to read carefully the exam question requirements. Do not jump into a quick start, only to later find out that you didn't understand what information the examiners were asking for. Read slowly and carefully. Take time to recall your knowledge. Respond to the question asked. Apply an exam strategy such as allocating your time among all question formats. Do not spend too much time on the multiple-choice testlets, leaving no time to spend on preparing your simulation responses. Write neatly and label all answer sections. Upon completion of any written communication requirement, proofread and edit your answer. Use the spell check function of the word processor. Answer questions quickly but precisely, avoid common mistakes, and increase your score.

## PURPOSE AND ORGANIZATION OF THIS REVIEW TEXTBOOK

This book is designed to help you prepare adequately for the Auditing and Attestation examination. There is no easy way to prepare for the successful completion of the CPA Examination; however, through the use of this manual, your approach will be systematic and logical.

The objective of this book is to provide study materials supportive to CPA candidates. While no guarantees are made concerning the success of those using this text, this book promotes efficient preparation by

1. Explaining how to **maximize your score** through analysis of examination grading and illustration of the solutions approach.

2. **Defining areas tested** through the use of the content specification outlines. Note that predictions of future exams are not made. You should prepare yourself for all possible topics rather than gambling on the appearance of certain questions.

3. **Organizing your study program** by comprehensively outlining all of the subject matter tested on the examination in six easy-to-use study modules. Each study module is a manageable task which facilitates your exam preparation. Turn to Chapter 5 and peruse the contents to get a feel for the organization of this book.

4. **Providing CPA candidates with examination questions** organized by topic (e.g., internal control, audit reports, etc.). Questions have also been developed for new areas and in simulation format.

5. **Explaining the AICPA unofficial answers** to the examination questions included in this text. The AICPA publishes unofficial answers for all questions from exams administered prior to 1996 and for any released questions from exams administered on or after May 1996. However, no explanation is made of the approach that should have been applied to the examination questions to obtain these unofficial answers.

As you read the next few paragraphs which describe the contents of this book, flip through the chapters to gain a general familiarity with the book's organization and contents. Chapters 2, 3, and 4 are to help you maximize your score.

Chapter 2  Examination Grading
Chapter 3  The Solutions Approach
Chapter 4  Taking the Examination

Chapters 2, 3, and 4 contain material that should be kept in mind throughout your study program. Refer back to them frequently. Reread them for a final time just before you sit for the exam.

Chapter 5 (Auditing and Attestation Modules) contains

1. AICPA Content Specification Outlines of material tested on the Auditing and Attestation Examination
2. Multiple-choice questions
3. Simulation style problems
4. AICPA unofficial answers with the author's explanations for the multiple-choice questions
5. Author answers to simulation problems
6. Multiple-topic simulations included in Appendix A

Also included at the end of this text is a complete Sample Auditing and Attestation CPA Examination. The sample exam is included to help candidates gain experience in taking a "realistic" exam. While studying the modules, the candidates can become accustomed to concentrating on fairly narrow topics. By working through the sample examination near the end of their study programs, candidates will be better prepared for taking the actual examination. Because some simulations require the use of research materials, it is useful to have the appropriate electronic research database (e.g., AICPA Resource: Accounting and Auditing) or printed versions of professional standards to complete the sample examination. AICPA Resource: Accounting and Auditing is available at discounted prices to student and faculty members of the AICPA. **Remember that this research material will not be available to answer the multiple-choice questions.**

### Other Textbooks

This text is a comprehensive compilation of study guides and outlines; it should not be necessary to supplement them with textbooks and other materials for most topics. You probably already have an auditing textbook. In such a case, you must make the decision whether to replace it and trade familiarity (including notes therein, etc.), with the cost and inconvenience of obtaining the newer text containing a more updated presentation.

Before spending time and money acquiring a new book, begin your study program with *CPA EXAMINATION REVIEW: AUDITING AND ATTESTATION* to determine your need for a supplemental text.

### Ordering Other Textual Materials

If you want to order AICPA materials, locate an AICPA educator member to order your materials, since educator members are entitled to a discount and may place Web site or telephone orders.

AICPA (CPA2Biz)                                    Address:    Order Department
                                                                        CPA2Biz
          Telephone:  888-777-7077                           P.O. Box 2209
          Web site:  www.CPA2Biz.com                    Jersey City, NJ 07303-2209

A variety of supplemental CPA products are available from John Wiley & Sons, Inc. By using a variety of learning techniques, such as software, computer-based learning, and audio CDs, the candidate is more likely to remain focused during the study process and to retain information for a longer period of time. Visit our Web site at **www.wiley.com/cpa** for other products, supplements, and updates.

### Working CPA Questions

The AICPA content outlines, study outlines, etc., will be used to acquire and assimilate the knowledge tested on the examination. This, however, should be only **one-half** of your preparation program. The other half should be spent practicing how to work questions. Some candidates probably spend over 90% of their time reviewing material tested on the CPA exam. Much more time should be allocated to working previous examination questions. Working examination questions serves two functions. First, it helps you develop a solutions approach as well as solutions that will maximize your score. Second, it provides the best test of your knowledge of the material.

The multiple-choice questions and answer explanations can be used in many ways. First, they may be used as a diagnostic evaluation of your knowledge. For example, before beginning to review audit sampling you may wish to answer 10 to 15 multiple-choice questions to determine your ability to answer CPA examination questions on audit sampling. The apparent difficulty of the questions and the correctness of your answers will allow you to determine the necessary breadth and depth of your review. Additionally, exposure to examination questions prior to review and study of the material should provide motivation. You will develop a feel for your level of proficiency and an understanding of the scope and difficulty of past examination diagnostic multiple-choice questions. Moreover, your review materials will explain concepts encountered in the diagnostic multiple-choice questions.

Second, the multiple-choice questions can be used as a poststudy or postreview evaluation. You should attempt to understand all concepts mentioned (even in incorrect answers) as you answer the questions. Refer to the explanation of the answer for discussion of the alternatives even though you selected the correct response. Thus, you should read the explanation of the unofficial answer unless you completely understand the question and all of the alternative answers.

Third, you may wish to use the multiple-choice questions as a primary study vehicle. This is probably the quickest but least thorough approach in preparing for the exam. Make a sincere effort to understand the question and to select the correct response before referring to the unofficial answer and explanation. In many cases, the explanations will appear inadequate because of your lack of familiarity with the topic. Always refer back to an appropriate study source, such as the outlines and text in this volume, your auditing textbook, AICPA pronouncements, etc.

The multiple-choice questions outnumber the simulations by greater than 10 to 1 in this book. This is similar to the proposed content of the new computer-based examination. One problem with so many multiple-choice questions is that you may overemphasize them. Candidates generally prefer to work multiple-choice questions because they are

1. Shorter and less time-consuming
2. Solvable with less effort
3. Less frustrating than simulations

Another problem with the large number of multiple-choice questions is that you may tend to become overly familiar with the questions. The result may be that you begin reading the facts and assumptions of previously studied questions into the questions on your examination. Guard against this potential problem by reading each multiple-choice question with **extra** care.

Beginning with the introduction of the computer-based examination, the AICPA began testing with simulations. Simulation problems prepared by the author and revised from prior CPA exam problems are incorporated in the modules to which they pertain. Also, Appendix A to the manual contains multiple-topic simulations. (See the listing of question material at the beginning of Chapter 5.)

The questions and solutions in this volume provide you with an opportunity to diagnose and correct any exam-taking weaknesses prior to sitting for the examination. Continually analyze your incorrect solutions to determine the cause of the error(s) during your preparation for the exam. Treat each incorrect solution as a mistake that will not be repeated (especially on the examination). Also attempt to generalize your weaknesses so that you may change, reinforce, or develop new approaches to exam preparation and exam taking.

After you have reviewed for the Auditing and Attestation section of the exam, work the complete Auditing and Attestation Sample Exam provided in Appendix B.

## SELF-STUDY PROGRAM

CPA candidates generally find it difficult to organize and to complete their own self-study programs. A major problem is determining **what** and **how** to study. Another major problem is developing the self-discipline to stick to a study program. Relatedly, it is often difficult for CPA candidates to determine how much to study (i.e., determining when they are sufficiently prepared).

The following suggestions will assist you in developing a **systematic, comprehensive,** and **successful** self-study program to help you complete the Auditing and Attestation exam. Remember that these are only suggestions. You should modify them to suit your personality, available study time, and other constraints. Some of the suggestions may appear trivial, but CPA candidates generally need all the assistance they can get to systemize their study programs.

### Study Facilities and Available Time

Locate study facilities that will be conducive to concentrated study. Factors which you should consider include

1. Noise distraction
2. Interruptions
3. Lighting
4. Availability (e.g., a local library is not available at 5:00 a.m.)
5. Accessibility (e.g., your kitchen table vs. your local library)
6. Desk or table space

You will probably find different study facilities optimal for different times (e.g., your kitchen table during early morning hours and local libraries during early evening hours).

Next review your personal and professional commitments from now until the exam to determine regularly available study time. Formalize a schedule to which you can reasonably commit yourself. At the end of this chapter you will find a detailed approach to managing your time available for the exam preparation program.

### Self-Evaluation

The *CPA EXAMINATION REVIEW: AUDITING AND ATTESTATION* self-study program is partitioned into six topics or modules. Since each module is clearly defined and should be studied separately, you have the task of preparing for the Auditing and Attestation exam by tackling six manageable tasks. Partitioning the overall project into six modules makes preparation psychologically easier, since you sense yourself completing one small step at a time rather than seemingly never completing one or a few large steps.

By completing the following "Preliminary Estimate of Your Present Knowledge of Subject" inventory, organized by the six modules in this program, you will tabulate your strong and weak areas at the beginning of your study program. This will help you budget your limited study time. Note that you should begin studying the material in each module by answering up to 1/4 of the total multiple-choice questions covering that module's topics. See instruction 4.A. in the next section. This "mini-exam" should constitute a diagnostic evaluation as to the amount of review and study you need.

### PRELIMINARY ESTIMATE OF YOUR PRESENT KNOWLEDGE OF SUBJECT

| No. | Module | Proficient | Fairly Proficient | Generally Familiar | Not Familiar |
|-----|--------|-----------|-------------------|--------------------|--------------|
| 1. | Engagement Planning | | | | |
| 2. | Internal Control | | | | |
| 3. | Evidence | | | | |
| 4. | Reporting | | | | |
| 5. | Audit Sampling | | | | |
| 6. | Auditing with Technology | | | | |

### Time Allocation

The study program below entails an average of 75 hours (Step 5. below) of study time. The breakdown of total hours is indicated in the left margin.

[2 1/2 hrs.]      1.  Study Chapters 2-4 in this volume. These chapters are essential to your efficient preparation program. (Time estimate includes candidate's review of the examples of the solutions approach in Chapters 2 and 3.)

[1/2 hr.]      2.  Begin by studying the introductory material at the beginning of Chapter 5.

3. Study one module at a time. The modules are listed above in the self-evaluation section.
4. For each module

[6 hrs.]    A. Work 1/4 of the multiple-choice questions (e.g., if there are 40 multiple-choice questions in a module, you should work every 4th question). Score yourself.

This diagnostic routine will provide you with an index of your proficiency and familiarity with the type and difficulty of questions.

Time estimate: 3 minutes each, not to exceed 1 hour total.

[20 hrs.]    B. Study the outlines and illustrations. Where necessary, refer to your auditing textbook and original authoritative pronouncements (this will occur more frequently for topics in which you have a weak background).

Time estimate: 2 hours minimum per module with more time devoted to topics less familiar to you.

[16 hrs.]    C. Work the remaining multiple-choice questions. Study the explanations of the multiple-choice questions you missed or had trouble answering.

Time estimate: 3 minutes to answer each question and 2 minutes to study the answer explanation of each question missed.

[16 hrs.]    D. Work at least 6 simulation problems. Work additional problems as time permits.

Time estimate: 20-30 minutes for each problem and 10 minutes to review the answer for each problem worked.

[7 hrs.]    E. Under simulated exam conditions, work the full simulations in Appendix A to the manual.

Time estimate: 45 minutes for each simulation and 20 minutes to review the answer.

[7 hrs.]    F. Work through the sample CPA examination presented at the end of this text. The exam should be taken in one sitting.

Take the examination under simulated exam conditions (i.e., in a strange place with other people present [your local municipal library or a computer lab]). Apply your solutions approach to each question and your exam strategy to the overall exam.

You should limit yourself to the time that you will have when taking the actual CPA exam section (4.5 hours for the Auditing and Attestation section). Spend time afterwards grading your work and reviewing your effort. It might be helpful to do this with other CPA candidates. Another person looking over your exam might be more objective and notice things such as clarity of writing assignments, etc.

Time estimate: To take the exam and review it later, approximately 7 hours.

5. The total suggested time of 75 hours is only an average. Allocation of time will vary candidate by candidate. Time requirements vary due to the diverse backgrounds and abilities of CPA candidates.

Allocate your time so you gain the most proficiency in the least time. Remember that while 75 hours will be required, you should break the overall project down into 6 or more manageable tasks. Do not study more than one module during each study session.

### Using Notecards

Below are one candidate's notecards on Auditing and Attestation topics which illustrate how key definitions, formulas, lists, etc. can be summarized on index cards for quick review. Since candidates can take these anywhere they go, they are a very efficient review tool.

| *Auditability* | | *Variable Sampling* | |
| --- | --- | --- | --- |
| *Refers to auditor's ability to audit.* | | | *Effect on* |
| *Requires:* | | *Increases in* | *sample size* |
| | | *Risk—incorrect acceptance* | *D* |
| *1. Adequate accounting records* | | *Risk—incorrect rejection* | *D* |
| *2. Permission from client to understand* | | *Tolerable misstatement* | *D* |
| *internal control process* | | *Expected population misstatement* | *I* |
| *3. Management Integrity* | | *Population size and variability* | *I* |

### Level of Proficiency Required

What level of proficiency must you develop with respect to each of the topics to pass the exam? You should work toward a minimum correct rate on the multiple-choice questions of 80%. Working toward a correct rate of 80% or higher will give you a margin.

Warning: Disproportional study time devoted to multiple-choice questions (relative to simulations) can be disastrous on the exam. You should work a substantial number of simulation problems under simulated exam conditions, even though multiple-choice questions are easier to work and are used to gauge your proficiency. The authors believe that practicing simulation problems will also improve your proficiency on the multiple-choice questions.

### Multiple-Choice Feedback

One of the benefits of working through previous exam questions is that it helps you to identify your weak areas. Once you have graded your answers, your strong areas and weak areas should be clearly evident. Yet, the important point here is that you should not stop at a simple percentage evaluation. The percentage only provides general feedback about your knowledge of the material contained within that particular module. The percentage **does not** give you any specific feedback regarding the concepts which were tested. In order to get this feedback, you should look at the questions missed on an individual basis because this will help you gain a better understanding of **why** you missed the question.

This feedback process has been facilitated by the fact that within each module where the multiple-choice answer key appears, two blank lines have been inserted next to the multiple-choice answers. As you grade the multiple-choice questions, mark those questions which you have missed. However, instead of just marking the questions right and wrong, you should now focus on marking the questions in a manner which identifies **why** you missed the question. As an example, a candidate could mark the questions in the following manner: ✓ for math mistakes, x for conceptual mistakes, and ? for areas which the candidate was unfamiliar with. The candidate should then correct these mistakes by reworking through the marked questions.

The objective of this marking technique is to help you identify your weak areas and thus, the concepts which you should be focusing on. While it is still important for you to get 80% correct when working multiple-choice questions, it is more important for you to understand the concepts. This understanding applies to both the questions answered correctly and those answered incorrectly. Remember, questions on the CPA exam will be different from the questions in the book; however, the concepts will be the same. Therefore, your preparation should focus on understanding concepts, not just getting the correct answer.

### Conditional Candidates

If you have received conditional status on the examination, you must concentrate on the remaining section(s). Unfortunately, many candidates do not study after conditioning the exam, relying on luck to get them through the remaining section(s). Conditional candidates will find that material contained in Chapters 1 – 4 and the information contained in the appropriate modules will benefit them in preparing for the remaining section(s) of the examination.

## PLANNING FOR THE EXAMINATION

### Overall Strategy

An overriding concern should be an orderly, systematic approach toward both your preparation program and your examination strategy. A major objective should be to avoid any surprises or anything else that would rattle you during the examination. In other words, you want to be in complete control as much as possible.

Control is of paramount importance from both positive and negative viewpoints. The presence of control on your part will add to your confidence and your ability to prepare for and take the exam. Moreover, the presence of control will make your preparation program more enjoyable (or at least less distasteful). On the other hand, a lack of organization will result in inefficiency in preparing and taking the examination, with a highly predictable outcome. Likewise, distractions during the examination (e.g., inadequate lodging, long drive) are generally disastrous.

In summary, establishing a systematic, orderly approach to taking the examination is of paramount importance. Follow these six steps:

1. Develop an overall strategy at the beginning of your preparation program (see below)
2. Supplement your overall strategy with outlines of material tested on the Auditing and Attestation section
3. Supplement your overall strategy with an explicitly stated set of question and problem-solving procedures—the solutions approach
4. Supplement your overall strategy with an explicitly stated approach to each examination session (see Chapter 4)
5. Evaluate your preparation progress on a regular basis and prepare lists of things "to do" (see Weekly Review of Preparation Program Progress below)
6. RELAX: You can pass the exam. About 40 to 45% of the candidates taking a section of the CPA examination pass. But if you take out the individuals that did not adequately prepare, these percentages increase substantially. You will be one of those who pass if you complete an efficient preparation program and execute well (i.e., solutions approach and exam strategy) while taking the exam.

The following outline is designed to provide you with a general framework of the tasks before you. You should tailor the outline to your needs by adding specific items and comments.

A. Preparation Program (refer to Self-Study Program discussed previously)

1. Obtain and organize study materials
2. Locate facilities conducive for studying and block out study time
3. Develop your solutions approach (including solving simulations and multiple-choice questions)
4. Prepare an examination strategy
5. Study the material tested recently and prepare answers to actual exam questions on these topics under examination conditions
6. Periodically evaluate your progress

B. Physical Arrangements

1. Apply to and obtain acceptance from your state board
2. Schedule your testing location and time

C. Taking the Examination (covered in detail in Chapter 4)

1. Become familiar with location of the testing center and procedures
2. Implement examination strategies and the solutions approach

### Weekly Review of Preparation Program Progress

The following pages contain a hypothetical weekly review of program progress. You should prepare a similar progress chart. This procedure, taking only 5 minutes per week, will help you proceed through a more efficient, complete preparation program.

Make notes of materials and topics

1. That you have studied
2. That you have completed
3. That need additional study

| Weeks to go | | Comments on progress, "to do" items, etc. |
|---|---|---|
| 8 | 1) | Read chapters 1 - 4 |
| | 2) | Applied solutions approach to Multiple-Choice Questions and Simulations on a sample basis |
| | 3) | Started Engagement Planning Mod |
| 7 | 1) | Mods read:  Engagement Planning and Internal Control |
| | 2) | Completed MC and Simulation Problems for Engagement Planning and Internal Control |
| 6 | 1) | Refined solutions approach to Engagement Planning and Internal Control Simulation Problems |
| | 2) | Read Evidence Mod |
| 5 | 1) | Continued Evidence Mod |
| | 2) | Completed MC Questions and Simulation Problems in Evidence Mod |
| | 3) | Prepared Audit programs for receivables and payroll cycles |
| | 4) | Contrasted Internal Control and Evidence Mods |
| 4 | 1) | Read Reporting Mod |
| | 2) | Prepared a standard unqualified report from memory |
| | 3) | Began MC questions, and Simulation Problems for Reporting Mod |
| | 4) | Reviewed Engagement Planning, Internal Control, and Evidence Mods |
| 3 | 1) | Finished Reporting Mod |
| | 2) | Memorized outlines for report modifications and formats |
| | 3) | Read Audit Sampling Mod |
| | 4) | Completed Simulation Problems in Audit Sampling |
| 2 | 1) | Read Auditing with Technology Mod |
| | 2) | Completed MC and Simulation Problems in Auditing with Technology |
| | 3) | Reviewed SAS and SSARS |
| | 4) | Reviewed all Mods |
| 1 | 1) | Reviewed all audit reports |
| | 2) | Reviewed MC Questions for all Mods |
| | 3) | Completed Simulations for all Mods from Appendix A |
| 0 | 1) | Completed and graded sample exam |
| | 2) | Reviewed all Mods, especially Reporting |

### *Time Management of Your Preparation*

As you begin your CPA exam preparation, you obviously realize that there is a large amount of material to cover over the course of the next two to three months. Therefore, it is very important for you to organize your calendar, and maybe even your daily routine, so that you can allocate sufficient time to studying. An organized approach to your preparation is much more effective than a last week cram session. An organized approach also builds up the confidence necessary to succeed on the CPA exam.

An approach which we have already suggested, is to develop weekly "to do" lists. This technique helps you to establish intermediate objectives and goals as you progress through your study plan. You can then focus your efforts on small tasks and not feel overwhelmed by the entire process. And as you accomplish these tasks you will see yourself moving one step closer to realizing the overall goal, succeeding on the CPA exam.

Note, however, that the underlying assumption of this approach is that you have found the time during the week to study and thus accomplish the different tasks. Although this is an obvious step, it is still a very important step. Your exam preparation should be of a continuous nature and not one that jumps around the calendar. Therefore, you should strive to find available study time within your daily schedule, which can be utilized on a consistent basis. For example, everyone has certain hours of the day which are already committed for activities such as jobs, classes, and, of course, sleep. There is also going to be the time you spend relaxing because CPA candidates should try to maintain some balance in their lives. Sometimes too much studying can be counterproductive. But there will be some time available to you for studying and working through the questions. Block off this available time and use it only for exam prep. Use the time to accomplish your weekly tasks and to keep yourself committed to the process. After awhile your preparation will develop into a habit and the preparation will not seem as overwhelming as it once did.

---

**NOW IS THE TIME
TO MAKE YOUR COMMITMENT**

---

# 2 EXAMINATION GRADING

All State Boards of Accountancy use the AICPA advisory grading service. As your grade is to be determined by this process, it is very important that you understand the AICPA grading process and its **implications for your preparation program and for the solution techniques you will use during the examination**. The AICPA has a full-time staff of CPA examination personnel under the supervision of the AICPA Board of Examiners, which has responsibility for the CPA examination.

This chapter contains a description of the AICPA grading process including a determination of the passing standard.

## Setting the Passing Standard of the Uniform CPA Examination

As a part of the development of any licensing process, the passing score on the licensing examination must be established. This passing score must be set to distinguish candidates who are qualified to practice from those who are not. After conducting a number of studies of methods to determine passing scores, the Board of Examiners decided to use candidate-centered methods to set passing scores for the computer-based Uniform CPA Examination. In candidate-centered methods, the focus is on looking at actual candidate answers and making judgments about which sets of answers represent the answers of qualified entry-level CPAs. To make these determinations, the AICPA convened panels of CPAs during 2003 to examine candidate responses and set the passing scores for multiple-choice questions and simulations. The data from these panels provide the basis for the development of question and problem points (relative weightings). **As with the previous pencil-and-paper exam, a passing score on the computer-based examination is 75%.**

## Grading the Examination

Most of the responses on the computer-based CPA examination are objective in nature. Obviously, this includes the responses to the multiple-choice questions. However, it also includes most of the responses to the requirements of simulations. Requirements of simulations include responses involving check boxes, entries into spreadsheets, form completion, graphical responses, drag and drop, and written communications. All of these responses, with the exception of written communications, are computer graded. Therefore, no consideration is given to any comments or explanations outside of the structured responses.

Graders are used to score the responses involving written communication, (e.g., a written memorandum). These responses are graded for the quality of the written communication, but not the technical accuracy. However, the response must address the requirement to be graded at all.

## Multiple-Choice Grading

Auditing and Attestation exams contain three multiple-choice testlets of 30 questions each. **Five of these questions will be pretest questions that will not be considered in the candidate's score.** Also, the possible score on a question and on a testlet will vary based on the difficulty of the questions. The makeup of the second testlet provided to a candidate will be determined based upon the candidate's performance on the first testlet, and the makeup of the third testlet will be determined by the candidate's performance on the first two testlets. Therefore, you should not be discouraged if you a get a difficult set of questions; it may merely mean that you performed very well on the previous testlet(s). Also, you will receive more raw points for hard and medium questions than for easy questions.

Your answers to the multiple-choice questions are graded by the computer. Your grade is based on the total number of correct answers weighted by their difficulty, and with no penalty for incorrect answers. As mentioned earlier, 5 of the multiple-choice questions are pretest items that are not included in the candidate's grade.

*Simulation Grading*

As indicated previously, a majority of the responses to the simulations will be computer graded.  They will typically involve checking a box, selecting a response from a list, or dragging and dropping an answer.  The responses involving written communications will be graded for writing skills.  These responses are scored based on the following criteria:

1. Organization:  structure, ordering of ideas, and linking one idea to another

   - Overview/thesis statement
   - Unified paragraphs (topic and supporting sentences)
   - Transitions and connectives

2. Development:  supporting evidence/information to clarify thoughts

   - Details
   - Definitions
   - Examples
   - Rephrasing

3. Expression:  use of standard business English

   - Grammar
   - Punctuation
   - Word usage
   - Capitalization
   - Spelling

**A communication response is not graded for technical accuracy.**  However, it must be on point to be graded at all.  For example, if the requirement is to write a memorandum to describe the components of internal control, the response must describe a group of components although the group does not have to be complete or technically accurate.  That is, the information must be helpful t the intended user.

As with the multiple-choice questions, a small percentage of the simulation requirements will be pretest items that will not be included in the candidate's grade.

Chapter 3 will provide detailed suggestions on ways that you may use the information about grading to maximize your score.

**NOW IS THE TIME
TO MAKE YOUR COMMITMENT**

# 3 THE SOLUTIONS APPROACH

The solutions approach is a systematic problem-solving methodology. The purpose is to assure efficient, complete solutions to CPA exam questions, some of which are complex and confusing relative to most undergraduate accounting questions. This is especially true with regard to the new simulation type problems. Unfortunately, there appears to be a widespread lack of emphasis on problem-solving techniques in accounting courses. Most accounting books and courses merely provide solutions to specific types of problems. Memorization of these solutions for examinations and preparation of homework problems from examples is "cookbooking." "Cookbooking" is perhaps a necessary step in the learning process, but it is certainly not sufficient training for the complexities of the business world. Professional accountants need to be adaptive to a rapidly changing complex environment. For example, CPAs have been called on to interpret and issue reports on new concepts such as price controls, energy allocations, and new taxes. These CPAs rely on their problem-solving expertise to understand these problems and to formulate solutions to them.

The steps outlined below are only one of many possible series of solution steps. Admittedly, the procedures suggested are **very** structured; thus, you should adapt the suggestions to your needs. You may find that some steps are occasionally unnecessary, or that certain additional procedures increase your own problem-solving efficiency. Whatever the case, substantial time should be allocated to developing an efficient solutions approach before taking the examination. You should develop your solutions approach by working questions and problems.

Note that the steps below relate to any specific question or problem; overall examination or section strategies are discussed in Chapter 4.

## Multiple-Choice Screen Layout

The following is a computer screenshot that illustrates the manner in which multiple-choice questions will be presented:

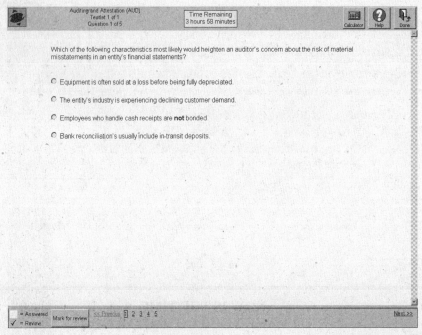

As indicated previously, multiple-choice questions will be presented in three individual testlets of 25 to 30 questions each. Characteristics of the computerized testlets of multiple-choice questions include the following:

1. You may move freely within a particular testlet from one question to the next or back to previous questions until you click the "Done" button. Once you have indicated that you have finished the testlet by clicking on the "Done" button, you can never return to that set of questions.
2. A button on the screen will allow you to mark a question for review if you wish to come back to it later.
3. A four-function computer calculator is available as a tool.
4. The time remaining for the entire exam section is shown on the screen.
5. The number of the questions out of the total in the testlet is shown on the screen.
6. The "Help" button will provide you with help in navigating and completing the testlet.

The screenshot above was obtained from the AICPA's tutorial at www.cpa-exam.org. Candidates are urged to complete the tutorial and other example questions on the AICPA's Web site to obtain additional experience with the computer-based testing.

### Multiple-Choice Question Solutions Approach Algorithm

1. **Work individual questions in order.**

   a. If a question appears lengthy or difficult, skip it until you can determine that extra time is available. Mark it for review to remind you to return to a question that you have skipped or need to review.

2. **Read the stem of the question without looking at the answers.**

   a. The answers are sometimes misleading and may cause you to misread or misinterpret the question.

3. **Read each question *carefully* to determine the topical area.**

   a. Study the requirements **first** so you know which data are important.
   b. Note keywords and important data.
   c. Identify pertinent information.
   d. Be especially careful to note when the requirement is an **exception** (e.g., "Which of the following is **not** a characteristic of variables sampling?").
   e. If a set of data is the basis for two or more questions, read the requirements of each of the questions first before beginning to work the first question (sometimes it is more efficient to work the questions out of order).
   f. Be alert to read questions as they are, not as you would like them to be. You may encounter a familiar looking item; do not jump to the conclusion that you know what the answer is without reading the question completely.

4. **Anticipate the answer before looking at the alternative answers.**

   a. Recall the applicable principle (e.g., circumstances requiring a consistency exception in the audit report).

5. **Read the answers and select the *best* alternative.**
6. **Click on the correct answer (or your educated guess).**
7. **After completing all of the questions including the ones marked for review click on the "Done" button to close out the testlet. Remember once you have closed out the testlet you can never return to it.**

### *Multiple-Choice Question Solutions Approach Example*

A good example of the multiple-choice solutions approach follows.

*Step 3:*

Topical area?  Auditor's assessment of control risk

*Step 4:*

Principle?  Assessing control risk at below the maximum means that the auditor believes the particular controls are effective

*Step 5:*

a. Incorrect  -   Would do if control risk at max
b. **Correct**  -   Which controls are relevant to FS
c. Incorrect  -   Would do if control risk at max
d. Incorrect  -   Auditor does not control inherent risk

**13.** Assessing control risk at below the maximum most likely would involve

a. Changing the timing of substantive tests by omitting interim-date testing and performing the tests at year-end.
b. Identifying specific internal control policies and procedures relevant to specific assertions.
c. Performing more extensive substantive tests with larger sample sizes than originally planned.
d. Reducing inherent risk for most of the assertions relevant to significant account balances.

Currently, all multiple-choice questions are scored based on the number correct, weighted by a difficulty rating (i.e., there is no penalty for guessing). The rationale is that a "good guess" indicates knowledge. Thus, you should answer all multiple-choice questions.

### Simulations

Simulations are case-based multiple-part problems designed to

- Test integrated knowledge
- More closely replicate real-world problems
- Assess research, written communication and other skills

Each simulation will be designed to take from 30 to 50 minutes.

The parts of simulations are separated by computer tabs. Typically they begin with directions and/or a situation and continue with various tabs requiring responses and possibly a resource tab. An example is shown below.

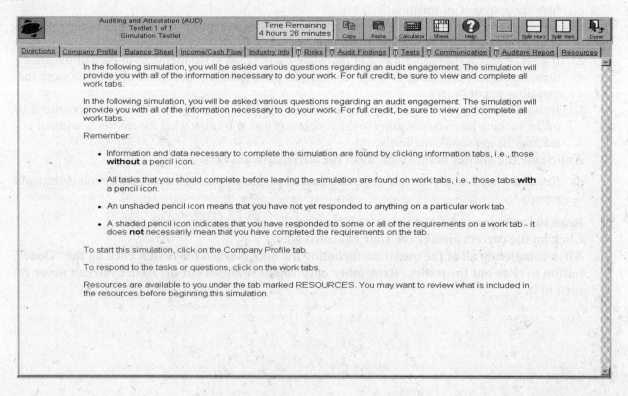

While the tabs without the pencils are informational in nature, the tabs with pencils require a response.

Any of the following types of responses might be required on simulation parts:

- Multiple selection
- Drop-down selection
- Numeric and monetary inputs
- Formula answers
- Check box response
- Enter spreadsheet formulas
- Research results
- Written communications

The screenshot below illustrates a part that requires the candidate to select an answer from a drop-down list.

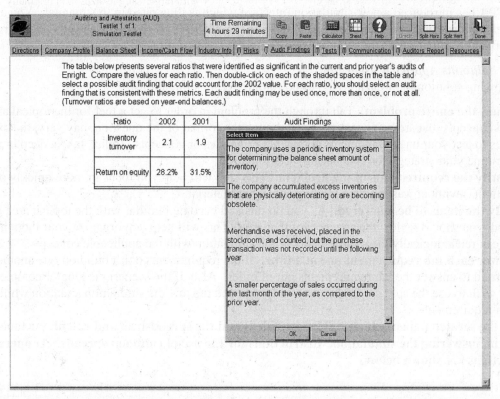

The following screenshot illustrates a part that requires multiple selection.

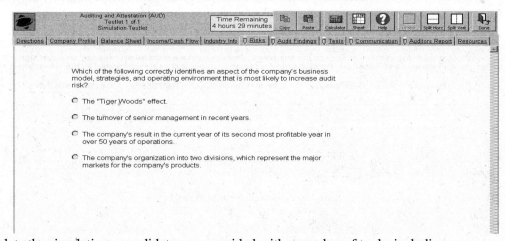

To complete the simulations, candidates are provided with a number of tools, including

- A four-function computer calculator
- Scratch spreadsheet (The spreadsheet will likely have the wizard functions disabled which means that candidates will have to construct spreadsheet formulas without assistance.)

- The ability to split windows horizontally or vertically to show two tabs on the screen (e.g., you can examine the situation tab in one window and a particular requirement in a second window)
- Access to professional literature databases to answer research requirements
- Copy and paste functions
- A spellchecker to correct written communications
- The research screen now has a "back" button to allow you to visit previously viewed screens.

In addition, the resource tab provides other resources that may be needed to complete the problem. For example, a resource tab might contain a present value table for use in answering a lease problem.

A window on the screen shows the time remaining for the entire section and the "Help" button provides instructions for navigating the simulation and completing the requirements.

The AICPA has introduced a new simulation interface which is illustrated in this manual. You are urged to complete the tutorial and other sample tests that are on the AICPA's Web site (www.cpa-exam.org) to obtain additional experience with the interface and computer-based testing.

### *Simulations Solutions Approach Algorithm*

The following solutions approach is suggested for answering simulations:

1. **Review the entire problem.** Tab through the problem in order to get a feel for the topical area and related concepts that are being tested. Even though the format of the question may vary, the exam continues to test your understanding of applicable principles or concepts. Relax, take a deep breath, and determine your strategy for conquering the simulation.
2. **Identify the requirements of the problem.** This step will help you focus in more quickly on the solution(s) without wasting time reading irrelevant material.
3. **Study the items to be answered.** As you do this and become familiar with the topical area being tested, you should review the concepts of that area. This will help you organize your thoughts so that you can relate logically the requirements of the simulation with the applicable concepts.
4. **Answer each tab requirement one at a time.** If the requirements don't build on one another, don't be afraid to answer the tab requirements out of order. Also, if the scenario is long or complex, you may wish to use the split screen function to enable you to view the simulation situation while answering a requirement.
5. **Use the scratch paper (which will be provided) and the spreadsheet and calculator tools to assist you in answering the simulation. Instructions for the use of common spreadsheet operators and functions are shown below.**

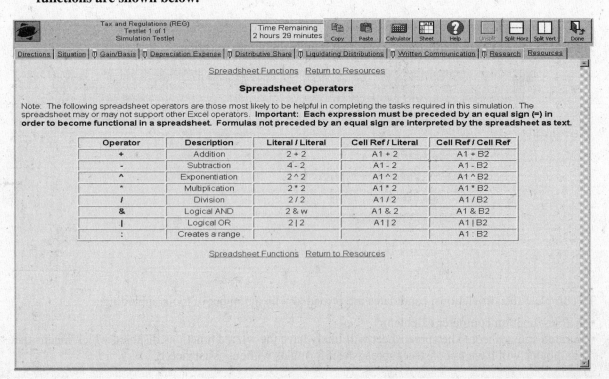

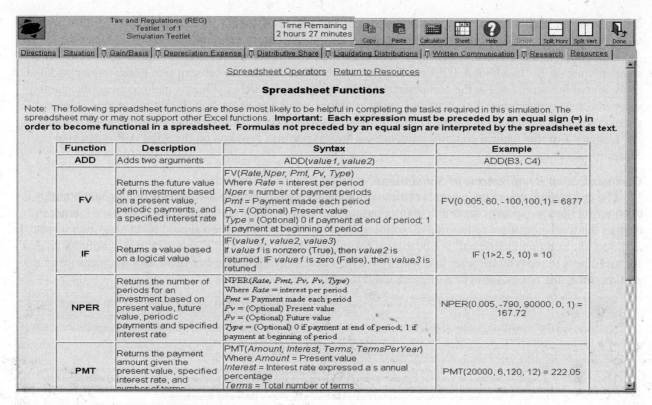

## Research Components of Simulations

All simulations will include a research component. Research components of simulations require candidates to search the professional literature in electronic format and interpret the results. In the auditing section the professional literature database includes

- Statements on Auditing Standards and Interpretations
- Statements on Attestation Standards and Interpretations
- Statements on Standards for Accounting and Review Services and Interpretations
- Statements on Standards for Quality Control

Shown below is a screenshot of the research page for the Auditing and Attestation section of the CPA examination.

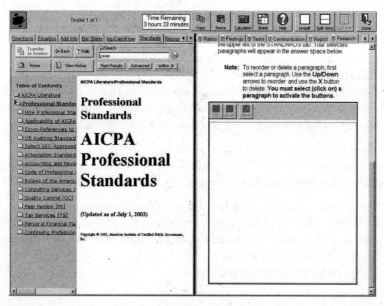

The professional literature may be searched using the table of contents or a keyword search. **If you use the search function, you must spell the term or terms correctly.** In using the table of contents, you simply click on the applicable standards and it expands to the next level of detail. By continuing to drill-down you will get the topic or professional standard that provides the solution to the requirement.

If possible, it is important to get experience using the AICPA Resource: Accounting and Auditing to sharpen your skills. In addition, CPA candidates can get a free six-month subscription to the online package of professional literature used in the computerized CPA examination. Other students and recent graduates may subscribe at a special price. Subscriptions are available at www.cpa-exam.org. If that is not available, you should use the printed copy of the professional standards to answer the simulation problems in the manual.

Chapter 5 of this manual contains guidance on how to perform research on the AICPA Professional Standards database.

### *Communication Requirements of Simulations*

The communications requirements of simulations will involve some real-world writing assignment that a CPA might have to perform, such as a memorandum to a client explaining an auditing issue, or a memorandum to the working papers addressing an auditing issue. The communication should be in your own words. In addition, the communication will not be graded for technical accuracy. If it is relevant, it will only be graded for usefulness to the intended user and writing skills. The following screenshot illustrates a screenshot of a part requiring the composition of a memorandum to a junior accountant.

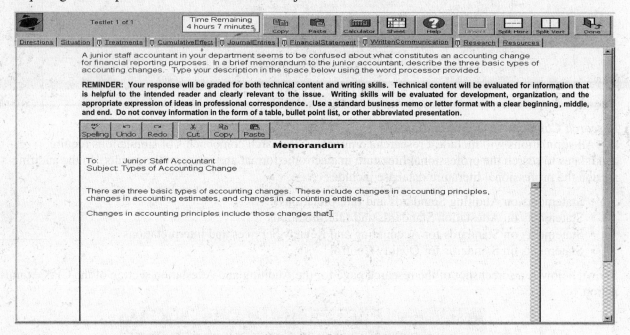

Candidates' writing skills will be graded according to the following criteria:
1. **Coherent organization**

   Candidates should organize their responses in a manner that is logical and easy to follow. Jumbled paragraphs and disorderly sentences will only confuse the grader and make his/her job more difficult. The following techniques will help improve written coherence.[1]

   - Use short paragraphs composed of short sentences
   - Indent paragraphs to set off lists, equations, key ideas, etc. when appropriate
   - Maintain coherence **within** paragraphs

     - Use a topic sentence at the beginning of each paragraph
     - Develop and support this topic throughout the rest of the paragraph
     - Present old or given information before discussing new information
     - Discuss ideas in chronological order
     - Use parallel grammatical structure

---

[1] *Adapted from **Writing for Accountants** by Aletha S. Hendrickson (Cincinnati, OH: Southwestern Publishing Co., 1993) pp.128-209.*

- Be consistent in person, verb tense, and number
- Substitute pronouns or synonyms for previously used keywords
- Use transitions (e.g., therefore, finally)

• Maintain coherence **between** paragraphs

- Repeat keywords from previous paragraph
- Use transitions

Candidates are strongly advised to keyword outline their responses **before** writing their communications.  This technique helps the candidate to focus on the flow of ideas s/he wants to convey before starting the actual writing task.

2.  **Conciseness**

Candidates should express themselves in as few words as possible.  Complex, wordy sentences are hard to understand.  Conciseness can be improved using the following guidelines.

- Write in short sentences
- Use a simple word instead of a long word if it serves the same purpose
- Avoid passive constructions (e.g., **was** evaluat**ed**)
- Use words instead of phrases
- Combine sentences, if possible
- Avoid empty fillers (e.g., **it is** apparent; **there seems to be**)
- Avoid multiple negatives (e.g., **no** reason for **not** using)

3.  **Clarity**

Written responses should leave no doubt in the reader's mind as to the meaning intended.  Clarity can be improved as follows:

- Do **not** use abbreviations
- Use correct terminology
- Use words with specific and precise meanings
- Write in short, well-constructed sentences
- Make sure subjects and verbs agree in number
- Make sure pronouns and their antecedents agree in number (e.g., the partnership must decide how **it** (not **they**) wants to split profits.)
- Avoid unclear reference to a pronoun's antecedent (e.g., the comptroller should inform the auditor that **he** must mail confirmations. -- Who does "he" refer to?)

4.  **Use of standard English**

Spelling, punctuation, and word usage should follow the norm used in most books, newspapers, and magazines.  Note the following common mistakes:

- Confusion of its/it's
  *The firm had **its** audit.*
  ***It's** (it is) an audit of the firm.*

- Confusion of there/their/they're
  ***There** will be an audit.*
  ***Their** audit was last week.*
  ***They're** (they are) auditing the firm.*

- Spelling errors
  *Separate **not** seperate*
  *Receivable **not** recievable*

The word processing software that you will use to write the communication on the exam will have a spell-checker function.  Use it.

5.  **Appropriateness for the reader**

Candidates will be asked to prepare a communication for a certain reader (e.g., a memorandum for a client).  Writing that is appropriate for the reader will take into account the reader's background, knowledge of the subject, interests, and concerns.  (When the intended reader is not specified, the candidate should write for a knowledgeable CPA.)

Intended readers may include those who are unfamiliar with most terms and concepts, and who seek financial information because of self-interest (i.e., clients, stockholders).  Try the following techniques for these readers:

- Avoid jargon, if possible (i.e., GAAP, etc.)
- Use parenthetical definitions

  - *unearned revenues (advance payments by customers)*
  - *marketable equity securities (short-term investments in stock)*

- Set off definitions as appositives

  *The lag, the time between the receipt and deposit of cash, needs to be shortened.*

- Incorporate a "you" attitude

The requirement of a question may also specify that the response should be directed to professionals who are knowledgeable of most terms and concepts.  Employ the following techniques with these readers:

- Use jargon
- Refer to authoritative sources (i.e., FASB pronouncements, SAS)
- Incorporate a "we" attitude

Again, preparing a keyword outline will assist you in meeting many of these requirements.  You should also reread each written communication in its entirety.  Writing errors are common during the exam, so take your time to proofread and edit your answers.  Again, make use of the spell check function of the word processing software if it is available.

## *Methods for Improving Your Writing Skills*

1. **Organization**

   Logical organization is very important  Again, this is where the keyword outline helps.

2. **Syntax, grammar, and style**

   By the time you sit for the CPA exam, you have at your disposal various grammatical constructs from which you may form sentences.  Believe it or not, you know quite a bit of English grammar; if you did not, you would never have made it this far in your studies.  So in terms of your grammar, relax!  You already know it.

   A frequent problem with writing occurs with the syntactic structure of sentences.  Although the Board of Examiners does not expect the rhetoric of Cicero, it does expect to read and understand your answer.

   a.   Basic syntactic structure (transitive and intransitive action verbs)

   Most English sentences are based on this simple dynamic:  that someone or something (the subject) does some action (the predicate).  These sentences involve action verbs and are grouped in the following categories:

   (1)   Subject-Verb

   *The AUDITOR WAITED for 3 weeks to get all the confirmations back.*

   (2)   Subject-Verb-Direct Object (The object receives the action of the verb.)

   *The ACCOUNTANT CALCULATED an AGING SCHEDULE.*

   (3)   Subject-Verb-Indirect Object-Direct Object (The direct object receives the action of the verb, but the indirect object is also affected by this action, though not in the same way as the direct object.)

   *Our CPA GAVE US our INCOME TAX RETURN well before the April 15 deadline.*

   b.   Syntactic structure (linking verbs)

   Linking verbs are verbs which, rather than expressing action, say something about the subject's state of being.  In sentences with linking verbs, the subject is linked to a work which describes it or renames it.

   (1)   Subject-Linking Verb-Nominative (The nominative renames the subject.)

   *In the field of Accounting, the FASB IS the standard-setting BOARD.*

(2)   Subject-Linking Verb-Adjective (The adjective describes the subject.)

> *An amortization SCHEDULE IS always HELPFUL in determining interest payments.*

c.   Subordinate clauses

(1)   Adverbial clauses (subordinating connector + sentence).  These clauses modify the action of the main clause.

> *When a related-party transaction occurs, it must be disclosed in the footnotes to the financial statements.*

(2)   Noun clauses (nominal connectors + sentence).  These clauses function as nouns in the main sentence.

> *In pension accounting, we know that excessive unrecognized gains and losses must be amortized.*

(3)   Adjective clauses [relative pronoun + verb + (object/nominative/adjective)].  These clauses function as noun modifiers.

> *The variance which shows the greatest amount of underapplied overhead is the production volume variance.*

d.   The above are patterns which form basic clauses (both dependent and independent).  In addition, numerous phrases may function as modifiers of the basic sentence elements.

(1)   Prepositional (a preposition + an object)

> *of the FASB*
> *on the data*
> *about a new type of depreciation*

(2)   Verbal

(a)   Verb + ing + a modifier (noun, verb, adverb, prepositional phrase)

i]   Used as an adjective

> *the discount requiring amortization*
> *the option maximizing operating income*

ii]   Used as a noun (gerund)

> *Consolidating the balance sheets of an entity's subsidiaries is difficult and time-consuming.*

(b)   Verb + ed + modifier (noun, adverb, prepositional phrase)

i]   Used as an adjective

> *The method of depreciation used for tax purposes is MACRS.*

(c)   Infinitive (to + verb + object)

i]   Used as a noun

> *The company needs to depreciate that asset over five years.*

4.   **Sentence clarity**

a.   When constructing your sentences, do not separate basic sentence elements with too many phrases.

> *The amortization of unrecognized gains and losses falling outside of a predetermined corridor value is another component of pension cost.*

> **Better:** *One component of pension cost is the amortization of unrecognized gains and losses which fall outside a predetermined corridor value.*

b.   Refrain from lumping prepositional and infinitive phrases together.

> *The Exposure Draft by the FASB on the accounting for the restructuring of an entity due to troubled debt is very recent.*

> **Better:** *Accounting for troubled debt restructuring is the topic of the most recent FASB Exposure Draft.*

c.   Make sure that your pronouns have a clear and obvious referent.

> *When internal auditors perform tests of controls or perform substantive tests of the details of transactions and balances, they serve a special function.*

> **Better:** *When performing tests of controls and substantive tests, internal auditors serve a special function.*

d.    Make sure that any adjectival verbal phrase clearly modifies a noun stated in the sentence.

> *To reach this decision, each product's incremental revenue was compared to its incremental costs.*

> **Better:** *To reach this decision, we compared each product's incremental revenue with its incremental costs.*

### Time Requirements for the Solutions Approach

Many candidates bypass the solutions approach, because they feel it is too time-consuming. Actually, the solutions approach is a time-saver and, more importantly, it helps you prepare better solutions to all questions and simulations.

Without committing yourself to using the solutions approach, try it step-by-step on several questions and simulations. After you conscientiously go through the step-by-step routine a few times, you will begin to adopt and modify aspects of the technique which will benefit you. Subsequent usage will become subconscious and painless. The important point is that you must try the solutions approach several times to accrue any benefits.

In summary, the solutions approach may appear foreign and somewhat cumbersome. At the same time, if you have worked through the material in this chapter, you should have some appreciation for it. Develop the solutions approach by writing down the steps in the solutions approach algorithm at the beginning of this chapter, and keep them before you as you work CPA exam questions and problems. Remember that even though the suggested procedures appear **very structured** and **time-consuming,** integration of these procedures into your own style of problem solving will help improve **your** solutions approach. The next chapter discusses strategies for the overall examination.

---

**NOW IS THE TIME**
**TO MAKE YOUR COMMITMENT**

---

# 4 TAKING THE EXAMINATION

This chapter is concerned with developing an examination strategy (e.g., how to cope with the environment at the test center, time management, etc.).

## EXAMINATION STRATEGIES

Your performance during the examination is final and not subject to revision. While you may sit for the examination again if you are unsuccessful, the majority of your preparation will have to be repeated, requiring substantial, additional amounts of time. Thus, examination strategies (discussed in this chapter) that maximize your exam-taking efficiency are very important.

### Getting "Psyched Up"

The CPA exam is quite challenging and worthy of your best effort. Explicitly develop your own psychological strategy to get yourself "up" for the exam. Pace your study program such that you will be able to operate at peak performance when you are actually taking the exam. A significant advantage of the new computerized exam is that if you have scheduled early in a testing window and do not feel well, you can reschedule your sitting. However, once you start the exam, you cannot retake it in the same testing window, so do not leave the exam early. Do the best you can.

### Lodging, Meals, Exercise

If you must travel to the test center, make advance reservations for comfortable lodging convenient to the test center. Do not stay with friends, relatives, etc. Both uninterrupted sleep and total concentration on the exam are a must. Consider the following in making your lodging plans:

1. Proximity to the test center
2. Availability of meals and snacks
3. Recreational facilities

Plan your meal schedule to provide maximum energy and alertness during the day and maximum rest at night. Do not experiment with new foods, drinks, etc., around your scheduled date. Within reasonable limits, observe your normal eating and drinking habits. Recognize that overconsumption of coffee during the exam could lead to a hyperactive state and disaster. Likewise, overindulgence in alcohol to overcome nervousness and to induce sleep the night before might contribute to other difficulties the following morning.

Tenseness should be expected before and during the examination. Rely on a regular exercise program to unwind at the end of the day. As you select your lodging for the examination, try to accommodate your exercise pleasure (e.g., running, swimming etc.).

To relieve tension or stress while studying, try breathing or stretching exercises. Use these exercises before and during the examination to start and to keep your adrenaline flowing. Remain determined not to have to sit for the section another time.

In summary, the examination is likely to be both rigorous and fatiguing. Expect it and prepare for it by getting in shape, planning methods of relaxation during the exam and in the evening before, and finally, building the confidence and competence to complete the exam (successfully).

### Test Center and Procedures

If possible, visit the test center before the examination to assure knowledge of the location. Remember: no surprises. Having a general familiarity with the facilities will lessen anxiety prior to the examination. Talking to a recent veteran of the examination will give you background for the general examination procedures. **You must arrive at the testing center 30 minutes before your scheduled time.**

Upon completion of check-in at the test location, the candidate

- Is seated at a designated workstation
- Begins the exam after proctor launches the session
- Is monitored by a Test Center Administrator
- Is videotaped

Upon completion of the examination, the candidate

- Signs out
- Collects his/her belongings
- Turns in scratch paper
- Is given a Post Exam Information sheet

If you have any remaining questions regarding examination procedure, call or write your state board or go to Prometric's Web site at www.prometric.com.

### Allocation of Time

Budget your time. Time should be carefully allocated in an attempt to maximize points per minute. While you must develop your own strategy with respect to time allocation, some suggestions may be useful. Allocate 5 minutes to reading the instructions. When you begin the exam you will be given an inventory of the total number of testlets and simulations, including the suggested times. Budget your time based on this inventory.

Plan on spending 1 1/2 minutes working each of the individual multiple-choice questions. The time allocated to the simulations will vary. On the Auditing and Attestation section you can expect longer simulations with suggested times of about 45 minutes.

### Techniques for Time Management

The Auditing and Attestation section contains three testlets of multiple-choice questions with 30 questions each. As you complete each testlet keep track of how you performed in relation to the AICPA suggested time. The Auditing and Attestation section will also have two long simulations. After you finish the multiple-choice testlets, budget your time for the simulations based on your remaining time and the AICPA suggested times. For example, if you have 2 hours remaining to complete two simulations that each have the same AICPA suggested time, budget 1/2 hour for each simulation. Remember that you alone control your progress towards successfully completing this exam.

### Examination Rules

1. Prior to the start of the examination, you will be required to sign a *Statement of Confidentiality*.
2. You will not be allowed to take any materials with you. Lockers will be provided for your personal effects. Any reference during the examination to books or other materials or the exchange of information with other persons shall be considered misconduct sufficient to bar you from further participation in the examination.
3. Penalties will be imposed on any candidate who is caught cheating before, during, or after the examination. These penalties may include expulsion from the examination, denial of applications for future examinations, and civil or criminal penalties.
4. You may not leave the examination room with any notes about the examination.

Refer to the brochure *Information for Uniform CPA Examination Candidates* for other rules.

## CPA EXAM CHECKLIST

**One week before you are scheduled to sit**

___ 1. Reread outlines (your own or those in this volume) of most important SASs, underlining buzzwords.

___ 2. If time permits, work through a few questions in your weakest areas so that techniques/concepts are fresh in your mind.

___ 3. Assemble notecards and key outlines of major topical areas into a manageable "last review" notebook to be taken with you to the exam.

**What to bring**

___ 1. *Notice to Schedule (NTS)*—You must bring the proper NTS with you.

___ 2. *Identification*—Bring two valid forms of ID. One must be government issued. The name on the ID must match exactly the name on the NTS. The CPA Candidate bulletin lists valid primary and secondary IDs.

___ 3. *Hotel confirmation*—(if you must travel).

___ 4. *Cash*—Payment for anything by personal check is rarely accepted.

___ 5. *Major credit card*—American Express, Master Card, Visa, etc.

___ 6. *Alarm clock*—This is too important an event to trust to a hotel wake-up call that might be overlooked.

___ 7. *Clothing*—Should be comfortable and layered to suit the possible temperature range in the testing room.

___ 8. *Earplugs*—Even though examinations are being given, there may be constant activity in the testing room (e.g., people walking around, rustling of paper, clicking of keyboards, people coughing, etc.). The use of earplugs may block out some of this distraction and help you concentrate better.

___ 9. *Other*—Any "Last review" materials.

## Evenings before exams

1. Reviewing the evening before the exam could earn you the extra points needed to pass a section. Just keep this last-minute effort in perspective and do **not** panic yourself into staying up all night trying to cover every possible point. This could lead to disaster by sapping your body of the endurance needed to attack questions creatively during the next day.

2. Reread key outlines or notecards, reviewing important topics in which you feel deficient.

3. Go over mnemonics and acronyms you have developed as study aids. Test yourself by writing out the letters on paper while verbally giving a brief explanation of what the letters stand for.

4. Reread key outlines of important SASs.

5. **Set your alarm and get a good night's rest!** Being well rested will permit you to meet each day's challenge with a fresh burst of creative energy. You should arrive 30 minutes before your scheduled time.

## Exam-taking strategy

1. Review the AICPA suggested times for the testlets and simulations to plan your time allocation during the exam.

2. The crucial technique to use for auditing and attestation simulation questions is to read each question **carefully,** noting keywords such as "most," "least," "primary," "special report," "interim report," etc. Then **read each choice** before you start eliminating inappropriate answers. In auditing and attestation, often the first or second answer may **sound** correct, but a later answer may be **more correct**! Be discriminating! Never choose answer (a) or (b) **before** reading (c) and (d).

3. If you are struggling with questions beyond your time limit, use the strategy of dividing simulation questions into two categories.

   a. Questions for which you **know** you lack knowledge to answer: Drawing from any resources you have, narrow answers down to as few as possible; then make an **educated guess**.

   b. Questions for which you feel you should be getting the correct answer: Mark the question for review. Your mental block may clear, or you may spot a simple error in logic that now can be corrected.

4. Remember: **never** change a first impulse question answer later unless you are **absolutely certain** you are right. It is a proven fact that your subconscious often guides you to the correct answer.

5. Begin the simulations, carefully monitoring your time. Read all requirement tabs and organize your thoughts around the key concepts, mnemonics, acronyms, and buzzwords that are responsive to the requirements. Use the solutions approach as highlighted in Chapter 1, including keyword outlines for any communication requirements.

6. Constantly compare your progress with the time remaining. **Never** spend excessive amounts of time on one testlet or simulation.

7. The cardinal rule is **never,** but **never,** leave an answer blank.

## HAVE YOU MADE YOUR COMMITMENT?

# 5 AUDITING AND ATTESTATION

## Introduction

## Module 1/Engagement Planning (ENPL)

## Module 2/Internal Control (IC)

## Module 3/Evidence (EVID)

## Module 4/Reporting (REPT)

# SUMMARY OF AUDITING AND ATTESTATION TOPICS TESTED

The Auditing & Attestation section of the CPA exam tests the candidate's knowledge primarily of generally accepted auditing standards (GAAS) and procedures as they relate to the CPA's functions in the examination of financial statements. However, the section also covers accounting and review services, other attestation services, and quality control standards. You will increase your chances for success if you have a recent copy of the codification of the Statements on Auditing Standards, Statements on Standards for Accounting and Review Services, Statements on Standards for Attestation Engagements, and Statements on Quality Control Standards. The codified versions, as opposed to the original pronouncements as issued, eliminates all superseded portions. The AICPA publishes the codification as the *AICPA Professional Standards*. Many university bookstores carry this source, as it is often required in undergraduate auditing courses. An auditing textbook is also helpful.

This chapter reviews topics tested on the Auditing section of the exam. Begin by performing a self-evaluation as suggested in the "self-study program" which appears in Chapter 1 of this volume. After studying each module in this volume, work all of the multiple-choice questions and the essay and simulation-style problems.

Recognize that most candidates have difficulty with audit sampling and auditing with technology due to limited exposure in their undergraduate programs and in practice. Thus, you should work through the outlines presented in each study module and work the related questions. Unfortunately, this entire volume would be required to provide comprehensive textbook coverage of topics tested on the exam.

## *AICPA Content Specification Outline*

The AICPA Content Specification Outline of the coverage of Auditing and Attestation appears below.

## AICPA CONTENT SPECIFICATION OUTLINE: AUDITING & ATTESTATION

I. Plan the Engagement, Evaluate the Prospective Client and Engagement, Decide Whether to Accept or Continue the Client and the Engagement, and Enter into an Agreement with the Client **(22%-28%)**

    A. Determine Nature and Scope of Engagement

        1. Auditing Standards Generally Accepted in the United States of America (GAAS)

        2. Standards for Accounting and Review Services

        3. Standards for Attestation Engagements

        4. Compliance Auditing Applicable to Governmental Entities and Other Recipients of Governmental Financial Assistance

        5. Other Assurance Services

        6. Appropriateness of Engagement to Meet Client's Needs

    B. Assess Engagement Risk and the CPA Firm's Ability to Perform the Engagement

        1. Engagement Responsibilities

        2. Staffing and Supervision Requirements

        3. Quality Control Considerations

        4. Management Integrity

        5. Researching Information Sources for Planning and Performing the Engagement

    C. Communicate with the Predecessor Accountant or Auditor

    D. Decide Whether to Accept or Continue the Client and Engagement

    E. Enter into an Agreement with the Client about the Terms of the Engagement

    F. Obtain an Understanding of the Client's Operations, Business, and Industry

    G. Perform Analytical Procedures

    H. Consider Preliminary Engagement Materiality

    I. Assess Inherent Risk and Risk of Misstatements from Errors, Fraud, and Illegal Acts by Clients

    J. Consider Other Planning Matters

        1. Using the Work of Other Independent Auditors

        2. Using the Work of a Specialist

        3. Internal Audit Function

        4. Related Parties and Related-Party Transactions

        5. Electronic Evidence

        6. Risks of Auditing Around the Computer

    K. Identify Financial Statement Assertions and Formulate Audit Objectives

        1. Significant Financial Statement Balances, Classes of Transactions, and Disclosures

        2. Accounting Estimates

    L. Determine and Prepare the Work Program Defining the Nature, Timing, and Extent of the Procedures to Be Applied

II. Consider Internal Control in Both Manual and Computerized Environments **(12%-18%)**

    A. Obtain an Understanding of Business Processes and Information Flows

    B. Identify Controls that Might Be Effective in Preventing or Detecting Misstatements

    C. Document an Understanding of Internal Control

    D. Consider Limitations of Internal Control

    E. Consider the Effects of Service Organizations on Internal Control

    F. Perform Tests of Controls

    G. Assess Control Risk

III. Obtain and Document Information to Form a Basis for Conclusions **(32%-38%)**

    A. Perform Planned Procedures

        1. Applications of Audit Sampling

        2. Analytical Procedures

        3. Confirmation of Balances and/or Transactions with Third Parties

        4. Physical Examination of Inventories and Other Assets

        5. Other Tests of Details

        6. Computer-Assisted Audit Techniques, Including Data Interrogation, Extraction, and Analysis

        7. Substantive Tests before the Balance Sheet Date

        8. Tests of Unusual Year-End Transactions

    B. Evaluate Contingencies

    C. Obtain and Evaluate Lawyers' Letters

    D. Review Subsequent Events

    E. Obtain Representations from Management

    F. Identify Reportable Conditions and Other Control Deficiencies

    G. Identify Matters for Communication with Audit Committees

    H. Perform Procedures for Accounting and Review Services Engagements

    I. Perform Procedures for Attestation engagements

IV. Review the Engagement to Provide Reasonable Assurance That Objectives Are Achieved and Evaluate Information Obtained to Reach and to Document Engagement Conclusions **(8%-12%)**

    A. Perform Analytical Procedures

    B. Evaluate the Sufficiency and Competence of Audit Evidence and Document Engagement Conclusions

    C. Evaluate Whether Financial Statements Are Free of Material Misstatements

    D. Consider Whether Substantial Doubt about an Entity's Ability to Continue as a Going Concern Exists

    E. Consider Other Information in Documents Containing Audited Financial Statements

    F. Review the Work Performed to Provide Reasonable Assurance That Objectives Are Achieved

V. Prepare Communications to Satisfy Engagement Objectives **(12%-18%)**

    A. Reports

        1. Reports on Audited Financial Statements

        2. Reports on Reviewed and Compiled Financial Statements

        3. Reports Required by *Government Auditing Standards*

        4. Reports on Compliance with Laws and Regulations

        5. Reports on Internal Control

        6. Reports on Prospective Financial Information

        7. Reports on Agreed-Upon Procedures

        8. Reports on the Processing of Transactions by Service Organizations

        9. Reports on Supplementary Financial Information

      10. Special Reports

      11. Reports on Other Assurance Services

      12. Reissuance of Reports

    B. Other Required Communications

        1. Errors and Fraud

        2. Illegal Acts

        3. Communication with Audit Committees

        4. Other Reporting Considerations Covered by Statements on Auditing Standards and Statements on Standards for Attestation Engagements

    C. Other Matters

        1. Subsequent Discovery of Facts Existing at the Date of the Auditor's Report

        2. Consideration after the Report Date of Omitted Procedures

## RESEARCHING AICPA PROFESSIONAL STANDARDS

    Research components of simulations in the Auditing and Attestation section will involve a research database that includes

- Statements on Auditing Standards and Interpretations
- Statements on Attestation Standards and Interpretations
- Statements on Standards for Accounting and Review Services and Interpretations
- Statements on Standards for Quality Control

### *The AICPA Professional Standards*

    The AICPA Professional Standards include standards and interpretations issued by senior technical committees of the AICPA (e.g., the Auditing Standards Board). Standards are developed through a due process that includes deliberation in meetings open to the public, public exposure of proposed standards, and a formal vote. Interpretations are not standards, but are issued by the committees to provide recommendations on the application of a particular standard. The codification of the AICPA Professional Standards is shown below.

**Codification of AICPA Professional Standards**

|                                                                                 | *Citation* |
|---------------------------------------------------------------------------------|------------|
| Statements on Auditing Standards                                                | AU Sec.    |
|    Introduction                                                   | 100        |
|    The General Standards                                          | 200        |
|    The Standards of Field Work                                    | 300        |
|    The First, Second, and Third Standards of Reporting            | 400        |
|    The Fourth Standard of Reporting                               | 500        |
|    Other Types of Reports                                         | 600        |
|    Special Topics                                                 | 700        |
|    Compliance Auditing                                            | 800        |
|    Special Reports of the Committee on Auditing Procedures        | 900        |
| Statements on Standards for Attestation Engagements                             | AT Sec.    |
|    Attestation Standards                                          | 101        |
|    Agreed-upon Procedures Engagements                             | 201        |
|    Financial Forecasts and Protections                            | 301        |
|    Reporting on Pro Forma Financial Information                   | 401        |
|    Reporting on an Entity's Internal Control Structure Over Financial Reporting | 501 |
|    Compliance Attestation                                         | 601        |
|    Management's Discussion and Analysis                           | 701        |
| Statements on Standards for Accounting and Review Services                      | AR Sec.    |
|    Compilation and Review of Financial Statements                 | 100        |
|    Reporting on Comparative Financial Statements                  | 200        |
|    Compilation Reports on Financial Statements Included in Certain Prescribed Forms | 300 |
|    Communications between Predecessor and Successor Accountants   | 400        |
|    Reporting on Compiled Financial Statements                     | 500        |
|    Reporting on Personal Financial Statements Included in Written Personal Financial Plans | 600 |
| Code of Professional Conduct                                                    | ET         |
| Bylaws of the AICPA                                                             | BL         |
| Quality Control                                                                 | QC         |

There are two ways to cite a professional standard

1. Using the original standard number (e.g., Statement on Auditing Standards No. 39, paragraph 12 and 14).
2. Using the section numbers (e.g., AU section 350.12 - .14).

## Database Searching

Searching a database consists of the following five steps:

1. Define the issue. What is the research question to be answered?
2. Select the database to search (e.g., the Statement on Auditing Standards and Interpretations).
3. Choose a keyword or table of contents search.
4. Execute the search. Enter the keyword(s) or click on the appropriate table of contents item and complete the search.
5. Evaluate the results. Evaluate the research to see if an answer has been found. If not, try a new search.

## Advanced Searches

When performing advanced searches it is useful to understand Boolean operators. Boolean operators allow you to make more precise queries of a database.

1. The Boolean "AND" narrows your search by retrieving only cites that contain every one of the keywords listed.

    *EXAMPLE:  Confirmation AND Receivables*

    This query would only retrieve cites that include both confirmation and receivables.
2. The Boolean "OR" actually expands your search by retrieving all cites that contain either or both of the keywords.

    *EXAMPLE:  Receivables OR Sales*

    This query would retrieve cites that include either receivables or sales or both.
3. The Boolean "NOT" narrows your search by retrieving only cites that containing the first keyword but not the second.

*EXAMPLE: Confirmation NOT Receivables*

This query would retrieve cites that include confirmation but not receivables.

## OVERVIEW OF THE ATTEST FUNCTION

In this overview section the general nature of the attest function is first discussed. Second, the general nature of the attest function as it relates to financial statement information is discussed. Third, a diagram is provided for understanding the nature of audits of financial statements. A section on generally accepted auditing standards (GAAS) and Statements on Auditing Standards (SAS) follows.

### Attest Function—General Nature

In an attest engagement a CPA is engaged to issue or does issue an examination, a review, or an agreed-upon procedures report on *subject matter*, or an *assertion* about subject matter, that is the responsibility of another party. An attestation engagement may be performed under either generally accepted accounting principles (for historical financial statements and related information) **or** the attestation standards (for other information). Both the ten generally accepted auditing standards and the eleven attestation standards are presented later in this chapter.

The need for independent third-party attestation arises due to possible differences between management and others (stockholders, the government, etc.) as to

1.  Beliefs regarding activities in which the firm should engage
2.  Beliefs regarding the manner in which these activities should be performed
3.  Reward structures (management's pay, at least in part, is a salary while investors receive interest dividends, and/or capital gains)

As a starting point to thinking about the attest function, consider both the preparation of financial statements and the performance of an audit of those financial statements. The preparation of financial statements may be viewed as consisting of inputs (source documents) being processed (through use of journals, ledgers, etc.) to arrive at an output (the financial information itself). Or shown diagrammatically

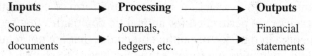

While CPAs often assist in the preparation of the financial statements, the attestation function conceptually begins with financial statements having been prepared by management. The purpose of a CPA financial statement audit is to provide assurance that financial statements which have been prepared by management follow appropriate criteria—usually generally accepted accounting principles, but sometimes other criteria such as the cash or tax bases of accounting.

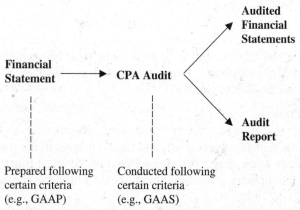

In performing an audit engagement, a CPA collects various types of evidence relating to the propriety of the recording of economic events and transactions. For financial statements, this evidence will support the assertions that the assets listed in the balance sheet actually exist, that the company has title to these assets, and that the valuations assigned to these assets have been established in conformity with generally accepted accounting principles. The evidence gathered will also show that the balance sheet contains all the liabilities of the company and that the notes to the financial statements include the needed disclosures. Similarly, a CPA will gather evidence about the income statement and the statement of cash flows. In short, the attest function provides assurance for the overall assertion that the financial statements follow generally accepted accounting principles.

It is helpful to generalize the discussion to information other than financial statements covered by the attestation standards as follows:

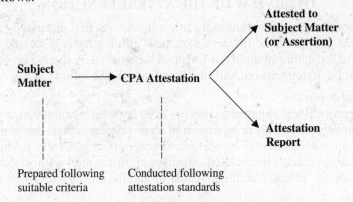

The attestation standards establish three forms of CPA attestation engagements—examinations, reviews, and the performance of agreed-upon procedures. An **examination**, referred to as an **audit** when it involves financial statements, normally results in a positive opinion, the highest form of assurance provided. When performing an examination, the CPAs select from all available evidence a combination that limits to a low level of risk the chance of material misstatement. A **review** is substantially less in scope than an audit and normally provides negative assurance ("nothing came to our attention") rather than a positive opinion with respect to whether the information follows the appropriate criteria. (Negative assurance is also referred to as "limited assurance.") For the third form of attestation engagement, a CPA and a specified party that wishes to use the information may mutually decide on specific **agreed-upon procedures** that the CPA will perform. Agreed-upon procedures engagements result in a report that describes the procedures performed and related findings.

CPAs may also provide nonattestation services to clients in the form of **compilation** and unaudited statement services. Compilation services are performed for nonpublic companies that seek assistance in the preparation of financial statements. In the case of public companies that are not required to have audits (primarily certain utilities, banks, etc., which do not report to the Securities Exchange Commission) similar assistance may be obtained through CPA preparation of **unaudited** statements. For both compilations and unaudited statements, note that the CPA's primary role is to prepare the financial statements, an accounting as opposed to an attestation function (in fact, in the case of compilations, independence is not required). Accordingly, in both cases the CPA's report disclaims any opinion and gives no assurances with respect to whether the statements comply with the appropriate criteria. (The Evidence and Reporting Modules discuss these forms of association in further detail.)

Finally, note that while attestation (i.e., reviewing and/or auditing) is often considered an area within accounting, it is probably more accurate to consider it a separate function that provides assurance (attests) to the accuracy of the outputs generated by the accounting process. One must be an accountant to be an auditor (or reviewer), but one is not necessarily an auditor if one is an accountant. In other words, auditors must be proficient as auditors as well as proficient as accountants.

### *Expansions of the Attest Function*

The overall need of individuals and organizations for credible information, combined with changes currently taking place in information technology, is leading to rapid changes in the role of the public accounting profession. CPA firms are already embracing a broader concept of the attest function that is being referred to as the **assurance function,** which includes providing assurance on a broad variety of types of financial or nonfinancial information.

To develop a strategic plan for expansion of the assurance function, in 1994 the AICPA formed a *Special Committee on Assurance Services*—also referred to as the Elliott Committee. Although the Committee's charge is lengthy, it largely relates to analyzing and reporting on the current state and future of the audit/ assurance function and trends shaping the function's environment.

The Elliott Committee defined assurance services as: "Independent professional services that improve the quality of information, or its context, for decision makers." Assurance services include all attestation (including audit) services, plus a variety of other services which will be developed in the future; note, however, that tax and consulting services are not considered assurance services.  The Elliott Committee developed the following chart to compare attestation, assurance, and consulting services:

|  | Attestation | Assurance | Consulting |
|---|---|---|---|
| **Result** | Written conclusion about the reliability of the written assertions of another party. | Better information for decision makers.  Recommendations might be a by-product. | Recommendations based on the objectives of the engagement. |
| **Objective** | Reliable information. | Better decision making. | Better outcomes. |
| **Parties to the engagement** | Not specified, but generally three (the third party is usually external); CPA generally paid by the preparer. | Generally three (although the other two might be employed by the same entity); CPA paid by the preparer or user. | Generally two; CPA paid by the user. |
| **Independence** | Required by standards. | Included in definition. | Not required. |
| **Substance of CPA output** | Conformity with established or stated criteria. | Assurance about reliability or relevance of information.  Criteria might be established, stated, or unstated. | Recommendations; not measured against formal criteria. |
| **Form of CPA output** | Written. | Some form of communication. | Written or oral. |
| **Critical information developed by** | Asserter. | Either CPA or asserter. | CPA. |
| **Information content determined by** | Preparer (client). | Preparer, CPA, or user. | CPA. |
| **Level of assurance** | Examination, review, or agreed-upon procedures. | Flexible; for example, it might be compilation level, explicit assurance about usefulness of the information for intended purpose, or implicit from the CPA's involvement. | No explicit assurance. |

The Elliott Committee has led the profession to consideration of expansion into a variety of areas, with current particular emphasis on the following:

- **Risk assessment**—Providing assurance that an entity's profile of business risks is comprehensive and that the company has appropriate systems in place to effectively manage those risks.
- **Business performance measurement**—Evaluating whether an entity's performance measurement system contains relevant and reliable measures for assessing the degree to which the entity's goals and objectives are achieved or how its performance compares to that of its competitors.
- **Information systems reliability**—Assessing whether an entity's internal information systems (financial and nonfinancial) provide reliable information for operating and financial decisions.
- **Electronic commerce**—Assessing whether systems and tools used in electronic commerce provide appropriate data integrity, security, privacy, and reliability.
- **Health care performance measurement**—Providing assurance about the effectiveness of health care services provided by health maintenance organizations, hospitals, doctors, and other providers.
- **ElderCare**—Assessing whether specified goals regarding care for the elderly are being met by various caregivers.

The Assurance Services Executive Committee (ASEC) identifies, develops, and communicates new assurance service opportunities for CPAs.  The committee is using the work of the Elliott Committee as a starting point.  The first service developed was WebTrust, a service aimed at providing assurance on Web sites—the Reporting Module provides a description of the service.

For purposes of the CPA exam, you might expect a multiple-choice question or an essay question about the nature of assurance services.  Both the Elliott Committee's "report" and publications of the Assurance Services Executive Committee are available electronically on the AICPA home page (http://www.aicpa.org).

### Diagram of an Audit

In the audit process an auditor gathers evidence to support a professional opinion.  Sufficient competent evidential matter must be gathered to adequately restrict **audit risk,** the risk of unknowingly failing to appropriately modify the audit report on materially misstated financial statements.[1]  The following diagram outlines the steps in the evidence collection and evaluation process in which an auditor forms an opinion:

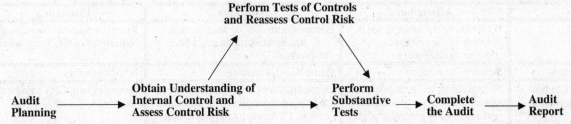

**Audit Planning.**  While planning continues throughout the audit, the objective of this first phase is to obtain an overall understanding of the entity being audited, and to develop an overall strategy for the expected conduct and scope of the audit.  A primary goal is to assess inherent risk—the likelihood of material misstatements, assuming no related internal control—related to various accounts as well as the level of risk associated with the overall engagement.  In addition, an important part of the planning process involves the initial identification of risk of material misstatement due to fraud.  Evidence gathered includes information about the entity's characteristics and the characteristics of its industry.  Also, analytical procedures are required at this stage to assist in planning the nature, timing, and extent of audit procedures.

**Internal Control—General.**  The second generally accepted auditing standard of fieldwork requires a consideration of internal control.  The auditor's study of internal control has the two primary purposes of helping the auditor (1) to plan the audit and (2) to assess control risk, the risk that a material misstatement will not be prevented or detected on a timely basis by internal control.  Based on the results obtained while obtaining an understanding of internal control primarily for planning purposes, the auditor decides whether to perform tests of controls to possibly allow a reassessment of control risk.

**Obtain Understanding of Internal Control and Assess Control Risk.**  The auditor obtains an understanding of internal control and documents this understanding using memoranda, questionnaires, checklists, flowcharts, and/or decision tables.  The emphasis at this stage is usually on obtaining an understanding of how internal control is purported to function to allow further planning of the audit.  Indeed, it is difficult to imagine planning an audit without understanding the essentials of the internal control.

While obtaining an understanding of the system, the auditor may or may not have chosen to perform **tests of controls** to evaluate the effectiveness of the design and operation of controls.  For example, for a continuing client, the auditor may understand the controls well enough to perform some tests.  If tests of controls have been performed, the auditor may be able to assess control risk at somewhat below the maximum level; if tests of controls have not been performed, control risk will be assessed at the maximum level.

Regardless of whether any tests of controls have been performed at this stage, the auditor must decide whether to perform (more) tests to possibly allow a lower assessed level of control risk and thereby restrict substantive testing.  For controls that seem weak, a decision will be made to rely in large part on substantive tests—analytical procedures, and/or tests of details of transactions and balances.  On the other hand, if controls seem capable of preventing, detecting, and correcting material misstatements, the auditor must decide whether it is more cost effective to perform tests of controls or to directly perform substantive tests.

**Perform Tests of Controls and Reassess Control Risk.**  The objective of tests of controls is to evaluate whether internal control operated effectively, thereby supporting a lower assessed level of control risk.  The ultimate purpose of assessing control risk is to contribute to the auditor's evaluation of the risk that material misstatements exist in the financial statements.  Tests of controls are concerned with how the control was applied, the consistency with which it was applied, and by whom it was applied throughout the period being audited.  These tests ordinarily include evidence obtained through (1) inquiry of personnel, (2) inspection of documents and reports, (3) observation of the application of the control, and (4) reperformance of the control.  When tests of controls justify a lower assessed level of control risk, the scope of substantive testing may be reduced.

**Substantive Tests—General.**  Substantive tests are used to "substantiate" account balances.  Substantive tests restrict detection risk, the risk that audit procedures will incorrectly lead to a conclusion that a material misstatement does not exist in an account balance when in fact such a misstatement does exist.  While tests of control, as noted above, provide evidence as to whether controls are operating effectively, substantive tests

---

[1]  *The concept of audit risk and its components of inherent risk, control risk, and detection risk is presented briefly in this section and is discussed in detail in Section A.1.a. of the* **Engagement Planning** *Module.*

provide evidence as to whether actual account balances are proper.  The auditor's reliance on substantive tests to achieve an audit objective may be derived from (1) analytical procedures, (2) tests of details of transactions and balances, or a combination of both.

**Substantive Tests—Analytical Procedures.**  Analytical procedures used as substantive tests are used to obtain evidential matter about particular assertions related to account balances or classes of transactions.  In these tests auditors gather evidence about relationships among various accounting and nonaccounting data such as industry and economic information.  When unexpected changes occur (or expected changes do **not** occur) in these relationships, an auditor investigates further and obtains an explanation.  Ratio analysis is a frequently used analytical procedure.  The auditor would, for example, calculate a ratio and compare it to criteria such as budgets, prior year data, and industry data.

**Substantive Tests—Tests of Details of Transactions and Balances.**  The objective of these tests is to detect misstatements in the financial statements.  The details supporting financial statement accounts are tested to obtain assurance that material misstatements do not exist.  Sending confirmations for year-end receivable accounts is an example.

**Completing the Audit.**  Auditors perform a number of procedures near the end of the audit.  For example, evidence is aggregated and evaluated for sufficiency.  Analytical procedures are performed (again) to assist the auditor in assessing conclusions reached and for evaluating overall financial statement presentation.  Final decisions are made as to required financial statement disclosures and as to the appropriate audit report.

**Audit Report.**  A standard unqualified audit report is issued by CPAs when their examination and the results thereof are satisfactory.  It is also known as a "clean opinion" and is reproduced below.  This standard unqualified report is modified as the audit examination deviates from normal, or as the financial statements fail to comply with generally accepted accounting principles (GAAP).

Variations of the audit report include

1.  Standard unqualified
2.  Unqualified with additional explanatory language
3.  Qualified
4.  Disclaimer
5.  Adverse

The purposes and examples of each are outlined and illustrated in the Reporting Module of this chapter.

Read the standard unqualified report carefully, and note the key points made in it.  Remember, the audit report is the primary product of the audit.

*Independent Auditor's Report*

TO:     Board of Directors and Stockholders
        ABC Company

We have audited the accompanying balance sheets of ABC Company as of December 31, 20X1 and 20X0, and the related statements of income, retained earnings, and cash flows for the years then ended.  These financial statements are the responsibility of the Company's management.  Our responsibility is to express an opinion on these financial statements based on our audits.

We conducted our audits in accordance with US generally accepted auditing standards.  Those standards require that we plan and perform the audit to obtain reasonable assurance about whether the financial statements are free of material misstatement.  An audit includes examining, on a test basis, evidence supporting the amounts and disclosures in the financial statements.  An audit also includes assessing the accounting principles used and significant estimates made by management, as well as evaluating the overall financial statement presentation.  We believe that our audits provide a reasonable basis for our opinion.

In our opinion, the financial statements referred to above present fairly, in all material respects, the financial position of ABC Company as of December 31, 20X1 and 20X0, and the results of its operations and its cash flows for the years then ended in conformity with US generally accepted accounting principles.

Joe Smith, CPA
February 23, 20X2

Some key points in the above report include

Required Title ("Independent" must be in title)
Addressee (company, board of directors and/or stockholders—**not** management)
Introductory paragraph

1.  We have audited
2.  Client's financial statements (statements listed)
3.  Financial statements are the responsibility of management
4.  The auditor's responsibility is to express an opinion

Scope paragraph

1.  Audit conducted in accordance with GAAS of the United States of America[2]
2.  Those standards require that we plan and perform audit to provide reasonable assurance statements free of material misstatement
3.  Audit involves

    a.  Examining on a test basis evidence supporting amounts and disclosures
    b.  Assessment of accounting principles
    c.  Assessment of significant estimates
    d.  Evaluation of overall presentation

4.  Audit provides reasonable basis for opinion

Opinion paragraph

1.  In our opinion
2.  Statements fairly present per US GAAP[2]

Manual or printed signature (firm name)
Date (normally last day of fieldwork)

### Generally Accepted Auditing Standards

CPAs are to perform their examinations of financial statements in compliance with generally accepted auditing standards. The figure on the following page summarizes the ten generally accepted auditing standards; for comparative purposes, the eleven attestation standards are also presented. You should memorize the ten generally accepted auditing standards (also by category) for the exam. The following mnemonics provide one way to remember the standards:

TIP (Training, Independence, Professional Care)
PIE (Planning, Internal Control, Evidence)
GODC (GAAP, Opinion, Disclosure, Consistency)

*NOTE: To form the third mnemonic (god with a soft c), one must reorder the reporting standards—1, 4, 3, 2.*

The attestation standards relate to all attestation services performed by CPAs. The generally accepted auditing standards may be considered to be the appropriate interpretations as they relate to audits of financial statements. After you have memorized the generally accepted auditing standards, you will find that studying the attestation standards is easy since most are similar. Be familiar with the attestations standards since a question on them is likely.

**ATTESTATION STANDARDS AND GENERALLY ACCEPTED AUDITING STANDARDS**

| *Attestation Standards* | *Generally Accepted Auditing Standards* |
|---|---|
| *General Standards* | |
| 1.  The engagement shall be performed by a practitioner or practitioners having adequate technical **training** and proficiency in the attest function. | 1.  The audit is to be performed by a person or persons having adequate technical **training** and proficiency as an auditor. |
| 2.  The engagement shall be performed by a practitioner or practitioners having adequate **knowledge** in the subject matter of the assertion. | |
| 3.  The practitioner shall perform an engagement only if he or she has reason to believe that the subject matter is capable of reasonably consistent evaluation against criteria that are suitable and available to users. | |
| 4.  In all matters relating to the engagement, an **independence** in mental attitude shall be maintained by the practitioner or practitioners. | 2.  In all matters relating to the assignment, an **independence** in mental attitude is to be maintained by the auditor or auditors. |
| 5.  Due **professional care** shall be exercised in the performance of the engagement. | 3.  Due **professional care** is to be exercised in the planning and performance of the audit and the preparation of the report. |

---

[2]  *SAS 93 introduced a requirement that the CPA indicate the country of the accounting principles and auditing standards. The actual wording suggested is either*
*•  US generally accepted accounting principles (auditing standards) or*
*•  Auditing standards (accounting principles) generally accepted in the United States of America.*
*Throughout the text we will use the first form.*

*Standards of Fieldwork*

1. The work shall be adequately **planned** and assistants, if any, shall be properly supervised.

2. Sufficient **evidence** shall be obtained to provide a reasonable basis for the conclusion that is expressed in the report.

1. The work is to be adequately **planned** and assistants, if any, are to be properly supervised.

2. **A sufficient understanding of internal control is to be obtained to plan the audit and to determine the nature, timing, and extent of tests to be performed.**

3. Sufficient competent **evidential matter** is to be obtained through inspection, observation, inquiries, and confirmations to afford a reasonable basis for an opinion regarding the financial statements under audit.

*Standards of Reporting*

1. The report shall identify the subject matter or the assertion being reported on and state the character of the engagement

2. The report shall state the practitioner's conclusion about the subject matter or the assertion in relation to the criteria against which the subject matter was evaluated.

3. The report shall state all of the practitioner's significant reservations about the engagement, the subject matter, and if applicable, the assertion related thereto.

4. The report shall state that the use of the report is restricted to specified parties under the following circumstances:

   • When the criteria used to evaluate the subject matter are determined by the practitioner to be suitable only for a limited number of parties who either participated in their establishment or can be presumed to have an adequate understanding of the criteria.
   • When the criteria used to evaluate the subject matter are available only to specified parties.
   • When reporting on subject matter and a written assertion has not been provided by the responsible party.
   • When the report is on an attest engagement to apply agreed-upon procedures to the subject matter.

1. The report shall state whether the financial statements are presented in accordance with **generally accepted accounting principles.**

2. The report shall identify those circumstances in which such principles have not been consistently observed in the current period in relation to the preceding period.

3. Informative **disclosures** in the financial statements are to be regarded as reasonably adequate unless otherwise stated in the report.

4. The report shall either contain an expression of **opinion** regarding the financial statements, taken as a whole, or an assertion to the effect that an opinion cannot be expressed. When an overall opinion cannot be expressed, the reasons therefor should be stated. In all cases where an auditor's name is associated with financial statements, the report should contain a clear-cut indication of the character of the auditor's work, if any, and the degree of responsibility the auditor is taking.

# PROFESSIONAL STANDARDS

The Professional Standards most directly related to the Auditing and Attestation section of the CPA exam (hereafter AUDIT) are

- Statements on Auditing Standards
- Public Company Accounting Oversight Board Pronouncements
- Statements on Standards for Attestation Engagements
- Statements on Standards for Accounting and Review Services
- Statements on Quality Control Standards

## Statements on Auditing Standards

The Auditing Standards Board issues Statements on Auditing Standards that are considered interpretations of GAAS. Outlines of the SAS (except superseded sections) are presented after Module 6 in their codified order with an AU prefix. The manner in which you use these outlines depends upon your educational and practical auditing background. If you have previously read the SAS, you may be able to use the outlines directly without rereading the material. If you are unfamiliar with the SAS, you will probably need to read them, and either simultaneously study the outline, or use the outline to review the major points. In some circumstances you may find that although you haven't read the detailed SAS, your educational and/or practical experience makes studying the outline adequate. At the beginning of each module in this chapter, a study program will refer you to the appropriate SAS. At this point you may read the SAS either before beginning the module or when finished. Many AUDIT exam questions can be directly answered by the SAS outlines. One week before, you can use the outlines as a good review for the AUDIT section. The module presentation provides a summary of the most important information, generally that which has received extremely heavy coverage on past exams.

The SASs (and attestation standards) use two categories of requirements to described auditor responsibility for following a particular requirement.

- **Unconditional requirement**—the auditor must comply with the requirement in all cases in which the circumstances exist. SASs use the words *must* or *is required* to indicate an unconditional requirement.
- **Presumptively mandatory requirement**—Similarly, the auditor must comply with the requirement, but, in rare circumstances, the auditor may depart from such a requirement. In such circumstances, the

auditor documents the departure, the justification for the departure, and how the alternative procedures performed in the circumstances were sufficient. SASs use the word *should* to indicate a presumptively mandatory requirement.

As discussed earlier in this book, the CPA exam requires the candidates to be able to conduct electronic research of the professional standards. While in most circumstances candidates should expect to use the index or a keyword search to find the relevant topic, knowledge of the overall codified layout of the standards may be helpful. The following table presents the SAS sections in their codified order:

**AU 100**   **SASs—Introduction**

110  Responsibilities and Functions
150  GAAS

161  Relationship between GAAS and Quality Control Standards

**AU 200**   **General Standards**

201  Nature
210  First General Standard—Training and Proficiency

220  Second Gen. Standard—Independence
230  Third Gen. Standard—Due Professional Care

**AU 300**   **Standards of Fieldwork**

310  Appointment of the Independent Auditor
311  Planning and Supervision
312  Audit Risk and Materiality
313  Substantive Tests Prior to the Balance Sheet Date
315  Predecessor/Successor Auditors
316  Fraud
317  Illegal Acts
319  Internal Control
322  Internal Auditors
324  Service Organization
325  Commun. of Control Related Matters
326  Evidence
328  Fair Value Measurements and Disclosures

329  Analytical Procedures
330  Confirmation
331  Inventories
333  Representation Letters
334  Related-Party Transactions
337  Inquiries of Lawyer
339  Audit Documentation
341  Going Concern
342  Accounting Estimates
350  Audit Sampling
380  Communication with Audit Committees
390  Omitted Procedures

**AU 400**   **Reporting Standards 1, 2, and 3**

410  Adherence to GAAP
411  Meaning of Present Fairly

420  Consistency
431  Adequacy of Disclosure

**AU 500**   **Reporting Standard 4 (Opinion)**

504  Association with Financial Statements
508  Reports on Audited Financial Statements
530  Dating the Audit Report
532  Restricting Use of Audit Report
534  Reporting on Financial Statements for Use in Other Countries
543  Other Auditors
544  Lack of Conformity with GAAP

550  Other Information in Documents Containing Audited Statements
551  Auditor-Submitted Documents
552  Condensed Financial Statements
558  Required Supplementary Information
560  Subsequent Events
561  Subsequent Discovery of Facts Existing at Date of Audit Report

**AU 600**   **Other Types of Reports**

622  Agreed-Upon Procedures
623  Special Reports

625  Reports on Application of Accounting Principles
634  Letters for Underwriters

**AU 700**   **Special Topics**

711  Filings under Federal Securities Statutes

722  Interim Financial Information

**AU 800**   **Compliance Auditing**

801  Compliance Auditing

**AU 900**   **Special Reports of the Committee on Auditing Procedure**

901  Public Warehouses

The following sections may be particularly important for typical exams:

- AU 312 Audit risk and materiality
- AU 316 Auditor responsibilities with respect to fraud
- Various sections are helpful for audit reports, including

   AU 508—Most comprehensive section on types of reports (includes most sample reports, including consistency)
   AU 341—Going concern considerations and reporting (going concern sample paragraph modification)
   AU 420—Consistency
   ALL AU 500 and AU 600 sections, but somewhat less frequently

- Communicating on internal control with audit committees

  AU 325—Significant deficiencies (reportable conditions) and material weaknesses
  AU 380—Other accounting and auditing matters
  AT 501—Examination on internal control over financial reporting

- AU 701 Compliance auditing

The Appendix to this chapter presents the individual Statements on Auditing Standards in the order issued.

## Public Company Accounting Oversight Board Pronouncements

In the summer of 2002, in reaction to a number of corporate frauds, Congress passed the Sarbanes-Oxley Act authorizing the creation of the Public Company Accounting Oversight Board (PCAOB) to oversee the accounting profession. Establishment of the PCAOB eliminated a significant portion of the accounting profession's system of self-regulation. The Public Company Accounting Oversight Board was established in 2002. The five member Board's duties include

- Registration of public accounting firms that prepare audit reports for financial statement issuers
- Establishment or adoption of auditing, quality control, ethics, independence and other standards relating to audit reports for issuers
- Conducting inspections of registered public accounting firms
- Performing other duties or functions to promote high professional standards for audits, enforcing compliance with the Sarbanes-Oxley Act, setting the budget, and managing operations

All accounting firms that audit SEC registrants must register with the Board. As part of that registration process, each firm pledges to cooperate with any inquiry made by the Board. The Board may impose monetary damages and may suspend firms and accountants from working on engagements for publicly traded companies. It may also make referrals to the Justice Department to consider criminal cases.

The Board is currently in the process of creating and adopting auditing standards for the above areas of its listed duties, including audits and reviews of public company financial statements. Information relating to the PCAOB is presented in Modules 1 through 4.

## Statements on Standards for Attestation Engagements (SSAEs)

The Statements on Standards for Attestation Engagements relate to attestation engagements on subject matter other than financial statements. Outlines of the SSAEs, which have an AT prefix, are presented following Module 6 and are discussed in the various modules, particularly Module 4. Their codified form may be summarized as

| | |
|---|---|
| AT 101 | Attest engagements |
| AT 201 | Agreed-upon procedures engagements |
| AT 301 | Financial forecasts and projections |
| AT 401 | Reporting on pro forma financial information |
| AT 501 | Reporting on an entity's internal control over financial reporting |
| AT 601 | Compliance attestation |
| AT 701 | Management's discussion and analysis |

## Statements on Standards for Accounting and Review Services (SSARSs)

The Statements on Standards for Accounting and Review Services provide the authoritative guidance on procedures and reporting of compilation and review engagements of nonpublic entity financial statements. The outlines of the SSARSs have an AR prefix and follow the SAS (AU) outlines. At the beginning of the AR outlines we provide a table that summarizes SSARSs and other nonpublic company review and compilation guidance authority.

## Statements on Quality Control Standards (SQCS)

The Statements on Quality Control Standards apply to the accounting and auditing practices (including all attest services) of all firms. They serve as the standards a firm should be measured against when being evaluated through a peer review—an engagement in which other CPAs evaluate the quality of the firm's auditing and attestation work. In addition to peer reviews conducted under the SCQSs, quality reviews are performed under the Public Company Accounting Oversight Board.

## APPENDIX

The following represents a chronological listing of the various Statements on Auditing Standards (SASs), the module in which they are primarily covered in this book, and either their codified section or, in the case of superseded SASs, the SAS that replaced them.

| SAS 1 section | | Module in this book | New codified SAS section no. |
|---|---|---|---|
| 100* | Introduction | Overview | |
| 200* | General GAAS | Overview | |
| 310 | Relationship between Appointment and Planning | EVID | |
| 320 | Internal Control | IC | Superseded by SAS 55 |
| 331 | Receivables and Inventories | EVID | |
| 332 | Long-Term Investments | EVID | |
| 400* | First 3 Reporting GAAS | REPT | |
| 500* | Fourth Reporting GAAS | REPT | |
| 901 | Public Warehouses | EVID | |
| SAS 2 | Audit Reports | REPT | Superseded by SAS 58 |
| SAS 3 | EDP and Internal Control | ATEC | Superseded by SAS 48 |
| SAS 4 | Firm Quality Controls | ENPL | Superseded by SAS 25 |
| SAS 5 | Meaning of Present Fairly | REPT | Superseded by SAS 69 |
| SAS 6 | Related-Party Transactions | EVID | Superseded by SAS 45 |
| SAS 7 | Predecessor-Successor Communications | EVID | Superseded by SAS 84 |
| SAS 8 | Other Information | REPT | 550 |
| SAS 9 | Effect of an Internal Audit Function | IC | Superseded by SAS 65 |
| SAS 10 | Limited Review | REPT | Superseded by SAS 24 |
| SAS 11 | Using Specialists | EVID | Superseded by SAS 73 |
| SAS 12 | Inquiry of Client's Lawyer | EVID | 337 |
| SAS 13 | Limited Review Reports | REPT | Superseded by SAS 24 |
| SAS 14 | Special Reports | REPT | Superseded by SAS 62 |
| SAS 15 | Comparative Financial Statements | REPT | Superseded by SAS 58 |
| SAS 16 | Detection of Errors and Irregularities | ENPL | Superseded by SAS 53 |
| SAS 17 | Illegal Acts by Clients | ENPL | Superseded by SAS 54 |
| SAS 18 | Replacement Costs | EVID | Deleted by Auditing Standards Board |
| SAS 19 | Client Representations | EVID | Superseded by SAS 85 |
| SAS 20 | Required Communications of Material Weaknesses in Internal Accounting Control | IC | Superseded by SAS 60 |
| SAS 21 | Segment Reporting | REPT | 435 |
| SAS 22 | Planning and Supervision | EVID | 311 |
| SAS 23 | Analytical Review Procedures | EVID | Superseded by SAS 56 |
| SAS 24 | Review of Interim Financial Information | EVID | Superseded by SAS 36 |
| SAS 25 | The Relationship of Generally Accepted Auditing Standards to Quality Control Standards | ENPL | 161 |
| SAS 26 | Association with Financial Statements | REPT | 504 |
| SAS 27 | Supplementary Information Required by the Financial Accounting Standards Board | REPT | Superseded by SAS 52 |
| SAS 28 | Supplementary Information on the Effects of Changing Prices | REPT | Withdrawn by SAS 52 |
| SAS 29 | Reporting on Information Accompanying the Basic Financial Statements in Auditor-Submitted Documents | REPT | 551 |
| SAS 30 | Reporting on Internal Accounting Control | REPT | Superseded by SSAE 2 |
| SAS 31 | Evidential Matter | EVID | 326 |
| SAS 32 | Adequacy of Disclosure in Financial Statements | REPT | 431 |
| SAS 33 | Supplementary Oil and Gas Reserve Information | REPT | Superseded by SAS 45 |
| SAS 34 | The Auditor's Considerations When a Question Arises about an Entity's Continued Existence | REPT | Superseded by SAS 59 |
| SAS 35 | Special Reports—Applying Agreed-Upon Procedures to Specified Elements, Accounts, or Items of a Financial Statement | REPT | Superseded by SAS 75 |
| SAS 36 | Review of and Performing Procedures on Interim Financial Information | EVID | Superseded by SAS 71 |
| SAS 37 | Filings under Federal Securities Statutes | REPT | 711 |
| SAS 38 | Letters for Underwriters | REPT | Superseded by SAS 49 |
| SAS 39 | Audit Sampling | AUDS | 350 |
| SAS 40 | Supplementary Mineral Reserve Information | EVID | Superseded by SAS 52 |
| SAS 41 | Working Papers | EVID | 339 |

*\* Contains multiple subsections*

|  |  | Module in<br>*this book* | New codified<br>*SAS section no.* |
|---|---|---|---|
| SAS 42 | Reporting on Condensed Financial Statements and Selected Financial Data | REPT | 552 |
| SAS 43 | Omnibus Statement on Auditing Standards | VARIOUS | ** |
| SAS 44 | Special-Purpose Reports on Internal Accounting Control at Service Organizations | IC | Superseded by SAS 70 |
| SAS 45 | Omnibus Statement on Auditing Standards—1983 | VARIOUS | ** |
| SAS 46 | Consideration of Omitted Procedures after the Report Date | EVID | 390 |
| SAS 47 | Audit Risk and Materiality in Conducting an Audit | ENPL<br>VARIOUS | 312 |
| SAS 48 | The Effects of Computer Processing on the Examination of Financial Statements | VARIOUS | ** |
| SAS 49 | Letters for Underwriters | REPT | Superseded by SAS 72 |
| SAS 50 | Reports on the Application of Accounting Principles | REPT | 625 |
| SAS 51 | Reporting on Financial Statements Prepared for Use in Other Countries | REPT | 534 |
| SAS 52 | Omnibus Statement on Auditing Standards | VARIOUS | ** |
| SAS 53 | The Auditor's Responsibility to Detect and Report Errors and Irregularities | ENPL | Superseded by SAS 82 |
| SAS 54 | Illegal Acts by Clients | ENPL | 317 |
| SAS 55 | Consideration of the Internal Control Structure in a Financial Statement Audit | IC | 319 |
| SAS 56 | Analytical Procedures | EVID | 329 |
| SAS 57 | Auditing Accounting Estimates | EVID | 342 |
| SAS 58 | Reports on Audited Financial Statements | REPT | 508 |
| SAS 59 | The Auditor's Consideration of an Entity's Ability to Continue as a Going Concern | EVID<br>REPT | 341 |
| SAS 61 | Communication with Audit Committees | IC | 380 |
| SAS 62 | Special Reports | REPT | 623 |
| SAS 63 | Compliance Auditing Applicable to Governmental Entities and Other Specified Recipients of Governmental Financial Assistance | EVID | Superseded by SAS 68 |
| SAS 64 | Omnibus Statement on Auditing Standards—1990 | VARIOUS | ** |
| SAS 65 | The Auditor's Consideration of the Internal Audit Function in an Audit of Financial Statements | IC | 322 |
| SAS 66 | Communication of Matters about Interim Financial Information Filed or to Be Filed with Specified Regulatory Agencies—an Amendment to SAS 36 | IC | Superseded by SAS 71 |
| SAS 67 | The Confirmation Process | EVID | 330 |
| SAS 68 | Compliance Auditing Applicable to Governmental Entities and Other Recipients of Governmental Financial Assistance | EVID | Superseded by SAS 74 |
| SAS 69 | The Meaning of *Present Fairly in Conformity with Generally Accepted Accounting Principles* in the Auditor's Report | REPT | 411 |
| SAS 70 | Reports on the Processing of Transactions by Service Organizations | ATEC | 324 |
| SAS 71 | Interim Financial Information | REPT | Superseded by SAS 100 |
| SAS 72 | Letters for Underwriters and Certain Other Requesting Parties | REPT | 634 |
| SAS 73 | Using the Work of a Specialist | EVID | 336 |
| SAS 74 | Compliance Auditing Considerations in Audits of Governmental Entities and Recipients of Governmental Financial Assistance | REPT | 801 |
| SAS 75 | Engagements to Apply Agreed-Upon Procedures to Specified Elements, Accounts, or Items of a Financial Statement | REPT | Superseded by SAS 93 |
| SAS 76 | Amendments to Statement on Auditing Standards No. 72, *Letters for Underwriters and Certain Other Requesting Parties* | REPT | 634 |

** *Outlines of the paragraphs of this statement have been inserted in the outlines of the sections that it superseded.*

| | | *Module in*<br>*this book* | *New codified*<br>*SAS section no.* |
|---|---|---|---|
| SAS 77 | Amendments to Statements on Auditing Standards No. 22, *Planning and Supervision*, No. 59, *The Auditor's Consideration of an Entity's Ability to Continue as a Going Concern*, and No. 62, *Special Reports* | VARIOUS | ** |
| SAS 78 | Amendments to Statements on Auditing Standards to Recognize the *Internal Control—Integrated Framework Report* | IC | 319 |
| SAS 79 | Amendment to Statement on Auditing Standards No. 58, *Reports on Audited Financial Statements* | REPT | 508 |
| SAS 80 | An Amendment to Statement on Auditing Standards No. 31, *Evidential Matter* | EVID | 326 |
| SAS 81 | Accounting for Certain Investments in Debt and Equity Securities | EVID | Superseded by SAS 92 |
| SAS 82 | Consideration of Fraud in a Financial Statement Audit | ENPL | Superseded by SAS 99 |
| SAS 83 | Establishing an Understanding with the Client | ENPL | 310 |
| SAS 84 | Communications between Predecessor and Successor Auditors | ENPL | 315 |
| SAS 85 | Management Representations | EVID | 333 |
| SAS 86 | Amendment to Statement on Auditing Standards No. 72, *Letters for Underwriters and Certain Other Requesting Parties* | REPT | 634 |
| SAS 87 | Restricting the Use of an Auditor's Report | REPT | 532 |
| SAS 88 | Service Organizations and Reporting on Consistency | VARIOUS | ** |
| SAS 89 | Audit Adjustments | VARIOUS | ** |
| SAS 90 | Audit Committee Communications | IC | 325 |
| SAS 91 | Federal GAAP Hierarchy | REPT | 411 |
| SAS 92 | Auditing Derivative Instruments, Hedging Activities, and Investments in Securities | EVID | 332 |
| SAS 93 | Omnibus Statement on Auditing Standards | VARIOUS | |
| SAS 94 | The Effect of Information Technology on the Auditor's Consideration of Internal Control in a Financial Statement Audit | IC | 319 |
| SAS 95 | Generally Accepted Auditing Standards | ENPL | 150 |
| SAS 97 | Amendment to Statement on Auditing Standards No. 50, *Reports on the Application of Accounting Principles* | REPT | 625 |
| SAS 98 | Omnibus Statement on Auditing Standards—2002 | VARIOUS | ** |
| SAS 99 | Consideration of Fraud in a Financial Statement Audit | ENPL | 316 |
| SAS 100 | Interim Financial Information | EVID<br>REPT | 722 |
| SAS 101 | Auditing Fair Value Measurements and Disclosures | EVID | 328 |
| SAS 102 | Defining Professional Requirements | Ch. 5 | |
| SAS 103 | Audit Documentation | EVID | |
| SAS 112 | Communicating Internal Control Matters Identified in an Audit | IC | |

** *Outlines of the paragraphs of this statement have been inserted in the outlines of the sections that it superseded.*

The Public Company Accounting Oversight Board has issued the following standards, the guidance from which is incorporated in Modules 1 through 4.

| *Standard* | *Title* |
|---|---|
| 1 | References in Auditor's Reports to the Standards of the PCAOB |
| 2 | An Audit of Internal Control over Financial Reporting Performed in Conjunction with an Audit of Financial Statements |
| 3 | Audit Documentation |
| 4 | Reporting on Whether a Previously Reported Material Weakness Continues to Exist |

## ENGAGEMENT PLANNING

The first standard of fieldwork states

> The work is to be adequately planned and assistants, if any, are to be properly supervised.

This module presents requirements on planning audits and various other services that CPAs provide. Generally, multiple-choice questions are used to test the candidate's knowledge of audit planning, auditor responsibility for the detection of misstatements (errors, fraud, and illegal acts), and the components of audit risk. A simulation may require you to examine a situation, evaluate areas of risk related to a company, and to design appropriate audit procedures in response to that situation.

### Study Program for the Engagement Planning Module

This module is organized in the following manner:

A. Planning the Engagement

1. Overall Audit Planning Requirements
2. Procedures Followed prior to Obtaining a New Client
3. Audit Planning Procedures

B. Other Responsibilities

1. General Attestation
2. Audit
3. Compilation and Review
4. Prospective Financial Statements
5. Quality Control
6. Public Company Accounting Oversight Board Requirements

The above outline is based on the AICPA CPA Exam Content Specification Outline.

The following SAS sections pertain to this module:

*AU section*

| | |
|---|---|
| 110 | Responsibilities and Functions of the Independent Auditor |
| 150 | Generally Accepted Auditing Standards |
| 161 | Relationship of Generally Accepted Auditing Standards to Quality Control Standards |
| 201 | Nature of the General Standards |
| 210 | Training and Proficiency of the Independent Auditor |
| 220 | Independence |
| 230 | Due Care in the Performance of Work |
| 310 | Relationship between the Auditor's Appointment and Planning |
| 311 | Planning and Supervision |
| 312 | Audit Risk and Materiality in Conducting an Audit |
| 313 | Substantive Tests prior to the Balance Sheet Date |
| 315 | Communications between Predecessor and Successor Auditors |
| 316 | Consideration of Fraud in a Financial Statement Audit |
| 317 | Illegal Acts by Clients |
| 326 | Evidential Matter |
| 329 | Analytical Procedures |
| AT 101 | Attestation Standards |

Although you should review the outlines of all of the above sections, the information presented in the outlines of AU 312, 315, 316, and 317 is particularly heavily examined. Also, an outline of *Statements of Quality Control* is presented later in this module.

### A. Planning the Engagement

Audit planning requirements are presented in various parts of the professional standards. In this section of the module we summarize that information in three subsections—(1) overall audit planning requirements, (2) procedures followed prior to obtaining a new client, and (3) audit planning procedures.

1. **Overall Audit Planning Requirements.** The auditor should plan the audit to obtain **reasonable,** not absolute, **assurance** that material misstatements are detected. An assessment of the risk of material misstatement (whether caused by error or fraud) should be made during planning. This assessment must include a specific assessment of the risk of material misstatement of the financial statements due

to fraud.  As indicated in the combined outline of AU 201-230, absolute assurance is not attainable because of the nature of audit evidence and the characteristics of fraud (see point D.3. of that outline).

a.  **Audit risk (AU 312).**  An audit must be designed to limit audit risk to an appropriately low level. Audit risk, which may be assessed in quantitative or nonquantitative terms, consists of (1) the risk that an account and its related assertions contains material misstatements (composed of two components, referred to as inherent risk and control risk) and (2) the risk that the auditor will not detect such misstatements (referred to as detection risk).  Mathematically, we may view this as follows:

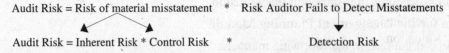

Audit Risk = Risk of material misstatement    *    Risk Auditor Fails to Detect Misstatements

Audit Risk = Inherent Risk * Control Risk    *                Detection Risk

**Inherent risk** refers to the likelihood of material misstatement of an assertion, assuming no related internal control.  This risk differs by account and assertion.  For example, cash is more susceptible to theft than an inventory of coal.  This risk is assessed using various analytical techniques, available information on the company and its industry, as well as by using overall auditing knowledge.

**Control risk** is the likelihood that a material misstatement will not be prevented or detected on a timely basis by internal control.  This risk is assessed using the results of tests of controls.

**Detection risk** is the likelihood that an auditor's procedures lead to an improper conclusion that no material misstatement exists in an assertion when in fact such a misstatement does exist. The auditor's substantive tests are primarily relied upon to restrict detection risk.

**Relationship among inherent risk, control risk, and detection risk.**  Inherent risk and control risk differ from detection risk in that they exist independently of the audit, whereas detection risk relates to the effectiveness of the auditor's procedures.  A number of questions are asked concerning the relationship among the three risks.  Although the auditor may make either separate or combined assessments of inherent risk and control risk, you may find the audit risk formula that separates the risks helpful for such questions.  First, assume that a given audit risk is to be accepted, say .05.  Then, the product of inherent risk, control risk and detection risk must be .05 as follows:

Audit Risk    =    Inherent Risk    *    Control Risk    *    Detection Risk

.05    =    Inherent Risk    *    Control Risk    *    Detection Risk

Accordingly, if any risk increases another must decrease to hold audit risk at .05.  Therefore, when a question asks for the relationship between control risk and detection risk, for example, you would reply that it is inverse.  Stated otherwise, if control risk (or inherent risk) increases, detection risk must decrease.

b.  **Materiality (AU 312).**  Materiality is "the magnitude of an omission or misstatement of accounting information that, in the light of surrounding circumstances, makes it probable that the judgment of a reasonable person relying on the information would have been changed or influenced by the omission or misstatement."  An auditor must consider materiality both in (1) planning the audit and designing audit procedures and (2) evaluating audit results.

Operationally, the measure of materiality may be either quantitative or nonquantitative.  The auditor plans the audit to obtain reasonable assurance of detecting misstatements that could be large enough, individually or when combined, to be quantitatively material to the financial statements.  Section 312 suggests that auditors may develop a level of materiality for each financial statement.  For example, the auditor may believe that misstatements aggregating approximately $100,000 would have a material effect on income, but that such misstatement would have to aggregate approximately $200,000 to materially affect financial position.  In such cases the lower measure would be used for any transactions affecting income.

After determining a materiality level for the various financial statements, the auditor then apportions the amount among the various accounts.  This apportionment may be based on factors such as the relative size of various accounts and on professional judgment.  The apportioned amount for each account is the "tolerable misstatement" discussed in the Audit Sampling Module (Section C).

The measures of materiality used for evaluation purposes will ordinarily differ from measures of materiality used for planning. This is the result of information encountered during the audit. For evaluation purposes, the auditor is aware of qualitative aspects of actual misstatements that s/he is not aware of during the planning stage. For example, an auditor will consider any fraud in which management is involved to be material, regardless of the amount involved.

c. **Financial statement assertions.** SAS 31 (AU 326) summarizes five assertions or representations made by management that are embodied in the accounts.

1. Presentation and disclosure
2. Existence or occurrence
3. Rights and obligations
4. Completeness
5. Valuation

In planning and performing an audit, the auditor considers these assertions for the various financial statement accounts. When all of these assertions have been met for an account, the account is in conformity with generally accepted accounting principles. Thus, errors and fraud may be viewed as having the effect of misstating one or more of the assertions. The Evidence Module presents further illustration of these assertions.

d. **Errors and fraud (AU 312 and 316).** An audit should be planned and performed to obtain reasonable assurance about whether the financial statements are free of material misstatements, whether caused by error or fraud. While both errors and fraud may result in misstatements or omissions in the financial statements, they differ in that fraud is intentional. The two types of fraud considered in an audit are (1) **fraudulent financial reporting** that makes the financial statements misleading and (2) **misappropriation of assets** (i.e., theft, defalcation). The Summary of Auditor Responsibility for Errors, Fraud, and Illegal Acts table presents overall auditor responsibilities.

**SUMMARY OF AUDITOR RESPONSIBILITY FOR ERRORS, FRAUD, AND ILLEGAL ACTS**

|  | *Errors* | *Fraud* | *Illegal acts* *Direct effect* | *Illegal acts* *Indirect effect* |
|---|---|---|---|---|
| *Definition* | Unintentional misstatements or omissions | Intentional misstatements or omissions | Violations of laws or governmental regulations having a material and direct effect on financial statement **amounts** | Violations of laws or governmental regulations **not** having a material and direct effect on financial statement **amounts** |
| *Examples* | Mistakes in processing accounting data, incorrect accounting estimates due to oversight, mistakes in application of accounting principles | Two types—**fraudulent financial reporting** (falsification of accounting records) and **misappropriation of assets** (embezzlement) | Tax laws, accrued revenue based on government contracts | Securities trading, occupational safety and health, food and drug administration, environmental protection, equal employment, price fixing |
| *Detection responsibility* | 1. Assess risk of misstatement 2. Based on assessment, design audit to provide reasonable assurance of detection of material misstatements 3. Exercise due care in planning, performing, and evaluating results of audit procedures, and proper degree of professional skepticism to achieve reasonable assurance of detection | (Same as for errors) | (Same as for errors) | 1. Be aware of possibility that they may have occurred 2. If specific information comes to attention on an illegal act with a possible material indirect financial statement effect, apply audit procedures necessary to determine whether illegal act has occurred |
| *Reporting responsibility* | 1. Modify audit report for remaining departures from GAAP or scope limitations 2. Report to audit committee (unless clearly inconsequential) 3. In audits in accordance with government auditing standards, consider notification of other parties (e.g., regulatory agencies) 4. Report in various other circumstances (e.g., Form 8-K, successor auditor, subpoena response) | (Same as for errors) | (Same as for errors) | (Similar to errors) |
| *Primary standards* | AU 312 | AU 316 | AU 316, 317 | AU 317 |

You should be very familiar with the information presented in the rather lengthy outline of AU 316, as well as the outline of AU 317 on illegal acts (discussed in detail in the following section). While we summarize some of the most important concepts from them, reading this section of the module alone is insufficient. Although AU 316 does not refer to "steps" involved related to fraud, and indeed in practice the "steps" don't follow one another nicely, we summarize the layout of its guidance in the table Consideration of Fraud.

**Consideration of Fraud**

| *Step* | | *Approach* |
|---|---|---|
| Step 1. | Staff discussion of the risk of material misstatement | • Brainstorm<br>• Consider incentives/pressures, opportunities<br>• Exercise professional skepticism |
| Step 2. | Obtain information needed to identify risks of material misstatement due to fraud | • Make inquiries of management and others<br>• Consider results of analytical procedures<br>• Consider fraud risk factors<br>• Consider other information |
| Step 3. | Identify risks that may result in a material misstatement due to fraud | For risks identified, consider<br>• Type of risk that may exist<br>• Significance of risk (magnitude)<br>• Likelihood of risk<br>• Pervasiveness of risk |
| Step 4. | Assess the identified risks after considering programs and controls | • Consider understanding of internal control<br>• Evaluate whether programs and controls address the identified risks<br>• Assess risks taking into account this evaluation |
| Step 5. | Respond to the results of the assessment | As risk increases<br>• Overall response: More experienced staff, more attention to accounting policies, less predictable procedures<br>• For specifically identified risks: Consider need to increase nature, timing, and extent of audit procedures<br><br>On all audits consider the possibility of management override of controls (adjusting journal entries, accounting estimates, unusual transactions) |
| Step 6. | Evaluate audit evidence | • Assess risk of fraud throughout the audit<br>• Evaluate analytical procedures performed as substantive tests and at overall review stage<br>• Evaluate risk of fraud near completion of fieldwork<br>• Respond to misstatements that may be due to fraud |
| Step 7. | Communicate about fraud | • Communicate all fraud to an appropriate level of management<br>• Communicate all management fraud to audit committee<br>• Communicate all material fraud to management and audit committee<br>• Determine if reportable conditions have been identified |
| Step 8. | Document consideration of fraud | • Document steps 1-7<br>• If improper revenue recognition not considered a risk, describe why |

AU 316 is the source of many questions. Here are some particularly important points included in the outline.

1.  Because an audit is planned and performed to obtain reasonable, not absolute, assurance, even a properly performed audit may miss material misstatements.
2.  The auditor must exercise professional skepticism—an attitude that includes a questioning mind and a critical assessment of audit evidence.
3.  Make certain you can distinguish between **fraudulent financial reporting** in which the financial statements are intentionally misstated (cooked books) and **misappropriation of assets** when its assets are stolen.
4.  Three conditions that are generally present when individuals commit fraud are incentive/pressure, opportunity, and attitude/rationalization.
5.  A staff discussion of the risk of material misstatement is required either prior to or in conjunction with obtaining information to identify risks of fraud.
6.  In planning the audit, the auditor should perform analytical procedures relating to revenue to identify unusual or unexpected relationships involving revenue accounts.

7.  The responses to the results of the assessment as risk are an overall response, a response that specifically addresses identified risks, and a response for the possibility of management override.  The response for management override (performed on all audits to some extent) includes

- Testing the appropriateness of journal entries and adjustments
- Reviewing accounting estimates for biases
- Evaluating the rationale for significant unusual transactions

8.  Fraud communication responsibility

- All fraud involving management must be communicated to the audit committee
- All material fraud should be communicated to the audit committee
- The auditor should reach an understanding with the audit committee regarding other communications

At this point study the outline of AU 316 in detail.

e.  **Illegal acts (AU 317).**  Illegal acts are also heavily examined.  AU 317 differentiates between illegal acts having a **direct and material effect** in the determination of financial statement amounts (i.e., result in adjusting entries) and those with an **indirect effect** on the financial statements (i.e., result in note disclosures).  The primary example of an illegal act with a direct and material effect is one related to tax laws.  Examples of indirect effect illegal acts include securities purchased or sold based on inside information, price-fixing, and antitrust violations; their indirect effect is normally the result of a need to disclose a contingent liability because of the allegation or determination of illegality.  As indicated in the earlier summary, the auditor's responsibility differs for the two types as follows:

*Direct*—Responsibility same as for errors and fraud (provide reasonable assurance of detection of material misstatements)

*Indirect*—An audit in accordance with GAAS does not include audit procedures specially designed to detect illegal acts with an indirect effect.  However, when procedures applied for other purposes identify possible illegal acts, the auditor should apply audit procedures to determine whether an illegal act has occurred.

When an auditor discovers an act that **might** be illegal, s/he should inquire of management at a level above those involved, if possible.  If management does not provide satisfactory information that there has been no illegal act, the auditor should

(1)  Consult with the client's legal counsel or other specialists
(2)  Apply additional procedures such as

- Examine supporting documents such as invoices, canceled checks, and agreements and compare them with accounting records
- Confirm significant information with the other involved party or with intermediaries, such as banks or lawyers
- Determine whether the transaction has been properly authorized
- Consider whether other similar transactions may have occurred and apply appropriate procedures

When, based on procedures such as the above, the auditor believes that an illegal act has or is likely to have occurred, the auditor should

(1)  Consider its financial statement effect
(2)  Consider its implications to other aspects of the audit, particularly the reliability of representations by management
(3)  Communicate it to the audit committee
(4)  Consider the need to modify the audit report as follows:

- Lack of disclosure is a departure from GAAP and either a qualified or an adverse opinion may be appropriate
- Client-imposed scope restrictions will generally lead to a disclaimer of opinion

- Circumstance-imposed scope restrictions may lead to either a qualified opinion or a disclaimer of opinion

Unless the act is clearly inconsequential, the audit committee should be provided with a description of the act, circumstances concerning its occurrence, and its effect on the financial statements. When senior management is involved, the auditor should communicate directly with the audit committee. When a client refuses to give appropriate consideration to handling the illegal act (even an immaterial one), the auditor should consider whether the refusal affects his or her ability to rely on management's representations and whether resignation is desirable.

2. **Procedures Followed prior to Obtaining a New Client.** CPAs must establish policies for deciding whether to accept (or continue serving) a client in order to minimize the likelihood of being associated with an organization whose management lacks integrity. Prior to acquiring a client, an auditor should attempt communication with the predecessor auditor and obtain a general understanding of the nature of the organization and its industry. The overall goal is to determine whether to attempt to acquire the client, and to gather adequate information so as to allow the auditor to develop a proposal to be presented to the prospective client.

   a. **Communications between predecessor and successor auditors (AU 315).** Make certain that you are very familiar with the information presented in the outline of AU 315. That standard requires a communication with the predecessor prior to acceptance of the engagement, and strongly recommends one after acceptance of the engagement (see section A.3.b. of this module). Particularly heavily examined are concepts such as the following:

      (1) Initiating the communication is the responsibility of the successor
      (2) If the prospective client refuses to permit the predecessor to respond, or limits the predecessor's response, the successor should inquire as to the reasons and consider the implications in deciding whether to accept the engagement
      (3) The successor's inquiries of the predecessor should include

         - Information bearing on **integrity** of management
         - **Disagreements** with management as to accounting principles, auditing procedures or other similarly significant matters
         - **Communications** to audit committee regarding fraud, illegal acts, and internal control related matters
         - Predecessor's understanding of the **reasons for the change** in auditors

   b. **Obtaining a general understanding of the client and industry.** AICPA industry audit and accounting guides and technical publications are available for the auditor to study most major industries.

      Concerning the company itself, an auditor will generally tour the client's facilities, and obtain an overall understanding of the client's organization, including the adequacy of its accounting records. In addition to communicating with the predecessor auditor, the potential successor will generally communicate with the company's audit committee, its lawyers, and possibly with other practitioners and bankers.

      The process typically ends with a proposal to the client. If this proposal is accepted, an engagement letter is ordinarily sent to the client.

   c. **Establishing an understanding with the client (engagement letters).** Auditors should establish an understanding with the client regarding the services to be performed. Although this understanding may be obtained orally or in writing, it must be documented in the working papers and is generally obtained through use of an engagement letter. The engagement letter is sent to the client, who indicates approval through returning a signed copy to the CPA.

      The understanding must include four general topics: (1) objectives of the engagement, (2) management's responsibilities, (3) auditor's responsibilities, and (4) limitations of the audit. If an auditor believes that an understanding has not been established, he or she should decline to accept or perform the audit.

      The following summary presents details of the required understanding with the client.

**SUMMARY OF DETAILS OF AN UNDERSTANDING WITH THE CLIENT**

| General | Details |
|---|---|
| 1. Objectives of the engagement | Expression of an opinion on the financial statements |
| 2. Management's responsibilities | • Establishing and maintaining effective internal control over financial reporting<br>• Identifying and ensuring that the entity complies with laws and regulations<br>• Making financial records and related information available to the auditor<br>• Providing a representation letter (see Evidence Module)<br>• Adjusting financial statements to correct material misstatements<br>• Affirming in representation letter that effect of uncorrected misstatements aggregated by auditor is immaterial |
| 3. Auditor's responsibilities | • Conducting audit in accordance with US GAAS<br>• Ensuring that audit committee is aware of any reportable conditions which came to auditor's attention |
| 4. Limitations of the audit | • Obtains reasonable, rather than absolute, assurance<br>• Material misstatement may remain undetected<br>• If auditor is unable to form or has not formed an opinion, auditor may decline to express an opinion or decline to issue a report |
| Other (not required) | • Arrangements regarding<br>  – Conduct of engagement (timing, client assistance, etc.)<br>  – Involvement of specialists or internal auditors<br>  – Predecessor auditor<br>  – Fees and billing<br>  – Additional services to be provided relating to regulatory requirements<br>  – Other additional services<br>• Any limitation or other arrangement regarding the liability of the auditor or the client<br>• Conditions under which access to the auditor's working papers may be granted to others |

3. **Audit Planning Procedures.** Subsequent to client acceptance of the proposal, an overall audit strategy must be developed. Factors included here are obtaining additional information from the predecessor auditor, performing analytical procedures, considering internal control, developing a written audit program, considering supervision needs, and considering the timing of audit procedures.

    a. **Developing an overall strategy (AU 311).** The nature, timing, and extent of planning will vary with the size and complexity of the audit client, experience with the client, and knowledge of the client's business. To develop an overall audit strategy, the auditor may consider the following client and audit considerations:

| | |
|---|---|
| *Client considerations* | 1. Business and industry<br>2. Accounting policies and procedures<br>3. Methods of processing accounting information (e.g., computer service center)<br>4. Financial statement items likely to need adjustment<br>5. Considerations requiring extension of audit procedures (e.g., risk of misstatement, related-party transactions) |
| *Audit considerations* | 6. Planned assessed level of control risk<br>7. Preliminary judgments about materiality levels<br>8. Nature of reports to be issued by CPA |

In addition, the auditor may consider performing the following review and inquiry procedures during planning.

| | |
|---|---|
| *Review of records* | 1. Correspondence, prior working papers, financial statements, etc.<br>2. Current year's interim financial statements |
| *Inquiries within CPA firm* | 3. Effects of nonaudit services<br>4. Extent of assistance from specialists and consultants<br>5. Timing of audit work<br>6. Staffing requirements |
| *Inquiries of client* | 7. Current business developments<br>8. Discussion of audit (e.g., type, scope, timing)<br>9. Effects of new accounting and auditing pronouncements<br>10. Coordinate client assistance, including that from internal auditors |

The CPA should obtain a level of knowledge of the client's business that will enable effective planning and performance of the audit in accordance with generally accepted auditing standards. This knowledge helps the auditor in

(1) **Identifying areas** that may need special consideration
(2) **Assessing conditions** under which accounting data are produced, processed, reviewed and accumulated
(3) **Evaluating accounting estimates** for reasonableness (e.g., valuation of inventories, depreciation, allowance for doubtful accounts, percentage of completion of long-term contracts)
(4) Evaluating the **reasonableness of management representations**
(5) Making judgments about the **appropriateness of the accounting principles** applied and the **adequacy of disclosures**

b.  **Communicate with predecessor auditors.** Earlier, we discussed the AU 315 requirement that potential successor auditors attempt communication with the predecessor **before** accepting a new client. We also emphasized that you should be very familiar with the outline of AU 315.

Although strongly recommended, no communication with the predecessor auditor is required **after** accepting a new client. This second communication relates primarily to the review of working papers related to opening balances and the consistency of application of accounting principles. With regard to working papers

(1) Areas generally examined include

   - Documentation of planning
   - Internal control
   - Audit results
   - Other matters of continuing accounting **and** auditing significance such as analyses of balance sheet accounts

(2) If in reviewing the working papers the successor identifies financial statement misstatements, the successor should request that the client inform the predecessor and arrange a meeting of the three parties.

In addition, AU 315 includes a section on "reaudits" of previously audited financial statements. Reaudits may be necessary, for example, when a change in auditors has occurred and the predecessor refuses to reissue his or her audit report on previous year financial statements that are to be reissued (e.g., as prior year statements in an SEC filing). In such cases the successor should request the working papers for the period of the reaudit; the extent to which the predecessor permits such access is considered a matter of judgment. Additional procedures beyond those performed by the predecessor are always considered necessary in such circumstances.

c.  **Analytical procedures.** AU 329 requires that analytical procedures be performed in planning the audit (as well as an overall review near completion of the audit). During the planning stage the objective of analytical procedures is to assist in planning the nature, timing, and extent of audit procedures that will be used to obtain evidence for specific accounts. Analytical procedures are discussed in further detail in the Evidence Module.

d.  **Consideration of internal control.** In all audits, the CPA must obtain a sufficient understanding of internal control to plan the audit. This understanding should include knowledge about the design of controls, and whether they have been placed in operation by the client. This understanding must be sufficient to allow the auditor to (1) identify types of potential misstatements, (2) consider factors affecting the risk of misstatements, and (3) design substantive tests. In addition, as listed above, the auditor must identify a planned assessed level of control risk for the various assertions. This is discussed further in the Internal Control Module. In the audit of a public company, the auditor must go further to provide an opinion on the effectiveness of internal control over financial reporting.

e.  **Audit program.** A written audit program must be developed and used for the audit.

f.  **Supervision requirements (AU 311).** Supervision includes instructing assistants, being informed on significant problems, reviewing audit work, and dealing with differences of opinion among audit personnel. The complexity of the audit and qualifications of audit assistants affect the degree of supervision needed. The work of each assistant should be reviewed (1) to determine whether it was adequately performed and (2) to evaluate whether the results are consistent with the conclusions to be presented in the audit report. Procedures should be established for documenting any disagreements of opinions among staff personnel; the basis for resolution of such disagreements should be documented.

g.  **Timing of audit procedures (AU 310, 313).** Tests of controls and substantive tests can be conducted at various times. The timing of tests of controls is very flexible; they are often performed at an interim period, and subsequently updated through year-end.

Auditors also have a certain amount of flexibility in planning the timing of substantive tests. Section 313 discusses three timing aspects.

(1) Factors to be considered before applying tests at an **interim date** before year-end
(2) Auditing procedures to be followed for the **remaining period** (the period after the interim date through year-end)
(3) Coordination of the timing of audit procedures

Before applying procedures at an interim date, an auditor should consider the incremental audit risk involved as well as whether performance of such interim procedures is likely to be cost-effective. As an illustration of a substantive test applied at an interim date, consider the possibility of confirming receivables as of November 30, one month prior to the client's year-end.

Appropriate auditing procedures must be applied to provide a reasonable basis for extending November 30 interim date results to the **remaining period** (December 1-31). When control risk is assessed at a level below the maximum, the auditor might be able to perform only limited substantive tests during the remaining period to obtain the assurance needed as of the balance sheet date.

Assessing control risk at below the maximum is not required in order to have a reasonable basis for extending audit procedures from the interim date to the balance sheet date. When control risk is assessed at the maximum, a greater extent of procedures must be performed to obtain the needed balance sheet date assurance. In such circumstances the auditor should consider whether the effectiveness of substantive tests used in the remaining period will be impaired. For example, it may be difficult to satisfy the completeness assertion (see the Evidence Module), since substantive tests performed on recorded receivable transactions might be unlikely to detect unrecorded receivable transactions. If the auditor concludes that the effectiveness of such substantive tests would be impaired, either additional assurance must be sought, or the accounts should be examined as of the balance sheet date.

The auditor who intends to apply audit tests at an interim date should consider whether the accounting system will provide information on remaining period transactions that is sufficient to investigate (1) significant unusual transactions, (2) other causes of significant fluctuation (or expected fluctuations that did not occur), and (3) changes in the composition of the account balances.

The substantive tests performed on the remaining period should be designed to cover the remaining period in such a way that their results, in combination with interim date substantive results and any assurance provided from the assessed level of control risk, achieve the audit objectives at the balance sheet date. Such tests ordinarily should compare information between the interim and year-end periods to identify unusual changes. This should include other analytical procedures and/or substantive tests of details to provide a reasonable basis for extending to the balance sheet date the audit conclusions relative to the assertions tested at the interim date.

Concerning the coordination of timing of audit procedures, a properly conducted audit will reflect the fact that the performance of certain procedures needs to be synchronized. This especially applies to (1) related-party transactions, (2) interrelated accounts and cutoffs, and (3) negotiable assets. For interrelated accounts and negotiable assets, the auditor is concerned that one might be substituted for another to allow the double counting of a given resource (e.g., sale of securities after they have been counted at year-end and inclusion of proceeds in year-end cash).

## B.  Other Responsibilities

1.  **General Attestation.** The overview section presented the eleven attestation standards and pointed out that they relate to attestation services with information other than historical financial information; the generally accepted auditing standards relate to audits of financial statements. You may wish to

quickly review the standards at this point. Note especially the third and fourth general standards and the fourth reporting standard.

The third general standard requires that the CPA perform the engagement only if there is reason to believe that the subject matter is capable of reasonably consistent evaluation against criteria that are suitable and available to users. The fourth general attestation standard requires an independence in mental attitude when performing any attestation engagement. The fourth standard of reporting requires that the report state that its use is restricted to specified parties under the following circumstances when

- The criteria used are suitable only for a limited number of parties
- The subject matter is available only to specified parties
- A written assertion has not been provided by the responsible party
- Reporting upon an agreed-upon procedures engagement

Next, review carefully the outline of AT 101, the general framework relating to the attestation standards. This information, which will arise at various points throughout the auditing modules, is becoming increasingly important as the profession begins reporting upon a wide variety of types of information.

2. **Audit.** While audit responsibilities are presented throughout the various modules, here we present information on the general audit standards. The three general audit standards (recall TIP—Training, Independence, Professional Care) are personal in nature in the sense that they are concerned with the auditor's qualifications and the quality of his/her work. Be aware of several overall points. First, training includes both formal education and professional experience. Second, independence requires both actual independence and the appearance of independence to third parties. It is important to realize that independence is required for all attest services relating to historical financial statements including audits and reviews. It is not required for nonattest engagements, such as compilations, tax or consulting services. Third, although infallibility is not assumed by the auditor, due professional care must be exerted at all levels. Due professional care requires each individual to observe the fieldwork and reporting standards, including a critical review at every level of supervision of the work done and the judgment exercised.

3. **Compilation and Review.** While the accountant's overall responsibilities with respect to compilations and reviews of financial statements are discussed in the Evidence and Reporting Modules, as indicated above, the accountant **need not** be independent to perform a compilation (a nonattestation or accounting service) but must be independent to perform a review (an attestation service). Also, the various *Statements on Standards for Accounting and Review Services,* which present the standards for compilations and reviews of nonpublic companies, must only be followed when a CPA has prepared financial statements for a client or has materially modified those that a client has prepared.

4. **Prospective Financial Statements.** Information on prospective financial information is presented in Section C of the Reporting Module and in the outline of AT 301. Three forms of accountant association are possible—compilation, examination, and application of agreed-upon procedures. As for compilations of other types of information, the accountant need not be independent. Also, there is no review form of association with prospective financial information.

5. **Quality Control**

   a. **Overview.** The quality control standards (outlined at the end of this section) apply to the accounting and auditing practice (including all attest services) of all firms. While the generally accepted auditing standards and the Code of Professional Conduct are primarily directed at the **individual practitioner** level, the quality control standards apply to the CPA **firm** itself.

   A major function of the quality control standards is to serve as the appropriate criteria for evaluating the results of **peer reviews**. A peer review involves a study of the adequacy of the firm's established quality control policies and tests to determine the extent of the firm's compliance with those policies. In large part, the tests consist of a review of working paper files and reports for selected engagements. The engagements are evaluated for compliance with professional standards and established quality control policies, including policies regarding promotions of employees, continuing education of firm personnel, staffing of engagements, client acceptance, and the employment of professional personnel.

Based on the peer reviewers' study and tests of the quality controls, they issue a report that includes an opinion as to the adequacy of the reviewed firm's quality control system. Suggestions for improvement to the system are outlined in a "letter of comments" issued by the peer reviewers to the reviewed firm. Peer reviews are educational in that they encourage firms to develop and implement strong systems of quality control. In addition, if a firm fails to take appropriate corrective action various sanctions may be imposed (e.g., additional continuing education requirement, admonishments, suspension from AICPA firm membership).

To this point there have been relatively few questions on quality control, generally no more than one or two multiple-choice questions per exam. Be familiar with the five quality control elements presented below and also what they imply.

b. **SQCS 2—System of Quality Control for a CPA Firm's Accounting and Auditing Practice**

(1) A system of quality control is a process to provide the firm with reasonable assurance that its personnel comply with applicable professional standards and the firm's standards of quality.

(2) The quality control policies and procedures applicable to a firm's accounting and auditing practices should encompass the following five elements:

    (a) **Independence, integrity, and objectivity**—Requires a continuing assessment of client relationships

        1] **Independence** encompasses an impartiality recognizing an obligation of fairness not only to management and business owners, but also those who may use the auditor's report

        2] **Integrity** requires personnel to be honest and candid, with service and the public trust not subordinated to personal gain and advantage

        3] **Objectivity** is a state of mind that imposes the obligation to be impartial, intellectually honest, and free of conflicts of interest

    (b) **Personnel management**—Includes effective hiring, assignment of personnel, professional development and advancement activities

    (c) **Acceptance and continuance of clients and engagements**—Provides reasonable assurance that likelihood of association with a client whose management lacks integrity is minimized

        1] Such policies should also provide reasonable assurance of undertaking only engagements that may reasonably be expected to be completed with professional competence, with the firm considering the risks associated with providing professional services

    (d) **Engagement performance**—Encompasses all phases of the design and execution of the engagement

        1] To extent appropriate, for each engagement should include—planning, performing, supervising, reviewing, documenting, and communicating results

        2] Where applicable, should address concurring partner review requirements applicable for SEC engagements

    *NOTE: Point (d)—including subpoints 1] and 2]—is the SQCS 4 amendment of SQCS 2.*

    (e) **Monitoring**—Provide firm with reasonable assurance that policies and procedures related to other elements are suitably designed and are being effectively applied.

        1] Includes relevance of policies and procedures, adequacy of materials, effectiveness of professional development programs, and compliance with firm's policies and procedures

    *NOTE: Make certain that you know the above quality control elements.*

(3) Administration of a quality control system

    (a) Although **all** firm personnel are responsible for complying with quality control policies and procedures, responsibility should be assigned to one or more individuals

    (b) Policies should be appropriately communicated

  (c) The extent of documentation needed is based on the size, structure, and nature of the firm's practice

c. **SQCS 3—Monitoring a CPA Firm's Accounting and Auditing Practice**

 (1) A firm's monitoring policies should provide reasonable assurance that each of the other elements of quality control is suitably designed and effectively applied.

 (2) For purposes of monitoring a CPA firm's accounting and auditing practice, the firm's monitoring procedures may include

  (a) Inspection procedures

  (b) Preissuance and postissuance review of selected engagements

  (c) Review of selected administrative and personnel records pertaining to quality control elements

  (d) Analysis and assessment of

   1] New professional pronouncements

   2] Result of independence confirmation

   3] Continuing professional education and development

   4] Decision related to acceptance and continuance of clients

   5] Interview of firm personnel

  (e) Determination of necessary corrective actions and improvements

  (f) Communication of quality control weaknesses

  (g) Follow-up of necessary modification to quality control

d. **SQCS 4—System of Quality Control for a CPA Firm's Accounting and Auditing Practice—** See point (d) above.

e. **SQCS 5—The Personnel Management Element of a Firm's System of Quality Control— Competencies Required by a Practitioner in Charge of an Attest Engagement**

 (1) Policies and procedures should be established to provide firm with reasonable assurance that

  (a) Those hired have appropriate characteristics (e.g., academic requirements, maturity, integrity, leadership)

  (b) Work is assigned to personnel with adequate training and proficiency

  (c) Personnel participate in appropriate general and industry specific continuing professional education

  (d) Personnel selected for advancement have appropriate qualifications

 (2) A practitioner in charge will ordinarily obtain necessary competencies through recent experience in accounting, auditing, and attestation engagements

  (a) In some cases experience will be from other areas (e.g., industry, government, academic)

   1] If necessary, experience should be supplemented by continuing professional education and consultation

 (3) The firm's quality control policies and procedures should address

  (a) Understanding of the role of a System of Quality Control and the Code of Professional Conduct

  (b) Understanding of service to be performed

  (c) Technical proficiency

  (d) Familiarity with industry

  (e) Professional judgement

  (f) Understanding of client's information technology system

  *NOTE: The above competencies are interrelated, and gaining one may be related to achieving another (e.g., familiarity with industry interrelates with ability to make professional judgments).*

 (4) The Uniform Accountancy Act provides that any CPA who is responsible for supervising attest or compilation services and signs (or authorizes signing) the accountant's report shall meet the competency requirements set out in the professional standards for such services

  (a) While CPAs are not required to follow the Act itself, states in general have passed similar or identical requirements

6. **Public Company Accounting Oversight Board Requirements.** The Sarbanes-Oxley Act of 2002 includes a set of reforms that toughened penalties for corporate fraud, restricted the types of consulting CPAs may perform for audit clients, and created the Public Company Accounting Oversight Board (PCAOB). It was this act, implemented by the PCAOB, that led to "integrated audits" in which auditors report on audits of both the financial statements and on internal control over financial reporting for public audit clients.

   The five-member PCAOB (which may include no more than two CPAs as members) has broad authority to oversee the public accounting profession by establishing or adopting auditing, attestation, quality control, ethics, and independence standards relating to the audits performed for SEC registrants (public companies). In addition, the PCAOB has the responsibility to

   • Register public accounting firms that audit public companies
   • Perform inspections of the practices of registered firms
   • Conduct investigations and disciplinary proceedings of registered firms
   • Sanction registered firms

   a. **Inspections performed by the PCAOB.** The Sarbanes-Oxley Act requires that the PCAOB perform inspections of CPA firms that include at least the following three general components:

      (1) An inspection and review of selected audit and review engagements
      (2) An evaluation of the sufficiency of the quality control system of the CPA firm and the manner of documentation and communication of the system
      (3) Performance of such other testing of the audit, supervisory, and quality control procedures as are considered necessary

      Although inspection performed by the PCAOB staff meet the AICPA's practice review requirement for the public auditing practices of CPA firms, they differ from peer reviews conducted by CPA firms. Inspections generally focus on selected quality control issues and may also consider other aspects of practice management, such as how partner compensation is determined. Most of the inspection process is focused on evaluating a CPA firm's performance on a sample of individual audit and review engagements. In selecting the engagements for inspection, the PCAOB staff uses a risk assessment process to identify those engagements that have a higher risk of lack of compliance with professional standards. When an audit is selected, the inspection focuses on the high-risk aspects of that engagement, such as revenue recognition and accounting estimates. When a lack of compliance with professional standards is identified, the PCAOB staff attempts to determine the cause, which may lead to identification of a defect in the firm's quality control system.

      Each inspection results in a written report that is transmitted to the SEC and appropriate regulatory authorities. Also included is a letter of comments by the PCAOB inspectors, and any responses by the CPA firm. While the content of most of the reports are made available to the public, discussion of criticisms of a firm's quality control system are not made public unless the firm does not address the criticism within twelve months.

   b. **PCAOB interim standards.** Until it is able to adopt its own standards, the PCAOB adopted as interim standards the following AICPA professional standards (in existence on April 16, 2003):

      • Auditing Standards
      • Attestation Standards
      • Quality Control Standards
      • Independence Standards
      • Code of Professional Conduct

      Therefore, both the PCAOB standards and most of those presented throughout the Auditing and Attestation modules apply to audits of public clients.

      In one of its first pronouncements, the PCAOB clarified the meanings of certain terms used in its standards as follows:

| Responsibility level | Meaning | Words used to indicate responsibility |
|---|---|---|
| Unconditional responsibility | Auditor must fulfill responsibilities | "Must" "Shall" "Is required" |
| Presumptively mandatory responsibility | Auditor must comply with requirements unless auditor demonstrates that alternative actions were sufficient to achieve the objectives of the standards | "Should" |
| Responsibility to consider | Auditor should consider; whether auditor follows depends on exercise of professional judgment in the circumstances | "Might" "Could" Other phrases indicating a responsibility to consider |

**MULTIPLE-CHOICE QUESTIONS (1-124)**

**1.** As the acceptable level of detection risk decreases, an auditor may
   a. Reduce substantive testing by relying on the assessments of inherent risk and control risk.
   b. Postpone the planned timing of substantive tests from interim dates to the year-end.
   c. Eliminate the assessed level of inherent risk from consideration as a planning factor.
   d. Lower the assessed level of control risk from the maximum level to below the maximum.

**2.** The risk that an auditor will conclude, based on substantive tests, that a material misstatement does **not** exist in an account balance when, in fact, such misstatement does exist is referred to as
   a. Sampling risk.
   b. Detection risk.
   c. Nonsampling risk.
   d. Inherent risk.

**3.** As the acceptable level of detection risk decreases, the assurance directly provided from
   a. Substantive tests should increase.
   b. Substantive tests should decrease.
   c. Tests of controls should increase.
   d. Tests of controls should decrease.

**4.** Which of the following audit risk components may be assessed in nonquantitative terms?

|     | Control risk | Detection risk | Inherent risk |
| --- | --- | --- | --- |
| a. | Yes | Yes | No |
| b. | Yes | No | Yes |
| c. | Yes | Yes | Yes |
| d. | No | Yes | Yes |

**5.** Inherent risk and control risk differ from detection risk in that they
   a. Arise from the misapplication of auditing procedures.
   b. May be assessed in either quantitative or nonquantitative terms.
   c. Exist independently of the financial statement audit.
   d. Can be changed at the auditor's discretion.

**6.** On the basis of the audit evidence gathered and evaluated, an auditor decides to increase the assessed level of control risk from that originally planned. To achieve an overall audit risk level that is substantially the same as the planned audit risk level, the auditor would
   a. Decrease substantive testing.
   b. Decrease detection risk.
   c. Increase inherent risk.
   d. Increase materiality levels.

**7.** Relationship between control risk and detection risk is ordinarily
   a. Parallel.
   b. Inverse.
   c. Direct.
   d. Equal.

**8.** Which of the following would an auditor most likely use in determining the auditor's preliminary judgment about materiality?
   a. The anticipated sample size of the planned substantive tests.
   b. The entity's annualized interim financial statements.
   c. The results of the internal control questionnaire.
   d. The contents of the management representation letter.

**9.** Which of the following statements is **not** correct about materiality?
   a. The concept of materiality recognizes that some matters are important for fair presentation of financial statements in conformity with GAAP, while other matters are **not** important.
   b. An auditor considers materiality for planning purposes in terms of the largest aggregate level of misstatements that could be material to any one of the financial statements.
   c. Materiality judgments are made in light of surrounding circumstances and necessarily involve both quantitative and qualitative judgments.
   d. An auditor's consideration of materiality is influenced by the auditor's perception of the needs of a reasonable person who will rely on the financial statements.

**10.** Which of the following elements underlies the application of generally accepted auditing standards, particularly the standards of fieldwork and reporting?
   a. Internal control.
   b. Corroborating evidence.
   c. Quality control.
   d. Materiality and relative risk.

**11.** In considering materiality for planning purposes, an auditor believes that misstatements aggregating $10,000 would have a material effect on an entity's income statement, but that misstatements would have to aggregate $20,000 to materially affect the balance sheet. Ordinarily, it would be appropriate to design auditing procedures that would be expected to detect misstatements that aggregate
   a. $10,000
   b. $15,000
   c. $20,000
   d. $30,000

**12.** Which of the following would an auditor most likely use in determining the auditor's preliminary judgment about materiality?
   a. The results of the initial assessment of control risk.
   b. The anticipated sample size for planned substantive tests.
   c. The entity's financial statements of the prior year.
   d. The assertions that are embodied in the financial statements.

**13.** Holding other planning considerations equal, a decrease in the amount of misstatement in a class of transactions that an auditor could tolerate most likely would cause the auditor to
   a. Apply the planned substantive tests prior to the balance sheet date.

b. Perform the planned auditing procedures closer to the balance sheet date.

c. Increase the assessed level of control risk for relevant financial statement assertions.

d. Decrease the extent of auditing procedures to be applied to the class of transactions.

**14.** When issuing an unqualified opinion, the auditor who evaluates the audit findings should be satisfied that the

a. Amount of known misstatement is documented in the management representation letter.

b. Estimate of the total likely misstatement is less than a material amount.

c. Amount of known misstatement is acknowledged and recorded by the client.

d. Estimate of the total likely misstatement includes the adjusting entries already recorded by the client.

**15.** Which of the following is an example of fraudulent financial reporting?

a. Company management changes inventory count tags and overstates ending inventory, while understating cost of goods sold.

b. The treasurer diverts customer payments to his personal due, concealing his actions by debiting an expense account, thus overstating expenses.

c. An employee steals inventory and the "shrinkage" is recorded in cost of goods sold.

d. An employee steals small tools from the company and neglects to return them; the cost is reported as a miscellaneous operating expense.

**16.** Which of the following best describes what is meant by the term "fraud risk factor?"

a. Factors whose presence indicates that the risk of fraud is high.

b. Factors whose presence often have been observed in circumstances where frauds have occurred.

c. Factors whose presence requires modification of planned audit procedures.

d. Reportable conditions identified during an audit.

**17.** Which of the following is correct concerning requirements about auditor communications about fraud?

a. Fraud that involves senior management should be reported directly to the audit committee **regardless** of the amount involved.

b. Fraud with a material effect on the financial statements should be reported directly by the auditor to the Securities and Exchange Commission.

c. Fraud with a material effect on the financial statements should ordinarily be disclosed by the auditor through use of an "emphasis of a matter" paragraph added to the audit report.

d. The auditor has no responsibility to disclose fraud outside the entity under any circumstances.

**18.** When performing a financial statement audit, auditors are required to explicitly assess the risk of material misstatement due to

a. Errors.

b. Fraud.

c. Illegal acts.

d. Business risk.

**19.** Audits of financial statements are designed to obtain assurance of detecting misstatement due to

|  | Errors | Fraudulent financial reporting | Misappropriation of assets |
|---|---|---|---|
| a. | Yes | Yes | Yes |
| b. | Yes | Yes | No |
| c. | Yes | No | Yes |
| d. | No | Yes | No |

**20.** An auditor is unable to obtain absolute assurance that misstatements due to fraud will be detected for all of the following **except**

a. Employee collusion.

b. Falsified documentation.

c. Need to apply professional judgment in evaluating fraud risk factors.

d. Professional skepticism.

**21.** The most difficult type of misstatement to detect is fraud based on

a. The overrecording of transactions.

b. The nonrecording of transactions.

c. Recorded transactions in subsidiaries.

d. Related-party receivables.

**22.** When considering fraud risk factors relating to management's characteristics, which of the following is **least likely** to indicate a risk of possible misstatement due to fraud?

a. Failure to correct known reportable conditions on a timely basis.

b. Nonfinancial management's preoccupation with the selection of accounting principles.

c. Significant portion of management's compensation represented by bonuses based upon achieving unduly aggressive operating results.

d. Use of unusually conservative accounting practices.

**23.** Which of the following conditions identified during fieldwork of an audit is most likely to affect the auditor's assessment of the risk of misstatement due to fraud?

a. Checks for significant amounts outstanding at year-end.

b. Computer generated documents.

c. Missing documents.

d. Year-end adjusting journal entries.

**24.** Which of the following is most likely to be a response to the auditor's assessment that the risk of material misstatement due to fraud for the existence of inventory is high?

a. Observe test counts of inventory at certain locations on an unannounced basis.

b. Perform analytical procedures rather than taking test counts.

c. Request that inventories be counted prior to year-end.

d. Request that inventory counts at the various locations be counted on different dates so as to allow the same auditor to be present at every count.

**25.** Which of the following is most likely to be an example of fraud?

a. Defalcations occurring due to invalid electronic approvals.

b. Mistakes in the application of accounting principles.

c. Mistakes in processing data.

d. Unreasonable accounting estimates arising from oversight.

**26.** Which of the following characteristics most likely would heighten an auditor's concern about the risk of intentional manipulation of financial statements?

    a. Turnover of senior accounting personnel is low.

    b. Insiders recently purchased additional shares of the entity's stock.

    c. Management places substantial emphasis on meeting earnings projections.

    d. The rate of change in the entity's industry is slow.

**27.** Which of the following statements reflects an auditor's responsibility for detecting misstatements due to errors and fraud?

    a. An auditor is responsible for detecting employee errors and simple fraud, but **not** for discovering fraud involving employee collusion or management override.

    b. An auditor should plan the audit to detect misstatements due to errors and fraud that are caused by departures from GAAP.

    c. An auditor is **not** responsible for detecting misstatements due to errors and fraud unless the application of GAAS would result in such detection.

    d. An auditor should design the audit to provide reasonable assurance of detecting misstatements due to errors and fraud that are material to the financial statements.

**28.** Disclosure of fraud to parties other than a client's senior management and its audit committee or board of directors ordinarily is not part of an auditor's responsibility. However, to which of the following outside parties may a duty to disclose fraud exist?

| | To the SEC when the client reports an auditor change | To a successor auditor when the successor makes appropriate Inquiries | To a government funding agency from which the client receives financial assistance |
|---|---|---|---|
| a. | Yes | Yes | No |
| b. | Yes | No | Yes |
| c. | No | Yes | Yes |
| d. | Yes | Yes | Yes |

**29.** Under Statements on Auditing Standards, which of the following would be classified as an error?

    a. Misappropriation of assets for the benefit of management.

    b. Misinterpretation by management of facts that existed when the financial statements were prepared.

    c. Preparation of records by employees to cover a fraudulent scheme.

    d. Intentional omission of the recording of a transaction to benefit a third party.

**30.** What assurance does the auditor provide that misstatements due to errors, fraud, and direct effect illegal acts that are material to the financial statements will be detected?

| | *Errors* | *Fraud* | *Direct effect illegal acts* |
|---|---|---|---|
| a. | Limited | Negative | Limited |
| b. | Limited | Limited | Reasonable |
| c. | Reasonable | Limited | Limited |
| d. | Reasonable | Reasonable | Reasonable |

**31.** Because of the risk of material misstatement, an audit of financial statements in accordance with generally accepted auditing standards should be planned and performed with an attitude of

    a. Objective judgment.

    b. Independent integrity.

    c. Professional skepticism.

    d. Impartial conservatism.

**32.** Which of the following most accurately summarizes what is meant by the term "material misstatement?"

    a. Fraud and direct-effect illegal acts.

    b. Fraud involving senior management and material fraud.

    c. Material error, material fraud, and certain illegal acts.

    d. Material error and material illegal acts.

**33.** Which of the following statements best describes the auditor's responsibility to detect conditions relating to financial stress of employees or adverse relationships between a company and its employees?

    a. The auditor is required to plan the audit to detect these conditions on all audits.

    b. These conditions relate to fraudulent financial reporting, and an auditor is required to plan the audit to detect these conditions when the client is exposed to a risk of misappropriation of assets.

    c. The auditor is required to plan the audit to detect these conditions whenever they may result in misstatements.

    d. The auditor is not required to plan the audit to discover these conditions, but should consider them if he or she becomes aware of them during the audit.

**34.** When the auditor believes a misstatement is or may be the result of fraud but that the effect of the misstatement is not material to the financial statements, which of the following steps is required?

    a. Consider the implications for other aspects of the audit.

    b. Resign from the audit.

    c. Commence a fraud examination.

    d. Contact regulatory authorities.

**35.** Which of the following statements is correct relating to the auditor's consideration of fraud?

    a. The auditor's interest in fraud consideration relates to fraudulent acts that cause a material misstatement of financial statements.

    b. A primary factor that distinguishes fraud from error is that fraud is always intentional, while errors are generally, but not always, intentional.

    c. Fraud always involves a pressure or incentive to commit fraud, and a misappropriation of assets.

    d. While an auditor should be aware of the possibility of fraud, management, and not the auditor, is responsible for detecting fraud.

**36.** Which of the following factors or conditions is an auditor least likely to plan an audit to discover?

    a.   Financial pressures affecting employees.

    b.   High turnover of senior management.

    c.   Inadequate monitoring of significant controls.

    d.   Inability to generate positive cash flows from operations.

**37.** At which stage(s) of the audit may fraud risk factors be identified?

|  | Planning | Obtaining understanding | Conducting fieldwork |
|---|---|---|---|
| a. | Yes | Yes | Yes |
| b. | Yes | Yes | No |
| c. | Yes | No | No |
| d. | No | Yes | Yes |

**38.** Management's attitude toward aggressive financial reporting and its emphasis on meeting projected profit goals most likely would significantly influence an entity's control environment when

    a.   External policies established by parties outside the entity affect its accounting practices.

    b.   Management is dominated by one individual who is also a shareholder.

    c.   Internal auditors have direct access to the board of directors and the entity's management.

    d.   The audit committee is active in overseeing the entity's financial reporting policies.

**39.** Which of the following is **least** likely to be required on an audit?

    a.   Test appropriateness of journal entries and adjustment.

    b.   Review accounting estimates for biases.

    c.   Evaluate the business rationale for significant unusual transactions.

    d.   Make a legal determination of whether fraud has occurred.

**40.** Which of the following is most likely to be an overall response to fraud risks identified in an audit?

    a.   Supervise members of the audit team less closely and rely more upon judgment.

    b.   Use less predictable audit procedures.

    c.   Only use certified public accountants on the engagement.

    d.   Place increased emphasis on the audit of objective transactions rather than subjective transactions.

**41.** Which of the following is **least** likely to be included in an auditor's inquiry of management while obtaining information to identify the risks of material misstatement due to fraud?

    a.   Are financial reporting operations controlled by and limited to one location?

    b.   Does it have knowledge of fraud or suspect fraud?

    c.   Does it have programs to mitigate fraud risks?

    d.   Has it reported to the audit committee the nature of the company's internal control?

**42.** Individuals who commit fraud are ordinarily able to rationalize the act and also have an

|  | Incentive | Opportunity |
|---|---|---|
| a. | Yes | Yes |
| b. | Yes | No |
| c. | No | Yes |
| d. | No | No |

**43.** What is an auditor's responsibility who discovers management involved in what is financially immaterial fraud?

    a.   Report the fraud to the audit committee.

    b.   Report the fraud to the Public Company Oversight Board.

    c.   Report the fraud to a level of management at least one below those involved in the fraud.

    d.   Determine that the amounts involved are immaterial, and if so, there is no reporting responsibility.

**44.** Which of the following is most likely to be considered a risk factor relating to fraudulent financial reporting?

    a.   Domination of management by top executives.

    b.   Large amounts of cash processed.

    c.   Negative cash flows from operations.

    d.   Small high-dollar inventory items.

**45.** Which of the following is most likely to be presumed to represent fraud risk on an audit?

    a.   Capitalization of repairs and maintenance into the property, plant, and equipment asset account.

    b.   Improper revenue recognition.

    c.   Improper interest expense accrual.

    d.   Introduction of significant new products.

**46.** An auditor who discovers that a client's employees paid small bribes to municipal officials most likely would withdraw from the engagement if

    a.   The payments violated the client's policies regarding the prevention of illegal acts.

    b.   The client receives financial assistance from a federal government agency.

    c.   Documentation that is necessary to prove that the bribes were paid does **not** exist.

    d.   Management fails to take the appropriate remedial action.

**47.** Which of the following factors most likely would cause a CPA to **not** accept a new audit engagement?

    a.   The prospective client has already completed its physical inventory count.

    b.   The CPA lacks an understanding of the prospective client's operation and industry.

    c.   The CPA is unable to review the predecessor auditor's working papers.

    d.   The prospective client is unwilling to make all financial records available to the CPA.

**48.** Which of the following factors would most likely heighten an auditor's concern about the risk of fraudulent financial reporting?

    a.   Large amounts of liquid assets that are easily convertible into cash.

    b.   Low growth and profitability as compared to other entities in the same industry.

    c.   Financial management's participation in the initial selection of accounting principles.

    d.   An overly complex organizational structure involving unusual lines of authority.

**49.** An auditor who discovers that a client's employees have paid small bribes to public officials most likely would withdraw from the engagement if the
  a. Client receives financial assistance from a federal government agency.
  b. Evidential matter that is necessary to prove that the illegal acts were committed does not exist.
  c. Employees' actions affect the auditor's ability to rely on management's representations.
  d. Notes to the financial statements fail to disclose the employees' actions.

**50.** Which of the following illegal acts should an audit be designed to obtain reasonable assurance of detecting?
  a. Securities purchased by relatives of management based on knowledge of inside information.
  b. Accrual and billing of an improper amount of revenue under government contracts.
  c. Violations of antitrust laws.
  d. Price fixing.

**51.** Which of the following relatively small misstatements most likely could have a material effect on an entity's financial statements?
  a. An illegal payment to a foreign official that was **not** recorded.
  b. A piece of obsolete office equipment that was **not** retired.
  c. A petty cash fund disbursement that was **not** properly authorized.
  d. An uncollectible account receivable that was **not** written off.

**52.** During the annual audit of Ajax Corp., a publicly held company, Jones, CPA, a continuing auditor, determined that illegal political contributions had been made during each of the past seven years, including the year under audit. Jones notified the board of directors about the illegal contributions, but they refused to take any action because the amounts involved were immaterial to the financial statements. Jones should reconsider the intended degree of reliance to be placed on the
  a. Letter of audit inquiry to the client's attorney.
  b. Prior years' audit programs.
  c. Management representation letter.
  d. Preliminary judgment about materiality levels.

**53.** The most likely explanation why the auditor's examination **cannot** reasonably be expected to bring all illegal acts by the client to the auditor's attention is that
  a. Illegal acts are perpetrated by management override of internal control.
  b. Illegal acts by clients often relate to operating aspects rather than accounting aspects.
  c. The client's internal control may be so strong that the auditor performs only minimal substantive testing.
  d. Illegal acts may be perpetrated by the only person in the client's organization with access to both assets and the accounting records.

**54.** If specific information comes to an auditor's attention that implies the existence of possible illegal acts that could have a material, but indirect effect on the financial statements, the auditor should next

  a. Apply audit procedures specifically directed to ascertaining whether an illegal act has occurred.
  b. Seek the advice of an informed expert qualified to practice law as to possible contingent liabilities.
  c. Report the matter to an appropriate level of management at least one level above those involved.
  d. Discuss the evidence with the client's audit committee, or others with equivalent authority and responsibility.

**55.** An auditor who discovers that client employees have committed an illegal act that has a material effect on the client's financial statements most likely would withdraw from the engagement if
  a. The illegal act is a violation of generally accepted accounting principles.
  b. The client does not take the remedial action that the auditor considers necessary.
  c. The illegal act was committed during a prior year that was not audited.
  d. The auditor has already assessed control risk at the maximum level.

**56.** Under the Private Securities Litigation Reform Act of 1995, Baker, CPA, reported certain uncorrected illegal acts to Supermart's board of directors. Baker believed that failure to take remedial action would warrant a qualified audit opinion because the illegal acts had a material effect on Supermart's financial statements. Supermart failed to take appropriate remedial action and the board of directors refused to inform the SEC that it had received such notification from Baker. Under these circumstances, Baker is required to
  a. Resign from the audit engagement within ten business days.
  b. Deliver a report concerning the illegal acts to the SEC within one business day.
  c. Notify the stockholders that the financial statements are materially misstated.
  d. Withhold an audit opinion until Supermart takes appropriate remedial action.

**57.** Before accepting an engagement to audit a new client, a CPA is required to obtain
  a. An understanding of the prospective client's industry and business.
  b. The prospective client's signature to the engagement letter.
  c. A preliminary understanding of the prospective client's control environment.
  d. The prospective client's consent to make inquiries of the predecessor auditor, if any.

**58.** Before accepting an audit engagement, a successor auditor should make specific inquiries of the predecessor auditor regarding
  a. Disagreements the predecessor had with the client concerning auditing procedures and accounting principles.
  b. The predecessor's evaluation of matters of continuing accounting significance.
  c. The degree of cooperation the predecessor received concerning the inquiry of the client's lawyer.
  d. The predecessor's assessments of inherent risk and judgments about materiality.

**59.** Before accepting an audit engagement, a successor auditor should make specific inquiries of the predecessor auditor regarding the predecessor's
   a.   Opinion of any subsequent events occurring since the predecessor's audit report was issued.
   b.   Understanding as to the reasons for the change of auditors.
   c.   Awareness of the consistency in the application of GAAP between periods.
   d.   Evaluation of all matters of continuing accounting significance.

**60.** Which of the following factors would most likely cause a CPA to decide not to accept a new audit engagement?
   a.   The CPA's lack of understanding of the prospective client's internal auditor's computer-assisted audit techniques.
   b.   Management's disregard of its responsibility to maintain an adequate internal control environment.
   c.   The CPA's inability to determine whether related-party transactions were consummated on terms equivalent to arm's-length transactions.
   d.   Management's refusal to permit the CPA to perform substantive tests before the year-end.

**61.** An auditor is required to establish an understanding with a client regarding the services to be performed for each engagement. This understanding generally includes
   a.   Management's responsibility for errors and the illegal activities of employees that may cause material misstatement.
   b.   The auditor's responsibility for ensuring that the audit committee is aware of any reportable conditions that come to the auditor's attention.
   c.   Management's responsibility for providing the auditor with an assessment of the risk of material misstatement due to fraud.
   d.   The auditor's responsibility for determining preliminary judgments about materiality and audit risk factors.

**62.** Which of the following is most likely to require special planning considerations related to asset valuation?
   a.   Inventory is comprised of diamond rings.
   b.   The client has recently purchased an expensive copy machine.
   c.   Assets costing less than $250 are expensed even when the expected life exceeds one year.
   d.   Accelerated depreciation methods are used for amortizing the costs of factory equipment.

**63.** Which of the following factors most likely would influence an auditor's determination of the auditability of an entity's financial statements?
   a.   The complexity of the accounting system.
   b.   The existence of related-party transactions.
   c.   The adequacy of the accounting records.
   d.   The operating effectiveness of control procedures.

**64.** To obtain an understanding of a continuing client's business in planning an audit, an auditor most likely would
   a.   Perform tests of details of transactions and balances.
   b.   Review prior year working papers and the permanent file for the client.
   c.   Read specialized industry journals.

   d.   Reevaluate the client's internal control environment.

**65.** Which of the following matters is generally included in an auditor's engagement letter?
   a.   Management's responsibility for the entity's compliance with laws and regulations.
   b.   The factors to be considered in setting preliminary judgments about materiality.
   c.   Management's vicarious liability for illegal acts committed by its employees.
   d.   The auditor's responsibility to search for significant internal control deficiencies.

**66.** During the initial planning phase of an audit, a CPA most likely would
   a.   Identify specific internal control activities that are likely to prevent fraud.
   b.   Evaluate the reasonableness of the client's accounting estimates.
   c.   Discuss the timing of the audit procedures with the client's management.
   d.   Inquire of the client's attorney as to whether any unrecorded claims are probable of assertion.

**67.** Which of the following statements would **least** likely appear in an auditor's engagement letter?
   a.   Fees for our services are based on our regular per diem rates, plus travel and other out-of-pocket expenses.
   b.   During the course of our audit we may observe opportunities for economy in, or improved controls over, your operations.
   c.   Our engagement is subject to the risk that material misstatements or fraud, if they exist, will **not** be detected.
   d.   After performing our preliminary analytical procedures we will discuss with you the other procedures we consider necessary to complete the engagement.

**68.** Which of the following documentation is **not** required for an audit in accordance with generally accepted auditing standards?
   a.   A written audit program setting forth the procedures necessary to accomplish the audit's objectives.
   b.   An indication that the accounting records agree or reconcile with the financial statements.
   c.   A client engagement letter that summarizes the timing and details of the auditor's planned fieldwork.
   d.   The basis for the auditor's conclusions when the assessed level of control risk is below the maximum level.

**69.** An engagement letter should ordinarily include information on the objectives of the engagement and

|     | CPA responsibilities | Client responsibilities | Limitation of engagement |
| --- | --- | --- | --- |
| a. | Yes | Yes | Yes |
| b. | Yes | No | Yes |
| c. | Yes | No | No |
| d. | No | No | No |

**70.** Arrangements concerning which of the following are **least** likely to be included in engagement letter?
  a.  A predecessor auditor.
  b.  Fees and billing.
  c.  CPA investment in client securities.
  d.  Other services to be provided in addition to the audit.

**71.** When an auditor believes that an understanding with the client has **not** been established, he or she should ordinarily
  a.  Perform the audit with increased professional skepticism.
  b.  Decline to accept or perform the audit.
  c.  Assess control risk at the maximum level and perform a primarily substantive audit.
  d.  Modify the scope of the audit to reflect an increased risk of material misstatement due to fraud.

**72.** Select the proper reply as to the allowable form of the understanding with a client when an audit is being performed
  a.  While preferably written, it may be oral; but in all cases it should be documented in the working papers.
  b.  While preferably written, it may be oral, in which case it need not be documented in the working papers.
  c.  The understanding must be obtained in written form and included in the working papers.
  d.  No requirement exists that the auditor obtain an understanding with the client.

**73.** A CPA wishes to determine how various publicly held companies have complied with the disclosure requirements of a new financial accounting standard. Which of the following information sources would the CPA most likely consult for information?
  a.  AICPA Codification of Statements on Auditing Standards.
  b.  AICPA *Accounting Trends and Techniques*.
  c.  SEC Quality Control Review.
  d.  SEC Statement 10-K Guide.

**74.** Which of the following procedures would an auditor most likely include in the planning phase of a financial statement audit?
  a.  Obtain an understanding of the entity's risk assessment process.
  b.  Identify specific internal control activities designed to prevent fraud.
  c.  Evaluate the reasonableness of the entity's accounting estimates.
  d.  Perform cutoff tests of the entity's sales and purchases.

**75.** An auditor obtains knowledge about a new client's business and its industry to
  a.  Make constructive suggestions concerning improvements to the client's internal control.
  b.  Develop an attitude of professional skepticism concerning management's financial statement assertions.
  c.  Evaluate whether the aggregation of known misstatements causes the financial statements taken as a whole to be materially misstated.

  d.  Understand the events and transactions that may have an effect on the client's financial statements.

**76.** Which of the following procedures would an auditor **least** likely perform in planning a financial statement audit?
  a.  Coordinating the assistance of entity personnel in data preparation.
  b.  Discussing matters that may affect the audit with firm personnel responsible for nonaudit services to the entity.
  c.  Selecting a sample of vendors' invoices for comparison to receiving reports.
  d.  Reading the current year's interim financial statements.

**77.** Ordinarily, the predecessor auditor permits the successor auditor to review the predecessor's working paper analyses relating to

|    | Contingencies | Balance sheet accounts |
|----|---------------|------------------------|
| a. | Yes           | Yes                    |
| b. | Yes           | No                     |
| c. | No            | Yes                    |
| d. | No            | No                     |

**78.** In auditing the financial statements of Star Corp., Land discovered information leading Land to believe that Star's prior year's financial statements, which were audited by Tell, require substantial revisions. Under these circumstances, Land should
  a.  Notify Star's audit committee and stockholders that the prior year's financial statements **cannot** be relied on.
  b.  Request Star to reissue the prior year's financial statements with the appropriate revisions.
  c.  Notify Tell about the information and make inquiries about the integrity of Star's management.
  d.  Request Star to arrange a meeting among the three parties to resolve the matter.

**79.** A successor auditor should request the new client to authorize the predecessor auditor to allow a review of the predecessor's

|    | Engagement letter | Working papers |
|----|-------------------|----------------|
| a. | Yes               | Yes            |
| b. | Yes               | No             |
| c. | No                | Yes            |
| d. | No                | No             |

**80.** Which of the following procedures would an auditor most likely perform in planning a financial statement audit?
  a.  Inquiring of the client's legal counsel concerning pending litigation.
  b.  Comparing the financial statements to anticipated results.
  c.  Examining computer generated exception reports to verify the effectiveness of internal control.
  d.  Searching for unauthorized transactions that may aid in detecting unrecorded liabilities.

**81.** Analytical procedures used in planning an audit should focus on
  a.  Reducing the scope of tests of controls and substantive tests.
  b.  Providing assurance that potential material misstatements will be identified.
  c.  Enhancing the auditor's understanding of the client's business.

d.   Assessing the adequacy of the available evidential matter.

**82.** The objective of performing analytical procedures in planning an audit is to identify the existence of
a.   Unusual transactions and events.
b.   Illegal acts that went undetected because of internal control weaknesses.
c.   Related-party transactions.
d.   Recorded transactions that were **not** properly authorized.

**83.** Which of the following nonfinancial information would an auditor most likely consider in performing analytical procedures during the planning phase of an audit?
a.   Turnover of personnel in the accounting department.
b.   Objectivity of audit committee members.
c.   Square footage of selling space.
d.   Management's plans to repurchase stock.

**84.** An auditor should design the written audit program so that
a.   All material transactions will be selected for substantive testing.
b.   Substantive tests prior to the balance sheet date will be minimized.
c.   The audit procedures selected will achieve specific audit objectives.
d.   Each account balance will be tested under either tests of controls or tests of transactions.

**85.** The audit program usually **cannot** be finalized until the
a.   Consideration of the entity's internal control has been completed.
b.   Engagement letter has been signed by the auditor and the client.
c.   Reportable conditions have been communicated to the audit committee of the board of directors.
d.   Search for unrecorded liabilities has been performed and documented.

**86.** Audit programs should be designed so that
a.   Most of the required procedures can be performed as interim work.
b.   Inherent risk is assessed at a sufficiently low level.
c.   The auditor can make constructive suggestions to management.
d.   The audit evidence gathered supports the auditor's conclusions.

**87.** In designing written audit programs, an auditor should establish specific audit objectives that relate primarily to the
a.   Timing of audit procedures.
b.   Cost-benefit of gathering evidence.
c.   Selected audit techniques.
d.   Financial statement assertions.

**88.** The in-charge auditor most likely would have a supervisory responsibility to explain to the staff assistants
a.   That immaterial fraud is **not** to be reported to the client's audit committee.
b.   How the results of various auditing procedures performed by the assistants should be evaluated.
c.   What benefits may be attained by the assistants' adherence to established time budgets.

d.   Why certain documents are being transferred from the current file to the permanent file.

**89.** The audit work performed by each assistant should be reviewed to determine whether it was adequately performed and to evaluate whether the
a.   Auditor's system of quality control has been maintained at a high level.
b.   Results are consistent with the conclusions to be presented in the auditor's report.
c.   Audit procedures performed are approved in the professional standards.
d.   Audit has been performed by persons having adequate technical training and proficiency as auditors.

**90.** With respect to planning an audit, which of the following statements is always true?
a.   It is acceptable to perform a portion of the audit of a continuing audit client at interim dates.
b.   An engagement should not be accepted after the client's year-end.
c.   An inventory count must be observed at year-end.
d.   Final staffing decisions must be made prior to completion of the planning stage.

**91.** The element of the audit planning process most likely to be agreed upon with the client before implementation of the audit strategy is the determination of the
a.   Evidence to be gathered to provide a sufficient basis for the auditor's opinion.
b.   Procedures to be undertaken to discover litigation, claims, and assessments.
c.   Pending legal matters to be included in the inquiry of the client's attorney.
d.   Timing of inventory observation procedures to be performed.

**92.** The "Special Committee on Assurance Services" defined assurance services as independent professional services that
a.   Include a written communication that expresses a conclusion.
b.   Improve the quality of information, or its context, for decision makers.
c.   Include audit services, attest services, and consulting services.
d.   Involve the examination of the credibility of a written assertion that is the responsibility of another party.

**93.** The group that was established in 1994 by the American Institute of Certified Public Accountants to analyze and report on the current state and future of the audit/assurance function and trends shaping its environment is the
a.   Commission on Auditors' Responsibilities.
b.   Committee of Sponsoring Organizations (COSO).
c.   Special Committee on Assurance Services.
d.   Accountancy Future Task Force (AFTF).

**94.** Which of the following is **not** a type of attest engagement?
a.   Agreed-upon procedures.
b.   Compilation.
c.   Examination.
d.   Review.

**95.** Which of the following is a conceptual difference between the attestation standards and generally accepted auditing standards?

    a.   The attestation standards do not apply to audits of historical financial statements, while the generally accepted auditing standards do.

    b.   The requirement that the practitioner be independent in mental attitude is omitted from the attestation standards.

    c.   The attestation standards do **not** permit an attest engagement to be part of a business acquisition study or a feasibility study.

    d.   **None** of the standards of fieldwork in generally accepted auditing standards are included in the attestation standards.

**96.** Which of the following is **not** an attestation standard?

    a.   Sufficient evidence shall be obtained to provide a reasonable basis for the conclusion that is expressed in the report.

    b.   The report shall identify the subject matter on the assertion being reported on and state the character of the engagement.

    c.   The work shall be adequately planned and assistants, if any, shall be properly supervised.

    d.   A sufficient understanding of internal control shall be obtained to plan the engagement.

**97.** On an audit engagement performed by a CPA firm with one office, at the minimum, knowledge of the relevant professional accounting and auditing standards should be held by

    a.   The auditor with final responsibility for the audit.

    b.   All professionals working upon the audit.

    c.   All professionals working upon the audit and the partner in charge of the CPA firm.

    d.   All professionals working in the office.

**98.** An attitude that includes a questioning mind and a critical assessment of audit evidence is referred to as

    a.   Due professional care.

    b.   Professional skepticism.

    c.   Reasonable assurance.

    d.   Supervision.

**99.** Professional skepticism requires that an auditor assume that management is

    a.   Honest, in the absence of fraud risk factors.

    b.   Dishonest until completion of audit tests.

    c.   Neither honest nor dishonest.

    d.   Offering reasonable assurance of honesty.

**100.** An unqualified attestation report ordinarily may refer to

    a.   Only the assertion.

    b.   Only the subject matter to which the assertion relates.

    c.   Either the assertion or the subject matter to which the assertion relates.

    d.   Neither the assertion nor the subject matter to which the assertion relates.

**101.** Which of the following is most likely to be unique to the audit work of CPAs as compared to work performed by practitioners of other professions?

    a.   Due professional care.

    b.   Competence.

    c.   Independence.

    d.   Complex body of knowledge.

**102.** The third general standard states that due care is to be exercised in the performance of an audit. This standard is ordinarily interpreted to require

    a.   Thorough review of the existing safeguards over access to assets and records.

    b.   Limited review of the indications of employee fraud and illegal acts.

    c.   Objective review of the adequacy of the technical training and proficiency of firm personnel.

    d.   Critical review of the judgment exercised at every level of supervision.

**103.** After fieldwork audit procedures are completed, a partner of the CPA firm who has not been involved in the audit performs a second or wrap-up working paper review. This second review usually focuses on

    a.   The fair presentation of the financial statements in conformity with GAAP.

    b.   Fraud involving the client's management and its employees.

    c.   The materiality of the adjusting entries proposed by the audit staff.

    d.   The communication of internal control weaknesses to the client's audit committee.

**104.** Which of the following statements is correct concerning an auditor's responsibilities regarding financial statements?

    a.   Making suggestions that are adopted about the form and content of an entity's financial statements impairs an auditor's independence.

    b.   An auditor may draft an entity's financial statements based on information from management's accounting system.

    c.   The fair presentation of audited financial statements in conformity with GAAP is an implicit part of the auditor's responsibilities.

    d.   An auditor's responsibilities for audited financial statements are **not** confined to the expression of the auditor's opinion.

**105.** Which of the following is an authoritative body designated to promulgate attestation standards?

    a.   Auditing Standards Board.

    b.   Governmental Accounting Standards Board.

    c.   Financial Accounting Standards Board.

    d.   General Accounting Office.

**106.** Which of the following best describes what is meant by the term generally accepted auditing standards?

    a.   Procedures to be used to gather evidence to support financial statements.

    b.   Measures of the quality of the auditor's performance.

    c.   Pronouncements issued by the Auditing Standards Board.

    d.   Rules acknowledged by the accounting profession because of their universal application.

**107.** The auditor with final responsibility for an engagement and one of the assistants have a difference of opinion about the results of an auditing procedure. If the assistant believes it is necessary to be disassociated from the matter's resolution, the CPA firm's procedures should enable the assistant to

- a. Refer the disagreement to the AICPA's Quality Review Committee.
- b. Document the details of the disagreement with the conclusion reached.
- c. Discuss the disagreement with the entity's management or its audit committee.
- d. Report the disagreement to an impartial peer review monitoring team.

**108.** When engaged to compile the financial statements of a nonpublic entity, an accountant is required to possess a level of knowledge of the entity's accounting principles and practices. This requirement most likely will include obtaining a general understanding of the

- a. Stated qualifications of the entity's accounting personnel.
- b. Design of the entity's internal controls placed in operation.
- c. Risk factors relating to misstatements arising from illegal acts.
- d. Internal control awareness of the entity's senior management.

**109.** An accountant is required to comply with the provisions of Statements on Standards for Accounting and Review Services when

I. Reproducing client-prepared financial statements, without modification, as an accommodation to a client.
II. Preparing standard monthly journal entries for depreciation and expiration of prepaid expenses.

- a. I only.
- b. II only.
- c. Both I and II.
- d. Neither I nor II.

**110.** If requested to perform a review engagement for a nonpublic entity in which an accountant has an immaterial direct financial interest, the accountant is

- a. Not independent and, therefore, may **not** be associated with the financial statements.
- b. Not independent and, therefore, may **not** issue a review report.
- c. Not independent and, therefore, may issue a review report, but may **not** issue an auditor's opinion.
- d. Independent because the financial interest is immaterial and, therefore, may issue a review report.

**111.** Kell engaged March, CPA, to submit to Kell a written personal financial plan containing unaudited personal financial statements. March anticipates omitting certain disclosures required by GAAP because the engagement's sole purpose is to assist Kell in developing a personal financial plan. For March to be exempt from complying with the requirements of SSARS 1, *Compilation and Review of Financial Statements*, Kell is required to agree that the

- a. Financial statements will **not** be presented in comparative form with those of the prior period.
- b. Omitted disclosures required by GAAP are **not** material.
- c. Financial statements will **not** be disclosed to a non-CPA financial planner.
- d. Financial statements will **not** be used to obtain credit.

**112.** An accountant has been engaged to review a nonpublic entity's financial statements that contain several departures from GAAP. If the financial statements are **not** revised and modification of the standard review report is **not** adequate to indicate the deficiencies, the accountant should

- a. Withdraw from the engagement and provide **no** further services concerning these financial statements.
- b. Inform management that the engagement can proceed only if distribution of the accountant's report is restricted to internal use.
- c. Determine the effects of the departures from GAAP and issue a special report on the financial statements.
- d. Issue a modified review report provided the entity agrees that the financial statements will **not** be used to obtain credit.

**113.** Statements on Standards for Accounting and Review Services (SSARS) require an accountant to report when the accountant has

- a. Typed client-prepared financial statements, without modification, as an accommodation to the client.
- b. Provided a client with a financial statement format that does **not** include dollar amounts, to be used by the client in preparing financial statements.
- c. Proposed correcting journal entries to be recorded by the client that change client-prepared financial statements.
- d. Generated, through the use of computer software, financial statements prepared in accordance with a comprehensive basis of accounting other than GAAP.

**114.** Statements on Standards for Accounting and Review Services establish standards and procedures for which of the following engagements?

- a. Assisting in adjusting the books of account for a partnership.
- b. Reviewing interim financial data required to be filed with the SEC.
- c. Processing financial data for clients of other accounting firms.
- d. Compiling an individual's personal financial statement to be used to obtain a mortgage.

**115.** The authoritative body designated to promulgate standards concerning an accountant's association with unaudited financial statements of an entity that is **not** required to file financial statements with an agency regulating the issuance of the entity's securities is the

- a. Financial Accounting Standards Board.
- b. General Accounting Office.
- c. Accounting and Review Services Committee.
- d. Auditing Standards Board.

**116.** Which of the following accounting services may an accountant perform **without** being required to issue a compilation or review report under the Statements on Standards for Accounting and Review Services?

I. Preparing a working trial balance.
II. Preparing standard monthly journal entries.

- a. I only.
- b. II only.
- c. Both I and II.
- d. Neither I nor II.

**117.** An examination of a financial forecast is a professional service that involves
   a.  Compiling or assembling a financial forecast that is based on management's assumptions.
   b.  Limiting the distribution of the accountant's report to management and the board of directors.
   c.  Assuming responsibility to update management on key events for one year after the report's date.
   d.  Evaluating the preparation of a financial forecast and the support underlying management's assumptions.

**118.** An accountant may accept an engagement to apply agreed-upon procedures to prospective financial statements provided that
   a.  Use of the report is restricted to the specified parties.
   b.  The prospective financial statements are also examined.
   c.  Responsibility for the adequacy of the procedures performed is taken by the accountant.
   d.  Negative assurance is expressed on the prospective financial statements taken as a whole.

**119.** The nature and extent of a CPA firm's quality control policies and procedures depend on

|      | The CPA firm's size | The nature of the CPA firm's practice | Cost-benefit considerations |
|------|---------------------|---------------------------------------|-----------------------------|
| a.   | Yes                 | Yes                                   | Yes                         |
| b.   | Yes                 | Yes                                   | No                          |
| c.   | Yes                 | No                                    | Yes                         |
| d.   | No                  | Yes                                   | Yes                         |

**120.** Would the following factors ordinarily be considered in planning an audit engagement's personnel requirements?

|      | Opportunities for on-the-job training | Continuity and periodic rotation of personnel |
|------|---------------------------------------|-----------------------------------------------|
| a.   | Yes                                   | Yes                                           |
| b.   | Yes                                   | No                                            |
| c.   | No                                    | Yes                                           |
| d.   | No                                    | No                                            |

**121.** Quality control for a CPA firm, as referred to in Statements on Quality Control Standards, applies to
   a.  Auditing services only.
   b.  Auditing and management advisory services.
   c.  Auditing and tax services.
   d.  Auditing and accounting and review services.

**122.** One of a CPA firm's basic objectives is to provide professional services that conform with professional standards. Reasonable assurance of achieving this basic objective is provided through
   a.  A system of quality control.
   b.  A system of peer review.
   c.  Continuing professional education.
   d.  Compliance with generally accepted reporting standards.

**123.** Which of the following is correct concerning PCAOB guidance that uses the term "should"?
   a.  The auditor must fulfill the responsibilities.
   b.  The auditor must comply with requirements unless s/he demonstrates that alternative actions were sufficient to achieve the objectives of the standard.
   c.  The auditor should consider performing the procedure; whether the auditor performs depends on the exercise of professional judgment in the circumstances.
   d.  The auditor has complete discretion as to whether to perform the procedure.

**124.** Which of the following sets of standards does the Public Company Accounting Oversight Board not have the authority to establish for audits of public companies?
   a.  Auditing standards.
   b.  Quality control standards.
   c.  Accounting standards.
   d.  Independence standards.

**SIMULATION PROBLEMS**

**Simulation Problem 1**                                     (50 to 60 minutes)

| Situation | Audit and Fraud Risk | Fraud Discussion | Research | Communication |
|---|---|---|---|---|

Green, CPA, is considering audit risk, including fraud risk, at the financial statement level in planning the audit of National Federal Bank (NFB) Company's financial statements for the year ended December 31, 2003. Audit risk at the financial statement level is influenced by the risk of material misstatements, which may be indicated by a combination of factors related to management, the industry, and the entity. In assessing such factors Green has gathered the following information concerning NFB's environment.

*Company profile*

NFB is a federally insured bank that has been consistently more profitable than the industry average by marketing mortgages on properties in a prosperous rural area, which has experienced considerable growth in recent years. NFB packages its mortgages and sells them to large mortgage investment trusts. Despite recent volatility of interest rates, NFB has been able to continue selling its mortgages as a source of new lendable funds.

NFB's board of directors is controlled by Smith, the majority stockholder, who also acts as the chief executive officer. Management at the bank's branch offices has authority for directing and controlling NFB's operations and is compensated based on branch profitability. The internal auditor reports directly to Harris, a minority shareholder, who also acts as chairman of the board's audit committee.

The accounting department has experienced little turnover in personnel during the five years Green has audited NFB. NFB's formula consistently underestimates the allowance for loan losses, but its controller has always been receptive to Green's suggestions to increase the allowance during each engagement.

*Recent developments*

During 2003, NFB opened a branch office in a suburban town thirty miles from its principal place of business. Although this branch is not yet profitable due to competition from several well-established regional banks, management believes that the branch will be profitable by 2005.

Also, during 2003, NFB increased the efficiency of its accounting operations by installing a new, sophisticated computer system.

| Situation | Audit and Fraud Risk | Fraud Discussion | Research | Communication |
|---|---|---|---|---|

Based only on the information above, indicate by marking the appropriate button whether the following factors indicate an increased or decreased audit risk. Also, indicate whether the factor is a fraud risk factor.

| *Factor* | *Increased audit risk* | *Decreased audit risk* | *Fraud risk factor* |
|---|:---:|:---:|:---:|
| 1.  Branch management authority | O | O | O |
| 2.  Government regulation | O | O | O |
| 3.  Company profitability | O | O | O |
| 4.  Demand for product | O | O | O |
| 5.  Interest rates | O | O | O |
| 6.  Availability of mortgage funds | O | O | O |
| 7.  Involvement of principal shareholder in management | O | O | O |
| 8.  Branch manager compensation | O | O | O |
| 9.  Internal audit reporting relationship | O | O | O |
| 10.  Accounting department turnover | O | O | O |
| 11.  Continuing audit relationship | O | O | O |
| 12.  Internal controls over accounting estimates | O | O | O |
| 13.  Response to proposed accounting adjustments | O | O | O |
| 14.  New unprofitable branch | O | O | O |
| 15.  New computer system | O | O | O |

| Situation | Audit and Fraud Risk | Fraud Discussion | Research | Communication |
|---|---|---|---|---|

Assume you are preparing for the audit personnel discussion of potential risks of material misstatement due to fraud for the NFB audit. While any matters below might be discussed, indicate by marking the appropriate **four** highest risks based on the information contained in the simulation description and requirements of professional standards.

| *Risk* | *High risk item* |
|---|---|
| 1. Computer fraud risk | ○ |
| 2. Risk related to management override of internal control | ○ |
| 3. Fraud by branch management | ○ |
| 4. Fraud by accounting personnel | ○ |
| 5. Misstatement of accounting estimates | ○ |
| 6. Fraud by loan processing clerks | ○ |
| 7. Fraud by internal auditors | ○ |
| 8. The risk of fraudulent misstatement of revenues | ○ |

| Situation | Audit and Fraud Risk | Fraud Discussion | Research | Communication |
|---|---|---|---|---|

Research the professional standards and locate the requirements regarding the required audit documentation of your consideration of fraud for the NFB audit. Excerpt the appropriate paragraphs.

| Situation | Audit and Fraud Risk | Fraud Discussion | Research | Communication |
|---|---|---|---|---|

Professional standards require auditors to have a staff discussion regarding fraud when planning the audit. Write a memorandum describing the purpose of this discussion.

To:     Audit Working Papers
From:   CPA Candidate
Re:     Staff discussion regarding fraud

---

**Simulation Problem 2**            (50 to 60 minutes)

| Situation | Nonattest Services | Auditing Standards | Research | Communication |
|---|---|---|---|---|

The director of the audit committee of Hanmei Corp., a nonpublic company, has indicated that the company may be interested in engaging your firm to perform various professional services. Consider each of the following potential services **by itself**, and determine whether a CPA firm may provide such a service. If a CPA firm may provide the service, fill in the circle under the first or second column of replies based upon whether independence is required. If the service may not be provided, fill in the circle under "May Not Provide." For each service you should have only one reply.

| Situation | Nonattest Services | Auditing Standards | Research | Communication |
|---|---|---|---|---|

| *Service* | *May provide, independence is required* | *May provide, independence is not required* | *May not provide* |
|---|---|---|---|
| 1. Provide an opinion on whether financial statements are prepared following the cash basis of accounting | ○ | ○ | ○ |

|  | | *Service* | *May provide, independence is required* | *May provide, independence is **not** required* | *May **not** provide* |
|---|---|---|:---:|:---:|:---:|
| 2. | | Compile a forecast for the coming year. | ○ | ○ | ○ |
| 3. | | Compile the financial statements for the past year and issue a publicly available report. | ○ | ○ | ○ |
| 4. | | Apply certain agreed-upon procedures to accounts receivable for purposes of obtaining a loan, and express a summary of findings relating to those procedures. | ○ | ○ | ○ |
| 5. | | Review quarterly information and issue a report that includes limited assurance. | ○ | ○ | ○ |
| 6. | | Perform an audit of the financial statements on whether they are prepared following generally accepted accounting principles. | ○ | ○ | ○ |
| 7. | | Perform a review of a forecast the company has prepared for the coming year. | ○ | ○ | ○ |
| 8. | | Compile the financial statements for the past year, but not issue a report since the financial statements are only for the company's use. | ○ | ○ | ○ |
| 9. | | Calculate the client's taxes and fill out the appropriate tax forms. | ○ | ○ | ○ |
| 10. | | Design a new payroll system for Hanmei and base billings on Hamnei's actual savings for the next three years. | ○ | ○ | ○ |

| Situation | Nonattest Services | Auditing Standards | Research | Communication |
|---|---|---|---|---|

Now assume that you have been hired to perform the audit of Hanmei's financial statements. When planning such an audit, you often may need to refer to various of the profession's auditing standards. For each of the following circumstances in Column A, select the topic from the Professional Standards that is likely to provide the most guidance in the planning of the audit. A topic may be selected once, more than once, or not at all.

### *Topic*

| | | | | |
|---|---|---|---|---|
| A. | Analytical Procedures | | F. | Illegal Acts by Clients |
| B. | Audit Risk and Materiality | | G. | Management Representations |
| C. | Communications between Predecessor and Successor Auditors | | H. | Part of the Audit Performed by Other Independent Auditors |
| D. | Consideration of Fraud in a Financial Statement Audit | | I. | Related Parties |
| E. | Consideration of Internal Control in a Financial Statement Audit | | | |

| *Transactions* | (A) | (B) | (C) | (D) | (E) | (F) | (G) | (H) | (I) |
|---|:---:|:---:|:---:|:---:|:---:|:---:|:---:|:---:|:---:|
| 1. Possible risk factors related to misappropriation of assets. | ○ | ○ | ○ | ○ | ○ | ○ | ○ | ○ | ○ |
| 2. The relationship between materiality used for planning versus evaluation purposes. | ○ | ○ | ○ | ○ | ○ | ○ | ○ | ○ | ○ |
| 3. Hanmei Corp. has transactions with the corporation president's brother. | ○ | ○ | ○ | ○ | ○ | ○ | ○ | ○ | ○ |
| 4. Comparing a client's unaudited results for the year with last year's audited results. | ○ | ○ | ○ | ○ | ○ | ○ | ○ | ○ | ○ |
| 5. Auditing and reporting guidance on the possible need to reaudit previous year results due to the disbanding of the firm that performed last year's audit. | ○ | ○ | ○ | ○ | ○ | ○ | ○ | ○ | ○ |
| 6. Requirements relating to identifying violations of occupational safety and health regulations. | ○ | ○ | ○ | ○ | ○ | ○ | ○ | ○ | ○ |

| *Transactions* | (A) | (B) | (C) | (D) | (E) | (F) | (G) | (H) | (I) |
|---|---|---|---|---|---|---|---|---|---|
| 7. Audit report considerations when audit of a subsidiary of the client will be performed by Williams & Co., CPAs. | ○ | ○ | ○ | ○ | ○ | ○ | ○ | ○ | ○ |
| 8. The need to "brainstorm" among audit team members about how accounts could be intentionally misstated. | ○ | ○ | ○ | ○ | ○ | ○ | ○ | ○ | ○ |
| 9. Details on considering operating effectiveness of controls. | ○ | ○ | ○ | ○ | ○ | ○ | ○ | ○ | ○ |
| 10. The importance of considering the possibility of overstated revenues (for example, through premature revenue recognition). | ○ | ○ | ○ | ○ | ○ | ○ | ○ | ○ | ○ |

| Situation | Nonattest Services | Auditing Standards | **Research** | | Communication |
|---|---|---|---|---|---|

An auditor should establish an understanding with the client regarding the nature of the services to be provided. Research the Professional Standards for (1) the information that an understanding with the client generally includes, and (2) other matters that it may include. You may simply paste the appropriate material to your solution but make certain the (1) items are clearly distinguished from (2) items.

| Situation | Nonattest Services | Auditing Standards | Research | **Communication** |
|---|---|---|---|---|

Write a memorandum to Caroline Smith, the Chairperson of Hanmei's audit committee describing why independence is required to perform an audit.

To:    Ms. Caroline Smith, Chairperson of the Audit Committee
From:  CPA Candidate
Re:    Independence

**MULTIPLE-CHOICE ANSWERS[*]**

| | | | | | | | | | | | |
|---|---|---|---|---|---|---|---|---|---|---|---|
| 1. | b | 23. | c | 45. | b | 67. | d | 89. | b | 111. | d |
| 2. | b | 24. | a | 46. | d | 68. | c | 90. | a | 112. | a |
| 3. | a | 25. | a | 47. | d | 69. | a | 91. | d | 113. | d |
| 4. | c | 26. | c | 48. | d | 70. | c | 92. | b | 114. | d |
| 5. | c | 27. | d | 49. | c | 71. | b | 93. | c | 115. | c |
| 6. | b | 28. | d | 50. | b | 72. | a | 94. | b | 116. | c |
| 7. | b | 29. | b | 51. | a | 73. | b | 95. | a | 117. | d |
| 8. | b | 30. | d | 52. | c | 74. | a | 96. | d | 128. | a |
| 9. | b | 31. | c | 53. | b | 75. | d | 97. | a | 119. | a |
| 10. | d | 32. | c | 54. | a | 76. | c | 98. | b | 120. | a |
| 11. | a | 33. | d | 55. | b | 77. | a | 99. | c | 121. | d |
| 12. | c | 34. | a | 56. | b | 78. | d | 100. | c | 122. | a |
| 13. | b | 35. | a | 57. | d | 79. | c | 101. | c | 123. | b |
| 14. | b | 36. | a | 58. | a | 80. | b | 102. | d | 124. | c |
| 15. | a | 37. | a | 59. | b | 81. | c | 103. | a | | |
| 16. | b | 38. | b | 60. | b | 82. | a | 104. | b | | |
| 17. | a | 39. | d | 61. | b | 83. | c | 105. | a | | |
| 18. | b | 40. | b | 62. | a | 84. | c | 106. | b | | |
| 19. | a | 41. | a | 63. | c | 85. | a | 107. | b | | |
| 20. | d | 42. | a | 64. | b | 86. | a | 108. | a | | |
| 21. | b | 43. | a | 65. | a | 87. | d | 109. | d | 1st: __/124 = __% |
| 22. | d | 44. | c | 66. | c | 88. | b | 110. | b | 2nd: __/124 = __% |

**MULTIPLE-CHOICE ANSWER EXPLANATIONS**

### A.1.a.  Audit Risk

**1.    (b)**   The requirement is to determine a likely auditor reaction to a decreased acceptable level of detection risk. Answer (b) is correct because postponement of interim substantive tests to year-end decreases detection risk by reducing the risk for the period subsequent to the performance of those tests; other approaches to decreasing detection risk include changing to more effective substantive tests and increasing their extent. Answer (a) is incorrect because increased, not reduced, substantive testing is required. Answer (c) is incorrect because inherent risk must be considered in planning, either by itself or in combination with control risk. Answer (d) is incorrect because tests of controls must be performed to reduce the assessed level of control risk.

**2.    (b)**   The requirement is to identify the risk that an auditor will conclude, based on substantive tests, that a material error does **not** exist in an account balance when, in fact, such error does exist. Answer (b) is correct because detection risk is the risk that the auditor will not detect a material misstatement that exists in an assertion. Detection risk may be viewed in terms of two components (1) the risk that analytical procedures and other relevant substantive tests would fail to detect misstatements equal to tolerable misstatement, and (2) the allowable risk of incorrect acceptance for the substantive tests of details. Answer (a) is incorrect because sampling risk arises from the possibility that, when a test of controls or a substantive test is restricted to a sample, the auditor's conclusions may be different from the conclusions he or she would reach if the tests were applied in the same way to all items in the account balance or class of transactions. When related to substantive tests sampling risk is only a part of the risk that the auditor's substantive tests will not detect a material misstatement. An-

swer (c) is incorrect because nonsampling risk includes only those aspects of audit risk that are not due to sampling. Answer (d) is incorrect because inherent risk is the susceptibility of an assertion to a material misstatement, assuming that there are no related controls.

**3.    (a)**   The requirement is to identify an effect of a decrease in the acceptable level of detection risk. Answer (a) is correct because as the acceptable level of detection risk decreases, the assurance provided from substantive tests should increase. To gain this increased assurance the auditors may (1) change the **nature** of substantive tests to more effective procedures (e.g., use independent parties outside the entity rather than those within the entity), (2) change the **timing** of substantive tests (e.g., perform them at year-end rather than at an interim date), and (3) change the **extent** of substantive tests (e.g., take a larger sample). Answer (b) is incorrect because the assurance provided from substantive tests increases, it does not decrease. Answers (c) and (d) are incorrect because the acceptable level of detection risk is based largely on the assessed levels of control risk and inherent risk. Accordingly, any tests of controls will already have been performed.

**4.    (c)**   The requirement is to determine whether inherent risk, control risk, and detection risk may be assessed in nonquantitative terms. Answer (c) is correct because all of these risks may be assessed in either quantitative terms such as percentages, **or** nonquantitative terms such as a range from a minimum to a maximum.

**5.    (c)**   The requirement is to determine a manner in which inherent risk and control risk differ from detection risk. Answer (c) is correct because inherent risk and control risk exist independently of the audit of the financial statements as functions of the client and its environment, whereas detection risk relates to the auditor's procedures and can be

---

[*]*Explanation of how to use this performance record appears on page 12.*

changed at his or her discretion. Answer (a) is incorrect because inherent risk and control risk are functions of the client and its environment and do not arise from misapplication of auditing procedures. Answer (b) is incorrect because inherent risk, control risk and detection risk may each be assessed in either quantitative or nonquantitative terms. Answer (d) is incorrect because inherent risk and control risk are functions of the client and its environment, they cannot be changed at the auditor's discretion. However, the assessed levels of inherent and control risk (not addressed in this question) may be affected by auditor decisions relating to the cost of gathering evidence to substantiate assessed levels below the maximum.

**6.** **(b)** The requirement is to determine the best way for an auditor to achieve an overall audit risk level when the audit evidence relating to control risk indicates the need to increase its assessed level. Answer (b) is correct because a decrease in detection risk will allow the auditor achieve an overall audit risk level substantially the same as planned. Answer (a) is incorrect because a decrease in substantive testing will increase, not decrease, detection risk and thereby increase audit risk. Answer (c) is incorrect because an increase in inherent risk will also increase audit risk. Answer (d) is incorrect because there appears to be no justification for increasing materiality levels beyond those used in planning the audit.

**7.** **(b)** The requirement is to determine the relationship between control risk and detection risk. Inverse is correct because as control risk increases (decreases) detection risk must decrease (increase).

### A.1.b. Materiality

**8.** **(b)** The requirement is to identify the information that an auditor would most likely use in determining a preliminary judgment about materiality. Answer (b) is correct because many materiality measures relate to an annual figure (e.g., net income, sales). Answer (a) is incorrect because the preliminary judgment about materiality is a factor used in determining the anticipated sample size, not the reverse as suggested by the reply. Answers (c) and (d) are incorrect because materiality will not normally be affected by the results of the internal control questionnaire or the contents of the management representation letters.

**9.** **(b)** The requirement is to identify the statement that is **not** correct concerning materiality. Answer (b) is the proper reply because the auditor considers materiality for planning purposes in terms of the **smallest,** not the **largest,** aggregate amount of misstatement that could be material to any one of the financial statements. Answers (a), (c), and (d) all represent correct statements about materiality.

**10.** **(d)** The requirement is to identify the elements which underlie the application of generally accepted auditing standards, particularly the standards of fieldwork and reporting. Answer (d) is correct because AU 150 states that materiality and relative risk underlie the application of all the standards. Answer (a) is incorrect because a consideration of internal control is one of the field standards, not an element underlying the standards. Answer (b) is incorrect because the second fieldwork standard, on evidence, relates most directly to corroborating evidence. Answer (c) is incorrect because while it is accurate that quality control standards encompass the firm's policies and procedures to pro-

vide reasonable assurance of conforming with professional standards, the standards are not related more directly to the fieldwork and reporting standards than to the general group of generally accepted auditing standards.

**11.** **(a)** The requirement is to determine the appropriate level of materiality for planning purposes when $10,000 would have a material effect on an entity's income statement, but $20,000 would materially affect the balance sheet. AU 312 states that the audit should be designed to obtain reasonable assurance about whether the financial statements are free of material misstatement. Because it will ordinarily be difficult to anticipate during the planning stage of an audit whether all misstatements will affect only one financial statement, the auditor is generally required to use the lower financial statement figure for most portions of planning. Therefore, answer (a), $10,000, is correct. Answers (b), (c), and (d) are all incorrect because they are dollar amounts which exceed the lowest level of materiality.

**12.** **(c)** The requirement is to identify the information that an auditor would be most likely to use in making a preliminary judgment about materiality. Answer (c) is correct because auditors often choose to use a measure relating to the prior year's financial statements (e.g., a percentage of total assets, net income, or revenue) to arrive at a preliminary judgment about materiality. Answer (a) is incorrect because materiality is based on the magnitude of an omission or misstatement and not on the initial assessment of control risk. Answer (b) is incorrect because while an auditor's materiality judgment will affect the anticipated sample size for planned substantive tests, sample size does not affect the materiality judgment. Answer (d) is incorrect because the assertions embodied in the financial statements remain the same from one audit to another. See AU 312 for information on materiality and AU 326 for information on financial statement assertions.

**13.** **(b)** The requirement is to identify the most likely effect of a decrease in the tolerable amount of misstatement (tolerable misstatement) in a class of transactions. Answer (b) is correct because AU 312 states that decreasing the tolerable amount of misstatement will require the auditor to do one or more of the following: (1) perform auditing procedures closer to the balance sheet date (answer [b]); (2) select a more effective auditing procedure; or (3) increase the extent of a particular auditing procedure. Answer (a) is incorrect because in such a circumstance substantive tests are more likely to be performed at or after the balance sheet date than prior to the balance sheet date. Answer (c) is incorrect because decreasing the tolerable amount of misstatement will not necessarily lead to an increase in the assessed level of control risk. Answer (d) is incorrect because the extent of auditing procedures will be increased, not decreased.

**14.** **(b)** The requirement is to identify the necessary condition for an auditor to be able to issue an unqualified opinion. Answer (b) is correct because if the estimate of likely misstatement is equal to or greater than a material amount a material departure from generally accepted accounting principles exists and thus AU 508 requires either a qualified or adverse opinion in such circumstances. Answer (a) is incorrect because the amount of known misstatement (if any) need not be documented in the management representation letter. Answer (c) is incorrect because it ordinarily is not necessary for the client to acknowledge and record immaterial known misstatements. Answer (d) is incorrect because the total likely misstatement need not include the adjusting entries already recorded by the client. See AU 312 for guidance on the evaluation of audit findings involving misstatements.

### A.1.d.   Errors and Fraud

**15.   (a)** The requirement is to identify the example of fraudulent financial reporting. Answer (a) is correct because fraudulent financial reporting involves intentional misstatements or omissions of amounts or disclosures in financial statements to deceive financial statement users and changing the inventory count tags results in such a misstatement. Answers (b), (c), and (d) are all incorrect because they represent the misappropriation of assets. See AU 316 which divides fraudulent activities into misstatement arising from fraudulent financial reporting and misstatements arising from misappropriation of assets (sometimes referred to as defalcation).

**16.   (b)** The requirement is to identify the best description of what is meant by a "fraud risk factor." Answer (b) is correct because AU 316 suggests that while fraud risk factors do not necessarily indicate the existence of fraud, they often have been observed in circumstances where frauds have occurred. Answer (a) is incorrect because the risk of fraud may or may not be high when a risk factor is present. Answer (c) is incorrect because the current audit program may in many circumstances appropriately address a fraud risk factor. Answer (d) is incorrect because a fraud risk factor may or may not represent a reportable condition—see AU 325 for information on reportable conditions.

**17.   (a)** The requirement is to identify the reply which represents an auditor communication responsibility relating to fraud. Answer (a) is correct because all fraud involving senior management should be reported directly to the audit committee. Answer (b) is incorrect because auditors are only required to report fraud to the Securities and Exchange Commission under particular circumstances. Answer (c) is incorrect because auditors do not ordinarily disclose fraud through use of an "emphasis of a matter" paragraph added to their report. Answer (d) is incorrect because under certain circumstances auditors must disclose fraud outside the entity.

**18.   (b)** The requirement is to identify the risk relating to material misstatement that auditors are required to assess. Answer (b) is correct because AU 312 and AU 316 require auditors to specifically assess the risk of material misstatements due to fraud and consider that assessment in designing the audit procedures to be performed. Answer (a) is incorrect because while AU 312 also requires an assessment of the overall risk of material misstatement (whether caused by error or fraud) there is no requirement to explicitly assess the risk of material misstatement due to errors. Answer (c) is incorrect because the auditor need not explicitly assess the risk of misstatement due to illegal acts (see AU 317 for information on illegal acts). Answer (d) is incorrect because no assessment of business risk is required.

**19.   (a)** The requirement is to determine whether audits are designed to provide reasonable assurance of detecting misstatements due to errors, fraudulent financial reporting,

and/or misappropriation of assets. Answer (a) is correct because AU 110 and AU 316 require that an audit obtain reasonable assurance that material misstatements, whether caused by error or fraud, be detected. Fraudulent financial reporting and the misappropriation of assets are the two major types of fraud with which an audit is relevant.

**20.   (d)** The requirement is to identify the reply which is not a reason why auditors are unable to obtain absolute assurance that misstatements due to fraud will be detected. Answer (d) is correct because while an auditor must exercise professional skepticism when performing an audit it does not represent a limitation that makes is impossible to obtain absolute assurance. Answers (a), (b), and (c) are all incorrect because they represent factors considered in the professional literature for providing reasonable, and not absolute assurance.

**21.   (b)** The requirement is to identify the type of fraudulent misstatement that is most difficult to detect. Answer (b) is correct because transactions that have not been recorded are generally considered most difficult because there is no general starting point for the auditor in the consideration of the transaction. Answers (a), (c), and (d) all represent recorded transactions which, when audited, are in general easier to detect.

**22.   (d)** The requirement is to identify the **least likely** indicator of a risk of possible misstatement due to fraud. Answer (d) is correct because one would expect unusually aggressive, rather than unusually conservative accounting practices to indicate a risk of misstatement due to fraud. Answers (a), (b), and (c) are all incorrect because they represent risk factors explicitly included in AU 316, which provides guidance on fraud.

**23.   (c)** The requirement is to determine the reply which represents information most likely to affect the auditor's assessment of the risk of misstatement due to fraud. Answer (c) is correct because AU 316 states that missing documents may be indicative of fraud. Answer (a) is incorrect because checks for significant amounts are normally expected to be outstanding at year-end. Answer (b) is incorrect because almost all audits involve computer generated documents and their existence is not considered a condition indicating possible fraud. Answer (d) is incorrect because while last-minute adjustments that significantly affect financial results may be considered indicative of possible fraud, year-end adjusting journal entries alone are to be expected.

**24.   (a)** The requirement is to identify the most likely response to the auditor's assessment that the risk of material misstatement due to fraud for the existence of inventory is high. Answer (a) is correct because observing test counts of inventory on an unannounced basis will provide evidence as to whether record inventory exists. Answer (b) is incorrect because replacing test counts with analytical procedures is not likely to be particularly effective. Answers (c) and (d) are incorrect because the inventories might well be counted at year-end, all on the same date, rather than prior to year-end and at differing dates.

**25.   (a)** The requirement is to identify the reply that is most likely to be an example of fraud. Answer (a) is most likely, since "defalcation" is another term for misstatements arising from misappropriation of assets, a major type of fraud. Answers (b), (c), and (d) are all incorrect because mistakes in the application of accounting principles or in processing data, and unreasonable accounting estimates arising from oversight are examples of misstatements rather than fraud.

**26.   (c)**   The requirement is to identify the characteristic most likely to heighten an auditor's concern about the risk of intentional manipulation of financial statements. Answer (c) is correct because the placement of substantial emphasis on meeting earnings projections is considered a risk factor. Answer (a) is incorrect because high turnover, not low turnover, is considered a risk factor. Answer (b) is incorrect because insider purchases of additional shares of stock are less likely to be indicative of intentional manipulation of the financial statements than is undue emphasis on meeting earnings projections. Answer (d) is incorrect because a rapid rate of change in an industry, not a slow rate, is considered a risk factor.

**27.   (d)**   The requirement is to identify an auditor's responsibility for detecting errors and fraud. Answer (d) is correct because AU 110 requires that an auditor design the audit to provide reasonable assurance of detecting misstatements due to errors and fraud that are material to the financial statements. Answer (a) is incorrect because audits provide reasonable assurance of detecting material errors and fraud. Answer (b) is incorrect because it doesn't restrict the responsibility to material errors and fraud. Answer (c) is incorrect because it is less precise than answer (d), which includes the AU 110 responsibility on errors and fraud.

**28.   (d)**   The requirement is to identify the circumstances in which an auditor may have a responsibility to disclose fraud to parties other than a client's senior management and its audit committee or board of directors. Answer (d) is correct because AU 316 states that such a responsibility may exist to the SEC when there has been an auditor change to a successor auditor or to comply with SEC 1995 Private Securities Reform Act communication requirement, when the successor auditor makes inquiries, and to a government agency from which the client receives financial assistance. In addition, that section states that an auditor may have such a disclosure responsibility in response to a subpoena, a circumstance not considered in this question.

**29.   (b)**   Errors refer to unintentional mistakes in financial statements such as misinterpretation of facts. Answers (a), (c), and (d) all represent fraud which are defined as intentional distortions of financial statements.

**30.   (d)**   The requirement is to identify the level of assurance an auditor provides with respect to detection of material errors, fraud, and direct effect illegal acts. Answer (d) is correct because AU 110 requires the auditor to design the audit to provide **reasonable assurance** of detecting material errors, fraud and direct effect illegal acts. (A "direct effect" illegal act is one that would have an effect on the determination of financial statement amounts.)

**31.   (c)**   The requirement is to identify the proper attitude of an auditor who is performing an audit in accordance with generally accepted auditing standards. Answer (c) is correct because the auditor should plan and perform the audit with an attitude of professional skepticism, recognizing that the application of the auditing procedures may produce evidential matter indicating the possibility of misstatements due to errors or fraud. Answer (a) is incorrect because while the CPA must exhibit objective judgment, "professional skepticism" more accurately summarizes the proper attitude during an audit. Answer (b) is incorrect because while a CPA must be independent and have integrity, this is not the "attitude" used to plan and perform the audit. Answer (d) is incorrect because the audit is not planned and performed with impartial conservatism.

**32.   (c)**   The requirement is to identify the meaning of the term "material misstatement" when used in the professional standards. Answer (c) is correct because AU 312 and AU 316 state that a material misstatement may occur due to errors, fraud, and illegal acts with a direct effect on financial statement amounts.

**33.   (d)**   The requirement is to identify an auditor's responsibility for detecting financial stress of employees or adverse relationships between a company and its employees. Answer (d) is correct because AU 316 states that, while the auditor is not required to plan the audit to discover information that is indicative of financial stress of employees or adverse relationships between the company and its employees, such conditions must be considered when an auditor becomes aware of them. Answers (a), (b), and (c) are all incorrect because the auditor does not plan the audit to detect these conditions.

**34.   (a)**   The requirement is to identify an auditor's responsibility when he or she believes that a misstatement is or may be the result of fraud, but that the effect of the misstatements is immaterial to the financial statements. Answer (a) is correct because AU 316 states that in such circumstances the auditor should evaluate the implications of the fraud, especially those dealing with the organizational position of the person(s) involved.

**35.   (a)**   The requirement is to identify the correct statements relating to the auditor's consideration of fraud. Answer (a) is correct because AU 316 states that the auditor's interest relates to fraudulent acts that cause a material misstatement of financial statements. Answer (b) is incorrect because errors are unintentional. Answer (c) is incorrect because fraud does not necessarily involve the misappropriation of assets (it may involve fraudulent financial reporting). Answer (d) is incorrect because an auditor must design an audit to obtain reasonable assurance of detecting misstatements, regardless of whether they are caused by errors or fraud.

**36.   (a)**   The requirement is to identify the factor or condition that an audit is least likely to be planned to discover. Answer (a) is correct because it represents a financial stress, and auditors are not required to plan audits to discover information that is indicative of financial stress of employees or adverse relationships between the entity and its employees. Answers (b), (c), and (d) are all incorrect because they represent examples of risk factors that should be considered in an audit and are included in AU 316.

**37.   (a)**   The requirement is to determine when audit risk factors may be identified. Answer (a) is correct because AU 316 states that fraud risk factors may be identified during planning, obtaining an understanding, or while conducting fieldwork; in addition, they may be identified while considering acceptance or continuance of clients and engagements.

**38.** **(b)** The requirement is to identify the circumstance in which it is most likely that management's attitude toward aggressive financial reporting and toward meeting projected profit goals would most likely significantly influence an entity's control environment. Answer (b) is correct because when management is dominated by one individual, that individual may be able to follow overly aggressive accounting principles.

**39.** **(d)** The requirement is to identify the procedure **least** likely to be required on an audit. Answer (d) is correct because fraud is a broad legal concept and auditors do not make legal determinations of whether fraud has occurred. Answers (a), (b), and (c) are incorrect because considering journal entries, estimates, and unusual transactions are ordinarily required audit procedures to address the risk of management override of controls. See AU 316 for information on the auditor's responsibility for the consideration of fraud in a financial statement audit.

**40.** **(b)** The requirement is to identify the most likely response when a risk of fraud has been identified on an audit. Answer (b) is correct because AU 316 indicates that overall responses to the risk of material misstatements due to fraud include (1) assigning personnel with particular skills relating to the area and considering the necessary extent of supervision to the audit, (2) increasing the consideration of management's selection and application of accounting principles, and (3) making audit procedures less predictable. Answer (a) is incorrect because closer supervision, not less close supervision, is more likely to be appropriate. Answer (c) is incorrect because individuals with specialized skills may be needed who are not CPAs. Answer (d) is incorrect because subjective transactions (e.g., accounting estimates) often provide more risk than objective transactions.

**41.** **(a)** The requirement is to identify the **least** likely inquiry of management relating to identifying the risk of material misstatement due to fraud. Answer (a) is correct because financial operations of many companies are not ordinarily controlled by and limited to one location. Answers (b), (c), and (d) are all incorrect because they are included in AU 316 as inquiries that should be made of management.

**42.** **(a)** The requirement is to identify the attributes ordinarily present when individuals commit fraud. Answer (a) is correct because AU 316 suggests that the three conditions generally present when fraud occurs are that individuals have an (1) incentive or pressure, (2) opportunity, and (3) ability to rationalize. Answers (b), (c), and (d) are all incorrect because they suggest that one of the three elements is not ordinarily present.

**43.** **(a)** The requirement is to determine an auditor's reporting responsibility when he or she has discovered that management is involved in a financially immaterial fraud. Answer (a) is correct because AU 316 requires that all management fraud, regardless of materiality, be reported to the Public Company Accounting Oversight Board. Answer (b) is incorrect because fraud is not directly reported to the Public Company Accounting Oversight Board. Answer (c) is incorrect because if anything, in addition to the audit committee, the fraud is reported to a level of management at least one level above those involved in a fraud. Answer (d)

is incorrect because there is a reporting responsibility for financially immaterial management fraud.

**44.** **(c)** The requirement is to identify the most likely risk factor relating to fraudulent financial reporting. Answer (c) is correct because negative cash flows from operations may result in pressure upon management to overstate the results of operations. Answer (a) is incorrect because one would expect a company's top executives to dominate management—domination by one or a few might be considered a risk factor. Answers (b) and (d) are incorrect because large amounts of cash being processed and small high-dollar inventory items are more directly related to the misappropriation of assets than they are to fraudulent financial reporting.

**45.** **(b)** The requirement is to identify the most likely fraud risk factor on an audit. Answer (b) is correct because the possibility of improper revenue recognition is ordinarily presumed on audits. Answers (a), (c), and (d) all represent potential risks, but risks that are not ordinarily presumed on an audit. See AU 316 for information on the auditor's responsibility for the consideration of fraud in a financial statement audit.

**46.** **(d)** The requirement is to identify the circumstances relating to the discovery of the payment of small bribes to municipal officials that is most likely to cause an auditor to withdraw from an engagement. Answer (d) is correct because AU 317 states that management failure to take the appropriate remedial action is particularly problematical since it may affect the auditor's ability to rely on management representation and may therefore lead to withdrawal. Answers (a), (b), and (c) all represent circumstances which the auditor will consider, but are not ordinarily considered as serious as failure to take the appropriate remedial action.

**47.** **(d)** The requirement is to identify the factor most likely to cause a CPA **not** to accept a new audit engagement. Answer (d) is correct because a part of the understanding an auditor must obtain with a client is that management is responsible for making all financial records and related information available (see AU 310). Accordingly, if the client refuses to make such information available the auditor is unlikely to accept the audit client. Answer (a) is incorrect because a circumstance-imposed scope limitations such as completion of the physical inventory count results in a situation in which the auditor may consider using alternative procedures (including making some test counts) to determine whether inventory counts are proper. Answer (b) is incorrect because an auditor may obtain an understanding of the client's operations and industry while performing the audit. Answer (c) is incorrect because while a review of the predecessor auditor's working papers is ordinarily desirable, it is not required.

**48.** **(d)** The requirement is to identify the factor most likely to heighten an auditor's concern about the risk of fraudulent financial reporting. Answer (d) is correct because AU 316, which presents a variety of risk factors, suggests that an overly complex organizational structure is such a risk factor. Answer (a) is incorrect because large amounts of liquid assets that are easily convertible into cash represent more of a risk relating to misappropriation of assets rather than to fraudulent financial reporting. Answer (b) is incorrect because high growth, rather than low growth, is considered a risk factor. Answer (c) is incorrect because one would expect financial management's participation in the initial selection of accounting principles.

**A.1.e. Illegal Acts**

**49. (c)** The requirement is to identify the situation in which an auditor would be most likely to withdraw from an engagement when he or she has discovered that a client's employees have paid small bribes to public officials. Answer (c) is correct because AU 317 states that resignation should be considered when an illegal act does not receive proper remedial action, because such inaction may affect the auditor's ability to rely on management representations and the effects of continued association with the client. Answer (a) is incorrect because the receipt of federal funds in such a situation is not as likely to result in auditor withdrawal as is answer (c). Answer (b) is incorrect because it seems inconsistent with the premise of the question in that, if no evidential matter exists, the auditor is unlikely to know that bribes have been paid. Answer (d) is incorrect because such small bribes will not ordinarily need to be disclosed. Alternatively, if the auditor believes that there is such a need, the lack of such disclosure represents a departure from generally accepted accounting principles and either a qualified or adverse opinion is appropriate.

**50. (b)** The requirement is to identify the illegal act that an audit should be designed to obtain reasonable assurance of detecting. Answer (b) is correct because the accrual and billing of an improper amount of revenue under government contracts is an illegal act with a direct effect on the determination of financial statement amounts, and audits are designed to detect such illegal acts. Answers (a), (c), and (d) are all incorrect because they represent illegal acts with an indirect financial statement effect and an audit provides no assurance that such acts will be detected or that any contingent liabilities that may result will be disclosed. See AU 317 for detailed guidance on auditor responsibility with respect to direct and indirect illegal acts.

**51. (a)** The requirement is to identify the small misstatement that is most likely to have a material effect on an entity's financial statements. Answer (a) is correct because an illegal payment of an otherwise immaterial amount may be material if there is a reasonable possibility that it may lead to a material contingent liability or a material loss of revenue.

**52. (c)** The requirement is to determine what an auditor might reconsider when a client's board of directors has refused to take any action relating to an auditor's disclosure that the company has made immaterial illegal contributions. Answer (c) is correct because in such a circumstance the failure to take remedial action may cause an auditor to decrease reliance on management representations. Answer (a) is incorrect because the reply by the attorney is likely to disclose any claims, litigation or assessments that the client has improperly omitted from the letter of audit inquiry. Answer (b) is incorrect because the prior years' audit programs are not being relied upon for this year's audit. Answer (d) is incorrect because the preliminary judgment about materiality levels would not be expected to change.

**53. (b)** The requirement is to identify a reason why audits cannot reasonably be expected to bring all illegal acts to the auditor's attention. Answer (b) is correct because illegal acts relating to the operating aspects of an entity are often highly specialized and complex and often are far removed from the events and transactions reflected in financial statements. Answer (a) is partially correct since management override represents a limitation of the effectiveness of internal control. Yet, auditors are more likely to identify such transactions because they relate to events and transactions reflected in the financial statements. Answer (c) is incorrect because many illegal acts are not subject to the client's internal control. Answer (d) is incorrect because illegal acts may be perpetrated without access to both assets and accounting records.

**54. (a)** The requirement is to determine an auditor's responsibility when information comes to his/her attention that implies the existence of possible illegal acts with a material, but indirect effect on the financial statements. Answer (a) is correct because AU 317 requires the auditor to apply audit procedures specifically designed to determine whether an illegal act has occurred when such information comes to his/her attention. Answers (b), (c), and (d) are all incorrect because they represent procedures the auditor would perform after initial procedures had confirmed the existence of the possible illegal act(s).

**55. (b)** The requirement is to determine the circumstance in which it is most likely that a CPA would withdraw from an audit engagement after having discovered that client employees have committed an illegal act. Answer (b) is correct because the auditor may conclude that withdrawal is necessary when the client does not take the remedial action, even when the illegal act is not material to the financial statements. Answers (a) and (c) are incorrect because whether generally accepted accounting principles have been violated and whether the illegal act occurred during a prior year that was not audited may or may not have an effect on the decision to withdraw from the engagement. Answer (d) is incorrect because the assessed level of control risk will not have a direct relationship on the decision to withdraw from the engagement.

**56. (b)** The requirement is to identify a CPA's responsibility under the Securities Litigation Reform Act of 1995 for uncorrected illegal acts which have been communicated to the board of directors which refuses to inform the SEC of their existence. Answer (b) is correct because CPAs are required under the law to deliver a report on those illegal acts to the SEC within one business day in such circumstances. Answer (a) in incorrect because there is no requirement to resign, although the auditor may decide to do so. Answer (c) is incorrect because the Act sets up reporting to the SEC, not to the stockholders. Answer (d) is incorrect because withholding of the audit opinion is not suggested in the Act.

**A.2.a. Communication between Predecessor and Successor Auditors**

**57. (d)** The requirement is to identify a requirement prior to accepting an engagement to audit a new client. Answer (d) is correct because AU 315 requires that an auditor attempt to obtain client permission to contact the predecessor prior to accepting a new engagement. Answers (a), (b), and (c) are incorrect because they may all be obtained subsequent to accepting an engagement.

**58.   (a)**   The requirement is to determine the nature of the inquiries that a successor auditor should make of the predecessor auditor prior to accepting an audit engagement. Answer (a) is correct because the inquiries should include specific questions to management on (1) disagreements with management as to auditing procedures and accounting principles (reply [a]), (2) facts that might bear on the integrity of management and (3) the predecessor's understanding as to the reasons for the change of auditors. Answers (b), (c), and (d) are incorrect because, if made at all, they will be after the engagement has been accepted.

**59.   (b)**   The requirement is to identify the correct statement regarding a successor auditor's inquiries of the predecessor auditor. Answer (b) is correct because the successor should request information such as (1) facts that might bear on the integrity of management, (2) disagreements with management as to accounting principles, auditing procedures, or other significant matters, and (3) the predecessor's understanding of the reasons for the change of auditors. Answers (a), (c), and (d) all relate to matters not required to be discussed prior to accepting an audit engagement.

### A.2.b.   Obtaining a General Understanding of the Client and Industry

**60.   (b)**   The requirement is to identify the factor most likely to cause a CPA to decide not to accept a new audit engagement. Answer (b) is correct because a certain level of internal control is essential for financial statement reporting, and management's disregard in this area may lead the CPA to reject the engagement. Answer (a) is incorrect both because a CPA may not need an understanding of the prospective client's internal auditor's computer-assisted audit technique to form an opinion on the financial statements, and because if such understanding is necessary, it can be obtained subsequent to engagement acceptance. Answer (c) is incorrect because AU 334 indicates that a CPA often will be unable to determine whether related-party transactions were consummated on terms equivalent to arm's-length transactions. Answer (d) is incorrect because while management's refusal to permit the performance of substantive tests before the year-end may present a problem, the auditor may be able to effectively perform such tests after year-end.

**61.   (b)**   The requirement is to identify the item ordinarily included when an auditor establishes an understanding with a client regarding the services to be performed. Answer (b) is correct because AU 380 requires that an auditor ensure that the audit committee is aware of any reportable conditions which come to the CPA's attention. Answer (a) is incorrect because while an understanding will include a statement that management is responsible for the entity's financial statements, an explicit statement about errors and illegal activities of employees is not ordinarily included. Answer (c) in incorrect because management does not provide the auditor with an assessment of the risk of material misstatement due to fraud. Answer (d) is incorrect because no such statement about an auditor's responsibility for determining preliminary judgments about materiality and audit risk factors is ordinarily included in establishing an understanding. See AU 310 for information on establishing an understanding with a client.

**62.   (a)**   The requirement is to identify the area that is most likely to require special audit planning considerations.

Answer (a) is correct because an inventory comprised of diamond rings is likely to require that the auditor plan ahead to involve a specialist to assist in valuation issues. Answer (b) is incorrect because valuation of an asset such as a new copy machine is not ordinarily expected to provide valuation difficulties. Answer (c) is incorrect because the expensing purchases of such small assets is ordinarily acceptable due to the immateriality of the transactions. Answer (d) is incorrect because accelerated depreciation methods are ordinarily acceptable.

**63.   (c)**   The requirement is to identify the factor that most likely would influence an auditor's determination of the auditability of an entity's financial statements. Answer (c) is correct because inadequate accounting records may cause an auditor to conclude that it is unlikely that sufficient competent evidential matter will be available to support an opinion on the financial statements; accordingly, an auditor may determine that the financial statements are not auditable. Answer (a) is incorrect because an auditor should be able to obtain the knowledge necessary to audit a complex accounting system. Answer (b) is incorrect because while related-party transactions may raise transaction valuation issues due to the lack of an "arm's length transaction," the problem is normally not so severe as to make the entity not auditable. Answer (d) is incorrect because a lack of operating effectiveness of controls may often be overcome through an increase in the scope of substantive tests.

**64.   (b)**   The requirement is to determine the manner in which an auditor plans an audit of a continuing client. Answer (b) is correct because a review of prior year working papers and the permanent file may provide useful information about the nature of the business, organizational structure, operating characteristics, and transactions that may require special attention. Answer (a) is incorrect because tests of details of transactions and balances occur subsequent to planning. Answer (c) is incorrect because while reading specialized industry journals will help the auditor to obtain a better understanding of the client's industry, it is likely to be less helpful than reviewing the working papers. Answer (d) is incorrect because a reevaluation of the client's internal control environment occurs subsequent to the ordinal planning of the audit.

### A.2.c.   Establishing an Understanding with the Client (Engagement Letters)

**65.   (a)**   The requirement is to identify the matter generally included in an auditor's engagement letter. Answer (a) is correct because AU 310, which outlines requirements for engagement letters, indicates that an engagement letter should include an indication that management is responsible for identifying and ensuring that the company complies with the laws and regulations applicable to its activities. Answer (b) is incorrect because such detailed information on materiality is not generally included in an engagement letter. Answer (c) is incorrect because management liability (if any) for illegal acts committed by employees is not generally included in an engagement letter. Answer (d) is incorrect because while an auditor is required to obtain an understanding of internal control, he or she is not required to search for significant internal control deficiencies.

**66.   (c)**   The requirement is to identify the most likely procedure during the initial planning phase of an audit. Answer (c) is correct because during initial planning the timing of procedures will be discussed due to the need for client assistance with many of these procedures. Answer (a) is incorrect because the consideration of internal control will often occur subsequent to the **initial** planning stage of an audit (see AU 319). Answer (b) is incorrect because the evaluation of reasonableness of the client's accounting estimates will occur after planning (see AU 342). Answer (d) is incorrect because the inquiry of a client's attorney will occur subsequently to initial planning (see AU 337). See AU 311 for information on planning.

**67.** **(d)** The requirement is to identify the statement that is **least** likely to appear in an auditor's engagement letter. Answer (d) is correct because auditors ordinarily will not discuss with management the details of procedures that are necessary to perform the audit. Answers (a), (b), and (c) are incorrect because engagement letters **will** include a statement on the risk of not detecting material errors and fraud, and **may** include information on fees and observed opportunities for economy.

**68.** **(c)** The requirement is to identify the item for which the generally accepted auditing standards do not require documentation. Answer (c) is correct because while a CPA firm will often include an engagement letter in the working papers, this is not required by the generally accepted auditing standards. Answer (a) is incorrect because AU 311 requires a written audit program. Answer (b) is incorrect because AU 339 requires that the working papers document the agreement or reconciliation of the accounting records with the financial statements. Answer (d) is incorrect because AU 319 requires documentation of the basis for an auditor's conclusions when the assessed level of control risk is below the maximum level.

**69.** **(a)** The requirement is to determine what types of items are ordinarily included in an engagement letter in addition to the objectives of the engagement. Answer (a) is correct because AU 311 also requires inclusion of information on CPA responsibilities, client responsibilities, and limitations of the engagement.

**70.** **(c)** The requirement is to determine the reply which is least likely to be included in an engagement letter. Answer (c) is correct because AU 311, which provides information on obtaining an understanding with the client, does not suggest any arrangement concerning CPA investment in client securities; indeed such investments are prohibited by the Code of Professional Conduct. Answers (a), (b), and (d) all represent arrangements which AU 311 suggests may be included in an engagement letter (or other form of understanding with a client).

**71.** **(b)** The requirement is to identify an auditor's responsibility when he or she believes that an understanding with the client has **not** been established. Answer (b) is correct because AU 311 requires that the CPA ordinarily decline to accept or perform the audit engagement in such circumstances. Answers (a), (c), and (d) are all incorrect because the audit will not ordinarily be performed.

**72.** **(a)** The requirement is to determine the allowable form(s) of an understanding with a client when an audit is being performed. Answer (a) is correct because AU 311 states that while a written understanding is preferable, it is not required; also, in all cases the understanding must be documented in the working papers. Answer (b) is incorrect because working paper documentation of the understanding is required in all circumstances. Answer (c) is incorrect because an oral understanding is acceptable. Answer (d) is incorrect because AU 311 includes a requirement that an auditor obtain an understanding with the client.

### A.3.a.  Developing an Overall Strategy

**73.** **(b)** The requirement is to identify the information source that a CPA would most likely consult for information on how various publicly held companies have complied with the disclosure requirements of a new financial accounting standard. Answer (b) is correct because AICPA *Accounting Trends and Techniques*, which is issued annually, summarizes such disclosures of 600 industrial and merchandising corporations. Answer (a) is incorrect because the AICPA Codification of Statements on Auditing Standards codifies the various Statements on Auditing Standards and does not include information on individual company compliance with disclosure requirements. Answer (c) is incorrect because Quality Control Review standards are established by the AICPA and because they do not include information on individual company compliance with disclosure requirements. Answer (d) is incorrect because Form 10-K itself provides information on preparing Form10-K and this form does not include information on individual company compliance with disclosure requirements.

**74.** **(a)** The requirement is to identify the procedure an auditor would most likely include in the planning phase of a financial statement audit. Answer (a) is correct because during the planning stage an auditor should obtain an understanding of each of the five components of internal control (including the element of risk assessment) sufficient to plan the audit (AU 319). Answer (b) is incorrect because an identification of specific internal control activities designed to prevent fraud may occur either during planning or subsequently. Answer (c) is incorrect because a valuation of the reasonableness of the entity's accounting estimates will ordinarily occur subsequent to the planning stage (see AU 342 for guidance on auditing accounting estimates). Answer (d) is incorrect because cutoff tests are performed subsequent to the planning of the audit. See AU 310 and AU 311 for information on planning the audit, and AU 319 for information on internal control responsibilities both during planning and subsequent stages of the audit.

**75.** **(d)** The requirement is to determine why an auditor obtains knowledge about a new client's business and its industry. Answer (d) is correct because obtaining a level of knowledge of the client's business and industry enables the CPA to obtain an understanding of the events, transactions, and practices that, in the CPA's judgment, may have a significant effect on the financial statements. Answer (a) is incorrect because providing constructive suggestions is a secondary, and not the primary, reason for obtaining knowledge about a client's business and industry. Answer (b) is incorrect because while a CPA must develop an attitude of professional skepticism concerning a client, this attitude is not obtained by obtaining knowledge about the client's business and industry. Answer (c) is incorrect because information on the business and industry of a client will provide only limited information in determining whether financial statements are materially misstated, and numerous other factors are considered in evaluating audit findings.

**76.   (c)**   The requirement is to identify the **least** likely procedure to be performed in planning a financial statement audit. Answer (c) is correct because selecting a sample of vendors' invoices for comparison to receiving reports will occur normally as a part of the evidence accumulation process, not as a part of the planning of an audit. Answer (a) is incorrect because coordination of the assistance of entity personnel in data preparation occurs during planning. Answer (b) is incorrect because while planning the audit, CPAs may discuss matters that affect the audit with firm personnel responsible for providing nonaudit services to the entity. Answer (d) is incorrect because any available current year interim financial statements will be read during the planning stage.

**A.3.b.   Communicate with Predecessor Auditors**

**77.   (a)**   The requirement is to identify whether a predecessor auditor should permit a successor auditor to review working paper analyses relating to contingencies, balance sheet accounts, or both. Answer (a) is correct because AU 315 states that a predecessor auditor should ordinarily permit the successor to review working papers, including documentation of planning, internal control, audit results, and other matters of continuing accounting and auditing significance, such as the working paper analysis of balance sheet accounts and those relating to contingencies.

**78.   (d)**   The requirement is to determine a successor auditor's responsibility when financial statements audited by a predecessor auditor are found to require substantial revisions. Answer (d) is correct because when a successor auditor becomes aware of information that indicates that financial statements reported on by the predecessor may require revision, the successor should request that the client arrange a meeting among the three parties to discuss and attempt to resolve the matter. Answer (a) is incorrect because the successor is not required to notify the audit committee and stockholders. Answer (b) is incorrect because the client should first communicate with the predecessor before revising the financial statements. Answer (c) is incorrect because a meeting of the three parties is arranged by the client and because the situation may or may not have anything to do with the integrity of management.

**79.   (c)**   The requirement is to determine whether a successor auditor should request a new client to authorize the predecessor auditor to allow a review of the predecessor's engagement letter, working papers, or both. Answer (c) is correct because AU 315 states that it is advisable that a successor auditor request to be allowed to review the predecessor's working papers

**A.3.c.   Analytical Procedures**

**80.   (b)**   The requirement is to identify the audit procedure that an auditor will most likely perform in planning a financial statement audit. Answer (b) is correct because AU 329 requires that an auditor perform analytical procedures such as comparing the financial statements to anticipated results during the planning stage of an audit. Answers (a), (c), and (d) are all incorrect because these procedures will all occur subsequent to planning.

**81.   (c)**   The requirement is to determine the proper focus of analytical procedures used in planning an audit. Answer (c) is correct because analytical procedures used in

planning should focus on (1) enhancing the auditor's understanding of the client's business and the transactions and events that have occurred since the last audit date, and (2) identifying areas that may represent specific risks relevant to the audit. Answer (a) is incorrect because while analytical procedures performed as substantive tests may affect the scope of other substantive tests and of tests of controls, analytical procedures used in planning generally do not. Answer (b) is incorrect because the general nature of analytical procedures used in planning provide only very limited assurance that potential misstatements will be identified; analytical procedures used as substantive tests provide a level of assurance that potential misstatements will be identified. Answer (d) is incorrect because analytical procedures performed at the review stage of audits more directly relate to assessing the adequacy of the available evidential matter.

**82.   (a)**   The requirement is to identify the objective of performing analytical procedures in planning an audit. Answer (a) is correct because AU 329 states that the objective of such procedures during planning is to identify such things as the existence of unusual transactions and events, amounts, ratios and trends that might indicate matters that have financial statement and audit planning ramifications. Answers (b), (c), and (d) are all incorrect because while analytical procedures may lead to the discovery of illegal acts, related-party transactions, and unauthorized transactions, this is not the primary objective.

**83.   (c)**   The requirement is to identify the type of nonfinancial information an auditor would most likely consider in performing analytical procedures during the planning phase of an audit. Answer (c) is correct because the square footage of selling space may be used in considering the overall reasonableness of sales. Answer (a) is incorrect because while the turnover of personnel in the accounting department may provide a measure of risk relating to the accounting function, it is not ordinarily used in performing analytical procedures. Similarly, answer (b) is incorrect because while the objectivity of audit committee members is an important consideration, it is not ordinarily used in performing analytical procedures. Answer (d) is also incorrect because management's plans to repurchase stock is not directly related to analytical procedures. See AU 329 for information on analytical procedures.

**A.3.e.   Audit Program**

**84.   (c)**   The requirement is to determine why an auditor should design a written audit program. Answer (c) is correct because an audit program sets forth in detail the audit procedures that are necessary to accomplish the objectives of the audit. Answer (a) is incorrect because audit programs address topics beyond selecting material transactions and this is not their primary focus. Answer (b) is incorrect because a program may include numerous substantive tests to be performed prior to the balance sheet date. Answer (d) is incorrect because immaterial accounts often are not tested and because tests of transactions, tests of balances, and analytical procedures are used to test account balances; account balances are not directly tested through tests of controls.

**85.   (a)**   The requirement is to determine a point at which an audit program may be finalized. Answer (a) is correct because the consideration of internal control helps the auditor to assess control risk and to plan the audit: accordingly, the audit program is not generally finalized prior to the consideration of internal control. Answer (b) is incorrect because, while generally desirable, engagement letters are not required on audits. Answer (c) is incorrect because reportable conditions may be communicated at various times subsequent to finalization of the audit program. Answer (d) is incorrect because audit programs are often finalized prior to the performance of the search for unrecorded liabilities.

**86.** **(d)** The requirement is to determine the manner in which audit programs should be designed. Answer (d) is correct because an audit program should be designed so that the audit evidence gathered is sufficient to support the auditor's conclusions. Answer (a) is incorrect because, often, most audit procedures will not be performed as interim work. Answer (b) is incorrect because inherent risk need not be assessed at a low level. Answer (c) is incorrect because while providing constructive suggestions to management is desirable, the audit program is not based on developing constructive suggestions.

**87.** **(d)** The requirement is to determine what specific audit objectives are addressed when designing an audit program. Answer (d) is correct because in obtaining evidential matter in support of financial statement assertions, the auditor develops specific audit objectives in the light of those assertions. Answers (a), (b), and (c) are all incorrect because these replies do not relate specifically to the audit objectives as do the financial statement assertions.

### A.3.f. Supervision Requirements (AU 311)

**88.** **(b)** The requirement is to identify the information that is most likely to be communicated by a supervisor to staff assistants. Answer (b) is correct because staff assistants must be aware of how their procedures should be evaluated in order to perform these procedures effectively. Answer (a) is incorrect because some immaterial fraud may be reported to the client's audit committee. Answer (c) is incorrect because the emphasis in an audit must be on performing the audit effectively and not merely on adhering to time budgets. Answer (d) is incorrect because decisions regarding transferring documents from the current file to the permanent file are generally of less importance than the procedure suggested by answer (b).

**89.** **(b)** The requirement is to determine why the work of each assistant should be reviewed. Answer (b) is correct because AU 311 suggests that the work performed by each assistant should be reviewed to determine whether it was adequately performed and to evaluate whether the results are consistent with the conclusions to be presented in the auditor's report. Answer (a) is incorrect because CPA firms, not individual auditors within the firms, have systems of quality control. Answer (c) is incorrect because the professional standards do not in general approve specific audit procedures. Answer (d) is incorrect because while determining that the audit has been performed by persons having adequate technical training and proficiency as auditors is important, it should be addressed prior to the commencement of fieldwork.

### A.3.g. Timing of Audit Procedures

**90.** **(a)** The requirement is to identify the statement that is always true with respect to planning an audit. Answer (a) is correct because it is acceptable for an auditor to perform a certain portion of the audit at an interim date; for example, performing a portion of planning prior to year-end is always acceptable for a continuing client. Also, when a new client has engaged an auditor prior to year-end, a portion of the audit may be conducted prior to year-end. Answer (b) is incorrect because an engagement may be accepted after the client's year-end. Answer (c) is incorrect because alternative procedures may be possible when an inventory count was not observed at year-end. Answer (d) is incorrect because final staffing decisions need not be made prior to completion of the planning stage of audits.

**91.** **(d)** The requirement is to identify the element of the audit planning process most likely to be agreed upon with the client before implementation of the audit strategy. Answer (d) is correct because the auditor will ordinarily observe the counting of inventory and this will require a degree of coordination between the performance of audit procedures and client count procedures. Answer (a) is incorrect because the client will not determine the evidence to be gathered to provide a sufficient basis for the auditor's opinion. Answers (b) and (c) are incorrect because these procedures will be determined subsequent to implementation of the audit strategy.

### B.1. General Attestation

**92.** **(b)** The requirement is to identify the definition of assurance services. Answer (b) is correct because the Special Committee on Assurance Services, also referred to as the Elliott Committee, defined assurance services as independent professional services that improve the quality of information, or its context, for decision makers. Answer (a) is incorrect because the definition does not include a statement on a written communication or a conclusion. Answer (c) is incorrect because not all consulting services are included as assurance services, and because the definition differs. Answer (d) is incorrect because it abstracts a portion of the definition of an attest engagement that is not included in the definition of an assurance service.

**93.** **(c)** The requirement is to identify the organization that was formed to analyze and report on the current state and future of the audit/assurance function and trends shaping its environment. Answer (c) is correct because it was the Special Committee on Assurance Services, also referred to as the "Elliott Committee," that was established to analyze and report on the current state and future of the audit/ assurance function and trends shaping its environment. Answer (a) is incorrect because the Commission on Auditors' Responsibilities, a similar but much earlier committee, was charged with developing conclusions and recommendation regarding the appropriate responsibilities of independent auditors in 1974. Answer (b) is incorrect because the Committee of Sponsoring Organizations is primarily concerned with internal control. Answer (d) is incorrect because no committee with that name has been established.

**94.** **(b)** The requirement is to identify the service that is **not** a type of attest engagement. Answer (b) is correct because compilations are not considered attest engagements. Answers (a), (c), and (d) are incorrect because AU 100 establishes agreed-upon procedures for engagements, examinations, and reviews as the three basic types of attest engagements.

**95.** **(a)**   The requirement is to identify a conceptual difference between the attestation standards and generally accepted auditing standards. Answer (a) is correct because AT 101 states that the attestation standards do not apply to audits of historical financial statements. Answer (b) is incorrect because an independent mental attitude is required for attestation engagements. Answer (c) is incorrect because an attest engagement may be related to a business acquisition study or a feasibility study. Answer (d) is incorrect because while there is no internal control fieldwork standard under the attestation standards, both a planning and an evidence standard of fieldwork are included.

**96.** **(d)**   The requirement is to identify the reply which is **not** an attestation standard. Answer (d) is correct because the attestation standards do not include a requirement that a sufficient understanding of internal control be obtained to plan the engagement. There is no internal control standard because the concept of internal control may not be relevant to certain assertions on which a CPA may be engaged to report (e.g., aspects of information about computer software). Answers (a), (b), and (c) are all incorrect because standards exist for evidence, reporting on the assertion or subject matter, and proper planning.

**97.** **(a)**   The requirement is to determine who, at a minimum, must have knowledge of the relevant professional accounting and auditing standards when an audit is being performed. Answer (a) is correct because AU 230 requires that, at a minimum, the auditor with final responsibility have such knowledge. Answers (b), (c), and (d) are all incorrect because they suggest a higher minimum requirement.

**98.** **(b)**   The requirement is to determine which concept requires an attitude that includes a questioning mind and a critical assessment of audit evidence. Answer (b) is correct because AT 230 states that professional skepticism includes these qualities. Answer (a) is incorrect because due professional care is a broader concept that concerns what the independent auditor does and how well he or she does it. Answer (c) is incorrect because reasonable assurance is based on the concept that an auditor is not an insurer and his or her report does not provide absolute assurance. Answer (d) is incorrect because supervision involves the directing of the efforts of assistants who are involved in accomplishing the objectives of the audit and determining whether those objectives were accomplished.

**99.** **(c)**   The requirement is to determine what presumption concerning management's honesty that professional skepticism requires. Answer (c) is correct because professional skepticism requires that an auditor neither assume dishonesty nor unquestioned honesty. Answers (a) and (b) are incorrect because neither honesty in the absence of fraud risk factor nor dishonesty are assumed. Answer (d) is incorrect because the concept of reasonable assurance is not directed towards management's honesty.

**100.** **(c)**   Answer (c) is correct because AT 100 indicates that an unqualified may ordinarily refer to that assertion or to the subject matter to which the assertion relates. Answer (a) is incorrect because it suggests reporting only on the assertion. Answer (b) is incorrect because it suggests reporting only on the subject matter. Answer (d) is incorrect because it suggests that reporting on neither the assertion nor the subject matter is appropriate. Note, however, that

AT 100 also states that when a deviation from the criteria being reported upon exists (e.g., a material weakness in internal control) the CPA should report directly upon the subject matter and not upon the assertion.

**B.2.   Audit**

**101.** **(c)**   The requirement is to identify the characteristic that is most likely to be unique to the audit work of CPAs as compared to work performed by practitioners of other professions. Answer (c) is correct because independence is absolutely required for the performance of audits; other professions do not in general require such independence. Answers (a), (b), and (d) are incorrect because the various professions require due professional care and competence and have a complex body of knowledge.

**102.** **(d)**   The requirement is to determine what is meant by the third general standard's requirement of due care in the performance of an audit. Answer (d) is correct because due care requires critical review at every level of supervision of the work done and the judgment exercised by those assisting in the audit. Answer (a) is incorrect because the due care standard does not directly address safeguards over access to assets and records. Answer (b) is incorrect because due care does not relate to a limited review of employee fraud and illegal acts. Answer (c) is incorrect because the first general standard addresses technical training and proficiency as an auditor.

**103.** **(a)**   The requirement is to identify the focus of a final wrap-up review performed by a second partner who has not been involved in the audit. Answer (a) is correct because this second or "cold" review aims at determining whether the financial statements result in fair presentation in conformity with GAAP and with whether sufficient competent evidential matter has been obtained. Answer (b) is incorrect because most frequently fraud involving the client's management and its employees have not been discovered and, even if they have been, the focus of the review is still on the fairness of presentation of the financial statements. Answers (c) and (d) are incorrect because decisions on materiality and communications with the audit committee are only two of the many matters the review may address in an effort to address fairness of presentation of the financial statements.

**104.** **(b)**   The requirement is to identify the correct statement concerning an auditor's responsibilities regarding financial statements. Answer (b) is correct because an auditor may draft an entity's financial statements based on information from management's accounting system. Answer (a) is incorrect because making suggestions does not necessarily impair an auditor's independence. Answer (c) is incorrect because fair presentation of financial statements is an implicit part of management's, not the auditor's, responsibilities. Answer (d) is incorrect because an auditor's responsibilities for the audited financial statements is confined to the expression of an opinion on them.

**105.** **(a)**   The requirement is to identify the listed authoritative body designated to promulgate attestation standards. Answer (a) is correct because only the Auditing Standards Board, the Accounting and Review Services Committee, and the Management Advisory Services Executive Committee have been authorized to promulgate attestation standards.

**106.** (b) The requirement is to identify the statement that best describes the meaning of generally accepted auditing standards. Answer (b) is correct because generally accepted auditing standards deal with measures of the quality of the performance of audit procedures. Answer (a) is incorrect because procedures relate to acts to be performed, not directly to the standards. Answer (c) is incorrect because generally accepted auditing standards have been issued by predecessor groups, as well as by the Auditing Standards Board. Answer (d) is incorrect because there may or may not be **universal** compliance with the standards.

**107.** (b) The requirement is to determine the proper method for handling a difference of opinion between auditors concerning interpretation of the results of an auditing procedure. Answer (b) is correct because the quality control standards require documentation of the considerations involved in the resolution of differences of opinion. Answer (a) is incorrect because the AICPA does not, in general, rule on disagreements of this nature. Answer (c) is incorrect because the disagreement relates to an auditing procedure and therefore in most such circumstances the entity's management or its audit committee will have no particular expertise. Answer (d) is incorrect because the disagreement need not necessarily be reported to a peer review "monitoring" team.

**B.3.  Responsibilities in Compilation and Review**

**108.** (a) The requirement is to determine an accountant's responsibility relating to knowledge of the client's accounting principles and practices when performing a compilation. Answer (a) is correct because to compile financial statements the accountant should possess a general understanding of the nature of the entity's business transactions, the form of its accounting records, the stated qualifications of its accounting personnel, the accounting basis on which the financial statements are to be presented, and the form and content of the financial statements. Answer (b) is incorrect because the accountant need not have a general understanding of the entity's controls. Answer (c) is incorrect because no such consideration of risk factors is envisioned in a compilation. Answer (d) is incorrect because no such consideration of internal control awareness of senior management is made.

**109.** (d) The requirement is to determine whether reproducing client-prepared financial statements without modification and preparing standard monthly journal entries are included in the provisions of Statements on Standards for Accounting and Review Services. Answer (d) is correct because AR 100 states that neither producing statements nor preparing standard monthly journal entries is included.

**110.** (b) The requirement is to determine the effect of an immaterial direct financial interest on accountant independence. Answer (b) is correct because even immaterial direct financial interests impair the independence that is required for the performance of reviews and other attestation services. Answer (a) is incorrect because a CPA who lacks independence may compile those financial statements when this lack of independence is disclosed in the compilation report. Answer (c) is incorrect because a review report may not be issued. Answer (d) is incorrect because the CPA is not independent.

**111.** (d) The requirement is to identify the correct statement about unaudited personal financial statements included

in a personal financial plan. Answer (d) is correct because AT 600 requires that the financial statements be used solely to assist the client and the client's advisor and not be used to obtain credit. Answer (a) is incorrect because financial statements may be presented in comparative form. Answer (b) is incorrect because omitted disclosures may be material. Answer (c) is incorrect because such financial statements may be disclosed to a non-CPA financial planner.

**112.** (a) The requirement is to determine a CPA's responsibilities when performing a review of a nonpublic entity's financial statements that contain uncorrected departures from GAAP and the CPA believes that the review report is not adequate to indicate the deficiencies. Answer (a) is correct because AR 100 states that in such circumstances the CPA should withdraw from the engagement and provide no further services with respect to those financial statements. Answers (b) and (d) are incorrect because restricting distribution is not adequate or appropriate in such a circumstance. Answer (c) is incorrect because the standards on special reports do not apply in this circumstance.

**113.** (d) The requirement is to identify the circumstance in which Statements on Standards for Accounting and Review Services require an accountant to prepare a report. A report is required when a CPA submits unaudited financial statements of a nonpublic entity to his or her client or others. Accordingly, answer (d) is correct because when a CPA prepares financial statements a compilation report (assuming that neither a review nor an audit has been performed) is required. Answers (a), (b), and (c) are all incorrect because they are all included as services that do not constitute a submission of financial statements to a client.

**114.** (d) The requirement is to identify the engagement for which Statements on Standards for Accounting and Review Services establish standards and procedures. Answer (d) is correct because the Statements apply when a CPA either compiles or reviews the financial statements of a nonpublic entity. Answer (a) is incorrect because the Statements do not apply when the CPA is assisting in adjusting the books of account for a partnership or other organization. Answer (b) is incorrect because the Statements only apply to nonpublic entities. Answer (c) is incorrect because the Statements do not apply when processing the financial data for clients of other accounting firms.

**115.** (c) The requirement is to identify the authoritative body designated to promulgate standards concerning an accountant's association with unaudited financial statements of an entity that is **not** required to file financial statements with an agency regulating the issuance of the entity's securities. Answer (c) is correct because the Accounting and Review Services Committee is so designated. Answer (a) is incorrect because the Financial Accounting Standards Board is the authoritative body designated to promulgate financial accounting standards. Answer (b) is incorrect because General Accounting Office is not one of the bodies designated by the AICPA to promulgate technical standards. Answer (d) is incorrect because the Auditing Standards Board is the authoritative body designated to promulgate statements on auditing standards. ET Appendix A presents the bodies designated to promulgate technical standards.

**116.** (c) The requirement is to determine which of the two listed accounting services an accountant may perform

**without** being required to issue a compilation or review report under the Statements on Standards for Accounting and Review Services. Answer (c) is correct because the Statements on Standards for Accounting and Review Services do not apply to preparing a working trial balance or to preparing standard monthly journal entries. See AR 100 for these and additional circumstances in which the standards do not apply. Accordingly, no compilation or review report needs to be issued when these services are provided.

### B.4.  Prospective Financial Statements

**117.  (d)**   The requirement is to identify what is included in the examination of a financial forecast. Answer (d) is correct because an examination of a forecast includes an evaluation of its preparation and the support underlying management's assumptions. As discussed in AT 200, an examination also includes evaluating the representation of the prospective financial statements for conformity with AICPA presentation guidelines and the issuance of an examination report. Answer (a) is incorrect because the service need not include the compiling or assembling of the financial forecast. Answer (b) is incorrect because distribution of financial forecasts need not be limited. Answer (c) is incorrect because the CPA assumes no responsibility to update management on key events. See AT 200 for information on prospective financial information.

**118.  (a)**   The requirement is to identify the circumstance in which an accountant may accept an engagement to apply agreed-upon procedures to prospective financial statements. Answer (a) is correct because AR 200 states that an accountant may accept an engagement to apply agreed-upon procedures to prospective financial statements provided that (1) the specified parties involved have participated in establishing the nature and scope of the engagement and take responsibility for the adequacy of the procedures to be performed, (2) use of the report is to be restricted to the specified parties involved, and (3) the prospective financial statements include a summary of significant assumptions. Answer (b) is incorrect because the prospective financial statements need not be examined. Answer (c) is incorrect because responsibility for the adequacy of the procedures is taken by the specified parties. Answer (d) is incorrect because a summary of findings may be provided based on the agreed-upon procedures.

### B.5.  Quality Control

**119.  (a)**   The requirement is to determine the factors that affect the nature and extent of a CPA firm's quality control policies and procedures. Answer (a) is correct because the nature and extent of a firm's quality control policies and procedures depend on a number of factors, including its size, the degree of operating autonomy allowed to its personnel and practice offices, the nature of its practice, its organization, and appropriate cost-benefit considerations.

**120.  (a)**   The requirement is to identify the factors that ordinarily would be considered in planning an audit engagement's personnel requirement. Answer (a) is correct because opportunities for on-the-job training and rotation of personnel among the various appropriate policies and procedures represent factors to be considered.

**121.  (d)**   The requirement is to determine the types of services to which *Statements on Quality Control Standards*

apply. Answer (d) is correct because the standards explicitly limit application to auditing and accounting and review services. Although the quality control standards may be applied to other segments of a firm's practice (e.g., management advisory services and tax), the standards do not require it.

**122.  (a)**   The requirement is to determine how a CPA firm obtains reasonable assurance of providing professional services that conform with professional standards. Answer (a) is correct because a system of quality control is designed to provide a CPA firm with reasonable assurance of meeting its responsibility to provide professional services that conform with professional standards. Answer (b) is incorrect because a peer review provides information on whether a CPA firm is following an appropriate system of quality control. Answer (c) is incorrect because it is less complete than answer (a) since continuing professional education helps achieve the specific quality control element of professional development. Answer (d) is incorrect because complying with generally accepted reporting standards is only one part of the basic objective of providing professional services that conform with professional standards.

### B.6.  Public Company Accounting Oversight Board Requirements

**123.  (b)**   The requirement is to identify the correct statement concerning PCAOB guidance that uses the term "should." Answer (b) is correct because the term "should" means that the auditor must comply with the requirements unless he or she can demonstrate that alternative actions were sufficient to achieve the objectives of the standards. Answer (a) is incorrect because terms such as "must," "shall," and "is required to" are used to indicate that the auditor must fulfill the responsibilities. Answer (c) is incorrect because terms such as "may," "might," and "could" are used when the auditor should consider performing the audit procedure. Answer (d) is incorrect because no particular terms are used for the situation in which the auditor has complete discretion whether to perform the procedure.

**124.  (c)**   The requirement is to determine the set of standards that the PCAOB does *not* have authority to establish. Answer (c) is correct because the FASB establishes accounting standards for both public and nonpublic companies. Answer (a) is incorrect because the PCAOB has authority to issue auditing standards. Answer (b) is incorrect because the PCAOB has the authority to issue quality control standards. Answer (d) is incorrect because the PCAOB has the authority to issue independence standards.

**SOLUTION TO SIMULATION PROBLEMS**

**Simulation Problem 1**

| Situation | Audit and Fraud Risk | Fraud Discussion | Research | Communication |
|---|---|---|---|---|

| Factor | Increased audit risk | Decreased audit risk | Fraud risk factor |
|---|---|---|---|
| 1. Branch management authority | ● | ○ | ● |
| 2. Government regulation | ○ | ● | ○ |
| 3. Company profitability | ○ | ● | ○ |
| 4. Demand for product | ○ | ● | ○ |
| 5. Interest rates | ● | ○ | ○ |
| 6. Availability of mortgage funds | ○ | ● | ○ |
| 7. Involvement of principal shareholder in management | ○ | ● | ○ |
| 8. Branch manager compensation | ● | ○ | ● |
| 9. Internal audit reporting relationship | ○ | ● | ○ |
| 10. Accounting department turnover | ○ | ● | ○ |
| 11. Continuing audit relationship | ○ | ● | ○ |
| 12. Internal controls over accounting estimates | ● | ○ | ● |
| 13. Response to proposed accounting adjustments | ○ | ● | ○ |
| 14. New unprofitable branch | ● | ○ | ● |
| 15. New computer system | ● | ○ | ○ |

| Situation | Audit and Fraud Risk | Fraud Discussion | Research | Communication |
|---|---|---|---|---|

| Risk | High risk item |
|---|---|
| 1. Computer fraud risk | ○ |
| 2. Risk related to management override of internal control[1] | ● |
| 3. Fraud by branch management | ● |
| 4. Fraud by accounting personnel | ○ |
| 5. Misstatement of accounting estimates | ● |
| 6. Fraud by loan processing clerks | ○ |
| 7. Fraud by internal auditors | ○ |
| 8. The risk of fraudulent misstatement of revenues[1] | ● |

| Situation | Audit and Fraud Risk | Fraud Discussion | Research | Communication |
|---|---|---|---|---|

To get the appropriate guidance you could search on Statement on Auditing Standards No. 99, or AU Section 316 and then scan the documentation requirements. Alternatively, a word search with "fraud" and "documenting" would get you right to the appropriate place in the literature. The excerpt from the literature is shown below.

---

[1] *Required points for these types of discussions.*

83. The auditor should document the following:

- The discussion among engagement personnel in planning the audit regarding the susceptibility of the entity's financial statements to material misstatement due to fraud, including how and when the discussion occurred, the audit team members who participated, and the subject matter discussed. (See paragraphs 14 through 17.)
- The procedures performed to obtain information necessary to identify and assess the risks of material misstatement due to fraud. (See paragraphs 19 through 34.)
- Specific risks of material misstatement due to fraud that were identified (see paragraphs 35 through 45), and a description of the auditor's response to those risks. (See paragraphs 46 through 56.)
- If the auditor has not identified in a particular circumstance, improper revenue recognition as a risk of material misstatement due to fraud, the reasons supporting the auditor's conclusion. (See paragraph 41.)
- The results of the procedures performed to further address the risk of management override of controls. (See paragraphs 58 through 67.)
- Other conditions and analytical relationships that caused the auditor to believe that additional auditing procedures or other responses were required and any further responses the auditor concluded were appropriate, to address such risks or other conditions. (See paragraphs 68 through 73.)
- The nature of the communications about fraud made to management, the audit committee, and others. (See paragraphs 79 through 82.)

| Situation | Audit and Fraud Risk | Fraud Discussion | Research | Communication |
| --- | --- | --- | --- | --- |

To:     Audit Working Papers
From:   CPA Candidate
Re:      Staff discussion regarding fraud

SAS No. 99, *Consideration of Fraud in a Financial Statement Audit*, requires the staff to have a discussion of how and where fraud might be perpetrated. The discussion must also emphasize the importance of maintaining professional skepticism during the audit. Participants to the discussion should include the partner in charge of the audit, along with other members of the audit staff.

---

**Simulation Problem 2**

| Situation | Nonattest Services | Auditing Standards | Research | Communication |
| --- | --- | --- | --- | --- |

| Service | May provide, independence is required | May provide, independence is not required | May not provide |
| --- | :---: | :---: | :---: |
| 1. Provide an opinion on whether financial statements are prepared following the cash basis of accounting | ● | ○ | ○ |
| 2. Compile a forecast for the coming year. | ○ | ● | ○ |
| 3. Compile the financial statements for the past year and issue a publicly available report. | ○ | ● | ○ |
| 4. Apply certain agreed-upon procedures to accounts receivable for purposes of obtaining a loan, and express a summary of findings relating to those procedures. | ● | ○ | ○ |
| 5. Review quarterly information and issue a report that includes limited assurance. | ● | ○ | ○ |
| 6. Perform an audit of the financial statements on whether they are prepared following generally accepted accounting principles. | ● | ○ | ○ |
| 7. Perform a review of a forecast the company has prepared for the coming year. | ○ | ○ | ● |
| 8. Compile the financial statements for the past year, but not issue a report since the financial statements are only for the company's use. | ○ | ● | ○ |
| 9. Calculate the client's taxes and fill out the appropriate tax forms. | ○ | ● | ○ |
| 10. Design a new payroll system for Hanmei and base billings on Hamnei's actual savings for the next three years. | ○ | ● | ○ |

| Situation | Nonattest Services | Auditing Standards | Research | Communication |
|---|---|---|---|---|

### *Transactions*

|   | | (A) | (B) | (C) | (D) | (E) | (F) | (G) | (H) | (I) |
|---|---|---|---|---|---|---|---|---|---|---|
| **1.** | Possible risk factors related to misappropriation of assets. | ○ | ○ | ○ | ● | ○ | ○ | ○ | ○ | ○ |
| **2.** | The relationship between materiality used for planning versus evaluation purposes. | ○ | ● | ○ | ○ | ○ | ○ | ○ | ○ | ○ |
| **3.** | Hanmei Corp. has transactions with the corporation president's brother. | ○ | ○ | ○ | ○ | ○ | ○ | ○ | ○ | ● |
| **4.** | Comparing a client's unaudited results for the year with last year's audited results. | ● | ○ | ○ | ○ | ○ | ○ | ○ | ○ | ○ |
| **5.** | Auditing and reporting guidance on the possible need to reaudit previous year results due to the disbanding of the firm that performed last year's audit. | ○ | ○ | ● | ○ | ○ | ○ | ○ | ○ | ○ |
| **6.** | Requirements relating to identifying violations of occupational safety and healt regulations. | ○ | ○ | ○ | ○ | ○ | ● | ○ | ○ | ○ |
| **7.** | Audit report considerations when audit of a subsidiary of the client will be performed by Williams & Co., CPAs. | ○ | ○ | ○ | ○ | ○ | ○ | ○ | ● | ○ |
| **8.** | The need to "brainstorm" among audit team members about how accounts coul be intentionally misstated. | ○ | ○ | ○ | ● | ○ | ○ | ○ | ○ | ○ |
| **9.** | Details on considering operating effectiveness of controls. | ○ | ○ | ○ | ○ | ● | ○ | ○ | ○ | ○ |
| **10.** | The importance of considering the possibility of overstated revenues (for example, through premature revenue recognition). | ○ | ○ | ○ | ● | ○ | ○ | ○ | ○ | ○ |

| Situation | Nonattest Services | Auditing Standards | Research | Communication |
|---|---|---|---|---|

AU 310.06-.07 provides the necessary information.

**1.** Information generally included          **AU310.06**

An understanding with the client regarding an audit of the financial statements generally includes the following matters:

- The objective of the audit is the expression of an opinion on the financial statements.
- Management is responsible for the entity's financial statements.
- Management is responsible for establishing and maintaining effective internal control over financial reporting
- Management is responsible for identifying and ensuring that the entity complies with the laws and regulations applicable to its activities.
- Management is responsible for making all financial records and related information available to the auditor.
- At the conclusion of the engagement, management will provide the auditor with a letter that confirms certain representations made during the audit.
- The auditor is responsible for conducting the audit in accordance with generally accepted auditing standards. Those standard require that the auditor obtain reasonable rather than absolute assurance about whether the financial statements are free of material misstatement, whether caused by error or fraud. Accordingly, a material misstatement may remain undetected. Also, an audit is not designed to detect error or fraud that is immaterial to the financial statements. If, for any reason, the auditor is unable to complete the audit or is unable to form or has not formed an opinion, he or she may decline to express an opinion or decline to issue a report as a result of the engagement.
- An audit includes obtaining an understanding of internal control sufficient to plan the audit and to determine the nature, timing,

and extent of audit procedures to be performed. An audit is not designed to provide assurance on internal control or to identify reportable conditions. However, the auditor is responsible for ensuring that the audit committee or others with equivalent authority or responsibility are aware of any reportable conditions which come to his or her attention.

- Management is responsible for adjusting the financial statements to correct material misstatements and for affirming to the auditor in the representation letter that the effect of any uncorrected misstatements fn3 aggregated by the auditor during the current engagement and pertaining to the latest period presented are immaterial, both individually and in the aggregate, to the financial statements taken as a whole.

2.   Other matters

**AU310.07**

An understanding with the client may also include other matters, such as the following:

- Arrangements regarding the conduct of the engagement (for example, timing, client assistance regarding the preparation of schedules, and the availability of documents).
- Arrangements concerning involvement of specialists or internal auditors, if applicable.
- Arrangements involving a predecessor auditor.
- Arrangements regarding fees and billing.
- Any limitation of or other arrangements regarding the liability of the auditor or the client, such as indemnification to the auditor for liability arising from knowing representations to the auditor by management. (Regulators, including the Securities and Exchange Commission, may restrict or prohibit such liability limitation arrangements.)
- Conditions under which access to the auditor's working papers may be granted to others.
- Additional services to be provided relating to regulatory requirements.
- Arrangement regarding other services to be provided in connection with the engagement.

| Situation | Nonattest Services | Auditing Standards | Research | Communication |
|---|---|---|---|---|

To:    Ms. Caroline Smith, Chairperson of the Audit Committee
From:  CPA Candidate
Re:    Independence

You have asked why independence is required to perform an audit in accordance with generally accepted auditing standards. The purpose of an audit is to lend credibility to your company's financial statements by acquiring an audit opinion. Only by maintaining our independence will users, such as stockholders and financial institutions, believe that our opinion is objective and not subject to bias.

## INTERNAL CONTROL

The second fieldwork standard states

> A sufficient understanding of internal control is to be obtained to plan the audit and to determine the nature, timing, and extent of tests to be performed.

AU 319 provides auditors with information on the relationship between a client's internal control[1] and financial statement audits. For purposes of audits, the consideration of internal control has two primary objectives: (1) aid in planning the remainder of the audit and (2) assess control risk (this assessment leads to the auditor's determination of the nature, timing, and extent of tests to be performed).

The following "Diagram of an Audit," originally presented in the auditing overview section, shows the relationship of internal control to an audit:

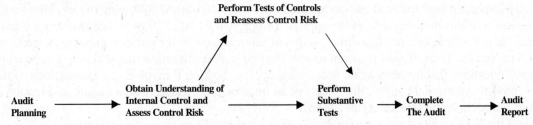

This module covers internal control and develops the relationships among internal control, tests of controls, and substantive tests. Every CPA examination includes questions on internal control and its relationship to various portions of the audit. Multiple-choice questions frequently require specification of a control that would, if present and operating properly, detect a stated weakness or error. Objective questions also have appeared regarding organization responsibility (e.g., who should distribute payroll checks?). A simulation may include a requirement to complete a flowchart of a transaction cycle, evaluate strengths and weaknesses of a system, and/or determine appropriate tests of controls and substantive tests.

### Study Program for the Internal Control Module

This module is organized and should be studied in the following manner:

A. The Nature of Internal Control

  1. Definition of Internal Control
  2. Major Components of Internal Control
  3. Related Topics

B. The Auditor's Consideration of Internal Control

  1. Obtain and Document Understanding of Internal Control
  2. Assess Control Risk
  3. Perform Tests of Controls
  4. Reassess Control Risk
  5. Summary

C. Public Company Audits of Internal Control

  1. Management's Responsibility
  2. Management's Assessment
  3. Control Definitions
  4. Evaluating Internal Control
  5. The Audit of Internal Control

D. Accounting Cycles

  1. Sales, Receivables, and Cash Receipts
  2. Purchases, Payables, and Cash Disbursements
  3. Inventories and Production

---

[1] *AU 319, "Consideration of Internal Control in a Financial Statement Audit," as modified in 1995 by Statement on Auditing Standards 78, uses the term "internal control." Other references (including prior auditing references) use "internal control structure" or "internal control system." We will use the terms interchangeably.*

    4.   Personnel and Payroll
    5.   Financing
    6.   Investing
    7.   Overall Internal Control Checklists

E.  Other Considerations
    1.   Communicating with the Audit Committee
    2.   Reporting on Internal Control
    3.   Effects of an Internal Audit Function
    4.   Reports on Processing of Transactions by Service Organizations

In Section A we begin with the key concepts related to an entity's internal control as presented in AU 319. It is especially important that you read and understand AU 319—the outline following the modules should be helpful. Section B of this module reviews the approach suggested by AU 319 by which auditors are to consider internal control when performing audits. Audits of internal control for public companies is presented in Section C. The Section D discussion is meant to provide you with information that will help you to respond to "applied type" questions that involve actual accounting cycles. Section E involves communications with audit committees, reports on internal control, the effects of an internal audit function on an audit, and reports on the processing of transactions by service organizations.

The following SAS sections pertain to internal control and are discussed in this module.

*AU Section*

| | |
|---|---|
| 319 | Consideration of Internal Control in a Financial Statement Audit |
| 322 | The Auditor's Consideration of the Internal Audit Function in an Audit of Financial Statements |
| 324 | Reports on the Processing of Transactions by Service Organizations |
| 325 | Communication of Internal Control Related Matters Noted in an Audit |
| 380 | Communication with Audit Committees |
| AT 501 | Reporting on an Entity's Internal Control over Financial Reporting |

## A.  The Nature of Internal Control

AU 319 presents information on (1) the nature of internal control and (2) the auditor's consideration of internal control. In this section we begin by discussing material related to the first area—the nature of internal control. Finally, we present several important, related topics.

### 1.  Definition of Internal Control

AU 319 uses the definition of internal control included in *Internal Control—Integrated Framework*, published by the Committee of Sponsoring Organizations of the Treadway Commission (the COSO Commission). It defines internal control as

> a process—effected by an entity's board of directors, management, and other personnel—designed to provide reasonable assurance regarding the achievement of objectives in the following categories: (a) reliability of financial reporting, (b) effectiveness and efficiency of operations, and (c) compliance with applicable laws and regulations.

The controls generally most relevant to audits are those that pertain to the entity's objective of preparing financial statements for external purposes [category (a) above]. Thus, typically, controls over **financial reporting** are relevant to the audit. Controls over operations and compliance objectives [categories (b) and (c) above] may be relevant if they pertain to data the auditor evaluates or uses in applying auditing procedures. For example, while controls relating to the number of salespersons hired often would not be relevant to the audit, if the auditor uses the number of salespersons in performing analytical procedures to help determine the reasonableness of sales (e.g., by calculating sales per salesperson), then the related controls become relevant.

While the safeguarding of assets against unauthorized acquisition, use, or disposition is an essential part of internal control, the auditor's responsibility with respect to safeguarding of assets is limited to those relevant to the reliability of financial reporting. For example, the company's use of passwords for limiting access to accounts receivable data files may be relevant to a financial statement audit, while controls to prevent the excess use of materials in production generally are not relevant to an audit.

2.  **Major Components of Internal Control**
    You need to know that AU 319 divides internal control into five components,[2] and the nature of each—(a) control environment, (b) risk assessment, (c) control activities, (d) information and communication, and (e) monitoring. Although you should study these in the outline of AU 319, we provide a brief summary of each of them at this point.

a.  **Control environment.** The control environment factors set the tone of an organization, influencing the control consciousness of its people. The seven control environment factors, which you may remember using the mnemonic IC HAMBO, are

    I  -  Integrity and ethical values
    C  -  Commitment to competence
    H  -  Human resource policies and practices
    A  -  Assignment of authority and responsibility
    M  -  Management's philosophy and operating style
    B  -  Board of directors or audit committee participation
    O  -  Organizational structure

b.  **Risk assessment.** For financial reporting purposes an entity's risk assessment is its identification, analysis, and management of risks relevant to the preparation of financial statements following GAAP (or some other comprehensive basis). The following are considered risks that may affect an entity's ability to properly record, process, summarize, and report financial data:

    (1)  Changes in the operating environment (e.g., increased competition)
    (2)  New personnel
    (3)  New information systems
    (4)  Rapid growth
    (5)  New technology
    (6)  New lines, products, or activities
    (7)  Corporate restructuring
    (8)  Foreign operations
    (9)  Accounting pronouncements

c.  **Control activities.** The third component of internal control is composed of the various policies and procedures that help ensure that necessary actions are taken to address risks to achieving the entity's objectives. Those policies and procedures include

    P  -  Performance reviews (reviews of actual performance against budgets, forecasts, one another, etc.)
    I  -  Information processing (controls that check accuracy, completeness, and authorization of transactions)
    P  -  Physical controls (activities that assure the physical security of assets and records)
    S  -  Segregation of duties (separate authorization, recordkeeping, and custody)

d.  **Information and communication.** The fourth component includes the accounting system, consisting of the methods and records established to **record, process, summarize, and report** entity transactions and to maintain accountability of the related assets and liabilities. To be effective, the information and communication system must accomplish the following goals for transactions:

    (1)  Identify and record all valid transactions
    (2)  Describe on a timely basis
    (3)  Measure the value properly
    (4)  Record in the proper time period
    (5)  Properly present and disclose
    (6)  Communicate responsibilities to employees

---

[2] *Prior to issuance of Statement on Auditing Standards 78, AU 319 divided internal control into three "elements": control environment, accounting system, and control procedures.*

e. **Monitoring.** Monitoring assesses the quality of internal control performance over time. Monitoring activities may be **ongoing, separate evaluations**, or a **combination** thereof. Ongoing monitoring activities are often designed into recurring activities such as sales and purchases. **Separate evaluations** are often performed by internal auditors or other personnel and often include communication of information about strengths and weaknesses and recommendations for improving internal control. Monitoring activities may also be performed by external parties (e.g., customers implicitly corroborate billing data by paying invoices).

3. **Related Topics**

   a. **Financial statement assertions.** As is discussed in further detail in the Evidence Module, assertions are management representations that are embodied in the account balance, transaction class, and disclosure components of financial statements. They include (1) presentation and disclosure, (2) existence or occurrence, (3) rights and obligations, (4) completeness, and (5) valuation. The AU 319 approach is one of suggesting that for each account or transaction class the auditor determines assertions of primary importance and then considers the related controls. A control often relates to less than all important assertions. Thus, a control over processing sales orders might, for example, be effective at determining the **existence** of receivables (e.g., there was a sale), but not directly address receivables **valuation** (because collection may be questionable), or **completeness** (whether all receivables have been recorded).

   b. **Limitations of internal control.** As we have suggested earlier, internal control provides reasonable, but not absolute, assurance that specific entity objectives will be achieved. Even the best internal control may break down due to

      (1) Human judgment in decision making can be faulty
      (2) Breakdowns can occur because of human failures such as simple errors or mistakes
      (3) Controls, whether manual or automated, can be circumvented by collusion
      (4) Management has the ability to override internal control
      (5) Cost constraints (the cost of internal control should not exceed the expected benefits expected to be derived)
      (6) Custom, culture, and the corporate governance system may inhibit fraud, but they are not absolute deterrents

      *NOTE: Be familiar with these limitations.*

   c. **Accounting vs. administrative control.** Before AU 319, the AICPA Professional Standards distinguished between administrative and accounting controls, stating that auditors generally emphasize the latter. While the distinction no longer remains for purposes of the professional standards, it does remain in certain laws, such as the Foreign Corrupt Practices Act.

   d. **Foreign Corrupt Practices Act.** A law passed by Congress in 1977 with provisions

      (1) Requiring every corporation registered under the Securities Exchange Act of 1934 to maintain a system of strong internal accounting control (as defined above),
      (2) Requiring corporations [defined in (1)] to maintain accurate books and records, and
      (3) Making it illegal for individuals or business entities to make payments to foreign officials to secure business.

      Violations of the Act can result in fines (up to $1 million for SEC registrants and $10,000 for individuals) and imprisonment (up to five years) of the responsible individuals. Thus, strong internal accounting control is required under federal law.

   e. **Committee of Sponsoring Organizations (COSO).** This committee is composed of representatives from various professional organizations, including the AICPA, the Institute of Management Accountants, the Financial Executives Institute, the Institute of Internal Auditors, and the American Accounting Association. COSO commissioned a study for the purpose of integrating various internal control concepts and definitions being used in the business community. The purposes of the study are to establish a common definition of internal control and to provide a standard against which business and other entities can assess internal control. The definition that COSO developed is included in AU 319.

f.  **Sarbanes-Oxley Act of 2002 (SOA).**  As indicated in Chapter 5, the SOA created a variety of new regulations and eliminated a significant portion of the accounting profession's system of self-regulation.  Three particularly relevant sections are

> **Section 302:**  Makes officers responsible for maintaining effective internal control and requires the principal executive and financial officers to disclose all significant internal control deficiencies to the company's auditors and audit committee.
>
> **Section 404:**  Requires that management acknowledge its responsibility for establishing adequate internal control over financial reporting and provide an assessment in the annual report of the effectiveness of internal control.  Also requires that CPAs attest to management's report on internal control as part of the audit of the financial statements—discussed further in section D.2 of this module.
>
> **Section 906:**  Requires that management certify reports filed with the SEC (primarily annual 10-K and quarterly 10-Qs) that the reports comply with relevant securities laws and also fairly present, in all material respects, the financial condition and results of operations of the company.

B.  **The Auditor's Consideration of Internal Control**

AU 319 presents the auditor's consideration of internal control (this begins at Section B in the SAS outline).  Recall that AU 319 identifies two major objectives of the auditor's consideration of internal control—(1) aid in planning the remainder of the audit and (2) assess control risk.

While auditor consideration of internal control may become quite involved, we will summarize the auditor's approach using four steps.

1.  Obtain and document understanding of internal control to plan the audit
2.  Assess control risk
3.  Perform (additional) tests of controls
4.  Reassess control risk

If the auditor is performing an audit of a public company, the approach to internal control will be somewhat different.  Section C covers the auditor's approach to the audit of a public company.

The relationships among these four steps are presented in the flowchart on the next page.  We now discuss them in detail.

1.  **Obtain and document understanding of internal control to plan the audit.**  In determining the level of understanding necessary to plan the audit, an auditor assesses the risk of misstatement using sources such as experience with the client, and an understanding of the industry in which the client operates.  The knowledge obtained for planning is used to

    - Identify types of potential misstatements
    - Consider factors that affect the risk of material misstatement
    - Design tests of controls, when applicable
    - Design substantive tests

    AU 319 provides information on the level of understanding necessary for the (a) control environment, (b) risk assessment, (c) control activities, (d) information and communication, and (e) monitoring.

    a.  **Control environment.**  The auditor must obtain sufficient knowledge to understand management's and the board of director's **attitude, awareness** and **actions** concerning the control environment.  The substance of the policies, procedures, and actions is more important than the form.  Thus, for example, a budget reporting system that provides adequate reports that are not used is of little value.

    b.  **Risk assessment.**  The auditor must obtain a sufficient knowledge to understand how management considers risks relevant to financial reporting objectives and decides about actions to address those risks.  This knowledge generally includes obtaining an understanding of how management identifies risks, estimates the significance of risks, assesses the likelihood of their occurrence, and relates them to financial reporting.

    c.  **Control activities.** The auditor should obtain an understanding of those control activities relevant to planning the audit.  While obtaining an understanding of the other components of internal control, the auditor obtains knowledge about some control activities.  For example, while obtaining an understanding of accounting for cash disbursements, an auditor is likely to become aware of whether bank accounts are reconciled (a control activity). An auditor should use professional judgment to determine the extent of additional knowledge needed to plan the audit. Ordinarily, audit planning does not require an understanding of control activities related to each account or to every assertion.

d. **Information and communication.** The auditor needs to obtain a level of knowledge of the information system and communication to understand (1) the major transaction classes, (2) how those transactions are initiated, (3) the available accounting records and support, (4) the manner of processing of transactions, (5) the financial reporting process used to prepare financial statements, and (6) the means the entity uses to communicate financial reporting roles and responsibilities.

e. **Monitoring.** The auditor should obtain sufficient knowledge of the major types of monitoring activities the entity uses to monitor internal control over financial reporting, including how those activities are used to initiate corrective action.

The following illustration summarizes the nature of the internal control components and the auditor's planning responsibility.

**SUMMARY FLOWCHART OF AU 319 CONSIDERATION
OF INTERNAL CONTROL DURING A FINANCIAL STATEMENT AUDIT**

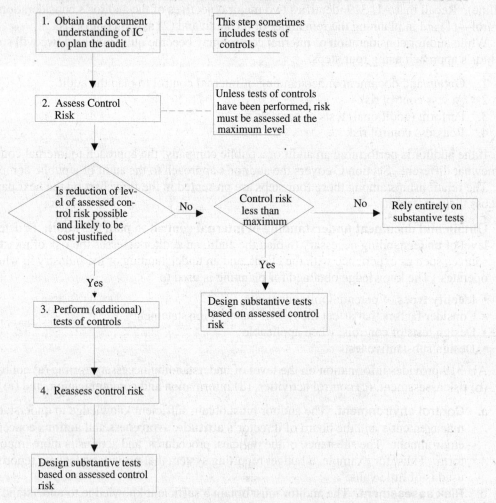

***Procedures for obtaining an understanding.*** The auditor relies primarily upon a combination of (1) previous experience with the entity, (2) inquiries, (3) inspection of documents and records, and (4) observation of entity activities to obtain the needed understanding of the internal control. At this point in the audit, these procedures are performed primarily to help the auditor to understand the design and whether the controls have been **placed in operation**. AU 319 distinguishes between determining that controls are placed in operation vs. evaluating their operating effectiveness. In determining whether controls have been placed in operation, the auditor determines that the entity is using them.  This is all that is necessary for planning the audit.

In evaluating operating effectiveness, the auditor goes further and considers (1) how the control was applied; (2) the consistency with which it was applied; and (3) by whom.  Tests of controls (described in detail in Section 3 below) address the effectiveness of the design and operation of a control.  Tests of controls are necessary to assess control risk below the maximum level.

AU 319 points out that while obtaining an understanding of the design of a control, including whether it has been placed in operation, an auditor may either by plan or by chance obtain some information on operating effectiveness.  For example, while making inquiries about the design of the client's budgeting system and whether it has been placed in operation, an auditor may have obtained evidence on the effectiveness of the control in preventing or detecting expense misclassifications.  Thus, its operating effectiveness has been tested.  In this manner, in essence, some **tests of controls** may have been concurrently performed with obtaining an understanding of internal control

## SUMMARY OF INTERNAL CONTROL COMPONENTS AND
## THE AUDITOR'S REQUIRED UNDERSTANDING TO PLAN THE AUDIT

|  | Summary of Components | Auditor's Required Understanding to Plan Audit |
|---|---|---|
| **Overall Internal Control for Financial Reporting** | Objective is to prepare financial statements for external purposes that are fairly presented in conformity with GAAP (or another comprehensive basis) | Obtain knowledge about design and whether controls have been placed in operation; the understanding should be adequate to allow the auditor to<br><br>(1)  Identify types of potential misstatements<br>(2)  Consider factors affecting risk of material misstatements<br>(3)  Design effective substantive tests |
| **Control Environment** | Factors<br><br>• Integrity and ethical values<br>• Commitment to competence<br>• Human resource policies and practices<br>• Assignment of authority and responsibility<br>• Management's philosophy and operating style<br>• Board of directors or audit committee participation<br>• Organizational structure | Obtain sufficient knowledge to understand management and board of directors<br><br>(1)  Attitudes<br>(2)  Awareness<br>(3)  Actions |
| **Risk Assessment** | The identification, analysis, and management of risks relevant to the preparation of financial statements following GAAP. | Obtain understanding of how management<br><br>(1)  Identifies risks<br>(2)  Estimates the significance of the risks<br>(3)  Assesses the likelihood of occurrence |
| **Control Activities** | Policies and procedures that pertain to<br><br>• Performance reviews<br>• Information processing<br>• Physical controls<br>• Segregation of duties | Obtain additional understanding as necessary to plan the audit.  Ordinarily, an understanding of control activities related to each account or to every assertion is not necessary. |
| **Information and Communication** | Methods to record, process, summarize, and report transactions, which include<br><br>• Identify and record all valid transactions<br>• Describe on a timely basis<br>• Measure the value properly<br>• Record in the proper time period<br>• Properly present and disclose<br>• Communicate responsibilities to employees | Obtain understanding of<br><br>(1)  Major transaction classes<br>(2)  How transactions are initiated<br>(3)  Available accounting records and support<br>(4)  Manner of processing of transactions<br>(5)  Financial reporting process used to prepare financial statements<br>(6)  Means the entity uses to communicate financial reporting roles and responsibilities |
| **Monitoring** | Methods to consider whether controls are operating as intended. | Obtain sufficient understanding of major types of monitoring activities |

***Documentation of understanding of internal control.*** The auditor's documentation of his/her understanding of internal control for purposes of planning the audit is influenced by the size and complexity of the entity, as well as the nature of the entity's internal control. For a small client a memorandum may be sufficient. For a larger client, flowcharts, questionnaires, and decision tables may be needed. The more complex the internal control and the more extensive the procedures performed by the auditor, the more extensive should be the documentation. The advantages and disadvantages of using questionnaires, memoranda, and/or flowchart methods are as follows:

| *Method* | *Advantages* | *Disadvantages* |
|---|---|---|
| Questionnaire | 1. Easy to complete<br>2. Comprehensive list of questions make it unlikely that important portions of internal control will be overlooked<br>3. Weaknesses become obvious (generally those questions answered with a "no") | 1. May be answered without adequate thought being given to questions<br>2. Questions may not "fit" client adequately |
| Memoranda | 1. Tailor-made for engagement<br>2. Requires a detailed analysis and thus forces auditor to understand functioning of structure | 1. May become very long and time-consuming<br>2. Weaknesses in structure not always obvious<br>3. Auditor may overlook important portions of internal control |
| Flowchart | 1. Graphic representation of structure<br>2. Usually makes it unlikely that important portions of internal control will be overlooked<br>3. Good for electronic systems<br>4. No long wording (as in case of memoranda) | 1. Preparation is time-consuming<br>2. Weaknesses in structure not always obvious (especially to inexperienced auditor) |

NOTE: *Flowcharts, including symbols, are discussed in the Auditing with Technology Module.*

In addition to questionnaires, memoranda, and flowcharts, auditors may prepare "decision tables" to document their understanding of internal control. Decision tables are graphic methods of describing the logic of decisions. Various combinations of **conditions** are matched to one of several **actions**. In an internal control setting, the various important controls are reviewed and, based on the combination of answers received, an action is taken, perhaps a decision on whether to perform tests of controls. The following extremely simplified table will provide you with the information you need for the CPA exam (note, for example, in the case of segregation of functions, a series of detailed segregation conditions—not one summary—would be used).

| *Conditions* | | *Rules* | | | | | | |
|---|---|:-:|:-:|:-:|:-:|:-:|:-:|:-:|
| | | 1 | 2 | 3 | 4 | 5 | 6 | 7 |
| (1) | Segregation of function adequate | y | y | y | y | n | n | n |
| (2) | Adequate documents | y | y | n | n | y | y | n |
| (3) | Independent checks on performance | y | n | y | n | y | n | - |

| *Actions* | | *Rules* | | | | | | |
|---|---|:-:|:-:|:-:|:-:|:-:|:-:|:-:|
| | | 1 | 2 | 3 | 4 | 5 | 6 | 7 |
| (1) | Perform all relevant tests of controls | x | | | | | | |
| (2) | Perform limited tests of controls | | x | x | | x | | |
| (3) | Perform no tests of controls | | | | x | | x | x |

Note that for decision rule 7, after the first two conditions have received "no's" it doesn't matter what the third condition is—tests of controls will not be used. Also, while a decision table is an efficient means of describing the logic of an internal control process, it does not provide an analysis of document flow as does a flowchart.

2. **Assess Control Risk.** To assess control risk is to evaluate the effectiveness of an entity's internal control in preventing and detecting material misstatements. This assessment is organized in terms of financial statement assertions (see Section A.3.a. in this module), often by transaction cycle. After

documenting an understanding of internal control, the auditor determines a **planned assessed level of control risk** for the various financial statement assertions. For controls known to be ineffective, the planned assessed level of control risk will necessarily be established at the maximum level and no tests of controls will be performed—no purpose is served by testing controls already known to be ineffective.

A decision must be made for controls that appear effective. First, an auditor may establish the planned assessed level of control risk at the maximum. No evidence on the operating effectiveness of the controls need then be gathered; that is, no tests of controls will be performed. This decision will be made when the auditor believes that performing extensive substantive tests is likely to be more cost effective than performing a combination of tests of controls and a decreased scope of substantive tests.

Alternatively, when controls appear effective, the planned assessed level of control risk may be established below the maximum level. This decision will be made when the auditor believes that a combination of tests of controls and a decreased scope of substantive tests is likely to be more cost effective than performing extensive substantive tests. Supporting such an assessment involves (1) identifying controls that are relevant to specific assertions that are likely to prevent or detect material misstatements, and (2) performing tests of controls to evaluate the effectiveness of those controls.

At this point in the audit, the auditor will have obtained the understanding of internal control necessary to plan the audit. During this process the effectiveness of some controls may have been tested (i.e., some tests of controls may have been performed). If these controls justify an **assessed level of control risk** at the planned level, no more tests of controls need be performed. Thus, there are three circumstances in which additional tests of controls **will not** be performed subsequent to obtaining an understanding to plan the audit.

(1)  Controls are believed to be ineffective, and therefore control risk is to be assessed at the maximum level
(2)  Controls are believed to be effective, but testing them is not cost efficient and therefore control risk is to be assessed at the maximum level
(3)  Controls are believed to be effective and evidence already obtained is adequate to support a planned assessed level of control risk that is below the maximum level

Yet, because in most circumstances the testing of the controls effectiveness will have been quite limited at this point, the **planned** level will often not have been met, and additional tests of controls will be required.

*NOTE:  Distinguish among* **control risk**, *the* **planned assessed level of control risk**, *and the* **assessed level of control risk**. *For any assertion, the actual effectiveness of a control at preventing or detecting misstatements, the* **control risk**, *is unknown. The auditor, based on the understanding of internal control, decides upon a* **planned assessed level of control risk** *that will allow the audit to be performed in an efficient manner. Based on the results of tests of controls, the auditor ultimately determines the* **assessed level of control risk** *that is supported by the evidence obtained. Unless tests of controls have been performed, this assessed level of control risk must be at the maximum level. Additional tests of controls will be performed if the* **assessed level of control risk** *is higher than the* **planned assessed level of control risk***.*

3.  **Perform (additional) tests of controls.** Tests of controls are used to test either the effectiveness of the design or operation of a control. Approaches include
    a.  **Inquiries** of appropriate personnel
    b.  **Inspection** of documents and reports
    c.  **Observation** of the application of controls
    d.  **Reperformance** of the control by the auditor (when evaluating operation)

To illustrate the nature of tests of controls, assume that the client has implemented the control of requiring a second person to review the quantities, prices, extensions, and footing of each sales invoice. The purpose of this control is to prevent material misstatements in the billing of customers and the recording of sales transactions. By using the first approach, inquiry, the auditor would discuss with appropriate client personnel the manner in which the control functions. Generally, because of the indirect nature of the information obtained, inquiry alone is not considered to provide credible enough evidence to support a reduced level of assessed control risk.

The remaining approaches, inspection, observation, and reperformance, may be illustrated by assuming that a sample of sixty sales invoices has been selected from throughout the year. The auditor might inspect the invoices and determine whether evidence exists that the procedures have been performed (e.g., invoices bearing initials of the individual who reviewed them). Another option is to observe applications of the procedures being applied to the invoices. Note that for controls that leave no documentary trail (e.g., segregation of functions in certain circumstances) inquiry and observation may become the only feasible approaches. Finally, the auditors may reperform the procedure by comparing quantities shown on each invoice to the quantities listed on the related shipping documents, by comparing unit prices to the client's price lists, and by verifying the extensions and footings.

*Timeliness of evidential matter.* For reasons of efficiency and practicality, auditors often perform tests of controls at a date prior to year-end. Also, pertaining to observation, note that for many situations only a limited number of observations of individuals performing controls are practical. The auditor must realize that generalizing tests of controls results beyond the periods sampled is risky. It is for this reason that auditors must consider whether additional tests should be performed over untested periods to provide assurance that controls functioned over the entire period. Relatedly, while auditors may consider evidential matter obtained from prior audits, they should obtain evidential matter in the current period to determine whether changes have occurred in internal control.

4. **Reassess control risk.** Based on the results of the tests of controls the auditor will reassess control risk related to the various assertions. As the "assessed level of control risk" **decreases**, the auditor may modify the **nature**, **timing**, and **extent** of substantive tests. The **nature** of substantive tests may be changed to a less effective test (e.g., using tests directed toward internal rather than external parties). The **timing** of tests may be changed in that a number of tests are performed at an interim date rather than at year-end. The **extent** of substantive tests may be decreased by selecting a smaller sample size. Conversely, as the assessed level of control risk increases, the auditor will require more effective tests, generally performed at year-end, using larger sample sizes. Thus, the relationship between the assessed level of control risk and detection risk is inverse. The auditor needs to document assertions in which the assessed level of control risk is at the maximum level, but not the basis for the conclusion. For those assertions where the assessed level of control risk is below the maximum, the auditor should document the basis for this conclusion that the design and operation of internal control supports that assessed level. The following table summarizes the documentation requirements both related to planning the audit and assessing control risk.

### SUMMARY OF INTERNAL CONTROL DOCUMENTATION REQUIREMENTS

|  | Assessed level of control risk | |
| --- | --- | --- |
|  | *Maximum* | *Below the maximum* |
| Document understanding of internal control obtained to plan the audit? | Yes | Yes |
| Document assessed level of control risk? | Yes | No |
| Document the basis for the control risk assessment? | No | Yes |

The entire approach for the consideration of internal control (understand, assess control risk, perform tests of controls, reassess control risk) may be illustrated through use of an example. Assume that you have been told by the controller that two secretaries are present and open all mail together each morning. These secretaries are supposed to prepare a list of all cash receipts, which is then to be forwarded to the accounts receivable clerk. The cash, according to the controller, is then given to the cashier who deposits it each day. Because you work in the area where the secretaries work, you have observed them following these procedures and conclude that the process seems to have been placed in operation. To keep the example simple, assume that based on this and other information you gathered while obtaining an understanding of internal control over receivables, controls seem strong. Assume that to this point you have performed no tests of controls. Thus, you must document your understanding of the structure and make a decision as to whether controls should be tested. Because no tests of controls have been performed, your initial assessment is that control risk is at the maximum level.

Subsequently, you decide to perform tests of controls with the objective of determining whether the structure is actually in operation and may be relied upon to limit control risk. Also, assume you have decided that, if the results of your tests of controls indicate that the controls are operating as described, one substantive test will be to confirm 30 of the firm's 250 accounts receivable to verify their existence. That is, despite strong internal control, substantive tests must generally still be performed.

However, now assume that when you performed your tests of controls by observing the opening of the mail, you discovered that the secretaries, in circumstances in which one is "busy," had decided to minimize their work by having the other individually perform the task periodically. Also, you discovered that the secretaries, when only a "limited" amount of cash is received, decided to omit the step of preparing a list of cash receipts and simply forwarded the receipts to the accounts receivable clerk who then forwarded them to the cashier who deposited them periodically.

You have discovered that the controls over cash receipts are **not** as strong as was indicated when you were gaining an understanding of internal control. In this situation, you might decide that a higher than acceptable likelihood exists that an embezzlement of cash receipts could occur; that is, control risk is high. You might then decide to increase the scope of your substantive tests; you could, for example, confirm more accounts than originally had been planned. You might also decide to expand your investigation of bad debt write-offs to determine that accounts have not been collected and subsequently have been fraudulently written off. Note that if you had originally obtained a more accurate description of the actual functioning of the internal control over cash receipts, you might have decided to omit the tests of controls and might have initially assessed control risk at the maximum level, thus resulting in complete reliance upon substantive tests.

5. **Summary.** The approach presented above may be summarized as follows:

    a. Obtain and document understanding of internal control to plan the audit

        (1) Study the control environment, risk assessment, control activities, information and communication, and monitoring

        (2) Decide whether to perform any tests of controls at this first stage

        (3) Document understanding of system—use flowcharts, memoranda, questionnaires, decision tables, etc.

    b. Assess control risk

        (1) If no tests of controls have been performed, control risk must be assessed at the maximum level

        (2) If tests of controls have been performed, a lower assessed level of control risk may be possible

        (3) Determine whether to perform additional tests of controls

    c. Perform tests of controls

        (1) Tests whether controls are operating effectively (through inquiry, inspection, observation, and reperformance)

        (2) Document results of tests by transaction type and assertion

    d. Reassess control risk

        (1) Based on results of tests of controls, assess control risk

        (2) If control risk is assessed at the maximum document that conclusion; if control risk is assessed at less than the maximum, document the basis for that conclusion

        (3) Plan substantive tests

## C. Public Company Audits of Internal Control

The Sarbanes-Oxley Act of 2002 created a requirement for an integrated audit of SEC registrants that provides assurance about the fairness of financial statements *and* about the effectiveness of internal control over financial reporting. The financial statement audit portion of the integrated audit is similar to any other financial statement audit, but its integrated nature means that auditors rely much more on internal control and less on substantive tests.

Section 404 of the Sarbanes-Oxley act of 2002 requires internal control reporting by management and the auditor.

- Section 404a: Requires management to include its assessment of internal control in the annual report filed with the SEC
- Section 404b: Requires the CPA firm to audit internal control and (1) report on management's assessment and (2) express an opinion on the effectiveness of internal control

Guidance to meet the auditor's responsibilities is provided by PCAOB Standard 2, *An Audit of Internal Control over Financial Reporting Performed in Conjunction with an Audit of Financial Statements* (Standard 2). Standard 2 emphasizes the need for an *integrated audit* that results in either separate reports or one combined report on the financial statements and the internal control over financial reporting (hereafter, internal control). The following serves both as an overall outline of Standard 2 and a summary of its most important points. In addition, this section provides an overall outline of PCAOB Standard 4, *Reporting on Whether a Previously Reported Material Weakness Continues to Exist.* Standard 4 provides guidance on this nonrequired service available for when, subsequent to a company's receipt of an adverse internal control audit report, management believes that it has eliminated the weakness and wishes to have a CPA's report so indicating.

1. **Management's responsibility.** Management is responsible for maintaining effective internal control and must prepare a report that

    a. States that it is management's responsibility to establish and maintain adequate internal control

    b. Identifies management's framework for evaluating internal control (e.g., the COSO internal control framework)

    c. Includes management's assessment of the effectiveness of the company's internal control over financial reporting as of the end of the most recent fiscal period, including a statement as to whether internal control over financial reporting is effective

    d. Includes a statement that the company's auditor has issued an attestation report on management's assessment

2. **Management's assessment.** Management's assessment process may be viewed as having the following stages:

    a. Understand the definition of internal control

    b. Establish control objectives (e.g., assure the complete recording of sales transactions) and select an internal control framework and related criteria

    c. Understand and evaluate internal control at the entity level

    d. Understand and evaluate internal control at the process and class of transactions level

    e. Evaluate overall internal control effectiveness by considering control deficiencies, significant deficiencies, and material weaknesses

    f. Correct significant deficiencies and material weaknesses, and correct other control deficiencies to the extent it is cost justified

    g. Document internal control

    h. Issue report on internal control

The auditor may provide only limited assistance to management in performing its assessment.

3. **Control Definitions.** The following definitions apply to reporting on internal control by both management and the auditor:

    a. Control deficiency—The design or operation of a control does not allow management or employees, in the normal course of performing their functions, to prevent or detect misstatements on a timely basis.

    b. Significant deficiency—A control deficiency (or a combination of control deficiencies) that adversely affects the company's ability to initiate, authorize, record, process, or report external financial data reliably in accordance with generally accepted accounting principles, such that there is more than a remote likelihood that a misstatement of the company's annual or interim financial statements that is more than inconsequential will not be prevented or detected.

    c. Material weakness—A significant deficiency (or a combination of significant deficiencies) that results in more than a remote likelihood that a material misstatement of the company's annual or interim financial statements will not be prevented or detected.

      Note that both significant deficiencies and material weaknesses involve *more than a remote likelihood.* The only difference in the definitions is the amount involved.

     • Significant deficiency—more than inconsequential misstatement

     • Material weakness—material misstatement

### SUMMARY OF DEFINITIONS

| | *Likelihood* | *Potential amount involved* |
|---|---|---|
| **Control deficiency** | Likelihood not included. Design or operation of control does not allow prevention or timely detection of misstatements. | Any misstatement (immaterial or material) |

| | *Likelihood* | *Potential amount involved* |
|---|---|---|
| **Significant deficiency** | More than remote | More than inconsequential misstatement |
| **Material weakness** | More than remote | Material misstatement |

The following exhibit illustrates that all material weaknesses are also significant deficiencies and control deficiencies, and all significant deficiencies are control deficiencies. However, all control deficiencies are not significant or material.

**Relationships among Control Deficiencies,
Significant Deficiencies and Material Weaknesses**

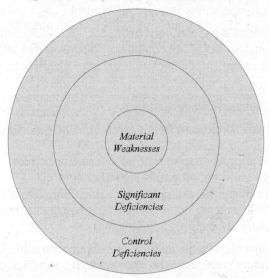

4. **Evaluating Internal Control.** In evaluating the significance of identified deficiencies, both quantitative and qualitative factors are considered. Also, the consideration of a control deficiency should include analysis of whether a compensating control exists to either prevent or detect the misstatement. If a compensating control does exist and is effective, the control deficiency is ordinarily not a significant deficiency or material weakness.

   *EXAMPLE*: *Compensating Control*

   *A reconciliation of a bank account performed by an individual otherwise independent of the cash function serves as a compensating control in that it may detect a variety of possible misstatements in both cash receipts and disbursements.*

   In evaluating internal control, it is often useful to classify major classes of transactions as being routine, nonroutine, or estimation transactions.

   a. **Routine transaction.** A transaction for a recurring financial activity recorded in the accounting records in the normal course of business, such as sales, purchases, cash receipts, cash disbursements and payroll.

   b. **Nonroutine transaction.** A transaction that occurs only periodically, such as counting and pricing inventory, calculating depreciation expense, or determining prepaid expenses.

   c. **Estimation transaction.** A transaction involving management's judgments or assumptions, such as determining the allowance for doubtful accounts, establishing warranty reserves, and assessing assets for impairment.

   Typically, nonroutine transactions and estimation transactions have more risk than do routine transactions. Accordingly, although routine transactions are carefully considered, particular emphasis is often applied to nonroutine transactions and estimation transactions. Also, when auditors use the work of others (e.g., internal auditors), it is often related to routine transactions.

5. **The Audit of Internal Control.** The auditor's responsibility for reporting on internal control may be viewed as consisting of the following six stages:

   • Plan the engagement
   • Evaluate management's assessment process
   • Obtain an understanding of internal control
   • Test and evaluate design effectiveness of internal control

- Test and evaluate operating effectiveness of internal control
- Form an opinion on the effectiveness of internal control

a. **Plan the engagement**

   (1) The auditor should recognize that the opinion on internal control is as to whether internal control is effective at a point in time—the as of date—as contrasted to a period of time (e.g., the entire year). The "as of date" is the last day of the company's fiscal period.

   (2) Similar to a typical audit of financial statements, the auditor should obtain an understanding of the company's industry, regulations affecting the company, the company's business, and recent changes in operations and internal control.

b. **Evaluate management's assessment process:** The auditor must determine whether management has tested controls over all relevant assertions related to all significant accounts and disclosures. Management's documentation must be adequate to support management's assessment.

   (1) Controls included are those related to

- Initiating, authorizing, recording, processing, and reporting significant accounts and disclosures
- Selecting and applying appropriate accounting principles
- Fraud through antifraud programs and other controls
- Various types of significant transactions, including overall company-level controls, IT general controls, and period-end financial reporting controls (e.g., consolidating adjustments, reclassifications, final adjustments)

   (2) After identifying controls, the auditor must evaluate the likelihood of their failure, the magnitude of any related misstatement, and the degree to which compensating controls achieve the same control objective

   (3) The auditor considers whether management has addressed both (a) design effectiveness and (b) operating effectiveness of controls

   (4) The auditor must examine the adequacy of management's documentation of internal control to determine that it provides reasonable support for management's assessment

   (5) The lack of effective antifraud programs is at least a significant deficiency

c. **Obtain an understanding of internal control:** The emphasis here switches from consideration of management's assessment, to the auditor's own tests.

   (1) During a CPA firm's first audit of the internal control of a client, "walk-throughs" for each major type of transition should be conducted.

- Walk-through involves literally tracing a transaction from its origination through the company's information systems until it is reflected in the financial reports
- Walk-throughs provide the auditor with evidence to

     1. Confirm the understanding of the flow of transactions and the design of controls
     2. Evaluate the effectiveness of the design of controls
     3. Confirm whether controls have been placed in operation

- While performing walk-through the auditor should ask questions such as

     1. What do you do when you find an error?
     2. What kind of errors have you found?
     3. What happened as a result of finding the errors?
     4. Have you ever been asked to override the process or controls?

- Unless significant changes have occurred in a subsequent year, the auditor may carry the documentation for walk-throughs forward each year, after updating it for changes that have occurred

   (2) The auditor must obtain an understanding of the design of controls in each component of internal control—control environment, risk assessment, control activities, information and communication, and monitoring. A "top down" approach is applied.

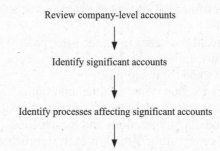

(3) Some controls (such as company-level controls) might have a pervasive effect on the achievement of many overall objectives of the control criteria. For example, information technology general controls over program development, program changes, computer operations, and access to programs and data help ensure that specific controls over the processing of transactions are operating effectively

(4) The auditors begin by considering *company-level controls,* because these controls have a pervasive impact on controls at the process, transaction, or application level. Company-level controls include

- Controls within the control environment, including tone at the top, assignment of authority and responsibility, consistent policies and procedures, and company-wide programs such as codes of conduct and fraud prevention
- Management's risk assessment process
- Centralized processing and controls
- Controls to monitor results of operations
- Controls to monitor other controls, such as internal audit, the audit committee, and self-assessment programs
- The period-end financial reporting process is always considered significant and includes: the consolidation procedures, use of spreadsheets, journal entries, significant nonroutine, nonsystematic transactions, and selection and application of accounting policies
- Drafting of the financial statements and disclosures
- Board of director approved policies that address business control and risk management

> *NOTE: Testing company-level controls alone is not sufficient for the purpose of expressing an opinion on internal control.*

The auditor uses the following process to link significant accounts to the controls that need to be tested:

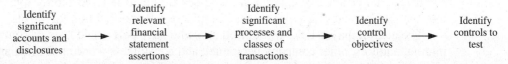

(5) Significant accounts—Accounts with a more than a remote likelihood that they could contain misstatements that individually, or when aggregated with others could have a material effect on the financial statements. Factors to consider in determining significance of accounts include

- Quantitative factors—some function of planning materiality
- Qualitative factors
- Size and composition
- Susceptibility of loss due to errors or fraud
- Volume of activity, complexity, and homogeneity of individual transactions
- Nature of the account
- Accounting and reporting complexity
- Exposure to losses
- Likelihood of significant contingent liabilities
- Existence of related-party transactions
- Changes from the prior period

(6) Identify relevant financial statement assertions as appropriate (e.g., completeness, valuation, existence, etc.)

(7) Identify significant processes (e.g., the sales process) and major classes of transactions that impact the significant accounts (e.g., the sales account may have two classes of transactions: (a) Internet sales and (b) in-store sales)

(8) Consider the transaction types: routine, nonroutine, or estimation

(9) Most processes involve tasks such as capturing input data, sorting and merging data, making calculations, updating transactions and master files, generating transactions, and summarizing and displaying or reporting data. For each significant process, the auditor should

- Understand the flow of transactions (initiation, authorization, recording, processing, reporting)
- Identify points at which a misstatement could arise
- Identify controls to address potential misstatement
- Identify controls to prevent or detect unauthorized acquisition, use, or disposition of the company's assets

(10) Considering control objectives and identifying controls to test

d. **Test and evaluate design effectiveness of internal control:** In this phase, the auditor identifies the company's control objectives for significant processes and classes of transactions. Then, s/he determines whether the related controls, if operating properly, could effectively prevent or detect material misstatements

e. **Test and evaluate operating effectiveness of internal control:** Tests of controls are performed that include a combination of inquiries of appropriate personnel, inspection of relevant documents, observation of the company's operations, and reperformance of the application of controls. These tests are performed over a period of time sufficient to determine whether, at the as of date, the controls operated effectively. The extent of procedures must be adequate to provide the auditor with a high level of assurance that the controls related to each relevant assertion are operating effectively.

It is important to note that the objective of tests of controls in an audit of internal control is to obtain evidence about the effectiveness of controls to support the auditor's opinion on whether management's assessment of the effectiveness of internal control, taken as a whole, is fairly stated as of a point in time (the "as of date"). The objective of tests of controls for a financial statement audit is to asses control risk.

Since an integrated audit requires tests of controls for all major accounts and relevant assertion, circumstances in which controls are found to be effective will ordinarily lead to a decrease in scope of substantive procedures in the audit of the financial statements. However, when significant deficiencies or material weaknesses are identified, the auditor must obtain assurance that such deficiencies have not resulted in undetected material misstatements.

The auditor may use the work of others, who have performed tests of controls, including internal auditors, other company personnel, and consultants working for management. However, in deciding what portion of the work of others may be used, the auditor should consider materiality of the accounts, the extent of the judgment required to test the control, the pervasiveness of the control, the judgment or estimation required in establishing the related account, and the potential for management override of the control. The auditor should not use the work of others to reduce tests of the control environment or to perform walk-throughs of transaction classes. In all audits the auditor must perform enough of the testing to provide the principal evidence for the audit opinion.

To rely on the work of others, the auditor should also evaluate the nature of the controls they reviewed, evaluate their competence and objectivity, and test some of the work. The auditor should perform more work directly related to high-risk areas and seek the work of others in areas of lesser risk.

f. **Form an opinion on the effectiveness of internal control:** In forming an opinion, the auditor evaluates all evidence, including (1) the adequacy of the assessment performed by management; (2) the results of the auditor's evaluation of the design; (3) the results of tests of operating effectiveness of controls; (4) misstatements discovered by substantive procedures performed during the financial statement audit; and (5) any identified control deficiencies.

- An unqualified audit opinion may be issued when no material weaknesses in internal control have been identified that exist at the as of date and when there have been no restrictions on the scope of the auditor's work
- When a deficiency has been identified, the auditor will consider whether any other controls effectively mitigate the risk of potential misstatement and create a situation in which the deficiency is not significant or, at least, does not constitute a material weakness
- In evaluating the potential amount of misstatement related to a control deficiency, the auditor considers not only misstatements identified, but the amount that could occur with more than a remote chance
- The auditor issues an adverse opinion if the client's internal control has one or more material weaknesses
- Scope limitations may result in either a qualified opinion or a disclaimer of opinion

(1) PCAOB Standard 2 states that a deficiency in any one of the following controls, would at least be a significant deficiency:

- Controls over the selection and application of accounting principles that are in conformity with generally accepted accounting principles
- Antifraud programs and controls
- Controls over nonroutine and nonsystematic transactions
- Controls over the period-end financial reporting process

The following circumstances are indicative of deficiencies that are at least significant deficiencies and provide strong indicators of the existence of a material weakness:

- Restatement of previously issued financial statements to reflect a correction
- Identification by the auditor of a material misstatement that was not initially identified by the company's internal control
- Ineffective oversight of external reporting by the audit committee
- An ineffective internal audit function
- An inadequate regulatory compliance function (in highly regulated industries)
- Significant deficiencies previously communicated that have gone uncorrected for a reasonable period of time
- An ineffective control environment

(2) A material weakness that has been remediated (eliminated) prior to year-end, and for which the auditor has evidence supporting the fact that it has been effectively remediated, will **not** result in modification of the auditor's report.

(3) The auditor's opinion has two distinct parts, which are both based on the control criteria selected by management: (1) the auditor's opinion on whether management's assessment of the effectiveness of internal control is appropriate, and (2) the auditor's opinion on whether the company maintained, in all material respect, effective internal control over financial reporting.

A scope restriction imposed by the circumstances requires the auditor to withdraw from the engagement, disclaim an opinion, or express a qualified opinion. When restrictions are imposed by management, the auditor should withdraw from the engagement or disclaim an opinion. When management's assessment is found to be inadequate, the auditor should modify the report for a scope limitation.

(4) The auditor must communicate in writing to the audit committee all significant deficiencies and material weaknesses of which the auditor becomes aware. This requirement exists even for those significant deficiencies and material weaknesses that have been corrected prior to year-end. The auditor also is required to communicate in writing to the company's management information about all control deficiencies that have not previously been communicated.

6. **Reporting on Whether a Previously Reported Material Weakness Continues to Exist.** When one or more internal control material weaknesses exist in an integrated audit, an internal control audit report with an adverse opinion is issued. After a company receives such an adverse opinion, management will ordinarily design and implement controls to remediate (eliminate) the weakness. In such a situation, the company's CPA firm may be hired to perform an engagement aimed at obtaining reason-

able assurance about whether the previously reported material weakness has been eliminated. The engagement, performed under PCAOB Standard 4, may be viewed as consisting of the following four stages:

- Plan the engagement
- Obtain an understanding of internal control
- Test and evaluate whether a material weakness continues to exist
- Form an opinion on whether a previously reported material weakness continues to exist

a.  **Plan the engagement**

    (1)  Planning considerations are similar to an audit of internal control, but are aimed at the material weakness.

    (2)  Management must

        (a)  Evaluate effectiveness of controls that address the material weakness(es)

        (b)  Present a written assertion in a report that will accompany the auditor's report that includes the following:

- IC is management's responsibility
- Identification of the control criteria that were used (e.g., COSO)
- Identification of the material weakness
- Identification of control objectives addressed
- A statement that material weakness no longer exists

        (c)  Support its assertion with sufficient evidence, including documentation

        (d)  Provide the auditor with written representations, including

- IC is management's responsibility
- Management has evaluated IC effectiveness
- Management's assertion that controls are effective in achieving the stated control objective(s) as of a specified date
- Management's assertion that the identified material weakness no longer exists
- Management believes that its assertions are supported by sufficient evidence
- Description of any material fraud and any other fraud, although not material that involves senior management or other employees with a significant IC role
- Whether subsequent to the date being reported on any identified controls were not operating effectively

    (3)  Relevant financial statement assertions, control criteria, and control objectives

        (a)  *Relevant financial statement assertions* are those that have a meaningful bearing on whether an account is properly stated (e.g., completeness, existence, or occurrence)

        (b)  *Control criteria* are those used for the annual assessment of IC (e.g., COSO)

        (c)  *Control objectives* provide a target against which to evaluate the effectiveness of controls (e.g., recorded sales of product X are real)

- A *stated control objective* is the control objective identified by management that, if achieved, would result in the material weakness no longer existing.

        (d)  Relationships

- *Control objectives* relate to *relevant financial statement assertions* and state a criterion for evaluating whether the company's control procedures provide reasonable assurance that a misstatement is prevented or detected on a timely basis; example of a control objective and a relevant financial statement assertion

|   *Control Objective*   |   | *Assertion* |
|-------------------------|---|-------------|
| Recorded sales are real | ⟶ | Existence or occurrence |

- The process of tailoring *control objectives* to the individual company allows the *control criteria* to be applied to the facts and circumstances in a reasonable and appropriate manner
- If a material weakness was reported, a necessary *control objective* (or objectives) was not achieved

b. **Obtain an understanding of internal control**

(1) A continuing auditor ordinarily has obtained this understanding through having previously performed the audit of internal control; this understanding must be updated

(2) A successor auditor (in an auditor change situation) may perform this type of engagement, but must obtain sufficient knowledge to conclude on the material weakness and must

   (a) Obtain understanding sufficient to report on the material weakness

   (b) Perform a walk-through for all major classes of transactions involved with the material weakness

   (c) Make inquiries of the predecessor auditor related to the material weakness

c. **Test and evaluate whether a material weakness continues to exist**

(1) The procedures are similar to those of an internal control audit, but are aimed at the material weakness being reported upon

(2) If management has not supported its assertion with sufficient evidence, the auditor cannot complete the engagement

(3) Procedures similar to those required under Standard 2 are performed to determine whether the material weakness has been eliminated

(4) The auditor may

   (a) Use the work of others (e.g., internal auditors)

   • But the auditor must obtain the *principal evidence* that the control objectives are achieved

   • As the importance of the control and the risk of the account increase, use of the work of others should decrease

   (b) Base the opinion in part on the work of another auditor

d. **Form an opinion on whether a previously reported material weakness continues to exist**

(1) The auditors' report concludes on whether the material weakness exists as of the date of management's assertions

   (a) The opinion is on whether a material weakness continues to exist—"In our opinion, the material weakness described above exists (or, no longer exists) as of the *date of management's assertion*"

   (b) Since a statement is made on existence or nonexistence of the material weakness, the standard does not distinguish between an unqualified opinion and an adverse opinion

   (c) Unlike an internal control audit report from Standard 2, the Standard 4 opinion is only upon existence of the material weakness, not also on management's assertion.

(2) Audit report modifications

   (a) Restrictions on the scope of the auditor's work, including failure to obtain written representations from management, result in a disclaimer or the auditor's withdrawal from the engagement

   (b) If other material weaknesses were included *in the internal control audit report*, this report should make clear that those weaknesses are not considered in this engagement

   (c) If important subsequent events indicate that the material weakness continues to exist, the auditor's opinion should so state

   (d) If management's report includes information in addition to that required, the auditor should disclaim an opinion on the additional information

   (e) The auditor is not required to issue a report as a result of the engagement—this particularly is the case if he or she concludes that the material weakness continues to exist

   • If this is the conclusion, and no report is being issued, the auditor should communicate in writing his/her conclusion that the material weakness still exists

   (f) The situation in which management believes that the previously reported material weakness has been reduced to what is only a significant deficiency is difficult

- Since only material weaknesses result in modification of the audit report, at one level it would seem that the auditor is able to issue a report indicating that the material weakness no longer exists
- However, Standard 2 sates that a significant deficiency that is not corrected after a reasonable period of time is a strong indicator of a material weakness
- The auditor must use judgment as to the proper course of action. Related, Standard 4 indicates that the auditor could reasonably decline to provide an opinion under such circumstances

   (g) If an auditor identifies a material weakness not previously identified, the audit committee must be informed in writing, but the audit report is not modified

- If the material weakness existed at the date of the original audit report on internal control the auditor must consider AU 561 on subsequent discovery of events existing at the date of the report to determine whether there is a disclosure responsibility arising from the original internal control audit engagement

## D.  Accounting Cycles

We now consider CPA exam questions that require an understanding of a transaction cycle. These questions may, for example, require a candidate to perform one or more of the following:

- Identify an audit test that will meet some specified objective (or financial statement assertion).
- Identify internal control strengths/weaknesses.
- Complete a flowchart which includes a number of symbols without descriptors.
- Evaluate an internal control questionnaire.

These questions may be difficult because a candidate (1) may not have an understanding of the various source documents and accounting records and how they relate to one another in an accounting system, and (2) does not know what types of detailed controls should exist. To help you prepare for these questions we are presenting information on both directional testing (which is also helpful for evidence questions) and a summary of transaction cycles.

***Directional Testing.*** As a starting point, you should understand the notion of **directional testing**. Directional testing has a **from** and **to**. The basic idea is that testing **from** source documents forward **to** recorded entries accomplishes a different objective than testing **from** recorded entries back **to** source documents.

Diagrammatically, directions testing suggests

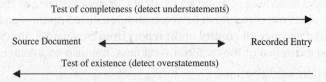

In sentence form, the rules are

1.  Tracing forward (source document to recorded entry) primarily tests completeness of recording, and has a primary objective of detecting understatements.
2.  Vouching (tracing backwards—recorded entry to source document) primarily tests existence and has a primary objective of detecting overstatements.

To understand the basic concept here, think about sales invoices (a source document) and the sales journal (the recorded entry).

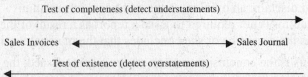

An auditor may select a group of sales invoices and compare them to the sales journal. On the other hand, the auditor may also vouch sales journal entries back to the sales invoices (and other support such as shipping documents, customer purchase orders). If an auditor is testing for **understated** sales, it would be best to start with possible sales, not those that were already recorded in the sales journal. Thus, for finding understatements of sales, a CPA would sample from the sales invoices (which are prepared when a sale occurs) in an effort to determine whether individual sales are being recorded. On the other hand, when testing for overstated sales, the CPA would test from the sales recorded in the sales journal back to sales invoices (as well as other source documents such as shipping documents, customer purchase orders). This is because for each recorded sale there should be support. We will apply the concept of directional testing in our discussion of the detailed transaction cycles.

*Financial Accounting Reporting Cycle.* In the overview section we suggested that an accounting system may be viewed as follows:

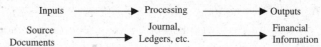

At this point review "The Financial Reporting Cycle" on the following page and simply look it over and note the various **source documents** (inputs), and **accounting records** such as journals and ledgers which are used to process the inputs (processing), and financial statements (outputs). Recall that our objectives are to (1) learn an approach for addressing questions pertaining to internal control weaknesses and for preparing internal control questionnaires, and (2) learn how to answer other questions pertaining to the effectiveness of audit tests.

When you consider a simulation question pertaining to internal control weaknesses an organized approach is to

(1) Read the problem to identify the type of transaction cycle
(2) Obtain an understanding of how the accounting system works by carefully reading the problem in detail (and possibly informally flowcharting it if the description is very detailed)
(3) Consider the control activities (PIPS—**P**erformance reviews, **I**nformation processing, **P**hysical controls, and **S**egregation of duties), but particularly segregation of duties
(4) Recall typical weaknesses (presented subsequently) for the transaction cycle involved to find additional internal control weaknesses

Steps 1 and 2 are clearly necessary since you need to understand the problem and its requirements. When performing the second step, realize that on an overall basis, controls are aimed at safeguarding both assets and financial records. Also, be aware of each department's operational objective (e.g., the shipping department ships goods). Also, know that one way to consider controls is to classify them by function.

*Functions of controls.* Although the word "controls" has different meanings in different contexts, from an internal control perspective controls within a business organization serve to ensure that information is processed correctly. Controls can in general be viewed as having a function of either (1) **preventing** misstatements, (2) **detecting and correcting** misstatements that have occurred, although a particular control may have elements of each. **Preventive** controls are typically most effective since they are designed to prevent a misstatement from occurring (e.g., two persons opening the mail which includes cash receipts may prevent embezzlement). **Detective** and **corrective** controls most frequently occur together. They detect and correct a misstatement that has already occurred (e.g., bank account reconciliation by an individual not otherwise involved with cash receipts or cash disbursements). While these controls are typically less expensive to implement than preventive controls, they may detect misstatements too late. They may detect that an employee embezzled $1,000,000, but may only be corrective in the sense that an embezzlement loss journal entry is made in cases where the employee has disappeared. For purposes of the CPA exam, ask yourself how effective each of the detective and corrective controls is—their effectiveness depends on the details of the system being examined.

*Segregation of duties.* When using the control activities to find internal control weaknesses (step 3), segregation of duties is especially important since many of the weaknesses relate to inadequate segregation. Recall that inadequate segregation exists whenever one individual is performing two or more of the following:

• Authorization,
• Recordkeeping, and
• Custodianship.

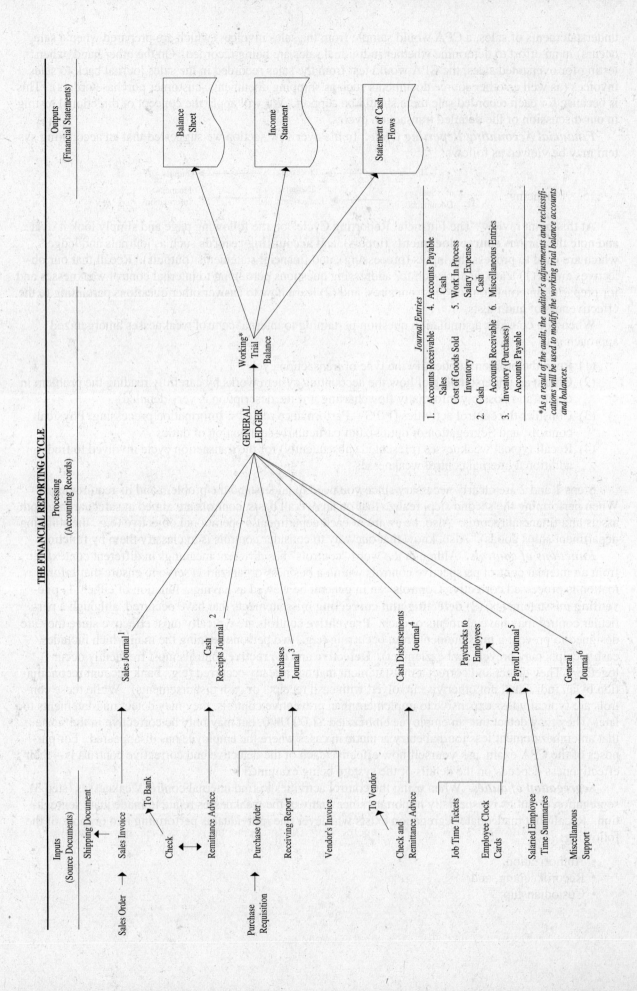

THE FINANCIAL REPORTING CYCLE

Inputs
(Source Documents)

Processing
(Accounting Records)

Outputs
(Financial Statements)

GENERAL
LEDGER

Working*
Trial
Balance

Balance
Sheet

Income
Statement

Statement of Cash
Flows

Shipping Document

Sales Invoice

Sales Order

Check

To Bank

Remittance Advice

Purchase Order

Purchase
Requisition

Receiving Report

Vendor's Invoice

Check and
Remittance Advice

To Vendor

Job Time Tickets

Employee Clock
Cards

Salaried Employee
Time Summaries

Miscellaneous
Support

Sales Journal[1]

Cash
Receipts Journal[2]

Purchases
Journal[3]

Cash Disbursements
Journal[4]

Paychecks to
Employees

Payroll Journal[5]

General
Journal[6]

Journal Entries

1. Accounts Receivable    4. Accounts Payable
   Sales                     Cash
   Cost of Goods Sold     5. Work In Process
   Inventory                 Salary Expense
2. Cash                      Cash
   Accounts Receivable    6. Miscellaneous Entries
3. Inventory (Purchases)
   Accounts Payable

*As a result of the audit, the auditor's adjustments and reclassifications will be used to modify the working trial balance accounts and balances.

For example, when a cashier (custodian) authorizes the write-off of bad debts (authorization), a weakness exists. Also, know that for good internal control reconciliation of an account with some other information should be performed by an individual otherwise independent of the function. To illustrate, the individual preparing checks should not perform the reconciliation of the bank account.

We now analyze in detail each of the following accounting cycles:

1. Sales, Receivables, and Cash Receipts
2. Purchases, Payables, and Cash Disbursements
3. Inventories and Production
4. Personnel and Payroll
5. Financing
6. Investing

1. **Sales, Receivables, and Cash Receipts.** The following is a possible flow of documents:

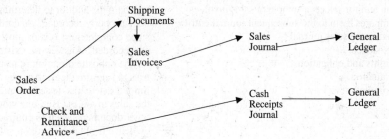

\* *Checks are sent to banks and remittance advices (or a list of remittance advices) are used to prepare journal entries.*

Assume that the firm's sales personnel prepare sales orders for potential sales (many other possibilities, such as the customer filling out the sales order, are found in practice). The sale is approved by the credit department, the goods are shipped, and the billing department (a part of accounting) prepares a sales invoice (a copy of which becomes the customer's "bill"). After the sales invoice is prepared, the sales journal, the general ledger, and the accounts receivable subsidiary ledger are posted. The customer pays the account with a check, and a remittance advice is enclosed to describe which invoice the check is paying. As a preventive control, two individuals open the mail that includes these customer remittances. The checks are listed and sent to the cashier who daily deposits them in the bank (recall that the checks should not go to the accounting department, as that would give the accounting department custody of assets [checks in this case] as well as recordkeeping responsibility). Another copy of the list of checks and the remittance advices is sent to accounting to be used to post the cash receipts journal, which is subsequently posted to the general and accounts receivable subsidiary ledgers.

### *Major Controls Frequently Missing in CPA Exam Questions*
Sales

    (1) Credit granted by a credit department
    (2) Sales orders and invoices prenumbered and controlled
    (3) Sales returns are presented to receiving clerk who prepares a receiving report which supports prenumbered sales return credit memoranda

Accounts Receivable

    (1) Subsidiary ledger reconciled to control ledger regularly
    (2) Individual independent of receivable posting reviews statements before sending to customers
    (3) Monthly statements sent to all customers
    (4) Write-offs approved by management official independent of recordkeeping responsibility (e.g., the treasurer is appropriate)

Cash Receipts

    (1) Cash receipts received in mail listed by individuals with no recordkeeping responsibility

        (a) Cash goes to cashier
        (b) Remittance advices go to accounting

(2)  Over-the-counter cash receipts controlled (cash register tapes)
(3)  Cash deposited daily
(4)  Employees handling cash are bonded
(5)  **Lockbox**, a post office box controlled by the company's bank at which cash remittances from customers are received.  The bank collects customer remittances, immediately credits the cash to the company's bank account, and forwards the remittance advices to the company.  A lockbox system is considered an extremely effective control because company employees have no access to cash and bank employees have no access to the company's accounting records.
(6)  Bank reconciliation prepared by individuals independent of cash receipts recordkeeping

### Sales, Receivables, and Cash Receipts CPA Exam Questions

*Question*

1.  Which assertion is being most directly addressed when an auditor selects a sample of sales invoices and compares them to the subsequent journal entries recorded in the sales journal?
    a.  Existence.
    b.  Rights and obligations.
    c.  Valuation.
    d.  Completeness.

*Answer*

(d)  This question is about directional testing.  The step will help the auditor to determine that **all** sales invoices have been properly recorded.  Accordingly answer (d) is correct since completeness relates most directly to whether **all** items are recorded.  Answer (a), existence, would be a good reply for the opposite direction of testing—from sales journal entries to sales invoices.  Answer (b), rights, would be to a limited extent also tested by tracing from the sales journal to the sales invoices.  But, one would also wish to examine other documents such as contracts relating to rights.  Little evidence is obtained here on valuation, answer (c), in that we have no evidence as to whether the account will be collected.

2.  When a client's physical count of inventories is lower than the inventory quantities shown on its perpetual records, the situation would most likely be caused by unrecorded
    a.  Sales.
    b.  Sales returns.
    c.  Purchases.
    d.  Purchase discounts.

(a)  The question is asking what situation could cause the actual inventory to be lower than the amount recorded in the perpetual records.  If sales had not been recorded, the perpetual records would not reflect the shipment of inventory; this would result in an overstatement of inventory in the accounting records.  Answers (b) and (c) would address cases for which the physical count is higher than the perpetual records since physical goods would be in inventory with no recordkeeping having been performed.  Purchase discounts, answer (d), relates to the cost of items as contrasted to the quantity.

3.  How would you test credit sales for understatement?

    ANSWER:  Compare a sample of approved sales orders to the subsequent posting in the sales journal (and through to the general ledger).  You are interested in finding out whether the approved sales order made it all the way to the general ledger.  Note that you may find overstatements by this audit procedure (e.g., a $10 sale recorded for a higher amount) but that the primary emphasis is in finding understatements.

4.  How would you test credit sales for overstatements?

    ANSWER:  Opposite of 3. above.

5.  Are you mainly testing for over or understatements of cash when you agree remittance advices to the cash receipts journal?

    ANSWER:  Understatements.  That is, did the cash that the firm received get recorded?

6.  What could cause a remittance advice with no subsequent cash receipt entry?

    ANSWER:  An embezzlement.

7.  Should there be a sales invoice for each sales order?

    ANSWER:  No.  Sales in process and sales not approved will not be invoiced.

### *Illustrative Simulation Problem*

Illustrative Simulation Problem A, which follows, involves internal control strengths and deficiencies over the revenue cycle.  Consider the following:

## Illustrative Simulation Problem A

**Items 1 through 11** present various internal control strengths or internal control deficiencies. For each item, select from the list below the appropriate response.

- A. Internal control strength for the revenue cycle (including cash receipts).
- B. Internal control deficiency for the revenue cycle (including cash receipts).
- C. Internal control strength unrelated to the revenue cycle.

### *Items to be answered*

1. Credit is granted by a credit department.

2. Sales returns are presented to a sales department clerk who prepares a written, prenumbered shipping report.

3. Statements sent monthly to customers.

4. Write-offs of accounts receivable are approved by the controller.

5. Cash disbursements over $10,000 require two signatures on the check.

6. Cash receipts received in the mail are received by a secretary with no recordkeeping responsibility.

7. Cash receipts received in the mail are forwarded unopened with remittance advices to accounting.

8. The cash receipts journal is prepared by the treasurer's department.

9. Cash is deposited weekly.

10. Support for disbursement checks is canceled after payment by the treasurer.

11. Bank reconciliation is prepared by individuals independent of cash receipts recordkeeping.

## Solution to Illustrative Simulation Problem A

1.  **(A)** The function of a credit department is to follow the company's credit policies to make decisions on the granting of credit.

2.  **(B)** Sales returns should be presented to the receiving clerk (not a sales department clerk) who should prepare a receiving report (not a shipping report).

3.  **(A)** Sending monthly statements to customers represents a control strength as errors and fraud may be discovered.

4.  **(B)** Write-offs of accounts receivable should be approved by a management official independent of recordkeeping responsibility, not by the controller who is responsible for recordkeeping. Frequently, the treasurer approves write-offs.

5.  **(C)** While requiring two signatures on large checks is a good control over expenditures, it relates much more directly to the purchases/disbursements cycle than to the revenue cycle.

6.  **(A)** Mailed cash receipts should be received by an individual with no recordkeeping responsibility—a secretary with no recordkeeping responsibility is appropriate. That individual should open the mail and prepare a list of the receipts. The cash should be forwarded with a copy of the listed receipts to a cashier (or the individual who makes deposits) and the remittance advices should be forwarded with another copy of the listed receipts to accounting.

7.  **(B)** As indicated in the answer explanation to item 6, the cash receipts should be opened by an individual with no recordkeeping responsibility. The cash should be forwarded with a copy of the listed receipts to a cashier (or the individual who makes deposits) and the remittance advices should be forwarded with another copy of the listed receipts to accounting.

8.  **(B)** The cash receipts journal should be prepared by the department responsible for recordkeeping—accounting—under the leadership of the controller.

9.  **(B)** Cash should ordinarily be deposited **daily**.

10.  **(C)** This control relates to the purchases/disbursements cycle.

11.  **(A)** Bank reconciliations should be prepared by individuals independent of cash receipts (and cash disbursements) recordkeeping.

2. **Purchases, Payables, and Cash Disbursements.** The following is a possible flow of documents:

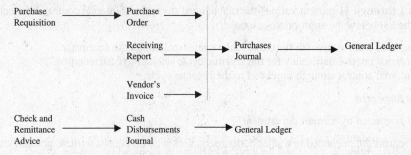

Assume that the purchase requisition is an internal document sent by the department in need of the supplies to the purchasing department. The purchasing department determines the proper quantity and vendor for the purchase and prepares a purchase order. One copy of the purchase order is sent to the vendor. Another copy is sent to the receiving department to allow receiving personnel to know that items received have been ordered; however, the copy of the purchase order sent to receiving will not have a quantity of items on it so as to encourage personnel to count the goods when they are received. When the goods are received, a receiving report is prepared by the receiving department and forwarded to the accounting department. A vendor's invoice or "bill" is received by the accounting department from the vendor. When the accounting department has the purchase order, receiving report, and vendor's invoice, the payment is approved and then recorded in the purchases journal since evidence exists that the item was ordered, received, and billed. A check and remittance advice is subsequently sent to the vendor in accordance with the terms of the sale. The purchase order, receiving report, and vendor's invoice are stamped paid to prevent duplicate payments.

### Major Controls Frequently Missing in CPA Exam Questions

Purchases

    (1)   Prenumbered purchase orders used
    (2)   Separate purchasing department makes purchases
    (3)   Purchasing personnel independent of receiving and recordkeeping
    (4)   Suppliers' monthly statements compared with recorded payables

Accounts Payable

    (1)   Accounts payable personnel independent of purchasing, receiving, and disbursements
    (2)   Clerical accuracy of vendors' invoices tested
    (3)   Purchase order, receiving report, and vendor's invoice matched

Cash Disbursements

    (1)   Prenumbered checks with a mechanical check protector used
    (2)   Two signatures on large check amounts
    (3)   Checks signed only with appropriate support (purchase order, receiving report, vendor's invoice). Treasurer signs checks and mails them
    (4)   Support for checks canceled after payment
    (5)   Voided checks mutilated, retained, and accounted for
    (6)   Bank reconciliations prepared by individual independent of cash disbursements recordkeeping
    (7)   Physical control of unused checks

### Purchases, Payables, and Cash Disbursement Short Answer Questions

    1.   Which documents need to be present before payment is approved?

        ANSWER:   Purchase order, receiving report, vendor's invoice. (This shows that the firm ordered the goods, received the goods, and has been billed for the goods.)

    2.   How can a firm control disbursements so that if a duplicate invoice is sent by the supplier the payment will not be made a second time?

        ANSWER:   Cancel the required supporting documents in 1. after the invoice is paid the first time.

    3.   What audit test could be used to determine whether recorded purchases represent valid business expenses?

ANSWER:   Compare a sample of recorded disbursements with properly approved purchase orders, purchase requisitions, vendor's invoices, and receiving reports.

4.   What audit procedure would test whether actual purchases are recorded?

ANSWER:   Select a sample of purchase requisitions and agree them to the purchase orders and to the purchases journal (as well as to subsequent general ledger posting).

5.   Should there be a purchase order for each purchase requisition?

ANSWER:   No.  Several requisitions may be summarized on one purchase order and some requisitions may not be approved.

The above are meant to assist you in obtaining an overall understanding of auditing procedures and internal control.  Note that entire courses (and majors) in systems analysis address these issues.  The purpose of the above is to give the individual who has a very limited systems background a starting point for analysis.

## *Problem*

Illustrative Simulation Problem B, a purchase/disbursements problem, is typical of a number of questions which have presented a flowchart with certain information on operations omitted—the candidate is to determine what description belongs in the blocks, circles, etc. which simply contain a number or letter.  This type of question does **not** require a knowledge of internal control weaknesses.  What is necessary is an understanding of how accounting systems generally work.

First, you must know the common flowchart symbols (presented in the Auditing with Technology Module under "Flowcharting").  This information will be helpful to you because when you see, for example, a trapezoid, you will know that a manual operation has been performed.  Additionally, for such problems, you should consider the department the missing information is in and that department's purpose (e.g., the purchasing department purchases appropriate goods from vendors at acceptable prices).  Finally, consider both the step preceding and succeeding the missing information to provide you with a clue as to what is being represented.

Starting with A in the purchasing department, we note that an approved requisition has been received from stores.  Step A represents some form of manual operation (due to the existence of a trapezoid) out of which a 5-copied purchase order as well as the requisition come.  The only possible manual operation here is the preparation of a 5-part purchase order.  At this point, the various copies are either filed or sent elsewhere (the circles represent connectors to other portions of the flowchart or possibly represent a document leaving the system).  In this case, we see the various copies being filed and sent to receiving and vouchers payable.  Step B represents a copy being sent elsewhere.  When we consider the fact that the purpose of the purchasing department is to purchase the items, it becomes obvious that this copy must be sent to the vendor—otherwise no order would occur.

Because a receiving report appears for the first time under step C, it obviously represents the preparation of a receiving report.  Next are connectors D and E.  We know that the use of the circle indicates that something—probably a document or form of some sort—has been received.  For D, a clue is given in that requisition 1 has also been received.  We know that this is from purchasing by recalling that requisition 1 and purchase order 5 were sent to vouchers payable—this is shown on the flowchart under purchasing.  Similarly, we know that receiving sent a copy of the receiving report to vouchers payable and that E and G relate to it.  Thus, through understanding the nature of the various symbols and by considering preceding and succeeding information, we are able to determine the nature of the omitted information.  The following is the complete solution to this problem:

*Purchases and Disbursements Flowchart*

| | | | |
|---|---|---|---|
| A. | Prepare purchase order | G. | Receiving report No. 1 |
| B. | To vendor | H. | Prepare and approve voucher |
| C. | Prepare receiving report | I. | Unpaid voucher file, filed by due date |
| D. | From purchasing | J. | Treasurer |
| E. | From receiving | K. | Sign checks and cancel voucher package documents |
| F. | Purchase order No. 5 | L. | Canceled voucher package |

Illustrative Simulation Problem C asks candidates to identify internal control strengths, not weaknesses.  Instead of solving that question prior to studying the solution, compare the points in the solution below with the flowchart.  While the strengths in the flowchart seem obvious, you may wish to spend some time reviewing them, especially if you have limited "real world" experience.  You also might wish to visualize a flowchart that omitted the strengths.  Make certain that you could identify the resulting weaknesses.

## Illustrative Simulation Problem B  (15 to 25 minutes)

The following illustrates a manual system for executing purchases and cash disbursements transactions.

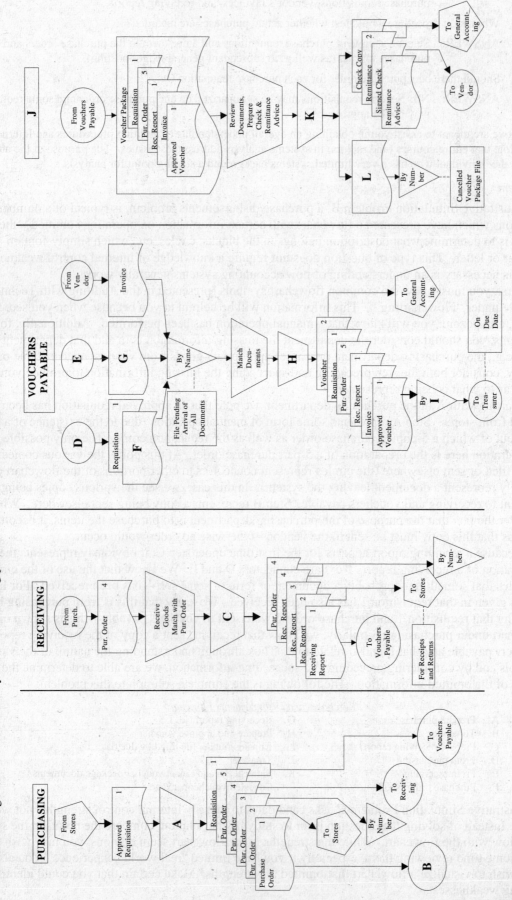

**Required:** Indicate what each of the letters (A) through (L) represent. Do not discuss adequacies or inadequacies in the system of internal control.

# Illustrative Simulation Problem C

This flowchart depicts the activities relating to the purchasing, receiving, and accounts payable departments of Model Company, Inc.

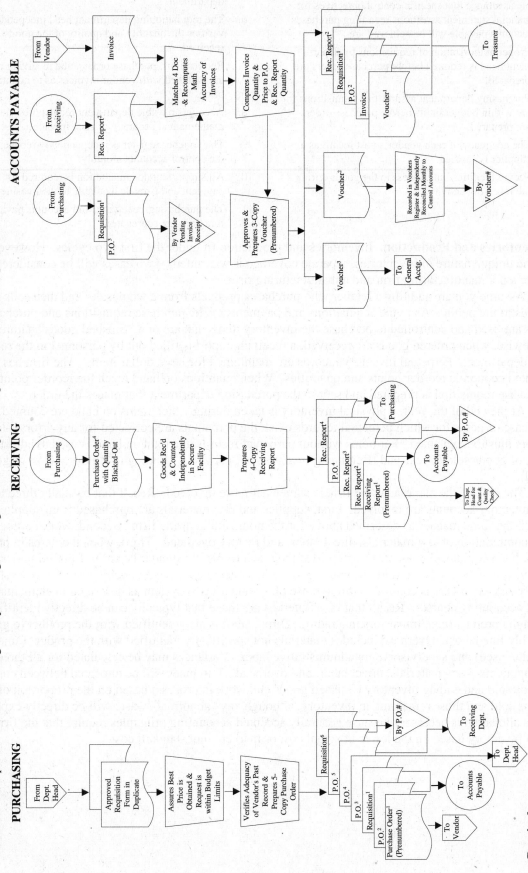

**Required:**

Based only on the flowchart, describe the internal control procedures (strengths) that most likely would provide reasonable assurance that specific internal control objectives for the financial statement assertions regarding purchases and accounts payable will be achieved. Do not describe weaknesses in internal control.

**Solution to Illustrative Simulation Problem C**

The controls that most likely would provide reasonable assurance that specific control objectives for the financial statement assertions regarding purchases and accounts payable will be achieved are

1. Proper authorization of requisitions by department head is required before purchase orders are prepared.

2. Purchasing department assures that requisitions are within budget limits before purchase orders are prepared.

3. The adequacy of each vendor's past record as a supplier is verified.

4. Secure facilities limit access to the goods during the receiving activity.

5. Receiving department makes a blind count of the goods received, independently of any other department.

6. The requisitioning department head independently verifies the quantity and quality of the goods received.

7. Requisitions, purchase orders, and receiving reports are matched with vendor invoices as to quantity and price.

8. Accounts payable department recomputes the mathematical accuracy of each invoice.

9. The voucher register is independently reconciled to the control accounts monthly.

10. All supporting documentation is required for payment and is made available to the treasurer.

11. The purchasing, receiving, and accounts payable functions are segregated.

3. **Inventories and Production.** Inventories and production fit under the first two cycles. However, due to the unique nature of inventories, separate coverage is warranted. Two cases will be considered here: a nonmanufacturing firm and a manufacturing firm.

Assume you are auditing a retailer who purchases products from a wholesaler and then sells the goods to the public. As in the acquisitions and payments cycle, purchase requisitions and purchase orders are used and controlled to purchase the inventory items that are of a "finished goods" nature. Likewise, when ordered goods are received, a receiving report is filled out by personnel in the receiving department. Perpetual inventory records are maintained for large dollar items. The firm has calculated economic reorder points and quantities. When quantities on hand reach the reorder point, a purchase requisition is prepared and sent to the purchasing department that places the order.

At the end of the year, a physical inventory is taken during which items on hand are counted. In the case of items for which perpetual records exist, the perpetuals are corrected for any errors—large errors must be explained. For items without perpetual records, the total on hand is used to adjust the cost of goods sold at year-end (Beginning inventory + Purchases – Ending inventory = Cost of goods sold).

The case of the manufacturing firm is somewhat more involved. Recall that basically three types of inventory accounts are involved. First, supplies and raw materials are purchased from suppliers in much the same manner as described above for the nonmanufacturing firm. Second, work in process is the combination of raw materials, direct labor, and factory overhead. Third, when the items in process have been completed, they are transferred at their cost (typically standard cost) to finished goods. Finally, when the goods are sold, the entry is to credit finished goods and to debit cost of goods sold.

Work in process is controlled through use of a standard cost system as described in elementary cost accounting courses. Recall that raw materials are those that typically can be directly identified with the product (e.g., transistors in a radio). Direct labor is also identified with the product (e.g., assembly line labor). Overhead includes materials not specifically identified with the product (amount of glue used) and supervisory, nonadministrative labor. Variances may be calculated for all three components—raw materials, direct labor, and overhead. Variances will be allocated between cost of goods sold and ending inventory (finished goods and work in process) based on the proportion of items sold and those remaining in inventory, although any "abnormal" waste will be directly expensed. This allocation is necessary because generally accepted accounting principles require that the firm report inventory based on the lower of actual cost or market—not standard cost.

### Major Inventory and Production Controls Frequently Missing in CPA Exam Questions

(1) Perpetual inventory records for large dollar items
(2) Prenumbered receiving reports prepared when inventory received; receiving reports accounted for
(3) Adequate standard cost system to cost inventory items
(4) Physical controls against theft
(5) Written inventory requisitions used
(6) Proper authorization of purchases and use of prenumbered purchase orders

### Inventories and Production CPA Exam Multiple-Choice Questions

**1.** To verify debits to the perpetual inventory records an auditor would sample from the recorded debits to a sample of
    a.  Purchase approvals.
    b.  Purchase requisitions.
    c.  Purchase invoices.
    d.  Purchase orders.

**1.** **(c)** The question is asking what an auditor would sample **to** when testing debits in the perpetual inventory records. The invoice from the vendor (purchase invoice) will include both the quantity and cost of items sent to the client company. Note that none of the other replies will include the quantities actually shipped. Answer (a) would address a question relating to internal control over purchases. Answer (b) would address: "When verifying that recorded purchases of inventory were requisitioned by stores, an auditor would be most interested in examining a sample of. . .?" Answer (d) would address: "When verifying that recorded purchases of inventory have been properly ordered, an auditor would be most interest in examining a sample of. . .?"

**2.** The best procedure to allow an auditor to determine that a client has completely included merchandise it owns in its ending inventory is to review and test the
    a.  Terms of the open purchase orders.
    b.  Purchase cutoff.
    c.  Commitments.
    d.  Purchase invoices received around year-end.

**2.** **(b)** The question is asking how best to address the completeness of inventory. Purchase cutoff procedures include the other choices and are thus more complete. Answers (a) and (c) would be good answers for a question such as "To determine the amount of future purchase commitments a client has, an auditor should test the. . .?" Answer (d) would address: "An effective procedure for determining that a proper year-end cutoff of purchases has occurred is to test the. . .?"

4. **Personnel and Payroll.** The following is a possible flow of documents:

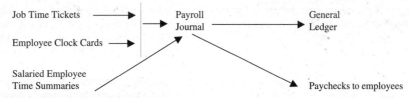

Assume that a separate personnel department maintains complete, up-to-date records for each employee. Included in such records is information on level of education, basic payroll information, experience, and authorization for any changes in pay rates. Assume that the firm's factory direct labor personnel use a time clock to punch in each morning and out each evening. Their employee clock card thus shows the total hours worked each day. These direct labor personnel also fill out job time tickets for each job they work on each day. At the end of each week their supervisor compares job time tickets with employee clock cards that have already been signed by the employees. Assume also that salaried and other employees fill out weekly time summaries indicating hours worked. All of the above information is sent to the payroll accounting department whose responsibility is to prepare the payroll journal and to prepare the unsigned payroll checks. The checks are then signed by the treasurer and distributed by an independent paymaster who has no other payroll functions. The summary payroll entry is then posted to the general ledger in the accounting department.

The internal auditing department periodically compares the payroll department's file on each employee with that in the personnel department's file to determine that no unauthorized changes in payroll records have been made. Employees with cash handling and recordkeeping responsibilities should be covered by fidelity bonds, a form of insurance which protects an employer against losses caused by dishonest employees (fidelity bonds also serve as a control when new employees are hired since the insurer will typically perform a background check on prospective employees).

## *Major Personnel and Payroll Controls Frequently Missing in CPA Exam Questions*

(1)   Segregate:   Timekeeping
                         Payroll Preparation
                         Personnel
                         Paycheck Distribution

(2)   Time clocks used where possible

(3)   Job time tickets reconciled to time clock cards

(4)   Time clock cards approved by supervisors (overtime and regular hours)

(5)   Treasurer signs paychecks

(6)   Unclaimed paychecks controlled by someone otherwise independent of the payroll function (locked up and eventually destroyed if not claimed).  In cases in which employees are paid cash (as opposed to checks) unclaimed pay should be deposited into a special bank account.

(7)   Personnel department promptly sends termination notices to the payroll department.

## *Personnel and Payroll CPA Exam Multiple-Choice Questions*

**1.**   From the perspective of good internal control, which of the following is the most appropriate individual to distribute payroll checks?

    a.   The payroll clerk.
    b.   A personnel employee.
    c.   Accounts receivable clerk.
    d.   Employee supervisors.

**1.**   **(c)**   When considering internal control, a person not otherwise involved in personnel or payroll procedures, an "independent paymaster," should distribute paychecks. Of the choices provided, the accounts receivable clerk [answer (c)] is best.  Answers (a) and (b) are improper because the payroll clerk prepares the payroll and the personnel department is involved in hiring and terminating employees.  Employee supervisors are inappropriate due to the potential problem of employees who have quit, but for which paychecks are still, improperly, being prepared.  Note that the key for this question is **not** that the accounts receivable clerk should distribute checks, but that an individual otherwise independent of the process should perform the function.  Previous CPA questions, for example, have included the receptionist as an appropriate individual to distribute checks.

**2.**   If an auditor is concerned about whether all individuals being paid are bona fide employees, would s/he sample from source documents to the payroll journal, or from the payroll journal to source documents?

**2.**   The direction of testing will be **from** the payroll journal that represents the population of employees who are being paid **to** support.  This support will include personnel records, employees' Form W-4, and clock cards or time tickets.  In addition, the auditor might observe the distribution of the paychecks, or observe employees listed in the payroll journal at work.  Note here that the auditor must sample from the population representing the firm's paid employees, here the payroll journal, to determine whether they are all bona fide.

## *Illustrative Simulation Problem*

Illustrative Simulation Problem D, which follows, provides an illustration of the relationship between controls and tests of controls in the payroll area.

### Illustrative Simulation Problem D

You are working in the payroll area of the Remlo Company Audit.  For each of the listed controls, select the **best** test of a control to determine whether the control is operating effectively.  Each test of a control may be used only once (or not at all).

### *Controls*

**1.**   The Human Resources Department authorizes all hires.

**2.**   The Human Resources Department authorizes all pay rate changes.

**3.**   Authorized **decreases** in pay rate have been reflected in subsequent remuneration.

**4.**   Factory workers on the payroll exist as working employees of the company.

5. The individual signing the payroll checks (the maker) is properly authorized.

6. Individual payroll checks are signed by the authorized check maker.

7. The payroll bank account is reconciled by an individual who is not involved in preparation of payroll checks.

8. Employee overtime is approved by the employee's supervisor.

9. Sales commissions are properly calculated.

*Tests of Controls*

A. Agree pay rate change authorizations to subsequent pay rates in the payroll journal.
B. Compare current employee time cards to the subsequent payroll journal.
C. Compare payroll budgets to the preceding period budget.
D. Compare the total payroll costs per the payroll journal to the amounts as posted to ledger accounts.
E. Confirm the payroll account using the Standard Form to Confirm Account Balance Information with Financial Institutions.
F. Confirm with the bank that all checks have been issued bearing the signature of the proper check maker.
G. Confirm with the bank the individual responsible for account reconciliation.
H. Examine employee time cards for proper authorization.
I. Observe and make inquiries about the performance of the reconciliation and payroll check preparation function.
J. Obtain a list of authorized check signers (makers) from the bank.
K. Recalculate employee gross pay using supporting information.
L. Select a sample of cancelled payroll checks and determine that the maker's signature is proper.
M. Select a sample of employees on the payroll and determine that each has a properly approved hiring authorization form in his or her personnel file.
N. Select a sample of employee names from the payroll register and briefly interview each on a surprise basis.
O. Select a sample of hiring authorization forms and agree each to an employee in the payroll journal.
P. Vouch changes in pay rates as per two periods to pay rate change authorizations.

## Solution to Illustrative Simulation Problem D

1. **(M)** To test whether all hires are authorized, selecting a sample of employees on the payroll to determine whether they have the proper documentation is the best approach. Notice that reply (o), selecting a sample of hiring authorization forms and agreeing each to employees in the payroll journal tests in the wrong direction. If one starts with a hiring authorization form one is not going to identify an employee without such a form. Reply (o) would more directly address whether those with hiring authorization forms are being paid—not typically a problem given individuals' tendency to complain is they are not paid.

2. **(P)** To test whether pay rate changes have been authorized, one must identify situations in which there is an actual change in pay and determine whether it was authorized. Reply (p) provides a good test since it identifies such a change and tests whether there is a pay rate change authorization.

3. **(A)** To determine whether authorized pay **decreases** have been properly processed, one must begin with the authorized decreases and test whether they have been recorded. In this case, the only documents likely to serve as the source documents are the pay rate change authorization forms.

4. **(N)** To determine whether factory workers being paid are actually at work, one would expect to test from source documents relating to paychecks (or the payroll journal) to some evidence that the person is on the job, whether it be evidence of work performed or the employee him or herself. Reply (n) is in the proper direction in that those on the payroll register are being paid, and should be on the job.

5. **(J)** The list of authorized check signers is maintained by the bank. Also, the board of directors may authorize signers. Since none of the replies deal with the Board of Directors the confirmation obtaining a list of authorized check signers from the bank is the best option.

6. **(L)** To determine whether the authorized check maker is signing the checks, one must examine individual checks. Notice that this control would ordinarily be tested following testing of the preceding control.

7. **(I)** Observation and inquiry about reconciliation and the payroll check preparation functions will serve to test this segregation.

8. **(H)** To determine whether overtime is approved by the employee's supervisor, one must understand the approval process. But in a question such as this, one must find a reply that implies authorization, as does reply (h).

9. **(K)** The proper calculation of sales commission requires a comparison of sales with pay. The general reply (k) on recalculating gross pay accomplishes this task.

5. **Financing.** This cycle includes issuance and repurchase of debt (bank loans, mortgages, bonds payable) and capital stock, and payment of interest and dividends. Debt and capital stock transactions should be authorized by the board of directors. Often an independent trustee issues bonds, monitors company compliance with the provisions of the debt agreement, and pays interest.

For capital stock transactions, corporations may either employ an independent stock registrar and a stock transfer agent, or handle their own transactions. Normally, internal control is stronger when a stock registrar and a stock transfer agent are utilized. A stock registrar's primary responsibility is to verify that stock is issued in accordance with the authorization of the board of directors and the articles of incorporation; the stock transfer agent's primary responsibility is maintaining detailed stockholder records and carrying out transfers of stock ownership.

### Major Financing Controls Frequently Missing in CPA Exam Questions

(1) Debt and equity transactions are properly approved by the company's board of directors.
(2) An independent trustee handles bond transactions.
(3) A stock registrar and a stock transfer agent handle capital stock transactions.
(4) Canceled stock certificates are defaced to prevent their reissuance.

6. **Investing.** This cycle includes investments in the debt and equity of other organizations, and purchases of property, plant, and equipment. Investments may be categorized as marketable securities and long-term investments. Purchases are recorded at cost, and reported at the lower of cost or market, as guided by SFAS 12.

### Major Investment Controls Frequently Missing in CPA Exam Questions

(1) Segregation of duties among the individuals authorizing purchases and sales of securities, maintaining custody of the securities, and maintaining the records of securities
(2) Use of an independent agent such as a stockbroker, bank or trust company to maintain custody of securities
(3) Securities **not** in the custody of an independent agent maintained in a bank safe-deposit box under the joint control of the treasurer and one other company official; both individuals must be present to gain access
(4) Registration of securities in the name of the company
(5) Detailed records of all securities and related revenue from interest and dividends
(6) Periodical physical inspection of securities by individuals with no responsibility for the authorization, custody, or recordkeeping for investments

Property, plant, and equipment acquisitions require board of directors' approval for purchases over a certain amount. Otherwise, the purchase is handled similarly to a merchandise purchase. As in the case of merchandise purchases, the item is recorded as an addition when some form of purchase authorization is present with a vendor's invoice and a receiving report. The company then selects an appropriate life and depreciation method (e.g., straight-line, sum-of-the-years' digits, double-declining balance). Depreciation entries are made in the general journal with a debit to depreciation expense (manufacturing overhead for manufacturing equipment) and a credit to accumulated depreciation. The company must also have controls to determine that repair and maintenance expenses have not been capitalized.

Asset retirements are recorded by removing the asset and accumulated depreciation from the general ledger—a gain (loss) may occur on the transaction. In the case of an exchange of assets, the firm has policies to determine that GAAP is properly followed in recording the transaction.

### Major Property, Plant, and Equipment Controls Frequently Missing in CPA Exam Questions

(1) Major asset acquisitions are properly approved by the firm's board of directors and properly controlled through capital budgeting techniques.
(2) Detailed records are available for property assets and accumulated depreciation.
(3) Written policies exist for capitalization vs. expensing decisions.
(4) Depreciation properly calculated.
(5) Retirements approved by an appropriate level of management.
(6) Physical control over assets to prevent theft.
(7) Periodic physical inspection of plant and equipment by individuals who are otherwise independent of property, plant, and equipment (e.g., internal auditors).

7. **Overall Internal Control Questionnaires (checklists).** The following internal control questionnaires (in checklist form) outline the controls that are typically necessary in various transaction cycles and

accounts. While the lists are clearly too lengthy to memorize, review them and obtain a general familiarity. **Candidates with little actual business experience will probably find them especially helpful for questions that require the preparation of an internal control questionnaire.** Study in detail the questionnaire checklists on cash receipts (#3), cash disbursements (#4), and on payroll (#14)—as indicated above, a large percentage of the internal control weakness type questions relate to these three areas.

The checklists are organized into subtopics—generally by category of balance sheet account (e.g., cash, receivables, fixed assets, liabilities, shareholders' equity, etc.). The related nominal accounts should be considered with the real accounts (e.g., depreciation and fixed assets, sales and accounts receivable).

1. General

Chart of accounts
Accounting procedures manual
Organizational chart to define responsibilities
Absence of entries direct to ledgers
Posting references in ledgers
Review of journal entries
Use of standard journal entries
Use of prenumbered forms
Support for all journal entries
Access to records limited to authorized persons
Rotation of accounting personnel
Required vacations
Review of system at every level
Appropriate revision of chart of accounts
Appropriate revision of procedures
Separation of recordkeeping from operations
Separation of recordkeeping from custodianship
Record retention policy
Bonding of employees
A conflict of interest policy

2. Cash funds

Imprest system
Reasonable amount
Completeness of vouchers
Custodian responsible for fund
Reimbursement checks to order of custodian
Surprise audits
No employee check cashing
Physically secure
Custodian has no access to cash receipts
Custodian has no access to accounting records

3. Cash receipts

Detail listing of mail receipts
Restrictive endorsement of checks
Special handling of postdated checks
Daily deposit
Cash custodians bonded
Cash custodians apart from negotiable instruments
Bank accounts properly authorized
Handling of returned NSF items
Comparison of duplicate deposit slips with cash book
Comparison of duplicate deposit slips with detail AR
Banks instructed not to cash checks to company
Control over cash from other sources
Separation of cashier personnel from accounting duties
Separation of cashier personnel from credit duties

Use of cash registers
Cash register tapes
Numbered cash receipt tickets
Outside salesmen cash control
Daily reconciliation of cash collections

4. Cash disbursements

Numbered checks
Sufficient support for check
Limited authorization to sign checks
No signing of blank checks
All checks accounted for
Detail listing of checks
Mutilation of voided checks
Specific approval for unusually large checks
Proper authorization of persons signing checks
Control over signature machines
Check listing compared with cash book
Control over interbank transfers
Prompt accounting for interbank transfers
Checks not payable to cash
Physical control of unused checks
Cancellation of supporting documents
Control over long outstanding checks
Reconciliation of bank account
Independence of person reconciling bank statement
Bank statement direct to person reconciling
No access to cash records or receipts by check signers

5. Investments

Proper authorization of transactions
Under control of a custodian
Custodian bonded
Custodian separate from cash receipts
Custodian separate from investment records
Safety-deposit box
Record of all safety-deposit visits
Access limited
Presence of two required for access
Periodic reconciliation of detail with control
Record of all aspects of all securities
Availability of brokerage advices, etc.
Periodic internal audit
Securities in name of company
Proper segregation of collateral
Physical control of collateral
Periodic appraisal of collateral
Periodic appraisal of investments
Adequate records of investments for application of equity method

6. Accounts receivable and sales

Sales orders prenumbered
Credit approval

Credit and sales departments independent
Control of back orders
Sales order and sales invoice comparison
Shipping invoices prenumbered
Names and addresses on shipping invoice
Review of sales invoices
Control over returned merchandise
Credit memoranda prenumbered
Matching of credit memoranda and receiving
   reports
Control over credit memoranda
Control over scrap sales
Control over sales to employees
Control over COD sales
Sales reconciled with cash receipts and AR
Sales reconciled with inventory change
AR statement to all customers
Periodic preparation of aging schedule
Control over collections of written-off receiv-
   ables
Control over AR write-offs (e.g., proper au-
   thorization)
Control over AR written off (i.e., review for
   possible collection)
Independence of sales, AR, receipts, billing,
   and shipping personnel

7.  Notes receivable

Proper authorization of notes
Detailed records of notes
Periodic detail to control comparison
Periodic confirmation with makers
Control over notes discounted
Control over delinquent notes
Physical safety of notes
Periodic count of notes
Control over collateral
Control over revenue from notes
Custodian of notes independent from cash and
   recordkeeping

8.  Inventory and cost of sales

Periodic inventory counts
Written inventory instructions
Counts by noncustodians
Control over count tags
Control over inventory adjustments
Use of perpetual records
Periodic comparison of G/L and perpetual
   records
Investigation of discrepancies
Control over consignment inventory
Control over inventory stored at warehouses
Control over returnable containers left with
   customers
Preparation of receiving reports
Prenumbered receiving reports
Receiving reports in numerical order
Independence of custodian from recordkeeping
Adequacy of insurance
Physical safeguards against theft
Physical safeguards against fire
Adequacy of cost system
Cost system tied into general ledger
Periodic review of overhead rates
Use of standard costs
Use of inventory requisitions
Periodic summaries of inventory usage
Control over intracompany inventory transfers

Purchase orders prenumbered
Proper authorization for purchases
Review of open purchase orders

9.  Prepaid expenses and deferred charges

Proper authorization to incur
Authorization and support of amortization
Detailed records
Periodic review of amortization policies
Control over insurance policies
Periodic review of insurance needs
Control over premium refunds
Beneficiaries of company policies
Physical control of policies

10. Intangibles

Authorization to incur
Detailed records
Authorization to amortize
Periodic review of amortization

11. Fixed assets

Detailed property records
Periodic comparison with control accounts
Proper authorization for acquisition
Written policies for acquisition
Control over expenditures for self-construction
Use of work orders
Individual asset identification plates
Written authorization for sale
Written authorization for retirement
Physical safeguard from theft
Control over fully depreciated assets
Written capitalization—expense policies
Responsibilities charged for asset and depre-
   ciation records
Written, detailed depreciation records
Depreciation adjustments for sales and retire-
   ments
Control over intracompany transfers
Adequacy of insurance
Control over returnable containers

12. Accounts payable

Designation of responsibility
Independence of AP personnel from purchas-
   ing, cashier, receiving functions
Periodic comparison of detail and control
Control over purchase returns
Clerical accuracy of vendors' invoices
Matching of purchase order, receiving report,
   and vendor invoice
Reconciliation of vendor statements with AP
   detail
Control over debit memos
Control over advance payments
Review of unmatched receiving reports
Mutilation of supporting documents at payment
Review of debit balances
Investigation of discounts not taken

13. Accrued liabilities and other expenses

Proper authorization for expenditure and incur-
   rence
Control over partial deliveries
Postage meter
Purchasing department
Bids from vendors
Verification of invoices

Imprest cash account
Detailed records
Responsibility charged
Independence from G/L and cashier functions
Periodic comparison with budget

14. Payroll

Authorization to employ
Personnel data records
Tax records
Time clock
Supervisor review of time cards
Review of payroll calculations
Comparison of time cards to job sheets
Imprest payroll account
Responsibility for payroll records
Compliance with labor statutes
Distribution of payroll checks
Control over unclaimed wages
Profit-sharing authorization
Responsibility for profit-sharing computations

15. Long-term liabilities

Authorization to incur
Executed in company name
Detailed records of long-term debt
Reports of independent transfer agent
Reports of independent registrar

Otherwise adequate records of creditors
Control over unissued instruments
Signers independent of each other
Adequacy of records of collateral
Periodic review of debt agreement compliance
Recordkeeping of detachable warrants
Recordkeeping of conversion features

16. Shareholders' equity

Use of registrar
Use of transfer agent
Adequacy of detailed records
Comparison of transfer agent's report with
    records
Physical control over blank certificates
Physical control over treasury certificates
Authorization for transactions
Tax stamp compliance for canceled certificates
Independent dividend agent
Imprest dividend account
Periodic reconciliation of dividend account
Adequacy of stockholders' ledger
Review of stock restrictions and provisions
Valuation procedures for stock issuances
Other paid-in capital entries
Other retained earnings entries

## E.  Other Considerations

1. **Communicating with the Audit Committee.** Recall that the existence of an audit committee is a factor in the control environment (see outline of AU 319). An audit committee is a group of outside (nonmanagement) directors whose functions typically include

- Nominating, terminating, and negotiating CPA firm audit fees
- Discussing broad, general matters concerning the type, scope, and timing of the audit with the public accounting firm
- Discussing internal control weaknesses with the public accounting firm
- Reviewing the financial statements and the public accounting firm's audit report
- Working with the company's internal auditors

CPAs communicate with audit committees on a variety of matters. We have discussed in the Engagement Planning Module that fraud and illegal acts must be communicated to the audit committee. In addition, AU 325 requires auditors to communicate **reportable conditions** to the audit committee. A reportable condition is a significant deficiency in the design or function of internal control that could adversely affect the organization's ability to record, process, summarize, and report financial data. These reportable conditions may be communicated orally (with the discussion documented in the working papers), or as is more frequently the case, in a written letter to the audit committee. Also, depending upon the significance of the matter being communicated, the CPA will decide whether to communicate the matter during the audit or after the audit is concluded. When a previously communicated reportable condition has not been corrected, the CPA **may** decide to recommunicate it because of changes in management or the audit committee, or due to the passage of time.

A reportable condition may be so significant as to be considered a **material weakness in internal control**. A material weakness is a condition that does not reduce to a relatively low level the risk that material misstatements might occur and not be detected within a timely period by employees in the normal course of performing their assigned functions. Auditors, unless a different arrangement is made with the client, are not required to classify reportable conditions as being material weaknesses.

The report issued on reportable conditions should indicate that it is intended solely for the audit committee, management, and others in the organization (unless requirements established by governmental authorities require such reports in which case the report may be provided). Because of the potential for misinterpretation, when no reportable conditions are noted, the auditor should **not** issue a report indicating that no such conditions were noted. Know that communicating information on weaknesses in internal control has long been considered a "secondary" purpose or a "by-product" of audits.

The following is an example of the form of a report that might be issued when reportable conditions have been found:

> In planning and performing our audit of the financial statements of the ABC Corporation for the year ended December 31, 20XX, we considered its internal control in order to determine our auditing procedures for the purpose of expressing our opinion on the financial statements and not to provide assurance on internal control. However, we noted certain matters involving internal control and its operation that we consider to be reportable conditions under standards established by the American Institute of Certified Public Accountants. Reportable conditions involve matters coming to our attention relating to significant deficiencies in the design or operation of internal control that, in our judgment, could adversely affect the organization's ability to record, process, summarize, and report financial data consistent with the assertions of management in the financial statements.
>
> [*Include paragraphs to describe the reportable conditions noted.*]
>
> This report is intended solely for the information and use of the audit committee (board of directors, board of trustees, or owners in owner-managed enterprises), management, and others within the organization (or specified regulatory agency or other specified third party).

Finally, AU 380 and AU 722 require the communication (orally or written) of certain information on SEC engagements, as well as engagements of other companies with active audit committees or boards of directors. The nature of the items, also presented in the outline of AU 380, may be summarized, using our categories, as follows:

### Audit-related matters

1. Auditor responsibility under GAAS audits
2. Significant audit adjustments
3. Uncorrected misstatements determined by management to be immaterial.
4. Auditor responsibility for other information in documents containing audited financial statements (see Reporting Module)

### Accounting matters—Determine audit committee is aware of

5. Significant accounting policies
6. Important management judgments and accounting estimates
7. Quality (e.g., aggressiveness) of accounting principles—only required for SEC registrant clients

### Auditor relationships with management

8. Disagreements with management
9. Management consultation with other accountants
10. Major issues discussed with management prior to retention
11. Difficulties encountered in performing the audit

At this point you should study the outline of AU 380.

AU 722 considers materially misstated **interim** information that has been filed with, or is about to be filed with, a regulatory agency such as the SEC, and on which management fails to take proper corrective action. The CPA is to contact the audit committee; if the audit committee also does not respond appropriately, the CPA should consider whether resignation is appropriate in the circumstances. See Section C of the outline of AU 722.

A simulation question might make the Professional Standards available and ask the candidate to prepare a report to the audit committee. While you might use either the index or keyword approach to identify the appropriate standards, bear in mind that the two primary sections here are AU 325 and AU 380 as follows:

| Section | Coverage |
|---------|----------|
| AU 325 | Communicating reportable conditions (significant deficiencies) and material weaknesses to the audit committee. |
| AU 380 | Communicating other information to the audit committee (i.e., accounting, audit, and the auditor's relationship with management). |

2. **Reporting on Internal Control.** AT 501 outlines examination and agreed-upon procedures forms of CPA association relating to a client's internal control over financial reporting association; reviews are not allowed. This service has gained increased importance since the Sarbanes-Oxley Act of 2002 requires that an examination be performed for SEC registrants as a part of the financial statement audit. The approach is one in which management includes a report in Form 10K (the annual report filed with the SEC) that indicates that it is responsible for establishing and maintaining internal control over financial reporting and includes an assessment of the effectiveness of internal control. Practitioners attest to, and report on, the assessment made by management.

CPAs may report on internal control if the following conditions are met:

(a) The responsible party assumes responsibility for the effectiveness of internal control

*NOTE: The "responsible party" concept is presented in AT 101. In general the responsible party is the person(s) responsible for the subject matter of the engagement (here internal control). Management is ordinarily the responsible party.*

(b) The responsible party evaluates the effectiveness of the entity's internal control using suitable criteria

(c) Sufficient evidential matter exists or could be developed

As part of the engagement, the CPA should obtain from the responsible party a written assertion about the effectiveness of the entity's internal control. The responsible party may present its written assertion either in a separate report that will accompany the CPA's report, or in a representation letter to the CPA. That assertion may state, for example, that internal control over financial reporting met the control criteria established by a particular commission.

Performing an examination of the effectiveness of an entity's internal control involves

1. Planning the engagement
2. Obtaining an understanding of internal control
3. Evaluating the design effectiveness of the controls
4. Testing and evaluating the operating effectiveness of the controls
5. Forming an opinion on the effectiveness of the entity's internal control (or the responsible party's assertion thereon) based on the control criteria.

Although the above steps are similar to those used in the auditors' consideration of internal control for financial statement audit purposes, the purpose and scope of the study differs. The purpose of the CPA's examination of the effectiveness of internal control is to express an opinion about whether the entity maintained, in all material respects, effective internal control as of a point in time based on the control criteria. In contrast, in a financial statement audit, the purpose of an auditor's consideration of internal control is to enable the auditor to plan the audit and determine the nature, timing, and extent of tests to be performed.

The CPA's report may either be (1) directly on whether the company maintained effective internal control over financial reporting, or (2) on the responsible party's assertion. The following is an unqualified report using the first approach and thereby directly upon internal control:

### Independent Practitioner's Report

*[Introductory paragraph]*

We have examined the effectiveness of Willis Company's internal control over financial reporting as of December 31, 200X, based on criteria established in *Internal Control—Integrated Framework* issued by the Sponsoring Organizations of the Treadway Commission. Management is responsible for maintaining effective internal control over financial reporting. Our responsibility is to express an opinion on the effectiveness of internal control based on our examination.

[*Scope paragraph*]

Our examination was conducted in accordance with attestation standards established by the American Institute of Certified Public Accountants and, accordingly, included obtaining an understanding of internal control over financial reporting, testing and evaluating the design and operating effectiveness of the internal control, and performing such other procedures as we considered necessary in the circumstances. We believe that our examination provides a reasonable basis for our opinion.

[*Inherent limitations paragraph*]

Because of inherent limitations on any internal control, misstatements due to error or fraud may occur and not be detected. Also, projections of any evaluation of the internal control over financial reporting to future periods are subject to the risk that the internal control may become inadequate because of changes in conditions, or that the degree of compliance with the policies or procedures may deteriorate.

[*Opinion paragraph*]

In our opinion, Willis Company maintained, in all material respects, effective internal control over financial reporting as of December 31, 200X, based upon criteria established in *Internal Control—Integrated Framework* issued by the Sponsoring Organizations of the Treadway Commission.

When the report is upon the responsible party's assertion, the primary changes are to modify the

(a) Last sentence of the introductory paragraph to state that the CPA's responsibility is to express an opinion on management's assertion.

(b) Opinion paragraph to state that management's assertion is fairly stated, in all material respects, based upon criteria (here the *Internal Control—Integrated Framework*).

When the opinion is modified, the first form of reporting, directly upon internal control, is required. The primary circumstances for which the opinion is modified for the existence of material weaknesses (rather than for "significant deficiencies") and for restrictions on the scope of the engagement. Recall that a material weakness involves a situation with more than a remote likelihood that a material misstatement of the financial statements will not be prevented or detected.

Agreed-upon procedures engagements result in a report presenting a description of the procedures performed and a summary of the CPA's findings. For this type of service, negative assurance is not considered appropriate. At this point you should read the outline of AT 501.

3. **Effects of an Internal Audit Function.** SAS 65 discusses the effect of an internal audit function on the CPA's audit. This section has been codified as AU 322.

Internal auditors have two primary effects on the audit: (1) their existence and work may **affect the nature, timing, and extent of audit procedures**, and (2) CPAs may use internal auditors to **provide direct assistance** in performing procedures. The CPA should assess both the **competence** and **objectivity** of internal auditors. Competence is evaluated by considering education, experience, professional certification, audit policies, and various work policies. Objectivity is assessed by considering organizational status within the company, and policies for assuring that internal auditors are objective with respect to the areas being audited. Section B of the outline of Section AU 322 presents more detailed information on the heavily tested area of internal auditor competence and objectivity.

Internal auditors may affect the CPA's understanding of internal control, control risk assessment, and substantive tests. You should know that for assertions with high audit risk, the internal auditor's work alone cannot eliminate the need for CPA's tests. A number of questions may be expected on this topic. At this point, you should study the section outline.

4. **Reports on Processing of Transactions by Service Organizations (AU 324).** Make certain that you understand that this section provides information for both **user auditors** and for **service auditors**.

User auditors audit an organization that uses a service organization. Consider a computer service organization that provides data processing services to an audit client. When the service organization performs such services, its controls interact with the audit client's internal control. In such circumstances three approaches are possible for the user auditor: (1) test the user organization's controls over activities of the service organization, (2) use the service auditor's report on the service organization's internal control policies, and (3) perform tests of controls at the service organization.

Two types of service auditor reports are described in detail in this section. The first addresses whether service organization controls have been placed in operation. The following is an example of such a report:

To the XYZ Loan Servicer:

We have examined the accompanying description of the loan servicing application of XYZ Loan Servicer. Our examination included procedures to obtain reasonable assurance about whether (1) the accompanying description presents fairly, in all material respects, the aspects of XYZ Loan Servicer's policies and procedures that may be relevant to a user organization's internal control, (2) the control structure policies and procedures included in the description were suitably designed to achieve the control objectives specified in the description, if those policies and procedures were complied with satisfactorily, and (3) such policies and procedures had been placed in operation as of December 31, 20X2. The control objectives were specified by the State of Arizona Loan Servicing Authority. Our examination was performed in accordance with standards established by the American Institute of Certified Public Accountants and included those procedures we considered necessary in the circumstances to obtain a reasonable basis for rendering an opinion.

We did not perform procedures to determine the operating effectiveness of policies and procedures for any period. Accordingly, we express no opinion on the operating effectiveness of any aspects of XYZ Loan Servicer's policies and procedures, individually or in the aggregate.

In our opinion, the accompanying description of the aforementioned application presents fairly, in all material respects, the relevant aspects of XYZ Loan Servicer's policies and procedures that had been placed in operation as of December 31, 20X2. Also, in our opinion, the policies and procedures, as described, are suitably designed to provide reasonable assurance that the specified control objectives would be achieved if the described policies and procedures were complied with satisfactorily.

The description of policies and procedures at XYZ Loan Servicer is as of December 31, 20X2, and any projection of such information to the future is subject to the risk that, because of change, the description may no longer portray the system in existence. The potential effectiveness of specific policies and procedures at the service organization is subject to inherent limitations and, accordingly, misstatements or fraud may occur and not be detected. Furthermore, the projection of any conclusions, based on our findings, to future periods is subject to the risk that changes may alter the validity of such conclusions.

This report is intended solely for use by the management of XYZ Loan Servicer, its customers, and the independent auditors of its customers.

The second, issued when the effectiveness of controls has been tested, includes the information presented in the first type of report plus an opinion on the operating effectiveness of those controls. Of the two reports, only the second type provides the user auditor a basis for reducing the assessment of control risk. At this point, you may wish to study the outline of AU 324.

**MULTIPLE-CHOICE QUESTIONS (1-165)**

**1.** Which of the following most likely would **not** be considered an inherent limitation of the potential effectiveness of an entity's internal control?
    a. Incompatible duties.
    b. Management override.
    c. Mistakes in judgment.
    d. Collusion among employees.

**2.** When considering internal control, an auditor should be aware of the concept of reasonable assurance, which recognizes that
    a. Internal control may be ineffective due to mistakes in judgment and personal carelessness.
    b. Adequate safeguards over access to assets and records should permit an entity to maintain proper accountability.
    c. Establishing and maintaining internal control is an important responsibility of management.
    d. The cost of an entity's internal control should **not** exceed the benefits expected to be derived.

**3.** Proper segregation of functional responsibilities calls for separation of the functions of
    a. Authorization, execution, and payment.
    b. Authorization, recording, and custody.
    c. Custody, execution, and reporting.
    d. Authorization, payment, and recording.

**4.** An entity's ongoing monitoring activities often include
    a. Periodic audits by the audit committee.
    b. Reviewing the purchasing function.
    c. The audit of the annual financial statements.
    d. Control risk assessment in conjunction with quarterly reviews.

**5.** The overall attitude and awareness of an entity's board of directors concerning the importance of internal control usually is reflected in its
    a. Computer-based controls.
    b. System of segregation of duties.
    c. Control environment.
    d. Safeguards over access to assets.

**6.** Management philosophy and operating style most likely would have a significant influence on an entity's control environment when
    a. The internal auditor reports directly to management.
    b. Management is dominated by one individual.
    c. Accurate management job descriptions delineate specific duties.
    d. The audit committee actively oversees the financial reporting process.

**7.** Which of the following factors are included in an entity's control environment?

|     | Audit committee | Integrity and ethical values | Organizational |
| --- | --- | --- | --- |
| a. | Yes | Yes | No |
| b. | Yes | No | Yes |
| c. | No | Yes | Yes |
| d. | Yes | Yes | Yes |

**8.** Which of the following is **not** a component of an entity's internal control?
    a. Control risk.
    b. Control activities.
    c. Monitoring.
    d. Control environment.

**9.** Which of the following is a provision of the Foreign Corrupt Practices Act?
    a. It is a criminal offense for an auditor to fail to detect and report a bribe paid by an American business entity to a foreign official for the purpose of obtaining business.
    b. The auditor's detection of illegal acts committed by officials of the auditor's publicly held client in conjunction with foreign officials should be reported to the Enforcement Division of the Securities and Exchange Commission.
    c. If the auditor of a publicly held company concludes that the effects on the financial statements of a bribe given to a foreign official are **not** susceptible of reasonable estimation, the auditor's report should be modified.
    d. Every publicly held company must devise, document, and maintain internal control sufficient to provide reasonable assurances that internal control objectives are met.

**10.** An auditor suspects that certain client employees are ordering merchandise for themselves over the Internet without recording the purchase or receipt of the merchandise. When vendors' invoices arrive, one of the employees approves the invoices for payment. After the invoices are paid, the employee destroys the invoices and the related vouchers. In gathering evidence regarding the fraud, the auditor most likely would select items for testing from the file of all
    a. Cash disbursements.
    b. Approved vouchers.
    c. Receiving reports.
    d. Vendors' invoices.

**11.** Which of the following procedures most likely would provide an auditor with evidence about whether an entity's internal control activities are suitably designed to prevent or detect material misstatements?
    a. Reperforming the activities for a sample of transactions.
    b. Performing analytical procedures using data aggregated at a high level.
    c. Vouching a sample of transactions directly related to the activities.
    d. Observing the entity's personnel applying the activities.

**12.** Which statement is correct concerning the relevance of various types of controls to a financial audit?
    a. An auditor may ordinarily ignore a consideration of controls when a substantive audit approach is taken.
    b. Controls over the reliability of financial reporting are ordinarily most directly relevant to an audit, but other controls may also be relevant.
    c. Controls over safeguarding of assets and liabilities are of primary importance, while controls over the reliability of financial reporting may also be relevant.
    d. All controls are ordinarily relevant to an audit.

**13.** In an audit of financial statements in accordance with generally accepted auditing standards, an auditor is required to
   a. Document the auditor's understanding of the entity's internal control.
   b. Search for significant deficiencies in the operation of internal control.
   c. Perform tests of controls to evaluate the effectiveness of the entity's internal control.
   d. Determine whether controls are suitably designed to prevent or detect material misstatements.

**14.** In obtaining an understanding of an entity's internal control relevant to audit planning, an auditor is required to obtain knowledge about the
   a. Design of the controls pertaining to internal control components.
   b. Effectiveness of controls that have been placed in operation.
   c. Consistency with which controls are currently being applied.
   d. Controls related to each principal transaction class and account balance.

**15.** An auditor should obtain sufficient knowledge of an entity's information system to understand the
   a. Safeguards used to limit access to computer facilities.
   b. Process used to prepare significant accounting estimates.
   c. Controls used to assure proper authorization of transactions.
   d. Controls used to detect the concealment of fraud.

**16.** When obtaining an understanding of an entity's internal control, an auditor should concentrate on the substance of controls rather than their form because
   a. The controls may be operating effectively but may **not** be documented.
   b. Management may establish appropriate controls but **not** enforce compliance with them.
   c. The controls may be so inappropriate that **no** reliance is contemplated by the auditor.
   d. Management may implement controls whose costs exceed their benefits.

**17.** Decision tables differ from program flowcharts in that decision tables emphasize
   a. Ease of manageability for complex programs.
   b. Logical relationships among conditions and actions.
   c. Cost benefit factors justifying the program.
   d. The sequence in which operations are performed.

**18.** During the consideration of internal control in a financial statement audit, an auditor is **not** obligated to
   a. Search for significant deficiencies in the operation of the internal control.
   b. Understand the internal control and the information system.
   c. Determine whether the control activities relevant to audit planning have been placed in operation.
   d. Perform procedures to understand the design of internal control.

**19.** The primary objective of procedures performed to obtain an understanding of internal control is to provide an auditor with
   a. Knowledge necessary for audit planning.
   b. Evidential matter to use in assessing inherent risk.
   c. A basis for modifying tests of controls.
   d. An evaluation of the consistency of application of management's policies.

**20.** Which of the following statements regarding auditor documentation of the client's internal control is correct?
   a. Documentation must include flowcharts.
   b. Documentation must include procedural write-ups.
   c. No documentation is necessary although it is desirable.
   d. No one particular form of documentation is necessary, and the extent of documentation may vary.

**21.** In obtaining an understanding of an entity's internal control, an auditor is required to obtain knowledge about the

|     | *Operating effectiveness of controls* | *Design of controls* |
| --- | --- | --- |
| a.  | Yes | Yes |
| b.  | No  | Yes |
| c.  | Yes | No  |
| d.  | No  | No  |

**22.** Control risk should be assessed in terms of
   a. Specific controls.
   b. Types of potential fraud.
   c. Financial statement assertions.
   d. Control environment factors.

**23.** After assessing control risk at below the maximum level, an auditor desires to seek a further reduction in the assessed level of control risk. At this time, the auditor would consider whether
   a. It would be efficient to obtain an understanding of the entity's information system.
   b. The entity's controls have been placed in operation.
   c. The entity's controls pertain to any financial statement assertions.
   d. Additional evidential matter sufficient to support a further reduction is likely to be available.

**24.** Assessing control risk at below the maximum level most likely would involve
   a. Performing more extensive substantive tests with larger sample sizes than originally planned.
   b. Reducing inherent risk for most of the assertions relevant to significant account balances.
   c. Changing the timing of substantive tests by omitting interim-date testing and performing the tests at year-end.
   d. Identifying specific controls relevant to specific assertions.

**25.** An auditor assesses control risk because it
   a. Is relevant to the auditor's understanding of the control environment.
   b. Provides assurance that the auditor's materiality levels are appropriate.
   c. Indicates to the auditor where inherent risk may be the greatest.
   d. Affects the level of detection risk that the auditor may accept.

**26.** When an auditor increases the assessed level of control risk because certain control activities were determined to be ineffective, the auditor would most likely increase the
   a.   Extent of tests of controls.
   b.   Level of detection risk.
   c.   Extent of tests of details.
   d.   Level of inherent risk.

**27.** When assessing control risk below the maximum level, an auditor is required to document the auditor's

|     | *Understanding of the entity's control environment* | *Basis for concluding that control risk is below the maximum level* |
| --- | --- | --- |
| a.  | Yes | No  |
| b.  | No  | Yes |
| c.  | Yes | Yes |
| d.  | No  | No  |

**28.** An auditor uses the knowledge provided by the understanding of internal control and the assessed level of control risk primarily to
   a.   Determine whether procedures and records concerning the safeguarding of assets are reliable.
   b.   Ascertain whether the opportunities to allow any person to both perpetrate and conceal fraud are minimized.
   c.   Modify the initial assessments of inherent risk and preliminary judgments about materiality levels.
   d.   Determine the nature, timing, and extent of substantive tests for financial statement assertions.

**29.** An auditor may compensate for a weakness in internal control by increasing the
   a.   Level of detection risk.
   b.   Extent of tests of controls.
   c.   Preliminary judgment about audit risk.
   d.   Extent of analytical procedures.

**30.** Which of the following statements is correct concerning an auditor's assessment of control risk?
   a.   Assessing control risk may be performed concurrently during an audit with obtaining an understanding of the entity's internal control.
   b.   Evidence about the operation of internal control in prior audits may not be considered during the current year's assessment of control risk.
   c.   The basis for an auditor's conclusions about the assessed level of control risk need not be documented unless control risk is assessed at the maximum level.
   d.   The lower the assessed level of control risk, the less assurance the evidence must provide that the control procedures are operating effectively.

**31.** Regardless of the assessed level of control risk, an auditor would perform some
   a.   Tests of controls to determine the effectiveness of internal control policies.
   b.   Analytical procedures to verify the design of internal control.
   c.   Substantive tests to restrict detection risk for significant transaction classes.
   d.   Dual-purpose tests to evaluate both the risk of monetary misstatement and preliminary control risk.

**32.** Before assessing control risk at a level lower than the maximum, the auditor obtains reasonable assurance that controls are in use and operating effectively. This assurance is most likely obtained in part by
   a.   Preparing flowcharts.
   b.   Performing substantive tests.
   c.   Analyzing tests of trends and ratios.
   d.   Inspection of documents.

**33.** An auditor generally tests the segregation of duties related to inventory by
   a.   Personal inquiry and observation.
   b.   Test counts and cutoff procedures.
   c.   Analytical procedures and invoice recomputation.
   d.   Document inspection and reconciliation.

**34.** The objective of tests of details of transactions performed as tests of controls is to
   a.   Monitor the design and use of entity documents such as prenumbered shipping forms.
   b.   Determine whether controls have been placed in operation.
   c.   Detect material misstatements in the account balances of the financial statements.
   d.   Evaluate whether controls operated effectively.

**35.** After obtaining an understanding of internal control and assessing control risk, an auditor decided to perform tests of controls. The auditor most likely decided that
   a.   It would be efficient to perform tests of controls that would result in a reduction in planned substantive tests.
   b.   Additional evidence to support a further reduction in control risk is **not** available.
   c.   An increase in the assessed level of control risk is justified for certain financial statement assertions.
   d.   There were many internal control weaknesses that could allow misstatements to enter the accounting system.

**36.** In assessing control risk, an auditor ordinarily selects from a variety of techniques, including
   a.   Inquiry and analytical procedures.
   b.   Reperformance and observation.
   c.   Comparison and confirmation.
   d.   Inspection and verification.

**37.** Which of the following types of evidence would an auditor most likely examine to determine whether controls are operating as designed?
   a.   Confirmations of receivables verifying account balances.
   b.   Letters of representations corroborating inventory pricing.
   c.   Attorneys' responses to the auditor's inquiries.
   d.   Client records documenting the use of computer programs.

**38.** Which of the following is **not** a step in an auditor's decision to assess control risk at below the maximum?
   a.   Evaluate the effectiveness of internal control with tests of controls.
   b.   Obtain an understanding of the entity's information system and control environment.
   c.   Perform tests of details of transactions to detect material misstatements in the financial statements.

d. Consider whether controls can have a pervasive effect on financial statement assertions.

**39.** To obtain evidential matter about control risk, an auditor selects tests from a variety of techniques including
   a. Inquiry.
   b. Analytical procedures.
   c. Calculation.
   d. Confirmation.

**40.** Which of the following is **least** likely to be evidence the auditor examines to determine whether controls are operating effectively?
   a. Records documenting usage of computer programs.
   b. Canceled supporting documents.
   c. Confirmations of accounts receivable.
   d. Signatures on authorization forms.

**41.** Which of the following procedures concerning accounts receivable would an auditor most likely perform to obtain evidential matter in support of an assessed level of control risk below the maximum level?
   a. Observing an entity's employee prepare the schedule of past due accounts receivable.
   b. Sending confirmation requests to an entity's principal customers to verify the existence of accounts receivable.
   c. Inspecting an entity's analysis of accounts receivable for unusual balances.
   d. Comparing an entity's uncollectible accounts expense to actual uncollectible accounts receivable.

**42.** The internal control provisions of the Sarbanes-Oxley Act of 2002 apply to which companies in the United States?
   a. All companies.
   b. SEC registrants.
   c. All public companies and nonpublic companies with more than $100,000,000 of net worth.
   d. All nonpublic companies.

**43.** The framework most likely to be used by management in its internal control assessment under requirements of the Sarbanes-Oxley Act of 2002 is the
   a. COSO internal framework.
   b. COSO enterprise risk management framework.
   c. FASB 37 internal control definitional framework.
   d. AICPA internal control analysis manager.

**44.** Which of the following is correct concerning the level of assistance auditors may provide in assisting management with its assessment of internal control?
   a. No assistance of any type may be provided.
   b. No limitations on assistance exist.
   c. Only very limited assistance may be provided.
   d. As less risk is assumed by the auditors, a higher level of assistance is appropriate.

**45.** Which of the following need **not** be included in management's report on internal control under Section 404a of the Sarbanes-Oxley Act of 2002?
   a. A statement that the company's auditor has issued an attestation report on management's assertion.
   b. Identification of the framework for evaluating internal control.
   c. Management's assessment of the effectiveness of internal control.

d. Management's statement of responsibility to establish and maintain internal control that has no significant deficiencies.

**46.** In an integrated audit, which of the following is defined as a weakness in internal control that allows more than a remote likelihood of misstatement that is more than inconsequential, but less than material?
   a. Control deficiency.
   b. Material weakness.
   c. Reportable condition.
   d. Significant deficiency.

**47.** A material weakness is a significant deficiency (or combination of significant deficiencies) that results in more than a remote likelihood that a misstatement of at least what amount will not be prevented or detected?
   a. An amount greater than zero.
   b. An amount greater than zero, but at least inconsequential.
   c. An amount greater than inconsequential.
   d. A material amount.

**48.** The minimum likelihood of loss involved in the consideration of a control deficiency is
   a. Remote.
   b. More than remote.
   c. Probable.
   d. Not explicitly considered.

**49.** Assume that a company has a control deficiency regarding the processing of cash receipts. Reconciliation of cash accounts by a competent individual otherwise independent of the cash function might make the likelihood of a significant misstatement due to the control deficiency remote. In this situation, reconciliation may be referred to as what type of control?
   a. Compensating.
   b. Preventive.
   c. Adjustive.
   d. Nonroutine.

**50.** According to Public Company Accounting Oversight Board Standard 2, what type of transaction involves establishing a loan loss reserve?
   a. Substantive transaction.
   b. Routine transaction.
   c. Nonroutine transaction.
   d. Estimation transaction.

**51.** A procedure that involves tracing a transaction from its origination through the company's information systems until it is reflected in the company's financial report is referred to as a(n)
   a. Analytical analysis.
   b. Substantive procedure.
   c. Test of a control.
   d. Walkthrough.

**52.** For purposes of an audit of internal control performed under Public Company Accounting Oversight Board standards, the "as of date" is ordinarily
   a. The first day of the year.
   b. The last day of the fiscal period.
   c. The last day of the auditor's fieldwork.
   d. The average date for the entire fiscal period.

**53.** Consider a public company whose purchases are made through the Internet and by telephone. Which of the following is correct?

    a.   These types of purchases represent control objectives for the audit of internal control.

    b.   These purchases are the assertions related to the purchase class of transactions.

    c.   These types of purchases represent two major classes of transactions within the purchases process.

    d.   These two types of transactions represent routine transactions that must always be investigated in extreme detail.

**54.** For a public company audit of internal control, walk-throughs provide the auditor with *primary evidence* to

| | Evaluate the effectiveness of the design of controls | Confirm whether controls have been placed in operation |
|---|---|---|
| a. | Yes | Yes |
| b. | Yes | No |
| c. | No | Yes |
| d. | No | No |

**55.** Which is **most** likely to be a question asked of employee personnel during a walk-through in an audit of the internal control of a public company?

    a.   Have you ever been asked to override the process?

    b.   Do you believe that you are underpaid?

    c.   What do you do when you find a fraudulent transaction?

    d.   Who trained you for this job?

**56.** How large must the *actual loss identified by the auditor* be for a control deficiency to possibly be considered a material weakness?

| | Immaterial | Material |
|---|---|---|
| a. | Yes | Yes |
| b. | Yes | No |
| c. | No | Yes |
| d. | No | No |

**57.** For purposes of an audit of internal control performed under Public Company Accounting Oversight Board requirements, an account is significant if there is more than a

    a.   Reasonably possible likelihood that it could contain immaterial or material misstatements.

    b.   Reasonably possible likelihood that it could contain material misstatements.

    c.   Remote likelihood that it could contain material misstatements.

    d.   Remote likelihood that it could contain more than inconsequential misstatements.

**58.** A control deficiency that is more than a significant deficiency is most likely to result in what form of audit opinion relating to internal control?

    a.   Adverse.

    b.   Qualified.

    c.   Unqualified.

    d.   Unqualified with explanatory language.

**59.** Which of the following is most likely to be considered a material weakness in internal control for purposes of an internal control audit of a public company?

    a.   An ineffective internal audit function.

    b.   Restatement of previously issued financial statements due to a change in accounting principles.

    c.   Inadequate segregation of recordkeeping from accounting.

    d.   Weaknesses in control activities.

**60.** Inability to evaluate internal control due to a circumstance-caused scope limitation relating to a significant account in a Sarbanes-Oxley 404 internal control audit is most likely to result in a(n)

    a.   Adverse opinion.

    b.   Qualified opinion.

    c.   Unqualified opinion with explanatory language.

    d.   All of the above are equally likely.

**61.** Which of the following is most likely to indicate a significant deficiency relating to a client's antifraud programs?

    a.   A broad scope of internal audit activities.

    b.   A "whistleblower" program that encourages anonymous submissions.

    c.   Audit committee passivity when conducting oversight functions.

    d.   Lack of performance of criminal background investigations for likely customers.

**62.** An auditor identified a material weakness in December. The client was informed and corrected it shortly after the "as of date" (December 31); the auditor agrees that the correction eliminates the material weakness as of January 31. The appropriate report under a PCAOB Standard 2 audit of internal control is

    a.   Adverse.

    b.   Unqualified.

    c.   Unqualified with explanatory language relating to the material weakness.

    d.   Qualified.

**63.** In an integrated audit, which of the following lead(s) to an adverse opinion on internal control?

| | Material weaknesses | Significant deficiencies |
|---|---|---|
| a. | Yes | Yes |
| b. | Yes | No |
| c. | No | Yes |
| d. | No | No |

**64.** In an integrated audit, what must the auditor communicate to the audit committee?

| | Known material weaknesses | All control deficiencies |
|---|---|---|
| a. | Yes | Yes |
| b. | Yes | No |
| c. | No | Yes |
| d. | No | No |

**65.** In which manner are significant deficiencies communicated by the auditors to the audit committee under Public Company Accounting Oversight Board Standard 2?

    a.   The communication may either be orally or in written form.

    b.   The communication must be oral, and not in written form.

    c.   The communication must be in written form.

    d.   No such communication is required as only material weaknesses must be communicated.

**66.** The existence of a material weakness resulted in an auditor's issuance of an adverse opinion as the result of an audit of a public company's internal control over financial reporting. Six months later the client believes that the material weakness has been remediated. Which of the following is **not** a correct statement relating to an auditor who is engaged to report on whether the previously reported material weakness continues to exist?

    a.  Management must present a written report to accompany the auditor's report on the material weakness.

    b.  If the auditor finds that the material weakness has been remediated, the auditor should withdraw the original report on internal control and replace it with an unqualified report.

    c.  The auditor may rely in part on work performed by internal auditors in arriving at a conclusion relating to the material weakness.

    d.  For the auditor to perform such an engagement, it is necessary that management provide documented support that the material weakness no longer exists.

**67.** Which of the following is correct when an auditor is engaged to report on whether a previously reported material weakness disclosed in an integrated audit continues to exist?

    a.  The auditor may issue a qualified opinion.

    b.  The auditor may decide not to issue a report.

    c.  The auditor's report must include a disclaimer of opinion.

    d.  The auditor may only issue an unqualified report if management's written assertion includes a statement that the material weakness continues to exist.

**68.** Which auditor actions are possible when that auditor incurs a scope limitation relating to a public company engagement on whether a previously reported material weakness continues to exist?

| | Withdrawal from the engagement | Qualified opinion |
|---|---|---|
| a. | Yes | Yes |
| b. | Yes | No |
| c. | No | Yes |
| d. | No | No |

**69.** An auditor is engaged to report on whether a previously reported material weakness disclosed in an integrated audit continues to exist. During the process, the auditor has discovered another material weakness that was not identified in the audit of internal control. The auditor's report on whether the material weakness continues to exist should indicate that the reported-upon material weakness no longer exists and should

    a.  Be qualified for the newly discovered material weakness.

    b.  Disclaim an opinion on the newly discovered material weakness.

    c.  Provide an adverse opinion on the newly discovered material weakness.

    d.  Not refer to the newly discovered material weakness.

**70.** Which of the following procedures would an auditor most likely perform to test controls relating to management's assertion about the completeness of cash receipts for cash sales at a retail outlet?

    a.  Observe the consistency of the employees' use of cash registers and tapes.

    b.  Inquire about employees' access to recorded but undeposited cash.

    c.  Trace deposits in the cash receipts journal to the cash balance in the general ledger.

    d.  Compare the cash balance in the general ledger with the bank confirmation request.

**71.** Sound internal control dictates that immediately upon receiving checks from customers by mail, a responsible employee should

    a.  Add the checks to the daily cash summary.

    b.  Verify that each check is supported by a prenumbered sales invoice.

    c.  Prepare a duplicate listing of checks received.

    d.  Record the checks in the cash receipts journal.

**72.** Tracing shipping documents to prenumbered sales invoices provides evidence that

    a.  No duplicate shipments or billings occurred.

    b.  Shipments to customers were properly invoiced.

    c.  All goods ordered by customers were shipped.

    d.  All prenumbered sales invoices were accounted for.

**73.** Which of the following controls most likely would reduce the risk of diversion of customer receipts by an entity's employees?

    a.  A bank lockbox system.

    b.  Prenumbered remittance advices.

    c.  Monthly bank reconciliations.

    d.  Daily deposit of cash receipts.

**74.** An auditor suspects that a client's cashier is misappropriating cash receipts for personal use by lapping customer checks received in the mail. In attempting to uncover this embezzlement scheme, the auditor most likely would compare the

    a.  Dates checks are deposited per bank statements with the dates remittance credits are recorded.

    b.  Daily cash summaries with the sums of the cash receipts journal entries.

    c.  Individual bank deposit slips with the details of the monthly bank statements.

    d.  Dates uncollectible accounts are authorized to be written off with the dates the write-offs are actually recorded.

**75.** Upon receipt of customers' checks in the mailroom, a responsible employee should prepare a remittance listing that is forwarded to the cashier. A copy of the listing should be sent to the

    a.  Internal auditor to investigate the listing for unusual transactions.

    b.  Treasurer to compare the listing with the monthly bank statement.

    c.  Accounts receivable bookkeeper to update the subsidiary accounts receivable records.

    d.  Entity's bank to compare the listing with the cashier's deposit slip.

**76.** Which of the following procedures most likely would **not** be a control designed to reduce the risk of misstatements in the billing process?

    a.  Comparing control totals for shipping documents with corresponding totals for sales invoices.

b. Using computer programmed controls on the pricing and mathematical accuracy of sales invoices.

c. Matching shipping documents with approved sales orders before invoice preparation.

d. Reconciling the control totals for sales invoices with the accounts receivable subsidiary ledger.

**77.** Which of the following audit procedures would an auditor most likely perform to test controls relating to management's assertion concerning the completeness of sales transactions?

a. Verify that extensions and footings on the entity's sales invoices and monthly customer statements have been recomputed.

b. Inspect the entity's reports of prenumbered shipping documents that have **not** been recorded in the sales journal.

c. Compare the invoiced prices on prenumbered sales invoices to the entity's authorized price list.

d. Inquire about the entity's credit granting policies and the consistent application of credit checks.

**78.** Which of the following controls most likely would assure that all billed sales are correctly posted to the accounts receivable ledger?

a. Daily sales summaries are compared to daily postings to the accounts receivable ledger.

b. Each sales invoice is supported by a prenumbered shipping document.

c. The accounts receivable ledger is reconciled daily to the control account in the general ledger.

d. Each shipment on credit is supported by a prenumbered sales invoice.

**79.** An auditor tests an entity's policy of obtaining credit approval before shipping goods to customers in support of management's financial statement assertion of

a. Valuation or allocation.

b. Completeness.

c. Existence or occurrence.

d. Rights and obligations.

**80.** Which of the following controls most likely would help ensure that all credit sales transactions of an entity are recorded?

a. The billing department supervisor sends copies of approved sales orders to the credit department for comparison to authorized credit limits and current customer account balances.

b. The accounting department supervisor independently reconciles the accounts receivable subsidiary ledger to the accounts receivable control account monthly.

c. The accounting department supervisor controls the mailing of monthly statements to customers and investigates any differences reported by customers.

d. The billing department supervisor matches prenumbered shipping documents with entries in the sales journal.

**81.** Which of the following controls most likely would be effective in offsetting the tendency of sales personnel to maximize sales volume at the expense of high bad debt write-offs?

a. Employees responsible for authorizing sales and bad debt write-offs are denied access to cash.

b. Shipping documents and sales invoices are matched by an employee who does not have authority to write off bad debts.

c. Employees involved in the credit-granting function are separated from the sales function.

d. Subsidiary accounts receivable records are reconciled to the control account by an employee independent of the authorization of credit.

**82.** Proper authorization of write-offs of uncollectible accounts should be approved in which of the following departments?

a. Accounts receivable.

b. Credit.

c. Accounts payable.

d. Treasurer.

**83.** Employers bond employees who handle cash receipts because fidelity bonds reduce the possibility of employing dishonest individuals and

a. Protect employees who make unintentional misstatements from possible monetary damages resulting from their misstatements.

b. Deter dishonesty by making employees aware that insurance companies may investigate and prosecute dishonest acts.

c. Facilitate an independent monitoring of the receiving and depositing of cash receipts.

d. Force employees in positions of trust to take periodic vacations and rotate their assigned duties.

**84.** During the consideration of a small business client's internal control, the auditor discovered that the accounts receivable clerk approves credit memos and has access to cash. Which of the following controls would be most effective in offsetting this weakness?

a. The owner reviews errors in billings to customers and postings to the subsidiary ledger.

b. The controller receives the monthly bank statement directly and reconciles the checking accounts.

c. The owner reviews credit memos after they are recorded.

d. The controller reconciles the total of the detail accounts receivable accounts to the amount shown in the ledger.

**85.** When a customer fails to include a remittance advice with a payment, it is common practice for the person opening the mail to prepare one. Consequently, mail should be opened by which of the following four company employees?

a. Credit manager.

b. Receptionist.

c. Sales manager.

d. Accounts receivable clerk.

**86.** To provide assurance that each voucher is submitted and paid only once, an auditor most likely would examine a sample of paid vouchers and determine whether each voucher is

a. Supported by a vendor's invoice.

b. Stamped "paid" by the check signer.

c. Prenumbered and accounted for.

d. Approved for authorized purchases.

**87.** In testing controls over cash disbursements, an auditor most likely would determine that the person who signs checks also
  a. Reviews the monthly bank reconciliation.
  b. Returns the checks to accounts payable.
  c. Is denied access to the supporting documents.
  d. Is responsible for mailing the checks.

**88.** In assessing control risk for purchases, an auditor vouches a sample of entries in the voucher register to the supporting documents. Which assertion would this test of controls most likely support?
  a. Completeness.
  b. Existence or occurrence.
  c. Valuation or allocation.
  d. Rights and obligations.

**89.** Which of the following controls is **not** usually performed in the vouchers payable department?
  a. Matching the vendor's invoice with the related receiving report.
  b. Approving vouchers for payment by having an authorized employee sign the vouchers.
  c. Indicating the asset and expense accounts to be debited.
  d. Accounting for unused prenumbered purchase orders and receiving reports.

**90.** With properly designed internal control, the same employee most likely would match vendors' invoices with receiving reports and also
  a. Post the detailed accounts payable records.
  b. Recompute the calculations on vendors' invoices.
  c. Reconcile the accounts payable ledger.
  d. Cancel vendors' invoices after payment.

**91.** An entity's internal control requires for every check request that there be an approved voucher, supported by a prenumbered purchase order and a prenumbered receiving report. To determine whether checks are being issued for unauthorized expenditures, an auditor most likely would select items for testing from the population of all
  a. Purchase orders.
  b. Canceled checks.
  c. Receiving reports.
  d. Approved vouchers.

**92.** Which of the following questions would most likely be included in an internal control questionnaire concerning the completeness assertion for purchases?
  a. Is an authorized purchase order required before the receiving department can accept a shipment or the vouchers payable department can record a voucher?
  b. Are purchase requisitions prenumbered and independently matched with vendor invoices?
  c. Is the unpaid voucher file periodically reconciled with inventory records by an employee who does not have access to purchase requisitions?
  d. Are purchase orders, receiving reports, and vouchers prenumbered and periodically accounted for?

**93.** For effective internal control, the accounts payable department generally should
  a. Stamp, perforate, or otherwise cancel supporting documentation after payment is mailed.

  b. Ascertain that each requisition is approved as to price, quantity, and quality by an authorized employee.
  c. Obliterate the quantity ordered on the receiving department copy of the purchase order.
  d. Establish the agreement of the vendor's invoice with the receiving report and purchase order.

**94.** Internal control is strengthened when the quantity of merchandise ordered is omitted from the copy of the purchase order sent to the
  a. Department that initiated the requisition.
  b. Receiving department.
  c. Purchasing agent.
  d. Accounts payable department.

**95.** A client erroneously recorded a large purchase twice. Which of the following internal control measures would be most likely to detect this error in a timely and efficient manner?
  a. Footing the purchases journal.
  b. Reconciling vendors' monthly statements with subsidiary payable ledger accounts.
  c. Tracing totals from the purchases journal to the ledger accounts.
  d. Sending written quarterly confirmations to all vendors.

**96.** With well-designed internal control, employees in the same department most likely would approve purchase orders, and also
  a. Reconcile the open invoice file.
  b. Inspect goods upon receipt.
  c. Authorize requisitions of goods.
  d. Negotiate terms with vendors.

**97.** In obtaining an understanding of a manufacturing entity's internal control over inventory balances, an auditor most likely would
  a. Analyze the liquidity and turnover ratios of the inventory.
  b. Perform analytical procedures designed to identify cost variances.
  c. Review the entity's descriptions of inventory policies and procedures.
  d. Perform test counts of inventory during the entity's physical count.

**98.** Which of the following controls most likely would be used to maintain accurate inventory records?
  a. Perpetual inventory records are periodically compared with the current cost of individual inventory items.
  b. A just-in-time inventory ordering system keeps inventory levels to a desired minimum.
  c. Requisitions, receiving reports, and purchase orders are independently matched before payment is approved.
  d. Periodic inventory counts are used to adjust the perpetual inventory records.

**99.** A client maintains perpetual inventory records in both quantities and dollars. If the assessed level of control risk is high, an auditor would probably
  a. Insist that the client perform physical counts of inventory items several times during the year.

b.  Apply gross profit tests to ascertain the reasonableness of the physical counts.

c.  Increase the extent of tests of controls of the inventory cycle.

d.  Request the client to schedule the physical inventory count at the end of the year.

**100.** Which of the following controls most likely addresses the completeness assertion for inventory?

a.  Work in process account is periodically reconciled with subsidiary records.

b.  Employees responsible for custody of finished goods do **not** perform the receiving function.

c.  Receiving reports are prenumbered and periodically reconciled.

d.  There is a separation of duties between payroll department and inventory accounting personnel.

**101.** Sound internal control dictates that defective merchandise returned by customers should be presented initially to the

a.  Salesclerk.
b.  Purchasing clerk.
c.  Receiving clerk.
d.  Inventory control clerk.

**102.** Alpha Company uses its sales invoices for posting perpetual inventory records. Inadequate controls over the invoicing function allow goods to be shipped that are not invoiced. The inadequate controls could cause an

a.  Understatement of revenues, receivables, and inventory.

b.  Overstatement of revenues and receivables, and an understatement of inventory.

c.  Understatement of revenues and receivables, and an overstatement of inventory.

d.  Overstatement of revenues, receivables, and inventory.

**103.** Which of the following is a question that the auditor would expect to find on the production cycle section of an internal control questionnaire?

a.  Are vendors' invoices for raw materials approved for payment by an employee who is independent of the cash disbursements function?

b.  Are signed checks for the purchase of raw materials mailed directly after signing without being returned to the person who authorized the invoice processing?

c.  Are all releases by storekeepers of raw materials from storage based on approved requisition documents?

d.  Are details of individual disbursements for raw materials balanced with the total to be posted to the appropriate general ledger account?

**104.** The objectives of internal control for a production cycle are to provide assurance that transactions are properly executed and recorded, and that

a.  Production orders are prenumbered and signed by a supervisor.

b.  Custody of work in process and of finished goods is properly maintained.

c.  Independent internal verification of activity reports is established.

d.  Transfers to finished goods are documented by a completed production report and a quality control report.

**105.** An auditor vouched data for a sample of employees in a payroll register to approved clock card data to provide assurance that

a.  Payments to employees are computed at authorized rates.

b.  Employees work the number of hours for which they are paid.

c.  Segregation of duties exist between the preparation and distribution of the payroll.

d.  Controls relating to unclaimed payroll checks are operating effectively.

**106.** Which of the following is a control that most likely could help prevent employee payroll fraud?

a.  The personnel department promptly sends employee termination notices to the payroll supervisor.

b.  Employees who distribute payroll checks forward unclaimed payroll checks to the absent employees' supervisors.

c.  Salary rates resulting from new hires are approved by the payroll supervisor.

d.  Total hours used for determination of gross pay are calculated by the payroll supervisor.

**107.** In determining the effectiveness of an entity's controls relating to the existence or occurrence assertion for payroll transactions, an auditor most likely would inquire about and

a.  Observe the segregation of duties concerning personnel responsibilities and payroll disbursement.

b.  Inspect evidence of accounting for prenumbered payroll checks.

c.  Recompute the payroll deductions for employee fringe benefits.

d.  Verify the preparation of the monthly payroll account bank reconciliation.

**108.** An auditor most likely would assess control risk at the maximum if the payroll department supervisor is responsible for

a.  Examining authorization forms for new employees.

b.  Comparing payroll registers with original batch transmittal data.

c.  Authorizing payroll rate changes for all employees.

d.  Hiring all subordinate payroll department employees.

**109.** Which of the following controls most likely would prevent direct labor hours from being charged to manufacturing overhead?

a.  Periodic independent counts of work in process for comparison to recorded amounts.

b.  Comparison of daily journal entries with approved production orders.

c.  Use of time tickets to record actual labor worked on production orders.

d.  Reconciliation of work-in-process inventory with periodic cost budgets.

**110.** In meeting the control objective of safeguarding of assets, which department should be responsible for

|  | *Distribution of paychecks* | *Custody of unclaimed paychecks* |
|---|---|---|
| a. | Treasurer | Treasurer |
| b. | Payroll | Treasurer |
| c. | Treasurer | Payroll |
| d. | Payroll | Payroll |

**111.** Proper internal control over the cash payroll function would mandate which of the following?
- a. The payroll clerk should fill the envelopes with cash and a computation of the net wages.
- b. Unclaimed pay envelopes should be retained by the paymaster.
- c. Each employee should be asked to sign a receipt.
- d. A separate checking account for payroll be maintained.

**112.** The purpose of segregating the duties of hiring personnel and distributing payroll checks is to separate the
- a. Authorization of transactions from the custody of related assets.
- b. Operational responsibility from the recordkeeping responsibility.
- c. Human resources function from the controllership function.
- d. Administrative controls from the internal accounting controls.

**113.** To minimize the opportunities for fraud, unclaimed cash payroll should be
- a. Deposited in a safe-deposit box.
- b. Held by the payroll custodian.
- c. Deposited in a special bank account.
- d. Held by the controller.

**114.** The auditor may observe the distribution of paychecks to ascertain whether
- a. Pay rate authorization is properly separated from the operating function.
- b. Deductions from gross pay are calculated correctly and are properly authorized.
- c. Employees of record actually exist and are employed by the client.
- d. Paychecks agree with the payroll register and the time cards.

**115.** Which of the following departments most likely would approve changes in pay rates and deductions from employee salaries?
- a. Personnel.
- b. Treasurer.
- c. Controller.
- d. Payroll.

**116.** Which of the following questions would an auditor most likely include on an internal control questionnaire for notes payable?
- a. Are assets that collateralize notes payable critically needed for the entity's continued existence?
- b. Are two or more authorized signatures required on checks that repay notes payable?
- c. Are the proceeds from notes payable used for the purchase of noncurrent assets?
- d. Are direct borrowings on notes payable authorized by the board of directors?

**117.** The primary responsibility of a bank acting as registrar of capital stock is to
- a. Ascertain that dividends declared do **not** exceed the statutory amount allowable in the state of incorporation.
- b. Account for stock certificates by comparing the total shares outstanding to the total in the shareholders subsidiary ledger.
- c. Act as an independent third party between the board of directors and outside investors concerning mergers, acquisitions, and the sale of treasury stock.
- d. Verify that stock is issued in accordance with the authorization of the board of directors and the articles of incorporation.

**118.** Where no independent stock transfer agents are employed and the corporation issues its own stocks and maintains stock records, canceled stock certificates should
- a. Be defaced to prevent reissuance and attached to their corresponding stubs.
- b. Not be defaced but segregated from other stock certificates and retained in a canceled certificates file.
- c. Be destroyed to prevent fraudulent reissuance.
- d. Be defaced and sent to the secretary of state.

**119.** Which of the following is **not** a control that is designed to protect investment securities?
- a. Custody over securities should be limited to individuals who have recordkeeping responsibility over the securities.
- b. Securities should be properly controlled physically in order to prevent unauthorized usage.
- c. Access to securities should be vested in more than one individual.
- d. Securities should be registered in the name of the owner.

**120.** Which of the following controls would a company most likely use to safeguard marketable securities when an independent trust agent is **not** employed?
- a. The investment committee of the board of directors periodically reviews the investment decisions delegated to the treasurer.
- b. Two company officials have joint control of marketable securities, which are kept in a bank safe-deposit box.
- c. The internal auditor and the controller independently trace all purchases and sales of marketable securities from the subsidiary ledgers to the general ledger.
- d. The chairman of the board verifies the marketable securities, which are kept in a bank safe-deposit box, each year on the balance sheet date.

**121.** A weakness in internal control over recording retirements of equipment may cause an auditor to
- a. Inspect certain items of equipment in the plant and trace those items to the accounting records.
- b. Review the subsidiary ledger to ascertain whether depreciation was taken on each item of equipment during the year.

c.   Trace additions to the "other assets" account to search for equipment that is still on hand but **no** longer being used.

d.   Select certain items of equipment from the accounting records and locate them in the plant.

**122.**   Which of the following questions would an auditor **least** likely include on an internal control questionnaire concerning the initiation and execution of equipment transactions?

a.   Are requests for major repairs approved at a higher level than the department initiating the request?

b.   Are prenumbered purchase orders used for equipment and periodically accounted for?

c.   Are requests for purchases of equipment reviewed for consideration of soliciting competitive bids?

d.   Are procedures in place to monitor and properly restrict access to equipment?

**123.**   Which of the following controls would be most effective in assuring that the proper custody of assets in the investing cycle is maintained?

a.   Direct access to securities in the safe-deposit box is limited to only one corporate officer.

b.   Personnel who post investment transactions to the general ledger are **not** permitted to update the investment subsidiary ledger.

c.   The purchase and sale of investments are executed on the specific authorization of the board of directors.

d.   The recorded balances in the investment subsidiary ledger are periodically compared with the contents of the safe-deposit box by independent personnel.

**124.**   A company holds bearer bonds as a short-term investment. Responsibility for custody of these bonds and submission of coupons for periodic interest collections probably should be delegated to the

a.   Chief Accountant.

b.   Internal Auditor.

c.   Cashier.

d.   Treasurer.

**125.**   Which of the following controls would an entity most likely use to assist in satisfying the completeness assertion related to long-term investments?

a.   Senior management verifies that securities in the bank safe-deposit box are registered in the entity's name.

b.   The internal auditor compares the securities in the bank safe-deposit box with recorded investments.

c.   The treasurer vouches the acquisition of securities by comparing brokers' advices with canceled checks.

d.   The controller compares the current market prices of recorded investments with the brokers' advices on file.

**126.**   Which of the following controls would an entity most likely use in safeguarding against the loss of marketable securities?

a.   An independent trust company that has no direct contact with the employees who have recordkeeping responsibilities has possession of the securities.

b.   The internal auditor verifies the marketable securities in the entity's safe each year on the balance sheet date.

c.   The independent auditor traces all purchases and sales of marketable securities through the subsidiary ledgers to the general ledger.

d.   A designated member of the board of directors controls the securities in a bank safe-deposit box.

**127.**   When there are numerous property and equipment transactions during the year, an auditor who plans to assess control risk at a low level usually performs

a.   Tests of controls and extensive tests of property and equipment balances at the end of the year.

b.   Analytical procedures for current year property and equipment transactions.

c.   Tests of controls and limited tests of current year property and equipment transactions.

d.   Analytical procedures for property and equipment balances at the end of the year.

**128.**   In general, material fraud perpetrated by which of the following are most difficult to detect?

a.   Cashier.

b.   Keypunch operator.

c.   Internal auditor.

d.   Controller.

**129.**   Which of the following matters would an auditor most likely consider to be a reportable condition to be communicated to the audit committee?

a.   Management's failure to renegotiate unfavorable long-term purchase commitments.

b.   Recurring operating losses that may indicate going concern problems.

c.   Evidence of a lack of objectivity by those responsible for accounting decisions.

d.   Management's current plans to reduce its ownership equity in the entity.

**130.**   In identifying matters for communication with an entity's audit committee, an auditor most likely would ask management whether

a.   The turnover in the accounting department was unusually high.

b.   It consulted with another CPA firm about accounting matters.

c.   There were any subsequent events of which the auditor was unaware.

d.   It agreed with the auditor's assessed level of control risk.

**131.**   Which of the following statements is correct concerning reportable conditions in an audit?

a.   An auditor is required to search for reportable conditions during an audit.

b.   All reportable conditions are also considered to be material weaknesses.

c.   An auditor may communicate reportable conditions during an audit or after the audit's completion.

d.   An auditor may report that **no** reportable conditions were noted during an audit.

**132.**   Which of the following statements is correct concerning an auditor's required communication with an entity's audit committee?

a. This communication is required to occur before the auditor's report on the financial statements is issued.

b. This communication should include discussion of any significant disagreements with management concerning the financial statements.

c. Any significant matter communicated to the audit committee also should be communicated to management.

d. Significant audit adjustments proposed by the auditor and recorded by management need **not** be communicated to the audit committee.

**133.** An auditor's letter issued on reportable conditions relating to an entity's internal control observed during a financial statement audit should

a. Include a brief description of the tests of controls performed in searching for reportable conditions and material weaknesses.

b. Indicate that the reportable conditions should be disclosed in the annual report to the entity's shareholders.

c. Include a paragraph describing management's assertion concerning the effectiveness of internal control.

d. Indicate that the audit's purpose was to report on the financial statements and **not** to provide assurance on internal control.

**134.** An auditor would **least** likely initiate a discussion with a client's audit committee concerning

a. The methods used to account for significant unusual transactions.

b. The maximum dollar amount of misstatements that could exist without causing the financial statements to be materially misstated.

c. Indications of fraud and illegal acts committed by a corporate officer that were discovered by the auditor.

d. Disagreements with management as to accounting principles that were resolved during the current year's audit.

**135.** Which of the following statements is correct about an auditor's required communication with an entity's audit committee?

a. Any matters communicated to the entity's audit committee also are required to be communicated to the entity's management.

b. The auditor is required to inform the entity's audit committee about significant misstatements discovered by the auditor and subsequently corrected by management.

c. Disagreements with management about the application of accounting principles are required to be communicated in writing to the entity's audit committee.

d. Weaknesses in internal control previously reported to the entity's audit committee are required to be communicated to the audit committee after each subsequent audit until the weaknesses are corrected.

**136.** Which of the following statements is correct concerning an auditor's required communication of reportable conditions?

a. A reportable condition previously communicated during the prior year's audit that remains uncorrected causes a scope limitation.

b. An auditor should perform tests of controls on reportable conditions before communicating them to the client.

c. An auditor's report on reportable conditions should include a restriction on the distribution of the report.

d. An auditor should communicate reportable conditions after tests of controls, but before commencing substantive tests.

**137.** Which of the following statements is correct concerning reportable conditions noted in an audit?

a. Reportable conditions are material weaknesses in the design or operation of specific internal control components.

b. The auditor is obligated to search for reportable conditions that could adversely affect the entity's ability to record and report financial data.

c. Reportable conditions should be recommunicated each year, even if management has acknowledged its understanding of such deficiencies.

d. The auditor may separately communicate those reportable conditions considered to be material weaknesses.

**138.** Which of the following representations should **not** be included in a report on internal control related matters noted in an audit?

a. Reportable conditions related to internal control design exist, but none are deemed to be a material weakness.

b. There are no significant deficiencies in the design or operation of internal control.

c. Corrective follow-up action is recommended due to the relative significance of material weaknesses discovered during the audit.

d. The auditor's consideration of internal control would not necessarily disclose all reportable conditions that exist.

**139.** Which of the following matters is an auditor required to communicate to an entity's audit committee?

I. Disagreements with management about matters significant to the entity's financial statements that have been satisfactorily resolved.

II. Initial selection of significant accounting policies in emerging areas that lack authoritative guidance.

a. I only.
b. II only.
c. Both I and II.
d. Neither I nor II.

**140.** Should an auditor communicate the following matters to an audit committee of a public entity?

| | *Significant audit adjustments recorded by the entity* | *Management's consultation with other accountants about significant accounting matters* |
|---|---|---|
| a. | Yes | Yes |
| b. | Yes | No |
| c. | No | Yes |
| d. | No | No |

**141.** A previously communicated reportable condition that has not been corrected should ordinarily be communicated again if

    a.   The deficiency has a material effect on the auditor's assessment of control risk.

    b.   The entity accepts that degree of risk because of cost-benefit considerations.

    c.   The weakness could adversely affect the entity's ability to report financial data.

    d.   There has been major turnover in upper-level management and the board of directors.

**142.** Which of the following statements concerning material weaknesses and reportable conditions is correct?

    a.   An auditor should identify and communicate material weaknesses separately from reportable conditions.

    b.   All material weaknesses are reportable conditions.

    c.   An auditor should report immediately material weaknesses and reportable conditions discovered during an audit.

    d.   All reportable conditions are material weaknesses.

**143.** Reportable conditions are matters that come to an auditor's attention that should be communicated to an entity's audit committee because they represent

    a.   Disclosures of information that significantly contradict the auditor's going concern assumption.

    b.   Material fraud or illegal acts perpetrated by high-level management.

    c.   Significant deficiencies in the design or operation of internal control.

    d.   Manipulation or falsification of accounting records or documents from which financial statements are prepared.

**144.** During the audit the independent auditor identified the existence of a weakness in the client's internal control and orally communicated this finding to the client's senior management and audit committee. The auditor should

    a.   Consider the weakness a scope limitation and therefore disclaim an opinion.

    b.   Document the matter in the working papers and consider the effects of the condition on the audit.

    c.   Suspend all audit activities pending directions from the client's audit committee.

    d.   Withdraw from the engagement.

**145.** In reporting on an entity's internal control over financial reporting, a practitioner should include a paragraph that describes the

    a.   Documentary evidence regarding the control environment factors.

    b.   Changes in internal control since the prior report.

    c.   Potential benefits from the practitioner's suggested improvements.

    d.   Inherent limitations of any internal control.

**146.** Brown, CPA, has accepted an engagement to examine and report on Crow Company's internal control. In what form may Crow present its written assertion?

  I. In a separate report that will accompany Brown's report.

  II. In a representation letter to Brown.

    a.   I only.

    b.   II only.

    c.   Either I or II.

    d.   Neither I nor II.

**147.** Which of the following best describes a CPA's engagement to report on an entity's internal control over financial reporting?

    a.   An attestation engagement to examine and report on the reliability of the effectiveness of its internal control.

    b.   An audit engagement to provide negative assurance on the entity's internal control.

    c.   A prospective engagement to project, for a period of time **not** to exceed one year, and report on the expected benefits of the entity's internal control.

    d.   A consulting engagement to provide constructive advice to the entity on its internal control.

**148.** An engagement to examine internal control will generally

    a.   Require procedures that duplicate those already applied in assessing control risk during a financial statement audit.

    b.   Increase the reliability of the financial statements that have already been audited.

    c.   Be more extensive in scope than the assessment of control risk made during a financial statement audit.

    d.   Be more limited in scope than the assessment of control risk made during a financial statement audit.

**149.** How do the scope, procedures, and purpose of an examination of internal control compare to those for obtaining an understanding of internal control and assessing control risk as part of an audit?

|   | Scope | Procedures | Purpose |
|---|-------|-----------|---------|
| a. | Similar | Different | Similar |
| b. | Different | Similar | Similar |
| c. | Different | Different | Different |
| d. | Different | Similar | Different |

**150.** When an independent auditor reports on internal control based on criteria established by governmental agencies, the report should

    a.   Not include the agency's name in the report.

    b.   Indicate matters covered by the study and whether the auditor's study included tests of controls with the procedures covered by the study.

    c.   Not express a conclusion based on the agency's criteria.

    d.   Assume responsibility for the comprehensiveness of the criteria established by the agency and include recommendations for corrective action.

**151.** When an examination has been performed on the effectiveness of entity's internal control over financial reporting and a material weakness has been noted, the practitioner's report should express an opinion on

    a.   The assertion.

    b.   The subject matter to which the assertion relates.

    c.   Neither of the above.

    d.   Both of the above.

**152.** In assessing the competence of an internal auditor, an independent CPA most likely would obtain information about the

a. Quality of the internal auditor's working paper documentation.

b. Organization's commitment to integrity and ethical values.

c. Influence of management on the scope of the internal auditor's duties.

d. Organizational level to which the internal auditor reports.

**153.** For which of the following judgments may an independent auditor share responsibility with an entity's internal auditor who is assessed to be both competent and objective?

|    | Assessment of inherent risk | Assessment of control risk |
|----|------|------|
| a. | Yes  | Yes  |
| b. | Yes  | No   |
| c. | No   | Yes  |
| d. | No   | No   |

**154.** The work of internal auditors may affect the independent auditor's

I. Procedures performed in obtaining an understanding of internal control.

II. Procedures performed in assessing the risk of material misstatement.

III. Substantive procedures performed in gathering direct evidence.

a. I and II only.

b. I and III only.

c. II and III only.

d. I, II, and III.

**155.** An internal auditor's work would most likely affect the nature, timing, and extent of an independent CPA's auditing procedures when the internal auditor's work relates to assertions about the

a. Existence of contingencies.

b. Valuation of intangible assets.

c. Existence of fixed asset additions.

d. Valuation of related-party transactions.

**156.** During an audit an internal auditor may provide direct assistance to an independent CPA in

|    | Obtaining an understanding of internal control | Performing tests of controls | Performing substantive tests |
|----|------|------|------|
| a. | No   | No   | No   |
| b. | Yes  | No   | No   |
| c. | Yes  | Yes  | No   |
| d. | Yes  | Yes  | Yes  |

**157.** When assessing the internal auditor's competence, the independent CPA should obtain information about the

a. Organizational level to which the internal auditors report.

b. Educational background and professional certification of the internal auditors.

c. Policies prohibiting the internal auditors from auditing areas where relatives are employed.

d. Internal auditors' access to records and information that is considered sensitive.

**158.** In assessing the competence and objectivity of an entity's internal auditor, an independent auditor would **least** likely consider information obtained from

a. Discussions with management personnel.

b. External quality reviews of the internal auditor's activities.

c. Previous experience with the internal auditor.

d. The results of analytical procedures.

**159.** If the independent auditors decide that the work performed by the internal auditor may have a bearing on their own procedures, they should consider the internal auditor's

a. Competence and objectivity.

b. Efficiency and experience.

c. Independence and review skills.

d. Training and supervisory skills.

**160.** In assessing the objectivity of internal auditors, an independent auditor should

a. Evaluate the quality control program in effect for the internal auditors.

b. Examine documentary evidence of the work performed by the internal auditors.

c. Test a sample of the transactions and balances that the internal auditors examined.

d. Determine the organizational level to which the internal auditors report.

**161.** Dunn, CPA, is auditing the financial statements of Taft Co. Taft uses Quick Service Center (QSC) to process its payroll. Price, CPA, is expressing an opinion on a description of the controls placed in operation at QSC regarding the processing of its customers' payroll transactions. Dunn expects to consider the effects of Price's report on the Taft engagement. Price's report should contain a(n)

a. Description of the scope and nature of Price's procedures.

b. Statement that Dunn may assess control risk based on Price's report.

c. Assertion that Price assumes no responsibility to determine whether QSC's controls are suitably designed.

d. Opinion on the operating effectiveness of QSC's internal controls.

**162.** Payroll Data Co. (PDC) processes payroll transactions for a retailer. Cook, CPA, is engaged to express an opinion on a description of PDC's internal controls placed in operation as of a specific date. These controls are relevant to the retailer's internal control, so Cook's report may be useful in providing the retailer's independent auditor with information necessary to plan a financial statement audit. Cook's report should

a. Contain a disclaimer of opinion on the operating effectiveness of PDC's controls.

b. State whether PDC's controls were suitably designed to achieve the retailer's objectives.

c. Identify PDC's controls relevant to specific financial statement assertions.

d. Disclose Cook's assessed level of control risk for PDC.

**163.** The auditor who audits the processing of transactions by a service organization may issue a report on controls

|    | Placed in operation | Operating effectiveness |
|----|------|------|
| a. | Yes  | Yes  |
| b. | Yes  | No   |
| c. | No   | Yes  |
| d. | No   | No   |

**164.** Computer Services Company (CSC) processes payroll transactions for schools. Drake, CPA, is engaged to report on CSC's policies and procedures placed in operation as of a specific date. These policies and procedures are relevant to the schools' internal control, so Drake's report will be useful in providing the schools' independent auditors with information necessary to plan their audits. Drake's report expressing an opinion on CSC's policies and procedures placed in operation as of a specific date should contain a(n)

    a.   Description of the scope and nature of Drake's procedures.

    b.   Statement that CSC's management has disclosed to Drake all design deficiencies of which it is aware.

    c.   Opinion on the operating effectiveness of CSC's policies and procedures.

    d.   Paragraph indicating the basis for Drake's assessment of control risk.

**165.** Lake, CPA, is auditing the financial statements of Gill Co. Gill uses the EDP Service Center, Inc. to process its payroll transactions. EDP's financial statements are audited by Cope, CPA, who recently issued a report on EDP's internal control. Lake is considering Cope's report on EDP's internal control in assessing control risk on the Gill engagement. What is Lake's responsibility concerning making reference to Cope as a basis, in part, for Lake's own opinion?

    a.   Lake may refer to Cope only if Lake is satisfied as to Cope's professional reputation and independence.

    b.   Lake may refer to Cope only if Lake relies on Cope's report in restricting the extent of substantive tests.

    c.   Lake may refer to Cope only if Lake's report indicates the division of responsibility.

    d.   Lake may **not** refer to Cope under the circumstances above.

**SIMULATION PROBLEMS**

**Simulation Problem 1**                              (35 to 40 minutes)

| Directions | | | | |
|---|---|---|---|---|
| | Situation | Internal Control | Research | Communication |

An auditor's working papers include the narrative description (situation tab) of the cash receipts and billing portions of Southwest Medical Center's internal control.

Evaluate the information in the situation on the worksheet (internal control tab) as being either (1) a strength, (2) a weakness, (3) not a strength or a weakness.

| | Situation | | | |
|---|---|---|---|---|
| Directions | | Internal Control | Research | Communication |

Southwest is a health care provider that is owned by a partnership of five physicians. It employs eleven physicians, including the five owners, twenty nurses, five laboratory and X-ray technicians, and four clerical workers. The clerical workers perform such tasks as reception, correspondence, cash receipts, billing, accounts receivable, bank deposits, and appointment scheduling. These clerical workers are referred to in the situation as office manager, clerk #1, clerk #2, and clerk #3. Assume that the narrative is a complete description of the system.

| | | Internal Control | | |
|---|---|---|---|---|
| Directions | Situation | | Research | Communication |

About two-thirds of Southwest's patients receive medical services only after insurance coverage is verified by the office manager and communicated to the clerks. Most of the other patients pay for services by cash or check when services are rendered, although the office manger extends credit on a case-by-case basis to about 5% of the patients.

When services are rendered, the attending physician prepares a prenumbered service slip for each patient and gives the slip to clerk #1 for pricing. Clerk #1 completes the slip and gives the completed slip to clerk #2 and a copy to the patient.

Using the information on the completed slip, clerk #2 performs one of the following three procedures for each patient:

- Clerk #2 files an insurance claim and records a receivable from the insurance company if the office manager has verified the patient's coverage, or
- Clerk #2 posts a receivable from the patient on clerk #2's PC if the office manager has approved the patient's credit, or
- Clerk #2 receives cash or a check from the patient as the patient leaves the medical center, and clerk #2 records the cash receipt.

At the end of each day, clerk #2 prepares a revenue summary.

Clerk #1 performs correspondence functions and opens the incoming mail. Clerk #1 gives checks from insurance companies and patients to clerk #2 for deposit. Clerk #2 posts the receipt of patients' checks on clerk #2's PC patient receivable records and insurance companies' checks to the receivables from the applicable insurance companies. Clerk #1 gives mail requiring correspondence to clerk #3.

Clerk #2 stamps all checks "for deposit only" and each day prepares a list of checks and cash to be deposited in the bank. (This list also includes the cash and checks personally given to clerk #2 by patients.) Clerk #2 keeps a copy of the deposit list and gives the original to clerk #3.

Clerk #3 personally makes the daily bank deposit and maintains a file of the daily bank deposits. Clerk #3 also performs appointment scheduling for all of the doctors and various correspondence functions. Clerk #3 also maintains a list of patients whose insurance coverage the office manager has verified.

When insurance claims or patient receivables are not settled within sixty days, clerk #2 notifies the office manager. The office manager personally inspects the details of each instance of nonpayment. The office manger converts insurance claims that have been rejected by insurance companies into patient receivables. Clerk #2 records these patient receivables on clerk #2's PC and deletes these receivables from the applicable insurance companies. Clerk #2 deletes the patient receivables that appear to be uncollectible from clerk #2's PC when authorized by the office manager. Clerk #2 prepares a list of patients with uncollectible balances and gives a copy of the list to clerk #3, who will not allow these patients to make appointments for future services.

Once a month an outside accountant posts clerk #2's daily revenue summaries to the general ledger, prepares a monthly trial balance and monthly financial statements, accounts for prenumbered service slips, files payroll forms and tax returns, and reconciles the monthly bank statements to the general ledger. This accountant reports directly to the physician who is the managing partner.

All four clerical employees perform their tasks on PCs that are connected through a local area network. Each PC is accessible with a password that is known only to the individual employee and the managing partner. Southwest uses a standard software package that was acquired from a software company and that cannot be modified by Southwest's employees. None of the clerical employees have access to Southwest's check writing abilities.

| Condition | Strength | Weakness | Neither |
|---|:---:|:---:|:---:|
| 1. Southwest is involved only in medical services and has not diversified its operations. | ○ | ○ | ○ |
| 2. Insurance coverage for patients is verified and communicated to the clerks by the office manager before medical services are rendered. | ○ | ○ | ○ |
| 3. The physician who renders the medical services documents the services on a prenumbered slip that is used for recording revenue and as a receipt for the patient. | ○ | ○ | ○ |
| 4. Cash collection is centralized in that Clerk #2 receives the cash (checks) from patients and records the cash receipt. | ○ | ○ | ○ |
| 5. Southwest extends credit rather than requiring cash or insurance in all cases. | ○ | ○ | ○ |
| 6. The office manager extends credit on a case-by-case basis rather than using a formal credit search and established credit limits. | ○ | ○ | ○ |
| 7. The office manager approves the extension of credit to patients and also approves the write-offs of uncollectible patient receivables. | ○ | ○ | ○ |
| 8. Clerk #2 receives cash and checks and prepares the daily bank deposit. | ○ | ○ | ○ |
| 9. Clerk #2 maintains the accounts receivable records and can add or delete information on the PC. | ○ | ○ | ○ |
| 10. Prenumbered service slips are accounted for on a monthly basis by the outside accountant who is independent of the revenue generating and revenue recording functions. | ○ | ○ | ○ |
| 11. The bank reconciliation is prepared monthly by the outside accountant who is independent of the revenue generating and revenue recording functions. | ○ | ○ | ○ |
| 12. Computer passwords are only known to the individual employees and the managing partner who has no duties in the revenue recording functions. | ○ | ○ | ○ |
| 13. Computer software cannot be modified by Southwest's employees. | ○ | ○ | ○ |
| 14. None of the employees who perform duties in the revenue generating and revenue recording are able to write checks. | ○ | ○ | ○ |

| | | | **Research** | |
|---|---|---|---|---|
| **Directions** | **Situation** | **Internal Control** | | **Communication** |

An auditor may discover certain audit adjustments, material and immaterial, that relate to the financial statements.  Search the Professional Standards to determine auditor responsibility for communicating these adjustments to the audit committee. You may simply paste the appropriate material to your solution.

| | | | | **Communication** |
|---|---|---|---|---|
| **Directions** | **Situation** | **Internal Control** | **Research** | |

Assume that in your audit of Southwest you assessed control risk at a low level for accounts receivable.  However, your substantive procedures have detected a large number of errors in the accounts.  Write a memorandum to the audit working papers describing the implications of this situation.

To:     Audit Working Papers
From: CPA Candidate
Re:     Implications of errors discovered in accounts receivable

**Simulation Problem 2**                                (25 to 35 minutes)

| Directions | | | |
|---|---|---|---|
| | Flowchart | Research | Communication |

The following flowchart (Flowchart tab) depicts part of a client's purchases and cash disbursements cycle.  Some of the flowchart symbols are labeled to indicate operations, controls, and records.  For each symbol numbered 1 through 12, select one response from the answer lists below.  Each response in the lists may be selected once or **not** at all.

| | Flowchart | | |
|---|---|---|---|
| Directions | | Research | Communication |

*Operations and controls*
A. Approve receiving report
B. Prepare and approve voucher
C. Prepare purchase order
D. Prepare purchase requisition
E. Prepare purchases journal
F. Prepare receiving report
G. Prepare sales journal
H. Prepare voucher
I.  Sign checks and cancel voucher package documents

*Connectors, documents, departments, and files*
J.  Accounts payable
K. Canceled voucher package
L.  From purchasing
M. From receiving
N. From vouchers payable
O. Purchase order No. 5
P.  Receiving report No. 1
Q. Stores
R. To vendor
S.  Treasurer
T.  Unpaid voucher file, filed by due date

| | | Research | |
|---|---|---|---|
| Directions | Flowchart | | Communication |

The Professional Standards state that internal control provides reasonable and not absolute assurance of achieving a client's control objectives.  Relatedly, the Professional Standards acknowledge that internal control has certain limitations.  Search the Professional Standards to find the location at which a number of limitations are discussed together.  You may simply paste the appropriate material to your solution.

| | | | Communication |
|---|---|---|---|
| Directions | Flowchart | Research | |

Internet controls either (1) prevent misstatements, or (2) detect material misstatements of financial statements.  Write a memorandum to the audit staff describing these two types of controls.

To:    Audit Staff
From:  CPA Candidate
Re:    Types of controls

| |
|---|
| |

---

**Simulation Problem 3**                                (40 to 50 minutes)

| Situation | | | |
|---|---|---|---|
| | Flowchart | Research | Communication |

You are working for Smith & Co. CPAs.  The following partially completed flowchart depicts part of Welcore Inc., your client's revenue cycle.  Some of the flowchart symbols are labeled to indicate controls and records.  For each symbol numbered **1** though **13**, select one response from all the answer lists below.  Each response in the lists may be selected once or **not** at all.

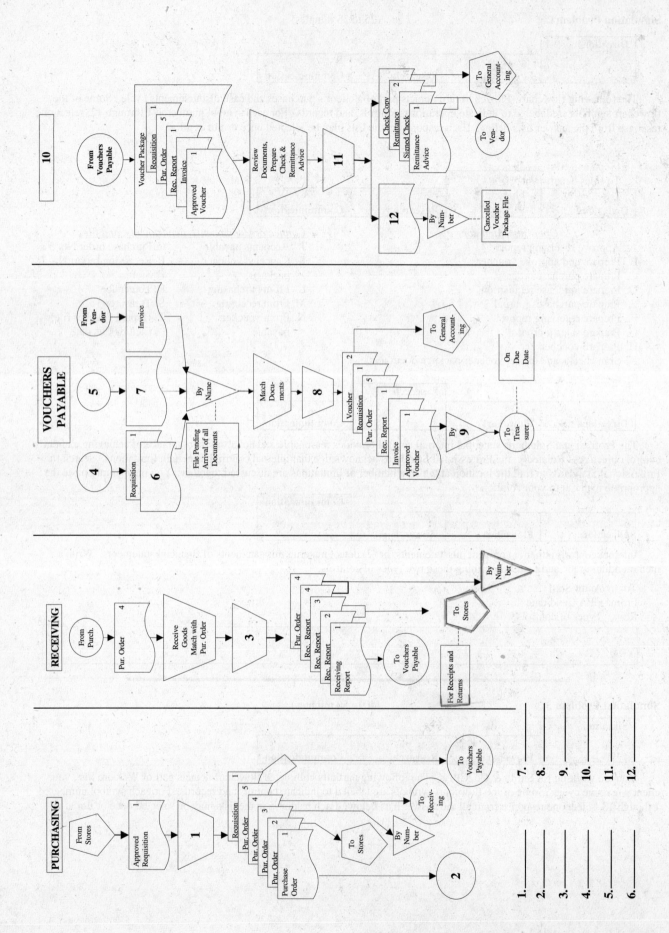

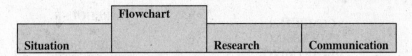

### Operations and controls

A. Enter shipping data
B. Verify agreement of sales order and shipping document
C. Write off accounts receivable
D. To warehouse and shipping department
E. Authorize account receivable write-off
F. Prepare aged trial balance
G. To sales department
H. Release goods for shipment
I. To accounts receivable department
J. Enter price data
K. Determine that customer exists
L. Match customer purchase order with sales order
M. Perform customer credit check
N. Prepare sales journal
O. Prepare sales invoice

### Documents, journals, ledgers, and files

P. Shipping document
Q. General ledger master file
R. General journal
S. Master price file
T. Sales journal
U. Sales invoice
V. Cash receipts journal
W. Uncollectible accounts file
X. Shipping file
Y. Aged trial balance
Z. Open order file

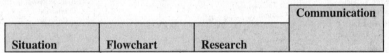

Now assume that the flowchart was originally prepared as a part of the necessary documentation for an audit of Welcore's financial statements. In the midst of discussions on this, the president of Welcore asked you about the possibilities of your issuing a publicly available report on its internal control over financial reporting. Use the Professional Standards to find a sample report on the effectiveness of Welcore's internal control over financial reporting. Create a report that might be issued to Welcore if internal control over financial reporting is found to be effective and an appropriate examination on internal control over financial reporting has been performed and no significant deficiencies are found. Prepare the report assuming the company is using the Internal Control—Integrated Framework Criteria established by the Committee of Sponsoring Organizations. Because the report is simply a draft, mark it as such and do not date it.

*NOTE: If you do not have access to professional standards indicate the keywords or section numbers that you would use to do your search. Then go to the solution which has excerpts from professional standards to complete the requirement.*

|  |  | | Communication |
| --- | --- | --- | --- |
| Situation | Flowchart | Research | |

Assume that Bill Warren, CFO of Welcore Inc., wants an explanation of how improvements in internal control will affect the audit of the company. Write a brief memorandum explaining how the audit might change based on improved internal control.

To:    Bill Warren, CFO
       Welcore Inc.
From: CPA Candidate
Re:    Effect of improvements in internal control

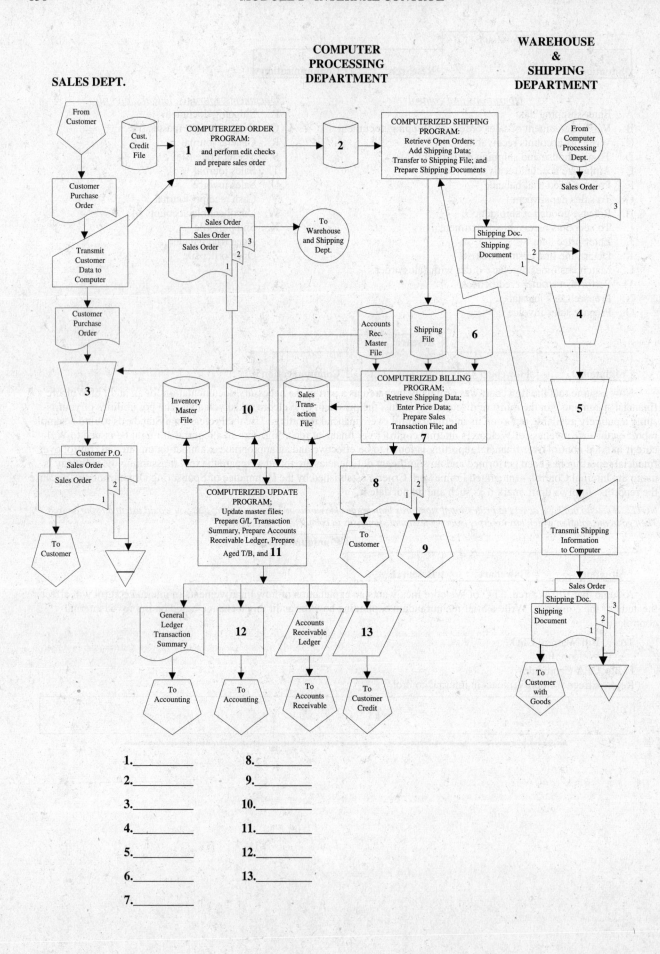

1._____    8._____

2._____    9._____

3._____    10._____

4._____    11._____

5._____    12._____

6._____    13._____

7._____

**Simulation Problem 4**                                    (45 to 50 minutes)

| Situation | | | |
|---|---|---|---|
| | Internal Control Evaluation | Purpose of Internal control | Research and Communication |

The following flowchart depicts the activities relating to the purchasing, receiving, and accounts payable departments of Model Company, Inc.  Assume that you are a supervising assistant assigned to the Model Company audit.

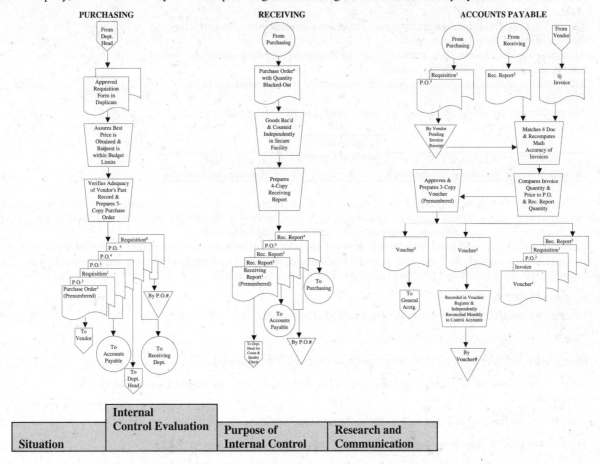

| | Internal Control Evaluation | | |
|---|---|---|---|
| Situation | | Purpose of Internal Control | Research and Communication |

Joe Werell, a beginning assistant, analyzed the flowchart and has supplemented the flowchart by making certain inquiries of the controller.  He has concluded that the internal control over purchasing, receiving, and accounts payable is strong and has provided the following list of what he refers to as internal control strengths.  Review his list and for each internal control strength indicate whether you agree or disagree that each represents a strength.  For those in which you disagree briefly explain why.

Internal Control Strengths
Prepared by Joe Werell

|  | Agree | Disagree |
|---|:---:|:---:|
| **Purchasing** | | |
| 1. The department head of the requisitioning department selects the appropriate supplier. | ○ | ○ |
| 2. Proper authorization of requisitions by department head is required before purchase orders are prepared. | ○ | ○ |
| 3. Purchasing department makes certain that low-cost supplier is always chosen. | ○ | ○ |
| 4. Purchasing department assures that requisitions are within budget limits before purchase orders are prepared. | ○ | ○ |
| 5. The adequacy of each vendor's past record as a supplier is verified. | ○ | ○ |
| **Receiving** | | |
| 6. Secure facilities limit access to the goods during the receiving activity. | ○ | ○ |
| 7. Receiving department compares its count of the quantity of goods received with that listed on its copy of the purchase order. | ○ | ○ |
| 8. A receiving report is required for all purchases, including purchases of services. | ○ | ○ |

|  | Agree | Disagree |
|---|:---:|:---:|
| 9. The requisitioning department head independently verifies the quantity and quality of the goods received. | ○ | ○ |
| 10. Requisitions, purchase orders, and receiving reports are matched with vendor invoices as to quantity and price. | ○ | ○ |

**Accounts Payable**

|  | Agree | Disagree |
|---|:---:|:---:|
| 11. Accounts payable department recomputes the mathematical accuracy of each invoice. | ○ | ○ |
| 12. The voucher register is independently reconciled to the control accounts monthly by the originators of the related vouchers. | ○ | ○ |
| 13. All supporting documentation is marked "paid" by accounts payable immediately prior to making it available to the treasurer. | ○ | ○ |
| 14. All supporting documentation is required for payment and is made available to the treasurer. | ○ | ○ |
| 15. The purchasing, receiving, and accounts payable functions are segregated. | ○ | ○ |

| Situation | Internal Control Evaluation | Purpose of Internal Control | Research and Communication |
|---|---|---|---|

Another assistant has been working in the revenue cycle area and has compiled a list of possible errors and fraud that may result in the misstatement of Model Company's financial statements, and a corresponding list of controls that, if properly designed and implemented, could assist in preventing or detecting the errors and fraud.

For each possible error and fraud numbered **1 through 15,** select one internal control from the answer list below that, if properly designed and implemented, most likely could assist management in preventing or detecting the errors and fraud. Each response in the list of controls may be selected once, more than once, or not at all.

### Possible Errors and Fraud

1. Invoices for goods sold are posted to incorrect customer accounts. _____

2. Goods ordered by customers are shipped, but are **not** billed to anyone. _____

3. Invoices are sent for shipped goods, but are **not** recorded in the sales journal. _____

4. Invoices are sent for shipped goods and are recorded in the sales journal, but are **not** posted to any customer account. _____

5. Credit sales are made to individuals with unsatisfactory credit ratings. _____

6. Goods are removed from inventory for unauthorized orders. _____

7. Goods shipped to customers do **not** agree with goods ordered by customers. _____

8. Invoices are sent to allies in a fraudulent scheme and sales are recorded for fictitious transactions. _____

9. Customers' checks are received for less than the customers' full account balances, but the customers' full account balances are credited. _____

10. Customers' checks are misappropriated before being forwarded to the cashier for deposit. _____

11. Customers' checks are credited to incorrect customer accounts. _____

12. Different customer accounts are each credited for the same cash receipt. _____

13. Customers' checks are properly credited to customer accounts and are properly deposited, but errors are made in recording receipts in the cash receipts journal. _____

14. Customers' checks are misappropriated after being forwarded to the cashier for deposit. _____

15. Invalid transactions granting credit for sales returns are recorded. _____

## Controls

A. Shipping clerks compare goods received from the warehouse with the details on the shipping documents.

B. Approved sales orders are required for goods to be released from the warehouse.

C. Monthly statements are mailed to all customers with outstanding balances.

D. Shipping clerks compare goods received from the warehouse with approved sales orders.

E. Customer orders are compared with the inventory master file to determine whether items ordered are in stock.

F. Daily sales summaries are compared with control totals of invoices.

G. Shipping documents are compared with sales invoices when goods are shipped.

H. Sales invoices are compared with the master price file.

I. Customer orders are compared with an approved customer list.

J. Sales orders are prepared for each customer order.

K. Control amounts posted to the accounts receivable ledger are compared with control totals of invoices.

L. Sales invoices are compared with shipping documents and approved customer orders before invoices are mailed.

M. Prenumbered credit memos are used for granting credit for goods returned.

N. Goods returned for credit are approved by the supervisor of the sales department.

O. Remittance advices are separated from the checks in the mailroom and forwarded to the accounting department.

P. Total amounts posted to the accounts receivable ledger from remittance advices are compared with the validated bank deposit slip.

Q. The cashier examines each check for proper endorsement.

R. Validated deposit slips are compared with the cashier's daily cash summaries.

S. An employee, other than the bookkeeper, periodically prepares a bank reconciliation.

T. Sales returns are approved by the same employee who issues receiving reports evidencing actual return of goods.

| Situation | Internal Control Evaluation | Purpose of Internal Control | Research and Communication |
|---|---|---|---|

Assume that in Internal Control Evaluation you have identified some circumstances that may be considered deficiencies in internal control—indeed some might be considered significant deficiencies (reportable conditions) or even material weaknesses. Write a memorandum addressed to Bill Jones, the job's senior, that abstracts from the professional standards the following:

1. Definition of material weakness and reportable condition.
2. Whether a preference exists in the standards on whether any communication need be in writing versus presented orally to the audit committee.
3. Whether deficiencies of which an audit committee is already aware must be communicated to the audit committee.

Assume that this is the audit of a nonpublic company for which no overall public reporting responsibility relating to internal control is required under the requirements of the Sarbanes-Oxley Act of 2002. Also, include an exact citation to the professional standards paragraph(s) in which you find the guidance.

*NOTE: If you do not have access to professional standards indicate the keywords or section numbers that you would use to do your search. Then, go to the solution which has excerpts for professional standards to complete the requirement.*

To: Mr. Bill Jones
From: CPA Candidate
Re: Reporting on internal control

## MULTIPLE-CHOICE ANSWERS

| | | | | | | | | | |
|---|---|---|---|---|---|---|---|---|---|
| 1. a __ __ | 35. a __ __ | 69. d __ __ | 103. c __ __ | 137. d __ __ |
| 2. d __ __ | 36. b __ __ | 70. a __ __ | 104. b __ __ | 138. b __ __ |
| 3. b __ __ | 37. d __ __ | 71. c __ __ | 105. b __ __ | 139. a __ __ |
| 4. b __ __ | 38. c __ __ | 72. b __ __ | 106. a __ __ | 140. a __ __ |
| 5. c __ __ | 39. a __ __ | 73. a __ __ | 107. a __ __ | 141. d __ __ |
| 6. b __ __ | 40. c __ __ | 74. a __ __ | 108. c __ __ | 142. b __ __ |
| 7. d __ __ | 41. a __ __ | 75. c __ __ | 109. c __ __ | 143. c __ __ |
| 8. a __ __ | 42. b __ __ | 76. d __ __ | 110. a __ __ | 144. b __ __ |
| 9. d __ __ | 43. a __ __ | 77. b __ __ | 111. c __ __ | 145. d __ __ |
| 10. a __ __ | 44. c __ __ | 78. a __ __ | 112. a __ __ | 146. c __ __ |
| 11. d __ __ | 45. d __ __ | 79. a __ __ | 113. c __ __ | 147. a __ __ |
| 12. b __ __ | 46. d __ __ | 80. d __ __ | 114. c __ __ | 148. c __ __ |
| 13. a __ __ | 47. d __ __ | 81. c __ __ | 115. a __ __ | 149. d __ __ |
| 14. a __ __ | 48. d __ __ | 82. d __ __ | 116. d __ __ | 150. b __ __ |
| 15. b __ __ | 49. a __ __ | 83. b __ __ | 117. d __ __ | 151. b __ __ |
| 16. b __ __ | 50. d __ __ | 84. c __ __ | 118. a __ __ | 152. a __ __ |
| 17. b __ __ | 51. d __ __ | 85. b __ __ | 119. a __ __ | 153. d __ __ |
| 18. a __ __ | 52. b __ __ | 86. b __ __ | 120. b __ __ | 154. d __ __ |
| 19. a __ __ | 53. c __ __ | 87. d __ __ | 121. d __ __ | 155. c __ __ |
| 20. d __ __ | 54. a __ __ | 88. b __ __ | 122. d __ __ | 156. d __ __ |
| 21. b __ __ | 55. a __ __ | 89. d __ __ | 123. d __ __ | 157. b __ __ |
| 22. c __ __ | 56. a __ __ | 90. b __ __ | 124. d __ __ | 158. d __ __ |
| 23. d __ __ | 57. c __ __ | 91. b __ __ | 125. b __ __ | 159. a __ __ |
| 24. d __ __ | 58. a __ __ | 92. d __ __ | 126. a __ __ | 160. d __ __ |
| 25. d __ __ | 59. a __ __ | 93. d __ __ | 127. c __ __ | 161. a __ __ |
| 26. c __ __ | 60. b __ __ | 94. b __ __ | 128. d __ __ | 162. a __ __ |
| 27. c __ __ | 61. c __ __ | 95. b __ __ | 129. c __ __ | 163. a __ __ |
| 28. d __ __ | 62. a __ __ | 96. d __ __ | 130. b __ __ | 164. a __ __ |
| 29. d __ __ | 63. b __ __ | 97. c __ __ | 131. c __ __ | 165. d __ __ |
| 30. a __ __ | 64. b __ __ | 98. d __ __ | 132. b __ __ | |
| 31. c __ __ | 65. c __ __ | 99. d __ __ | 133. d __ __ | |
| 32. d __ __ | 66. b __ __ | 100. c __ __ | 134. b __ __ | 1st: __/165= __% |
| 33. a __ __ | 67. b __ __ | 101. c __ __ | 135. b __ __ | 2nd: __/165= __% |
| 34. d __ __ | 68. b __ __ | 102. c __ __ | 136. c __ __ | |

## MULTIPLE-CHOICE ANSWER EXPLANATIONS

### A.1. Definition of Internal Control

**1. (a)** The requirement is to identify the reply that most likely would **not** be considered an inherent limitation of the potential effectiveness of an entity's internal control. Answer (a) is correct because incompatible duties may generally be divided among individuals in such a manner as to control the problem. Answers (b), (c), and (d) are all incorrect because management override, mistakes of judgment, and collusion among employees are all inherent limitations of internal control.

**2. (d)** The requirement is to identify the meaning of the concept of reasonable assurance. Answer (d) is correct because reasonable assurance recognizes that the cost of internal control should not exceed the benefits expected to be derived.

**3. (b)** The requirement is to identify the functions that should be segregated for effective internal control. Answer (b) is correct because authorizing transactions, recording transactions, and maintaining custody of assets should be segregated.

### A.2. Major Components of Internal Control

**4. (b)** The requirement is to identify the most likely type of *ongoing* monitoring activity. Answer (b) is correct because ongoing monitoring involves assessing the design and operation of controls on a timely basis and taking necessary corrective actions and such an approach may be followed in reviewing the purchasing function. Answer (a) is incorrect because periodic audits are not ordinarily performed by the audit committee, a subcommittee of the Board of Directors. Answer (c) is incorrect because the audit of the annual financial statements is not ordinarily considered monitoring as presented in the professional standards. Answer (d) is incorrect because the meaning of the reply, control risk assessment in conjunction with quarterly reviews, is uncertain.

**5. (c)** The requirement is to identify where the overall attitude and awareness of an entity's board of directors concerning the importance of internal control is normally reflected. Answer (c) is correct because the control environment reflects the overall attitude, awareness, and actions of the board of directors, management, owners, and others concerning the importance of control and its emphasis in the entity.

**6. (b)** The requirement is to identify the circumstance in which management philosophy and operating style would have a significant influence on an entity's control environment. Answer (b) is correct because management philosophy and operating style, while always important, is particularly so when management is dominated by one or a few individuals because it may impact numerous other factors. Answer (a) is incorrect because the impact of the internal auditor reporting directly to management is likely to be less than that of answer (a). Answer (c) is incorrect because while accurate management job descriptions are desirable, they do not have as significant of an effect on management philosophy and operating style as does domination by an individual. Answer (d) is incorrect because an active audit committee might temper rather than lead to a more significant influence of management philosophy and operating style.

**7.** **(d)** The requirement is to determine which of the factors listed are included in an entity's control environment. Answer (d) is correct because the audit committee, integrity and ethical values, and organization structure are all included.

**8.** **(a)** The requirement is to identify the reply that is **not** a component of an entity's internal control. Answer (a) is correct because while auditors assess control risk as a part of their consideration of internal control, it is not a component of an entity's internal control. Answers (b), (c), and (d) are incorrect because the control environment, risk assessment, control activities, information and communication, and monitoring are the five components of an entity's internal control (AU 319).

**A.3. Related Topics**

**9.** **(d)** The Foreign Corrupt Practices Act makes payment of bribes to foreign officials illegal and requires publicly held companies to maintain systems of internal control sufficient to provide reasonable assurances that internal control objectives are met.

**B.1. Obtain and Document Understanding of Internal Control to Plan the Audit**

**10.** **(a)** The requirement is to determine the most likely population from which an auditor would sample when vendors' invoices and related vouchers relating to purchases made by employees have been destroyed. Answer (a) is correct because the disbursement will be recorded and the auditor may thus sample from that population. Answers (b) and (d) are incorrect because the related vouchers and vendors' invoices are destroyed. Answer (c) is incorrect because there is no recording of the receipt of the merchandise.

**11.** **(d)** The requirement is to identify the procedure an auditor would perform to provide evidence about whether an entity's internal control activities are suitably designed to prevent or detect material misstatements. Answer (d) is correct because AU 319 indicates an auditor will observe the entity's personnel applying the procedures to determine whether controls have been placed in operation. Answer (a) is incorrect because reperforming the activities is a test of control to help assess the operating effectiveness of a control. Answer (b) is incorrect because analytical procedures are not performed to determine whether controls are suitably designed. Answer (c) is incorrect because vouching a sample of transactions is a substantive test not directly aimed at determining whether controls are suitably designed. See AU 319 for a discussion of an auditor's responsibility for determining whether controls have been placed in operation vs. their operating effectiveness.

**12.** **(b)** The requirement is to identify the correct statement relating to the relevance of various types of controls to a financial statement audit. Answer (b) is correct because, generally, controls that are relevant to an audit pertain to the entity's objective of preparing financial statements for external purposes. Answer (a) is incorrect because AU 319 makes clear that an auditor may not ignore consideration of controls under any audit approach. Answer (c) is incorrect because control over financial reporting are of primary importance. Answer (d) is incorrect because many operational and compliance related controls are not ordinarily relevant to an audit.

**13.** **(a)** The requirement is to identify the statement that represents a requirement when an audit of financial statements in accordance with generally accepted accounting principles is performed. Answer (a) is correct because AU 319 requires that the auditor document the understanding of the entity's internal control. Answer (b) is incorrect because while an auditor might find significant deficiencies in the operation of internal control, no such search is required. Answer (c) is incorrect because an auditor might use a substantive approach in performing an audit and thereby perform few (if any) tests of controls. Answer (d) is incorrect because while auditors must obtain knowledge of internal control sufficiently to identify types of potential misstatements, they are not required to obtain the detailed knowledge of internal control suggested by this reply.

**14.** **(a)** The requirement is to identify the knowledge that an auditor must obtain when obtaining an understanding of an entity's internal control sufficient for audit planning. Answer (a) is correct because an auditor must obtain an understanding that includes knowledge about the design of relevant controls and records and whether the client has placed those controls in operation. Answers (b) and (c) are incorrect because auditors may choose not to obtain information on operating effectiveness of controls and their consistency of application. Answer (d) is incorrect because there is no such explicit requirement relating to controls; see AU 319 for the necessary understanding of internal control.

**15.** **(b)** AU 319 states that the auditor should obtain sufficient knowledge of the information (including accounting) system to understand the financial reporting process used to prepare the entity's financial statements, including significant accounting estimates and disclosures. It also states that this knowledge is obtained to help the auditor to understand (1) the entity's classes of transactions, (2) how transactions are initiated, (3) the accounting records and support, and (4) the accounting processing involved from initiation of a transaction to its inclusion in the financial statements.

**16.** **(b)** The requirement is to determine why an auditor should concentrate on the substance of procedures rather than their form when obtaining an understanding of an entity's controls. Answer (b) is correct because management may establish appropriate controls but not act on them, thus creating a situation in which the form differs from the substance. Answer (a) is incorrect because documentation is not directly related to the issue of substance over form. Answer (c) is incorrect because inappropriate controls is only a part of an auditor concern; for example, a control may be appropriate, but it may not be operating effectively. Answer (d) is incorrect because while an auditor might suggest to management that the cost of certain controls seems to exceed their likely benefit, this is not the primary reason auditors are concerned with the substance of controls.

**17. (b)** Decision tables include various combinations of conditions that are matched to one of several actions. In an internal control setting, the various important controls are reviewed and, based on the combination of answers received, an action such as a decision on whether to perform tests of controls is determined. Program flowcharts simply summarize the steps involved in a program. Answer (a) is incorrect because decision tables do not emphasize the ease of manageability for complex programs. Answer (c) is incorrect because while decision tables may be designed using various cost benefit factors relating to the various conditions and actions, they do not justify the program. Answer (d) is incorrect because program flowcharts, not decision tables, emphasize the sequence in which operations are performed.

**18. (a)** The requirement is to identify the procedure that is not required to be included in an auditor's consideration of internal control. Answer (a) is correct because the auditor need not obtain evidence relating to operating effectiveness when control risk is to be assessed at the maximum level. Answer (b) is incorrect because an auditor must obtain an understanding of the internal control environment and the information system. Answers (c) and (d) are incorrect because an auditor is obligated to obtain information on the design of internal control and on whether control activities have been placed in operation.

**19. (a)** The requirement is to identify the primary objective of procedures performed to obtain an understanding of internal control. Answer (a) is correct because the auditor obtains a sufficient understanding of internal control to plan the audit of the entity's financial statements. Answer (b) addresses inherent risk, the susceptibility of an assertion to material misstatement, assuming that there are no related controls. Answer (b) is incorrect since the concept of inherent risk assumes **no** internal control and is therefore not the primary objective. Answer (c) is incorrect because answer (a) is more complete and because decisions on modifying tests of controls are often made at a later point in the audit. Answer (d) is incorrect because the consistency of application of management's policies relates more directly to tests of controls than to obtaining an understanding of internal control.

**20. (d)** The requirement is to determine the correct statement with respect to the auditor's required documentation of the client's internal control. An auditor may document his/her understanding of the structure and his/her conclusions about the design of that structure in the form of answers to a questionnaire, narrative memorandums, flowcharts, decision tables, or any other form that the auditor considers appropriate in the circumstances. Answers (a) and (b) are, thus, incorrect because they suggest restrictions which do not exist in practice. Answer (c) is incorrect since at a minimum a list of reasons for nonreliance must be provided.

**21. (b)** In obtaining an understanding of internal control, the auditor should perform procedures to provide sufficient knowledge of the design of the relevant controls and whether they have been placed in operation. Information on operating effectiveness need not be obtained unless control risk is to be assessed at a level below the maximum.

**B.2. Assess Control Risk**

**22. (c)** The requirement is to identify the terms in which control risk should be assessed. Answer (c) is correct because AU 319 requires that control risk be assessed in terms of financial statement assertions.

**23. (d)** The requirement is to identify a situation in which an auditor may desire to seek a further reduction in the assessed level of control risk. Answer (d) is correct because such a reduction is only possible when additional evidential matter, evaluated by performing additional tests of controls, is available. Answer (a) is incorrect because auditors at this point will ordinarily already have obtained the understanding of the information system to plan the audit. Furthermore, an understanding of internal control is needed on all audits. Answer (b) is incorrect because auditors must determine that controls have been placed in operation in all audits. Answer (c) is incorrect because a significant number of controls always pertain to financial statement assertions.

**24. (d)** Assessing control risk below the maximum level involves (1) identifying specific controls relevant to specific assertions that are likely to prevent or detect material misstatements in those assertions, and (2) performing tests of controls to evaluate the effectiveness of such controls. Answer (a) is incorrect because assessing control risk below the maximum may lead to less extensive, not more extensive substantive tests. Answer (b) is incorrect because the actual level of inherent risk is not affected by the level of control risk. Also, one would not expect a change in the assessed level of control risk to result in a change in the assessed level of inherent risk. Answer (c) is incorrect because assessing control risk below the maximum may lead to interim-date substantive testing rather than year-end testing.

**25. (d)** The requirement is to determine why an auditor assesses control risk. Answer (d) is correct because the assessed levels of control risk and inherent risk are used to determine the acceptable level of detection risk for financial statement assertions.

**26. (c)** Increases in the assessed level of control risk lead to decreases in the acceptable level of detection risk. Accordingly, the auditor will need to increase the extent of substantive tests such as tests of details. Answer (a) is incorrect because tests of controls are performed to reduce the assessed level of control risk only when controls are believed to be effective. Answer (b) is incorrect because the level of detection risk must be decreased, not increased. Answer (d) is incorrect because the level of inherent risk pertains to the susceptibility of an account to material misstatement independent of related controls.

**27. (c)** The requirement is to determine whether the auditor must document either the understanding of the control environment, the basis for concluding that control risk is below the maximum, or both, when assessing control risk below the maximum level. Answer (c) is correct because an auditor must always document the understanding of internal control component, and, when control risk is assessed below the maximum, the basis of that assessment.

**28. (d)** The requirement is to determine the primary purpose for which an auditor uses the knowledge provided by the understanding of internal control and the assessed level of control risk. Answer (d) is correct because the auditor uses such knowledge in determining the nature, timing, and extent of substantive tests for financial statement assertions. Answer (a) is incorrect because it is incomplete. For example, while auditors are concerned with the safeguarding of assets, they also need to determine whether the financial statement information is accurate. Answer (b) is incorrect for reasons similar to (a) in that determining whether opportunities are available for committing and concealing fraud is incomplete since this knowledge is also used to ascertain whether the chance of errors is minimized. Answer (c) is incorrect because knowledge provided by the understanding of internal control and the assessed level of control risk is not used to modify initial assessments of inherent risk and preliminary judgments about materiality levels. This knowledge is unrelated to those processes.

**29. (d)** The requirement is to identify a way that an auditor may compensate for a weakness in internal control. Answer (d) is correct because increasing analytical procedures decreases detection risk in a manner which may counterbalance the condition in internal control. In effect, the weakness in internal control is compensated for by increased substantive testing. See the outline of AU 312 for the relationships among audit risk and its component risks—inherent risk, control risk, and detection risk. Answer (a) is incorrect because increasing both control risk (through a weakness in internal control) and detection risk increases audit risks. In addition, control risk and detection risk do not compensate for one another. Answer (b) is incorrect because increasing the extent of tests of controls is unlikely to be effective since the condition is known to exist. Answer (c) is incorrect because it is not generally appropriate to increase the judgment as to audit risk based on the results obtained.

**30. (a)** The requirement is to identify the correct statement concerning an auditor's assessment of control risk. Answer (a) is correct because AU 319 states that assessing control risk may be performed concurrently during an audit with obtaining an understanding of internal control. Answer (b) is incorrect because evidence about the operation of internal control obtained in prior audits may be considered during the current year's assessment of control risk. Answer (c) is incorrect because the basis for an auditor's conclusions about the assessed level of control risk needs to be documented when control risk is assessed at levels **other than** the maximum level. Answer (d) is incorrect because a lower level of control risk requires more assurance that the control procedures are operating effectively.

**31. (c)** The requirement is to determine the correct statement concerning the assessed level of control risk. Answer (c) is correct because ordinarily the assessed level of control risk **cannot** be sufficiently low to **eliminate** the need to perform any substantive tests to restrict detection risk for significant transaction classes. Answer (a) is incorrect because tests of controls are unnecessary when control risk is assessed at the maximum level. Answer (b) is incorrect because analytical procedures are not designed to verify the design of internal control. Answer (d) is incorrect because dual-purpose tests (i.e., those that serve as both substantive tests and tests of controls) are not required to be performed, and because the term "preliminary control risk" is unclear.

### B.3.   Perform (Additional) Tests of Controls

**32. (d)** The requirement is to identify the type of audit test most likely to provide assurance that controls are in use and operating effectively. Answer (d) is correct because inspection of documents is a form of a test of controls, and such tests are used to obtain reasonable assurance that controls are in use and operating effectively. Answer (a) is incorrect because auditors prepare flowcharts to document a company's internal control, not to obtain assurance that controls are in use and operating effectively. Answer (b) is incorrect because substantive tests relate to the accuracy of accounts and assertions rather than testing controls directly. Answer (c) is incorrect because analyzing tests of trends and ratios is an analytical procedure that does not directly test controls.

**33. (a)** The requirement is to identify the appropriate procedures for testing the segregation of duties related to inventory. Answer (a) is correct because AU 319 suggests that when no audit trail exists (as is often the case for the segregation of duties) an auditor should use the observation and inquiry techniques.

**34. (d)** The requirement is to identify the objective of tests of details of transactions performed as tests of controls. Answer (d) is correct because the purpose of tests of controls is to evaluate whether internal control operates effectively. Answer (a) is incorrect because while monitoring the design and use of entity documents may be viewed as a test of controls, it is not the objective. Answer (b) is incorrect because determining whether internal control is placed in operation is not directly related to tests of controls; see AU 319 for the distinction between "placed in operation" and "operating effectiveness." Answer (c) is incorrect because substantive tests, not tests of controls, are focused on detection of material misstatements in the account balances of the financial statements.

**35. (a)** The requirement is to identify a circumstance in which an auditor may decide to perform tests of controls. Answer (a) is correct because tests of controls will be performed when they are expected to result in a cost effective reduction in planned substantive tests. Answer (b) is incorrect because tests of controls are only performed when they are likely to support a further reduction in the assessed level of control risk. Answer (c) is incorrect because tests of controls are designed to decrease the assessed level of control risk, not increase it. Answer (d) is incorrect because internal control weaknesses normally result in more substantive testing and less tests of controls.

**36. (b)** The requirement is to identify the most appropriate procedures for assessing control risk. Auditors perform tests of controls to obtain evidence on the operating effectiveness of controls to assess control risk. Answer (b) is correct because tests of controls include inquiries of appropriate entity personnel, inspection of documents and reports, observation of the application of the policy or procedure, and reperformance of the application of the policy or procedure.

**37. (d)** The requirement is to identify the type of evidence an auditor most likely would examine to determine whether controls are operating as designed. Answer (d) is correct because inspection of client records documenting the use of computer programs will provide evidence to help the auditor evaluate the effectiveness of the design and operation of internal control; the client's control over use of its computer programs in this case is documentation of the use of the programs. In order to test this control, the auditor will inspect the documentation records. See AU 319 for information on the nature of tests of controls. Answer (a) is incorrect because the confirmation process is most frequently considered a substantive test, not a test of a control. Answer (b) is incorrect because letters of representations provide corroborating information on various management representations obtained throughout the audit and therefore only provides limited evidence on internal control. Answer (c) is incorrect because attorneys' responses to auditor inquiries most frequently pertain to litigation, claims, and assessments.

**38. (c)** The requirement is to identify the procedure that is **not** a step in an auditor's decision to assess control risk at a level below the maximum. Answer (c) is correct because performing tests of details of transactions to detect material misstatements pertains more directly to detection risk rather than inherent or control risk. Answer (a) is incorrect because auditors evaluate the effectiveness of internal control with tests of controls. Answer (b) is incorrect because obtaining an understanding of the entity's information system and control environment is a preliminary step for considering control risk. Answer (d) is incorrect because auditors will consider the effect of internal control on the various financial statement assertions.

**39. (a)** The requirement is to identify an approach that auditors use to obtain evidential matter about control risk. Answer (a) is correct because auditors test controls to provide evidence for their assessment of control risk through inquiries of appropriate personnel, inspection of documents and records, observation of the application of controls, and reperformance of the application of the policy or procedure. Answers (b), (c), and (d) are incorrect because analytical procedures, calculation, and confirmation relate more directly to substantive testing and are not primary methods to test controls for purposes of assessing control risk.

**40. (c)** The requirement is to identify the **least** likely type of evidence the auditor will examine to determine whether controls are operating effectively. Answer (c) is correct because confirmation of accounts receivable is a substantive test, not a test of a control. Answer (a) is incorrect because records documenting the usage of computer programs may be tested to determine whether access is appropriately controlled. Answer (b) is incorrect because examining canceled supporting documents may help the auditor to determine that the structure will not allow duplicate billing to result in multiple payments. Answer (d) is incorrect because proper signatures will help the auditor to determine whether the authorization controls are functioning adequately.

**41. (a)** The requirement is to identify the accounts receivable auditing procedure that an auditor would most likely perform to obtain support for an assessed level of control risk below the maximum. Since an auditor uses the results of tests of controls to support an assessed level of control risk below the maximum, we are attempting to identify a test of a control. Answer (a) is correct because observing an entity's employee prepare the schedule of past due accounts receivable is a test of a control to evaluate the

effectiveness the process of preparing an accurate schedule of past due accounts; if the process is found to be effective it may lead to a reduction in the assessed level of control risk. Answer (b) is incorrect because the confirmation of accounts receivable is a substantive test, not a test of a control. Answer (c) is incorrect because the inspection of accounts receivable for unusual balances and comparing uncollectible accounts expense to actual accounts expense is ordinarily an analytical procedure performed as a substantive test. Answer (d) is incorrect because comparing uncollectible accounts expense to actual uncollectible accounts is ordinarily a substantive test.

### C.1. Management's Responsibility

**42. (b)** The requirement is to identify the type of companies to which the internal control provisions of the Sarbanes-Oxley Act of 2002 apply. Answer (b) is correct because the provisions apply to public companies that are registered with the Securities and Exchange Commission. Answer (a) is incorrect because nonpublic companies are not directly affected by the control provisions. Answer (c) is incorrect; there is no $100,000,000 requirement. Answer (d) is incorrect because nonpublic companies are not directly affected by the internal control provisions of the act.

**43. (a)** The requirement is to identify the most likely framework to be used by management in its internal control assessment. Answer (a) is correct as the COSO internal control framework is by far the most frequently used one. Answer (b) is incorrect because while a COSO enterprise risk management framework does exist, it is not ordinarily used by management in its internal control assessment. Answers (c) and (d) are incorrect because there is no such thing as a "FASB 37 internal control definitional framework" or an "AICPA internal control analysis manager."

### C.2. Management's Assessment

**44. (c)** The requirement is to identify the correct statement concerning the level of assistance that auditors may provide in assisting management with its assessment of internal control. Answer (c) is correct since only limited assistance may be provided so as not to create a situation in which the auditors are auditing their own work. Answer (a) is incorrect since some assistance may be provided. Answer (b) is incorrect because there are limitations on the level of assistance. Answer (d) is incorrect because the tie between risk and assistance seems inappropriate and in the wrong direction; also, this type of tradeoff between risk and assistance is not included in PCAOB Standard 2.

**45. (d)** The requirement is to identify which of the following need **not** be included in management's report on internal control under Section 404a of the Sarbanes-Oxley Act of 2002. Answer (d) is correct because, while the report must indicate that it is management's responsibility to establish and maintain adequate internal control, it need not also indicate that such control has no significant deficiencies. Answers (a), (b), and (c) are all incorrect because they include information that must be contained in management's report.

### C.3. Control Definitions

**46. (d)** The requirement is to identify the term that is defined as a weakness in internal control that allows more than a remote likelihood of misstatement that is more than inconsequential but less than material. Answer (d) is correct because this is the definition of a significant deficiency. Answer (a) is incorrect because a *control deficiency* exists when the design or operation of a control does not allow management, or employees, in the normal course of performing their functions to prevent or detect misstatements on a timely basis. Answer (b) is incorrect because a *material weakness* is a significant deficiency, or a combination of significant deficiencies that results in *more than a remote likelihood* that a *material misstatement* of the annual or interim financial statements will not be prevented or detected. Answer (c) is incorrect because the term reportable condition is not used in the standards for integrated audits.

**47. (d)** The requirement is to identify the amount involved with a material weakness. Answer (d) is correct because a material amount is involved. Answers (a), (b), and (c) are all incorrect because they suggest smaller amounts.

**48. (d)** The requirement is to identify the minimum likelihood of loss involved in the consideration of a control deficiency. Answer (d) is correct because a control deficiency is a condition in which the operation of a control does not allow management, or employees, in the normal course of performing their functions to prevent or detect misstatements on a timely basis—it does not explicitly consider likelihood of loss. Answer (a) is incorrect because the minimum likelihood of loss is not considered. Answer (b) is incorrect because the control deficiency occurrence of loss need not be more than remote. Answer (c) is incorrect because whether the minimum likelihood of loss is probable is not considered.

**C.4. Evaluating Internal Control**

**49. (a)** The requirement is to identify the type of control that reconciliation of cash accounts represents. Answer (a) is correct in that it is a compensating control which supplements a basic underlying control, in this case basic information processing controls related to cash. Answer (b) is incorrect because a preventive control prevents errors or fraud from occurring. Answer (c) is incorrect because the term "adjustive" control is not ordinarily used. Answer (d) is incorrect because "nonroutine" is ordinarily considered a type of transaction (e.g., the year-end close process), not a type of control.

**50. (d)** The requirement is to identify the type of transaction that establishing loan loss reserves is. Answer (d) is correct because *estimation transactions* are activities involving management's judgments or assumptions, such as determining the allowance for doubtful accounts, establishing warranty reserves, and assessing assets for impairment. Answer (a) is incorrect because the term substantive transaction is not used in PCAOB standards. Answer (b) is incorrect because routine transactions are those for recurring activities, such as sales, purchases, cash receipts and disbursements, and payroll. Answer (c) is incorrect because nonroutine transactions occur only periodically, such as the taking of physical inventory, calculating depreciation expense, or adjusting for foreign currencies; nonroutine transactions generally are not a part of the routine flow of transactions.

**C.5. The Audit of Internal Control**

**51. (d)** The requirement is to identify the procedure that involves tracing a transaction from origination through the company's information systems until it is reflected in the company's financial report. Answer (d) is correct because this is the approach followed in a walk-through. Answer (a) is incorrect because analytical analysis is a general term that simply suggests a general analysis. Answer (b) is incorrect because a substantive procedure addresses the correctness of a particular financial statement amount or disclosure. Answer (c) is incorrect because a test of a control addresses the operating effectiveness of a control.

**52. (b)** The requirement is to identify the "as of date" for purposes of an audit of internal control performed under PCAOB standards. Answer (b) is correct because the "as of date" is the last day of the fiscal period; it is this date on which the auditor concludes as to the effectiveness of internal control. Answers (a) and (c) are incorrect because neither the first day of the year nor the last day of the auditor's fieldwork is the appropriate date on which to evaluate internal control. Answer (d) is incorrect because the "as of date" is a particular date, not an average.

**53. (c)** The requirement is to identify the correct statement concerning a company that makes purchases both through the Internet and by telephone. Answer (c) is correct because both types of purchases are a part of the purchases process and represent major classes of transactions, as per PCAOB Standard 2. Answer (a) is incorrect because the purchase types themselves are not control objectives for internal control (control objectives address issues such as the completeness of the recording of sales). Answer (b) is incorrect because purchases are not assertions. Answer (d) is incorrect because purchase transactions may or may not be investigated in extreme detail.

**54. (a)** The requirement is to identify the circumstance(s) in which walk-throughs provide the auditor with primary evidence. A walk-through involves literally tracing a transaction from its origination through the company's information systems until it is reflected in the financial reports. Answer (a) is correct because a walk-through provides evidence to (1) confirm the auditor's understanding of the flow of transactions and the design of controls, (2) evaluate the effectiveness of the design of controls, and (3) to confirm whether controls have been placed in operation. Answer (b) is incorrect because walk-throughs provide the auditors with primary evidence to confirm whether controls have been placed in operation. Answer (c) is incorrect because walk-throughs provide primary evidence to evaluate the effectiveness of design in internal control. Answer (d) is incorrect both because walk-throughs provide primary evidence to (1) evaluate the effectiveness of the design of controls and (2) confirm whether the controls have been placed in operation.

**55. (a)** The requirement is to identify the most likely question to be asked of employee personnel during a walk-through. Answer (a) is correct because a question on whether an employee has ever been asked to override the process is included in the example questions to be asked by the auditor. Answer (b) is incorrect because auditors do not in general ask whether the employee believes he or she is underpaid. Answer (c) is incorrect because a direct question on fraudulent transactions like this, while possible, ordinarily is not suggested. Answer (d) is incorrect because the auditor will not usually ask who trained the person. Note that all four questions might be asked, but only one is among those recommended in Standard 2.

**56. (a)** The requirement is to identify how large the actual loss identified must be for a control deficiency to possibly be considered a material weakness. Answer (a) is correct because a material weakness is determined by whether there is more than a remote likelihood of a material loss occurring due to the control deficiency; the actual loss identified need not be material. Answer (b) is incorrect because it suggests that a material amount identified will not be considered a material weakness. Answer (c) is incorrect because it states that when the identified amount is immaterial it is never a material weakness. Answer (d) is incorrect because it suggests that when an immaterial or material actual loss is discovered, the situation would not be assessed as a possible material weakness.

**57. (c)** The requirement is to identify the circumstance that makes an account significant for purposes of a PCAOB audit of internal control. Answer (c) is correct because Standard 2 requires only more than a remote likelihood of material misstatement. Answer (a) is incorrect because the standard requires only a remote likelihood and because it is limited to material misstatements. Answer (b) is incorrect because the standard requires more than a remote likelihood, not more than a reasonably possible likelihood. Answer (d) is incorrect because material misstatements are involved, not misstatements that are more than inconsequential.

**58. (a)** The requirement is to identify the appropriate report when a control deficiency that is more than a significant deficiency is identified. Answer (a) is correct because a control deficiency that is more than a significant deficiency is a material weakness, and because a material weakness leads to an adverse opinion on internal control. Answer (b) is incorrect because qualified opinions are not issued when a material weakness exists. Answer (c) is incorrect because an unqualified opinion is not issued when a material weakness exists. Answer (d) is incorrect because explanatory language added to an unqualified report is not appropriate when a material weakness exists.

**59. (a)** The requirement is to identify the deficiency that is most likely to be considered a material weakness in internal control for purposes of an internal control audit of a public company. Answer (a) is correct because an ineffective internal audit function is among the list of circumstances that PCAOB Standard 2 suggests are significant deficiencies and strong indicators of the existence of a material weakness. Restatement of previously issued financial statements as a result of a *change in accounting principles* is ordinarily not considered even a significant deficiency. Answer (c) is incorrect because the reply "inadequate segregation of recordkeeping from accounting" makes no real sense because accounting is involved with recordkeeping. Answer (d) is incorrect because control activity weaknesses often do not represent material weaknesses.

**60. (b)** The requirement is to identify the most appropriate report when a circumstance-caused scope limitation results in inability to evaluate internal control for a significant account involved in the audit. Answer (b) is correct because

PCAOB Standard 2 indicates that either a qualified opinion or a disclaimer is appropriate, and because the disclaimer is not listed as an option. Answer (a) is incorrect because an adverse opinion is not appropriate. Answer (c) is incorrect because an unqualified opinion with explanatory language is not appropriate when the auditor is unable to evaluate internal control for a significant account. Answer (d) is incorrect because answers (a) and (c) are not appropriate.

**61. (c)** The requirement is to identify the most likely significant deficiency relating to a client's antifraud programs. Answer (c) is correct because an active audit committee, not a passive audit committee is needed. Answer (a) is incorrect because a broad scope of internal audit activities is ordinarily a strength, not a deficiency. Answer (b) is incorrect because a whistleblower program that encourages anonymous submissions is required. Answer (d) is incorrect because it is not ordinarily necessary to perform criminal background investigations for likely customers.

**62. (a)** The requirement is to identify the appropriate audit report when a material weakness is corrected subsequent to year-end, but before the audit report is issued. Answer (a) is correct because PCAOB Standard 2 requires an adverse audit report when a material weakness exists at year-end, the "as of date." Answer (b) is incorrect because an unqualified opinion is not appropriate. Answer (c) is incorrect because an unqualified opinion with explanatory language is not adequate. Answer (d) is incorrect because a qualified opinion is not appropriate when a material weakness exists at year-end.

**63. (b)** The requirement is to specify whether material weaknesses and/or significant deficiencies lead to an adverse opinion on internal control in an integrated audit. Answer (b) is correct because only material weaknesses lead to an adverse opinion. Answer (a) is incorrect because significant deficiencies do not result in an adverse opinion. Answer (c) is incorrect because material weaknesses do result in adverse opinions but significant deficiencies do not. Answer (d) is incorrect because material weaknesses do result in adverse opinions.

**64. (b)** The requirement is to specify what types of deficiencies must be communicated by the auditor to the audit committee. Answer (b) is correct because the auditor must communicate material weaknesses and other significant deficiencies, but not all control deficiencies. Answer (a) is incorrect because control deficiencies that are not significant need not be communicated to the audit committee (unless the auditor has made an agreement to communicate them). Answers (c) and (d) are incorrect because known material weaknesses must be communicated to the audit committee and control deficiencies that are not significant deficiencies need not be communicated.

**65. (c)** The requirement is to determine the manner in which significant deficiencies are communicated by the auditor to the audit committee under PCAOB Standard 2. Answer (c) is correct because the Standard requires a written communication. Answer (a) is incorrect because a written communication is required. Answer (b) is incorrect because the communication must be in a written form, not in an oral form. Answer (d) is incorrect because both material weaknesses and significant deficiencies must be communicated.

**66. (b)** The requirement is to identify the reply that is **not** correct relating to auditor reporting on client remediation of a material weakness identified in an audit of a public company's internal control. Answer (b) is correct because while an auditor may issue a report indicating that the material weakness no longer exists, the original report is not withdrawn. Answer (a) is not correct because management must present such a written statement. Answer (c) is not correct because auditors may rely in part upon the work performed by internal auditors. Answer (d) is not correct because it is necessary for management to provide documented support that the material weakness no longer exists. PCAOB Standard 4 provides auditor reporting guidance for reporting on whether a previously reported material weakness continues to exist.

**67. (b)** The requirement is to identify the correct statement with respect to reporting on whether a previously reported material weakness disclosed in an integrated audit continues to exist. Answer (b) is correct because an auditor may decide not to issue an audit report—for example, if the auditor believes that the material weakness remains or if a scope restriction is involved this is an available option. Answer (a) is incorrect because unqualified opinions are not allowed in such engagements. Answer (c) is incorrect because a disclaimer of opinion is not ordinarily required, although one may occur due to a scope limitation. Answer (d) is incorrect because one would expect management's written assertion to include a statement that the material weakness does not continue to exist, not that it exists. PCAOB Standard 4 provides auditor reporting guidance for reporting on whether a previously reported material weakness continues to exist.

**68. (b)** The requirement is to identify proper auditor actions when a scope limitation arises in an engagement to report on whether a previously reported material weakness continues to exist. Answer (b) is correct because while withdrawal from the engagement is allowed, qualified opinions are not allowed; in addition (not included in this question), a scope limitation may result in a disclaimer of opinion. Answer (a) is incorrect because a qualified opinion is not appropriate. Answer (c) is incorrect because withdrawal from the engagement is sometimes appropriate, and a qualified opinion is not. Answer (d) is incorrect because withdrawal from the engagement is sometimes appropriate. PCAOB Standard 4 provides auditor reporting guidance for reporting on whether a previously reported material weakness continues to exist.

**69. (d)** The requirement is to identify an auditor's reporting responsibility when he or she has identified a material weakness while performing an engagement to report upon whether a previously reported material weakness continues to exist. Answer (d) is correct because Standard No. 2 states that the report need not refer to the newly discovered material weakness. Answer (a) is incorrect because the auditor need not report on the newly discovered material weakness and because qualified opinions are not provided in this type of auditor's report. Answer (b) is incorrect because the auditor need not report on the newly discovered material weakness. Answer (c) is incorrect because the auditor need not report on the newly discovered material weakness. PCAOB Standard 4 provides auditor reporting guidance for reporting on whether a previously reported material weakness continues to exist. That standard requires the auditor to report any newly discovered material weaknesses to the audit committee. Also, the auditor may have a responsibility with respect to the internal control audit report under AU 561, *Subsequent Discovery of Facts Existing at the Date of the Auditor's Report.*

### D.1. Sales, Receivables, and Cash Receipts

**70. (a)** The requirement is to identify the procedure an auditor most likely would perform to test controls relating to management's assertion about the completeness of cash receipts for cash sales at a retail outlet. Answer (a) is correct because the use of cash registers and tapes helps assure that all such sales are recorded. Answer (b) is incorrect because the cash has already been recorded. Answer (c) is incorrect because the procedure only deals with recorded deposits, and therefore the completeness assertion is not addressed as directly as in answer (a). Answer (d) is incorrect because one would not expect the cash balance in the general ledger to agree with the bank confirmation request amount due to items in transit and outstanding at the point of reconciliation.

**71. (c)** The requirement is to identify the proper procedure to be performed immediately upon receipt of checks by mail. Sound internal control requires the use of adequate documentation to ensure that all transactions are properly recorded. This helps the company attain the financial statement assertion of completeness. Answer (c) is correct because the preparation of a duplicate listing of checks received provides the company with a source document of all the checks received that day. One list is then forwarded to the employee responsible for depositing the checks at the end of the day and the other list is sent to the accounting department so that they can post the amount to the cash receipts journal. Answer (a) is incorrect because the daily cash summary will ordinarily be prepared at the end of the day when all checks have been received. Answer (b) is incorrect because checks need not be compared to a sales invoice. Answer (d) is incorrect because the employee opening the mail should not also perform the recordkeeping function of recording the checks in the cash receipts journal.

**72. (b)** The requirement is to determine the type of evidence obtained when tracing shipping documents to prenumbered sales invoices. Answer (b) is correct because the shipping documents relate to shipments to customers, and tracing them to sales invoices will provide evidence on whether sales invoices were prepared. Answer (a) is incorrect because duplicate shipments or billings will not in general be detected by tracing individual shipping documents to prenumbered sales invoices. Answer (c) is incorrect because an auditor will trace from customer orders to shipping documents to determine whether all goods ordered were shipped. Answer (d) is incorrect because an auditor will account for the sequence of sales invoices to determine whether all sale invoices were accounted for.

**73. (a)** The requirement is to identify the control most likely to reduce the risk of diversion of customer receipts by an entity's employees. Answer (a) is correct because a bank lockbox system eliminates employee contact with cash receipts, and thereby greatly reduces the risk of diversion by employees. Answer (b) is incorrect because remittance advices are ordinarily prenumbered using the numbering schemes of the various customers and not of the client; also, even if a prenumbering system is instituted, difficulties remain in assuring that all receipts are recorded. Answer (c) is incorrect because a monthly bank reconciliation is only likely to be effective when receipts are deposited and then abstracted. Answer (d) is incorrect because while the daily deposit of cash receipts may reduce the risk of employee diversion of receipts, the procedure is not as effective as the bank lockbox system, which eliminates employee contact with the receipts.

**74.   (a)**   The requirement is to identify the best listed procedure for detecting the lapping of cash receipts by the client's cashier through use of customer checks received in the mail. Answer (a) is correct because lapping will result in a delay in the recording of specific remittance credits on the financial records, but the checks will be deposited in the bank as they are received. Answer (b) is incorrect because the daily cash summaries will include the same sums as the cash receipts journal entries. Answer (c) is incorrect because the bank deposit slips will be identical to any details included in the monthly bank statements. Answer (d) is incorrect because while the write-off of a receivable may help the individual involved in the lapping to avoid repayment, no lag is to be expected between authorization of the write-off and the date it is actually recorded.

**75.   (c)**   The requirement is to determine the individual or organization to which a list of remittances should be forwarded to in addition to the cashier. Answer (c) is correct because the accounts receivable bookkeeper will use the listing to update the subsidiary accounts receivable records. Answer (a) is incorrect because internal auditors will not normally investigate each day's listing of remittances for unusual transactions. Answer (b) is incorrect because the treasurer will not in general compare daily listings to the monthly bank statement. Answer (d) is incorrect because the list will not be sent to the bank.

**76.   (d)**   The requirement is to identify the procedure that most likely would **not** be a control designed to reduce the risk of errors in the billing process. Answer (d) is correct because the reconciliation of the control totals for sales invoices with the accounts receivable subsidiary ledger will follow billing; thus billing errors will have already occurred. Answer (a) is incorrect because identification of differences in shipping documents and sales invoices will allow for a correction of any errors and proper billing. Answer (b) is incorrect because computer programmed controls will assure the accuracy of the sales invoice. Answer (c) is incorrect because the matching of shipping documents with the approved sales orders will allow the preparation of a correct invoice.

**77.   (b)**   The requirement is to identify the audit procedure an auditor most likely would perform to test controls relating to management's assertion concerning the completeness of sales transactions. Answer (b) is correct because inspection of shipping documents that have **not** been recorded in the sales journal will possibly reveal items that have been sold (as evidenced by a shipping document) but for some reason have not been recorded as sales. Answers (a), (c), and (d) are all incorrect because verification of extension and footings, comparing invoiced prices, and inquiring about credit granting policies all relate more directly to the valuation assertion than to the completeness assertion. See AU 326 for information on financial statement assertions.

**78.   (a)**   The requirement is to identify the control that most likely would assure that all billed sales are correctly posted to the accounts receivable ledger. Answer (a) is correct because the daily sales summary will include all "billed" sales for a particular day. Comparing this summary to the postings to the accounts receivable ledger will provide evidence on whether billed sales are correctly posted. Answer (b) is incorrect because comparing sales invoices to shipping documents provides evidence on whether invoiced sales have been shipped. Answer (c) is incorrect because reconciling the accounts receivable ledger to the control account will not provide assurance that all billed sales were posted in that both the receivable ledger and the control account may have omitted the sales. Answer (d) is incorrect because comparing shipments with sales invoices provides evidence on whether all shipments have been invoiced, not on whether all billed sales are correctly posted.

**79.   (a)**   The requirement is to determine the financial statement assertion being most directly tested when an auditor tests an entity's policy of obtaining credit approval before shipping goods to customers. Answer (a) is correct because testing credit approval helps assure that goods are shipped to customers who are likely to be able to pay; accordingly the valuation assertion for receivables is being directly tested. Answer (b) is incorrect because completeness deals with whether all transactions and accounts are recorded. Answer (c) is incorrect because existence deals with whether assets exist at a given date and whether recorded transactions have occurred during a given period. Answer (d) is incorrect because rights and obligations deal with whether assets are the rights of the entity and liabilities are the obligations of the entity at a given date.

**80.   (d)**   The requirement is to identify the control that most likely would help ensure that **all** credit sales transactions are recorded. Answer (d) is correct because the matching of shipping documents with entries in the sales journal will provide assurance that all shipped items (sales) have been completely recorded. Answer (a) is incorrect because comparison of approved sales orders to authorized credit limits and balances will help ensure that customer credit limits are not exceeded, rather than the complete recording of credit sales. Answer (b) is incorrect because reconciliation of the accounts receivable subsidiary ledger to the accounts receivable control account will provide only a limited amount of control over the complete recording of sales. The control is incomplete since, for example, a sale that has not been recorded in either the subsidiary or control accounts will not be detected. Answer (c) is incorrect because monthly statements generally will not be sent to customers to whom no sales have been recorded.

**81.   (c)**   The requirement is to identify the control that will be most effective in offsetting the tendency of sales personnel to maximize sales volume at the expense of high bad debt write-offs. Answer (c) is correct because segregation of the authorization of credit from the sales function will allow an independent review of the creditworthiness of customers. Answer (a) is incorrect because while denying access to cash by employees responsible for sales and bad debt write-offs may deter embezzlements, the problem of high bad debt write-offs is likely to remain. Answer (b) is incorrect because while so segregating the matching of shipping documents and sales invoices may help assure that items are shipped properly and subsequently recorded, it will not significantly affect bad debts. Answer (d) is incorrect because while independent reconciliation of control and subsidiary accounts receivable records may defer embezzlements, bad debt write-offs will not be affected.

**82. (d)** The requirement is to determine the department that should approve bad debt write-offs. The department responsible for bad debt write-offs should be independent of the sales, credit, and the recordkeeping for that function, and should have knowledge relating to the accounts. Answer (d) is correct because, in addition to being independent of the various functions, the treasurer's department is likely to have knowledge to help make proper decisions of this nature. Answers (a) and (b), accounts receivable and the credit department, are incorrect because neither department is independent of this function. Answer (c) is incorrect because while accounts payable is independent of the function, its personnel are less likely than those of the treasurer's department to have the necessary information relating to the accounts that should be written off.

**83. (b)** The requirement is to identify a reason that employers bond employees who handle cash receipts. Answer (b) is correct because employee knowledge that bonding companies often prosecute those accused of dishonest acts may deter employees' dishonest acts. Answer (a) is incorrect because bonding protects the employer from dishonest acts, not the employee from unintentional errors. Answer (c) is incorrect because the bonding company does not serve the role of independent monitoring of cash. Answer (d) is incorrect because while rotation of positions and forcing employees to take periodic vacations are effective controls for preventing fraud, they are not accomplished through bonding.

**84. (c)** The requirement is to identify the control which would offset a weakness that allowed the accounts receivable clerk to approve credit memos and to have access to cash. Note that such a weakness may lead to a fraud in which the accounts receivable clerk receives and keeps cash payments while issuing a fraudulent credit memo as the basis for a credit to the customer's account. Answer (c) is correct because the owner's review of credit memos could help establish that fraudulent memos had not been issued for receivables which had in actuality been collected by the clerk; for example, when reviewing credit memos the owner would expect to see a receiving report for sales returns for which credit memos have been generated. Answer (a) is incorrect because the bookkeeper may be able to maintain the records in such a manner as to avoid billing errors related to the fraud, and therefore a review of billings and postings may not reveal such fraud. Answer (b) is incorrect because month-end reconciliation of checking accounts with the monthly bank statement will not reflect cash that has been improperly diverted by the accounts receivable clerk. Answer (d) is incorrect because the accounts receivable clerk should be able to maintain the detail and ledger amount in balance and thereby avoid detection.

**85. (b)** The requirement is to determine who should prepare a remittance advice when the customer fails to include one with a remittance. Remittances should be opened by an individual such as a receptionist who is independent of the sales function. That individual will prepare any needed remittance advices. The credit manager [answer (a)], and the sales manager [answer (c)], are incorrect because they

perform an authorization function related to sales. Answer (d) is incorrect because the accounts receivable clerk performs a recordkeeping function for sales.

**D.2. Purchases, Payables, and Cash Disbursements**

**86. (b)** The requirement is to identify the audit procedure relating to paid vouchers that will provide assurance that each voucher is submitted and paid only once. Answer (b) is correct because when the check signer stamps vouchers "paid" it is unlikely to be paid a second time since that individual will notice the stamp on the voucher the second time it is submitted for payment.

**87. (d)** The requirement is to determine the appropriate responsibility for the person who signs checks. Answer (d) is correct because the individual who signs checks should be responsible for mailing them so as to avoid a variety of fraud in which the checks are improperly converted into cash by company employees. Answer (a) is incorrect because the individual who reconciles the bank accounts should have no other responsibilities with respect to cash. Answer (b) is incorrect because accounts payable does not need the checks and, if they receive them, those checks may be converted into cash which is then stolen. Answer (c) is incorrect because the person who signs the checks should determine that proper supporting documents exist and should cancel that documentation after the payment is made.

**88. (b)** The requirement is to determine the financial statement assertion that a test of controls of vouching a sample of entries in the voucher register to the supporting documents most directly addresses. Answer (b) is correct because the existence or occurrence assertion addresses whether recorded entries are valid and the direction of this test is from the recorded entry in the voucher register to the supporting documents. Answer (a) is incorrect because completeness addresses whether all transactions and accounts are included and would involve tests tracing from support for purchases to the recorded entry. Answers (c) and (d) are incorrect because vouching the entries provides only limited evidence on valuation and rights. See AU 326 for information on management's financial statement assertions.

**89. (d)** The requirement is to determine the control that is **not** usually performed in the vouchers payable department. Answer (d) is correct because the vouchers payable department will not in general have access to unused prenumbered purchase orders and receiving reports. Answer (a) is incorrect because the vouchers payable department will match the vendor's invoice with the related receiving report to determine that the item for which the company has been billed has been received. Answer (b) is incorrect because the vouchers payable department will approve vouchers for payment when all documentation is proper and present. Answer (c) is incorrect because the vouchers payable department will code the voucher with accounts to be debited.

**90. (b)** The requirement is to identify the function that is consistent with matching vendors' invoices with receiving reports. Answer (b) is correct because while matching invoices and receiving reports, the employee might effectively recompute the calculations on the vendors' invoices to determine that the amounts are proper. Answers (a) and (c) are incorrect. The individual who matches the invoices and receiving reports will often also approve them for payment. Therefore, this individual should not also post accounts payable records or reconcile the accounts payable ledger. Answer (d) is incorrect because the individual who controls the signing of the checks should cancel the invoices after payment.

**91. (b)** The requirement is to identify the population from which items should be selected to determine whether checks are being issued for unauthorized expenditures. Answer (b) is correct because a sample of canceled checks should be selected and compared with the approved vouchers, a prenumbered purchase order and prenumbered receiving reports. A canceled check that does not have such support may have been unauthorized. Answers (a), (c), and (d) are all incorrect because selecting items from purchase orders, receiving reports, or approved vouchers will not reveal circumstances in which a check was issued without that supporting document. For example, when selecting a sample from purchase orders, one would not discover a situation in which a check had been issued without a purchase order.

**92. (d)** The requirement is to determine which question would most likely be included in an internal control questionnaire concerning the completeness assertion for purchases. Answer (d) is correct because prenumbering and accounting for purchase orders, receiving reports, and vouchers will allow a company to determine that purchases are completely recorded. For example, in examining a receiving report the client might discover that the purchase was not recorded. Answer (a) is incorrect because requiring a purchase order before a shipment is accepted will address whether or not the shipment has been ordered. Answer (b) is incorrect because matching purchase requisitions with vendor invoices does not directly address whether the purchase is recorded. Answer (c) is incorrect because the unpaid voucher file represents items that have already been recorded, and thus will not directly address the completeness of the recording of purchases.

**93. (d)** The requirement is to identify the proper control pertaining to the accounts payable department. Answer (d) is correct because the accounts payable department should establish the agreement of the vendor's invoice with the purchase order and receiving report to provide assurance that the item was both ordered and received. Answer (a) is incorrect because the individual signing the check (e.g., the treasurer), not the accounts payable department, should stamp, perforate, or otherwise cancel supporting documentation after a check is signed. Answer (b) is incorrect because purchase requisitions will not normally include detailed price information. Answer (c) is incorrect because the quantity ordered on the receiving department copy of the purchase order will already be obliterated when the purchase order is completed by the purchasing department.

**94. (b)** The requirement is to determine which copy of the purchase order should omit indication of the quantity of merchandise ordered. Answer (b) is correct because if the receiving department personnel are unaware of the quantities ordered, they will provide an independent count of quantities received. Answer (a) is incorrect because the department that initiated the requisition needs the merchandise, and therefore, should know what has been ordered. Answer (c) is incorrect because the purchasing agent is involved with

purchasing the items and therefore must be aware of the quantity involved. Answer (d) is incorrect because the accounts payable department must reconcile the quantity received and the quantity billed to the quantity that was authorized to be purchased per the purchase order.

**95. (b)** The requirement is to identify the audit procedure which would most likely detect a client error in recording a large purchase. Answer (b) is correct because reconciling the vendors' monthly statements with the subsidiary ledger for payables should disclose a difference in the month following the error. Answer (a), footing the purchases journal, is unlikely to detect the error since the journal's totals will have been mathematically accumulated properly. Answer (c) is incorrect because the incorrect total will be reflected in both the purchases journal and in the ledger accounts. Answer (d) is incorrect because such confirmations will only detect the error quarterly which is neither timely nor efficient.

**96. (d)** The requirement is to identify a function that is compatible with the approval of purchase orders. Answer (d) is correct because the purchases department will normally approve purchase orders (generated from user departments or stores) and negotiate terms of purchase with vendors. Answer (a) is incorrect because while the purchases department may reconcile the open invoice file, this is primarily a recordkeeping function that will often be performed by the accounting department. Answer (b) is incorrect because most frequently the receiving department will inspect goods upon receipt. Answer (c) is incorrect because user groups or stores will authorize requisitions of goods. Keep in mind the principle of segregation of functions. Recordkeeping, authorization, and custodial functions should all be segregated.

### D.3. Inventories and Production

**97. (c)** The requirement is to identify the most likely procedure an auditor would perform in obtaining an understanding of a manufacturing entity's internal control for inventory balances. Answer (c) is correct because a review of the entity's descriptions of inventory policies and procedures will help the auditor to obtain the necessary understanding about the design of relevant policies, procedures, and records, and whether they have been placed in operation by the entity. Answers (a) and (b) are incorrect because analyses of liquidity and turnover ratios are analytical procedures designed to identify cost variances that will help the auditor primarily to determine the nature, timing and extent of auditing procedures that will be used to obtain evidential matter for specific account balances or classes of transactions. Answer (d) is incorrect because test counts of inventory are generally obtained as a substantive procedure.

**98. (d)** The requirement is to identify the control that most likely would be used to maintain accurate inventory records. Answer (d) is correct because periodic inventory counts will assure that perpetual inventory records are accurate and, because employees will know that inventory differences are investigated, they will be less likely to steal any inventory. Answer (a) is incorrect because comparing the perpetual inventory records with current costs of items will reveal situations in which costs have changed, but is unlikely to help in the maintenance of accurate inventory records. Answer (b) is incorrect because while a just-in-time inventory ordering system may help assure that inventory records are accurate (as well as kept at low levels), such a system generally also requires periodic inventory counts to maintain accurate inventory records. Answer (c) is incorrect because matching requisitions, receiving reports, and purchase orders only helps assure that items received are paid for; the matching process does not assure accurate inventory records.

**99. (d)** The requirement is to determine a likely effect on the audit of inventory if the assessed level of control risk is high. Answer (d) is correct because a high assessed level of control risk may result in changing the timing of substantive tests to year-end rather than at an interim date. If the assessed level of control risk is low, the auditor could perform interim substantive tests and rely upon internal control to provide valid year-end records. However, because the assessed level of control risk is high, the controls cannot be relied upon. Also, the nature of substantive tests may change from less effective to more effective procedures (e.g., use of independent parties outside the entity rather than internal) and an increase in the extent of procedures (e.g., larger sample sizes). Answer (a) is incorrect because, as indicated, an auditor will generally seek a year-end count of inventory. Answer (b) is incorrect because gross profit tests will not in general have the required precision when control risk is high. Answer (c) is incorrect because tests of controls are likely to substantiate an auditor's view that control risk is high, and it is therefore unlikely that their performance will be cost-effective.

**100. (c)** The requirement is to identify the control which is most likely to address the completeness assertion for inventory. Answer (c) is correct because by prenumbering receiving reports and by reconciling them with inventory records, one is able to test completeness by determining whether all receipts have been recorded. Answer (a) is incorrect because reconciling the subsidiary records with the work in process will only identify discrepancies between the records, it will not identify whether all transactions that should be in the inventory records are represented in the records. Answer (b) is incorrect because while the segregation of receiving from custody of finished goods is important, it less directly addresses completeness than does answer (a). Answer (d) is incorrect because separating the duties between the payroll department and inventory accounting personnel does not directly address completeness of inventory.

**101. (c)** The requirement is to determine the proper internal control for handling customer returns of defective merchandise. Answer (c) is correct because the receiving department can count the goods, and list them on a sales return notice to determine that all such returns are properly recorded. This serves as a control because the normal procedures of the receiving function include establishing the original accountability and recordkeeping for items received. Answers (a), (b), and (d) all represent functions not typically involved in the receiving function and thus involve a higher risk relating to establishing accountability.

**102. (c)** The requirement is to identify the effect on revenues, receivables, and inventory of inadequate controls over the invoicing function that allows goods to be shipped without being invoiced. Items shipped without invoicing will result in a situation in which the accounting department is unaware of the sale. Therefore, debits to accounts receiv-

able and credits to sales will not be recorded, resulting in an understatement of both revenues and receivables. Similarly, because accounting is unaware of the sale, no entry to reduce inventory will be made, resulting in an overstatement of inventory.

**103. (c)** The requirement is to identify the question that an auditor would expect to find on the **production** cycle section of an internal control questionnaire. Answer (c) is correct because approved requisitions will help maintain control over raw materials released to be used in the production cycle. Answers (a), (b), and (d) are all incorrect because approval of vendors' invoices for payment, mailing of checks after signing, and comparing individual disbursements to totals all pertain more directly to the disbursement cycle.

**104. (b)** The requirement is to determine an objective of internal control for a production cycle in addition to providing assurance that transactions are properly executed and recorded. Answer (b) is correct because, in addition to providing assurance as to proper execution and recording, an objective for the production cycle (as well as other cycles) is the safeguarding of assets, here work in process and finished goods. Answers (a), (c), and (d) are incorrect because they represent detailed controls established to help achieve the overall objectives. They are all much more specific than the overall objectives.

**D.4. Personnel and Payroll**

**105. (b)** The requirement is to identify a purpose of vouching data for a sample of employees in a payroll register to approved clock card data. Answer (b) is correct because the clock card data provides the auditor with evidence on whether employees worked the number of hours for which the payroll register indicates they were paid. Answer (a) is incorrect because clock card data often does not include authorized pay rates. Answer (c) is incorrect because the procedure does not directly address the segregation of duties since no information is provided concerning the distribution of the payroll. Answer (d) is incorrect because unclaimed payroll checks are not being analyzed.

**106. (a)** The requirement is to identify the control that most likely could help prevent employee payroll fraud. Answer (a) is correct because prompt notification of the payroll supervisor concerning terminations will lead to timely removal of terminated employees from the payroll. Accordingly, no payroll checks will be prepared for such terminated employees. Answer (b) is incorrect because unclaimed payroll checks should not be returned to the supervisors who might inappropriately cash them. Answer (c) is incorrect because since the payroll department is involved in recordkeeping, it should not approve salary rates. Answer (d) is incorrect because calculation of total hours by the payroll supervisor is unlikely to prevent employee payroll fraud.

**107. (a)** The requirement is to determine the best procedure for determining the effectiveness of an entity's controls relating to the existence or occurrence assertion for payroll transactions. Answer (a) is correct because proper segregation of duties between personnel and payroll disbursement eliminates many frauds in which "phantom" employees are being paid. Answer (b) is incorrect because accounting for the prenumbered payroll checks addresses completeness more directly than it does existence or occurrence. Answer (c) is incorrect because recomputing payroll deductions for employee fringe benefits, without additional analysis, provides only a very limited test of existence or occurrence. Answer (d) is incorrect because verifying the preparation of the monthly payroll account bank reconciliation is unlikely to provide evidence on the existence or occurrence assertion, although some possibility does exist if signatures on checks are analyzed in detail.

**108. (c)** The requirement is to identify the situation in which it is most likely that an auditor would assess control risk for payroll at the maximum. Answer (c) is correct because the payroll department, which is essentially a recordkeeping function, should not also authorize payroll rate changes. Under strong internal control recordkeeping, authorization, and custody over assets should be segregated. Answer (a) is incorrect because examining authorization forms for new employees is consistent with the payroll department's recordkeeping function. Answer (b) is incorrect because comparing payroll registers with original batch transmittal data is a control relating to recordkeeping. Answer (d) is incorrect because while the actual hiring of employees is normally done in the personnel department, allowing the payroll department supervisor to hire subordinates, with proper approval, is not as inconsistent with payroll's recordkeeping function as is authorizing rate changes for all employees.

**109. (c)** The requirement is to identify the control most likely to prevent direct labor hours from being charged to manufacturing overhead. Answer (c) is correct because time tickets may be coded as to whether direct labor on various projects was involved. Accordingly, using time tickets will help identify direct labor costs. Answer (a) is incorrect because while periodic counts of work in process may provide a control over physical units of production, the counts will not in general provide assurance that direct labor hours are properly charged to the product rather than to manufacturing overhead. Answer (b) is incorrect because comparing daily journal entries with production orders will not in general identify costs that have been omitted from direct labor due to the level of aggregation of the entries. Answer (d) is incorrect because the reconciliation of work in process inventory with budgets will provide only very limited detection ability relating to the charging of direct labor to manufacturing overhead.

**110. (a)** The requirement is to determine the individual(s) who should distribute paychecks and have custody of unclaimed paychecks. Answer (a) is correct because these custody functions should not be performed by the payroll department which is a recordkeeping function. Under proper internal control recordkeeping, custody, and authorization of transactions should be segregated.

**111. (c)** If payment of wages were to be in cash, each employee receiving payment should be required to sign a receipt for the amount of pay received. Thus, there would be control over the total amount disbursed as well as amounts disbursed to each individual employee. Answer (a) is incorrect because if a signed receipt is not received from each employee paid, there would be no proof of payment. Even though the pay envelopes include both cash and a computation of net wages, the employees should have the opportunity to count the cash received before signing a payroll receipt. Answer (b) is incorrect because unclaimed pay

envelopes should not be retained by the paymaster, but rather deposited in a bank account by the cashier. Answer (d) is incorrect because the wage payment will be made in cash and not by check. Accordingly, a receipt must be obtained for each cash payment.

**112. (a)** The requirement is to identify the purpose of segregating the duties of hiring personnel and of distributing payroll checks. Answer (a) is correct because the hiring of personnel is an authorization function while the distribution of checks is a custody function. Thus, in order to properly segregate authorization from custody, these duties should not be performed by the same individual. The combination of these two functions in the same position would create the possibility of the addition of a fictitious employee to the payroll and subsequent misappropriation of paychecks. Answer (b) is incorrect because the functions involved are not primarily operational or recordkeeping. Answer (c) is incorrect because the treasury function, and not the controllership function, will normally be responsible for distributing payroll checks. Answer (d) is incorrect because segregation of duties does not directly address administrative controls vs. internal accounting controls.

**113. (c)** The requirement is to determine the best method to minimize the opportunities for fraud for unclaimed cash in a **cash** payroll system. For a **cash** payroll the best control is to get the unclaimed cash out of the firm's physical control and into the bank. Answer (a) is incorrect because maintaining the accountability for cash which is in a safe-deposit box is difficult. Answers (b) and (d) are incorrect because the cash need not be kept by the firm.

**114. (c)** The requirement is to identify a reason why an auditor may observe the distribution of paychecks. Answer (c) is correct because an employee's presence to collect the paycheck provides evidence that the employee actually exists and is currently employed by the client. Answer (a) is incorrect because the distributions of payroll checks would not reveal whether payrate authorization is properly separated from the operating function. Answer (b) is incorrect because the paycheck distribution does not provide information on whether deductions from gross pay have been calculated properly. Answer (d) is incorrect because observation of the paycheck distribution process does not of itself provide assurance that the paychecks agree with the related payroll register and time cards.

**115. (a)** The requirement is to determine the department most likely to approve change in pay rates and deductions from employee salaries. Answer (a) is correct because the personnel department, which has the primary objective of planning, controlling and coordinating employees, will determine that proposed salary increases (often recommended by supervisors of employees) are consistent with the company's salary guidelines and will approve changes in deductions. Answers (b) and (c) are incorrect because the treasurer and controller will in general initiate the pay rate change process for only those employees within their departments and will not generally approve changes for employees outside their departments. Answer (d) is incorrect because the payroll functions is a recordkeeping function which will modify employee pay rates based on approved changes from personnel. Payroll should not have authority regarding pay rates and deductions.

## D.5. Financing

**116. (d)**   The requirement is to determine the most likely question that would be included on an internal control questionnaire for notes payable. Answer (d) is correct because companies frequently require that direct borrowings on notes payable be authorized by the board of directors; accordingly, auditors will determine whether proper policy has been followed. Answer (a) is incorrect because internal control questionnaires do not in general include questions on whether assets that collateralize notes payable are critically needed. Answer (b) is incorrect because the internal control questionnaire for disbursements is more likely to address the required authorized signatures on checks than will the internal control questionnaire for notes payable. Answer (c) is incorrect because while it is often good business practice to use proceeds from long-term notes to purchase noncurrent assets, this is not required and is not included on an internal control questionnaire.

**117. (d)**   The requirement is to identify the primary responsibility of a bank acting as registrar for capital stock. Answer (d) is correct because the primary responsibility of the stock registrar is to prevent any overissuance of stock, and thereby verify that the stock is issued properly. Answer (a) is incorrect because registrar will not in general determine that the dividend amounts are proper. Answer (b) is incorrect because the transfer agent will maintain records of total shares outstanding as well as detailed stockholder records, and carry out transfers of stock ownership. Answer (c) is incorrect because registrars do not perform the role described relating to mergers, acquisitions, and the sale of treasury stock.

**118. (a)**   Canceled stock certificates should be defaced and attached to corresponding stubs as is done with voided checks. The objective of the control is to prevent reissuance. Answer (b) is incorrect because failure to deface permits reissuance. Answer (c) is incorrect because destruction of the certificates would preclude their control (i.e., their existence after defacing provides assurance that they cannot be reissued). If the certificates were destroyed, one or more might be reissued without any proof that such occurred. Answer (d) is incorrect because the Secretary of State has no interest in receiving defaced and canceled stock certificates.

## D.6. Investing

**119. (a)**   The requirement is to identify the reply which is **not** a control that is designed to protect investment securities. Answer (a) is not a control since the custody of securities should be assigned to individuals who **do not** have accounting responsibility for securities; as with other assets, authorization, recordkeeping, and custody should be separated. Answer (b) is incorrect because securities should be properly controlled physically in order to prevent unauthorized usage. Answer (c) is incorrect because access to securities should ordinarily be vested in two individuals so as to assure their safekeeping. Answer (d) is incorrect because securities should be registered in the name of the owner.

**120. (b)**   The requirement is to identify the best control for safeguarding marketable securities when an independent trust agent is not employed. Answer (b) is correct because requiring joint control over securities maintained in a safe-deposit box assures that, absent collusion, assets are safeguarded. Answer (a) is incorrect because a review of investment decisions by the investment committee will have a very limited effect on *safeguarding* marketable securities. Answer (c) is incorrect because the simple tracing of marketable securities from the subsidiary ledgers to the general ledger does not directly safeguard marketable securities since, for example, unrecorded transactions may occur. Answer (d) is incorrect because, even if the chairman of the board did verify marketable securities on the balance sheet date, the control will only be effective at that point in time.

**121. (d)**   The requirement is to identify the best audit procedure when a weakness in internal control over reporting of retirements exists. Answer (d) is correct because selecting certain items of equipment from the accounting records and attempting to locate them will reveal situations in which the accounting records still have them recorded subsequent to their retirement. Answer (a) is incorrect because inspecting items that still exist is not likely to lead to discovery of unrecorded retirements. Answer (b) is incorrect because depreciation may continue to be taken on equipment that has been retired, but not recorded. Answer (c) is incorrect because it is doubtful that such retirements have been reclassified as "other assets."

**122. (d)**   The requirement is to identify the question that is **least** likely to be included on an internal control questionnaire concerning the initiation and execution of equipment transactions. Answer (d) is correct because procedures to monitor and properly restrict access to equipment do not relate directly to the initiation and execution of equipment transactions. Answer (a) is incorrect because requests for major repairs relate to initiation of a transaction which should be controlled. Answer (b) is incorrect because prenumbered purchase orders may be used to control all purchases, including purchases of equipment. Answer (c) is incorrect because the significant amounts of money involved with purchases of equipment suggest the need for the solicitation of competitive bids.

**123. (d)**   The requirement is to identify the control that would be most effective in assuring that the proper custody of assets in the investing cycle is maintained. Answer (d) is correct because comparing recorded balances in the investment subsidiary ledger with physical counts will help assure that recorded assets are those over which the company has custody. This is an example of the control activity of comparison of assets with recorded accountability. Answer (a) is incorrect because internal control is improved when two individuals, not one, must be present for entry to the safe-deposit box. Answer (b) is incorrect because while the segregation of duties within the recordkeeping may in certain circumstances be desirable, it does not directly address custody over assets. Answer (c) is incorrect because only extremely major investments generally need be authorized by the board of directors.

**124. (d)**   The requirement is to determine who should have responsibility for custody of short-term bearer bond investments and the submission of coupons for periodic collections of interest. The treasurer authorizes such transactions. Answer (a) is incorrect because the chief accountant, who is in charge of the recordkeeping function, should not also maintain custody of the bonds. Answer (b) is incorrect because the internal auditor should not be directly involved as such involvement would make an independent review of the system impossible. Answer (c) is incorrect because the cashier function is more directly involved with details such as endorsing, depositing, and maintaining records of cash receipts.

**125.  (b)**   The requirement is to identify the control that would be most likely to assist an entity in satisfying the completeness assertion related to long-term investments. Answer (b) is correct because completeness deals with whether all transactions are recorded, and the comparison of securities in the bank safe-deposit box with recorded investments may reveal securities which are in the safe-deposit box but are not recorded.  Answer (a) is incorrect because verification of security registration helps establish the rights assertion not the completeness assertion.  Answer (c) is incorrect because vouching the acquisition of securities by comparing brokers' advices with canceled checks helps to establish the existence assertion not the completeness assertion.  Answer (d) is incorrect because a comparison of the current market prices of recorded investments with brokers' advices addresses the valuation assertion not the completeness assertion.

**126.  (a)**   The requirement is to identify the best control for safeguarding marketable securities against loss.  Answer (a) is correct because use of an independent trust company allows the effective separation of custody and recordkeeping for the securities.  Answer (b) is incorrect because a verification of marketable securities at the balance sheet date may have only a limited effect on safeguarding the securities throughout the year.  Answer (c) is incorrect because tracing all purchases and sales of marketable securities will not affect securities that have disappeared for which no entries have been made.  Also, it is unlikely that an entity will rely upon the independent auditor in this manner.  Answer (d) is incorrect because maintenance of control over custody by a member of the board of directors may provide less complete control than the use of an independent trust company.

**127.  (c)**   The requirement is to determine the appropriate combination of audit tests when there are numerous property and equipment transactions during the year and the auditor plans to assess control risk at a low level.  Answer (c) is correct because, to justify an assessment of control risk at a low level, tests of controls will be required.  This will allow auditors to perform only limited tests of current year property and equipment transactions.  Answer (a) is incorrect because tests of controls will be performed to allow the auditor to perform limited, not extensive, tests of property and equipment balances at the end of the year.  Answers (b) and (d) are incorrect because analytical procedures on either year-end balances or transactions will not justify a low assessed level of control risk.

### D.7.   Overall Internal Control Questionnaires (Checklists)

**128.  (d)**   The requirement is to determine the type of fraud which is most difficult to detect.  Answer (d), a fraud committed by the controller, is most difficult to detect because the controller is in control of the recordkeeping function and thus may be able to commit a fraud and then manipulate the accounting records so as to make its discovery unlikely.  Answer (a) is incorrect because while a cashier may be able to embezzle funds, s/he will not have access to the accounting records and thus discovery of the embezzlement will be likely.  Answer (b) is incorrect because a key-

punch operator will not in general have access to assets. Answer (c) is incorrect because an internal auditor will not generally be able to manipulate the accounting records and generally has limited access to assets.

### E.1.   Communicating with the Audit Committee

**129.  (c)**   The requirement is to identify the matter an auditor would most likely consider to be a reportable condition to be communicated to the audit committee.  AU 325 defines a reportable condition as a significant deficiency in the design or operation of internal control which could adversely affect the organization's ability to record, process, summarize, and report financial data consistent with the assertions of management.  Answer (c) is correct because a lack of objectivity by those responsible for accounting decisions may result in misstated financial statements.  Answers (a), (b), and (d) are all incorrect because a failure to renegotiate unfavorable long-term purchase commitments, recurring operating losses, and plans to reduce ownership equity do not fall within the definition of a reportable condition.

**130.  (b)**   The requirement is to determine the matter that an auditor would communicate to an audit committee.  Answer (b) is correct because AU 380 requires that when the auditor is aware of such consultation with another CPA, s/he should discuss with the audit committee his/her views about significant matters that were the subject of such consultation; accordingly, such a discussion with management is to be expected.  While the information suggested in answers (a), (c), and (d) may all be communicated to the audit committee, they are not included as required disclosures under AU 380.  See AU 380 for the various matters that must be communicated to the audit committee.

**131.  (c)**   The requirement is to identify the correct statement concerning reportable conditions identified in an audit. Answer (c) is correct because an auditor may communicate reportable conditions either during an audit or after the audit's completion.  Answer (a) is incorrect because an auditor need not search for reportable conditions.  Answer (b) is incorrect because all reportable conditions are not also material weaknesses.  Answer (d) is incorrect because an auditor may not issue a written report that **no** reportable conditions were noted during an audit.

**132.  (b)**   The requirement is to identify the correct statement concerning an auditor's required communication with an entity's audit committee.  Answer (b) is correct because the communication should include such information on disagreements.  See AU 380 for this and other required communications with the audit committee.  Answer (a) is incorrect because the communication may occur before or after issuance of the auditor's report.  Answer (c) is incorrect because not all matters need be communicated to management.  Answer (d) is incorrect because significant adjustments need to be communicated to the audit committee.

**133.  (d)**   The requirement is to identify the statement that should be included in an auditor's letter on reportable conditions.  Answer (d) is correct because AU 325 indicates that such a letter to the audit committee should (1) indicate that the audit's purpose was to report on the financial statements and **not** to provide assurance on internal control, (2) include the definition of a reportable condition, and (3) restrict distribution of the report.

**134. (b)** The requirement is to identify the discussion that it is least likely that an auditor will initiate with a client's audit committee. Answer (b) is correct because auditors do not generally initiate a discussion on materiality, although they do occasionally respond to such questions. See AU 380 for auditor communications with audit committees.

**135. (b)** The requirement is to identify the correct statement about an auditor's required communication with an entity's audit committee. Answer (b) is correct because the communication must include significant misstatements discovered, even if corrected by management. Answer (a) is incorrect because while such communications may be communicated to management, there is no such requirement. Answer (c) is incorrect because disagreements with management, as well as the other required disclosures, may be communicated either orally or in writing. Answer (d) is incorrect because an auditor must use judgment in determining whether to recommunicate such weaknesses in internal control. Also, see AU 380 for the matters communicated to the audit committee.

**136. (c)** The requirement is to identify the correct statement concerning an auditor's required communication of reportable conditions. Answer (c) is correct because distribution of an auditor's report on reportable conditions should be restricted to management and the audit committee. Answer (a) is incorrect because lack of correction of a reportable condition does not necessarily result in a scope limitation. Answer (b) is incorrect because tests of controls need not be performed relating to reportable conditions. Answer (d) is incorrect because although timely communication of reportable conditions may be important, depending upon the nature of the reportable condition identified, the auditor may choose to communicate it either after the audit is concluded or during the course of the audit.

**137. (d)** The requirement is to identify the correct statement about reportable conditions noted in an audit. Answer (d) is correct because the auditor may choose or the client may request the auditor to separately identify and communicate as material weaknesses those reportable conditions that, in the auditor's judgment are considered to be material weaknesses in internal control. Answer (a) is incorrect because not all reportable conditions are also material weaknesses in internal control. Answer (b) is incorrect because the auditor is not obligated to search for reportable conditions. Answer (c) is incorrect because the auditor may decide a matter does not need to be recommunicated.

**138. (b)** The requirement is to determine the representation that should **not** be included in a report on internal control related matters noted in an audit. Answer (b) is correct because a report on internal control related matters is not necessary when there are no significant deficiencies in internal control. The limited degree of assurance provided by such a report could be misinterpreted if a report were issued stating there are no significant deficiencies. Answer (a) is incorrect because an auditor may separately identify and communicate material weaknesses. Answer (c) is incorrect because an auditor may recommend corrective follow-up action. Answer (d) is incorrect because an auditor may disclose the fact that the consideration of internal control would **not** necessarily disclose all reportable conditions that exist.

**139. (a)** The requirement is to determine whether disagreements with management and initial selection of significant accounting policies need to be communicated to an entity's audit committee. Answer (a) is correct because disagreements should be communicated directly to the audit committee. Answer (b) is incorrect because direct communication by the auditor is not required for selection of accounting principles. Management may engage in this communication with the committee. Answer (c) is incorrect because the auditor only needs to make sure that management has communicated with the committee concerning initial selection of significant accounting policies in emerging areas that lack authoritative guidance. Answer (d) is incorrect because disagreements should be communicated directly to the audit committee.

**140. (a)** The requirement is to determine the information that an auditor should communicate to an audit committee of a public entity. Answer (a) is correct because both significant audit adjustments and management's consultation with other accountants about significant accounting matters should be communicated to an audit committee. See AU 380 for these and other matters that should be so communicated.

**141. (d)** The requirement is to identify when an auditor should recommunicate a previously communicated reportable condition that has not been corrected. Answer (d) is correct because such reportable conditions should be communicated again when there have been changes in management or the audit committee, or when a period of time has passed and the auditor believes it appropriate and timely to again report them. Answer (a) is incorrect because while the deficiency may affect the assessment of control risk, this will not in and of itself require the auditor to communicate the matter again. Answer (b) is incorrect because the entity's acceptance of the risk does not directly impact whether such a matter should be communicated again. Answer (c) is incorrect because it represents a portion of the definition of a reportable condition, and does not bear directly upon when such a condition should be communicated again.

**142. (b)** The requirement is to identify the correct statement regarding material weaknesses and reportable conditions. Answer (b) is correct because AU 325 defines a material weakness as a reportable condition in which the control structure does not reduce to a relatively low level the risk that material misstatements might occur and not be detected. Accordingly, all material weaknesses are reportable conditions. Answer (a) is incorrect because though material weaknesses may be reported separately from reportable conditions, there is no such requirement. Answer (c) is incorrect because while the auditor may choose to communicate material weakness and reportable conditions immediately, the communication may occur at other times. Answer (d) is incorrect because not all reportable conditions are considered material weaknesses.

**143. (c)** The requirement is to identify the meaning of a reportable condition that should be reported to an entity's audit committee. Answer (c) is correct because a reportable condition is a matter that represents a significant deficiency in the design or operation of internal control, which could adversely affect the organization's ability to record, process, summarize, and report financial data consistent with the assertions of management in the financial statements. Answer (a) is incorrect because a reportable condition need not address the entity's going concern status; also, the financial statements, not the auditors, have a going concern assumption. Answers (b) and (d) are incorrect because fraud, illegal acts, and the manipulation of accounting records need not be involved when a reportable condition exists.

**144. (b)** The requirement is to determine an auditor's responsibility after s/he has discovered and orally communicated information on a weakness in internal control to the client's senior management and its audit committee. Note that AU 325 suggests that the form of the communication to management and the board of directors or its audit committee is optional; it may be written or oral. Answer (b) is correct because the auditor, as outlined throughout AU 319, considers and documents his/her understanding of internal control to assist in planning and determining the proper nature, timing, and extent of substantive tests. Answer (a) is incorrect because no scope limitation is indicated although an internal control condition does exist. Similarly, answers (c) and (d) are incorrect because audit activities need not be suspended and the auditor need not withdraw from the engagement.

### E.2.   Reporting on Internal Control

**145. (d)** The requirement is to identify the statement that should be included in a CPA's report on a client's internal control over financial reporting. Answer (d) is correct because AT 501 requires that the report include a comment on the inherent limitations of any internal control.

**146. (c)** The requirement is to determine whether a written assertion about the effectiveness of its internal control may be in the form of a separate report, a representation letter, or both when a CPA is examining a client's internal control. Answer (c) is correct because AT 501 allows the written assertion to be either in a separate report or in a representation letter.

**147. (a)** The requirement is to identify the statement that best describes a CPA's engagement to report on an entity's internal control over financial reporting. Answer (a) is correct because AT 501, an attestation standard, describes engagements examining and reporting on the effectiveness of internal control. Answer (b) is incorrect because no such negative assurance is provided based on an "audit" of the entity's internal control. Answer (c) is incorrect because such engagements do not project expected benefits of the entity's internal control. Answer (d) is incorrect because such engagements are attestation engagements, not consulting engagements.

**148. (c)** The requirement is to determine the correct statement regarding an engagement to examine internal control. Answer (c) is correct because the procedures relating to internal control will be more extensive when reporting on internal control as compared to procedures performed for a financial statement audit. This difference occurs because during financial statement audits the auditor may decide not to perform tests of controls and may simply assess control risk at the maximum level. Conversely, in an engagement to report on internal control an auditor must perform additional tests of controls. Answer (a) is incorrect because such duplication of procedures may not be necessary. Answer (b) is incorrect because a report on internal control will not in general increase the reliability of the financial statements.

Answer (d) is incorrect because, as indicated, the scope of procedures relating to internal control is more extensive, not more limited, than the assessment of control risk made during a financial statement audit.

**149. (d)** The requirement is to identify the relationship between an examination of internal control and obtaining an understanding of internal control and assessing control risk as part of an audit. Answer (d) is correct because, while the scope and purpose differ between the two types of engagements, the procedures followed are similar. See AT 501 for information on reporting on management's written assertion on internal control.

**150. (b)** The requirement is to describe the contents of a report on the study of internal control that is based on criteria established by governmental agencies. Answer (b) is correct because the report should indicate matters covered by the consideration and whether the auditor's consideration included tests of controls with the procedures covered by his/her consideration. Additionally, the report should describe the objectives and limitations of internal control and the accountant's evaluation thereof; state the accountant's conclusion, based on the agency's criteria; and describe the purpose of the report and state that it should not be used for any other purpose. Answer (a) is incorrect because the agency's name should be included. Answer (c) is incorrect because a conclusion may be made relative to the agency's criteria. Answer (d) is incorrect because the accountant should not assume responsibility for the comprehensiveness of the criteria.

**151. (b)** AT 501 states that when a deviation from the control criteria being reported upon exists (here a material weakness in internal control) the CPA should report directly upon the subject matter and not upon the assertion.

### E.3.   Effects of an Internal Audit Function

**152. (a)** The requirement is to identify the most likely information a CPA would obtain in assessing the competence of an internal auditor. Answer (a) is correct because in assessing competence, an internal auditor will consider the quality of working paper documentation as well as a variety of other factors outlined in AU 322. Answer (b) is incorrect because an organization's commitment to integrity and ethical values, while important, does not bear as directly upon internal auditor competence. Answers (c) and (d) are incorrect because the influence of management and the organizational level to which the internal auditor reports are factors used to assess internal auditor objectivity. AU 322 provides overall guidance on the use of internal auditors.

**153. (d)** The requirement is to determine whether the independent auditor may share responsibility with an entity's internal auditor for assessing inherent risk and control risk. AU 322 requires that judgments about inherent and control risk always be those of the independent auditor. It also requires that judgments about the materiality of misstatements, the sufficiency of tests performed, the valuation of significant accounting estimates, and other matters affecting the auditor's report should always be those of the independent auditor. See AU 322 for information on the external auditor's consideration of the internal audit function.

**154.** **(d)** The work of internal auditors may affect the nature, timing and extent of the audit, including (1) procedures the auditor performs when obtaining an understanding of the entity's internal control, (2) procedures the auditor performs when assessing risk, and (3) substantive procedures the auditor performs.

**155.** **(c)** The requirement is to identify the circumstance in which an internal auditor's work would most likely affect the nature, timing, and extent of a CPA's auditing procedures. When considering the effect of the internal auditors' work, the CPA considers (1) the materiality of financial statement amounts, (2) the risk of material misstatement of the assertions, and (3) the degree of subjectivity involved in the evaluation of the audit evidence. Answer (c) is correct because the existence of fixed asset additions involves little subjectivity. Answers (a) and (b) are incorrect because the existence of contingencies and the valuation of intangible assets are subjective and the risk of misstatement may be high. Answer (d) is incorrect because the valuation of related-party transactions may be very subjective due to the lack of an "arm's-length" transaction.

**156.** **(d)** AU 322 states that internal auditors may assist the CPA in obtaining an understanding of internal control, in performing tests of controls, and in performing substantive tests.

**157.** **(b)** The requirement is to identify the type of information used by a CPA to assess the competence of internal auditors. Answer (b) is correct because, along with various other factors, AU 322 indicates that the CPA should obtain evidence on the educational background and professional certification of the internal auditors when considering competence. Answers (a) and (c) are incorrect because analysis of organizational level to which the internal auditors report and policies on relatives are considered when assessing internal auditor objectivity. Answer (d) is incorrect because access to sensitive records will not provide a CPA with information on competence.

**158.** **(d)** The requirement is to identify the **least** likely source of information to the CPA on an entity's internal auditor's competence and objectivity. Answer (d) is correct because analytical procedures do not ordinarily provide information on the internal auditor. See AU 329 for information on analytical procedures.

**159.** **(a)** The requirement is to identify the characteristics of an internal auditor which must be considered by an independent auditor who decides that the internal auditor's work might have a bearing on his/her procedures. Answer (a) is correct because independent auditors must consider internal auditor competence, objectivity, and work performance. Answer (b) is incorrect because an independent auditor is less concerned about internal auditor efficiency, although internal auditor experience will be considered in the assessment of competence. Answers (c) and (d), while partially correct, are less complete than answer (a).

**160.** **(d)** The requirement is to determine how a CPA should assess the objectivity of an internal auditor. Answer (d) is correct because when assessing the objectivity of an internal auditor the CPA should consider organizational status and policies for maintaining objectivity. Answers (a), (b), and (c) are all incorrect because evaluating the quality control program, and examining and testing an internal

auditor's work all relate more directly to assessing internal auditor competence rather than to objectivity. See AU 322 for these and other factors considered when assessing internal auditor competence.

### E.4. Reports on the Processing of Transactions by Service Organizations

**161.** **(a)** The requirement is to identify the information provided in a service auditor's report which includes an opinion on a description of controls placed in operation. Answer (a) is correct since such a report includes a description of the scope and nature of the CPA's procedures. Answers (b), (c), and (d) are all incorrect because they suggest information not included in such a report. See AU 324 for information on the audit of service organizations.

**162.** **(a)** The requirement is to identify a CPA's reporting responsibility when reporting on internal control placed in operation for a service organization that processes payroll transactions. Answer (a) is correct because since the CPA is only expressing an opinion on whether controls have been placed in operation, a disclaimer should be provided on operating effectiveness. Answer (b) is incorrect because no specific statement is made with respect to earlier objectives. Answer (c) is incorrect because controls relevant to financial statement assertions are not so identified. Answer (d) is incorrect because the assessed level of control risk is not disclosed. See AU 324 for information on processing of transactions by service organizations.

**163.** **(a)** The requirement is to determine whether an auditor who audits the processing of transactions by a service organization may issue a report on either, or both, of whether controls have been placed in operation and control operating effectiveness. Answer (a) is correct because AU 324 indicates that such "service auditors" may issue either of the two types of reports.

**164.** **(a)** The requirement is to identify the proper information to be included in a service auditor's report on whether a client's controls have been placed in operation. Answer (a) is correct because such a report should include a description of the scope and nature of the client's procedures.

**165.** **(d)** The requirement is to determine the propriety of a computer "user" auditor (Lake) making reference to a service auditor's (Cope) report. Answer (d) is correct because the user auditor should not make reference to the report of the service auditor. See AU 324 for reports on the processing of transactions by service organizations.

**SOLUTIONS TO SIMULATION PROBLEMS**

**Simulation Problem 1**

| | Internal Control | | |
|---|---|---|---|
| Directions | Situation | | Research | Communication |

| | *Condition* | *Strength* | *Weakness* | *Neither* |
|---|---|:---:|:---:|:---:|
| 1. | Southwest is involved only in medical services and has not diversified its operations. | ○ | ○ | ● |
| 2. | Insurance coverage for patients is verified and communicated to the clerks by the office manager before medical services are rendered. | ● | ○ | ○ |
| 3. | The physician who renders the medical services documents the services on a prenumbered slip that is used for recording revenue and as a receipt for the patient. | ● | ○ | ○ |
| 4. | Cash collection is centralized in that Clerk #2 receives the cash (checks) from patients and records the cash receipt. | ○ | ● | ○ |
| 5. | Southwest extends credit rather than requiring cash or insurance in all cases. | ○ | ○ | ● |
| 6. | The office manager extends credit on a case-by-case basis rather than using a formal credit search and established credit limits. | ○ | ● | ○ |
| 7. | The office manager approves the extension of credit to patients and also approves the write-offs of uncollectible patient receivables. | ○ | ● | ○ |
| 8. | Clerk #2 receives cash and checks and prepares the daily bank deposit. | ○ | ● | ○ |
| 9. | Clerk #2 maintains the accounts receivable records and can add or delete information on the PC. | ○ | ● | ○ |
| 10. | Prenumbered service slips are accounted for on a monthly basis by the outside accountant who is independent of the revenue generating and revenue recording functions. | ● | ○ | ○ |
| 11. | The bank reconciliation is prepared monthly by the outside accountant who is independent of the revenue generating and revenue recording functions. | ● | ○ | ○ |
| 12. | Computer passwords are only known to the individual employees and the managing partner who has no duties in the revenue recording functions. | ● | ○ | ○ |
| 13. | Computer software cannot be modified by Southwest's employees. | ● | ○ | ○ |
| 14. | None of the employees who perform duties in the revenue generating and revenue recording are able to write checks. | ● | ○ | ○ |

| | | Research | | |
|---|---|---|---|---|
| Directions | Situation | Internal Control | | Communication |

AU 380.09-.10 provides requirements with respect to communication of audit adjustments to the audit committee as follows:

Audit Adjustments

**AU380.09**

The auditor should inform the audit committee about adjustments arising from the audit that could, in his judgment, either individually or in the aggregate, have a significant effect on the entity's financial reporting process. For purposes of this section, an audit adjustment, whether or not recorded by the entity, is a proposed correction of the financial statements that, in the auditor's judgment, may not have been detected except through the auditing procedures performed. Matters underlying adjustments proposed by the auditor but not recorded by the entity could potentially cause future financial statements to be materially misstated, even though the auditor has concluded that the adjustments are not material to the current financial statements.

**AU380.10**

The auditor also should inform the audit committee about uncorrected misstatements aggregated by the auditor during the current engagement and pertaining to the latest period presented that were determined by management to be immaterial, both individually and in the aggregate, to the financial statements taken as a whole.

| | | | | Communication |
|---|---|---|---|---|
| **Directions** | **Situation** | **Internal Control** | **Research** | |

To:      Audit Working Papers
From:  CPA Candidate
Re:      Implications of errors discovered in accounts receivable

In the course of performing our substantive audit procedures for the audit of Southwest's accounts receivable, we detected a large number of errors. Having assessed control risk at a low level, we should reassess control risk for the assertions regarding accounts receivable and then reevaluate the sufficiency of our substantive procedures.

---

**Simulation Problem 2**

| | Flowchart | | |
|---|---|---|---|
| **Directions** | | **Research** | **Communication** |

1. **(C)** *Prepare purchase order*—A trapezoid represents a manual operation. Here, a purchase order enters the flowchart after this step; accordingly, a purchase order is being prepared.

2. **(R)** *To vendor*—A circle represents a connector, a symbol indicating that a document is entering or leaving that portion of the flowchart. Here a copy of the purchase order is sent to the vendor to order the goods. This must be the case because, otherwise, the vendor would not be informed of the order.

3. **(F)** *Prepare receiving report*—A trapezoid represents a manual operation. Here, a receiving report enters the flowchart after this step; accordingly, a receiving report is being prepared. Also, note above this step that goods are received, the point at which one would expect preparation of a receiving report.

4. **(L)** *From purchasing*—A circle represents a connector, a symbol indicating that a document is entering or leaving that portion of the flowchart. The document here is from purchasing because below the connector is requisition No. 1, which purchasing has sent with the purchase order No. 5 to vouchers payable, as evidenced by the connector in the bottom far right under purchasing.

5. **(M)** *From receiving*—A circle represents a connector, a symbol indicating that a document is entering or leaving that portion of the flowchart. The document here is from receiving because under the receiving portion of the flowchart, approximately 3/4 of the way down, we see a connector indicating that receiving report No. 1 is being sent to vouchers payable. Also, toward the bottom under the vouchers payable portion of the flowchart, we see that receiving report No. 1 is indeed in the system.

6. **(O)** *Purchase order No. 5*—We know from item 4 that this document was sent from purchasing, and we know that purchasing has sent to vouchers payable requisition No. 1 and purchase order No. 5. Since requisition No. 1 is labeled on the flowchart, this must be purchase order No. 5.

7. **(P)** *Receiving report No. 1*—We know from item 5 that this document was sent from receiving, and since we know that receiving has sent receiving report No. 1 to vouchers payable this must be that document.

8. **(B)** *Prepare and approve voucher*—A trapezoid represents a manual operation. Here, an approved voucher enters the flowchart after this step; accordingly, a voucher is being prepared and approved in this step.

9. **(T)** *Unpaid voucher file, filed by due date*—The triangle symbol represents a file. Entering this file are the approved but unpaid vouchers with the support of their invoices, receiving reports, purchase orders and purchase requisitions. Because these vouchers are sent to the treasurer in order of due date (the bottom, right symbol under vouchers payable) this file is the unpaid voucher file, filed by due date.

10. **(S)** *Treasurer*—Because the unpaid vouchers (the "voucher package") was sent from vouchers payable to the treasurer, this is the treasurer.

11. **(I)** *Sign checks and cancel voucher package documents*—A trapezoid represents a manual operation. Here, the operation prior to 11 involves a review of documents and preparation of a check and a remittance advice. After this operation the documents changed are a "canceled voucher package file" and a "signed check"; accordingly, checks are being signed and the voucher package is being canceled.

12. **(K)** *Canceled voucher package*—After step 11, the check copy, remittance advice No. 1, the signed check, and remittance advice No. 2 exit on the far right. Accordingly, item 12 is the voucher package, now canceled as evidenced by the description below the triangular file symbol.

| | | Research | |
|---|---|---|---|
| **Directions** | **Flowchart** | | **Communication** |

AU 319.21-.24 provide a discussion of limitations of an entity's internal control as follows:

Limitations of an Entity's Internal Control          **AU319.21**

Internal control, no matter how well designed and operated, can provide only reasonable assurance of achieving an entity's control objectives. The likelihood of achievement is affected by limitations inherent to internal control. These include the realities that human judgment in decision making can be faulty and that breakdowns in internal control can occur because of human failures such as simple errors or mistakes. For example, errors may occur in designing, maintaining, or monitoring automated controls. If an entity's IT personnel do not completely understand how an order entry system processes sales transactions, they may erroneously design changes to the system to process sales for a new line of products. On the other hand, such changes may be correctly designed but misunderstood by individuals who translate the design into program code. Errors also may occur in the use of information produced by IT. For example, automated controls may be designed to report transactions over a specified dollar limit for management review, but individuals responsible for conducting the review may not understand the purpose of such reports and, accordingly, may fail to review them or investigate unusual items.

**AU319.22**

Additionally, controls, whether manual or automated, can be circumvented by the collusion of two or more people or inappropriate management override of internal control. For example, management may enter into side agreements with customers that alter the terms and conditions of the entity's standards sales contract in ways that would preclude revenue recognition. Also, edit routines in a software program that are designed to identify and report transactions that exceed specified credit limits may be overridden or disabled.

**AU319.23**

Internal control is influenced by the quantitative and qualitative estimates and judgments made by management in evaluating the cost-benefit relationship of an entity's internal control. The cost of an entity's internal control should not exceed the benefits that are expected to be derived. Although the cost-benefit relationship is a primary criterion that should be considered in designing internal control, the precise measurement of costs and benefits usually is not possible.

**AU319.24**

Custom, culture, and the corporate governance system may inhibit fraud, but they are not absolute deterrents. An effective control environment, too, may help reduce the risk of fraud. For example, an effective board of directors, audit committee, and internal audit function may constrain improper conduct by management. Alternatively, the control environment may reduce the effectiveness of other components. For example, when the nature of management incentives increases the risk of material misstatement of financial statements, the effectiveness of control activities may be reduced.

| Directions | Flowchart | Research | Communication |
| --- | --- | --- | --- |

To:    Audit Staff
From: CPA Candidate
Re:    Types of controls

Financial reporting controls may be viewed as having a function of either (1) preventing misstatements, or (2) detecting and correcting misstatements. Preventive controls are usually more effective because they reduce the possibility of a misstatement occurring. While detective controls are generally less expensive, they may be ineffective if they detect misstatements too late.

**Simulation Problem 3**

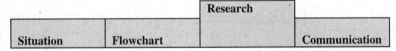

1.  **(M)**  *Perform customer credit check*—The customer credit file is being accessed, making it likely that a credit check is occurring.

2.  **(Z)**  *Open order file*—The processing to the right of #2 begins with "open orders," making this an open order file.

3.  **(L)**  *Match customer purchase order with sales order*—Two copies of the sales order are being combined with the customer purchase order through a manual operation (the trapezoid).

4.  **(B)**  *Verify agreement of sales order and shipping document*—This manual operation (trapezoid) includes two copies of the shipping document being combined with the sales order.

5.  **(H)**  *Release goods for shipment*—The department is the warehouse and shipping department, and out of this operation is "shipping information"; accordingly goods are being released for shipment.

6.  **(S)**  *Master price file*—The operation below #6 includes entering price data; since the first two files being accessed are the accounts receivable master file and the shipping file, this third file must include prices.

7.  **(O)**  *Prepare sales invoice*—Since a document is being prepared through this computerized billing program, it is the sales invoice.

8.  **(U)**  *Sales invoice*—A sales invoice is normally sent to the customer.

9.  **(I)**  *To accounts receivable department*—This copy of the sales invoice informs accounts receivable that the sale has been both processed and shipped.

10. **(Q)**  *General ledger master file*—Because the processing step below includes updating of master files, this is the general ledger master file.

11. **(N)**  *Prepare sales journal*—Sales transactions are being processed; accordingly a sales journal is prepared.

12. **(T)**  *Sales journal*—From above, a sales journal was prepared; the accounting department will receive the sales journal.

13. **(Y)**  *Aged trial balance*—In the processing step above, an aged trial balance of accounts receivable is prepared; the credit department will receive such a report.

| | | Research | |
|---|---|---|---|
| Situation | Flowchart | | Communication |

The first step is to determine the manner in which you wish to identify the pertinent research in the area. Since this is not an audit report on whether a company's financial statements follow generally accepted accounting principles, the approach outlined in the Reporting Module for preparing a report is not used. If a keyword or index search is to be used, words such as "internal control report" or "illustration internal control report" may be helpful. But in reviewing the requirements for the question watch for hints—you find such hints to include "internal control over financial reporting" and "examination on internal control over financial reporting" which may be helpful. But internal control is a difficult area to research in that the term occurs frequently throughout the standards. If you know that reporting on internal control is included in the attestation standards, you have a significant head start in either a keyword search or in searching sections, since the attestation standards have few sections. Here AT 501 involves reporting on internal control. It provides the following report illustration:

.48  The following is the form of report a practitioner should use when he or she expresses an opinion directly on the effectiveness of an entity's internal control as of a specified date.

***Independent Accountant's Report***

[*Introductory paragraph*]

We have examined the effectiveness of Welcore Inc.'s internal control over financial reporting as of December 31, 20X1, based on [*identify criteria*]. Welcore Inc.'s management is responsible for maintaining effective internal control over financial reporting. Our responsibility is to express an opinion on the effectiveness of internal control based on our examination.

[*Scope paragraph*]

Our examination was conducted in accordance with attestation standards established by the American Institute of Certified Public Accountants and, accordingly, included obtaining an understanding of the internal control over financial reporting, testing, and evaluating the design and operating effectiveness of the internal control, and performing such other procedures as we considered necessary in the circumstances. We believe that our examination provides a reasonable basis for our opinion.

[*Inherent limitations paragraph*]

Because of inherent limitations in any internal control, misstatements due to error or fraud may occur and not be detected. Also, projections of any evaluation of the internal control over financial reporting to future periods are subject to the risk that the internal control may become inadequate because of changes in conditions, or that the degree of compliance with the policies or procedures may deteriorate.

[*Opinion paragraph*]

In our opinion, Welcore Inc. maintained, in all material respects, effective internal control over financial reporting as of December 31, 20X1, based on [*identify criteria*]

[*Signature*]

[*Date*]

One might prepare the following report for Welcore Inc.:

**Draft**

### *Independent Accountant's Report*

To Board of Directors of Welcore Inc.

We have examined the effectiveness of Welcore Inc.'s internal control over financial reporting as of December 31, 20X1, based on the Internal Control—Integrated Frameword Criteria established by the Committee of Sponsoring Organizations. Welcore Inc.'s management is responsible for maintaining effective internal control over financial reporting. Our responsibility is to express an opinion on the effectiveness of internal control based on our examination.

Our examination was conducted in accordance with attestation standards established by the American Institute of Certified Public Accountants and, accordingly, included obtaining an understanding of the internal control over financial reporting, testing, and evaluating the design and operating effectiveness of the internal control, and performing such other procedures as we considered necessary in the circumstances. We believe that our examination provides a reasonable basis for our opinion.

Because of inherent limitations in any internal control, misstatements due to error or fraud may occur and not be detected. Also, projections of any evaluation of the internal control over financial reporting to future periods are subject to the risk that the internal control may become inadequate because of changes in conditions, or that the degree of compliance with the policies or procedures may deteriorate.

In our opinion, Welcore Inc. maintained, in all material respects, effective internal control over financial reporting as of December 31, 20X1, based on the Internal Control—Integrated Framework Criteria established by the Committee of Sponsoring Organizations.

[*Signature*]

[*Date*]

| Situation | Flowchart | Research | Communication |
|-----------|-----------|----------|---------------|

To:    Bill Warren, CFO
        Welcore Inc.
From:  CPA Candidate
Re:     Effect of improvements in internal control

You have requested a description of the effects of improved internal control on our audit. Improved internal control may affect the audit in at least two related ways. First, it may change the combination of audit tests performed and thereby lead to a more efficient audit. In auditing the financial statements of a company, auditors perform two types of tests: tests of the effectiveness of internal control (referred to as test of controls) and substantive tests of financial statement balances and transactions. As internal control improves, more reliance can be placed on tests of controls and a result may be a more efficient audit. Second, because an improvement in internal control is likely to decrease the occurrence of material misstatements, there may be a reduction in the required overall scope of audit procedures that may also lead to a more efficient audit.

---

**Simulation Problem 4**

| Situation | Internal Control Evaluation | Purpose of Internal Control | Research and Communication |
|-----------|-----------------------------|-----------------------------|----------------------------|

**1.** Disagree. Someone independent of requisitioning should select the supplier.

**2.** Agree.

**3.** Disagree. Often, factors in addition to cost are considered (e.g., quality, dependability).

**4.** Agree.

**5.** Agree.

6.   Agree.

7.   Disagree. A comparison of quantities is not possible because quantity is blacked out on the purchase order provided to receiving.

8.   No receiving report is ordinarily necessary for purchases of services.

9.   Agree.

10.  Agree.

11.  Agree.

12.  Disagree. The reconciliation should be performed by an independent party.

13.  Disagree. Documentation should be marked "paid" by the individual making the payment.

14.  Agree.

15.  Agree.

| Situation | Internal Control Evaluation | Purpose of Internal Control | Research and Communication |
| --- | --- | --- | --- |

1.   **(C)** Invoices posted to incorrect customer accounts will be detected by analyzing customer responses to monthly statements that include errors, particularly statements with errors not in favor of the customer.

2.   **(G)** The comparison of shipping documents with sales invoices will detect goods that have been shipped but not billed when no sales invoice is located for a particular shipping document.

3.   **(F)** To provide assurance that all invoiced goods that have been shipped are recorded as sales, daily sales summaries should be compared with invoices. For example, a sale that has not been recorded will result in a sales summary that does not include certain sales invoices.

4.   **(K)** A comparison of the amounts posted to the accounts receivable ledger with the control total for invoices will provide assurance that all invoices have been posted to a customer account.

5.   **(I)** Comparing customer orders with an approved customer list will provide assurance that credit sales are made only to customers that have been granted credit.

6.   **(B)** Requiring an approved sales order before goods are released from the warehouse will provide assurance that goods are not removed for unauthorized orders.

7.   **(D)** A comparison by shipping clerks of goods received from the warehouse with the approved sales orders will provide assurance that goods shipped to customers agree with goods ordered by customers.

8.   **(L)** A comparison of sales invoices with shipping documents and approved sales orders will detect invoices that do not have the proper support. Accordingly, it will help prevent the recording of fictitious transactions.

9.   **(P)** Comparing amounts posted to the accounts receivable ledger with the validated bank deposit will detect improper postings to accounts receivable since any differences in amounts will be investigated.

10.  **(C)** Misappropriations of customers' checks will be detected when customers indicate that they have made payments for items shown as payable on their monthly statement. Note that replies O and P will only detect this misappropriation in the unlikely event that the perpetrator does not dispose of the remittance advice.

11.  **(C)** Mispostings of payments made will be detected when customers indicate that they have made payments for items shown as payable on their monthly statement.

12.  **(P)** Crediting more than one account for a cash receipt will be detected when the total of amounts posted to the accounts receivable ledger is compared with the validated bank deposit slip.

13.  **(S)** An independent reconciliation of the bank account will reveal improper total recording of receipts in the cash receipts journal because unlocated differences between bank and book balances will occur and be investigated.

14.  **(P)** Comparing total amounts posted to the accounts receivable ledger with the validated bank deposit slip will detect a difference between total cash receipts and the amount credited to the accounts receivable ledger.

15.  **(N)** Requiring the approval of the supervisor of the sales department for goods received will provide assurance that invalid transactions granting credit for sales returns are not recorded. Note that using prenumbered credit memos (reply M) will only be effective if the sequence is accounted for and if credit memos may be compared in some form to actual returns.

| Situation | Internal Control Evaluation | Purpose of Internal Control | Research and Communication |
| --- | --- | --- | --- |

   The first step is to determine the manner in which the candidate wishes to identify the pertinent research in the area. If a keyword or index search is to be used, words such as "internal control report" or "reportable condition" may be helpful. But internal control is a difficult area to research in that the term occurs frequently throughout the standards. Concerning internal control it is probably best to memorize the fact that the auditor's responsibility for reporting on internal control reportable conditions is included in AU 325 (also, know that other communications to the audit committee are included in AU 380). Attest reports on internal control over financial reporting (not an issue in this question) are in AT 501.

1. AU 325 includes the following definition for a reportable condition and a material weakness:

   Reportable condition—matters coming to the auditor's attention that, in his judgment, should be communicated to the audit committee because they represent significant deficiencies in the design or operation of internal control, which could adversely affect the organization's ability to initiate, record, process, and report financial data consistent with the assertions of management in the financial statements.

   Material weakness—a reportable condition in which the design or operation of one or more of the internal control components does not reduce to a relatively low level the risk that misstatements caused by error or fraud in amounts that would be material in relation to the financial statements being audited may occur and not be detected within a timely period by employees in the normal course of performing their assigned functions.

2. AU 325 states that it is preferable that the communication be in writing, although it does not require that the communication be in writing.

   09  Conditions noted by the auditor that are considered reportable under this section or that are the result of agreement with the client should be reported, preferably in writing. If information is communicated orally, the auditor should document the communication by appropriate memoranda or notations in the working papers.

3. AU 325 indicates that if the audit committee has acknowledged the existence of such deficiencies, the auditor may decide that the matter does not need to be reported. But, periodically, the auditor should consider whether it is appropriate and timely to report such matters.

   06  The existence of reportable conditions related to internal control design or operation may already be known and, in fact, may represent a conscious decision by management—a decision of which the audit committee is aware—to accept that degree of risk because of cost or other considerations. It is the responsibility of management to make the decisions concerning costs to be incurred and related benefits. Provided the audit committee has acknowledged its understanding and consideration of such deficiencies and the associated risks, the auditor may decide the matter does not need to be reported. Periodically, the auditor should consider whether, because of changes in management, the audit committee, or simply because of the passage of time, it is appropriate and timely to report such matters.

Given the above information, one may write a memorandum as follows:

To:  Mr. Bill Jones
From:  [*Your name*]
Re:  Reporting on internal control
Date:  [*Today's date*]

I researched the Professional Standards on the following three issues:

a. Definitions of material weaknesses and reportable conditions.
b. Whether a communication on reportable conditions must be in writing.
c. Whether a reportable condition must be communicated when the audit committee is already aware of it.

The guidance for all three of these matters is included in AU section 325.

### Definitions of material weaknesses and reportable conditions

The definitions for a reportable condition and a material weakness are presented in AU section 325 as

Reportable condition—matters coming to the auditor's attention that, in his judgment, should be communicated to the auditor committee because they represent significant deficiencies in the design or operation of internal control, which could adversely affect the organizations' ability to initiate, record, process, and report financial data consistent with the assertions of management in the financial statements. (sec. 325.02)

Material weakness—a reportable condition in which the design or operation of one or more of the internal control components does not reduce to a relatively low level the risk that misstatements caused by error or fraud in amounts that would be material in relation to the financial statements being audited may occur and not be detected within a timely period by employees in the normal course of performing their assigned functions. (sec. 325.15)

### Must a communication on reportable conditions be in writing?

No. The communication may be written or oral. AU section 325.09 states that it is preferable that it be written. Nonetheless, if information is communicated orally, such communication should be documented in the working papers using appropriate memoranda or notations.

### Must a reportable condition of which the audit committee is aware be communicated?

No. AU section 325.06 indicates that if the audit committee has acknowledged its understanding and consideration of such deficiencies and the associated risks, an auditor may decide that the matter need not be reported. However, the paragraph also warns that periodic communication should be considered because of changes in management, the audit committee, or simply because of the passage of time.

# EVIDENCE

The entire financial statement audit may be described as a process of evidence accumulation and evaluation. This process enables the auditor to formulate an informed opinion as to whether the financial statements are presented fairly in accordance with US generally accepted accounting principles. The following "Diagram of an Audit" was first presented and explained in the auditing overview section.

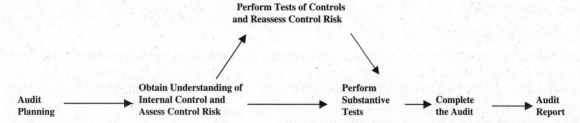

This module covers "evidential matter" as a concept and discusses types of evidential matter generated through performance of substantive tests (both analytical procedures and tests of details of transactions and balances) and discusses completing the audit.

Numerous questions on evidence appear on each CPA exam. Multiple-choice questions frequently ask the candidate to select the audit procedure most likely to detect misstatements that have occurred in given accounting records and to distinguish among various concepts such as

1. Competent vs. sufficient evidence
2. Analytical procedures vs. tests of details of transactions and balances
3. Audit objectives vs. audit procedures

A simulation question may require the candidate to select appropriate audit procedures for a particular account and to research the professional standards on some aspect of that account (e.g., when are negative confirmation requests appropriate). Alternatively, the candidate may be required to calculate various ratios using a spreadsheet and to then interpret those ratios.

## Study Program for Evidence Module

This module is organized and should be studied in the following manner:

A. Evidence—General

    1. Competent and Sufficient Evidential Matter
    2. Types of Evidence

B. Evidence—Specific (Substantive Tests)

    1. Types of Substantive Tests
    2. Substantive Test Audit Programs
    3. Documentation

C. Other Specific Evidence Topics

    1. Cash
    2. Receivables
    3. Inventory
    4. Investment Securities
    5. Property, Plant, and Equipment
    6. Prepaid Assets
    7. Payables (Current)
    8. Long-Term Debt
    9. Owners' Equity

    10. Revenue
    11. Expenses
    12. Client Representation Letters
    13. Using the Work of a Specialist
    14. Inquiry of a Client's Lawyer
    15. Fair Values
    16. Related-Party Transactions
    17. Going Concern Considerations
    18. Subsequent Events
    19. Omitted Procedures

D. Completing the Audit

    1. Procedures Completed near the End of the Audit
    2. Evaluate Audit Findings

E.  Compilation and Review Procedures

1.  Compilation Procedures
2.  Review Procedures
3.  Review of Public Company Interim Financial Information
4.  Overall Comments

F.  Other Related Topics

1.  Operational Auditing

This module covers information included in the Evidence and Procedures Section of the AICPA Content Specification Outline with the following exceptions:  (1) Use of the Computer in Performing the Audit is covered in the Auditing with Technology Module; and (2) Use of Statistical Sampling in Performing the Audit is covered in the Audit Sampling Module.

The following SAS sections pertain to audit evidence:

*AU Section*

| | |
|---|---|
| 326 | Evidential Matter |
| 328 | Auditing Fair Value Measurements and Disclosures |
| 329 | Analytical Procedures |
| 330 | The Confirmation Process |
| 331 | Inventories |
| 332 | Auditing Derivative Instruments, Hedging Activities, and Investments in Securities |
| 333 | Client Representations |
| 334 | Related-Party Transactions |
| 336 | Using the Work of a Specialist |
| 337 | Inquiry of a Client's Lawyer Concerning Litigation, Claims, and Assessments |
| 339 | Working Papers |
| 341 | The Auditor's Consideration of an Entity's Ability to Continue as a Going Concern |
| 342 | Auditing Accounting Estimates |
| 390 | Consideration of Omitted Procedures After the Report Date |
| 558 | Supplementary Information Required by the FASB |
| 560 | Subsequent Events |
| 561 | Subsequent Discovery of Facts Existing at the Date of the Auditor's Report |
| 722 | Review of Interim Financial Information |
| 801 | Compliance Auditing Applicable to Governmental Entities and Other Recipients of Governmental Financial Assistance |

Read the various sections and study the outlines for each of the above SAS separately.  After studying each outline, attempt to summarize in your own words the "sum and substance" of the pronouncement.  If you cannot explain the pronouncement in your own words, you do not understand it.  Go back and study it again.

**A.  Evidence—General**

The second attestation standard, as well as the third audit fieldwork standard, both require the collection of sufficient evidence to provide a reasonable basis for the conclusion to be issued in the report.  As background pertaining to financial statements, bear in mind that when management prepares financial statements that purport to be in conformity with generally accepted accounting principles, certain assertions (implicit or explicit) are made.  Section 326 identifies and classifies these assertions as

*Presentation and disclosure*—Components of financial statements are properly classified, described, and disclosed (e.g., inventories are properly classified on the balance sheet)

*Existence or occurrence*—Assets and liabilities exist at a given date and transactions have occurred during a given period (e.g., inventories physically exist)

*Rights and obligations*—Assets are rights of the entity and liabilities are obligations at a given date (e.g., firm has legal title to inventory)

*Completeness*—All transactions and accounts are included (e.g., all inventory items included on balance sheet)

*Valuation or allocation*—Components of financial statements included at appropriate amounts (e.g., inventories are properly stated at lower of cost or market)

(PERCV—as in, "I perceive the need to pass the CPA exam.")

Note the relationship between existence and completeness. The existence assertion relates to whether the recorded amount is bona fide (e.g., recorded receivables are legitimate). Completeness, on the other hand, addresses the issue of whether all transactions have been recorded (e.g., are all receivables recorded?). An auditor must test for both existence and completeness. This concept of "directional testing" is discussed in Section C of the Internal Control Module.

The Statement on Attestation Standards suggests two basic types of evidence collection procedures: (1) search and verification, and (2) internal inquiries and comparisons. Search and verification procedures include procedures such as inspecting assets, confirming receivables, and observing the counting of inventory. Internal inquiry and comparison procedures include discussions with firm representatives and analytical procedures such as ratio analysis.

As described in greater detail in the Reporting Module, accountants perform (1) **examinations,** (2) **reviews,** (3) **agreed-upon procedures,** and (4) **compilation** accounting engagements. Of these forms of association, an examination offers the highest level of assurance. (An "audit" is considered to be an examination of financial statements.) In examinations, accountants select from among all available audit procedures to determine whether the appropriate assertions (generally PERCV in the case of financial statements) have been met.

A review offers limited assurance (also referred to as negative assurance) with respect to information. It is composed primarily of internal inquiries and comparisons. However, when evidence with respect to an assertion seems incomplete or inaccurate, search and verification procedures may be performed.

Agreed-upon procedures result in a report in which a summary of findings is provided. The extent of the procedures is specified by the user, but must exceed the attester's mere reading of the assertions.

Compilations, which are considered accounting and not attestation services, result in a report that provides no explicit assurance on the information. While the accountant who performs a compilation should understand the nature of the client's business and its accounting records, s/he is not required to make any inquiries or perform any other verification procedures beyond reading the information. As is the case with all other forms of association, material known misstatements or omissions must be disclosed in the accountant's report that is expanded to disclose the situation.

Three presumptions (asked directly and indirectly on several previous exams) relate to the validity of evidence: (1) evidence from independent sources provides more assurance than evidence secured solely from within the entity, (2) information from direct personal knowledge is more persuasive than information obtained indirectly, and (3) assertions developed under effective internal control are more reliable than those developed in the absence of internal control.

1. **Competent and Sufficient Evidential Matter.** The amount of evidence necessary depends upon the form of accountant association—examination, review, agreed-upon procedures, compilation. Competent evidential matter may be thought of as being reliable. Section 326 states that to be competent, evidential matter must be both **valid** and **relevant** (know these criteria). The concept of **sufficient** evidence refers to the quantity of evidence that an accountant must gather. Sufficient evidence has been gathered when attestation risk (audit risk in the case of financial statement examinations—see the Engagement Planning Module) is considered to be at an acceptable level.

   Section 326 suggests that in the great majority of cases the auditor finds it necessary to rely on evidence that is persuasive rather than convincing. An acceptable level of audit risk does not indicate that **all** uncertainty be eliminated for sufficient evidence to have been gathered. The auditor must be able to form an opinion within a reasonable length of time, at a reasonable cost. However, the difficulty or expense involved in testing a particular item is not in itself a valid reason for omitting a test. Auditors use professional judgment to determine the extent of tests necessary to obtain sufficient evidence. In exercising this professional judgment, auditors consider both the materiality of the item in question (e.g., dollar size) as well as the inherent risk of the item (e.g., cash, due to its liquidity, may have a higher inherent risk than do certain property, plant, and equipment items).

   The following example distinguishes between competent vs. sufficient evidence. Assume that an auditor has highly credible evidence on one account receivable for $400 out of a total receivable balance of $1,000,000. While this evidence is competent, most auditors would suggest that it is not sufficient evidence for the $1,000,000 balance; to be sufficient, more evidence verifying the account's **total** value must be collected.

Obtaining sufficient competent evidence is particularly difficult when auditing client ac-counting estimates (e.g., allowance for doubtful accounts, loss reserves, pension expenses).  AU 342 suggests that the auditor's objectives relating to estimates are to determine that all estimates (1) have been developed, (2) are reasonable, and (3) follow GAAP.  Typically these estimates are needed because the valuation of some accounts is based on future events or because certain evi-dence cannot be accumulated on a timely, cost-effective basis.  Know that the three basic ap-proaches for evaluating the reasonableness of these estimates are (1) to review and test manage-ment's process of deriving the estimate (consider the reasonableness and accuracy of manage-ment's approach), (2) develop one's own expectation of the accounting estimate and compare it to management's, and (3) review subsequent events or transactions occurring prior to the completion of fieldwork which bear on the estimate.

2. **Types of Evidence.**  Recall from the Engagement Planning Module (Section A.1.a.) that at the ac-count level audit risk has three components—inherent risk, control risk, and detection risk.  Inher-ent risk refers to the fact that certain accounts are riskier than others (e.g., cash has more inherent risk than an inventory of coal).  Most frequently inherent risk is assessed by auditors performing overall review techniques and using overall auditing knowledge.  As is discussed in detail in the Internal Control Module, control risk is assessed through the auditor's consideration of internal control.

Detection risk is restricted by the auditor's substantive tests.  As the acceptable level of detec-tion risk decreases, the assurance provided by substantive tests must increase.  This increased as-surance may be obtained by modifying the nature, timing and/or extent of substantive tests as fol-lows:

- *Nature*—Use more effective procedures, such as tests directed toward independent parties rather than toward parties within the entity.
- *Timing*—Perform tests at year-end rather than at an interim date.
- *Extent*—Use a larger sample size.

AU 326 distinguishes between underlying accounting data and all corroborating (supporting) information available to the auditor.  **Underlying accounting data** includes books of original en-try (journals), general and subsidiary ledgers, related accounting manuals, and informal and memorandum records such as worksheets supporting cost allocations, computations, and recon-ciliations.

*Corroborating evidence* is the supporting documentation that is the basis for a transaction be-ing recorded in the journals and ledgers.  While every text seems to have its own list of types of corroborating evidence, the following list seems adequate (memorize them by remembering the first letter of each category—AICPA S).

Authoritative documents
Interrelationships
Calculations
Physical existence
Authoritative statements—by client and by third parties
Subsequent events

*NOTE:  Some sources include internal control in such lists—this makes the mnemonic AICPA IS.*

*Authoritative documents* such as truck titles, vendors' invoices, etc., support ownership and transaction occurrence.

*Interrelationships* within the data such as interest expense and accrued interest payable, un-usual items, etc., provide assurance as to the reasonableness of items and the absence of mate-rial misstatements due to errors.

*Calculations* by auditor such as calculation of depreciation expense, tax liabilities, etc., sup-port the application of GAAP.

*Physical existence* is determined by observation and count.

*Authoritative statements* by a client provide support for the treatment of certain items in the recording and aggregation of transaction data.  Authoritative statements by third parties such as confirmations provide evidence concerning the existence of transactions with third parties.

*Subsequent events* confirm the status of estimates and assertions at the financial statement date. For example, subsequent collection of receivables gives evidence as to their valuation and collectibility. Court award of a lawsuit pending at year-end is evidence of the year-end payable or receivable.

Since the competency of evidence depends upon the financial statement assertion under consideration (recall PERCV), the auditor must use professional judgment when deciding which type of evidence is most appropriate in a specific situation. Conceptually, the auditor should attempt to gather a sufficient quantity of competent evidence at a minimum cost.

*Audit procedures* (acts to be performed) are undertaken by the auditor to obtain the corroborating evidence discussed above. The professional standards and auditing textbooks have used a variety of terms to describe the procedures used by auditors. The following is a list of frequently used terms that represent distinct audit procedures:

*Inspection* (of documents and reports)
*Observation* (of an activity—e.g., inventory count, internal control procedure)
*Inquiry* (of appropriate client personnel)
*Confirmation* (of information—e.g., accounts receivable)
*Reperformance* (of an activity—e.g., refoot an invoice, recalculate depreciation)
*Physical Examination* (of an asset—e.g., marketable securities, fixed assets)
*Analytical Procedures* (comparing interrelationships)
*Vouch* (from recorded entry to support)
*Trace* (from support to recorded entry)

The first four audit procedures above are directly from the third field standard on evidence. The last five are derived from AU 326 and several auditing texts.

While the above list of audit procedures is meant to be comprehensive, numerous other terms have been used in both the professional standards and in auditing texts. Some of the more frequent terms that you will find in written audit programs include the following:

Agree (schedule balances to general ledger)
Analyze (account transactions)
Compare (beginning balances with last year's audited figures)
Count (cash, inventory, etc.)
Examine (authoritative documents)
Foot (totals)
Prove (totals)
Read (minutes of directors' meetings)
Reconcile (cash balance)
Review (disclosure, legal documents)
Scan (for unusual items)

## B. Evidence—Specific (Substantive Tests)

As noted earlier, the objective of an audit is to express an opinion on whether the firm's financial statements are fairly presented in conformity with generally accepted accounting principles. Substantive tests are designed to assist the auditor in reaching this goal by ascertaining whether the specific balances of financial statement accounts are in conformity with generally accepted accounting principles. While tests of controls are used to test the "means" of processing (the internal control system), substantive tests are used to directly test the "ends" of processing—the financial statements.

When evaluating evidence, the objective is to obtain an estimate of the total error in the financial statements and to determine whether it exceeds a material amount. The auditor estimates the likely error in the financial statements and attempts to determine whether an unacceptably high audit risk exists. Note here that in the evaluation of audit evidence, because of information obtained during the audit, the auditor **may** revise his/her preliminary estimate of materiality (see discussion in the Engagement Planning Module).

1. **Types of Substantive Tests.** Substantive tests are of two types: (1) Analytical procedures, (2) Tests of details of transactions and balances.

a.  **Analytical procedures.** Analytical procedures consist of evaluations of financial information
    made by a study of plausible relationships among financial and nonfinancial data.  Analytical pro-
    cedures are used for the following purposes:

    *Planning*—Determine the nature, timing, and extent of tests (Required)
    *Substantive testing*—Substantiate accounts for which overall comparisons are helpful
    *Overall review*—Assess conclusions reached and evaluate overall financial statement presentation
    (Required)

    NOTE: *GAAS requires the use of analytical procedures during the planning stage and the final review stage. Analyti-*
    *cal procedures are **not** a required substantive test.*

    The following table summarizes some important characteristics of analytical procedures per-
    formed at the three stages of an audit:

| Stage of audit | Required? | Purpose | Comment |
|---|---|---|---|
| Planning | Yes | To assist in planning the nature, timing and extent of other auditing procedures | Generally use data aggregated at a high level |
| Substantive Testing | No | To obtain evidential matter about particular assertions related to account balances or classes of transactions | Effectiveness depends upon (a) Nature of assertion (b) Plausibility and predictability of relations (c) Reliability of data (d) Precision of expectation |
| Overall Review | Yes | To assist in assessing the conclusions reached and in the evaluation of the overall financial statement presentation | Includes reading financial statements to consider (a) Adequacy of evidence gathered for unusual or unexpected balances identified during planning or during course of audit (b) Unusual or unexpected balances or relationships not previously identified |

    Perhaps the most familiar example of analytical procedures used in auditing is the calculation of
    ratios.  However, analytical procedures range from simple comparisons of information through the
    use of complex models such as regression and time series analysis.  The typical approach is

    (1) Develop an expectation for the account balance
    (2) Determine the amount of difference from the expectation that can be accepted without inves-
        tigation
    (3) Compare the company's account balance (or ratio) with the expected account balance
    (4) Investigate significant differences from the expected account balance

    When developing an expectation, the auditor must attempt to identify plausible relationships.
    These expectations may be derived from

    (1) The information itself in prior periods
    (2) Anticipated results such as budgets and forecasts
    (3) Relationships among elements of financial information within the period
    (4) Industry information
    (5) Relevant **nonfinancial** information

    Relationships differ in their predictability.  Be familiar with the following principles:

    (1) Relationships in a dynamic or unstable environment are less predictable than those in a stable
        environment.
    (2) Relationships involving balance sheet accounts are less predictable than income statement ac-
        counts (because balance sheet accounts represent balances at one arbitrary point in time).
    (3) Relationships involving management discretion are sometimes less predictable (e.g., decision
        to incur maintenance expense rather than replace plant).

    Recall from earlier in this module (section A) that the reliability of evidence varies based on
    whether it is obtained from (1) independent sources, (2) personal knowledge, or (3) developed un-
    der strong internal control.  In addition, in the case of analytical procedures be aware that use of

data that has been subjected to audit testing and data available from a variety of sources increases the reliability of the data used in the analysis.

Principal limitations concerning analytical procedures include

(1) The guidelines for evaluation may be inadequate (e.g., Why is an industry average good? Why should the ratio be the same as last year?)

(2) It is difficult to determine whether a change is due to a misstatement or is the result of random change in the account.

(3) Cost-based accounting records hinder comparisons between firms of different ages and/or asset compositions.

(4) Accounting differences hinder comparisons between firms (e.g., if one firm uses LIFO and another uses FIFO the information is not comparable).

(5) Analytical procedures present only "circumstantial" evidence in that a "significant" difference will lead to additional audit procedures as opposed to direct detection of a misstatement.

b. **Tests of details of transactions and balances.** These tests are used to examine the actual details making up the various account balances. For example, if receivables total $1,000,000 at year-end, tests of details may be made of the individual components of the total account. Assume the $1,000,000 is the accumulation of 250 individual accounts. As a test of details, an auditor might decide to confirm a sample of these 250 accounts. Based on the results of the auditor's consideration of internal control and tests of controls, the auditor might determine that 60 accounts should be confirmed. Thus, when responses are received and when the balances have been reconciled, the auditor has actually tested the detail supporting the account; the **existence** of the accounts has been confirmed. As an additional test (and also as an alternative procedure when confirmation replies have not been received from debtors), the auditor may examine cash receipts received subsequent to year-end on individual accounts. This substantive test provides evidence pertaining to both the **existence** and the **valuation** of the account.

*NOTE: In gathering sufficient competent evidential matter, auditors seek an efficient and effective combination of (1) tests of controls, (2) analytical procedures, and (3) tests of details of transactions to afford a reasonable basis for an opinion.*

2. **Substantive Test Audit Programs.** An audit program is a detailed list of the audit procedures to be performed in the course of an audit. It is helpful to understand the nature of audit programs for various accounts to help reply to a variety of multiple choice questions and, possibly, to a simulation. The professional standards require a written audit program for each audit.

As noted earlier under "Evidence—Specific (Substantive Tests)," financial statements that purport to be in conformity with generally accepted accounting principles contain certain assertions: presentation and disclosure, existence or occurrence, rights and obligations, completeness, and valuation or allocation (PERCV). Auditors gather evidence to form an opinion with respect to these assertions. The experienced auditor should be able to prepare an audit program for an audit area (e.g., inventory) to test whether these assertions are supportable. The process is one in which specific audit objectives are developed (also either explicitly or implicitly) based on the assertions being made in the financial statements. Finally, audit procedures to meet these audit objectives are formulated and listed in an audit program. These relationships may be illustrated as

Financial Statements

↓

Assertions

↓

Audit Objectives

↓

Audit Procedures

↓

Audit Program

For purposes of the CPA exam, consider two possible approaches for auditing an account

   (1)  Direct tests of ending balance ("tests of balances"), and
   (2)  Tests of inputs and outputs during the year ("tests of details of transactions").

An auditor may emphasize the first approach to directly test ending balances for high turnover accounts such as cash, accounts receivable, accounts payable, etc. (e.g., confirm year-end balances). The second approach, tests of transactions (inputs and outputs during the year), is used most extensively for lower turnover accounts (e.g., fixed assets, long-term debt, etc.). For example, for fixed assets, a low turnover account, the emphasis will be on vouching additions or retirements—not on auditing the entire account for a continuing audit engagement. Bear in mind, however, that during an audit it is **not** an either/or proposition—a **combination of approaches** with an emphasis of one approach over the other will generally be used.

   The tables that appear at the end of this section present summarized substantive audit programs for the major balance sheet accounts. Although the programs are constructed to present the pertinent procedures under only one assertion, be aware that many audit procedures provide support for multiple assertions. For example, while cutoffs are listed under the "rights and obligations" assertion, cutoffs also apply to the existence and completeness assertions. The purpose is to use the PERCV assertions to organize your thoughts about audit programs. When you think about a program you need not worry about which assertion an audit procedure "best fits under." However, recall from Section A of this module and Section C of the Internal Control Module on directional testing, that some objective questions may ask which assertion a procedure applies most directly to (e.g., analysis of inventory turnover rates most directly applies to valuation). You must use your understanding of the assertions for the specific procedure presented in that type of question. Section C of this module should help you understand the nature of various audit procedures.

   In reviewing the summary audit procedures, you will find a number of similarities between areas. We have provided the following "overall framework" to help you identify the similarities.

*Overall:*  The following are typical procedures included in a substantive audit program:

### Presentation and Disclosure:

   *Review disclosure.* Always include a general disclosure requirement related to overall compliance with GAAP.

   *Inquire about disclosures.* Consider specific disclosure requirements for the account, as well as for related accounts. Example: for receivables, you would recall from your accounting courses such possibilities as factoring, pledging, or discounting.

### Existence or Occurrence:

   *Confirmation.* Often an account will lend itself to confirmation (e.g., bank for cash, debtor for receivables, stock registrar and transfer agent for stock authorized and outstanding).

   *Observation.* Always consider whether you can observe the item itself and/or a legal document representing the item. Examples: cash on hand, inventory, loan agreements.

   *Trace/Vouch transactions.* This step relates directly to "directional testing" as presented in Section C of the Internal Control Module. Example: for receivables the auditor may examine shipping documents, invoices, and credit memos.

### Rights and Obligations:

   *Cutoffs.* Auditors must consider whether transactions have been reported in the proper period. Think about the transactions affecting the account to determine the proper cutoff. For example, cash cutoffs will relate to receipts and disbursements of cash, while receivables will relate to credit sales and cash receipts.

   *NOTE: Be careful here. Cutoffs also apply directly to the existence/occurrence and completeness assertions. If a multiple-choice question is asked, the specific details of the question determine the most directly related assertion.*

   *Authorization.* Consider whether there are transactions that require specific authorization. Authorization of transactions relates to whether proper rights and obligations have been established. This step is not always included, but programs for accounts such as receivables, debt, and owners' equity accounts are affected.

*Completeness:*

*Analytical procedures.* Always include a step on analytical procedures. Also, mention specific procedures for the account being audited. Section C of this module provides examples for the various accounts.

*Omissions.* Consider how transactions (adjustment) could improperly have been omitted from the account. Examples here include inventory count sheets not included, accruals not made, debt not recorded.

*Valuation:*

*Foot schedules.* Consider the actual schedules involved with the account and include a step to foot and cross-foot them.

*Agree schedules balances to general ledger balances.*

*Agree financial statement balances to schedules.* Because financial statements are derived from accounting information, the general and subsidiary ledgers as well as other accounting records must be summarized. Examples: accounts receivable, inventory count sheets.

*Consider valuation method of account.* You should consider the accounting method used, and whether it has been properly applied. Most accounts have a number of steps here. Examples: Receivables must be valued net of an appropriate allowance, inventory costing methods (e.g., LIFO, FIFO), and application of the lower of cost or market rule. Always integrate your accounting knowledge with auditing procedures here.

*Consider related accounts.* When you are considering an audit program for a balance sheet account, know that it ordinarily will include procedures used to audit the related income statement accounts. Examples: analytical procedures for bad debt expense may provide evidence as to the valuation of receivables; recalculating interest expense may provide evidence as to the existence of long-term debt; and recalculating depreciation and applying analytical procedures to repairs and maintenance expense may provide evidence as to the completeness and/or valuation of property, plant, and equipment.

*Audit objectives.* The CPA exam may ask for the auditor's "objectives" in the audit of an account. In general there will be one or more "objectives" relating to each of the financial statement assertions. For example, in the case of long-term debt, the following could serve as objectives:

1. Determine whether internal control over long-term debt is adequate
2. Determine whether long-term debt disclosures comply with GAAP (presentation and disclosure)
3. Determine whether recorded long-term debt exists at year-end (existence or occurrence)
4. Determine whether long-term debt represents an obligation to the firm at year-end (rights and obligations)
5. Determine whether all long-term debt has been completely recorded at year-end (completeness)
6. Determine whether all long-term debt has been properly valued at year-end (valuation)

*Areas in which a SAS prescribes procedures.* The Professional Standards include a number of areas in which specific procedures are either required or suggested. A simulation question may require you to find them. Although you need not memorize the AU section, know that such procedures have been presented in areas such as the following:

**Specific types of transactions**

| | |
|---|---|
| Illegal Acts | AU 317 |
| Related Parties | AU 334 |
| Litigation (Loss Contingencies) | AU 337 |

**Information with which "limited" procedures are required**

| | |
|---|---|
| Other Information in Documents Containing Audited Statements | AU 550 |
| Interim Reviews | AU 722 |
| Compilations | AR 100 |
| Reviews | AR 100 |

**Supplemental information required by the FASB**

| | |
|---|---|
| General Procedures | AU 558 |

**Areas in which "audit" procedures are required**

| | |
|---|---|
| Receivables | AU 330 |
| Inventories | AU 331 |
| Investment Securities | AU 332 |
| Subsequent Events | AU 560 |

**Other**
Other Auditors Involved                                                                  AU 543
Public Warehouses                                                              AU 901, AU 331

While we discuss these areas throughout the various modules, the Summary of Prescribed Audit Procedures: Other Areas (see the following pages) presents lists of the primary procedures for several of the areas for which you may expect an exam question. Do not try to memorize the procedures for each of the areas. Instead, review them well before the exam and then again shortly before the exam. A simulation question might ask you to find certain of these procedures and paste them to your answer.

### SUMMARY AUDIT PROCEDURES[1]:  CASH, RECEIVABLES, INVENTORY

| | *Cash* | *Receivables* | *Inventory* |
|---|---|---|---|
| **Presentation and Disclosure** | 1. Review disclosures for compliance with GAAP <br> 2. Inquire about compensating balance requirements and restrictions | 1. Review disclosures for compliance with GAAP <br> 2. Inquire about pledging, discounting <br> 3. Review loan agreements for pledging, factoring | 1. Review disclosures for compliance with GAAP <br> 2. Inquire about pledging <br> 3. Review purchase commitments |
| **Existence or Occurrence** | 3. Confirmation <br> 4. Count cash on hand <br> 5. Prepare bank transfer schedule | 4. Confirmation <br> 5. Inspect notes <br> 6. Vouch (examine shipping documents, invoices, credit memos) | 4. Confirmation of consigned inventory and inventory in warehouses <br> 5. Observe inventory count |
| **Rights and Obligations** | 6. Review cutoffs (receipts and disbursements) <br> 7. Review passbooks, bank statements | 7. Review cutoffs (sales, cash receipts, sales returns) <br> 8. Inquire about factoring of receivables | 6. Review cutoffs (sales, sales returns, purchases, purchase returns) |
| **Completeness** | 8. Perform analytical procedures <br> 9. Review bank reconciliation <br> 10. Obtain bank cutoff statement to verify reconciling items on bank reconciliation | 9. Perform analytical procedures | 7. Perform test counts and compare with client's counts/summary <br> 8. Inquire about consigned inventory <br> 9. Perform analytical procedures <br> 10. Account for all inventory tags and count sheets |
| **Valuation** | 11. Foot summary schedules <br> 12. Reconcile summary schedules to general ledger <br> 13. Test translation of any foreign currencies | 10. Foot subsidiary ledger <br> 11. Reconcile subsidiary ledger to general ledger <br> 12. Examine subsequent cash receipts <br> 13. Age receivables to test adequacy of allowance for doubtful accounts <br> 14. Discuss adequacy of allowance for doubtful accounts with management and compare to historical experience | 11. Foot and extend summary schedules <br> 12. Reconcile summary schedules to general ledger <br> 13. Test inventory costing method <br> 14. Determine that inventory is valued at lower of cost or market <br> 15. Examine inventory quality (salable condition) <br> 16. Test inventory obsolescence |

### SUMMARY AUDIT PROCEDURES:
### MARKETABLE SECURITIES, PROPERTY, PLANT, AND EQUIPMENT, PREPAIDS

| | *Marketable securities* | *Property, plant, equipment* | *Prepaids* |
|---|---|---|---|
| **Presentation and Disclosure** | 1. Review disclosures for compliance with GAAP <br> 2. Inquire about pledging <br> 3. Review loan agreements for pledging <br> 4. Review management's classification of securities | 1. Review disclosures for compliance with GAAP <br> 2. Inquire about liens and restrictions <br> 3. Review loan agreements for liens and restrictions | 1. Review disclosures for compliance with GAAP <br> 2. Review adequacy of insurance coverage |
| **Existence or Occurrence** | 5. Confirmation of securities held by third parties <br> 6. Inspect and count <br> 7. Vouch (to available documentation) | 4. Inspect additions <br> 5. Vouch additions <br> 6. Review any leases for proper accounting <br> 7. Perform search for unrecorded retirements | 3. Confirmation of deposits and insurance <br> 4. Vouch (examine) insurance polices (miscellaneous support for deposit) |
| **Rights and Obligations** | 8. Review cutoffs (examine transactions near year-end) | 8. Review minutes for approval of additions | (See existence or occurrence) |
| **Completeness** | 9. Perform analytical procedures <br> 10. Reconcile dividends received to publish records | 9. Perform analytical procedures <br> 10. Vouch major entries to repairs and maintenance expense | 5. Perform analytical procedures |
| **Valuation** | 11. Foot summary schedules <br> 12. Reconcile summary schedules to general ledger <br> 13. Test amortization of premiums and discounts <br> 14. Determine the market value for trading and available-for-sale securities <br> 15. Review audited financial statements of major investees | 11. Foot summary schedules <br> 12. Reconcile summary schedules to general ledger <br> 13. Recalculate depreciation | 6. Foot summary schedules <br> 7. Reconcile summary schedules to general ledger <br> 8. Recalculate prepaid portions |

---

[1]  *Audit procedures are described in detail in Section C.*

# SUMMARY OF PRESCRIBED AUDIT PROCEDURES: OTHER AREAS

| Professional Standard Section | Illegal acts | Related parties— identifying transactions | Related parties— determining existence | Litigation, claims, and assessments | Required supplemental information | Subsequent events |
|---|---|---|---|---|---|---|
| | AU 317 | AU 334 | AU 334 | AU 337 | AU 558 | AU 560 |
| **1. Discuss with Management** | a. Policies for prevention<br>b. Policies for identifying, evaluating, and accounting<br>c. Inquire as to existence<br><br>*NOTE: Audits do not include procedures designed specifically to detect illegal acts. However, normal audit procedures may bring illegal acts to the auditor's attention.* | a. Inquire as to existence | a. Policies for identifying and accounting<br>b. Obtain list of related parties<br>c. Inquire as to existence | a. Policies for identifying, evaluating, and accounting for<br>b. Obtain description | a. Measurement methods, significant assumptions, consistency with prior periods | a. Contingent liabilities<br>b. Significant changes in capital stock, debt, working capital<br>c. Current status of estimated items<br>d. Unusual items after balance sheet date |
| **2. Examine** | a. Consider laws and regulations<br>b. Normal tests of controls (compliance tests) and substantive test examination procedures | a. SEC filings<br>b. Minutes of Board of Directors and others<br>c. Conflict of interest statements | a. SEC filings<br>b. Pensions, other trusts, and identifying officers thereof<br>c. Stockholder listings (for closely held firms)<br>d. Prior year audit workpapers | a. Correspondence and invoices from lawyers<br>b. Minutes—stockholders, directors, others<br>c. Read contracts, agreements. Etc.<br>d. Other documents. | a. Compare with financial statements and other information | a. Latest interim statements<br>b. Minutes of stockholders, directors, etc. |
| **3. Other Procedures** | a. Coordinate with loss contingency procedures<br>b. Consideration of internal control<br>c. Read minutes<br>d. Overall substantive tests<br>e. Include in representation letter | a. Review business with major customers, suppliers, etc.<br>b. Consider services being provided (received) at unreasonable prices<br>c. Review accounting records for large, unusual transactions<br>d. Review confirmations<br>e. Review invoices from lawyers<br>f. Consideration of internal control<br>g. Provide audit personnel with names of known related parties | a. Contact predecessor and other auditors<br>b. Review material investment transactions<br>c. Know that such transactions are more likely for firms in financial difficulty | a. Letters of audit inquiry to clients's lawyers | a. Add to representation letter<br>b. Perform further inquiries if information seems incorrect<br>c. Apply any other required procedures for specific area being considered | a. Include in representation letter<br>b. Coordinate with loss contingency procedures<br>c. Cutoff procedures (sales, purchases) |

**SUMMARY AUDIT PROCEDURES:**
**PAYABLES (CURRENT), LONG-TERM DEBT, OWNERS' EQUITY**

| | *Payables (current)* | *Long-term debt* | *Owners' equity* |
|---|---|---|---|
| **Presentation and Disclosure** | 1. Review disclosures for compliance with GAAP<br>2. Review purchase commitments | 1. Review disclosures for compliance with GAAP<br>2. Inquire about pledging of assets<br>3. Review debt agreements for pledging and events causing default | 1. Review disclosures for compliance with GAAP<br>2. Review information on stock options, dividend restrictions |
| **Existence or Occurrence** | 3. Confirmation<br>4. Inspect copies of notes and note agreements<br>5. Vouch payables (examine purchase order, receiving reports, invoices) | 4. Confirmation<br>5. Inspect copies of notes and note agreements<br>6. Trace receipt of funds (and payment) to bank account and cash receipts journal | 3. Confirmation with registrar and transfer agent (if applicable)<br>4. Inspect stock certificate book (when no registrar or transfer agent)<br>5. Vouch capital stock entries |
| **Rights and Obligations** | 6. Review cutoffs (purchases, purchase returns, disbursements) | 7. Review cutoffs (examine transactions near year-end)<br>8. Review minutes for proper authorization (and completeness) | 6. Review minutes for proper authorization<br>7. Inquire of legal counsel on legal issues<br>8. Review Articles of Incorporation and bylaws for propriety of equity securities |
| **Completeness** | 7. Perform analytical procedures<br>8. Perform search for unrecorded payables (examine unrecorded invoices, receiving reports, purchase orders)<br>9. Inquire of management as to completeness | 9. Perform analytical procedures<br>10. Inquire of management as to completeness<br>11. Review bank confirmations for unrecorded debt | 9. Perform analytical procedures<br>10. Inspect treasury stock certificates |
| **Valuation** | 10. Foot subsidiary ledger<br>11. Reconcile subsidiary ledger to general ledger<br>12. Recalculate interest expense (if any)<br>13. For payroll, review year-end accrual<br>14. Recalculate other accrued liabilities | 12. Foot summary schedules<br>13. Reconcile summary schedules to general ledger<br>14. Vouch entries to account<br>15. Recalculate interest expense and accrued interest payable | 11. Agree amounts to general ledger<br>12. Vouch dividend payments<br>13. Vouch all entries to retained earnings<br>14. Recalculate treasury stock transactions |

3. **Documentation (SAS 103 and PCAOB 3).** Make certain that you are familiar with the information in the outline of SAS 103. You should know that

   a. Audit documentation should be prepared so as to enable an experienced auditor, with no previous connection to the audit, to understand procedures performed, audit evidence obtained, and conclusions reached.

   b. While it is not necessary to document every matter considered during an audit, oral explanations alone (absent working paper documentation) are not sufficient to support the work of the auditor.

   c. Audit documentation should include a written audit program (or set of audit programs) for every audit.

   d. Documentation relating to documents inspected by the auditor should allow an experienced auditor to determine which ones were tested.

   e. The auditor should identify any information that contradicts or is inconsistent with auditor's final conclusion regarding significant matter and how the matter was addressed in forming a conclusion, but need not retain documentation that is incorrect or superseded. Documentation of the contradiction or inconsistency may include procedures performed, records documenting consultations, differences in professional judgment among team members or between team members and others consulted.

   f. If information is added to the working papers after the issuance of the audit report, documentation should include (1) when and by whom changes were made and reviewed, (2) specific reasons for changes, and (3) the effect, if any, of the changes on the auditor's conclusion.

   g. The documentation completion period is 60 days following the report release date. That means that changes resulting from the process of assembling and completing the audit file may be made within 60 days following the date the audit report was released to the client. The fact that these changes have been made need not be documented. Examples of such changes include routine file-assembling procedures, deleting discarded documentation, sorting, and signing off file completion checklists. However, the auditor may not add new information to the working papers unless it is documented per f. above.

   h. After the documentation completion date, the auditor should not delete or discard audit documentation. Additions are treated as per f. above.

i.  The retention period (how long audit documentation must be kept) should not be less than five years from the report release date (longer if legal and regulatory requirements so require).

j.  Audit documentation is the property of the auditor and is confidential.

PCAOB Standard 3 contains documentation requirements for audits and reviews of public companies—you should review the outline of Standard 3, which follows the AU Outlines. The requirements differ from AICPA standards in these significant ways.

1.  The documentation must demonstrate that the engagement complied with PCAOB standards

2.  The documentation completion period is 45 days (not 60 days) following the report release date

3.  The retention period is seven years (rather than five years)

Additionally, candidates should be aware of the following terms:

*Working Trial Balance*—A listing of ledger accounts with current year-end balances (as well as last year's ending balances), with columns for adjusting and reclassifying entries as well as for final balances for the current year. Typically both balance sheet and income statement accounts are included.

*Lead Schedules*—Schedules that summarize like accounts, the total of which is typically transferred to the working trial balance. For example, a client's various cash accounts may be summarized on a lead schedule with only the total cash being transferred to the working trial balance.

*Index*—The combination of numbers and/or letters given to a workpaper page for identification and organization purposes. For example, cash workpaper may be indexed A-1.

*Cross-Reference*—When the same information is included on two workpapers, auditors indicate on each workpaper the index of the other workpaper containing the identical information. For example, if Schedule A-1 includes a bank reconciliation with total outstanding checks listed, while Schedule A-2 has a detailed list of these outstanding checks plus the total figure, the totals on the two workpapers will be cross-referenced to one another.

*Current Workpaper Files*—Files that contain corroborating information pertaining to the current year's audit program (e.g., cash confirmation)

*Permanent Workpaper Files*—Files that contain information that is expected to be used by the auditor on many future audits of a client (e.g., copies of articles of incorporation and bylaws, schedules of ratios by year, analyses of capital stock accounts, debt agreements, and internal control)

## C.  Other Specific Evidence Topics

### 1.  Cash

#### a.  Special audit considerations for cash

(1) **Kiting.** Kiting is a form of fraud that overstates cash by causing it to be simultaneously included in two or more bank accounts. Kiting is possible because a check takes several days to clear the bank on which it is drawn (the "float period"). Following is an example of how kiting can be used to conceal a prior embezzlement in a company that has two bank accounts (one in Valley State Bank and one in First City Bank).

| Date | Situation |
|------|-----------|
| 12/15 | Bookkeeper writes himself a $10,000 check on the Valley account, and cashes it—no journal entry is made |
| 12/16 | Bookkeeper loses the money gambling in Bullhead City |
| 12/31 | Bookkeeper, fearing the auditors will detect the fraud, conceals the shortage by |

1.  Writing a $10,000 unrecorded check on First City account and depositing it in the Valley account. This will cover up the shortage because Valley will credit the account for the $10,000, and the check will not clear the First City account until January—no journal entry is made until after year-end.
2.  When the First City bank reconciliation is prepared at 12/31, the check is not listed as outstanding.

Kiting may be detected by preparing a bank transfer schedule, by preparing a four-column bank reconciliation for the Valley account, or by obtaining a cutoff statement for the First City account.

(2) **Bank transfer schedule.**  A bank transfer schedule shows the dates of all transfers of cash among the client's various bank accounts.  Know that its primary purpose is to help auditors to **detect kiting**.  The schedule is prepared by using bank statements for the periods before and after year-end **and** by using the firm's cash receipts and disbursements journals.  The following is an example of a bank transfer schedule that will help an auditor to detect the kiting described in (1) above:

|  |  | *Date* | | | *Date* | |
| *Amount* | *Bank drawn on* | *Books* | *Bank* | *Bank deposited in* | *Books* | *Bank* |
| $10,000 | First City | 1/2 | 1/2 | Valley | 1/2 | 12/31 |

Note that analysis of the schedule reveals that at December 31, the cash is double counted:  it is included in both the Valley account (the bank gave credit for the deposit on 12/31) and in the First City account.

(3) **Bank reconciliations.**  Auditors generally prepare either a two- or a four-column bank reconciliation for the difference between the cash per bank and per books.  The four-column approach (also called a proof of cash) **will** allow the auditor to reconcile

   (a)  All cash receipts and disbursements recorded on the books to those on the bank statement and

   (b)  All deposits and disbursements recorded on the bank statement to the books

A four-column reconciliation **will not** allow the auditor to verify whether

   (a)  Checks written have been for the wrong amounts and so recorded on both the books and the bank statement and

   (b)  Unrecorded checks or deposits exist that have not cleared the bank

In the earlier kiting example, note that the Valley four-column reconciliation will detect the kiting because the 12/15 credit for the check used in the embezzlement will have been included in the Valley bank statement disbursements, but not on the books as of 12/31.  This is because the embezzlement will result in a $10,000 unreconciled difference between the book and bank totals in the disbursements column of the reconciliation.  The First City reconciliation, by itself, will not assist in detection of the kiting because both book and bank entries occur after year-end.

(4) **Bank cutoff statements.**  A cutoff statement is a bank statement for the first 8-10 business days after year-end.  Know that its primary purpose is to help auditors to **verify reconciling items** on the year-end bank reconciliation.  Tests performed using a cutoff statement include verifying that outstanding checks have been completely and accurately recorded as of year-end, and that deposits in transit have cleared within a reasonable period.  The statement is sent directly by the bank to the auditor.  In the above kiting example, the cutoff statement for the First City account will allow the auditor to detect the fraud since it will include the December 31 unrecorded check.

(5) **Standard confirmation form.**  Auditors use a standard form to obtain information from financial institutions (Standard Form to Confirm Account Balance Information with Financial Institutions).  The form requests information on two types of balances—**deposits** and **loans**. The form requests financial institutions to indicate any exceptions to the information noted, and to confirm any additional account or loan balance information that comes to their attention while completing the form.  Know that the form is designed to substantiate evidence primarily on the **existence** assertion, and not to discover or provide assurance about accounts not listed on the form (evidence on the completeness assertion is not elicited).

b.  **Typical substantive audit procedures for cash**

(1) **Review disclosures for compliance with generally accepted accounting principles.**

(2) **Inquire of management concerning compensating balance requirements and restrictions on cash.**  A compensating balance is an account with a bank in which a company has agreed to maintain a specified minimum amount; compensating balances are typically required under the terms of bank loan agreements.  Such restrictions on cash, when material, should be disclosed in the financial statements.

(3) **Send confirmation letters to financial institutions** to verify existence of the amounts on deposit.  See Section a.(5) above.

(4) **Count cash on hand at year-end** to verify its existence.

(5) **Prepare a bank transfer schedule for the last week of the audit year and the first week of the following year** to disclose misstatements of cash balances resulting from **kiting**. See Section a. above.

(6) **Review the cutoff of cash receipts and cash disbursements around year-end** to verify that transactions affecting cash are recorded in the proper period.

(7) **Review passbooks and bank statements** to verify that book balances represent amounts to which the client has rights.

(8) **Perform analytical procedures** to test the reasonableness of cash balances. Tests here may include comparisons to prior year cash balances.

(9) **Review year-end bank reconciliations** to verify that cash has been properly stated as of year-end. See Section a. above.

(10) **Obtain a bank cutoff statement** to verify whether the reconciling items on the year-end bank reconciliation have been properly reflected. See Section a. above.

(11) **Foot summary schedules of cash and agree their total to the amount which will appear on the financial statements.**

(12) **Reconcile summary schedules of cash to the general ledger.**

(13) **Test translation of any foreign currencies.**

2. **Receivables (AU 330)**

   a. **Special audit considerations for receivables**

      (1) **Lapping.** Lapping is an embezzlement scheme in which cash collections from customers are stolen and the shortage is concealed by delaying the recording of subsequent cash receipts. A simplified lapping scheme is shown below.

| Date | Situation | Bookkeeping entry | | |
|------|-----------|-------------------|---|---|
| 1/7 | Jones pays $500 on account | No entry, bookkeeper cashes check and keeps proceeds | | |
| 1/8 | Smith pays $200 on account | Cash | 500 | |
| | Adam pays $300 on account |    Accounts Receivable—Jones | | 500 |
| 1/9 | Brock pays $500 on account | Cash | 500 | |
| | |    Accounts Receivable—Smith | | 200 |
| | |    Accounts Receivable—Adams | | 300 |
| 1/10 | Bookkeeper determines Brock is unlikely to purchase from company in the future | Allowance for Doubtful Accts. | 500 | |
| | |    Accounts Receivable—Brock | | 500 |

Lapping most frequently occurs when one individual has responsibility for both recordkeeping and custody of cash. Although the best way to control lapping is to segregate duties and thereby make its occurrence difficult, it may be detected by using the following procedures:

(a) Analytical procedures—calculate age of receivables and turnover of receivables (lapping increases the age and decreases turnover)

(b) Confirm receivables—investigate all exceptions noted, emphasize accounts that have been written off and old accounts. For all accounts watch for postings of cash receipts which have taken an unusually long time. For example, when a reply to a confirmation suggests that the account was paid on December 29, investigate when the posting occurred.

(c) Deposit slips

   1] Obtain authenticated deposit slips from bank and compare names, dates, and amounts on remittance advices to information on deposit slips (where possible)

   2] Perform surprise inspection of deposits, and compare deposit slip with remittances

(d) Bookkeeping system

   1] Compare remittance advices with information recorded

   2] Verify propriety of noncash credits to accounts receivable

   3] Foot cash receipts journal, customers' ledger accounts, and accounts receivable control account

   4] Reconcile individual customer accounts to accounts receivable control account

   5] Compare copies of monthly statements with customer accounts

(2) **Confirmations.** Confirmation of accounts receivable is a generally accepted auditing procedure. Auditors are to confirm receivables unless (1) accounts receivable are immaterial, (2) confirmations would be ineffective as an audit procedure, or (3) the combined assessment of inherent and control risk is low, and that assessment, with other substantive evidence, is sufficient to reduce audit risk to an acceptably low level.

Receivable confirmations primarily test the **existence** assertion, and only to a limited extent the completeness and valuation assertions. Know the difference between the **positive** and **negative** forms of confirmation request.

The positive form requests a reply from debtors. Some positive forms request the recipient to indicate either agreement or disagreement with the information stated on the request. Other positive forms, "blank forms," do not state the amount (or other information), but request the respondent to fill in the balance or furnish other information.

The negative form requests the recipient to respond only if he or she disagrees with the information stated on the request. Negative confirmation requests may be used when

(a) The combined assessed level of inherent risk and control risk is low,
(b) A large number of small balances is involved, and
(c) The auditor has no reason to believe that recipients are unlikely to give them adequate consideration.

Note that when no reply is received to the negative form, the assumption is made that the debtor agrees with the amount and that evidence as to the existence assertion has been collected. When no reply is received to a positive confirmation, a second request is normally mailed to the debtor; if no reply to the second request is received, the auditor normally performs **alternative procedures** (e.g., examination of shipping documents, subsequent cash receipts, sales agreements). However, the auditor may consider **not performing alternative procedures** when (1) no unusual qualitative factors or systematic characteristics related to responses have been identified, and (2) the nonresponses in total, when projected as 100% misstatements to the population, are immaterial.

b. **Typical substantive audit procedures for receivables**
   (1) **Review disclosures for compliance with generally accepted accounting principles.**
   (2) **Inquire of management about pledging, or discounting of receivables** to verify that appropriate disclosure is provided.
   (3) **Review loan agreements for pledging and factoring of receivables** to verify that appropriate disclosure is provided.
   (4) **Confirm accounts and notes receivable by direct communication with debtors** to verify the existence of the accounts. See Section a. above.
   (5) **Inspect notes on hand and confirm those not on hand by direct communication with holders.** For notes receivable, the auditor will generally be able to inspect the actual note. This procedure is particularly important in situations in which the note is negotiable (i.e., salable) to third parties.
   (6) **Vouch receivables to supporting customer orders, sales orders, invoices, shipping documents, and credit memos** to verify the existence of accounts.
   (7) **Review the cutoff of sales and cash receipts around year-end** to verify that transactions affecting accounts receivable are recorded in the proper period. A sale is properly recorded when title passes on the items being sold. Title passes for items sold FOB shipping point when the item is shipped from inventory; title passes for items sold FOB destination when the item is received by the purchaser. You should realize that a proper credit sales cutoff generally affects at least four components of the financial statements: accounts receivable, sales, cost of goods sold, and inventory. Cash receipts should be recorded when the check (or cash) is received from a customer.
   (8) **Inquire about factoring of receivables** to verify that the client maintains rights to the accounts.
   (9) **Perform analytical procedures for accounts receivable, sales, notes receivable, and interest revenue.** Typical ratios include: (a) the gross profit rate, (b) accounts receivable

turnover, (c) the ratio of accounts receivable to credit sales, (d) the ratio of accounts written off to the ending accounts receivable, and (e) the ratio of interest revenue to notes receivable.

(10) **Foot the accounts and notes receivable subsidiary ledgers** to verify clerical accuracy.

(11) **Reconcile subsidiary ledgers to the general ledger control accounts** to verify clerical accuracy.

(12) **Examine cash receipts subsequent to year-end** to test the adequacy of the allowance for doubtful accounts.

(13) **Age accounts receivable** to test the adequacy of the allowance for doubtful accounts. An **aging schedule** is used to address the receivable **valuation** assertion. Such a schedule summarizes receivables by their age (e.g., 0-30 days since sale, 31-60 days since sale...). Estimates of the likely amount of bad debts in each age group are then made (typically based on historical experience) to estimate whether the amount in the allowance for doubtful accounts is adequate at year-end.

(14) **Discuss the adequacy of the allowance for doubtful accounts with management and the credit department and compare it to historical experience** to verify valuation.

3. **Inventory (AU 331)**

   a. **Special audit consideration for inventory**

      (1) **Observation.** Observation by the auditor of the client's counting of inventory (which primarily addresses the **existence** assertion) is a generally accepted auditing procedure and departure from it must be justified. You should be familiar with various situations that may affect the auditor's observation.

         (a) When a client uses statistical methods in determining inventory quantities, the auditor must be satisfied that the sampling plan has statistical validity.

         (b) The existence of good internal control may allow an effective count to be made prior to year-end. In such circumstances, the auditor will rely upon internal control and tests of updating of inventory through year-end to determine that year-end inventory is properly stated.

         (c) For a first-year client the auditor will probably not have been present for the count of the beginning inventory, a necessary input to determining cost of goods sold. If adequate evidence is available (e.g., acceptable predecessor workpapers), no report modification may be necessary. When adequate evidence is not available, the auditor may be required to qualify his/her audit report due to the scope limitation. Any resulting misstatement affects both current and prior year income and is therefore likely to result in qualification of the opinion on the income statement. The balance sheet at year-end will be unaffected due to the self-correcting nature of such an error.

         (d) Related to (c), a first-year client may have engaged the auditor subsequent to year-end and the auditor may also have missed the year-end inventory count. In addition, other events may make it impossible for the auditor to be present for the client's count of inventory. In such circumstances, alternate procedures may sometimes be used to establish the accuracy of the count (e.g., good internal control); however, these alternate procedures **must include some physical counts of inventory items** and must include appropriate tests of intervening transactions.

   b. **Typical substantive audit procedures for inventory**

      (1) **Review disclosures for compliance with generally accepted accounting principles.**

      (2) **Inquire of management about pledging of inventory** and verify the adequacy of disclosure.

      (3) **Review purchase and sales commitments** to verify whether there may be a need to either accrue a loss and/or provide disclosure. Generally, commitments are not disclosed in the financial statements unless uneconomic commitments result in a need to accrue significant losses (due to current price changes).

      (4) **Confirm consigned inventory and inventory in warehouses.** Some companies store inventory items in public warehouses. In such a situation, the auditor should **confirm** in writing with the custodian that the goods are being held. Additionally, if such holdings are significant, the auditor should apply one or more of the following procedures:

(a) Review the client's control procedures relating to the warehouseman
(b) Obtain a CPA's report on the warehouseman's internal control
(c) Observe physical counts of the goods
(d) If warehouse receipts have been pledged as collateral, confirm with lenders details of the pledged receipts

(5) **Observe the taking of the physical inventory and make test counts** to verify the existence (and to a limited extent the ownership) of inventory. See Section a. above.

(6) **Review cutoffs of sales, sales returns, purchases, and purchase returns around year-end** to verify that transactions affecting inventory are recorded in the proper period. Know here that the objective is to include in inventory those items for which the client has legal title.

(7) **Perform test counts during the observation of the taking of the inventory and compare them to the client's counts and subsequently to the accumulated inventory** to verify the accuracy of the count and its accumulation. See Section a. above.

(8) **Inquire of management as to the existence of consigned inventory** to verify the adequacy of its disclosure. Know that inventory consigned out remains the property of the client until it is sold. Inventory consigned to the client must not be included in the physical count since it belongs to the consignor.

(9) **Perform analytical procedures** to test the reasonableness of inventory. Analytical procedures include calculation of gross profit margins by product, and inventory turnover rates.

(10) **Account for all inventory tags and count sheets** to verify that inventory has been completely recorded.

(11) **Foot and extend summary inventory schedules** to verify clerical accuracy.

(12) **Reconcile inventory summary schedules to the general ledger** to verify clerical accuracy.

(13) **Test the inventory cost method** to verify that it is in conformity with generally accepted accounting principles. Here the auditor will determine the method of pricing used and whether it is acceptable and consistent with the prior years (e.g., LIFO, FIFO).

(14) **Test the pricing of inventory** to verify that it is valued at the lower of cost or market. As a general rule, inventories should not be carried in excess of their net realizable value. In certain circumstances a specialist may be needed to assist in valuation of inventory (see Section 11, **Using the Work of a Specialist**, below).

(15) **Examine inventory quality and condition** to assess whether there may be evidence suggesting that it is in unsatisfactory condition.

(16) **Perform any necessary additional tests of inventory obsolescence** to verify the valuation of inventory.

4. **Investment Securities (AU 332)**

(Review outline of AU 332 at this point)

a. **Special audit considerations for investment securities**

(1) **GAAP requirements.** Recall the criteria for deciding whether the cost adjusted for fair value, equity, or consolidated basis should be used for the investments (see outlines of APB 18 and SFAS 94). Also recall the distinction in accounting treatment under SFAS 115 for debt securities and equity securities where significant influence does not exist. Accounting for derivative instruments is presented in SFAS 133.

(2) **Audit approach.** Evidence related to the **existence** assertion is obtained by inspecting any securities that are held by a client (often in a safe deposit box) and by confirming securities held by custodians (e.g., a bank or trust company). A client employee should be present during the inspection to avoid confusion over any missing securities. In examining the security certificates, the auditor determines whether securities held are identical to the recorded securities (certificate numbers, number of shares, face value, etc.).

Evidence pertaining to **valuation** (carrying amount) for long-term investments for an investee may be obtained by examining investee (a) audited financial statements, (b) unaudited financial statements (insufficient evidence in and of itself), (c) market quotations, and (d) other evidential matter.

(3) **Simultaneous verification.** Because of the liquid nature of securities, the auditor's inspection is generally performed at year-end simultaneously with the audit of cash, bank loans (e.g., a revolving credit agreement), and other related items.

(4) **Client controls.** The liquid nature of marketable securities makes certain controls, such as the following, desirable:

   (a) The treasurer should authorize purchases and sales up to a certain value. After that value has been reached, transactions should be authorized by the board of directors.
   (b) Two individuals should be present when access to the securities is necessary.
   (c) Recorded balances for investments should periodically be compared with the actual securities held by individuals independent of the function.

b. **Typical substantive audit procedures for investment securities**

(1) **Review disclosures for compliance with generally accepted accounting principles.**

(2) **Inquire of management about pledging of investment securities** and verify that appropriate disclosure is provided.

(3) **Review loan agreements for pledging of investment securities** and verify that appropriate disclosure is provided.

(4) **Review management's classification of securities held for investment.**

(5) **Obtain confirmation of securities in the custody of others** to verify their existence.

(6) **Inspect and count securities on hand and compare serial numbers with those shown on the records and, if appropriate, with prior year audit working papers.** This procedure addresses the existence of the securities and provides evidence that no fraud involving "substitution" (e.g., unauthorized sale and subsequent repurchase) of securities has occurred during the year. When an auditor is unable to inspect and count securities held in a safe-deposit box at a bank until after the balance sheet date, a bank representative should be asked to confirm that there has been no access between the balance sheet date and the security count date.

(7) **Vouch purchases and sales of securities during the year.** This audit procedure will provide evidence relating to all financial statement assertions. Included here will be recomputation of gains and losses on security sales.

(8) **Review the cutoff of cash receipts and disbursements around year-end** to verify that transactions affecting investment securities transactions are recorded in the proper period.

(9) **Perform analytical procedures** to test the reasonableness of investment securities. A typical analytical procedure is to verify the relationship between interest and dividend income to the related securities. The auditor will also be able to recompute the interest and dividend income if so desired.

(10) **Reconcile amounts of dividends received to published dividend records.**

(11) **Foot and extend summary investment security schedules** to verify clerical accuracy.

(12) **Reconcile summary inventory schedules to the general ledger** to verify clerical accuracy.

(13) **Test amortization of premiums and discounts** to verify that investments are properly valued.

(14) **Determine the market value of securities classified as trading or available-for-sale at the date of the balance sheet.**

(15) **Review audited financial statements of major investments** to test whether they are properly valued at year-end.

5. **Property, Plant, and Equipment (PP&E)**

a. **Special audit considerations for PP&E**

(1) **Accounting considerations.** Many PP&E acquisitions involve trades of used assets. Recall APB 29 which requires that no gain be recognized when a plant asset is exchanged for a similar plant asset; gains are properly recognized for dissimilar trades.

   Assets constructed by a company for its own use should be recorded at the cost of direct material, direct labor, and applicable overhead. Recall that interest may be capitalized.

(2) **Overall approach.** The reasonableness of the entire account balance must be audited in detail for a client that has not previously been audited. When a predecessor auditor exists, the successor will normally review that auditor's workpapers.

For a continuing audit client, the audit of PP&E consists largely of an analysis of the year's acquisitions and disposals (an input and output approach). Subsequent to the first year, the account's slow rate of turnover generally permits effective auditing of the account in less time than accounts of comparable size.

(3) **Relationship with repairs and maintenance.** A number of CPA questions address this area. A PP&E acquisition may improperly be recorded in the repair and maintenance expense account. Therefore, an analysis of repairs and maintenance may detect **understatements** of PP&E. Alternatively, an analysis of PP&E may disclose repairs and maintenance that have improperly been capitalized, thereby resulting in **overstatements** of PP&E.

(4) **Unrecorded retirements.** Disposals may occur due to retirements or thefts of PP&E items. Simple retirements of equipment are often difficult to detect since no journal entry may have been recorded to reflect the event. Unrecorded or improperly recorded retirements (and thefts) may be discovered through examination of changes in insurance policies, consideration of the purpose of recorded acquisition, examination of property tax files, discussions, observation, or through an examination of debits to accumulated depreciation and of credits to miscellaneous revenue accounts. Inquiry of the plant manager may disclose unrecorded retirements and/or obsolete equipment.

b. **Typical substantive audit procedures for PP&E**

(1) **Review disclosures for compliance with generally accepted accounting principles.**

(2) **Inquire of management concerning any liens and restrictions on PP&E.** PP&E may be pledged as security on a loan agreement. Such restrictions are disclosed in the notes to the financial statements.

(3) **Review loan agreements for liens and restrictions on PP&E** and verify that appropriate disclosure is provided.

(4) **Inspect major acquisitions of PP&E** to verify their existence.

(5) **Vouch additions and retirements to PP&E** to verify their existence and the client's rights to them. Typically large PP&E transactions support will include original documents such as contracts, deeds, construction work orders, invoices, and authorization by the directors.

(6) **Review any leases for proper accounting** to determine whether the related PP&E assets should be capitalized.

(7) **Perform search for unrecorded retirements and for obsolete equipment.** See Section a. above.

(8) **Review minutes of the board of directors (and shareholders)** to verify that additions have been properly approved.

(9) **Perform analytical procedures** to test the reasonableness of PP&E. Typical analytical procedures involve a (a) comparison of total cost of PP&E divided by cost of goods sold, (b) comparison of repairs and maintenance on a monthly and annual basis, and (c) comparison of acquisitions and retirements for the current year with prior years.

(10) **Obtain or prepare an analysis of repairs and maintenance expense and vouch transactions** to discover items that should have been capitalized. See Section a. above.

(11) **Foot PP&E summary schedules** to verify clerical accuracy.

(12) **Reconcile summary PP&E schedules to the general ledger** to verify clerical accuracy.

(13) **Recalculate depreciation** to verify its clerical accuracy. In addition, the existence of recurring losses on retired assets may indicate that depreciation charges are generally insufficient.

6. **Prepaid Assets**

a. **Special audit considerations for prepaid assets**

(1) **Overall.** Prepaid assets typically consist of items such as insurance and deposits. Insurance policies may be examined and the prepaid portion of any expenditure may be recalculated. Additionally, policies may be confirmed with the company's insurance agent and/or payments may be vouched. Deposits and other prepaid amounts are typically immaterial. When they are considered material, an auditor may confirm their existence, recalculate prepaid portions, and examine any available support.

(2) **Self-insurance.** The lack of insurance on an asset (or inadequate insurance) will not typically result in report modification, although this may be disclosed in the notes to the financial

statements.  Also, an auditor may serve an advisory role by pointing out assets that, unknown to management, may have inadequate insurance.

b.  **Typical substantive audit procedures for prepaid assets**

(1) **Review disclosures for compliance with generally accepted accounting principles.**

(2) **Review the adequacy of insurance coverage.**

(3) **Confirm deposits and insurance with third party** to verify their existence.

(4) **Vouch additions to accounts (examine insurance policies and miscellaneous other support for deposit)** to verify existence.

(5) **Perform analytical procedures** to test the reasonableness of prepaid assets.  A primary procedure here is comparison with prior year balances and obtaining explanations for any significant changes.

(6) **Foot prepaid summary schedules** to verify clerical accuracy.

(7) **Reconcile summary schedules to the general ledger** to verify proper valuation.

(8) **Recalculate prepaid portions of prepaid assets** to verify proper valuation.

7. **Payables (Current)**

a.  **Special audit considerations for payables**

(1) **Confirmation.**  Confirmations may be sent to vendors.  However, such confirmation procedures are sometimes omitted due to the availability of externally generated evidence (e.g., both purchase agreements and vendors' invoices) and due to the inability of confirmations to adequately address the completeness assertion.  (Auditors are primarily concerned about the possibility of understated payables; a major payable will not in general be confirmed if the client completely omits it from the trial balance of payables.)

Accounts payable confirmations are most frequently used in circumstances involving (1) bad internal control, (2) bad financial position, and (3) situations when vendors do not send month-end statements.  However, when an auditor has chosen to confirm payables despite the existence of vendor statements, the confirmation will generally request the vendor to send the month-end statement to the auditor.  For this reason, the balance per the client's books is not included on such a confirmation.

Confirmations are sent to (1) major suppliers, (2) disputed accounts, and (3) a sample of other suppliers.  Major suppliers are selected because they represent a possible source of large understatement:  the client will normally have established large credit lines.  The size of the **recorded** payable at year-end is of less importance than for receivables.  While as a practical matter large year-end recorded balances will normally be confirmed, the emphasis on detecting understated payables may lead the auditor to also confirm accounts with relatively low recorded year-end balances.  Also, if the payables to be confirmed are selected from a list of vendors instead of from the recorded year-end payables, the completeness assertion as well as the existence assertion may be addressed.

(2) **The search for unrecorded liabilities.**  The search for unrecorded liabilities is an effort to discover any liabilities that may have been omitted from recorded year-end payables.  Typical procedures include the following:

(a) Examination of vendors' invoices and statements both immediately prior to and following year-end.

(b) Examination, **after year-end**, of the following to test whether proper cutoffs have occurred:

1] Cash disbursements
2] Purchases
3] Unrecorded vouchers (receiving reports, vendors' invoices, purchase orders)

(c) Analytical procedures

(d) Internal control is analyzed to evaluate its likely effectiveness in preventing and detecting the occurrence of such misstatements.

b.  **Typical substantive audit procedures for payables**

(1) **Review disclosures for compliance with generally accepted accounting principles.**

(2) **Review purchase commitments** to determine whether there may be a need to either accrue a loss and/or provide disclosure (see also step 3 of inventory program).

(3) **Confirm accounts payable by direct correspondence with vendors.** Confirmation of payables provides evidence relating to the occurrence, obligation, completeness, and valuation assertions. See Section a. above.

(4) **Inspect copies of notes and note agreements.**

(5) **Vouch balances payable to selected creditors by inspecting purchase orders, receiving reports, and invoices** to verify existence, valuation, and to a lesser extent, completeness.

(6) **Review the cutoff of purchases, purchase returns, and disbursements around year-end** to verify that transactions are recorded in the proper period.

(7) **Perform analytical procedures** to test the reasonableness of payables. Examples here are ratios such as accounts payable divided by purchases, and accounts payable divided by total current liabilities.

(8) **Perform search for unrecorded payables** to determine whether liabilities have been completely recorded. See Section a. above.

(9) **Inquire of management as to the completeness of payables.**

(10) **Foot the subsidiary accounts payable ledger** to test clerical accuracy.

(11) **Reconcile the subsidiary ledger to the general ledger control account** to verify clerical accuracy.

(12) **Recalculate interest expense on interest-bearing debt.**

(13) **Recalculate year-end accrual for payroll.** A typical procedure here is to allocate the total days in the payroll subsequent to year-end between the old and new years and to determine whether the accrual is reasonable.

(14) **Recalculate other accrued liabilities.** The approach for accruals is largely one of (1) testing computations made by the client in setting up the accrual, and (2) determining that the accruals have been treated consistently with the past. Note that the audit approach here is somewhat different than for accounts payable that, because one or more transactions usually directly indicate the year-end liability, do not require such a computation. Examples of accounts requiring accrual include property taxes, pension plans, vacation pay, service guarantees, commissions, and income taxes payable.

8. **Long-Term Debt**

    a. **Special audit considerations for long-term debt**

       (1) **Overall approach.** Despite the fact that this account's turnover rate is low, considerable analysis is performed on its ending balance. Confirmations are frequently used; recall that when the debt is owed to banks, confirmation is obtained with the standard bank confirmation. In addition, minutes of director and/or stockholder meetings will be reviewed to determine whether new borrowings have been properly authorized.

         The proceeds of any new borrowings are traced to the cash receipts journal, deposit slips, and bank statements. Repayments are traced to the cash disbursements journal, canceled checks, and canceled notes. If a debt trustee is used, it will be possible to obtain information through use of a confirmation whether the repayments have been made.

    b. **Typical substantive audit procedures for long-term debt**

       (1) **Review disclosures for compliance with generally accepted accounting principles.**

       (2) **Inquire of management concerning pledging of assets related to debt.**

       (3) **Review debt agreements for details on pledged assets and for events that may result in default on the loan.**

       (4) **Confirm long-term debt with payees or appropriate third parties.**

       (5) **Obtain and inspect copies of debt agreements** to verify whether provisions have been met and disclosed.

       (6) **Trace receipt of funds (and payments) to the bank account and to the cash receipts journal** to verify that the funds were properly received (or disbursed) by the company.

       (7) **Review the cutoff of cash receipts and disbursements around year-end** to verify that transactions affecting debt are recorded in the proper period.

(8) **Review minutes of board of directors' and/or shareholders' meetings** to verify that transactions have been properly authorized.

(9) **Perform analytical procedures** to verify the overall reasonableness of long-term debt and interest expense.

(10) **Inquire of management as to the completeness of debt.**

(11) **Review bank confirmations for any indication of unrecorded debt.**

(12) **Foot summary schedules of long-term debt** to test clerical accuracy.

(13) **Reconcile summary schedules of long-term debt to the general ledger** to verify clerical accuracy.

(14) **Vouch entries in long-term debt accounts.**

(15) **Recalculate interest expense and accrued interest payable.**

9. **Owners' Equity**

   a. **Special audit considerations for owners' equity**

      (1) **Control of capital stock transactions.** Clients use one of two approaches for capital stock transactions. First, a stock certificate book may be used which summarizes shares issued through use of "stubs" which remain after a certificate has been removed. The certificates for outstanding shares are held by the stockholders; canceled certificates (for repurchased stock or received when a change in stock ownership occurs) are held by the client. When a stock certificate book is used auditors reconcile outstanding shares, par value, etc., with the "stubs" in the book. Confirmations are sometimes sent to stockholders.

      The second approach, typically used by large clients, is to engage a registrar and a stock transfer agent to manage the company's stock transactions. The primary responsibility of the registrar is to verify that stock which is issued is properly authorized. Stock transfer agents maintain detailed stockholder records and carry out transfers of stock ownership. The number of shares authorized, issued, and outstanding will usually be confirmed to the auditor directly by the registrar and stock transfer agent.

      (2) **Retained earnings.** Little effort will be exerted in auditing the retained earnings of a continued client. The audit procedures for dividends will allow the auditor to verify the propriety of that debit to retained earnings. The entry to record the year's net income (loss) is readily available. Finally, the nature of any prior period adjustments is examined to determine whether they meet the criteria for an adjustment to retained earnings. Recall that the type of adjustment typically encountered is a correction of prior years' income.

   b. **Typical substantive audit procedures for stockholders' equity**

      (1) **Review disclosures for compliance with generally accepted accounting principles.**

      (2) **Review Articles of Incorporation, bylaws, and minutes for provisions relating to stock options, and dividends restriction.**

      (3) **Confirm stocks authorized, issued, and outstanding with the independent registrar and stock transfer agent (if applicable).**

      (4) **For a corporation that acts as its own stock registrar and transfer agent, reconcile the stock certificate book to transactions recorded in the general ledger.**

      (5) **Vouch transactions and trace receipt of funds (and payment) to the bank account and to the cash receipts journal** to verify that the funds were properly received (or disbursed) by the company.

      (6) **Review minutes of the board of directors' and/or shareholders' meetings** to verify that stock transactions have been properly authorized.

      (7) **Inquire of the client's legal counsel** to obtain information concerning any unresolved legal issues.

      (8) **Review the Articles of Incorporation and bylaws for the propriety of equity transactions.**

      (9) **Perform analytical procedures** to test the reasonableness of dividends.

      (10) **Inspect treasury stock certificates** to verify that transactions have been completely recorded and that client has control of certificates.

      (11) **Agree amounts that will appear on the financial statements to the general ledger.**

      (12) **Vouch dividend payments** to verify that amounts have been paid.

      (13) **Vouch all entries affecting retained earnings.**

(14) **Recalculate treasury stock transactions.**

10. **Revenue**

   a. **Special audit considerations for revenue**

     (1) **Overall approach.** Most revenue accounts are verified in conjunction with the audit of a related asset or liability account. For example

| *Balance Sheet Account* | *Revenue Account* |
|---|---|
| Accounts receivable | Sales |
| Notes receivable | Interest |
| Investments | Interest, dividends, gains on sales |
| Property, plant, and equipment | Rent, gains on sales |

     (2) Module 7 discusses revenue recognition. Most frequently sales are recorded during the period in which title has passed, or services have been rendered to customers who have made firm, enforceable commitments to purchase such goods or services. SEC Staff Accounting Bulletin 101 provides a more specific, helpful overall set of criteria for revenue recognition.

       (a) Persuasive evidence of an arrangement exists.
       (b) Delivery has occurred or services have been rendered.
       (c) The seller's price to the buyer is fixed or determinable.
       (d) Collectibility is reasonably assured.

     (3) **Potential problem areas for revenues**

       (a) **Bill and hold transactions.** Transactions in which a customer agrees to purchase goods but the seller retains physical possession until the customer requests shipment to designated locations. Because delivery has not yet occurred, such transactions do not ordinarily qualify. The primary requirements to qualify for revenue recognition are that the buyer make an absolute commitment to purchase, has assumed the risks and rewards of the product, and is unable to accept delivery because of some compelling reason.

       (b) **Side agreements.** Agreements used to alter the terms and conditions of recorded sales transactions, often to convince customers to accept delivery of goods and services. Side agreements are frequently hidden from the board of directors and may create obligations that relieve the customer of the risks and rewards of ownership. Accordingly, side agreement terms *may* preclude revenue recognition.

       (c) **Channel stuffing (trade loading).** A marketing practice that suppliers sometimes use to boost sales by inducing distributors to buy substantially more inventory than they can promptly resell. Inducements may range from deep discounts on the inventory to threats of losing the distributorship if inventory is not purchased. Channel stuffing may result in the need to increase the level of anticipated sales returns.

       (d) **Related-party transactions.** A variety of potential misstatements may occur due to transactions with related parties. For example, sales of the same inventory back and forth among affiliated companies may "freshen" receivables.

   b. **Substantive test approach for revenues not verified in the audit of balance sheet accounts**

     (1) Perform analytical procedures related to revenue accounts.
     (2) Obtain or prepare analyses of selected revenue accounts.
     (3) Vouch selected transactions and determine that they represent proper revenue for the period.

11. **Expenses**

   a. **Special audit considerations for expenses**

     (1) **Overall approach.** Most expense accounts are verified in conjunction with the audit of a related asset or liability account. For example

| *Balance Sheet Account* | *Expense Account* |
|---|---|
| Accounts receivable | Uncollectible accounts |
| Inventories | Purchases, cost of goods sold, payroll |
| Property, plant, and equipment | Depreciation, repairs, and maintenance |
| Accrued liabilities | Commissions, fees, product warranty expenses |

b. **Substantive test approach for expenses not verified in the audit of balance sheet accounts**

    (1) Perform analytical procedures related to the expense accounts.

    (2) Obtain or prepare analyses of selected expense accounts.

    (3) Vouch selected transactions.

12. **Client Representation Letters (AU 333).** Review the outline and note that representation letters are required for audits. In reviewing the outline be generally familiar with the various representations obtained by auditors. Expect multiple-choice questions on matters such as the following:

    a. The representation letter should be addressed to the auditor, in a letter dated no earlier than the date of the auditor's report.

    b. The representation letter should be signed by the chief executive officer and the chief financial officer.

    c. Representations from management are not a substitute for the application of other necessary auditing procedures.

    d. Representations should be obtained for all periods being reported upon, even if management was not present during all of those periods.

    e. Management refusal to furnish written representations **precludes** an unqualified opinion, and ordinarily results in a disclaimer, although a qualified opinion may be appropriate in some circumstances.

13. **Using the Work of a Specialist (AU 336).** Read the outline of this standard. Auditors increasingly are finding it necessary to use the work of specialists in areas such as postemployment and postretirement benefits, environmental cleanup obligations, fair value disclosures and derivatives, as well as in more traditional areas such as the valuation of inventory (e.g., diamonds). This standard provides guidance both in situations in which an auditor (1) uses the work of specialists that have already performed services for a client (including client employees and specialists hired by the client such as the consulting services personnel of the CPA firm) and (2) engages specialists to perform various procedures. In all cases, the auditors should evaluate the specialist's professional qualifications, understand the objectives and scope of the specialist's work, the appropriateness of using the specialist's work, and the form and content of the specialist's findings. Several other key points from AU 336 include

    a. AU 336 applies whenever auditors use a specialist's work as evidence in performing substantive tests to evaluate financial statement assertions. For purposes of this standard, internal auditors are **not** considered specialists.

    b. To assess the qualifications of the specialist, the CPA should consider specialist professional certification, reputation, and experience in the type of work under consideration.

    c. While the work of a specialist who is a client employee may be used, the standard requires the CPA to evaluate the relationship and consider whether it might impair the specialist's objectivity. If objectivity may be impaired, additional procedures should be performed, possibly including using another specialist.

    d. The specialist is not referred to in the auditor's report unless such a reference would help report users to understand the need for an explanatory paragraph or a departure from an unmodified opinion. (If the work of the specialist is consistent with the client's financial statements, no reference is permitted.)

14. **Inquiry of a Client's Lawyer (AU 337).** Read the key points in the outline. The client's lawyer is the primary source for corroboration of information obtained from the client concerning loss contingencies. Therefore, the client prepares a list and describes claims, litigation, assessments, and unasserted claims pending against the firm. This information is sent by the auditor to the attorney who is to review it and provide additional input, if possible.

    Refusal of the lawyer to reply is a scope limitation that may affect the audit report. If the lawyer is unable to estimate the effect of litigation, claims, and assessments on the financial statements, it may result in an uncertainty that would also have an effect on the audit report. In the case of unasserted claims that the client has not disclosed, the lawyer is **not** required to note them in his/her reply to the auditor. However, the lawyer is generally required to inform the client of the omission and to consider withdrawing if the client fails to inform the auditor. The following is a sample lawyer's letter:

In connection with an examination of our financial statements at (balance sheet date) and for the (period) then ended, management of the Company has prepared, and furnished to our auditors (name and address of auditors), a description and evaluation of certain contingencies, including those set forth below involving matters with respect to which you have been engaged and to which you have devoted substantive attention on behalf of the Company in the form of legal consultation or representation. These contingencies are regarded by management of the Company as material for this purpose (management may indicate a materiality limit if an understanding has been reached with the auditor). Your response should include matters that existed at (balance sheet date) and during the period from that date to the date of your response.

**Pending or Threatened Litigation (excluding unasserted claims)**

[Ordinarily the information would include the following: (1) the nature of the litigation, (2) the progress of the case to date, (3) how management is responding or intends to respond to the litigation (for example, to contest the case vigorously or to seek an out-of-court settlement), and (4) an evaluation of the likelihood of an unfavorable outcome and an estimate, if one can be made, of the amount or range of potential loss.] Please furnish to our auditors such explanation, if any, that you consider necessary to supplement the foregoing information, including an explanation of those matters as to which your views may differ from those stated and an identification of the omission of any pending or threatened litigation, claims, and assessments or a statement that the list of such matters is complete.

**Unasserted Claims and Assessments (considered by management to be probable of assertion, and that, if asserted, would have at least a reasonable possibility of an unfavorable outcome)**

[Ordinarily management's information would include the following: (1) the nature of the matter, (2) how management intends to respond if the claim is asserted, and (3) an evaluation of the likelihood of an unfavorable outcome and an estimate, if one can be made, of the amount or range of potential loss.] Please furnish to our auditors such explanation, if any, that you consider necessary to supplement the foregoing information, including an explanation of those matters as to which your views may differ from those stated.

We understand that, in the course of performing legal services for us with respect to a matter recognized to involve an unasserted possible claim or assessment that may call for financial statement disclosure, if you have formed a professional conclusion that we should disclose or consider disclosure concerning such possible claim or assessment, as a matter of professional responsibility to us, you will so advise us and will consult with us concerning the question of such disclosure and the applicable requirements of Statement of Financial Accounting Standards No. 5. Please specifically confirm to our auditors that our understanding is correct.

Please specifically identify the nature of and reasons for any limitation on your response.

[The auditor may request the client to inquire about additional matters, for example, unpaid or unbilled charges or specified information on certain contractually assumed obligations of the company, such as guarantees of indebtedness of others.]

(Section 337, Appendix)

15. **Fair Values (AU 328).** Generally accepted accounting principles require companies to use "fair value" for measuring, presenting, and disclosing various accounts (e.g., investments, intangible assets, impaired assets, derivatives). Fair value is generally considered to be the amount at which an asset (or liability) could be bought or sold in a current transaction between willing parties.

The determination of fair value is easiest when there are published price quotations in an active market (e.g., a stock exchange). Determining fair value is more difficult when an active market does not exist for items such as various investment properties or complex derivative financial instruments. In such circumstances fair value may be calculated through the use of a valuation model (e.g., a model based on forecasts and discounting of future cash flows). Auditing fair values is similar to that of other estimates (see topic A.1 of this module) in that a combination of three approaches is often used—(1) review and test management's process, (2) independently develop as estimate, or (3) review subsequent events.

When reviewing management's process (approach 1), the auditors consider whether the assumptions used by management are reasonable, whether the valuation model seems appropriate, and whether management has used relevant information that is reasonably available. Developing one's own estimate (approach 2) offers the advantage of allowing the auditors to compare that estimate with that developed by management. Reviewing subsequent events (approach 3) allows the auditors to use information obtained subsequent to year-end to help evaluate the reasonableness of management's estimate. Often auditors will use a combination of the approaches. Regardless of the approach(es) followed, the auditors should evaluate whether the disclosures of fair values required by GAAP have been properly presented.

16. **Related-Party Transactions (AU 334).** Review the outline of AU 334. The main issue with related-party transactions concerns the price at which a transaction occurs. This price may not be the one that would have resulted from an "arm's-length bargaining." Note the procedures suggested in Section 334 for discovering related-party transactions. Further note that it is generally not possible for the auditor to determine whether such a transaction would have occurred if no related party had existed, and, if so, the price thereof.

17. **Going Concern Considerations (AU 341).** The use of accruals by generally accepted accounting principles relies on an assumption that an entity will continue indefinitely as a going concern. For example, capitalizing assets and depreciating them over future periods is justified on the basis that the costs will be "matched" against future revenues. While audits do not contain specific procedures to test the appropriateness of this going concern assumption, procedures performed for other objectives (i.e., the PERCV objectives) may identify conditions and events indicating substantial doubt as to whether an entity will remain a going concern. AU 341 suggests that such procedures include (1) analytical procedures, (2) the review of subsequent events, (3) (non)compliance with debt agreements, (4) reading of minutes, (5) inquiry of legal counsel, and (6) confirmation of arrangements with various organizations to maintain financial support. When such procedures indicate that substantial doubt may exist as to whether an entity will remain a going concern, the auditor must obtain management's plans (including significant prospective financial information) for dealing with the situation and assess the likelihood that these plans can be implemented. As we will discuss in further detail in the Reporting Module, when substantial doubt remains, the auditor must determine that it is properly disclosed in the notes to the financial statements and must either add an explanatory paragraph to his/her unqualified audit report or must disclaim an opinion. At this point you should review the outline of AU 341.

18. **Subsequent Events and Subsequent Discovery of Facts Existing at the Date of the Audit Report (AU 560, 561).** These two sections deal with accounting issues (e.g., how to measure and disclose certain events) as well as audit responsibility with respect to subsequent events. Section 560 classifies subsequent events into two types.

a. Those events that provide additional evidence with respect to conditions that existed at the date of the balance sheet (for which the financial statements are to be adjusted for any changes in estimates)

b. Those events that provide evidence with respect to conditions that did **not** exist at the date of the balance sheet but arose subsequent to that date (for which there is to be footnote disclosure)

The following diagram depicts the two types of subsequent events.

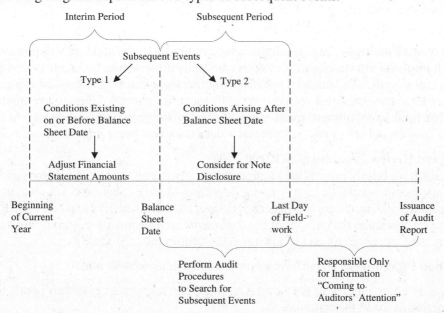

Section 560 also deals with the auditing issues involved when these types of events are noted prior to release of the audit report. Be familiar with the audit procedures that may reveal the existence of subsequent events—see Section C. In the Reports Module we discuss dating of the audit report when a subsequent event has occurred.

Section 561 deals with the auditing of events existing at the report date that are not discovered until after the release of the financial statements. Read carefully the outline of the auditor's responsibilities with respect to these events—a number of questions have been asked concerning subsequent events.

19. **Omitted Procedures Discovered after the Report Date (AU 390).** Subsequent to issuance of an audit report, an auditor may realize that one or more necessary procedures were omitted from the audit. When this occurs, the auditor should first assess its importance. If omission is considered important (i.e., it affects present ability to support the previously expressed opinion) and if the auditor believes individuals are relying or are likely to rely on the financial statements, the procedures or alternate procedures should be promptly applied. If the procedure is then applied and misstatements are detected, the auditor should review his/her responsibilities under AU 561 on subsequent discovery of facts existing at the date of the auditor's report. If the client does not allow the auditor to apply the necessary procedure(s), the auditor should consult his/her attorney as to appropriate action.

## D.  Completing the Audit

1.  **Procedures Completed near the End of the Audit.** A number of audit procedures (most discussed in sections B and C) are involved in completing the audit. These procedures, completed on or near the last day of fieldwork, include

    * Search for unrecorded liabilities
    * Review of minutes of meetings of shareholders, board of directors, and the audit committee
    * Perform final review stage analytical procedures
    * Perform procedures, including the inquiry of client's lawyers, to identify loss contingencies
    * Perform review for subsequent events
    * Obtain representation letter
    * Evaluate audit findings (see 2. below)
    * Review adequacy of disclosures using a **disclosure checklist** that lists all specific disclosures required by GAAP and the SEC, if appropriate
    * Review of working papers performed by manager, partner, and possibly a **second partner review** performed by a partner who is not otherwise involved in the engagement but to provide an independent review of the work performed. The review process helps provide assurance that audit risk is an appropriately low level, working paper documentation is adequate, and that the evidence supports the opinion being rendered
    * Communicate with the audit committee

2.  **Evaluate Audit Findings.** Throughout the course of the audit, the auditors will propose adjusting entries for all **material misstatements** (whether caused by error or fraud) that are discovered in the client's financial records. Any material misstatement that the auditors find must be corrected; otherwise, they cannot issue an unqualified opinion on the financial statements. Unrecorded misstatements are combined as **total likely misstatement** in the financial statements and considered. At this point turn to Section D of the outline of AU 312 to review details on how these misstatements are considered.

## E.  Compilation and Review Procedures (AR 100 - 600)

In this module, we briefly present the requirements for performing (1) compilations and (2) reviews of financial statements of a nonpublic entity. In the Reporting Module (Section C.1.b.) we discuss the related reporting procedures. Because compilations and reviews are often heavily tested on the CPA exam, it is important that you also study the outlines of the *Statements on Standards for Accounting and Review Services*—they have an AR prefix and follow the AU Outlines (after Module 6).

1.  **Compilation Procedures.** To perform a compilation the accountant must

    a.  Possess an understanding of the accounting principles and practices in the client's industry to enable performance of the compilation
    b.  Possess a general understanding of the client's

      (1)   Business transactions,

      (2)   Accounting records,

      (3)   Accounting personnel qualifications,

      (4)   Financial statement accounting basis, and

      (5)   Financial statement form and content.

  c.  Read the compiled statements and consider whether they appear to be appropriate and free from obvious material errors

      The accountant is not required to make inquiries or perform other procedures to verify, corroborate, or review the information supplied by the client.  However, whenever an accountant becomes aware of information that is incorrect, incomplete, or otherwise unsatisfactory, the accountant should obtain additional or revised information.  If the entity refuses to provide (or correct) such information, the accountant should withdraw from the compilation.  Finally, recall from the Overview Section that independence is not required when performing a compilation.

2.  **Review Procedures.**  To perform a review, an accountant must

  a.  Possess an understanding of the accounting principles and practices in the client's industry and an understanding of the entity's business that will provide him/her, through the performance of inquiry and analytical procedures, a reasonable basis for expressing limited assurance that no material modifications need to be made to the financial statements

  b.  Possess a general understanding of the client's

      (1)   Organization

      (2)   Operating characteristics

      (3)   Assets, liabilities, revenues and expenses

  c.  Analytical procedures should include

      (1)   Developing expectations by identifying plausible relationships that are expected to exist based on the accountant's understanding of entity and industry.

      (2)   comparing recorded amounts, or ratios, to expectations.

         (a)   Expectations developed for a review are ordinarily less encompassing than those for an audit

         (b)   In a review the accountant is ordinarily not required to corroborate management's responses, although the accountant should consider those responses for reasonableness and consistency with other information

  d.  Inquiries

      (1)   To management members that have financial/accounting responsibility about

         (a)   Whether financial statements prepared following GAAP

         (b)   Accounting principles followed

         (c)   Unusual or complex situations that might affect financial statements

         (d)   Significant transactions near end of reporting period

         (e)   Status of uncorrected misstatement identified during previous engagement

         (f)   Questions arising in course of applying review procedures

         (g)   Subsequent events

         (h)   Significant journal entries and other adjustments

         (i)   Communications from regulatory agencies

      (2)   Concerning actions taken at meetings (shareholder, board of directors, committees of directors, or comparable meetings) that may affect financial statements

      (3)   Read the financial statements to consider, on the basis of information coming to accountant's attention, whether statements appear to conform to GAAP

      (4)   Obtain reports from other accountants, if any, that have audited or reviewed significant components of reporting entity.

  e.  Read the financial statements to determine whether they seem to follow GAAP

  f.  Obtain reports from other accountants who have audited or reviewed components

  g.  Obtain a representation letter signed by management

3.  **Review of Public Company Interim Financial Information.**  For each of the first three quarters of their reporting year, SEC registrants report interim results reviewed by their public accountants.  In addition, certain large SEC registrants must disclose summarized interim financial information in their annual reports, either as supplementary information or as an "unaudited" note to the annual financial statements.

    The objective of a review of interim financial information is to provide the accountant with a basis for communicating whether he or she is aware of any material modifications that should be made to the interim financial information for it to conform with generally accepted accounting principles.  The procedures for a public company interim review are similar to those presented in the previous section for nonpublic companies, although an interim review for public companies includes the following additional requirements:

    -   Consideration of internal control adequate to (1) identify types of potential misstatements and their likelihood and (2) select appropriate inquiries and analytical procedures
    -   Inclusion of procedures relating to (1) revenue, (2) reconciliation of interim financial information to the accounting records, and (3) inquiry of management concerning fraud.

4.  **Overall Comments.**  The CPA exam multiple-choice questions concerning compilation and review procedures have most frequently provided a list of procedures and asked which one is not a compilation or review procedure.  The answer is usually a procedure relative to a detailed consideration of internal control or a detailed test of balances such as sending a receivable confirmation.  In addition, several times the exam has expected candidates to know that use of an engagement letter is more likely (although not required) when performing a review as compared to a compilation.

## F.  Other Related Topics

**Operational Auditing.**  Operational audits, generally performed by internal auditors, typically evaluate the **effectiveness** and **efficiency** of various operational processes.  As such they are similar to "performance audits" as presented in the outline of *Government Auditing Standards*.  In fact, the topic "operational auditing" was dropped from the AICPA Content Specification Outline when compliance auditing was added.

As an example of an operational audit, consider an auditor's examination of the sales, receivables, and cash receipts cycle to consider whether policies and procedures concerning the effectiveness and efficiency of related management decision-making processes.  A financial statement audit, on the other hand, would deal more directly with controls relating to the entity's ability to record, process, summarize, and report financial data consistent with the assertions in the financial statements.

**MULTIPLE-CHOICE QUESTIONS (1-186)**

**1.** Which of the following types of audit evidence is the most persuasive?
    a. Prenumbered client purchase order forms.
    b. Client work sheets supporting cost allocations.
    c. Bank statements obtained from the client.
    d. Client representation letter.

**2.** Which of the following presumptions is correct about the reliability of evidential matter?
    a. Information obtained indirectly from outside sources is the most reliable evidential matter.
    b. To be reliable, evidential matter should be convincing rather than persuasive.
    c. Reliability of evidential matter refers to the amount of corroborative evidence obtained.
    d. Effective internal control provides more assurance about the reliability of evidential matter.

**3.** Which of the following statements relating to the competence of evidential matter is always true?
    a. Evidential matter gathered by an auditor from outside an enterprise is reliable.
    b. Accounting data developed under satisfactory conditions of internal control are more relevant than data developed under unsatisfactory internal control conditions.
    c. Oral representations made by management are **not** valid evidence.
    d. Evidence gathered by auditors must be both valid and relevant to be considered competent.

**4.** Which of the following types of audit evidence is the **least** persuasive?
    a. Prenumbered purchase order forms.
    b. Bank statements obtained from the client.
    c. Test counts of inventory performed by the auditor.
    d. Correspondence from the client's attorney about litigation.

**5.** In evaluating the reasonableness of an entity's accounting estimates, an auditor normally would be concerned about assumptions that are
    a. Susceptible to bias.
    b. Consistent with prior periods.
    c. Insensitive to variations.
    d. Similar to industry guidelines.

**6.** Which of the following procedures would an auditor ordinarily perform first in evaluating management's accounting estimates for reasonableness?
    a. Develop independent expectations of management's estimates.
    b. Consider the appropriateness of the key factors or assumptions used in preparing the estimates.
    c. Test the calculations used by management in developing the estimates.
    d. Obtain an understanding of how management developed its estimates.

**7.** In evaluating the reasonableness of an accounting estimate, an auditor most likely would concentrate on key factors and assumptions that are
    a. Consistent with prior periods.
    b. Similar to industry guidelines.
    c. Objective and **not** susceptible to bias.
    d. Deviations from historical patterns.

**8.** In evaluating an entity's accounting estimates, one of an auditor's objectives is to determine whether the estimates are
    a. Not subject to bias.
    b. Consistent with industry guidelines.
    c. Based on objective assumptions.
    d. Reasonable in the circumstances.

**9.** In testing the existence assertion for an asset, an auditor ordinarily works from the
    a. Financial statements to the potentially unrecorded items.
    b. Potentially unrecorded items to the financial statements.
    c. Accounting records to the supporting evidence.
    d. Supporting evidence to the accounting records.

**10.** A client uses a suspense account for unresolved questions whose final accounting has not been determined. If a balance remains in the suspense account at year-end, the auditor would be most concerned about
    a. Suspense debits that management believes will benefit future operations.
    b. Suspense debits that the auditor verifies will have realizable value to the client.
    c. Suspense credits that management believes should be classified as "Current liability."
    d. Suspense credits that the auditor determines to be customer deposits.

**11.** Which of the following would **not** be considered an analytical procedure?
    a. Estimating payroll expense by multiplying the number of employees by the average hourly wage rate and the total hours worked.
    b. Projecting an error rate by comparing the results of a statistical sample with the actual population characteristics.
    c. Computing accounts receivable turnover by dividing credit sales by the average net receivables.
    d. Developing the expected current year sales based on the sales trend of the prior five years.

**12.** What type of analytical procedure would an auditor most likely use in developing relationships among balance sheet accounts when reviewing the financial statements of a nonpublic entity?
    a. Trend analysis.
    b. Regression analysis.
    c. Ratio analysis.
    d. Risk analysis.

**13.** An auditor may achieve audit objectives related to particular assertions by
    a. Performing analytical procedures.
    b. Adhering to a system of quality control.
    c. Preparing auditor working papers.
    d. Increasing the level of detection risk.

**14.** An entity's income statements were misstated due to the recording of journal entries that involved debits and credits to an unusual combination of expense and revenue accounts. The auditor most likely could have detected this fraudulent financial reporting by

a. Tracing a sample of journal entries to the general ledger.

b. Evaluating the effectiveness of internal control.

c. Investigating the reconciliations between controlling accounts and subsidiary records.

d. Performing analytical procedures designed to disclose differences from expectations.

**15.** Auditors try to identify predictable relationships when using analytical procedures. Relationships involving transactions from which of the following accounts most likely would yield the highest level of evidence?

a. Accounts receivable.

b. Interest expense.

c. Accounts payable.

d. Travel and entertainment expense.

**16.** Analytical procedures used in the overall review stage of an audit generally include

a. Gathering evidence concerning account balances that have **not** changed from the prior year.

b. Retesting control procedures that appeared to be ineffective during the assessment of control risk.

c. Considering unusual or unexpected account balances that were **not** previously identified.

d. Performing tests of transactions to corroborate management's financial statement assertions.

**17.** Which of the following tends to be most predictable for purposes of analytical procedures applied as substantive tests?

a. Relationships involving balance sheet accounts.

b. Transactions subject to management discretion.

c. Relationships involving income statement accounts.

d. Data subject to audit testing in the prior year.

**18.** A basic premise underlying the application of analytical procedures is that

a. The study of financial ratios is an acceptable alternative to the investigation of unusual fluctuations.

b. Statistical tests of financial information may lead to the discovery of material misstatements in the financial statements.

c. Plausible relationships among data may reasonably be expected to exist and continue in the absence of known conditions to the contrary.

d. These procedures **cannot** replace tests of balances and transactions.

**19.** For all audits of financial statements made in accordance with generally accepted auditing standards, the use of analytical procedures is required to some extent

| | In the planning stage | As a substantive test | In the review stage |
|---|---|---|---|
| a. | Yes | No | Yes |
| b. | No | Yes | No |
| c. | No | Yes | Yes |
| d. | Yes | No | No |

**20.** An auditor's analytical procedures most likely would be facilitated if the entity

a. Segregates obsolete inventory before the physical inventory count.

b. Uses a standard cost system that produces variance reports.

c. Corrects material weaknesses in internal control before the beginning of the audit.

d. Develops its data from sources solely within the entity.

**21.** Analytical procedures performed in the overall review stage of an audit suggest that several accounts have unexpected relationships. The results of these procedures most likely would indicate that

a. Irregularities exist among the relevant account balances.

b. Internal control activities are **not** operating effectively.

c. Additional tests of details are required.

d. The communication with the audit committee should be revised.

**22.** Which of the following comparisons would an auditor most likely make in evaluating an entity's costs and expenses?

a. The current year's accounts receivable with the prior year's accounts receivable.

b. The current year's payroll expense with the prior year's payroll expense.

c. The budgeted current year's sales with the prior year's sales.

d. The budgeted current year's warranty expense with the current year's contingent liabilities.

**23.** To be effective, analytical procedures in the overall review stage of an audit engagement should be performed by

a. The staff accountant who performed the substantive auditing procedures.

b. The managing partner who has responsibility for all audit engagements at that practice office.

c. A manager or partner who has a comprehensive knowledge of the client's business and industry.

d. The CPA firm's quality control manager or partner who has responsibility for the firm's peer review program.

**24.** Which of the following is the best example of a substantive test?

a. Examining a sample of cash disbursements to test whether expenses have been properly approved.

b. Confirmation of balances of accounts receivable.

c. Comparison of signatures on checks to a list of authorized signers.

d. Flowcharting of the client's cash receipts system.

**25.** The objective of tests of details of transactions performed as substantive tests is to

a. Comply with generally accepted auditing standards.

b. Attain assurance about the reliability of the accounting system.

c. Detect material misstatements in the financial statements.

d. Evaluate whether management's policies and procedures operated effectively.

**26.** In the context of an audit of financial statements, substantive tests are audit procedures that

a. May be eliminated under certain conditions.

b. Are designed to discover significant subsequent events.

c. May be either tests of transactions, direct tests of financial balances, or analytical tests.

d. Will increase proportionately with the auditor's reliance on internal control.

**27.** The auditor will most likely perform extensive tests for possible understatement of
a. Revenues.
b. Assets.
c. Liabilities.
d. Capital.

**28.** Which of the following procedures would an auditor most likely perform in auditing the statement of cash flows?
a. Compare the amounts included in the statement of cash flows to similar amounts in the prior year's statement of cash flows.
b. Reconcile the cutoff bank statements to verify the accuracy of the year-end bank balances.
c. Vouch all bank transfers for the last week of the year and first week of the subsequent year.
d. Reconcile the amounts included in the statement of cash flows to the other financial statements' balances and amounts.

**29.** In determining whether transactions have been recorded, the direction of the audit testing should be from the
a. General ledger balances.
b. Adjusted trial balance.
c. Original source documents.
d. General journal entries.

**30.** Which statement is correct concerning the deletion of audit documentation?
a. Superseded audit documentation should always be deleted from the audit file.
b. After the audit file has been completed, the auditor should not delete or discard audit documentation.
c. Auditors should use professional skepticism in determining which audit documentation should be deleted.
d. Audit documentation should never be deleted from the audit file.

**31.** Ignoring any particular legal or regulatory requirement, audit documentation should be retained
a. A minimum of five years.
b. As long as lead schedules have relevance to forthcoming audits.
c. Until 3 years after the client selects another auditor.
d. Working papers must be maintained indefinitely.

**32.** Which of the following pairs of accounts would an auditor most likely analyze on the same working paper?
a. Notes receivable and interest income.
b. Accrued interest receivable and accrued interest payable.
c. Notes payable and notes receivable.
d. Interest income and interest expense.

**33.** An auditor's working papers serve mainly to
a. Provide the principal support for the auditor's report.
b. Satisfy the auditor's responsibilities concerning the Code of Professional Conduct.

c. Monitor the effectiveness of the CPA firm's quality control procedures.
d. Document the level of independence maintained by the auditor.

**34.** The permanent file of an auditor's working papers generally would **not** include
a. Bond indenture agreements.
b. Lease agreements.
c. Working trial balance.
d. Flowchart of internal control.

**35.** An auditor ordinarily uses a working trial balance resembling the financial statements without footnotes, but containing columns for
a. Cash flow increases and decreases.
b. Audit objectives and assertions.
c. Reclassifications and adjustments.
d. Reconciliations and tick marks.

**36.** Which of the following is least likely to be a factor in the auditor's decision about the extent of the documentation of a particular audit area?
a. The risk of material misstatement.
b. The extent of the judgment involved in performing the procedures.
c. The nature and extent of exceptions identified.
d. Whether or not the client has an internal audit function.

**37.** Which of the following is required documentation in an audit in accordance with generally accepted auditing standards?
a. A flowchart or narrative of the accounting system describing the recording and classification of transactions for financial reporting.
b. An audit program setting forth in detail the procedures necessary to accomplish the engagement's objectives.
c. A planning memorandum establishing the timing of the audit procedures and coordinating the assistance of entity personnel.
d. An internal control questionnaire identifying controls that assure specific objectives will be achieved.

**38.** Which of the following factors most likely would affect an auditor's judgment about the quantity, type, and content of the auditor's working papers?
a. The assessed level of control risk.
b. The likelihood of a review by a concurring (second) partner.
c. The number of personnel assigned to the audit.
d. The content of the management representation letter.

**39.** The audit working paper that reflects the major components of an amount reported in the financial statements is the
a. Interbank transfer schedule.
b. Carryforward schedule.
c. Supporting schedule.
d. Lead schedule.

**40.** Which of the following documentation is required for an audit in accordance with generally accepted auditing standards?

a. A flowchart or an internal control questionnaire that evaluates the effectiveness of the entity's controls.

b. A client engagement letter that summarizes the timing and details of the auditor's planned field-work.

c. An indication in the working papers that the accounting records agree or reconcile with the financial statements.

d. The basis for the auditor's conclusions when the assessed level of control risk is at the maximum level for all financial statement assertions.

**41.** For public company audits, no deletions of audit documentation are allowed after the
a. Client's year-end.
b. Documentation completion date.
c. Last date of significant fieldwork.
d. Report release date.

**42.** Under the requirements of the PCAOB, audit documentation must contain sufficient information to allow what type of auditor to understand the nature, timing, extent, and results of procedures performed?
a. An experienced audit team member.
b. An experienced auditor having no previous connection with the engagement.
c. Any certified public accountant.
d. An auditor qualified as a peer review specialist.

**43.** Audit documentation for audits performed under the requirements of the Public Company Accounting Oversight Board should be retained for
a. The shorter of five years, or the period required by law.
b. Seven years.
c. The longer of seven years, or the period required by law.
d. Indefinitely.

**44.** Which of the following sets of information does an auditor usually confirm on one form?
a. Accounts payable and purchase commitments.
b. Cash in bank and collateral for loans.
c. Inventory on consignment and contingent liabilities.
d. Accounts receivable and accrued interest receivable.

**45.** The usefulness of the standard bank confirmation request may be limited because the bank employee who completes the form may
a. Not believe that the bank is obligated to verify confidential information to a third party.
b. Sign and return the form without inspecting the accuracy of the client's bank reconciliation.
c. Not have access to the client's cutoff bank statement.
d. Be unaware of all the financial relationships that the bank has with the client.

**46.** An auditor most likely would limit substantive audit tests of sales transactions when control risk is assessed as low for the existence or occurrence assertion concerning sales transactions and the auditor has already gathered evidence supporting
a. Opening and closing inventory balances.
b. Cash receipts and accounts receivable.
c. Shipping and receiving activities.
d. Cutoffs of sales and purchases.

---

**Items 47 and 48** are based on the following:

The information below was taken from the bank transfer schedule prepared during the audit of Fox Co.'s financial statements for the year ended December 31, 2005. Assume all checks are dated and issued on December 30, 2005.

| Check no. | Bank accounts From | To | Disbursement date Per books | Per bank | Receipt date Per books | Per bank |
|---|---|---|---|---|---|---|
| 101 | National | Federal | Dec. 30 | Jan. 4 | Dec. 30 | Jan. 3 |
| 202 | County | State | Jan. 3 | Jan. 2 | Dec. 30 | Dec. 31 |
| 303 | Federal | American | Dec. 31 | Jan. 3 | Jan. 2 | Jan. 2 |
| 404 | State | Republic | Jan. 2 | Jan. 2 | Jan. 2 | Dec. 31 |

**47.** Which of the following checks might indicate kiting?
a. #101 and #303.
b. #202 and #404.
c. #101 and #404.
d. #202 and #303.

**48.** Which of the following checks illustrate deposits/transfers in transit at December 31, 2005?
a. #101 and #202.
b. #101 and #303.
c. #202 and #404.
d. #303 and #404.

---

**49.** An auditor should trace bank transfers for the last part of the audit period and first part of the subsequent period to detect whether
   a. The cash receipts journal was held open for a few days after the year-end.
   b. The last checks recorded before the year-end were actually mailed by the year-end.
   c. Cash balances were overstated because of kiting.
   d. Any unusual payments to or receipts from related parties occurred.

**50.** To gather evidence regarding the balance per bank in a bank reconciliation, an auditor would examine all of the following **except**
   a. Cutoff bank statement.
   b. Year-end bank statement.
   c. Bank confirmation.
   d. General ledger.

**51.** Which of the following cash transfers results in a misstatement of cash at December 31, 2005?

|  | Bank Transfer Schedule | | | |
|  | Disbursement | | Receipt | |
| Transfer | Recorded in books | Paid by bank | Recorded in books | Received by bank |
| a. | 12/31/05 | 1/4/06 | 12/31/05 | 12/31/05 |
| b. | 1/4/06 | 1/5/06 | 12/31/05 | 1/4/06 |
| c. | 12/31/05 | 1/5/06 | 12/31/05 | 1/4/06 |
| d. | 1/4/06 | 1/11/06 | 1/4/06 | 1/4/06 |

**52.** A cash shortage may be concealed by transporting funds from one location to another or by converting negotiable assets to cash. Because of this, which of the following is vital?
   a. Simultaneous confirmations.
   b. Simultaneous bank reconciliations.
   c. Simultaneous verification.
   d. Simultaneous surprise cash count.

**53.** The primary purpose of sending a standard confirmation request to financial institutions with which the client has done business during the year is to
   a. Detect kiting activities that may otherwise **not** be discovered.
   b. Corroborate information regarding deposit and loan balances.
   c. Provide the data necessary to prepare a proof of cash.
   d. Request information about contingent liabilities and secured transactions.

**54.** An auditor observes the mailing of monthly statements to a client's customers and reviews evidence of follow-up on errors reported by the customers. This test of controls most likely is performed to support management's financial statement assertion(s) of

|  | Presentation and disclosure | Existence occurrence |
| a. | Yes | Yes |
| b. | Yes | No |
| c. | No | Yes |
| d. | No | No |

---

**Items 55 and 56** are based on the following:

*Miles Company*
**BANK TRANSFER SCHEDULE**
*December 31, 2005*

| Check no. | Bank accounts | | Amount | Date disbursed per | | Date deposited per | |
|  | From | To |  | Books | Bank | Books | Bank |
| 2020 | 1st Natl. | Suburban | $32,000 | 12/31 | 1/5♦ | 12/31 | 1/3▲ |
| 2021 | 1st Natl. | Capital | 21,000 | 12/31 | 1/4♦ | 12/31 | 1/3▲ |
| 3217 | 2nd State | Suburban | 6,700 | 1/3 | 1/5 | 1/3 | 1/6 |
| 0659 | Midtown | Suburban | 5,500 | 12/30 | 1/5♦ | 12/30 | 1/3▲ |

**55.** The tick mark ♦ most likely indicates that the amount was traced to the
   a. December cash disbursements journal.
   b. Outstanding check list of the applicable bank reconciliation.
   c. January cash disbursements journal.
   d. Year-end bank confirmations.

**56.** The tick mark ▲ most likely indicates that the amount was traced to the
   a. Deposits in transit of the applicable bank reconciliation.
   b. December cash receipts journal.
   c. January cash receipts journal.
   d. Year-end bank confirmations.

---

**57.** Which of the following statements is correct concerning the use of negative confirmation requests?
   a. Unreturned negative confirmation requests rarely provide significant explicit evidence.
   b. Negative confirmation requests are effective when detection risk is low.
   c. Unreturned negative confirmation requests indicate that alternative procedures are necessary.
   d. Negative confirmation requests are effective when understatements of account balances are suspected.

**58.** When an auditor does **not** receive replies to positive requests for year-end accounts receivable confirmations, the auditor most likely would
   a. Inspect the allowance account to verify whether the accounts were subsequently written off.
   b. Increase the assessed level of detection risk for the valuation and completeness assertions.
   c. Ask the client to contact the customers to request that the confirmations be returned.
   d. Increase the assessed level of inherent risk for the revenue cycle.

**59.** In confirming a client's accounts receivable in prior years, an auditor found that there were many differences between the recorded account balances and the confirmation replies. These differences, which were not misstatements, required substantial time to resolve. In defining the sampling unit for the current year's audit, the auditor most likely would choose

    a. Individual overdue balances.
    b. Individual invoices.
    c. Small account balances.
    d. Large account balances.

**60.** Confirmation is most likely to be a relevant form of evidence with regard to assertions about accounts receivable when the auditor has concerns about the receivables'

    a. Valuation.
    b. Classification.
    c. Existence.
    d. Completeness.

**61.** An auditor should perform alternative procedures to substantiate the existence of accounts receivable when

    a. No reply to a positive confirmation request is received.
    b. No reply to a negative confirmation request is received.
    c. Collectibility of the receivables is in doubt.
    d. Pledging of the receivables is probable.

**62.** Which of the following procedures would an auditor most likely perform for year-end accounts receivable confirmations when the auditor did **not** receive replies to second requests?

    a. Review the cash receipts journal for the month prior to the year-end.
    b. Intensify the study of internal control concerning the revenue cycle.
    c. Increase the assessed level of detection risk for the existence assertion.
    d. Inspect the shipping records documenting the merchandise sold to the debtors.

**63.** In which of the following circumstances would the use of the negative form of accounts receivable confirmation most likely be justified?

    a. A substantial number of accounts may be in dispute and the accounts receivable balance arises from sales to a few major customers.
    b. A substantial number of accounts may be in dispute and the accounts receivable balance arises from sales to many customers with small balances.
    c. A small number of accounts may be in dispute and the accounts receivable balance arises from sales to a few major customers.
    d. A small number of accounts may be in dispute and the accounts receivable balance arises from sales to many customers with small balances.

**64.** To reduce the risks associated with accepting e-mail responses to requests for confirmation of accounts receivable, an auditor most likely would

    a. Request the senders to mail the original forms to the auditor.
    b. Examine subsequent cash receipts for the accounts in question.
    c. Consider the e-mail responses to the confirmations to be exceptions.
    d. Mail second requests to the e-mail respondents.

**65.** To reduce the risks associated with accepting fax responses to requests for confirmations of accounts receivable, an auditor most likely would

    a. Examine the shipping documents that provide evidence for the existence assertion.
    b. Verify the sources and contents of the faxes in telephone calls to the senders.
    c. Consider the faxes to be nonresponses and evaluate them as unadjusted differences.
    d. Inspect the faxes for forgeries or alterations and consider them to be acceptable if none are noted.

**66.** In auditing accounts receivable, the negative form of confirmation request most likely would be used when

    a. The total recorded amount of accounts receivable is immaterial to the financial statements taken as a whole.
    b. Response rates in prior years to properly designed positive confirmation requests were inadequate.
    c. Recipients are likely to return positive confirmation requests without verifying the accuracy of the information.
    d. The combined assessed level of inherent risk and control risk relative to accounts receivable is low.

**67.** Under which of the following circumstances would the use of the blank form of confirmations of accounts receivable most likely be preferable to positive confirmations?

    a. The recipients are likely to sign the confirmations without devoting proper attention to them.
    b. Subsequent cash receipts are unusually difficult to verify.
    c. Analytical procedures indicate that few exceptions are expected.
    d. The combined assessed level of inherent risk and control risk is low.

**68.** In confirming accounts receivable, an auditor decided to confirm customers' account balances rather than individual invoices. Which of the following most likely would be included with the client's confirmation letter?

    a. An auditor-prepared letter explaining that a nonresponse may cause an inference that the account balance is correct.
    b. A client-prepared letter reminding the customer that a nonresponse will cause a second request to be sent.
    c. An auditor-prepared letter requesting the customer to supply missing and incorrect information directly to the auditor.
    d. A client-prepared statement of account showing the details of the customer's account balance.

**69.** Which of the following statements would an auditor most likely add to the negative form of confirmations of accounts receivable to encourage timely consideration by the recipients?

    a. "This is **not** a request for payment; remittances should **not** be sent to our auditors in the enclosed envelope."

b. "Report any differences on the enclosed statement directly to our auditors; **no** reply is necessary if this amount agrees with your records."

c. "If you do **not** report any differences within fifteen days, it will be assumed that this statement is correct."

d. "The following invoices have been selected for confirmation and represent amounts that are overdue."

**70.** Which of the following strategies most likely could improve the response rate of the confirmation of accounts receivable?

a. Including a list of items or invoices that constitute the account balance.

b. Restricting the selection of accounts to be confirmed to those customers with relatively large balances.

c. Requesting customers to respond to the confirmation requests directly to the auditor by fax or e-mail.

d. Notifying the recipients that second requests will be mailed if they fail to respond in a timely manner.

**71.** An auditor most likely would make inquiries of production and sales personnel concerning possible obsolete or slow-moving inventory to support management's financial statement assertion of

a. Valuation or allocation.

b. Rights and obligations.

c. Existence or occurrence.

d. Presentation and disclosure.

**72.** While observing a client's annual physical inventory, an auditor recorded test counts for several items and noticed that certain test counts were higher than the recorded quantities in the client's perpetual records. This situation could be the result of the client's failure to record

a. Purchase discounts.

b. Purchase returns.

c. Sales.

d. Sales returns.

**73.** To gain assurance that all inventory items in a client's inventory listing schedule are valid, an auditor most likely would trace

a. Inventory tags noted during the auditor's observation to items listed in the inventory listing schedule.

b. Inventory tags noted during the auditor's observation to items listed in receiving reports and vendors' invoices.

c. Items listed in the inventory listing schedule to inventory tags and the auditor's recorded count sheets.

d. Items listed in receiving reports and vendors' invoices to the inventory listing schedule.

**74.** To measure how effectively an entity employs its resources, an auditor calculates inventory turnover by dividing average inventory into

a. Net sales.

b. Cost of goods sold.

c. Operating income.

d. Gross sales.

**75.** Which of the following auditing procedures most likely would provide assurance about a manufacturing entity's inventory valuation?

a. Testing the entity's computation of standard overhead rates.

b. Obtaining confirmation of inventories pledged under loan agreements.

c. Reviewing shipping and receiving cutoff procedures for inventories.

d. Tracing test counts to the entity's inventory listing.

**76.** A client maintains perpetual inventory records in both quantities and dollars. If the assessed level of control risk is high, an auditor would probably

a. Increase the extent of tests of controls of the inventory cycle.

b. Request the client to schedule the physical inventory count at the end of the year.

c. Insist that the client perform physical counts of inventory items several times during the year.

d. Apply gross profit tests to ascertain the reasonableness of the physical counts.

**77.** An auditor concluded that no excessive costs for idle plant were charged to inventory. This conclusion most likely related to the auditor's objective to obtain evidence about the financial statement assertions regarding inventory, including presentation and disclosure and

a. Valuation and allocation.

b. Completeness.

c. Existence or occurrence.

d. Rights and obligations.

**78.** An auditor selected items for test counts while observing a client's physical inventory. The auditor then traced the test counts to the client's inventory listing. This procedure most likely obtained evidence concerning management's assertion of

a. Rights and obligations.

b. Completeness.

c. Existence or occurrence.

d. Valuation.

**79.** An auditor most likely would analyze inventory turnover rates to obtain evidence concerning management's assertions about

a. Existence or occurrence.

b. Rights and obligations.

c. Presentation and disclosure.

d. Valuation or allocation.

**80.** An auditor usually examines receiving reports to support entries in the

a. Voucher register and sales returns journal.

b. Sales journal and sales returns journal.

c. Voucher register and sales journal.

d. Check register and sales journal.

**81.** When auditing inventories, an auditor would **least** likely verify that

a. The financial statement presentation of inventories is appropriate.

b. Damaged goods and obsolete items have been properly accounted for.

c.   All inventory owned by the client is on hand at the time of the count.

d.   The client has used proper inventory pricing.

**82.**   An auditor who physically examines securities should insist that a client representative be present in order to

a.   Detect fraudulent securities.

b.   Lend authority to the auditor's directives.

c.   Acknowledge the receipt of securities returned.

d.   Coordinate the return of securities to the proper locations.

**83.**   In establishing the existence and ownership of a long-term investment in the form of publicly traded stock, an auditor should inspect the securities or

a.   Correspond with the investee company to verify the number of shares owned.

b.   Inspect the audited financial statements of the investee company.

c.   Confirm the number of shares owned that are held by an independent custodian.

d.   Determine that the investment is carried at the lower of cost or market.

**84.**   When an auditor is unable to inspect and count a client's investment securities until after the balance sheet date, the bank where the securities are held in a safe-deposit box should be asked to

a.   Verify any differences between the contents of the box and the balances in the client's subsidiary ledger.

b.   Provide a list of securities added and removed from the box between the balance sheet date and the security-count date.

c.   Confirm that there has been **no** access to the box between the balance sheet date and the security-count date.

d.   Count the securities in the box so the auditor will have an independent direct verification.

**85.**   In testing long-term investments, an auditor ordinarily would use analytical procedures to ascertain the reasonableness of the

a.   Completeness of recorded investment income.

b.   Classification between current and noncurrent portfolios.

c.   Valuation of marketable equity securities.

d.   Existence of unrealized gains or losses in the portfolio.

**86.**   Analysis of which account is **least** likely to reveal evidence relating to recorded retirement of equipment?

a.   Accumulated depreciation.

b.   Insurance expense.

c.   Property, plant, and equipment.

d.   Purchase returns and allowances.

**87.**   Which of the following explanations most likely would satisfy an auditor who questions management about significant debits to the accumulated depreciation accounts?

a.   The estimated remaining useful lives of plant assets were revised upward.

b.   Plant assets were retired during the year.

c.   The prior year's depreciation expense was erroneously understated.

d.   Overhead allocations were revised at year-end.

**88.**   In testing for unrecorded retirements of equipment, an auditor most likely would

a.   Select items of equipment from the accounting records and then locate them during the plant tour.

b.   Compare depreciation journal entries with similar prior year entries in search of fully depreciated equipment.

c.   Inspect items of equipment observed during the plant tour and then trace them to the equipment subsidiary ledger.

d.   Scan the general journal for unusual equipment additions and excessive debits to repairs and maintenance expense.

**89.**   An auditor analyzes repairs and maintenance accounts primarily to obtain evidence in support of the audit assertion that all

a.   Noncapitalizable expenditures for repairs and maintenance have been recorded in the proper period.

b.   Expenditures for property and equipment have been recorded in the proper period.

c.   Noncapitalizable expenditures for repairs and maintenance have been properly charged to expense.

d.   Expenditures for property and equipment have **not** been charged to expense.

**90.**   The auditor is most likely to seek information from the plant manager with respect to the

a.   Adequacy of the provision for uncollectible accounts.

b.   Appropriateness of physical inventory observation procedures.

c.   Existence of obsolete machinery.

d.   Deferral of procurement of certain necessary insurance coverage.

**91.**   Treetop Corporation acquired a building and arranged mortgage financing during the year. Verification of the related mortgage acquisition costs would be least likely to include an examination of the related

a.   Deed.

b.   Canceled checks.

c.   Closing statement.

d.   Interest expense.

**92.**   In testing plant and equipment balances, an auditor may inspect new additions listed on the analysis of plant and equipment. This procedure is designed to obtain evidence concerning management's assertions of

|     | Existence or occurrence | Presentation and disclosure |
|-----|-------------------------|-----------------------------|
| a.  | Yes                     | Yes                         |
| b.  | Yes                     | No                          |
| c.  | No                      | Yes                         |
| d.  | No                      | No                          |

**93.**   In auditing intangible assets, an auditor most likely would review or recompute amortization and determine whether the amortization period is reasonable in support of management's financial statement assertion of

a.   Valuation or allocation.

b.   Existence or occurrence.

c.   Completeness.

d.   Rights and obligations.

**94.** When auditing prepaid insurance, an auditor discovers that the original insurance policy on plant equipment is not available for inspection. The policy's absence most likely indicates the possibility of a(n)

    a. Insurance premium due but **not** recorded.
    b. Deficiency in the coinsurance provision.
    c. Lien on the plant equipment.
    d. Understatement of insurance expense.

**95.** Which of the following procedures would an auditor most likely perform in searching for unrecorded liabilities?

    a. Trace a sample of accounts payable entries recorded just before year-end to the unmatched receiving report file.
    b. Compare a sample of purchase orders issued just after year-end with the year-end accounts payable trial balance.
    c. Vouch a sample of cash disbursements recorded just after year-end to receiving reports and vendor invoices.
    d. Scan the cash disbursements entries recorded just before year-end for indications of unusual transactions.

**96.** When using confirmations to provide evidence about the completeness assertion for accounts payable, the appropriate population most likely would be

    a. Vendors with whom the entity has previously done business.
    b. Amounts recorded in the accounts payable subsidiary ledger.
    c. Payees of checks drawn in the month after the year-end.
    d. Invoices filed in the entity's open invoice file.

**97.** Auditor confirmation of accounts payable balances at the balance sheet date may be unnecessary because

    a. This is a duplication of cutoff tests.
    b. Accounts payable balances at the balance sheet date may not be paid before the audit is completed.
    c. Correspondence with the audit client's attorney will reveal all legal action by vendors for nonpayment.
    d. There is likely to be other reliable external evidence to support the balances.

**98.** Which of the following is a substantive test that an auditor most likely would perform to verify the existence and valuation of recorded accounts payable?

    a. Investigating the open purchase order file to ascertain that prenumbered purchase orders are used and accounted for.
    b. Receiving the client's mail, unopened, for a reasonable period of time after the year-end to search for unrecorded vendors' invoices.
    c. Vouching selected entries in the accounts payable subsidiary ledger to purchase orders and receiving reports.
    d. Confirming accounts payable balances with known suppliers who have zero balances.

**99.** In auditing accounts payable, an auditor's procedures most likely would focus primarily on management's assertion of

    a. Existence or occurrence.
    b. Presentation and disclosure.
    c. Completeness.
    d. Valuation or allocation.

**100.** When a CPA observes that the recorded interest expense seems to be excessive in relation to the balance in the bonds payable account, the CPA might suspect that

    a. Discount on bonds payable is understated.
    b. Bonds payable are understated.
    c. Bonds payable are overstated.
    d. Premium on bonds payable is overstated.

**101.** An auditor most likely would inspect loan agreements under which an entity's inventories are pledged to support management's financial statement assertion of

    a. Presentation and disclosure.
    b. Valuation or allocation.
    c. Existence or occurrence.
    d. Completeness.

**102.** In auditing long-term bonds payable, an auditor most likely would

    a. Perform analytical procedures on the bond premium and discount accounts.
    b. Examine documentation of assets purchased with bond proceeds for liens.
    c. Compare interest expense with the bond payable amount for reasonableness.
    d. Confirm the existence of individual bond holders at year-end.

**103.** The auditor can best verify a client's bond sinking fund transactions and year-end balance by

    a. Confirmation with individual holders of retired bonds.
    b. Confirmation with the bond trustee.
    c. Recomputation of interest expense, interest payable, and amortization of bond discount or premium.
    d. Examination and count of the bonds retired during the year.

**104.** An auditor usually obtains evidence of stockholders' equity transactions by reviewing the entity's

    a. Minutes of board of directors meetings.
    b. Transfer agent's records.
    c. Canceled stock certificates.
    d. Treasury stock certificate book.

**105.** When control risk is assessed as low for assertions related to payroll, substantive tests of payroll balances most likely would be limited to applying analytical procedures and

    a. Observing the distribution of paychecks.
    b. Footing and crossfooting the payroll register.
    c. Inspecting payroll tax returns.
    d. Recalculating payroll accruals.

**106.** Which of the following circumstances most likely would cause an auditor to suspect an employee payroll fraud scheme?

    a. There are significant unexplained variances between standard and actual labor cost.
    b. Payroll checks are disbursed by the same employee each payday.

c. Employee time cards are approved by individual departmental supervisors.

d. A separate payroll bank account is maintained on an imprest basis.

**107.** In auditing payroll, an auditor most likely would

a. Verify that checks representing unclaimed wages are mailed.

b. Trace individual employee deductions to entity journal entries.

c. Observe entity employees during a payroll distribution.

d. Compare payroll costs with entity standards or budgets.

**108.** In performing tests concerning the granting of stock options, an auditor should

a. Confirm the transaction with the Secretary of State in the state of incorporation.

b. Verify the existence of option holders in the entity's payroll records or stock ledgers.

c. Determine that sufficient treasury stock is available to cover any new stock issued.

d. Trace the authorization for the transaction to a vote of the board of directors.

**109.** During an audit of an entity's stockholders' equity accounts, the auditor determines whether there are restrictions on retained earnings resulting from loans, agreements, or state law. This audit procedure most likely is intended to verify management's assertion of

a. Existence or occurrence.

b. Completeness.

c. Valuation or allocation.

d. Presentation and disclosure.

**110.** When a client company does **not** maintain its own stock records, the auditor should obtain written confirmation from the transfer agent and registrar concerning

a. Restrictions on the payment of dividends.

b. The number of shares issued and outstanding.

c. Guarantees of preferred stock liquidation value.

d. The number of shares subject to agreements to repurchase.

**111.** An audit program for the examination of the retained earnings account should include a step that requires verification of the

a. Market value used to charge retained earnings to account for a two-for-one stock split.

b. Approval of the adjustment to the beginning balance as a result of a write-down of an account receivable.

c. Authorization for both cash and stock dividends.

d. Gain or loss resulting from disposition of treasury shares.

**112.** An auditor most likely would perform substantive tests of details on payroll transactions and balances when

a. Cutoff tests indicate a substantial amount of accrued payroll expense.

b. The assessed level of control risk relative to payroll transactions is low.

c. Analytical procedures indicate unusual fluctuations in recurring payroll entries.

d. Accrued payroll expense consists primarily of unpaid commissions.

**113.** An auditor usually tests the reasonableness of dividend income from investments in publicly held companies by computing the amounts that should have been received by referring to

a. Dividend record books produced by investment advisory services.

b. Stock indentures published by corporate transfer agents.

c. Stock ledgers maintained by independent registrars.

d. Annual audited financial statements issued by the investee companies.

**114.** The most likely risk involved with a bill and hold transaction at year-end is a(n)

a. Accrued liability may be overstated as of year-end.

b. Buyer may have made an absolute purchase commitment.

c. Sale may inappropriately have been recorded as of year-end.

d. Buyer may have assumed the risk and reward of the purchased product.

**115.** Which of the following accounts is the practice of "channel stuffing" for sales most likely to most directly affect, and thereby result in additional audit procedures?

a. Accrued liabilities.

b. Allowance for sales returns.

c. Cash.

d. Marketable investments.

**116.** Recorded entries in which of the following accounts are most likely to relate to the property, plant, and equipment completeness assertion?

a. Allowance for doubtful accounts.

b. Marketable securities.

c. Property, plant, and equipment.

d. Repairs and maintenance expense.

**117.** For which of the following matters should an auditor obtain written management representations?

a. Management's cost-benefit justifications for **not** correcting internal control weaknesses.

b. Management's knowledge of future plans that may affect the price of the entity's stock.

c. Management's compliance with contractual agreements that may affect the financial statements.

d. Management's acknowledgment of its responsibility for employees' violations of laws.

**118.** To which of the following matters would materiality limits **not** apply in obtaining written management representations?

a. The availability of minutes of stockholders' and directors' meetings.

b. Losses from purchase commitments at prices in excess of market value.

c. The disclosure of compensating balance arrangements involving related parties.

d. Reductions of obsolete inventory to net realizable value.

**119.** The date of the management representation letter should coincide with the date of the
   a.   Balance sheet.
   b.   Latest interim financial information.
   c.   Auditor's report.
   d.   Latest related-party transaction.

**120.** Which of the following matters would an auditor most likely include in a management representation letter?
   a.   Communications with the audit committee concerning weaknesses in internal control.
   b.   The completeness and availability of minutes of stockholders' and directors' meetings.
   c.   Plans to acquire or merge with other entities in the subsequent year.
   d.   Management's acknowledgment of its responsibility for the detection of employee fraud.

**121.** The current chief executive and financial officers have only been employed by ABC Company for the past five months of year 2. ABC Company is presenting comparative financial statements on Years 1 and 2, both of which were audited by William Jones, CPA. For which year(s) should Jones obtain written representations from these two individuals?

|      | Year 1 | Year 2 |
|------|--------|--------|
| a.   | No     | No     |
| b.   | No     | Yes    |
| c.   | Yes    | No     |
| d.   | Yes    | Yes    |

**122.** Which of the following statements ordinarily is included among the written client representations obtained by the auditor?
   a.   Compensating balances and other arrangements involving restrictions on cash balances have been disclosed.
   b.   Management acknowledges responsibility for illegal actions committed by employees.
   c.   Sufficient evidential matter has been made available to permit the issuance of an unqualified opinion.
   d.   Management acknowledges that there are **no** material weaknesses in the internal control.

**123.** When considering the use of management's written representations as audit evidence about the completeness assertion, an auditor should understand that such representations
   a.   Complement, but do **not** replace, substantive tests designed to support the assertion.
   b.   Constitute sufficient evidence to support the assertion when considered in combination with reliance on internal control.
   c.   Are **not** part of the evidential matter considered to support the assertion.
   d.   Replace reliance on internal control as evidence to support the assertion.

**124.** A written representation from a client's management which, among other matters, acknowledges responsibility for the fair presentation of financial statements, should normally be signed by the
   a.   Chief executive officer and the chief financial officer.

   b.   Chief financial officer and the chairman of the board of directors.
   c.   Chairman of the audit committee of the board of directors.
   d.   Chief executive officer, the chairman of the board of directors, and the client's lawyer.

**125.** A limitation on the scope of the auditor's examination sufficient to preclude an unqualified opinion will always result when management
   a.   Prevents the auditor from reviewing the working papers of the predecessor auditor.
   b.   Engages the auditor after the year-end physical inventory count is completed.
   c.   Fails to correct a reportable condition of internal control that had been identified during the prior year's audit.
   d.   Refuses to furnish a management representation letter to the auditor.

**126.** A purpose of a management representation letter is to reduce
   a.   Audit risk to an aggregate level of misstatement that could be considered material.
   b.   An auditor's responsibility to detect material misstatements only to the extent that the letter is relied on.
   c.   The possibility of a misunderstanding concerning management's responsibility for the financial statements.
   d.   The scope of an auditor's procedures concerning related-party transactions and subsequent events.

**127.** "There have been no communications from regulatory agencies concerning noncompliance with, or deficiencies in, financial reporting practices that could have a material effect on the financial statements." The foregoing passage is most likely from a
   a.   Report on internal control.
   b.   Special report.
   c.   Management representation letter.
   d.   Letter for underwriters.

**128.** Which of the following statements is correct concerning an auditor's use of the work of a specialist?
   a.   The work of a specialist who is related to the client may be acceptable under certain circumstances.
   b.   If an auditor believes that the determinations made by a specialist are unreasonable, only a qualified opinion may be issued.
   c.   If there is a material difference between a specialist's findings and the assertions in the financial statements, only an adverse opinion may be issued.
   d.   An auditor may **not** use a specialist in the determination of physical characteristics relating to inventories.

**129.** In using the work of a specialist, an auditor may refer to the specialist in the auditor's report if, as a result of the specialist's findings, the auditor
   a.   Becomes aware of conditions causing substantial doubt about the entity's ability to continue as a going concern.

b.   Desires to disclose the specialist's findings, which imply that a more thorough audit was performed.

c.   Is able to corroborate another specialist's earlier findings that were consistent with management's representations.

d.   Discovers significant deficiencies in the design of the entity's internal control that management does **not** correct.

**130.** Which of the following statements is correct about the auditor's use of the work of a specialist?

a.   The specialist should **not** have an understanding of the auditor's corroborative use of the specialist's findings.

b.   The auditor is required to perform substantive procedures to verify the specialist's assumptions and findings.

c.   The client should **not** have an understanding of the nature of the work to be performed by the specialist.

d.   The auditor should obtain an understanding of the methods and assumptions used by the specialist.

**131.** In using the work of a specialist, an auditor referred to the specialist's findings in the auditor's report. This would be an appropriate reporting practice if the

a.   Client is **not** familiar with the professional certification, personal reputation, or particular competence of the specialist.

b.   Auditor, as a result of the specialist's findings, adds an explanatory paragraph emphasizing a matter regarding the financial statements.

c.   Client understands the auditor's corroborative use of the specialist's findings in relation to the representations in the financial statements.

d.   Auditor, as a result of the specialist's findings, decides to indicate a division of responsibility with the specialist.

**132.** In using the work of a specialist, an understanding should exist among the auditor, the client, and the specialist as to the nature of the specialist's work. The documentation of this understanding should cover

a.   A statement that the specialist assumes **no** responsibility to update the specialist's report for future events or circumstances.

b.   The conditions under which a division of responsibility may be necessary.

c.   The specialist's understanding of the auditor's corroborative use of the specialist's findings.

d.   The auditor's disclaimer as to whether the specialist's findings corroborate the representations in the financial statements.

**133.** Which of the following is **not** a specialist upon whose work an auditor may rely?

a.   Actuary.

b.   Appraiser.

c.   Internal auditor.

d.   Engineer.

**134.** A lawyer's response to an auditor's inquiry concerning litigation, claims, and assessments may be limited to matters that are considered individually or collectively material to the client's financial statements. Which parties should reach an understanding on the limits of materiality for this purpose?

a.   The auditor and the client's management.

b.   The client's audit committee and the lawyer.

c.   The client's management and the lawyer.

d.   The lawyer and the auditor.

**135.** The refusal of a client's attorney to provide information requested in an inquiry letter generally is considered

a.   Grounds for an adverse opinion.

b.   A limitation on the scope of the audit.

c.   Reason to withdraw from the engagement.

d.   Equivalent to a reportable condition.

**136.** Which of the following is an audit procedure that an auditor most likely would perform concerning litigation, claims, and assessments?

a.   Request the client's lawyer to evaluate whether the client's pending litigation, claims, and assessments indicate a going concern problem.

b.   Examine the legal documents in the client's lawyer's possession concerning litigation, claims, and assessments to which the lawyer has devoted substantive attention.

c.   Discuss with management its policies and procedures adopted for evaluating and accounting for litigation, claims, and assessments.

d.   Confirm directly with the client's lawyer that all litigation, claims, and assessments have been recorded or disclosed in the financial statements.

**137.** The primary reason an auditor requests letters of inquiry be sent to a client's attorneys is to provide the auditor with

a.   The probable outcome of asserted claims and pending or threatened litigation.

b.   Corroboration of the information furnished by management about litigation, claims, and assessments.

c.   The attorneys' opinions of the client's historical experiences in recent similar litigation.

d.   A description and evaluation of litigation, claims, and assessments that existed at the balance sheet date.

**138.** Which of the following is **not** an audit procedure that the independent auditor would perform concerning litigation, claims, and assessments?

a.   Obtain assurance from management that it has disclosed all unasserted claims that the lawyer has advised are probable of assertion and must be disclosed.

b.   Confirm directly with the client's lawyer that all claims have been recorded in the financial statements.

c.   Inquire of and discuss with management the policies and procedures adopted for identifying, evaluating, and accounting for litigation, claims, and assessments.

d.   Obtain from management a description and evaluation of litigation, claims, and assessments existing at the balance sheet date.

**139.** The scope of an audit is **not** restricted when an attorney's response to an auditor as a result of a client's letter of audit inquiry limits the response to

a. Matters to which the attorney has given substantive attention in the form of legal representation.
b. An evaluation of the likelihood of an unfavorable outcome of the matters disclosed by the entity.
c. The attorney's opinion of the entity's historical experience in recent similar litigation.
d. The probable outcome of asserted claims and pending or threatened litigation.

**140.** A CPA has received an attorney's letter in which no significant disagreements with the client's assessments of contingent liabilities were noted. The resignation of the client's lawyer shortly after receipt of the letter should alert the auditor that
a. Undisclosed unasserted claims may have arisen.
b. The attorney was unable to form a conclusion with respect to the significance of litigation, claims, and assessments.
c. The auditor must begin a completely new examination of contingent liabilities.
d. An adverse opinion will be necessary.

**141.** Which of the following statements extracted from a client's lawyer's letter concerning litigation, claims, and assessments most likely would cause the auditor to request clarification?
a. "I believe that the possible liability to the company is nominal in amount."
b. "I believe that the action can be settled for less than the damages claimed."
c. "I believe that the plaintiff's case against the company is without merit."
d. "I believe that the company will be able to defend this action successfully."

**142.** When auditing the fair value of an asset or liability, valuation issues ordinarily arise at the point of

| | Initial recording | Subsequent to initial recording |
|---|---|---|
| a. | Yes | Yes |
| b. | Yes | No |
| c. | No | Yes |
| d. | No | No |

**143.** Which of the following is **least** likely to be an approach followed when auditing the fair values of assets and liabilities?
a. Review and test management's process of valuation.
b. Confirm valuations with audit committee members.
c. Independently develop an estimate of the value of the account.
d. Review subsequent events relating to the account.

**144.** Which of the following auditing procedures most likely would assist an auditor in identifying related-party transactions?
a. Inspecting correspondence with lawyers for evidence of unreported contingent liabilities.
b. Vouching accounting records for recurring transactions recorded just after the balance sheet date.
c. Reviewing confirmations of loans receivable and payable for indications of guarantees.
d. Performing analytical procedures for indications of possible financial difficulties.

**145.** After determining that a related-party transaction has, in fact, occurred, an auditor should
a. Add a separate paragraph to the auditor's standard report to explain the transaction.
b. Perform analytical procedures to verify whether similar transactions occurred, but were **not** recorded.
c. Obtain an understanding of the business purpose of the transaction.
d. Substantiate that the transaction was consummated on terms equivalent to an arm's-length transaction.

**146.** When auditing related-party transactions, an auditor places primary emphasis on
a. Ascertaining the rights and obligations of the related parties.
b. Confirming the existence of the related parties.
c. Verifying the valuation of the related-party transactions.
d. Evaluating the disclosure of the related-party transactions.

**147.** Which of the following statements is correct concerning related-party transactions?
a. In the absence of evidence to the contrary, related-party transactions should be assumed to be outside the ordinary course of business.
b. An auditor should determine whether a particular transaction would have occurred if the parties had **not** been related.
c. An auditor should substantiate that related-party transactions were consummated on terms equivalent to those that prevail in arm's-length transactions.
d. The audit procedures directed toward identifying related-party transactions should include considering whether transactions are occurring, but are **not** being given proper accounting recognition.

**148.** An auditor most likely would modify an unqualified opinion if the entity's financial statements include a footnote on related-party transactions
a. Disclosing loans to related parties at interest rates significantly below prevailing market rates.
b. Describing an exchange of real estate for similar property in a nonmonetary related-party transaction.
c. Stating that a particular related-party transaction occurred on terms equivalent to those that would have prevailed in an arm's-length transaction.
d. Presenting the dollar volume of related-party transactions and the effects of any change in the method of establishing terms from prior periods.

**149.** Which of the following conditions or events most likely would cause an auditor to have substantial doubt about an entity's ability to continue as a going concern?
a. Significant related-party transactions are pervasive.
b. Usual trade credit from suppliers is denied.
c. Arrearages in preferred stock dividends are paid.
d. Restrictions on the disposal of principal assets are present.

**150.** Cooper, CPA, believes there is substantial doubt about the ability of Zero Corp. to continue as a going concern for a reasonable period of time. In evaluating Zero's plans for dealing with the adverse effects of future conditions and events, Cooper most likely would consider, as a mitigating factor, Zero's plans to

    a. Discuss with lenders the terms of all debt and loan agreements.

    b. Strengthen controls over cash disbursements.

    c. Purchase production facilities currently being leased from a related party.

    d. Postpone expenditures for research and development projects.

**151.** Which of the following conditions or events most likely would cause an auditor to have substantial doubt about an entity's ability to continue as a going concern?

    a. Cash flows from operating activities are negative.

    b. Research and development projects are postponed.

    c. Significant related-party transactions are pervasive.

    d. Stock dividends replace annual cash dividends.

**152.** Which of the following auditing procedures most likely would assist an auditor in identifying conditions and events that may indicate substantial doubt about an entity's ability to continue as a going concern?

    a. Inspecting title documents to verify whether any assets are pledged as collateral.

    b. Confirming with third parties the details of arrangements to maintain financial support.

    c. Reconciling the cash balance per books with the cutoff bank statement and the bank confirmation.

    d. Comparing the entity's depreciation and asset capitalization policies to other entities in the industry.

**153.** Which of the following audit procedures would most likely assist an auditor in identifying conditions and events that may indicate there could be substantial doubt about an entity's ability to continue as a going concern?

    a. Review compliance with the terms of debt agreements.

    b. Confirmation of accounts receivable from principal customers.

    c. Reconciliation of interest expense with debt outstanding.

    d. Confirmation of bank balances.

**154.** Davis, CPA, believes there is substantial doubt about the ability of Hill Co. to continue as a going concern for a reasonable period of time. In evaluating Hill's plans for dealing with the adverse effects of future conditions and events, Davis most likely would consider, as a mitigating factor, Hill's plans to

    a. Accelerate research and development projects related to future products.

    b. Accumulate treasury stock at prices favorable to Hill's historic price range.

    c. Purchase equipment and production facilities currently being leased.

    d. Negotiate reductions in required dividends being paid on preferred stock.

**155.** The adverse effects of events causing an auditor to believe there is substantial doubt about an entity's ability to continue as a going concern would most likely be mitigated by evidence relating to the

    a. Ability to expand operations into new product lines in the future.

    b. Feasibility of plans to purchase leased equipment at less than market value.

    c. Marketability of assets that management plans to sell.

    d. Committed arrangements to convert preferred stock to long-term debt.

**156.** Which of the following procedures would an auditor most likely perform in obtaining evidence about subsequent events?

    a. Determine that changes in employee pay rates after year-end were properly authorized.

    b. Recompute depreciation charges for plant assets sold after year-end.

    c. Inquire about payroll checks that were recorded before year-end but cashed after year-end.

    d. Investigate changes in long-term debt occurring after year-end.

**157.** Which of the following events occurring after the issuance of an auditor's report most likely would cause the auditor to make further inquiries about the previously issued financial statements?

    a. An uninsured natural disaster occurs that may affect the entity's ability to continue as a going concern.

    b. A contingency is resolved that had been disclosed in the audited financial statements.

    c. New information is discovered concerning undisclosed lease transactions of the audited period.

    d. A subsidiary is sold that accounts for 25% of the entity's consolidated net income.

**158.** Zero Corp. suffered a loss that would have a material effect on its financial statements on an uncollectible trade account receivable due to a customer's bankruptcy. This occurred suddenly due to a natural disaster ten days after Zero's balance sheet date, but one month before the issuance of the financial statements and the auditor's report. Under these circumstances,

| | The financial statements should be adjusted | The event requires financial statement disclosure, but no adjustment | The auditor's report should be modified for a lack of consistency |
|---|---|---|---|
| a. | Yes | No | No |
| b. | Yes | No | Yes |
| c. | No | Yes | Yes |
| d. | No | Yes | No |

**159.** After an audit report containing an unqualified opinion on a nonpublic client's financial statements was issued, the client decided to sell the shares of a subsidiary that accounts for 30% of its revenue and 25% of its net income. The auditor should

    a. Determine whether the information is reliable and, if determined to be reliable, request that revised financial statements be issued.

b.   Notify the entity that the auditor's report may **no** longer be associated with the financial statements.

c.   Describe the effects of this subsequently discovered information in a communication with persons known to be relying on the financial statements.

d.   Take **no** action because the auditor has **no** obligation to make any further inquiries.

**160.**  A client acquired 25% of its outstanding capital stock after year-end and prior to completion of the auditor's fieldwork.  The auditor should

a.   Advise management to adjust the balance sheet to reflect the acquisition.

b.   Issue pro forma financial statements giving effect to the acquisition as if it had occurred at year-end.

c.   Advise management to disclose the acquisition in the notes to the financial statements.

d.   Disclose the acquisition in the opinion paragraph of the auditor's report.

**161.**  Which of the following procedures would an auditor most likely perform to obtain evidence about the occurrence of subsequent events?

a.   Confirming a sample of material accounts receivable established after year-end.

b.   Comparing the financial statements being reported on with those of the prior period.

c.   Investigating personnel changes in the accounting department occurring after year-end.

d.   Inquiring as to whether any unusual adjustments were made after year-end.

**162.**  Which of the following procedures should an auditor generally perform regarding subsequent events?

a.   Compare the latest available interim financial statements with the financial statements being audited.

b.   Send second requests to the client's customers who failed to respond to initial accounts receivable confirmation requests.

c.   Communicate material weaknesses in internal control to the client's audit committee.

d.   Review the cutoff bank statements for several months after the year-end.

**163.**  On February 25, a CPA issued an auditor's report expressing an unqualified opinion on financial statements for the year ended January 31.  On March 2, the CPA learned that on February 11, the entity incurred a material loss on an uncollectible trade receivable as a result of the deteriorating financial condition of the entity's principal customer that led to the customer's bankruptcy.  Management then refused to adjust the financial statements for this subsequent event.  The CPA determined that the information is reliable and that there are creditors currently relying on the financial statements.  The CPA's next course of action most likely would be to

a.   Notify the entity's creditors that the financial statements and the related auditor's report should **no** longer be relied on.

b.   Notify each member of the entity's board of directors about management's refusal to adjust the financial statements.

c.   Issue revised financial statements and distribute them to each creditor known to be relying on the financial statements.

d.   Issue a revised auditor's report and distribute it to each creditor known to be relying on the financial statements.

**164.**  An auditor is considering whether the omission of a substantive procedure considered necessary at the time of an audit may impair the auditor's present ability to support the previously expressed opinion.  The auditor need **not** apply the omitted procedure if the

a.   Financial statements and auditor's report were not distributed beyond management and the board of directors.

b.   Auditor's previously expressed opinion was qualified because of a departure from GAAP.

c.   Results of other procedures that were applied tend to compensate for the procedure omitted.

d.   Omission is due to unreasonable delays by client personnel in providing data on a timely basis.

**165.**  On March 15, 2002, Kent, CPA, issued an unqualified opinion on a client's audited financial statements for the year ended December 31, 2001.  On May 4, 2002, Kent's internal inspection program disclosed that engagement personnel failed to observe the client's physical inventory.  Omission of this procedure impairs Kent's present ability to support the unqualified opinion.  If the stockholders are currently relying on the opinion, Kent should first

a.   Advise management to disclose to the stockholders that Kent's unqualified opinion should **not** be relied on.

b.   Undertake to apply alternative procedures that would provide a satisfactory basis for the unqualified opinion.

c.   Reissue the auditor's report and add an explanatory paragraph describing the departure from generally accepted auditing standards.

d.   Compensate for the omitted procedure by performing tests of controls to reduce audit risk to a sufficiently low level.

**166.**  Six months after issuing an unqualified opinion on audited financial statements, an auditor discovered that the engagement personnel failed to confirm several of the client's material accounts receivable balances.  The auditor should first

a.   Request the permission of the client to undertake the confirmation of accounts receivable.

b.   Perform alternative procedures to provide a satisfactory basis for the unqualified opinion.

c.   Assess the importance of the omitted procedures to the auditor's ability to support the previously expressed opinion.

d.   Inquire whether there are persons currently relying, or likely to rely, on the unqualified opinion.

**167.**  Which of the following procedures is **least** likely to be performed before the balance sheet date?

a.   Testing of internal control over cash.

b.   Confirmation of receivables.

c.   Search for unrecorded liabilities.

d.   Observation of inventory.

**168.** Which of the following most likely would be detected by an auditor's review of a client's sales cutoff?
- a. Shipments lacking sales invoices and shipping documents.
- b. Excessive write-offs of accounts receivable.
- c. Unrecorded sales at year-end.
- d. Lapping of year-end accounts receivable.

**169.** Cutoff tests designed to detect credit sales made before the end of the year that have been recorded in the subsequent year provide assurance about management's assertion of
- a. Presentation.
- b. Completeness.
- c. Rights.
- d. Existence.

**170.** Which of the following procedures would an auditor most likely perform during an audit engagement's overall review stage in formulating an opinion on an entity's financial statements?
- a. Obtain assurance from the entity's attorney that all material litigation has been disclosed in the financial statements.
- b. Verify the clerical accuracy of the entity's proof of cash and its bank cutoff statement.
- c. Determine whether inadequate provisions for the safeguarding of assets have been corrected.
- d. Consider whether the results of audit procedures affect the assessment of the risk of material misstatement due to fraud.

**171.** Which of the following procedures is ordinarily performed by an accountant in a compilation engagement of a nonpublic entity?
- a. Reading the financial statements to consider whether they are free of obvious mistakes in the application of accounting principles.
- b. Obtaining written representations from management indicating that the compiled financial statements will **not** be used to obtain credit.
- c. Making inquiries of management concerning actions taken at meetings of the stockholders and the board of directors.
- d. Applying analytical procedures designed to corroborate management's assertions that are embodied in the financial statement components.

**172.** Davis, CPA, accepted an engagement to audit the financial statements of Tech Resources, a nonpublic entity. Before the completion of the audit, Tech requested Davis to change the engagement to a compilation of financial statements. Before Davis agrees to change the engagement, Davis is required to consider the

| | Additional audit effort necessary to complete the audit | Reason given for Tech's request |
|---|---|---|
| a. | No | No |
| b. | Yes | Yes |
| c. | Yes | No |
| d. | No | Yes |

**173.** May an accountant accept an engagement to compile or review the financial statements of a not-for-profit entity if the accountant is unfamiliar with the specialized industry accounting principles, but plans to obtain the required level of knowledge before compiling or reviewing the financial statements?

| | Compilation | Review |
|---|---|---|
| a. | No | No |
| b. | Yes | No |
| c. | No | Yes |
| d. | Yes | Yes |

**174.** Which of the following statements is correct concerning both an engagement to compile and an engagement to review a nonpublic entity's financial statements?
- a. The accountant does not contemplate obtaining an understanding of internal control.
- b. The accountant must be independent in fact and appearance.
- c. The accountant expresses no assurance on the financial statements.
- d. The accountant should obtain a written management representation letter.

**175.** One of the conditions required for an accountant to submit a written personal financial plan containing unaudited financial statements to a client without complying with the requirements of SSARS 1, *Compilation and Review of Financial Statements*, is that the
- a. Client agrees that the financial statements will **not** be used to obtain credit.
- b. Accountant compiled or reviewed the client's financial statements for the immediate prior year.
- c. Engagement letter acknowledges that the financial statements will contain departures from generally accepted accounting principles.
- d. Accountant expresses limited assurance that the financial statements are free of any material misstatements.

**176.** When providing limited assurance that the financial statements of a nonpublic entity require **no** material modifications to be in accordance with generally accepted accounting principles, the accountant should
- a. Assess the risk that a material misstatement could occur in a financial statement assertion.
- b. Confirm with the entity's lawyer that material loss contingencies are disclosed.
- c. Understand the accounting principles of the industry in which the entity operates.
- d. Develop audit programs to determine whether the entity's financial statements are fairly presented.

**177.** Which of the following procedures would an accountant **least** likely perform during an engagement to review the financial statements of a nonpublic entity?
- a. Observing the safeguards over access to and use of assets and records.
- b. Comparing the financial statements with anticipated results in budgets and forecasts.
- c. Inquiring of management about actions taken at the board of directors' meetings.
- d. Studying the relationships of financial statement elements expected to conform to predictable patterns.

**178.** Which of the following procedures should an accountant perform during an engagement to review the financial statements of a nonpublic entity?

a. Communicating reportable conditions discovered during the assessment of control risk.

b. Obtaining a client representation letter from members of management.

c. Sending bank confirmation letters to the entity's financial institutions.

d. Examining cash disbursements in the subsequent period for unrecorded liabilities.

**179.** Smith, CPA, has been asked to issue a review report on the balance sheet of Cone Company, a nonpublic entity, and not on the other related financial statements. Smith may do so only if

a. Smith compiles and reports on the related statements of income, retained earnings, and cash flows.

b. Smith is **not** aware of any material modifications needed for the balance sheet to conform with GAAP.

c. The scope of Smith's inquiry and analytical procedures is **not** restricted.

d. Cone is a new client and Smith accepts the engagement after the end of Cone's fiscal year.

**180.** An accountant should perform analytical procedures during an engagement to

| | Compile a nonpublic entity's financial statements | Review a nonpublic entity's financial statements |
|---|---|---|
| a. | No | No |
| b. | Yes | Yes |
| c. | Yes | No |
| d. | No | Yes |

**181.** Which of the following inquiry or analytical procedures ordinarily is performed in an engagement to review a nonpublic entity's financial statements?

a. Analytical procedures designed to test the accounting records by obtaining corroborating evidential matter.

b. Inquiries concerning the entity's procedures for recording and summarizing transactions.

c. Analytical procedures designed to test management's assertions regarding continued existence.

d. Inquiries of the entity's attorney concerning contingent liabilities.

**182.** Which of the following procedures would most likely be included in a review engagement of a nonpublic entity?

a. Preparing a bank transfer schedule.

b. Inquiring about related-party transactions.

c. Assessing internal control.

d. Performing cutoff tests on sales and purchases transactions.

**183.** Which of the following would the accountant most likely investigate during the review of financial statements of a nonpublic entity if accounts receivable did **not** conform to a predictable pattern during the year?

a. Sales returns and allowances.

b. Credit sales.

c. Sales of consigned goods.

d. Cash sales.

**184.** When performing an engagement to review a nonpublic entity's financial statements, an accountant most likely would

a. Confirm a sample of significant accounts receivable balances.

b. Ask about actions taken at board of directors' meetings.

c. Obtain an understanding of internal control.

d. Limit the distribution of the accountant's report.

**185.** Operational auditing is primarily oriented toward

a. Future improvements to accomplish the goals of management.

b. The accuracy of data reflected in management's financial records.

c. The verification that a company's financial statements are fairly presented.

d. Past protection provided by existing internal control.

**186.** A typical objective of an operational audit is to determine whether an entity's

a. Internal control is adequately operating as designed.

b. Operational information is in accordance with generally accepted governmental auditing standards.

c. Financial statements present fairly the results of operations.

d. Specific operating units are functioning efficiently and effectively.

**SIMULATION PROBLEMS**

**Simulation Problem 1**                              (30 to 35 minutes)

| Directions | | | | |
|---|---|---|---|---|
| | Audit Objectives—Investments | Audit Objectives—Accounts Receivable | Research | Communication |

To support financial statement assertions, an auditor develops specific audit objectives. The auditor then designs substantive tests to satisfy or accomplish each objective.

**Items 1 through 7** represent audit objectives for the investments and accounts receivable. To the right of each set of audit objectives is a listing of possible audit procedures for that account. For each audit objective, select the audit procedure that would primarily respond to the objective. Select only one procedure for each audit objective. A procedure may be selected only once, or not at all.

| | Audit Objectives—Investments | | | |
|---|---|---|---|---|
| Directions | | Audit Objectives—Accounts Receivable | Research | Communication |

### Audit procedures for investments

A. Trace opening balances in the subsidiary ledger to prior year's audit working papers.
B. Determine that employees who are authorized to sell investments do not have access to cash.
C. Examine supporting documents for a sample of investment transactions to verify that prenumbered documents are used.
D. Determine that any impairments in the price of investments have been properly recorded.
E. Verify that transfers from the current to the noncurrent investment portfolio have been properly recorded.
F. Obtain positive confirmations as of the balance sheet date of investments held by independent custodians.
G. Trace investment transactions to minutes of the Board of Directors meetings to determine that transactions were properly authorized.

### Audit objectives for investments                                  (A) (B) (C) (D) (E) (F) (G)

1. Investments are properly described and classified in the financial statements.  ○ ○ ○ ○ ○ ○ ○

2. Recorded investments represent investments actually owned at the balance sheet date.  ○ ○ ○ ○ ○ ○ ○

3. Trading investments are properly valued at fair market value at the balance sheet date.  ○ ○ ○ ○ ○ ○ ○

| | | Audit Objectives—Accounts Receivable | | |
|---|---|---|---|---|
| Directions | Audit Objectives—Investments | | Research | Communication |

### Audit procedures for accounts receivable

A. Analyze the relationship of accounts receivable and sales and compare it with relationships for preceding periods.
B. Perform sales cutoff tests to obtain assurance that sales transactions and corresponding entries for inventories and cost of goods sold are recorded in the same and proper period.
C. Review the aged trial balance for significant past due accounts.
D. Obtain an understanding of the business purpose of transactions that resulted in accounts receivable balances.
E. Review loan agreements for indications of whether accounts receivable have been factored or pledged.
F. Review the accounts receivable trial balance for amounts due from officers and employees.
G. Analyze unusual relationships between monthly accounts receivable balances and monthly accounts payable balances.

### Audit objectives for accounts receivable                          (A) (B) (C) (D) (E) (F) (G)

4. Accounts receivable represent all amounts owed to the entity at the balance sheet date.  ○ ○ ○ ○ ○ ○ ○

5. The entity has legal right to all accounts receivable at the balance sheet date.  ○ ○ ○ ○ ○ ○ ○

6. Accounts receivable are stated at net realizable value.  ○ ○ ○ ○ ○ ○ ○

7. Accounts receivable are properly described and presented in the financial statements.  ○ ○ ○ ○ ○ ○ ○

| | | | Research | |
|---|---|---|---|---|
| Directions | Audit Objectives—Investments | Audit Objectives—Accounts Receivable | | Communication |

Your client has suggested to you that his previous auditor did not confirm accounts receivable. Search the Professional Standards to determine whether there are any circumstances in which an auditor need not request the confirmation of accounts receivable. You may simply paste the appropriate material to your solution.

| Directions | Audit Objectives— Investments | Audit Objectives— Accounts Receivable | Research | Communication |
|---|---|---|---|---|

Assume that you are preparing accounts receivable confirmations for a client. You are concerned that some of the companies whose accounts were selected from the client's records may be fictitious. Write a memorandum to the audit files describing how you will detect fictitious companies.

To:  Audit Working Papers
From: CPA Candidate
Re:  Procedures to detect fictitious companies

---

**Simulation Problem 2**  (40 to 50 minutes)

| Directions | Audit Implications | Confirmations | Inventory Observation | Research | Communication |
|---|---|---|---|---|---|

In the following simulation you are asked to reply to various statements concerning situations that may arise in an audit.

| Directions | Audit Implications | Confirmations | Inventory Observation | Research | Communication |
|---|---|---|---|---|---|

In applying audit procedures and evaluating the results of those procedures, auditors may encounter specific information that may raise a question concerning the existence of illegal acts and related-party transactions. Indicate whether each of the following is more likely related to an illegal act (IA) or a related-party transaction (RP).

|  | *Statement* | *IA* | *RP* |
|---|---|---|---|
| 1. | A note payable has an interest rate well below the market rate at the time at which the loan was obtained. | ○ | ○ |
| 2. | The company has a properly documented loan but the loan has no scheduled repayment terms. | ○ | ○ |
| 3. | Unexplained payments have been made to government officials. | ○ | ○ |
| 4. | The company exchanged certain real estate property for similar real estate property. | ○ | ○ |
| 5. | Large cash receipts near year-end have been received based on cash sales for which there is no documentation. | ○ | ○ |

| Directions | Audit Implications | Confirmations | Inventory Observation | Research | Communication |
|---|---|---|---|---|---|

An auditor may use confirmations of accounts receivable. Reply as to whether the following statements are correct or incorrect with respect to the confirmation process when applied to accounts receivable.

|  | *Statement* | *Correct* | *Incorrect* |
|---|---|---|---|
| 1. | The confirmation requests should be mailed to respondents by the CPAs. | ○ | ○ |
| 2. | A combination of positive and negative request forms must be used if receivables are significant. | ○ | ○ |
| 3. | Second requests are ordinarily sent for positive form confirmations requests when the first request is not returned. | ○ | ○ |
| 4. | Confirmations address existence more than they address completeness. | ○ | ○ |
| 5. | Confirmation of accounts receivable is a generally accepted auditing standard | ○ | ○ |
| 6. | Absent a few circumstances, there is a presumption that the auditor will confirm accounts receivable. | ○ | ○ |

| | Statement | Correct | Incorrect |
|---|---|---|---|
| 7. | Auditors should always confirm the total balances of accounts rather than individual portions (e.g., if the balance is made up of three sales, all three should be confirmed). | O | O |
| 8. | Auditors may ignore individually immaterial accounts when confirming accounts receivable | O | O |
| 9. | The best way to evaluate the results of the confirmation process is to total the misstatements identified and to compare that total to the account's tolerable error amounts. | O | O |
| 10. | Accounts receivable are ordinarily confirmed on a standard form developed by the American Institute of Certified Public Accountants and the Financial Executives Institute. | O | O |

| Directions | Audit Implications | Confirmations | Inventory Observation | Research | Communication |
|---|---|---|---|---|---|

Auditors often observe the counting of their clients' inventories. Reply as to whether the following statements are correct or incorrect with respect to the inventory observation.

| | Statement | Correct | Incorrect |
|---|---|---|---|
| 1. | With strong internal control, the inventory count may be at the end of the year or at other times | O | O |
| 2. | When a client has many inventory locations, auditors ordinarily need not be present at each location. | O | O |
| 3. | All auditor test counts must be documented in the working papers. | O | O |
| 4. | Auditors' observation of the counting of their clients' inventories addresses the existence of inventory, and not the completeness of the count. | O | O |
| 5. | When the client manufactures a product, direct labor and overhead ordinarily become a part of inventory item costs. | O | O |
| 6. | Inventory is ordinarily valued at the lower of standard cost or market. | O | O |
| 7. | Inventory items present as "consigned in" should not be included in the clients' inventory value. | O | O |
| 8. | Auditor recording of test counts ordinarily replaces the need for client "tagging" of inventory. | O | O |
| 9. | Ordinarily, an auditor need not count all items in the inventory. | O | O |
| 10. | At the completion of the count, an auditor will ordinarily provide the client with copies of his or her inventory test counts to help assure inventory accuracy. | O | O |

| Directions | Audit Implications | Confirmations | Inventory Observation | Research | Communication |
|---|---|---|---|---|---|

When audit clients may become involved with financial derivative transactions, auditors need to determine that client financial statements meet the completeness assertion with respect to determining that all of the client's derivatives are properly reported. Search the Professional Standards to identify suggested substantive procedures for completeness as it relates to financial derivatives.

| Directions | Audit Implications | Confirmations | Inventory Observation | Research | Communication |
|---|---|---|---|---|---|

Write a memorandum to the audit working papers about the importance of controlling the mailing of confirmations.

To: Audit Working Papers
From: CPA Candidate
Re: Audit confirmations

**Simulation Problem 3**                              (40 to 50 minutes)

| Audit Procedures | | | |
|---|---|---|---|
| | Assessing Audit Risk | Research | Communication |

   **Items 1 through 6** represent the items that an auditor ordinarily would find on a client-prepared bank reconciliation. The accompanying **List of Auditing Procedures** represents substantive auditing procedures. For each item, select one or more procedures, as indicated, that the auditor most likely would perform to gather evidence in support of that item. The procedures on the **List** may be selected once, more than once, or not at all.

*Assume*

- The client prepared the bank reconciliation on 10/2/05
- The bank reconciliation is mathematically accurate.
- The auditor received a cutoff bank statement dated 10/7/05 directly from the bank on 10/11/05
- The 9/30/05 deposit in transit, outstanding checks #1281, #1285, #1289, and #1292, and the correction of the error regarding check #1282 appeared on the cutoff bank statement.
- The auditor assessed control risk concerning the financial statement assertions related to cash at the maximum.

### List of Auditing Procedures

| | |
|---|---|
| A. Trace to cash receipts journal. | F. Inspect bank debit memo. |
| B. Trace to cash disbursements journal. | G. Ascertain reason for unusual delay. |
| C. Compare to 9/30/01 general ledger. | H. Inspect supporting documents for reconciling item **not** appearing on cutoff statement. |
| D. Confirm directly with bank. | |
| E. Inspect bank credit memo. | I. Trace items on the bank reconciliation to cutoff statement. |
| | J. Trace items on the cutoff statement to bank reconciliation. |

### General Company
### BANK RECONCILIATION
### 1ST NATIONAL BANK OF US BANK ACCOUNT
*September 30, 2005*

| | | | | | |
|---|---|---|---|---|---|
| **1.** | Select 2 Procedures | — | Balance per bank | | $ 28,375 |
| **2.** | Select 5 Procedures | — | Deposits in transit | | |
| | | | 9/29/05 | $4,500 | |
| | | | 9/30/05 | 1,525 | 6,025 |
| | | | | | 34,400 |
| **3.** | Select 5 Procedures | — | Outstanding checks | | |
| | | | # 988    8/31/05 | 2,200 | |
| | | | #1281    9/26/05 | 675 | |
| | | | #1285    9/27/05 | 850 | |
| | | | #1289    9/29/05 | 2,500 | |
| | | | #1292    9/30/05 | 7,225 | (13,450) |
| | | | | | 20,950 |
| **4.** | Select 1 Procedure | — | Customer note collected by bank | | (3,000) |
| **5.** | Select 2 Procedures | — | Error: Check #1282, written on 9/26/05 for $270 was erroneously charged by bank as $720; bank was notified on 10/2/05 | | 450 |
| **6.** | Select 1 Procedure | — | Balance per books | | $ 18,400 |

| Audit Procedures | Addressing Audit Risk | | |
|---|---|---|---|
| | | Research | Communication |

   **Items 1 through 12** represent possible errors and fraud that you suspect may be present at General Company. The accompanying *List of Auditing Procedures* represents procedures that the auditor would consider performing to gather evidence concerning possible errors and fraud. For each item, select one or two procedures, as indicated, that the auditor most likely would perform to gather evidence in support of that item. The procedures on the list may be selected once, more than once, or not at all.

### Possible misstatements due to errors and fraud

**1.** The auditor suspects that a kiting scheme exists because an accounting department employee who can issue and record checks seems to be leading an unusually luxurious lifestyle. (**Select only 1 procedure**)

**2.** An auditor suspects that the controller wrote several checks and recorded the cash disbursements just before year-end but did not mail the checks until after the first week of the subsequent year. (**Select only 1 procedure**)

3. The entity borrowed funds from a financial institution. Although the transaction was properly recorded, the auditor suspects that the loan created a lien on the entity's real estate that is not disclosed in its financial statements. (**Select only 1 procedure**)

4. The auditor discovered an unusually large receivable from one of the entity's new customers. The auditor suspects that the receivable may be fictitious because the auditor has never heard of the customer and because the auditor's initial attempt to confirm the receivable has been ignored by the customer. (**Select only 2 procedures**)

5. The auditor suspects that fictitious employees have been placed on the payroll by the entity's payroll supervisor, who has access to payroll records and to the paychecks. (**Select only 1 procedure**)

6. The auditor suspects that selected employees of the entity received unauthorized raises from the entity's payroll supervisor, who has access to payroll records. (**Select only 1 procedure**)

7. The entity's cash receipts of the first few days of the subsequent year were properly deposited in its general operating account after the year-end. However, the auditor suspects that the entity recorded the cash receipts in its books during the last week of the year under audit. (**Select only 1 procedure**)

8. The auditor suspects that vouchers were prepared and processed by an accounting department employee for merchandise that was neither ordered nor received by the entity. (**Select only 1 procedure**)

9. The details of invoices for equipment repairs were not clearly identified or explained to the accounting department employees. The auditor suspects that the bookkeeper incorrectly recorded the repairs as fixed assets. (**Select only 1 procedure**)

10. The auditor suspects that a lapping scheme exists because an accounting department employee who has access to cash receipts also maintains the accounts receivable ledger and refuses to take any vacation or sick days. (**Select only 2 procedures**)

11. The auditor suspects that the entity is inappropriately increasing the cash reported on its balance sheet by drawing a check on one account and not recording it as an outstanding check on that account and simultaneously recording it as a deposit in a second account. (**Select only 1 procedure**)

12. The auditor suspects that the entity's controller has overstated sales and accounts receivable by recording fictitious sales to regular customers in the entity's books. (**Select only 2 procedures**)

*List of Auditing Procedures*

A. Compare the details of the cash receipts journal entries with the details of the corresponding daily deposit slips.

B. Scan the debits to the fixed asset accounts and vouch selected amounts to vendors' invoices and management's authorization.

C. Perform analytical procedures that compare documented authorized pay rates to the entity's budget and forecast.

D. Obtain the cutoff bank statement and compare the cleared checks to the year-end bank reconciliation.

E. Prepare a bank transfer schedule.

F. Inspect the entity's deeds to its real estate.

G. Make inquiries of the entity's attorney concerning the details of real estate transactions.

H. Confirm the terms of borrowing arrangements with the lender.

I. Examine selected equipment repair orders and supporting documentation to determine the propriety of the charges.

J. Send requests to confirm the entity's accounts receivable on a surprise basis at an interim date.

K. Send a second request for confirmation of the receivable to the customer and make inquiries of a reputable credit agency concerning the customer's creditworthiness.

L. Examine the entity's shipping documents to verify that the merchandise that produced the receivable was actually sent to the customer.

M. Inspect the entity's correspondence files for indications of customer disputes for evidence that certain shipments were on consignment.

N. Perform edit checks of data on the payroll transaction tapes.

O. Inspect payroll check endorsements for similar handwriting.

P. Observe payroll check distribution on a surprise basis.

Q. Vouch data in the payroll register to documented authorized pay rates in the human resources department's files.

R. Reconcile the payroll checking account and determine if there were unusual time lags between the issuance and payment of payroll checks.

S. Inspect the file of prenumbered vouchers for consecutive numbering and proper approval by an appropriate employee.

T. Determine that the details of selected prenumbered vouchers match the related vendors' invoices.

U. Examine the supporting purchase orders and receiving reports for selected paid vouchers.

| Audit Procedures | Addressing Audit Risk | Research | Communication |
| --- | --- | --- | --- |

Now assume that the note collected by the bank is from a "related party." Search the Professional Standards to determine procedures that should be performed concerning a related-party transaction that has been identified.

*NOTE: If you do not have access to professional standards indicate the keywords or section numbers that you would use to do your search.*

| Audit Procedures | Addressing Audit Risk | Research | Communication |
|---|---|---|---|

General Company wishes to put a note in the company's financial statements indicating that the terms of the related-party loan is comparable to those between unrelated parties.  Write a brief memorandum to Joe Smith, the CEO of General Company, explaining the implications of this proposed action.

To:     Joe Smith, CEO
          General Company
From:  CPA Candidate
Re:     Related-party loan disclosure

**Additional Simulations**

## MULTIPLE-CHOICE ANSWERS

| # | | # | | # | | # | | # | | # | |
|---|---|---|---|---|---|---|---|---|---|---|---|
| 1. | c | 33. | a | 65. | b | 97. | d | 129. | a | 161. | d |
| 2. | d | 34. | c | 66. | d | 98. | c | 130. | d | 162. | a |
| 3. | d | 35. | c | 67. | a | 99. | c | 131. | b | 163. | b |
| 4. | a | 36. | d | 68. | d | 100. | b | 132. | c | 164. | c |
| 5. | a | 37. | b | 69. | c | 101. | a | 133. | c | 165. | b |
| 6. | d | 38. | a | 70. | a | 102. | c | 134. | d | 166. | c |
| 7. | d | 39. | d | 71. | a | 103. | b | 135. | b | 167. | c |
| 8. | d | 40. | c | 72. | d | 104. | a | 136. | c | 168. | c |
| 9. | c | 41. | b | 73. | c | 105. | d | 137. | b | 169. | b |
| 10. | a | 42. | b | 74. | b | 106. | a | 138. | b | 170. | d |
| 11. | b | 43. | c | 75. | a | 107. | d | 139. | a | 171. | a |
| 12. | c | 44. | b | 76. | b | 108. | d | 140. | a | 172. | b |
| 13. | a | 45. | d | 77. | a | 109. | d | 141. | b | 173. | d |
| 14. | d | 46. | b | 78. | b | 110. | b | 142. | a | 174. | a |
| 15. | b | 47. | b | 79. | d | 111. | c | 143. | b | 175. | a |
| 16. | c | 48. | b | 80. | a | 112. | c | 144. | c | 176. | c |
| 17. | c | 49. | c | 81. | c | 113. | a | 145. | c | 177. | a |
| 18. | c | 50. | d | 82. | c | 114. | c | 146. | d | 178. | b |
| 19. | a | 51. | b | 83. | c | 115. | b | 147. | d | 179. | c |
| 20. | b | 52. | c | 84. | c | 116. | d | 148. | c | 180. | d |
| 21. | c | 53. | b | 85. | a | 117. | c | 149. | b | 181. | b |
| 22. | b | 54. | c | 86. | d | 118. | a | 150. | d | 182. | b |
| 23. | c | 55. | b | 87. | b | 119. | c | 151. | a | 183. | b |
| 24. | b | 56. | a | 88. | a | 120. | b | 152. | b | 184. | b |
| 25. | c | 57. | a | 89. | d | 121. | d | 153. | a | 185. | a |
| 26. | c | 58. | c | 90. | c | 122. | a | 154. | d | 186. | d |
| 27. | c | 59. | b | 91. | a | 123. | a | 155. | c | | |
| 28. | d | 60. | c | 92. | b | 124. | a | 156. | d | | |
| 29. | c | 61. | a | 93. | a | 125. | d | 157. | c | | |
| 30. | b | 62. | d | 94. | c | 126. | c | 158. | d | | |
| 31. | a | 63. | d | 95. | c | 127. | c | 159. | d | 1st: | __/186 = __% |
| 32. | a | 64. | a | 96. | a | 128. | a | 160. | c | 2nd: | __/186 = __% |

## MULTIPLE-CHOICE ANSWER EXPLANATIONS

### A.1. Competent and Sufficient Evidential Matter

**1.** **(c)** The requirement is to identify the most persuasive type of evidence. Answer (c) is correct because a bank statement represents evidence prepared outside of the entity and is considered an evidential matter source which provides the auditor with a high level of assurance. Answers (a), (b), and (d) are incorrect because prenumbered client purchase order forms, client work sheets and a representation letter all represent internally generated documents, generally considered less persuasive than externally generated documents. See AU 326 for information on the persuasiveness of evidential matter.

**2.** **(d)** The requirement is to identify a correct presumption about the reliability of evidential matter. Answer (d) is correct because AU 326 indicates that effective internal control provides more assurance about the reliability of evidential matter than an ineffective control structure. AU 329 also indicates that evidential matter obtained from independent sources provides greater assurance of reliability than that secured from solely within the entity, and that the independent auditor's direct personal knowledge is more persuasive than information obtained indirectly. Answer (a) is incorrect because information obtained directly is considered more reliable than that obtained indirectly. Answer (b) is incorrect because evidential matter is normally persuasive rather than convincing. Answer (c) is incorrect because

reliability of evidential matter relates to the competence of evidential matter.

**3.** **(d)** The requirement is to determine the correct statement with respect to the competence of evidential matter. To be competent, evidence must be both valid and relevant. Answer (a) is incorrect because while externally generated evidence is generally considered to provide greater assurance of reliability, there are important exceptions, (e.g., the confirmation is erroneously returned with no exception when one actually exists). Answer (b) is incorrect because while evidence so gathered is typically considered to provide greater assurance concerning reliability, no similar generalization can be made about its relevance. Answer (c) is incorrect because oral representations from management, when corroborated by other forms of evidence, are considered valid evidence.

**4.** **(a)** The requirement is to identify the **least** persuasive type of evidence. Answer (a) is correct because evidence secured solely from within the entity, here prenumbered purchase order forms, is considered less persuasive than evidence obtained from independent sources. Answer (b) is incorrect because a bank statement (even though received from the client) is externally created and therefore more persuasive than evidential matter secured solely from within the entity. Answer (c) is incorrect because evidence obtained directly by the auditor through observation is considered relatively persuasive. Answer (d) is incorrect because correspondence from the client's attorney about litigation is obtained directly from independent sources and is therefore more persuasive than evidential matter secured from within the entity.

**5.   (a)**   The requirement is to identify an area of concern to auditors when evaluating the reasonableness of an entity's accounting estimates. Answer (a) is correct because AU 342 states that in evaluating the reasonableness of estimates auditors normally concentrate on assumptions that are subjective and susceptible to bias. Answer (b) is incorrect because all things being equal, an auditor would expect assumptions that are consistent with prior periods. Answer (c) is incorrect because assumptions that are insensitive to variations in underlying data have little predictive ability. Answer (d) is incorrect because, often, one would expect assumptions similar to industry guidelines.

**A.2.   Types of Evidence**

**6.   (d)**   The requirement is to identify the procedure an auditor would perform first in evaluating management's accounting estimates for reasonableness. Answer (d) is correct because in evaluating reasonableness, the auditor should first obtain an understanding of how management developed the estimate. Answers (a), (b), and (c) are all incorrect because developing independent expectations, considering appropriateness of key factors or assumptions, and testing calculations occur after obtaining the understanding. See AU 342 for information on auditing accounting estimates.

**7.   (d)**   The requirement is to identify a factor that an auditor would concentrate upon when evaluating the reasonableness of an accounting estimate. Answer (d) is correct because AU 342 states that the auditor normally concentrates on key factors and assumptions that are deviations from historical patterns, as well as those that are significant to the accounting estimate, sensitive to variations, and subjective and susceptible to misstatement and bias. Answer (a) is incorrect because deviations from historical patterns, not consistent patterns, are concentrated upon. Answer (b) is incorrect because factors and assumptions that are similar to industry guidelines are often reasonable. Answer (c) is incorrect because subjective factors and assumptions that are susceptible to bias are concentrated upon, not objective ones that are **not** susceptible to bias. See AU 342 for information on the manner in which auditors consider accounting estimates.

**8.   (d)**   The requirement is to identify one of an auditor's objectives when evaluating an entity's accounting estimates. Answer (d) is correct because when evaluating accounting estimates an auditor's objectives are to obtain sufficient competent evidential matter that (1) all material accounting estimates have been developed, (2) those accounting estimates are reasonable, and (3) those accounting estimates are in conformity with GAAP.

**9.   (c)**   The requirement is to determine the proper test for the existence assertion of an asset. Answer (c) is correct because testing **from** accounting records **to** the supporting evidence discloses whether recorded transactions occurred and whether the asset exists. Answer (a) is incorrect because testing for the completeness assertion addresses whether there are unrecorded items. Also, the aggregated nature of the financial statements makes the use of poten-

tially unrecorded items unlikely as a method of identifying unrecorded items. Answer (b) is incorrect because testing potentially unrecorded items to the financial statements addresses the completeness assertion. Answer (d) is incorrect because testing from the supporting evidence to the accounting records addresses the completeness assertion. See the outline of AU 326 for information on the financial statement assertions.

**10.   (a)**   The requirement is to determine which balance remaining in a "suspense" account would be of most concern to an auditor. Answer (a) is correct because suspense debits that management believes will benefit future operations must be audited carefully to determine whether they have value and should be classified as an asset. Answer (b) is incorrect because when an auditor has already determined that a suspense debit has value it becomes a relatively straightforward issue of the item's proper classification. Answer (c) is incorrect because the conservative approach taken in audits is likely to cause the auditor to have somewhat more concern about suspense purported to be assets [i.e., answer (a)], than for those classified as current liabilities. Answer (d) is incorrect because when the auditor determines that the suspense credits represent customer deposits, establishing a proper accounting will ordinarily be relatively simple.

**B.1.a.   Analytical Procedures**

**11.   (b)**   The requirement is to identify the procedure that would **not** be considered an analytical procedure. Analytical procedures consist of evaluations of financial information made by a study of plausible relationships among both financial and nonfinancial data. Answer (b) is correct because projecting an error rate from a statistical sample to an actual population is not a comparison of a plausible relationship. Answers (a), (c), and (d) are all incorrect because they all include a study of plausible relationships.

**12.   (c)**   The requirement is to identify the type of analytical procedure an auditor would most likely use in developing relationships among balance sheet accounts when reviewing the financial statements of a nonpublic entity. Answer (c) is correct because balance sheet accounts may be analyzed through a number of ratios (e.g., current ratio). Answer (a) is incorrect because trend analysis is often more appropriate for income statement analysis. Answer (b) is incorrect because regression analysis, while used in practice, is not used as frequently as is ratio analysis. Answer (d) is incorrect because risk analysis in and of itself is not a type of analytical procedure. See AR 100 for information on reviews of nonpublic entities.

**13.   (a)**   The requirement is to identify how an auditor may achieve audit objectives related to particular assertions. Answer (a) is correct because an auditor may perform analytical procedures to achieve an audit objective related to a particular assertion. Answer (b) is incorrect because a system of quality control provides the CPA firm with reasonable assurance of conforming with professional standards. Answer (c) is incorrect because while working papers provide support for the audit report and aid in the conduct and supervision of the audit, they do not in and of themselves achieve audit objectives (see AU 339 for information on audit working papers). Answer (d) is incorrect because increasing the level of detection risk does not in and of itself achieve audit objectives.

**14. (d)** The requirement is to identify the procedure most likely to detect a fraud involving misstatement of income statements due to the recording of journal entries with unusual combinations of debits and credits to expense and revenue accounts. Answer (d) is correct because an objective of analytical procedures is identification of unusual transactions and events, and amounts, ratios and trends that might indicate misstatements. Answer (a) is incorrect because the limited number of journal entries traced to the general ledger in a sample is unlikely to include the erroneous journal entries. Answer (b) is incorrect because while an evaluation of the effectiveness of internal control might help detect such misstatements, it is somewhat doubtful due to the fact that it is likely that few journal entries are involved. Answer (c) is incorrect because there is no indication that the fraud involves differences between controlling accounts and subsidiary records.

**15. (b)** The requirement is to identify the account that would yield the highest level of evidence through the performance of analytical procedures. As higher levels of assurance are desired from analytical procedures, more predictable relationships are required to develop the auditor's expectation. Relationships involving income statement accounts tend to be more predictable than relationships involving only balance sheet accounts, and relationships involving transactions not subject to management discretion are generally more predictable. Answer (b) is correct because interest expense relates to the income statement, and because interest expense is subject to only limited management discretion, given the existence of the related debt. Answers (a) and (c) are incorrect because accounts receivable and accounts payable are balance sheet accounts. Answer (d) is incorrect because travel and entertainment expense is normally subject to management discretion. See AU 329 for more information on the use of analytical procedures.

**16. (c)** The requirement is to determine what is included when analytical procedures are used in the overall review stage of an audit. Answer (c) is correct because the overall review stage includes reading the financial statements and notes and considering the adequacy of evidence gathered in response to unusual or unexpected balances. Answer (a) is incorrect because analytical procedures are not particularly aimed at gathering evidence on account balances that have not changed. Answer (b) is incorrect because analytical procedures do not directly test control procedures. Answer (d) is incorrect because tests of transactions to corroborate management's financial statement assertions are performed when considering internal control and for substantive tests of transactions. See AU 329 for information on analytical procedures and AU 319 for information on tests of controls performed both when considering internal control and as substantive tests.

**17. (c)** The requirement is to determine the most predictable relationship for purposes of analytical procedures applied as substantive tests. Answer (c) is correct because AU 329 indicates that relationships involving income statement accounts tend to be more predictable than relationships involving only balance sheet accounts. Answer (a) is incorrect because, as indicated, relationships involving income

statements are considered more predictable. Answer (b) is incorrect because relationships involving transactions subject to management discretion are often less predictable. For example, management might incur maintenance expense rather than replace plant and equipment, or they may delay advertising expenditures. Answer (d) is incorrect because prior year data is sometimes not a reliable predictor of subsequent year's data.

**18. (c)** The requirement is to identify a basic premise underlying the application of analytical procedures. Answer (c) is correct because, as indicated in AU 329, a basic premise underlying the application of analytical procedures is that plausible relationships among data may reasonably be expected to exist and continue in the absence of known conditions to the contrary. Answer (a) is incorrect because the study of financial ratios is an approach to identifying unusual fluctuations, not an acceptable alternative to investigating them. Answer (b) is incorrect because analytical procedures may be either statistical or nonstatistical. Answer (d) is incorrect because analytical procedures may be used as substantive tests, and may result in modification of the scope of tests of balances and transactions.

**19. (a)** The requirement is to identify the stages of an audit for which the use of analytical procedures is required. AU 329 requires the use of analytical procedures at both the planning and overall review stages of the audit, but not as a substantive test.

**20. (b)** The requirement is to determine the reply that would facilitate an auditor's analytical procedures. Answer (b) is correct because use of a standard cost system (a form of budgeting) produces variance reports that will allow the auditor to compare the financial information with the standard cost system data to identify unusual fluctuations. See AU 329 for the approach used. Answer (a) is incorrect because segregating obsolete inventory before the inventory count is related to the auditor's physical inventory observation and will not necessarily affect analytical procedures. Answer (c) is incorrect because correcting a material weakness in internal control before the beginning of the audit generally will have minimal, if any, effect on the historical information used for analytical procedures. Answer (d) is incorrect because data from independent sources outside the entity is more likely to be reliable than purely internal sources.

**21. (c)** The requirement is to identify the most likely effect on an audit of having performed analytical procedures in the overall review stage of an audit which suggest that several accounts have unexpected relationships. Answer (c) is correct because when unexpected relationships exist, additional tests of details are generally required to determine whether misstatements exist. Answer (a) is incorrect because irregularities (fraud) may or may not exist. Answer (b) is incorrect because internal control activities may or may not be operating effectively. Answer (d) is incorrect because ordinarily the situation need not be communicated to the audit committee.

**22. (b)** The requirement is to identify the comparison an auditor most likely would make in evaluating an entity's costs and expenses. Answer (b) is correct because payroll expense is an income statement expense and because it may be expected to have a relationship with that of the prior year.

Answer (a) is incorrect because the accounts receivable account is not a cost or expense. Answer (c) is incorrect because comparing budgeted sales with actual sales of the current year is more likely to be performed than comparing budgeted sales with those of prior years. Answer (d) is incorrect because comparing the budgeted current year's warranty expense with the current year's contingent liabilities is less direct than that in answer (b), and because one would be more likely to compare current year budgeted warranty expense with actual warranty expense.

**23.** **(c)** The requirement is to identify the best individual to perform analytical procedures in the overall review stage of an audit. At this stage of an audit the objective of analytical procedures is to assist the auditor in assessing the conclusions reached and in the evaluation of the overall financial statement presentation. Answer (c) is correct because an experienced individual with business and industry knowledge is likely to be able to fulfill this function. Answer (a) is incorrect because a staff accountant who has performed the substantive auditing procedures may not be able to objectively perform the analytical procedure and may not have the necessary experience to perform the function. Answer (b) is incorrect because the managing partner of the office may not be close enough to the audit to perform the function effectively. Answer (d) is incorrect because the individual in charge of quality control and the peer review program should be as independent as possible of the audits he or she is considering. See AU 329 for guidance on analytical procedures.

### B.1.b. Tests of Details of Transactions and Balances

**24.** **(b)** The requirement is to identify the best example of a substantive test. Answer (b) is correct because confirmation of balances of accounts receivable will provide a test of the ending account balance and is therefore a detailed test of a balance, a type of substantive test—see AU 330 for information on the confirmation process. Answers (a) and (c) are incorrect because examining approval of cash disbursements and comparison of signatures on checks to a list of authorized check signers are tests of controls; see AU 319 for information on tests of controls. Answer (d) is incorrect because flowcharting a client's cash receipts system is a method used to document the auditor's understanding of internal control.

**25.** **(c)** The requirement is to identify the objective of tests of details of transactions performed as substantive tests. Answer (c) is correct because AU 319 states that the objective of tests of details of transactions performed as substantive tests is to detect material misstatements in the financial statements. Answer (a) is incorrect because while performing tests of details of transactions as substantive tests complies with generally accepted auditing standards, this is not their objective. Answers (b) and (d) are incorrect because neither attaining assurance about the reliability of the accounting system nor the evaluation of the operating effectiveness of management's policies and procedures are the objective of tests of details of transactions performed as substantive tests.

**26.** **(c)** The requirement is to find the statement which describes substantive audit tests. Answer (c) is correct because substantive tests are defined as tests of transactions, direct tests of financial balances, or analytical procedures.

Answer (a) is incorrect because substantive tests may not be eliminated due to the limitations of internal control. Answer (b) is incorrect since substantive tests primarily directly test ending financial statement balances, not subsequent events. Answer (d) is incorrect because substantive tests **decrease** with increased reliance on internal control. See outlines of AU 312 and 319 for a discussion of the various interrelationships among audit tests.

**27.** **(c)** The requirement is to determine the account for which the auditor is most likely to perform extensive tests for possible understatement. An analysis of past audits, in which existing financial statement errors were not discovered prior to the issuance of the financial statements, reveals that the great majority of the errors resulted in overstated profits. Therefore, the risk to a CPA is that the client is overstating profits. Answer (c) is correct because it is the only item whose understatement results in overstated profits. Answers (a), (b), and (d) are incorrect because understatement of these items would result in understated profits.

### B.2. Preparing Substantive Test Audit Programs

**28.** **(d)** The requirement is to determine the most likely approach for auditing the statement of cash flows. Answer (d) is correct because the statement of cash flows includes accounts considered during the audit of the balance sheet and income statements and, accordingly, the most frequent approach is to reconcile amounts. Answers (a), (b), and (c) are all incorrect because they suggest approaches not typically followed when auditing the statement of cash flows.

**29.** **(c)** The requirement is to determine the direction of audit testing to determine whether transactions have been recorded. Answer (c) is correct because to determine whether transactions have been recorded the auditor will test **from** the original source documents **to** the recorded entries. Answers (a), (b), and (d) are incorrect because when testing from the general ledger, the adjusted trial balance, or from general journal entries the auditor is dealing with the entries that have been recorded, not whether all transactions have been recorded.

### B.3. Documentation

**30.** **(b)** The requirement is to identify the correct statement concerning the deletion of audit documentation. Answer (b) is correct because after the audit file has been completed (ordinarily 60 days or less after the issuance of the audit report), no portions of audit documentation should be deleted. Answer (a) is incorrect because after completion of the audit file no documentation should be deleted or discarded. Answer (c) is incorrect because professional skepticism is not the basis for determining deletions. Answer (d) is incorrect because prior to the file completion date most superseded documentation may be deleted (an exception is that information that reflects a disparate point of view should be retained).

**31.** **(a)** The requirement is to determine how long audit documentation must be retained. Answer (a) is correct because SAS 103 requires that they be maintained a minimum of five years. Answers (b), (c) and (d) all present other, incorrect time periods.

**32.    (a)**    The requirement is to identify the most likely pair of accounts to be analyzed on the same working paper. Answer (a) is correct because an auditor will often consider interest income with notes receivable because the interest is earned on those notes and therefore closely related. Answer (b) is incorrect because interest receivable relates to an asset account (notes receivable) while accrued interest payable relates to a liability account (notes payable) and accordingly one would expect separate working papers. Answer (c) is incorrect because notes payable and receivable are entirely separate accounts. Answer (d) is incorrect because interest income relates to interest-bearing securities while interest expense relates to debt accounts.

**33.    (a)**    The requirement is to identify a primary purpose of an auditor's working papers. SAS 103 states that working papers serve mainly to provide the principal support for the auditor's report and to aid the auditor in the conduct and supervision of the audit.

**34.    (c)**    The requirement is to identify the **least** likely item to be included in the permanent file of an auditor's working papers. Answer (c) is correct because permanent files include information affecting a number of years' audits, and the working trial balance relates most directly to the current and, to a limited extent, the subsequent year's audit. Answers (a), (b), and (d) are all incorrect because bond indenture agreements, lease agreements, and a flowchart of internal control affect more years' audits than does a specific year's working trial balance.

**35.    (c)**    The requirement is to determine a difference between an auditor's working trial balance and financial statements without footnotes. Answer (c) is correct because a working trial balance includes columns for reclassification and adjustments. Answers (a), (b), and (d) are all incorrect because while they suggest information that might be included on a working trial balance, they will not be included in the form of additional columns.

**36.    (d)**    SAS 103 states that the degree of documentation for a particular audit area should be affected by (1) the risk of material misstatement, (2) extent of judgment, (3) nature of the auditing procedures, (4) significance of the evidence obtained, (5) nature and extent of the exceptions identified, and (6) the need to document a conclusion that is not obvious from the documentation of the work.

**37.    (b)**    The requirement is to identify the required documentation in an audit. Answer (b) is correct because AU 311 requires a written audit program setting forth in detail the procedure necessary to accomplish the engagement's objectives. Answer (a) is incorrect because while flowcharts and narratives are acceptable methods of documenting an auditor's understanding of internal control, they are not required. Answer (c) is incorrect because a planning memorandum is not required. Answer (d) is incorrect because completion of an internal control questionnaire is not required.

**38.    (a)**    The requirement is to identify a factor that would most likely affect the auditor's judgment about the quantity, type, and content of the working papers. Answer (a) is correct because the Professional Standards state that the assessed level of control risk will affect the quantity, type and content of working papers. SAS 103 provides a listing of this and other factors. For example, the quantity, type and content of working papers will be affected by whether tests of controls have been performed.

**39.    (d)**    The requirement is to identify the type of audit working paper that reflects the major components of an amount reported in the financial statements. Answer (d) is correct because lead schedules aggregate the major components to be reported in the financial statements. Answer (a) is incorrect because an interbank transfer schedule summarizes transfers between banks among accounts. Answer (b) is incorrect because the term "carryforward schedule" is not frequently used. Answer (c) is incorrect because supporting schedules present the details supporting the information on a lead schedule. For example, a detailed bank reconciliation for a cash account might serve as a supporting schedule for an account on the cash lead schedule.

**40.    (c)**    The requirement is to identify the documentation that is required for an audit in accordance with generally accepted auditing standards. Answer (c) is correct because SAS 103 requires that the working papers show that the accounting records agree or reconcile with the financial statements. Answer (a) is incorrect because neither a flowchart nor an internal control questionnaire is required. Answer (b) is incorrect because the *Professional Standards* do not require the use of an engagement letter. Answer (d) is incorrect because when control risk is assessed at the maximum level, the auditor's understanding of internal control needs to be documented, but the basis for the conclusion that it is at the maximum level need not be documented.

**41.    (b)**    The requirement is to identify the point at which no deletions of audit documentation are allowed. Answer (b) is correct because PCAOB Standard 3 indicates that audit documentation may not be deleted after the documentation completion date (not more than 45 days after the report release date). Answer (a) is incorrect because documentation may be deleted between the client's year-end date and the documentation completion date. Answer (c) is incorrect because the last date of significant fieldwork is prior to the documentation completion date. Answer (d) is incorrect because the report release date is up to 45 days prior to the documentation completion date.

**42.    (b)**    The requirement is to determine the type of auditor that should be able to understand audit documentation of the nature, timing, extent, and results of audit procedures performed. Answer (b) is correct because PCAOB Standard 3 requires that audit documentation be understandable to an experienced auditor having no prior connection with the engagement. Answer (a) is incorrect because the requirement is not limited to audit team members. Answer (c) is incorrect because the requirement is more limited than to any certified public accountant. Answer (d) is incorrect both because there is no certification of a peer review specialist and because this is not a requirement.

**43.    (c)**    The requirement is to identify the period for which audit documentation should be retained for public company audits. Answer (c) is correct because PCAOB Standard 3 requires that audit documentation be retained for the longer of seven years or the period required by law. Answer (a) is incorrect both because of the seven-year requirement, and because it is the longer of seven years or the period required by law. Answer (b) is incorrect because while seven years is the general requirement, a longer period may be required by law. Answer (d) is incorrect because audit documentation need not be retained indefinitely.

### C.1. Evidence—Cash

**44. (b)** The requirement is to identify the information that an auditor usually confirms on one form. Answer (b) is correct because the standard form to confirm account balance information with financial institution requests information on both the cash in bank and collateral for loans. Answers (a), (c), and (d) are all incorrect because they suggest pairs of information that are not usually confirmed on one form.

**45. (d)** The requirement is to determine a reason that the usefulness of the standard bank confirmation request may be limited. Answer (d) is correct because the bank employee who completes the form often will not have access to all the financial relationships that the bank has with the client. Answer (a) is incorrect because bank employees who complete the form realize that they may verify confidential information with the auditor. Answer (b) is incorrect because while it is correct that the employee who completes the confirmation form will not generally inspect the accuracy of the bank reconciliation, this does not limit the confirmation's usefulness. Answer (c) is incorrect because the employee who completes the form does not need to have access to the client's cutoff bank statement to complete the confirmation.

**46. (b)** The requirement is to determine the type of evidence that is likely to result in an auditor limiting substantive audit tests of sales transactions when control risk is assessed as low for the existence or occurrence assertion for sales. Answer (b) is correct because an auditor may analyze the completeness of sales using cash receipts and accounts receivable (for example, an auditor may add year-end receivables to cash receipts and subtract beginning receivables to obtain an estimate of sales). Answer (a) is incorrect because the opening and closing inventory balances will only provide indirect evidence on sales through calculation of the cost of goods sold. Answer (c) is incorrect because while shipping as of year-end will help assure an accurate cutoff of sales, the receiving activity has no necessary relationship to the sales figure. Answer (d) is incorrect because while the cutoff of sales will provide evidence on the completeness of sales, the purchases portion of the reply is not appropriate.

**47. (b)** The requirement is to determine the two checks that might indicate kiting, a form of fraud that overstates cash by simultaneously including it in two or more bank accounts. Answer (b) is correct because checks #202 and #404 include cash in two accounts at year-end. The cash represented by check #202 is included in both State Bank and County Bank cash as of December 31. This is because its receipt is recorded prior to year-end, but its disbursement is recorded after year-end. (For the cash receipts journal to remain in balance prior to year-end, some account must have been credited on December 30 to offset the debit to cash.) Check #404 also represents a situation in which the cash is included in two accounts as of year-end; the check may represent a situation in which a shortage in the account is concealed through deposit of the check that is not recorded on the books at year-end. Check #101 does not result in a misstatement of cash since the books recorded both the debit and credit portions of the entry before year-end,

while both banks recorded them after year-end. Check #303 represents a situation in which funds are disbursed on the Federal account as of year-end, but not received into the American account (per bank or per books) until after year-end; check #303 accordingly understates cash and the nature of the debit for the entry on December 31 is unknown. Answer (a) is incorrect because neither check #101 nor #303 overstates cash. Answer (c) is incorrect because check #101 does not overstate cash. Answer (d) is incorrect because check #303 understates cash.

**48. (b)** The requirement is to determine the checks which represent deposits in transit at December 31, 2001. Deposits in transit are those that have been sent to the bank prior to year-end, but have not been received by the bank as of year-end. Answer (b) is correct because both check #101 and check #303 have been disbursed per books as of year-end, but have not yet been received by the bank as of December 31. Checks #202 and #404 have been received by the bank as of year-end and accordingly are not in transit. Answer (a) is incorrect because check #202 has been received before year-end. Answer (c) is incorrect because both checks #202 and #404 have been received before year-end. Answer (d) is incorrect because check #404 has been received before year-end.

**49. (c)** The requirement is to identify why auditors trace bank transfers for the last part of the audit period and the first part of the subsequent period. Answer (c) is correct because auditors use a bank transfer schedule to analyze transfers so as to detect kiting that overstates cash balances. Answers (a) and (b) are incorrect because the process of analyzing transfers is not an efficient way to determine whether the cash receipts journal was held open or when the year's final checks were mailed. Auditors use a bank cutoff statement rather than a bank transfer schedule to help detect these situations. Answer (d) is incorrect because the process of analyzing transfers is unlikely to identify any unusual payments or receipts from related parties.

**50. (d)** The requirement is to determine the source of evidence which does **not** contain information on the balance per bank in a bank reconciliation. Answer (d) is correct because the general ledger contains only the client's cash balance, not the balance per bank. Answer (a) is incorrect because the beginning balance on a cutoff statement represents the year-end bank balance. Answer (b) is incorrect because the primary purpose of a year-end bank statement is to present information on the balance per bank. Answer (c) is incorrect because the first question on a standard bank confirmation form requests information on the year-end balance per bank.

**51. (b)** The requirement is to identify the cash transfer which will result in a misstatement of year-end cash. Answer (b) is correct because the receipt is recorded on the books prior to year-end, while the disbursement is recorded subsequent to year-end. Therefore, the cash on the books is overstated. Answers (a), (c), and (d) are incorrect because they do not reveal a cutoff error. Answer (a) is incorrect because both the disbursement and receipt are recorded on the books prior to year-end; note that one would expect to see an outstanding check on the disbursing bank reconciliation as of year-end. Answer (c) is incorrect because both the disbursement and receipt are recorded on the books prior to year-end; one would expect the disbursing bank reconciliation to show an outstanding check and the receiving bank to show a deposit in transit as of year-end. Answer (d) is incorrect because the entire transaction is recorded after year-end.

**52. (c)** The requirement is to determine an approach for detecting the concealing of a cash shortage by transporting funds from one location to another or by converting negotiable assets to cash. Answer (c) is correct because the timing of the performance of auditing procedures involves the proper synchronizing of their application and thus comprehends the possible need for simultaneous examination of, for example, cash on hand and in banks, securities owned, bank loans, and other related items.

**53. (b)** The requirement is to identify the primary purpose of sending a standard confirmation request to financial institutions with which the client has done business during the year. Answer (b) is correct because CPAs generally provide the account information on the form and ask for balance corroboration. The form explicitly states that the CPAs do not request, nor expect, the financial institution to conduct a comprehensive, detailed, search of its records for other accounts. Answer (a) is incorrect because a standard confirmation request will not detect kiting, a manipulation causing an amount of cash to be included simultaneously in the balance of two or more bank accounts. Answer (c) is incorrect because bank statements available from the client allow the CPA to prepare a proof of cash. Answer (d) is incorrect because the standard form does not request information about contingent liabilities and secured transactions.

**54. (c)** The requirement is to determine the assertion (or assertions) being tested by a test of a control in which an auditor observes the mailing of monthly statements to a client's customers and reviews evidence of follow-up on errors reported by the customers. Answer (c) is correct because observing the mailing of monthly statements and follow-up of errors will provide evidence to the auditor as to whether the receivables **exist** at a given date; the tests do not directly address the presentation and disclosure assertion since little evidence is obtained about whether financial statement components are properly classified, described and disclosed. See AU 326 for a discussion of the various financial statement assertions. Answer (a) is incorrect because the presentation and disclosure assertion is not addressed. Answer (b) is incorrect because the presentation and disclosure assertion is not addressed and because the existence or occurrence assertion is addressed. Answer (d) is incorrect because the existence or occurrence assertion is addressed.

**55. (b)** The requirement is to determine the most likely audit step summarized by the tick mark placed under "date disbursed per bank." Answer (b) is correct because the checks were written in December but cleared in January and should therefore be listed as outstanding on the year-end outstanding check list of the applicable bank reconciliation. Answer (a) is incorrect because the tick marks are beside the date per bank, and not per books. Answer (c) is incorrect because the December cash disbursements journal, and not the January cash disbursements journal, will include these disbursements. Answer (d) is incorrect because the year-end bank confirmations do not include information on outstanding checks.

**56. (a)** The requirement is to determine the most likely audit step summarized by the tick mark placed under "date deposited per bank." Answer (a) is correct because deposits recorded on the books as of 12/31 should be included as deposits in transit on the applicable bank reconciliation. Answer (b) is incorrect because the tick mark is placed beside the "bank" column, and not the books column. Answer (c) is incorrect because the December cash receipts journal, and not the January cash receipts journal should include the deposit. Answer (d) is incorrect because the year-end bank confirmations will not include deposits in transit.

**C.2. Evidence—Receivables**

**57. (a)** The requirement is to identify the correct statement concerning the use of negative confirmation requests. Answer (a) is correct because AU 330 states that unreturned negative confirmation requests rarely provide significant evidence concerning financial statements assertions other than certain aspects of the existence assertion. Answer (b) is incorrect because positive, not negative, confirmation requests are normally used when a low level of detection risk is to be achieved. Answer (c) is incorrect because alternative procedures are not generally performed on unreturned negative confirmation requests since it is assumed that the respondent did not reply because of agreement with the balance on the confirmation request. Answer (d) is incorrect because respondents may not reply when misstatements are in their favor. See AU 330 for information on the confirmation process.

**58. (c)** The requirement is to identify the most likely action taken by an auditor when no reply is received to positive confirmation requests. Answer (c) is correct because asking the client to contact customers to ask that confirmation requests be returned may increase response rates. Answer (a) is incorrect because the lack of a reply to a confirmation request does not necessarily indicate that the account needs to be written off. Answer (b) is incorrect because accounts receivable confirmations deal more directly with existence than with valuation or completeness and because alternative procedures may provide the auditor with the desired assurance with respect to the nonrespondents. Answer (d) is incorrect because the assessed level of inherent risk will not normally be modified due to confirmation results. See AU 330 for information on the confirmation process.

**59. (b)** The requirement is to determine the best sampling unit for confirmation of accounts receivable when many differences between the recorded account balances and the confirmation replies have occurred in the past. Answer (b) is correct because the misstatements may have occurred because respondents are not readily able to confirm account balances. AU 330 suggests that in such circumstances certain respondents' accounting systems may facilitate the confirmation of single transactions (individual invoices) rather than of entire account balances.

**60. (c)** The requirement is to identify the assertion most directly addressed by accounts receivable confirmations. Section 326 presents information on financial statement assertions. Answer (c) is correct because a confirmation addresses whether the entity replying to the confirmation believes that a debt exists. Answer (a) is incorrect because while confirmations provide limited information on valuation, they do not directly address whether the entity replying will pay the debt (or whether the account has been factored). Answer (b) is incorrect because limited classification information is received via confirmations. Answer (d) is incorrect because confirmations are generally sent to recorded receivables, and are of limited assistance in the determination of whether all accounts are recorded (completeness).

**61.** **(a)** The requirement is to determine when alternative procedures should be performed in order to substantiate the existence of accounts receivable. Answer (a) is correct because the auditor should employ alternative procedures for nonresponses to positive confirmations to satisfy himself/herself as to the existence of accounts receivable. Those procedures may include examination of evidence of subsequent cash receipts, cash remittance advices, sales and shipping documents, and other records. Answer (b) is incorrect because with negative confirmations the debtor is asked to respond only if s/he disagrees with the information on the confirmation; thus, no reply is assumed to indicate agreement. Answers (c) and (d) are incorrect because while **additional** procedures may be required when collectibility is questionable, **alternative** procedures are those used in lieu of confirmation.

**62.** **(d)** The requirement is to identify the most likely alternate procedure when replies have not been received to either first or second accounts receivable confirmation requests. Answer (d) is correct because the inspection of shipping records will provide evidence that the merchandise was actually shipped to the debtor. Answer (a) is incorrect because, a review of the cash receipts journal **prior** to year-end is unlikely to provide evidence on account recorded as unpaid as of year-end. Also, the procedure would only detect one specific type of misstatement, that in which payments were recorded in the cash receipts journal, but not credited to the customers' accounts. Answer (b) is incorrect because the lack of a reply to the confirmation provides no particular evidence that the scope of procedures related to internal control should be modified. Answer (c) is incorrect because the lack of a reply need not necessarily lead to a presumption that the account is misstated. See AU 330 for procedures typically performed for year-end accounts receivable confirmation requests for which no reply is received.

**63.** **(d)** The requirement is to identify the circumstances in which use of the negative form of accounts receivable confirmation most likely would be justified. Negative confirmations are used when (1) the combined assessed level of inherent and control risk is low, (2) a large number of small balances is involved, and (3) the auditor has no reason to believe that the recipients of the requests are unlikely to give them consideration. Positive confirmations are used when those conditions are not met as well as in other circumstances in which it seems desirable to request a positive response, such as when accounts are in dispute. Answer (d) is best because small balances are involved and few accounts are in dispute. Answer (a) is incorrect because it refers to a substantial number of accounts in dispute and sales are to a few major customers. Answer (b) is incorrect because it refers to a substantial number of accounts in dispute. Answer (c) is incorrect because it refers to sales to a few major customers.

**64.** **(a)** The requirement is to identify a method to reduce the risk associated with accepting e-mail responses to accounts receivable confirmation requests. Answer (a) is correct because a response by mail will confirm the e-mail response. Answer (b) is incorrect because while such subsequent cash receipts will ordinarily be examined, this represents an alternative, complementary approach to confirmation. Answer (c) is incorrect because the auditor need not consider e-mail responses to be confirmations with exception. Answer (d) is incorrect because a second request is more likely to elicit either no response or another e-mail response. See AU 330 for information on the confirmation process.

**65.** **(b)** The requirement is to determine the most likely procedure to reduce the risks associated with accepting fax responses to requests for confirmations of accounts receivable. Answer (b) is correct because verification of the sources and contents through telephone calls will address whether the information on the fax (which may have been sent from almost anywhere) is correct. Answer (a) is incorrect because an examination of the shipping documents is less complete than is verification of the entire balance. Answer (c) is incorrect because such faxes need not be treated as nonresponses. Answer (d) is incorrect because inspection of the faxes is unlikely to reveal forgeries or alterations, even when such circumstances have occurred.

**66.** **(d)** The requirement is to identify the circumstance in which the negative form of confirmation request most likely would be used. Answer (d) is correct because AU 330 states that negative confirmations may be used when (1) the combined assessed level of inherent and control risk is low [answer (d)], (2) a large number of small balances is involved, and (3) the auditor has no reason to believe that the recipients of the requests are unlikely to give them consideration. Answer (a) is incorrect because when the accounts receivable are immaterial, a decision may be made to send no confirmations. Answer (b) is incorrect because an inadequate rate is not an acceptable reason to send negative confirmations. Answer (c) is incorrect because negative confirmations are only of value when the auditor has no reason to believe that the recipients of the requests are unlikely to give them consideration.

**67.** **(a)** The requirement is to identify the circumstance in which an auditor would use the blank form of confirmations (one which includes no amount and asks the respondent to supply the amount due) rather than positive confirmations. Answer (a) is correct because if a recipient simply signs a blank confirmation and returns it the confirmation will have no amount on it and the auditor will know that additional procedures are necessary. Answers (b) and (c) are incorrect because there is no necessary relationship between the use of blank confirmations and subsequent cash receipt verification difficulty and analytical procedures results. Answer (d) is incorrect because when the combined assessed level of inherent risk and control risk is low it is unlikely to lead to the blank form of confirmation. In fact, when that risk is low, and when adequate other substantive tests of details, no confirmation may be necessary. See AU 334 for information on the confirmation process.

**68.** **(d)** The requirement is to identify the most likely information that would be included in a client's confirmation letter that is being used to confirm accounts receivable balances rather than individual invoices. Answer (d) is correct since including details of the account is likely to make it easier for the customer to respond in a meaningful manner. Answer (a) is incorrect because no such auditor-prepared letter will be included and because only in the case of the negative form of confirmation does a nonresponse lead to an inference that the account balance is correct. Answer (b) is incorrect because confirmation requests do not ordinarily include a letter suggesting that a second request will be sent. Answer (c) is incorrect because the auditor does not enclose a letter requesting that the information be supplied. See AU 330 for information on the confirmation process.

**69.** **(c)** The requirement is to identify a statement that an auditor would be most likely to add to the negative form of confirmation of accounts receivable to encourage a timely consideration by the recipient. Answer (c) is correct because providing such information might increase timely consideration in that the recipient may realize the importance of a reply when the information is incorrect. Answers (a) and (b) are incorrect because while a confirmation request may include these statements, the statements are unlikely to encourage timely consideration of the request. Answer (d) is incorrect because many accounts that are not overdue are sampled, and because even for those overdue such a statement is not ordinarily included with the confirmation request.

**70.** **(a)** The requirement is to identify the strategy most likely to improve the response rate for confirmation of accounts receivable. Answer (a) is correct because including a list of items or invoices that constitute the account balance makes it easier for the potential respondent to reply. Answer (b) is incorrect because customers with relatively large balances may or may not be more likely to reply. Answers (c) and (d) are incorrect because there is no research available indicating that requesting a fax or e-mail reply, or threatening a second request is likely to improve response rate.

**C.3. Evidence—Inventory**

**71.** **(a)** The requirement is to determine the financial statement most directly related to the procedure of making inquiries concerning possible obsolete or slow-moving inventory. Answer (a) is correct because inquiries concerning possible obsolete or slow-moving inventory deal with whether the inventory is being carried at the proper value and this is most directly related to the valuation assertion. The other assertions are less directly related. Answer (b) is incorrect because the rights and obligations assertion deals with whether assets are the rights of the entity and liabilities are the obligations of the entity at a given date. Answer (c) is incorrect because the existence or occurrence assertion deals with whether assets or liabilities exist at a given date and whether recorded transactions have occurred during a given period. Answer (d) is incorrect because the presentation and disclosure assertion deals with whether particular components of the financial statements are properly classified, described, and disclosed. See AU 326 for information on the financial statement assertions.

**72.** **(d)** The requirement is to identify the type of omitted journal entry that would result in inventory test counts that are higher than the recorded quantities in the client's perpetual records. Answer (d) is correct because a failure to

record sales returns results in a situation in which the item is returned by a customer and included in the inventory count, but not recorded in the perpetual records; accordingly the test counts are higher than the recorded quantities. Answer (a) is incorrect because purchase discounts do not affect quantities in inventory. Answers (b) and (c) are incorrect because a failure to record purchase returns or sales result in a situation in which less inventory will be counted (since the items are no longer physically in inventory) than is recorded on the perpetual records.

**73.** **(c)** The requirement is to identify a procedure that will provide assurance that all inventory items in a client's inventory listing schedule are valid. Answer (c) is correct because tracing **from** the inventory listing schedule **to** inventory tags and **to** the auditor's recorded count sheets will provide assurance that the listed items actually exist. Answer (a) is incorrect because tracing from inventory tags to items in the inventory listing schedule tests the completeness of the inventory listing sheet, not whether all of the items it lists are valid. Answer (b) is incorrect because it does not directly test the client's inventory listing schedule. Answer (d) is incorrect because tracing items listed in receiving reports and vendors' invoices to the inventory listing schedule will provide assurance on the completeness of the inventory listing sheet; it will also be a difficult procedure to accomplish due to the fact that a number of these items will not be in inventory due to sales. See AU 326 for information on the testing of the various financial statement assertions.

**74.** **(b)** The requirement is to identify the factor that average inventory is divided into to calculate inventory turnover. Answer (b) is correct because the average inventory is divided into the cost of goods sold to calculate the inventory turnover.

**75.** **(a)** The requirement is to identify the auditing procedure that most likely would provide assurance about a manufacturing entity's inventory valuation. Answer (a) is correct because testing the overhead computation will provide evidence on whether inventory has been included in the financial statements at the appropriate amount. Answer (b) is incorrect because obtaining confirmation of inventories pledged under loan agreements relates more directly to the presentation assertion. Answers (c) and (d) are incorrect because reviewing shipping and receiving cutoff procedures for inventories and tracing test counts to the inventory listing relate more directly to the existence and completeness assertions.

**76.** **(b)** The requirement is to identify an action that an auditor might take when the assessed level of control risk is high for inventory. Answer (b) is correct because a high level of control risk will generally result in a low acceptable level of detection risk, which may be achieved by changing the timing of substantive tests to year-end, changing the nature of substantive tests to more effective procedures, and/or by changing the extent of substantive tests. Answer (a) is incorrect because control risk has been assessed and tests of controls, if any, will already have been completed. Answer (c) is incorrect because a year-end count of inventory is more appropriate when control risk is high. Answer (d) is incorrect because gross profit tests will generally provide less assurance than is required in circumstances such as this when control risk is assessed at a high level.

**77.    (a)**    The requirement is to identify the financial statement assertion (other than presentation and disclosure) most directly related to an auditor's conclusion that no excessive costs for idle plant were charged to inventory. Answer (a) is correct because the valuation or allocation assertion deals with whether the inventory has been included in the financial statements at the appropriate amount, and therefore that no excessive costs were charged to inventory. Answer (b) is incorrect because the completeness assertion deals with whether all inventory items that should be presented are so included. Answer (c) is incorrect because existence or occurrence deals with whether the inventory actually exits at the given date. Answer (d) is incorrect because rights and obligations deal with whether the inventory is owned by the client. For more information on management's financial statement assertions, see AU 326.

**78.    (b)**    The requirement is to identify the financial statement assertion most directly related to an auditor's tracing of inventory test counts to the client's inventory listing. Answer (b) is correct because the completeness assertion deals with whether all transactions are included. Tracing from the inventory items observed to the inventory listing will help determine whether all the transactions are included and the inventory listing is complete. Answer (a) is incorrect because the rights and obligations assertion deals with whether assets are the rights of the entity and this is not being tested when an auditor traces test counts to an inventory listing. Answer (c) is incorrect because existence or occurrence deals with whether the inventory existed at the date of the count. To test existence the auditor would sample from the inventory listing and compare quantities to the test counts. Answer (d) is incorrect because valuation deals with whether the inventory is properly included in the balance sheet at the appropriate dollar amount and this is not being tested here. See AU 326 for more information on management's financial statement assertions.

**79.    (d)**    The requirement is to determine the assertion most directly related to an auditor's analysis of inventory turnover rates. Answer (d) is correct because an analysis of inventory turnover rates will provide the auditor with evidence on slow-moving, excess, defective, and obsolete items included in inventories. These items may be improperly valued.

**80.    (a)**    The requirement is to determine which types of entries will be supported when the auditor examines receiving reports. Answer (a) is correct because receiving reports will be prepared when goods are received through purchase (as recorded in the voucher register) and when goods are received through sales returns (as recorded in the sales returns journal). Answers (b), (c), and (d) are incorrect because entries in sales journals result in items being shipped, not received. Note, however, that answers (b), (c), and (d) are partially correct because the sales returns journal, voucher register, and check register all result from transactions related to the receipt of goods.

**81.    (c)**    The requirement is to identify the response which does **not** represent one of the independent auditor's objectives regarding the examination of inventory. Answer (c) is correct because verifying that all inventory owned by the client is on hand at the time of the count is not an objective. For example, purchased items in transit at year-end, for which title has passed, should be included in

inventory. Similarly, inventory out on consignment should also be included in inventory. Answer (a) is incorrect because proper presentation of inventory pertains to the presentation and disclosure assertion and therefore would be subject to auditor verification. Answers (b) and (d) are incorrect because proper accounting for damaged and obsolete items and proper inventory pricing pertain to the valuation assertion and therefore would be subject to auditor verification. See AU 326 for details on financial statement assertions.

**C.4.   Evidence—Investment Securities**

**82.    (c)**    The requirement is to determine why an auditor should insist that a client representative be present when he or she physically examines securities. Answer (c) is correct because requiring that a client representative acknowledge the receipt of the securities will eliminate any question concerning the CPA's responsibility for any subsequent misplacement or misappropriation of the securities. Answer (a) is incorrect because the client's representative will not in general help the CPA to detect fraudulent securities. Answers (b) and (d) are incorrect because while the client's representative will help the CPA to gain access to the securities and may coordinate their return, these are not the auditor's primary purpose.

**83.    (c)**    The requirement is to identify the best procedure other than inspection to establish the existence and ownership of a long-term investment in a publicly traded stock. Answer (c) is correct because confirmation of the number of shares owned that are held by an independent custodian is effective at testing existence. Answer (a) is incorrect because auditors do not in general correspond with the investee company and because that company may or may not have detailed information on the identity of shareholders at any point in time. Answer (b) is incorrect because while inspection of the audited financial statements of the investee company may provide limited information on valuation of the investment, it does not directly address existence; note that this procedure is of limited use here since the stock is publicly traded and obtaining its value through stock price quotations should not be difficult. Answer (d) is incorrect because this procedure addresses the valuation of the securities. In addition, under SFAS 115, investments are no longer carried at the lower of cost or market. See AU 326 for more information on management's financial statement assertions.

**84.    (c)**    The requirement is to determine the best procedure when an auditor has been unable to inspect and count a client's investment securities (held in a safe-deposit box) until after the balance sheet date. Answer (c) is correct because banks maintain records on access to safe-deposit boxes. Thus, the confirmation of no access during the period will provide the auditor with evidence that the securities in the safe-deposit box at the time of the count were those available at year-end. Answers (a) and (b) are incorrect because the bank will not generally be able to provide a list of securities added and removed from the box (typically, only records on access are maintained by the bank). Therefore, the bank will have no information on reconciling items between the subsidiary ledger and the securities on hand. Answer (d) is incorrect because it is the responsibility of the auditor and the client, not the bank, to count the securities maintained in a safe-deposit box.

**85.** **(a)** The requirement is to determine the most likely use of analytical procedures when testing long-term investments. Answer (a) is correct because the predictable relationship between long-term investments and investment income creates a situation in which analytical procedures may provide substantial audit assurance. Answer (b) is incorrect because the classification between current and noncurrent portfolios may be expected to fluctuate in an unpredictable manner as investment goals and the environment change. Answers (c) and (d) are incorrect because the valuation of marketable equity securities at the lower of cost or market and unrealized gains or losses do not result in a predictable relationship on which analytical procedures may provide effective results.

**C.5. Evidence—Property, Plant, and Equipment**

**86.** **(d)** The requirement is to identify the account whose analysis is **least** likely to reveal evidence relating to **recorded** retirements of equipment. Answer (d) is correct because the purchase returns and allowances account deals with returns and allowances for purchases of merchandise, not equipment. Answer (a) is incorrect because analysis of accumulated depreciation will reveal the retirement through charges made to the accumulated depreciation account. Answer (b) is incorrect because companies will ordinarily modify insurance coverage when assets are retired. Answer (c) is incorrect because the property, plant, and equipment account will reflect the retirement.

**87.** **(b)** The requirement is to identify a likely explanation for a situation in which significant debits have been posted to the accumulated depreciation expense. Answer (b) is correct because debits to accumulated depreciation are properly recorded upon retirement of a plant asset. Answer (a) is incorrect because changing the useful lives of plant assets does not affect accumulated depreciation. Answer (c) is incorrect because understatement of the prior year's depreciation expense does not result in an adjustment to accumulated depreciation. Answer (d) is incorrect because overhead allocations do not ordinarily affect accumulated depreciation.

**88.** **(a)** The requirement is to identify the best procedure for testing unrecorded retirements of equipment. Answer (a) is correct because selecting items from the accounting records and attempting to locate them will reveal unrecorded retirements when the item cannot be located. Answer (b) is incorrect because depreciation entries will continue when retirements have not been recorded. Answer (c) is incorrect because the direction of the test is incorrect since beginning with the item is unlikely to reveal a situation in which an unrecorded retirement has occurred. Answer (d) is incorrect because scanning the general journal for **recorded** entries is unlikely to reveal **unrecorded** retirements of equipment.

**89.** **(d)** The requirement is to determine why an auditor analyzes repairs and maintenance accounts. Answer (d) is correct because clients often erroneously charge expenditures for property and equipment acquisitions as expenses rather than capitalize them as assets. An analysis of repairs and maintenance accounts will reveal such errors. Answer (a) is incorrect because while auditors will want to determine that noncapitalizable expenses for repairs and maintenance have been recorded in the proper period, analyzing only the recorded entries is an incomplete test since

entries occurring after year-end will also need to be examined. Answer (b) is incorrect because procedures relating to the property and equipment account will be performed to determine whether such entries have been recorded in the proper period. Answer (c) is incorrect because analyzing the repairs and maintenance accounts only considers recorded entries and not whether all noncapitalizable expenditures for repairs and maintenance have been properly charged to expense.

**90.** **(c)** The requirement is to determine the information an auditor is most likely to seek from the plant manager. The plant manager comes into day-to-day contact with the machinery when producing a product; that contact is likely to provide information on its condition and usefulness. Answers (a) and (d) are incorrect because the plant manager will generally not have detailed knowledge as to the adequacy of the provision for uncollectible accounts or the amount of insurance which is desirable. Answer (b) is incorrect because the plant manager will have limited knowledge concerning physical inventory observation procedures and their appropriateness.

**91.** **(a)** The requirement is to identify the document least likely to provide evidence regarding mortgage acquisition costs. Deeds generally consist of a legal conveyance of rights to use real property. Frequently the sales price is not even specified and the related mortgage acquisition costs are much less likely to be stated in a deed. Answer (b) is incorrect because cancelled checks would provide verification of mortgage acquisition costs. Answer (c) is incorrect because the closing statement would provide a detailed listing of the costs of acquiring the real property, including possible mortgage acquisition costs. Answer (d) is incorrect because examination of interest expense would also relate to the mortgage acquisition costs.

**92.** **(b)** The requirement is to determine the assertion(s) involved when an auditor is inspecting new additions on a list of property, plant, and equipment. Answer (b) is correct because an auditor who inspects new additions relating to property and equipment balances addresses existence or occurrence, but not presentation and disclosure; presentation and disclosure relates more directly to proper classification and note disclosures rather than account balances.

**C.6. Evidence—Prepaid Assets**

**93.** **(a)** The requirement is to determine the financial statement assertion most directly related to the procedure of reviewing or recomputing amortization of intangible assets. Answer (a) is correct because the amortization of intangible assets deals with whether the accounts are properly valued, the valuation assertion. The other assertions are less directly related. Answer (b) is incorrect because the existence or occurrence assertion deals with whether assets or liabilities exist at a given date and whether recorded transactions have occurred during a given period. Answer (c) is incorrect because the completeness assertion deals with whether all transactions and accounts that should be presented in the financial statements are so included. Answer (d) is incorrect because the rights and obligations assertion deals with whether assets are the rights of the entity and liabilities are the obligations of the entity at a given date. See AU 326 for information on the financial statement assertions.

**94.** **(c)** The requirement is to determine the most likely reason for the absence of the original insurance policy on plant equipment. Answer (c) is correct because the holder of the lien may also in certain circumstances maintain the original insurance policy. Answer (a) is incorrect because an insurance premium which is due but not recorded is unlikely to account for the lack of the original insurance policy. Answer (b) is incorrect because while coinsurance provisions are outlined in the policy, they are unlikely to be a reason that the policy is not available for inspection. Answer (d) is incorrect because there is no obvious relationship between the understatement of insurance expense and the presence or absence of an insurance policy.

### C.7. Evidence—Payables (Current)

**95.** **(c)** The requirement is to identify the best audit procedures for identifying unrecorded liabilities. Answer (c) is correct because unrecorded liabilities eventually become due and must be paid. Accordingly, a review of cash disbursements after the balance sheet date is an effective procedure for detecting unrecorded payables. Answer (a) is incorrect because tracing a sample of accounts payable that have been recorded is not likely to result in identification of unrecorded liabilities. Answer (b) is incorrect because purchase orders issued after year-end will not result in liabilities as of year-end. Answer (d) is incorrect because disbursement entries recorded before year-end generally relate to accounts payable that have been paid before year-end.

**96.** **(a)** The requirement is to identify the appropriate population when using accounts payable confirmations directed towards obtaining evidence on the completeness assertion. Answer (a) is correct because to address completeness the auditor attempts to determine that all accounts payable are reflected, and a company potentially may be liable to any of its vendors. Answer (b) is incorrect because confirming based on recorded amounts addresses existence more directly than completeness. Answer (c) is incorrect because basing the sample on payees after year-end only deals with those payables that have been paid as of that point. Answer (d) is incorrect because open invoices are a less complete population than are vendors. See AU 330 for information on the confirmation process, and AU 326 for information on management's financial statement assertions.

**97.** **(d)** The requirement is to determine why confirmation of accounts payable is unnecessary. Accounts payable are usually not confirmed because there is better evidence available to the auditor, (i.e., examination of cash payments subsequent to the balance sheet date). If the auditor reviews all cash payments for a sufficient time after the balance sheet date for items pertaining to the period under audit and finds no such payments which were not recorded as liabilities at year-end, the auditor is reasonably assured that accounts payable were not understated. Answer (a) is a nonsense answer. Answer (b) is incorrect because AP balances could be paid during year-end audit work after the balance sheet date. Answer (c) is incorrect because whether or not legal action has been taken against the client is irrelevant to the confirmation procedure.

**98.** **(c)** The requirement is to identify the substantive test to be performed to verify the existence and valuation of recorded accounts payable. Answer (c) is correct because the vouching of various payable accounts to purchase orders

and receiving reports will provide evidence that the debt was incurred and the related goods received, thereby providing evidence on the existence of the debt and its amount, or valuation. Answer (a) is incorrect because determining whether prenumbered purchase orders are used and accounted for relates more directly to the completeness with which purchases and accounts payable were recorded. Answers (b) and (d) are incorrect because the question addresses the existence and valuation of **recorded** accounts payable, not unrecorded payables or payables with a zero balance.

**99.** **(c)** The requirement is to determine management's accounts payable assertion that an auditor will primarily focus on. Experience has indicated that overstated income is more of a risk than is understated income. Answer (c) is correct because the completeness assertion focuses upon whether payables have been omitted, thereby overstating income. Answer (a) is incorrect because the existence assertion deals with whether recorded accounts payable are overstated, thereby understating income. Answer (b) is incorrect because payables often require no particularly troublesome presentations and disclosures. Answer (d) is incorrect because payables are most frequently simply valued at the cost of the related acquisition. See AU 326 for more information on management's financial statement assertions.

### C.8. Evidence—Long-Term Debt

**100.** **(b)** The requirement is to identify a likely reason for a recorded interest expense that seems excessive in relation to the balance in the bonds payable account. Answer (b) is correct because understated bonds payable will result in a lower account balance than is proper and thereby create a situation in which the interest expense appears excessive. Answers (a) and (d) are incorrect because an understated discount or an overstated premium on bonds payable result in situations in which the recorded interest expense seems lower than expected since the net bonds payable are overstated. Answer (c) is incorrect because understatements, not overstatements, of bonds payable will result in what appears to be an excessive rate of interest expense.

**101.** **(a)** The requirement is to determine the financial statement assertion most directly related to an auditor's inspection of loan agreements under which an entity's inventories are pledged. Answer (a) is correct because the presentation and disclosure assertion deals with whether particular components of the financial statements—such as loan agreement covenants—are properly classified, described, and disclosed. The other assertions are less directly related. Answer (b) is incorrect because the valuation or allocation assertion deals with whether asset, liabilities, revenue, and expense components have been included in the financial statements at the appropriate amounts. Answer (c) is incorrect because the existence or occurrence assertion deals with whether assets or liabilities exist at a given date and whether recorded transactions have occurred during a given period. Answer (d) is incorrect because the completeness assertion deals with whether all transactions and accounts that should be presented in the financial statements are so included. See AU 326 for information on the financial statement assertions.

**102.** **(c)** The requirement is to identify a procedure an auditor would perform in auditing long-term bonds payable.

Answer (c) is correct because comparing interest expense with the bond payable amount will provide evidence as to reasonableness. Such a procedure may reveal either interest not expensed or debt not properly recorded. Answer (a) is incorrect because analytical procedures will not in general be performed on bond premiums and discounts since these accounts may easily be verified by examining details of the entry recording the debt issuance and any subsequent amortization. Answer (b) is incorrect because an examination of the documentation of assets purchased with bond proceeds is only necessary when such a use of the funds is a requirement of the debt issuance. Answer (d) is incorrect because confirmation of bonds outstanding will often be with the trustee rather than with individual bondholders.

**103. (b)** The requirement is to determine how an auditor can best verify a client's bond sinking fund transactions and year-end balance. Answer (b) is correct because confirmation with the bond trustee represents externally generated evidence received directly by the auditor. Such evidence is considered very reliable. Answer (a) is incorrect because individual holders of retired bonds will have no information on actual bond sinking fund transactions or year-end balances. Answer (c) is incorrect because, while recomputing interest expense, interest payable, and amortization of bond discount or premiums are desirable procedures, they do not directly address bond sinking fund transactions and year-end balances. Answer (d) is similar to answer (c) in that it is desirable but does not address the actual bond sinking fund transactions and year-end balance.

**C.9. Evidence—Owners' Equity**

**104. (a)** The requirement is to determine how an auditor ordinarily obtains evidence of stockholders' equity transactions. Answer (a) is correct because the board of directors will, in general, authorize changes in stockholders' equity. Answer (b) is less complete in that for small clients there may be no transfer agent, and because the transfer agent deals most directly with transfers of outstanding stock. Answer (c) is incorrect because canceled stock certificates are ordinarily available only for small clients. Answer (d) is incorrect because companies do not ordinarily have a "treasury stock certificate book."

**105. (d)** The requirement is to identify the most likely audit procedure, in addition to analytical procedures, when control risk for payroll is assessed as low. Answer (d) is correct because accrual of payroll at year-end is not an entry made frequently throughout the year and accordingly recording of the entry is often not controlled by the payroll portion of the internal control structure. Answers (a), (b), and (c) are incorrect because observing the distribution of paychecks, the footing and crossfooting of the payroll register, and inspection of payroll tax returns are recurring operations that will have been considered when assessing control risk at a low level.

**106. (a)** The requirement is to identify the circumstance that most likely would cause an auditor to suspect an employee payroll fraud scheme. Answer (a) is correct because significant unexplained variances between standard and actual labor cost may lead an auditor to suspect fraud. Answer (b) is incorrect because one would expect payroll checks to be distributed by the same employees each payday. Answer (c) is incorrect because time cards are ordinar-

ily approved by individual departmental supervisors. Answer (d) is incorrect because the maintenance of a separate payroll bank account is considered a control, not an indication of fraud.

**107. (d)** The requirement is to identify the procedure that an auditor most likely would perform when auditing payroll. Answer (d) is correct because a comparison of payroll costs with entity standards or budgets will generally be included in the audit program as a test of overall payroll reasonableness. Answer (a) is incorrect because unclaimed wages will not be mailed unless an employee so requests and this often will not be tested by an auditor. Answer (b) is incorrect because total employee deductions will be traced to journal entries. Answer (c) is incorrect because observing entity employees during a payroll distribution is generally only included in an audit program when internal control is weak; accordingly, it is more likely that a comparison of payroll costs with entity standards or budgets [answer (d)] will be included.

**108. (d)** The requirement is to identify the procedure that is most likely when an auditor is performing tests concerning the granting of stock options. Answer (d) is correct because authorizing the issuance of stock options is ordinarily a decision made by the board of directors. Answer (a) is incorrect because the Secretary of State of the state of incorporation will not have this information on stock options. Answer (b) is incorrect because the existence of the option holders is not ordinarily a significant question. Answer (c) is incorrect because stock to be issued relating to options may be either from treasury stock or new issuances; accordingly, sufficient treasury stock need not be available.

**109. (d)** The requirement is to identify the assertion to which determining whether there are restrictions on retained earnings relates most directly. Answer (d) is correct because such restrictions will result in disclosures and thus the presentation and disclosure assertion is most directly being verified. Answer (a) is incorrect because the existence or occurrence assertion addresses whether assets or liabilities of the entity exist at a given date and whether recorded transactions have occurred during a given period. Answer (b) is incorrect because the completeness assertion addresses whether all transactions and accounts that should be presented in the financial statements are so included. Answer (c) is incorrect because the valuation or allocation assertion addresses whether asset, liability, revenue, and expense components have been included in the financial statements at appropriate amounts. See AU 326 for a discussion of financial statement assertions.

**110. (b)** The requirement is to identify the information an auditor should confirm with a client's transfer agent and registrar. Answer (b) is correct because when a client employs a transfer agent and registrar, there will be no stock certificate book to examine, and accordingly, information on shares issued and outstanding should be confirmed. Answers (a), (c), and (d) are incorrect because the transfer agent and registrar often will not have information on dividend restrictions, guarantees of preferred stock liquidation values, and the number of shares subject to agreements to repurchase.

**111. (c)** The requirement is to determine a likely step in the audit program for retained earnings. The legality of a dividend depends in part on whether it has been properly authorized (state laws differ on specific requirements). Thus, the auditor must determine that proper authorization exists, as both cash and stock dividends affect retained earnings. Answer (a) is incorrect since only a memo entry is required for a stock split. Answer (b) is incorrect because the write-down of an account receivable will not, in general, be recorded in retained earnings. Answer (d) is incorrect because gains from the disposition of treasury shares are recorded in paid-in capital accounts.

**112.  (c)**    The requirement is to determine when an auditor would be most likely to perform substantive tests of details on payroll transactions and balances. Answer (c) is correct because analytical procedures result in further investigation when unexpected differences occur. This investigation will generally involve substantive tests of details of transactions and balances. AU 329 provides detailed information on analytical procedures. Answer (a) is incorrect because a substantial amount of accrued payroll expense as indicated by a cutoff test will not necessarily result in additional substantive tests. Answer (b) is incorrect because a low assessed level of control risk is likely to result in less substantive testing. Answer (d) is incorrect because the nature of accrued payroll expense being unpaid commissions need not necessarily result in more substantive testing.

**113.  (a)**    The requirement is to determine a source an auditor uses to test the reasonableness of dividend income from investments in publicly held companies. Answer (a) is correct because dividend record books produced by investment advisory services provide summaries of dividends paid for various securities, and an auditor is able to compare the reasonableness of a client's recorded dividend income from investments with this information. Answers (b) and (c) are incorrect because auditors do not, in general, determine the reasonableness of dividend income by examining stock "indentures" or "stock ledgers." Answer (d) is incorrect because while annual financial statements of investee companies may include such information, examining such financial statements is not generally an efficient approach for testing the reasonableness of dividend income. Also, the current year financial statements of the investees often are not available when the auditor is performing the current audit.

### C.10.  Revenue

**114.  (c)**    The requirement is to identify the most likely risk involved with a bill and hold transaction at year-end. Answer (c) is correct because a bill and hold transaction results in the recording of a sale prior to delivery of the goods—accordingly, sales may be inappropriately recorded. Answer (a) is incorrect because accrued liabilities are not ordinarily affected by bill and hold transactions. Answers (b) and (d) are incorrect because an absolute purchase commitment and the assuming of risk and reward relating to the product represent conditions which increase the likelihood that recording of a sale for such a transaction is appropriate.

**115.  (b)**    The requirement is to identify the most likely listed effect of "channel stuffing." Answer (b) is correct because channel stuffing is a marketing practice that suppliers sometimes use to boost sales by inducing distributors to buy substantially more inventory than they can promptly resell; accordingly, increased sales returns in the future are

likely. Answers (a), (c) and (d) are incorrect because accrued liabilities, cash, and marketable investments are less likely to be affected by channel stuffing, which results in entries increasing accounts receivable, cost of good sold, and sales, while decreasing inventory.

### C.11.  Expenses

**116.  (d)**    The requirement is to identify the account in which a recorded entry is most likely to relate to the property, plant, and equipment completeness assertion. The completeness assertion addresses whether all transactions have been recorded in an account (here, property, plant, and equipment). Answer (d) is correct because the purchase of property, plant, and equipment may inappropriately have been recorded in the repairs and maintenance account rather than in property, plant, and equipment; this is a frequent bookkeeping error since the individual recording the entry may frequently see similar invoices which do represent repairs and maintenance expense. Answers (a), (b), and (c) are all incorrect because the allowance for doubtful accounts, marketable securities, and sales have no apparent relationship to the completeness of recording of property, plant, and equipment.

### C.12.  Client Representation Letters

**117.  (c)**    The requirement is to identify the matter on which an auditor should obtain written management representations. Answer (c) is correct because written representations are ordinarily obtained on noncompliance with aspects of contractual agreements that may affect the financial statements. Answer (a) is incorrect because auditors do not ordinarily obtain a cost-benefit justification from management related to internal control weaknesses. Answer (b) is incorrect because written representations are not ordinarily obtained on such future plans. Answer (d) is incorrect because management may or may not be responsible for employee violations of laws, and because such a representation is not ordinarily obtained. See AU 333 for information on client representations.

**118.  (a)**    The requirement is to determine a matter to which materiality limits do **not** apply in obtaining written management representations. Answer (a) is correct because materiality considerations do not apply to management's acknowledgment of its responsibility for fair presentation of financial statements, the availability of all financial records, the completeness and availability of all minutes and meetings of stockholders, directors, and committees of directors, and communication from regulatory agencies. Answers (b), (c), and (d) are all incorrect because materiality considerations relate to losses from purchase commitments, compensating balances, and obsolete inventory. AU 333 discusses client representations.

**119.  (c)**    The requirement is to determine the proper date for a client's representation letter. AU 333 states that the representation letter should be dated as of the date of the auditor's report.

**120.  (b)**    The requirement is to identify the matter that an auditor most likely would include in a management representation letter. Auditors will generally request assurance as to the completeness and availability of minutes of stockholders' and directors' meetings. See AU 333 for written representations ordinarily obtained by the auditor.

**121. (d)** The requirement is to determine the year(s) on which a CPA must obtain written representations from management, when comparative financial statements are being issued, but current management has only been employed for a portion of one of those years. AU 333 states that if current management was not present during all periods reported upon, the auditor should nevertheless obtain written representations from current management on all such periods.

**122. (a)** The requirement is to identify the information ordinarily included among the written client representations obtained by the auditor. Answer (a) is correct because AU 333 includes information on compensating balances in the list of representations normally obtained. Answer (b) is incorrect because management need not acknowledge a responsibility for employee illegal actions. Answer (c) is incorrect because the auditor, not the client, determines whether sufficient evidential matter has been made available. Answer (d) is incorrect because, for purposes of a financial statement audit, management need not attempt to determine whether material weaknesses in internal control exist.

**123. (a)** The requirement is to determine the correct statement with respect to the use of a management representation letter as audit evidence about the completeness assertion. Answer (a) is correct because such written representations are meant to complement, but not replace, substantive tests. Answer (b) is incorrect because the complementary nature of such representations is **not** considered sufficient, even when combined with reliance upon internal control. The inherent limitations of internal control do not permit the auditor to **replace** substantive tests with complete reliance on internal control. Answer (c) is incorrect because the written representations are considered complementary evidence in support of various assertions. Answer (d) is incorrect because such written representations are not considered to be replacements for reliance upon internal control.

**124. (a)** The requirement is to determine who should sign a letter of representation. AU 333 states that, normally, the chief executive officer and the chief financial officers should sign the letter of representation.

**125. (d)** The requirement is to identify the scope limitation which **in all cases** is sufficient to preclude an unqualified opinion. Answer (d) is correct because the professional standards state that management refusal to furnish written representations constitutes a limitation on the scope of the auditor's examination sufficient to preclude an unqualified opinion. Answer (a) is incorrect because management's refusal to allow the auditor to review the predecessor's work may not necessarily result in report modification. Answer (b) is incorrect because alternate procedures may be available that will make report modification unnecessary when the auditor has been engaged after completion of the year-end physical count. Answer (c) is incorrect because management may choose not to correct a reportable condition of internal control without a resulting limitation on the scope of the audit.

**126. (c)** The requirement is to identify a purpose of a management representation letter. Answer (c) is correct because a management representation letter is meant to reduce the possibility of a misunderstanding concerning management's responsibility for the financial statements. An-

swer (a) is incorrect because reducing audit risk to an aggregate level of misstatement that could be considered material is not a logically sound statement. Answer (b) is incorrect because the management representation letter does not modify an auditor's responsibility to detect material misstatements. Answer (d) is incorrect because management representation letters are not a substitute for other procedures.

**127. (c)** The requirement is to identify the most likely source of a statement suggesting that there have been no communications from regulatory agencies. Answer (c) is correct because information such as this is ordinarily included in a management representation letter. Answers (a), (b), and (d) are incorrect because such a disclosure is not ordinarily included in a report on internal control, a special report, or a letter for an underwriter. See AU 333 for guidance on representation letters.

### C.13. Using the Work of a Specialist

**128. (a)** The requirement is to identify the correct statement concerning an auditor's use of the work of a specialist. Answer (a) is correct because the work of a specialist who is related to the client may be acceptable under certain circumstances. Answer (b) is incorrect because if the auditor believes that the findings of the specialist are unreasonable, it is generally appropriate to obtain the findings of another specialist. Answer (c) is incorrect because a material difference between a specialist's findings and those included in the financial statements may result in the need for an explanatory paragraph, a qualified opinion, a disclaimer, or an adverse opinion. Answer (d) is incorrect because an auditor may use a specialist in the determination of various physical characteristics of assets.

**129. (a)** The requirement is to identify a circumstance in which an auditor may refer to the findings of a specialist in the auditor's report. Answer (a) is correct because the auditor may refer to the specialist when the specialist's findings result in inclusion of an explanatory paragraph to an audit report, in this case on going concern status. Answers (b), (c), and (d) are all incorrect because a specialist is only referred to in an audit report when that specialist's findings identify a circumstance requiring modification of the audit report. Auditors do not modify audit reports to simply inform the user that a specialist was involved.

**130. (d)** The requirement is to identify the statement that is correct about the auditor's use of the work of a specialist. Answer (d) is correct because the auditor should obtain an understanding of the nature of the work performed by the specialist. Answer (a) is incorrect because ordinarily a specialist will have a basic understanding of the auditor's corroborative use of the findings. Answer (b) is incorrect because the auditor need not perform substantive procedures to verify the specialist's assumptions and findings. Answer (c) is incorrect because the client may have an understanding of the nature of the work performed by the specialist. See AU 336 (revised in 1994 by SAS 73) for information on the auditor's use of the work of a specialist.

**131. (b)** The requirement is to identify the circumstance in which an auditor may appropriately refer to the findings of a specialist. Answer (b) is correct because an auditor may refer to a specialist when the report is being modified due to the specialist's findings.  Answers (a) and (c) are incorrect because a client's familiarity with a specialist or understanding of the auditor's use of the findings of a specialist does not result in modification of the audit report. Answer (d) is incorrect because an auditor does not divide responsibility with a specialist.

**132.**  **(c)**    The requirement is to identify the statement that an auditor must document when using the work of a specialist.  Answer (c) is correct because the specialist's understanding of the auditor's corroborative use of his or her findings must be documented.  See AU 336 for this and other documentation requirements.  Answer (a) is incorrect because no statement concerning an update of the specialist's report is required to be documented.  Answer (b) is incorrect because a division of responsibility relates to circumstances in which other auditors, not specialists, are involved.  Answer (d) is incorrect because an auditor will not normally issue a disclaimer related to whether the specialist's findings corroborate the representations in the financial statements.  The specialist's report is only referred to when there is a material difference between the specialist's findings and the representations in the financial statements.  See AU 336 for information on the effect of a specialist's work on an auditor's report.

**133.**  **(c)**    The requirement is to determine which individual is **not** considered a **specialist** upon whose work an independent auditor may rely.  The professional standards relating to using the work of a specialist do not apply to using the work of an internal auditor.  Answers (a), (b), and (d), actuary, appraiser, and engineer, respectively, are all examples of specialists per the professional standards.  Note here that the question and its reply do not imply that a CPA cannot use the work of an internal auditor.  What is being suggested is that an internal auditor is not considered a specialist under the professional standards.

### C.14.  Inquiry of a Client's Lawyer

**134.**  **(d)**    The requirement is to identify which parties should reach an understanding on the limits of materiality for purposes of a lawyer's response to an auditor's inquiry concerning litigation, claims, and assessments.  Answer (d) is correct because AU 337 states that a lawyer's response to an inquiry may be limited to material items, provided the lawyer and the auditor have reached an understanding on the limits of materiality for this purpose.  Answer (a) is incorrect because it includes the client's management.  Answer (b) is incorrect because it includes the client's audit committee and omits the auditor.  Answer (c) is incorrect because it includes the client's management and omits the auditor.

**135.**  **(b)**    The requirement is to identify the correct statement concerning the refusal of a client's attorney to provide information requested in an inquiry letter.  Answer (b) is correct because AU 337 indicates that this is a limitation on the scope of the audit.  Answer (a) is incorrect because the lack of information is unlikely to lead to an adverse opinion since no information has been provided indicating that the financial statements are misstated.  Answer (c) is incorrect because withdrawal is not generally necessary due to the client's attorney's failure to provide information.  Answer (d) is incorrect because reportable conditions pertain to weaknesses in internal control.

**136.**  **(c)**    The requirement is to identify the audit procedure that an auditor most likely would perform concerning litigation, claims, and assessments.  Answer (c) is correct because auditors must discuss with management its policies and procedures for evaluating and accounting for litigation, claims and assessments.  See AU 337 for this and other requirements.  Answer (a) is incorrect because the client's lawyer is not ordinarily asked to make an assessment about whether the client has a going concern problem (see AU 341 for information on an auditor's consideration of a client's ability to continue as a going concern).  Answer (b) is incorrect because an auditor will not ordinarily examine legal documents in the client's lawyer's possession.  Answer (d) is incorrect because an auditor will not ordinarily confirm with the client's lawyer that all litigation, claims, and assessment have been recorded.

**137.**  **(b)**    The requirement is to identify the primary reason that an auditor should request a client to send a letter of inquiry to its attorneys.  Answer (b) is correct because a letter of audit inquiry to the client's attorney is the auditor's primary means of obtaining corroboration of the information furnished by management concerning litigation, claims, and assessments.  Answer (a) is incorrect because it will often be impossible to determine the probable outcome of asserted claims and pending or threatened litigation.  Answer (c) is incorrect because no such opinions on historical experiences are generally available.  Answer (d) is incorrect because the description of litigation, claims, and assessments is generally prepared by the client.

**138.**  **(b)**    The requirement is to identify the procedure that is **not** performed regarding litigation, claims, and assessments.  Answer (b) is correct because the CPA does not confirm directly with the client's lawyer that all claims have been recorded in the financial statements.  Answers (a), (c), and (d) are all incorrect because they represent information obtained from management regarding litigation, claims, and assessments as summarized in AU 337.

**139.**  **(a)**    The requirement is to identify the appropriate limitation for an attorney's response to a client's letter of audit inquiry.  Answer (a) is correct because AU 337 states that an attorney may appropriately limit his response to matters to which s/he has given substantive attention in the form of legal consultation or representation.  Answers (b), (c), and (d) are incorrect because AU 337 presents a variety of other requests in addition to information on the likelihood of an unfavorable outcome of the matters disclosed by the entity, similar litigation, and probable outcomes.

**140.**  **(a)**    If a client's lawyer resigned shortly after the receipt of an attorney's letter which indicated no significant disagreements with the client's assessment of contingent liabilities, the auditor should inquire why the attorney resigned.  The auditor's concern is whether any undisclosed unasserted claims have arisen.  Per AU 337, a lawyer may be required to resign if his advice concerning reporting for litigation, claims, and assessments is disregarded by the client.  Accordingly, the resignation shortly after issuance of an attorney's letter may indicate a problem.  Answer (b) is incorrect because the attorney issued a letter indicating no significant disagreement with the client's assessment of contingent liabilities.  Answers (c) and (d) are incorrect because AU 337 only suggests that the auditor should consider the need for inquiries (i.e., AU 337 does not require a complete new exam of contingent liabilities or an adverse opinion).

**141.** **(b)** The requirement is to identify the lawyer's letter comment that is most likely to cause the auditor to request clarification. Answer (b) is correct because a statement that the action can be settled for less than the damages claimed is unclear as to the details of the attorney's belief. Answers (a), (c), and (d) are all incorrect because they represent responses that may be clearly interpreted by the auditor. See AU 337, interpretation 7, for information on assessing lawyer's evaluations of the likely outcome of litigation.

### C.15.  Fair Values

**142.** **(a)** The requirement is to determine whether valuation issues arise at initial recording, subsequent to initial recording, or at both times when considering fair value of an asset or liability. Answer (a) is correct because AU 328 makes clear that valuation issues arise at both times. Answers (b), (c), and (d) are all incorrect because they suggest that there are no valuation issues at one or both of these time periods.

**143.** **(b)** The requirement is to identify the **least** likely approach for auditing the fair values of assets and liabilities. Answer (b) is correct because it is doubtful that audit committee members will have information on the valuation. Answers (a), (c), and (d) are all incorrect because they represent the three approaches presented for auditing fair values (as well as other estimates).

### C.16.  Related-Party Transactions

**144.** **(c)** The requirement is to identify the auditing procedure that would most likely assist an auditor in identifying related-party transactions. Answer (c) is correct because reviewing confirmations of loans receivable and payable for indications of guarantees may reveal unusual transactions that involve related parties. See AU 334 for procedures related to identifying transactions with related parties. Answer (a) is incorrect because inspecting the correspondence with lawyers for evidence of unreported contingent liabilities does not generally relate directly to related-party transactions. Answer (b) is incorrect because nonrecurring transactions are more indicative of related-party transactions. Answer (d) is incorrect because analytical procedures performed to identify possible financial difficulties do not relate directly to related-party transactions.

**145.** **(c)** The requirement is to determine an auditor's responsibility after having determined that a related-party transaction has occurred. Answer (c) is correct because after identifying the existence of such an act, the auditor should obtain an understanding of the business purpose of the transaction. See AU 334 for this and other responsibilities. Answer (a) is incorrect because the mere existence of a related-party transaction may or may not lead to audit report modification. Answer (b) is incorrect because the performance of analytical procedures is not required. Answer (d) is incorrect because except for routine transactions, it will generally not be possible to determine whether the transaction would have taken place, or whether it was consummated on terms equivalent to an arm's-length transaction.

**146.** **(d)** The requirement is to identify the correct statement concerning related-party transactions. Answer (d) is

correct because AU 334 requires that the auditor should place primary emphasis on the adequacy of disclosure. Answer (a) is incorrect because ascertaining rights and obligations is only part of the auditor's total responsibility and not the primary emphasis. Answer (b) is incorrect because while auditors attempt to determine the existence of related parties, this is not the primary emphasis. Answer (c) is incorrect because verifying the valuation of related-party transactions will often not be possible.

**147.** **(d)** The requirement is to identify the correct statement concerning related-party transactions. Answer (d) is correct because AU 334 requires that procedures directed toward identifying related-party transactions should be performed, even if the auditor has no reason to suspect their existence. Answer (a) is incorrect because, in the absence of evidence to the contrary, related-party transactions need not be assumed to be outside the ordinary course of business. Answer (b) is incorrect because the auditor will not in general be able to determine whether a particular transaction would have occurred if the parties had **not** been related. Answer (c) is incorrect because, if proper disclosures are made, the related-party transactions are not required to be recorded on terms equivalent to arm's-length transactions.

**148.** **(c)** The requirement is to identify the circumstance in which an auditor most likely would modify an unqualified opinion if the entity's financial statements include a footnote on related-party transactions. Answer (c) is correct because it generally will not be possible to determine whether a particular transaction was consummated on terms equivalent to those with unrelated parties. Therefore, the auditor may be required to express a qualified or an adverse opinion when such an unsubstantiated disclosure is included. Answers (a), (b), and (d) are all incorrect because they represent situations that may be disclosed in related-party transaction disclosures.

### C.17.  Going Concern Considerations

**149.** **(b)** The requirement is to identify the condition or event most likely to cause an auditor to have substantial doubt about an entity's ability to continue as a going concern. Answer (b) is correct because denial of usual trade from suppliers is ordinarily an indicator that the company is in weak financial condition. Answer (a) is incorrect because while such related-party transactions may be considered risky, there is less likely to be a question concerning going concern status than suggested by answer (a). Answer (c) is incorrect because the payment of such stock dividends does not indicate financial weakness. Answer (d) is incorrect because restrictions on the disposal of principal assets is a condition often present in various loan agreements.

**150.** **(d)** The requirement is to identify the most likely mitigating factor a CPA would consider when a client's ability to continue as a going concern is in question. Answer (d) is correct because the ability to postpone expenditures for research and development projects may mitigate the circumstance. See AU 341 for this and other mitigating factors. Answer (a) is incorrect because there is no guarantee that Zero's discussions with its lenders will lead to a restructuring of the debt and loan agreements. Only existing or committee agreements to restructure the debt would be considered a mitigating factor. Answer (b) is incorrect because weak internal control over cash disbursements may or may not have caused the going concern problem. Answer (c) is incorrect because an entity with a going concern problem is unlikely to be able to purchase such production facilities.

**151. (a)** The requirement is to identify the condition or event that is most likely to cause an auditor to have substantial doubt about an entity's ability to continue as a going concern. Answer (a) is correct because AU 341 includes negative cash flows as one of its examples of such conditions and events. Answer (b) is incorrect because while the postponement of research and development projects may sometimes be due to extreme financial difficulties, often it is not. Answers (c) and (d) are incorrect because neither significant related-party transactions nor stock dividends need not indicate substantial doubt about an entity's ability to continue as a going concern. See AU 341 for information on an auditor's consideration of an entity's ability to continue as a going concern.

**152. (b)** The requirement is to identify the condition or event that might indicate to an auditor substantial doubt about an entity's ability to continue as a going concern. Answer (b) is correct because confirmation with related and third parties of the details of arrangements to provide or maintain financial support is a procedure that would assist an auditor in identifying a question concerning going concern status. See AU 341 for this and other such conditions and events indicating doubt about an entity's ability to continue as a going concern. Answer (a) is incorrect because the pledging of assets as collateral is a normal business transaction and it need not necessarily indicate a question of going concern status. Answer (c) is incorrect because reconciling the cash balances with the cutoff bank statement is an acceptable audit procedure, but will not normally identify a going concern question. Answer (d) is incorrect because comparing an entity's depreciation and asset capitalization policies will not normally indicate a question of going concern status.

**153. (a)** The requirement is to identify the audit procedure most likely to assist an auditor in identifying conditions and events that may indicate there could be substantial doubt about an entity's ability to continue as a going concern. Answer (a) is correct because a review of compliance with terms of debt and loan agreements may reveal conditions of non-compliance due to poor financial condition. See the outline of AU 341 for a list of procedures that may identify such conditions and events. Answers (b), (c), and (d) are all incorrect because, while they might in some circumstances reveal a question concerning the company's ability to continue as a going concern, they are not considered to be as effective as answer (a).

**154. (d)** The requirement is to identify the factor which a CPA would most likely consider as mitigating substantial doubt about the ability of an entity to continue as a going concern. Answer (d) is correct because management's ability to negotiate reductions of required dividends will decrease required cash outflows, and thereby increase the likelihood that the entity will be able to continue as a going concern. AU 341 provides examples of information that might mitigate such concern. Answers (a), (b), and (c) are all incorrect because they involve spending cash, rather than reducing outflows of cash.

**155. (c)** The requirement is to identify the circumstance most likely to mitigate an auditor's substantial doubt about an entity's ability to continue as a going concern. Answer (c) is correct because the marketable assets that management intends to sell may potentially provide the necessary financial resources to mitigate the substantial doubt about the entity's ability to continue as a going concern. Answer (a) is incorrect because the ability to expand operations into new product lines is a suspect circumstance, given the substantial doubt about the entity's ability to continue as a going concern. Answer (b) is incorrect because it also requires cash resources which may not be available. Answer (d) is incorrect because converting preferred stock to long-term debt will not generally alleviate a question concerning an entity's ability to continue as a going concern.

### C.18. Subsequent Events

**156. (d)** The requirement is to identify the most likely procedure to be performed in obtaining evidence about subsequent events. Answer (d) is correct because changes in long-term debt occurring after year-end may require note disclosure. Answers (a) and (b) are incorrect because auditors will not generally test changes in employee pay rates after year-end or recompute depreciation expense for plant assets sold. Answer (c) is incorrect because payroll checks issued near year-end may frequently be cashed after year-end and their investigation will not in general be directly related to obtaining evidence about subsequent events. See AU 560 for the responsibilities of auditors with respect to subsequent events.

**157. (c)** The requirement is to identify the event occurring after the issuance of an auditor's report that would most likely cause the auditor to make further inquiries about the previously issued financial statements. Answer (c) is correct because when an auditor becomes aware of information which relates to the financial statements previously reported upon, but which was not known at the date of the report, he or she should undertake to determine whether the information is reliable and whether the facts existed at the date of the audit report; in this circumstance it seems that the lease transactions existed as of the date of the audit report. Answer (a) is incorrect because the natural disaster occurred subsequent to the issuance of the audit report. Answer (b) is incorrect because the contingency had been properly disclosed. Answer (d) is incorrect because the sale of the subsidiary occurred subsequent to the issuance of the audit report.

**158. (d)** The requirement is to determine proper accounting and auditing treatment of uncollectibility of an account receivable resulting from a customer's bankruptcy due to a natural disaster occurring after a client's balance sheet date. Answer (d) is correct because a customer's major casualty loss after year-end will result in a financial statement note disclosure with no adjustment and no audit report modification due to consistency.

**159. (d)** The requirement is to determine an auditor's responsibility when subsequent to issuance of an audit report a client sells the shares of a major subsidiary. Answer (d) is correct because no action need be taken since the event arose after the issuance of the auditor's report. Answers (a), (b), and (c) are all incorrect because they outline responsibilities which are not appropriate in this circumstance.  See AU 561 for a discussion of auditor responsibility when subsequent to the issuance of the auditor's report the auditor becomes aware of a fact that **existed at the date of the auditor's report**.

**160. (c)**    The requirement is to determine the auditor's responsibility with respect to a client acquisition of 25% of its outstanding capital stock after year-end and prior to the completion of the auditor's fieldwork.  Answer (c) is correct because the transaction described is a type 2 subsequent event (since the acquisition provided evidence of a condition which came into existence after year-end) and therefore the proper accounting approach would be note disclosure rather than adjustment.  Answer (a) is incorrect because adjustments are only appropriate for type 1 subsequent events (events which provide evidence that the condition was in existence at year-end).  Answer (b) is incorrect because the auditor does not issue financial statements for the client.  Answer (d) is incorrect because the opinion paragraph of the report need not be modified; if any report modification were considered necessary, it would be an explanatory paragraph emphasizing the matter.

**161. (d)**    The requirement is to identify a procedure that an auditor would perform to obtain evidence about the occurrence of subsequent events.  Answer (d) is correct because an auditor will inquire of officers and other executives having responsibility for financial and accounting matters whether any unusual adjustments have been made during the period from the balance sheet date to the date of inquiry.  See AU 560 for auditing procedures performed to identify subsequent events.

**162. (a)**    The requirement is to determine a procedure that an auditor should generally perform regarding subsequent events.  Answer (a) is correct because the *Professional Standards* state that the auditor generally should compare the latest available interim financial statements with the financial statements being audited.  See AU 560 for this and other requirements.  Answer (b) is incorrect because second accounts receivable confirmation requests will be sent well before the auditor's review of subsequent events.  Answer (c) is incorrect because the communication of material weaknesses is not a subsequent event procedure.  See AU 325 for the required communication of **reportable conditions**.  Answer (d) is incorrect because auditors generally only receive cutoff statements for the period immediately after year-end, not for multiple months.

**C.19. Omitted Procedures Discovered After the Report Date**

**163. (b)**    The requirement is to identify an auditor's responsibility when a client refuses to adjust recently issued financial statements for a subsequent event related to the bankruptcy of the entity's principal customer.  Answer (b) is correct because if the client refuses to make disclosures, AU 561 requires the auditor to notify each member of the board of directors of such refusal and that he or she will take steps to prevent future reliance upon the audit report.  Ordinarily the auditor will then notify the clients and regulatory agencies that the report should no longer be associated with the financial statements, and when possible, notify persons known to be relying upon the financial statements.  Answer (a) is incorrect because it is less likely that all of the creditors will be informed.  Answer (c) is incorrect because

the financial statements are the responsibility of management, and the auditor will not revise or distribute them.  Answer (d) is incorrect because no revised report will be issued.

**164. (c)**    The requirement is to identify the circumstance in which an auditor who finds that he or she has omitted a substantive procedure at the time of an audit may decide not to apply that procedure.  Answer (c) is correct because when results of other procedures tend to compensate for the procedure it may be omitted.  Answer (a) is incorrect because, even when distribution of the financial statement has been limited to management and the board of directors, it may be necessary to perform the procedure.  Answer (b) is incorrect because the type of report issued does not affect the need to perform the procedure.  Answer (d) is incorrect because delays by the client in providing data is not an acceptable reason not to perform that procedure.

**165. (b)**    The requirement is to determine professional responsibility when, subsequent to issuance of an audit report, an auditor has determined that a necessary audit procedure has been omitted.  Answer (b) is correct because an auditor must apply procedures that would provide a satisfactory basis for the opinion issued.  Answer (a) is incorrect because stockholders need not be informed at this point that the audit report should **not** be relied upon.  Answer (c) is incorrect because the auditor's report will not be reissued unless the financial statements are restated.  Answer (d) is incorrect because tests of controls will not compensate for the omitted procedure.  See AU 390 for overall procedures relating to considering omitted procedures after an audit report has been issued.

**166. (c)**    The requirement is to identify an auditor's first responsibility upon discovering six months after completion of an audit that engagement personnel failed to confirm several of the client's material accounts receivable balances.  Answer (c) is correct because the auditor must first assess the importance of the omitted procedures to the auditor's ability to support the previously expressed opinion.  Answers (a) and (b) are incorrect because prior to attempting any such confirmation or performing alternative procedures, an assessment of whether the procedures are needed is to be performed.  Answer (d) is incorrect because a consideration of whether anyone is relying on, or is likely to rely on, the unqualified opinion is made after assessing the importance of the omitted procedure.

**D.    Completing the Audit**

**167. (c)**    The requirement is to determine the procedure **least** likely to be performed before the balance sheet date.  Answer (c) is correct because the search for unrecorded liabilities relies upon a review of documents unrecorded at year-end, as well as inspection of purchases and disbursements recorded after year-end, to determine whether a proper cutoff of transactions between periods has occurred.  Answer (a) is incorrect because auditors are able to test internal control over cash prior to year-end.  Answers (b) and (d) are incorrect because in cases of good internal control, receivables may be confirmed and inventory observed prior to year-end.

**168. (c)**    The requirement is to determine the most likely type of transaction that would be detected by an auditor's review of a client's sales cutoff.  Answer (c) is correct because the auditor's review will include a study of sales recorded late in December and early in January.  This will be accomplished by reviewing the period when the revenue was earned by shipment of goods or performance of services, as compared to the period in which the revenue was recorded.  Accordingly, the review of sales recorded in January may reveal unrecorded sales for the preceding year.  Answer (a) is incorrect because shipments lacking sales invoices and shipping documents will be very difficult to identify; also, this reply is more limited than answer (c).  Answer (b) is incorrect because excessive write-offs of accounts receivable will not usually be detected when testing the sales cutoff.  Answer (d) is incorrect because it is unlikely that lapping in the application of cash receipts will be detected by sales cutoff testing.  More frequently, procedures such as confirmations, analytical procedures, and an analysis of deposit tickets reveal lapping.

**169. (b)**   The requirement is to identify the assertion being tested by cutoff tests designed to detect credit sales made before the end of the year that have improperly been recorded in the subsequent year.  Answer (b) is correct because the completeness assertion deals with whether all transactions have been included in the proper period.  Answer (a) is incorrect because the presentation or disclosure assertion deals with whether particular components of the financial statements are properly classified, described, and disclosed.  Answer (c) is incorrect because the rights and obligations assertion deals with whether assets are the rights of the entity and liabilities are the obligations of the entity at a given date.  Answer (d) is incorrect because the existence or occurrence assertion deals with whether assets or liabilities of the entity exist at a given date and whether recorded transactions have occurred during a given period.  In this question, the existence assertion would be tested if the auditor sampled from sales recorded prior to year-end to determine whether the sale occurred before or after year-end.

### D.1.  Procedures Completed near the End of the Audit

**170. (d)**   The requirement is to identify the procedure an auditor would most likely perform during the overall review stage of formulating an opinion on an entity's financial statements.  Answer (d) is correct because a consideration of results relating to the assessment of the risk of material misstatement due to fraud may reveal that the audit has inadequately addressed that risk; in such a case additional procedures would be required.  Answer (a) is incorrect because such assurance from the entity's attorney is ordinarily obtained prior to the overall review stage of an audit.  Answer (b) is incorrect because the verification of the accuracy of the proof of cash is ordinarily performed prior to the overall review and because little verification of the bank cutoff statement is usually necessary since it is ordinarily received directly by the auditor from the bank.  Answer (c) is incorrect because such provisions for the safeguarding of assets may be corrected well after the conclusion of the audit.

### E.1.  Compilation Procedures

**171. (a)**   The requirement is to identify the procedure an accountant ordinarily performs in a compilation engagement of a nonpublic entity.  Answer (a) is correct because the

accountant is required, at a minimum, to read the financial statements to consider whether they are free from obvious material errors.

**172. (b)**   The requirement is to determine whether either or both of (1) the additional audit effort necessary to complete the audit and (2) the reason for the change in the engagement should be considered by a CPA whose client has requested that an audit engagement be changed to a compilation.  Answer (b) is correct because AR 100 states that additional necessary audit effort and the reason for the change—as well as the additional cost to complete the audit—be considered.

**173. (d)**   The requirement is to determine whether an accountant can accept a compilation or a review engagement when s/he is unfamiliar with a prospective client's specialized industry accounting principles, but s/he plans to obtain the required level of knowledge prior to the engagement.  Answer (d) is correct because an accountant may accept either a compilation or a review engagement in such circumstances.

**174. (a)**   The requirement is to determine the correct statement concerning both an engagement to compile and an engagement to review a nonpublic entity's financial statements.  Answer (a) is correct because neither a compilation nor a review contemplates obtaining an understanding of internal control.  Answer (b) is incorrect because when performing a compilation the accountant need not be independent; independence is required for reviews.  Answer (c) is incorrect because a review provides limited assurance.  Answer (d) is incorrect because the accountant is not required to obtain a written management representation letter for a compilation; a management representation letter is required for a review.

**175. (a)**   The requirement is to identify a condition required for an accountant to submit a written personal financial plan containing unaudited financial statements to a client without complying with the compilation and review requirements presented in SSARS 1.  Answer (a) is correct because AR 600 allows such an exception when the plan (1) is to be used to assist the client and the client's advisors in developing financial goals and objectives, (2) will not be used to obtain credit, and (3) when nothing comes to the accountant's attention that would lead him/her to believe that the statements will be used for credit or for any other purposes.  Answer (b) is incorrect because any work performed on the prior year statements is not applicable to the statements of the current year.  Answer (c) is incorrect because the engagement letter need not acknowledge departures from GAAP.  Answer (d) is incorrect because no assurance is provided in such reports.

### E.2.  Review Procedures

**176. (c)**   The requirement is to determine the listed requirement when an accountant is providing limited assurance that the financial statements of a nonpublic entity require **no** material modifications to be in accordance with generally accepted accounting principles.  Accountants perform reviews to provide such limited assurance.  Answer (c) is correct because obtaining an understanding of the accounting principles in the industry is required for reviews.  See AR 100 for this and other requirements.  Answer (a) is incorrect because reviews do not require the accountant to assess the risk of material misstatement. Answer (b) is incorrect because reviews generally do not include any communication with the entity's lawyer. Answer (d) is incorrect because an "audit" program is not required since a review is being performed.

**177. (a)** The requirement is to identify the procedure **least** likely to be performed in a review of the financial statements of a nonpublic entity. Answer (a) is correct because a review of a nonpublic entity's financial statements does not specifically address observing the safeguards over access to and use of assets and records. Answers (b), (c), and (d) are all incorrect because they are included in the procedures suggested for a review by AR 100.

**178. (b)** The requirement is to identify the procedures that an accountant would perform during an engagement to review the financial statements of a nonpublic entity. Answer (b) is correct because AR 100 requires that the CPA obtain a representation letter. Answers (a), (c), and (d) are incorrect because they are not included in AR 100 which presents a list of procedures performed during a review.

**179. (c)** The requirement is to identify the circumstances in which a CPA may issue a review report on the balance sheet of a nonpublic entity, and not report on the related financial statements. Answer (c) is correct because an accountant may issue a review report on one financial statement and not on the other related statements if the scope of the inquiry and analytical procedures has not been restricted. Answer (a) is incorrect because the CPA need not compile or report on the related statements of income, retained earnings, and cash flows when reviewing only the balance sheet. Answer (b) is incorrect because, when material modifications are needed, a CPA may still report on the balance sheet, but must indicate the modifications in the review report. Answer (d) is incorrect because the client need not be new.

**180. (d)** The requirement is to determine whether analytical procedures need to be performed on a compilation and/or a review engagement. Answer (d) is correct because a compilation does not require performance of analytical procedures, while a review does.

**181. (b)** The requirement is to determine the type of inquiry or analytical procedures ordinarily performed in an engagement to review a nonpublic entity's financial statements. Answer (b) is correct because an accountant will make inquiries concerning the entity's procedures for recording, classifying, and summarizing transactions, and accumulating information for disclosure in the financial statements. Answer (a) is incorrect because the analytical procedures and other procedures involved in a review do not in general obtain corroborating evidential matter as do the procedures of an audit. Answer (c) is incorrect because the procedures for reviews are not specially designed to test management's assertion regarding continued existence. Answer (d) is incorrect because inquiries of the entity's attorney are not normally required when a review is being performed.

**182. (b)** The requirement is to determine the most likely procedures to be included in a review engagement of a nonpublic entity. Answer (b) is correct because a review consists primarily of inquiries and analytical procedures. Answer (a) is incorrect because a bank transfer schedule is generally not prepared for a review engagement. Answer (c) is incorrect because a review does not include assessing the control structure. Answer (d) is incorrect because cutoff tests on sales and purchases are not normally performed on a review. Note that the procedures included in answers (a), (c), and (d) are typically performed in an audit.

**183. (b)** The requirement is to determine the type of transaction the accountant is most likely to investigate during a review when the year's accounts receivable did **not** conform to a predictable pattern. Answer (b) is correct because accounts receivable are generated from credit sales and an accountant would therefore investigate them. Answer (a) is incorrect because sales returns and allowances would be less likely to cause large shifts in accounts receivable than credit sales. Answer (c) is incorrect because it is less complete than answer (b) since sales of consigned goods represent only one possible type of sale that might impact accounts receivable. Answer (d) is incorrect because cash sales do not affect accounts receivable.

**184. (b)** The requirement is to identify the most likely procedure to be included in a review of a nonpublic entity's financial statements. Answer (b) is correct because AR 100 states that reviews ordinarily include inquires concerning actions taken at board of directors' meetings. Answer (a) is incorrect because reviews consist primarily of inquiry and analytical procedures and do not generally include confirmation of accounts receivable. Answer (c) is incorrect because a review of a nonpublic entity does not normally include obtaining an understanding of internal control or assessing control risk. Answer (d) is incorrect because distribution of a review report need not be limited. See AR 100 for specific procedures included in reviews.

## F. Operational Auditing

**185. (a)** The requirement is to identify the correct statement with respect to the primary orientation of operational auditing. Answer (a) is correct because operational audits deal primarily with evaluating the efficiency and effectiveness with which operations function, often with the intention of making improvements to accomplish the goals of management. Answers (b) and (c) are incorrect because financial statement audits are oriented toward such determinations, not operational audits. Answer (d) is incorrect because examinations of internal control are not performed on operational audits.

**186. (d)** The requirement is to identify a typical objective of an operational audit. Answer (d) is correct because operational audits typically address efficiency and effectiveness. Answer (a) is incorrect because while the adequacy of internal control design may be addressed during an operational audit, this is less complete than answer (d). Answer (b) is incorrect because operational audits may or may not be related to compliance with generally accepted governmental auditing standards. Answer (c) is incorrect because financial statement audits, not operational audits, address whether results of operations are fairly presented.

**SOLUTIONS TO SIMULATION PROBLEMS**

**Simulation Problem 1**

| Directions | Audit Objectives—Investments | Audit Objectives—Accounts Receivable | Research | Communication |
|---|---|---|---|---|

| *Audit objectives for investments* | (A) | (B) | (C) | (D) | (E) | (F) | (G) |
|---|---|---|---|---|---|---|---|
| 1. Investments are properly described and classified in the financial statements. | ○ | ○ | ○ | ○ | ● | ○ | ○ |
| 2. Recorded investments represent investments actually owned at the balance sheet date. | ○ | ○ | ○ | ○ | ○ | ● | ○ |
| 3. Trading investments are properly valued at fair market value at the balance sheet date. | ○ | ○ | ○ | ● | ○ | ○ | ○ |

**Explanation of solutions**

**1.** **(E)** The verification of transfers from the current to the noncurrent investment portfolio will provide assurance that the investments are properly classified in the financial statements.

**2.** **(F)** Positive confirmation replies as of the balance sheet date for investments held by independent custodians will provide assurance that the recorded investments are in fact owned by the audit client.

**3.** **(D)** Because trading investments should be valued at fair market value, determining whether any impairments in the price of investments have been recorded will provide assurance that investments are properly valued.

| Directions | Audit Objectives—Investments | Audit Objectives—Accounts Receivable | Research | Communication |
|---|---|---|---|---|

| *Audit objectives for accounts receivable* | (A) | (B) | (C) | (D) | (E) | (F) | (G) |
|---|---|---|---|---|---|---|---|
| 4. Accounts receivable represent all amounts owed to the entity at the balance sheet date. | ○ | ● | ○ | ○ | ○ | ○ | ○ |
| 5. The entity has legal right to all accounts receivable at the balance sheet date. | ○ | ○ | ○ | ○ | ● | ○ | ○ |
| 6. Accounts receivable are stated at net realizable value. | ○ | ○ | ● | ○ | ○ | ○ | ○ |
| 7. Accounts receivable are properly described and presented in the financial statements. | ○ | ○ | ○ | ○ | ○ | ● | ○ |

**Explanation of solutions**

**4.** **(B)** Performance of sales cutoff tests will provide assurance that sales transactions and the related receivables are recorded in the proper period. Thus, sales cutoff tests will provide assurance that all amounts owed to the entity at the balance sheet date are recorded in that period.

**5.** **(E)** A review of loan agreements, paying special attention to accounts receivable that have been factored, will provide assurance as to whether the entity has a legal right to all accounts receivable at the balance sheet date.

**6.** **(C)** An analysis of the aged trial balance for significant past due accounts will provide evidence with respect to accounts that may be uncollectible. Accordingly, the procedure will address the net realizable value of accounts receivable.

**7.** **(F)** Because material amounts due from officers and employees should be segregated from other receivables, a review of the trial balance for amounts due from officers and employees will provide assurance that accounts receivable are properly described and presented in the financial statements.

| Directions | Audit Objectives—Investments | Audit Objectives—Accounts Receivable | Research | Communication |
|---|---|---|---|---|

AU 330.34 states that

Confirmation of accounts receivable is a generally accepted auditing procedure. As discussed in paragraph .06, it is generally presumed that evidence obtained from third parties will provide the auditor with higher-quality audit evidence than is typically available from within the entity. Thus, there is a presumption that the auditor will request the confirmation of accounts receivable during an audit unless one of the following is true:

- Accounts receivable are immaterial to the financial statements
- The use of confirmations would be ineffective.[4]
- The auditor's combined assessed level of inherent and control risk is low, and the assessed level, in conjunction with the evidence expected to be provided by analytical procedures or other substantive tests of details is sufficient to reduce audit risk to an acceptably low level for the applicable financial statement assertions. In many situations both confirmation of accounts receivable and other substantive tests of details evidence are necessary to reduce audit risk to an acceptably low level for the applicable financial statement assertions.

.35 An auditor who has not requested confirmations in the examination of accounts receivable should document how he or she overcame this presumption.

[4] *For example, if, based on prior years' audit experience or on experience with similar engagements, the auditor concludes that response rates to properly designed confirmation requests will be inadequate, or if responses are known or expected to be unreliable, the auditor may determine that the use of confirmations would be ineffective.*

| Directions | Audit Objectives—Investments | Audit Objectives—Accounts Receivable | Research | Communication |
|---|---|---|---|---|

To:   Audit Working Papers
From: CPA Candidate
Re:   Procedures to detect fictitious companies

    There is a risk that some of the accounts receivable on the company's financial statements may be from fictitious companies. To detect such companies, we are going to verify names and addresses in telephone directories or on Web sites. If we detect even one fictitious company, we will reassess fraud risk for the engagement.

---

**Simulation Problem 2**

| Directions | Audit Implications | Confirmations | Inventory Observation | Research | Communication |
|---|---|---|---|---|---|

| | *Statement* | *IA* | *RP* |
|---|---|---|---|
| 1. | A note payable has an interest rate well below the market rate at the time at which the loan was obtained. | ○ | ● |
| 2. | The company has a properly documented loan but the loan has no scheduled repayment terms. | ○ | ● |
| 3. | Unexplained payments have been made to government officials. | ● | ○ |
| 4. | The company exchanged certain real estate property for similar real estate property. | ○ | ● |
| 5. | Large cash receipts near year-end have been received based on cash sales for which there is no documentation. | ● | ○ |

| Directions | Audit Implications | Confirmations | Inventory Observation | Research | Communication |
|---|---|---|---|---|---|

| | *Statement* | *Correct* | *Incorrect* |
|---|---|---|---|
| 1. | The confirmation requests should be mailed to respondents by the CPAs. | ● | ○ |
| 2. | A combination of positive and negative request forms must be used if receivables are significant. | ○ | ● |
| 3. | Second requests are ordinarily sent for positive form confirmations requests when the first request is not returned. | ● | ○ |
| 4. | Confirmations address existence more than they address completeness. | ● | ○ |
| 5. | Confirmation of accounts receivable is a generally accepted auditing standard. | ○ | ● |
| 6. | Absent a few circumstances, there is a presumption that the auditor will confirm accounts receivable. | ● | ○ |
| 7. | Auditors should always confirm the total balances of accounts rather than individual portions (e.g., if the balance is made up of three sales, all three should be confirmed). | ○ | ● |
| 8. | Auditors may ignore individually immaterial accounts when confirming accounts receivable. | ○ | ● |
| 9. | The best way to evaluate the results of the confirmation process is to total the misstatements identified and to compare that total to the account's tolerable error amounts. | ○ | ● |
| 10. | Accounts receivable are ordinarily confirmed on a standard form developed by the American Institute of Certified Public Accountants and the Financial Executives Institute. | ○ | ● |

| Directions | Audit Implications | Confirmations | Inventory Observation | Research | Communication |
|---|---|---|---|---|---|

| | *Statement* | *Correct* | *Incorrect* |
|---|---|---|---|
| 1. | With strong internal control, the inventory count may be at the end of the year or at other times. | ● | ○ |
| 2. | When a client has many inventory locations, auditors ordinarily need not be present at each location. | ● | ○ |
| 3. | All auditor test counts must be documented in the working papers. | ○ | ● |
| 4. | Auditors' observation of the counting of their clients' inventories addresses the existence of inventory, and not the completeness of the count. | ○ | ● |
| 5. | When the client manufactures a product, direct labor and overhead ordinarily become a part of inventory item costs. | ● | ○ |
| 6. | Inventory is ordinarily valued at the lower of standard cost or market. | ○ | ● |
| 7. | Inventory items present as "consigned in" should not be included in the client's inventory value. | ● | ○ |
| 8. | Auditor recording of test counts ordinarily replaces the need for client "tagging" of inventory. | ○ | ● |
| 9. | Ordinarily, an auditor need not count all items in the inventory. | ● | ○ |
| 10. | At the completion of the count, an auditor will ordinarily provide the client with copies of his or her inventory test counts to help assure inventory accuracy. | ○ | ● |

| Directions | Audit Implications | Confirmations | Inventory Observation | Research | Communication |
|---|---|---|---|---|---|

AU 332.22 discusses completeness as it relates to derivative instruments.

.22  Completeness assertions address whether all of the entity's derivatives and securities are reported in the financial statements through recognition or disclosure. They also address whether all derivatives and securities transactions are reported in the financial statements as a part of earnings, other comprehensive income, or cash flows or through disclosure. The extent of substantive procedures for completeness may properly vary in relation to the assessed level of control risk. In addition, the auditor should consider that since derivatives may not involve an initial exchange of tangible consideration, it may be difficult to limit audit risk for assertions about the completeness of derivatives to an acceptable level with an assessed level of control risk at the maximum. Paragraph .19 provides guidance on the auditor's determination of the nature, timing, and extent of substantive procedures to be performed. Examples of substantive procedures for completeness assertions about derivatives and securities are

- Requesting the counterparty to a derivative or the holder of a security to provide information about it, such as whether there are any side agreements or agreements to repurchase securities sold.
- Requesting counterparties or holders who are frequently used, but with whom the accounting records indicate there are presently no derivatives or securities, to state whether they are counterparties to derivatives with the entity or holders of its securities. fn 13
- Inspecting financial instruments and other agreements to identify embedded derivatives.
- Inspecting documentation in paper or electronic form for activity subsequent to the end of the reporting period.
- Performing analytical procedures. For example, a difference from an expectation that interest expense is a fixed percentage of a note based on the interest provisions of the underlying agreement may indicate the existence of an interest rate swap agreement,
- Comparing previous and current account detail to identify assets that have been removed from the accounts and testing those items further to determine that the criteria for sales treatment have been met.
- Reading other information, such as minutes of meetings of the board of directors or finance, asset/liability, investment, or other committees.

(You might have chosen to paste paragraphs 332.23-.24 also.)

| Directions | Audit Implications | Confirmations | Inventory Observation | Research | Communication |
|---|---|---|---|---|---|

To:    Audit Working Papers
From: CPA Candidate
Re:    Audit confirmations

In preparing audit confirmations, it is very important for the audit staff to control the mailing of the confirmations. If client officers or employees are allowed to intercept the confirmations, they could mitigate any evidence that could be derived from the audit procedure.

---

**Simulation Problem 3**

| Audit Procedures | Assessing Audit Risk | Research | Communication |
|---|---|---|---|

**1.** **(D, I)** The balance per bank may be traced to a standard form used to confirm account balance information with financial institutions and to the cutoff statement (on which will appear the beginning balance).

**2.** **(A, G, H, I, J)** One of the deposits in transit does not appear on the cutoff bank statement (the 9/29/05 deposit for $4,500). Accordingly, that deposit should be traced to the cash receipts journal (procedure A), the reason for the delay should be investigated (procedure G), and supporting documents should be inspected (procedure H). Both deposits should be traced to and from the bank reconciliation and the cutoff statement (procedures I and J).

**3.** **(B, G, H, I, J)** One of the checks does not appear on the cutoff statement (check #988 dated 8/31/05 for $2,200). Accordingly, that check should be traced to the cash disbursements journal (procedure B), the reason for the delay should be investigated (procedure G), and supporting documents should be inspected (procedure H). All checks should be traced to and from the bank reconciliation and cutoff statement (procedures I and J).

**4.** **(E)** The credit memo from the bank for the note collected should be investigated.

**5.** **(E, I)** The credit for the check that was charged by the bank for an incorrect amount should be investigated on both the bank credit memo and on the cutoff statement.

**6.** **(C)** The only source of the balance per books is the cash general ledger account as of 9/30/05.

| Audit Procedures | Addressing Audit Risk | Research | Communication |
|---|---|---|---|

**1.** **(E)** Kiting involves manipulations causing an amount of cash to be included simultaneously in the balance of two or more bank accounts. Kiting schemes are based on the float period—the time necessary for a check deposited in one bank to clear the bank on which it was drawn. To detect kiting, a bank transfer schedule is prepared to determine whether cash is improperly included in two accounts.

**2.** **(D)** A comparison of the cleared checks to the year-end bank reconciliation will identify checks that were not mailed until after the first week of the subsequent year because most of those checks will not be returned with the cutoff statement and will appear to remain outstanding an abnormally long period of time.

**3.** **(H)** Among the terms confirmed for such a borrowing arrangement will be information on liens.

**4.** **(K,L)** A reply to the second request, or information from the credit agency, may confirm the existence of the new customer. Also, examination of shipping documents will reveal where the goods were shipped, and ordinarily to which party.

**5.** **(P)** Observing the payroll check distribution on a surprise basis will assist in detection since the auditor will examine details related to any paychecks not picked up by employees.

**6.** **(Q)** Vouching data in the payroll register to document authorized pay rates will reveal situations in which an employee is earning income at a rate that differs from the authorized rate.

**7.** **(A)** A comparison of the details of the cash receipts journal to the details on the daily deposit slips will reveal a circumstance since the details will have been posted to accounts during the last week of the year under audit.

**8.** **(U)** When vouchers are processed for merchandise not ordered or received, there will be no supporting purchase orders and receiving reports and this will alert the auditor to the problem.

**9.** **(B)** Scanning the debits to the fixed asset accounts and vouching selected amounts will reveal repairs that have improperly been capitalized.

**10**. **(A,J)** Lapping involves concealing a cash shortage by delaying the recording of journal entries for cash receipts. Since lapping includes differences between the details of postings to the cash receipts journal and corresponding deposit slips, comparing these records will reveal it. Also, confirmation requests may identify lapping when payments of receivables (as indicated by confirmation replies) appear to have taken too much time to be processed.

**11.** **(E)** Increasing cash by drawing a check in this manner is a form of kiting (see answer 1). Preparation of a bank transfer schedule will assist the auditor in identifying such transactions.

**12.** **(J,L)** Confirmations will identify overstated accounts receivable when customers disagree with the recorded balance due. Also, the related overstated sales will not have shipping documents indicating that a shipment has occurred.

| Audit Procedures | Addressing Audit Risk | Research | Communication |
|---|---|---|---|

The first step is to determine the manner in which the candidate wishes to identify the pertinent research in the area. If a keyword or index search is to be used, words such as "identified related-party transactions" or "identified related-party" may be helpful. Even using "related party" will get the candidate to AU 334 which provides the needed information. AU 334 indicates the following with respect to identified related-party transactions:

.09 After identifying related-party transactions, the auditor should apply the procedures he considers necessary to obtain satisfaction concerning the purpose, nature, and extent of these transactions and their effect on the financial statements. The procedures should be directed toward obtaining and evaluating sufficient competent evidential matter and should extend beyond inquiry of management. Procedures that should be considered include the following:

    a. Obtain an understanding of the business purpose of the transaction.

    b. Examine invoices, executed copies of agreements, contracts, and other pertinent documents, such as receiving reports and shipping documents.

    c. Determine whether the transaction has been approved by the board of directors or other appropriate officials.

    d. Test for reasonableness the compilation of amounts to be disclosed, or considered for disclosure, in the financial statements.

    e. Arrange for the audits of intercompany account balances to be performed as of concurrent dates, even if the fiscal years differ, and for the examination of specified, important, and representative related-party transactions by the auditors for each of the parties, with appropriate exchange of relevant information.

    f. Inspect or confirm and obtain satisfaction concerning the transferability and value of collateral.

.10 When necessary to fully understand a particular transaction, the following procedures, which might not otherwise be deemed necessary to comply with generally accepted auditing standards, should be considered.

    a. Confirm transaction amount and terms, including guarantees and other significant data, with the other party or parties to the transaction.

    b. Inspect evidence in possession of the other party or parties to the transaction.

    c. Confirm or discuss significant information with intermediaries, such as banks, guarantors, agents, or attorneys, to obtain a better understanding of the transaction.

    d. Refer to financial publications, trade journals, credit agencies, and other information sources when there is reason to believe that unfamiliar customers, suppliers, or other business enterprises with which material amounts of business have been transacted may lack substance.

    e. With respect to material uncollected balances, guarantees, and other obligations, obtain information about the financial capability of the other party or parties to the transaction. Such information may be obtained from audited financial statements, unaudited financial statements, income tax returns, and reports issued by regulatory agencies, taxing authorities, financial publications, or credit agencies. The auditor should decide on the degree of assurance required and the extent to which available information provides such assurance.

| Audit Procedures | Addressing Audit Risk | Research | Communication |
|---|---|---|---|

To:    Joe Smith, CEO
          General Company
From: CPA Candidate
Re:    Related-party loan disclosure

By their nature, related-party transactions are not at arm's length—they do not involve independent bargaining. Except for routine transactions, it is generally not possible to determine whether a particular transaction would have occurred if the parties were not related, or assuming it would have occurred, what the terms would have been. Therefore, it is difficult to support representations that the transaction's terms are similar to those that would have occurred between unrelated parties. Accordingly, we do not recommend that this representation be included in the notes to the financial statements.

# REPORTING

The report represents the end product of the auditor's association with the client's financial statements. The following "Diagram of an Audit," originally presented in the auditing overview section, shows the relationship of the audit report to the entire financial statement audit.

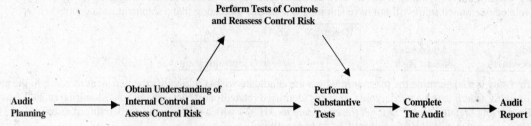

This module covers the topics listed in the Reporting area of the AICPA Content Specification Outline and subsequent events (which the AICPA includes in the Audit Evidence and Procedures area of the Outline). The emphasis in this module is upon audit reports, but it also includes information on other reports (e.g., compilation reports, review reports, attestation reports).

Candidate knowledge of reports is tested on every examination. While most of the report questions refer to audit reports, a significant number refer to the other types of reports that CPAs issue. Multiple-choice questions present a circumstance that calls for a departure from the standard short form report and ask specifically what type of report is to be issued. A simulation question may require preparation of a report using electronic access to the appropriate professional standards.

## Study Program for the Reporting Module

This module is organized and should be studied in the following manner:

A. Financial Statement Audit Reports—General
B. Financial Statement Audit Reports—Detailed

    1. Circumstances Resulting in Departure from the Auditor's Standard Report
    2. Report Preparation

C. Accountant Association other than Audits

    1. Other Forms of Accountant Association with Historical Financial Statements
    2. Other Reports—Statements on Auditing Standards Based
    3. Other Reports—Attestation Standards Based

D. Reporting on Compliance

    1. Compliance Attestation Engagements
    2. Compliance Auditing of Federal Financial Assistance Programs

All of the following sections of Statements on Auditing Standards apply to reports.

*AU Section*

| | |
|---|---|
| 341 | The Auditor's Consideration of an Entity's Ability to Continue as a Going Concern |
| 410 | Adherence to GAAP |
| 411 | The Meaning of "Present Fairly" |
| 420 | Consistency of Application of GAAP |
| 431 | Adequacy of Informative Disclosure |
| 435 | Segment Information |
| 504 | Association with Financial Statements |
| 508 | Reports on Audited Financial Statements |
| 530 | Dating the Independent Auditor's Report |
| 534 | Reporting on Financial Statements Prepared for Use in Other Countries |
| 543 | Part of Examination Made by Other Independent Auditors |
| 550 | Other Information in Documents Containing Audited Financial Statements |
| 551 | Information in Auditor-Submitted Documents |
| 552 | Reporting on Condensed Financial Statements and Selected Financial Data |
| 558 | Required Supplementary Information |
| 560 | Subsequent Events |

The following attestation standards outlines (all have AT prefixes) apply to this module:

## Statements on Standards for Attestation Engagements (SSAE)

AT 501, *Reporting on an Entity's Internal Control over Financial Reporting,* is included in the Internal Control Module.

Finally, you should read the outlines of the Statements on Standards for Accounting and Review Services, following the outlines of the Statements on Auditing Standards.

## Statements on Standards for Accounting and Review Services (SSARS)

The AU, AT, and AR sections listed earlier are very detailed. In this module, we present an overview of this information contained in those sections. In order to simplify the discussion, the topics are covered in a sequence that is different than the order in which they are presented in the codified professional standards. The best way to cover this material is to first read the background material presented in Section A of this module. Then, read each subsequent section together with the SAS outline presented later in this volume. The purpose of this module is to give you an overview of the information that will make it easier for you to understand the actual professional standards. But you should also carefully study the various outlines.

This module covers the topics listed in the Reporting area of the AICPA Content Specification Outline plus subsequent events that the AICPA includes in the Audit Evidence and Procedures area of the Outline.

## A.  Financial Statement Audit Reports—General

1.  **Overall issues**

    a.  **Forms of association.** It is useful to think about four primary forms of accountant association with information; examinations, reviews, agreed-upon procedures, and compilations.

        **Examinations** (referred to as audits in the case of financial statements) provide a positive opinion with reasonable assurance on whether assertions follow the appropriate criteria. The unqualified report for financial statement audits includes three paragraphs: introductory, scope, and opinion.

        **Reviews** provide a report that includes limited assurance. Limited assurance is also referred to as "negative assurance" because a phrase such as "I am not aware of any material modifications that should be made" is included in the report. The first paragraph of the report states that a review in accordance with AICPA standards was performed. The second paragraph indicates the limited scope of the review and the third paragraph provides the limited assurance. The procedures of a review are largely limited to internal inquiries and analytical procedures and are thus significantly more limited than an examination (see Evidence Module).

**Agreed-upon procedures** result in a report that provides a summary of findings. Because agreed-upon procedures will ordinarily be less in scope than examination, the report disclaims a positive opinion on the financial statements.

**Compilations** are considered an accounting service (not attestation) because no assurance is provided in the report. The first paragraph states that a compilation in conformity with AICPA standards has been performed, the second paragraph states that no opinion or assurance is provided.

b. **Restricted-use reports vs. general-use reports (AU 532).** Reports issued by auditors differ in that some are available for only "restricted use" while others are available for "general use."

**Restricted-use** auditors' reports are intended only for specified parties. Ordinarily "specified parties" are those parties to the agreement (e.g., management, the board of directors, the audit committee, others within the organization, and sometimes, regulatory agencies). The following three circumstances result in a restricted-use auditors' report and should be issued:

(1) The subject is based on criteria in contractual agreements or regulatory provisions that are not in accordance with GAAP or another comprehensive basis of accounting
(2) Agreed-upon procedures engagements
(3) "By-products" of an audit (for example, internal control reportable conditions letters [AU 325], and communications with audit committees [AU 380])

An auditor's report that is restricted should contain a separate paragraph at the end of the report that includes

(1) A statement that the report is intended solely for the information and use of the specified parties
(2) An identification of the specified parties to whom use is restricted
(3) A statement that the report is not intended to be and should not be used by anyone other than the specified parties

**General-use** auditors' reports are not restricted to specified parties. These reports are on information that is ordinarily understandable by a broader set of individuals than is the information reported upon in restricted-use reports. For example, audit reports on financial statements prepared in accordance with GAAP provide an illustration of what is ordinarily a general-use report.

2. **Financial Statement Audit Reports—Nonpublic Companies.** Most CPA exam questions pertain to audits of financial statements. The following standard short-form report for a nonpublic company was originally presented in the overview section:

*Independent Auditor's Report*

To: Board of Directors and Stockholders
ABC Company

We have audited the accompanying balance sheets of ABC Company as of December 31, 20X2 and 20X1, and the related statements of income, retained earnings, and cash flows for the years then ended. These financial statements are the responsibility of the Company's management. Our responsibility is to express an opinion on these financial statements based on our audits.

We conducted our audits in accordance with US generally accepted auditing standards. Those standards require that we plan and perform the audit to obtain reasonable assurance about whether the financial statements are free of material misstatement. An audit includes examining, on a test basis, evidence supporting the amounts and disclosures in the financial statements. An audit also includes assessing the accounting principles used and significant estimates made by management, as well as evaluating the overall financial statement presentation. We believe that our audits provide a reasonable basis for our opinion.

In our opinion, the financial statements referred to above present fairly, in all material respects, the financial position of ABC Company as of December 31, 20X2 and 20X1, and the results of its operations and its cash flows for the years then ended in conformity with US generally accepted accounting principles.

                                                                        Joe Smith, CPA
                                                                        February 23, 20X3

Some key details relating to the above report include

Title ("Independent" must be in title)
Addressee (company, board of directors and/or stockholders—**not** management)
Introductory paragraph

1. We have audited
2. Client's financial statements (statements listed)

   *NOTE: SFAS 130 establishes standards for the reporting and display of comprehensive income and its components when a full set of financial statements is being issued. While it does not require a specific format, the statement provides illustrations that display comprehensive income and its components in three manners.*

   *1. A separate statement*
   *2. As an add-on to the statement of income*
   *3. Integrated with the statement of changes in equity*

   *When a separate statement of comprehensive income is presented (method 1. above), the introductory paragraph of the auditor's report should refer to that statement.*

3. Financial statements are the responsibility of management
4. The auditor's responsibility is to express an opinion

Scope paragraph

1. Audit conducted in accordance with US generally accepted auditing standards
2. Those standards require that we plan and perform audit to provide reasonable assurance statements free of material misstatement
3. Audit involves

   Examining on a test basis evidence supporting amounts and disclosures
   Assessment of accounting principles
   Assessment of significant estimates
   Evaluation of overall presentation

4. Audit provides reasonable basis for opinion

Opinion paragraph

1. In our opinion
2. Statements present fairly per US generally accepted accounting principles.

Manual or printed signature (Firm name)
Date (normally last day of fieldwork)

Remember that the generally accepted auditing standards include four reporting standards (GAAP, Opinion, Disclosure, Consistency—the GODC mnemonic presented in the Overview Section). Read Sections 410, 411, and 431. Note especially in Section 411 that the term "present fairly" in the opinion paragraph is normally to be interpreted within the framework of GAAP. That is, if financial statements are in conformity with GAAP, they normally are presented fairly. Nevertheless, there may be unusual circumstances in which a generally accepted accounting principle may cause the financial statements to be misleading (e.g., new legislation); in such a case, the principle is not to be followed.

Section 411 addresses the issue of the authority of various sources of GAAP. The section establishes a four-level hierarchy of "established accounting principles."

1. Accounting principles promulgated by a body designated by the AICPA Council to establish such principles, pursuant to Rule 203 of the Code of Professional Conduct (i.e., FASB and GASB)—we refer to this category as "authoritative body pronouncements"
2. Pronouncements of bodies composed of expert accountants, exposed for public comment
3. Pronouncements of bodies composed of expert accountants, **not** exposed for public comment
4. Widely recognized practices and pronouncements

In addition, the above four categories are supplemented by "other accounting literature."

The following hierarchy that is duplicated from the outline of AU 411 indicates where the various types of pronouncements fit into each of the categories for nongovernmental entities, state and local governments, and the federal government.

**GAAP HIERARCHY SUMMARY**

| Category | Nongovernmental Entities | State and Local Governments | Federal Government |
|---|---|---|---|
| A. **Authoritative Body Pronouncements** | FASB *Statements* and *Interpretations*<br>APB *Opinions*<br>AICPA *Accounting Research Bulletins* | GASB *Statements* and *Interpretations*<br>FASB and AICPA pronouncements applicable by a GASB *Statement* or *Interpretation* | FASAB *Statements* and *Interpretations*<br>AICPA, FASB, and GASB pronouncements made applicable by a FASAB *Statement* or *Interpretation* |
| B. **Pronouncements of Bodies Composed of Expert Accountants, Exposed for Public Comment** | FASB *Technical Bulletins*<br>AICPA *Industry Audit and Accounting Guides* and *Statements of Position* (cleared by FASB) | GASB *Technical Bulletins*<br>AICPA *Industry Audit and Accounting Guides* and *Statements of Position* (cleared by GASB) | FASAB *Technical Bulletins*<br>AICPA *Industry Audit and Accounting Guides* and *Statements of Position* (cleared by FASAB) |
| C. **Pronouncements of Bodies Composed of Expert Accountants, *Not* Exposed for Public Comment** | *Consensus Positions of the FASB Emerging Issues Task Force*<br>AICPA *Practice Bulletins* (cleared by FASB) | *Consensus Positions of the GASB Emerging Issues Task Force*<br>AICPA *Practice Bulletins* (cleared by GASB) | *Technical Releases* of the Accounting and Auditing Policy Committee of the FASAB<br>AICPA *Practice Bulletins* (cleared by the FASAB) |
| D. **Widely Recognized Practices and Pronouncements** | FASB staff *"Questions and Answers"*<br>AICPA *Accounting Interpretations*<br>Widely accepted industry practices | GASB staff *"Questions and Answers"*<br>Widely accepted industry practices | FASAB staff *Implementation Guides*<br>Widely accepted federal government practices |
| E. **Other Accounting Literature** | FASB *Concepts Statements*<br>APB *Statements*<br>AICPA *Issues Papers* and *Technical Practice Aids*<br>International Accounting Standards Committee *Statements*<br>GASB *Statements, Interpretations,* and *Technical Bulletins*<br>Pronouncements of other professional associations or regulatory agencies<br>Accounting textbooks, handbooks, and articles | GASB *Concepts Statements*<br>Pronouncements in (A) through (D) of nongovernmental hierarchy not specifically made applicable<br>APB *Statements*<br>FASB *Concepts Statements*<br>AICPA *Issues Papers* and *Technical Practice Aids*<br>International Accounting Standards Committee *Statements*<br>Pronouncements of other professional associations or regulatory agencies<br>Accounting textbooks, handbooks, and articles | FASAB *Concepts Statements*<br>Pronouncements in (A) through (D) of GASB and FASB not specifically made applicable<br>FASB and GASB *Concepts Statements*, AICPA *Issues Papers*, and *Technical Practice Aids*<br>International Accounting Standards Committee *Statements*<br>Pronouncements of other professional associations or regulatory agencies<br>Accounting textbooks, handbooks, and articles |

In cases of conflict between the accounting treatment suggested by the categories, the higher category normally prevails over lower categories. For conflicts within a category the treatment most closely approximating the transaction's economic substance prevails (i.e., substance over form).

Section 431 addresses the adequacy of financial statement disclosures. Disclosures are to be regarded as reasonably adequate unless otherwise stated in the audit report. When the auditor issues a qualified or an adverse opinion, the report should provide, **if practicable,** the information causing the departure from an unqualified report. Thus, if the client omits information in the notes concerning a loan agreement's restriction of future dividends, the auditor would provide the additional information. However, if the client has omitted a statement of cash flows, the auditor would not be required to prepare it, since it is not practicable to easily and directly obtain this information from the client's records.

As indicated earlier in this module, the date of the report is normally the last day of fieldwork. AU 530 discusses an often-tested exception to this rule. When a subsequent event requiring note disclosure has occurred after the close of fieldwork but prior to issuance of the audit report, the auditor may either dual date the report or change its date to that of the subsequent event. For example, assume that March 2 was the last day of significant fieldwork. A dual dated report would be dated as "March 2, 20X2, except for note X for which the date is March 6, 20X2." Alternatively, the auditor may change the report date to March 6. This latter option is generally less desirable since the auditor's responsibility with respect to other possible subsequent events is extended to the date of the report—here March 6.

AU 530 also addresses the proper date of an audit report when a CPA is asked to either furnish additional copies of a previously issued report or to reissue a previously issued report (e.g., for inclusion in a report filed with the SEC).  In both circumstances, the date is not normally changed from that originally used.  However, if the CPA has become aware of an event requiring note disclosure (as contrasted to requiring an adjusting entry), the financial statements should disclose the event in a separate unaudited note to the financial statements.  The note should be captioned in a manner such as "Event (Unaudited) Subsequent to the Date of the Independent Auditor's Report."  When the event is such that the financial statements require adjustment, the auditor should reissue the report as dual dated (as discussed above).

3. **Financial Statement Audit Reports—Public Companies.**  The Sarbanes-Oxley Act of 2002 created a requirement for an integrated audit that provides assurance about the fairness of financial statements and about the effectiveness of internal control over financial reporting—the internal control module discusses audit reports on internal control.  The audit report on financial statements is different from that of a nonpublic company in the following ways:

1. The report includes the title "Report of Independent Registered Public Accounting Firm"
2. The report refers to the standards of the PCAOB rather than generally accepted auditing standards
3. The report includes a paragraph referring to the auditor's report on internal control (this reference is obviously only required when the reports on the financial statements and internal control are separate)
4. The report should contain the city and state or country of the office that issued the report.

The following is a sample audit report on the financial statements of a public company.

### Report of Independent Registered Public Accounting Firm

We have audited the accompanying balance sheets of X Company as of December 31, 20X3 and 20X2, and the related statements of operations, stockholders' equity, and cash flows for each of the three years in the period ended December 31, 20X3.  These financial statements are the responsibility of the Company's management.  Our responsibility is to express an opinion on these financial statements based on our audits.

We conducted our audits in accordance with the standards of the Public Company Accounting Oversight Board (United States).  Those standards require that we plan and perform the audit to obtain reasonable assurance about whether the financial statements are free of material misstatement.  An audit includes examining, on a test basis, evidence supporting the amounts and disclosures in the financial statements.  An audit also includes assessing the accounting principles used and significant estimates made by management, as well as evaluating the overall financial statement presentation.  We believe that our audits provide a reasonable basis for our opinion.

In our opinion, the financial statements referred to above present fairly, in all material respects, the financial position of the Company as of [at] December 31, 20X3 and 20X2, and the results of its operations and its cash flows for each of the three years in the period ended December 31, 20X3, in conformity with US generally accepted accounting principles.

We also have audited, in accordance with the standards of the Public Company Accounting Oversight Board (United States), the effectiveness of X Company's internal control over financial reporting as of December 31, 20X3, based on criteria established in Internal Control—Integrated Framework issued by the Committee of Sponsoring Organizations of the Treadway Commission and our report dated February 24, 20X4, expressed an unqualified opinion thereon.

[Signature]
[City and State or Country]
[Date]

The examples in the following portions of this module follow the format for nonpublic company audit reports.  At this point, the rules for modifying reports of public companies are the same as those for nonpublic companies—one simply begins with a slightly different standard report.  Accordingly, this material applies to both public and nonpublic company audit reports.

B. **Financial Statement Audit Reports—Detailed**

1. **Circumstances Resulting in Departure from the Auditor's Standard Report.**
   The AICPA does not present a list of necessary conditions for an auditor to render a standard, unqualified report.  The approach is one of presenting circumstances that may require departure from the standard report.  These situations may be divided into circumstances requiring additional explanatory language be added to an unqualified report, and those which result in other than an unqualified report as follows:

   Circumstances requiring unqualified report with additional explanatory language

   a. Opinion based, in part, on report of another auditor

    b.  Unusual circumstances requiring a departure from promulgated GAAP
    c.  Substantial doubt about ability to remain a going concern (may also lead to a disclaimer)
    d.  Inconsistency in application of GAAP
    e.  Certain circumstances affecting comparative statements
    f.  Required quarterly data for SEC reporting companies
    g.  Supplementary information required by FASB or GASB
    h.  Other information in document containing audited financial statements
    i.  Emphasis of a matter

Circumstances requiring **other** than an unqualified report

    j.  Departure from GAAP
    k.  Scope limitation
    l.  Lack of independence

You should be familiar with the effect that each of the above circumstances has on an audit report. The following pages contain a summary of some of the most important "must know" material. While the outlines of the various audit report sections present the information in more detail, we provide you with a more structured, organized approach to these topics than is possible with the outlines alone. Section B.2. of this module presents examples of the actual modifications made to audit reports to reflect the circumstances.

a.  **Opinion based, in part, on report of another auditor (AU 543, 508).** Opinions based, in part, on the report of another auditor may differ from the standard report. This situation arises when two or more auditors are involved in the audit of a single entity. An example of this is the case in which one CPA firm audits the entire firm except for a subsidiary in a distant location. The auditor who audited the single subsidiary will generally issue a report on the subsidiary. The auditor who audited the remainder of the firm could give a report on that portion of the entity examined. However, there will generally be a preference (and indeed often a legal requirement) for an audit report on the overall entity.

    The overall audit report must be signed by the principal auditor. The principal auditor is designated based on the materiality of the portion of financial statements examined, knowledge of the overall financial statements, and the importance of the components audited. The principal auditor is required to

    (1)  Make inquiries regarding the other auditor's reputation (e.g., contact AICPA, state society of CPAs, other practitioners, bankers, etc.)
    (2)  Obtain representation from the other auditor concerning independence
    (3)  Ascertain that the other auditor knows US auditing standards, SEC standards (if appropriate), and knows that the financial statements he or she audited are a component of, and to be included with, the financial statements on which the principal auditor will report

If the results of any of the above inquiries are unsatisfactory, the principal auditor must either modify the overall audit report (qualify or disclaim), or audit the component. If the results of the inquiries are satisfactory, the following summarizes the principal auditor's required decisions and responsibilities:

## PRINCIPAL-OTHER AUDITOR RELATIONSHIP

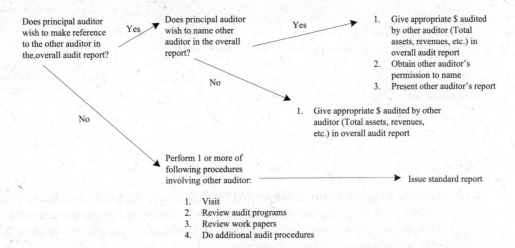

The decision to make reference to the other auditor indicates **divided** (or **shared**) **responsibility** between the auditors and is **not** considered an audit report qualification.  The decision **not** to make reference to the other report indicates that the principal auditor assumes responsibility for the work of the other auditor.  Reasons for assuming responsibility include

1.   The other auditor is an affiliate of the principal auditor
2.   The principal auditor hired the other auditor
3.   The portion audited by the other auditor is not material
4.   Other miscellaneous reasons as the principal auditor (or client) desires

Finally, note that in situations in which the other auditor's report is other than unqualified, the materiality of the matter (causing a departure from the standard report of the other auditor) to the overall financial statements determines whether the principal auditor's report must be modified.

b.  **Unusual circumstances requiring a departure from promulgated GAAP (AU 508).**
This circumstance occurs when an auditor agrees with the client that a departure from GAAP is justified due to unusual circumstances (e.g., new legislation or a new type of transaction).  The situation here is one in which following GAAP would result in misleading financial statements.  This situation is **not,** for example, one in which a client reports its fixed assets at current values instead of historical cost (less depreciation); inflation hasn't been unusual in that it has affected the financial statements of all companies.  When an unusual circumstance does occur, and when following GAAP would result in misleading financial statements, GAAP should be departed from and the auditor should issue an unqualified report with an explanatory paragraph describing the departure.

c.  **Substantial doubt about ability to remain a going concern (AU 341).**  Auditors must make a judgment as to whether there is substantial doubt about the ability of a client to continue as a going concern for a reasonable period of time—a period not to exceed **one year** from the **date** of the **financial statements**.

The Evidence Module (Section C.17.) included discussion of the audit approach for considering going concern status.  Although an audit is not required to include procedures aimed solely at identifying a going concern question, results obtained from procedures performed throughout the audit should be evaluated to determine whether they suggest substantial doubt.  When substantial doubt is raised, an auditor considers whether management's plans for dealing with the conditions and events causing the uncertainty are likely to negate the problem.  If after evaluating management's plans substantial doubt still exists, the auditor should either add an explanatory paragraph to an unqualified report (following the opinion paragraph) or disclaim an opinion.  In either case the report must explicitly include the phrases "substantial doubt" and "going concern."  If analysis of management's plans convinces the auditor that substantial doubt does not exist, he or she still must consider the adequacy of financial statement note disclosures related to the matter.  The following diagram summarizes the entire decision process.

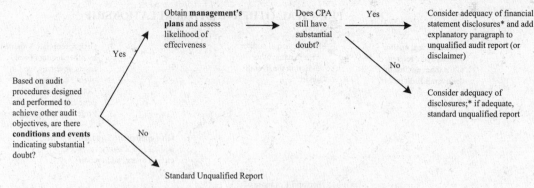

*\* If disclosures are not adequate, a departure from GAAP exists which may lead to a qualified or adverse opinion*

**d.   Inconsistency in application of GAAP (AU 420, 508).**   A change in accounting principle that has a material effect on the comparability of a company's financial statements ordinarily results in a report with an unqualified opinion followed by an explanatory paragraph.  Review APB 20 on accounting changes when studying this section.

The general rule is that changes in accounting principles result in the addition of explanatory language, while changes in accounting estimates, corrections of clerical errors, and minor reclassifications of accounts from one year to the next do not.  Changes in business entities and changes among carrying bases (cost, equity, consolidated) for continuing subsidiaries result in explanatory language; creation, cessation, purchase, or disposition of subsidiaries do not result in explanatory language.

Bear in mind that consistency pertains to the accounting treatment for items **between periods**. Also, in comparative reports for changes that are not accounted for by retroactive restatement, the explanatory paragraph is retained as long as the year of change is presented.  Retroactive changes require the explanatory paragraph only in the year of the change.

Here are several other important points relating to consistency.

(1)  Differing accounting principles may be used for different portions of an account.  For example, a client may choose to use FIFO for valuation of a portion of its inventory and LIFO for the remainder.  Similarly, for fixed assets, differing depreciation methods may be used for differing classes (types) of assets.

(2)  A change that is immaterial this year, but is expected to become material in the future, **does not** result in explanatory language if the client has properly disclosed it in the notes to the financial statements.

(3)  If the auditor does not concur with a change in principle, or if the change has not been properly accounted for, a qualified or adverse opinion is required because this represents a departure from GAAP.

(4)  The audit report does not mention consistency when there has been no change in principle.

The most frequent changes in principle relating to consistency are summarized below.

|  |  | *Consistency explanatory paragraph* |
|---|---|---|
| *Type of change* | | |
| I.   Change in Accounting Principle | | |
|    1.  GAAP to GAAP | | Yes |
|    2.  Non-GAAP to GAAP | | Yes |
|    3.  GAAP to non-GAAP | | Yes* |
|    4.  For newly acquired assets in an existing class of assets (whether 1, 2, or 3 above) | | Yes |
|    5.  For a new class of asset (whether 1, 2, or 3 above) | | No |

| Type of change | Consistency explanatory paragraph |
|---|---|
| II.   Change in Accounting Estimate | |
| 1.  Judgmental adjustments | No |
| 2.  Inseparable estimate and principle change | Yes |
| III.  Change in Entity | |
| 1.  Changes between carrying basis (cost, equity, consolidated) | Yes |
| 2.  Pooling | No |
| 3.  Changes in subsidiaries (creation, cessation, purchase, or disposition) | No |
| IV.  Correction of Error | |
| 1.  Error in principle (I.2., above) | Yes |
| 2.  Error not involving application of a principle | No |
| V.   Change in Statement Format | |
| 1.  Classifications and reclassifications | No |

*Note that Section I.3. will also result in a departure from GAAP exception.

e.  **Certain circumstances affecting comparative financial statements (AU 508).** When comparative statements are issued (i.e., financial statements for two or more periods are presented), the auditor must report on the statements for all years presented. One overall report, dated as of the last day of fieldwork for the most recent audit, addressing the years presented, is issued. Two major situations may result in an unqualified report with explanatory language.

(1) An opinion on the prior period financial statements may differ from the opinion previously issued. For example, an auditor previously may have qualified the opinion on the prior period statements because of a departure from GAAP, and the prior period statements may be restated in the current period to follow GAAP. In such a circumstance the auditor's updated report on the prior period statements should indicate that the statements have been restated and should express an unqualified opinion with respect to the restated statements. Whenever an updated report has an opinion different from that previously expressed, the auditor should disclose all substantive reasons for the different opinion in a separate explanatory paragraph preceding the opinion paragraph. The explanatory paragraph should disclose

(a) The date of the previous report
(b) The type of opinion previously expressed
(c) The circumstances causing the auditor to express a different opinion
(d) That the updated opinion is different from the previous opinion

(2) When a predecessor auditor has examined the prior period statements, a decision needs to be made as to whether the predecessor's report is to be reissued. If the report is **not** to be reissued, the successor auditor's report should indicate in the introductory paragraph

(a) That the financial statements of the prior period were examined by other auditors
(b) The date of the predecessor's report
(c) The type of report issued by the predecessor
(d) The substantive reasons therefore, if it was other than a standard unqualified report

If the predecessor's report is to be reissued, the predecessor should read the current statements, compare the prior period statements to the current statements, and obtain from the successor a letter of representation as to whether any material matters concerning the prior period statements have arisen.

Regardless of whether the predecessor's report is being reissued, the opinion paragraph of the successor auditor's report refers only to the second year.

f.  **Required quarterly data for SEC reporting companies (AU 722).** Certain SEC reporting companies are required to include unaudited quarterly information in their annual reports or other documents filed with the SEC that contain audited financial statements. Auditors are engaged to perform review procedures either at the conclusion of each quarter, or at the end of the year when the information is included with the annual information. When dealing with the annual financial statements, omission, misstatement, or auditor inability to review the quarterly information all lead to inclusion of an explanatory paragraph in the annual audit report. Be aware that the information is to be reviewed, not audited. Therefore, its misstatement will **not** lead to a qualified or an adverse opinion.

g. **Supplementary information required by the FASB or GASB (AU 558).** This information is treated identically to the required quarterly data for SEC reporting companies (see the prior section). Omission, misstatement, or auditor inability to review the information will lead to the inclusion of an explanatory paragraph in the audit report.

h. **Other information in a document containing audited financial statements (AU 550-552).** Several types of information are included here. Section 550 deals with other information in documents containing audited statements. This refers to the case where the audited financial statements are included in a published annual report that includes other information (e.g., president's letter, graphs, pictures). The auditor is required to read the annual report and note any inconsistencies between the financial statements and the other information provided. If the audited financial statements are inconsistent with the other information, one or both of the following must be true:

(1) Financial statements are incorrect—this will lead to a qualified opinion or an adverse opinion since it is a departure from GAAP (see Section j. below).

(2) Other information is incorrect—this will lead to an unqualified report with an explanatory paragraph, and/or withholding use of the audit report and/or withdrawal from the engagement.

Finally, the auditor may note no inconsistency, but may believe that the other information **seems** incorrect. In such cases the auditor is to discuss the matter with the client, consult with other parties such as legal counsel, and use judgment as to the resolution of the matter.

Section 551 deals with reporting on information in auditor-submitted documents. When an **auditor submits a document** containing audited financial statements, s/he has the responsibility to report on **all** the information included in the document. The auditor should either disclaim an opinion on this additional information or audit the information and issue an opinion on it. If the information is to be audited, the measure of materiality is in relation to the financial statements taken as a whole. The disclaimer or opinion may either be included in the overall audit report or presented as a separate report.

Section 552 addresses the situation for which selected financial data, derived from audited financial statements, are presented in a client prepared document (e.g., annual report) that also includes the audited financial statements. The auditor may report only on the financial data that is derived from the audited financial statements. In this situation, an explanatory paragraph is added in which the auditor states whether the selected financial data are fairly stated in all material respects in relation to the financial statements.

i. **Emphasis of a matter (AU 508).** The auditor may wish to emphasize a matter (through adding an explanatory paragraph) regarding the financial statements, but, nevertheless, may intend to render an unqualified opinion. Examples include cases in which the entity is a component of a larger entity, or in which significant related party transactions exist, or the auditor wishes to draw attention to an important subsequent event. Such information is included in an explanatory paragraph.

Until 1996, significant uncertainties affecting the financial statements (e.g., a significant lawsuit, which nevertheless did not raise a question concerning going concern status) were considered a distinct circumstance that might result in the addition of an explanatory paragraph to an audit report. Standards relating to uncertainty modifications were eliminated, and now an auditor may wish to emphasize an uncertainty through inclusion under the emphasis of a matter paragraph.

*NOTE: The following sections require other than an unqualified report.*

j. **Departures from generally accepted accounting principles (AU 508).** Departures from GAAP result in either a qualified opinion or an adverse opinion; both types of reports include an explanatory paragraph preceding the opinion paragraph. Examples of departures from GAAP include the use of an unacceptable inventory valuation method (e.g., current sales value) or incorrectly treating a capital lease as an operating lease.

The type of report depends on the materiality of the departure. **Know** that materiality depends on

(1) Dollar magnitude of effects
(2) Significance of item to enterprise
(3) Pervasiveness of misstatement
(4) Impact of misstatement on financial statements taken as a whole

As the effects of such departures become more material, the likelihood of an adverse opinion increases. If the departure from GAAP consists of inadequate disclosure of required information, the correct information, if available, should be included in an explanatory paragraph that **precedes** the qualified or adverse opinion paragraph. When the information is not available, the explanatory paragraph of the report should so state.

When an adverse opinion is being issued, an auditor may be asked to add a comment in the audit report indicating that certain identified accounts or disclosures in the financial statements are fairly presented. The auditor should not comply with this type of request since such "piecemeal opinions" are considered inappropriate because they might overshadow or contradict the overall adverse opinion.

Be familiar with two specific circumstances relating to departures from GAAP: omission of the statement of cash flows and incorrect segment disclosures. When a company presents financial statements that purport to present financial position **and** results of operations (e.g., balance sheet **and** an income statement) a statement of cash flows must also be presented. The omission of a statement of cash flows in such a circumstance is a departure form GAAP that requires issuance of a qualified opinion (an adverse opinion is not recommended). Additionally, the auditor need not present the missing statement of cash flows in an explanatory paragraph of the audit report.

The second circumstance involves incorrect (or omitted) segment disclosures required under SFAS 131 issued by the Financial Accounting Standards Board. Inaccurate (or omitted) segment disclosures constitute a departure from GAAP and lead to a qualified opinion or an adverse opinion. When a client changes operating segments from one year to the next for acceptable reasons, no consistency modification or other report modification is necessary.

An auditor considers segment disclosures (as other disclosures) in relation to the financial statements taken as a whole. Accordingly, the auditor is not required to apply procedures as extensive as would be necessary to express an opinion on the segment information itself. The procedures performed include

| Procedures to evaluate identification of segments: | Procedures to evaluate adequacy of segment disclosures: |
| --- | --- |
| • Inquire about methods of identifying segments<br>• Review corroborating evidence<br>• Assess whether SFAS 131 procedures were appropriately followed to determine segments<br>• Obtain management's written representation that segments appropriately identified | • Perform analytical procedures<br>• Evaluate adequacy with regard to general information, information about segments, reconciliations of revenues, losses, etc.<br>• Review reconciliations of totals of segment revenues, etc.<br>• If an entity has had a reorganization of its structure, assess whether segment disclosures for prior periods have been restated. |

k. **Scope limitations (AU 508).** Scope limitations result in either a qualified opinion or a disclaimer. In both cases, the opinion paragraph indicates that the opinion modification is based on the possible effects on the financial statements, and not due to the scope limitation itself, and the explanatory paragraph is added preceding the opinion paragraph. The type of report issued depends on the importance of the omitted procedures. This assessment is affected by the nature and magnitude of the potential effects of the matters in question and by their significance to the financial statements (e.g., number of accounts involved). An auditor may issue a disclaimer whenever he or she is unable to form an opinion or has not formed an opinion as to the fairness of presentation of the financial statements.

Two types of scope limitations must be considered: client-imposed and circumstance imposed. Client-imposed limitations result when a client will not allow the auditor to perform an audit procedure (e.g., confirm receivables). Circumstance-imposed limitations occur in situations **other** than the client saying, "No, I will not allow you to perform that procedure." For example, weak internal control may make it impossible for the auditor to perform the audit. This is considered a circumstance-imposed limitation. The following diagram summarizes the effect of scope limitations on the report.

**SCOPE LIMITATION DECISIONS**

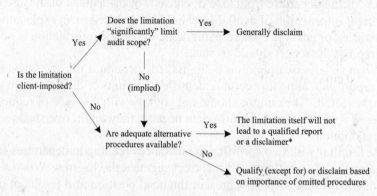

*The alternative procedures used should not be mentioned in the report.*

Know that scope limitations may result in different opinions on individual financial statements. For example, if the auditor of a first-year client has been unable to verify the accuracy of the beginning inventory, the scope limitation will affect the current year's income statement (through cost of goods sold) but not the year-end balance sheet. In such a situation, the auditor might issue an unqualified opinion on the balance sheet and a disclaimer on the income statement.

Note the distinction between scope limitations and limited reporting objectives. Consider two circumstances. First, the auditor may, when requested, report on only one statement (e.g., the balance sheet). If access to information underlying the financial statements is not limited, such a situation does not involve a scope limitation. The auditor may report on the financial statement.

Second, as is the case with issuance of an adverse opinion, when issuing a disclaimer the auditor may not include a "piecemeal opinion" that identifies certain accounts that are properly stated.

Several multiple-choice questions have required knowledge of the "circumstance for which it is **not** appropriate to refer a reader of an auditor's report to a financial statement note for details." The proper answer is generally a scope limitation since details of audit scope are not presented in the financial statement notes.

l.  **Lack of independence (AU 504).** When an auditor is not independent, a disclaimer must be issued stating that the auditor is not independent. No mention of the reason for the lack of independence nor any audit procedures followed is to be given in the report. These circumstances might occur when the CPA firm has neglected to sell an equity (e.g., common stock) interest in the client being audited.

*Summary.* Know that circumstances a. through i. may result in unqualified reports with additional explanatory language. Circumstance c., doubt about ability to remain a going concern, may also result in a disclaimer of opinion. The circumstances requiring other than an unqualified opinion may be summarized as

| *Circumstances* | *Type of opinion* |
|---|---|
| j.   Departure from GAAP | Qualified or adverse |
| k.   Scope limitation | |
|    1.   Client-imposed | "Generally disclaim," otherwise qualified |
|    2.   Circumstance-imposed | Qualified or disclaimer |
| l.   Lack of independence | Disclaimer |

The actual wording of the required modifications to the reports is discussed in the next section.

2. **Report Preparation.** A simulation question may require the candidate to prepare an audit report that reflects certain departures from the standard form. The research component of the question may make available the professional standards.

When preparing a report it is helpful to consider an approach of beginning with the standard short-form report and modifying it as appropriate for the circumstances presented. While the various SASs present numerous types of reports that are other than the standard short form, it is **not** necessary to memorize them. Use the following approach to prepare (or evaluate) reports:

Step 1.    Determine whether the question requires an audit report on whether the financial statements follow GAAP.

Step 2.    Find the standard report and cut/paste it to your solution space.

Step 3.    Determine the circumstance(s) involved and the overall type of report to be issued.

Step 4.    Research the Professional Standards to identify appropriate report modifications for the circumstance(s) and overall type of report to be issued.

Step 5.    Cut/paste the appropriate modifications to the standard report, and complete the report as necessary.

**Step 1.**    *Determine whether the question requires an audit report on whether the financial statements follow GAAP.*

Ask yourself whether it is an audit of financial statements that is involved. If that is the case, continue. Other options are discussed later in this module (e.g., review, compilations or agreed-upon procedures engagements, attestation reports, and reports on financial statements that follow another comprehensive basis of accounting).

**Step 2.**    *Find the standard report and cut/paste it to your solution space.*

Because the Professional Standards most frequently only present modifications of the standard report, a useful approach is to begin with the standard report[1]. The first major section of AU 508 (The Auditor's Standard Report) presents two standard reports—one for use when the audit report is only on a single year, and one for when it is on two years. It is best to quickly determine whether your report will deal with one or more years and paste the appropriate report to your solution space. The report for two years follows:

*Independent Auditor's Report*

We have audited the accompanying balance sheets of X Company as of December 31, 20XX and 20X1, and the related statements of income, retained earnings, and cash flows for the years then ended. These financial statements are the responsibility of the Company's management. Our responsibility is to express an opinion on these financial statements based on our audits.

We conducted our audits in accordance with auditing standards generally accepted in the United States of America. Those standards require that we plan and perform the audit to obtain reasonable assurance about whether the financial statements are free of material misstatement. An audit includes examining, on a test basis, evidence supporting the amounts and disclosures in the financial statements. An audit also includes assessing the accounting principles used and significant estimates made by management, as well as evaluating the overall financial statement presentation. We believe that our audits provide a reasonable basis for our opinion.

In our opinion, the financial statements referred to above present fairly, in all material respects, the financial position of X Company as of December 31, 20XX and 20X1, and the results of its operations and its cash flows for the years then ended in conformity with accounting principles generally accepted in the United States of America.

[*Signature*]

[*Date*]

**Step 3.**    *Determine the circumstance(s) involved and the overall type of report to be issued.*

To accomplish this, use the information presented earlier in this module. Those primary circumstances discussed earlier in this module include

Circumstances requiring unqualified report with additional explanatory language

a.    Opinion based, in part, on report of another auditor.

---

[1]   *In certain circumstances, however, you may find that the report is not needed (e.g., the standards for reporting when "other auditors" exist provide a complete report).*

   b.  Unusual circumstances requiring a departure from promulgated GAAP.
   c.  Substantial doubt about ability to remain a going concern (may also lead to a disclaimer)
   d.  Inconsistency in application of GAAP.
   e.  Certain circumstances affecting comparative statements.
   f.  Required quarterly data for SEC reporting companies.
   g.  Supplementary information required by FASB or GASB.
   h.  Other information in document containing audited financial statements.
   i.  Emphasis of a matter.

   Circumstances requiring **other** than an unqualified report

   j.  Departure from GAAP.
   k.  Scope limitation.
   l.  Lack of independence.

   It is helpful if you recall the type of report to be issued—for example, a departure from GAAP leads to either a qualified report or an adverse report.

Step 4.  ***Research the Professional Standards to identify appropriate report modifications for the circumstance(s) and overall type of report to be issued.***

   You may use keywords, or your knowledge of the standards to find information on the relevant report modifications that are necessary. Primary sections on audit report include

   AU 508—Most comprehensive section on types of reports.
   AU 341—Going concern reporting (and procedures).
   AU 420—Consistency
   All AU 500 and AU 600 sections, but somewhat less frequently.

   Assume the situation is a departure from GAAP, and you believe that a qualified opinion is appropriate. AU 508 provides the following illustration:

### Independent Auditor's Report

*[Same first and second paragraphs as the standard report]*

   The Company has excluded from property and debt in the accompanying balance sheets, certain lease obligations that, in our opinion, should be capitalized in order to conform with US generally accepted accounting principles. If these lease obligations were capitalized, property would be increased by $__ and $__, long-term debt by $__ and  $__, and retained earnings by $__ and $__ as of December 31, 20X2 and 20X1, respectively. Additionally, net income would be decreased by $__ and $__ and earnings per share would be decreased by $__ and $__, respectively for the years then ended.

   In our opinion, except for the effects of not capitalizing certain lease obligations as discussed in the preceding paragraph, the financial statements referred to above present fairly, in all material respects, the financial position of X Company as of December 31, 20XX and 20X1, and the results of its operations and its cash flows for the years then ended in conformity with accounting principles generally accepted in the United States of America.

   Expect the simulation to have more than one circumstance involved. For example, in addition to a departure from GAAP, "other auditors" might be involved.

Step 5.  ***Cut/paste the appropriate modifications to the standard report, and tailor the report as necessary.***

   The approach is to cut/paste the above two paragraphs into the standard report—in this case replacing the opinion paragraph with the two above paragraphs. At this point you must tailor the report as necessary. For example, you should expect to replace the above leasing departure from GAAP with the departure(s) relevant to the simulation you are replying to. Also, consider

   • Make certain that you retain the title of the report with the word independent.
   • Add an addressee to the report (ordinarily to the audit committee, board of directors, and/or company).
   • Fill in the appropriate year(s) in place of those in the report (e.g., 20X2).
   • Key in the name of the CPA firm as the signature.

- Date the report as of the completion of fieldwork, unless subsequent events result in "dual dating" of the audit report—see outline of AU 530, or discussion under point A.2. of this module.

The following "Summary of Departures from Standard Report" is included to provide an overall perspective of changes required in audit reports, as well as to help with a multiple choice question which might ask in general terms about paragraphs that need to be modified.

### SUMMARY OF DEPARTURES FROM STANDARD REPORT

| *Circumstance* | *Introductory paragraph modified* | *Scope paragraph modified* | *Opinion paragraph modified* | *Explanatory paragraph added* |
|---|---|---|---|---|
| UNQUALIFIED WITH EXPLANATORY LANGUAGE | | | | |
| a.  Other Auditor—Make reference | Yes | Yes | Yes | No |
| b.  Justified GAAP departure | | | | |
| c.  Going concern | | | | |
| d.  Inconsistency | | | | |
| e.  Report reissued | No | No | No | Yes |
| f.  Required SEC quarterly data | | | | |
| g.  Supplementary information | | | | |
| h.  Other information | | | | |
| i.  Emphasis of a matter | | | | |
| e.  Predecessor report not reissued | Yes | No | No | No |
| | | | | |
| QUALIFIED OPINIONS | | | | |
| j.  Departure from GAAP | No | No | Yes | Yes |
| k.  Scope limitation | No | Yes | Yes | Yes |
| DISCLAIMER | | | | |
| c.  Going concern* | Yes | Yes | Yes | Yes |
| k.  Scope limitation | Yes | Omit | Yes | Yes |
| l.  Lack of independence | | (A one-paragraph disclaimer is issued) | | |
| ADVERSE | | | | |
| j.  Departure from GAAP | No | No | Yes | Yes |

*No sample report presented in Professional Standards

## C.  Accountant Association other than Audits

As indicated in the overview section, accountants become involved with financial information on engagements less than "full" audits. These forms may be categorized as: (1) other forms of accountant association with historical financial statements, and (2) other reports.

1. **Other Forms of Accountant Association with Historical Financial Statements.** Here we discuss four primary "other" forms of accountant association. The candidate should be very familiar with each of these forms of association.

   a. **Unaudited statements (AU 504).** For those relatively few public firms that are not required to have an annual audit, the option of unaudited statements exists. In this case, a simple disclaimer of opinion is generally issued; also, each page of the financial statements should be marked "unaudited." As a minimum, the auditor must read the financial statements for obvious material misstatements. If the auditor is aware of any significant departures from GAAP, s/he should suggest that the statements be revised and, failing that, should include such information in the disclaimer.

   b. **Compiled or reviewed statements (AR 100-600).** The compilation and review standards outlined in AR 100-600 are designed for CPA association with the financial statements of **nonpublic entities**. Make certain that you read the outlines of those sections (**especially AR 100 and AR 200**) and then review the important points highlighted in this section which deal with compilation and review reports—compilation and review procedures have been presented in Sections E.1. and E.2. of the Evidence Module. Be familiar with both the compilation and review reports (provided below) as multiple-choice questions may require knowledge of the specific information included in each report. Know that they are from ARE 100 and ARE 200 in the event that a situation requires that you use the professional standards to prepare a compilation or a review report.

When a CPA prepares financial statements for a client, he or she must—at a minimum—comply with the compilation requirements. More formally, the standards state that a CPA should not **submit unaudited financial statements** of a nonpublic entity to a client or others unless, at a minimum, he or she has complied with the compilation requirements. To submit unaudited financial statements is to present to a client or third party one or more financial statements that the accountant has prepared either manually or through the use of computer software. However, the following are **not** considered submission of financial statements and therefore do **not** require adherence to the compilation standards:

- Reading client-prepared financial statements
- Typing or reproducing financial statements without notification
- Proposing journal entries and disclosures and providing a client with a financial statement format without dollar amounts

**Compilations.** The form of communication by an accountant for a compilation depends upon whether those financial statements are expected to be used by a third party. When those financial statements are to be used by a third party, a compilation report must be issued by the accountant. When the use of those financial statements is limited to the client, the accountant may either issue a compilation report or may document an understanding with the client through the use of an engagement letter, preferably signed by management, regarding the services to be performed and the limitations on the use of those financial statements.

A compilation report should be dated as of the date of the completion of the compilation, signed in the name of the firm, and should state that

- A compilation has been performed in accordance with Statements on Standards for Accounting and Review Services issued by the AICPA.
- A compilation is limited to presenting in the form of financial statements information that is the representation of management.
- The financial statements have not been audited or reviewed and accordingly, the accountant does not express an opinion or any other form of assurance on them.

The following is a standard compilation report:

I (we) have compiled the accompanying balance sheet of XYZ Company as of December 31, 20XX, and the related statements of income, retained earnings, and cash flows for the year then ended, in accordance with Statements on Standards for Accounting and Review Services issued by the American Institute of Certified Public Accountants.

A compilation is limited to presenting in the form of financial statements information that is the representation of management (owners). I (we) have not audited or reviewed the accompanying financial statements and, accordingly, do not express an opinion or any other form of assurance on them.

Compiled financial statements may omit note disclosures; the following is added as a third paragraph to the compilation report:

Management has elected to omit substantially all of the disclosures (and the statement of cash flows) required by US generally accepted accounting principles. If the omitted disclosures were included in the financial statements, they might influence the user's conclusions about the company's financial position, results of operations, and cash flows. Accordingly, these financial statements are not designed for those who are not informed about such matters.

When a CPA is aware of a departure from GAAP (other than omission of note disclosures), a sentence is added to the end of the second paragraph indicating that "We did become aware of a departure from GAAP that is explained in the following paragraph." A third paragraph of the report then describes the matter.

The following paragraph is added to the compilation report if the financial statements have been prepared on a comprehensive basis other than GAAP:

These financial statements (including related disclosures) are presented in accordance with the requirements of (name of body), which differ from US generally accepted accounting principles. Accordingly, these financial statements are not designed for those who are not informed about such differences.

Several other important points include

1.  Because compilations are not considered attest services, a CPA need not be independent to perform a compilation (a final paragraph stating "I am [we are] not independent with respect to XYZ Company" is added to the report).
2.  Each page of the financial statements should include a reference such as "See Accountant's Compilation Report," or, in the case of comparative statements, "See Accountant's Report."
3.  A CPA should not report on compiled comparative financial statements in which one year, but not all years, omit note disclosures.
4.  A CPA engaged to compile financial statements that follow a prescribed form adopted by the client's industry trade association need not advise the association of the omission of GAAP related disclosures.
5.  A CPA may be engaged to compile one financial statement, such as a balance sheet, and not the others.
6.  When a CPA performs more than one service (e.g., a compilation and an audit) the only report that should be issued is that for the highest level of service rendered.

**Reviews.** A review report should be dated as of the completion of the review procedures, signed in the name of the firm, and should state that

1.  A review was performed in accordance with Statements on Standards for Accounting and Review Services issued by the AICPA.
2.  All information included in the financial statements is the representation of the management (owners) of the entity.
3.  A review consists principally of inquiries of company personnel and analytical procedures applied to financial data.
4.  A review is substantially less in scope than an audit, the objective of which is the expression of an opinion regarding the financial statements taken as a whole and, accordingly, no such opinion is expressed.
5.  The accountant is not aware of any material modification that should be made to the financial statements in order for them to be in conformity with GAAP, other than those modifications, if any, indicated in the report.

The following is a standard report:

I (we) have reviewed the accompanying balance sheet of XYZ Company as of December 31, 20XX, and the related statements of income, retained, earnings, and cash flows for the year then ended, in accordance with Statements on Standards for Accounting and Review Services issued by the American Institute of Certified Public Accountants. All information included in these financial statements is the representation of the management (owners) of XYZ Company.

A review consists principally of inquiries of company personnel and analytical procedures applied to financial data. It is substantially less in scope than an examination in accordance with US generally accepted auditing standards, the objective of which is the expression of an opinion regarding the financial statements taken as a whole. Accordingly, I (we) do not express such an opinion.

Based on my (our) review, I am (we are) not aware of any material modification that should be made to the accompanying financial statements in order for them to be in conformity with US generally accepted accounting principles.

When the CPA is aware of a departure from GAAP, the matter is described in a fourth paragraph. Also, the third paragraph includes the following term (which we have italicized):

Based on my (our) review, *with the exception of the matter described in the following paragraph,...*

Several other important points on reviews include

1.  Because reviews are attest services, the CPA must be independent to perform a review.
2.  Each page of the financial statements should include a reference such as "See Accountant's Review Report," or, in the case of comparative statements, "See Accountant's Report."
3.  If the client restricts the scope of review procedures or refuses to provide the CPA with a representation letter (required on reviews and audits), the review is incomplete and no review report may be issued.

4.  Although a CPA *may choose* to describe uncertainties (including going concern uncertainties) and changes in accounting principles in a review report, there is no such requirement.
5.  When current year financial statements have been reviewed and prior year financial statements were audited, the CPA may either reissue the audit report and issue a review report, *or* may refer to the audit in the review report.  In referring to the audit in the review report, the CPA should indicate that the statements were audited, the date of the previous opinion, reasons for any departures from an unqualified form, and that no auditing procedures were performed after the date of the previous report.  (When the current year financial statements have been compiled, the same procedures are followed.)
6.  When the current year financial statements have been audited and prior year financial statements were reviewed the audit report should include a statement indicating the type of service performed, the date of the report, a description of any material modifications noted in the report, and a statement that the service was less in scope than an audit and does not provide a basis for the expression of an opinion on the financial statements. (When prior year financial statements have been compiled, the same procedures are followed.)
7.  An audit engagement may be changed to a review engagement (or a review to a compilation) if the reason for the client's request is considered reasonable.

The "Compilation and Review Report Summary" that appears below presents the essentials of compilation and review reports.

**COMPILATION AND REVIEW REPORT SUMMARY**

|  | *Compilation report* | *Review report* |
|---|---|---|
| **First paragraph** | 1. A compilation has been performed in accordance with SSARS* issued by the AICPA | 1. A review was performed in accordance with SSARS issued by the AICPA.<br>2. All information included in the financial statements is the representation of the management of the entity. |
| **Second paragraph** | 2. A compilation is limited to presenting in the form of financial statements information that is the representation of management (owners).<br>3. I have not audited or reviewed the accompanying financial statements and, accordingly, do not express an opinion or any other form of assurance on them. | 3. A review consists principally of inquiries of company personnel and analytical procedures applied to financial data.<br>4. It is substantially less in scope than an audit, the objective of which is the expression of an opinion regarding the financial statements taken as a whole. |
| **Third paragraph** | [Standard report has only two paragraphs] | 5. I am not aware of any material modifications that should be made to the financial statements in order for them to be in conformity with GAAP. |
| **Circumstances in which additional paragraphs are added** | a. Departures from GAAP—A paragraph is added describing the departure.<br>b. Client omission of note disclosures—A paragraph is added stating that management has elected to omit substantially all of the disclosures required by GAAP and that if the omitted disclosures were included they might influence the user's conclusions.<br>c. Lack of CPA independence—Paragraph added stating "I am not independent with respect to [company name]." | a. Departures from GAAP—A paragraph is added describing the departure.  If the CPA does not consider this sufficient s/he is to consider resignation.<br><br>NOTES:<br>Client omission of disclosures is considered a departure from GAAP for reviews.<br>A CPA must be independent to perform a review. |

\* *Statements on Standards for Accounting and Review Services*

c.  **Reviewed interim (quarterly) statements (AU 722).**  The review form of association discussed above is also appropriate for companies wishing to have their interim (quarterly) financial information reviewed.  The following is the standard review report:

*Independent of Independent Registered Public Accounting Firm*

We have reviewed the accompanying [*describe the interim financial information*] of ABC Company and consolidated subsidiaries as of September 30, 20X1, and for the three-month and nine-month periods then ended.  This interim financial information is the responsibility of the company's management.

We conducted our review in accordance with standards of the Public Company Accounting Oversight Board.  A review of interim financial information consists principally of applying analytical procedures and making inquiries of persons responsible for financial and accounting matters.  It is substantially less in scope than an audit conducted in accordance with generally accepted auditing standards, the objective of which is the expression of an opinion regarding the financial statements taken as a whole.  Accordingly, we do not express such an opinion.

Based on our review, we are not aware of any material modifications that should be made to the accompanying interim financial information for it to be in conformity with US generally accepted accounting principles.

Section E.3 of the Evidence Module and the outline of AU 722 discuss the nature of these reviews in more detail.

d. **Condensed financial statements (AU 552).**  A client who must file a set of audited financial statements at least annually with a regulatory agency may choose to prepare condensed financial statements for other purposes.  In such cases the auditor's report on condensed statements should disclose

    (1)  That the auditor has expressed an opinion on the complete audited financial statements
    (2)  The date of the audit report on the complete statements
    (3)  The type of opinion expressed on the complete statements
    (4)  Whether the condensed statements are fairly stated in relation to the complete financial statements

e. **Financial statements prepared for use in other countries (AU 534).**  An auditor may be asked to report on the financial statements of a United States client that follow the accounting principles of a foreign country.  The general rule is that in such circumstances the auditor must follow US general and fieldwork standards to the extent that they are appropriate.  Certain procedures, however, may **not** be appropriate (e.g., procedures related to the tax deferral account in a country which does not allow tax deferral).  Also, the auditor may be requested to apply the other country's auditing standards.  This may be done if US standards have been followed and if the auditor is familiar with the standards of the other country.

The report issued depends on whether it is for use primarily outside the US (the most frequent case) or within the US.  If it is intended primarily for outside the US, a modified US report may be issued which:  (1) describes the basis followed, (2) states that US standards (and other national standards if appropriate) were followed, and (3) states whether the statements present fairly and consistently the basis followed.  If, however, the auditor has made certain that s/he understands the responsibilities relating to the standard report of the other country, then such report may be issued.  Financial statements for use primarily outside of the US may be distributed to limited US individuals and organizations (such as banks) if differences between the US and the foreign country standards are understood.

If distribution within the US is **more than limited,** the auditor should use the US standard report and modify it as necessary for any departures from GAAP.  Additionally, for distribution outside the US, a report may be prepared as indicated in the prior paragraph.

2. **Other Reports—Statements on Auditing Standards Based.**  In addition to guidance on financial statement audits, the Statements on Auditing Standards (those with AU prefix in the outlines that follow Module 6) also present guidance on a number of engagements not discussed earlier in this module, including

    a.  Special reports
    b.  Letters for underwriters
    c.  Application of accounting principles

a. **Special reports (AU 623).**  AU 623 presents guidance on five basic types of reports.  You should have a general familiarity with each.  Your approach here should be to study the information in this section in combination with the outline of AU 623.  Here we present only summary information and sample reports; details are presented in the outline of AU 623.

The first type of special report deals with reporting on financial statements that follow a comprehensive basis other than GAAP (e.g., cash basis, tax basis, or a basis prescribed by a regulatory agency).  In general, the report issued parallels the standard audit report, with a fourth paragraph added indicating the basis being followed, and that it is a comprehensive basis of accounting other than GAAP.  When the basis is prescribed by a regulatory agency, an additional paragraph limiting distribution to the company and to the regulatory agency is added at the end of the report.

Terms such as "balance sheet" and "income statement" are **not** used for statements that follow a comprehensive basis other than GAAP. Instead, an other comprehensive basis of accounting may use, for example, "statement of assets and liabilities arising from cash transactions." (The use of such terms will require the auditor to qualify the opinion.)

The following is the suggested standard form for cash-basis statements:

## Financial Statements Prepared on the Cash Basis

### Independent Auditor's Report

We have audited the accompanying statements of assets and liabilities arising from cash transactions of XYZ Company as of December 31, 20X2 and 20X1, and the related statements of revenue collected and expenses paid for the years then ended. These financial statements are the responsibility of the Company's management. Our responsibility is to express an opinion on these financial statements based on our audits.

We conducted our audits in accordance with US generally accepted auditing standards. Those standards require that we plan and perform the audit to obtain reasonable assurance about whether the financial statements are free of material misstatement. An audit includes examining, on a test basis, evidence supporting the amounts and disclosures in the financial statements. An audit also includes assessing the accounting princi-

ples used and significant estimates made by management, as well as evaluating the overall financial statement presentation. We believe that our audits provide a reasonable basis for our opinion.

As described in Note X, these financial statements were prepared on the basis of cash receipts and disbursements, which is a comprehensive basis of accounting other than US generally accepted accounting principles.

In our opinion, the financial statements referred to above present fairly, in all material respects, the assets and liabilities arising from cash transactions of XYZ Company as of December 31, 20X2 and 20X1, and its revenue collected and expenses paid during the years then ended, on the basis of accounting described in Note X.

A comprehensive-basis report prepared solely for filing with a regulatory agency, following a basis prescribed by that agency, would be similar to the above report, but would also add the following as a final paragraph:

> This report is intended solely for the information and use of the board of directors and management of XYZ Insurance Company and for filing with the [name of regulatory agency] and should not be used for any other purpose.

The second type of special report is that on special elements, accounts, or items. An auditor may, if allowed to perform the procedures s/he believes necessary, issue an opinion on one or more accounts (e.g., receivables or rentals). However, if a specified element is, or is based upon, an entity's net income or stockholders' equity, the CPA should have audited the complete financial statements in order to express an opinion. On the other hand, if the auditor is hired to perform only agreed-upon procedures, a summary of findings is provided.

The overall area of agreed-upon procedure engagements is discussed below in section C.2.f, and in the outline of AT 201. At this point simply read the reports.

## Special Elements Report Examples

### Report Relating to Accounts Receivable

#### Independent Auditor's Report

We have audited the accompanying schedule of accounts receivable of ABC Company as of December 31, 20X2. This schedule is the responsibility of the Company's management. Our responsibility is to express an opinion on this schedule based on our audit.

We conducted our audit in accordance with US generally accepted auditing standards. Those standards require that we plan and perform the audit to obtain reasonable assurance about whether the schedule of accounts receivable is free of material misstatement. An audit includes examining, on a test basis, evidence supporting the amounts and disclosures in the schedule of accounts receivable. An audit also includes assessing the accounting principles used and significant estimates made by management, as well as evaluating the overall schedule presentation. We believe that our audit provides a reasonable basis for our opinion.

In our opinion, the schedule of accounts receivable referred to above presents fairly, in all material respects, the accounts receivable of ABC Company as of December 31, 20X2, in conformity with US generally accepted accounting principles.

NOTE: *As is the case with all special reports, an additional paragraph is added limiting distribution when a basis which is not GAAP or another comprehensive basis is used.*

### Independent Accountant's Report on Applying Agreed-Upon Procedures

To the Board of Directors and Management of
X Company:

We have performed the procedures enumerated below, which were agreed to by the Board of Directors and Management of X Company, solely to assist you in connection with the proposed acquisition of Y Company as of December 31, 20XX. This agreed-upon procedures engagement was conducted in accordance with attestation standards established by the American Institute of Certified Public Accountants. The sufficiency of these procedures is solely the responsibility of the parties specified in this report. Consequently, we make no representation regarding the sufficiency of the procedures described below either for the purpose for which this report has been requested or for any other purpose.

The procedures and the associated findings are as follows:

**Accounts Receivable**

1. We added the individual customer account balances shown in an aged trial balance of accounts receivable (identified as exhibit A) and compared the resultant total with the balance in the general ledger account.

[*Present Findings.*]

2. We mailed confirmations directly to the customers representing the 150 largest customer account balances selected from the accounts receivable trial balance, and we received responses as indicated below. We also traced the items constituting the outstanding customer account balance to invoices and supporting shipping documents for customers from which there was no reply. As agreed, any individual differences in a customer account balance of less than $300

were to be considered minor, and no further procedures were performed.

[*Present Findings.*]

We were not engaged to, and did not, perform an examination, the objective of which would be the expression of an opinion on cash and accounts receivable. Accordingly, we do not express such an opinion. Had we performed additional procedures, other matters might have come to our attention that would have been reported to you.

This report is intended solely for the information and use of the board of directors and management of X Company and is not intended to be and should not be used by anyone other than these specified parties.

[*Signature*]
[*Date*]

The third type of special report is one that results from an engagement in which the auditor is hired to test whether a client is in compliance with some form of agreement. For example, an auditor may provide negative assurance to a bank on whether a client is in conformity with restrictions contained in a debt agreement. This type of report may only be issued when the CPA has performed an audit of the financial statements. Section D of this Module discusses other compliance reports; those reports relate to audits performed under *Government Auditing Standards* and reports providing positive assurance on compliance with contractual agreements or regulatory provisions when no financial statement audit has been performed.

**Compliance Report Examples**
**Contractual Compliance**
**Independent Auditor's Report**

*Compliance Report as a Separate Report*

We have audited, in accordance with US generally accepted auditing standards, the balance sheet of XYZ Company as of December 31, 20X1, and the related statement of income, retained earnings, and cash flows for the year then ended, and have issued our report thereon dated February 16, 20X2.

In connection with our audit, nothing came to our attention that caused us to believe that the Company failed to comply with the terms, covenants, provisions, or conditions of sections, XX to XX, inclusive, of the Indenture dated July 21, 19X8, with ABC Bank insofar as they relate to accounting matters. However, our audit was not directed primarily toward obtaining knowledge of such noncompliance.

This report is intended solely for the information and use of the boards of directors and managements of XYZ Company and ABC Bank and should not be used for any other purpose.

*Compliance Report Included in Unqualified Report*

Standard Unqualified Report

Then add these two paragraphs

The fourth type of special report is for client special-purpose financial presentations that have been prepared by the client to comply with an agreement (e.g., a loan agreement). The information presented is more substantial than specified elements, but is different in some ways, and generally less complete than required by a comprehensive basis of accounting. Unless the report is to be filed with a regulatory agency such as the SEC and to be included in a publicly available document (e.g., a prospectus), a paragraph limiting distribution is added to the report.

**Special-Purpose Financial Presentation Examples**

*Loan Agreement*
*(GAAP not followed)*

[Introductory paragraph refers to specific report]
[Standard scope paragraph]

The accompanying special-purpose financial statements were prepared for the purpose of complying with Section 4 of a loan agreement between DEF Bank and the Company as discussed in Note X, and are not intended to be a presentation in conformity with US generally accepted accounting principles.

In our opinion, the special-purpose financial statements referred to above present fairly, in all material respects, the assets and liabilities of ABC Company at December 31, 20X1 and 20X0, and the revenues, expenses and cash flows for the years then ended, on the basis of accounting described in Note X.

This report is intended solely for the information and use of the boards of directors and managements of ABC Company and DEF Bank and should not be used for any other purpose.

***Schedule of Apartment Revenues and Expenses Included in a Document to Be Distributed to the General Public***

[Introductory paragraph refers to specific report]

[Standard scope paragraph]

The accompanying Historical Summaries were prepared for the purpose of complying with the rules and regulations of the Securities and Exchange Commission (for inclusion in the registration statement on Form S-11 of DEF Corporation) as described in Note X and are not intended to be a complete presentation of the Apartments' revenues and expenses.

In our opinion, the Historical Summaries referred to above present fairly, in all material respects, the gross income and direct operating expenses described in Note X of ABC Apartments for each of the three years in the period ended December 31, 20XX, in conformity with US generally accepted accounting principles.

The fifth special report is that for which a client is required to present information on prescribed forms or schedules. For example, a state corporate commission may require all corporations within its jurisdiction to report assets, liabilities, and equities per a standard form. If that form calls for the auditor to make an assertion that s/he believes to be unjustified, s/he is to either reword the form or attach a separate report to the form.

The "Special Reports Summary" presents the essential elements of each type of special report. In the past, the most frequently examined report formats have been the comprehensive basis and agreed-upon procedures applied to specified elements.

b. **Letters for underwriters (AU 634).** When a public company wishes to issue new securities to the public, the underwriters of the securities will generally ask the company's auditor to provide "comfort" on the financial and accounting data in the prospectus that is not covered by an accountant's report of some form (e.g., an audit report on the financial statements). In comfort letters, the CPAs will provide positive assurance that they are independent and that their audit followed SEC standards. They will provide negative assurance or a summary of findings on various types of accounting related matters such as the following: unaudited condensed and summarized interim information, pro forma financial information, change subsequent to the balance sheet date, and on various tables of data. At this point quickly review the outline of AU 634.

c. **Application of accounting principles (AU 625).** CPAs may be asked by specified users (e.g., management, the board of directors and others) to report on the application of accounting principles to new transactions and products, or to increase the specified users' knowledge of certain financial reporting issues. This section applies to public accountants when they get a request from a prospective client for a **written or oral** report on the accounting treatment of a prospective or completed transaction.

Before providing a report on accounting principles, AU 625 requires the accountants to take steps to make sure they have a complete understanding of the form and substance of the transaction, including consulting with the company's current auditors. They should also review existing accounting principles and consult appropriate references and experts to provide an adequate basis for their conclusions. Also, such reports should not be issued on a hypothetical transaction that does not involve facts or circumstances relating to the specific company. Use of such reports is restricted to the specified parties involved.

3. **Other Reports—Attestation Standards Based.** CPAs[2] also become involved with a variety of other types of information which result in the following reports:

   a. Attestation engagements—general (AT 101)
   b. Agreed-upon procedures engagements (AT 201)
   c. Financial forecasts and projections (AT 301)
   d. Pro forma financial information (AT 401)
   e. Management discussion and analysis (AT 701)
   f. WebTrust
   g. SysTrust

Points a. and b. provide overall general guidance for attestation engagements of all types. For example, the overall eleven attestation standards are presented in AT 101, and the overall standards for agreed-upon procedures engagements in AT 201.

The remaining points (c. through g.) relate to specific guidance for attestation engagements related to a particular topic (e.g., AT 301 [topic c. above] relates to providing assurance on forecasts). Thus,

---

[2] *The attestation standards use the term "practitioner" throughout.*

# SPECIAL REPORTS SUMMARY*

| | Comprehensive basis | Specified Elements — a. Opinion | Specified Elements — b. Agreed-upon procedures | Compliance Reports — a. Within standard report | Compliance Reports — b. Separate report | Special Purpose Presentation |
|---|---|---|---|---|---|---|
| **Introductory Paragraph** | 1. Standard report except for, in first sentence<br>(a) names of statements<br>(b) name reporting basis used | 1. Standard report except for, in first sentence<br>(a) names of accounts<br>(b) name reporting basis used | 1. We have performed agreed-upon procedures<br>2. Report solely to assist (specified parties)<br>3. AICPA attestation standards followed<br>4. Sufficiency of procedures responsibility of users<br>5. No representation made as to sufficiency of procedures | 1. Standard report | 1. Standard report except for, add "and have issued our report thereon dated ___ " (to end of first sentence) | 1. Standard report except for, in first sentence<br>(a) names of statements |
| **Scope Paragraph** | 1. Standard report | 1. Standard report except for naming of accounts | | 1. Standard report | | 1. Standard report except for names of accounts |
| **Explanatory Paragraph** | 1. Mention basis and refer to note which describes | 1. Description of reporting basis if not given in scope paragraph | 1. Enumerate procedures and findings | 1. No explanatory paragraph | 1. No explanatory paragraph | 1. Mention basis and refer to note which describes |
| **Opinion (Assurance) Paragraph** | *Opinion*<br>1. Standard report except for<br>(a) Names of statements<br>(b) Refer to reporting basis used | *Opinion*<br>1. Standard report except for<br>(a) Names of accounts<br>(b) Name reporting basis used | *Assurance*<br>1. We did not perform an audit and do not express an opinion<br>2. If additional procedures had been performed other matters might have come to our attention<br>   An additional paragraph follows indicating report intended solely for specified parties | *Opinion and negative assurance*<br>2 paragraphs:<br>A. Standard opinion para<br>B. Negative assurance on compliance para<br>1. Nothing came to our attention to lead us to believe not in compliance<br>2. Exam was not directed primarily toward obtaining knowledge of such noncompliance | *Negative assurance*<br>1. Nothing came to our attention to lead us to believe not in compliance<br>2. Exam was not directed primarily toward obtaining knowledge of such noncompliance | *Opinion*<br>1. Standard report except for<br>(a) Names of statements<br>(b) Refer to reporting basis used |
| **How to Report Departures from Reporting Criteria\*\*** | 1. Same as standard report | 1. Add comment to opinion para and add explanatory para describing<br>2. If significant client interpretations of criteria have been made, add explanatory para describing | 1. Prepare schedules summarizing accounts<br>2. Add comment to negative assurance para and add explanatory para describing | 1. Add comment to negative assurance para and add explanatory para describing | 1. Add comment to negative assurance para and explanatory para describing | 1. Same as standard report |

\* Note that no report form has been proposed for the Special Report based on Prescribed Forms or Schedules. Prospective financial statements are summarized in the outline section [following the SAS [AU] outlines].

\*\* All special reports include an additional paragraph when distribution is limited (see outline of AU 623).

the individual performing an attestation engagement for a financial forecast has two sources of guidance—the general and the specific.  In situations in which an attestation engagement is being performed on a type of information for which a detailed standard has not been provided, the CPA uses that information provided in AT 101 and AT 201.  In addition to the above detailed types of engagements, recall that auditors may issue reports on internal control over financial reporting (AT 501); this topic is summarized in the Internal Control Module.  Also, information on compliance attestation (AT 601) is presented later in this module.

a.  **Attestation engagements—general (AT 101).**  AT 101 provides the framework for all attest engagements.  Attestation standards apply to engagements in which CPAs are engaged to issue or do issue an examination, a review, or an agreed-upon procedures report on subject matter, or an assertion about subject matter, that is the responsibility of another party.  It is important to distinguish between the subject matter and the assertion about the subject matter.

The **subject matter** of an attestation engagement may take many forms, including

- Historical or prospective performance or condition (e.g., historical prospective financial information, performance measurements, and backlog data),
- Physical characteristics (e.g., narrative descriptions, square footage of facilities),
- Historical events (e.g., price of a market basket of goods on a certain date),
- Analyses (e.g., breakeven analyses),
- Systems or processes (e.g., internal control), or
- Behavior (e.g., corporate governance, compliance with laws and regulations, and human resource practices).

An **assertion** is a declaration about whether the subject matter is presented in accordance with certain criteria.  For example, management might assert that the price of a market basket of goods at its store was the lowest in the city as of a certain date.  While such an assertion is generally obtained, in those circumstances in which it is not, the attest report must be restricted in those few circumstances in which a written assertion is not obtained.

CPAs may ordinarily report on either the assertion about the subject matter, **or** on the subject matter itself either as of a point in time or for a period of time.  Continuing with our market basket engagement example, if reporting on the assertion, the CPAs' opinion would include assurance about management's assertion concerning the prices.  Alternatively, when reporting on the subject matter, the CPAs' opinion would include assurance directly on the price of that market basket.  An exception to allowing reporting on either the subject matter or on the assertion is when the examination reveals material departures from the suitable criteria.  In such circumstance the CPA should report directly upon the subject matter, and not on the assertion.

If the CPAs are reporting on an assertion about the subject matter, the assertion is presented with the subject matter or in the CPAs' report.  If the CPAs are reporting **directly** on the subject matter, the assertion normally is included only in a representation letter that the CPAs obtain from the responsible party.

Recall the eleven attestation standards presented in Chapter 5.  Those standards provide a general framework for all such engagements.  You should consider several important concepts related to those standards, including criteria and types of engagements.

**Criteria.**  Criteria are standards or benchmarks that are used to evaluate the subject matter of the engagements.  Criteria are important in reporting the CPAs' conclusion to the users because they convey the basis on which the conclusion was formed.  For example, generally accepted accounting principles are ordinarily used as the frame of reference—criteria—to evaluate the financial statements.

A CPA must evaluate the criteria being followed.  As indicated in the third general standard, the criteria used in an attestation engagement must be **suitable** and **available** to the users.  **Suitable criteria** must have an appropriate combination of the following characteristics:  objective, measurable, complete, and relevant.  The following are general rules relating to criteria suitability:

- Criteria are ordinarily suitable if they are developed by regulatory agencies or other bodies composed of experts that use due process, including exposing the proposed criteria for public comment.

- Criteria developed by management or industry groups without due process may be suitable, but the CPA should carefully evaluate them in relation to the characteristics described in the previous paragraph.
- Criteria that are overly subjective should not be used in an attestation engagement. For example, an assertion that a particular software product is the *best on the market* is too subjective for an attestation engagement. There are no generally accepted criteria for what constitutes the *best* software product. Some criteria may be suitable in evaluating subject matter for only those specified parties who established them (e.g., management and the CPA) and are not suitable for general use.

In addition to meeting the requirement that they be *suitable*, the criteria must also be available to users. This requirement of availability actually has two parts in that not only must the criteria be available, they must be understandable to users. Criteria should be available in one or more of the following ways:

- Publicly
- Inclusions—with the subject matter or in the assertion
- Inclusion in CPA's report
- Well understood by most users (e.g., the distance between A and B is 20 feet)
- Available only to specified parties (in this case the CPA's report is restricted to those parties)

**Forms of engagements.** As indicated in Chapter 5, the forms of attestation engagements are **examinations, reviews,** or the performance of **agreed-upon procedures**.

An examination is designed to provide the highest level of assurance that CPAs provide—the same level of assurance about other types of subject matter as an audit provides for financial statements. When performing an examination, CPAs select from all available procedures to gather sufficient evidence to allow the issuance of a report with a positive opinion about whether the subject matter being examined follows some established or stated criteria. Sufficient evidence exists when it is enough to drive attestation risk to an appropriate **low level**.

At the completion of the examination, the CPAs issue an appropriate report. The following is an example of a standard unqualified examination report **directly on the subject matter:**

> *Independent Accountant's Report*
>
> We have examined the accompanying schedule of investment performance statistics of Yorn Investment Fund for the year ended December 31, 20X2. This schedule is the responsibility of Yorn Investment Fund's management. Our responsibility is to express an opinion on this schedule based on our examination.
>
> Our examination was conducted in accordance with attestation standards established by the American Institute of Certified Public Accountants and, accordingly, included examining, on a test basis, evidence supporting the schedule and performing such other procedures as we considered necessary in the circumstances. We believe our examination provides a reasonable basis for our opinion.
>
> In our opinion, the schedule of investment performance statistics referred to above presents, in all material respects, the performance of Yorn Investment Fund for the year ended December 31, 20X2, in conformity with the measurement and disclosure criteria set forth by the Association of Investment Management Research, Inc., as described in Note 1.
>
> *Jane Zhang, CPA, LLP*
> January 22, 20X3

This standard report, however, is not appropriate in all cases. The following illustrates circumstances that result in modification of the standard unqualified report.

| *Situation* | *Report modification* |
|---|---|
| 1. Criteria are agreed upon or only available to specified users. | A statement of limitations on the use of the report. |
| 2. Departure of subject matter from criteria. | Qualified or adverse opinion depending on materiality of the departure. |
| 3. Limitation on scope of engagement. | Qualified opinion or disclaimer. |
| 4. When reporting on subject matter and a written assertion is not obtained from the responsible party. | A statement of limitations on the use of the report. |

**Reviews.** A review engagement involves performing limited procedures, such as inquiries and analytical procedures. In performing a review, the CPAs endeavor to gather sufficient evidence to drive attestation risk to a **moderate level**. Accordingly, the resulting report provides only limited assurance that the information is fairly presented.  **Limited assurance** is also referred to as **negative assurance** because the CPAs' report disclaims an opinion on the reviewed information, but includes a statement such as "We are not aware of any material modifications that should be made in order for the information to be in conformity with the criteria."  Of course, when uncorrected material departures from the criteria are noted, the report must be modified to so indicate. The following is an example of an unmodified review report **directly on the subject matter:**

### Independent Accountant's Report

We have examined the accompanying schedule of investment performance statistics of King Investment Fund for the year ended December 31, 20X2.  This schedule is the responsibility of King Investment Fund's management.

Our examination was conducted in accordance with attestation standards established by the American Institute of Certified Public Accountants.  A review is substantially less in scope than an examination, the objective of which is the expression of an opinion on the schedule.  Accordingly, we do not express such an opinion.

Based on our review, nothing came to our attention that caused us to believe that the accompanying schedule of investment performance statistics of King Investment Fund for the year ended December 31, 20X2, is not presented, in all material respects, in accordance with the measurement and disclosure criteria set forth by the Association of Investment Management Research, Inc., as described in Note 1.

*George Williams & Associates, LLP*
January 15, 20X3

The following lists circumstances that result in modification of the CPAs' review report.

| Situation | Report modification |
|---|---|
| 1. Criteria are agreed upon or only available to specified users. | A statement of limitations on the use of the report. |
| 2. Departure of subject matter from criteria. | Modified report describing the departure. |
| 3. Limitation on scope of the engagement. | Report cannot be issued. |
| 4. When reporting on subject matter and a written assertion is not obtained from the responsible party. | A statement of limitations on the use of the report. |

At this point you should carefully study the outline of AT 101.

b.  **Agreed-upon procedures engagements.**  AT 201 provides guidance for agreed-upon procedures engagements.  The section applied to both engagements relating to historical financial information (e.g., specified elements of a financial statement—section 2.a. of this module) and engagements related to information other than historical financial statements.  Agreed-upon procedures reports include a list of procedures performed (or reference thereto) and the related findings. Because specified parties have agreed upon the nature of the procedures, the reports for such engagements are intended only for those parties.  Consequently, reports on agreed-upon procedures are referred to as **restricted use** reports, as contrasted to **general use** reports, such as those on examinations and reviews.  As previously indicated, examination and review reports ordinarily may be used by all third parties.  Only when the criteria have been agreed upon by the parties involved and such criteria are not generally understandable to those not involved with the information must an examination or review report be restricted.  Examples of the later type of engagement include the application of agreed-upon procedures to an entity's internal control over financial reporting, compliance with various laws and regulations, or on a schedule of statistical production data.  At this point you should carefully study the outline of AT 201.

c.  **Financial forecasts and projections (AT 301).**  AT 301 presents three forms of accountant association with forecasts or projections—compilation, examination, and application of agreed-upon procedures.

The following are the standard report forms suggested for compilation and examination of forecasts or projections:

### Compilation Report

We have compiled the accompanying forecasted balance sheet, statements of income, retained earnings, and cash flows of XYZ Company as of December 31, 20XX, and for the year then ending, in accordance with standards established by the American Institute of Certified Public Accountants.

A compilation is limited to presenting in the form of a forecast information that is the representation of management and does not include evaluation of the support for the assumptions underlying the forecast.  We have not examined the forecast and, accordingly, do not express an opinion or any other form of assurance on the accompanying statements or assumptions.  Furthermore, there will usually be differences between the forecasted and actual results, because events and circumstances frequently do not occur as expected, and those differences may be material.  We have no responsibility to update this report for events and circumstances occurring after the date of this report.

*Examination Report*

We have examined the accompanying forecasted balance sheet, statements of income, retained earnings, and cash flows for XYZ Company as of December 31, 20XX, and for the year then ended. XYZ Company's management is responsible for the forecast. Our responsibility is to express an opinion on the forecast based on our examination.

Our examination was conducted in accordance with attestation standards established by the American Institute of Certified Public Accountants and, accordingly, included such procedures as we considered necessary to evaluate both the assumptions used by management and the preparation and pre-

sentation of the forecast. We believe that our examination provides a reasonable basis for our opinion.

In our opinion, the accompanying forecast is presented in conformity with guidelines for presentation of a forecast established by the American Institute of Certified Public Accountants, and the underlying assumptions provide a reasonable basis for management's forecast. However, there will usually be differences between the forecasted and actual results, because events and circumstances frequently do not occur as expected, and those differences may be material. We have no responsibility to update this report for events and circumstances occurring after the date of this report.

Departures from the standard report for forecasts/projections are very similar to those for historical financial statement audit reports. While it is not necessary that you read the entire Statement (on forecasts/projections), you should at this point turn to the outline of AT 301. Several **extremely** important points relative to that outline are

(1) An accountant should not be associated with forecasts/projections that do not disclose assumptions.

(2) Forecasts may be for general or limited use, while projections are for limited use only (see Section A.1. of outline for AT 301 for discussion).

(3) Independence is **not** required for compilations (recall this is also the case for financial statement compilations).

(4) Concerning assurance provided: Know that a compilation report provides no assurance (again, this is also the case with financial statement compilations); an examination report provides positive assurance with respect to the reasonableness of assumptions; and an agreed-upon procedures report provides a summary of findings.

d. **Reporting on pro forma financial information (AT 401).** High levels of business combinations and various types of changes in capitalization created a significant demand for auditor association with "pro forma financial information" which adjusts earlier historical financial information prospectively for the effects of an actual or proposed transaction (or event). Accountants may either review or examine the information. The following is an example of an examination report:

**Pro Forma Financial Information**

*Independent Auditor's Report*

We have examined the pro forma adjustments reflecting the transaction described in Note 1 and the application of those adjustments to the historical amounts in the accompanying pro forma condensed balance sheet of X Company as of December 31, 20X0, and the pro forma condensed statement of income for the year then ended. The historical condensed financial statements are derived from the historical financial statements of X Company, which were audited by us, and of Y Company, which were audited by other accountants, appearing elsewhere herein. Such pro forma adjustments are based upon management's assumptions described in Note 2. X Company's management is responsible for the pro forma financial information. Our responsibility is to express an opinion on the pro forma financial information based on our examination.

Our examination was conducted in accordance with attestation standards established by the American Institute of Certified Public Accountants and, accordingly, included such procedures as were considered necessary in the circumstances. We believe that our examination provides a reasonable basis for our opinion.

The objective of this pro forma financial information is to show what the significant effects on the historical financial information might have been had the transaction [or event] occurred at an earlier date. However, the pro forma condensed financial statements are not necessarily indicative of the results of operations or related effects on financial position that would have been attained had the above-mentioned transaction [or event] actually occurred earlier.

[Additional paragraph(s) may be added to emphasize certain matters relating to the attest engagement of the subject matter.]

In our opinion, management's assumptions provide a reasonable basis for presenting the significant effects directly attributable to the above-mentioned transaction described in Note 1, the related pro forma adjustments give appropriate effect to those assumptions, and the pro forma column reflects the proper application of those adjustments to the historical financial statement amounts in the pro forma condensed balance sheet as of December 31, 20X0, and the pro forma condensed statement of income for the year then ended.

Review reports, as is the case with reviews of historical financial information, indicate that they are less in scope than examinations, and provide negative assurance (e.g., "I am not aware of any material modifications that should be made. . .").

Scope restrictions, departures from AICPA standards, etc., are treated in a manner similar to that for reviews and audits of historical financial statements. At this point, review the outline of the section that precedes the SAS outline.

e.  **Management discussion and analysis.**  AT 701 provides guidance for performing review and examination of management's discussion and analysis (MD&A).  MD&A is included in reports filed with the SEC (e.g., Form 10K and 10Q) and in annual reports sent directly to shareholders.  In addition, a number of companies that do not report to the SEC prepare such information.  This service allows a CPA to provide assurance ("negative assurance" for a review, and "reasonable assurance" for an examination) on a client's MD&A.  At this point you should review carefully the outline of AT 701, including the summary tables that follow that outline.

f.  **Trust Services.**  Trust Services—jointly developed with the Canadian Institute of Chartered Accountants (CICA)—are designed to provide information system business assurance and advisory services that instill confidence in an organization, system, or other entity by improving the quality or context of information for decision makers.  They were developed by the AICPA's Assurance Services Executive Committee (discussed in Overview).

Trust Services view a system as consisting of five key components organized to achieve a specified objective—infrastructure, software, people, procedures, and data.  It may be as simple as a personal-computer based payroll application with only one user, or as complex as a multi-application, multicomputer banking system accessed by many users both within and outside the banks involved.

In a Trust Services engagement, management prepares and communicates a system description that can be included on the company's website, attached to the practitioners' report, or communicated to users in some other manner.  It must clearly articulate the boundaries of the system so as to allow individuals to understand both the scope of management's assertions related to it and the CPA's report.

In performing a Trust Services engagement the CPA (practitioner) performs procedures to determine that management's description of the system is fairly stated, and obtains evidence that the controls over the system are designed and operating effectively to meet the Trust Services **Principles** and **Criteria**—the suitable criteria required for an attest engagement.  The CPA reports on whether the system meets one or more of the following **principles** over a particular reporting period:

1.  **Security.**  The system (infrastructure, software, people, procedures, and data) is protected against unauthorized access (both physical and logical).
2.  **Availability.**  The system is available for operation and use as committed or agreed.
3.  **Processing Integrity.**  System processing is complete, accurate, timely and authorized.
4.  **Online Privacy.**  Private information obtained as a result of electronic commerce is collected, used, disclosed, and retained as committed or agreed.
5.  **Confidentiality.**  Information designated as confidential is protected as committed or agreed.

For each principle reported upon by the auditor, the auditor considers each of the following four criteria:

1.  **Policies.**  The entity has defined and documented its policies relevant to the particular principle.  These policies are written statements that communicate management's intent, objectives, requirements, responsibilities, and/or standards for a particular subject.
2.  **Communications.**  The entity has communicated its defined policies to authorized users.
3.  **Procedures.**  The entity utilizes procedures to achieve the objectives in accordance with its defined policies.
4.  **Monitoring.**  The entity monitors the system and takes action to maintain compliance with its defined policies.

Key points related to a Trust Services engagement

1.  Management ordinarily provides the CPA with a written assertion on the system and the CPA may report either on management's assertion or the subject matter of the engagement (one or more of the principles).  When the CPA reports on the assertion, the assertion should accompany the CPA's report or the first paragraph of the report should contain a statement of the assertion.  The CPA's report and management's assertion should specify the period covered—that may be for a period of time (ordinarily one year or less) or at a point in time.

2. If one or more criteria relating to a principle have not been achieved, the CPA issues a qualified or adverse report. If management refuses to provide a written assertion, a disclaimer of opinion is ordinarily appropriate.

3. When reporting on more than one principle, the CPA may issue either a combined report on all principles, or individual reports.

4. Either an examination or an agreed-upon procedures engagement may be performed for a Trust Services engagement.

5. At present CPAs offer two types of trust services—WebTrust and SysTrust.

   a. **WebTrust** provides assurance on electronic commerce (including websites). The CPA is engaged to examine *both* that a client *complied* with the Trust Services criteria (e.g., the company uses procedures in accordance with its defined policies) and that it *maintained effective controls* over the system based on Trust Services criteria (e.g., the company's procedures are effective).

   b. **SysTrust** provides assurance on any defined electronic system. In a SysTrust engagement the CPA is engaged to examine only that a client *maintained effective controls* over the system based on the Trust Services criteria.

6. Both WebTrust and SysTrust are designed to incorporate a seal management process by which a seal (logo) may be included on a client's website as an electronic representation of the practitioner's unqualified WebTrust report. If the client wishes to use the seal (logo), the engagement must be updated at least annually. Also, the initial reporting period must include at least two months. Following are sample reports for WebTrust and SysTrust.

---

**Independent Practitioner's WebTrust Report on Consumer Protection**

To the Management of ABC Company:

We have examined ABC Company's compliance with the AICPA/CICA Trust Services Criteria for consumer protection, and based on these criteria, the effectiveness of controls over the On-line Privacy and Processing Integrity of the Customer Order Placement System during the period January 1, 20X2, through June 30, 20X2. The compliance with these criteria and maintaining the effectiveness of these controls is the responsibility of ABC Company's management. Our responsibility is to express an opinion based on our examination.

Within the context of AICPA/CICA Trust Services, consumer protection addresses the controls over personally identifiable information and the processing of electronic commerce transactions. The AICPA/CICA Trust Services On-line Privacy and Processing Integrity Criteria are used to evaluate whether ABC Company's controls over consumer protection of its Customer Order Placement System are effective. Consumer protection does not address the quality of ABC Company's goods, nor their suitability for any customer's intended purpose.

Our examination was conducted in accordance with attestation standards established by the American Institute of Certified Public Accountants and, accordingly, included (1) obtaining an understanding of ABC Company's relevant on-line privacy and processing integrity controls; (2) testing and evaluating the operating effectiveness of the controls; (3) testing compliance with the On-line Privacy and Processing Integrity Criteria; and (4) performing such other procedures as we considered necessary in the circumstances. We believe that our examination provides a reasonable basis for our opinion.

In our opinion, ABC Company complied, in all material respects, with the criteria for consumer protection and maintained, in all material respects, effective controls over the Customer Order Placement System to provide reasonable assurance that

- Personal information obtained as a result of electronic commerce was collected, used, disclosed, and retained as committed or agreed, and
- System processing was complete, accurate, timely and authorized during the period of January 1, 20X2, through June 30, 20X2, based on the AICPA/CICA Trust Services Criteria for consumer protection.

Because of inherent limitations in controls, error or fraud may occur and not be detected. Furthermore, the projection of any conclusions, based on our findings, to future periods is subject to the risk that the validity of such conclusions may be altered because of changes made to the system or controls, the failure to make needed changes to the system or controls, or a deterioration in the degree of effectiveness of the controls.

The WebTrust Seal of Assurance on ABC Company's website constitutes a symbolic representation of the contents of this report and it is not intended, nor should it be construed, to update this report or provide any additional assurance.

This report does not include any representation as to the quality of ABC Company's goods nor their suitability for any customer's intended purpose.

[Name of CPA Firm, City, State, Date]

---

**Independent Practitioner's SysTrust Report**

To the Management of ABC Company:

We have examined the effectiveness of ABC Company's control described in Schedule X, over the security of its Cash Disbursements System during the period January 1, 20X2, to June 30, 20X2, based on the AICPA/CICA Trust Services Security Criteria. Maintaining the effectiveness of these controls is the responsibility of ABC Company's management. Our responsibility is to express an opinion based on our examination.

Our examination was conducted in accordance with attestation standards established by the American Institute of Certified Public Accountants and, accordingly, included (1) obtaining an understanding of ABC Company's relevant on-line privacy and processing integrity controls; (2) testing and evaluating the operating effectiveness of the controls; (3) testing compliance with the On-line Privacy and Processing Integrity Criteria; and (4) performing such other procedures as we considered necessary in the circumstances. We believe that our examination provides a reasonable basis for our opinion.

In our opinion, ABC Company maintained, in all material respects, effective controls described in Schedule X, over the security of the Cash Disbursements System to provide reasonable assurance that the Cash Disbursements System was protected against unauthorized access (both physical and logical) during the period January 1, 20X2 to June 30, 20X2, based on the AICPA/CICA Trust Services Security Criteria.

Because of inherent limitations in controls, error or fraud may occur and not be detected. Furthermore, the projection of any conclusions, based on our findings, to future periods is subject to the risk that the validity of such conclusions may be altered because of changes made to the system or controls, the failure to make needed changes to the system or controls, or a deterioration in the degree of effectiveness of the controls.

The SysTrust Seal on ABC Company's website constitutes a symbolic representation of the contents of this report and it is not intended, nor should it be construed, to update this report or provide any additional assurance.

[Name of CPA Firm, City, State, Date]

---

## D. Reporting on Compliance

Compliance auditing involves testing and reporting on whether an organization has complied with the requirements of various laws, regulations, contracts, and grants. Congress and various regulatory agencies have adopted compliance auditing requirements for a variety of governmental and other organizations. While not a new type of auditing, it has become more significant in the last decade. A primary purpose of compliance auditing is to provide assurance that requirements of various federal programs have been met. Currently, the major engagements are (1) compliance attestation engagements, or (2) compliance auditing of federal financial assistance programs.

1. **Compliance Attestation Engagements.** AT 601 provides guidance to CPAs on providing assurance —either through agreed-upon procedures or through examination engagements—concerning an organization's compliance with requirements of certain laws, regulations, rules, contracts, or grants (referred to as compliance with **specified requirements**). The following are examples of agreed-upon procedures engagements (which occur much more frequently than examinations):

   *EXAMPLE 1: The Federal Depository Insurance Corporation (FDIC) Improvement Act of 1991 requires that CPAs be engaged by certain financial institutions to perform agreed-upon procedures engagements to test financial institution compliance with certain "safety and soundness" laws designated by the FDIC.*

   *EXAMPLE 2: The Environmental Protection Agency (EPA) requires that CPAs (or internal auditors) be engaged to perform agreed-upon procedures engagements to test certain entities' compliance with an EPA regulation that gasoline contains at least 2.0% oxygen.*

   As an alternative to performing agreed-upon procedures in engagements such as the above, a CPA may perform agreed-upon procedures on the portion of the internal control that is designed to provide reasonable assurance of compliance with such specified requirements. Using the second illustration, a control over compliance engagement would analyze controls related to providing management with reasonable assurance that gasoline contains at least 2.0% oxygen.

   Basic to compliance attestation engagements **is a written management assertion** concerning compliance. In this assertion, management ordinarily states that it believes that the company is in compliance with the specified requirements or acknowledges certain instances of noncompliance. This written assertion is included in a representation letter addressed by management to the auditor, and may also be included in a separate management report. For example, in the second earlier example, the written management assertion relates to its compliance with the EPA regulation; alternatively, structured on internal control, the assertion relates to internal control over compliance with the EPA regulation. The CPA performs procedures to test whether the written assertion is correct. AT 601 establishes standards for agreed-upon procedures engagements on compliance and internal control, and for examination engagements on compliance. The statement does not permit review engagements.

a. **Agreed-upon procedures engagements**

    (1) **Applicability**—These engagements may be related either to management's assertion about compliance with specified requirements or to management's assertion about the effectiveness of its internal control over compliance.

    (2) **Engagement scope**—The scope of these engagements is often fixed by the regulatory agency involved (e.g., the EPA in the second example presented earlier). The CPA is required to obtain an understanding of the compliance requirements addressed in management's assertion and must obtain a representation letter from management.

    (3) **Reporting**—As with other agreed-upon procedures engagements, the report is a limited distribution report, in this case restricted to the audit committee, management, and the parties for whom the procedures were performed (e.g., the EPA). The accountant provides a summary of findings in the report. The report must include any material noncompliance noted, regardless of whether the CPA became aware of it as a direct result of the procedures performed or in some other manner (e.g., through a discussion with an internal auditor). The following is an example of an agreed-upon procedures report:

---

**Independent Practitioner's Report**

To XYZ Company:

    We have performed the procedures enumerated below, which were agreed to by the Minnesota Department of Education, solely to assist the specified parties in evaluating XYZ Company's compliance with Section F.2. of Minnesota Department of Education Regulation 76A of *Employment Health Requirements* during the period ended December 31, 20XX. Management is responsible for XYZ Company's compliance with those requirements. This agreed-upon procedures engagement was conducted in accordance with attestation standards established by the American Institute of Certified Public Accountants. The sufficiency of these procedures is solely the responsibility of those parties specified in this report. Consequently, we make no representation regarding the sufficiency of the procedures described below either for the purpose for which this report has been requested or for any other purpose.

[Include paragraphs to enumerate procedures and findings.]

    We were not engaged to, and did not, perform an examination, the objective of which would be the expression of an opinion on compliance. Accordingly, we do not express such an opinion. Had we performed additional procedures, other matters might have come to our attention that would have been reported to you.

    This report is intended solely for the information of the audit committee, management, and the parties listed in the first paragraph, and is not intended to be and should not be used by anyone other than those specified parties.

---

b. **Examination engagements**

    (1) **Applicability**—These engagements relate to management's written assertion about the entity's compliance with specified requirements. (AT 601 does not provide guidance for examinations of the internal control over compliance. General guidance for such engagements is provided in AT 101.)

    (2) **Engagement scope**—The procedures and scope of an examination of compliance are similar to those of an audit of financial statements. Following are the major stages:

        (a) Obtain understanding of specified compliance requirements

        (b) Plan the engagement

        (c) Consider relevant portions of internal control over compliance (when control risk is to be assessed below maximum, tests of controls must be performed)

        (d) Obtain sufficient evidence through substantive tests of compliance with specified requirements

        (e) Consider whether any subsequent events affect compliance

        (f) Form opinion about whether management's assertion about the entity's compliance with specified requirements is fairly stated in all material respects based on established or agreed-upon criteria

(3) **Reporting**—The CPA's report may either be (1) directly upon compliance, or (2) on management's assertion. The following is an unqualified report directly upon compliance:

---

**Independent Practitioner's Report**

To XYZ Company:

We have examined XYZ Company's compliance with Section F.2. of Minnesota Department of Education Regulation 76A of *Employment Health Requirements* during the period ended December 31, 20XX. Management is responsible for XYZ Company's compliance with those requirements. Our responsibility is to express an opinion on XYZ Company's compliance based on our examination.

Our examination was conducted in accordance with attestation standards established by the American Institute of Certified Public Accountants, and, accordingly, included examining, on a test basis, evidence about XYZ Company's compliance with those requirements and performing such other procedures as we considered necessary in the circumstances. We believe that our examination provides a reasonable basis for our opinion. Our examination does not provide a legal determination on XYZ Company's compliance with specified requirements.

In our opinion, XYZ Company complied, in all material respects, with the aforementioned requirements for the year ended December 31, 20XX.

This report is intended solely for the information and use of XYZ Company and the State of Minnesota and is not intended to be and should not be used by anyone other than these specified parties.

---

As is the case with other attestation reports, if an opinion other than unqualified is being issued the CPA should follow the first reporting option, reporting directly upon compliance. The following table presents the primary circumstances:

| Circumstance | Examination Report Effect |
|---|---|
| 1.   Entity did not comply | Qualified or adverse opinion with an explanatory paragraph added before the opinion paragraph. |
| 2.   Material uncertainty relating to future events makes determination of compliance insusceptible to reasonable estimation | Qualified opinion or disclaimer of opinion with an explanatory paragraph added before the opinion paragraph |
| 3.   Scope restriction | When client-imposed, generally disclaim an opinion; when circumstance-imposed, consider qualified opinion or disclaimer of opinion. |
| 4.   Involvement of another CPA firm | When the principal CPA does not wish to take responsibility for the other CPA's work, the other CPA's report is referred to. |

2. **Compliance Auditing of Federal Financial Assistance Programs.** A major factor causing the demand for compliance auditing is the need for accountability over the financial assistance provided by the federal government. AU 801 provides requirements related to auditing entities that have received governmental financial assistance. In addition, guidance is provided by *Government Auditing Standards* (GAS), also referred to as the "yellow book," published by the Comptroller General of the United States (the top executive within the General Accounting Office). GAS presents what it refers to as "generally accepted government auditing standards"; the importance of GAS on the CPA exam is emphasized by its inclusion in *Information for CPA Candidates* as a publication that should be studied (its outline follows the AU 901 outline). In this section we present a brief overview of the important information so as to allow you to more efficiently review the outlines of AU 801 and GAS. Make certain that you allocate sufficient time for these fairly lengthy outlines.

GAS divides audits into two broad types—financial and performance. These two types of audits are further subdivided as follows:

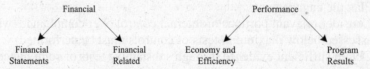

Most of the examined material on compliance auditing has been on three types of financial audits.

a.   Audits conducted in accordance with GAAS.
b.   Audits conducted in accordance with Government Auditing Standards (GAS).
c.   Audits conducted in accordance with the Single Audit Act of 1984.

a. **Audits conducted in accordance with GAAS**

(1) **Applicability**—This form of audit is generally performed for governmental entities for which no law requires either a GAS or Single Audit. It is also performed for certain nongovernmental entities that have received federal financial assistance.

(2) **Audit scope**—Recall from Section A of the Engagement Planning Module that auditors have a responsibility to design all audits to provide reasonable assurance of detecting misstatements resulting from violations of laws and regulations that have a direct and material effect on line item amounts (hereafter "direct effect") in the financial statements; this responsibility remains the same for these audits. Because entities that receive financial aid must comply with a number of laws that, if violated, result in illegal acts with a direct effect on the financial statements, an audit must provide reasonable assurance of their detection.

To identify laws having a direct effect on an organization's financial statements, auditors (1) discuss laws with management, other administrators, and government auditors, (2) review relevant grant and loan agreements, (3) review minutes of the legislative body of the governmental organization, and (4) obtain written representations from management about the completeness of laws identified. They then assess the risk that financial statement amounts might be materially misstated by violations of laws and design and perform appropriate substantive **tests of compliance** with the laws.

The objectives, scope, methodology, and results of the audit should be summarized in audit working papers in a legible manner and should contain evidence of supervisory reviews of the work conducted. These working papers should "stand alone" without the need for any supplementary explanations to describe the nature of the audit and should include a written audit program, with proper cross-referencing to the working papers.

(3) **Reporting**—The standard audit report is normally issued. If material noncompliance is detected, it must be disclosed in the financial statements or treated as a departure from GAAP in the audit report, thus requiring a qualified or an adverse opinion. **No** compliance report (see next section) is issued, and a report on internal control is only issued when reportable conditions have been identified.

b. **Audits conducted in accordance with government auditing standards (GAS)**

(1) **Applicability**—These audits are required for certain organizations that receive federal financial assistance. Whether a governmental organization is so required depends upon requirements of the federal financial assistance programs in which it participates and whether it is required to have a Single Audit (see c. below).

(2) **Audit scope**—The scope is identical to GAAS audits as described in the preceding section.

(3) **Reporting**—GAS require reporting on the **financial statements** (i.e., the "audit report"), **internal control,** and on **compliance with laws and regulations**. This requirement may be met by issuing (1) one combined report, (2) two reports (internal and compliance combined) or (3) three separate reports.

*NOTE: The reporting on compliance and internal control differs from ordinary financial statement audits in that no report on compliance is issued and a report on internal control (to the audit committee) is only issued when reportable conditions have been identified.*

**Reporting on financial statements.** The report on the financial statements is similar to the standard audit report, but also includes a number of modifications.

**Paragraphs 1-3**—Similar to the standard audit report presented in section A.2. of this module, although the scope paragraph indicates that the audit was conducted in accordance with GAAS **and** Government Auditing Standards.

**Paragraph 4**—Refers to issuance of another report on internal control over financial reporting and tests of compliance.

**Paragraph 5**—

• The audit was performed for the purpose of forming an opinion on the General-Purpose Financial Statements

• The accompanying Schedule of Expenditures of Federal Awards is not a required part of the General-Purpose Financial Statements

- The Schedule of Expenditures of Federal Awards has been subjected to auditing procedures applied in the audit of the General-Purpose Financial Statements, and, in our opinion, is fairly stated, in all material respects, in relation to the General-Purpose Financial Statements taken as a whole.

**Reporting on internal control.** When performing an audit in accordance with GAS, this portion of the combined report must disclose any reportable conditions identified during the audit. The report also includes an identification and discussion of the implications of those reportable conditions that are considered to be material weaknesses. Other items included in the report include

- An indication that management is responsible for establishing and maintaining internal control.
- A description of the scope of the auditors' work in obtaining an understanding of internal control and in assessing control risk.
- A description of deficiencies in internal control not significant enough to be reportable conditions, or a reference to a separate letter to management that reported these conditions.

**Reporting on compliance with laws and regulations.** This portion of the combined report is based on the tests of compliance with laws and regulations that have a direct and material effect on the amount in the financial statements; these tests are required by GAAS. The report describes the scope of the tests of compliance with laws and regulations and presents the auditors' findings. Violations of such laws and regulations that might result in a material misstatement of the financial statements are referred to as material instances of **noncompliance**. Even when any financial statement misstatements are corrected, the auditors must still modify their report on compliance (and internal control) to include a description of such material instances of noncompliance. Auditors also should report any other fraudulent or illegal acts, unless those acts are clearly inconsequential. In a GAS audit, the auditors are sometimes required to report fraudulent or illegal acts directly to a governmental agency or another third party (e.g., a particular government agency that has provided funding may require such disclosure).

The following is a sample combined report on compliance and internal control when reportable instances of noncompliance and reportable conditions have been identified:

---

[*Addressee*]

We have audited the financial statements of Example Entity, as of and for the year ended June 30, 20X1, and have issued our report thereon dated August 15, 20X1. We conducted our audit in accordance with US generally accepted auditing standards and the standards applicable to financial audits contained in *Government Auditing Standards*, issued by the Comptroller General of the United States.

**Compliance**

As part of obtaining reasonable assurance about whether Example Entity's financial statements are free of material misstatement, we performed tests of its compliance with certain provisions of laws, regulations, contracts, and grants, noncompliance with which could have a direct effect on the determination of financial statement accounts. However, providing an opinion on compliance with those provisions was not an objective of our audit and, accordingly, we do not express such an opinion. The results of our tests disclosed instances of noncompliance that are required to be reported under *Government Auditing Standards* which are described in the accompanying Schedule of Findings and Questioned Costs as *items* [*List related finding reference numbers, for example, 97-2 and 97-5*].

**Internal control over financial reporting**

In planning and performing our audit, we considered Example Entity's internal control over financial reporting in order to determine our auditing procedures for the purpose of expressing our opinion on the financial statements and not to provide assurance on the internal control over financial reporting. However, we noted certain matters involving the internal control over financial reporting and its operation that we consider to be reportable conditions. Reportable conditions involve matters coming to our attention relating to significant deficiencies in the design or operation of the internal control over financial reporting that, in our judgment, could adversely affect Example Entity's ability to record, process, summarize, and report financial data consistent with the assertions of management in the financial statements. Reportable conditions are described in the accompanying Schedule of Findings and Questioned Costs as *items* [*List related finding reference numbers, for example, 97-1, 97-4, and 97-8*].

A material weakness is a condition in which the design or operation of one or more of the internal control components does not reduce to a relatively low level the risk that misstatements in amounts that would be material in relation to the financial statements being audited may occur, and not be detected within a timely period by employees in the normal course of performing their assigned functions. Our consideration of internal control over financial reporting would not necessarily disclose all matters in internal control that might be reportable conditions and, accordingly, would not necessarily disclose all reportable conditions that are also considered to be material weaknesses. However, we believe none of the reportable conditions described above are a material weakness.

This report is intended for the information of the audit committee, management, and federal awarding agencies and pass-through entities. However, this report is a matter of public record and its distribution is not limited.

[*Signature*]

[*Date*]

c. **Audits conducted in accordance with the Single Audit Act.** Audits in accordance with the Single Audit Act of 1984 (as amended in 1996) are more extensive than GAAS or GAS audits. This act, passed by Congress, is implemented by the Office of Management and Budget (OMB) through its Circular A-133 and its related Compliance Supplement. Circular A-133 is the OMB's key policy document that implements the Single Audit Act. The Compliance Supplement is the document that provides guidance to auditors who are engaged to test for compliance with program requirements.

Audits in accordance with the Single Audit Act include requirements that supplement the GAS audit procedures. The auditors' report(s) may be presented in the form of either combined or separate reports, but should include the following:

(1) **Opinion (or disclaimer) on whether financial statements conform to GAAP.**

(2) **Opinion on schedule of expenditures of federal awards.** The schedule summarized program expenditures for all programs. The auditors' report includes an opinion as to whether the information is presented fairly, in all material respects, in relation to the financial statements taken as a whole.

(3) **Report on internal control related to the financial statements and major programs.** Under the single audit requirements, auditors are responsible for understanding internal control over major programs and reporting the results of their tests; reportable conditions and material weaknesses must be disclosed. Auditors are required to obtain an understanding of the recipient's internal control over financial reporting and over federal programs sufficient to **plan** the audit to support a low assessed level of control risk for major programs. While this provision does not require that auditors **achieve** a low assessed level of risk, it does require auditors to test the controls over federal programs to determine whether they are effective.

The internal control report (or internal control portion of a combined report) includes the following:

**First paragraph**

- Management is responsible for establishing and maintaining effective internal control over compliance with requirements of laws.
- We considered internal control over compliance that could have a direct and material effect on a major federal program.

**Second paragraph**

- Our consideration would not necessarily disclose all material weaknesses
- Definition of material weakness (condition that does not reduce to a relatively low level the risk of noncompliance)
- Material weaknesses noted (or statement that none were noted)

**Third paragraph**

- Other matters (less than material weaknesses) noted

**Fourth paragraph**

- Report is for information of audit committee, management, and federal awarding agencies
- Report is a matter of public record and its distribution is not limited

**Opinion paragraph**

- Entity complied, in all material respects, with types of requirements described above for each of its major programs.
- Auditing procedures disclosed immaterial instances of noncompliance described in the accompanying Schedule of Findings and Questioned Costs

(4) **Report on major financial assistance program compliance.** A major program is one that is determined by using a risk-based approach that considers both the amount of the program's expenditures and the risk of material noncompliance. In general, the major programs must constitute at least 50% of the total federal expenditures by the organization.

Under the Single Audit Act, compliance procedures are performed for the specific requirements of all major programs. The specific requirements that must be audited are those that, if not complied with, could have a material effect on a major program. These requirements relate to such matters as activities allowed, allowable costs, cash management, and eligibility. In testing compliance under the Single Audit Act, a lower level of planning materiality is used because auditors must consider compliance from the perspective of a material effect on each major federal assistance program. When evaluating whether an instance of noncompliance with law is material, auditors should consider the frequency of noncompliance and whether it results in a material amount of questioned costs. Questioned costs are those costs not allowed by the program, not adequately supported with documentation, unnecessary, or unreasonable.

The compliance report (or compliance portion of a combined report) in general follows the format of the standard unqualified report, with modifications including the following:

### Introductory paragraph

- We have audited compliance with requirements of Circular A-133
- Compliance is responsibility of management
- Our responsibility is to express an opinion on compliance

### Scope paragraph

- Conducted audit in compliance with US GAAS; *Government Auditing Standards*, and OMB Circular A-133

### Opinion paragraph

- Entity complied, in all material respects, with types of requirements described above for each of its major programs.
- Auditing procedures disclosed immaterial instances of noncompliance described in the accompanying Schedule of Findings and Questioned Costs

(5) **A summary report on audit results relating to financial statements, internal control, and compliance.** This report includes a summary of the auditors' findings relating to the financial statements, internal control, compliance matters, questioned costs, or suspected fraud.

The following schedule summarizes procedures and reporting requirements under GAAS, GAS, and the Single Audit Act.

**SUMMARY OF PROCEDURES AND REPORTING UNDER GENERALLY ACCEPTED AUDITING STANDARDS (GAAS), GOVERNMENT AUDITING STANDARDS (GAS), AND THE SINGLE AUDIT ACT**

|  | *GAAS Audit* | *GAS Audit* | *Single Audit Act Audit* |
|---|---|---|---|
| Audit procedures | GAAS requirements, including tests of compliance on laws and regulations having a direct and material effect on financial statement amounts | Same as GAAS | Same as GAAS, plus<br><br>• Tests of compliance for major federal assistance programs<br>• Tests of internal control over major federal assistance programs |
| Reports issued | Opinion on financial statements | Same as GAAS, plus<br><br>• Combined report on compliance with applicable laws and regulations and internal control | Same as GAS, plus combined or separate reports on<br><br>• Schedule of expenditures of federal awards<br>• Internal control of major programs<br>• Compliance of major programs<br><br>Summary of audit results relating to financial statements, internal control, and compliance |

## MULTIPLE-CHOICE QUESTIONS (1-181)

**1.** The existence of audit risk is recognized by the statement in the auditor's standard report that the auditor
- a. Obtains reasonable assurance about whether the financial statements are free of material misstatement.
- b. Assesses the accounting principles used and also evaluates the overall financial statement presentation.
- c. Realizes some matters, either individually or in the aggregate, are important while other matters are not important.
- d. Is responsible for expressing an opinion on the financial statements, which are the responsibility of management.

**2.** When an accountant performs more than one level of service (for example, a compilation and a review, or a compilation and an audit) concerning the financial statements of a nonpublic entity, the accountant generally should issue the report that is appropriate for
- a. The lowest level of service rendered.
- b. The highest level of service rendered.
- c. A compilation engagement.
- d. A review engagement.

**3.** Which of the following is **least** likely to be a restricted use report?
- a. A report on internal control reportable conditions noted in an audit.
- b. A required communication with the audit committee.
- c. A report on financial statements prepared following a comprehensive basis of accounting other than generally accepted accounting principles.
- d. A report on compliance with aspects of contractual agreements.

**4.** Which of the following statements is correct concerning an auditor's responsibility for controlling the **distribution by the client** of a restricted-use report?
- a. An auditor must inform the client that a restricted-use report is not intended for distribution to non-specified parties.
- b. When an auditor is aware that a client has distributed a restricted-use report to inappropriate third parties, the auditor should immediately inform the client to cease and desist.
- c. An auditor controls distribution through insisting that the client not duplicate the restricted-use report for any purposes.
- d. An auditor is not responsible for controlling the distribution of such reports.

**5.** Which of the following statements is a basic element of the auditor's standard report?
- a. The disclosures provide reasonable assurance that the financial statements are free of material misstatement.
- b. The auditor evaluated the overall internal control.
- c. An audit includes assessing significant estimates made by management.
- d. The financial statements are consistent with those of the prior period.

**6.** In May 2003, an auditor reissues the auditor's report on the 2001 financial statements at a continuing client's request. The 2001 financial statements are not restated and the auditor does not revise the wording of the report. The auditor should
- a. Dual date the reissued report.
- b. Use the release date of the reissued report.
- c. Use the original report date on the reissued report.
- d. Use the current period auditor's report date on the reissued report.

**7.** Which paragraphs of an auditor's standard report on financial statements should refer to generally accepted auditing standards (GAAS) and generally accepted accounting principles (GAAP)?

|    | GAAS | GAAP |
|----|------|------|
| a. | Opening | Scope |
| b. | Scope | Scope |
| c. | Scope | Opinion |
| d. | Opening | Opinion |

**8.** An auditor expressed a qualified opinion on the prior year's financial statements because of a lack of adequate disclosure. These financial statements are properly restated in the current year and presented in comparative form with the current year's financial statements. The auditor's updated report on the prior year's financial statements should
- a. Be accompanied by the auditor's original report on the prior year's financial statements.
- b. Continue to express a qualified opinion on the prior year's financial statements.
- c. Make **no** reference to the type of opinion expressed on the prior year's financial statements.
- d. Express an unqualified opinion on the restated financial statements of the prior year.

**9.** An auditor's responsibility to express an opinion on the financial statements is
- a. Implicitly represented in the auditor's standard report.
- b. Explicitly represented in the opening paragraph of the auditor's standard report.
- c. Explicitly represented in the scope paragraph of the auditor's standard report.
- d. Explicitly represented in the opinion paragraph of the auditor's standard report.

**10.** Which of the following phrases should be included in the opinion paragraph when an auditor expresses a qualified opinion?

|    | When read in conjunction with Note X | With the foregoing explanation |
|----|------|------|
| a. | Yes | No |
| b. | No | Yes |
| c. | Yes | Yes |
| d. | No | No |

**11.** How does an auditor make the following representations when issuing the standard auditor's report on comparative financial statements?

|     | Examination of evidence on a test basis | Consistent application of accounting principles |
|-----|-----------------------------------------|-------------------------------------------------|
| a.  | Explicitly                              | Explicitly                                      |
| b.  | Implicitly                              | Implicitly                                      |
| c.  | Implicitly                              | Explicitly                                      |
| d.  | Explicitly                              | Implicitly                                      |

**12.** The fourth standard of reporting requires the auditor's report to contain either an expression of opinion regarding the financial statements taken as a whole or an assertion to the effect that an opinion cannot be expressed. The objective of the fourth standard is to prevent

    a. An auditor from expressing different opinions on each of the basic financial statements.

    b. Restrictions on the scope of the audit, whether imposed by the client or by the inability to obtain evidence.

    c. Misinterpretations regarding the degree of responsibility the auditor is assuming.

    d. An auditor from reporting on one basic financial statement and **not** the others.

**13.** Which of the following **best** describes the reference to the expression "taken as a whole" in the fourth generally accepted auditing standard of reporting?

    a. It applies equally to a complete set of financial statements and to each individual financial statement.

    b. It applies only to a complete set of financial statements.

    c. It applies equally to each item in each financial statement.

    d. It applies equally to each material item in each financial statement.

**14.** Several sources of GAAP consulted by an auditor are in conflict as to the application of an accounting principle. Which of the following should the auditor consider the most authoritative?

    a. FASB Technical Bulletins.

    b. AICPA Accounting Interpretations.

    c. FASB Statements of Financial Accounting Concepts.

    d. AICPA Technical Practice Aids.

**15.** Wilson, CPA, completed the fieldwork of the audit of Abco's December 31, 2001 financial statements on March 6, 2002. A subsequent event requiring adjustment to the 2001 financial statements occurred on April 10, 2002, and came to Wilson's attention on April 24, 2002. If the adjustment is made without disclosure of the event, Wilson's report ordinarily should be dated

    a. March 6, 2002.

    b. April 10, 2002.

    c. April 24, 2002.

    d. Using dual dating.

**16.** An auditor issued an audit report that was dual dated for a subsequent event occurring after the completion of fieldwork but before issuance of the auditor's report. The auditor's responsibility for events occurring subsequent to the completion of fieldwork was

    a. Extended to subsequent events occurring through the date of issuance of the report.

    b. Extended to include all events occurring since the completion of fieldwork.

    c. Limited to the specific event referenced.

    d. Limited to include only events occurring up to the date of the last subsequent event referenced.

**17.** A financial statement audit report issued for the audit of a public company concludes that the financial statements follow

    a. Generally accepted accounting principles.

    b. Public Company Accounting Oversight Board standards.

    c. Generally accepted auditing standards.

    d. International accounting standards.

**18.** Which of the following is not correct concerning information included in an audit report of financial statements issued under the requirements of the Public Company Accounting Oversight Board?

    a. The report should include the title "Report of Independent Registered Public Accounting Firm."

    b. The report should refer to the standards of the PCAOB.

    c. The report should include a paragraph referring to the auditor's report on compliance with laws and regulations.

    d. The report should contain the city and state or country of the office that issued the report.

**19.** A principal auditor decides not to refer to the audit of another CPA who audited a subsidiary of the principal auditor's client. After making inquiries about the other CPA's professional reputation and independence, the principal auditor most likely would

    a. Add an explanatory paragraph to the auditor's report indicating that the subsidiary's financial statements are **not** material to the consolidated financial statements.

    b. Document in the engagement letter that the principal auditor assumes no responsibility for the other CPA's work and opinion.

    c. Obtain written permission from the other CPA to omit the reference in the principal auditor's report.

    d. Contact the other CPA and review the audit programs and working papers pertaining to the subsidiary.

**20.** The introductory paragraph of an auditor's report contains the following sentences:

> We did not audit the financial statements of EZ Inc., a wholly owned subsidiary, which statements reflect total assets and revenues constituting 27% and 29%, respectively, of the related consolidated totals. Those statements were audited by other auditors whose report has been furnished to us, and our opinion, insofar as it relates to the amounts included for EZ Inc., is based solely on the report of the other auditors.

These sentences

    a. Indicate a division of responsibility.

    b. Assume responsibility for the other auditor.

    c. Require a departure from an unqualified opinion.

    d. Are an improper form of reporting.

**21.** In which of the following situations would an auditor ordinarily issue an unqualified audit opinion without an explanatory paragraph?

a. The auditor wishes to emphasize that the entity had significant related-party transactions.

b. The auditor decides to make reference to the report of another auditor as a basis, in part, for the auditor's opinion.

c. The entity issues financial statements that present financial position and results of operations, but omits the statement of cash flows.

d. The auditor has substantial doubt about the entity's ability to continue as a going concern, but the circumstances are fully disclosed in the financial statements.

**22.** An auditor may issue the standard audit report when the
a. Auditor refers to the findings of a specialist.
b. Financial statements are derived and condensed from complete audited financial statements that are filed with a regulatory agency.
c. Financial statements are prepared on the cash receipts and disbursements basis of accounting.
d. Principal auditor assumes responsibility for the work of another auditor.

**23.** In the auditor's report, the principal auditor decides not to make reference to another CPA who audited a client's subsidiary. The principal auditor could justify this decision if, among other requirements, the principal auditor
a. Issues an unqualified opinion on the consolidated financial statements.
b. Learns that the other CPA issued an unqualified opinion on the subsidiary's financial statements.
c. Is unable to review the audit programs and working papers of the other CPA.
d. Is satisfied as to the independence and professional reputation of the other CPA.

**24.** When financial statements contain a departure from GAAP because, due to unusual circumstances, the statements would otherwise be misleading, the auditor should explain the unusual circumstances in a separate paragraph and express an opinion that is
a. Unqualified.
b. Qualified.
c. Adverse.
d. Qualified or adverse, depending on materiality.

**25.** An auditor concludes that there is substantial doubt about an entity's ability to continue as a going concern for a reasonable period of time. If the entity's financial statements adequately disclose its financial difficulties, the auditor's report is required to include an explanatory paragraph that specifically uses the phrase(s)

|  | *"Reasonable period of time, not to exceed 1 year"* | *"Going concern"* |
|---|---|---|
| a. | Yes | Yes |
| b. | Yes | No |
| c. | No | Yes |
| d. | No | No |

**26.** Mead, CPA, had substantial doubt about Tech Co.'s ability to continue as a going concern when reporting on Tech's audited financial statements for the year ended June 30, 2001. That doubt has been removed in 2002. What is Mead's reporting responsibility if Tech is presenting its

financial statements for the year ended June 30, 2002, on a comparative basis with those of 2002?
a. The explanatory paragraph included in the 2002 auditor's report should **not** be repeated.
b. The explanatory paragraph included in the 2002 auditor's report should be repeated in its entirety.
c. A different explanatory paragraph describing Mead's reasons for the removal of doubt should be included.
d. A different explanatory paragraph describing Tech's plans for financial recovery should be included.

**27.** When an auditor concludes there is substantial doubt about a continuing audit client's ability to continue as a going concern for a reasonable period of time, the auditor's responsibility is to
a. Issue a qualified or adverse opinion, depending upon materiality, due to the possible effects on the financial statements.
b. Consider the adequacy of disclosure about the client's possible inability to continue as a going concern.
c. Report to the client's audit committee that management's accounting estimates may need to be adjusted.
d. Reissue the prior year's auditor's report and add an explanatory paragraph that specifically refers to "substantial doubt" and "going concern."

**28.** Green, CPA, concludes that there is substantial doubt about JKL Co.'s ability to continue as a going concern. If JKL's financial statements adequately disclose its financial difficulties, Green's auditor's report should

|  | *Include an explanatory paragraph following the opinion paragraph* | *Specifically use the words "going concern"* | *Specifically use the words "substantial doubt"* |
|---|---|---|---|
| a. | Yes | Yes | Yes |
| b. | Yes | Yes | No |
| c. | Yes | No | Yes |
| d. | No | Yes | Yes |

**29.** In which of the following circumstances would an auditor most likely add an explanatory paragraph to the standard report while **not** affecting the auditor's unqualified opinion?
a. The auditor is asked to report on the balance sheet, but **not** on the other basic financial statements.
b. There is substantial doubt about the entity's ability to continue as a going concern.
c. Management's estimates of the effects of future events are unreasonable.
d. Certain transactions **cannot** be tested because of management's records retention policy.

**30.** After considering an entity's negative trends and financial difficulties, an auditor has substantial doubt about the entity's ability to continue as a going concern. The auditor's considerations relating to management's plans for dealing with the adverse effects of these conditions most likely would include management's plans to
a. Increase current dividend distributions.
b. Reduce existing lines of credit.

c. Increase ownership equity.

d. Purchase assets formerly leased.

**31.** For which of the following events would an auditor issue a report that omits any reference to consistency?

a. A change in the method of accounting for inventories.

b. A change from an accounting principle that is **not** generally accepted to one that is generally accepted.

c. A change in the useful life used to calculate the provision for depreciation expense.

d. Management's lack of reasonable justification for a change in accounting principle.

**32.** An auditor would express an unqualified opinion with an explanatory paragraph added to the auditor's report for

| | An unjustified accounting change | A material weakness in the internal control |
|---|---|---|
| a. | Yes | Yes |
| b. | Yes | No |
| c. | No | Yes |
| d. | No | No |

**33.** Under which of the following circumstances would a disclaimer of opinion **not** be appropriate?

a. The auditor is unable to determine the amounts associated with an employee fraud scheme.

b. Management does **not** provide reasonable justification for a change in accounting principles.

c. The client refuses to permit the auditor to confirm certain accounts receivable or apply alternative procedures to verify their balances.

d. The chief executive officer is unwilling to sign the management representation letter.

**34.** Digit Co. uses the FIFO method of costing for its international subsidiary's inventory and LIFO for its domestic inventory. Under these circumstances, the auditor's report on Digit's financial statements should express an

a. Unqualified opinion.

b. Opinion qualified because of a lack of consistency.

c. Opinion qualified because of a departure from GAAP.

d. Adverse opinion.

**35.** In the first audit of a new client, an auditor was able to extend auditing procedures to gather sufficient evidence about consistency. Under these circumstances, the auditor should

a. Not report on the client's income statement.

b. Not refer to consistency in the auditor's report.

c. State that the consistency standard does **not** apply.

d. State that the accounting principles have been applied consistently.

**36.** When management does **not** provide reasonable justification that a change in accounting principle is preferable and it presents comparative financial statements, the auditor should express a qualified opinion

a. Only in the year of the accounting principle change.

b. Each year that the financial statements initially reflecting the change are presented.

c. Each year until management changes back to the accounting principle formerly used.

d. Only if the change is to an accounting principle that is **not** generally accepted.

**37.** When an entity changes its method of accounting for income taxes, which has a material effect on comparability, the auditor should refer to the change in an explanatory paragraph added to the auditor's report. This paragraph should identify the nature of the change and

a. Explain why the change is justified under generally accepted accounting principles.

b. Describe the cumulative effect of the change on the audited financial statements.

c. State the auditor's explicit concurrence with or opposition to the change.

d. Refer to the financial statement note that discusses the change in detail.

**38.** An entity changed from the straight-line method to the declining balance method of depreciation for all newly acquired assets. This change has no material effect on the current year's financial statements, but is reasonably certain to have a substantial effect in later years. If the change is disclosed in the notes to the financial statements, the auditor should issue a report with a(n)

a. "Except for" qualified opinion.

b. Explanatory paragraph.

c. Unqualified opinion.

d. Consistency modification.

**39.** When reporting on comparative financial statements, an auditor ordinarily should change the previously issued opinion on the prior year's financial statements if the

a. Prior year's financial statements are restated to conform with generally accepted accounting principles.

b. Auditor is a predecessor auditor who has been requested by a former client to reissue the previously issued report.

c. Prior year's opinion was unqualified and the opinion on the current year's financial statements is modified due to a lack of consistency.

d. Prior year's financial statements are restated following a pooling of interests in the current year.

**40.** Jewel, CPA, audited Infinite Co.'s prior year financial statements. These statements are presented with those of the current year for comparative purposes without Jewel's auditor's report, which expressed a qualified opinion. In drafting the current year's auditor's report, Crain, CPA, the successor auditor, should

I. Not name Jewel as the predecessor auditor.

II. Indicate the type of report issued by Jewel.

III. Indicate the substantive reasons for Jewel's qualification.

a. I only.

b. I and II only.

c. II and III only.

d. I, II, and III.

**41.** Before reissuing the prior year's auditor's report on the financial statements of a former client, the predecessor auditor should obtain a letter of representations from the

|   | Former client's management | Successor auditor |
|---|---|---|
| a. | Yes | Yes |
| b. | Yes | No |
| c. | No | Yes |
| d. | No | No |

**42.** When single-year financial statements are presented, an auditor ordinarily would express an unqualified opinion in an unmodified report if the
- a. Auditor is unable to obtain audited financial statements supporting the entity's investment in a foreign affiliate.
- b. Entity declines to present a statement of cash flows with its balance sheet and related statements of income and retained earnings.
- c. Auditor wishes to emphasize an accounting matter affecting the comparability of the financial statements with those of the prior year.
- d. Prior year's financial statements were audited by another CPA whose report, which expressed an unqualified opinion, is **not** presented.

**43.** A client is presenting comparative (two-year) financial statements. Which of the following is correct concerning reporting responsibilities of a continuing auditor?
- a. The auditor should issue one audit report that is on both presented years.
- b. The auditor should issue two audit reports, one on each year.
- c. The auditor should issue one audit report, but only on the most recent year.
- d. The auditor may issue either one audit report on both presented years, or two audit reports, one on each year.

**44.** The predecessor auditor, who is satisfied after properly communicating with the successor auditor, has reissued a report because the audit client desires comparative financial statements. The predecessor auditor's report should make
- a. Reference to the report of the successor auditor only in the scope paragraph.
- b. Reference to the work of the successor auditor in the scope and opinion paragraphs.
- c. Reference to both the work and the report of the successor auditor only in the opinion paragraph.
- d. No reference to the report or the work of the successor auditor.

**45.** Unaudited financial statements for the prior year presented in comparative form with audited financial statements for the current year should be clearly marked to indicate their status and
- I. The report on the prior period should be reissued to accompany the current period report.
- II. The report on the current period should include as a separate paragraph a description of the responsibility assumed for the prior period's financial statements.
  - a. I only.
  - b. II only.
  - c. Both I and II.
  - d. Either I or II.

**46.** What is an auditor's responsibility for supplementary information, such as segment information, which is outside the basic financial statements, but required by the FASB?

- a. The auditor has **no** responsibility for required supplementary information as long as it is outside the basic financial statements.
- b. The auditor's only responsibility for required supplementary information is to determine that such information has **not** been omitted.
- c. The auditor should apply certain limited procedures to the required supplementary information, and report deficiencies in, or omissions of, such information.
- d. The auditor should apply tests of details of transactions and balances to the required supplementary information, and report any material misstatements in such information.

**47.** If management declines to present supplementary information required by the Governmental Accounting Standards Board (GASB), the auditor should issue a(n)
- a. Adverse opinion.
- b. Qualified opinion with an explanatory paragraph.
- c. Unqualified opinion.
- d. Unqualified opinion with an additional explanatory paragraph.

**48.** What is an auditor's reporting responsibility concerning information accompanying the basic financial statements in an auditor-submitted document?
- a. The auditor should report on all the accompanying information included in the document.
- b. The auditor should report on the accompanying information only if the auditor participated in its preparation.
- c. The auditor should report on the accompanying information only if the auditor did **not** participate in its preparation.
- d. The auditor should report on the accompanying information only if it contains obvious material misstatements.

**49.** If information accompanying the basic financial statements in an auditor-submitted document has been subjected to auditing procedures, the auditor may include in the auditor's report on the financial statements an opinion that the accompanying information is fairly stated in
- a. Accordance with US generally accepted auditing standards.
- b. Conformity with US generally accepted accounting principles.
- c. All material respects in relation to the basic financial statements taken as a whole.
- d. Accordance with attestation standards expressing a conclusion about management's assertions.

**50.** An auditor concludes that there is a material inconsistency in the other information in an annual report to shareholders containing audited financial statements. If the auditor concludes that the financial statements do **not** require revision, but the client refuses to revise or eliminate the material inconsistency, the auditor may
- a. Revise the auditor's report to include a separate explanatory paragraph describing the material inconsistency.
- b. Issue an "except for" qualified opinion after discussing the matter with the client's board of directors.

    c.    Consider the matter closed since the other informa-
         tion is **not** in the audited financial statements.

    d.    Disclaim an opinion on the financial statements af-
         ter explaining the material inconsistency in a sepa-
         rate explanatory paragraph.

**51.** When audited financial statements are presented in a
client's document containing other information, the auditor
should

    a.    Perform inquiry and analytical procedures to ascer-
         tain whether the other information is reasonable.

    b.    Add an explanatory paragraph to the auditor's re-
         port without changing the opinion on the financial
         statements.

    c.    Perform the appropriate substantive auditing proce-
         dures to corroborate the other information.

    d.    Read the other information to determine that it is
         consistent with the audited financial statements.

**52.** An auditor includes a separate paragraph in an otherwise unmodified report to emphasize that the entity being
reported on had significant transactions with related parties.
The inclusion of this separate paragraph

    a.    Is considered an "except for" qualification of the
         opinion.

    b.    Violates generally accepted auditing standards if
         this information is already disclosed in footnotes to
         the financial statements.

    c.    Necessitates a revision of the opinion paragraph to
         include the phrase "with the foregoing explana-
         tion."

    d.    Is appropriate and would **not** negate the unquali-
         fied opinion.

**53.** An auditor concludes that a client's illegal act, which
has a material effect on the financial statements, has not
been properly accounted for or disclosed. Depending on the
materiality of the effect on the financial statements, the
auditor should express either a(n)

    a.    Adverse opinion or a disclaimer of opinion.

    b.    Qualified opinion or an adverse opinion.

    c.    Disclaimer of opinion or an unqualified opinion
         with a separate explanatory paragraph.

    d.    Unqualified opinion with a separate explanatory
         paragraph or a qualified opinion.

**54.** Which of the following phrases would an auditor most
likely include in the auditor's report when expressing a
qualified opinion because of inadequate disclosure?

    a.    Subject to the departure from US generally ac-
         cepted accounting principles, as described above.

    b.    With the foregoing explanation of these omitted
         disclosures.

    c.    Except for the omission of the information dis-
         cussed in the preceding paragraph.

    d.    Does **not** present fairly in all material respects.

**55.** In which of the following circumstances would an auditor be most likely to express an adverse opinion?

    a.    The chief executive officer refuses the auditor ac-
         cess to minutes of board of directors' meetings.

    b.    Tests of controls show that the entity's internal
         control is so poor that it **cannot** be relied upon.

    c.    The financial statements are **not** in conformity
         with the FASB Statements regarding the capitali-
         zation of leases.

    d.    Information comes to the auditor's attention that
         raises substantial doubt about the entity's ability to
         continue as a going concern.

**56.** When an auditor qualifies an opinion because of inadequate disclosure, the auditor should describe the nature of
the omission in a separate explanatory paragraph and modify
the

| | Introductory paragraph | Scope paragraph | Opinion paragraph |
|---|---|---|---|
| a. | Yes | No | No |
| b. | Yes | Yes | No |
| c. | No | Yes | Yes |
| d. | No | No | Yes |

**57.** If a publicly held company issues financial statements
that purport to present its financial position and results of
operations but omits the statement of cash flows, the auditor
ordinarily will express a(n)

    a.    Disclaimer of opinion.

    b.    Qualified opinion.

    c.    Review report.

    d.    Unqualified opinion with a separate explanatory
         paragraph.

**58.** In which of the following situations would an auditor
ordinarily choose between expressing an "except for" qualified opinion or an adverse opinion?

    a.    The auditor did not observe the entity's physical
         inventory and is unable to become satisfied as to
         its balance by other auditing procedures.

    b.    The financial statements fail to disclose informa-
         tion that is required by generally accepted ac-
         counting principles.

    c.    The auditor is asked to report only on the entity's
         balance sheet and not on the other basic financial
         statements.

    d.    Events disclosed in the financial statements cause
         the auditor to have substantial doubt about the en-
         tity's ability to continue as a going concern.

**59.** In which of the following situations would an auditor
ordinarily choose between expressing a qualified opinion or
an adverse opinion?

    a.    The auditor did **not** observe the entity's physical
         inventory and is unable to become satisfied about
         its balance by other auditing procedures.

    b.    Conditions that cause the auditor to have substan-
         tial doubt about the entity's ability to continue as a
         going concern are inadequately disclosed.

    c.    There has been a change in accounting principles
         that has a material effect on the comparability of
         the entity's financial statements.

    d.    The auditor is unable to apply necessary proce-
         dures concerning an investor's share of an inves-
         tee's earnings recognized on the equity method.

**60.** In the first audit of a client, an auditor was not able to
gather sufficient evidence about the consistent application of
accounting principles between the current and the prior year,
as well as the amounts of assets or liabilities at the beginning
of the current year. This was due to the client's record retention policies. If the amounts in question could materially
affect current operating results, the auditor would

    a.    Be unable to express an opinion on the current
         year's results of operations and cash flows.

b. Express a qualified opinion on the financial statements because of a client-imposed scope limitation.
c. Withdraw from the engagement and refuse to be associated with the financial statements.
d. Specifically state that the financial statements are **not** comparable to the prior year due to an uncertainty.

**61.** In which of the following circumstances would an auditor **not** express an unqualified opinion?
a. There has been a material change between periods in accounting principles.
b. Quarterly financial data required by the SEC has been omitted.
c. The auditor wishes to emphasize an unusually important subsequent event.
d. The auditor is unable to obtain audited financial statements of a consolidated investee.

**62.** Due to a scope limitation, an auditor disclaimed an opinion on the financial statements taken as a whole, but the auditor's report included a statement that the current asset portion of the entity's balance sheet was fairly stated. The inclusion of this statement is
a. Not appropriate because it may tend to overshadow the auditor's disclaimer of opinion.
b. Not appropriate because the auditor is prohibited from reporting on only one basic financial statement.
c. Appropriate provided the auditor's scope paragraph adequately describes the scope limitation.
d. Appropriate provided the statement is in a separate paragraph preceding the disclaimer of opinion paragraph.

**63.** Park, CPA, was engaged to audit the financial statements of Tech Co., a new client, for the year ended December 31, 2001. Park obtained sufficient audit evidence for all of Tech's financial statement items except Tech's opening inventory. Due to inadequate financial records, Park could not verify Tech's January 1, 2001 inventory balances. Park's opinion on Tech's 2001 financial statements most likely will be

|     | Balance sheet | Income statement |
|-----|---------------|------------------|
| a.  | Disclaimer    | Disclaimer       |
| b.  | Unqualified   | Disclaimer       |
| c.  | Disclaimer    | Adverse          |
| d.  | Unqualified   | Adverse          |

**64.** An auditor who qualifies an opinion because of an insufficiency of evidential matter should describe the limitations in an explanatory paragraph. The auditor should also refer to the limitation in the

|     | Scope paragraph | Opinion paragraph | Notes to the financial statements |
|-----|------|------|------|
| a.  | Yes  | No   | Yes  |
| b.  | No   | Yes  | No   |
| c.  | Yes  | Yes  | No   |
| d.  | Yes  | Yes  | Yes  |

**65.** Harris, CPA, has been asked to audit and report on the balance sheet of Fox Co. but not on the statements of income, retained earnings, or cash flows. Harris will have access to all information underlying the basic financial statements. Under these circumstances, Harris may
a. Not accept the engagement because it would constitute a violation of the profession's ethical standards.
b. Not accept the engagement because it would be tantamount to rendering a piecemeal opinion.
c. Accept the engagement because such engagements merely involve limited reporting objectives.
d. Accept the engagement but should disclaim an opinion because of an inability to apply the procedures considered necessary.

**66.** When disclaiming an opinion due to a client-imposed scope limitation, an auditor should indicate in a separate paragraph why the audit did not comply with generally accepted auditing standards. The auditor should also omit the

|     | Scope paragraph | Opinion paragraph |
|-----|------|------|
| a.  | No   | Yes  |
| b.  | Yes  | Yes  |
| c.  | No   | No   |
| d.  | Yes  | No   |

**67.** An auditor decides to issue a qualified opinion on an entity's financial statements because a major inadequacy in its computerized accounting records prevents the auditor from applying necessary procedures. The opinion paragraph of the auditor's report should state that the qualification pertains to
a. A client-imposed scope limitation.
b. A departure from generally accepted auditing standards.
c. The possible effects on the financial statements.
d. Inadequate disclosure of necessary information.

**68.** A scope limitation sufficient to preclude an unqualified opinion always will result when management
a. Prevents the auditor from reviewing the working papers of the predecessor auditor.
b. Engages the auditor after the year-end physical inventory is completed.
c. Requests that certain material accounts receivable **not** be confirmed.
d. Refuses to acknowledge its responsibility for the fair presentation of the financial statements in conformity with GAAP.

**69.** An auditor may **not** issue a qualified opinion when
a. An accounting principle at variance with GAAP is used.
b. The auditor lacks independence with respect to the audited entity.
c. A scope limitation prevents the auditor from completing an important audit procedure.
d. The auditor's report refers to the work of a specialist.

**70.** An auditor may express an opinion on an entity's accounts receivable balance even if the auditor has disclaimed an opinion on the financial statements taken as a whole provided the
a. Report on the accounts receivable discloses the reason for the disclaimer of opinion on the financial statements.

b.  Distribution of the report on the accounts receivable is restricted to internal use only.
c.  Auditor also reports on the current asset portion of the entity's balance sheet.
d.  Report on the accounts receivable is presented separately from the disclaimer of opinion on the financial statements.

**71.** March, CPA, is engaged by Monday Corp., a client, to audit the financial statements of Wall Corp., a company that is not March's client. Monday expects to present Wall's audited financial statements with March's auditor's report to 1st Federal Bank to obtain financing in Monday's attempt to purchase Wall. In these circumstances, March's auditor's report would usually be addressed to
a.  Monday Corp., the client that engaged March.
b.  Wall Corp., the entity audited by March.
c.  1st Federal Bank.
d.  Both Monday Corp. and 1st Federal Bank.

**72.** When an auditor expresses an adverse opinion, the opinion paragraph should include
a.  The principal effects of the departure from generally accepted accounting principles.
b.  A direct reference to a separate paragraph disclosing the basis for the opinion.
c.  The substantive reasons for the financial statements being misleading.
d.  A description of the uncertainty or scope limitation that prevents an unqualified opinion.

**73.** An auditor should disclose the substantive reasons for expressing an adverse opinion in an explanatory paragraph
a.  Preceding the scope paragraph.
b.  Preceding the opinion paragraph.
c.  Following the opinion paragraph.
d.  Within the notes to the financial statements.

**74.** When an independent CPA assists in preparing the financial statements of a publicly held entity, but has **not** audited or reviewed them, the CPA should issue a disclaimer of opinion. In such situations, the CPA has **no** responsibility to apply any procedures beyond
a.  Documenting that internal control is **not** being relied on.
b.  Reading the financial statements for obvious material misstatements.
c.  Ascertaining whether the financial statements are in conformity with GAAP.
d.  Determining whether management has elected to omit substantially all required disclosures.

**75.** When an independent CPA is associated with the financial statements of a publicly held entity but has **not** audited or reviewed such statements, the appropriate form of report to be issued must include a(n)
a.  Regulation S-X exemption.
b.  Report on pro forma financial statements.
c.  Unaudited association report.
d.  Disclaimer of opinion.

**76.** Green, CPA, is aware that Green's name is to be included in the interim report of National Company, a publicly held entity. National's quarterly financial statements are contained in the interim report. Green has not audited or reviewed these interim financial statements. Green should request that

I.  Green's name not be included in the communication.
II. The financial statements be marked as unaudited with a notation that **no** opinion is expressed on them.

a.  I only.
b.  II only.
c.  Both I and II.
d.  Either I or II.

**77.** When compiled financial statements are accompanied by an accountant's report, that report should state that
a.  A compilation includes assessing the accounting principles used and significant management estimates, as well as evaluating the overall financial statement presentation.
b.  The accountant compiled the financial statements in accordance with Statements on Standards for Accounting and Review Services.
c.  A compilation is substantially less in scope than an audit in accordance with GAAS, the objective of which is the expression of an opinion.
d.  The accountant is not aware of any material modifications that should be made to the financial statements to conform with GAAP.

**78.** Miller, CPA, is engaged to compile the financial statements of Web Co., a nonpublic entity, in conformity with the income tax basis of accounting. If Web's financial statements do **not** disclose the basis of accounting used, Miller should
a.  Disclose the basis of accounting in the accountant's compilation report.
b.  Clearly label each page "Distribution Restricted— Material Modifications Required."
c.  Issue a special report describing the effect of the incomplete presentation.
d.  Withdraw from the engagement and provide **no** further services to Web.

**79.** When an accountant is engaged to compile a nonpublic entity's financial statements that omit substantially all disclosures required by GAAP, the accountant should indicate in the compilation report that the financial statements are
a.  Not designed for those who are uninformed about the omitted disclosures.
b.  Prepared in conformity with a comprehensive basis of accounting other than GAAP.
c.  Not compiled in accordance with Statements on Standards for Accounting and Review Services.
d.  Special-purpose financial statements that are **not** comparable to those of prior periods.

**80.** An accountant may compile a nonpublic entity's financial statements that omit all of the disclosures required by GAAP only if the omission is

I.  Clearly indicated in the accountant's report.
II. Not undertaken with the intention of misleading the financial statement users.

a.  I only.
b.  II only.
c.  Both I and II.
d.  Either I or II.

**81.** When unaudited financial statements of a nonpublic entity are presented in comparative form with audited financial statements in the subsequent year, the unaudited financial statements should be clearly marked to indicate their status and

I. The report on the unaudited financial statements should be reissued.
II. The report on the audited financial statements should include a separate paragraph describing the responsibility assumed for the unaudited financial statements.

    a. I only.
    b. II only.
    c. Both I and II.
    d. Either I or II.

**82.** Clark, CPA, compiled and properly reported on the financial statements of Green Co., a nonpublic entity, for the year ended March 31, 2001. These financial statements omitted substantially all disclosures required by generally accepted accounting principles (GAAP). Green asked Clark to compile the statements for the year ended March 31, 2002, and to include all GAAP disclosures for the 2002 statements only, but otherwise present both years' financial statements in comparative form. What is Clark's responsibility concerning the proposed engagement?

    a. Clark may **not** report on the comparative financial statements because the 2001 statements are **not** comparable to the 2002 statements that include the GAAP disclosures.
    b. Clark may report on the comparative financial statements provided the 2002 statements do **not** contain any obvious material misstatements.
    c. Clark may report on the comparative financial statements provided an explanatory paragraph is added to Clark's report on the comparative financial statements.
    d. Clark may report on the comparative financial statements provided Clark updates the report on the 2001 statements that do **not** include the GAAP disclosures.

**83.** Which of the following statements should **not** be included in an accountant's standard report based on the compilation of an entity's financial statements?

    a. A statement that the compilation was performed in accordance with standards established by the American Institute of CPAs.
    b. A statement that the accountant has **not** audited or reviewed the financial statements.
    c. A statement that the accountant does **not** express an opinion but expresses only limited assurance on the financial statements.
    d. A statement that a compilation is limited to presenting, in the form of financial statements, information that is the representation of management.

**84.** How does an accountant make the following representations when issuing the standard report for the compilation of a nonpublic entity's financial statements?

|  | The financial statements have _not been audited_ | The accountant has compiled the _financial statements_ |
|---|---|---|
| a. | Implicitly | Implicitly |
| b. | Explicitly | Explicitly |
| c. | Implicitly | Explicitly |
| d. | Explicitly | Implicitly |

**85.** An accountant's compilation report should be dated as of the date of

    a. Completion of fieldwork.
    b. Completion of the compilation.
    c. Transmittal of the compilation report.
    d. The latest subsequent event referred to in the notes to the financial statements.

**86.** An accountant has compiled the financial statements of a nonpublic entity in accordance with Statements on Standards for Accounting and Review Services (SSARS). Does SSARS require that the compilation report be printed on the accountant's letterhead and that the report be manually signed by the accountant?

|  | Printed on the _accountant's letterhead_ | Manually signed _by the accountant_ |
|---|---|---|
| a. | Yes | Yes |
| b. | Yes | No |
| c. | No | Yes |
| d. | No | No |

**87.** Which of the following is correct relating to compiled financial statements when third-party reliance upon those statements is anticipated?

    a. A compilation report must be issued.
    b. Omission of note disclosures is unacceptable.
    c. A written engagement letter is required.
    d. Each page of the financial statements should have a restriction such as "Restricted for Management's Use Only."

**88.** Which communication option(s) may be used when an accountant submits compiled financial statements to be used only by management?

|  | Compilation report | Written engagement letter |
|---|---|---|
| a. | Yes | Yes |
| b. | Yes | No |
| c. | No | Yes |
| d. | No | No |

**89.** A compilation report is **not** required when compiled financial statements are expected to be used by

    a. Management only.
    b. Management and third parties.
    c. Third parties only.
    d. A compilation report is required whenever financial statements are compiled.

**90.** In reviewing the financial statements of a nonpublic entity, an accountant is required to modify the standard report for which of the following matters?

|  | Inability to assess the risk of material misstatement _due to fraud_ | Discovery of significant deficiencies in the design of the entity's _internal control_ |
|---|---|---|
| a. | Yes | Yes |
| b. | Yes | No |
| c. | No | Yes |
| d. | No | No |

**91.** Moore, CPA, has been asked to issue a review report on the balance sheet of Dover Co., a nonpublic entity. Moore will not be reporting on Dover's statements of income, retained earnings, and cash flows. Moore may issue the review report provided the

a. Balance sheet is presented in a prescribed form of an industry trade association.

b. Scope of the inquiry and analytical procedures has not been restricted.

c. Balance sheet is not to be used to obtain credit or distributed to creditors.

d. Specialized accounting principles and practices of Dover's industry are disclosed.

**92.** Baker, CPA, was engaged to review the financial statements of Hall Co., a nonpublic entity. During the engagement Baker uncovered a complex scheme involving client illegal acts that materially affect Hall's financial statements. If Baker believes that modification of the standard review report is **not** adequate to indicate the deficiencies in the financial statements, Baker should

a. Disclaim an opinion.

b. Issue an adverse opinion.

c. Withdraw from the engagement.

d. Issue a qualified opinion.

**93.** Each page of a nonpublic entity's financial statements reviewed by an accountant should include the following reference:

a. See Accompanying Accountant's Footnotes.

b. Reviewed, No Material Modifications Required.

c. See Accountant's Review Report.

d. Reviewed, **No** Accountant's Assurance Expressed.

**94.** Financial statements of a nonpublic entity that have been reviewed by an accountant should be accompanied by a report stating that a review

a. Provides only limited assurance that the financial statements are fairly presented.

b. Includes examining, on a test basis, information that is the representation of management.

c. Consists principally of inquiries of company personnel and analytical procedures applied to financial data.

d. Does **not** contemplate obtaining corroborating evidential matter or applying certain other procedures ordinarily performed during an audit.

**95.** An accountant who had begun an audit of the financial statements of a nonpublic entity was asked to change the engagement to a review because of a restriction on the scope of the audit. If there is reasonable justification for the change, the accountant's review report should include reference to the

| | Scope limitation that caused the changed engagement | Original engagement that was agreed to |
|---|---|---|
| a. | Yes | No |
| b. | No | Yes |
| c. | No | No |
| d. | Yes | Yes |

**96.** Gole, CPA, is engaged to review the 2001 financial statements of North Co., a nonpublic entity. Previously, Gole audited North's 2000 financial statements and expressed an unqualified opinion. Gole decides to include a separate paragraph in the 2001 review report because North plans to present comparative financial statements for 2001 and 2000. This separate paragraph should indicate that

a. The 2001 review report is intended solely for the information of management and the board of directors.

b. The 2000 auditor's report may **no** longer be relied on.

c. No auditing procedures were performed after the date of the 2000 auditor's report.

d. There are justifiable reasons for changing the level of service from an audit to a review.

**97.** An accountant's standard report on a review of the financial statements of a nonpublic entity should state that the accountant

a. Does **not** express an opinion or any form of limited assurance on the financial statements.

b. Is **not** aware of any material modifications that should be made to the financial statements for them to conform with GAAP.

c. Obtained reasonable assurance about whether the financial statements are free of material misstatement.

d. Examined evidence, on a test basis, supporting the amounts and disclosures in the financial statements.

**98.** Financial statements of a nonpublic entity that have been reviewed by an accountant should be accompanied by a report stating that

a. The scope of the inquiry and analytical procedures performed by the accountant has not been restricted.

b. All information included in the financial statements is the representation of the management of the entity.

c. A review includes examining, on a test basis, evidence supporting the amounts and disclosures in the financial statements.

d. A review is greater in scope than a compilation, the objective of which is to present financial statements that are free of material misstatements.

**99.** During a review of the financial statements of a nonpublic entity, an accountant becomes aware of a lack of adequate disclosure that is material to the financial statements. If management refuses to correct the financial statement presentations, the accountant should

a. Issue an adverse opinion.

b. Issue an "except for" qualified opinion.

c. Disclose this departure from generally accepted accounting principles in a separate paragraph of the report.

d. Express only limited assurance on the financial statement presentations.

**100.** An accountant who reviews the financial statements of a nonpublic entity should issue a report stating that a review

a. Is substantially less in scope than an audit.

b. Provides negative assurance that internal control is functioning as designed.

c. Provides only limited assurance that the financial statements are fairly presented.

d. Is substantially more in scope than a compilation.

**101.** The objective of a review of interim financial information of a public entity is to provide an accountant with a basis for reporting whether

a. Material modifications should be made to conform with generally accepted accounting principles.

b. A reasonable basis exists for expressing an updated opinion regarding the financial statements that were previously audited.

c. Condensed financial statements or pro forma financial information should be included in a registration statement.

d. The financial statements are presented fairly in accordance with generally accepted accounting principles.

**102.** An independent accountant's report is based on a review of interim financial information. If this report is presented in a registration statement, a prospectus should include a statement clarifying that the

a. Accountant's review report is **not** a part of the registration statement within the meaning of the Securities Act of 1933.

b. Accountant assumes **no** responsibility to update the report for events and circumstances occurring after the date of the report.

c. Accountant's review was performed in accordance with standards established by the Securities and Exchange Commission.

d. Accountant obtained corroborating evidence to determine whether material modifications are needed for such information to conform with GAAP.

**103.** A modification of the CPA's report on a review of the interim financial statements of a publicly held company would be necessitated by which of the following?

a. An uncertainty.

b. Lack of consistency.

c. Reference to another accountant.

d. Inadequate disclosure.

**104.** Which of the following procedures ordinarily should be applied when an independent accountant conducts a review of interim financial information of a publicly held entity?

a. Verify changes in key account balances.

b. Read the minutes of the board of directors' meetings.

c. Inspect the open purchase order file.

d. Perform cut-off tests for cash receipts and disbursements.

**105.** Which of the following is **least** likely to be a procedure included in an accountant's review of interim financial information of a public entity?

a. Compare disaggregated revenue data by month to that of the previous interim period.

b. Read available minutes of meetings of stockholders.

c. Observe counting of physical inventory.

d. Inquire of management concerning significant journal entries and other adjustments.

**106.** An accountant's review report on interim financial information of a public entity is most likely to include a

a. Statement that the interim financial information was examined in accordance with standards of the Public Company Accounting Oversight Board .

b. Statement that the interim financial information is the responsibility of the entity's shareholders.

c. Description of the procedures for a review.

d. Statement that a review of interim financial information is less in scope than a compilation conducted in accordance with AICPA standards.

**107.** An auditor may report on condensed financial statements that are derived from complete financial statements if the

a. Condensed financial statements are distributed to stockholders along with the complete financial statements.

b. Auditor described the additional procedures performed on the condensed financial statements.

c. Auditor indicates whether the information in the condensed financial statements is fairly stated in all material respects in relation to the complete financial statements from which it has been derived.

d. Condensed financial statements are presented in comparative form with the prior year's condensed financial statements.

**108.** An auditor is engaged to report on selected financial data that are included in a client-prepared document containing audited financial statements. Under these circumstances, the report on the selected data should

a. Be limited to data derived from the audited financial statements.

b. Be distributed only to senior management and the board of directors.

c. State that the presentation is a comprehensive basis of accounting other than GAAP.

d. Indicate that the data are **not** fairly stated in all material respects.

**109.** Before reporting on the financial statements of a US entity that have been prepared in conformity with another country's accounting principles, an auditor practicing in the US should

a. Understand the accounting principles generally accepted in the other country.

b. Be certified by the appropriate auditing or accountancy board of the other country.

c. Notify management that the auditor is required to disclaim an opinion on the financial statements.

d. Receive a waiver from the auditor's state board of accountancy to perform the engagement.

**110.** The financial statements of KCP America, a US entity, are prepared for inclusion in the consolidated financial statements of its non-US parent. These financial statements are prepared in conformity with the accounting principles generally accepted in the parent's country and are for use only in that country. How may KCP America's auditor report on these financial statements?

I. A US-style report (unmodified).

II. A US-style report modified to report on the accounting principles of the parent's country.

III. The report form of the parent's country.

|    | *I*  | *II* | *III* |
|----|------|------|-------|
| a. | Yes  | No   | No    |
| b. | No   | Yes  | No    |
| c. | Yes  | No   | Yes   |
| d. | No   | Yes  | Yes   |

**111.** Field is an employee of Gold Enterprises. Hardy, CPA, is asked to express an opinion on Field's profit participation in Gold's net income. Hardy may accept this engagement only if
   a.   Hardy also audits Gold's complete financial statements.
   b.   Gold's financial statements are prepared in conformity with GAAP.
   c.   Hardy's report is available for distribution to Gold's other employees.
   d.   Field owns controlling interest in Gold.

**112.** When an auditor reports on financial statements prepared on an entity's income tax basis, the auditor's report should
   a.   Disclaim an opinion on whether the statements were examined in accordance with generally accepted auditing standards.
   b.   Not express an opinion on whether the statements are presented in conformity with the comprehensive basis of accounting used.
   c.   Include an explanation of how the results of operations differ from the cash receipts and disbursements basis of accounting.
   d.   State that the basis of presentation is a comprehensive basis of accounting other than GAAP.

**113.** Helpful Co., a nonprofit entity, prepared its financial statements on an accounting basis prescribed by a regulatory agency solely for filing with that agency. Green audited the financial statements in accordance with generally accepted auditing standards and concluded that the financial statements were fairly presented on the prescribed basis. Green should issue a
   a.   Qualified opinion.
   b.   Standard three-paragraph report with reference to footnote disclosure.
   c.   Disclaimer of opinion.
   d.   Special report.

**114.** An auditor's special report on financial statements prepared in conformity with the cash basis of accounting should include a separate explanatory paragraph before the opinion paragraph that
   a.   Justifies the reasons for departing from generally accepted accounting principles.
   b.   States whether the financial statements are fairly presented in conformity with another comprehensive basis of accounting.
   c.   Refers to the note to the financial statements that describes the basis of accounting.
   d.   Explains how the results of operations differ from financial statements prepared in conformity with generally accepted accounting principles.

**115.** An auditor's report would be designated a special report when it is issued in connection with
   a.   Interim financial information of a publicly held company that is subject to a limited review.
   b.   Compliance with aspects of regulatory requirements related to audited financial statements.
   c.   Application of accounting principles to specified transactions.
   d.   Limited use prospective financial statements such as a financial projection.

**116.** Delta Life Insurance Co. prepares its financial statements on an accounting basis insurance companies use pursuant to the rules of a state insurance commission. If Wall, CPA, Delta's auditor, discovers that the statements are **not** suitably titled, Wall should
   a.   Disclose any reservations in an explanatory paragraph and qualify the opinion.
   b.   Apply to the state insurance commission for an advisory opinion.
   c.   Issue a special statutory basis report that clearly disclaims any opinion.
   d.   Explain in the notes to the financial statements the terminology used.

**117.** A CPA is permitted to accept a separate engagement (**not** in conjunction with an audit of financial statements) to audit an entity's

|     | Schedule of accounts receivable | Schedule of royalties |
|-----|-----|-----|
| a.  | Yes | Yes |
| b.  | Yes | No |
| c.  | No  | Yes |
| d.  | No  | No |

**118.** Financial information is presented in a printed form that prescribes the wording of the independent auditor's report. The form is not acceptable to the auditor because the form calls for statements that are inconsistent with the auditor's responsibility. Under these circumstances, the auditor most likely would
   a.   Withdraw from the engagement.
   b.   Reword the form or attach a separate report.
   c.   Express a qualified opinion with an explanation.
   d.   Limit distribution of the report to the party who designed the form.

**119.** A registration statement filed with the SEC contains the reports of two independent auditors on their audits of financial statements for different periods. The predecessor auditor who audited the prior period financial statements generally should obtain a letter of representation from the
   a.   Successor independent auditor.
   b.   Client's audit committee.
   c.   Principal underwriter.
   d.   Securities and Exchange Commission.

**120.** Which of the following statements is correct concerning letters for underwriters, commonly referred to as comfort letters?
   a.   Letters for underwriters are required by the Securities Act of 1933 for the initial public sale of registered securities.
   b.   Letters for underwriters typically give negative assurance on unaudited interim financial information.
   c.   Letters for underwriters usually are included in the registration statement accompanying a prospectus.
   d.   Letters for underwriters ordinarily update auditors' opinions on the prior year's financial statements.

**121.** Comfort letters ordinarily are signed by the client's
   a.   Independent auditor.
   b.   Underwriter of securities.
   c.   Audit committee.
   d.   Senior management.

**122.** Comfort letters ordinarily are addressed to
- a. Creditor financial institutions.
- b. The client's audit committee.
- c. The Securities and Exchange Commission.
- d. Underwriters of securities.

**123.** When an accountant issues to an underwriter a comfort letter containing comments on data that have **not** been audited, the underwriter most likely will receive
- a. Negative assurance on capsule information.
- b. Positive assurance on supplementary disclosures.
- c. A limited opinion on pro forma financial statements.
- d. A disclaimer on prospective financial statements.

**124.** When an independent audit report is incorporated by reference in a SEC registration statement, a prospectus that includes a statement about the independent accountant's involvement should refer to the independent accountant as
- a. Auditor of the financial reports.
- b. Management's designate before the SEC.
- c. Certified preparer of the report.
- d. Expert in auditing and accounting.

**125.** Which of the following matters is covered in a typical comfort letter?
- a. Negative assurance concerning whether the entity's internal control procedures operated as designed during the period being audited.
- b. An opinion regarding whether the entity complied with laws and regulations under Government Auditing Standards and the Single Audit Act of 1984.
- c. Positive assurance concerning whether unaudited condensed financial information complied with generally accepted accounting principles.
- d. An opinion as to whether the audited financial statements comply in form with the accounting requirements of the SEC.

**126.** When unaudited financial statements are presented in comparative form with audited financial statements in a document filed with the Securities and Exchange Commission, such statements should be

| | Marked as "unaudited" | Withheld until audited | Referred to in the auditor's report |
|---|---|---|---|
| a. | Yes | No | No |
| b. | Yes | No | Yes |
| c. | No | Yes | Yes |
| d. | No | Yes | No |

**127.** In connection with a proposal to obtain a new audit client, a CPA in public practice is asked to prepare a report on the application of accounting principles to a specific transaction. The CPA's report should include a statement that
- a. The engagement was performed in accordance with Statements on Standards for Accounting and Review Services.
- b. Responsibility for the proper accounting treatment rests with the preparers of the financial statements.
- c. The evaluation of the application of accounting principles is hypothetical and may **not** be used for opinion-shopping.

- d. The guidance is provided for management's use only and may **not** be communicated to the prior or continuing auditor.

**128.** In connection with a proposal to obtain a new client, an accountant in public practice is asked to prepare a written report on the application of accounting principles to a specific transaction. The accountant's report should include a statement that
- a. Any difference in the facts, circumstances, or assumptions presented may change the report.
- b. The engagement was performed in accordance with Statements on Standards for Consulting Services.
- c. The guidance provided is for management use only and may **not** be communicated to the prior or continuing auditors.
- d. Nothing came to the accountant's attention that caused the accountant to believe that the accounting principles violated GAAP.

**129.** Blue, CPA, has been asked to render an opinion on the application of accounting principles to a specific transaction by an entity that is audited by another CPA. Blue may accept this engagement, but should
- a. Consult with the continuing CPA to obtain information relevant to the transaction.
- b. Report the engagement's findings to the entity's audit committee, the continuing CPA, and management.
- c. Disclaim any opinion that the hypothetical application of accounting principles conforms with generally accepted accounting principles.
- d. Notify the entity that the report is for the restricted use of management and outside parties who are aware of all relevant facts.

**130.** Which of the following statements is **not** included in an accountant's report on the application of accounting principles?
- a. The engagement was performed following standards established by the American Institute of Certified Public Accountants.
- b. The report is based on a hypothetical transaction not involving facts or circumstances of this particular entity.
- c. The report is intended solely for the information and use of specified parties.
- d. Responsibility for the proper accounting treatment rests with the preparers of the financial statements.

**131.** Which of the following services would be most likely to be structured as an attest engagement?
- a. Advocating a client's position in tax matter.
- b. A consulting engagement to develop a new database system for the revenue cycle.
- c. An engagement to issue a report addressing an entity's compliance with requirements of specified laws.
- d. The compilation of a client's forecast information.

**132.** A practitioner is issuing a standard unqualified examination report under the attestation standards. The CPA's conclusion may be on

|    | *Subject matter* | *Management's written assertion* |
|----|------------------|----------------------------------|
| a. | Yes              | Yes                              |
| b. | Yes              | No                               |
| c. | No               | Yes                              |
| d. | No               | No                               |

**133.** Conditions exist that result in a material deviation from the criteria against which the subject matter was evaluated during an examination. The CPA's conclusion may be on

|    | *Subject matter* | *Written assertion* |
|----|------------------|---------------------|
| a. | Yes              | Yes                 |
| b. | Yes              | No                  |
| c. | No               | Yes                 |
| d. | No               | No                  |

**134.** When performing an attestation engagement, which of the following is **least** likely to be present?
    a.   Assertion.
    b.   Practitioner independence.
    c.   Subject matter.
    d.   Suitable criteria.

**135.** Suitable criteria in an attestation engagement may be available

|    | *Publicly* | *In CPA's report* |
|----|------------|-------------------|
| a. | Yes        | Yes               |
| b. | Yes        | No                |
| c. | No         | Yes               |
| d. | No         | No                |

**136.** Which of the following is **least** likely to result in a restricted use attest report?
    a.   Criteria suitable only for a limited number of parties.
    b.   Subject matter available only to specified parties.
    c.   A written assertion has not been obtained.
    d.   Criteria developed by an industry association.

**137.** Which of the following is **least** likely to be included in an agreed-upon procedures attestation engagement report?
    a.   The specified party takes responsibility for the sufficiency of procedures.
    b.   Use of the report is restricted.
    c.   Limited assurance on the information presented.
    d.   A summary of procedures performed.

**138.** A summary of findings rather than assurance is most likely to be included in
    a.   Agreed-upon procedures report.
    b.   Compilation report.
    c.   Examination report.
    d.   Review report.

**139.** Which of the following is **not** correct concerning "specified parties" of an agreed-upon procedures report under either the auditing or attestation standards?
    a.   They must agree on the procedures to be performed.
    b.   They must take responsibility for the adequacy of the procedures performed.
    c.   They must sign an engagement letter.
    d.   After completion of the engagement, another party may be added as a specified user.

**140.** When an accountant examines projected financial statements, the accountant's report should include a separate paragraph that
    a.   Describes the limitations on the usefulness of the presentation.
    b.   Provides an explanation of the differences between an examination and an audit.
    c.   States that the accountant is responsible for events and circumstances up to one year after the report's date.
    d.   Disclaims an opinion on whether the assumptions provide a reasonable basis for the projection.

**141.** An accountant's compilation report on a financial forecast should include a statement that
    a.   The forecast should be read only in conjunction with the audited historical financial statements.
    b.   The accountant expresses only limited assurance on the forecasted statements and their assumptions.
    c.   There will usually be differences between the forecasted and actual results.
    d.   The hypothetical assumptions used in the forecast are reasonable in the circumstances.

**142.** Accepting an engagement to examine an entity's financial projection most likely would be appropriate if the projection were to be distributed to
    a.   All employees who work for the entity.
    b.   Potential stockholders who request a prospectus or a registration statement.
    c.   A bank with which the entity is negotiating for a loan.
    d.   All stockholders of record as of the report date.

**143.** A CPA in public practice is required to comply with the provisions of the Statements on Standards for Attestation Engagements (SSAE) when

|    | *Testifying as an expert witness in accounting and auditing matters given stipulated facts* | *Compiling a client's financial projection that presents a hypothetical course of action* |
|----|---------------------------------|---------------------------------|
| a. | Yes                             | Yes                             |
| b. | Yes                             | No                              |
| c. | No                              | Yes                             |
| d. | No                              | No                              |

**144.** An accountant's compilation report on a financial forecast should include a statement that the
    a.   Compilation does **not** include evaluation of the support of the assumptions underlying the forecast.
    b.   Hypothetical assumptions used in the forecast are reasonable.
    c.   Range of assumptions selected is one in which one end of the range is less likely to occur than the other.
    d.   Prospective statements are limited to presenting, in the form of a forecast, information that is the accountant's representation.

**145.** Which of the following is a prospective financial statement for general use upon which an accountant may appropriately report?
    a.   Financial projection.
    b.   Partial presentation.
    c.   Pro forma financial statement.
    d.   Financial forecast.

**146.** Given one or more hypothetical assumptions, a responsible party may prepare, to the best of its knowledge and belief, an entity's expected financial position, results of operations, and changes in financial position. Such prospective financial statements are known as
   a. Pro forma financial statements.
   b. Financial projections.
   c. Partial presentations.
   d. Financial forecasts.

**147.** An accountant may accept an engagement to apply agreed-upon procedures to prospective financial statements provided that
   a. The prospective financial statements are also examined.
   b. Responsibility for the adequacy of the procedures performed is taken by the accountant.
   c. Negative assurance is expressed on the prospective financial statements taken as a whole.
   d. Distribution of the report is restricted to the specified parties.

**148.** When an accountant examines a financial forecast that fails to disclose several significant assumptions used to prepare the forecast, the accountant should describe the assumptions in the accountant's report and issue a(n)
   a. "Except for" qualified opinion.
   b. "Subject to" qualified opinion.
   c. Unqualified opinion with a separate explanatory paragraph.
   d. Adverse opinion.

**149.** An accountant's report on a review of pro forma financial information should include a
   a. Statement that the entity's internal control was not relied on in the review.
   b. Disclaimer of opinion on the financial statements from which the pro forma financial information is derived.
   c. Caveat that it is uncertain whether the transaction or event reflected in the pro forma financial information will ever occur.
   d. Reference to the financial statements from which the historical financial information is derived.

**150.** Which of the following is **not** an objective of a CPA's examination of a client's management discussion and analysis (MD&A) prepared pursuant to Securities and Exchange Commission rules and regulations?
   a. The historical amounts have been accurately derived, in all material respects, from the entity's financial statements.
   b. The presentation is in conformity with rules and regulations adopted by the Securities and Exchange Commission.
   c. The underlying information, determinations, estimates and assumptions of the entity provide a reasonable basis for the disclosures contained herein.
   d. The presentation includes the required elements of MD&A.

**151.** Which of the following is an assertion embodied in management's discussion and analysis (MD&A)?
   a. Valuation.
   b. Reliability.
   c. Consistency with the financial statements.
   d. Rights and obligations.

**152.** Which of the following statements is correct relating to an auditor's review engagements on an entity's management discussion and analysis (MD&A)?
   a. A review consists principally of applying analytical procedures and search and verification procedures.
   b. The review report of a public entity should be restricted to the use of specified parties.
   c. No consideration of internal control is necessary.
   d. The report issued will ordinarily include a summary of findings, but no negative assurance.

**153.** Which of the following is a term for an attest engagement in which a CPA assesses a client's commercial Internet site for predefined criteria such as those over online privacy?
   a. ElectroNet.
   b. EDIFACT.
   c. TechSafe.
   d. WebTrust.

**154.** Trust Service engagements are performed under the provisions of
   a. Statements on Assurance Standards.
   b. Statements on Standards for Attestation Engagements.
   c. Statements on Standards for Trust Engagements
   d. Statements on Auditing Standards.

**155.** The WebTrust seal of assurance relates most directly to
   a. Financial statements maintained on the Internet.
   b. Health care facilities.
   c. Risk assurance procedures.
   d. Web sites.

**156.** A CPA's examination report relating to a WebTrust engagement is most likely to include
   a. An opinion on whether the site is "hackproof."
   b. An opinion on whether the site meets the WebTrust criteria.
   c. Negative assurance on whether the site is electronically secure.
   d. No opinion or other assurance, but a summary of findings relating to the Web site.

**157.** An engagement in which a CPA considers security, availability, processing integrity, online privacy, and/or confidentiality over any type of defined electronic system is most likely to considered which of the following types of engagements?
   a. Internal control over financial reporting.
   b. SysTrust.
   c. Web siteAssociate.
   d. WebTrust.

**158.** A client's refusal to provide a written assertion in a Trust Services engagement is most likely to result in which of the following types of opinions?
   a. Adverse.
   b. Disclaimer.
   c. Qualified.
   d. Unqualified with explanatory language.

**159.** Which of the following types of engagements is **not** permitted under the professional standards for reporting on an entity's compliance?

a. Agreed-upon procedures on compliance with the specified requirements of a law.
b. Agreed-upon procedures on the effectiveness of internal control over compliance with a law.
c. Review on compliance with specified requirements of a law.
d. Examination on compliance with specified requirements of a law.

**160.** Mill, CPA, was engaged by a group of royalty recipients to apply agreed-upon procedures to financial data supplied by Modern Co. regarding Modern's written assertion about its compliance with contractual requirements to pay royalties. Mill's report on these agreed-upon procedures should contain a(n)
a. Disclaimer of opinion about the fair presentation of Modern's financial statements.
b. List of the procedures performed (or reference thereto) and Mill's findings.
c. Opinion about the effectiveness of Modern's internal control activities concerning royalty payments.
d. Acknowledgment that the sufficiency of the procedures is solely Mill's responsibility.

**161.** A CPA's report on agreed-upon procedures related to an entity's compliance with specified requirements should contain
a. A statement of limitations on the use of the report.
b. An opinion about whether management's assertion is fairly stated.
c. Negative assurance that control risk has not been assessed.
d. An acknowledgment of responsibility for the sufficiency of the procedures.

**162.** When reporting on an examination of a company's compliance with requirements of specified laws, the practitioner has identified an instance of material noncompliance. Management has agreed to include this instance in its written assertion. The examination report should include
a. No modification from the standard form.
b. An opinion paragraph that is unqualified, and an explanatory paragraph.
c. A qualified or adverse opinion.
d. A disclaimer of opinion.

**163.** In auditing a not-for-profit entity that receives governmental financial assistance, the auditor has a responsibility to
a. Issue a separate report that describes the expected benefits and related costs of the auditor's suggested changes to the entity's internal control.
b. Assess whether management has identified laws and regulations that have a direct and material effect on the entity's financial statements.
c. Notify the governmental agency providing the financial assistance that the audit is **not** designed to provide any assurance of detecting misstatements and fraud.
d. Render an opinion concerning the entity's continued eligibility for the governmental financial assistance.

**164.** Hill, CPA, is auditing the financial statements of Helping Hand, a not-for-profit organization that receives financial assistance from governmental agencies. To detect mis-

statements in Helping Hand's financial statements resulting from violations of laws and regulations, Hill should focus on violations that
a. Could result in criminal prosecution against the organization.
b. Involve reportable conditions to be communicated to the organization's trustees and the funding agencies.
c. Have a direct and material effect on the amounts in the organization's financial statements.
d. Demonstrate the existence of material weaknesses.

**165.** A governmental audit may extend beyond an examination leading to the expression of an opinion on the fairness of financial presentation to include

| | Program results | Compliance | Economy & efficiency |
|---|---|---|---|
| a. | Yes | Yes | No |
| b. | Yes | Yes | Yes |
| c. | No | Yes | Yes |
| d. | Yes | No | Yes |

**166.** When auditing an entity's financial statements in accordance with Government Auditing Standards (the "yellow book"), an auditor is required to report on

I. Noteworthy accomplishments of the program.
II. The scope of the auditor's testing of internal controls.

a. I only.
b. II only.
c. Both I and II.
d. Neither I nor II.

**167.** When auditing an entity's financial statements in accordance with Government Auditing Standards (the "yellow book"), an auditor is required to report on

I. Recommendations for actions to improve operations.
II. The scope of the auditor's tests of compliance with laws and regulations.

a. I only.
b. II only.
c. Both I and II.
d. Neither I nor II.

**168.** Which of the following statements is a standard applicable to financial statement audits in accordance with Government Auditing Standards (the "yellow book")?
a. An auditor should report on the scope of the auditor's testing of compliance with laws and regulations.
b. An auditor should assess whether the entity has reportable measures of economy and efficiency that are valid and reliable.
c. An auditor should report recommendations for actions to correct problems and improve operations.
d. An auditor should determine the extent to which the entity's programs achieve the desired results.

**169.** Which of the following statements is a standard applicable to financial statement audits in accordance with Government Auditing Standards (the "yellow book")?
a. An auditor should report on the scope of the auditor's testing of internal controls.
b. All instances of abuse, waste, and mismanagement should be reported to the audit committee.

c.   An auditor should report the views of responsible officials concerning the auditor's findings.

d.   Internal control activities designed to detect or prevent fraud should be reported to the inspector general.

**170.**  In reporting under Government Auditing Standards, an auditor most likely would be required to report a falsification of accounting records directly to a federal inspector general when the falsification is

a.   Discovered after the auditor's report has been made available to the federal inspector general and to the public.

b.   Reported by the auditor to the audit committee as a significant deficiency in internal control.

c.   Voluntarily disclosed to the auditor by low-level personnel as a result of the auditor's inquiries.

d.   Communicated by the auditor to the auditee and the auditee fails to make a required report of the matter.

**171.**  Although the scope of audits of recipients of federal financial assistance in accordance with federal audit regulations varies, these audits generally have which of the following elements in common?

a.   The auditor is to determine whether the federal financial assistance has been administered in accordance with applicable laws and regulations.

b.   The materiality levels are lower and are determined by the government entities that provided the federal financial assistance to the recipient.

c.   The auditor should obtain written management representations that the recipient's internal auditors will report their findings objectively without fear of political repercussion.

d.   The auditor is required to express both positive and negative assurance that illegal acts that could have a material effect on the recipient's financial statements are disclosed to the inspector general.

**172.**  An auditor most likely would be responsible for communicating significant deficiencies in the design of internal control

a.   To the Securities and Exchange Commission when the client is a publicly held entity.

b.   To specific legislative and regulatory bodies when reporting under Government Auditing Standards.

c.   To a court-appointed creditors' committee when the client is operating under Chapter 11 of the Federal Bankruptcy Code.

d.   To shareholders with significant influence (more than 20% equity ownership) when the reportable conditions are deemed to be material weaknesses.

**173.**  Wolf is auditing an entity's compliance with requirements governing a major federal financial assistance program in accordance with Government Auditing Standards. Wolf detected noncompliance with requirements that have a material effect on the program. Wolf's report on compliance should express

a.   No assurance on the compliance tests.

b.   Reasonable assurance on the compliance tests.

c.   A qualified or adverse opinion.

d.   An adverse or disclaimer of opinion.

**174.**  Reporting on internal control under Government Auditing Standards differs from reporting under generally accepted auditing standards in that Government Auditing Standards requires a

a.   Written report describing the entity's controls specifically designed to prevent fraud, abuse, and illegal acts.

b.   Written report describing each reportable condition observed including identification of those considered material weaknesses.

c.   Statement of negative assurance that internal control procedures **not** tested have an immaterial effect on the entity's financial statements.

d.   Statement of positive assurance that controls designed to detect material errors and fraud were tested.

**175.**  Which of the following is a documentation requirement that an auditor should follow when auditing in accordance with Government Auditing Standards?

a.   The auditor should obtain written representations from management acknowledging responsibility for correcting instances of fraud, abuse, and waste.

b.   The auditor's working papers should contain sufficient information so that supplementary oral explanations are **not** required.

c.   The auditor should document the procedures that assure discovery of all illegal acts and contingent liabilities resulting from noncompliance.

d.   The auditor's working papers should contain a caveat that all instances of material misstatements and fraud may **not** be identified.

**176.**  In performing a financial statement audit in accordance with Government Auditing Standards, an auditor is required to report on the entity's compliance with laws and regulations. This report should

a.   State that compliance with laws and regulations is the responsibility of the entity's management.

b.   Describe the laws and regulations that the entity must comply with.

c.   Provide an opinion on overall compliance with laws and regulations.

d.   Indicate that the auditor does **not** possess legal skills and **cannot** make legal judgments.

**177.**  In reporting under Government Auditing Standards, an auditor most likely would be required to communicate management's misappropriation of assets directly to a federal inspector general when the fraudulent activities are

a.   Concealed by management by circumventing specific internal controls designed to safeguard those assets.

b.   Reported to the entity's governing body and the governing body fails to make a required report to the federal inspector general.

c.   Accompanied by fraudulent financial reporting that results in material misstatements of asset balances.

d.   Perpetrated by several levels of management in a scheme that is likely to continue in future years.

**178.**  In auditing compliance with requirements governing major federal financial assistance programs under the Single Audit Act, the auditor's consideration of materiality differs from materiality under generally accepted auditing standards. Under the Single Audit Act, materiality is

    a.   Calculated in relation to the financial statements taken as a whole.

    b.   Determined separately for each major federal financial assistance program.

    c.   Decided in conjunction with the auditor's risk assessment.

    d.   Ignored, because all account balances, regardless of size, are fully tested.

**179.** Kent is auditing an entity's compliance with requirements governing a major federal financial assistance program in accordance with the Single Audit Act. Kent detected noncompliance with requirements that have a material effect on that program. Kent's report on compliance should express a(n)

    a.   Unqualified opinion with a separate explanatory paragraph.

    b.   Qualified opinion or an adverse opinion.

    c.   Adverse opinion or a disclaimer of opinion.

    d.   Limited assurance on the items tested.

**180.** When performing an audit of a city that is subject to the requirements of the Uniform Single Audit Act of 1984, an auditor should adhere to

    a.   Governmental Accounting Standards Board *General Standards.*

    b.   Governmental Finance Officers Association *Governmental Accounting, Auditing, and Financial Reporting Principles.*

    c.   General Accounting Office Government Auditing Standards.

    d.   Securities and Exchange Commission *Regulation S-X.*

**181.** A CPA has performed an examination of the general-purpose financial statements of Big City. The examination scope included the additional requirements of the Single Audit Act. When reporting on Big City's internal accounting and administrative controls used in administering a federal financial assistance program, the CPA should

    a.   Communicate those weaknesses that are material in relation to the general-purpose financial statements.

    b.   Express an opinion on the systems used to administer major federal financial assistance programs and express negative assurance on the systems used to administer nonmajor federal financial assistance programs.

    c.   Communicate those weaknesses that are material in relation to the federal financial assistance program.

    d.   Express negative assurance on the systems used to administer major federal financial assistance programs and express **no** opinion on the systems used to administer nonmajor federal financial assistance programs.

**SIMULATION PROBLEMS**

**Simulation Problem 1**                                          (20 to 25 minutes)

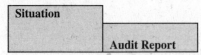

   The audit of Park Publishing Co., for the year ended September 30, 20X2, is near completion.  Your senior, Dave Moore, at Tyler & Tyler CPAs, has asked you to draft the audit report, considering the following:

- During fiscal year 20X2, Park changed its depreciation method.  The engagement partner concurred with this change in accounting principle and its justification, and Moore wants it properly reflected in the auditors' report; the change is discussed in Note 7 to the financial statements.
- The 20X2 financial statements are affected by an uncertainty concerning a lawsuit over patent infringement, the outcome of which cannot presently be estimated.  Moore has suggested the need for an explanatory paragraph in the auditors' report related to this matter which is discussed in Note 4 to the financial statements.
- The last day of fieldwork is October 25, 20X2, while the date the report is expected to be delivered to the client is October 28, 20X2.
- The financial statements for the year ended September 30, 20X1, are to be presented for comparative purposes.  Tyler & Tyler previously audited these statements and expressed a standard unqualified opinion.

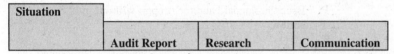

   Prepare Tyler & Tyler, CPAs, auditor's report on the consolidated financial statements of Park Publishing Company.

---

**Simulation Problem 2**                                          (30 to 40 minutes)

   **Assume that items 1 through 8** are situations that Jones, CPA, has encountered during his audit of Welles Incorporated.  List A represents the types of opinions the auditor ordinarily would issue and List B represents the report modifications (if any) that would be necessary.  For each situation, select one response from List A and one from List B.  Select as the **best** answers for each item the action the auditor would normally take.  The types of opinions in List A and the report modifications in List B may be selected once, more than once, or not at all.

   *Assume*

- The auditor is independent
- The auditor previously expressed an unqualified opinion on the prior year's financial statements.
- Only single-year (not comparative) statements are presented for the current year.
- The conditions for an unqualified opinion exist unless contradicted by the facts.
- The conditions stated in the items to be answered are material, unless otherwise indicated.
- Each item to be answered is independent of the others.
- No report modifications are to be made except in response to the factual situation.
- The auditor will not treat a situation as an "emphasis of a matter" in what remains an unqualified audit report unless it is one of those circumstances specifically illustrated in the Professional Standards as an example of a matter an auditor may wish to emphasize.

Audit Report

| Situation | | Research | Communication |
|---|---|---|---|

**List A**
*Types of opinions*

A. Either an "except for" qualified opinion or an adverse opinion

B. Either a disclaimer of opinion or an "except for" qualified opinion

C. Either an adverse opinion or a disclaimer of opinion

D. An "except for" qualified opinion

E. An unqualified opinion

F. An adverse opinion

G. A disclaimer of opinion

**List B**
*Report modifications*

H. Describe the circumstances in an explanatory paragraph **without modifying** the three standard paragraphs.

I. Describe the circumstances in an explanatory paragraph and **modify** the **opinion** paragraph.

J. Describe the circumstances in an explanatory paragraph and **modify** the **scope** and **opinion** paragraphs.

K. Describe the circumstances in an explanatory paragraph and **modify** the **introductory**, **scope**, and **opinion** paragraphs.

L. Describe the circumstances within the **scope** paragraph without adding an explanatory paragraph.

M. Describe the circumstances within the **opinion** paragraph without adding an explanatory paragraph.

N. Describe the circumstances within the **scope** and **opinion** paragraphs without adding an explanatory paragraph.

O. Describe the circumstances within the **introductory**, **scope**, and **opinion** paragraphs without adding an explanatory paragraph.

P. Issue the standard auditor's report **without modification.**

|  | *Types of opinions* (A-G) | *Report Modifications* (H-P) |
|---|---|---|

1. Jones hired an actuary to assist in corroborating Welles' complex pension calculations concerning accrued pension liabilities that account for 35% of the client's total liabilities. The actuary's findings are reasonably close to Welles' calculations and support the financial statements.

2. Welles holds a note receivable consisting of principal and accrued interest payable in 20X4. The note's maker recently filed a voluntary bankruptcy petition, but Welles failed to reduce the recorded value of the note to its net realizable value, which is approximately 20% of the recorded amount.

3. Jones was engaged to audit a client's financial statements after the annual physical inventory count. The accounting records were not sufficiently reliable to enable him to become satisfied as to the year-end inventory balances.

4. Jones found an immaterial adjustment relating to inventory. Welles has refused to adjust the financial statements to reflect this immaterial item.

5. Welles' financial statements do not disclose certain long-term lease obligations. Jones determined that the omitted disclosures are required by FASB.

6. Jones decided not to take responsibility for the work of another CPA who audited a wholly owned subsidiary of Welles. The total assets and revenues of the subsidiary represent 27% and 28%, respectively, of the related consolidated totals.

7. Welles changed its method of accounting for the cost of inventories from FIFO to LIFO. Jones concurs with the change although it has a material effect on the comparability of the financial statements.

8. Due to losses and adverse key financial ratios, Jones has substantial doubt about Welles' ability to continue as a going concern for a reasonable period of time. The client has adequately disclosed its financial difficulties in a note to its financial statements, which do **not** include any adjustments that might result from the outcome of this uncertainty. Also, Jones has ruled out the use of a disclaimer of opinion.

| Situation | Audit Report | Research | | Communication |
|-----------|--------------|----------|--|---------------|

Research the Professional Standards and identify the matters that are ordinarily the subjects of a successor auditor's inquiry of the predecessor auditor prior to accepting the new engagement. You may paste the appropriate information from the Professional Standards as your solution.

| Situation | Audit Report | Research | Communication |
|-----------|--------------|----------|---------------|

The CEO of Welles is concerned about the audit report modification due to a change in accounting principle. Write a memorandum to her explaining the purpose of this modification of the audit report.

To:     CEO, Welles Inc.
From:   CPA Candidate

**Additional Simulations**

Appendix A—Simulation 4  (Part b.) involves Reporting
Appendix A—Simulation 5 (item 8) involves Reporting
Appendix A—Simulation 6 (item 8) involves Reporting

## MULTIPLE-CHOICE ANSWERS

| | | | | | | | | | |
|---|---|---|---|---|---|---|---|---|---|
| 1. | a | 38. | c | 75. | d | 112. | d | 149. | d |
| 2. | b | 39. | a | 76. | d | 113. | d | 150. | b |
| 3. | c | 40. | d | 77. | b | 114. | c | 151. | c |
| 4. | d | 41. | a | 78. | a | 115. | b | 152. | b |
| 5. | c | 42. | d | 79. | a | 116. | a | 153. | d |
| 6. | c | 43. | a | 80. | c | 117. | a | 154. | b |
| 7. | c | 44. | d | 81. | d | 118. | b | 155. | d |
| 8. | d | 45. | d | 82. | a | 119. | a | 156. | b |
| 9. | b | 46. | c | 83. | c | 120. | b | 157. | b |
| 10. | d | 47. | d | 84. | b | 121. | a | 158. | b |
| 11. | d | 48. | a | 85. | b | 122. | d | 159. | c |
| 12. | c | 49. | c | 86. | d | 123. | a | 160. | b |
| 13. | a | 50. | a | 87. | a | 124. | d | 161. | a |
| 14. | a | 51. | d | 88. | a | 125. | d | 162. | c |
| 15. | a | 52. | d | 89. | a | 126. | a | 163. | b |
| 16. | c | 53. | b | 90. | d | 127. | b | 164. | c |
| 17. | a | 54. | c | 91. | b | 128. | a | 165. | b |
| 18. | c | 55. | c | 92. | c | 129. | a | 166. | b |
| 19. | d | 56. | d | 93. | c | 130. | b | 167. | b |
| 20. | a | 57. | b | 94. | c | 131. | c | 168. | a |
| 21. | b | 58. | b | 95. | c | 132. | a | 169. | a |
| 22. | d | 59. | b | 96. | c | 133. | b | 170. | d |
| 23. | d | 60. | a | 97. | b | 134. | a | 171. | a |
| 24. | a | 61. | d | 98. | b | 135. | a | 172. | b |
| 25. | c | 62. | a | 99. | c | 136. | d | 173. | c |
| 26. | a | 63. | b | 100. | a | 137. | c | 174. | b |
| 27. | b | 64. | c | 101. | a | 138. | a | 175. | b |
| 28. | a | 65. | c | 102. | a | 139. | c | 176. | a |
| 29. | b | 66. | d | 103. | d | 140. | a | 177. | b |
| 30. | c | 67. | c | 104. | b | 141. | c | 178. | b |
| 31. | c | 68. | d | 105. | c | 142. | c | 179. | b |
| 32. | d | 69. | b | 106. | c | 143. | c | 180. | c |
| 33. | b | 70. | d | 107. | c | 144. | a | 181. | c |
| 34. | a | 71. | a | 108. | a | 145. | d | | |
| 35. | b | 72. | b | 109. | a | 146. | b | | |
| 36. | b | 73. | b | 110. | d | 147. | d | 1st:   __/181 = __% |
| 37. | d | 74. | b | 111. | a | 148. | d | 2nd:   __/181 = __% |

## MULTIPLE-CHOICE ANSWER EXPLANATIONS

### A.1. Overall Issues

**1. (a)** The requirement is to identify the statement in the standard audit report that indicates the existence of audit risk. Answer (a) is correct because the existence of audit risk is recognized by the statement in the auditor's standard report that the auditor obtained "reasonable assurance." Answer (b) is incorrect because while the standard report does indicate that the CPA assesses the accounting principles used and the overall financial statement presentation, this does not indicate the existence of audit risk. Answer (c) is incorrect because while the standard report does indicate that the audit relates to whether the financial statements are free of material misstatement, it does not discuss materiality and the audit risk associated with materiality. Answer (d) is incorrect because while the financial statements are the responsibility of management and the CPA's responsibility is to express an opinion, the indication that the CPA expresses an opinion does not address audit risk and is less precise than the statement that the auditor obtains reasonable assurance.

**2. (b)** The requirement is to determine an accountant's reporting responsibility when more than one level of service

concerning the financial statements of a nonpublic entity has been performed. Answer (b) is correct because AR 100 requires that the accountant report on the highest level of service rendered. Answer (a) is incorrect because the highest, and not the lowest, level is reported on. Answer (c) is incorrect because regardless of the other type of service performed, the compilation level is always the lowest level and therefore should not be the basis of the report. Answer (d) is incorrect because in circumstances in which an audit has been performed, an audit report, not a review report, is appropriate.

**3. (c)** The requirement is to identify the report that is **least** likely to be a restricted-use report. Answer (c) is correct because AU 623 indicates that reports on most comprehensive basis financial statements are not restricted. Answers (a) and (b) are incorrect because reports on reportable conditions and reports to audit committees are restricted under AU 325 and AU 380, respectively. Answer (d) is incorrect because AU 623 restricts such reports on compliance. Also, see AU 532 for information on restricting the use of an audit report.

**4.** **(d)** The requirement is to determine an auditor's responsibility for controlling the distribution by the client of a restricted-use report. Answer (d) is correct because AU 532 states that an auditor is not responsible for controlling the distribution of such reports. Answer (a) is incorrect because while an auditor should consider informing a client that restricted-use reports are not intended for such distribution, there is no such requirement. Answer (b) is incorrect because the auditor need not inform the client to cease and desist. Answer (c) is incorrect because an auditor need not insist that the client not duplicate the restricted-use report.

### A.2. Financial Statement Audit Reports—Nonpublic Companies

**5.** **(c)** The requirement is to identify the statement that is included in the auditor's standard report. Answer (c) is correct because the auditor's standard report states that an audit includes assessing significant estimates made by management; see AU 508 for this and other required elements included in a standard report.

**6.** **(c)** The requirement is to determine the proper date of a reissued audit report on financial statements that have **not** been restated. Answer (c) is correct because use of the original date on the reissued audit report removes any implication that records, transactions or events after the date of the audit report have been examined or reviewed.

**7.** **(c)** The requirement is to identify which paragraph of an auditor's standard audit report should refer to generally accepted auditing standards and generally accepted accounting principles. Answer (c) is correct because the scope paragraph indicates that generally accepted auditing standards have been followed, while the opinion paragraph indicates that the financial statements follow generally accepted accounting principles.

**8.** **(d)** The requirement is to determine auditor reporting responsibility when prior period financial statements which received a qualified opinion due to a lack of adequate disclosure have been restated to eliminate the lack of disclosure. Answer (d) is correct because AU 508 states that an auditor should express an unqualified opinion on the restated financial statements of the prior year (with an explanatory paragraph describing the circumstance). Answer (a) is incorrect because the auditor's original report is not reissued. Answer (b) is incorrect because the qualified opinion is eliminated. Answer (c) is incorrect because reference to the type of opinion expressed is included in the reissued report's explanatory paragraph.

**9.** **(b)** The requirement is to identify the correct statement concerning an auditor's responsibility to express an opinion on the financial statements. Answer (b) is correct because the opening (introductory) paragraph of the auditor's standard report states that the auditor's responsibility is to express an opinion on the financial statements based on the audit. Answer (a) is incorrect because of the explicit statement in the introductory paragraph. Answers (c) and (d) are incorrect because the introductory paragraph, not the scope or opinion paragraphs, includes the statement on the auditor's responsibility.

**10.** **(d)** The requirement is to determine whether the terms "when read in conjunction with Note X," and "with the foregoing explanation" should be included in the opinion paragraph of a qualified opinion. AU 508 states that an audit report with a qualified opinion should **not** include either phrase in the opinion paragraph.

**11.** **(d)** The requirement is to determine the representations made explicitly and implicitly when issuing the standard auditor's report on comparative financial statements. Answer (d) is correct because the standard audit report explicitly states that the examination of evidence is made on a test basis and implicitly assumes consistent application of accounting principles. Answer (a) is incorrect because consistency of application of accounting principles is not indicated explicitly. Answer (b) is incorrect because examination of evidence on a test basis is referred to explicitly. Answer (c) is incorrect because examination of evidence on a test basis is explicitly referred to and because consistent application of accounting principles is not explicitly referred to.

**12.** **(c)** The requirement is to determine the objective of the fourth reporting standard which requires either an opinion regarding the financial statements taken as a whole or an assertion to the effect that an opinion cannot be expressed. Answer (c) is correct because the standard states that the objective is to prevent misinterpretation of the degree of responsibility that the auditor is assuming when his/her name is associated with financial statements. Answer (a) is incorrect because differing opinions may be issued on each of the financial statements (e.g., if the count of the beginning inventory has not been observed, an auditor may disclaim an opinion on the income statement and yet express an unqualified opinion on the balance sheet). Answer (b) is incorrect because the objective does not relate directly to scope limitations. Answer (d) is incorrect because an auditor may report on only one statement.

**13.** **(a)** The requirement is to determine the meaning of the expression "taken as a whole" in the fourth generally accepted auditing standard of reporting. AU 508 states that "taken as a whole" applies equally to a complete set of financial statements and to an individual financial statement.

**14.** **(a)** The requirement is to identify the most authoritative source of GAAP among those listed in a circumstance in which a conflict exists in the proper application of an accounting principle. AU 411 presents a GAAP hierarchy that includes FASB Technical Bulletins in the second level, AICPA Accounting Interpretations in the third, and FASB Statements of Financial Accounting Concepts and Technical Practice Aids in the fifth. Accordingly, answer (a) is correct because FASB Technical Bulletins are the most highly ranked of the sources presented.

**15.** **(a)** The requirement is to determine the appropriate date for an audit report when a subsequent event requiring adjustment of financial statements, without disclosure of the event, comes to the auditor's attention. AU 530 states that the date of completion of fieldwork should be used in such circumstances.

**16.** **(c)** The requirement is to determine an auditor's responsibility for subsequent events when an audit report has been dual dated for a subsequent event. Answer (c) is correct because, when dual dating is used, auditor responsibility for events subsequent to the completion of fieldwork is limited to the specific event referred to in the notes to the financial statement. Answers (a), (b), and (d) are all incorrect because they establish more responsibility than required by the professional standards. Note, however, that if the auditor chooses to date the report as of the date of the subsequent event, his/her responsibility for other subsequent events extends to the date of the audit report.

### A.3.    Financial Statement Audit Reports—Public Companies

**17.    (a)**    The requirement is to determine the accounting principles that a public company audit report refers to. Answer (a) is correct because the financial statements follow generally accepted accounting principles. Answer (b) is incorrect because, while the audit is performed in accordance with PCAOB standards, the financial statements do not follow those standards. Answer (c) is incorrect because the financial statements do not follow generally accepted auditing standards. Answer (d) is incorrect because the financial statements ordinarily follow generally accepted accounting principles, not International Accounting Standards.

**18.    (c)**    The requirement is to identify the incorrect statement concerning information included in an audit report of financial statements issued under the requirements of the PCAOB. Answer (c) is correct since the report should refer to the auditor's report on internal control, not on compliance with laws and regulations. Answer (a) is incorrect because the report should include the title "Report of Independent Registered Public Accounting Firm." Answer (b) is incorrect because the report should refer to the standards of the PCAOB. Answer (d) is incorrect because the report should contain the city and state or country of the office that issued the report.

### B.1.a.    Opinion Based, in Part, on Report of Another Auditor

**19.    (d)**    The requirement is to determine a principal auditor's responsibility, in addition to making inquiries of the other auditor's reputation and independence, after having decided **not** to refer to the audit of the other auditor. Answer (d) is correct because when a decision is made **not** to make reference to the other audit—that is, to take responsibility for that auditor's work—the principal auditor should consider (1) visiting the other auditor, (2) reviewing the audit programs of the other auditor, (3) reviewing the working papers of the other auditor, and (4) performing additional audit procedures. Answer (a) is incorrect because no explanatory paragraph is added to the audit report. Answer (b) is incorrect because the principal auditor is assuming responsibility for the other auditor's work when a decision is made not to refer to the other auditor's report. Answer (c) is incorrect because written permission is not required when the principal auditor is taking responsibility for the work of the other auditor.

**20.    (a)**    The requirement is to determine the meaning of sentences added to an introductory paragraph of an auditor's report that states that another auditor audited a portion of the entity. Answer (a) is correct because AU 508 provides that such a statement indicates a division of responsibility. Answer (b) is incorrect because when the other auditor is referred to the CPA, the CPA is not assuming responsibility for the other auditor. Answer (c) is incorrect because an

unqualified opinion may be issued. Answer (d) is incorrect because the sentences are proper.

**21.    (b)**    The requirement is to determine the situation in which an auditor would ordinarily issue an unqualified audit opinion without an explanatory paragraph. Answer (b) is correct because when an auditor makes reference to the report of another auditor, each of the three standard paragraphs of the report are modified, but no additional paragraph is added to the report. Answer (a) is incorrect because emphasizing that the entity had significant related-party transactions is normally accomplished through the addition of an explanatory paragraph. Answer (c) is incorrect because the omission of a statement of cash flows when an entity issues financial statements that present financial position and result of operations results in a qualified audit opinion with an explanatory paragraph. Answer (d) is incorrect because substantial doubt about the entity's ability to continue as a going concern normally results in either an unqualified opinion with an explanatory paragraph or a disclaimer of opinion.

**22.    (d)**    The requirement is to identify the situation in which an auditor may issue the standard audit report. Answer (d) is correct because a standard report may be issued in circumstances in which the principal auditor assumes responsibility for the work of another auditor. Answer (a) is incorrect because the standard report does not include reference to a specialist. Thus, reference to a specialist within a report by definition causes modification of the standard report. Answer (b) is incorrect because the auditor is required to issue a modified report on condensed financial statements per AU 552. Answer (c) is incorrect because audit reports on financial statements prepared on a comprehensive basis other than GAAP are considered to be "special reports" which require departures from the standard form.

**23.    (d)**    The requirement is to determine a principal auditor's reporting responsibility when a decision has been made to not make reference to another CPA who has audited a client's subsidiary. Answer (d) is correct because, regardless of whether the other auditor is referred to, the principal auditor must be satisfied as to the independence and professional reputation of the other CPA. Answer (a) is incorrect because the principal auditor need not issue an unqualified opinion on the consolidated financial statements. Answer (b) is incorrect because it is not necessary that the other CPA issue an unqualified opinion on the subsidiary's financial statements. Answer (c) is incorrect because the principal auditor should consider reviewing the audit programs and working papers of the other CPA when a decision is made to not make reference to that CPA.

### B.1.b.    Unusual Circumstances Requiring a Departure from Promulgated GAAP

**24.    (a)**    The requirement is to determine the type of opinion to be issued when financial statements depart from GAAP due to the existence of unusual circumstances which would cause the financial statements to be misleading had GAAP been followed. Answer (a) is correct because the auditor should issue an unqualified opinion and should include a separate explanatory paragraph explaining the departure from GAAP. Answers (b), (c), and (d) are incorrect because when the auditor believes that the departure is justified, neither a qualified nor adverse opinion is appropriate.

### B.1.c. Substantial Doubt about Ability to Remain a Going Concern

**25. (c)** The requirement is to determine whether the term "reasonable period of time, not to exceed one year" and/or "going concern" is included in an explanatory paragraph relating to going concern status. Answer (c) is correct because while the term "going concern" must be included, the first term is not included in such a report.

**26. (a)** The requirement is to determine an auditor's reporting responsibility when reporting on comparative financial statements in which the first year presented originally received a going concern modification on a matter that has now been resolved, thus removing the auditor's substantial doubt. Answer (a) is correct because if substantial doubt has been removed in the current period, the explanatory paragraph included in the auditor's report on the financial statements of the prior period should not be repeated. Answers (b), (c), and (d) are all incorrect because they suggest the need for an explanatory paragraph.

**27. (b)** The requirement is to determine the auditor's responsibility when s/he concludes that there is substantial doubt about an entity's ability to continue as a going concern for a reasonable period of time. Answer (b) is correct because when the auditor concludes there is substantial doubt, s/he should consider the possible effects on the financial statements, and the adequacy of the related disclosures. Answer (a) is incorrect because either an unqualified opinion with an explanatory paragraph or a disclaimer is generally appropriate, not a qualified or adverse opinion. Answer (c) is incorrect because the substantial doubt of going concern status does not require adjusting accounting estimates. Answer (d) is incorrect because the prior year's audit report need not be reissued with an explanatory paragraph.

**28. (a)** The requirement is to determine an auditor's reporting responsibility when there is substantial doubt about a client's ability to continue as a going concern. Answer (a) is correct because the audit report must include an explanatory paragraph following the opinion paragraph, and must use the terms "going concern" and "substantial doubt."

**29. (b)** The requirement is to identify the situation in which an explanatory paragraph may be added to an unqualified report. Answer (b) is correct because substantial doubt about the entity's ability to continue as a going concern leads to either an unqualified report with an explanatory paragraph or a disclaimer of opinion. Answer (a) is incorrect because an auditor may issue an opinion on a balance sheet without reporting on the other basic financial statements. Answer (c) is incorrect because unreasonable estimates lead to either a qualified or an adverse opinion. Answer (d) is incorrect because inadequate management record retention policies are a scope limitation that may result in a qualified opinion or a disclaimer.

**30. (c)** The requirement is to identify the management plan an auditor would most likely positively consider when a question concerning an entity's ability to continue as a going concern exists. Answer (c) is correct because increasing the ownership equity will bring in funds to possibly overcome the negative trends and financial difficulties. Answers (a), (b), and (d) are all incorrect because increasing dividend distributions, reducing lines of credit, and purchasing assets will all use funds, they will not provide funds. See AU 341 for guidance on an auditor's consideration of an entity's ability to continue as a going concern.

### B.1.d. Inconsistency in Application of GAAP

**31. (c)** The requirement is to identify the circumstances in which an auditor would issue a report that omits any reference to consistency. Answer (c) is correct because, as discussed in AU 508, a change in the useful life of assets is a change in estimate, and a change in estimate does not result in a consistency modification. Answers (a) and (b) are incorrect because they both represent a change in accounting principle, and a change in accounting principle requires a consistency modification. Answer (d) is incorrect because management's lack of reasonable justification for a change in accounting principle is a departure from generally accepted accounting principles, and the description of the departure will discuss the inconsistency.

**32. (d)** The requirement is to determine whether an unjustified accounting change, a material weakness in internal control, or both, would cause an auditor to express an unqualified opinion with an explanatory paragraph. Answer (d) is correct because an unjustified accounting change will result in either a qualified or an adverse opinion and a material weakness will ordinarily result in no report modification (see AU 325 for information on the treatment of material weaknesses); accordingly, an unqualified opinion with an explanatory paragraph added to the auditor's report is not appropriate in either case.

**33. (b)** The requirement is to identify the circumstance in which a disclaimer of opinion is **not** appropriate. Answer (b) is correct because when management does **not** provide reasonable justification of a change in accounting principles either a qualified or an adverse opinion is appropriate, not a disclaimer. Answers (a), (c), and (d) are all incorrect because they represent scope limitations that lead to either a qualified opinion or a disclaimer of opinion.

**34. (a)** The requirement is to determine the effect on an audit report of a client's decision to use differing inventory costing methods for various portions of its inventory. Answer (a) is correct because a standard unqualified opinion may ordinarily be issued (see AU 420 for a discussion of the consistency standard). Answer (b) is incorrect because there is no lack of consistency between accounting periods. Answer (c) is incorrect because there is no departure from GAAP. Answer (d) is incorrect because adverse opinions are only issued when a departure from GAAP exists that makes the financial statements misleading.

**35. (b)** The requirement is to identify an auditor's reporting responsibility when performing a first audit of a new client and when the auditor was able to extend auditing procedures to gather sufficient evidence about consistency. Answer (b) is correct because, when the auditor has obtained assurance as to the consistency of application of accounting principles between the current and preceding year, no mention of consistency is included in the audit report. Answer (a) is incorrect because the auditor may report on the client's income statement. Answer (c) is incorrect because the consistency standard does apply. Answer (d) is incorrect because the auditor does not refer to consistency when accounting principles have been applied consistently.

**36.   (b)**   The requirement is to determine auditor reporting responsibility when management does not provide reasonable justification for a change in accounting principle and presents comparative financial statements.  Answer (b) is correct because the auditor should continue to express his/her exception with the financial statements for the year of change as long as they are presented and reported on.  Answer (a) is incorrect because the auditor must express his/her exception for as long as the financial statements for the year of change are presented and reported on.  Answer (c) is incorrect because the auditor need not qualify the report until management changes back to the accounting principle formerly used.  Answer (d) is incorrect because the qualification is necessary despite the fact that the principle is generally accepted.

**37.   (d)**   The requirement is to determine the information that must be presented when a client has changed accounting principles.  Answer (d) is correct because in addition to identifying the nature of the change, the auditor must refer to the financial statement note that discusses the change in detail.  Answer (a) is incorrect because while the auditor must believe that the change is justified, it is not necessary to explain it in the report.  Answer (b) is incorrect because the cumulative effect of the change need not be described in the audit report.  Answer (c) is incorrect because the auditor need not make explicit concurrence with the change.

**38.   (c)**   The requirement is to determine the proper reporting option for a change in accounting principles with an immaterial current year effect, but which is expected to have a substantial effect in subsequent years.  Answer (c) is correct because the auditor need not recognize the change in the audit report and may issue a standard unqualified opinion.

**B.1.e.   Certain Circumstances Affecting Comparative Financial Statements**

**39.   (a)**   The requirement is to identify the circumstance in which an auditor reporting on comparative financial statements would ordinarily change the previously issued opinion on the prior year's financial statements.  Answer (a) is correct because when an auditor has previously expressed a qualified or an adverse opinion on financial statements of a prior period and those financial statements have been restated, the auditor's updated report is changed.  Answer (b) is incorrect because, ordinarily, the reissued report by a predecessor auditor will be the same as that originally issued.  Answer (c) is incorrect because the prior year's opinion will remain unqualified if the current year's audit report is modified due to a lack of consistency.  Answer (d) is incorrect because restatement of prior year's financial statements following a pooling of interest will not lead to a change in the previously issued opinion.

**40.   (d)**   The requirement is to determine the information to be included in an audit report on comparative financial statements when a predecessor auditor's report is not being reissued.  Answer (d) is correct because the introductory paragraph of the successor's report should indicate (1) that the financial statements of the prior period were audited by another auditor (whose name is not presented), (2) the date of the predecessor's report, (3) the type of report issued by the predecessor, and (4) if the report was other than a standard report, the substantive reasons therefor.

**41.   (a)**   The requirement is to determine whether the predecessor auditor should obtain a representation letter from management, the successor auditor, or both, before reissuing the prior year's audit record.  Answer (a) is correct because the predecessor auditor should obtain a representation letter from both management (AU 333) and the successor auditor (AU 508).

**42.   (d)**   The requirement is to identify the circumstance in which a standard unqualified report may be issued when single-year financial statements are presented.  Answer (d) is correct because when the prior year's financial statements are not being presented, the CPA need not refer to them or include the predecessor auditor's report.  See AU 508 for information on reissuance of a predecessor's report when comparative financial statements are being issued.  Answer (a) is incorrect because inability to audit an investment in a foreign affiliate is a scope limitation that is likely to result in either a qualified opinion or a disclaimer.  Answer (b) is incorrect because a qualified opinion is appropriate when an entity declines to present a statement of cash flows with its balance sheet and related statements of income and retained earnings.  Answer (c) is incorrect because the emphasis of an accounting matter by an auditor results in inclusion of an explanatory paragraph to the unqualified audit report.

**43.   (a)**   The requirement is to identify the correct form of an audit report on comparative financial statements when a continuing auditor has audited the two years of financial statements being presented.  Answer (a) is correct because one audit report should be issued that includes the years involved.  Answer (b) is incorrect because one report, not two reports, should be issued.  Answer (c) is incorrect because both years should be reported upon.  Answer (d) is incorrect because auditors do not have the option of issuing two audit reports in this circumstance.

**44.   (d)**   The requirement is to determine the manner in which a predecessor auditor who has reissued a report for comparative financial statements should refer to the successor auditor.  AU 508 indicates that the predecessor auditor should not refer in the reissued report to the report or work of the successor auditor.

**45.   (d)**   The requirement is to determine the proper reporting procedure for comparative financial statements for which the prior year is unaudited, and the current year is audited.  AU 504 states that when unaudited financial statements are presented in comparative form with audited financial statements, the report on the prior period may be reissued to accompany the current period report.  In addition, the report on the current period may include a separate paragraph describing responsibility assumed for the prior period financial statements.  If these statements are filed with the SEC, the statements should be clearly marked as "unaudited" but should not be referred to in the auditor's report.

**B.1.g.   Supplementary Information Required by FASB or GASB**

**46.   (c)**   The requirement is to identify an auditor's responsibility for supplementary information required by the FASB that is placed outside the basic financial statements.  Answer (c) is correct because AU 558 requires that the auditor apply limited procedures to the information and report deficiencies in, or the omission of, the information. Answer (a) is incorrect because the auditor does have some responsibility for the supplementary information. Answer (b) is incorrect because the auditor must apply limited procedures to information presented and report deficiencies in the information in addition to determining whether it has been omitted. Answer (d) is incorrect because tests of details of transactions and balances need not be performed.

**47.** (**d**)   The requirement is to determine the proper audit report when management declines to present supplementary information required by the Governmental Accounting Standards Board. Answer (d) is correct because omission of required supplementary information, which when presented is not considered audited, leads to an unqualified opinion with an explanatory paragraph. Answers (a) and (b) are incorrect because neither an adverse opinion nor a qualified opinion is appropriate since the supplementary information is not audited. Answer (c) is incorrect because it is incomplete since an unqualified opinion with an additional explanatory paragraph is required.

**B.1.h.   Other Information in a Document Containing Audited Financial Statements**

**48.** (**a**)   The requirement is to identify the auditor's reporting responsibility concerning information accompanying the basic financial statements in an auditor-submitted document. Answer (a) is correct because the auditor should report on all the information included in the document. Answers (b) and (c) are incorrect because the auditor should report on the accompanying information regardless of whether he or she participated in its preparation. Answer (d) is incorrect because the auditor should report on the accompanying information regardless of whether it contains misstatements. See AU 551 for information on auditor-submitted documents.

**49.** (**c**)   The requirement is to identify the correct statement that may be included in an auditor's report when information accompanying the basic financial statements in an auditor-submitted document has been subjected to auditing procedures. Answer (c) is correct because the report indicates whether the accompanying information is fairly stated in all material respects in relation to the basic financial statements taken as a whole. Answer (a) is incorrect because the information is not presented in accordance with generally accepted auditing standards. Answer (b) is incorrect because the information is in addition to that required by generally accepted accounting principles. Answer (d) is incorrect because it is not in accordance with attestation standards.

**50.** (**a**)   The requirement is to identify the auditor's reporting responsibility for a material inconsistency between the audited financial statements and the other information in an annual report to shareholders containing audited financial statements. Answer (a) is correct because AU 550 states that if a material inconsistency exists and the client refuses to revise the other information, the auditor should include an explanatory paragraph that explains the inconsistency. The auditor may also withhold the use of the audit report or the auditor may withdraw from the engagement. Answer (b) is incorrect because the financial statements are not misstated. Answer (c) is incorrect because the auditor must review the other information to ensure that it is consistent with the fi-

nancial statements. Answer (d) is incorrect because the financial statements are not misstated and therefore a disclaimer of opinion is inappropriate.

**51.** (**d**)   The requirement is to determine an auditor's responsibility when audited financial statements are presented in a client's document containing other information. Answer (d) is correct because the auditor is required to read the other information to determine that it is consistent with the audited financial statements. Answers (a) and (c) are incorrect because no such inquiry, analytical procedures, or other substantive auditing procedures are required. Answer (b) is incorrect because, unless the information seems incorrect or inconsistent with the audited financial statements, no explanatory paragraph needs to be added to the auditor's report.

**B.1.i.   Emphasis of a Matter**

**52.** (**d**)   The requirement is to identify the proper statement about an audit report that includes a separate paragraph in an otherwise unmodified report that emphasizes that the entity being reported on had significant transactions with related parties. Answer (d) is correct because AU 508 allows such emphasis of a matter and states that it does not negate the unqualified opinion. Answer (a) is incorrect because the report is considered unqualified. Answer (b) is incorrect because such emphasis of a matter does not violate generally accepted auditing standards if this information is disclosed in notes to the financial statements. Answer (c) is incorrect because the report should **not** include the phrase "with the foregoing explanation."

**B.1.j.   Departures from GAAP**

**53.** (**b**)   The requirement is to identify the appropriate types of audit reports when an illegal act with a material effect on the financial statements has not been properly accounted for or disclosed. Answer (b) is correct because omission of required disclosures, a departure from generally accepted accounting principles, leads to either a qualified or an adverse opinion. Answer (a) is incorrect because a disclaimer of opinion is not appropriate when the auditor knows of such misstatements. Answer (c) is incorrect because neither a disclaimer of opinion nor an unqualified opinion with a separate explanatory paragraph is appropriate. Answer (d) is incorrect because an unqualified opinion with a separate explanatory paragraph is not appropriate.

**54.** (**c**)   The requirement is to identify the phrase that an auditor would include in an audit report with a qualified opinion because of inadequate disclosure. AU 508 indicates that the phrase "except for the omission of the information discussed in the opinion paragraph" is the proper phrase. Answers (a), (b), and (d) are all incorrect because they are phrases not allowed in reports with qualified opinions.

**55.** (**c**)   The requirement is to identify the circumstance that would most likely result in an auditor expressing an adverse opinion. Answer (c) is correct because departures from GAAP, such as inappropriately reporting leases, result in either a qualified or an adverse opinion. Answer (a) is incorrect because client refusal to provide access to minutes is a client imposed scope limitation that will normally result in a disclaimer of opinion. Answer (b) is incorrect because weak internal control will not in general result in an adverse opinion; if controls are so weak that an audit cannot effectively be completed, a disclaimer of opinion or withdrawal may be appropriate. Answer (d) is incorrect because substantial doubt about going concern status results in either an unqualified opinion with an explanatory paragraph or a disclaimer of opinion.

**56. (d)** The requirement is to identify the paragraphs of an audit report that are modified when an auditor qualifies an opinion because of inadequate disclosure. In addition to requiring the inclusion of a separate explanatory paragraph, AU 508 indicates that only the opinion paragraph should be modified.

**57. (b)** The requirement is to determine the appropriate report modification that results when the management of a publicly held company issues financial statements that purport to present its financial position and results of operations but omits the statement of cash flows. Answer (b) is correct because failure to include a statement of cash flows will lead the auditor to qualify the opinion.

**58. (b)** The requirement is to identify the circumstance in which an auditor will choose between expressing an "except for" qualified opinion and an adverse opinion. Answer (b) is correct because omissions of required information, a departure from generally accepted accounting principles, leads to either a qualified or an adverse opinion. Answer (a) is incorrect because a scope limitation such as the failure to observe a client's physical inventory leads to either a qualified opinion or a disclaimer of opinion. Answer (c) is incorrect because an auditor may issue an unqualified opinion on one statement. Answer (d) is incorrect because substantial doubt about an entity's ability to continue as a going concern leads to either an unqualified report with explanatory language or a disclaimer of opinion.

**59. (b)** The requirement is to identify the situation in which an auditor will ordinarily choose between expressing a qualified opinion or an adverse opinion. Answer (b) is correct because departures from generally accepted accounting principles result in either a qualified opinion or an adverse opinion—such lack of disclosure is a departure from generally accepted accounting principles. Answer (a) is incorrect because the inability to observe the physical inventory and inability to become satisfied about its balance represents a scope limitation that will result in either a qualified opinion or a disclaimer of opinion. Answer (c) is incorrect because a change in accounting principles leads to an unqualified opinion with an explanatory paragraph added to the report. Answer (d) is incorrect because inability to apply necessary procedures represents a scope limitation that will result in either a qualified opinion or a disclaimer of opinion. See AU 508 for information on audit reports.

**B.1.k. Scope Limitations**

**60. (a)** The requirement is to identify the type of opinion that should be issued on the financial statements when an auditor has been unable to obtain sufficient evidence relating to the consistent application of accounting principles between the current and prior year. Answer (a) is correct because the scope limitation will affect the year's beginning balances and thereby affect the current year's results of operations and cash flows. Answer (b) is incorrect because the year-end balance sheet will be unaffected by the scope limitation (any retained earnings misstatement of the preceding

year will be offset in the current year). Answer (c) is incorrect because the auditor need not withdraw in such circumstances. Answer (d) is incorrect because this situation represents a scope limitation, and not an uncertainty.

**61. (d)** The requirement is to identify the circumstance in which an auditor would **not** express an unqualified opinion. Answer (d) is correct because an inability to obtain the audited financial statements of a consolidated investee represents a scope limitation, and a significant scope limitation results in either a qualified opinion or a disclaimer of opinion. Answer (a) is incorrect because a material change between periods in accounting principles will result in an explanatory paragraph being added to a report with an unqualified opinion. Answer (b) is incorrect because the omission of the SEC required quarterly financial data, which is considered "unaudited," results in a report with an unqualified opinion with an explanatory paragraph. Answer (c) is incorrect because an auditor's emphasis of an unusually important subsequent event results in a report with an unqualified opinion with an explanatory paragraph.

**62. (a)** The requirement is to determine the propriety of including a statement that the current asset portion of an entity's balance sheet was fairly stated in an audit report that disclaims an opinion on the overall financial statements. Answer (a) is correct because expressions of opinion as to certain identified items in financial statements (referred to as "piecemeal opinions") should not be expressed when the auditor has disclaimed an opinion or has expressed an adverse opinion. Such opinions tend to overshadow or contradict the disclaimer or adverse opinion. Answer (b) is incorrect because an auditor may report on one basic financial statement. Answers (c) and (d) are incorrect because providing such assurance is **not** appropriate.

**63. (b)** The requirement is to identify the type of opinion that should be issued on the balance sheet and the income statement when an auditor did not observe a client's taking of the beginning physical inventory and was unable to become satisfied about its accuracy by using other auditing procedures. Answer (b) is correct because the scope limitation will not affect the year-end balance sheet account balances. However, because evidence with respect to the beginning inventory is lacking, verification of cost of goods sold, an income statement element, is impossible. Although year-end retained earnings will not be affected, both the current and prior years' retained earnings statements will be affected (by an offsetting amount) by the cost of goods sold misstatement. If no other problems arise, the auditor will be able to issue an unqualified opinion on the balance sheet and a disclaimer on the income statement (and on the retained earnings statement). Answer (a) is incorrect because an unqualified opinion may be issued on the balance sheet. Answer (c) is incorrect because an unqualified opinion may be issued on the balance sheet with a disclaimer on the income statement. Answer (d) is incorrect because a disclaimer should be issued on the income statement.

**64. (c)** The requirement is to determine whether the scope paragraph, opinion paragraph, and/or notes to the financial statements should refer to an audit scope limitation. Answer (c) is correct because the suggested report presented for a scope limitation includes modification of both the scope and opinion paragraphs. In addition, it is not appropriate for the scope of the audit to be explained in a note to the financial statements

**65. (c)** The requirement is to identify a CPA's responsibility when asked to report on only one financial statement. Answer (c) is correct because the auditor may accept the engagement because the situation involves limited reporting objectives, not a limitation on the scope of audit procedures. Answers (a), (b), and (d) are incorrect because the auditor is able to accept such an engagement and because the auditor is able to apply the procedures considered necessary.

**66. (d)** The requirement is to determine whether either the scope paragraph, the opinion paragraph, or both should be deleted when an auditor is disclaiming an opinion due to a client-imposed scope limitation. Answer (d) is correct because the scope paragraph is omitted in this situation and the opinion paragraph is modified to disclaim an opinion. Answer (a) is incorrect because it suggests that the scope paragraph is not omitted but that the opinion paragraph is omitted. Answer (b) is incorrect because it states that the opinion paragraph is omitted. Answer (c) is incorrect because it states that the scope paragraph is not omitted.

**67. (c)** The requirement is to identify the information included in the opinion paragraph of an auditor's report that is qualified due to a major inadequacy in the computerized accounting records. Answer (c) is correct because the opinion paragraph indicates that the exception is due to the possible effects on the financial statements. Answer (a) is incorrect because the opinion paragraph will not include a reference to client-imposed scope limitations. Answer (b) is incorrect because no indication of a departure from generally accepted auditing standards is provided in the opinion paragraph and this situation is not a departure from GAAS. Answer (d) is incorrect because there is no indication that there is inadequate disclosure of necessary information.

**68. (d)** The requirement is to identify the circumstance in which a scope limitation is sufficient to preclude an unqualified opinion. Answer (d) is correct because AU 333 states that management's refusal to furnish such a written representation constitutes a limitation on the scope of an audit sufficient to preclude an unqualified opinion. Answers (a), (b), and (c) are all incorrect because while they represent scope limitations, they may sometimes not result in a report that is other than unqualified.

**B.1.l. Lack of Independence**

**69. (b)** The requirement is to identify the situation in which an auditor may **not** issue a qualified opinion. Answer (b) is correct because the auditor who lacks independence must disclaim an opinion, not qualify an opinion. Answer (a) is incorrect because a departure from GAAP will result in either a qualified opinion or an adverse opinion. Answer (c) is incorrect because scope limitations result in either a qualified opinion or a disclaimer of opinion. Answer (d) is incorrect because a specialist may be referred to when an auditor is issuing a qualified opinion, an adverse opinion, or a disclaimer of opinion.

**B.2. Report Preparation**

**70. (d)** The requirement is to identify the manner in which an auditor may express an opinion on an entity's accounts receivable when that auditor has disclaimed an opin-

ion on the financial statements taken as a whole. Answer (d) is correct because such a report is considered a "specified elements, accounts, or items report," and should include the opinion on the accounts receivable separately from the disclaimer of opinion on the financial statement. Answer (a) is incorrect because reason for the disclaimer of opinion need not be provided. Answer (b) is incorrect because distribution of such a report is not restricted to internal use only. Answer (c) is incorrect because the auditor need not report on the current asset portion of the entity's balance sheet to issue such a report.

**71. (a)** The requirement is to determine the proper addressee of a report in a circumstance in which one company has hired a CPA to audit another company's financial statements. Answer (a) is correct because while audit reports are ordinarily addressed to the company whose financial statements are being audited, when a CPA audits the financial statements of a company that is not his or her client (as is the case here) the report is addressed to the company that hired the CPA.

**72. (b)** The requirement is to identify the information that should be included in the opinion paragraph of an audit report with an adverse opinion. Answer (b) is correct because the opinion paragraph should include a direct reference to a separate paragraph disclosing the basis for the opinion. Answer (a) is incorrect because the principal effects, if available, should be described in a separate explanatory paragraph, and not in the opinion paragraph. Answer (c) is incorrect because while a separate explanatory paragraph provides a description of the substantive reasons for the adverse opinion, the opinion paragraph does not. Answer (d) is incorrect because neither an uncertainty nor a scope limitation leads to an adverse opinion.

**73. (b)** The requirement is to determine the proper placement of an explanatory paragraph disclosing the substantive reasons for expressing an adverse opinion. AU 508 requires that such paragraphs precede the opinion paragraph.

**C.1.a. Unaudited Statements**

**74. (b)** The requirement is to determine the CPA's responsibility when s/he assists in preparing financial statements of a publicly held entity, but has **not** audited or reviewed them. Answer (b) is correct because the CPA must, at a minimum, read the financial statements for obvious material misstatements. Answer (a) is incorrect because no documentation with respect to internal control is necessary. Answer (c) is incorrect because the limited scope of procedures being performed does not allow the CPA to ascertain whether the financial statements are in conformity with generally accepted accounting principles. Answer (d) is incorrect because omitting all required disclosures is not expected for a publicly held entity in these circumstances.

**75. (d)** The requirement is to identify the appropriate form of report to issue when the CPA is associated with the financial statements of a publicly held entity but has **not** audited or reviewed such statements. Answer (d) is correct because the standards require the CPA to disclaim an opinion on the financial statements when the accountant has not audited or reviewed such statements. Answer (a) is incorrect because Regulation S-X exemption is not a form of audit report. Answer (b) is incorrect because pro forma information is not involved. Answer (c) is incorrect because there is no such report as an unaudited association report.

**76. (d)** The requirement is to identify a CPA's responsibility when his/her name is to be included in the interim report of a publicly held entity and the CPA has not audited or reviewed the interim financial statements. Answer (d) is correct because when an accountant is aware that his/her name is to be included in a client-prepared written communication of a public entity containing financial statements that have not been audited or reviewed, he/she should request (1) that his/her name not be included in the communication **or** (2) that the statements be marked as unaudited and note that there is no opinion expressed on them.

### C.1.b. Compilations

**77. (b)** The requirement is to identify the statement that should be included in a compilation report. Answer (b) is correct because compilation reports indicate that the accountant compiled the financial statements in accordance with Statements on Standards for Accounting and Review Services.

**78. (a)** The requirement is to determine how a CPA should indicate that a client's compiled financial statements were prepared in conformity with the income tax basis of accounting when the financial statements provide no such disclosure. Answer (a) is correct because if the basis of accounting is not disclosed in the financial statements, the accountant should disclose the basis in the compilation report. Answer (b) is incorrect because each page of the financial statements should only include the reference "See Accountant's Compilation Report." Answer (c) is incorrect because the auditor is not required to issue a special report. See AU 623 for information on special reporting. Answer (d) is incorrect because the auditor does not have to withdraw from the engagement.

**79. (a)** The requirement is to determine how the compilation report should be modified to indicate that the entity's financial statements do not include all disclosures required by GAAP. Answer (a) is correct because AR 100 states that while the accountant may compile such financial statements, the accountant must clearly indicate in the compilation report that substantially all disclosures required by GAAP have been omitted. Answer (b) is incorrect because the financial statements are not compiled on a comprehensive basis other than GAAP. Answer (c) is incorrect because a compilation may be performed on financial statements lacking such disclosures. Answer (d) is incorrect because these financial statements are not considered "special-purpose financial statements."

**80. (c)** The requirement is to determine when a CPA may compile and be associated with financial statements that omit disclosures required by GAAP. Answer (c) is correct because the CPA may compile such financial statements provided that the omission of substantially all disclosures (1) is clearly indicated in the audit report and (2) is not, to the CPA's knowledge, undertaken with the intention of misleading those who might reasonably be expected to use the financial statements.

**81. (d)** The requirement is to determine the proper reporting procedure for comparative financial statements for which the prior year is unaudited, and the current year is

audited. AU 504 states that when unaudited financial statements are presented in comparative form with audited financial statements, the report on the prior period may be reissued to accompany the current period report. In addition, the report on the current period may also include a separate paragraph describing responsibility assumed for the prior period financial statements. If these statements are filed with the SEC, the statements should be clearly marked as "unaudited" but should not be referred to in the auditor's report.

**82. (a)** The requirement is to determine a CPA's responsibility when the first year of compiled comparative financial statements omit substantially all disclosures required by generally accepted accounting principles, while the second year's statements include such disclosures. Answer (a) is correct because the CPA may **not** report on the comparative financial statements because of a lack of comparability. Answers (b), (c), and (d) are all incorrect because they allow such reporting to occur under certain circumstances.

**83. (c)** The requirement is to identify the statement that should **not** be included in a CPA's financial statement compilation report. Answer (c) is correct because a compilation report provides no assurance on the financial statements.

**84. (b)** The requirement is to determine the representations made explicitly and implicitly when issuing a standard compilation report on a nonpublic entity's financial statements. Answer (b) is correct because the report explicitly states that the financial statements have not been audited and that the accountant has compiled them.

**85. (b)** The requirement is to determine the appropriate date for an auditor's compilation report. AR 100 requires that the date of completion of the compilation should be used.

**86. (d)** The requirement is to determine whether an accountant's compilation report must be printed on the accountant's letterhead, manually signed by the accountant, or both. Answer (d) is correct because the professional standards require neither that the report be printed on the accountant's letterhead, nor that it be manually signed by the accountant. Answers (a), (b), and (c) are all incorrect because they include an inappropriate "yes" to one or both issues. See AR 100 for information on reporting on a compilation of financial statements.

**87. (a)** The requirement is to identify the correct statement concerning compiled financial statements that are to be made available to third parties. Answer (a) is correct because a compilation report must be issued when third-party reliance upon compiled financial statements is anticipated. Answer (b) is incorrect because note disclosures may be omitted. Answer (c) is incorrect because while advisable, use of an engagement letter is not required in such circumstances. Answer (d) is incorrect because no such restriction is necessary.

**88. (a)** The requirement is to identify the correct statement concerning appropriate communication option(s) when compiled financial statements are only going to be used by management. Answer (a) is correct because when an accountant submits to a client compiled financial statements that are not expected to be used by a third party, either a compilation report or a written engagement letter (or both) may be used. Answer (b), (c), and (d) are all incorrect because they suggest that either a compilation report, a written engagement letter, or both are unacceptable.

**89. (a)** The requirement is to identify the circumstance in which a compilation report is not required. Answer (a) is correct because when financial statements are only for management, no compilation report is required. Answers (b) and (c) are incorrect because when third parties are expected to use compiled financial statements, a compilation report is required. Answer (d) is incorrect because a compilation report is not always required.

### C.1.b. Reviews

**90. (d)** The requirement is to identify whether a review report is modified due to either inability to assess the risk of material misstatement due to fraud, a discovery of internal control deficiencies, or both. Answer (d) is correct because neither of these circumstances requires modification of a review report. Answers (a), (b), and (c) are all incorrect because they suggest that one or the other of these circumstances results in modification of a review report. A departure from GAAP is the primary cause of a review report modification. AR 100 provides guidance on review reports.

**91. (b)** The requirement is to identify the circumstance in which a CPA may issue a review report on a single financial statement. Answer (b) is correct because an accountant may issue a review report on a financial statement, such as a balance sheet, and not report on the other related financial statements if the scope of his or her inquiry and analytical procedures has not been restricted. Answer (a) is incorrect because the balance sheet need not be presented in prescribed form. Answer (c) is incorrect because the balance sheet may be used to obtain credit or to distribute to creditors. Answer (d) is incorrect because specialized accounting principles and practices in an industry may or may not need to be disclosed depending upon the circumstances.

**92. (c)** The requirement is to identify a CPA's responsibility when he or she believes that modification of the standard review report is **not** adequate to indicate deficiencies in financial statements affected by illegal acts. Answer (c) is correct because whenever a CPA believes that modification of the standard report is not adequate to indicate the deficiencies in the financial statements, he or she should withdraw from the review engagement and provide no further services with respect to those financial statements.

**93. (c)** The requirement is to identify the reference that should be included in each page of a nonpublic entity's reviewed financial statements. AR 100 requires that each page of the financial statements include a reference such as "See Accountant's Review Report."

**94. (c)** The requirement is to identify the statement that is included in an accountant's review report on the financial statements of a nonpublic entity. Answer (c) is correct because a review report includes a statement that a review consists principally of inquires of company personnel and analytical procedures applied to financial data. See AR 100 for information that should be included in a review report.

**95. (c)** The requirement is to determine a CPA's reporting responsibility when an audit engagement for a nonpublic

entity has been changed to a review engagement because of what the CPA believes to be a reasonable restriction on the scope of the audit. Answer (c) is correct because in such circumstances the CPA should neither include reference to the original engagement nor to the scope limitation.

**96. (c)** The requirement is to identify the correct statement relating to a CPA's report on comparative statements when the current year has been reviewed and the previous year has been audited. Answer (c) is correct because when a separate paragraph is being added to the CPA's review report the CPA should clearly indicate the difference in the levels of assurance for the two years. In this situation, AR 200 requires the auditor to indicate that the previous year's financial statements were audited, the date of the report, the type of opinion expressed and if the opinion was other than unqualified, the substantive reasons for that opinion, and that no auditing procedures were performed after the date of the previous report. Answer (a) is incorrect because the review report is not solely intended for management or the board of directors. Answer (b) is incorrect because the prior year's audit report may still be appropriate. Answer (d) is incorrect because this statement does not need to be included within the review report.

**97. (b)** The requirement is to identify the statement included in the standard report issued by an accountant after reviewing the financial statements of a nonpublic entity. Answer (b) is correct because the report states that the accountant is not aware of any material modifications that should be made to the financial statements in order for them to be in conformity with generally accepted accounting principles. AR 100 presents the required disclosures for a review report.

**98. (b)** The requirement is to identify the information presented in a review report of financial statements of a nonpublic entity. Answer (b) is correct because the report indicates that all information included in the financial statements is the representation of the management of the entity.

**99. (c)** The requirement is to determine an accountant's reporting responsibility when associated with a nonpublic entity's reviewed statements which contain a material departure from generally accepted accounting principles. Answer (c) is correct because AR 100 requires the inclusion of a separate paragraph describing the departure. Answers (a) and (b) are incorrect because an adverse opinion or an "except for" qualified opinion may only be issued when an audit has been performed. Answer (d) is incorrect because expressing limited assurance (as is normally provided in reviews) on the financial statements is not adequate to disclose the departure.

**100. (a)** The requirement is to identify the reply which is correct concerning the content of a review report. Answer (a) is correct because a review report indicates that a review is substantially less in scope than an audit. Answer (b) is incorrect because a review report provides no information on internal control. Answer (c) is incorrect because while a review report states that the accountant is not aware of any material modifications that should be made to the financial statements, it does not provide limited assurance that the financial statements are fairly presented. Answer (d) is incorrect because while a review report does state that a review is substantially less in scope than an audit, it does not refer to a compilation.

### C.1.c.   Reviewed Interim (Quarterly) Statements

**101. (a)** The requirement is to identify the objective of a review of interim financial information. Answer (a) is correct because AU 722 states that the objective of a review of interim financial information is to provide a basis for reporting on whether material modification should be made for such information to conform with generally accepted accounting principles. Answer (b) is incorrect because no updated opinion is being issued. Answer (c) is incorrect because condensed statements or pro forma financial information are not being considered in this question. Answer (d) is incorrect because the statements may or may not be presented in conformity with generally accepted accounting principles.

**102. (a)** The requirement is to identify the correct statement with respect to an independent accountant's review report on interim financial information presented in a registration statement. Answer (a) is correct because an accountant's review report is **not** a part of the registration statement within the meaning of Section 11 of the Securities Act of 1933. Answer (b) is incorrect because under certain conditions an accountant is required to update the report. Answers (c) and (d) are incorrect because the prospectus includes neither a statement that the review was performed in accordance with SEC standards, nor a statement that the accountant obtained corroborating evidence.

**103. (d)** The requirement is to determine the circumstances which will lead to a modification of an interim report. Departures from generally accepted accounting principles, which include adequate disclosure, require modification of the accountant's report. Normally neither an uncertainty [answer (a)] nor a lack of consistency [answer (b)] would cause a report modification. Reference to another accountant [answer (c)] is not considered a modification.

**104. (b)** The requirement is to identify the procedure that would ordinarily be applied when an accountant conducts a review of the interim financial information of a publicly held entity. Answer (b) is correct because the accountant will ordinarily read the minutes of meetings of stockholders, the board of directors, and committees of the board of directors to identify actions that may affect the interim financial information. AU 722 describes the nature of procedures for conducting a review of interim financial information. Answers (a), (c), and (d) are all incorrect because they represent verification procedures typically beyond the scope of a review of interim financial information.

**105. (c)** The requirement is to identify the least likely procedure to be included in an accountant's review of interim financial information of a public entity. Answer (c) is correct because a review consists principally of performing analytical procedures and making inquiries, not procedures such as observation, inspection, and confirmation. Answers (a), (b), and (d) are all incorrect because they include review procedures, as presented in AU 722.

**106. (c)** The requirement is to identify the most likely information included in a review report. Answer (c) is correct because AU 722 requires that the report include a description of procedures performed. Answer (a) is incorrect

because the information was reviewed, not examined, in accordance with standards of the PCAOB. Answer (b) is incorrect because the interim financial information is the responsibility of the entity's management, not the shareholders. Answer (d) is incorrect because a review is less in scope than an audit, not than a compilation.

### C.1.d.   Condensed Financial Statements

**107. (c)** The requirement is to determine the circumstance under which an auditor may report on condensed financial statements that are derived from complete audited financial statements. Answer (c) is correct because a report may be issued when the information in the condensed financial statements is fairly stated in all material respects in relation to the financial statements. Answer (a) is incorrect because the condensed financial statements need not be distributed with the complete financial statements. Answer (b) is incorrect because the report need not indicate the nature of any additional procedures. Answer (d) is incorrect because prior year condensed financial information is not necessary. See AU 552 for information on condensed financial statements.

**108. (a)** The requirement is to determine the appropriate response relating to selected financial data that are included in a client's prepared document containing audited financial statements. Answer (a) is correct because the selected data should be limited to data derived from the audited financial statements. Answer (b) is incorrect because distribution of the report need not be limited to senior management and the board of directors. Answer (c) is incorrect because the selected data need not follow a comprehensive basis of accounting other than GAAP. Answer (d) is incorrect because the report will ordinarily state that the selected data are fairly stated in all material respects in relation to the consolidated financial statements.

### C.1.e.   Financial Statements Prepared for Use in Other Countries

**109. (a)** The requirement is to identify audit reporting requirements when reporting on financial statements of a US entity prepared in accordance with another country's accounting principles. Answer (a) is correct because AU 534 states that the auditor should understand the accounting principles generally accepted in the other country. Answer (b) is incorrect because the auditor does not have to obtain certification outside of the United States. Answer (c) is incorrect because the auditor does not have to disclaim an opinion. Answer (d) is incorrect because the auditor does not have to receive a waiver from the auditor's State Board of Accountancy.

**110. (d)** The requirement is to determine the appropriate types of reports that may be issued when the financial statements of a US subsidiary are prepared following the principles of a non-US parent company's country for inclusion in that parent company's non-US consolidated financial statements. AU 534 allows either a modified US style report or the report form of the parent's country. A US style unmodified report is not appropriate.

### C.2.a.   Special Reports

**111. (a)** The requirement is to identify a requirement for a CPA to express an opinion on a profit participation plan relating to an entity's net income. Answer (a) is correct because if a specified element is, or is based upon, an entity's net income or stockholders' equity, the CPA should have audited the complete financial statements in order to express an opinion on the element. Answer (b) is incorrect because the financial statements need not be prepared in conformity with GAAP, as other bases of accounting may be followed. Answer (c) is incorrect because the report need not be made available for distribution to other employees. Answer (d) is incorrect because the individual in the profit participation plan need not own a controlling interest in the company.

**112. (d)** The requirement is to determine the information that should be included in an audit report on financial statements prepared on the income tax basis of accounting. AU 623 presents the form of the report to be issued. Answer (d) is correct because AU 623 requires that the report indicate that the income tax basis of accounting is a comprehensive basis of accounting other than GAAP.

**113. (d)** The requirement is to identify the appropriate type of audit report to be issued for a nonprofit entity's financial statements prepared following an accounting basis prescribed by a regulatory agency solely for filing with that agency. Answer (d) is correct because audit reports for such financial statements are considered special reports. Answer (a) is incorrect because an unqualified report may be issued if there are no departures from the prescribed basis. The report would not be qualified because the financial statements were prepared using an accounting basis prescribed by a regulatory agency. Answer (b) is incorrect because the report issued has five paragraphs. Answer (c) is incorrect because a disclaimer of opinion need not be issued.

**114. (c)** The requirement is to identify the disclosure included in a separate explanatory paragraph of an auditor's special report on financial statements prepared in conformity with the cash basis of accounting. Answer (c) is correct because the explanatory paragraph refers to the note to the financial statements that describes the basis of accounting. AU 623 presents complete details on such special reports. Answer (a) is incorrect because the report need not justify the reasons for following a basis other than generally accepted accounting principles. Answer (b) is incorrect because the explanatory paragraph contains no statement on fair presentation, and because the opinion paragraph states whether the presentation is in conformity with the basis described in the appropriate financial statement note. Answer (d) is incorrect because no explanation of how the results of operations differ from financial statements prepared in conformity with generally accepted accounting principles is necessary.

**115. (b)** The requirement is to identify the example of a "special report." AU 623 defines reports on compliance with aspects of regulatory requirements related to audited financial statements as special reports. [The other types of special reports include (1) other comprehensive basis financial statements, (2) specified elements, (3) financial presentations to comply with contracts, and (4) financial information presented in prescribed forms.]

**116. (a)** The requirement is to determine the type of report to issue when a client who uses a comprehensive basis of accounting has not appropriately titled its financial sta-

ments. Answer (a) is correct because any such exceptions or reservation should be described in an explanatory paragraph and possibly a qualified (or adverse) opinion should be issued. Answer (b) is incorrect because no such application to the state insurance commission is necessary. Answer (c) is incorrect because a disclaimer of opinion is not appropriate when known misstatements exist. Answer (d) is incorrect because, as indicated, more than describing the terminology is necessary.

**117. (a)** The requirement is to determine whether a CPA is permitted to accept an engagement to audit either a schedule of accounts receivable, a schedule of royalties, or both. Answer (a) is correct because auditors may audit "specified elements, accounts or items of a financial statement," including either a schedule of accounts receivable or a schedule of royalties. Answer (b) is incorrect because an auditor may audit a schedule of royalties. Answer (c) is incorrect because an auditor may audit a schedule of accounts receivable. Answer (d) is incorrect because an auditor may audit both a schedule of accounts receivable and a schedule of royalties.

**118. (b)** The requirement is to identify an auditor's reporting responsibility when a printed form prescribes the wording of the independent auditor's report that will accompany it, but that wording is not acceptable to the auditor. AU 623 suggests that the auditor reword the report (or attach a separate report) when involved with this type of "special report."

**C.2.b. Letters for Underwriters**

capsule information, a comfort letter will generally provide negative assurance. Answer (b) is incorrect because CPAs do not provide positive assurance on supplementary disclosures. Answer (c) is incorrect because no "limited opinion" is issued on pro forma or other information. Answer (d) is incorrect because no disclaimer will be included on the prospective financial statements.

**124. (d)** The requirement is to determine the appropriate reference to an independent accountant in a prospectus (relating to an SEC registration statement) that includes a statement about his/her involvement with an independent audit report. AU 711 indicates that the independent accountant is an expert in auditing and accounting.

**125. (d)** The requirement is to identify the information included in a typical comfort letter. Answer (d) is correct because in a comfort letter auditors provide an opinion as to whether the audited financial statements comply in form with the accounting requirements of the SEC. Answer (a) is incorrect because negative assurance concerning whether the entity's internal control procedures operated as designed during the period is not provided. Answer (b) is incorrect because a comfort letter does not include an opinion on whether the entity complied with Government Auditing Standards and the Single Audit Act. Answer (c) is incorrect because negative, not positive, assurance is provided on unaudited condensed financial information.

**126. (a)** The requirement is to determine the proper treatment of unaudited financial statements presented in comparative form with audited financial statements in a document filed with the Securities and Exchange Commission. Answer (a) is correct because those statements should be marked "unaudited," not withheld until they are audited, and not referred to in the auditor's report.

**127. (b)** The requirement is to identify the requirement relating to a CPA's report when reporting on the application of accounting principles to a specific transaction. Answer (b) is correct because AU 625 requires that the report include a statement that responsibility for the proper accounting treatment rests with the preparers of the financial statements. Answer (a) is incorrect because the report states that the engagement was performed in accordance with applicable AICPA standards, not Statements on Standards for Accounting and Review Services. Answer (c) is incorrect as no such statement about opinion-shopping is included. Answer (d) is incorrect because the information may be communicated to a prior or continuing auditor.

### C.2.c. Application of Accounting Principles

**128. (a)** The requirement is to determine an auditor's reporting responsibility when asked by a prospective client to render an opinion on the application of accounting principles to a specific transaction. Answer (a) is correct because AU 625 indicates that the report must include a statement that any difference in the facts, circumstances, or assumptions presented may change the report, as well as various other disclosures. Answer (b) is incorrect because the report indicates that the engagement was performed in accordance with AICPA standards, not Statements on Standards for Consulting Services. Answer (c) is incorrect because the report need **not** indicate that the guidance is for management use only and may not be communicated to the prior or con-

tinuing auditors. Answer (d) is incorrect because the report does not include negative assurance ("nothing came to our attention"). See AU 625 for performance and reporting standards relating to reports on the application of accounting principles.

**129. (a)** The requirement is to determine an auditor's responsibility when asked to render an opinion on the application of accounting principles to a specific transaction by an entity that is audited by another CPA. Answer (a) is correct because the accountant must consult with the continuing CPA to attempt to obtain information relevant to the transaction. Answer (b) is incorrect because the engagement's findings need not be reported to all of the groups listed—the entity's audit committee, the continuing CPA, and management. Answer (c) is incorrect because the accountant need not disclaim an opinion. Answer (d) is incorrect because the report's distribution need not be restricted to management and outside parties who are aware of all relevant facts.

**130. (b)** Answer (b) is correct because AU 625 indicates that an accountant should not undertake such an engagement when the report would be based on such a hypothetical transaction. Answers (a), (c), and (d) are all incorrect because they include information included in an accountant's report on the application of accounting principles.

### C.3.a. Attestation Engagements—General

**131. (c)** The requirement is to select the service that is most likely to be structured as an attest engagement. Answer (c) is correct because CPAs may provide assurance as to compliance with requirements of specified laws through a variety of services, including agreed-upon procedures engagements and various compliance audits. Answers (a) and (b) are incorrect because advocating a client's tax position and consulting on a new database system are examples of professional services **not** typically structured as attest services. Answer (d) is incorrect because compilations are not a form of attest engagement.

**132. (a)** The requirement is to identify the correct statement. When a standard unqualified examination report is being issued, that report may be upon the subject matter or the written assertion. Answers (b), (c), and (d) are all incorrect because they suggest that the report may not be upon either the subject matter, the written assertion, or both.

**133. (b)** The requirement is to determine whether a CPA's conclusion may be upon the subject matter, the written assertion, or both when conditions exist that result in a material deviation from the criteria against which the subject matter was evaluated during an examination. Answer (b) is correct because in such circumstances the conclusion should be directly upon the subject matter. Answer (a) is incorrect because it suggests that the conclusion may be upon the written assertion. Answer (c) is incorrect because it states that the conclusion may not be upon the subject matter and may be upon the written assertion. Answer (d) is incorrect because it states that the conclusion may not be upon the subject matter.

**134. (a)** The requirement is to determine the element that is **least** likely to be present when a practitioner performs an attest engagement. Answer (a) is correct because while an assertion is generally present, it is not ordinarily required. Answers (b), (c), and (d) are all incorrect because practitioner independence, subject matter, and suitable criteria are all required.

**135. (a)**  The requirement is to determine whether suitable criteria in an attestation engagement may be available publicly, and/or in the CPA's report.  Answer (a) is correct because suitable criteria may be available publicly in the CPA's report, included with the subject matter or in the assertion, well understood by users (e.g., the distance between A and B is twenty feet) or available only to specified parties. Answers (b), (c), and (d) are all incorrect because they suggest that suitable criteria may not be available publicly, in the CPA's report, or both.

**136. (d)**  The requirement is to identify the situation that is **least** likely to result in a restricted use attest report.  Answer (d) is correct because criteria developed by an industry association may or may not result in a restricted use attest report.  Answers (a), (b), and (c) always result in a restricted use report.

**137. (c)**  The requirement is to identify the information that is **least** likely to be included in an agreed-upon procedures attestation report.  Answer (c) is correct because an agreed-upon procedures report provides a summary of procedures performed and findings, not limited assurance.  Answer (a) is incorrect because the specified party does not take responsibility for the sufficiency of procedures.  Answer (b) is incorrect because the report's use is restricted. Answer (d) is incorrect because a summary of procedures performed is included.

**138. (a)**  The requirement is to identify the type of report that is most likely to include a summary of findings rather than assurance.  Answer (a) is correct because agreed-upon procedures reports include a summary of findings.  Answer (b) is incorrect because a compilation report does not provide a summary of findings.  Answer (c) is incorrect because an examination report includes positive assurance and not a summary of findings.  Answer (d) is incorrect because a review report includes limited (negative) assurance, not a summary of findings.

### C.3.b.  Agreed-upon Procedures Engagements

**139. (c)**  The requirement is to identify the statement that is **not** correct concerning "specified parties" of an agreed-upon procedures report under either the auditing or attestation standards.  Answer (c) is correct because while a practitioner should establish a clear understanding regarding the terms of the engagement, preferably in an engagement letter, no such engagement letter is required.  Answers (a) and (b) are incorrect because the specified parties must agree on the procedures to be performed and take responsibility for their adequacy.  Answer (d) is incorrect because an additional party may be added as a specified party after completion of the engagement.

### C.3.c.  Financial Forecasts and Projections

**140. (a)**  The requirement is to determine the information to be included in a separate paragraph included in an accountant's report on the examination of projected financial statements.  Answer (a) is correct because AT 301 requires that such a report include a separate paragraph that describes the limitations on the usefulness of the presentation.  See AT 301 for information that should be included in an exami-

nation report of prospective financial statements.  Answer (b) is incorrect because the report includes no such statement attempting to distinguish between an examination and an audit.  Answer (c) is incorrect because the report includes no such disclosure and because the accountant is **not** responsible for events and circumstances up to one year after the report's date.  Answer (d) is incorrect because the report suggests that the assumptions do provide a reasonable basis.

**141. (c)**  The requirement is to identify the statement which should be included in an accountant's compilation report on financial forecasts.  Answer (c) is correct because when the accountant is preparing a standard compilation report on prospective financial statements, AT 301 requires that the accountant include a statement indicating that the prospective results may not be achieved.

**142. (c)**  The requirement is to identify the appropriate distribution of an entity's financial projection.  A financial projection is sometimes prepared to present one or more hypothetical courses of action for evaluation in response to a question such as "What would happen if...?"  It is based on a responsible party's assumptions reflecting conditions it expects would exist and the course of action it expects would be taken, given one or more hypothetical assumptions.  Projections are "limited use" financial statements meant for the responsible party (generally management) and third parties with whom the responsible party is negotiating directly. Answer (c) is correct because a bank might be expected to receive such a projection.  Answers (a), (b), and (d) are all incorrect because projections are meant for "limited use" and not to be broadly distributed to groups such as all employees or potential or current stockholders.  AT 301 provides overall guidance on the area of financial forecasts and projections.

**143. (c)**  The requirement is to determine whether either testifying as an expert witness, compiling a financial projection, or both are engagements governed by the provisions of the Statement on Standards for Attestation Statements.  Answer (c) is correct because the attestation standards explicitly exclude expert witness work, but include the compilation of a financial projection; note that in most areas compilations are not included in attestation standard coverage, but in the area of prospective financial statement (forecasts as well as projections) coverage is included.  Answer (a) is incorrect because it states that expert witness work is included.  Answer (b) is incorrect both because it states that expert witness work is included and that compiling a projection is not included.  Answer (d) is incorrect because it states that compilations of projections are not included.

**144. (a)**  The requirement is to identify the statement that should be included in a compilation report on a financial forecast.  Answer (a) is correct because the report should state that the compilation does **not** include evaluation of the support of the assumptions underlying the forecast.  Answer (b) is incorrect because no such statement is included in a compilation report, and because hypothetical assumptions pertain to financial projections, not financial forecasts. Answer (c) is incorrect because the report makes no statement concerning the range of assumptions.  Answer (d) is incorrect because the statement is not included in the report, and because the prospective statements are management's, not the accountant's, representation.

**145. (d)** The requirement is to identify the type of general use prospective financial statement on which the accountant may appropriately report. Answer (d) is correct because financial forecasts are considered prospective financial statements, and they are appropriate for general use. Answer (a) is incorrect because financial projections are only appropriate for the party responsible for preparing them or for third parties with whom the responsible party is negotiating directly. Answers (b) and (c) are incorrect because partial presentations and pro forma financial statements are not considered prospective financial statements.

**146. (b)** The requirement is to identify the type of prospective financial statement that includes one or more hypothetical ("what if?") assumptions. Answer (b) is correct because financial projections include one or more hypothetical assumptions. Answer (a) is incorrect because pro forma financial presentations are designed to demonstrate the effect of a future or hypothetical transaction by showing how it might have affected the historical financial statements if it had been consummated during the period covered by those statements. Answer (c) is incorrect because partial presentations are presentations that do not meet the minimum presentation guidelines of AT 301. Answer (d) is incorrect because financial forecasts present, to the best of the responsible party's knowledge and belief, an entity's expected financial position, results of operations, and changes in financial information.

**147. (d)** The requirement is to determine an accountant's responsibility when he or she accepts an engagement to apply agreed-upon procedures to prospective financial statements. Answer (d) is correct because distribution of such a report is to be restricted to the specified parties involved. AT 301 also requires that the specified parties participate in establishing and taking responsibility for the adequacy of the procedures, and that the prospective financial statements include a summary of significant assumptions. Answer (a) is incorrect because the prospective financial statements need not be examined. Answer (b) is incorrect because responsibility for the adequacy of the procedures is taken by the specified parties, not by the accountant. Answer (c) is incorrect because when the accountant reports on the results of applying agreed-upon procedures he or she should not express any form of negative assurance on the prospective financial statements taken as a whole.

**148. (d)** The requirement is to determine the appropriate type of audit report to be issued when an accountant examines a financial forecast that fails to disclose several significant assumptions used to prepare the forecast. AT 301 states that an adverse opinion is appropriate when significant assumptions are not disclosed.

**C.3.d. Pro Forma Financial Information**

**149. (d)** The requirement is to determine the statement that should be included in an accountant's report on a review of pro forma financial information. Answer (d) is correct because the report must include a reference to the financial statements from which the historical financial information is derived and a statement as to whether such financial statements were audited or reviewed.

**C.3.e. Management Discussion and Analysis**

**150. (b)** The requirement is to determine the reply that is **not** an objective of a CPA's examination of a client's MD&A. Answer (b) is correct because an examination of a client's MD&A does not directly address overall conformity with such rules and regulations. Answers (a), (c), and (d) are the three objectives of an MD&A examination agreement.

**151. (c)** The requirement is to identify an assertion embodied in MD&A. Answer (c) is correct because the attestation standards on MD&A indicate that consistency with the financial statements is an assertion—in addition, occurrence, completeness, and presentation and disclosure are embodied assertions. Answers (a), (b), and (d) are all incorrect because valuation, reliability, and rights and obligations are not considered to be assertions embodied in the MD&A.

**152. (b)** Answer (b) is correct because the MD&A review of a public entity should be restricted to the use of specified parties. Answer (a) is incorrect because a review consists principally of applying analytical procedures, rather than also including search and verification procedures. Answer (c) is incorrect because a consideration of relevant portion of internal control is necessary to identify types of potential misstatements and to select the inquiries and analytical procedures. Answer (d) is incorrect because a review report ordinarily provides negative assurance, not a summary of findings.

**C.3.f. Trust Services**

**153. (d)** The requirement is to identify the proper term for an attest engagement in which a CPA assesses a client's commercial Internet site for predefined criteria such as those over online privacy. Answer (d) is correct because the AICPA's Trust Services Principles relate to this area, and WebTrust is the most likely product—see www.aicpa.org. Answers (a), (b), and (c) all represent names of products not included in the professional standards.

**154. (b)** The requirement is to identify the standards under which Trust Services engagements are performed. Answer (b) is correct because the Statements on Standards for Attestation engagements address such engagements. More information on Trust Services engagements (WebTrust and SysTrust) is available on the AICPA's Web site— www.aicpa.org. Answers (a) and (c) are incorrect because such standards do not exist. Answer (d) is incorrect because Statements on Auditing Standards do not address Trust Services engagements.

**155. (d)** The requirement is to identify what the WebTrust seal of assurance relates most directly to. Answer (d) is correct because the WebTrust seal is designed to provide assurance on Web site security, availability, processing integrity, online privacy and confidentiality. Answers (a), (b), and (c) are all incorrect since WebTrust isn't specially aimed at financial statements, health care facilities, or risk assurance procedures.

**156. (b)** The requirement is to determine the type of opinion or assurance most likely to be included in a CPA's report relating to WebTrust engagements. Answer (b) is correct because the WebTrust examination report provides an opinion on whether the site meets the Trust Services criteria for one or more of the Trust Services Principles.  Answer (a) is incorrect because no opinion on being "hack-proof" is issued.  Answer (c) is incorrect because negative assurance is not provided.  Answer (d) is incorrect because an agreed-upon procedures engagement, not an examination engagement results in a summary of findings.

**157.  (b)**   The requirement is to identify the type of engagement that considers security, availability, processing integrity, online privacy and/or confidentiality over any type of defined electronic system.  Answer (b) is correct because SysTrust engagements consider any type of defined electronic system.  Answer (a) is incorrect because an engagement to consider internal control over financial reporting does not directly address these attributes.  Answer (c) is incorrect because there is no such engagement as a Web site Associate.  Answer (d) is incorrect because WebTrust deals more directly with company Web sites.

**158.  (b)**   The requirement is to identify the most likely report when a client refuses to provide a written assertion in a Trust Services engagement.  Answer (b) is correct because this represents a scope limitation, and client imposed scope limitations are most likely to result in a disclaimer of opinion.  Answer (a) is incorrect because an adverse opinion is appropriate when a CPA believes that the information is so misstated as to be misleading.  Answer (c) is incorrect because client imposed scope limitations generally result in disclaimers, not qualified opinions.  Answer (d) is incorrect because an unqualified opinion is most likely not appropriate in such a circumstance.

### D.1.a.  Compliance Attestation Engagements—Agreed-upon Procedures Engagements

**159.  (c)**   The requirement is to identify the type of association **not** permitted under the compliance attestation standards.  AT 601 does not allow the CPA to perform a review over compliance.

**160.  (b)**   The requirement is to identify the information provided in an agreed-upon procedures report on compliance with contractual requirements to pay royalties.  Answer (b) is correct because agreed-upon procedures reports include a list of the procedures performed (or reference thereto) and findings.  Answer (a) is incorrect because no such disclaimer of opinion is provided in an agreed-upon procedures report.  Answer (c) is incorrect because no opinion is included in an agreed-upon procedures report.  Answer (d) is incorrect because an agreed-upon procedures report includes a statement disclaiming an opinion on the sufficiency of procedures, not an acknowledgement of the sufficiency of the procedures.  See AT 201 for guidance on agreed-upon procedures engagements.

**161.  (a)**   The requirement is to identify the statement that is included in a CPA's report on agreed-upon procedures on management's assertion about an entity's compliance with specified requirements.  Answer (a) is correct because such an agreed-upon procedures report includes a statement of limitations on the use of the report because it is intended solely for the use of specified parties.  See AT 601 for information that should be included in such an agreed-upon procedures report.  Answer (b) is incorrect because no "opinion" is included.  Answer (c) is incorrect because a summary of findings, not negative assurance is provided.

Answer (d) is incorrect because the CPA makes no representation regarding the sufficiency of procedures.

### D.1.b.  Compliance Attestation Engagements—Examination Engagements

**162.  (c)**   The requirement is to identify the correct statement concerning an examination report when management has properly disclosed an instance of material noncompliance.  AT 601 states that the opinion should be qualified or adverse.  Note that AT 601 requires the CPA's report to relate directly to the subject matter when the opinion is modified.

### D.2.a.  Compliance Auditing of Federal Financial Assistance Programs—GAAS Audits

**163.  (b)**   The requirement is to determine an auditor's responsibility when auditing a not-for-profit entity that receives governmental financial assistance.  Answer (b) is correct because AU 801 requires that the auditor assess whether management has identified laws and regulations that have a direct and material effect on the entity's financial statements; AU 801 also presents procedures to be followed in assessing such laws and regulations.  Answer (a) is incorrect because such a separate report describing expected benefits and costs does not need to be issued.  Answer (c) is incorrect because the CPA will not notify the governmental agency that the audit is not designed to provide assurance.  Answer (d) is incorrect because the CPA does not express an opinion on the entity's continued eligibility for governmental financial assistance.  AU 801 presents requirements relating to compliance auditing for governmental entities and recipients of governmental financial assistance.

**164.  (c)**   The requirement is to determine the focus of an auditor's attention in detecting misstatements resulting from violations of laws and regulations when auditing a not-for-profit organization that receives financial assistance from governmental agencies.  Answer (c) is correct because the focus of such procedures should be on violations that have a direct and material effect on the amounts in the organization's financial statements (AU 801).  Answers (a), (b), and (d) all represent a focus that is not as accurate as that provided in answer (c).

**165.  (b)**   The requirement is to determine the proper scope of a governmental audit.  The General Accounting Office's "yellow book" suggests that in addition to financial statements, such an audit may include consideration of (1) program results, (2) compliance with laws and regulations, and (3) economy and efficiency.

**166.  (b)**   The requirement is to identify whether an auditor performing an audit in accordance with Government Auditing Standards (the "yellow book") is required to report on noteworthy accomplishments of the program, the scope of the auditor's testing of internal controls, or both.  Answer (b) is correct because the "yellow book" requires reporting only upon the scope of the auditor's testing of internal controls.  Answers (a), (c), and (d) all include an incorrect combination of reporting replies.

**167.  (b)**   The requirement is to identify whether an auditor performing an audit in accordance with Government Auditing Standards (the "yellow book") is required to report on recommendations for actions to improve operations, the scope of tests of compliance with laws and regulations, or both. Answer (b) is correct because the "yellow book" requires reporting upon the scope of the auditor's tests of compliance with laws and regulations. Answers (a), (c), and (d) all include an incorrect combination of reporting replies.

### D.2.b.    Compliance Auditing of Federal Financial Assistance Programs—GAS Audits

**168. (a)**    The requirement is to identify the correct statement with respect to a financial statement audit conducted in accordance with Government Auditing Standards (the "yellow book"). Answer (a) is correct because the auditor issues a report on compliance with laws and internal control, and a report on the financial information. Answer (b) is incorrect because a financial statement audit does not address economy and efficiency in the manner suggested. Answer (c) is incorrect because recommendations for actions to correct problems and improve operations are not ordinarily included. Answer (d) is incorrect because a financial statement audit does not address whether programs are achieving the desired results.

**169. (a)**    The requirement is to identify the correct statement with respect to a financial statement audit conducted in accordance with Government Auditing Standards (the "yellow book"). Answer (a) is correct because the auditor issues a report on compliance with laws and internal control, and a report on the financial information. Answer (b) is incorrect because not all instances of abuse, waste and mismanagement are so reported. Answer (c) is incorrect because the views of officials are not reported. Answer (d) is incorrect because internal control activities designed to detect or prevent fraud are not reported to the inspector general.

**170. (d)**    The requirement is to identify the circumstance in which an auditor is required to report a falsification of accounting records directly to a federal inspector general. Answer (d) is correct because under Government Auditing Standards a falsification of accounting records must ordinarily be communicated by the auditor to the auditee and, if the auditee fails to make appropriate disclosure, by the auditor to a federal inspector general. Answers (a), (b), and (c) all provide inaccurate descriptions of auditor reporting responsibility. See Government Auditing Standards (the "yellow book") for information on reporting under Government Auditing Standards.

**171. (a)**    The requirement is to identify a common aspect of various types of audits of recipients of federal financial assistance in accordance with federal audit regulations. Answer (a) is correct because audits of recipients of federal financial assistance include reports on (1) the financial statements, and (2) a separate or combined report on internal control and on compliance with laws and regulations. Answer (b) is incorrect because materiality levels are not ordinarily lower or always determined by the governmental entity. Answer (c) is incorrect because the auditor need not obtain such written management representations. Answer (d) is incorrect because requirements for reporting illegal acts may vary depending upon the type of audit being performed. AU 801 provides requirements related to auditing entities that have received governmental financial assistance. In addition, guidance is provided by Government Auditing Standards (GAS), also referred to as the "yellow book," published by the Comptroller General of the United States.

**172. (b)**    The requirement is to identify to whom an auditor most likely would be responsible for communicating significant deficiencies in the design of internal control. Answer (b) is correct because in audits under Government Auditing Standards, significant deficiencies in the design of internal control are communicated to legislative and regulatory bodies (AU 801). Answer (a) is incorrect because the Securities and Exchange Commission does not ordinarily receive information on such deficiencies. Answer (c) is incorrect because while a court-appointed creditors' committee might in some circumstances receive information on such deficiencies, this practice is not as frequent as is done under Government Auditing Standards. Answer (d) is incorrect because shareholders do not normally receive reports on reportable conditions or material weaknesses (see AU 325).

**173. (c)**    The requirement is to determine the opinion which an auditor should express in a report on compliance when s/he has detected material instances of noncompliance within the program. AU 801 defines these instances of material noncompliance as failures to follow requirements, or violations of regulations or grants which cause the auditor to conclude that the total of the misstatements resulting from these failures or violations is material to the financial statements. Therefore, answer (c) is correct because the auditor should issue a qualified or an adverse opinion. Answer (a) is incorrect because the auditor is required under Governmental Auditing Standards to provide reasonable assurance on the entity's compliance with the applicable laws and regulations. Answer (b) is incorrect because the auditor must disclose the instances of noncompliance. Answer (d) is incorrect because the auditor should not disclaim an opinion as a result of noncompliance.

**174. (b)**    The requirement is to determine a way in which reporting on internal control under Government Auditing Standards differs from reporting under generally accepted auditing standards. Answer (b) is correct because AU 801 requires that audits under  include a written report identifying material weaknesses. AU 325 makes the identification of material weaknesses optional on other audits. Answer (a) is incorrect because neither type of report requires a description of procedures specially designed to prevent fraud, abuse, and illegal acts. Answer (c) is incorrect because neither report provides assurance on controls not tested which have an immaterial effect on the entity's financial statements. Answer (d) is incorrect because neither report provides positive assurance that controls designed to detect material errors and fraud were tested. See AU 801 for reporting on internal control under Government Auditing Standards.

**175. (b)**    The requirement is to determine a documentation requirement that an auditor should follow when auditing in accordance with  (also referred to as the "yellow book"). Answer (b) is correct because Government Auditing Standards requires that the auditor's working papers contain sufficient information so that supplementary oral explanations are **not** required.

**176. (a)**    The requirement is to identify the statement that should be included in an auditor's report on an entity's compliance with laws and regulations when performing an audit in accordance with Government Auditing Standards.

Answer (a) is correct because such compliance reports require a statement that management is responsible for compliance with laws, regulations, contracts, and grants. See AU 801 for this requirement and others.

**177.  (b)**  The requirement is to determine when an auditor reporting under  would most likely be required to communicate management's misappropriation of assets directly to a federal inspector general.  Answer (b) is correct because Government Auditing Standards requires that when a governing body fails to make a required report on such acts the auditors should communicate the matter to the external body specified in the law or regulation.  Answer (a) is incorrect because such concealment will not necessarily lead to communication to a federal inspector general.  Answer (c) is incorrect because material misstatement does not necessarily lead to such communication.  Answer (d) is incorrect because the expected duration of the scheme is not what leads to reporting to a federal inspector general.

**D.2.c.  Compliance Auditing of Federal Financial Assistance Programs—Single Audit Act**

**178.  (b)**  The requirement is to identify the auditor's proper measure of materiality for major federal financial assistance programs under the Single Audit Act.  AU 801 requires that it be determined separately for each major program.

**179.  (b)**  The requirement is to identify the appropriate compliance report under the Single Audit Act when a CPA has detected noncompliance with requirements that have a material effect on that program.  AU 801 states that under such circumstances the auditor should express a qualified or adverse opinion.

**180.  (c)**  The requirement is to identify the source of authoritative guidance for performing audits of a city that is subject to the requirements of the Uniform Single Audit Act of 1984.  Answer (c) is correct because while the AICPA's generally accepted auditing standards must be followed to the extent they are pertinent, the General Accounting Office Government Auditing Standards must also be adhered to.  The other replies all relate to standards not directly related to the Uniform Single Audit Act.

**181.  (c)**  The requirement is to identify the correct statement which would communicate weaknesses in internal control used in administering a federal financial assistance program when a CPA has examined the general purpose financial statements of a municipality.  The AICPA Accounting and Audit Guide, *Audits of State and Local Governmental Units*, requires the communication of weaknesses that are material in relation to the federal financial assistance program.

**SOLUTIONS TO SIMULATION PROBLEMS**

**Simulation Problem 1**

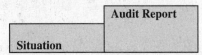

As we have suggested in Module 4, when preparing a report it is helpful to consider an approach of beginning with the standard short-form report and modifying it as appropriate for the circumstances presented. The following approach for preparing a report is likely to be helpful:

Step 1.   Determine whether the question requires an audit report on whether the financial statements follow GAAP.
Step 2.   Find the standard report and cut/paste it to your solution space.
Step 3.   Determine the circumstance(s) involved and the overall type of report to be issued.
Step 4.   Research the Professional Standards to identify appropriate report modifications for the circumstances(s) and overall type of report to be issued.
Step 5.   Cut/paste the appropriate modifications to the standard report, and complete report as necessary.

*Step 1:*   Yes, the type of report is an audit report on whether the financial statements follow GAAP.

*Step 2:*   You should recall that standard audit reports are presented early in AU 508—one for a one-year report and one for comparative statements. Since Tyler & Tyler is reporting upon comparative statements, the comparative form audit report will be appropriate. We paste that report from AU 508 as follows:

.08        The form of the auditor's standard report on comparative financial statements is as follows:

### Independent Auditor's Report

We have audited the accompanying balance sheets of X Company as of December 31, 20X2 and 20X1, and the related statements of income, retained earnings, and cash flows for the years then ended. These financial statements are the responsibility of the Company's management. Our responsibility is to express an opinion on these financial statements based on our audits.

We conducted our audits in accordance with auditing standards generally accepted in the United States of America. Those standards require that we plan and perform the audit to obtain reasonable assurance about whether the financial statements are free of material misstatement. An audit includes examining, on a test basis, evidence supporting the amounts and disclosures in the financial statements. An audit also includes assessing the accounting principles used and significant estimates made by management, as well as evaluating the overall financial statement presentation. We believe that our audits provide a reasonable basis for our opinion.

In our opinion, the financial statements referred to above present fairly, in all material respects, the financial position of X company as of [at] December 31, 20X2 and 20X1, and the results of its operations and its cash flows for the years then ended in conformity with accounting principles generally accepted in the United States of America

[Signature]

[Date]

*Step 3*:   Determining the circumstances involved requires a careful reading of the text of the simulation.

The simulation's first bullet describes a change in depreciation method. This will result in a consistency modification being added to the report. The overall modification is to simply add a paragraph on this following the opinion paragraph.

The second bullet describes an uncertainty that the senior wishes to emphasize. This is treated in the standards in the area of "emphasis of a matter." Again this paragraph will not affect the opinion paragraph. It may be placed either before or after the opinion paragraph.

*Step 4*:   We need to research the Professional Standards to find both a consistency modification and an emphasis of a matter modification. If you are unfamiliar with the reporting requirements in the area, you may also need to spend time determining the proper treatments. You may recall that AU 508 provides most audit report modifications and is ordinarily a good place to begin searching. Searching terms such as "lack of consistency" or "consistency explanatory paragraph" may help you find the following in AU 508.17:

.17        Following is an example of an appropriate explanatory paragraph:

As discussed in Note X to the financial statements, the Company changed its method of computing depreciation in 20X2.

Conveniently, the illustration is about depreciation, the circumstances included in this simulation. Make certain that when this is not the case to remember to modify it appropriately.

Searching for "emphasis of a matter" in that section provides the following:

**Emphasis of a Matter**

.19        In any report on financial statements, the auditor may emphasize a matter regarding the financial statements.

Such explanatory information should be presented in a separate paragraph of the auditor's report.  Phrases such as "with the foregoing [following] explanation" should not be used in the opinion paragraph if an emphasis paragraph is included in the auditor's report.   Emphasis paragraphs are never required; they may be added solely at the auditor's discretion.  Examples of matters the auditor may wish to emphasize are

- That the entity is a component of a larger business enterprise.
- That the entity has had significant transactions with related parties.
- Unusually important subsequent events.
- Accounting matters, other than those involving a change or changes in accounting principles, affecting the comparability of the financial statements with those of the preceding period.

Here there is no sample paragraph, although we do receive some guidance on phrases not to use ("With the foregoing [following] explanation").

In sum, we find that we have two explanatory paragraphs to be added to the report, with no modification of the opinion. The consistency modification must follow the opinion paragraph, while the emphasis of a matter paragraph may either precede or follow the opinion paragraph.

*Step 5*:    We now make the necessary modifications to the standard report:

### *Independent Auditor's Report*

**To the Board of Directors of Park Publishing Co.:**

We have audited the accompanying balance sheets of **Park Publishing Co.** X Company as of **September 30,** December 31, 20X2 and 20X1, and the related statements of income, retained earnings, and cash flows for the years then ended.  These financial statements are the responsibility of the Company's management.  Our responsibility is to express an opinion on these financial statements based on our audits.

We conducted our audits in accordance with auditing standards generally accepted in the United States of America.  Those standards require that we plan and perform the audit to obtain reasonable assurance about whether the financial statements are free of material misstatement.  An audit includes examining, on a test basis, evidence supporting the amounts and disclosures in the financial statements.  An audit also includes assessing the accounting principles used and significant estimates made by management, as well as evaluating the overall financial statement presentation.  We believe that our audits provide a reasonable basis for our opinion.

In our opinion, the financial statements referred to above present fairly, in all material respects, the financial position of **Park Publishing Co.** X Company as of [at] **September 30,** December 31, 20X2 and 20X1, and the results of its operations and its cash flows for the years then ended in conformity with accounting principles generally accepted in the United State of America.

**As discussed in Note 4 to the financial statements, the company is involved in a lawsuit over patent infringement, the outcome of which cannot presently be estimated.**

**As discussed in Note 7 to the financial statements, the Company changed its method of computing depreciation in 20X2.**

**Tyler & Tyler, CPAs** [Signature]
**October 25, 20X2** [Date]

Your solution need not highlight changes and should simply include the correct report.

---

## Simulation Problem 2

| Situation | Audit Report | Research | Communication |
|---|---|---|---|

| | | | | *Assets*<br>*(A-G)* | *Liabilities*<br>*(H-P)* |
|---|---|---|---|---|---|
| **1.** | Jones hired an actuary to assist in corroborating Welles' complex pension calculations concerning accrued pension liabilities that account for 35% of the client's total liabilities.  The actuary's findings are reasonably close to Welles' calculations and support the financial statements. | | | E | P |
| **2.** | Welles holds a note receivable consisting of principal and accrued interest payable in 20X4.  The note's maker recently filed a voluntary bankruptcy petition, but Welles failed to reduce the recorded value of the note to its net realizable value, which is approximately 20% of the recorded amount. | | | A | I |
| **3.** | Jones was engaged to audit a client's financial statements after the annual physical inventory count.  The accounting records were not sufficiently reliable to enable him to become satisfied as to the year-end inventory balances. | | | B | J |

|   |   | Assets *(A-G)* | Liabilities *(H-P)* |
|---|---|:---:|:---:|
| 4. | Jones found an immaterial adjustment relating to inventory. Welles has refused to adjust the financial statements to reflect this immaterial item. | **E** | **P** |
| 5. | Welles' financial statements do not disclose certain long-term lease obligations. Jones determined that the omitted disclosures are required by FASB. | **A** | **I** |
| 6. | Jones decided not to take responsibility for the work of another CPA who audited a wholly owned subsidiary of Welles. The total assets and revenues of the subsidiary represent 27% and 28%, respectively, of the related consolidated totals. | **E** | **O** |
| 7. | Welles changed its method of accounting for the cost of inventories from FIFO to LIFO. Jones concurs with the change although it has a material effect on the comparability of the financial statements. | **E** | **H** |
| 8. | Due to losses and adverse key financial ratios, Jones has substantial doubt about Welles' ability to continue as a going concern for a reasonable period of time. The client has adequately disclosed its financial difficulties in a note to its financial statements, which do **not** include any adjustments that might result from the outcome of this uncertainty. Also, Jones has ruled out the use of a disclaimer of opinion. | **E** | **H** |

## Explanation of solutions

1.    **(E,P)** When an auditor hires a specialist to assist in corroborating a client estimate (here complex pension calculations), and that specialist's findings are reasonably close to those of the client, no report modification is required or permitted. Since the specialist's findings support the financial statements in this situation, a standard unqualified audit report is appropriate. When major unresolved differences between the findings of management and the specialist exist, report modification is appropriate.

2.    **(A,I)** When the client's financial statements materially depart from generally accepted accounting principles, either a qualified opinion or an adverse opinion is appropriate, depending on the magnitude of the misstatement. The value of the client's note receivable has been impaired and therefore the client should write the note receivable down to its net realizable value. The auditor will have to determine whether to issue a qualified opinion or an adverse opinion on the basis of the materiality of the misstatement. Factors the auditor will consider include the significance of the account, the pervasiveness of the misstatement and the misstatement's effect on the financial statement taken as whole. The audit report, for either opinion, will include an explanatory paragraph to describe the substantive reasons for the modification, and the opinion paragraph will be modified.

3.    **(B,J)** A situation where the auditor is unable to obtain sufficient competent evidential matter is referred to as a scope limitation. A scope limitation may require the auditor to either qualify his or her opinion or to disclaim an opinion altogether. Since the auditor was unable to observe the inventory count or to obtain evidence through alternative procedures, the auditor will have to decide whether to issue a qualified opinion or a disclaimer of opinion. The decision will be based on the auditor's judgment as to the nature and magnitude of the potential effects of the matters in question and by their significance to the financial statements. A qualified opinion will describe the circumstances in an explanatory paragraph and will modify the scope and opinion paragraphs. A disclaimer of opinion will omit the scope paragraph and will include modification of the opinion paragraph.

4.    **(E,P)** An auditor need not modify a report for an immaterial item that the client declines to reflect.

5.    **(A,I)** Since the client's financial statements omitted required disclosures on certain long-term lease obligations, they are not prepared in accordance with generally accepted accounting principles. As a result, the auditor should express either a qualified opinion or an adverse opinion. The decision to express either a qualified or adverse opinion is based on the significance of the lack of disclosure, the pervasiveness of the misstatement, and the overall effect the lack of disclosure has on the financial statements. The audit report, for either opinion, will include an explanatory paragraph to describe the substantive reasons for the modification, and the opinion paragraph will be modified.

6.    **(E,O)** When a principal auditor decides not to take responsibility for the work of another auditor, the principal auditor should make reference to the work of the other auditor in the audit report. The audit report should clearly indicate the division of responsibility between the two auditors in the introductory, scope, and opinion paragraphs. Reference to the other auditor in the audit report does not prevent the principal auditor from issuing an unqualified opinion. The reference to the other auditor is designed to emphasize the divided responsibilities between the two auditors.

7.    **(E,H)** When an auditor agrees with a change in accounting principles, a lack of consistency results in an unqualified opinion with an explanatory paragraph following the opinion paragraph. There is no modification of the three standard paragraphs.

8.    **(E,H)** The auditor has substantial doubt about the client's ability to remain a going concern for a reasonable period of time. The audit report should emphasize this concern to the financial statement users. As a result, the auditor's report will include an unqualified opinion with an explanatory paragraph following the opinion paragraph.

| Situation | Audit Report | Research | | Communication |

The necessary information, presented in AU 315.09, is as follows:

The successor auditor should make specific and reasonable inquiries of the predecessor auditor regarding matters that will assist the successor auditor in determining whether to accept the engagement. Matters subject to inquiry should include

- Information that might bear on the integrity of management.
- Disagreements with management as to accounting principles, auditing procedures, or other similarly significant matters.
- Communications to audit committees or others with equivalent authority and responsibility regarding fraud, illegal acts by clients, and internal control related matters.
- The predecessor auditor's understanding as to the reasons for the change of auditors.

The successor auditor may wish to consider other reasonable inquiries.

| Situation | Audit Report | Research | Communication |

To:     CEO, Welles Inc.
From:   CPA Candidate

You have requested an explanation of the audit report modification for a change in accounting principle. This modification to our report is merely a one-sentence paragraph that emphasizes the fact that the company has changed accounting principles and gives our concurrence with the change. It in no way affects our unqualified opinion on your company's financial statements.

If you have any additional questions please contact us.

## AUDIT SAMPLING

Sampling is essential throughout audits as auditors attempt to gather sufficient competent evidence in a cost efficient manner.  The following "Diagram of an Audit" was originally presented in the auditing overview section.

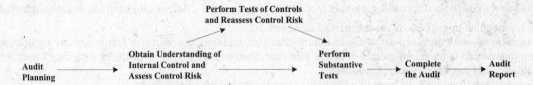

Audit sampling is used for both tests of controls (attributes sampling) and for tests of details of transactions and balances (usually, variables sampling).  In both attributes sampling and variables sampling, the plans may be either nonstatistical or statistical.  The chart at the bottom of this page summarizes methods of audit sampling.

Audit sampling has been tested on most recent auditing examinations, usually in the form of multiple-choice questions.  One might anticipate additional questions dealing with concepts such as sampling risk, non-sampling risk, tolerable misstatement, and the projection of sample results to an overall population.  Also, as in the past, one might expect exam questions dealing with the relationships between statistical concepts and basic audit concepts such as assessing control risk, materiality, and audit decision making.  One might expect a portion of a simulation to require candidates to calculate or interpret statistical results.

### Detailed Audit Sampling Techniques

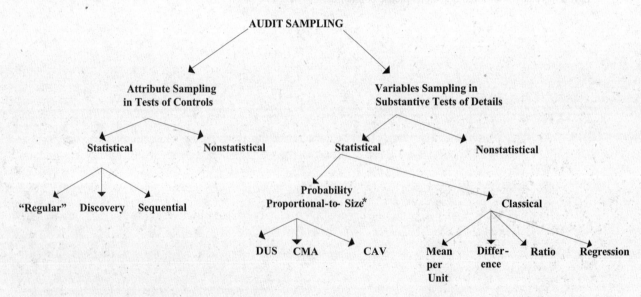

\* *Probability-proportional-to-size sampling may also be used for attributes sampling.  A number of variations of probability-proportional-to-size sampling exist, including dollar-unit sampling and monetary-unit sampling.*

## Study Program for Audit Sampling Module

This module is organized and should be studied in the following manner:

A.  Basic Audit Sampling Concepts

1.  Definition of Sampling
2.  General Approaches to Audit Sampling—Nonstatistical and Statistical
3.  Uncertainty and Audit Sampling
4.  Types of Audit Tests in Which Sampling May Be Used
5.  Types of Statistical Sampling Plans

B.  Sampling in Tests of Controls

1.  Sampling Risk
2.  Statistical Sampling for Tests of Controls

3. Nonstatistical Sampling for Tests of Controls

C. Sampling in Substantive Tests of Details

1. Sampling Risk
2. Probability-Proportional-to-Size (PPS) Sampling
3. Classical Variables Sampling
4. Comparison of PPS Sampling to Classical Variables Sampling

The material in this module is primarily structured around both AU 350 and the *Audit Sampling* guide. It is presented in outline form to allow an efficient review of the material. Additionally, SAS 107 on audit risk and materiality relates to this area.

**A. Basic Audit Sampling Concepts**

1. **Definition of Sampling**

   a. **Audit sampling** is the application of an audit procedure to less than 100% of the items within an account balance or class of transactions for the purpose of evaluating some characteristic of the balance or class (AU 350).

   b. The AICPA Audit and Accounting Guide, *Audit Sampling*, lists procedures that **do not** involve sampling as follows:

      (1) Inquiry and observation

         (a) Interview management and employees
         (b) Obtain an understanding of internal control
         (c) Obtain written representations from management
         (d) Scan accounting records for unusual items
         (e) Observe behavior of personnel and functioning of business operations
         (f) Observe cash-handling procedures
         (g) Inspect land and buildings

      (2) Analytical procedures
      (3) Procedures applied to every item in a population

         (a) For example, some audit plans include the audit of all "large" accounts and a portion of the small accounts. In such situations only the "small" accounts would be subject to sampling.

      (4) Tests of controls where application is not documented

         (a) Procedures that depend on segregation of duties or that otherwise provide no documentary evidence

      (5) Procedures from which the auditor does not intend to extend a conclusion to the remaining items in the account

         (a) For example, tracing several transactions through accounting system to obtain understanding

      (6) Untested balances

2. **General Approaches to Audit Sampling—Nonstatistical and Statistical**

   a. Both involve judgment in planning, executing the sampling plan, and evaluating the results of the sample
   b. Both can provide sufficient competent evidential matter
   c. Statistical sampling helps the auditor to

      (1) Design an efficient sample
      (2) Measure the sufficiency of the evidential matter obtained
      (3) Evaluate the sample results

(a) The auditor can objectively **quantify sampling risk** to limit it to a level considered acceptable. (This has been the proper reply to numerous multiple-choice questions on the advantages of sampling.)

d. Costs of statistical sampling

(1) Training auditors
(2) Designing samples
(3) Selecting items to be tested

3. **Uncertainty and Audit Sampling**—Eliminating all uncertainty, even if possible, would delay release of audited information and greatly increase audit cost

a. **Audit risk** is a combination of the risk that a material misstatement will occur and the risk that it will not be detected by the auditor. It consists of (1) the risk (inherent risk and control risk) that the balance or class and related assertions contain misstatements that could be material when aggregated with other misstatements, and (2) the risk (detection risk) that the auditor will not detect such misstatement. Recall our discussion of audit risk in the Engagement Planning Module (Section A.1.a.).

(1) **Audit risk** may be expressed using the following model:

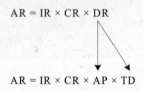

$$AR = IR \times CR \times DR$$

$$AR = IR \times CR \times AP \times TD$$

where:  
| | | |
|---|---|---|
| AR | = | Audit risk |
| IR | = | Inherent risk |
| CR | = | Control risk |
| DR | = | Detection risk |
| AP | = | Analytical procedures risk and other relevant substantive tests |
| TD | = | Test of details allowable risk of incorrect acceptance for this substantive test |

*NOTE: The second equation is presented in the Appendix to AU 350. This model separates detection risk into the two components of AP and TD.*

(2) **Nonsampling risk** includes all aspects of audit risk that are not due to sampling. It is controlled by adequate planning and supervision of audit work and proper adherence to quality control standards. The following are examples of nonsampling risk:

(a) The failure to select appropriate audit procedures
(b) The failure to recognize misstatements in documents examined
(c) Misinterpreting the results of audit tests

(3) **Sampling risk** is the risk that the auditor's conclusion, based on a sample, might be different from the conclusion that would be reached if the test were applied in the same way to the entire population (AU 350).

(a) Tests of controls sampling risks include the risk of assessing control risk too high and the risk of assessing control risk too low. These risks are discussed in section B.1. of this outline.

(b) Substantive test sampling risks include the risk of incorrect rejection and the risk of incorrect acceptance. These risks are discussed in section C.1. of this outline.

*NOTE: A number of exam multiple-choice questions have required candidates to identify the response that is an example of nonsampling risk. For example, illustrations of three of the above sampling risks may be presented with one of nonsampling risk. To identify nonsampling risk, think of it as the risk of "human" type errors (e.g., failure to detect a misstatement).*

4. **Types of Audit Tests in Which Sampling May Be Used**

a. **Tests of controls** are directed toward the design or operation of a control to assess its effectiveness in preventing or detecting material misstatements in a financial statement assertion.

    b.  **Substantive tests** are used to obtain evidence about the validity and propriety of the accounting treatment of transactions and balances.

    c.  **Dual-purpose tests** are those in which a single sample is used to test a control **and** to serve as a substantive test of a recorded balance or class of transactions. When a dual-purpose test is used, auditors select the sample size as the higher of that required for the two purposes. For example, if the test of control test required thirty-five items, and the substantive test required forty, both tests would be performed using the forty items.

5.  **Types of Statistical Sampling Plans**

    a.  **Attributes sampling** (used in tests of controls) reaches a conclusion in terms of a rate of occurrence—discussed in section B. below.

    b.  **Variables sampling** (used in substantive testing) reaches a conclusion in dollar amounts (or possibly in units).

        (1)  **Probability-proportional-to-size (PPS) sampling**—discussion in section C.2.

        (2)  **Classical variables sampling techniques**—discussed in section C.3.

Below is an outline organized around the audit guide's steps involved in attributes and variables sampling.

**AUDIT AND ACCOUNTING GUIDE SAMPLING STEPS**

| *Attributes Sampling (used in Tests of Controls)* | *Variables Sampling (used in Substantive Testing)* |
|---|---|
| 1.  **Determine** the objectives of the test | **Determine** the objectives of the test |
| 2.  **Define** the deviation conditions | **Define** the population<br>   a.  Define the sampling unit<br>   b.  Consider the completeness of the population<br>   c.  Identify individually significant items |
| 3.  **Define** the population<br>   a.  Define the period covered by the test<br>   b.  Define the sampling unit<br>   c.  Consider the completeness of the population | **Select** an audit sampling technique |
| 4.  **Determine** the method of selecting the sample<br>   a.  Random-number sampling<br>   b.  Systematic sampling<br>   c.  Other sampling | **Determine** the sample size<br>   a.  Consider the variation within the population<br>   b.  Consider the acceptable level of risk<br>   c.  Consider the tolerable misstatement<br>   d.  Consider the expected amount of misstatement<br>   e.  Consider the population size |
| 5.  **Determine** the sample size<br>   a.  Consider the acceptable risk of assessing control risk too low<br>   b.  Consider the tolerable rate<br>   c.  Consider the expected population deviation rate<br>   d.  Consider the effect of population size<br>   e.  Consider a sequential or a fixed sample-size approach | **Determine** the method of selecting the sample |

| *Attributes Sampling (used in Tests of Controls)* | *Variables Sampling (used in Substantive Testing)* |
|---|---|
| 6.  **Perform** the sampling plan | **Perform** the sampling plan |
| 7.  **Evaluate** the sample results<br>   a.  Calculate the deviation rate<br>   b.  Consider sampling risk<br>   c.  Consider the qualitative aspects of the deviations<br>   d.  Reach an overall conclusion | **Evaluate** the sample results<br>   a.  Project the misstatement to the population and consider sampling risk<br>   b.  Consider the qualitative aspects of the misstatements and reach an overall conclusion |
| 8.  **Document** the sampling procedure | **Document** the sampling procedure |

*NOTE: Be familiar with the preceding steps as the CPA exam questions have required candidates to list and explain them.*

**B. Sampling in Tests of Controls**

    1.  **Sampling Risk**

        a.  **Risk of assessing control risk too high (alpha risk, type I error)** is the risk that the assessed level of control risk based on the sample is **greater** than the true operating effectiveness of the control structure policy or procedure. Know that this risk relates to **audit efficiency**. If the auditor assesses control risk too high, substantive tests will consequently be expanded beyond the necessary level, leading to audit inefficiency.

        b.  **Risk of assessing control risk too low (beta risk, type II error)** is the risk that the assessed level of control risk based on the sample is **less** than the true operating effectiveness of the control structure policy or procedure. Know that this risk relates to **audit effectiveness**. If the auditor assesses control risk too low, substantive tests will not be expanded to the necessary level to ensure an effective audit. Because materially misstated financial statements may result from this situation, controlling this risk is generally considered of greater audit concern than controlling the risk of assessing control risk too high. The table below illustrates the two aspects of sampling risk for tests of controls.

| *The test of controls sample indicates:* | **TRUE OPERATING EFFECTIVENESS OF THE CONTROLS IS** | |
| --- | --- | --- |
| | *Adequate for planned assessed level of control risk* | *Inadequate for planned assessed level of control risk* |
| **Extent of operating effectiveness is adequate** | Correct Decision | Incorrect Decision (risk of assessing control risk too low) |
| **Extent of operating effectiveness is inadequate** | Incorrect Decision (risk of assessing control risk too high) | Correct Decision |

    2.  **Statistical (Attributes) Sampling for Tests of Controls**

        a.  **Steps involved in attributes sampling**

            (1)  **Determine the objectives of the test**—Remember that tests of controls are designed to provide reasonable assurance that internal control is operating effectively. For example, attributes sampling might test controls for voucher processing, billing systems, payroll systems, inventory pricing, fixed-asset additions, and depreciation computations.

               (a)  Attributes sampling is generally used when there is a trail of documentary evidence.

            (2)  **Define the deviation conditions**—An auditor should identify characteristics (attributes) that would indicate operation of the internal control procedures. The auditor next defines the possible deviation conditions. A deviation is a departure from the prescribed internal control policy or procedure.

> EXAMPLE: *If the prescribed procedure to be tested requires the cancellation of each paid voucher, a paid but uncanceled voucher would constitute a deviation.*

            (3)  **Define the population**—For tests of controls, the population is the class of transactions being tested. Conclusions based on sample results can be projected only to the population from which the sample was selected. Three steps are involved in defining the population.

               (a)  **Define the period covered by the test**—Ideally, tests of controls should be applied to transactions executed during the entire period under audit. In some cases it is more efficient to test transactions at an interim date and use supplemental procedures to obtain reasonable assurance regarding the remaining period.

               (b)  **Define the sampling unit**—The sampling unit is one of the individual elements constituting the population. In our earlier example, the sampling unit is the voucher.

(c) **Consider the completeness of the population**—The auditor actually selects sampling units from a physical representation of the population (in our example, the recorded paid vouchers). Because subsequent statistical conclusions relate to the physical representation, the auditor should consider whether it includes the entire population.

(4) **Determine the method of selecting the sample**—The sample should be representative of the population. All items in the population should have an opportunity to be selected. Methods include

(a) **Random-number sampling**—Every sampling unit has the same probability of being selected, and every combination of sampling units of equal size has the same probability of being selected. Random numbers can be generated using a random number table or a computer program.

(b) **Systematic sampling**—Every nth (population size/sample size) item is selected after a random start. When a random starting point is used, this method provides every sampling unit in the population an equal chance of being selected. If the population is arranged randomly, systematic selection is essentially the same as random number selection.

1] One problem with systematic sampling is that the population may be systematically ordered; for example, the identification number of all large items ends with a nine. A biased sample may result since nine's may be selected either too frequently **or** never. This limitation may be overcome by using multiple random starts or by using an interval that does not coincide with the pattern in the population.

2] An advantage of systematic sampling, as compared to random-number sampling, is that the population items do not have to be consecutively numbered for the auditor to use this method.

(c) **Haphazard sampling**—A sample consisting of units selected without any conscious bias, that is, without any special reason for including or omitting items from the sample. It does not consist of sampling units selected in a "careless" manner, but in a manner that the auditor hopes to be representative of the population. Haphazard sampling is not used for statistical sampling because it does not allow the auditor to measure the probability of selecting a given combination of sampling units.

(d) **Block sampling**—A sample consisting of contiguous units

> EXAMPLE: *An auditor selects three blocks of ten vouchers for examination.*

The advantage of block sampling is the ease of sample unit selection. The disadvantage is that the sample selected may not be representative of the overall population. Because of this disadvantage, use of this method is **generally the least desirable** method.

(5) **Determine the sample size**—A series of decisions must be made.

(a) **Allowable risk of assessing control risk too low.** Since the auditor uses the results of tests of controls as the source of evidence for assessing control risk at levels below the maximum, a low allowable risk is normally selected.

1] Risk levels between 1% and 10% are normally used.
2] There is an inverse relationship (e.g., as one increases the other decreases) between the risk of assessing control risk too low and sample size.

(b) **Tolerable rate (tolerable deviation rate)**—The maximum rate of deviation from a prescribed control structure policy or procedure that an auditor is willing to accept without modifying the planned assessed level of control risk.

1] The auditor's determination of the tolerable deviation rate is a function of

a] The planned assessed level of control risk, and
b] The degree of assurance desired by the sample.

2] When the auditor's planned assessed level of control risk is low, and the degree of assurance desired from the sample is high, the tolerable rate should be low.

a] This will be the case, for example, when the auditor does not perform other tests of controls for an assertion.

(c) **Expected population deviation rate (expected rate of occurrence)**—An estimate of the deviation rate in the entire population

1] If the expected population deviation rate exceeds the tolerable rate, tests (tests of controls/attributes sampling) will not be performed.

2] Although the risk of assessing control risk too high is often not explicitly controlled when determining attributes sample size, it can be controlled to some extent by specifying a conservative (larger) expected deviation rate.

3] There is a direct relationship (e.g., as one increases, the other also increases) between the expected deviation rate and sample size.

4] The expected population deviation rate is

a] Typically determined by using last year's deviation rate adjusted judgmentally for current year changes in the control procedure, or by determining the deviation rate in a small preliminary sample.

b] Used only to determine sample size and not to evaluate sample results, so the estimate need not be exact.

5] Because a deviation from a control procedure does not necessarily result in a misstatement (e.g., an unapproved invoice may still represent a valid business expenditure), the rate of misstatements is generally lower than the deviation rate.

(d) **Population effect**—Increases in the size of the population normally increase the sample size. However, it is generally appropriate to treat any population of more than 5,000 sample units as if it were infinite.

(e) When (a) through (d) above have been quantified, the sample size can be easily determined through the use of sample size tables. For the CPA exam **remember the following relationships**:

**ATTRIBUTES SAMPLING**
**SUMMARY OF RELATIONSHIPS TO SAMPLE SIZE**

| *Increases in* | *Effect on Sample Size* |
|---|---|
| Risk of assessing control risk too low | Decrease |
| Tolerable rate | Decrease |
| Expected population deviation rate | Increase |
| Population | Increase (slightly for large samples) |

(f) **Fixed vs. sequential sample size approach**—Audit samples may be designed using either a fixed or a sequential sample size approach. Supplementing traditional attributes (fixed size) sampling approaches are

1] **Sequential (stop-or-go) sampling**—a sampling plan for which the sample is selected in several steps, with the need to perform each step conditional on the results of the previous steps. That is, the results may either be so poor as to indicate that the control may not be relied upon, or so good as to justify reliance at each step.

2] **Discovery sampling**—a procedure for determining the sample size required to have a stipulated probability of observing at least one occurrence when the expected population deviation rate is at a designated level. It is most appropriate when the expected deviation rate is zero or near zero. If a deviation is detected, the auditor must either (1) use an alternate approach, or (2) if the deviation is of sufficient importance, audit all transactions.

(6) **Perform the sampling plan**—The auditor should apply the appropriate audit procedures to all items in the sample to determine if there are any deviations from the prescribed control procedures. Each deviation should be analyzed to determine whether it is an isolated or recurring type of occurrence.

(a) The auditor should select extra sample items (more than the needed sample size) so that voided, unused, or inapplicable documents can be excluded from the sample and be replaced.

(b) If the auditor is unable to examine a selected item (e.g., a document has been misplaced), it should be considered a deviation for evaluation purposes. Furthermore, the auditor should consider the reasons for this limitation and its implications for the audit.

(c) In some cases the auditor may find enough deviations early in the sampling process to indicate that a control cannot be relied upon. The auditor need not continue the tests in such circumstances.

(7) **Evaluate the sample results**—Once audit procedures have been performed on all sample items, the sample results must be evaluated and projected to the entire population from which the sample was selected.

(a) Calculate the sample deviation rate.

   1] Deviation rate $= \dfrac{\text{Number of observed deviations}}{\text{Sample size}}$

   2] The deviation rate is the auditor's best estimate of the true (but unknown) deviation rate in the population.

(b) For the risk of assessing control risk too low that is being used, determine the **upper deviation limit** (upper occurrence limit, achieved upper precision limit).

   1] The auditor uses the number of deviations noted, and the appropriate sampling table (not presented here) to calculate the upper deviation limit.

      a] This upper deviation limit represents the sample deviation rate plus an **allowance for sampling risk**.

(c) Compare the upper deviation limit to the tolerable rate specified in designing the sample.

   1] If the upper deviation limit is less than or equal to the tolerable rate, the sample results support reliance on the control procedure tested.

> EXAMPLE: *Assume that the auditor established the following criteria for an attributes sampling plan:*
>
> *Population size: over 5,000 units*
> *Allowable risk of assessing control risk too low: 5%*
> *Tolerable deviation rate: 6%*
> *Estimated population deviation rate: 2.5%*

By referencing the appropriate sample size table (not included here) the auditor determined that the required sample size was 150 units.

The auditor applied appropriate audit procedures to the 150 sample units and found eight deviations.

   a] The sample deviation rate $= 8/150 = 5.3\%$
   b] The upper deviation limit found from the table (not presented) for a 5% risk of assessing control risk too low and eight deviations $= 9.5\%$
   c] The allowance for sampling risk $= 9.5 - 5.3 = 4.2\%$
   d] The conclusions that can be drawn include

      i] There is a 5% chance of the true population deviation rate being greater than or equal to 9.5%.
      ii] Since the upper deviation limit (9.5%) exceeds the tolerable deviation rate (6%), the sample results indicate that control risk for the control procedure being tested is higher than planned, and, therefore, the scope of resulting substantive tests must be increased.

(d) In addition to the frequency of deviations found, the auditor should consider the qualitative aspects of each deviation.

   1] The nature and cause of each deviation should be analyzed. For example, are the deviations due to a misunderstanding of instructions or to carelessness?

          2] The possible relationship of the deviations to other phases of the audit should be considered. For example, the discovery of fraud ordinarily requires broader consideration than does the discovery of an error.

    (e) Reach an overall conclusion by applying audit judgment

        1] If all evidence obtained, including sample results, supports the auditor's planned assessed level of control risk, the auditor generally does not need to modify planned substantive tests.

        2] If the planned level is not supported, the auditor will

            a] Test other related controls, or

            b] Modify the related substantive tests to reflect increased control risk assessment.

    (8) **Document the sampling procedure.** Each of the prior seven steps, as well as the basis for overall conclusions, should be documented in the workpapers.

3. **Nonstatistical Sampling for Tests of Controls**—The steps involved in the design and implementation of a nonstatistical sampling plan are similar to statistical plans. Differences in determining sample size, sample selection, and evaluating sample results are discussed below.

  a. **Determine sample size**—As in statistical sampling, the major factors are the risk of assessing control risk too low, the tolerable rate, and the expected population deviation rate.

    (1) In nonstatistical sampling it is not necessary to quantify these factors.
    (2) The auditor should still consider the effects on sample size as described in section B.2.a.(5).

  b. **Sample selection**—Any of the sample selection methods discussed under statistical sampling (B.2.) may be used (i.e., random-numbers, systematic, haphazard, or, less desirably, block).

  c. **Evaluate sample results**—In nonstatistical sampling it is impossible to determine an upper deviation limit or to quantify sampling risk.

    (1) The auditor should relate the deviation rate in the sample to the tolerable rate established in the design stage to determine whether an adequate allowance for sampling risk has been provided to draw the conclusion that the sample provides an acceptably low level of risk.

      (a) **Rule of thumb**—If the deviation rate in a properly designed sample does not exceed the expected population deviation rate used in determining sample size, the auditor can generally "accept" the population and conclude that the control is operating effectively.

    (2) As in statistical sampling, the qualitative aspects of deviations should be considered in addition to the frequency of deviations.
    (3) Again the auditor must use his/her professional judgment to reach an overall conclusion as to the assessed level of control risk for the assertion(s) related to the internal control procedure tested.

C. **Sampling in Substantive Tests of Details**

1. **Sampling Risk**

  a. **Risk of incorrect rejection (alpha risk, type I error)** is the risk that the sample supports the conclusion that the recorded account balance is materially misstated when it is not materially misstated. Know that like the risk of assessing control risk too high, this risk relates to **audit efficiency**. If the sample results incorrectly indicate that an account balance is materially misstated, the performance of additional audit procedures will generally lead to the correct conclusion.

  b. **Risk of incorrect acceptance (beta risk, type II error)** is the risk that the sample supports the conclusion that the recorded account balance is not materially misstated when it is materially misstated. Know that like the risk of assessing control risk too low, this risk relates to **audit effectiveness**. If the sample results indicate that an account balance is not misstated, when it is misstated, the auditor will not perform additional procedures and the financial statements may include such misstatements.

c. Although the two risks are mutually exclusive (the auditor cannot incorrectly decide to reject an account balance at the same time s/he incorrectly decides to accept an account balance), both risks may be considered in the sample design stage. The following table illustrates both aspects of sampling risk for substantive tests.

|  | THE POPULATION ACTUALLY IS | |
| --- | --- | --- |
| *The Substantive Test Sample Indicates* | *Not Materially Misstated* | *Materially Misstated* |
| **The population is not materially misstated** | Correct Decision | Incorrect Decision (risk of incorrect acceptance) |
| **The population is materially misstated** | Incorrect Decision (risk of incorrect rejection) | Correct Decision |

*The following portions of this outline summarize the steps involved in substantive testing (section C.1.d.), probability-proportional-to-size sampling (section C.2.), and classical variables sampling (section C.3.). Finally, PPS and classical variables sampling are compared (section C.4.).*

d. **Steps involved in variables sampling**

   (1) **Determine the objectives of the test**—Remember that variables sampling is used primarily for substantive testing and that its conclusion is generally stated in dollar terms (although conclusions in terms of units [e.g., inventory] are possible). Variables sampling might test, for example, the recorded amount of accounts receivable, inventory quantities and amounts, payroll expense, and fixed asset additions.

   (2) **Define the population**—The population consists of the items constituting the account balance or class of transactions of interest. Three areas need be considered.

      (a) **Sampling unit**—The sampling unit is any of the individual elements that constitute the population.

         EXAMPLE: *If the population to be tested is defined as total accounts receivable, the sampling unit used to confirm the balance of accounts receivable could be each individual account receivable.*

      (b) **Consider the completeness of the population**—Since sampling units are selected from a physical representation (e.g., a trial balance of receivables), the auditor should consider whether the physical representation includes the entire population.

      (c) **Identify individually significant items**—Items that are individually significant for which sampling risk is not justified should be tested separately and not be subjected to sampling. These are items in which potential misstatements could individually equal or exceed tolerable misstatement.

   (3) **Select an audit sampling technique**—Either nonstatistical or statistical sampling may be used. If statistical sampling is used, either probability-proportional-to-size sampling (PPS) or classical variables techniques are appropriate.

   (4) **Determine the sample size**—Five items need to be considered.

      (a) **Variation within the population**—Increases in variation (standard deviation in classical sampling) result in increases in sample size.

      (b) **Acceptable level of risk**—The risk of incorrect acceptance is related to audit risk (see SAS 107 outline and Engagement Planning Module Section A.2.). The auditor may also control the risk of incorrect rejection so as to allow an efficiently performed audit. Increases in these risks result in decreases in sample size.

         NOTE: *The risk of incorrect rejection is **not** typically controlled when using PPS sampling, but is controlled when using classical methods.*

      (c) **Tolerable misstatement (error)**—An estimate of the maximum monetary misstatement that may exist in an account balance or class of transactions, when combined with misstatements in other accounts, without causing the financial statements to be materially misstated. As tolerable misstatement increases, sample size decreases.

      (d) **Expected amount of misstatement (error)**—Expected misstatement is estimated using an understanding of the business, prior year information, a pilot sample, and/or the results of the review and evaluation of internal control. As expected misstatement increases, a larger sample size is required.

(e) **Population size**—Sample size increases as population size increases. The effect is more significant in classical variables sampling than PPS sampling.

**VARIABLES SAMPLING**
**SUMMARY OF RELATIONSHIPS TO SAMPLE SIZE**

| *Increases in* | *Effect on sampling size* |
|---|---|
| Risk—Incorrect Acceptance | Decrease |
| Risk—Incorrect Rejection | Decrease |
| Tolerable Misstatement (Error) | Decrease |
| Expected Misstatement (Error) | Increase |
| Population | Increase |
| Variation (standard deviation) | Increase |

*NOTE: Memorize the above relationships. As an aid remember that, in both variables sampling and attributes sampling, increases in risk and in the "tolerables" (tolerable misstatement and tolerable rate) lead to decreases in sample size. For the risks especially, this result is intuitively appealing in that when one expects more risk in many contexts when one does less work. Increases in the other factors increase sample size.*

(5) **Determine the method of selecting the sample**—Generally random number or systematic sampling.

(6) **Perform the sampling plan**—Perform appropriate audit procedures to determine an audit value for each sample item.

(7) **Evaluate the sample results**—The auditor should project the results of the sample to the population. The total projected misstatement, after any adjustments made by the entity, should be compared with the tolerable misstatement and the auditor should consider whether the risk of misstatement in excess of the tolerable amount is at an acceptably low level. Also, qualitative factors (such as the nature of the misstatements and their relationship to other phases of the audit) should be considered. For example, when fraud has been discovered, a simple projection of them will not in general be sufficient as the auditor will need to obtain a thorough understanding of them and of their likely effects.

(8) **Document the sampling procedure**—Each of the prior seven steps, as well as the basis for overall conclusions, should be documented.

e. **Comments on nonstatistical sampling**—Both statistical and nonstatistical sampling require judgment. The major differences between statistical and nonstatistical sampling in substantive testing are in the steps for determining sample size and evaluating sample results.

(1) **Determination of sample size**—Be aware of the relationships summarized in section C.1.d.(4)(e). Also, know that the statistical tables **may** be used to assist in the determination of sample size.

(2) **Evaluation of sample results**—The auditor should project misstatements found in the sample to the population and consider sampling risk.

(a) Projecting misstatements can be accomplished by

    1] Dividing the total dollar amount of misstatement in the sample by the fraction of total dollars from the population included in the sample, or

    2] Multiplying the average difference between audit and book values for sample items times the number of units in the population.

(b) If tolerable misstatement exceeds projected misstatement by a large amount, the auditor may be reasonably sure that an acceptably low level of sampling risk exists. Sampling risk increases as projected misstatement approaches tolerable error.

(c) When sampling results do not support the book value, the auditor can

    1] Examine additional sampling units,
    2] Apply alternative auditing procedures, or
    3] Ask the client to investigate and, if appropriate, make necessary adjustments.

(d) Qualitative aspects of misstatements need to be considered as well as frequency and amounts of misstatements.

2. **Probability-Proportional-to-Size (PPS) Sampling [dollar-unit, cumulative monetary amount (CMA) sampling]**

   a.  Uses attributes sampling theory to express a conclusion in dollar amounts. PPS sampling has gained popularity in practice because it is easier to apply than classical variables sampling.

   b.  Steps in PPS sampling

     (1)  **Determine the objectives of the test**—PPS tests the reasonableness of a recorded account balance or class of transactions. PPS is primarily applicable in testing account balances and transactions for **overstatements**.

     (2)  **Define the population**—The population is the account balance or class of transactions being tested.

        (a)  **Define the sampling unit**—The sampling units in PPS are the individual dollars in the population. The auditor ordinarily examines each individual account or transaction (called a **logical unit**) that includes a sampled dollar.

        (b)  **Consider the completeness of the population**—As with other sampling plans, the auditor must assure him/herself that the physical representation of the population being tested includes the entire population.

        (c)  **Identify individually significant items**—PPS automatically includes in the sample any unit that is individually significant.

     (3)  **Select an audit sampling technique**—Here we have selected PPS.

     (4)  **Determine the sample size**—A PPS sample divides the population into sampling intervals and selects a logical unit from each sampling interval.

        (a)  Sample size $= \dfrac{\text{Book value of population x Reliability factor}}{\text{Tolerable error} - (\text{Expected error x Expansion factor})}$

$$\text{Sampling interval} = \dfrac{\text{Book value of population}}{\text{Sample size}}$$

Expansion Factors (from the *Audit Sampling* guide) for expected misstatements

| | \multicolumn{9}{c}{*Risk of Incorrect Acceptance*} |
|---|---|---|---|---|---|---|---|---|---|
| | 1% | 5% | 10% | 15% | 20% | 25% | 30% | 37% | 50% |
| Factor | 1.9 | 1.6 | 1.5 | 1.4 | 1.3 | 1.25 | 1.2 | 1.15 | 1.0 |

Reliability Factors (from the *Audit Sampling* guide) for misstatements of overstatement. (Use 0 errors for determining Reliability Factor.)

| Number of Overstatements | \multicolumn{9}{c}{*Risk of Incorrect Acceptance*} |
|---|---|---|---|---|---|---|---|---|---|
| | 1% | 5% | 10% | 15% | 20% | 25% | 30% | 37% | 50% |
| 0 | 4.61 | 3.00 | 2.31 | 1.90 | 1.61 | 1.39 | 1.21 | 1.00 | .70 |
| 1 | 6.64 | 4.75 | 3.89 | 3.38 | 3.00 | 2.70 | 2.44 | 2.14 | 1.68 |
| 2 | 8.41 | 6.30 | 5.33 | 4.72 | 4.28 | 3.93 | 3.62 | 3.25 | 2.68 |
| 3 | 10.05 | 7.76 | 6.69 | 6.02 | 5.52 | 5.11 | 4.77 | 4.34 | 3.68 |

        (b)  Observations

           1]  The size of the **sampling interval** is related to the risk of incorrect acceptance and tolerable misstatement. The auditor controls the risk of incorrect rejection by making an allowance for expected misstatements. The auditor specifies a planned allowance for sampling risk so that the estimate of projected misstatement plus the allowance for sampling risk will be less than or equal to tolerable misstatement.

           2]  If no misstatements are expected, the sampling interval is determined by dividing tolerable misstatement by a factor that corresponds to the risk of incorrect acceptance (i.e., the reliability factor).

           3]  A reliability factor table such as the one above has been included with CPA exam questions.

     (5)  **Determine the method of selecting the sample**—PPS samples are generally selected using **systematic sampling** with a random start. All logical units (e.g., accounts) with dollar amounts greater than or equal to the sampling interval are certain to be selected.

(6) **Perform the sampling plan**—The auditor must apply appropriate audit procedures to determine an audit value for each logical unit included in the sample.

(7) **Evaluate the sample results**—Misstatements found should be projected to the population and an allowance for sampling risk should be calculated. When the sample contains misstatements, the **upper limit on misstatements** is the total of projected misstatement and the allowance for sampling risk (with its two subcomponents).

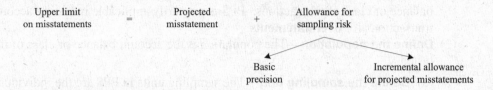

**Projected misstatement** is calculated for each logical unit containing misstatements and totaled. The approach differs based on whether the book value of the specific logical unit is less than or greater than the size of the sampling interval.

*Logical unit less than sampling interval*—Multiply the percentage the account is misstated (misstatement/book value, referred to as the "taint") times the sampling interval. For example, an account with a book value of $100 has an audited value of $95, and a sampling interval of $3,000. The tainting percentage of 5% ($5 misstatement/$100) is multiplied times the $3,000 sampling interval, or

$$\$5/\$100 \times \$3,000 = \$150 \text{ projected misstatement.}$$

*Logical unit greater than sampling interval*—The actual amount of misstatement is considered to be the projected misstatement. For example, consider an account with a book value of $4,000, an audited value of $40, and a sampling interval of $3,000; the projected misstatement is $3,960 ($4,000 – $40). Similarly, if the audited value is $3,300, the projected misstatement is $700 ($4,000 – $3,300).

*NOTE: Questions have required candidates to calculate a projected misstatement for one or more accounts. If more than one account is involved, the various projected misstatements are simply totaled.*

*For completeness' sake we also present computations of basic precision and the incremental allowance for projected misstatements. That information has not been heavily examined to this point.*

**Basic precision** is found by multiplying the reliability factor [see section C.2.b.(4)] times the sampling interval.

**Incremental allowance for projected misstatements** is determined by ranking the misstatements for logical units that are less than the sampling interval from highest to lowest and considering the incremental changes in reliability factors for the actual number of misstatements found. The table of Reliability Factors presented earlier [section C.2.b.(4)] presents values for zero through three misstatements. The *Audit Sampling* guide presents additional values for situations in which more misstatements are detected. One must subtract 1.00 from each incremental change to isolate the incremental allowance for projected misstatements.

(a) **Decision rule:** Compare the upper limit on misstatements to tolerable misstatement

    1] If the upper limit on misstatements is less than or equal to tolerable misstatement, the sample results support the conclusion that the population is not misstated by more than tolerable misstatement at the specified risk of incorrect acceptance.

    2] If the upper limit on misstatements is greater than the tolerable misstatement, the sample results do not support the conclusion that the population is not misstated by more than the tolerable misstatement. This may be due to the fact that (a) the population is misstated, (b) the auditor's expectation of misstatement was low and resulted in too small of a sample, or (c) the sample is not representative of the population.

    3] The auditor should consider qualitative aspects of errors found as well as quantitative factors.

(b) **Observation:** If no misstatements are found, projected misstatement and the incremental allowance for projected misstatements will equal zero, leaving the basic precision as the only nonzero component of the upper limit on misstatements.  No further calculations are needed since the tolerable misstatement will be greater than this amount.

(8) **Document the sampling procedure**—Each of the prior seven steps, as well as the basis for overall conclusions, should be documented.

The following example illustrates the probability-proportional-to-size method:

### Probability-Proportional-to-Size Sampling Example

Step 1.   Objective of test—determine reasonableness of accounts receivable
Step 2.   Define population—individual dollars in account
Step 3.   Select sampling technique—probability-proportional-to-size
Step 4.   Determine sample size

Given:

| | |
|---|---|
| Tolerable misstatement (TM) | $50,000 |
| Risk of incorrect acceptance | .05 |
| Expected misstatement (EM) | $10,000 |

$$\text{Calculation sample size} = \frac{\text{Book value of population} \times \text{Reliability factor}}{\text{Total misstatement} - (\text{Expected misstatement} \times \text{Expansion factor})}$$

$$= \frac{\$1,000,000 \times 3}{\$50,000\,(10,000 \times 1.6)} \approx 88$$

$$\text{Sampling interval} = \frac{\text{Book value of population}}{\text{Sample size}}$$

$$= \frac{\$1,000,000}{88} \approx \$11,333.33$$

Step 5.   Determine method of selecting sample—systematic
Step 6.   Perform sampling plan
Step 7.   Evaluate and project results

Projected misstatement—Assume 3 misstatements

| *Book value* | *Audited value* | *Misstatement* | *Taint %* | *Sampling interval* | *Projected misstatement* |
|---|---|---|---|---|---|
| $   100 | $ 95.00 | $   5.00 | 5% | $11,333 | $   567 |
| 11,700 | 212.00 | 11,488.00 | --* | NA | 11,488 |
| 65 | 58.50 | 6.50 | 10% | 11,333 | 1,133 |
| | | | | Projected misstatement | $13,188 |

\* *Not applicable; book value larger than sampling interval.*

*NOTE:  Make certain that you understand details of the projected misstatement computation as it has been required on various CPA examination questions.*

| Basic precision | = | Reliability factor | × | Sampling interval |
|---|---|---|---|---|
| | = | 3.0 | × | $11,333.33 |
| | = | $34,000.00 | | |

Incremental allowance for projected misstatements

| *Reliability factor* | *Increment* | *(Increm - 1)* | *Projected misstatements* | *Incremental allowance* |
|---|---|---|---|---|
| 3.00 | -- | -- | -- | -- |
| 4.75 | 1.75 | .75 | $1,133 | $  850 |
| 6.30 | 1.55 | .55 | 567 | 312 |
| | Incremental allowance for projected misstatements | | | $1,162 |

| Upper limit on misstatements | = | Projected misstatement | + | Basic precision | + | Incremental allowance for projected misstatements |
|---|---|---|---|---|---|---|
| | = | $13,188 | + | $34,000 | + | $1,162 |
| | = | $48,350   (Accept, this is less than tolerable misstatement) | | | | |

3. **Classical Variables Sampling**

   a. **Classical variables sampling models** use normal distribution theory to evaluate selected characteristics of a population on the basis of a sample of the items constituting the population.

      (1) For any normal distribution, the following fixed relationships exist concerning the area under the curve and the distance from the mean in standard deviations. This table assumes a two-tailed approach that is appropriate since classical variables sampling models generally test for both overstatement and understatement.

| Distance in Stan. Dev.<br>(Reliability coefficient) | Area under the Curve<br>(Reliability level) |
|---|---|
| ± 1.0 | 68% |
| 1.64 | 90% |
| 1.96 | 95% |
| 2.0 | 95.5% |
| 2.7 | 99% |

*  Most frequently tested on CPA exam

   Example where the mean = 250 and the standard deviation = 10:

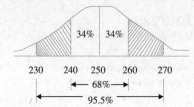

      (2) For large samples (greater than or equal to thirty) the distribution of sample means tends to be normally distributed about its own mean which is equal to the true population mean, even if the population is not normally distributed (Central Limit Theorem). Since many populations sampled in auditing are not normally distributed, this is important.

      (3) **The standard deviation** in the above model measures the dispersion among the respective amounts of a particular characteristic, for all items in the population for which a sample estimate is developed.

   b. **Variations of classical variables sampling**

      (1) **Mean-per-unit estimation** is a classical variables sampling technique that projects the sample average to the total population by multiplying the sample average by the number of items in the population.

         (a) Determine audit values for each sample item
         (b) Calculate the average audit amount
         (c) Multiply this average audit amount times the number of units in the population to obtain the estimated population value

      (2) **Difference estimation** is a classical variables sampling technique that uses the average difference between audited amounts and individual recorded amounts to estimate the total audited amount of a population and an allowance for sampling risk.

         (a) Determine audit values for each sample item
         (b) Calculate the difference between the audit value and book value for each sample item
         (c) Calculate the average difference
         (d) Determine the estimated population value by multiplying the average difference by the total population units and adding or subtracting this value from the recorded book value

      (3) **Ratio estimation** is a classical variables sampling technique that uses the ratio of audited amounts to recorded amounts in the sample to estimate the total dollar amount of the population and an allowance for sampling risk.

         (a) Determine audit values for each sample item
         (b) Calculate the ratio between the sum of sample audit values and sample book values

(c) Determine the estimated population value by multiplying the total population book value times this ratio

(4) **The regression approach** is similar to the difference and ratio approaches. This approach has the effect of using both the average ratio and the average difference in calculating an estimate of the total amount for the population.

(5) **Difference and ratio estimation** are used as alternatives to mean-per-unit estimation. The auditor should use these approaches when applicable because they require a smaller sample size (i.e., they are more efficient than mean-per-unit estimation).

   (a) One factor in the calculation of sample size for classical variables sampling models is the estimated standard deviation. If the standard deviation of differences or ratios is smaller than the standard deviation of audit values, these two methods will produce a smaller sample size.

   1] Difference estimation will be used if the differences between sample audit values and book values are a relatively constant dollar amount, regardless of account size.
   2] Ratio estimation will be used if the differences are a constant percentage of book values.

   (b) In order to use either difference or ratio estimation, the following constraints must be met:

   1] The individual book values must be known and must sum to the total book value.
   2] There must be more than a few differences (twenty is often suggested as a minimum) between audit and book values.

   (c) These two methods will usually be more efficient than mean-per-unit estimation when stratification of the population is not possible.

(6) **Stratification** separates a population into relatively homogeneous groups to reduce the sample size by minimizing the effect of variation of items (i.e., the standard deviation) in the population.

   (a) Although stratification may be applied with any of the classical methods, it is most frequently used with the mean-per-unit estimation method.
   (b) Know that the primary objective of stratification is to decrease the effect of variance in the total population and thereby reduce sample size.

c. **Variables sampling steps applied to classical variables sampling**

(1) **Determine the objectives of the test**—Recall that variables sampling models are designed to draw conclusions in dollar amounts.
(2) **Define the population**—The population consists of the items constituting the account balance or class of transactions.

   (a) **Sampling unit**—As with PPS sampling, the sampling unit is any of the individual elements that constitute the population. For example, the sampling unit in receivables is often an individual customer's account.
   (b) **Consider the completeness of the population**—As discussed in PPS, the auditor must consider whether the physical representation includes the entire population.
   (c) **Identify individually significant items**—Items which are individually significant for which sampling risk is not justified, should be tested separately and not be subject to sampling. These are items for which potential error could individually equal or exceed tolerable misstatement. Note that in PPS these items were automatically selected.

(3) **Select an audit sampling technique**—Here we would select among mean-per-unit, difference, ratio, and regression estimation.
(4) **Determine the sample size**—The following factors are included in the sample size calculation:

   (a) **The population size** is directly related to sample size.

(b) **Estimated standard deviation**—An estimate must be made of the dispersion of audit values for the units constituting the population.  This value can be estimated by

    1]  Calculating the standard deviation of recorded amounts,
    2]  Auditing a small pilot sample, or
    3]  Using the standard deviation found in the previous audit.

(c) **Tolerable misstatement**—An estimate of the maximum monetary misstatement that may exist in an account balance or class of transactions, when combined with error in other accounts, without causing the financial statements to be materially misstated.

(d) **Risk of incorrect rejection (alpha risk)**—Since the risk of incorrect rejection is inversely related to sample size, the auditor must weigh the costs of a larger sample size against the potential additional costs associated with expanded audit procedures following the initial rejection resulting from a sample size that was too small.

(e) **Risk of incorrect acceptance (beta risk)**—In specifying an acceptable level of risk of incorrect acceptance, the auditor considers the level of audit risk that s/he is willing to accept.  Recall this discussion in section A.1.a. of the Engagement Planning Module.

(f) **Planned allowance for sampling risk (desired precision)**—The allowance is a function of the auditor's estimates of tolerable misstatement, risk of incorrect rejection, and risk of incorrect acceptance.  The risk of incorrect acceptance is not explicitly included in the sample size equation, but the allowance for sampling risk controls the level of risk the auditor is assuming.

    Various approaches are used to calculate the planned allowance for sampling risk.  Since these approaches are not frequently examined, we will not present them.  Depending upon the risk assumed (incorrect acceptance and rejection) the planned allowance for sampling risk is either equal to or less than the tolerable misstatement.  For example, when a 5% and 10% risk of incorrect acceptance and rejection respectively are established, the planned allowance for sampling risk is established at 1/2 the amount of the tolerable misstatement.

(g) **Sample size equation**

$$ n \quad = \quad \left( \frac{N \times SD \times U_R}{A} \right)^2 $$

| | | |
|---|---|---|
| n | = | Sample size |
| N | = | Population size |
| SD | = | Estimated population standard deviation |
| $U_R$ | = | The standard normal deviate for the acceptable risk of incorrect rejection |
| A | = | Planned allowance for sampling risk |

(h) The above formula assumes sampling with replacement and may be adjusted by a finite correction factor (thereby reducing sample size) when sampling without replacement.

$$ n' = \frac{n}{1 + n/N} \qquad n' = \text{Sample size adjusted for finite correction factor} $$

(5) **Determine the method of selecting the sample**—Classical samples are generally selected using random sampling or stratified random sampling.

(6) **Perform the sampling plan**—Perform appropriate audit procedures to determine an audit value for each item

(a) If the auditor is unable to examine selected items (i.e., accounts receivable confirmations are not returned), s/he should perform alternative procedures that provide sufficient evidence to form a conclusion.

(7) **Evaluate and project the sample results**—As was the case with sample selection, the actual evaluation and projection of sample results is affected by the method used.  Additionally, the various auditing textbooks do not agree on the approach for evaluating sample results.  We provide a summarized approach. Assume a population of 10,000 accounts with a book value of $1,000,000; this represents an average book value of $100 ($1,000,000 / 10,000 accounts).  Further, assume that a sample has been selected and the following results obtained:

Average book value of items in sample        $101
Average audited value of items in sample     $ 98

**Projected misstatement and estimated total audited value (ETAV).**   As was the case with PPS sampling a projected misstatement may be calculated.

### Mean-Per-Unit Method

ETAV = Population size × Average audited value

= 10,000 × $98 = $980,000

**Projected misstatement** = $1,000,000 – $980,000 = $20,000 overstatement

### Difference Estimation Method

Average difference (in sample):  Average BV – Average AV.

$101 – $98 = $3

**Projected misstatement:**  10,000 accounts × $3 = $30,000 overstatement

**ETAV** = $1,000,000 – $30,000 = $970,000

### Ratio Estimation Method

ETAV = (Sample Avg. AV/Sample Avg. BV) × Population BV

= ($98 / $101) × $1,000,000 = $970,297

**Projected Misstatement** = $1,000,000 – $970,297 = $29,703 overstatement

*NOTE:  The difference and ratio estimation methods use the book value of the sample items in the analysis, while the mean-per-unit method **does not**.*

**Considering sampling risk.**  When statistical sampling is used, the auditors utilize statistical formulas to determine whether the account balance should be accepted.  In essence, these formulas help the auditor to determine whether the projected misstatement may reveal a materially misstated account.  One approach is to construct an adjusted allowance for sampling risk (plus or minus) around the estimated audited population value.  (The CPA exam does not generally require such a computation.)

If the book value falls within this interval, the auditors will accept that the population is materially correct.  If not, the auditors will conclude that there is an unacceptably high risk that the inventory account is materially misstated.  When a conclusion is reached that an account is materially misstated, the auditors may decide to (1) increase the sample size of the test, (2) perform other audit tests of the account, or (3) work with the client's personnel to locate other misstated items in the account.

4.  **Comparison of PPS Sampling to Classical Variables Sampling**

   a.  Advantages of PPS sampling

   (1)  Generally easier to use
   (2)  Size of sample not based on variation of audited amounts
   (3)  Automatically results in a stratified sample
   (4)  Individually significant items are automatically identified
   (5)  Usually results in a smaller sample size if no misstatements are expected
   (6)  Can be easily designed and sample selection can begin before the complete population is available

   b.  Advantages of classical variables sampling

   (1)  May result in a smaller sample size if there are many differences between audited and book values
   (2)  Easier to expand sample size if that becomes necessary
   (3)  Selection of zero balances does not require special sample design considerations
   (4)  Inclusion of negative balances does not require special sample design considerations

**MULTIPLE-CHOICE QUESTIONS (1-58)**

**1.** An advantage of using statistical over nonstatistical sampling methods in tests of controls is that the statistical methods
- a. Can more easily convert the sample into a dual-purpose test useful for substantive testing.
- b. Eliminate the need to use judgment in determining appropriate sample sizes.
- c. Afford greater assurance than a nonstatistical sample of equal size.
- d. Provide an objective basis for quantitatively evaluating sample risk.

**2.** An advantage of statistical sampling over nonstatistical sampling is that statistical sampling helps an auditor to
- a. Eliminate the risk of nonsampling errors.
- b. Reduce the level of audit risk and materiality to a relatively low amount.
- c. Measure the sufficiency of the evidential matter obtained.
- d. Minimize the failure to detect errors and fraud.

**3.** The likelihood of assessing control risk too high is the risk that the sample selected to test controls
- a. Does **not** support the auditor's planned assessed level of control risk when the true operating effectiveness of the control structure justifies such an assessment.
- b. Contains misstatements that could be material to the financial statements when aggregated with misstatements in other account balances or transactions classes.
- c. Contains proportionately fewer monetary errors or deviations from prescribed controls than exist in the balance or class as a whole.
- d. Does **not** support the tolerable error for some or all of management's assertions.

**4.** The risk of incorrect acceptance and the likelihood of assessing control risk too low relate to the
- a. Allowable risk of tolerable misstatement.
- b. Preliminary estimates of materiality levels.
- c. Efficiency of the audit.
- d. Effectiveness of the audit.

**5.** Which of the following best illustrates the concept of sampling risk?
- a. A randomly chosen sample may **not** be representative of the population as a whole on the characteristic of interest.
- b. An auditor may select audit procedures that are **not** appropriate to achieve the specific objective.
- c. An auditor may fail to recognize errors in the documents examined for the chosen sample.
- d. The documents related to the chosen sample may **not** be available for inspection.

**6.** In assessing sampling risk, the risk of incorrect rejection and the risk of assessing control risk too high relate to the
- a. Efficiency of the audit.
- b. Effectiveness of the audit.
- c. Selection of the sample.
- d. Audit quality controls.

**Items 7 and 8** are based on the following information:

The diagram below depicts the auditor's estimated deviation rate compared with the tolerable rate, and also depicts the true population deviation rate compared with the tolerable rate.

|  | *True State of Population* | |
|---|---|---|
|  | **Deviation rate exceeds tolerable rate** | **Deviation rate is less than tolerable rate** |
| *Auditor's estimate based on* *sample results* **Deviation rate exceeds tolerable rate** | I. | II. |
| **Deviation rate is less than tolerable rate** | III. | IV. |

**7.** In which of the situations would the auditor have properly concluded that control risk is at or below the planned assessed level?
- a. I.
- b. II.
- c. III.
- d. IV.

**8.** As a result of tests of controls, the auditor assesses control risk too high and thereby increases substantive testing. This is illustrated by situation
- a. I.
- b. II.
- c. III.
- d. IV.

**9.** While performing a test of details during an audit, an auditor determined that the sample results supported the conclusion that the recorded account balance was materially misstated. It was, in fact, not materially misstated. This situation illustrates the risk of
- a. Assessing control risk too high.
- b. Assessing control risk too low.
- c. Incorrect rejection.
- d. Incorrect acceptance.

**10.** The size of a sample designed for dual purpose testing should be
- a. The larger of the samples that would otherwise have been designed for the two separate purposes.
- b. The smaller of the samples that would otherwise have been designed for the two separate purposes.
- c. The combined total of the samples that would otherwise have been designed for the two separate purposes.
- d. More than the larger of the samples that would otherwise have been designated for the two separate purposes, but less than the combined total of the samples that would otherwise have been designed for the two separate purposes.

**11.** The expected population deviation rate of client billing errors is 3%. The auditor has established a tolerable rate of 5%. In the review of client invoices the auditor should use

a.   Stratified sampling.
b.   Variable sampling.
c.   Discovery sampling.
d.   Attribute sampling.

**12.** Which of the following sampling methods would be used to estimate a numerical measurement of a population, such as a dollar value?

a.   Attribute sampling.
b.   Stop-or-go sampling.
c.   Variables sampling.
d.   Random-number sampling.

**13.** For which of the following audit tests would an auditor most likely use attribute sampling?

a.   Making an independent estimate of the amount of a LIFO inventory.
b.   Examining invoices in support of the valuation of fixed asset additions.
c.   Selecting accounts receivable for confirmation of account balances.
d.   Inspecting employee time cards for proper approval by supervisors.

**14.** An underlying feature of random-based selection of items is that each

a.   Stratum of the accounting population be given equal representation in the sample.
b.   Item in the accounting population be randomly ordered.
c.   Item in the accounting population should have an opportunity to be selected.
d.   Item must be systematically selected using replacement.

**15.** Which of the following statistical selection techniques is **least** desirable for use by an auditor?

a.   Systematic selection.
b.   Stratified selection.
c.   Block selection.
d.   Sequential selection.

**16.** Which of the following statistical sampling plans does **not** use a fixed sample size for tests of controls?

a.   Dollar-unit sampling.
b.   Sequential sampling.
c.   PPS sampling.
d.   Variables sampling.

**17.** If certain forms are not consecutively numbered

a.   Selection of a random sample probably is not possible.
b.   Systematic sampling may be appropriate.
c.   Stratified sampling should be used.
d.   Random number tables cannot be used.

**18.** When performing a test of a control with respect to control over cash receipts, an auditor may use a systematic sampling technique with a start at any randomly selected item. The biggest disadvantage of this type of sampling is that the items in the population

a.   Must be systematically replaced in the population after sampling.
b.   May systematically occur more than once in the sample.
c.   Must be recorded in a systematic pattern before the sample can be drawn.

d.   May occur in a systematic pattern, thus destroying the sample randomness.

**19.** What is the primary objective of using stratification as a sampling method in auditing?

a.   To increase the confidence level at which a decision will be reached from the results of the sample selected.
b.   To determine the occurrence rate for a given characteristic in the population being studied.
c.   To decrease the effect of variance in the total population.
d.   To determine the precision range of the sample selected.

**20.** As a result of tests of controls, an auditor assessed control risk too low and decreased substantive testing. This assessment occurred because the true deviation rate in the population was

a.   Less than the risk of assessing control risk too low, based on the auditor's sample.
b.   Less than the deviation rate in the auditor's sample.
c.   More than the risk of assessing control risk too low, based on the auditor's sample.
d.   More than the deviation rate in the auditor's sample.

**21.** Which of the following factors is(are) considered in determining the sample size for a test of controls?

|     | *Expected deviation rate* | *Tolerable deviation rate* |
|-----|-----------------|-----------------|
| a.  | Yes             | Yes             |
| b.  | No              | No              |
| c.  | No              | Yes             |
| d.  | Yes             | No              |

**22.** Which of the following statements is correct concerning statistical sampling in tests of controls?

a.   Deviations from control procedures at a given rate usually result in misstatements at a higher rate.
b.   As the population size doubles, the sample size should also double.
c.   The qualitative aspects of deviations are **not** considered by the auditor.
d.   There is an inverse relationship between the sample size and the tolerable rate.

**23.** In determining the sample size for a test of controls, an auditor should consider the likely rate of deviations, the allowable risk of assessing control risk too low, and the

a.   Tolerable deviation rate.
b.   Risk of incorrect acceptance.
c.   Nature and cause of deviations.
d.   Population size.

**24.** Which of the following combinations results in a decrease in sample size in a sample for attributes?

|     | *Risk of assessing control risk too low* | *Tolerable rate* | *Expected population deviation rate* |
|-----|----------------|----------------|----------------|
| a.  | Increase       | Decrease       | Increase       |
| b.  | Decrease       | Increase       | Decrease       |
| c.  | Increase       | Increase       | Decrease       |
| d.  | Increase       | Increase       | Increase       |

**25.** An auditor is testing internal control procedures that are evidenced on an entity's vouchers by matching random numbers with voucher numbers. If a random number matches the number of a voided voucher, that voucher ordinarily should be replaced by another voucher in the random sample if the voucher

     a.   Constitutes a deviation.
     b.   Has been properly voided.
     c.   Cannot be located.
     d.   Represents an immaterial dollar amount.

**26.** An auditor plans to examine a sample of twenty purchase orders for proper approvals as prescribed by the client's control procedures. One of the purchase orders in the chosen sample of twenty cannot be found, and the auditor is unable to use alternative procedures to test whether that purchase order was properly approved. The auditor should

     a.   Choose another purchase order to replace the missing purchase order in the sample.
     b.   Consider this test of control invalid and proceed with substantive tests since internal control **cannot** be relied upon.
     c.   Treat the missing purchase order as a deviation for the purpose of evaluating the sample.
     d.   Select a completely new set of twenty purchase orders.

**27.** When assessing the tolerable rate, the auditor should consider that, while deviations from control procedures increase the risk of material misstatements, such deviations do not necessarily result in errors. This explains why

     a.   A recorded disbursement that does **not** show evidence of required approval may nevertheless be a transaction that is properly authorized and recorded.
     b.   Deviations would result in errors in the accounting records only if the deviations and the errors occurred on different transactions.
     c.   Deviations from pertinent control procedures at a given rate ordinarily would be expected to result in errors at a higher rate.
     d.   A recorded disbursement that is properly authorized may nevertheless be a transaction that contains a material error.

**28.** The objective of the tolerable rate in sampling for tests of controls of internal control is to

     a.   Determine the probability of the auditor's conclusion based upon reliance factors.
     b.   Determine that financial statements taken as a whole are not materially in error.
     c.   Estimate the reliability of substantive tests.
     d.   Estimate the range of procedural deviations in the population.

**29.** The tolerable rate of deviations for a test of a control is generally

     a.   Lower than the expected rate of errors in the related accounting records.
     b.   Higher than the expected rate of errors in the related accounting records.
     c.   Identical to the expected rate of errors in related accounting records.
     d.   Unrelated to the expected rate of errors in the related accounting records.

**30.** If the auditor is concerned that a population may contain exceptions, the determination of a sample size sufficient to include at **least** one such exception is a characteristic of

     a.   Discovery sampling.
     b.   Variables sampling.
     c.   Random sampling.
     d.   Dollar-unit sampling.

**31.** In determining the number of documents to select for a test to obtain assurance that all sales have been properly authorized, an auditor should consider the tolerable rate of deviation from the control activity. The auditor should also consider the

   I. Likely rate of deviations.
   II. Allowable risk of assessing control risk too high.

     a.   I only.
     b.   II only.
     c.   Both I and II.
     d.   Either I or II.

**32.** An auditor should consider the tolerable rate of deviation when determining the number of check requests to select for a test to obtain assurance that all check requests have been properly authorized. The auditor should also consider

| | The average dollar value of the check requests | The allowable risk of assessing control risk too low |
|---|---|---|
| a. | Yes | Yes |
| b. | Yes | No |
| c. | No | Yes |
| d. | No | No |

**33.** Which of the following statements is correct concerning statistical sampling in tests of controls?

     a.   As the population size increases, the sample size should increase proportionately.
     b.   Deviations from specific internal control procedures at a given rate ordinarily result in misstatements at a lower rate.
     c.   There is an inverse relationship between the expected population deviation rate and the sample size.
     d.   In determining tolerable rate, an auditor considers detection risk and the sample size.

**34.** What is an auditor's evaluation of a statistical sample for attributes when a test of fifty documents results in three deviations if tolerable rate is 7%, the expected population deviation rate is 5%, and the allowance for sampling risk is 2%?

     a.   Modify the planned assessed level of control risk because the tolerable rate plus the allowance for sampling risk exceeds the expected population deviation rate.
     b.   Accept the sample results as support for the planned assessed level of control risk because the sample deviation rate plus the allowance for sampling risk exceeds the tolerable rate.
     c.   Accept the sample results as support for the planned assessed level of control risk because the tolerable rate less the allowance for sampling risk equals the expected population deviation rate.
     d.   Modify the planned assessed level of control risk because the sample deviation rate plus the allowance for sampling risk exceeds the tolerable rate.

**Items 35 and 36** are based on the following:

An auditor desired to test credit approval on 10,000 sales invoices processed during the year. The auditor designed a statistical sample that would provide 1% risk of assessing control risk too low (99% confidence) that not more than 7% of the sales invoices lacked approval. The auditor estimated from previous experience that about 2 1/2% of the sales invoices lacked approval. A sample of 200 invoices was examined and 7 of them were lacking approval. The auditor then determined the achieved upper precision limit to be 8%.

**35.** In the evaluation of this sample, the auditor decided to increase the level of the preliminary assessment of control risk because the
   a.   Tolerable rate (7%) was less than the achieved upper precision limit (8%).
   b.   Expected deviation rate (7%) was more than the percentage of errors in the sample (3 1/2%).
   c.   Achieved upper precision limit (8%) was more than the percentage of errors in the sample (3 1/2%).
   d.   Expected deviation rate (2 1/2%) was less than the tolerable rate (7%).

**36.** The allowance for sampling risk was
   a.   5 1/2%
   b.   4 1/2%
   c.   3 1/2%
   d.   1%

**37.** Which of the following statements is correct concerning statistical sampling in tests of controls?
   a.   The population size has little or **no** effect on determining sample size except for very small populations.
   b.   The expected population deviation rate has little or **no** effect on determining sample size except for very small populations.
   c.   As the population size doubles, the sample size also should double.
   d.   For a given tolerable rate, a larger sample size should be selected as the expected population deviation rate decreases.

**38.** When an auditor has chosen a random sample and is using nonstatistical attributes sampling, that auditor
   a.   Need not consider the risk of assessing control risk too low.
   b.   Has committed a nonsampling error.
   c.   Will have to use discovery sampling to evaluate the results.
   d.   Should compare the deviation rate of the sample to the tolerable deviation rate.

**39.** How would increases in tolerable misstatement and assessed level of control risk affect the sample size in a substantive test of details?

|     | Increase in tolerable misstatement | Increase in assessed level of control risk |
| --- | --- | --- |
| a.  | Increase sample size | Increase sample size |
| b.  | Increase sample size | Decrease sample size |
| c.  | Decrease sample size | Increase sample size |
| d.  | Decrease sample size | Decrease sample size |

**40.** Which of the following courses of action would an auditor most likely follow in planning a sample of cash disbursements if the auditor is aware of several unusually large cash disbursements?
   a.   Set the tolerable rate of deviation at a lower level than originally planned.
   b.   Stratify the cash disbursements population so that the unusually large disbursements are selected.
   c.   Increase the sample size to reduce the effect of the unusually large disbursements.
   d.   Continue to draw new samples until all the unusually large disbursements appear in the sample.

**41.** Which of the following sample planning factors would influence the sample size for a substantive test of details for a specific account?

|     | Expected amount of misstatements | Measure of tolerable misstatement |
| --- | --- | --- |
| a.  | No  | No  |
| b.  | Yes | Yes |
| c.  | No  | Yes |
| d.  | Yes | No  |

**42.** When planning a sample for a substantive test of details, an auditor should consider tolerable misstatement for the sample. This consideration should
   a.   Be related to the auditor's business risk.
   b.   Not be adjusted for qualitative factors.
   c.   Be related to preliminary judgments about materiality levels.
   d.   Not be changed during the audit process.

**43.** A number of factors influences the sample size for a substantive test of details of an account balance. All other factors being equal, which of the following would lead to a larger sample size?
   a.   Greater reliance on internal control.
   b.   Greater reliance on analytical procedures.
   c.   Smaller expected frequency of errors.
   d.   Smaller measure of tolerable misstatement.

**44.** In estimation sampling for variables, which of the following must be known in order to estimate the appropriate sample size required to meet the auditor's needs in a given situation?
   a.   The qualitative aspects of errors.
   b.   The total dollar amount of the population.
   c.   The acceptable level of risk.
   d.   The estimated rate of misstatements in the population.

**45.** An auditor established a $60,000 tolerable misstatement for an asset with an account balance of $1,000,000. The auditor selected a sample of every twentieth item from the population that represented the asset account balance and discovered overstatements of $3,700 and understatements of $200. Under these circumstances, the auditor most likely would conclude that
   a.   There is an unacceptably high risk that the actual misstatements in the population exceed the tolerable misstatement because the total projected misstatement is more than the tolerable misstatement.
   b.   There is an unacceptably high risk that the tolerable misstatement exceeds the sum of actual overstatements and understatements.

c. The asset account is fairly stated because the total projected misstatement is less than the tolerable misstatement.

d. The asset account is fairly stated because the tolerable misstatement exceeds the net of projected actual overstatements and understatements.

**46.** Which of the following statements is correct concerning probability-proportional-to-size (PPS) sampling, also known as dollar unit sampling?

a. The sampling distribution should approximate the normal distribution.

b. Overstated units have a lower probability of sample selection than units that are understated.

c. The auditor controls the risk of incorrect acceptance by specifying that risk level for the sampling plan.

d. The sampling interval is calculated by dividing the number of physical units in the population by the sample size.

**47.** Hill has decided to use probability-proportional-to-size (PPS) sampling, sometimes called dollar-unit sampling, in the audit of a client's accounts receivable balances. Hill plans to use the following PPS sampling table:

**TABLE**
**Reliability Factors for Overstatements**

| Number of over- | Risk of incorrect acceptance | | | | |
|---|---|---|---|---|---|
| statements | *1%* | *5%* | *10%* | *15%* | *20%* |
| 0 | 4.61 | 3.00 | 2.31 | 1.90 | 1.61 |
| 1 | 6.64 | 4.75 | 3.89 | 3.38 | 3.00 |
| 2 | 8.41 | 6.30 | 5.33 | 4.72 | 4.28 |
| 3 | 10.05 | 7.76 | 6.69 | 6.02 | 5.52 |
| 4 | 11.61 | 9.16 | 8.00 | 7.27 | 6.73 |

*Additional information*

| | |
|---|---|
| Tolerable misstatements (net of effect of expected misstatements) | $ 24,000 |
| Risk of incorrect acceptance | 20% |
| Number of misstatements | 1 |
| Recorded amount of accounts receivable | $240,000 |
| Number of accounts | 360 |

What sample size should Hill use?

a. 120
b. 108
c. 60
d. 30

**48.** In a probability-proportional-to-size sample with a sampling interval of $5,000, an auditor discovered that a selected account receivable with a recorded amount of $10,000 had an audit amount of $8,000. If this were the only error discovered by the auditor, the projected error of this sample would be

a. $1,000
b. $2,000
c. $4,000
d. $5,000

**49.** An auditor is determining the sample size for an inventory observation using mean-per-unit estimation, which is a variables sampling plan. To calculate the required sample size, the auditor usually determines the

| | Variability in the dollar amounts of inventory items | Risk of incorrect acceptance |
|---|---|---|
| a. | Yes | Yes |
| b. | Yes | No |
| c. | No | Yes |
| d. | No | No |

**50.** In statistical sampling methods used in substantive testing, an auditor most likely would stratify a population into meaningful groups if

a. Probability-proportional-to-size (PPS) sampling is used.

b. The population has highly variable recorded amounts.

c. The auditor's estimated tolerable misstatement is extremely small.

d. The standard deviation of recorded amounts is relatively small.

**51.** The use of the ratio estimation sampling technique is most effective when

a. The calculated audit amounts are approximately proportional to the client's book amounts.

b. A relatively small number of differences exist in the population.

c. Estimating populations whose records consist of quantities, but **not** book values.

d. Large overstatement differences and large understatement differences exist in the population.

**52.** In the application of statistical techniques to the estimation of dollar amounts, a preliminary sample is usually taken primarily for the purpose of estimating the population

a. Variability.
b. Mode.
c. Range.
d. Median.

**53.** Using statistical sampling to assist in verifying the year-end accounts payable balance, an auditor has accumulated the following data:

| | Number of accounts | Book balance | Balance determined by the auditor |
|---|---|---|---|
| Population | 4,100 | $5,000,000 | ? |
| Sample | 200 | $ 250,000 | $300,000 |

Using the ratio estimation technique, the auditor's estimate of year-end accounts payable balance would be

a. $6,150,000
b. $6,000,000
c. $5,125,000
d. $5,050,000

**54.** Use of the ratio estimation sampling technique to estimated dollar amounts is **inappropriate** when

a. The total book value is known and corresponds to the sum of all the individual book values.

b. A book value for each sample item is unknown.

c. There are some observed differences between audited values and book values.

d. The audited values are nearly proportional to the book values.

**55.** An auditor is performing substantive tests of pricing and extensions of perpetual inventory balances consisting of a large number of items. Past experience indicates numerous pricing and extension errors. Which of the following statistical sampling approaches is most appropriate?

   a.   Unstratified mean-per-unit.

   b.   Probability-proportional-to-size.

   c.   Stop or go.

   d.   Ratio estimation.

**56.** The major reason that the difference and ratio estimation methods would be expected to produce audit efficiency is that the

   a.   Number of members of the populations of differences or ratios is smaller than the number of members of the population of book values.

   b.   Beta risk may be completely ignored.

   c.   Calculations required in using difference or ratio estimation are less arduous and fewer than those required when using direct estimation.

   d.   Variability of the populations of differences or ratios is less than that of the populations of book values or audited values.

**57.** Which of the following statements is correct concerning the auditor's use of statistical sampling?

   a.   An auditor needs to estimate the dollar amount of the standard deviation of the population to use classical variables sampling.

   b.   An assumption of PPS sampling is that the underlying accounting population is normally distributed.

   c.   A classical variables sample needs to be designed with special considerations to include negative balances in the sample.

   d.   The selection of zero balances usually does **not** require special sample design considerations when using PPS sampling.

**58.** Which of the following most likely would be an advantage in using classical variables sampling rather than probability-proportional-to-size (PPS) sampling?

   a.   An estimate of the standard deviation of the population's recorded amounts is **not** required.

   b.   The auditor rarely needs the assistance of a computer program to design an efficient sample.

   c.   Inclusion of zero and negative balances generally does **not** require special design considerations.

   d.   Any amount that is individually significant is automatically identified and selected.

**SIMULATION PROBLEMS**

**Simulation Problem 1**                    (30 to 35 minutes)

| Situation | | |
|---|---|---|
| | Analysis | Research |

The following is a computer printout generated by audit software using probability-proportional-to-size (PPS) sampling:

Winz Corporation
Receivable Sampling Evaluation Results
December 31, 20X2

Population book value = $2,400,00;   Tolerable misstatement = $280,000

*Projected Misstatement*

| Book value | Audited value | Misstatement | Tainting percentage | Sampling interval | Projected misstatement |
|---|---|---|---|---|---|
| $1,000 | $ 0 | $1,000 | 100% | $80,000 | $ 1,000 |
| 750 | 600 | 150 | 20% | $80,000 | 16,000 |
| 85,000 | 60,000 | 25,000 | NA | NA | 25,000 |
| | | | | | $42,000 |

Basic Precision = 3.0 * $80,000                                   $240,000

*Incremental Allowance*

| Reliability factor | Increment | (Increment −1) | Projected misstatement | Incremental allowance |
|---|---|---|---|---|
| 3.00 | | | | |
| 4.75 | 1.75 | .75 | $16,000 | $12,000 |
| 6.30 | 1.55 | .55 | 1,000 | 550 |
| | | | | $12,550 |

The software uses factors from the following PPS sampling table:

**TABLE**
**Reliability Factors for Overstatements**

| Number of overstatements | Risk of incorrect acceptance | | | | |
|---|---|---|---|---|---|
| | 1% | 5% | 10% | 15% | 20% |
| 0 | 4.61 | 3.00 | 2.31 | 1.90 | 1.61 |
| 1 | 6.64 | 4.75 | 3.89 | 3.38 | 3.00 |
| 2 | 8.41 | 6.30 | 5.33 | 4.72 | 4.28 |
| 3 | 10.05 | 7.76 | 6.69 | 6.02 | 5.52 |
| 4 | 11.61 | 9.16 | 8.00 | 7.27 | 6.73 |

| | Analysis | |
|---|---|---|
| Situation | | Research |

Answer the following questions relating to the above worksheet:

| *Questions* | *Answers* |
|---|---|
| 1. What was the planned sample size? | A.  30 items |
| 2. What is the total misstatement in the sample? | B.  60 items |
| | C.  76 items |
| 3. What is the most likely total misstatement in the population? | D.  90 items |
| | E.  0 |
| 4. Calculate the upper limit on misstatement. | F.  $ 12,550 |
| 5. Calculate the allowance for sampling risk. | G.  $ 26,150 |
| | H.  $ 42,000 |
| 6. Would one "accept" or "reject" the population as being materially correct? | I.  $ 54,550 |
| | J.  $ 80,000 |
| 7. What is the risk of incorrect acceptance? | K.  $252,550 |
| | L.  $280,000 |
| | M.  $294,550 |
| | N.  $354,550 |
| | O.  Accept |
| | P.  Reject |
| | Q.  5% |
| | R.  20% |
| | S.  100% |

| | Research | |
|---|---|---|
| Situation | Analysis | |

Audit risk includes both sampling and nonsampling risk. Search the Professional Standards to identify the nature of sampling risk versus nonsampling risk. You may simply paste the appropriate material to your solution.

---

**Simulation Problem 2**                                    (35 to 45 minutes)

| Situation | | | | | |
|---|---|---|---|---|---|
| | Characteristics | Calculation | Spreadsheet | Research | Communication |

Edwards has decided to use probability-proportional-to-size (PPS) sampling, sometimes called dollar-unit sampling, in the audit of his client Jane2 Inc.'s accounts receivable balance. Few, if any, misstatements of account balance overstatement are expected.

| | Characteristics | | | | |
|---|---|---|---|---|---|
| Situation | | Calculation | Spreadsheet | Research | Communication |

Reply as to whether you believe the following statements are correct or incorrect concerning PPS sampling:

|   | *Correct* | *Incorrect* |
|---|---|---|
| 1. Size of a PPS sample is not based on the estimated variation of audited amounts. | O | O |
| 2. PPS sampling results in a stratified sample. | O | O |
| 3. Individually significant items are automatically identified. | O | O |
| 4. PPS sampling results in a smaller sample size when numerous small misstatements are expected. | O | O |
| 5. If no misstatements are expected, PPS sampling will usually result in a smaller sample size than classical variables sampling methods. | O | O |
| 6. One does not need a book value for individual items to evaluate a PPS sample. | O | O |
| 7. A PPS sample eliminates the need to project results to the overall population. | O | O |
| 8. PPS sampling is "preferred" by the professional standards. | O | O |

| | | Calculation | | | |
|---|---|---|---|---|---|
| Situation | Characteristics | | Spreadsheet | Research | Communication |

Calculate the sampling interval Edwards should use given the following information:

| | |
|---|---|
| Tolerable misstatements | $ 50,000 |
| Sample size | 100 |
| Number of misstatements allowed | $ 10,000 |
| Recorded amount of accounts receivable | $300,000 |

Sampling interval =

A.   $   1,000
B.   $   3,000
C.   $   2,500
D.   $   4,200
E.   $ 10,000
F.   $ 62,000
G.   $300,000

| | | | Spreadsheet | | |
|---|---|---|---|---|---|
| Situation | Characteristics | Calculation | | Research | Communication |

Complete the spreadsheet to calculate total projected misstatement if the following three misstatements were discovered in a PPS sample:

| | *Recorded amount* | *Audit amount* | *Sampling interval* |
|---|---|---|---|
| 1st misstatement | $ 400 | $ 320 | $1,000 |
| 2nd misstatement | 500 | 0 | 1,000 |
| 3rd misstatement | 3,000 | 2,500 | 1,000 |

Projected misstatement =

    a.   $   723
    b.   $ 1,080
    c.   $ 1,533
    d.   $ 1,700
    e.   $ 2,169
    f.   $16,200
    g.   $18,234
    h.   $32,520

| | A | B | C | D | E | F | G |
|---|---|---|---|---|---|---|---|
| 1 | Jane2 Inc. | | | | | | |
| 2 | Accounts Receivable | | | | | | |
| 3 | December 31, 20X2 | | | | | | |
| 4 | | | | | | | |
| 5 | | Recorded amount | Audited amount | Difference | Tainting % | Sampling interval | |
| 6 | 1st misstatement | 400 | 320 | *80* | *20%* | 1,000 | *200* |
| 7 | 2nd misstatement | 500 | 0 | *500* | *100%* | 1,000 | *1000* |
| 8 | 3rd misstatement | 3,000 | 2,500 | *500* | | 1,000 | *500* |

*1700*

| Situation | Characteristics | Calculation | Spreadsheet | **Research** | | **Communication** |
|---|---|---|---|---|---|---|

Auditors must consider both the concepts of materiality and tolerable misstatement. Search the Professional Standards to identify the relationship between tolerable misstatement and materiality. You may simply paste the appropriate material to your solution.

| Situation | Characteristics | Calculation | Spreadsheet | Research | **Communication** |
|---|---|---|---|---|---|

Write a memorandum to the audit working papers describing the importance of projection sample results to the population.

To:      Audit Working Papers
From:  CPA Candidate

MULTIPLE-CHOICE ANSWERS

| | | | | |
|---|---|---|---|---|
| 1. d __ __ | 13. d __ __ | 25. b __ __ | 37. a __ __ | 49. a __ __ |
| 2. c __ __ | 14. c __ __ | 26. c __ __ | 38. d __ __ | 50. b __ __ |
| 3. a __ __ | 15. c __ __ | 27. a __ __ | 39. c __ __ | 51. a __ __ |
| 4. d __ __ | 16. b __ __ | 28. d __ __ | 40. b __ __ | 52. a __ __ |
| 5. a __ __ | 17. b __ __ | 29. b __ __ | 41. b __ __ | 53. b __ __ |
| 6. a __ __ | 18. d __ __ | 30. a __ __ | 42. c __ __ | 54. b __ __ |
| 7. d __ __ | 19. c __ __ | 31. a __ __ | 43. d __ __ | 55. d __ __ |
| 8. b __ __ | 20. d __ __ | 32. c __ __ | 44. c __ __ | 56. d __ __ |
| 9. c __ __ | 21. a __ __ | 33. b __ __ | 45. a __ __ | 57. a __ __ |
| 10. a __ __ | 22. d __ __ | 34. d __ __ | 46. c __ __ | 58. c __ __ |
| 11. d __ __ | 23. a __ __ | 35. a __ __ | 47. d __ __ | 1st: __/58 = __% |
| 12. c __ __ | 24. c __ __ | 36. b __ __ | 48. b __ __ | 2nd: __/58 = __% |

**MULTIPLE-CHOICE ANSWER EXPLANATIONS**

## A.2. General Approaches to Audit Sampling— Nonstatistical and Statistical

**1. (d)** The requirement is to identify an advantage of statistical sampling over nonstatistical sampling. Answer (d) is correct because statistical sampling helps the auditor to: (1) design an efficient sample, (2) measures the sufficiency of the evidential matter obtained, and (3) evaluate the sample results (AICPA *Audit Sampling Guide*). Answer (a) is incorrect because dual-purpose tests, which both test a control and serve as substantive test, may be performed with either a statistical or a nonstatistical sample. Answer (b) is incorrect because both statistical and nonstatistical sampling require the use of judgment, although that judgment is quantified when statistical sampling is used. Answer (c) is incorrect because either statistical or nonstatistical sampling may provide equal assurance to the auditor.

**2. (c)** The requirement is to identify an advantage of statistical sampling over nonstatistical sampling. Answer (c) is correct because statistical sampling helps the auditor to: (1) design an efficient sample, (2) measure the sufficiency of the evidential matter obtained, and (3) evaluate the sample results (AICPA *Audit Sampling Guide*). Answer (a) is incorrect because the risk of nonsampling errors is not directly affected by whether statistical or nonstatistical sampling is used. Answer (b) is incorrect because either statistical or nonstatistical sampling can be used to reduce the level of audit risk to a low level; the materiality level should not be affected by the type of sampling used. Answer (d) is incorrect because either statistical or nonstatistical sampling may be used to minimize the failure to detect errors and fraud.

## A.3. Uncertainty and Audit Sampling

**3. (a)** The requirement is to determine the meaning of the likelihood of assessing control risk too high in a test of controls. Answer (a) is correct because the risk of assessing control risk too high is the risk that the sample does **not** support the auditor's planned assessed level of control risk when the true operating effectiveness of the control structure justifies such an assessment. Answer (b) is incorrect because the risk of assessing control risk too high relates to the deviation rate from a control procedure in a population, not to monetary misstatements. Answer (c) is incorrect because the risk of assessing control risk too high does not directly relate to monetary misstatements. Answer (d) is incorrect because tolerable error (misstatement) relates to variables sampling applied to substantive testing and not to tests of

controls and because the meaning of "support the tolerable error" is uncertain.

**4. (d)** The requirement is to determine the nature of the risk of incorrect acceptance and the risk of assessing control risk too low. Answer (d) is correct because the risk of incorrect acceptance and the risk of assessing control risk too low relate to the effectiveness of an audit in detecting an existing material misstatement or deviation. Answer (a) is incorrect because the term "allowable risk of tolerable misstatement" is not used in the professional standards. Answer (b) is incorrect because preliminary estimates of materiality levels relate most directly to the risk of incorrect acceptance, and only indirectly to the risk of assessing control risk too low. Answer (c) is incorrect because the risk of incorrect rejection and the risk of assessing control risk too high relate to the efficiency of the audit.

**5. (a)** The requirement is to determine which answer represents the concept of sampling risk. Sampling risk arises from the possibility that an auditor's conclusions based upon a sample would differ from the conclusions which would be drawn from examining the entire population (i.e., the risk that the sample examined is not representative of the population). Answers (b), (c), and (d) are all incorrect because they relate to errors which could occur even if 100% of the population were examined, that is, nonsampling risk.

**6. (a)** The requirement is to determine what is related to the risk of incorrect rejection and the risk of assessing control risk too high. Answer (a) is correct because AU 350 states that the risk of incorrect rejection and the risk of assessing control risk too high relate to the efficiency of the audit. These two errors generally result in an auditor performing unnecessary additional procedures. Answer (b) is incorrect because the risk of incorrect acceptance and the risk of assessing control risk too low relate to the effectiveness of an audit. Answer (c) is incorrect because the risks do not relate directly to the actual selection of the sample. Answer (d) is incorrect because the audit quality controls do not directly mention either of these risks.

**7. (d)** The requirement is to determine the situation in which an auditor has properly concluded that control risk is at or below the planned assessed level. Answer (d) is correct because to support the planned level, the deviation rate must be less than the tolerable rate and the auditor must conclude that the deviation rate is less than the tolerable rate. Answer (a) is incorrect because it represents a situation in which the auditor appropriately decides that the deviation rate exceeds the tolerable rate. Answer (b) is incorrect because it represents a situation in which an auditor erroneously concludes that the deviation rate exceeds the tolerable rate when it actually does not. Answer (c) is incorrect because the auditor erroneously concludes that the deviation rate is less than the tolerable rate when it actually exceeds it.

**8.   (b)**   The requirement is to determine the situation in which the auditor assesses control risk too high and thereby increases substantive testing. Answer (b) is correct because to assess control risk too high, an auditor must estimate that the deviation rate exceeds the tolerable rate when it actually is less than the tolerable rate. Answer (a) is incorrect because it represents a situation in which the auditor appropriately decides that the deviation rate exceeds the tolerable rate. Answer (c) is incorrect because the auditor erroneously concludes that the deviation rate is less than the tolerable rate when it actually exceeds the tolerable rate. Answer (d) is incorrect because to properly rely on internal control, the deviation rate must be less than the tolerable rate and the auditor must conclude that the deviation rate is less than the tolerable rate.

**9.   (c)**   The requirement is to determine the type of risk demonstrated when an auditor concludes that an account is misstated when in fact it is not. Answer (c) is correct because the risk of incorrect rejection is the risk that the sample supports the conclusion that the recorded account balance is materially misstated when the account is not misstated. Answers (a) and (b) are incorrect because the risk of assessing control risk too high and the risk of assessing control risk too low relate to tests of controls, and not to substantive tests of details. Answer (d) is incorrect because the risk of incorrect acceptance is the risk that the sample support the conclusion that the account is not misstated when in fact it is misstated.

### A.4. Types of Audit Tests in Which Sampling May Be Used

**10.   (a)**   The requirement is to identify the correct statement with respect to the size of a sample required for dual purpose testing. Answer (a) is correct because the auditor should select the larger of the required sample sizes.

### A.5. Types of Statistical Sampling Plans

**11.   (d)**   The requirement is to identify the type of sampling involved in a review of client invoices in which an expected population deviation rate and an established tolerable rate are provided. Answer (d) is correct because attribute sampling is used to reach a conclusion about a population in terms of a rate of occurrence (*Audit Sampling Guide*). Answer (a) is incorrect because stratified sampling is generally used to reach a dollar-based conclusion in variables sampling approaches. Answer (b) is incorrect because, as indicated, variables sampling deals with a dollar amount conclusion, not deviation rates. Answer (c) is incorrect because discovery sampling is only used in cases in which the auditor expects deviation rates to be extremely low (approaching zero).

**12.   (c)**   The requirement is to identify the sampling method that would be used to estimate a numerical measurement such as a dollar value of a population. Answer (c) is correct because sampling for variables addresses such numerical measurements. Answer (a) is incorrect because

attributes sampling deals with deviation rates. Answer (b) is incorrect because stop-or-go sampling (also referred to as sequential sampling) is a form of attributes sampling. Answer (d) is incorrect because random-number sampling is simply a sample selection technique that may be used with either an attributes or a variables form of sampling; accordingly, a numerical measurement such as a dollar value is not necessary for random-number sampling.

**13.   (d)**   The requirement is to determine the audit test for which an auditor would most likely use attribute sampling. Answer (d) is correct because attribute sampling is used to reach a conclusion about a population in terms of a rate of occurrence. Here the rate of occurrence will be the rate of (un)approved time cards. Answers (a), (b), and (c) are all incorrect because they all relate more directly to variables sampling which is generally used to reach conclusion about a population in terms of a dollar amount. See the AICPA Audit and Accounting Guide, *Audit Sampling* and AU 350 for more information on audit sampling.

### General Sampling Questions

**14.   (c)**   The requirement is to determine the correct statement with respect to random sampling. Answer (c) is correct because every item in the accounting population should have an opportunity to be selected. Answer (a) is incorrect because with stratified random sampling, each stratum need not be given equal representation. Answer (b) is incorrect because while sample units should be randomly selected, there is no requirement that the accounting population be randomly ordered. Answer (d) is incorrect because random sampling, by its very nature, is not systematic. Additionally, random sampling may be performed without replacement.

**15.   (c)**   The requirement is to determine the least desirable statistical selection technique. Answer (c), block selection, is correct because, ideally, a sample should be selected from the entire set of data to which the resulting conclusions are to be applied. When block sampling is used, the selection of blocks often precludes items from being so selected. In most cases, systematic [answer (a)], stratified [answer (b)], and sequential [answer (d)] selection techniques all provide a better representation of the entire population than does block selection.

**16.   (b)**   The requirement is to identify the type of sampling plan that does **not** use a fixed sample size for tests of controls. Answer (b) is correct because sequential sampling results in the selection of a sample in several steps, with each step conditional on the result of the previous steps. Therefore, sample size will vary depending upon the number of stages that prove necessary. Answers (a), (c), and (d) are all incorrect because dollar-unit sampling, PPS sampling, and variables sampling all use a fixed sample size.

**17.   (b)**   The requirement is to identify the correct statement concerning a statistical sampling application where the population consists of forms which are not consecutively numbered. Answer (b) is correct because systematic sampling is a procedure where a random start is obtained and then every n*th* item is selected. For example, a sample of forty from a population of a thousand would require selecting every 25th item after obtaining a random start between items 1 through 25. Answer (a) is incorrect because selection of a random sample is possible even though the population is not consecutively numbered. Answer (c) is incorrect because there is no special reason for using stratified sampling. Stratified sampling breaks down the population into subpopulations and applies different selection methods to each subpopulation. This selection method is used when the population consists of different types of items (e.g., large balances and small balances). Answer (d) is incorrect because random number tables can be used even though the forms are not consecutively numbered. If random numbers are selected for which there are no forms, they are ignored. This is the same as if there were 86,000 items in a consecutively numbered population and random numbers selected between 86,000 and 99,999 are ignored.

**18. (d)** Answer (d) is correct because systematic items occurrence in a population **may** destroy a sample's randomness. Answer (a) is incorrect because items need not be replaced in the population, and therefore is not a disadvantage of systematic sampling. Answer (b) is incorrect because an individual item will not occur more than once in a sample when systematic sampling is being used (because the auditor selects every nth item). Answer (c) is incorrect because systematic sampling refers to the type of sampling selection plan used and not the manner in which items in the population are recorded. Also, as indicated in (d) above, a systematic pattern in the population is a hindrance to systematic sampling.

**19. (c)** Stratified sampling is a technique of breaking the population down into subpopulations and applying different sample selection methods to the subpopulations. Stratified sampling is used to minimize the variance within the overall population [answer (c)]. Recall that as variance increases, so does the required sample size (because of the extreme values). Thus, stratification allows the selection of subpopulations to reduce the effect of dispersion in the population.

**B.1. Tests of Controls—Sampling Risk**

**20. (d)** The requirement is to identify the circumstance that would cause an auditor to assess control risk too low and decrease substantive testing inappropriately. Answer (d) is correct because when the true deviation rate in the population exceeds that in the sample, the auditor may assess control risk too low. The AICPA *Audit Sampling Guide* discusses tests of controls and attributes sampling in its second chapter. Answers (a) and (c) are incorrect because the true deviation rate and the risk of assessing control risk too low do not have such a relationship, either positive or negative. Answer (b) is incorrect because a deviation rate in the population that is less than the deviation rate in the auditor's sample may lead the auditor to assess control risk too high.

**21. (a)** The requirement is to determine whether the expected deviation rate, the tolerable deviation rate, or both affect the sample size for a test of controls. Answer (a) is correct because attribute sampling formulas and tables used in auditing generally require the auditor to specify an expected deviation rate, a tolerable deviation rate and the risk of assessing control risk too low. See AICPA *Audit Sampling Guide* and AU 350 for more information on audit sampling.

**22. (d)** The requirement is to identify the correct statement about sampling for attributes. Answer (d) is correct

because the sample size increases as the tolerable rate decreases, an inverse relationship. Answer (a) is incorrect because many deviations do not necessarily result in a misstatement. Answer (b) is incorrect because a doubling of the population size will result in less than a doubling of the required sample size. Answer (c) is incorrect because auditors must consider the qualitative aspects of deviations.

**23. (a)** The requirement is to identify the information needed in addition to the likely rate of deviations and the allowable risk of assessing control risk too low to determine the sample size for a test of controls in an attributes sampling plan. Answer (a) is correct because the tolerable deviation rate is also needed. Answer (b) is incorrect because the risk of incorrect acceptance relates to variables sampling applied to substantive testing, not attributes sampling applied to tests of controls. Answer (c) is incorrect because the auditor will examine the nature and cause of deviations after the sample has been selected. Answer (d) is incorrect because auditors often do not consider population size when performing attributes sampling applied to tests of controls.

**24. (c)** The requirement is to determine when a sample size would be decreased when sampling for attributes. Answer (c) is correct because the sample size will decrease when the risk of assessing control risk too low is increased, the tolerable rate is increased, and the expected population deviation rate is decreased (Audit and Accounting Guide *Audit Sampling*). Answers (a), (b), and (d) are all incorrect because they include combinations of changes that would not necessarily decrease sample size.

**25. (b)** The requirement is to identify the correct statement with respect to treatment of a voided voucher that has been selected in a sample. Answer (b) is correct because the AICPA *Audit Sampling Guide* states that the auditor should obtain reasonable assurance that the voucher has been properly voided, and should then replace it with another voucher. Answer (a) is incorrect because the voided voucher is not normally considered to be a deviation. Answer (c) is incorrect because the auditor must obtain reasonable assurance that the misplaced voucher has been voided. Answer (d) is incorrect because the level of materiality normally does not directly affect the decision.

**26. (c)** The requirement is to determine the proper method of handling a sample item which cannot be located for evaluation purposes. Answer (c) is correct because an auditor would ordinarily consider the selected item to be a deviation. Answers (a) and (d) are incorrect since a possible cause for the missing purchase order could be a breakdown in one of the controls of the system. Thus, in selecting a new sample item(s) the auditor may be ignoring a portion of the population which is in error and may be artificially skewing the results of the tests performed on the sample. Answer (b) is incorrect because there is no reason to believe that the entire test is invalid and cannot be relied upon.

**27. (a)** The requirement is to determine why deviations from control procedures do not necessarily result in errors. Answer (a) is correct because it provides an example of a situation in which a deviation from a control procedure exists (lack of documentation of transaction approval), although the entry was authorized and proper. Thus, such a deviation does not necessarily result in an error in the financial statements. Answer (b) is incorrect because a deviation from control procedure and an error may occur in the same transaction. Answer (c) is incorrect since the fact that all deviations do not lead to errors will result in a lower error rate. Answer (d) is incorrect because while it represents a correct statement, it does not follow from the point of the question which is based on the idea that deviations do not directly result in errors.

**28.   (d)**   The requirement is to determine the objective of the tolerable rate in sampling. Tolerable rate is calculated to determine the range of procedural deviations in the population. Answer (a) is incorrect because probabilities relate more directly to reliability. Answer (b) is incorrect because errors on financial statements in materiality terms relate to variables sampling. Answer (c) is incorrect because the tolerable rate does not relate directly to substantive tests.

**29.   (b)**   The requirement is to determine the correct relationship between the tolerable rate of deviations and the expected rate of deviations for a test of a control. The tolerable rate of deviations is the maximum rate of deviations from a prescribed control procedure that an auditor would be willing to accept and, unless the expected error rate is lower, reliance on internal control is not justified. Answer (a) is incorrect because if the tolerable rate of deviations is less than the expected rate, the auditor would not plan to rely on internal control and would therefore omit tests of controls. Answer (c) is incorrect because testing of controls is inappropriate if the expected rate of errors equals the tolerable rate of deviations (mathematically, the precision of zero makes the sample size equal to population size). Answer (d) is incorrect because, as indicated above, to perform tests of controls one must assume that the tolerable rate of deviations is more than the expected error rate.

**30.   (a)**   The requirement is to determine the type of sampling which is most directly related to finding at least one exception. Discovery sample sizes and related discovery sampling tables are constructed to measure the probability of at least one error occurring in a sample if the error rate in the population exceeds the tolerable rate. Answer (b) is incorrect because variables sampling need not include at least one exception (mean per unit sampling, for example, needs no errors). Answer (c) is incorrect since random sampling only deals with the technique used to select items to be included in the sample. Answer (d) is incorrect because dollar-unit sampling results are not directly related to finding at least one exception.

**31.   (a)**   The requirement is to determine whether an auditor should consider the likely rate of deviation, the allowable risk of assessing control risk too high, or both, when performing a test of a control. Answer (a) is correct because an auditor will consider the likely rate of deviations, but will not ordinarily consider the allowable risk of assessing control risk too high when following the approach outlined in the AICPA *Audit Sampling Guide*.

**32.   (c)**   The requirement is to determine whether an auditor would consider the average dollar value of check requests, the allowable risk of assessing control risk too low, or both, when testing whether check requests have been properly authorized. Answer (c) is correct because a test of authorization such as this is an attributes test which requires the auditor to determine an allowable risk of assessing control risk too low, but does not deal directly with dollar values. Answers (a), (b) and (d) are all incorrect because they include incorrect combinations of the replies. See AU 350 and the AICPA *Audit Sampling Guide* for information on sampling.

### B.2.   Statistical (Attributes) Sampling for Tests of Controls

**33.   (b)**   The requirement is to identify the correct statement concerning statistical sampling in tests of controls. Answer (b) is correct because while deviations from pertinent control procedures increase the risk of material misstatements, any specific deviation need not necessarily result in a misstatement. For example, a recorded disbursement that does not show evidence of required approval might nevertheless be a transaction that is properly authorized and recorded (AICPA *Audit Sampling Guide*). Answer (a) is incorrect because increases in population size result in small increases in sample size. Answer (c) is incorrect because a direct relationship, not an inverse relationship, exists between the expected population deviation rate and the sample size—that is, increases in the expected population deviation rate result in an increase in the required sample size. Answer (d) is incorrect because when determining the tolerable rate, the auditor does not yet have the required sample size.

**34.   (d)**   The requirement is to determine the proper evaluation of a statistical sample for attributes when a test of 50 documents results in 3 deviations, given a tolerable rate of 7%, an expected population deviation rate of 5%, and an allowance for sampling risk of 2%. Answer (d) is correct because when the deviation rate plus the allowance for sampling risk exceeds the tolerable rate, the assessed level of control risk may increase. Here the deviation rate of 6% (3 deviations/50 documents) plus the allowance for sampling risk of 2% equals 8% and exceeds the tolerable rate of 7%. Answer (a) is incorrect because the tolerable rate plus the allowance for sampling risk will always exceed the expected population deviation rate when tests of controls are being performed. Answer (b) is incorrect because when the sample deviation rate plus the allowance for sampling risk exceeds the tolerable rate the sample results do not support the planned assessed level of control risk. Answer (c) is incorrect because the tolerable rate less the allowance for sampling risk should be compared with the actual deviation rate.

**35.   (a)**   The requirement is to determine the circumstance in which an auditor would decide to increase the level of the preliminary assessment of control risk. Answer (a) is correct because the assessment of control risk will increase when the achieved upper precision limit (here 8%) exceeds the tolerable rate (here 7%). Answer (b) is incorrect because the expected deviation rate was 2 1/2%, not 7%. Also, if the expected deviation rate is higher than the percentage of error in the sample, the preliminary assessment does not need to be increased. Answer (c) is incorrect because the achieved upper precision limit will always exceed the percentage of errors in the sample. Answer (d) is incorrect because, in circumstances in which the auditor decides to sample the population, the expected deviation rate will always be less than the tolerable rate.

**36.   (b)**   The requirement is to determine the allowance for sampling risk of the presented sample. When considering the allowance for sampling risk, one may consider both the planned allowance for sampling risk or the adjusted allowance based on the sample results. Answer (b) is correct because both the planned and adjusted allowance for sampling risk are 4 1/2% (7% – 2.5% for planning purposes, and 8% – 3.5% [7/200] as adjusted).

**37.   (a)**   The requirement is to identify the correct statement concerning statistical sampling for tests of controls. Answer (a) is correct because population size has little or **no** effect on sample size. Answer (b) is incorrect because the population deviation rate has a significant effect on sample size. Answer (c) is incorrect because sample size increases to a much lesser extent than doubling as the population size doubles. Answer (d) is incorrect because for a given tolerable rate, a smaller, and not a larger, sample size should be selected as the expected population deviation rate decreases.

**B.3.   Nonstatistical Sampling for Tests of Controls**

**38.   (d)**   The requirement is to identify the proper statement concerning a random sample when nonstatistical attributes sampling is being used. Answer (d) is correct because the deviation rate of the sample should be compared to the tolerable deviation rate regardless of whether statistical or nonstatistical sampling is being used. Answer (a) is incorrect because the risk of assessing control risk too low should be considered, although it may be done judgmentally. Answer (b) is incorrect because nonsampling error relates to "human" type errors such as not identifying a deviation, and not specifically to the use of nonstatistical sampling. Answer (c) is incorrect because discovery sampling will not be used to evaluate the results.

**C.1.   Tests of Details—Sampling Risk**

**39.   (c)**   The requirement is to determine whether either or both of an increase in tolerable misstatement and an increase in the assessed level of control risk increase sample size in a substantive test of details. Answer (c) is correct because while an increase in tolerable misstatement decreases sample size for a substantive test of details, an increase in the assessed level of control risk increases the sample size for a substantive test of details because a lower level of detection risk is required.

**40.   (b)**   The requirement is to determine the proper course of action when an auditor is planning a sample of cash disbursements and he or she is aware of several unusually large cash disbursements. Given the description of the several disbursements as "unusually large," an auditor will generally test them. Answer (b) is therefore correct because stratifying the population will allow the auditor to ensure inclusion of the disbursements. The sampling procedure (selecting less than all items) will then be applied only to the smaller disbursements. Answer (a) is incorrect because the existence of the large disbursements will have no necessary relationship to the tolerable rate of deviation when attributes sampling is being used. Answer (c) is incorrect because while increasing the sample size might be appropriate in some variables sampling applications (we are not told in this problem whether attributes or variables sampling is being followed), the fact that the disbursements are described as "unusually large" leads one to include them. Answer (d) is incorrect because an auditor will not draw numerous samples to assure inclusion of the large disbursements.

**41.   (b)**   The requirement is to determine whether either or both of the expected amount of misstatement and the measure of tolerable misstatement influence sample size for a substantive test of details. Answer (b) is correct because both the expected amount of misstatement and the tolerable

misstatement affect sample size (AICPA *Audit Sampling Guide*). Increases in the expected amount of misstatements increase sample size, while increases in the tolerable misstatement decrease sample size.

**42.   (c)**   The requirement is to determine the correct statement concerning the auditor's consideration of tolerable misstatement. Answer (c) is correct because the consideration of tolerable misstatement is related to preliminary judgments in a manner such that when the auditor's preliminary judgments about tolerable misstatement levels for accounts or transaction types are combined for the entire audit plan, the preliminary judgments about materiality levels for the financial statements are not exceeded. Answer (a) is incorrect because the auditor's judgment of business risk related to a client is not directly related to tolerable misstatement. Answer (b) is incorrect because tolerable misstatement may be adjusted for qualitative factors. Answer (d) is incorrect because tolerable misstatement may be changed during the audit process, especially as misstatements are identified and the auditor considers the nature of the misstatements.

**43.   (d)**   The requirement is to determine the factor that would lead to larger sample size in a substantive test of details. Answer (d) is correct because the sample size required to achieve the auditor's objective at a given risk of incorrect acceptance increases as the auditor's assessment of tolerable misstatement for the balance or class decreases. Answer (a) is incorrect because a greater reliance on internal control will lead to a smaller sample size in a substantive test of details. Answer (b) is incorrect because greater reliance upon analytical procedures will result in a need for less reliance on substantive tests of details and therefore will result in a smaller sample. Answer (c) is incorrect because a smaller expected frequency of errors will generally include properly functioning internal control and will therefore result in a smaller sample for substantive tests of details.

**44.   (c)**   The requirement is to identify the factor which must be known in order to estimate the appropriate sample size when using variables sampling. Answer (c) is correct because the auditor must set an acceptable level of risk for both variables sampling and attribute sampling. Answer (a) is incorrect because while the auditor will consider the qualitative aspects of errors when evaluating the sample, they need not be considered in determining an appropriate sample size. Answer (b) is incorrect because a primary objective of variables sampling is to estimate the audited dollar amount of the population. Also, in some forms of variables sampling, knowledge of book values is not necessary (e.g., mean-per-unit). Answer (d) is incorrect because a rate of error in the population relates to attribute sampling.

**45.   (a)**   The requirement is to identify an auditor's most likely response to a circumstance in which there is a tolerable misstatement of $60,000, and the auditor has discovered misstatement of a net overstatement of $3,500 ($3,700 – $200) when 1/20 of the account has been included in the sample. Because auditors must project the misstatements to the entire population, one would expect a misstatement of approximately $70,000 (20 times the misstatement of $3,500). Since this exceeds the tolerable misstatement, there is little question that the risk of material misstatement is too high and that the misstatement in the population exceeds the tolerable misstatement, therefore answer (a) is correct. Answer (b) is incorrect because it seems that the sum of actual overstatement and understatement is likely to exceed the tolerable misstatement.  Also, answer (b) makes little sense since there probably is no such thing as "an unacceptably high risk" that the tolerable misstatement exceeds the sum of actual overstatements and understatements; in such a circumstance the auditor simply accepts the population as being materially correct.  Answers (c) and (d) are incorrect because the total projected misstatement must be calculated as indicated above.  See AU 350 and the *Audit Sampling Guide* for information on sampling.

### C.2.  Probability-Proportional-to-Size (PPS) Sampling

**46.   (c)**    The requirement is to identify the correct statement regarding probability-proportional-to-size (PPS) sampling.  Answer (c) is correct because when using PPS sampling, the auditor controls the risk of incorrect acceptance by specifying a risk level when planning the sample.  Answer (a) is incorrect because PPS sampling does not assume a normal distribution.  Answer (b) is incorrect because the book value of the unit determines how probable it is that it will be included in the sample, not whether it is over or understated.  Answer (d) is incorrect because the sampling interval is calculated by dividing the book value of the population by the sample size.

**47.   (d)**    The requirement is to determine the sample size that should be used in a probability-proportional-to-size (PPS) sample.  One approach is to first calculate a sampling interval and use it to determine an appropriate sample size.  Using this approach, when provided with the tolerable misstatement already adjusted for expected misstatements (as is the situation in this problem), one divides that total by the number of expected misstatements column for the appropriate risk of incorrect acceptance (the fact that some overstatements are expected is not used).  Here that computation is $24,000/1.61 = $14,906.83.  Sample size is computed by dividing the recorded amount by the sampling interval, here $240,000/14,906.83, for a sample size of 16.  An alternate approach is to use the reliability factor for the expected number of overstatements.  In that case the computations become $24,000/3.00 = $8,000.  Sample size is $240,000/$8,000 = 30.  In either case answer (d) is the closest and therefore the correct reply.

**48.   (b)**    The requirement is to determine the projected error (misstatement) of a probability-proportional-to-size (PPS) sample with a sampling interval of $5,000, when an auditor has discovered that an account with a recorded amount of $10,000 had an audit amount of $8,000.  Answer (b) is correct since, when an account's recorded amount exceeds the sampling interval, the projected error equals the actual misstatement, here $2,000 ($10,000 – $8,000).

### C.3.  Classical Variables Sampling

**49.   (a)**    The requirement is to determine whether an auditor uses the variability in dollar values, the risk of incorrect acceptance, or both, in a mean-per-unit estimation variables sampling plan.  Answer (a) is correct because both factors are included in a sampling plan.  Answers (b), (c) and (d) are all incorrect because they suggest that one or both factors are not considered.  See AU 350 and the AICPA *Audit Sampling Guide* for information on sampling.

**50.   (b)**    The requirement is to identify the circumstance in which an auditor most likely would stratify a population into meaningful groups.  Answer (b) is correct because stratified sampling is used to minimize the effect on sample size of variation within the overall population and results in the largest savings for populations with high variability.  Answer (a) is incorrect because while PPS sampling may in essence stratify a population, the items selected, other than those larger than the sampling interval, are not in "meaningful groups."  Answer (c) is incorrect because the tolerable misstatement in and of itself will not lead to stratification.  Answer (d) is incorrect because stratification is used primarily when there is a relatively large standard deviation, not a relatively small standard deviation.

**51.   (a)**    The requirement is to determine when ratio estimation sampling is most effective.  The ratio estimation sampling technique uses the ratio between the audited to book amounts as a measure of standard deviation in its sample size computation.  Answer (a) is correct because when audit differences are approximately proportional to account size the standard deviation of the ratio is small and this results in a relatively small required sample size.  Answer (b) is incorrect because a relatively large number of differences between book and audited values must exist to calculate a reliable standard deviation under the ratio method.  Answer (c) is incorrect because while the ratio estimation sampling technique may be used with quantities, it offers no particular advantage over other methods.  Answer (b) is incorrect because the absolute size of differences does not make the ratio estimation method most effective.

**52.   (a)**    The requirement is to determine the purpose of taking a preliminary sample when one uses statistical techniques.  It is necessary to obtain an estimate of a population's standard deviation (variability) when calculating the required sample size and when using sampling techniques.  Answers (b), (c), and (d) are incorrect because, in most statistical techniques used by auditors, the mode (most frequent balance), the median (middle balance) and the range (difference between the highest and lowest values) are not used.

**53.   (b)**    The requirement is to determine the estimated audited accounts payable balance using the ratio estimation technique.  Answer (b) is correct because the ratio estimation technique estimates the audited value by multiplying the audited value/book value of the sample times the population book value.  In this case, ($300,000/$250,000) × $5,000,000 = $6,000,000.

**54.   (b)**    The ratio estimation sampling technique is based on comparing the ratio of the book value to the audited value of the sampled items.  Answer (b) is correct because this method cannot be used when there is no book value to make the comparison.  The circumstances described in answers (a) and (c) are necessary for ratio point and interval estimation.  Answer (d) describes the circumstances in which the use of ratio estimation will be efficient in terms of required sample size.

**55.   (d)**    The requirement is to determine the most appropriate sampling approach for substantive tests of pricing and extensions of perpetual inventory balances consisting of a large number of items for which past experience indicates numerous expected pricing and extension errors.  Answer (d) is correct because ratio estimation is appropriate when testing a population for which a large number of errors of this nature is expected (Audit and Accounting Guide, *Audit Sampling*). Answer (a) is incorrect because the unstratified mean-per-unit method will typically provide a larger sample size than the ratio estimation method to achieve the same level of sampling risk. Thus, the ratio estimation method would be more appropriate. Answer (b) is incorrect because probability-proportional-to-size sampling is most efficient for testing populations with relatively low expected error rates. Answer (c) is incorrect because "stop or go" or "sequential" sampling is most frequently used in attribute sampling.

**56. (d)** Difference and ratio estimation methods are statistical sampling methods. They measure the difference between audit and book values or the ratio of audit to book values. As these differences should not be great, the population of these differences will have little variance. In statistical sampling, the less variation in a population, the smaller the required sample to provide an estimate of the population. In other words, difference and ratio estimation methods are more efficient because the differences between audit and book values are expected to vary less than the actual items in the population. Answer (a) is incorrect because the number of members in the population for differences or ratio methods would be the same as the number of items in the population for a direct estimation method. In difference sampling, many items would be zero because audit and book are the same, and in ratio sampling, many of the members would be one for the same reason. Answer (b) is incorrect because beta risk can never be ignored, as beta risk is the risk of accepting an incorrect (unacceptable) population. Answer (c) is incorrect because the calculations required in difference and ratio sampling are similar to those used in direct estimation sampling.

**57. (a)** The requirement is to identify the correct statement concerning the auditor's use of statistical sampling. Answer (a) is correct because an estimate of the variation of the population, the standard deviation, is needed to use classical variables sampling (AICPA Audit and Accounting Guide, *Audit Sampling*). Answer (b) is incorrect because PPS sampling does not make an assumption that the underlying population is normally distributed. Answers (c) and (d) are incorrect because classical variables sample selected accounts and therefore need not include special considerations to those with a negative balance.

### C.4. Comparison of PPS Sampling to Classical Variables Sampling

**58. (c)** The requirement is to identify an advantage in using classical variables sampling rather than probability-proportional-to-size sampling. Answer (c) is correct because the inclusion of zero and negative balances generally does **not** require special design considerations when using classical sampling, while it does when using probability-proportional-to-size sampling (AICPA *Audit Sampling Guide*). Answer (a) is incorrect because classical variables sampling does require an estimate of the standard deviation of the population's recorded amounts. Answer (b) is incorrect because the computational process involved with classical variables sampling may make use of a computer program desirable. Answer (d) is incorrect because probability-proportional-to-size sampling, not classical sampling, automatically stratifies individually significant items.

**SOLUTIONS TO SIMULATION PROBLEMS**

**Simulation Problem 1**

| | Analysis | |
|---|---|---|
| Situation | | Research |

**1. (A)** Thirty items. Calculated by dividing the population book value ($2,400,000) by the sampling interval size ($80,000). Accordingly $2,400,000/80,000 = 30 items.

**2. (G)** $26,150. Calculated by summing the misstatements ($1,000 + $150 + $25,000 = $26,150).

**3. (H)** $42,000. Projected misstatement represents the most likely total misstatement in the population ($42,000).

**4. (M)** $294,550. The upper limit on misstatement is the sum of projected misstatement, basic precision, and the incremental allowance ($42,000 + $240,000 + $12,550 = $294,550).

**5. (K)** $252,550. The allowance for sampling risk is the sum of basic precision and the incremental allowance ($240,000 + $12,550 = $252,550).

**6. (Reject)** Reject because the upper limit on misstatement ($294,550) exceeds the tolerable misstatement ($280,000).

**7. (5%)** Because basic precision uses a 3.0 factor, the test is being performed at 5%.

| | | Research |
|---|---|---|
| Situation | Analysis | |

AU 350.09-.11 discusses sampling and nonsampling risk as follows:

.09 Audit risk includes both uncertainties due to sampling and uncertainties due to factors other than sampling. These aspects of audit risk are sampling risk and nonsampling risk, respectively.

.10 Sampling risk arises from the possibility that when a test of controls or a substantive test is restricted to a sample, the auditor's conclusions may be different from the conclusion he would reach if the test were applied in the same way to all items in the account balance or class of transactions. That is, a particular sample may contain proportionately more or less monetary misstatements or deviations from prescribed controls than exist in the balance or class as a whole. For a sample of a specific design, sampling risk varies inversely with sample size: the smaller the sample size, the greater the sampling risk.

.11 Nonsampling risk includes all the aspects of audit risk that are not due to sampling. An auditor may apply a procedure to all transactions or balances and still fail to detect a material misstatement. Nonsampling risk includes the possibility of selecting audit procedures that are not appropriate to achieve the specific objective. For example, confirming receivables cannot be relied on to reveal unrecorded receivables. Nonsampling risk also arises because the auditor may fail to recognize misstatements included in documents that he examines, which would make that procedure ineffective even if he were to examine all items. Nonsampling risk can be reduced to a negligible level through such factors as adequate planning and supervision.

---

**Simulation Problem 2**

| | Characteristics | | | | |
|---|---|---|---|---|---|
| Situation | | Calculation | Spreadsheet | Research | Communication |

|  | Correct | Incorrect |
|---|:---:|:---:|
| 1. Size of a PPS sample is not based on the estimated variation of audited amounts. | ● | ○ |
| 2. PPS sampling results in a stratified sample. | ● | ○ |
| 3. Individually significant items are automatically identified. | ● | ○ |
| 4. PPS sampling results in a smaller sample size when numerous small misstatement are expected. | ○ | ● |
| 5. If no misstatements are expected, PPS sampling will usually result in a smaller sample size than classical variables sampling methods. | ● | ○ |
| 6. One does not need a book value for individual items to evaluate a PPS sample. | ○ | ● |
| 7. A PPS sample eliminates the need to project results to the overall population. | ○ | ● |
| 8. PPS sampling is "preferred" by the professional standards. | ○ | ● |

| Situation | Characteristics | Calculation | Spreadsheet | Research | Communication |
|---|---|---|---|---|---|

**(B) $3,000.** Sampling interval is equal to the recorded amount of accounts receivable ($300,000) divided by sample size (100). Accordingly, $300,000 ÷ 100 = $3,000.

| Situation | Characteristics | Calculation | Spreadsheet | Research | Communication |
|---|---|---|---|---|---|

**(D) $1,700.** The projected misstatement is calculated as

| | Recorded amount | Audit amount | Sampling interval | Difference | Tainting % | Projected misstatement |
|---|---|---|---|---|---|---|
| 1st misstatement | $ 400 | $ 320 | $1,000 | $80 | 20% | $ 200 |
| 2nd misstatement | 500 | 0 | 1,000 | 500 | 100% | 1,000 |
| 3rd misstatement | 3,000 | 2,500 | 1,000 | 1,000 | N/A | 500 |
| | | | | | | $1,700 |

| | A | B | C | D | E | F | G |
|---|---|---|---|---|---|---|---|
| 1 | Jane2 Inc. | | | | | | |
| 2 | Accounts Receivable | | | | | | |
| 3 | December 31, 20X2 | | | | | | |
| 4 | | | | | | | |
| 5 | | Recorded amount | Audited amount | Difference | Tainting % | Sampling interval | Projected misstatement |
| 6 | 1st misstatement | $ 400 | $ 320 | $ 80 | 20% | $ 1,0 | $ 200 |
| 7 | 2nd misstatement | 500 | -- | 500 | 100% | 1,0 | 1,000 |
| 8 | 3rd misstatement | 3,000 | 2,500 | 500 | N/A | 1,0 | 500 |
| 9 | | | | | | | $ 1,700 |

| Situation | Characteristics | Calculation | Spreadsheet | Research | Communication |
|---|---|---|---|---|---|

AU 350.18 discusses the relationship between tolerable misstatement and materiality as follows:

.18 Evaluation in monetary terms of the results of a sample for a substantive test of details contributes directly to the auditor's purpose since such an evaluation can be related to his judgment of the monetary amount of misstatements that would be material. When planning a sample for a substantive test of details, the auditor should consider how much monetary misstatement in the related account balance or class of transactions may exist without causing the financial statements to be materially misstated. This maximum monetary misstatement for the balance or class is called tolerable misstatement for the sample. Tolerable misstatement is a planning concept and is related to the auditor's preliminary judgments about materiality levels in such a way that tolerable misstatement, combined for the entire audit plan, does not exceed those estimates.

| Situation | Characteristics | Calculation | Spreadsheet | Research | Communication |
|---|---|---|---|---|---|

To:   Audit Working Papers
From: CPA Candidate

When audit sampling is used, a sample from a population is selected to make a conclusion about some characteristic of the population. Accordingly, to make a conclusion about the population, the results of the sample must be extended or projected to the population. This provides us with an estimate of the relevant characteristic of the population.

## AUDITING WITH TECHNOLOGY

Computers have become the primary means used to process financial accounting information and have resulted in a situation in which auditors must be able to use and understand current information technology (IT) to audit a client's financial statements. Accordingly, knowledge of computer terminology, computer systems, and related audit procedures is tested both on the Business Environment & Comments section and on the Auditing and Attestation section of the CPA exam. The following "Diagram of an Audit" was first presented and explained in the auditing overview section:

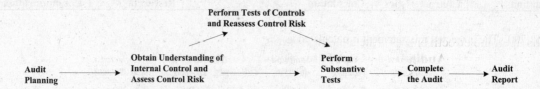

Computer processing (historically referred to as electronic data processing or EDP) does not necessitate modification of the diagram. However, the auditor's consideration of internal control includes an assessment of computerized as well as manual controls. Also, audit procedures may include computerized and manual procedures for considering internal control and for performing substantive tests.

The various professional pronouncements addressing computer processing include

- SAS 110 (SAS 55 and SAS 78) and an AICPA Audit Guide, both titled *Consideration of Internal Control in a Financial Statement Audit.*
- AICPA Auditing Procedures Studies: *Consideration of Internal Control in a Computer Environment: A Case Study; Auditing with Computers; Auditing in Common Computer Environments; Audit Implications of EDI.*

Because much of the IT information you need to know for auditing relates to IT systems, we have duplicated the material that appears in Module 39 of the *CPA Examination Review: Regulation* title as a supplement to this volume. The coverage here is limited to audit considerations.

### Study Program for Auditing with Technology Module

This module is organized as follows:

A. The Auditor's Consideration of Internal Control When a Computer Is Present

   1.  General
   2.  Computerized Audit Tools (CAAT) for Tests of Controls

B. Computerized Audit Tools

   1.  Generalized Audit Software
   2.  Electronic Spreadsheets
   3.  Automated Workpaper Software
   4.  Database Management Systems
   5.  Text Retrieval Software
   6.  Public Databases
   7.  Word Processing Software

### A. The Auditor's Consideration of Internal Control When a Computer Is Present

   1.  **General**

The auditor's responsibilities with respect to internal control over computer systems remain the same as with manual systems, that is, to obtain an understanding adequate (1) to aid in planning the remainder of the audit and (2) to assess control risk. Yet the auditor's consideration of internal control may be affected in that computer systems may

     a.  Result in transaction trails that exist for a short period of time or only in computer-readable form
     b.  Include program errors that cause uniform mishandling of transactions—clerical errors become much less frequent.
     c.  Include computer controls that need to be tested in addition to the segregation of functions.

    d.  Involve increased difficulty in detecting unauthorized access.

    e.  Allow increased management supervisory potential resulting from more timely reports.

    f.  Include less documentation of initiation and execution of transactions.

    g.  Include computer controls that affect the effectiveness of related manual control activities that use computer output.

As is the case for all controls, the auditor needs to test operating effectiveness only when control risk is to be assessed below the maximum. General application controls may be tested through inquiry, observation, and inspection techniques. In addition, application controls may be tested using reperformance techniques outlined in the following section. Because general controls affect all computer applications, the auditor's initial focus should be on them since the effectiveness of specific application controls depends upon the effectiveness of the general controls.

2. **Computerized Audit Tools (CAAT) for Tests of Controls**

Tests of controls may be divided into the following categories of techniques: (a) program analysis, (b) program testing, (c) continuous testing, and (d) review of operating systems and other systems software.

    a.  **Techniques for program analysis.** These techniques allow the auditor to gain an understanding of the client's program. Because these techniques ordinarily are relatively time-consuming and require a high level of computer expertise, they are infrequently used in financial statement audits.

        (1)  **Code review**—This technique involves actual analysis of the logic of the program's processing routines. The primary advantage is that the auditor obtains a detailed understanding of the program. Difficulties with the approach include the fact that it is extremely time-consuming, it requires a very high level of computer expertise, and difficulties involved with making certain that the program being verified is in fact the program in use throughout the accounting period.

        (2)  **Comparison programs**—These programs allow the auditor to compare computerized files. For example, they can be used in a program analysis to determine that the auditor has the same version of the program that the client is using.

        (3)  **Flowcharting software**—Flowcharting software is used to produce a flowchart of a program's logic and may be used both in mainframe and microcomputer environments. A difficulty involved is that the flowcharts of large programs become extremely involved.

        (4)  **Program tracing and mapping**—Program tracing is a technique in which each instruction executed is listed along with control information affecting that instruction. Program mapping identifies sections of code that can be "entered" and thus are executable. These techniques allow an auditor to recognize logic sequences or dormant section of code that may be a potential source of abuse. The techniques are infrequently used because they are extremely time-consuming

        (5)  **Snapshot**—This technique in essence "takes a picture" of the status of program execution, intermediate results, or transaction data at specified processing points in the program processing. This technique helps an auditor to analyze the processing logic of specific programs.

    b.  **Techniques for program testing.** Program testing involves the use of auditor-controlled actual or simulated data. The approach provides direct evidence about the operation of programs and programmed controls. Historically, knowledge of these techniques has been tested relatively frequently on the CPA exam.

        (1)  **Test data**—A set of dummy transactions is developed by the auditor and processed by the client's computer programs to determine whether the controls which the auditor intends to test (not necessarily all controls) to restrict control risk are operating effectively. Some of these dummy transactions may include errors to test effectiveness of programmed controls and to determine how transactions are handled (e.g., time tickets with invalid job numbers). When using test data, each control generally need only be tested once. Several possible problems include

            (a)  Making certain the test data is not included in the client's accounting records.

            (b)  Determining that the program tested is actually used by the client to process data.

            (c)  Adequately developing test data for every possible control.

(d) Developing adequate data to test key controls may be extremely time-consuming.

(2) **Integrated test facility (ITF)**—This method introduces dummy transactions into a system in the midst of live transactions and is usually built into the system during the original design. One way to accomplish this is to incorporate a simulated or subsidiary into the accounting system with the sole purpose of running test data through it. The test data approach is similar and therefore its limitations are also similar, although the test data approach does not run simultaneously through the live system. The running of dummy transactions in the midst of live transactions makes the task of keeping the two transaction types separate more difficult.

(3) **Parallel simulation**—Parallel simulation processes actual client data through an **auditor's generalized audit software program** and frequently, although not necessarily, the auditor's computer (generalized audit software is discussed in Section G. of this module). After processing the data the auditor compares the output obtained with output obtained from the client. The method verifies processing of **actual** transactions (as opposed to test data and ITF that use dummy transactions) and allows the auditor to verify actual client results. This method allows an auditor to simply test portions of the system to reduce the overall time and concentrate on key controls. The limitations of this method include

(a) The time it takes to build an exact duplicate of the client's system
(b) Incompatibility between auditor and client software
(c) Tracing differences between the two sets of outputs to differences in the programs may be difficult
(d) The time involved in processing large quantities of data

(4) **Controlled reprocessing**—Controlled reprocessing, a variation of parallel simulation, processes actual client data through a copy of the **client's application program**. As with parallel simulation, this method uses actual transactions and the auditor compares the output obtained with output obtained from the client. Limitations of this method include

(a) Determining that the copy of the program is identical to that currently being used by the client.
(b) Keeping current with changes in the program
(c) The time involved in reprocessing large quantities of data

c.  **Techniques for continuous (or concurrent) testing.** Advanced computer systems, particularly those utilizing EDI, sometimes do not retain permanent audit trails, thus requiring capture of audit data as transactions are processed. Such systems may require audit procedures that are able to identify and capture audit data as transactions occur.

(1) **Embedded audit modules and audit hooks**—Embedded audit modules are programmed routines incorporated into an application program that are designed to perform an audit function such as a calculation, or logging activity. Because embedded audit modules require that the auditor be involved in system design of the application to be monitored, this approach is often not practical. An audit hook is an exit point in an application program that allows an auditor to subsequently add an audit module (or particular instructions) by activating the hook to transfer control to an audit module.

(2) **Systems control audit review files (SCARF)**—A SCARF is a log, usually created by an embedded audit module, used to collect information for subsequent review and analysis. The auditor determines the appropriate criteria for review and the SCARF selects that type of transaction, dollar limit, or other characteristic.

(3) **Extended records**—This technique attaches additional data that would not otherwise be saved to regular historic records and thereby helps to provide a more complicated audit trail. The extended record information may subsequently be analyzed.

(4) **Transaction tagging**—Tagging is a technique in which an identifier providing a transaction with a special designation is added to the transaction record. The tag is often used to allow logging of transactions or snapshot of activities.

    d.  **Techniques for review of operating systems and other systems software.** Systems software may perform controls for computer systems. Related audit techniques range from user-written programs to the use of purchasing operating systems monitoring software.

        (1)  **Job accounting data/operating systems logs**—These logs, created by either the operating system itself or additional software packages that track particular functions, include reports of the resources used by the computer system. Because these logs provide a record of the activity of the computer system, the auditor may be able to use them to review the work processed, to determine whether unauthorized applications were processed, and to determine that authorized applications were processed properly.

        (2)  **Library management software**—This software logs changes in programs, program modules, job control language, and other processing activities. Auditors may review these logs.

        (3)  **Access control and security software**—This software supplements the physical and control measures relating to the computer and is particularly helpful in online environments or in systems with data communications because of difficulties of physically securing computers. Access control and security software restricts access to computers to authorized personnel through techniques such as only allowing certain users with "read-only" access or through use of encryption. An auditor may perform tests of the effectiveness of the use of such software.

3.  Information technology (IT) provides potential benefits of effectiveness and efficiency because it enables an entity to

    a.  Consistently apply predefined business rules and perform complex calculations on large volumes of transactions.

    b.  Enhance timeliness, availability, and accuracy of information

    c.  Facilitate the additional analysis of information

    d.  Enhance the ability to monitor the performance of the entity's activities and its policies and procedures.

    e.  Reduce risk that controls will be circumvented

    f.  Enhance ability to achieve effective segregation of duties by implementing security controls in applications, databases, and operating systems.

4.  IT poses specific risks to internal control including

    a.  Systems or programs may inaccurately process information

    b.  Unauthorized access to data may lead to destruction of data or inappropriate changes to data

    c.  Unauthorized changes to data in master files

    d.  Unauthorized changes to systems or programs

    e.  Failure to make necessary changes to systems or programs

    f.  Inappropriate manual intervention

    g.  Potential loss of data

5.  Use of an IT specialist

    a.  In determining whether specialized IT skills are needed to design and perform the audit, the auditor considers factors such as

        (1)  Complexity of entity's systems and IT controls

        (2)  Significance of changes made to existing systems, or implementation of new systems

        (3)  Extent to which data is shared among systems

        (4)  Extent of entity's participation in electronic commerce

        (5)  Entity's use of emerging technologies

        (6)  Significance of audit evidence available only in electronic form

    b.  Procedures an auditor may assign to a professional possessing IT skills

        (1)  Inquiring of entity's IT personnel on how data and transaction are initiated, recorded, processed, and reported, and how IT controls are designed

        (2)  Inspecting systems documentation

        (3)  Observing operation of IT controls

        (4)  Planning and performing of tests of IT controls

6. Documenting the understanding of internal control

    a. For an information system with a large volume of transactions that are electronically initiated, recorded, processed, or reported, may include flowcharts, questionnaires, or decision tables

    b. For an information system with limited or no use of IT, or for which few transactions are processed (e.g., long-term debt) a memorandum may be sufficient

    c. When an auditor is performing only substantive tests to restrict detection risk to an acceptable level, the auditor should obtain evidence about the accuracy and completeness of the information

7. Effects of IT on assessment of control risk

    a. In determining whether to assess control risk at the maximum level or at a lower level, the auditor should consider

        (1) Nature of the assertion
        (2) Volume of transactions
        (3) Nature and complexity of systems, including use of IT
        (4) Nature of available evidential matter, including evidence in electronic form

    b. In designing tests of automated controls

        (1) The inherent consistency of IT processing may allow the auditor to reduce the extent of testing (e.g., use a smaller sample)
        (2) Computer-assisted audit techniques may be needed for automated controls

8. Effects of IT on restriction of detection risk

    a. An auditor may assess control risk at the maximum and perform substantive tests to restrict detection risk when he or she believes that the substantive tests by themselves would be more efficient than performing tests of controls; for example

        (1) Client has only a limited number of transaction related to fixed assets and long-term debt and the auditor can readily obtain corroborating evidence in the form of documents and confirmations.

    b. When evidence is entirely or almost entirely electronic, the auditor in some circumstances may need to perform tests of controls. This is because it may be impossible to design effective substantive tests that by themselves provide sufficient evidence in circumstances such as when the client

        (1) Uses IT to initiate order using predetermined decisions rules and to pay related payables based on system-generating information, and no other documentation is produced.
        (2) Provides electronic service to customers (e.g., Internet service provider or telephone company) and uses IT to log service provided, initiate bills, process billing, and automatically record amounts in accounting records.

## B. Computerized Audit Tools

A variety of computerized audit tools (which may also be viewed as computer assisted audit techniques) are available for administering, planning, performing,, and reporting of an audit. We present a summary of major types

### 1. Generalized Audit Software (GAS)

The auditor may use various types of software on PCs (or other computers) and may include customized programs, utility software, and generalized audit software for performing tests of controls and substantive tests. Customized programs are written specifically for a client. Commercially produced utility software is used for sorting, merging, and other file maintenance tasks. Generalized audit software also performs such file maintenance tasks but generally requires a more limited understanding of the client's hardware and software features. The following is a list of functions performed by GAS (it is based on the AICPA Auditing Procedure Study *Auditing with Computers*):

    a. Record extraction—Extract (copy) records that meet certain criteria, such as

        (1) Accounts receivable balances over the credit limit

    (2) Inventory items with negative quantities or unreasonably large quantities
    (3) Uncosted inventory items
    (4) Transactions with related parties

  b.  Sorting (e.g., ascending or descending order)
  c.  Summarization, such as

    (1) By customer account number
    (2) Inventory turnover statistics
    (3) Duplicate sales invoices

  d.  Field statistics, such as

    (1) Net value
    (2) Total of all debt (credit values)
    (3) Number of records
    (4) Average value
    (5) Maximum (minimum) value
    (6) Standard deviation

  e.  File comparison, such as

    (1) Compare payroll details with personnel records
    (2) Compare current and prior period inventory files

  f.  Gap detection/duplicate detection—Find missing or duplicate records
  g.  Sampling
  h.  Calculation
  i.  Exportation—Select an application that has been performed using GAS and export to another file format (for additional analysis)

2.  **Electronic Spreadsheets**

    Electronic spreadsheets, often included in generalized audit software, may be used for applications such as analytical procedures and performing mathematical procedures. Also, auditors often use microcomputer electronic spreadsheets to prepare working trial balances, lead, and other schedules. Such spreadsheets may significantly simplify the computational aspects of tasks such as incorporating adjustments and reclassifications on a worksheet and are relatively easy to use, inexpensive, and can be saved and easily modified in the future. Disadvantages include the need for auditor training, and the fact that original spreadsheet development takes a significant amount of time.

3.  **Automated Workpaper Software**

    Automated workpaper software, generally microcomputer based, is increasingly being used by auditors. Originally used to generate trial balances, lead schedules, and other workpapers, advances in computer technology (e.g., improvements in scanning) make possible an electronic workpaper environment. Ordinarily, this type of software is easy to use and inexpensive. The primary disadvantage is the time required to enter the data for the first year being audited.

4.  **Database Management Systems**

    We have discussed database management systems in Section C. of this module. Database management software may be used to perform analytical procedures, mathematical calculations, generation of confirmation requests, and to prepare customized automated workpapers. An auditor may, for example, download relevant client files into his or her database and analyze the data as desired. Advantages of this approach include a great opportunity for the auditor to rearrange, edit, analyze, and evaluate a data file in a manner well beyond that possible to be performed manually and the ability to download client data without time-consuming data entry. Disadvantages include auditor training (more than with spreadsheets) and the need for adequate client documentation of applications.

5.  **Text Retrieval Software**

    Text retrieval software (also referred to as text database software) enables access to such databases as the AICPA Professional Standards and various FASB and SEC pronouncements. This software allows an auditor to research technical issues quickly and requires minimal training. Disadvantages include the fact that some training is required and that some professional literature is not currently available in software form.

6.  **Public Databases**

Public databases may be used to obtain accounting information related to particular companies and industries as well as other publicly available information on, for example, electronic bulletin boards, that an auditor may use.  Current developments for companies and their industries may be obtained from the Internet.  The **Internet** provides online access to newspaper and journal articles.  In addition, many companies and industry associations have World Wide Web **home pages** that describe current developments and statistics.

7.  **Word Processing Software**

Auditors use word processing software in a variety of communication-related manners including the consideration of internal control, developing audit programs, and reporting.

**MULTIPLE-CHOICE QUESTIONS (1-33)**

1.   An advantage of using systems flowcharts to document information about internal control instead of using internal control questionnaires is that systems flowcharts
    a.   Identify internal control weaknesses more prominently.
    b.   Provide a visual depiction of clients' activities.
    c.   Indicate whether control procedures are operating effectively.
    d.   Reduce the need to observe clients' employees performing routine tasks.

2.   A flowchart is most frequently used by an auditor in connection with the
    a.   Preparation of generalized computer audit programs.
    b.   Review of the client's internal control.
    c.   Use of statistical sampling in performing an audit.
    d.   Performance of analytical procedures of account balances.

3.   Matthews Corp. has changed from a system of recording time worked on clock cards to a computerized payroll system in which employees record time in and out with magnetic cards.  The computer system automatically updates all payroll records.  Because of this change
    a.   A generalized computer audit program must be used.
    b.   Part of the audit trail is altered.
    c.   The potential for payroll-related fraud is diminished.
    d.   Transactions must be processed in batches.

4.   Which of the following is correct concerning batch processing of transactions?
    a.   Transactions are processed in the order they occur, regardless of type.
    b.   It has largely been replaced by on-line real-time processing in all but legacy systems.
    c.   It is more likely to result in an easy-to-follow audit trail than is on-line transaction processing.
    d.   It is used only in nondatabase applications.

5.   An auditor would be most likely to assess control risk at the maximum level in an electronic environment with automated system-generated information when
    a.   Sales orders are initiated using predetermined, automated decision rules.
    b.   Payables are based on many transactions and large in dollar amount.
    c.   Fixed asset transactions are few in number, but large in dollar amount.
    d.   Accounts receivable records are based on many transactions and are large in dollar amount.

6.   In a highly automated information processing system tests of control
    a.   Must be performed in all circumstances.
    b.   May be required in some circumstances.
    c.   Are never required.
    d.   Are required in first year audits.

7.   Which of the following is **least** likely to be considered by an auditor considering engagement of an information technology (IT) specialist on an audit?
    a.   Complexity of client's systems and IT controls.
    b.   Requirements to assess going concern status.
    c.   Client's use of emerging technologies.
    d.   Extent of entity's participation in electronic commerce.

8.   Which of the following strategies would a CPA most likely consider in auditing an entity that processes most of its financial data only in electronic form, such as a paperless system?
    a.   Continuous monitoring and analysis of transaction processing with an embedded audit module.
    b.   Increased reliance on internal control activities that emphasize the segregation of duties.
    c.   Verification of encrypted digital certificates used to monitor the authorization of transactions.
    d.   Extensive testing of firewall boundaries that restrict the recording of outside network traffic.

9.   Which of the following is **not** a major reason for maintaining an audit trail for a computer system?
    a.   Deterrent to fraud.
    b.   Monitoring purposes.
    c.   Analytical procedures.
    d.   Query answering.

10.   Computer systems are typically supported by a variety of utility software packages that are important to an auditor because they
    a.   May enable unauthorized changes to data files if **not** properly controlled.
    b.   Are very versatile programs that can be used on hardware of many manufacturers.
    c.   May be significant components of a client's application programs.
    d.   Are written specifically to enable auditors to extract and sort data.

11.   An auditor would most likely be concerned with which of the following controls in a distributed data processing system?
    a.   Hardware controls.
    b.   Systems documentation controls.
    c.   Access controls.
    d.   Disaster recovery controls.

12.   Which of the following types of evidence would an auditor most likely examine to determine whether internal control is operating as designed?
    a.   Gross margin information regarding the client's industry.
    b.   Confirmations of receivables verifying account balances.
    c.   Client records documenting the use of computer programs.
    d.   Anticipated results documented in budgets or forecasts.

13.   An auditor anticipates assessing control risk at a low level in a computerized environment.  Under these circumstances, on which of the following activities would the auditor initially focus?
    a.   Programmed control activities.
    b.   Application control activities.
    c.   Output control activities.
    d.   General control activities.

**14.** After the preliminary phase of the review of a client's computer controls, an auditor may decide not to perform tests of controls (compliance tests) related to the controls within the computer portion of the client's internal control. Which of the following would **not** be a valid reason for choosing to omit such tests?

a. The controls duplicate operative controls existing elsewhere in the structure.

b. There appear to be major weaknesses that would preclude reliance on the stated procedure.

c. The time and dollar costs of testing exceed the time and dollar savings in substantive testing if the tests of controls show the controls to be operative.

d. The controls appear adequate.

**15.** Auditing by testing the input and output of a computer system instead of the computer program itself will

a. Not detect program errors which do **not** show up in the output sampled.

b. Detect all program errors, regardless of the nature of the output.

c. Provide the auditor with the same type of evidence.

d. Not provide the auditor with confidence in the results of the auditing procedures.

**16.** Which of the following client electronic data processing (EDP) systems generally can be audited without examining or directly testing the EDP computer programs of the system?

a. A system that performs relatively uncomplicated processes and produces detailed output.

b. A system that affects a number of essential master files and produces a limited output.

c. A system that updates a few essential master files and produces no printed output other than final balances.

d. A system that performs relatively complicated processing and produces very little detailed output.

**17.** An auditor who wishes to capture an entity's data as transactions are processed and continuously test the entity's computerized information system most likely would use which of the following techniques?

a. Snapshot application.

b. Embedded audit module.

c. Integrated data check.

d. Test data generator.

**18.** Which of the following computer-assisted auditing techniques processes client input data on a controlled program under the auditor's control to test controls in the computer system?

a. Test data.

b. Review of program logic.

c. Integrated test facility.

d. Parallel simulation.

**19.** To obtain evidence that on-line access controls are properly functioning, an auditor most likely would

a. Create checkpoints at periodic intervals after live data processing to test for unauthorized use of the system.

b. Examine the transaction log to discover whether any transactions were lost or entered twice due to a system malfunction.

c. Enter invalid identification numbers or passwords to ascertain whether the system rejects them.

d. Vouch a random sample of processed transactions to assure proper authorization.

**20.** An auditor most likely would introduce test data into a computerized payroll system to test controls related to the

a. Existence of unclaimed payroll checks held by supervisors.

b. Early cashing of payroll checks by employees.

c. Discovery of invalid employee I.D. numbers.

d. Proper approval of overtime by supervisors.

**21.** When an auditor tests a computerized accounting system, which of the following is true of the test data approach?

a. Several transactions of each type must be tested.

b. Test data are processed by the client's computer programs under the auditor's control.

c. Test data must consist of all possible valid and invalid conditions.

d. The program tested is different from the program used throughout the year by the client.

**22.** Which of the following statements is **not** true of the test data approach when testing a computerized accounting system?

a. The test need consist of only those valid and invalid conditions which interest the auditor.

b. Only one transaction of each type need be tested.

c. The test data must consist of all possible valid and invalid conditions.

d. Test data are processed by the client's computer programs under the auditor's control.

**23.** Which of the following is **not** among the errors that an auditor might include in the test data when auditing a client's computer system?

a. Numeric characters in alphanumeric fields.

b. Authorized code.

c. Differences in description of units of measure.

d. Illogical entries in fields whose logic is tested by programmed consistency checks.

**24.** Which of the following computer-assisted auditing techniques allows fictitious and real transactions to be processed together without client operating personnel being aware of the testing process?

a. Integrated test facility.

b. Input controls matrix.

c. Parallel simulation.

d. Data entry monitor.

**25.** Which of the following methods of testing application controls utilizes a generalized audit software package prepared by the auditors?

a. Parallel simulation.

b. Integrated testing facility approach.

c. Test data approach.

d. Exception report tests.

**26.** In creating lead schedules for an audit engagement, a CPA often uses automated work paper software. What client information is needed to begin this process?

a. Interim financial information such as third quarter sales, net income, and inventory and receivables balances.

b.   Specialized journal information such as the invoice and purchase order numbers of the last few sales and purchases of the year.

c.   General ledger information such as account numbers, prior year account balances, and current year unadjusted information.

d.   Adjusting entry information such as deferrals and accruals, and reclassification journal entries.

**27.** Using microcomputers in auditing may affect the methods used to review the work of staff assistants because

a.   The audit fieldwork standards for supervision may differ.

b.   Documenting the supervisory review may require assistance of consulting services personnel.

c.   Supervisory personnel may **not** have an understanding of the capabilities and limitations of microcomputers.

d.   Working paper documentation may not contain readily observable details of calculations.

**28.** An auditor would **least** likely use computer software to

a.   Access client data files.

b.   Prepare spreadsheets.

c.   Assess computer control risk.

d.   Construct parallel simulations.

**29.** A primary advantage of using generalized audit software packages to audit the financial statements of a client that uses a computer system is that the auditor may

a.   Access information stored on computer files while having a limited understanding of the client's hardware and software features.

b.   Consider increasing the use of substantive tests of transactions in place of analytical procedures.

c.   Substantiate the accuracy of data through self-checking digits and hash totals.

d.   Reduce the level of required tests of controls to a relatively small amount.

**30.** Auditors often make use of computer programs that perform routine processing functions such as sorting and merging. These programs are made available by electronic data processing companies and others and are specifically referred to as

a.   Compiler programs.

b.   Supervisory programs.

c.   Utility programs.

d.   User programs.

**31.** Smith Corporation has numerous customers. A customer file is kept on disk storage. Each customer file contains name, address, credit limit, and account balance. The auditor wishes to test this file to determine whether credit limits are being exceeded. The best procedure for the auditor to follow would be to

a.   Develop test data that would cause some account balances to exceed the credit limit and determine if the system properly detects such situations.

b.   Develop a program to compare credit limits with account balances and print out the details of any account with a balance exceeding its credit limit.

c.   Request a printout of all account balances so they can be manually checked against the credit limits.

d.   Request a printout of a sample of account balances so they can be individually checked against the credit limits.

**32.** An auditor most likely would test for the presence of unauthorized computer program changes by running a

a.   Program with test data.

b.   Check digit verification program.

c.   Source code comparison program.

d.   Program that computes control totals.

**33.** An entity has the following invoices in a batch:

| Invoice # | Product | Quantity | Unit price |
|-----------|---------|----------|------------|
| 201 | F10 | 150 | $ 5.00 |
| 202 | G15 | 200 | $10.00 |
| 203 | H20 | 250 | $25.00 |
| 204 | K35 | 300 | $30.00 |

Which of the following numbers represents the record count?

a.   1

b.   4

c.   810

d.   900

**SIMULATION PROBLEM**

**Simulation Problem 1**                              (40 to 45 minutes)

| Situation | | | | |
|---|---|---|---|---|
| | Technology | Controls | Research | Communication |

Computer processing has become the primary means used to process financial accounting information in most businesses. Consistent with this situation, CPAs must have knowledge of audit techniques using computers and of computer terminology.

| | Technology | | | |
|---|---|---|---|---|
| Situation | | Controls | Research | Communication |

Select the type of audit technique being described in **items 1 through 5**. Computer audit techniques may be used once, more than once, or not at all.

### Computer audit technique

A. Auditing "around" the computer     E. Processing output control
B. I/O audit approach     F. Test data
C. Integrated test facility     G. Write extract routine
D. Parallel simulation

### Description

| | (A) (B) (C) (D) (E) (F) (G) |
|---|---|
| 1. Auditing by manually testing the input and output of a computer system. | ○ ○ ○ ○ ○ ○ ○ |
| 2. Dummy transactions developed by the auditor and processed by the client's computer programs, generally for a batch processing system. | ○ ○ ○ ○ ○ ○ ○ |
| 3. Fictitious and real transactions are processed together without the client's operating personnel knowing of the testing process. | ○ ○ ○ ○ ○ ○ ○ |
| 4. May include a simulated division or subsidiary into the accounting system with the purpose of running fictitious transactions through it. | ○ ○ ○ ○ ○ ○ ○ |
| 5. Uses a generalized audit software package prepared by the auditors. | ○ ○ ○ ○ ○ ○ ○ |

| | | Controls | | |
|---|---|---|---|---|
| Situation | Technology | | Research | Communication |

For **items 1 through 5** select the type of computer control that is described in the definition that is presented. Each control may be used once, more than once, or not at all.

### Control

H. Backup and recovery     M. Hash total
I. Boundary protection     N. Missing data check
J. Check digit     O. Personal identification codes
K. Control digit     P. Visitor entry logs
L. File protection ring

### Description

| | (H) (I) (J) (K) (L) (M) (N) (O) (P) |
|---|---|
| 1. A control that will detect blanks existing in input data when they should not. | ○ ○ ○ ○ ○ ○ ○ ○ ○ |
| 2. A control to ensure that jobs run simultaneously in a multiprogramming environment cannot change the allocated memory of another job. | ○ ○ ○ ○ ○ ○ ○ ○ ○ |
| 3. A digit added to an identification number to detect certain types of data transmission or transposition errors. | ○ ○ ○ ○ ○ ○ ○ ○ ○ |
| 4. A terminal control to limit access to programs or files to authorized users. | ○ ○ ○ ○ ○ ○ ○ ○ ○ |
| 5. A total of one field for all the records of a batch where the total is meaningless for financial purposes. | ○ ○ ○ ○ ○ ○ ○ ○ ○ |

| | | | Research | |
|---|---|---|---|---|
| Situation | Technology | Controls | | Communication |

The use of sophisticated information technology may provide both benefits and risks relating to internal control. Find one place in the Professional Standards that lists IT benefits and risks relating to internal control. You may simply paste the appropriate material to your solution.

| Situation | Technology | Controls | Research | Communication |
|-----------|------------|----------|----------|---------------|

Write a memorandum to the audit working paper describing the risk of "auditing around the computer."

To:      Audit Working Papers
From:    CPA Candidate

MULTIPLE-CHOICE ANSWERS

| | | | | | | | | | | | |
|---|---|---|---|---|---|---|---|---|---|---|---|
| 1. b | __ __ | 7. b | __ __ | 13. d | __ __ | 19. c | __ __ | 25. a | __ __ | 31. b | __ __ |
| 2. b | __ __ | 8. a | __ __ | 14. d | __ __ | 20. c | __ __ | 26. c | __ __ | 32. c | __ __ |
| 3. b | __ __ | 9. c | __ __ | 15. a | __ __ | 21. b | __ __ | 27. d | __ __ | 33. b | __ __ |
| 4. c | __ __ | 10. a | __ __ | 16. a | __ __ | 22. c | __ __ | 28. c | __ __ | | |
| 5. c | __ __ | 11. c | __ __ | 17. b | __ __ | 23. a | __ __ | 29. a | __ __ | 1st: __/33 = __% |
| 6. b | __ __ | 12. c | __ __ | 18. d | __ __ | 24. a | __ __ | 30. c | __ __ | 2nd: __/33 = __% |

MULTIPLE-CHOICE ANSWER EXPLANATIONS

## A. Auditor's Consideration of Internal Control When a Computer Is Present

**1. (b)** The requirement is to identify an advantage of using systems flowcharts to document information about internal control instead of using internal control questionnaires. Answer (b) is correct because flowcharts provide a visual depiction of clients' activities which make it possible for auditors to quickly understand the design of the system. Answer (a) is incorrect because while the flow of operations is visually depicted, internal control weaknesses are not as obvious. Answer (c) is incorrect because while a flowchart describes a system, the flowchart alone does not indicate whether that system is operating effectively. Answer (d) is incorrect because auditors still need to determine whether the system has been placed in operation and therefore the need to observe employees performing routine tasks remains.

**2. (b)** The requirement is to determine when a flowchart is most frequently used by an auditor. Answer (b) is correct because flowcharts are suggested as being appropriate for documenting the auditor's consideration of internal control. Answer (a) is incorrect because auditors do not frequently write their own generalized computer audit programs, the most likely time a flowchart would be used with respect to such software. Answers (c) and (d) are incorrect because statistical sampling and analytical procedures do not in general require the use of flowcharts.

**3. (b)** The requirement is to identify the correct statement with respect to a computerized, automatically updating payroll system in which magnetic cards are used instead of a manual payroll system with clock cards. Answer (b) is correct because the automatic updating of payroll records alters the audit trail which, in the past, included steps pertaining to manual updating. Answer (a) is incorrect because although an auditor may choose to use a generalized computer audit program, it is not required. Answer (c) is incorrect because no information is presented that would necessarily indicate a change in the likelihood of fraud. Answer (d) is incorrect because given automatic updating, a large portion of the transactions are not processed in batches.

**4. (c)** The requirement is to identify the correct statement concerning the batch processing of transactions. Batch processing involves processing transactions through the system in groups of like transactions (batches). Answer (c) is correct because the similar nature of transactions involved with batch processing ordinarily makes it relatively easy to follow the transactions throughout the system. Answer (a) is incorrect because transactions are processed by type, not in the order they occur regardless of type. Answer (b) is incorrect because many batch applications still exist and might be expected to exist well into the future. Answer (d) is incor-

rect because batch processing may be used for database applications.

**5. (c)** The requirement is to determine when an auditor would be most likely to assess control risk at the maximum level in an electronic environment with automated system-generated information. Answer (c) is correct because the few transactions involved in fixed assets make it most likely to be one in which a substantive approach of restricting detection risk is most likely to be effective and efficient. Answer (a) is incorrect because an auditor might be expected to perform tests of controls to assess control risk below the maximum when automated decision rules are involved for an account (sales) which ordinarily has many transactions. Answers (b) and (d) are incorrect because the numerous transactions in payables and receivables make it likely that control risk will be assessed below the maximum.

**6. (b)** The requirement is to identify the most accurate statement with respect to tests of controls of a highly automated information processing system. Answer (b) is correct because SAS 110 states that in some such circumstances substantive tests alone will not be sufficient to restrict detection risk to an acceptable level. Answer (a) is incorrect because tests of controls need not be performed in all such circumstances. Answer (c) is incorrect because such tests are sometimes required. Answer (d) is incorrect because tests of controls are not in such circumstances in all first year audits.

**7. (b)** The requirement is to identify the least likely circumstance in which an auditor would consider engagements of an IT specialist on an audit. Answer (b) is correct because the requirement to assess going concern status remains the same on all audits, and thus does not directly affect engagement of an IT specialist. Answers (a), (c), and (d) are all incorrect because complexity, the use of emerging technologies, and participation in electronic commerce are all factors which SAS 110 suggests make it more likely that an IT specialist will be engaged.

**8. (a)** The requirement is to identify a strategy that a CPA most likely would consider in auditing an entity that processes most of its financial data only in electronic form. Answer (a) is correct because continuous monitoring and analysis of transaction processing with an embedded audit module might provide an effective way of auditing these processes—although some question exists as to how many embedded audit modules CPAs have actually used in practice. Answer (b) is incorrect because there may well be a decrease in reliance on internal control activities that emphasize this segregation of duties since so many controls are in the hardware and software of the application. Answer (c) is incorrect because digital certificates deal with electronic commerce between companies, a topic not directly addressed by this question, and because such certificates provide limited evidence on authorization. Answer (d) is incorrect because while firewalls do control network traffic, this is not the most significant factor in the audit of electronic form financial data.

**9.   (c)**   The requirement is to identify the reply that is **not** a major reason for maintaining an audit trail for a computer system. Answer (c) is correct because analytical procedures use the outputs of the system, and therefore the audit trail is of limited importance. Answer (a) is incorrect because an audit trail may deter fraud since the perpetrator may realize that his or her act may be detected. Answer (b) is incorrect because an audit trail will help management to monitor the computer system. Answer (d) is incorrect because an audit trail will make it much easier to answer queries.

**10.   (a)**   The requirement is to identify a reason that utility software packages are important to an auditor. Answer (a) is correct because client use of such packages requires that the auditor include tests to determine that no unplanned interventions using utility routines have taken place during processing (Audit and Accounting Guide, *Computer Assisted Audit Techniques*). Answer (b) is incorrect because a client's use of such programs implies that they are useful on his/her computer hardware, and therefore any flexibility is not of immediate relevance to the auditor. Answer (c) is incorrect because the primary purpose of utility programs is to support the computer user's applications (*Computer Assisted Audit Techniques*). Answer (d) is incorrect because utility software programs have a variety of uses in addition to enabling auditors to extract and sort data (*Computer Assisted Audit Techniques*).

**11.   (c)**   The requirement is to identify the types of controls with which an auditor would be most likely to be concerned in a distributed data processing system. A distributed data processing system is one in which there is a network of remote computer sites, each having a computer connected to the main computer system, thus allowing access to the computers by various levels of users. Accordingly, answer (c) is correct because numerous individuals may access the system, thereby making such controls of extreme importance. Answers (a), (b), and (d), while requiring concern, are normally considered less critical than proper access controls for this situation.

**12.   (c)**   The requirement is to identify the type of evidence an auditor would examine to determine whether internal control is operating as designed. Answer (c) is correct because the inspection of documents and records such as those related to computer programs represents an approach for obtaining an understanding of internal control. Answer (a) is incorrect because examining gross margin information is more likely to be performed during the performance of analytical procedures. Answer (b) is incorrect because confirming of receivables is a substantive test. Answer (d) is incorrect because anticipated results documented in budgets or forecasts are much more frequently used in the performance of analytical procedures.

**13.   (d)**   The requirement is to determine the procedures on which the auditor would initially focus when anticipating assessing control risk at a low level. Answer (d) is correct because auditors usually begin by considering general con-

trol procedures. Since the effectiveness of specific application controls is often dependent on the existence of effective general controls over all computer activities, this is usually an efficient approach. Answers (a), (b), and (c) are all incorrect because they represent controls that are usually tested subsequent to the general controls.

**14.   (d)**   The requirement is to determine an **inappropriate** reason for omitting tests of controls related to computer control procedures. Answer (d) is correct because the fact that the controls **appear** adequate is not sufficient justification for reliance; tests of controls must be performed before the auditor can actually rely upon a control procedure to reduce control risk. Answer (a) is incorrect because when controls duplicate other controls the auditor who wishes to rely upon internal control need not test both sets. Answer (b) is incorrect because if weak controls are not to be relied upon, the auditor need not test their effectiveness. Answer (c) is incorrect because tests of controls may be omitted if their cost exceeds the savings from reduced substantive testing resulting from reliance upon the controls.

**15.   (a)**   The requirement is to determine the correct statement with respect to testing inputs and outputs of a computer system instead of testing the actual computer program itself. Answer (a) is correct because portions of the program which have errors not reflected on the output will be missed. Thus, if a "loop" in a program is not used in one application, it is not tested. Answer (b) is incorrect because the lack of an understanding of the entire program precludes the detection of all errors. Answer (c) is incorrect because while auditing inputs and outputs can provide valuable evidence, it will often be different than the evidence obtained by testing the program itself. Answer (d) is incorrect because such auditing of inputs and outputs may well satisfy the auditor.

**16.   (a)**   The requirement is to identify the type of computer system that can be audited without examining or directly testing computer programs (i.e., auditing around the system). Auditing around the system is possible if the system performs uncomplicated processes and produces detailed output (i.e., is a fancy bookkeeping machine). Answers (b), (c), and (d) all describe more complicated computer systems that produce only limited output. In these more complicated systems, the data and related controls are within the system, and thus the auditor must examine the system itself. Auditors must identify and evaluate the accounting controls in all computer systems. Further, complex computer systems require auditor specialized expertise to perform the necessary procedures.

**17.   (b)**   The requirement is to determine an audit technique to determine whether an entity's transactions are processed and to continuously test the computerized information system. Answer (b) is correct because an embedded audit module is inserted within the client's information system to continuously test the processing of transactions. Answer (a) is incorrect because a snapshot application analyzes the information system at one point in time. Answer (c) is incorrect because an integrated data check simply tests data at one point in time. Answer (d) is incorrect because a test data generator provides a sample of possible circumstances in which data might be improperly processed.

**18. (d)** The requirement is to identify the computer-assisted audit technique that processes client input data on a controlled program under the auditor's control to test controls in a computer system Answer (d) is correct because parallel simulation processes actual client data through an auditor's generalized audit software program. Answer (a) is incorrect because test data is a set of dummy transactions developed by the auditor and processed by the client's programs to determine whether the controls which the auditor intends to test are operating effectively. Answer (b) is incorrect because a review of program logic is an approach in which an auditor reviews the steps by which the client's program processes data. Answer (c) is incorrect because an integrated test facility introduces dummy transactions into a client's system in the midst of live transactions.

### B. Computerized Audit Tools

**19. (c)** The requirement is to determine the best way to obtain evidence that on-line access controls are properly functioning. Answer (c) is correct because entering invalid identification numbers or passwords will provide the auditor with evidence on whether controls are operating as designed. Answer (a) is incorrect because directly testing access controls is more direct than testing data through checkpoints at intervals. Answer (b) is incorrect because a transaction log will not in general, by itself, identify whether transactions were lost or entered twice. Answer (d) is incorrect because vouching proper authorization is only one measure of whether controls are properly functioning.

**20. (c)** The requirement is to identify the situation in which it is most likely that an auditor would introduce test data into a computerized payroll system. Test data is a set of dummy transactions developed by the auditor and processed by the client's computer programs. These dummy transactions are used to determine whether the controls which the auditor tests are operating effectively. Answer (c) is correct because test data with invalid employee I.D. numbers could be processed to test whether the program detects them. Answer (a) is incorrect because the unclaimed payroll checks are held by the supervisors and no testing of the computer program is involved. Answer (b) is incorrect because no computer processing is generally involved when payroll checks are "cashed early" by employees. Answer (d) is incorrect because to test whether the approval of overtime is proper, one must determine what criteria are used for the decision and must then determine whether supervisors are following those criteria; it is less likely that this will all be included in a computer program than a test for invalid employee ID numbers.

**21. (b)** The requirement is to identify the correct statement regarding the test data approach. Answer (b) is correct because the test data approach consists of processing a set of dummy transactions on the client's computer system. The test data approach is used to test the operating effectiveness of controls the auditor intends to rely upon to assess control risk at a level lower than the maximum. Answer (a) is incorrect because only one transaction of each type is generally tested. Answer (c) is incorrect because it is not possible to include **all** possible valid and invalid conditions. Answer (d) is incorrect because the program that should be tested is the client's program which is used throughout the year.

**22. (c)** The requirement is to identify the statement which is **not** true of the test data approach. Answer (c) is correct (not true) because it is impossible or not cost beneficial to test **all** possible valid and invalid conditions. Answer (a) is incorrect because the auditor should test those valid and invalid conditions in which s/he is interested. Answer (b) is incorrect because only one transaction of each type need be tested in a computer control system in which the controls either work or do not work. Answer (d) is incorrect because test data is run using the client's computer programs under the auditor's control.

**23. (a)** The requirement is to determine which reply is not among the errors which are generally detected by test data. An auditor uses test data to determine whether purported controls are actually functioning. Answer (a) is correct because one would not use test data to test numeric characters in alphanumeric fields; numeric characters are accepted in alphanumeric fields and thus do not represent error conditions. Answer (b) is incorrect because authorization codes may be tested by inputting inappropriate codes. Answer (c) is incorrect because differing descriptions of units of measure may be inputted to test whether they are accepted. Answer (d) is incorrect because illogical combinations may be inputted to test whether they are detected by the system.

**24. (a)** The requirement is to identify the computer-assisted auditing technique which allows fictitious and real transactions to be processed together without client operating personnel being aware of the testing process. Answer (a) is correct because the integrated test facility approach introduces dummy transactions into a system in the midst of live transactions. Accordingly, client operating personnel may not be aware of the testing process. Answer (b) is incorrect because an input control matrix would simply indicate various controls in the form of a matrix. Answer (c) is incorrect because the parallel simulation technique requires the processing of actual client data through an auditor's software program. In this case, the client would be aware of the testing process since the auditor would need to request copies of data run on the actual system so that the data could then be run on the auditor's software program. Additionally, only valid transactions would be tested under parallel simulation. Answer (d) is incorrect because the client would generally be aware of an auditor using a data entry monitor (screen) to input transactions.

**25. (a)** The requirement is to determine the auditing technique which utilizes generalized audit software. Answer (a) is correct because the parallel simulation method processes the client's data using the CPA's software. Answers (b) and (c) are incorrect because the client's hardware and software are tested using test data designed by the CPA. Answer (d) is incorrect because although a CPA may test a client's exception reports in various manners, generalized software is unlikely to be used. Exception reports are generally tested via CPA-prepared test data containing all the possible error conditions. The test data are then run on the client's hardware and software to ascertain whether the exception reports are "picking up" the CPA's test data.

**26. (c)** The requirement is to identify the information that must be available to begin creating automated lead schedules. A lead schedule is used to summarize like accounts (e.g., if a client has five cash accounts those accounts may be summarized on a lead schedule). Answer (c) is correct because lead schedules include information such as account numbers, prior year account balances, and current year unadjusted information. Answer (a) is incorrect because interim information is not necessary. Answer (b) is incorrect because invoice and purchase order numbers are not summarized on lead schedules. Answer (d) is incorrect because adjusting entry information is identified subsequent to the creation of lead schedules.

**27.** **(d)** The requirement is to identify an effect on audit work review methods of using microcomputers in auditing. Answer (d) is correct because microcomputers typically produce a number of the "working papers" in computer disk form and because many computations, etc. will be performed directly by the computer with few details of the calculations conveniently available. Answer (a) is incorrect because the fieldwork standards remain the same regardless of whether or not computers are being utilized. Answer (b) is incorrect because one would not normally expect consulting services personnel to help with documentation. Answer (c) is incorrect because supervisory personnel must have an understanding of the capability and limitations of microcomputers before they are utilized on audits.

**28.** **(c)** The requirement is to determine an auditor's **least** likely use of computer software. Answer (c) is correct because an auditor will judgmentally assess control risk related to both the computer and manual systems after having performed the various tests of controls. Answer (a) is incorrect because computer software will be used to access client data files. Answers (b) and (d) are incorrect because software is used to prepare spreadsheets and to perform parallel simulations.

**29.** **(a)** The requirement is to identify a primary advantage of using generalized audit software packages to audit the financial statements of a client that uses a computer system. Answer (a) is correct because generalized audit software allows an auditor to perform audits tests on a client's computer files. Answer (b) is incorrect because generalized audit software packages may assist the auditor with either substantive tests of transactions or analytical procedures. Answer (c) is incorrect because while generalized audit software might be used to perform such operations, this is not their primary advantage. Answer (d) is incorrect because generalized audit software packages have no direct relationship to the performance of tests of controls.

**30.** **(c)** The requirement is to determine the type of computer programs which auditors use to assist them in functions such as sorting and merging. Answer (c) is correct because a utility program is a standard routine for performing commonly required processing such as sorting, merging, editing, and mathematical routines. Answer (a) is incorrect because compiler programs translate programming languages such as COBOL or FORTRAN to machine language. Answer (b) is incorrect because supervisory programs or "operating systems" consist of a series of programs that perform functions such as scheduling and supervising the application programs, allocating storage, controlling peripheral devices, and handling errors and restarts. Answer (d) is incorrect because user or "application programs" perform specific data processing tasks such as general ledger, accounts payable, accounts receivable, and payroll. Application programs make use of utility routines.

**31.** **(b)** The requirement is to determine the best approach for determining whether credit limits **are being exceeded** when accounts receivable information is stored on disk. Answer (b) is correct because a program to compare actual account balances with the predetermined credit limit and thereby prepare a report on whether any actual credit limits are being exceeded will accomplish the stated objective. Answer (a) is incorrect because while test data will indicate whether the client's program **allows** credit limits to be exceeded, it will not indicate whether credit limits **are actually being exceeded**. Answer (c) is incorrect because a manual check of all account balances will be very time consuming. Answer (d) is incorrect because a sample will provide less complete information than the audit of the entire population which is indicated in answer (b).

**32.** **(c)** The requirement is to identify how an auditor would test for the presence of unauthorized computer program changes. Answer (c) is correct because comparing source code of the program with a correct version of the program will disclose unauthorized computer program changes. Answer (a) is incorrect because test data is generally used to test specific controls and it will generally be less effective for detecting unauthorized changes than will source code comparison. Answer (b) is incorrect because check digits are primarily used as an input control to determine that input data is proper. Answer (d) is incorrect because properly computing control totals is only one possible unauthorized change that might be made to a program.

**33.** **(b)** The requirement is to identify the number that represents the record count. Answer (b) is correct because the record count represents the number of records in a file, in this case 4.

**SOLUTION TO SIMULATION PROBLEM**

**Simulation Problem 1**

| Situation | Technology | Controls | Research | Communication |
|---|---|---|---|---|

| *Description* | (A) | (B) | (C) | (D) | (E) | (F) | (G) |
|---|---|---|---|---|---|---|---|
| 1. Auditing by manually testing the input and output of a computer system. | ● | ○ | ○ | ○ | ○ | ○ | ○ |
| 2. Dummy transactions developed by the auditor and processed by the client's computer programs, generally for a batch processing system. | ○ | ○ | ○ | ○ | ○ | ● | ○ |
| 3. Fictitious and real transactions are processed together without the client's operating personnel knowing of the testing process. | ○ | ○ | ● | ○ | ○ | ○ | ○ |
| 4. May include a simulated division or subsidiary into the accounting system with the purpose of running fictitious transactions through it. | ○ | ○ | ● | ○ | ○ | ○ | ○ |
| 5. Uses a generalized audit software package prepared by the auditors. | ○ | ○ | ○ | ● | ○ | ○ | ○ |

**Explanation of solutions**

1. **(A)** Auditing "around" the computer involves examining inputs into and outputs from the computer while ignoring processing, as contrasted to auditing "through" the computer which in some manner directly utilizes the computer's processing ability.

2. **(F)** Test data is a set of dummy transactions developed by the auditor and processed by the client's computer programs to determine whether the controls that the auditor intends to rely upon are functioning as expected.

3. **(C)** An integrated test facility introduces dummy transactions into a system in the midst of live transactions and is often built into the system during the original design.

4. **(C)** An integrated test facility approach may incorporate a simulated division or subsidiary into the accounting system with the sole purpose of running test data through it.

5. **(D)** Parallel simulation involves processing actual client data through an auditor's software program to determine whether the output equals that obtained when the client processed the data.

| Situation | Technology | Controls | Research | Communication |
|---|---|---|---|---|

| *Description* | (H) | (I) | (J) | (K) | (L) | (M) | (N) | (O) | (P) |
|---|---|---|---|---|---|---|---|---|---|
| 1. A control that will detect blanks existing in input data when they should not. | ○ | ○ | ○ | ○ | ○ | ○ | ● | ○ | ○ |
| 2. A control to ensure that jobs run simultaneously in a multiprogramming environment cannot change the allocated memory of another job. | ○ | ● | ○ | ○ | ○ | ○ | ○ | ○ | ○ |
| 3. A digit added to an identification number to detect certain types of data transmission or transposition errors. | ○ | ○ | ● | ○ | ○ | ○ | ○ | ○ | ○ |
| 4. A terminal control to limit access to programs or files to authorized users. | ○ | ○ | ○ | ○ | ○ | ○ | ○ | ● | ○ |
| 5. A total of one field for all the records of a batch where the total is meaningless for financial purposes. | ○ | ○ | ○ | ○ | ○ | ● | ○ | ○ | ○ |

**Explanation of solutions**

1. **(N)** A missing data check tests whether blanks exist in input data where they should not (e.g., an employee's division number). When the data is missing, an error message is output.

2. **(I)** Boundary protection is necessary because most large computers have more than one job running simultaneously (a multiprogramming environment). To ensure that these simultaneous jobs cannot destroy or change the allocated memory of another job, the systems software contains boundary protection controls.

3. **(J)** A check digit is an extra digit added to an identification number to detect certain types of data transmission or transposition errors. It is used to verify that the number was entered into the computer system correctly; one approach is using a check digit that is calculated as a mathematical combination of the other digits.

4. **(O)** Personal identification codes require individuals to in some manner identify themselves to determine that only authorized users access programs or files.

**5. (M)** A hash total is the total of one field for all the records of a batch where the total is a meaningless total for financial purposes, such as a mathematical sum of employee social security numbers to determine that all employees have been processed.

| Situation | Technology | Controls | Research | Communication |
|-----------|------------|----------|----------|---------------|

SAS 110.18-.19 provides lists of benefits and risks relating to internal control and the use of information technology as follows:

.18 IT provides potential benefits of effectiveness and efficiency for an entity's internal control because it enables an entity to

- Consistently apply predefined business rules and perform complex calculations in processing large volumes of transactions or data.
- Enhance the timeliness, availability, and accuracy of information.
- Facilitate the additional analysis of information.
- Enhance the ability to monitor the performance of the entity's activities and its policies and procedures.
- Reduce the risk that controls will be circumvented.
- Enhance the ability to achieve effective segregation of duties by implementing security controls in applications, databases, and operating systems.

.19 IT also poses specific risks to an entity's internal control including

- Reliance on systems or programs that are inaccurately processing data, processing inaccurate data, or both.
- Unauthorized access to data that may result in destruction of data or improper changes to data, including the recording of unauthorized or nonexistent transactions or inaccurate recording of transactions.
- Unauthorized changes to data in master files.
- Unauthorized changes to systems or programs.
- Failure to make necessary changes to systems or programs.
- Inappropriate manual intervention.
- Potential loss of data.

| Situation | Technology | Controls | Research | Communication |
|-----------|------------|----------|----------|---------------|

To:    Audit Working Papers
From:  CPA Candidate

Auditing around the computer is a phrase used to describe a situation in which we do not test the controls in the system itself. Instead we focus on the input and output.

Auditing around the computer can only be justified in a situation in which the client has an unsophisticated computer system with no effective controls. When this technique is used there is a risk that we will not identify how errors or fraud could occur. Accordingly, we should never use the technique when we do not understand the system and its risks.

## OUTLINES OF PROFESSIONAL STANDARDS

This section presents outlines of (1) the **Statements on Standards for Attestation Engagements,** (2) the **Statements on Auditing Standards**, and (3) the **Statements on Standards for Accounting and Review Services**. When codified sequence differs from chronological sequence, we have presented the outlines in codified sequence. Study these outlines in conjunction with the related topical material (e.g., ethics, reports, etc.).

## STATEMENTS ON STANDARDS FOR ATTESTATION ENGAGEMENTS

*Overview*. The Statements on Standards for Attestation Engagements are issued by three organizations: (1) the Auditing Standards Board, (2) the Accounting and Review Services Committee, and (3) the Management Advisory Services Executive Committee.

### AT 101 Attestation Standards

*Overall Objectives and Approach*—This section is composed of (1) definitions and underlying concepts and (2) the eleven attestation standards with related explanations. This information is the general framework for attest services. Subsequent AT sections take the information included in AT 101 as a starting point and provide additional guidance, generally a particular type of service (e.g., reporting on internal control, or compliance with laws and regulations).

The scope of the section includes engagements in which a CPA is engaged to issue or does issue an examination, a review, or an agreed-upon procedures report on subject matter—or an assertion about the subject matter—that is the responsibility of another party. However, only limited guidance is provided relating to agreed-upon procedures engagements, which are discussed in detail in AT 201. Be aware that services explicitly **excluded** from this section's coverage include services and engagements performed

- Under Statements on Auditing Standards (see the AU outlines)
- Under Statements on Standards for Accounting and Review Services (see the AR outlines)
- Under Statements on Standards for Consulting Services
- Advocating a client's position (e.g., matters being reviewed by the Internal Revenue Service)
- Preparing tax returns or providing tax advice.

The following outline has four sections. Section A defines and provides underlying concepts relating to attest engagements. Sections B, C, and D present the general, fieldwork, and reporting standards, respectively. Note that the attest standards are included in *italics* as numbered subheadings under Sections B, C, and D. Finally, while the standards use the term "practitioner" in most places, we will use the term "CPA."

A. Definitions and underlying concepts
   1. **Subject matter**—May take many forms, including
       a. Historical or prospective performance or condition (e.g., prospective financial statements)
       b. Physical characteristics (e.g., narrative descriptions, square footage of facilities)
       c. Historical events (e.g., price of goods at a certain date)
       d. Analyses (e.g., breakeven analyses)
       e. Systems and processes (e.g., internal control)
       f. Behavior (e.g., corporate governance, compliance with laws and regulations, human resource practices)
   2. **Assertion**—Any declaration or set of declarations about whether the subject matter is based on or in conformity with the criteria selected
       a. A CPA may report on a **written assertion** or on the **subject matter**
       b. When a written assertion is not obtained the use of the report should be restricted
   3. **Responsible party**—The party responsible for the subject matter
       a. A CPA should obtain written acknowledgement or other evidence of responsible party's responsibility
       b. Most frequently, the responsible party is top management
B. General standards
   1. First general standard—The engagement shall be performed by a practitioner having adequate technical training and proficiency in the attest function
   2. Second general standard—The engagement shall be performed by a practitioner having adequate knowledge of the subject matter

3. Third general standard—The practitioner shall perform the engagement only if he or she has reason to believe that the subject matter is capable of reasonably consistent evaluation against criteria that are suitable and available to users
  a. Suitable criteria
    (1) Are the standards or benchmarks used to measure and present the subject matter and against which the CPA evaluates the subject matter

    *NOTE: To illustrate the suitable criteria concept, think of financial statements—the suitable criteria are frequently generally accepted accounting principles. We use this illustration because most are familiar with generally accepted accounting principles. Recognize that historical financial statements are not included under the attestation standards.*

    (2) Although trade-offs exist, suitable criteria must be
      (a) Objective
      (b) Measurable
      (c) Complete
      (d) Relevant
  b. Guidelines on suitable criteria
    (1) Criteria established or developed by groups composed of experts that follow due process (e.g., FASB) are ordinarily considered suitable
    (2) Criteria established or developed by management, industry associations, or other groups that do not follow due process may or may not be suitable
    (3) Some criteria are suitable only to a limited number of parties who participated in their establishment or have an understanding of them
      (a) In such circumstance use of the report should be restricted to those parties
  c. Criteria should be available in one or more of the following ways
    (1) Publicly
    (2) Inclusion with the subject matter or in the assertion
    (3) Inclusion in CPA's report
    (4) Well understood by most users (e.g., The distance between A and B is twenty feet)
    (5) Available only to specified parties
      (a) In this circumstance the CPA's report should be restricted to those parties
4. Fourth general standard—In all matters relating to the engagement, an independence in mental attitude shall be maintained by the practitioner

**C.** Standards of fieldwork
  1. First fieldwork standard—The work shall be adequately planned and assistants, if any, shall be properly supervised
  2. Second fieldwork standard—Sufficient evidence shall be obtained to provide a reasonable basis for the conclusion that is expressed in the report
    a. Presumptions
      (1) Evidence from independent sources provides greater assurance than evidence secured solely from within the entity
      (2) Information obtained from direct personal knowledge is more persuasive than information obtained indirectly
      (3) The more effective the controls over subject matter, the more assurance they provide about the subject matter or assertion

    *NOTE: Recall that the above presumptions are also presented in AU 326.*

  3. Types of attest engagements
    a. **Examination**—CPA selects from all available procedures and provides a high level of assurance to limit attestation risk to an appropriately low level
    b. **Review**—CPA generally limits procedures to inquiries and analytical procedures and provides a moderate level of assurance to limit attestation risk to moderate level
    c. **Agreed-upon procedures**—Presented in AT 201

**D.** Standards of reporting
  1. First reporting standard—The report shall identify the subject matter or the assertion being reported on and state the character of the engagement

2.  Second reporting standard—The report shall state the practitioner's conclusion about the subject matter or the assertion in relation to the criteria against which the subject matter was evaluated
3.  Third reporting standard—The report shall state all of the practitioner's significant reservations about the engagement, the subject matter, and if applicable, the assertion related thereto
4.  Fourth reporting standard—The report shall state that the use of the report is restricted to specified parties under the following circumstances [abridged]:
    a.  Criteria are suitable only for a limited number of parties
    b.  Subject matter is available only to specified parties
    c.  Written assertion has not been provided by the responsible party
    d.  Agreed-upon procedures engagements
5.  An examination report on subject matter [assertion] should include
    a.  Title with word "independent"
    b.  Identification of subject matter [assertion]
    c.  Subject matter [assertion] is the responsibility of the responsible party
    d.  CPA's responsibility is to express opinion on subject matter [assertion]
    e.  Examination conducted in accordance with attestation standard established by AICPA
    f.  Examination provides reasonable basis for opinion
    g.  Opinion on whether subject matter [assertion] follows criteria
    h.  Statement restricting use of report as per fourth reporting standard (D.4. above)
    i.  Manual or printed signature of firm
    j.  Date of report
6.  A review report on subject matter [assertion] should include
    a.  Title with word "independent"
    b.  Identification of subject matter [assertion]
    c.  Subject matter [assertion] is the responsibility of the responsible party
    d.  Review conducted in accordance with attestation standards established by AICPA
    e.  Review substantially less in scope than an examination, the objective of which is expression of an opinion, and accordingly, no such opinion is expressed
    f.  Statement about whether CPA is aware of any material modifications needed for subject matter [assertion] to comply with criteria
    g.  Statement restricting use of report as per fourth reporting standard (D.4. above)
    h.  Manual or printed signature of firm
    i.  Date of report

E.  Attest documentation
    1.  Purposes
        a.  Principal support for practitioner's report
        b.  Aid in conduct and supervision of engagement
    2.  Should be sufficient to
        a.  Enable members of engagement team with supervision and review responsibilities to understand nature, timing, extent, and results of attest procedures performed and information obtained
        b.  Indicate who performed and reviewed the work

## AT 201 Agreed-upon Procedures Engagements

*Overall Objectives and Approach*—This section sets forth attestation requirements and provides guidance for a CPA's performance of agreed-upon procedures (AUP) engagements. Recall that auditors currently perform three types of attestation engagements—examinations and reviews (emphasized in AT 101) and agreed-upon procedures. Because many of the concepts in AT 201 carry over from AT 101, make certain that you are familiar with that information.

A.  An agreed-upon procedures engagement is one in which a CPA is engaged by a client to issue a report of findings based on specific procedures performed on subject matter
    1.  The client engages the CPA to assist specified parties in evaluating subject matter or an assertion
        a.  Specified parties and the CPA agree upon the procedures that the specified parties believe appropriate
        b.  Specified parties assume responsibility for the sufficiency of the procedures
        c.  CPA's report should indicate that its use is restricted to those specified parties

*EXAMPLE: Assume that representatives of a bank ask that specified procedures be performed on balance sheet accounts that are to serve as collateral for a loan to a CPA's client. Those representatives would ordinarily be considered specified parties.*

   2.  A CPA may perform an AUP engagement provided that
     a.  CPA is independent
     b.  Party that wishes to engage CPA is
       (1)  Responsible for subject matter, or has a reasonable basis for providing a written assertion about the subject matter **or**
       (2)  **Not** responsible for the subject matter but is able to provide CPA, or have a third party who is responsible for the subject matter provide evidence of third party's responsibility for the subject matter
     c.  CPA and specified parties agree on procedures to be performed
     d.  Specified parties take responsibility for sufficiency of procedures
     e.  Subject matter involved is subject to reasonably consistent measurement
     f.  Criteria used to determine findings are agreed upon between CPA and specified parties
     g.  Procedures applied are expected to result in reasonably consistent findings using the criteria
     h.  Evidential matter is expected to provide reasonable basis for expressing findings
     i.  Where applicable, CPA and specified parties agree on materiality limits
     j.  Use of report restricted to specified parties
     k.  For AUP engagements on prospective financial information, the statements include a summary of significant findings
   3.  A written assertion is generally **not** required
   4.  CPA should establish an understanding with client about a variety of matters including—nature of engagement, identification of subject matter, specified parties, use restrictions, etc.
 **B.**  Procedures, findings, and working papers
   1.  Responsibility
     a.  Specified parties—sufficiency of agreed-upon procedures
     b.  CPA—perform procedures and report findings in accordance with attest standards and have adequate knowledge of subject matter
   2.  Procedures performed may be limited or extensive
     a.  But mere reading of an assertion or specified information about subject matter does not constitute a sufficient procedure to report on AUP
     b.  CPA should not agree to perform procedures so overly subjective and possibly open to varying interpretations; examples are
       (1)  Reading work performed by others solely to describe their findings
       (2)  Evaluating competency or objectivity of another party
       (3)  Obtaining understanding about a particular subject
       (4)  Interpreting documents outside scope of CPA's expertise
     c.  In certain circumstances a specialist may be called to assist the CPA in performing one or more procedures
   3.  Report should be in form of findings, and should **not** include negative assurance
   4.  The concept of materiality limits does not in general apply, unless agreed to by the specified parties
   5.  Working papers should indicate that work was adequately planned and supervised and that adequate evidential matter was obtained
**C.**  Reporting
   1.  Required elements
     a.  Title with word "independent"
     b.  Identification of specified parties
     c.  Identification of subject matter (or written assertion related thereto) and character of engagement
     d.  Subject matter responsibility of responsible party
     e.  Procedures performed agreed to by specified parties
     f.  AUP engagements conducted in accordance with attestation standards established by AICPA
     g.  Sufficiency of procedures responsibility of specified parties
     h.  List of procedures performed and related findings
     i.  Description of agreed-upon materiality limits (if any)

    j.   CPA not engaged to perform examination, disclaimer on subject matter, statement that if additional procedures had been performed other matters might come to CPA's attention

    k.   Statement restricting use of report to specified parties

    l.   For AUP on prospective financial information, items required under AT 301

    m.  Where applicable, description of nature of assistance provided by specialist

    n    Manual or printed signature of CPA's firm

    o.   Date of report

2.  Explanatory language may be included, such as

    a.   Stipulated facts, assumptions, interpretations

    b.   Condition of records, controls, etc.

    c.   Explanation that CPA has no responsibility to update report

    d.   Explanation of sampling risk

3.  Report should be dated as of date of completion of agreed-upon procedures

4.  If CPA's procedures restricted, CPA should describe restrictions in report or withdraw

5.  Additional specified parties may be added if they agree to take responsibility for sufficiency of procedures

**D.** Other

1.  CPA may wish to, but is not required to, obtain representation letter from responsible party

2.  A CPA who has performed another form of attest or nonattest engagement may be requested to change engagement to AUP engagement

    a.   Before changing to AUP, the CPA should consider

        (1)  Possibility that procedures performed for other engagement not appropriate for AUP

        (2)  Reason for request

        (3)  Additional effort required

        (4)  If applicable, reasons for changing from general-use report to restricted-use report

    b.   In all circumstances, if original engagement substantially complete, CPA should consider propriety of accepting a change in the engagement

3.  AUP reports may be combined with reports on other services (e.g., audit of financial statements) providing types of services clearly distinguished and report remains restricted

## AT 301 Financial Forecasts and Projections

*Overall Objectives and Approach*—This section sets forth standards and provides guidance for CPAs who are engaged to issue examination, compilation, or agreed-upon procedures reports on prospective financial information. As a starting point, it is important that you understand the basic information presented in Section A of the outline. That information is used throughout the remainder of the outline. Sections B, C, and D of the outline provide information on the three basic forms of CPA association with prospective financial information—compilations, examinations, and agreed-upon procedures. (CPAs do **not** perform reviews on prospective information.) Recognize that standards for the compilation form of association is not included in AT sections other than AT 301.

**A.** Definition and basic concepts

1.  Prospective financial statements—Partial presentations, financial forecasts, and financial projections

    a.   Types

        (1)  **Prospective forecasts**—Either financial forecasts or financial projections, including summaries of significant assumptions and accounting policies

        (2)  **Partial presentations**—A presentation of prospective financial information that excludes one or more of the items required for prospective financial statements (see b. below)

        (3)  **Financial forecasts**—Prospective financial statements that present the responsible party's beliefs about the entity's expected financial position, results of operations, and cash flows

        (4)  **Financial projection**—Prospective financial statements that present expected results, to the best of the responsible party's knowledge and belief **given one or more hypothetical assumptions**. A projection is a "what would happen if. . .? statement.

    b.   Minimum disclosures

        (1)  **Financial statement information:** sales, gross profit (or cost of goods sold), unusual or infrequently occurring items, provision for income taxes, discontinued operations, extraordinary items, income from continuing operations, net income, earnings per share, and significant cash flows

(2) **Background information:** purpose of prospective statements, assumptions, and significant accounting policies

(3) **Assumptions**

*NOTE: Omission of group 1 items creates a "partial presentation" not considered in the Statement. Omission of group 2 items in the presence of group 1 items results in a presentation subject to the provisions of this Statement. The accountant should not compile or examine statements lacking disclosure of assumptions (group 3).*

   c. **Pro forma statements** (those which show how a hypothetical transaction might have affected historical statements) and accountant financial analysis of a particular project are not included under provisions of this statement

   d. Financial forecasts and projections may both be in the form of single point estimates or ranges (in which case a paragraph discussing the estimates or ranges is added to report)

   e. Uses of prospective financial statements

     (1) **General**—May be used by persons with whom the responsible party is not negotiating directly (e.g., in an offering statement for debt or equity interests). Only a forecast is appropriate for general use

     (2) **Limited**—May only be used by responsible party or by responsible party and third parties with whom responsible party is negotiating directly. A forecast or a projection is appropriate for limited use

2. Accountant independence—an accountant need **not** be independent to perform a compilation, but must be independent to perform an examination or agreed-upon procedures

3. The accountant's report should not indicate that engagement included "preparation" of prospective financial statements

**B.** Compilations of prospective financial statements

1. Compilation procedures

   a. Assemble, to extent necessary, based on responsible party's assumptions

   b. **Perform required compilation procedures**

     (1) Establish understanding with client (preferably in writing) about services to be performed

     (2) Inquire about accounting principles used

     (3) Ask how responsible party identifies key factors and assumptions

     (4) List (or obtain a list of) significant assumptions and consider its completeness

     (5) Consider whether there are obvious inconsistencies in assumptions

     (6) Test mathematical accuracy

     (7) Read statements for conformity with AICPA guidelines and determine that assumptions are not obviously inappropriate

     (8) If a significant portion of prospective period has expired, inquire about actual results

     (9) Obtain written client representation letter (signed by responsible party at highest level of authority)

    (10) Attempt to obtain additional or revised information when above procedures make errors seem likely

2. Compilation reports (see the standard report in the Reporting Module)

   a. A compilation report on prospective financial information should include

     (1) Identification of prospective financial statements

     (2) Statements compiled in accordance with attestation standards established by AICPA

     (3) Compilation limited in scope and does not enable accountant to express opinion or any other form of assurance on prospective financial statements

     (4) Prospective results may not be achieved

     (5) Accountant assumes no responsibility to update the report after its issuance

   b. Circumstances resulting in departure from standard compilation report

     (1) Presentation deficiencies or disclosure omissions, other than a significant assumption (clearly indicate deficiency in report)

     (2) Comprehensive basis statements which do not disclose the basis used (disclose the basis in the report)

     (3) Summary of significant accounting policies omitted (a paragraph is needed which discloses that the policies have been omitted)

**C.** Examinations of prospective financial statements
1.  Examination procedures
    a.  Evaluate preparation
    b.  Perform examination procedures
        (1) Reach an **understanding with client** (ordinarily confirmed in an engagement letter)
        (2) **Evaluate the support for underlying assumptions** (consider available support, consistency, reliability of underlying historical information, logical arguments or theory)
        (3) **Obtain written representation letter** (signed by responsible party at highest level of authority)
    c.  Evaluate presentation for conformity with AICPA presentation guidelines (especially, that presentations reflect assumptions)
2.  The examination report on prospective financial statements should include
    a.  Title with the word independent
    b.  Identification of prospective financial statements
    c.  Identification of responsible party
    d.  CPA's responsibility is to express opinion on the prospective financial information
    e.  Examination conducted in accordance with attestation standards established by AICPA
    f.  Examination provides reasonable basis for opinion
    g.  Opinion on whether subject matter (assertion) follows criteria
    h.  Caveat that prospective results may not be obtained
    i.  CPA assumes no responsibility to update report
    j.  Manual or printed signature of firm
    k.  Date of report
3.  Circumstances resulting in departure from standard examination report
    a.  Departure from AICPA presentation guidelines (result in a qualified or adverse opinion)
    b.  Unreasonable assumptions (adverse opinion)
    c.  Scope limitation (disclaimer)
    d.  Emphasis of a matter (unqualified)
    e.  Evaluation based in part on report of another auditor (unqualified—divided responsibility)
**D.** Application of agreed-upon procedures to prospective financial statements
1.  An accountant engaged to perform agreed-upon procedures on prospective financial statements should follow SSAE 4 guidance (included in outline of AU 622)
2.  An agreed-upon procedures engagement may be performed if
    a.  The accountant is independent
    b.  The accountant and specified users agree on procedures
    c.  The specified users take responsibility for sufficiency of the agreed-upon procedures
    d.  The prospective financial statements include a summary of significant assumptions
    e.  The prospective financial statements to which the procedures are applied are subject to reasonably consistent estimation or measurement
    f.  Criteria to be used (accounting principles, policies and assumptions) are agreed upon between the accountant and the specified users
    g.  Procedures are expected to result in reasonably consistent findings using the criteria
    h.  Evidential matter to which the procedures are applied is expected to exist to provide a reasonable basis for expressing the findings in the accountant's report
    i.  Where applicable, there is agreement on any materiality limits
    j.  Use of the report is restricted to the specified users (although an accountant may perform an engagement pursuant to which his or her report will be matter of public record)
3.  The procedures may be as limited or as extensive as specified users desire, but must exceed mere reading of the prospective financial statements
4.  The report on agreed-upon procedures should be in the form of procedures and findings and include
    a.  Title with word "independent"
    b.  Identification of specified parties
    c.  Reference to the prospective financial statements and the character of the engagement
    d.  Statement that procedures were agreed to by specified parties
    e.  Identification of responsible party

f.  Reference to attestation standards established by AICPA
g.  Sufficiency of procedures responsibility of specified parties and a disclaimer of responsibility for sufficiency of those procedures
h.  List of procedures performed (or reference thereto) and related findings
i.  Where applicable, a description of any agreed-upon materiality limits
j.  Statement that CPA did not perform an examination of prospective financial statements; a disclaimer of opinion; if the CPA had performed additional procedures, other matters might have come to his or her attention that would have been reported
k.  A statement of restriction on the use of report because it is intended to be used solely by the specified parties
l.  Various other restrictions
m.  A caveat that prospective results may not be achieved
n.  A statement that accountant assumes no responsibility to update report
o.  Description of nature of assistance provided by a specialist (if applicable)
p.  Manual or printed signature of practitioner's firm
q.  The report should be dated as of the completion of the agreed-upon procedures

## AT 401 Reporting on Pro Forma Financial Information

*Overall Objective and Approach*—This section presents guidance on appropriate procedures and for reporting on certain pro forma financial information. As a starting point, this section **does not** apply to circumstances in which (1) pro forma information is presented within the same document, but not with financial statements (see the outline of AU 550) or (2) financial statements footnote information includes pro forma information (e.g., to show a revision of debt maturities, or a revision of earnings per share for a stock split).

This section **does** apply to pro forma financial information, presented with the basic financial statements, used to show the effects of an underlying transaction or event (hereafter, simply transaction). Such transactions include possible (1) business combinations, (2) changes in capitalization, (3) disposition of a significant portion of a business, and (4) proposed sale of securities and the application of proceeds. For example, a company which is considering issuing debt might prepare pro forma financial information to indicate what the effect of granting a loan in the prior period would have been. The pro forma financial information must be included with the historical financial statements. Thus, financial statements would generally have a column for historical information, and one for pro forma information.

This section divides much of the procedural and reporting advice into three areas—(1) determining that the assumptions are reasonable, (2) determining that the assumptions lead to the adjustments, and (3) determining that the adjustments have been properly reflected in the "pro forma column." The outline is divided into (a) procedural requirements and (b) reporting requirements.

**A.**  Procedural requirements
1.  The overall approach is to apply pro forma adjustments to historical financial information
2.  An accountant may agree to report on an **examination** or a **review** of pro forma financial information if the following conditions are met
    a.  The document with the pro forma financial information includes (or incorporates by reference) complete financial statements for the most recent period
    b.  The historical financial statements on which the pro forma financial information is based have been audited or reviewed
        (1)  The level of assurance for the pro forma financial information should be limited to the level of assurance provided on the historical financial statements

        > EXAMPLE: *When the historical financial statements have been audited, the pro forma financial information may be examined or reviewed. When the historical financial statements have been reviewed, the pro forma financial information may only be reviewed.*

    c.  The accountant must have an appropriate level of knowledge of the accounting and financial reporting practices of each significant part of the combined entity

        > EXAMPLE: *In a business combination between Company A and Company B, the accountant reporting on the pro forma financial information must obtain the knowledge relating to both companies, even if s/he has only audited one of them.*

3.  The objective of an accountant's examination or review procedures relates to whether
    a.  Management's assumptions are reasonable

b.   The pro forma adjustments appropriately follow from the assumptions
c.   The pro forma financial information column of numbers reflects proper application of the adjustments

*NOTE: When performing an examination, or review, reasonable assurance and negative assurance, respectively, are provided.*

4.   The following procedures should be applied to assumptions and pro forma adjustments for either an examination or a review
a.   Obtain knowledge of each part of the combined entity in a business combination
b.   Obtain an understanding of the underlying transaction (e.g., read contracts, minutes of meetings, make inquiries)
c.   Procedures applied to the assumptions
(1)  Discuss with management
(2)  Evaluate whether they are presented in a clear and comprehensive manner and are consistent with one another
d.   Procedures applied to the adjustments and their accumulation
(1)  Obtain sufficient evidence in support of adjustments
(2)  Evaluate whether pro forma adjustments are included for all significant effects of the transaction
(3)  Evaluate whether adjustments are consistent with one another and with the data used to develop them
(4)  Determine that computation of pro forma adjustments are mathematically correct and properly accumulated
e.   Obtain written representations from management concerning their
(1)  Responsibility for the assumptions
(2)  Belief that the assumptions are reasonable, that adjustments give effect to the assumptions, and that pro forma column reflects application of those adjustments
(3)  Belief that significant effects attributable to the transactions are properly disclosed
f.   Read the pro forma financial information and determine that the following disclosures are presented
(1)  Underlying transaction, pro forma adjustments, significant assumptions, and significant uncertainties
(2)  The source of the historical financial information on which the pro forma financial information is based has been appropriately identified

**B.**  Reporting on pro forma financial information
1.   Overall issues
a.   The report on the pro forma financial information may be added to the accountant's report on the historical financial information, or it may appear separately
b.   The report on pro forma financial information should be dated as of the completion of the appropriate procedures
(1)  When the reports on the historical and the pro forma financial information are combined, and when the completion of the pro forma procedures is after the completion of fieldwork for the audit or review of the historical financial information, the report should be dual dated
(a)  For example, "March 1, 20X8, except for the paragraphs referring to the pro forma financial information, for which the date is March 20, 20X8"
2.   The CPA's report on pro forma financial information should include
a.   Title with word "independent"
b.   Identification of pro forma financial information
c.   Reference to financial statements from which historical information derived
d.   Identification of responsible party
e.   CPA's responsibility is to express opinion on the pro forma financial
f.   Examination conducted in accordance with attestation standards established by AICPA
g.   Examination provides reasonable basis for opinion
h.   Objective of pro forma financial information and limitations
i.   Opinion on whether subject matter (assertion) follows criteria
j.   Manual or printed signature of CPA's firm

    k.   Date of the examination report

*NOTE: A review report is similar to the above, but presents negative assurance instead of an opinion.*

  3.  The accountant may qualify the opinion, render an adverse opinion, disclaim or withdraw due to circumstances such as scope limitation, uncertainties about the assumptions, conformity with presentation with assumptions or other reservations

## AT 501 Reporting on an Entity's Internal Control over Financial Reporting

*Overall Objective and Approach*—This section provides guidance on examining and reporting on an entity's internal control over financial reporting as of a point in time (or on an assertion thereon). AT 501 outlines the nature of a "responsible party." For purposes of this section, the "responsible party" is composed of the management personnel who accept responsibility for the effectiveness of the entity's internal control. Despite this definition, the terms "responsible party" and "management" are used virtually interchangeably in this section.

    The responsible party prepares a written assertion about the effectiveness of the entity's internal control measured against **suitable criteria,** also referred to as **control criteria**. The CPA then performs an examination or agreed-upon procedures engagement. The opinion for the CPA's report may be on either the internal control itself, or on the responsible party's assertion.

    Section A of this outline presents overview information. Section B outlines five steps performed in an examination engagement. Sections C through E deal with various aspects of reporting. Finally, Section F compares an auditor's consideration of internal control for purposes of an audit with that of examining an entity's internal control.

**A.** Overview information
1. The responsible party may present its written assertion about the effectiveness of its IC in either a
   a. Separate report that will accompany the CPA's report
   b. Representation letter to the CPA
2. The responsible party's written assertion will be as of a point in time, normally the end of the entity's fiscal year
   a. Refusal to provide a written assertion ordinarily causes the CPA to withdraw from the engagement
      (1) An exception exists for examinations required by law or regulation, in which case the CPA would disclaim an opinion (unless evidential matter indicates an adverse opinion being appropriate)
3. The following conditions must be met before an internal examination may be performed
   a. Responsible party (management) accepts responsibility for the effectiveness of IC
   b. Sufficient evidential matter exists or can be developed to support the responsible party's evaluation
4. The responsible party may select the definition for IC presented in AU 319, or another definition
5. Limitations of IC
   a. Human judgment can be faulty
   b. Breakdowns can occur due to simple error or mistake
   c. Controls can be circumvented by collusion of one or more people or management override of internal control
   d. Effectiveness of IC may be adversely affected by changes in
      (1) Ownership control
      (2) Management or other personnel
      (3) Entity's market or industry
**B.** When performing an examination engagement five steps are involved: (1) Planning the engagement, (2) Obtaining an understanding of IC, (3) Evaluating the design effectiveness of IC, (4) Testing and evaluating operating effectiveness, and (5) Forming an opinion
1. **Planning the engagement**
   a. When developing an overall strategy consider
      (1) Industry factors (e.g., financial reporting practices, economic conditions, laws)
      (2) Entity's operating characteristics, capital structure and distribution methods
      (3) Knowledge of entity's IC obtained during other engagements
      (4) Management's method of evaluating IC
      (5) Preliminary judgments about materiality levels, inherent risk and other factors relating to the determination of material weaknesses

          (6) Type and extent of available evidential matter

          (7) Nature of specific IC policies and procedures

          (8) Preliminary judgments about IC effectiveness

      b. If the entity has operations in multiple locations, it **may** not be necessary to understand and test controls at each location

   2. **Obtaining an understanding of IC**

      a. Obtained by inquiries of management and others in organization, inspection of documents, and observation of activities and operations

   3. **Evaluating IC *design effectiveness***

      a. This section presents the AU 319 information on the components of IC (control environment, risk assessment, information and communication system, control activities and monitoring)—see Section A of the outline of AU 319 for this information

      b. Evaluating the design effectiveness is concerned with whether the policies and procedures are suitably designed to prevent or detect material misstatements in specific financial statement assertions

   4. **Testing and evaluating IC *operating effectiveness***

      a. Tests of operating effectiveness

          (1) Are concerned with how policy or procedure was applied, the consistency with which it was applied, and by whom it was applied

          (2) Include inquiries of appropriate personnel, inspection of relevant documents, observation of operations, and reperformance or reapplication of IC procedure

      b. The process is similar to that performed on audits in assessing control risk. One difference here is that tests of controls are performed in all "important" areas, whereas in audits, auditors may choose to omit tests of controls and increase the scope of substantive tests.

   5. **Forming an opinion**

      a. All evidence obtained is used to evaluate the design and operating effectiveness of IC

**C.** Deficiencies in an entity's IC

   1. Definitions (from SAS 112)

      a. **Control deficiency**—A control deficiency exists when the design or operation of a control does not allow management or employees, in the normal course of performing their assigned functions, to prevent or detect misstatements on a timely basis; subtypes of control deficiencies:

          (1) **Deficiency in design**—Exists when

             (a) A control necessary to meet the control objective is missing or

             (b) An existing control is not properly designed so that even if the control operates as designed the control objective is not always met.

          (2) **Deficiency in operation**—Exists when a properly designed control does not operate as designed, or when the person performing the control does not possess the necessary authority or qualifications to perform the control effectively.

      b. **Significant deficiency**—A control deficiency, or combination of control deficiencies, that adversely affects the entity's ability to initiate, authorize, record, process, or report financial data reliably in accordance with generally accepted accounting principles such that there is more than a remote likelihood that a misstatement of the entity's financial statements that is more than *inconsequential* will not be prevented or detected.

          (1) A misstatement is *inconsequential* if a reasonable person would conclude that the misstatement, either individually or when aggregated with other misstatements, would clearly be immaterial.

      c. **Material weakness**—A significant deficiency, or combination of significant deficiencies, that results in more than a remote likelihood that a material misstatement of the financial statements will not be prevented or detected.

         Relationship among terms:

         • All material weaknesses and significant deficiencies are control deficiencies.

         • All material weaknesses are significant deficiencies.

   2. Evaluating control deficiencies

      a. The significance of a control deficiency depends on the potential for a misstatement, not on whether a misstatement actually has occurred.

(1) Related, absence of an identified misstatement does not provide evidence that identified control deficiencies are not significant deficiencies or material weaknesses.

b. The **likelihood** and **magnitude** of possible misstatements should be considered together when assessing the severity of a deficiency.

    (1) **Likelihood** factors relating to possible misstatement:

        (a) Nature of accounts, disclosures and assertions (e.g., suspense accounts and related-party transactions involve high likelihoods)

        (b) Susceptibility of related assets or liabilities to loss or fraud

        (c) Subjectivity and complexity involved

        (d) Frequency or any known or detected exceptions related to effectiveness of control.

        (e) Interaction with other controls and control deficiencies

        (f) Possible future consequences of the deficiency.

    (2) **Magnitude** factors relating to possible misstatement

        (a) Financial statement amounts or total transactions exposed to deficiency.

        (b) Volume of activity in account exposed to deficiency in current period or expected in future periods.

*NOTE: The maximum amount by which an account can be overstated is generally its recorded amount; but, because of the potential for unrecorded amounts, the recorded amount is not a limitation on the potential understatement.*

c. A control with a nonneglible deviation rate is a deficiency, regardless of the reason for the deviation(s).

d. Control deficiencies in the following areas are ordinarily at least significant deficiencies

    (1) Controls over selection and application of accounting policies that follow GAAP

    (2) Antifraud programs and controls

    (3) Controls over nonroutine and nonsystematic transactions

e. The following are at least significant deficiencies and a strong indicator of a material weakness

    (1) Ineffective oversight of entity financial reporting and internal control by those charged with governance

    (2) Restatement of previously issued financial statements to reflect a correction

    (3) Identification of a material misstatement not identified by entity's internal control

    (4) Ineffective internal audit or risk assessment function

    (5) For complex organizations in highly regulated industries, an ineffective regulatory compliance function

    (6) Identification of any fraud by senior management

    (7) Failure by management or those charged with governance to assess the effect of a significant deficiency that has been communicated by the auditor and to either correct it or conclude that it will not be corrected

    (8) An ineffective control environment

**D.** Reporting standards

  1. Examination reports should include

    a. Title that with the word "independent"

    b. Identification of subject matter (internal control over financial reporting)

    c. Identification of responsible party

    d. CPA's responsibility is to express opinion on effectiveness of IC

    e. Examination conducted in accordance with attestation standards established by AICPA

    f. Examination provides reasonable basis for opinion

    g. Inherent limitations of internal control (misstatements may occur and not be detected)

    h. Opinion on whether subject matter (assertion) follows criteria

    i. Statement restricting use of report (when internal control criteria suitable for only a limited number of parties or not generally available)

    j. Manual or printed signature of CPA's firm

    k. Date of the examination report

*NOTE: Generally the practitioner may report on either management's assertion or on the subject matter. However, when material deviation from the criteria exist, the practitioner should ordinarily express his/her conclusion on the subject matter, not on management's assertion. For example, if in the area of internal control a material weakness exists, the auditor would ordinarily report directly on internal control, not on management's assertion concerning internal control.*

**E.** Report modification conditions
1. Material weaknesses
    a. When one or more exist(s), to most effectively communicate with the reader of the report, the practitioner should express opinion directly on the effectiveness of IC, **not** on management's assertion
    b. If management includes material weakness in its assertion, practitioner should both modify the opinion paragraph by including a reference to the material weakness and add an explanatory paragraph that describes the weakness
        (1) Either a qualified or an adverse opinion may be issued (adverse when material weaknesses are so pervasive to ICS that it does not achieve the control objectives)
    c. If management does **not** include material weakness in its assertion (i.e., disagrees with practitioner about its importance), the practitioner should include an appropriate description of the weakness
        (1) If management's assertion accompanies the practitioner's report and states that the cost of correcting the weakness would exceed the benefits, the practitioner should disclaim an opinion on management's cost-benefit statement
2. Scope limitations
    a. Result in either a qualified opinion or a disclaimer depending on his/her assessment of the importance of the omitted procedures
    b. When significant scope limitations are imposed by the client, the practitioner generally should issue a disclaimer
3. Opinion based in part on the report of another practitioner
    a. The requirements are similar to those of AU 543 on other auditors in that a standard report is issued if the practitioner wishes to take responsibility for the work of other practitioners and the report is modified if s/he does not wish to take responsibility
4. Subsequent events
    a. Subsequent events related to IC should be described in management's written assertion and in the practitioner's report
5. A practitioner may report on whether controls are suitable for a specific purpose (e.g., provide reasonable assurance of preventing and detecting misstatements for purposes of a regulatory agency's regulations)
6. Management's assertion based on criteria specified by a regulatory agency
    a. If such criteria have been subjected to due process procedures (e.g., broad distribution for public comment) the report's distribution need not be limited
    b. If not subjected to due process procedures, report's distribution should be limited to regulatory agency and those within the entity
**F.** Relationship of examination of an entity's IC to consideration of IC for audit opinion
1. Purposes
    a. **Examination of IC**—Express an opinion about whether management's assertion that the entity maintained an effective IC as of a point in time is fairly stated in all material respects, based on the control criteria
    b. **Audit opinion**—Enable auditor to plan the audit and determine the nature, timing and extent of tests to be performed
2. The consideration of IC for purposes of an audit is more limited
3. In neither an audit nor examination of IC does a CPA indicate whether an entity is in compliance with the Foreign Corrupt Practices Act of 1977

## AT 601 Compliance Attestation

*Overall Objectives and Approach*—This section provides guidance on the CPA's (referred to as the "practitioner's") responsibilities with respect to attestation engagements to test compliance with specified requirements which arise through laws, regulations, contracts, rules, or grants. As indicated in part A.2. of the outline, not included in this section are engagements in accordance with *Government Auditing Standards* and various related acts (see AU 801) and several other areas.

The emphasis in this section is upon agreed-upon procedures engagements, although procedures and reporting responsibilities for examination engagements are also presented. Guidance for three types of engagements is provided: (1) agreed-upon procedures engagements on compliance with **specified requirements,** (2) agreed-upon procedures engagements on the effectiveness of an entity's **internal control over compli-**

**ance,** and (3) examination engagements on compliance with **specified requirements**. (Reviews are not permitted for any of these engagements; general guidance for examinations of the internal control over compliance is in AT 101.)

Section A of the outline presents general information. Sections B and C provide information on agreed-upon procedures and examination engagements respectively. Section D provides guidance on the required management representation letter that must be obtained on all of these engagements.

**A.** Introduction and general requirements
1. This section provides guidance for engagements related to **management's written assertion** about either
   a. An entity's compliance with requirements of specified laws, regulations, rules, contracts, or grants (hereafter, compliance with specified requirements) or
   b. Effectiveness of internal control over compliance with specified requirements
      (1) Management's assertions may be either financial or nonfinancial in nature
      (2) Engagements should comply with SSAE 1, *Attestation Standards,* which provides the overall attestation "umbrella" under which this more specific guidance exists
2. Section does **not** apply to
   a. GAAS audit responsibility
   b. Auditor reports on compliance based solely on an audit (see AU 623 outline)
   c. *Government Auditing Standards* and other governmental type engagements such as Single Audit Act engagements (see AU 801 outline)
   d. Letters for Underwriter (see AU 634 outline)
   e. Internal control engagements for a broker or dealer required by SEC Act of 1934
3. Allowed scope of services
   a. Three types of engagements are permitted
      (1) Agreed-upon procedures related to management's assertion about compliance with specified requirements
      (2) Agreed-upon procedures related to management's assertion about the effectiveness of an entity's internal control over compliance

      NOTE: *This type of engagement differs from an AT 501 engagement on internal control in that AT 501 is about management's internal control over financial reporting and this section is on management's internal control over compliance with specified requirements.*

      (3) Examination of management's assertion about compliance with specified requirements
   b. Review engagements are **not** permitted
4. Conditions for engagement performance
   a. Overall, management must
      (1) Accept responsibility for compliance with requirements **and** effectiveness of internal control over compliance
      (2) Evaluate compliance with specified requirements (or effectiveness of internal control over compliance)
      (3) Provide to the practitioner its written assertion about compliance with specified requirements (or effectiveness of internal control over compliance)
         (a) The written assertion must be in a separate management report if a general distribution **examination** report is to be issued (**all agreed-upon procedures** engagements and examinations with only a representation letter written assertion result in limited distribution reports)
      (4) For examinations
         (a) Assertion must be capable of evaluation against reasonable criteria that are expected to result in findings that are capable of reasonably consistent estimation
         (b) Sufficient evidential matter must support management's evaluation
   b. Management must identify applicable compliance requirements, establish policies to provide reasonable assurance of compliance, evaluate compliance, and produce specific reports that satisfy requirements.
**B.** Agreed-upon procedures engagements
1. The **objective** of an agreed-upon procedures engagement is to present specific findings to assist users in evaluating management's assertion about an entity's compliance with specified requirements or

about the effectiveness of an entity's internal control over compliance based on procedures agreed upon by the users of the report

    a.   The practitioner may be engaged to perform agreed-upon procedures about compliance with specified requirements **or** about effectiveness of internal control over compliance

2.  Ordinarily the accountant will communicate directly to obtain acknowledgment as to procedures from specified users; when this is not possible accountant may

    a.   Compare procedures to written requirements of specified users

    b.   Discuss procedures to be applied with representatives of the specified users, and/or

    c.   Review relevant contracts or communication from specified users

3.  The report on agreed-upon procedures should include

    a.   Title with word "independent"

    b.   Identification of specified parties

    c.   Identification of subject matter (internal control over financial reporting)

    d.   Identification of responsible party

    e.   Subject matter is responsibility of responsible party

    f.   Procedures agreed to by the specified parties

    g.   Examination conducted in accordance with attestation standards established by AICPA

    h.   Sufficiency of procedures responsibility of specified parties

    i.   List of procedures performed and related findings

    j.   Where applicable, description of materiality limits

    k.   CPA not engaged to perform an examination (and other limitations)

    l.   Restriction of use of report to specified parties

    m.   Where applicable, reservations or restrictions concerning procedures or findings

    n.   Where applicable, description of nature of assistance provided by specialist

    o.   Manual or printed signature of CPA's firm

    p.   Date of the examination report

**C.**  Examination engagements

1.  The audit risk model (AU 312) is adapted to compliance as follows:

    a.   Attestation risk—Risk practitioner unknowingly fails to modify opinion on management's assertion, composed of

       (1) Inherent risk—Risk of material noncompliance assuming no internal control

       (2) Control risk—Risk material noncompliance could occur and not be prevented or detected on a timely basis by internal control

       (3) Detection risk—Practitioner's procedures lead to conclusion that material noncompliance does not exist when it does

2.  Materiality differs from GAAS audit in that it is affected more by

    a.   Nature of assertion and compliance requirements, which may or may not be quantifiable in monetary terms

    b.   Nature and frequency of noncompliance identified with appropriate consideration of sampling risk

    c.   Qualitative considerations, including needs and expectations of report's users

       (1) In some cases practitioner may provide a supplemental report of all or certain noncompliance discovered

3.  Procedures to be followed

    a.   Obtain understanding of specified compliance requirements

    b.   Plan the engagement

       (1) Testing compliance at every location may be unnecessary

       (2) Practitioner may decide to use work of a specialist and to consider and use work of internal auditors

    c.   Consider relevant portions of internal control over compliance

       (1) When control risk to be assessed below maximum, perform tests of controls

    d.   Obtain sufficient evidence including testing compliance with specified requirements

    e.   Consider subsequent events

       (1) Responsibility similar to that of audits (see outline of AU 560)

    f.   Form opinion about whether entity compiled, in all material respects, with specified requirements (or management's assertion abort such compliance is fairly stated in all material respects)

4. Report should include
   a. Title with word "independent"
   b. Identification of compliance requirements
   c. Compliance is the responsibility of management
   d. Practitioner's responsibility is to express an opinion on compliance
   e. Examination was made in accordance with the attestation standards of AICPA, and included examining evidence about compliance
   f. Examination provides reasonable basis for opinion
   g. Examination does not provide a legal determination of compliance
   h. Opinion on whether entity complied, in all material respects, with specified requirements (or whether management's assertion about compliance is fairly stated) based on established or agreed-upon criteria
   i. Limitation on use when prepared in conformity with criteria specified by regulatory agency
   j. Manual or printed signature of firm
   k. Date of examination report
5. Report modifications
   a. Material noncompliance
      (1) Practitioner should state an opinion on compliance with specified requirements, not on management's assertion
      (2) If management discloses noncompliance and appropriately modifies its assertion, practitioner should modify opinion paragraph by including a reference to the noncompliance and add an explanatory paragraph (before the opinion paragraph) that describes the noncompliance
      (3) Depending upon significance either a qualified or an adverse opinion is appropriate
   b. Material uncertainty—may lead to a qualified opinion or a disclaimer of opinion
**D.** Management's representations
1. On all engagements a representation letter must be obtained from management
2. Management's refusal to furnish a representation letter is a scope limitation sufficient to require withdrawal in an agreed-upon procedures engagement and a qualified opinion or disclaimer in an examination engagement
3. When management's assertion is included in a report with other information the practitioner's only responsibility is to read that other information and consider whether it is materially inconsistent with the information appearing in management's report or whether it contains a material misstatement of fact

## AT 701 Management's Discussion and Analysis

*Overall Objectives and Approach*—This section presents guidance on management's discussion and analysis (MD&A) presented pursuant to the Securities and Exchange Commission's (SEC) rules and regulations (also, nonregistrants may voluntarily choose to present such information). It presents guidance for performing either a review or an examination on such information. The SEC does **not** require registrants to have MD&A information either reviewed or examined—the only current requirement is that an auditor meet the AU 550 requirement by reading all information accompanying the audited financial statements for consistency with those statements. While the section is extremely lengthy, in this outline we present only its most major points. You should be familiar with all of the information in the outline and the accompanying summary tables.

**A.** Review
1. Overall considerations
   a. Objective is to report whether any information came to practitioner's attention leading him/her to believe
      (1) MD&A presentation does **not** include, in all material respects, the SEC **required elements,** including a discussion of the entity's
         (a) Financial condition
         (b) Changes in financial condition and results of operations
         (c) Liquidity and capital resources
      (2) Historical amounts included in MD&A **not** accurately derived from financial statements
      (3) Underlying information, determinations, estimates and assumptions do **not** provide a reasonable basis for MD&A disclosures

b. Consists principally of applying analytical procedures and making inquiries of persons responsible for financial accounting and operational matters; does **not** contemplate
   (1) Tests of accounting records through inspection, observation, or confirmation
   (2) Obtaining corroborative evidential matter
   (3) Applications of other examination type procedures
c. A review of annual MD&A may be performed when practitioner has audited the historical financial statements of latest period to which MD&A relates, and other periods have been audited
d. A review of interim information may be performed if a quarterly review (or audit) of interim information has been performed

2. The review approach is similar to that for financial statements (analytical procedures and inquiry emphasis)
3. The review report of a public company (or a nonpublic company that is making a public offering) should be restricted to the use of specified parties
4. See MD&A General and Reporting Summaries at the end of this outline for guidance on planning, internal control, procedures, and reports

**B.** Examination
   1. Overall considerations
      a. Objectives are to express an opinion on whether
         (1) Presentation includes SEC **required elements,** including a discussion of the entity's
            (a) Financial condition
            (b) Changes in financial condition and results of operations
            (c) Liquidity and capital resources
         (2) Historical amounts accurately derived from financial statements
         (3) Underlying information, determinations, estimates, and assumptions provide a reasonable basis for MD&A disclosures
      b. Engagement may be performed when practitioner has audited the historical financial statements of the latest period to which MD&A relates, and other periods have been audited
   2. Practitioner should obtain reasonable assurance of detecting both intentional and unintentional misstatements, and adequately restrict attestation risk and its components—inherent risk, control risk, detection risk
   3. The assertions embodied in MD&A include
      a. Occurrence
      b. Consistency with financial statements
      c. Completeness
      d. Presentation and disclosure

   *NOTE: Points 1. and 2. above are the MD&A adaptations of "audit risk" and point 3. is the MD&A adaptation of the financial statement assertions—see AU 312.*

   4. See MD&A General and Reporting Summaries below for guidance on planning, internal control, procedures, and reports

## MD&A SUMMARY—GENERAL SUMMARY

| | Review | Examination |
|---|---|---|
| *Planning* | 1. Obtain understanding of SEC MD&A rules and regulations<br>2. Develop an overall strategy for the analytical procedures and inquiries to be performed to provide negative assurance | 1. Same as for reviews<br>2. Develop an overall strategy for the expected scope and performance of the engagement to obtain reasonable assurance to express an opinion |
| *Internal Control* | Consider relevant portions to identify types of potential misstatement and to select the inquires and analytical procedures—no tests of controls performed | Obtain understanding to plan the engagement and assess control risk (tests of controls may be performed) |
| *Procedures (test assertions)* | 1. Read MD&A, compare to financial statements, recompute increases, decreases, and percentages<br>2. Compare nonfinancial amounts to financial statements or other records<br>3. Consider consistency of MD&A explanations with information obtained during financial statement review or audit; make any necessary further inquiries<br>4. Compare MD&A to SEC requirements<br>5. Obtain and read available prospective financial information, inquire concerning this information<br>6. Obtain public communications and minutes of meetings and compare to MD&A<br>7. Make inquiries of officers with responsibility for operating areas and financial accounting matters as to their plans and expectations for the future<br>8. Inquire as to prior SEC experience<br>9. Consider whether there are additional matters that should be disclosed in MD&A based on results of preceding procedures | 1. Same as review<br><br>2. Same as review, but also perform tests on other records<br><br>3. Same as review, but investigate further explanations that cannot be substantiated by information in audit working papers<br>4. Same as review<br>5. Same as review, plus evaluate whether the underlying information, determinations, estimates, and assumptions provide a reasonable basis for MD&A disclosures<br>6. Same as review, plus consider obtaining other types of publicly available information for comparison to MD&A<br>7. Same as review<br><br>8. Same as review<br>9. Test completeness of results<br>10. Examine documents in support of existence, occurrence, or expected occurrence of events, transactions, etc. |
| *Report* | Includes negative assurance | Includes an opinion (reasonable assurance) |
| *Other* | 1. Must consider events subsequent to balance sheet<br>2. Must obtain management written representations | 1. Same as review<br>2. Same as review |

## MD&A SUMMARY—REPORTING SUMMARY

| | Review | Examination |
|---|---|---|
| *Report should include* | 1. Title with word independent<br>2. Identification of MD&A and period covered<br>3. Management responsible for MD&A<br>4. Reference to audit report on financial statements and, if nonstandard, reasons therefor<br>5. Review conducted in accordance with attestation standards and description of scope of examination established by AICPA; a description of review procedures<br>6. Review substantially less in scope than an examination<br>7. Paragraph stating that preparation of MD&A requires interpretations, and actual future results may vary<br>8. If nonpublic entity, MD&A intended to follow SEC rules<br>9. Statement about whether any information came to practitioner's attention concerning misstatements relating to (1) required elements, (2) historical amounts accurately derived, (3) underlying information provides reasonable basis (negative assurance provided)<br>10. Restriction on distribution if public company<br>11. Manual or printed signature<br>12. Date of a review | 1. Same as review<br>2. Same as review<br>3. Same as review<br>4. Same as review<br>5. Examination conducted in accordance with attestation standards established by AICPA and description of scope of examination<br>6. Practitioner believes examination provides reasonable basis for opinion<br>7. Same as review<br><br>8. Same as review<br>9. Practitioner's opinion on (1) presentation includes required elements, (2) historical amounts accurately derived, (3) underlying information provides reasonable basis<br><br>10. (No such requirement)<br>11. Same as review<br>12. Same as review |
| *Report modified for* | 1. Exclusion of a material required element<br>2. Historical financial amounts not accurately derived from financial statements<br>3. Underlying information has no reasonable basis<br>4. Practitioner decides to refer to report of another practitioner<br>5. Practitioner reviews MD&A after it has already been filed with SEC | 1. through 5., same as review, but also when there is a restriction on the scope of the engagement |
| *Other* | 1. Must consider events subsequent to balance sheet<br>2. Must obtain management written representations | 1. Same as review<br>2. Same as review |

## STATEMENTS ON AUDITING STANDARDS

*Overview*.  The Statements on Auditing Standards (SAS) are issued by the Auditing Standards Board.  The SAS which have been issued are codified into the following **overall** categories:

| *Section* | *Title* |
|---|---|
| AU 100 | Introduction |
| AU 200 | The General Standards |
| AU 300 | The Standards of Fieldwork |
| AU 400 | The First, Second, and Third Standards of Reporting |
| AU 500 | The Fourth Standard of Reporting |
| AU 600 | Other Types of Reports |
| AU 700 | Special Topics |
| AU 800 | Compliance Auditing |
| AU 900 | Special Reports of the Committee on Auditing Procedure |

Included following AU 901 is the outline of *Government Auditing Standards*, published by the Comptroller General of the United States.  *Government Auditing Standards*, which is listed in *Information for Uniform CPA Examination Candidates* as a publication which candidates should study, provides background material upon which much of AU 801 is based.

### 110 Responsibilities and Functions of the Independent Auditor (SAS 1)

*Overall Objectives and Approach*—This section presents the objective of audits,  compares the responsibilities of the auditor with those of management, and discusses the professional requirements necessary for an auditor.

A.  Objective of a financial statement audit—the expression of an opinion on the fairness with which the financial statements present financial position, results of operations, and cash flows in conformity with GAAP

B.  Responsibilities
   1.  Management—adopting sound accounting policies and internal control that will record, process, summarize, and report financial data that is consistent with management's assertions in the financial statements
   2.  Auditor—expression of an opinion on the financial statements

   NOTE:  *A number of exam questions have addressed the idea that management's role includes the preparation of the statements while that of the auditor is expressing an opinion.*

C.  An independent auditor must have adequate levels of education and experience

### 150 Generally Accepted Auditing Standards (SAS 1, 43)

*Overall Objectives and Approach*—This section (a) distinguishes between auditing standards and auditing procedures, (b) presents the 10 generally accepted auditing standards (GAAS), and (c) discusses the status of Statements on Auditing Standards (SAS), interpretative publications, and other auditing publications.

A.  A CPA plans, conducts, and reports the results of an audit in accordance with GAAS
   1.  Auditing standards—provide a measure of audit quality and objectives to be achieved in an audit
   2.  Auditing procedures—acts the auditor performs during an audit to comply with GAAS

B.  General standards
   1.  Training—the examination is to be performed by a person or persons having adequate technical **training** and proficiency as an auditor
   2.  Independence—in all matters relating to the assignment, an **independence** in mental attitude is to be maintained by the auditor or auditors
   3.  Professional Care—due **professional care** is to be exercised in the performance of the examination and the preparation of the report

C.  Standards of fieldwork
   1.  Planning—the work is to be adequately **planned** and assistants, if any, are to be properly supervised
   2.  Internal Control—a sufficient understanding of **internal control** is to be obtained to plan the audit and to determine the nature, timing, and extent of tests to be performed
   3.  Evidential matter—sufficient competent **evidential matter** is to be obtained through inspection, observation, inquiries, and confirmations to afford a reasonable basis for an opinion regarding the financial statements under examination

**D.** Standards of reporting
1. **G**enerally accepted accounting principles—the report shall state whether the financial statements are presented in accordance with **generally accepted accounting principles**
2. **C**onsistency—the report shall identify those circumstances in which such principles have not been **consistently** observed in the current period in relation to the preceding period
3. **D**isclosures—informative **disclosures** in the financial statements are to be regarded as reasonably adequate unless otherwise stated in the report
4. **O**pinion—the report shall either contain an expression of **opinion** regarding the financial statements, taken as a whole, or an assertion to the effect that an opinion cannot be expressed. When an overall opinion cannot be expressed, the reasons therefore should be stated. In all cases where an auditor's name is associated with financial statements, the report should contain a clear-cut indication of the character of the auditor's examination, if any, and the degree of responsibility s/he is taking

*NOTE: You need not memorize the exact wording, but know the 10 standards. Recall TIP, PIE, and GODC (reordered standards of reporting—1, 4, 3, 2).*

**E.** GAAS and Statements on Auditing Standards (SAS)
1. An auditor must identify those applicable to his/her audit and exercise professional judgment in applying SAS
2. Materiality and audit risk underlie application of GAAS and SAS
3. An auditor must be prepared to justify departures from SAS
4. **Interpretative publications** consist of Auditing Interpretations, AICPA Audit and Accounting Guides and AICPA Auditing Statements of Position
   a. Are recommendations, not auditing standards
   b. An auditor who does not apply should be prepared to explain how he or she complied with the SAS provisions addressed by such guidance
5. **Other auditing publications** include other AICPA auditing publications, *Journal of Accountancy* and *CPA Letter* articles, continuing education programs, texts, etc.
   a. Have no authoritative status, but may help auditor to apply SAS

**161 The Relationship of Generally Accepted Auditing Standards to Quality Control Standards (SAS 25)**
*Overall Objectives and Approach*—This section states that a CPA firm has a responsibility to adopt a system of quality control that will provide it with reasonable assurance that its personnel comply with generally accepted auditing standards in its audit standards. For details on the actual quality control standards that have been promulgated, see the Engagement Planning Module.

**A.** Rule 202 of the Code of Professional Conduct requires that individual CPAs comply with GAAS
1. GAAS relate to the conduct of individual audits; quality control standards relate to the conduct of a firm's audit practice as a whole
2. Deficiencies or instances of noncompliance with quality control policies and procedures do not, in and of themselves, indicate that an audit was not performed in accordance with GAAS
**B.** CPA firms should comply with GAAS and establish quality control policies and procedures
1. The nature and extent of quality control policies and procedures depends on the firm's
   a. Size
   b. Autonomy of personnel and practice offices
   c. Nature of the firm's practice
   d. Firm's organizational structure
   e. Appropriate cost-benefit considerations
**C.** GAAS and quality control standards are related
1. GAAS related to the conduct of **individual audits**
2. Quality control standards relate to **overall audit practice**
3. GAAS and quality control standards may affect both the conduct of individual audits and the conduct of a firm's entire audit practice

**201 through 230  The General Standards (SAS 1)**
*Overall Objectives and Approach*—These brief sections present information on the general group (training, independence, professional care) of GAAS. We combine discussion of these sections.

**A.** The general standards are personal in nature and are concerned with the qualifications of the auditor and the quality of the auditor's work

**B.** Training—the examination is to be performed by a person or persons having adequate technical training and proficiency as an auditor
1. Both proper **education** and **professional experience** are necessary
2. A CPA must exercise **objectivity** and **professional judgment** when performing an audit

**C.** Independence—in all matters relating to the assignment, an **independence** in mental attitude is to be maintained by the auditor or auditors
1. The CPA should not only be **independent in fact,** but should also **appear independent** (i.e., avoid situations that may lead outsiders to doubt his/her independence)
2. To stress the CPA's independence, many companies follow the practice of having the independent auditor appointed by the board of directors or the stockholders

**D.** Professional Care—due **professional care** is to be exercised in the planning and performance of the audit and the preparation of the report
1. At a minimum, the auditor with final responsibility for the engagement should know the relevant accounting and auditing standards and should be knowledgeable about the client
2. Due professional care requires the auditor to exercise professional skepticism
   a. Professional skepticism is an attitude that includes a questioning mind and a critical assessment of audit evidence
   b. The auditor neither assumes that management is dishonest nor assumes unqualified honesty
3. The auditor's objective is to obtain sufficient competent evidential matter to provide a reasonable basis for forming an opinion
   a. This is referred to as providing "reasonable assurance" (rather than "absolute assurance")
   b. Because of the characteristics of fraud, a properly planned and performed audit may not detect a material misstatement; characteristics include
      (1) Collusion among management, employees, or third parties
      (2) Withheld, misrepresented, or falsified documentation
      (3) Ability of management to override or instruct others to override what otherwise appear to be effective controls

## 310 and 311  Planning (SAS 1, 22)

***Overall Objectives and Approach***—These sections present information on planning.  Section 310 discusses advantages of early appointment of the auditor, while Section 311 presents actual planning considerations

**A.** Planning—the work is to be adequately **planned** and assistants, if any, are to be properly supervised
1. Early appointment of the auditor enables the auditor to plan work so that it may be done expeditiously and to determine the extent to which it can be done before year-end
2. When appointed close to year-end or after year-end, the auditor should make certain whether an adequate examination and the expression of an unqualified opinion is possible

**B.** Establishing an understanding with the client
1. The auditor should establish an understanding (preferably in writing, often through an engagement letter) regarding the services to be performed, including
   a. Objectives of the engagement
   b. Management's responsibilities
   c. Auditor's responsibilities
   d. Limitations of the engagements
2. The understanding generally includes
   a. Objective of audit is expression of an opinion on the financial statements
   b. Management responsible for financial statements
   c. Management responsible for establishing and maintaining effective internal control over financial reporting
   d. Management responsible for ensuring compliance with laws and regulations
   e. Management responsible for making financial records and related information available to auditor
   f. Management will provide representation letter
   g. Management responsible for adjusting financial statements to correct material misstatements and for affirming to auditor that effects of uncorrected misstatements aggregated by auditor are immaterial
   h. Auditor responsible for conducting audit in accordance with GAAS, and

        (1) Obtain reasonable and not absolute assurance that financial statements are free of material misstatement, whether due to error or fraud

        (2) Material misstatement may remain undetected

        (3) If for any reason auditor is unable to complete audit or to form an opinion auditor may decline to express an opinion or issue a report

    i. Audit includes obtaining an understanding of internal control sufficient to plan the audit and to determine the nature, timing, and extent of audit procedures

        (1) An audit is **not** designed to provide assurance on internal control or to identify reportable conditions

        (2) However, if reportable conditions are identified, the auditor must ensure that the audit committee is aware of them

  3. An understanding might also include other matters such as

    a. Arrangement on conduct of engagement (timing, client assistance, etc.)

    b. Arrangement on involvement of specialists or internal auditors

    c. Arrangement on involvement of predecessor auditor

    d. Arrangements on fees and billing

    e. Any limitation of liability

    f. Conditions under which access to auditor's working papers may be granted

    g. Additional services provided relating to regulatory requirements

    h. Arrangement regarding other services

**C.** Approach for planning the audit

  1. Overall considerations

    a. Entity's type of business and industry

    b. Entity's accounting policies and procedures

    c. Methods used to process accounting information, including the use of service centers

    d. Planned assessed level of control risk

    e. Preliminary materiality judgments

    f. Financial statement items likely to require adjustment

    g. Conditions likely to require extension of audit tests

    h. Nature of reports to be issued for the audit

  2. Audit procedures applicable to planning the examination

    a. Review correspondence, prior year's workpapers, statements, etc.

    b. Determine the effect of nonaudit services to the client on the examination

    c. Inquire about current business developments

    d. Read current interim statements

    e. Discuss type, scope, timing, etc., of examination with client

    f. Consider effects of applicable authoritative pronouncements

    g. Coordinate client's preparation of data needed by auditor

    h. Determine need for consultants, specialists, and internal auditors

    i. Establish timing of audit work

    j. Establish and coordinate staff requirements

*NOTE: Be familiar with the above.*

  3. **A written audit program should be prepared**

    a. Instructs assistants on the work to be done

    b. Details audit procedures which are necessary

    c. Reflects the results of planning considerations and procedures

    d. May require modifications due to changing conditions

  4. Knowledge of the entity's business helps the auditor in

    a. Identifying problem areas

    b. Assessing conditions in which accounting data are developed

    c. Evaluating reasonableness of estimates

    d. Evaluating reasonableness of management representations

    e. Evaluating appropriateness of GAAP

  5. The auditor should consider the manner in which the computer is used in processing data

  6. The auditor must adequately understand and audit computer operations

**D.** Supervision
1. Assistants should be adequately supervised
2. When a difference about an auditing or accounting issue arises among firm personnel, such difference should be documented in the workpapers and, if necessary, the subordinate whose views are **not** being followed should be allowed to disassociate himself/herself from the resolution of the matter

> EXAMPLE: *Assume that an assistant does not believe that an adequate number of receivable confirmations have been sent. The assistant and the others involved should document their views in the working papers. Also, from the perspective of the CPA firm, know that it is important that the working papers document the manner in which (including reasons) the issue was resolved.*

## 312 Audit Risk and Materiality in Conducting an Audit (SAS 47)

*Overall Objectives and Approach*—This section presents information on how the CPA should consider both audit risk and materiality when conducting an audit. The components of audit risk discussed in this section are particularly important. The section discusses the auditor's consideration of audit risk and materiality while (1) planning the audit and (2) evaluating audit findings. For both planning the audit and evaluating findings, considerations at the financial statement and individual account balance levels are discussed.

**A.** Definitions and key concepts
1. **Audit risk**—The risk that the auditor may unknowingly fail to modify his/her opinion on financial statements that are materially misstated

   *NOTE: Not included in this definition are business risks relating to losses from litigation, adverse publicity, or other such events. Also not included is the risk of an inappropriate audit report for matters unrelated to misstatements (e.g., scope limitations, going concern).*

2. **Materiality** (per SFAC 2)—The magnitude of omission or misstatement of accounting information that, in light of surrounding circumstances, makes it **probable that the judgment of a reasonable person relying on the information would have been changed or influenced**
   a. Financial statements are materially misstated when they contain **misstatements** whose effect (individually or in the aggregate) is important enough to cause them to not be fairly presented, in all material respects, in conformity with GAAP

3. **Errors**—**Unintentional** misstatements or omissions of amounts or disclosures in financial statements, including
   a. Mistakes
   b. Unreasonable accounting estimates arising from oversight or misinterpretation of facts
   c. Mistakes in application of accounting principles

4. **Fraud**—Although a broad legal concept, the auditor's interest relates to **fraudulent acts that cause a misstatement of financial statements**
   a. Types of fraud include misstatements arising from
      (1) **Fraudulent financial reporting**
      (2) **Misappropriation of assets**

      *NOTE: See outline of AU 316 for details on fraud.*

   b. When fraud is detected, the auditor should consider the implications for the integrity of management or employees and the possible effect on other aspects of the audit
      (1) Misstatements involving relatively small amounts may be material since they may lead to a material contingent liability (e.g., an illegal payment)
   c. The auditor should consider audit risk and materiality both in (a) planning the audit and designing auditing procedures and (b) in evaluating whether the financial statements taken as a whole conform with GAAP

**B.** **Planning the Audit:** Consider audit risk and materiality at the **financial statement level**
1. **Audit risk consideration at the financial statement level**
   a. Audit risk should be established at an appropriately low level—it may be assessed in either quantitative or nonquantitative terms
   b. An assessment of the risk of misstatement (whether caused by error or fraud) should be made during planning
      (1) The auditor should **specifically assess the risk of misstatement due to fraud;** higher risk ordinarily requires
         (a) More experienced personnel or more extensive supervision
         (b) Nature of procedures—more persuasive evidence

          (c)  Timing of procedures—closer to year-end
          (d)  Extent of procedures—expanded

  c.  In an audit of a client with multiple locations, the auditor should consider
      (1)  Nature and amount of assets at various locations
      (2)  Degree of centralized records or information processing
      (3)  Effectiveness of control environment
      (4)  Frequency, timing, and scope of monitoring
      (5)  Judgments about materiality of location

**2.**  **Materiality considerations at the financial statement level**

  a.  While an auditor may determine an appropriate materiality level to include for each financial statement, for planning purposes the lowest amount so obtained would ordinarily be considered material to any one of the financial statements

> *EXAMPLE: If $100,000 would have a material effect on income, but $200,000 would materially affect financial position, the lower amount would normally be used in planning. This lower amount is normally used because in planning, the auditor will not in general be able to distinguish the types of misstatements which will be detected, and because the statements are interrelated. A $100,000 misstatement may thus materially affect the income statement and immaterially affect the balance sheet.*

  b.  During planning, materiality is largely a **quantitative** concept, although throughout the performance of the audit the auditor must be alert for misstatements that could be **qualitatively** material

> *NOTE: The need for relying largely on quantitative considerations is because of difficulties in anticipating likely qualitative characteristics of misstatements which will subsequently be discovered.*

  c.  Theoretically, if the auditor's judgment about materiality at the planning stage was based on the same information available to him/her while evaluating audit findings, materiality for planning and evaluation purposes would be the same
      (1)  The planning vs. evaluation materiality levels will, however, ordinarily differ because circumstances encountered on the audit will influence the judgment
      (2)  If significantly lower materiality levels become appropriate in evaluating audit findings, the auditor should reevaluate the sufficiency of the auditing procedures s/he has performed

**C.**  **Planning the Audit:**  Consider audit risk and materiality at the **individual account-balance or class-of-transactions level** (hereafter, "account level")

  **1.**  Holding other planning considerations equal, either a decrease in the level of audit risk acceptable to the auditor or a decrease in the amount considered material will cause
    a.  Selection of a more effective auditing procedure
    b.  Performance of auditing procedures closer to balance sheet date
    c.  Increasing extent of a particular auditing procedure

  **2.**  Audit risk at the account level must be controlled to allow an overall financial statement low level of risk

  **3.**  Audit risk
    a.  Components
      (1)  **Inherent risk**—Risk of material misstatement, when aggregated with other misstatements, assuming there is no related internal control. This risk varies by account and assertion (e.g., cash is more susceptible to theft than an inventory of coal)
      (2)  **Control risk**—Risk that internal control will not prevent or detect misstatements which could be material when aggregated with other misstatements
      (3)  **Detection risk**—Risk that auditing procedures will not detect a misstatement which could be material when aggregated with other misstatements

> *NOTE: Know that, at the account level, audit risk is composed of these 3 risks. Conceptually, audit risk exists for the 5 assertions presented in AU 326 for each account.*

    b.  Relationships among components
      (1)  Inherent and control risks exist independently of the audit while detection risk relates to auditor's procedures

> *NOTE: Auditors **assess** inherent and control risk, and **restrict** detection risk.*

      (2)  **Acceptable detection risk should vary inversely with the inherent and control risks**

    c.  Professional judgment is used to assess inherent risk and control risk
      (1)  Separate or combined assessments are acceptable

(2)  If either is assumed to be at less than maximum level of risk, the basis for the assessment should be disclosed (e.g., questionnaires, checklists)

4.  It is **not appropriate to use assessments of inherent risk and control risk to eliminate substantive tests**

   a.  **Substantive tests for material accounts are necessary**

D.  Evaluating audit findings

1.  The auditor should consider the effects of misstatements, both individually and in the aggregate, that are not corrected by the client

   a.  In evaluating the effects of misstatements, the auditor should consider both qualitative and quantitative consideration

   b.  The aggregation should include the auditor's best estimate of the total misstatements (likely misstatements), not just the identified misstatements (known misstatements)

2.  The **total likely misstatement** is composed of

   a.  **Known misstatement** (passed adjustments)—identified misstatements

   b.  **Projected misstatement,** less misstatements used in its calculation—This is the "projected misstatement" from sampling applications (see part C of Audit Sampling module)

   c.  **Other estimated misstatements**—The total of misstatements estimated by techniques other than audit sampling, such as analytical procedures

   > EXAMPLE:  *Assume an auditor has used a number of substantive tests to audit in detail 25% of the dollar value of an account and has discovered $1,000 of misstatements.  Furthermore assume that other estimated misstatements are equal to $6,000.  The total likely misstatements is calculated as*
   >
   > | | | | |
   > |---|---|---|---|
   > | a. | Known misstatements | $ 1,000 | |
   > | b. | Projected misstatement, less known misstatements used in its calculation | $ 3,000 | ($4,000 – $1,000) |
   > | c. | Other estimated misstatement | $ 6,000 | |
   > | | Total likely misstatement | $10,000 | |
   >
   > *Note that in b. above the known misstatement is subtracted so as to not double count it in the calculation of total likely misstatement.*

3.  When total **likely misstatement** is material, the auditor should request management to eliminate the material misstatement

   a.  Failure by management to eliminate the misstatement will result in either a qualified or adverse opinion on the financial statements

4.  When total likely misstatements immaterial

   a.  The auditor should recognize that the financial statements may still be materially misstated due to further misstatement remaining undetected and that audit risk is unacceptably high

   b.  If total likely misstatement is sufficiently low, the auditor will decide that audit risk is acceptably low

5.  The auditor should document a conclusion as to whether the aggregated misstatements cause the financial statements to be materially misstated

6.  Inherent subjectivity generally makes the likelihood of material misstatement greater in accounts which include accounting estimates as compared to those based essentially on factual data (e.g., transactions)

   a.  Examples

      (1)  **Estimates:**  Inventory obsolescence, uncollectible receivables, warranty obligations

      (2)  **Essentially factual data:**  cash balance, notes payable, outstanding common stock

   b.  If the auditor believes that the estimate is unreasonable, s/he should treat the difference between that estimate and the **closest reasonable estimate** in the calculation of total likely misstatement

   c.  See AU 342 for further guidance on accounting estimates

## 313 Substantive Tests prior to the Balance Sheet Date (SAS 45)

*Overall Objectives and Approach*—This section presents guidance related to performing substantive tests at a date prior to the balance sheet date ("interim testing").  For example, in certain circumstances an auditor might wish to audit an account as of November 30, and then apply certain procedures for the period through December 31, the balance sheet date.  In addition to discussing the effect of interim procedures on audit risk, the section provides guidance on (1) factors to be considered prior to applying such procedures at an interim date,

(2) extending interim date audit conclusions to the balance sheet date, and (3) coordinating the timing of auditing procedures.

**A.** Overall relationship of interim substantive testing to audit risk
   1. Potentially increases audit risk (the risk that the auditor may **unknowingly fail to modify his/her opinion** on financial statements that are materially misstated—see outline of AU 312)
   2. Potential for increased audit risk increases as interim period is lengthened
   3. Effective substantive tests to cover the remaining period should be designed to control for the potentially increased audit risk
**B.** Performing substantive tests at an interim date
   1. Factors to be considered before performing tests at an interim date
      a. Difficulty in controlling the incremental audit risk due to performing test early
      b. Cost of subsequent tests necessary in remaining period (period after principal substantive tests through year-end)
      c. Effectiveness of remaining period substantive tests, especially when control risk is assessed at the maximum
         (1) In some circumstances a reasonable basis for extending audit conclusions from an interim date to the balance sheet date when control risk is assessed at the maximum level
      d. Existence of rapidly changing business conditions which might cause management to misstate financial statements
      e. Predictability of year-end balances
   2. **Extending interim date audit conclusions** to balance sheet date
      a. **Compare interim balances with year-end balances for unusual changes** and perform other analytical procedures and/or substantive tests of detail
      b. Consider implications of interim period errors in determining scope of remaining period tests
   3. Coordinate timing of audit procedures such as
      a. Related-party transactions
      b. Interrelated accounts and accounting cutoffs (e.g., cash with marketable securities)
      c. Negotiable assets (e.g., cash) and liabilities (e.g., loans)

### 315 Communications between Predecessor and Successor Auditors (SAS 84)

*Overall Objectives and Approach*—This section presents guidance on communications between predecessor and successor auditors when a change of auditors has taken place or is in process. The section presents information on (a) several definitions and key concepts, (b) a **required** communication by the potential successor **before** accepting the engagement, (c) **other** advisable communications **after** the successor auditor has accepted the engagement, and (d) audits of financial statements that have been previously audited (**reaudits**).

**A.** Definitions and key concepts
   1. **Predecessor auditor**—Auditor who has reported on the most recent audited financial statements or was engaged to perform but did not complete an audit of any subsequent financial statements and has resigned, declined to stand for reappointment, or been notified that his/her services have been, or may be terminated
   2. **Successor auditor**—Auditor who is considering accepting an engagement to audit financial statements or an auditor who has accepted such an engagement
   3. The responsibility for beginning the communication process is with the successor
   4. The communication may be written or oral
**B.** **Required** communications **before** successor accepts engagement
   1. The successor should obtain prospective client's permission to contact the predecessor
      a. If the prospective client refuses permission, the successor should inquire as to the reasons and consider the implications of such refusal in deciding whether to accept the engagement
   2. Successor's inquiries of the predecessor should include
      a. Information bearing on **integrity** of management
      b. **Disagreements** with management as to accounting principles, auditing procedures, or other similarly significant matters
      c. **Communications** to audit committee regarding fraud, illegal acts, and internal control related matters
      d. Predecessor's understanding of the **reasons for change** in auditors

3. Predecessor should respond promptly and fully to reasonable inquiries; however, unusual circumstances (e.g., litigation, disciplinary proceedings) may lead to a limited response

C. **Other** advisable communications **after acceptance** of the engagement

1. Successor should request client to authorize predecessor to allow a review of the predecessor auditor's
   working papers

   a. Although the review of working papers affects nature, timing, and extent of procedures with re-
      spect to **opening balances** and **consistency** of accounting principles, all conclusions reached are
      solely the responsibility of the successor

   b. The predecessor may wish to request the successor to sign a consent and acknowledgment letter
      from the client to document this authorization and reduce misunderstandings about the scope of
      the communication being authorized

      (1) **Consent letter**—From predecessor auditor to client (then signed by client) acknowledging
          client's permission to allow communication with the successor

      (2) **Acknowledgment letter**—From predecessor to successor (then signed by successor), indicat-
          ing that successor **will not**

          (a) Comment as to whether predecessor's engagement was performed in accordance with
              GAAS

          (b) Provide expert testimony on predecessor's audit

          (c) Use audit procedures in predecessor auditor's working papers as evidential matter

2. Predecessor should determine working papers to be made available, and should ordinarily include

   a. Documentation of planning

   b. Internal control

   c. Audit results

   d. Other matters of continuing accounting and auditing significance, such as analysis of balance
      sheet accounts

3. Extent to which predecessor permits access to working papers is a matter of judgment

4. Audit evidence includes

   a. Most recent financial statements

   b. Predecessor auditor's report

   c. Results of successor's review of predecessor auditor's working papers

5. If the successor auditor discovers financial misstatements, the successor should request client to inform predecessor auditor and arrange meeting of the three parties

   a. AU 561 provides further information

   b. If client refuses to inform predecessor, the successor should

      (1) Evaluate implications on current audit

      (2) Decide whether to resign

      (3) Consider need to consult with legal counsel concerning future action

D. Audits of financial statements that have been previously audited (**reaudits**)

1. If an auditor is asked to audit financial statements that have been previously audited (a reaudit), the
   auditor as a successor should follow procedures presented above in this outline; additional audit procedures are necessary in the reaudit

2. The successor should request working papers for period under reaudit, and the period prior to the
   reaudit period; the extent to which the predecessor permits access to working papers is a matter of
   judgment

3. If material, the successor performing the reaudit should perform some physical counts of inventory at
   a date subsequent to the period of reaudit; additional procedures may include

   a. Tests of prior transactions

   b. Review of records of prior counts

   c. Application of analytical procedures such as gross profit tests

## 316 Consideration of Fraud in a Financial Statement Audit (SAS 99)

*Overall Objectives and Approach*—It is an auditor's responsibility to plan and perform the audit to obtain reasonable assurance about whether the financial statements are free of material misstatement, whether caused by
error or fraud. Concerning fraud, the emphasis in the Professional Standards is on situations in which it causes
material misstatements, **not** on making determinations of whether legally fraud has occurred in any particular
situation.

This section deals with the auditor's responsibility as it relates to the risk of material misstatement due to fraud. Its major sections describe

A. Characteristics of fraud
B. Professional skepticism
C. Staff discussion of the risk of material misstatement
D. Obtaining the information needed to identify risks of material misstatement due to fraud
E. Identifying risks that may result in a material misstatement due to fraud
F. Assessing the identified risks after considering the client's programs and controls
G. Responding to the results of the assessment
H. Evaluating audit evidence
I. Communicating about fraud to management, the audit committee, and others
J. Documenting the auditor's consideration of fraud

In considering the outline, you might think of point A. as including background information, with point B. discussing the concept of professional skepticism. Although a simplification, the remaining sections may be viewed as "steps" to be performed relating to fraud.

Following point J. of the outline is a summary of AU 316's fraud risk factors and information on antifraud programs and controls. Those items are included as appendices to AU 316.

**A.** Characteristics of fraud
  1. Fraud is intentional, errors are unintentional
     a. Although fraud is considered an intentional act, when a misstatement exists, intent is often difficult to determine
  2. **Types of intentional misstatements**
     a. **Fraudulent financial reporting**—intentional misstatements, omissions of amounts or disclosures
     b. **Misappropriation of assets**—theft of an entity's assets, also referred to as defalcation
  3. Three conditions are generally present when fraud occurs
     a. **Incentive/pressure**—a reason to commit fraud
     b. **Opportunity**—for example, ineffective controls, override of controls
     c. **Attitude/rationalization**—ability to justify the fraud to oneself
  4. Management has a unique ability to perpetrate fraud because it can directly or indirectly manipulate accounting records and present fraudulent financial information; it may
     a. Override controls
     b. Direct or solicit employees to carry out fraud
  5. Although fraud is ordinarily concealed, certain conditions (e.g., missing documents) may suggest the possibility of fraud
  6. An auditor is unable to provide absolute assurance of detecting fraud
**B.** Professional Skepticism
  1. Professional skepticism is an attitude that includes a questioning mind and a critical assessment of audit evidence
  2. An audit should be conducted with a mindset that recognizes the possibility of material misstatement due to fraud, even if
     a. Past experience with the client has not revealed fraud, and
     b. Regardless of the auditor's belief about management's honesty and integrity
  3. An auditor should not be satisfied with less than persuasive evidence because of a belief that management is honest
**C.** Staff discussion of the risk of material misstatement
  1. Prior to or in conjunction with obtaining information to identify risks of fraud (part D of this outline), the audit team should discuss the potential for a material misstatement due to fraud, including
     a. "Brainstorming" among team members about how and where the financial statements might be susceptible to fraud, how management could perpetrate and conceal fraudulent financial reporting, and how assets could be misappropriated
     b. Emphasizing the importance of maintaining the proper state of mind regarding the potential for material misstatement due to fraud
  2. The discussion should

    a.  Include consideration of known factors affecting **incentives/pressures** for fraud, **opportunities,** and culture or environment that enables management to **rationalize** committing fraud

    b.  Emphasize the need to maintain a questioning mind and to exercise professional skepticism

    c.  Include key members of the audit team

        (1)  If multiple locations are involved there could be multiple discussions in different locations

        (2)  It may be useful to include any specialists assigned to the audit team in the discussion

**D.** Obtaining the information needed to identify risks of material misstatement due to fraud; procedures should include

    1.  Inquiries of management and others

        a.  Examples of inquiries of management

            (1)  Does it have knowledge of fraud or suspected fraud

            (2)  Have there been allegations of fraud or suspected fraud

            (3)  Its understanding of fraud risks

            (4)  Programs and controls established to mitigate fraud risks

            (5)  Control over multiple locations

            (6)  Communications to employees about business practices and ethical behavior

            (7)  Whether management has reported to the audit committee the nature of the company's internal control

        b.  Inquiries of the audit committee, internal audit function, and others should include their views about risks of fraud and their knowledge of any fraud or suspected fraud

    2.  Considering the results of analytical procedures performed in planning the audit

        a.  When unexpected results occur, consider the risk of material misstatement due to fraud

        b.  Perform analytical procedures on revenue to identify unusual or unexpected relationships

        *NOTE: Make certain that you know that analytical procedures relating to revenue must be performed during planning of the audit.*

        c.  Because analytical procedures performed during planning often use data aggregated at a high level, results obtained often only provide a broad initial indication about whether a material misstatement exists

    3.  Considering fraud risk factors

        a.  **Fraud risk factors** are events or conditions that indicate **incentives/pressures** to perpetrate fraud, **opportunities** to carry out fraud, or **attitude/rationalizations** to justify a fraudulent action

        *NOTE: Recall that **incentives/pressures, opportunities,** and **attitudes/rationalizations** are the conditions generally present in individuals who commit fraud presented in A.3 of the outline.*

        b.  The auditor should use professional judgment in determining whether a risk factor is present and in identifying and assessing the risk of material misstatement due to fraud

        c.  While fraud risk factors do **not** necessarily indicate the existence of fraud, they often are present when fraud exists

        d.  Fraud risk factors are presented following point I. of this outline

    4.  Consider other information: the discussion among audit team members, reviews of interim financial statements, consideration of identified inherent risks

**E.** Identifying risks that may result in a material misstatement due to fraud

    1.  It is helpful at this stage to consider the three conditions present when a material misstatement due to fraud ordinarily occurs—incentives/pressures, opportunities, and attitudes/rationalizations

        a.  But fraud may exist even if all three haven't been identified

    2.  The auditor should evaluate whether identified risks of material misstatement due to fraud can be related to specific accounts, assertions, or whether they relate more pervasively to the financial statements as a whole

    3.  The identification of a risk of material misstatement due to fraud includes consideration of

        a.  Type of risk that may exist (fraudulent financial reporting or misappropriation of assets)

        b.  Significance of risk (magnitude)

        c.  Likelihood of risk

        d.  Pervasiveness of risk (overall financial statements, or a particular assertion or account)

    4.  A presumption of improper revenue recognition is a fraud risk

    5.  The auditor should always address the risk of management override of controls

*NOTE: Make certain that you know points 4. and 5. above are required for all audits. That is, the auditor should ordinarily presume that there is a risk of material misstatement due to fraud relating to revenue recognition and of management override.*

**F.** Assessing the identified risks after considering programs and controls
  1. AU 319 requires the auditor to obtain an understanding of internal control sufficient to plan the audit; this understanding allows the auditor to
    a. Identify types of potential misstatements
    b. Consider factors that affect the risk of material misstatement
    c. Design tests of controls when applicable
    d. Design substantive tests
  2. As a part of obtaining an understanding of internal control sufficient to plan the audit, the auditor should evaluate whether the client's programs and controls that address the identified risks of material misstatement due to fraud have been suitably designed and placed in operation
  3. After the auditor has evaluated the client's programs and controls in this area, the auditor's assessment of the risk of material misstatement due to fraud should consider these results
  4. Appendix 2 to this section provides programs and controls
**G.** Responding to the results of the assessment—as risk increases
  1. **Overall responses**
    a. Assign personnel with more experience and have more supervision
    b. More carefully consider significant accounting policies
    c. Make auditing procedures less predictable
  2. **Responses that address specifically identified risks**
    a. General types of responses
      (1) Nature—more reliable evidence or additional corroborative information
      (2) Timing—perform at or near end of reporting period, but apply substantive procedures to transactions occurring throughout the year
      (3) Extent—increase sample sizes, perform more detailed analytical procedures
    b. Examples of modification of the nature, timing, and extent of procedures
      (1) Perform procedures on a surprise or unannounced basis (e.g., inventory observations, counting of cash)
      (2) Request inventory counts at end of reporting period
      (3) Make oral inquiries of major customers and suppliers in addition to written confirmations
      (4) Perform substantive analytical procedures using disaggregated data
      (5) Interview personnel in areas where risk of material misstatement due to fraud has been identified
      (6) Discuss the situation with any other auditors involved with audit (e.g., an "other auditor" who audits subsidiary)
    c. Additional examples of responses for a high risk of **fraudulent financial reporting** may result in increased
      (1) Analysis of revenue recognition
      (2) Consideration of inventory quantities
      (3) Consideration of management estimates (e.g., allowance for doubtful accounts)
    d. Additional responses for a high risk of **misappropriation of assets**
      (1) If a particular asset is susceptible to misappropriation, obtain understanding of controls and/or physical inspection may be appropriate
      (2) More precise analytical procedures may be used
  3. **Responses to further address the risk of management override of controls**
    a. **Examine journal entries and other adjustments** for evidence of possible material misstatement due to fraud
    b. **Review accounting estimates** for biases, including a retrospective review of previous year estimates so as to provide guidance on management's past performance in this area
    c. **Evaluate the business rationale** for significant unusual transactions

*NOTE: 1. through 3. above are distinct types of responses—(1) overall responses, (2) responses that address specifically identified risks, and (3) responses for management override of controls. Although differing combinations of each might be expected on an audit, those for management override are ordinarily required on an audit.*

**H.** Evaluating audit evidence
  1. The assessment of risks of material misstatement should be ongoing throughout the audit
  2. Conditions identified during fieldwork may change or support a judgment concerning the assessment
     a. Discrepancies in accounting records; examples
        (1) Transactions not recorded in a complete or timely manner, or improperly recorded
        (2) Unsupported or unauthorized balances or transactions
        (3) Significant last-minute adjustments
        (4) Evidence of employee inappropriate access to systems
     b. Conflicting or missing audit evidence; examples
        (1) Missing, unavailable, or altered documents
        (2) Unexplained items on reconciliations
        (3) Inconsistent, vague, or implausible responses to inquiries
        (4) Unusual discrepancies between records and confirmation replies
        (5) Missing inventory or physical assets
        (6) Unavailable or missing electronic evidence, inconsistent retention policies
     c. Problematic or unusual relationships between auditor and management; examples
        (1) Denial of access to records, facilities, employees, customers, vendors, and others
        (2) Undue time pressures
        (3) Management complaints, intimidation
        (4) Unusual delays in providing information
        (5) Tips or complaints about alleged fraud
        (6) Unwillingness to facilitate auditor access to electronic files
        (7) Denial of access to IT operations staff and facilities
        (8) Unwillingness to add or revise disclosures in financial statements
  3. The auditor should evaluate whether analytical procedures performed as substantive tests or in the overall review stage indicate a previously unrecognized risk of material misstatement due to fraud
     a. If not already performed, the auditor should perform analytical procedures at the overall review stage of the audit; unusual situations include
        (1) Large amounts of income recorded in the last week or two of the year
        (2) Income inconsistent with trends in cash flows from operations
     b. Examples of unusual or unexpected analytical relationships

| *Change* | *Possible cause* |
| --- | --- |
| Net income to cash flows may appear unusual | Fictitious revenue and receivables |
| Changes in inventory, payables, sales, or cost of goods sold as compared to preceding period | Theft of inventory, but inability to manipulate all related accounts |
| Company profitability inconsistent with industry trends | Numerous possible misstatements |
| Bad debt write-offs high | Theft of cash receipts |
| Sales volume per accounting records differs from production statistics | Misstatement of sales |

  4. The auditor should evaluate risks of material misstatement due to fraud at or near completion of fieldwork
     a. This is primarily a qualitative consideration based on the auditor's judgment
  5. When audit procedures identify misstatements, the auditor should consider whether such misstatements may indicate fraud
  6. When misstatements are or may be the result of fraud, but the effects are not material to the financial statements, the auditor should evaluate the implications
     a. A misappropriation of cash from a small petty cash fund normally would have little significance
     b. A misappropriation involving management may be indicative of a more pervasive problem and may require the auditor to consider the impact on the nature, timing, and extent of tests of balances or transactions, and the assessment of the effectiveness of controls
  7. If the auditor believes the misstatements may be the result of fraud and has determined it could be material to the financial statements, but has been unable to evaluate whether the effect is material, the auditor should
     a. Attempt to obtain audit evidence to determine whether fraud has occurred and its effect
     b. Consider implications for other aspects of the audit

      c.   Discuss the matter and an approach for further investigation with an appropriate level of management at least one level above those involved, and with senior management and the audit committee

      d.   If appropriate, suggest the client consult with legal counsel

  8.  The risk of fraud may be so high as to cause the auditor to consider withdrawing from engagement; factors affecting decision

      a.   Implications about integrity of management

      b.   Diligence and cooperation of management or the board of directors

**I.**  Communicating about fraud to management, the audit committee, and others

  1.  Whenever there is evidence that fraud may exist, the matter should be brought to an appropriate level of management, even if the matter might be considered inconsequential

      a.   All fraud involving senior management, and any fraud (by anyone) that causes a material misstatement should be reported directly to the audit committee

      b.   The auditor should reach an understanding with the audit committee regarding communications about misappropriations perpetrated by lower-level employees

  2.  If risks have continued control implications, the auditor should determine whether they represent reportable conditions and need to be communicated to the audit committee—see outline of AU 325

  3.  The auditor may choose to communicate other risks of fraud

  4.  Disclosure of fraud beyond senior management and its audit committee is not ordinarily a part of the auditor's responsibility, unless

      a.   Required by specific legal and regulatory requirements

      b.   To a successor auditor—see outline of AU 315

      c.   In response to a subpoena

      d.   To a funding agency or other specified agency in accordance with requirements of audits of entities that receive governmental financial assistance

**J.**  Documenting the auditor's consideration of fraud; document the following:

  1.  Discussion among audit team of risk of material misstatement due to fraud, including how and when discussion occurred, participants, and subject matter

  2.  Procedures performed to obtain information to identify and assess risks of material misstatement due to fraud

  3.  Specific risks of material misstatement due to fraud that were identified and auditor's response to those risks

  4.  If auditor has **not** identified improper revenue recognition as a risk of material misstatement due to fraud, the reasons for that conclusion

  5.  Results of procedures performed to further assess risk of management override of controls

  6.  Other conditions and analytical relationships or other responses required and any further responses the auditor concluded were appropriate to address such risks or conditions

  7.  Nature of communications about fraud made to management, the audit committee, and others

## APPENDIX 1: EXAMPLES OF FRAUD RISK FACTORS

### Misstatements Arising from Fraudulent Financial Reporting

| *Incentives/Pressures* | *Opportunities* | *Attitudes/Rationalizations* |
|---|---|---|
| 1. Threatened financial stability or profitability<br>• High degree of competition or sales saturation<br>• High vulnerability to rapid changes (e.g., technology, interest rates)<br>• Declines in customer demand, business failures in industry<br>• Operating losses<br>• Negative cash flows from operations<br>• Rapid growth or unusual profitability<br>• New accounting, statutory, or regulatory requirements<br><br>2. Excessive pressure on management to meet requirements or third-party expectations due to<br>• Profitability or trend level expectations<br>• Need for additional debt or equity financing<br>• Marginal ability to meet exchange listing requirements<br>• Likely poor financial results on pending transactions<br><br>3. Management or directors' financial situation threatened by<br>• Significant financial interests in company<br>• Significant portions of compensation contingent on results of company<br>• Personal guarantees of debts of company<br><br>4. Excessive pressure to meet financial target set up by directors or management | 1. Industry provides opportunities for<br>• Related-party transactions beyond ordinary<br>• Company can dictate terms or conditions to suppliers or customers (may result in inappropriate transactions)<br>• Accounts based on significant estimates<br>• Significant, unusual, or highly complex transactions<br>• Significant operations across international borders with differing business environments and cultures<br>• Significant bank accounts in tax haven jurisdictions<br><br>2. Ineffective monitoring of management allows<br>• Domination of management by a single person or small group without controls<br>• Ineffective board of director or audit committee oversight<br><br>3. Complex or unstable organizational structure<br>• Difficulty in determining organization or individuals with control of company<br>• Overly complex structure<br>• High turnover of senior management, counsel, or board members<br><br>Internal control deficient<br>• Inadequate monitoring of controls<br>• High turnover rate or ineffective accounting, internal audit, or information technology staff<br>• Ineffective accounting and information systems | Relating to board members, management, or employees<br>• Ineffective communications, implementation, support, or enforcement of ethics<br>• Nonfinancial management excessive participation in selecting accounting principles or determining estimates<br>• Known history of violations of securities or other laws<br>• Excessive interest in maintaining or increasing stock price<br>• Aggressive or unrealistic forecasts<br>• Failure to correct reportable conditions on a timely basis<br>• Interest by management of employing inappropriate means to minimize earnings for tax reasons<br>• Recurring management attempts to justify marginal or inappropriate accounting based on materiality<br>• Strained relationship with current or predecessor auditor |

### Misstatements Arising from Misappropriation of Assets

| | | |
|---|---|---|
| 1. Personal financial obligations<br><br>2. Adverse relationship between company and employees<br>• Known or anticipated layoffs<br>• Changes in compensation<br>• Promotions, compensation, or other rewards inconsistent with expectations | 1. Characteristics of assets<br>• Large amounts of cash on hand or processed<br>• Small, high-value, or high-demand inventory items<br>• Easily convertible assets (bearer bonds, diamonds, computer chips)<br>• Small marketable fixed assets<br><br>2. Inadequate internal control, including inadequate<br>• Segregation of duties<br>• Job application screening of employees with access to assets<br>• Recordkeeping for assets<br>• Authorization or approval of transactions<br>• Reconciliation of assets<br>• Documentation of transactions (e.g., credits for merchandise returns)<br>• No requirements for mandatory vacations<br>• Management understanding of information technology<br>• Access controls over automated records | Attitudes or behavior of those with access to assets susceptible to misappropriation<br>• Disregard for need for monitoring or reducing risks<br>• Disregard for internal control<br>• Behavior indicating displeasure or dissatisfaction with company or its treatment of employees<br>• Changes in behavior or lifestyle that indicate assets may have been misappropriated |

## APPENDIX 2: PROGRAMS AND CONTROLS RELATED TO FRAUD

This appendix includes a discussion of examples of programs and controls that management can implement to help deter, prevent, and detect fraud, which may be briefly summarized as

**A.** Creating a culture of honesty and high ethics
  1. Setting tone at the top
  2. Creating a positive workplace environment
  3. Hiring and promoting appropriate employees
  4. Proper training
  5. Proper discipline for those committing fraud

**B.** Management's evaluation of processes and controls to mitigate risk of and reduce opportunities for fraud include policies and procedures to
  1. Identify and measure fraud risks
  2. Mitigate fraud risks
  3. Implement and monitor appropriate controls and other measures

**C.** Develop an appropriate oversight process
  1. Effective audit committee or board of directors
  2. Effective internal auditors
  3. Assistance from independent auditors

## 317 Illegal Acts by Clients (SAS 54)

*Overall Objectives and Approach*—This section presents guidance on the nature and extent of consideration given to client illegal acts during audits. The guidance relates both to considering the possibility of illegal acts, and to the responsibility when such illegal acts are detected.

**A.** Overall definition of illegal acts and summary of auditor responsibility
  1. Illegal acts—violations of laws or governmental regulations
     a. Illegal acts by clients are acts attributable to entity under audit acts of management, or employees acting on behalf of entity
     b. Illegal acts by clients **do not include personal misconduct** by entity's personnel that is unrelated to business
  2. Determination of legality of act is normally beyond auditor's professional competence and depends on legal judgment
  3. The further removed illegal act is from the events and transactions ordinarily reflected in financial statements the less likely it is that the auditor will become aware
     a. Examples of illegal acts more likely to be detected (those with a direct and material effect on determination of financial statement amounts)
        (1) Tax laws affecting accruals
        (2) Revenue accrued on governmental contracts
     b. Examples of illegal acts less likely to be detected (those with an indirect effect on financial statements—often a contingent liability)
        (1) Laws related to securities trading
        (2) Occupational safety and health
        (3) Price fixing

     *NOTE: a. items typically relate to financial and accounting aspects; b. items typically relate more to an entity's operating aspects. The auditor's responsibility for illegal acts having a direct and material effect on determination of financial statement amounts (a.) is the same as for errors and fraud—to design the audit to provide reasonable assurance of their detection when they are material; see AU 316. An auditor does not ordinarily have a sufficient basis for recognizing possible violations of those illegal acts having only indirect effects (b.).*

     c. **The remainder of this section is only on illegal acts having material but indirect effect on the financial statements (b. above).**

**B.** Auditor's consideration of possibility of illegal acts **on all audits**
  1. Summary of the auditor's responsibility
     a. Be aware of possibility of such illegal acts

    b.  If specific information comes to the auditor's attention concerning the existence of illegal acts, apply audit procedures specifically directed to ascertaining whether such an illegal act has occurred

    c.  An audit provides no assurance that illegal acts will be detected or that any contingent liabilities that may result will be disclosed

2.  **Audit procedures when there is no evidence** concerning the existence of possible illegal acts

    a.  Audits normally do not include procedures designed to detect illegal acts, but other procedures may identify such acts (e.g., reading minutes, inquiries to management and legal counsel, substantive tests)

    b.  The auditor should make inquiries of management concerning the client's compliance with laws and regulations. Where applicable, the auditor should inquire of management concerning

        (1)  Client's policies related to prevention of illegal acts

        (2)  Directives issued by client and representations obtained by client from management on compliance with laws

    c.  The auditor should ordinarily also obtain written representations from management concerning the absence of violations of laws whose effects should be considered for disclosure in the financial statements or as a basis for recording a loss contingency

*NOTE: The section states that audits **do not** include procedures designed to detect illegal acts (a. above) and then suggests several inquiry-type procedures (b. and c. above).*

3.  **Information** that **may suggest** the possibility of **illegal acts**

    a.  Unauthorized, improperly recorded, or unrecorded transactions

    b.  Investigation by a governmental agency

    c.  Reports of regulatory agencies citing law violations

    d.  Large payments for unspecified services to consultants, affiliates, or employees

    e.  Excessive sales commissions

    f.  Unusually large payment to cash, bearer, transfers to numbered bank accounts

    g.  Unexplained payments to government officials or employees

    h.  Failure to file tax returns or pay other fees

4.  Audit procedures required **when the auditor becomes aware** of information concerning a **possible illegal act**

    a.  Obtain an understanding of the act and its implications

        (1)  Inquire of management at a level above those involved

    b.  If management **does not** provide satisfactory information that there has been no illegal act

        (1)  Consult client's legal counsel or other specialists (client arranges this consultation)

        (2)  Apply additional necessary procedures such as

            (a)  Examine supporting documents

            (b)  Confirm significant information

            (c)  Determine whether transaction authorized

            (d)  Consider whether other similar transactions have occurred and apply procedures to identify

**C.**  Auditor's response to detected illegal acts

*NOTE: This section only relates to audits in which the procedures followed in B. above have revealed that an illegal act is likely to have occurred.*

1.  If necessary contact legal counsel

2.  Consider financial statement effect

    a.  Quantitative and qualitative aspects

    b.  Determine that act adequately disclosed in financial statements

        (1)  Consider possible loss contingency (e.g., threat of expropriation of assets, enforced discontinuance of operations in another country, and litigation)

3.  Consider implications of illegal act on other aspects of audit (e.g., reliability of management representations)

**D.**  Communication with audit committee

1.  **Determine that audit committee is informed,** unless clearly inconsequential

2.  Communication should include

    a.  **Description of act**

    b.  **Circumstances of occurrence**

    c. **Effects on financial statements**
3. If senior management is involved, auditor should communicate directly with audit committee
4. **Communication may be written or oral (if oral, document)**

**E.** Effect on auditor's report
1. Improper accounting, a qualified or adverse opinion due to the departure from GAAP
2. If auditor precluded from obtaining sufficient information (i.e., a scope limitation exists), generally disclaim
3. If client refuses to accept report, withdraw and indicate reasons in writing to audit committee or board of directors
4. When circumstances (not the client) make it impossible to determine legality, the auditor should consider the effect on the report

    *NOTE: In this circumstance either a "circumstance imposed" scope limitation or an "uncertainty" may be involved. See the outline of AU 508.*

**F.** Other considerations
1. Withdrawal may be necessary, even when client does not take remedial actions for illegal acts having an immaterial effect on the financial statements (auditor may wish to contact legal counsel)
2. Situations in which there may be a duty to notify parties outside the client
    a. Form 8-K disclosures (change of auditors)
    b. Disclosure to successor auditor (AU 315)
    c. Disclosure in response to subpoena
    d. Disclosure to funding agency for entities receiving governmental financial assistance
3. Additional responsibilities may exist for audits of governmental units under the Single Audit Act of 1984

## 319 Consideration of Internal Control in a Financial Statement Audit (SAS 55, SAS 78, and SAS 94)

*Overall Objectives and Approach*—This section provides guidance on the auditor's responsibility with respect to a client's internal control. It describes internal control using the framework developed by the Committee of Sponsoring Organizations of the Treadway Commission (COSO), as being composed of five elements— (1) control environment, (2) risk assessment, (3) control activities, (4) information and communication, and (5) monitoring.

Auditors consider internal control for two primary purposes—(1) to **plan the audit** by performing procedures to obtain an understanding of the design of controls relevant to audit planning and to policies and to determine whether they have been placed in operation and (2) to **assess control risk**. Recall that control risk combined with inherent risk and detection risk are the components of audit risk—see outline of AU 312 and Section B.1.a. of the Engagement Planning Module for more on this.

This is among the most complex of the various AU sections. Know that its major concepts are summarized in Sections A and B of the Internal Control Module. Information technology (IT) information on internal control is also presented in the Auditing with Technology Module, particularly Section F. In the event that you have difficulties following this outline we suggest that you first read the module presentations.

**A.** Internal control
1. Internal control is a process effected by an entity's board of directors, management, and other personnel designed to provide reasonable assurance regarding the achievement of objectives in the following categories: (a) reliability of financial reporting, (b) effectiveness and efficiency of operations, and (c) compliance with applicable laws and regulations.
    a. The controls generally most relevant to an audit are those that pertain to the entity's objective of preparing financial statements for external purposes [(a) above]
    b. Operations and compliance objectives [(b) and (c) above] may be relevant if they pertain to data the auditor evaluates or uses in applying auditing procedures (e.g., production statistics for analytical procedures)
2. Internal control consists of five interrelated components
    a. Control environment
    b. Risk assessment
    c. Control activities
    d. Information and communication
    e. Monitoring

3. The auditor's consideration of internal control over **safeguarding of assets** against unauthorized acquisition is generally limited to those relevant to the reliability of financial reporting

   a. Example of a portion of internal control **not** normally considered: A commercial airline's system of automated controls to maintain flight schedules ordinarily would not be relevant to a financial statement audit.

4. The auditor's primary consideration is whether a specific control affects financial statement assertions rather than its classification into any particular component

5. Effects of information technology (IT)—overall

   a. May affect any of the five components of internal control (2. above)

   b. May affect the manner in which transactions are initiated, recorded, processed, and reported

   c. Automated systems ordinarily have a combination of manual and automated controls (e.g., controls embedded in computer programs)

6. IT provides potential benefits of effectiveness and efficiency because it enables an entity to

   a. Consistently apply predefined business rules and perform complex calculations on large volumes of transactions

   b. Enhance timelines, availability, and accuracy of information

   c. Facilitate the additional analysis of information

   d. Enhance the ability to monitor the performance of the entity's activities and its policies and procedures

   e. Reduce risk that controls will be circumvented

   f. Enhance ability to achieve effective segregation of duties by implementing security controls in applications, databases, and operating systems

7. IT poses specific risks to internal control including

   a. Reliance on systems or programs that inaccurately process information

   b. Unauthorized access to data may lead to destruction of data or inappropriate changes to data

   c. Unauthorized changes to data in master files

   d. Unauthorized changes to systems or programs

   e. Failure to make necessary changes to systems or programs

   f. Inappropriate manual intervention

   g. Potential loss of data

8. Limitations of internal control

   a. Human judgment in decision making can be faulty

      (1) Example: Errors may occur in designing, maintaining, or monitoring automated controls due to IT personnel not completely understanding the order entry system

   b. Breakdowns can occur because of human failures such as simple error or mistake

   c. Controls, whether manual or automated, can be circumvented by collusion

   d. Management has the ability to override internal control

   e. The cost of internal control should not exceed the benefits expected to be derived

   f. Custom, culture, and the corporate governance system may inhibit fraud, but they are not absolute deterrents

**B.** Obtaining an understanding of internal control

1. Overall—Auditor should obtain an understanding of each of the five components of internal control sufficient to plan the audit by performing procedures to obtain knowledge of the design of controls relevant to the preparation of financial statements and whether they have been **placed in operation;** such knowledge should be used to

   a. Identify types of potential misstatements

   b. Consider factors that affect the risk of material misstatement

   c. Design tests of controls, when applicable

   d. Design substantive tests

   *NOTE: Distinguish between determining that controls have been "placed in operation" (which is required for both audit planning and assessing control risk) and evaluating their "operating effectiveness" (which is detailed below in Section C.2. and is only required for assessing control risk). An auditor may simply observe that the client is using a control to determine that the control has been placed in operation. Operating effectiveness is concerned with (1) how the control was applied, (2) the consistency with which it was applied, and (3) by whom.*

2. The auditor also considers his/her assessment of inherent risk, judgments about materiality, and the complexity and sophistication of the entity's operations and systems in designing substantive tests

3. In determining whether specialized IT skills are needed to design and perform the audit, the auditor considers factors such as
   a. Complexity of entity's systems and IT controls
   b. Significance of changes made to existing systems, or implementation of new systems
   c. Extent to which data is shared among systems
   d. Extent of entity's participation in electronic commerce
   e. Entity's use of emerging technologies
   f. Significance of audit evidence available only in electronic form
4. Procedures an auditor may assign to a professional possessing IT skills
   a. Inquiring of entity's IT personnel on how data and transactions are initiated, recorded, processed, and reported and how IT controls are designed
   b. Inspecting systems documentation
   c. Observing operation of IT controls
   d. Planning and performing of tests of IT controls
5. **Control of environment**
   a. Factors—IC HAMBO
      (1) **I**ntegrity and ethical values
      (2) **C**ommitment to competence
      (3) **H**uman resource policies and practices
      (4) **A**ssignment of authority and responsibility
      (5) **M**anagement's philosophy and operating style
      (6) **B**oard of directors or audit committee participation
      (7) **O**rganizational structure
   b. Understanding needed by auditor—Understand management's and the board of directors' attitudes, awareness and actions, considering both the substance of controls and their collective effect
6. **Risk assessment**
   a. An entity's risk assessment for financial reporting purposes is its identification, analysis, and management of risks relevant to the proper preparation of financial statements; risks relevant to financial reporting include
      (1) Changes in operating environment
      (2) New personnel
      (3) New or revamped information systems
      (4) Rapid growth
      (5) New technology
      (6) New business models, products, or activities
      (7) Corporate restructuring
      (8) Expanded foreign operations
      (9) New accounting pronouncements
   b. Understanding needed by auditor—Understand how management considers risks relevant to financial reporting objectives and decides about actions to address those risks

   *NOTE: Know that an entity's risk assessment differs from an auditor's risk assessment during an audit. The purpose of an entity's risk assessment is to identify, analyze, and manage risks that affect entity objectives. This differs from an auditor's assessments of inherent risk and control risk to evaluate the likelihood that material misstatements could occur in the financial statements (see AU 312).*

7. **Control activities**
   a. Control activities that may be relevant to an audit may be categorized as policies and procedures that pertain to
      (1) Performance reviews (e.g., reviews of actual performance versus budgets)
      (2) Information processing—The two broad groupings of control activities are general controls (which apply to overall systems), and application controls (which apply to individual applications)
      (3) Physical controls—These controls include the physical security of assets (including adequate safeguards such as secured facilities) over access to assets and records
      (4) Segregation of duties (i.e., separation of authorization of transactions, recording of transactions, and maintaining custody of assets).

    b.  Understanding needed by auditor

        (1)  As auditor obtains understanding of the other components, s/he is also likely to obtain knowledge about some control activities (e.g., in obtaining understanding about information system's processing of cash, the auditor may become aware of whether bank accounts are reconciled)

        (2)  The auditor should consider whether it is necessary to devote additional attention to obtaining an understanding of the control activities to plan the audit

        (3)  Ordinarily, audit planning does **not** require an understanding of the control activities related to each account balance, transaction class, or disclosure item.

        (4)  Some entities and auditors may view controls in terms of application controls and general controls

            (a)  Application controls apply to individual applications (e.g., an edit check of input data)

            (b)  General controls relate to multiple applications (e.g., controls over data center and network operations

8.  **Information and communication**

    a.  The information system relevant to financial reporting includes the accounting system and consists of the methods and records established to record, process, summarize, and report entity transactions; communication involves providing an understanding of individual roles and responsibilities pertaining to internal control over financial reporting

    b.  Understanding needed by auditor—the auditor should obtain a sufficient knowledge to understand

        (1)  Classes of transactions

        (2)  Procedures, both automated and manual, by which transactions are initiated, recorded, processed, and reported

        (3)  Accounting records (electronic or manual), supporting information, and accounts

        (4)  How the information system captures other events and conditions that are significant to the financial statements

        (5)  Financial reporting process used to prepare financial statements, including significant accounting estimates and disclosures

    c.  The auditor should understand automated and manual procedures used to prepare financial statements, and how misstatements occur; such procedures include those to

        (1)  Enter transaction totals into the general ledger

        (2)  Initiate, record, and process journal entries in the general ledger

        (3)  Record recurring and nonrecurring adjustments to financial statements

9.  **Monitoring**

    a.  Monitoring is a process that assesses the quality of internal control performance over time, and involves assessing the design and operation of controls on a timely basis and taking necessary corrective actions.

        (1)  Monitoring is accomplished through ongoing activities, separate evaluations, or a combination of the two

    b.  Understanding needed by auditor—the auditor should obtain a sufficient knowledge of types of activities entity uses to monitor internal control, including how those activities are used to initiate corrective actions

10.  Procedures to obtain understanding of internal control

    a.  Previous experience

    b.  Inquiries of management, supervisory, and staff personnel

    c.  Inspection of entity activities and operations

    d.  Observation of entity activities and operations

11.  **Documenting the understanding of internal control**

    a.  For an information system with a large volume of transactions that are electronically initiated, recorded, processed, or reported, may include flowcharts, questionnaires, or decision tables

    b.  For an information system with limited or no use of IT, or for which few transactions are processed (e.g., long-term debt), a memorandum may be sufficient

*NOTE:  At this point you should be able to summarize*
    *1. The required knowledge of each of the 5 internal control components (3. through 7. above)*
    *2. The procedures to obtain this knowledge (8. above)*
    *3. The required level of documentation for purposes of planning the audit (9. above)*

## C. Assessing control risk

1. Overall—control risk is the risk of material misstatement not being prevented or detected by internal control

*NOTE: Recall that auditors consider control risk for two purposes—(1) to aid in planning the audit, and (2) to assess control risk (which is what this section of the outline is about).*

2. Assessing control risk at below the maximum involves
    a. Identifying controls relevant to assertions that are likely to prevent or detect misstatements
    b. Performing **tests of controls** to evaluate effectiveness of controls

    *NOTE: Prior to issuance of this section, tests of controls were referred to as "compliance tests."*

3. Control risk should be assessed in terms of the financial statement assertions—PERCV
    **P**resentation and disclosure
    **E**xistence or occurrence
    **R**ights and obligations
    **C**ompleteness
    **V**aluation

    *NOTE: For more on PERCV assertions see the Evidence Module and the outline of AU 326.*

    a. Controls such as the control environment and information system often have a pervasive effect on a number of accounts, and therefore can often affect many assertions

    *EXAMPLE: An auditor's conclusion that a highly effective control environment exists may influence decisions about the number of the entity's locations at which auditing procedures are to be performed, and whether to perform certain procedures for some accounts at an interim date.*

    b. Some controls have a specific effect on an individual assertion in a particular account

    *EXAMPLE: A control to ensure that employee personnel are properly counting the annual physical inventory may relate to the existence assertion for inventory.*

    c. When an auditor is performing only substantive tests to restrict detection risk to an acceptable level, the auditor should obtain evidence about the accuracy and completeness of the information
    d. In determining whether to assess control risk at the maximum level or at a lower level, the auditor should consider
        (1) Nature of the assertion
        (2) Volume of transactions
        (3) Nature and complexity of systems, including use of IT
        (4) Nature of available evidential matter, including evidence in electronic form

4. It may be impossible to design effective substantive tests that by themselves provide sufficient evidence in circumstances such as when the client
    a. Uses IT to initiate orders using predetermined decision rules and to pay related payables based on system-generated information, and no other documentation is produced
    b. Provides electronic services to customers (e.g., Internet service provider or a telephone company) and uses IT to log services provided, initiate bills, process billing, and automatically record amounts in accounting records
    c. In circumstances such as the above, some tests of controls need to be performed

5. **Tests of controls**—procedures directed toward either the effectiveness of the **design** or **operation** (operating effectiveness) of control
    a. Approaches
        (1) **Inquiries** of appropriate personnel
        (2) **Inspection** of documents and reports indicating performance of policy or procedure
        (3) **Observation** of the application of the policy or procedure
        (4) **Reperformance** of the application of the policy or procedure by the auditor (used for testing operation of system, not for testing design)

    *NOTE: Generally, inquiries **alone** will not provide sufficient evidential matter to support a conclusion about the effectiveness of the design or operation of a specific control. Also be able to recall the above four approaches.*

    b. The conclusion reached is referred to as the "assessed level of control risk"
        (1) It is based on effectiveness of design and of operation

      (2) Lower assessments of risk require more evidential matter support

      (3) The assessed levels of control risk and inherent risk determine the acceptable level of detection risk

      (4) As acceptable level of detection risk decreases, the assurance provided by substantive tests should increase; the auditor may modify the nature, timing and/or extent of tests

         (a) **Nature**—a change from less effective to more effective tests (e.g., use tests directed toward independent parties outside the entity rather than tests directed toward parties or documents within the entity)

         (b) **Timing**—less reliance on interim testing

         (c) **Extent**—more substantive tests (larger samples)

   c. In designing tests of automated controls,

      (1) The inherent consistency of IT processing may allow auditor to reduce the extent of testing

      (2) Computer-assisted audit techniques may be needed for automated controls

  6. **Documentation**—as reliance increases, required documentation of effectiveness of design and operation increases

**D.** Other points

  1. **Relationship of understanding internal control to assessing control risk**

   a. Auditors often plan to perform some tests of control concurrently with obtaining the understanding of internal control

   b. Audit tests aimed at obtaining an understanding of internal control may also address effectiveness of design and operation (tests thus become tests of controls)

   c. Additional tests of controls may be performed to justify a lower assessed level of control risk

  2. **Evidential matter to support assessment of control risk**

   a. No one specific test of controls is always appropriate, and the auditor selects among inquiry, inspection, observation, and reperformance

   b. When no documentation is available to substantiate performance (e.g., inspection is not possible), observation, inquiry, or computer-assisted audit techniques may be used

      (1) The auditor must be aware that procedures observed may not be performed in same manner when auditor is not present

      (2) When evidential matter has been gathered at an interim period, the importance of the related assertion, length of remaining period, and other evidence should be used to help auditor determine if remainder of period should be tested

      (3) **Inquiry alone** generally **will not provide sufficient evidential matter** to support a conclusion about the effectiveness of the design or operation of a specific control procedure

  3. **Control risk and detection risk (substantive tests)**

   a. The **ultimate purpose of assessing control risk** is to contribute to the auditor's evaluation of the risk that material misstatements exist in the financial statements

   b. As the assessed level of control risk decreases, the acceptable level of detection risk increases (an "inverse" relationship)

   c. Ordinarily, the assessed level of control risk cannot be so low as to eliminate need for substantive tests for all assertions relevant to significant accounts

   d. Recall that substantive tests are (1) tests of detail of transactions and balances and (2) analytical procedures

   e. In some circumstances the results of tests of details of transactions may also serve as tests of controls

      (1) Although the objective of tests of details of transactions for substantive tests is to detect material misstatements in financial statements, such tests may also provide evidential matter on whether a control has operated effectively

      *NOTE: Such tests are often referred to as "dual-purpose" tests.*

## 322 The Auditor's Consideration of the Internal Audit Function in an Audit of Financial Statements (SAS 65)

*Overall Objectives and Approach*—This section presents guidance on how CPAs (1) **consider the effect of work** of internal auditors on the nature, timing, and extent of audit procedures and (2) use internal auditors to **provide direct assistance** on the audit. When considering internal auditors' work, the CPA must assess both

**competence** and **objectivity**. Internal auditors may affect CPA understanding of internal control, control risk assessment, and substantive tests.

**A.** Obtaining an understanding of the internal auditing function
1. CPA should obtain an understanding of the internal auditing function sufficient to aid in planning the audit
2. The CPA should make inquiries concerning internal auditors'
   a. Organizational status within the entity
   b. Application of professional standards
   c. Audit plan
   d. Access to records, including any scope limitations placed on internal auditors
   e. Charter, mission statement, etc.
3. Consider relevant activities (those pertaining to entity's ability to record, process, summarize, and report financial data) using knowledge from prior-year audits, reviewing internal audit function allocation of its audit resources, and by reading internal auditors' reports
4. If CPA concludes internal auditors' activities are not relevant to audit, those activities need not be considered further unless CPA wishes to obtain internal auditors' direct assistance on audit (part D of this outline)
   > *EXAMPLE: A CPA is not typically interested in internal auditors' evaluation of management decision-making processes.*

**B.** Assessing **competence** and **objectivity** of internal auditors
1. When assessing **competence** CPA should consider internal auditors'
   a. Education and experience
   b. Professional certification and continuing education
   c. Audit policies, programs, and procedures
   d. Practices regarding assignments
   e. Supervision and review activities
   f. Quality of working paper documentation, reports, and recommendations
   g. Evaluation of performance
2. When assessing **objectivity** CPA should consider internal auditors'
   a. Organizational status, including whether
      (1) Internal auditors report to officer of sufficient status
      (2) Internal auditors have direct access to board of directors, audit committee, or owner-manager
      (3) Board of directors, audit committee, or owner/manager oversees internal auditors' employment decisions
   b. Policies to maintain internal auditors' objectivity about areas audited, such as policies prohibiting internal auditors from auditing areas where
      (1) Relatives are employed in important or audit-sensitive positions
      (2) An internal auditor was recently assigned or is scheduled to be assigned
3. Sources of information for assessing competence and objectivity
   a. Previous experience
   b. Discussions with management
   c. Recent external quality review of internal auditors' activities
   d. Professional internal auditing standards

**C.** Effect of internal auditors' work on the audit
1. Effect of internal auditors' work on the nature, timing, and extent of audit (effect on 3 stages of audit)
   a. **Understanding of internal control**—Internal auditors may have developed useful information for CPA (e.g., flowcharts, evidence on whether controls have been placed in operation)
   b. **Risk assessment**
      (1) **Financial statement level**—May affect many financial statement assertions (e.g., CPA and internal auditors may coordinate work to reduce number of entity's locations CPA performs auditing procedures)
      (2) **Account-balance or class-or-transaction level**—May affect nature, timing, and extent of tests
   c. **Substantive procedures**—CPA has ultimate responsibility for opinion
      (1) Responsibility for opinion cannot be shared with internal auditors

          (2) In determining extent of effect, CPA should consider materiality, risk of misstatement, and subjectivity of evidence

          (3) For assertions with high risk of material misstatement, internal auditors' work cannot alone eliminate need for CPA testing

               (a) Examples: Assertion on valuation of accounting estimates, related-party transactions, contingencies, uncertainties, subsequent events

          (4) For assertions related to immaterial financial statement amounts where risk of material misstatements is low, CPA in some circumstances may not need to do additional procedures

               (a) Examples: Existence of cash, prepaid assets, fixed asset additions

  2. Work of internal auditors and CPA should be coordinated through periodic meetings, scheduling audit work, access of internal auditors' working papers, reviewing audit reports, and discussions

  3. When evaluating the effectiveness of internal auditors' **work** the CPA should

    a. Consider whether

      (1) Scope of work appropriate

      (2) Audit programs appropriate

      (3) Adequate documentation in working papers

      (4) Appropriate conclusions in reports

      (5) Reports consistent with results of work

    b. Test internal auditors' work through examining controls, transactions, or balances either examined by internal auditors or similar to those examined by internal auditors

**D.** Using internal auditors to **provide direct assistance,** CPA should

  1. Consider internal auditors' competence and objectivity

  2. Supervise, review, evaluate, and test internal auditors' work performed

## 324 Reports on the Processing of Transactions by Service Organizations (SAS 70)

*Overall Objectives and Approach*—This section provides guidance on (1) performing audits of organizations that use a service organization and (2) reporting on the processing of transactions by a service organization. As an example of a service organization, consider a data processing company that processes the payroll information of other organizations (user organizations). Other service organizations include trust departments of banks that invest and hold assets for employee benefit plans for various entities, and mortgage bankers that service mortgages for others. The following terms are used throughout the standard:

*User organization*—The entity whose financial statements are being audited (this organization hired the service auditor).

*User auditor*—The auditor who reports on the financial statements of the user organization.

*Service organization*—The entity that provides services to the client organization.

*Service auditor*—The auditor who reports on the processing of transactions by the service organization.

Section A of this outline presents information on the user auditor's consideration of the service organization's effect on the audit of the user organization. Section B discusses overall responsibilities of service auditors and indicates that they may be engaged to perform two principal types of engagements, although others are possible. Section C discusses the first, reports on service organization controls placed in operation. Section D discusses the second, reports on controls placed in operation **and** tests of operating effectiveness.

**A.** **User auditors**—Consideration of the effect of a service organization on the internal control of a user organization

  1. A service organization's services are part of an entity's information system if they affect

    a. Transaction initiation

    b. Accounting records, supporting information and accounts

    c. Accounting processing from transaction initiation to inclusion in financial statements, **or**

    d. Financial reporting process used to prepare financial statements

  2. The significance of controls of the service organization for the user organization depends on

    a. Nature and materiality of transactions processed

    b. Degree of interaction of activities with those of user organization

  3. In **planning the audit** when a service organization is involved, information about the nature of services provided may be available from

    a. User manuals

    b. Technical manuals

    c.  Contract between user and service organization

    d.  Reports by service auditors, internal auditors, or regulatory authorities on service organization controls

4.  If services are highly standardized, the auditor's experience with the service organization may be helpful in planning the audit

5.  If the user auditor is unable to obtain sufficient evidence, a scope limitation exists that may lead to a qualified opinion or a disclaimer

6.  **Assessing control risk** of the user organization

    a.  The following types of evidential matter may assist the user auditor

        (1)  Tests of user organization's controls over activities of service organization

        (2)  Service auditor's report on controls tests of operating effectiveness (see Section D of this outline)

        (3)  Tests of controls by user auditor at the service organization

    b.  The user auditor is responsible for evaluating the evidence presented by the service auditor and for determining its effect on the assessment of control risk at the user organization

7.  When using a service auditor's report, the user auditor should

    a.  Make inquiries concerning service auditor's professional reputation

    b.  If necessary, supplement understanding of service auditor's procedures by discussing them with the service auditor

    c.  **Not** make reference to the report of the service auditor in his/her audit report

*NOTE: This ends the discussion of the user auditor. The remainder of the outline is about the service auditor.*

**B.**  Service auditor—Overall responsibilities

1.  The service auditor should be independent of the service organization

2.  When the service auditor becomes aware of service organization errors, fraud, and/or illegal acts, s/he should communicate them to the board of directors and follow procedures required in AU 316 and AU 317

3.  The two types of reports described below are

    a.  **Reports on controls placed in operation**—Because no tests of controls performed, report itself is not intended to provide user auditor with basis for reducing assessments of control risk

    b.  **Reports on controls placed in operation and tests of operating effectiveness**—Because tests of controls performed, may provide user auditor with a basis for reducing assessment of control risk

*NOTE: When considering this area, bear in mind that **control objectives** are designated by the service organization or by outside parties (e.g., a regulatory agency, or a user group). Controls are then designed to achieve the specified control objectives. Management prepares a description of the control objectives and policies and procedures. The CPA provides assurance on whether the description presents fairly policies and procedures placed in operation and whether the controls were suitably designed to provide reasonable assurance that control objectives will be achieved if the controls are complied with satisfactorily. In addition, in the second type report, assurance is provided on operating effectiveness of the controls in meeting the control objectives.*

4.  Regardless of the type of report issued, a **letter of representations** must be obtained from management

**C.**  Service auditors—Reports on controls placed in operation

*NOTE: This section of the outline is on the report listed in Section B.3.a. of this outline.*

1.  The report issued is on controls placed in operation as of a specified date, **not** for a period of time

    a.  If significant changes have occurred before the beginning of fieldwork, those changes should be included in the service organization's description of its controls

        (1)  If they are not included in the service organization's description, they should be included in the CPA's report

2.  The report should include

    a.  Reference to the covered applications, services, products or other aspects of the service organization

    b.  Description of scope and nature of auditor's procedures

    c.  Identification of the party specifying the control objectives

    d.  Purpose of service auditor's engagement is to provide reasonable assurance that

     (1)   Service organization's description presents fairly, in all material respects, the controls relevant to a user organization's internal control

     (2)   The controls were suitably designed to achieve specified control objectives

     (3)   Controls placed in operation as of a specific date

  e.  Disclaimer on operating effectiveness of controls

  f.  Opinion on whether description **presents fairly** controls placed in operation, and whether controls were **suitably designed** to provide **reasonable assurance that control objectives would be achieved** if controls were complied with satisfactorily

  g.  Statement of inherent limitations of service organization controls and the risk of projecting them into future periods

  h.  Identification of parties for whom report is intended

3.  To express an opinion the approach is

  a.  Service organization identifies and describes control objectives and relevant controls

  b.  Service auditor considers linkage of controls to stated control objectives

  c.  Service auditor obtains sufficient evidence to reach an opinion

4.  The control objectives may be designed by the service organization, outside regulatory authorities, user groups, or others

5.  A service auditor should inquire of management as to whether any subsequent events through the date of the service auditor's report have occurred that would have a significant effect on user organizations

**D.**  Service auditors—Reports on controls placed in operation **and** tests of operating effectiveness

*NOTE: This section of the outline is on the report listed in Section B.3.b. of this outline.*

1.  The procedures described under Section C above are appropriate, but they are supplemented for procedures directed toward tests of operating effectiveness

2.  The report issued is similar to that for controls placed in operation (part C.2. of this outline), but it also includes a description of tests of controls performed and an opinion on the operating effectiveness of controls

3.  Modifications of the report

  a.  If the service auditor believes the description is inaccurate or insufficiently complete for user auditors, his/her report should so state

  b.  If the controls require certain user controls to be effective, those controls should be delineated in the description of controls and the auditor's report should so indicate

  c.  Significant deficiencies in the design or operation of the service organization's controls will result in report modification

  d.  To express an opinion on whether controls are suitably designed to achieve specified control objectives it is necessary that

     (1)   The service organization identify and describe the control objectives and relevant controls

     (2)   The service auditor consider the linkage of controls to control objectives

     (3)   The service auditor obtain sufficient evidence for an opinion

## 325 Communicating Internal Control Related Matters Identified in an Audit (SAS 112)

***Overall Objectives and Approach***—This section provides guidance for CPAs on communicating internal control (IC) related matters identified in a financial statement audit by

- Defining the terms significant deficiency and material weakness
- Providing guidance on evaluating the severity of control deficiencies, and
- Requiring that the auditor communicate in writing significant deficiencies and material weaknesses to management and *those charged with governance.*

*Those charged with governance* include the board of directors, a committee of the board of directors (e.g., an audit committee), a committee of management (e.g., a finance committee), partners, or equivalent persons or some combination of these parties. In smaller organizations management and those charged with governance may be the same people (e.g., the owner in an owner-managed entity).

**A.**  Definitions and overall requirements

1.  Internal control is a process—effected by those charged with governance, management, and other personnel—designed to provide reasonable assurance about the achievement of the entity's objectives

with regard to *reliability of financial reporting*, *effectiveness and efficiency of operations*, and *compliance with applicable laws and regulations*.

    a.   The controls relevant to an audit of financial statements generally are those that pertain to the reliability of financial reporting.

2.   Internal control deficiencies

    a.   **Control deficiency**—a control deficiency exists when the design or operation of a control does not allow management or employees, in the normal course of performing their assigned functions, to prevent or detect misstatements on a timely basis; subtypes of control deficiencies:

        (1)  **Deficiency in design**—Exists when

            (a)  A control necessary to meet the control objective is missing or

            (b)  An existing control is not properly designed so that even if the control operates as designed the control objective is not always met.

        (2)  **Deficiency in operation**—Exists when a properly designed control does not operate as designed, or when the person performing the control does not possess the necessary authority or qualifications to perform the control effectively.

    b.   **Significant deficiency**—A control deficiency, or combination of control deficiencies, that adversely affects the entity's ability to initiate, authorize, record, process, or report financial data reliably in accordance with generally accepted accounting principles such that there is more than a remote likelihood that a misstatement of the entity's financial statements that is more than *inconsequential* will not be prevented or detected.

        (1)  A misstatement is *inconsequential* if a reasonable person would conclude that the misstatement, either individually or when aggregated with other misstatements, would clearly be immaterial.

    c.   **Material weakness**—A significant deficiency, or combination of significant deficiencies, that results in more than a remote likelihood that a material misstatement of the financial statements will not be prevented or detected.

        Relationship among terms:

          •  All material weaknesses and significant deficiencies are control deficiencies.

          •  All material weaknesses are significant deficiencies.

3.   Overall: In an audit of financial statements, the auditor is not required to perform procedures to identify deficiencies in internal control or to express an opinion on the effectiveness of internal control.

    a.   However, during an audit of financial statements the auditor may become aware of control deficiencies.

**B.**  Evaluating control deficiencies identified as part of the audit

1.   The significance of a control deficiency depends on the potential for a misstatement, not on whether a misstatement actually has occurred.

    a.   Related, absence of an identified misstatement does not provide evidence that identified control deficiencies are not significant deficiencies or material weaknesses.

2.   The **likelihood** and **magnitude** of possible misstatements should be considered together when assessing the severity of a deficiency.

    a.   **Likelihood** factors relating to possible misstatement:

        (1)  Nature of accounts, disclosures and assertions (e.g., suspense accounts and related-party transactions involve high likelihoods)

        (2)  Susceptibility of related assets or liabilities to loss or fraud

        (3)  Subjectivity and complexity involved

        (4)  Frequency or any known or detected exceptions related to effectiveness of control.

        (5)  Interaction with other controls and control deficiencies

        (6)  Possible future consequences of the deficiency.

    b.   **Magnitude** factors relating to possible misstatement

        (1)  Financial statement amounts or total transactions exposed to deficiency.

        (2)  Volume of activity in account exposed to deficiency in current period or expected in future periods.

*NOTE: The maximum amount by which an account can be overstated is generally its recorded amount; but, because of the potential for unrecorded amounts, the recorded amount is not a limitation on the potential understatement.*

3.  In determining whether a control deficiency (or combination of control deficiencies) is a significant deficiency or a material weakness, the auditor also should evaluate possible mitigating effects of effective compensating controls that have been tested and evaluated.

    a.  Compensating controls may mitigate the effects of a control deficiency, but do not eliminate the control deficiency.

    b.  Example of control deficiency and a compensating control: A lack of segregation in accounts payable (control deficiency) may be mitigated by owner approval of all disbursements over $1,000 (compensating control)

4.  A control with a nonnegligible deviation rate is a deficiency, regardless of the reason for the deviation(s).

5.  Control deficiencies in the following areas are ordinarily at least significant deficiencies

    a.  Controls over selection and application of accounting policies that follow GAAP

    b.  Antifraud programs and controls

    c.  Controls over nonroutine and nonsystematic transactions

    d.  Control over the period-end financial reporting process

6.  The following are at least significant deficiencies and a strong indicator of a material weakness

    a.  Ineffective oversight of entity financial reporting and internal control by those charged with governance

    b.  Restatement of previously issued financial statements to reflect a correction

    c.  Identification of a material misstatement not identified by entity's internal control

    d.  Ineffective internal audit or risk assessment function

    e.  For complex organizations in highly regulated industries, an ineffective regulatory compliance function

    f.  Identification of any fraud by senior management

    g.  Failure by management or those charged with governance to assess the effect of a significant deficiency that has been communicated by the auditor and to either correct it or conclude that it will not be corrected

        (1)  If management decides not to correct (e.g., because cost/benefit considerations), the significant deficiency should continue to be communicated in subsequent audits.

C.  Communication—Form, Timing, and Content

    1.  Form—Communication of significant deficiencies and material weaknesses should be in writing to management and those charged with governance, even if communicated in previous audits and not yet remediated.

    2.  Timing—Best if by date of report release date (the date the auditor grants permission to use the audit report), but should not be later than 60 days following report release date

        a.  May be communicated earlier if early communication is important

        b.  The auditor communicates significant deficiencies and material weaknesses even if management has made a conscious decision not to remediate them (e.g., based on its view that remediation is not cost effective).

    3.  Content—The following should be included in any report on significant deficiencies (and material weaknesses, where relevant)

        a.  The purpose of the audit was to express opinion on financial statements and not to express an opinion on IC

        b.  State that the auditor is not expressing an opinion on IC

        c.  Include definition of significant deficiencies and material weaknesses (if relevant)

        d.  Identify which matters are considered significant deficiencies, and material weaknesses (if any)

        e.  State that the communication is intended solely for management, those charged with governance, and others within the organization and is not intended for any other

    4.  Additional reporting guidance

        a.  An auditor may include additional statements in the report regarding the inherent limitations of internal control

        b.  When no material weaknesses have been identified, a written report so indicating may be issued

        c.  When no significant deficiencies have been noted, no written report should be issued stating this fact

        d.  The auditor may choose to communicate other matters (e.g., suggestions for increased operational efficiency, control deficiencies that are not significant deficiencies)

(1) Such a communication may either be oral or written; if oral, it should be documented in the working papers.

**D.** An appendix provides detailed examples of deficiencies in the design of controls and failures in the operation of internal control.

## 326 Evidential Matter (SAS 31 and SAS 80)

*Overall Objectives and Approach*—This section presents information related to the third standard of fieldwork which requires that sufficient competent evidential matter be obtained. The statement suggests that management makes various assertions, either implicitly or explicitly, that are embodied in the financial statements. The role of the auditor is to obtain sufficient competent evidence to determine that the various assertions have been met. These assertions are **extremely** important since they have been integrated into a number of subsequent sections (e.g., AU 319, which requires that control risk be assessed by assertion).

After discussing the financial statement assertions, the section presents information related to the competency and sufficiency of audit evidence.

**A.** Assertions (explicit or implicit) are representations made by management and include several types
1. **Existence or occurrence** assertions address whether
   a. Assets or liabilities existed at a specific date (e.g., inventories on the balance sheet are available for sale)
   b. Recorded transactions occurred during the period (e.g., sales on the income statement are the results of exchanges of goods or services for a valid asset)
2. **Completeness** assertions address whether all appropriate transactions and appropriate accounts are included in the financial statements (e.g., all purchases have been recorded and are included in financial statements)
3. **Rights and obligations** assertions address whether assets are rights of the entity and liabilities are obligations of the entity as of the balance sheet date (e.g., capital leases)
4. **Valuation or allocation** assertions address whether asset, liability, revenue, and expense elements are shown in the financial statements at the proper amounts (e.g., accounts receivable at net realization value and fixed assets at cost less accumulated depreciation)
5. **Presentation and disclosure** assertions address whether elements of financial statements are properly classified, described, and disclosed (e.g., extraordinary items meet the criteria of APB 30)

   *NOTE: Know these "PERCV" assertions (reordered as Presentation, Existence, Rights, Completeness, and Valuation). In the text we use them to help us prepare audit programs.*

**B.** Assertions are used to develop audit objectives and to design substantive tests
1. The relationship between audit objectives and audit procedures is not always one-to-one
   a. An audit objective may require application of more than one procedure
   b. An audit procedure may relate to more than one objective
2. While methods of applying audit procedures may be influenced by electronically processed information, the auditor's objectives do **not** change
   a. The existence of electronic processing may make inspection, inquiry, or confirmation impossible without using information technology
3. Professional judgment of the auditor considering specific circumstances determines the nature, timing, and extent of the procedures to be used on a given audit
   a. Procedures used should be adequate to fulfill specific audit objectives
   b. Evidential matter secured should be sufficient for auditor to assess validity of specific assertions contained in the elements of the financial statements
4. When significant information is transmitted, processed, maintained, or accessed electronically, the auditor may determine that it is not practical or possible to reduce detection risk to an acceptable level by performing only substantive tests for one or more assertions; in such circumstances, the auditor should
   a. Perform tests of controls or
   b. Consider the effect on the audit report

   *NOTE: The above point is an important one in that it suggests that in some cases relying entirely upon substantive tests may not be possible in an audit.*

**C.** Evidential matter supporting the financial statements consists of
1. **Underlying accounting data** including books of original entry, general and subsidiary ledgers, accounting manuals, and supporting records such as spreadsheets and worksheets
   a. Presence of the above alone is not sufficient support for the financial statements; however, in the absence of evidence regarding propriety and accuracy of this underlying data, an opinion is not justified
   b. Auditor tests underlying accounting data using analysis and review by
      (1) Retracing procedural steps of accounting process including worksheets, allocations, etc.
      (2) Recalculating allocations, etc.
      (3) Reconciling related types and applications of common information
   c. If system is properly designed and maintained, above tests will provide persuasive evidence regarding presentation of financial statements in conformity with GAAP
2. **Corroborating evidence** which provides additional support and includes
   a. Documentary items (e.g., checks, invoices, contracts, records of electronic funds transfers, minutes of meetings)
   b. Confirmations and other written representations
   c. Information gathered by the auditor through inquiry, observation, inspections, and physical examination
   d. Other information available or developed by auditor which allows him/her to form conclusions using valid reasoning
3. Certain electronic evidence may not be retrievable after a specified period of time if files are changed and if backup files do not exist
   a. Auditor should consider time information exists in determining the nature, timing, and extent of substantive tests and tests of controls
**D.** Competent evidential matter is valid and relevant
1. Since the validity of evidence is influenced so heavily by circumstances, the generalizations below are subject to exceptions
   a. External evidential matter gathered from unbiased outsiders gives greater assurance than internally obtained evidence
   b. Financial statements processed from accounting data under conditions of adequate internal control are more reliable than those processed in entities with weak internal control
   c. Corroborating evidential matter obtained directly is more persuasive than that obtained indirectly
      (1) For example, physical examination, observation, computation, and inspection

   NOTE: *Know that competent evidence is valid and relevant. Also, the above three generalizations concerning validity of evidence have been examined.*

**E.** Sufficient competent evidential matter must be obtained to give the auditor a basis for forming an opinion
1. Auditors use professional judgment to assess whether the quantities and types of evidential matter are sufficient
   a. Usually it is necessary to rely on persuasive rather than convincing evidence for both
      (1) Individual financial statement assertions, and
      (2) The assertion that the financial statements taken as a whole present financial position, results of operations, and its cash flows in accordance with GAAP

## 328 Auditing Fair Value Measurements and Disclosures

*Overall Objectives and Approach*—Generally accepted accounting principles require companies to use fair value for measuring, representing, and disclosing a number of the companies' assets, liabilities, and components of equity. Examples include complex derivative financial instruments, marketable securities with quoted market prices, and nonmarketable securities that must be priced using a valuation model. This section provides auditing guidance related to auditing fair value measurements and disclosures.

Fair value measurements may arise both at the initial recording of transactions and later when values change. Fair value measurements may be relatively simple in situations in which active markets exist, but more complex when no such markets exist. When there are no active markets the measurements are often imprecise, as they often involve uncertainty in both the amount and timing of future cash flows. They also may be based on assumptions about future conditions, transactions, or events.

A. The auditor's evaluation of the conformity of fair value measurements and disclosures with GAAP should include a(n)
1. Evaluation of management's intent and ability to carry out certain courses of action by considering matters such as
   a. Management's history of carrying out its stated intentions for assets and liabilities
   b. Written plans and other documentation, including budgets, minutes, and other such items
   c. Management's stated reasons for choosing a particular course of action
   d. Management's ability to carry out a particular course of action
2. Evaluation of whether the entity's fair value measurements are applied consistently
3. Consideration whether to use the work of a specialist to help with the above issues
B. The three general approaches for auditing estimates are appropriate for testing fair value measurements and disclosures
1. Review and test management's process of deriving the estimate by testing management's significant assumptions, the valuation, and the underlying data to evaluate whether
   a. The assumptions are reasonable
   b. Fair value was determined using an appropriate model
   c. Management used relevant information that was reasonably available
2. Develop the auditor's own expectation of the estimate and compare it to management's estimate of fair value
3. Review subsequent events and transactions occurring after period end may help the auditor with respect to fair value measurements
C. Other
1. Measurements become more complex, and uncertainty increases with the
   a. Length of the forecast period
   b. Number of significant and complex assumptions
   c. Degree of subjectivity associated with assumptions
   d. Degree of uncertainty with the future occurrence of events
   e. Lack of objective data when highly subjective factors are used
2. The auditor should evaluate whether disclosures about fair values are in conformity with GAAP
3. The auditor should consider the effects of subsequent events
4. Management representations may be obtained on
   a. Appropriateness of measurement methods
   b. Completeness and adequacy of disclosures
   c. Whether subsequent events require adjustment to the fair value measurements
5. The auditor should determine that the audit committee is informed about the process used by management to form sensitive accounting estimates, including fair value estimates as per AU 380

### 329 Analytical Procedures (SAS 56)
*Overall Objectives and Approach*—This section presents information on analytical procedures. It suggests that analytical procedures are normally used at three stages of the audit: (1) planning, (2) substantive testing, and (3) overall review at the conclusion of an audit. They are required during the planning and overall review stages. In addition, the section presents information on the manner in which analytical procedures are applied.

A. Analytical procedures consist of **evaluations of financial information made by a study of plausible relationships among financial and nonfinancial data**
1. **Basic premise—Plausible relationships** among data may be expected to exist in the absence of known conditions to the contrary
2. Analytical procedures used for **3 purposes:**
   a. **Planning** nature, timing, and extent of other auditing procedures
   b. **Substantive tests** about particular assertions
   c. **Overall review** in the final stage of audit

   *NOTE: The section requires the use of analytical procedures in a. and c. above.*

3. The auditor **compares recorded amounts to expectations** developed from sources such as
   a. **Prior period** financial information
   b. **Anticipated results** such as projections or forecasts

    c.  **Relationships among elements** of financial information within the period

    d.  **Industry** information

    e.  **Relevant nonfinancial information** (e.g., number of employees, volume of goods produced)

**B.**  Analytical procedures for **planning**

   1.  The purpose is to assist in planning the nature, timing, and extent of other substantive tests and therefore should

    a.  Enhance auditor's understanding of client's business and events since the last audit

    b.  Identify high risk areas (e.g., **unusual transactions**)

   2.  Generally use data aggregated at a high level

**C.**  Analytical procedures for **substantive tests**

   1.  Especially effective for assertions for which detailed evidence does not make misstatement apparent (e.g., comparing aggregate wages paid to number of employees)

   2.  Auditors must understand the reasons that relationships are plausible

    a.  For higher assurance more predictable relationships are required to develop an expectation

    b.  Principles involving **usual** predictability of relationships:

      (1)  Relationships in a **dynamic** or unstable environment are **less predictable** than those in a stable environment

      (2)  Relationships involving **balance sheet accounts are less predictable** than income statement accounts (because balance sheet accounts represent balances at one arbitrary point in time)

      (3)  Relationships involving management discretion are sometimes less predictable (e.g., decision to incur maintenance expense rather than replace plant)

       *NOTE: Know the above three principles.*

   3.  The following factors generally **increase the reliability** of data used to develop an expectation

    a.  Data generated from **independent sources outside entity**

    b.  **Internal data** developed by **sources independent** of amount being audited

    c.  **Internal data** developed under **effective internal control**

    d.  **Data subjected to audit testing** in current or prior year

    e.  **Expectations developed** using data from a **variety of sources**

   4.  Expectations developed at a detailed level generally have a greater chance of detecting misstatement

    a.  Monthly amounts will generally be more effective than annual amounts

    b.  Comparisons by line of business usually more effective than company-wide comparisons

   5.  The auditor should use the materiality amount and level of assurance desired from the procedure to determine the amount of difference from expectation that can be accepted without further investigation

   6.  When an analytical procedure is used as the principal substantive test for a significant assertion, the auditor should document

    a.  The expectation and factors considered in its development

    b.  Results of comparison of the expectation to the recorded amounts (or ratios)

    c.  Any additional procedures performed in response to significant unexpected differences and results of such additional procedures

**D.**  Analytical procedures in **overall review**

   1.  Purposes are to assist auditor in

    a.  **Assessing the conclusions** reached

    b.  **Evaluating the overall financial statement presentation**

   2.  Should include reading the financial statements and notes to consider

    a.  Adequacy of data gathered in response to unusual or unexpected balances identified during preliminary analysis

    b.  Unusual or unexpected balances or relationships not identified during the audit

## 330 The Confirmation Process (SAS 67)

***Overall Objectives and Approach***—This section provides guidance on the confirmation process. Confirmation is defined as "the process of obtaining and evaluating direct communication from a third party in response to a request for information about a particular item affecting financial statement assertions."

    The first portion of the outline discusses the relationship of the confirmation process to the auditor's assessment of audit risk. This portion of the section builds on AU 312 and AU 326 on audit risk and financial statement assertions, respectively. Recall that audit risk has three components—inherent risk, control risk and detection risk. The five management assertions relating to financial statements are presentation, existence/occurrence, rights/obligations, completeness, and valuation. If you are not familiar with these sections you may wish to study them prior to studying Section A (both are discussed in the Engagement Planning Module).

Section B of this outline discusses overall issues related to the confirmation process. Sections C and D discuss alternative procedures and the evaluation of confirmation results. Finally, the outline addresses the confirmation of accounts receivable.

**A.** Relationship of confirmation procedures to the auditor's assessment of audit risk and financial statement assertions.
   1. The greater the combined assessed levels of inherent risk and control risk, the greater the assurance needed from substantive tests
       a. In these situations the auditor might use confirmation procedures
       b. When the client has entered into an unusual or complex transaction the auditor should consider confirming the terms
       c. Procedures **in addition to confirmation** may be necessary to achieve a low level of audit risk (e.g., perform sales cutoff tests in addition to confirming receivables)
   2. Confirmation may not be necessary if inherent and control risks are assessed as low
       a. For example, when inherent and control risks are low for cash, the auditor might inspect client-provided bank statements rather than confirm cash balances
   3. Assertions addressed by confirmations
       a. Confirmation requests sent to a sample selected from recorded accounts are more likely to address existence than completeness; examples are
          (1) Receivables and payables samples selected from a trial balance
          (2) The standard form for cash confirmations is sent to recorded accounts and is not designed to test completeness
       b. To address completeness an appropriate population must be used (e.g., a list of vendors for payables)
       c. Confirmations may provide information on rights/obligations as well as existence (e.g., confirmation of goods held on consignment with the consignee)
       d. Confirmations generally provide only limited evidence relating to the valuation assertion

**B.** The confirmation process
   1. Steps involved in confirmation
       a. Select items to be confirmed
       b. Design confirmation request
       c. Send confirmation request
       d. Obtain response
       e. Evaluate the information provided
   2. Forms of confirmation requests
       a. **Positive form**
          (1) Two methods are possible
              (a) Request the respondent to indicate whether s/he agrees with the amount (or other information) included on the request
              (b) Do not include the amount (or other information) on the request and ask respondent to fill in the information (referred to as the "blank" positive form)
                  1] Use of the blank positive form may result in a lower response rate, although it may decrease the risk that respondents sign and return the confirmation without verifying the information
       b. **Negative form**
          (1) Request recipient to respond only if s/he disagrees with the information stated on the request
          (2) Negatives may be used when
              (a) Combined assessed level of inherent and control risk is low,
              (b) Large number of small balances are involved, and
              (c) The auditor has no reason to believe that recipients are unlikely to give them consideration
          (3) Unreturned negatives rarely provide significant evidence other than for certain aspects of existence

3. When using confirmations the auditor should consider
   a. **Prior experience**—response rates, misstatements identified, and inaccurate replies
   b. **Nature of information being confirmed**—consider whether respondents may reply effectively and understand the information being confirmed
   c. **Appropriate respondent**—consider who should receive the confirmation request so as to help assure a meaningful response
4. The auditor should maintain control over the confirmation requests and the responses
   a. Oral replies (e.g., by telephone)—when significant, the auditor should request written confirmation
   b. Fax replies—consider verifying source and contents through a telephone call and by asking that the original request be mailed (in addition to the fax replies) to the auditor
   c. Second, and sometimes third requests should be sent when positive requests used

C. Alternative procedures
   1. Should generally be performed when no reply to a positive confirmation request has been received
   2. Omission of alternative procedures may be acceptable when
      a. No unusual factors related to nonresponses have been noted (e.g., they don't all relate to year-end transactions) and
      b. The total of nonresponses in aggregate, when projected as 100% misstatements, and all other unadjusted differences noted in the audit are still immaterial

D. When evaluating confirmation results the auditor should consider
   1. The reliability of the confirmations and alternative procedures
   2. The nature of any exceptions
   3. Evidence provided by other procedures
   4. Whether additional evidence is needed

E. Accounts receivable should be confirmed unless
   1. They are immaterial,
   2. The use of confirmations would be ineffective, or
   3. The combined assessment of inherent and control risk is low and that assessment, with other substantive tests, reduces audit risk to an acceptably low level

*NOTE: Accounts receivable should normally be confirmed and the auditor who has not confirmed them should document how s/he overcame that presumption.*

## 331 Inventories (SAS 1)

***Overall Objectives and Approach***—This section establishes the observation of inventories as a **generally accepted auditing procedure**. An auditor who omits the observation of inventories must be able to justify the decision (in the working papers—not in the report). The section discusses a number of complications that may arise when observing the client's inventory count, and establishes procedures which may be necessary when inventories are held in public warehouses.

A. Inventories—held by clients
   1. It is normally necessary for the CPA to be present when inventory quantities are determined by means of a physical count
   2. When perpetual records are well maintained and checked by the client periodically by comparisons with physical counts, the auditor may perform observation procedures either during or after the end of the period under audit
   3. When a client uses statistical sampling to determine inventory quantities, the auditor must determine that
      a. It is reasonable and has statistical validity
      b. It has been properly applied
      c. The results are reasonable in the circumstances
   4. When a CPA has not observed the counting of inventory
      a. It will **always** be necessary to make some physical counts of inventory and apply appropriate tests of intervening transactions subsequent to the client's count

   > *EXAMPLE: Assume the client counted inventory on December 31, and the auditor was not present. At some point, say January 15, the auditor must make some physical counts and reconcile the January 15 quantities back to those of December 31.*

5. When a CPA is satisfied as to the current inventory, s/he may satisfy him/herself as to a **prior period's inventory** (e.g., the beginning inventory for the year under audit) by
   a. Tests of prior transactions
   b. Review of prior count records
   c. Gross profit tests

**B.** Inventories—held in public warehouses
1. Direct confirmation in writing from custodian is ordinarily obtained
2. If such inventories represent a significant portion of current or total assets, auditor should
   a. Review and test owner's control procedures for investigating and evaluating performance of the warehouseman
   b. Obtain report from independent accountant as to the reliability of internal control over custody of goods and, if applicable, pledging of receipts
      (1) Alternatively, test the structure to gain assurance that information received is reliable
   c. Observe physical counts where reasonable and practical
   d. Confirm pertinent details of pledged receipts with lenders, if any

## 332 Auditing Derivative Instruments, Hedging Activities, and Investments in Securities

*Overall Objectives and Approach*—This section presents guidance on auditing derivative instruments, hedging activities, and investments in securities. This guidance, which applies to both debt and equity securities, pertains to various accounting pronouncements, including

- SFAS 115, *Accounting for Certain Investments in Debt and Equity Securities*
- SFAS 133, *Accounting for Derivative Instruments and Hedging Activities*
- APB 18, *The Equity Method of Accounting for Investments*

**A.** Overall
1. The auditor may need special skill or knowledge to plan and perform auditing procedures for certain assertions about derivatives and securities
2. Auditors must design procedures to obtain reasonable assurance of detecting material misstatements of assertions about derivatives and securities

**B.** Inherent risk assessment—Examples of factors that affect inherent risk
1. Management's objectives
   a. For example, using hedges subject to the risk of market conditions may increase risk
2. Complexity of the features of the derivative or security
3. Whether the transaction that gave rise to the derivative or security involved the exchange of cash
   a. Those not involving an initial exchange of cash are more risky for valuation and disclosure
4. The entity's experience with the derivative or security
5. Whether a derivative is freestanding or an embedded feature of an agreement
   a. Embedded are more risky because they may be less likely to be identified by management
6. Whether external factors affect the assertion (e.g., credit risk, market risk, basis risk, legal risk)
7. Evolving nature of derivatives and applicable GAAP
8. Significant reliance on outside parties increases risk
9. GAAP may require developing assumptions about future conditions, which increases risk

**C.** Control risk assessment
1. Examples of controls include
   a. Monitoring by a control staff that is independent of derivative activities
   b. Prior to exceeding limits, senior management approval of transactions
   c. Senior management addresses limit excesses and divergences from approved derivatives strategies
   d. Derivatives positions accurately transmitted to risk measurement systems
   e. Appropriate reconciliations
   f. Constraints defined
   g. Regular review of controls by senior management, an independent group, or a designated individual
   h. Review of limits
2. When a service organization is involved, it may be a part of the entity's information system, and thereby the auditor should consider procedures from a variety of sources, such as
   a. User manuals

     b.  System overviews

     c.  Technical manuals

     d.  Contract between entity and service organization

     e.  Reports of auditors, regulatory agencies

     f.  Inquiry of personnel at the entity or service organization

     *NOTE: See AU 324 for more information on service organizations.*

   3.  If the auditor plans to assess control risk below the maximum, he or she should identify specific controls applicable to assertions and gather evidential matter about their operating effectiveness (i.e., perform tests of controls)

**D.**  Designing substantive procedures

   1.  Existence or occurrence assertion *example* procedures

     a.  Confirm (security issuer, security holder, broker-dealer)

     b.  Inspect security or derivative contract

     c.  Read executed partnership or similar agreements

     d.  Inspect supporting documentation for subsequent realization or settlement after end of reporting period

     e.  Perform analytical procedures

   2.  Completeness

     a.  Request counterparties or holders to state whether there are any side agreements or agreements to repurchase old securities sold

     b.  Request frequently used counterparties or holders with whom accounting records indicate there are no *current* derivatives or securities to state whether any exist

     c.  Inspect financial instruments and other agreements to identify embedded derivatives

     d.  Perform analytical procedures

     e.  Compare previous account detail with current account detail

     f.  Read other information (e.g., minutes of board of directors, other committees)

   3.  Rights and obligations

     a.  Confirm significant terms with counterparty or holder

     b.  Inspect underlying agreements

     c.  Consider findings of other audit procedures (e.g., reading minutes of meetings)

   4.  Valuation

     a.  Determine whether GAAP specifies the method to be used to determine the fair value of the derivatives and securities, and, if so, whether they have been properly handled.

     b.  The section also identifies sources of fair value information for derivatives and securities, the hierarchy of such sources, procedures to follow when market prices are not available, and the auditor's overall responsibility.

   5.  Presentation and disclosure

     a.  Since certain derivatives have particular presentation and disclosure requirements, the auditor must be aware of them

**E.**  Hedging activities

   1.  A hedge is a defensive strategy to protect an entity against the risk of adverse price or interest-rate movements on certain of its assets, liabilities, or anticipated transactions

   2.  In an audit, the auditor should gather evidence to determine whether management

     a.  Complied with GAAP hedge accounting requirements

     b.  Originally expected that the hedging relationship would be highly effective

     c.  Periodically assessed the hedge's ongoing effectiveness

   3.  For a cash flow hedge of a forecasted transaction, management must determine the probability of occurrence; probability should be supported by circumstances such as

     a.  Frequency of similar past transactions

     b.  Financial and operational ability of entity to carry out transaction

     c.  Extent of loss that could result if the transaction does not occur

     d.  Likelihood transaction with substantially different characteristics might be used to achieve same business purposes

## 333 Management Representations
*Overall Objectives and Approach*—This section establishes a requirement that auditors obtain written representations from management (representation letters) as part of any audit and provides related guidance.

A. Reliance upon management's representations
1. Written representations by management to an auditor (in a representation letter)
   a. **Confirm** representations explicitly or implicitly provided throughout the audit
   b. Indicate and document the continuing appropriateness of such representations, and
   c. Reduce the possibility of misunderstanding
2. Although written representations are **not** a substitute for other necessary audit procedures, in some cases they provide additional evidential matter
   a. For example, as to management's intent to discontinue a line of business
3. If a representation is contradicted by other audit evidence, the auditor should investigate the circumstances and consider whether reliance upon other representations during the audit is appropriate and justified

B. Written representation obtained
1. Representations should be obtained for **all** financial statements and periods covered by the auditor's report
2. Representations should be tailored by engagement, but should include the following matters:
   a. Financial statements
      (1) Management acknowledges its responsibility for the financial statements being prepared in conformity with GAAP
      (2) Management believes financial statements presented in conformity with GAAP
      (3) Management believes effects of uncorrected financial statement misstatements are immaterial, both individually and in the aggregate
   b. Completeness of information
      (1) Availability of all financial records and related data
      (2) Completeness and availability of all minutes of meetings of stockholders, directors, and committees of directors
      (3) Communications from regulatory agencies
      (4) Absence of unrecorded transactions
   c. Recognition, measurement, and disclosure
      (1) Management's acknowledgement of its responsibility to design and implement programs and controls to prevent or detect fraud
      (2) Information concerning fraud or suspected fraud affecting the company
      (3) Information concerning any allegations of fraud or suspected fraud affecting the company, for example, because of communications from employees, former employees, analysts, regulators, short sellers, or other investors
      (4) Plans or intentions that may affect carrying value or classification of assets or liabilities
      (5) Information about related-party transactions and receivable or payables
      (6) Guarantee (written or oral) under which the entity is contingently liable
      (7) All significant estimates and material concentrations known to management are disclosed as per AICPA Statement of Position 94-6, *Disclosure of Certain Significant Risk and Uncertainties*
      (8) Violations or possible violations of laws whose effects should be considered for disclosure or as basis for recording loss contingency
      (9) Unasserted claims or assessments that entity's lawyer has advised are probable of assertion and must be disclosed as per SFAS 5, *Accounting for Contingencies*
      (10) Satisfactory title to assets, liens on assets, and assets pledged as collateral
      (11) Compliance with aspects of contractual agreements that may affect financial statements

C. Details of Representations
1. Representations may be limited to matters considered either individually or collectively **material** to the financial statements, provided management and the auditor have an agreement on materiality
   a. But no materiality limitations should exist for management's responsibility for the financial statements, the availability of financial records, the completeness of records, or communications from regulatory agencies—all included in B.2. above

2. Written representation should be
   a. **Addressed to** the **auditor**
   b. **Dated no earlier than** the date of the **auditor's report**
   c. **Signed** by **chief executive officer** and **chief financial officer**
      (1) Representations should be obtained from current management for all periods reported upon, even if current management was not present during all those periods
D. Scope limitations
   1. **Management refusal** to furnish written representations constitutes a **scope limitation** that **precludes an unqualified opinion** and ordinarily is sufficient to cause a **disclaimer of opinion**
      a. Based on nature of representations not obtained, a qualified opinion may be appropriate

## 334 Related Parties (SAS 45)

*Overall Objectives and Approach*—This section presents guidance on **accounting** and **auditing** considerations for related-party transactions. The subsection on audit procedures, after providing some general advice, provides guidance on (1) identifying **conditions** in which related-party transactions are likely, (2) identifying **parties** that are related to the entity, (3) identifying **transactions** with related parties, and (4) **examining related-party transactions** that have been **identified**. The section closes with information on required disclosures.

A. Accounting (including disclosures) considerations for related-party transactions
   1. SFAS 57 provides accounting requirements for related-party disclosures
      a. Nature of relationship(s)
      b. Description of transaction(s)
      c. Dollar amount of transactions
      d. Amounts due to/from related parties, including terms

   *NOTE: See outline of SFAS 57 for more details.*

   2. Transactions should reflect their substance (rather than merely their legal form)
   3. Except for routine transactions, it will generally **not be possible** to determine whether a particular transaction would have taken place, or what its terms would have been
      a. If management makes such a representation, **and if it is unsubstantiated,** it may result in either a qualified or an adverse opinion due to a departure from GAAP—see outline of AU 508 and Reporting Module for information on departures from GAAP

   *NOTE: Points 3. and 3.a. have been asked several times in multiple-choice questions.*

   4. Example transactions that may be indicative of related-party transactions
      a. Borrowing or lending at interest rates above or below the market rate
      b. Selling real estate at a price significantly different from its appraised value
      c. Exchanging property for similar property in a nonmonetary transaction
      d. Making loans with no scheduled repayment terms

   *NOTE: Several multiple-choice questions have asked for a situation in which the existence of related parties is likely, and have used one of the above as the correct reply.*

B. **Auditing considerations** for related-party transactions
   1. An audit cannot be expected to provide assurance that all related-party transactions will be discovered
      a. Nevertheless, an auditor should be aware of the possible existence of material related-party transactions
         (1) Experience has shown, for example, that business structure and operating style are occasionally deliberately designed to obscure such transactions.
   2. **Conditions in which related-party transactions are likely**
      a. Lack of sufficient working capital or credit to continue the business
      b. An urgent desire for favorable EPS trends
      c. Overly optimistic EPS forecast
      d. Dependence on a few products, customers, or transactions
      e. Declining industry profitability
      f. Excess capacity
      g. Significant litigation

    h.  Significant obsolescence
3.  Procedures to identify **parties** that are related to the entity
    a.  Evaluate the client's procedures for related-party transactions
    b.  Ask client for names of all related parties and whether there have been any transactions with these parties
    c.  Review SEC filings
    d.  Determine names of officers of all employee trusts
    e.  Review stockholder listings of closely held companies
    f.  Review prior workpapers for the names of related parties
    g.  Inquire of predecessor and/or principal auditors
    h.  Review material investment transactions
4.  Procedures to identify **transactions** with related parties
    a.  Provide audit personnel with related-party names
    b.  Review Board of Directors' minutes (and other committees)
    c.  Review SEC filings
    d.  Review client "conflict of interest" statements obtained by company from management
    e.  Review nature of transactions with major customers, suppliers, etc.
    f.  Consider whether unrecorded transactions exist
    g.  Review accounting records for large, nonrecurring transactions
    h.  Review confirmations of compensating balances for indications that balances are maintained for or by related parties
    i.  Review legal invoices
    j.  Review confirmations of loans receivable and payable for guarantees
5.  Procedures (beyond management inquiry) for **examining** related-party transactions that have been **identified**
    a.  Obtain understanding of the purpose of the transaction
    b.  Examine supporting documents
    c.  Verify existence of required approval
    d.  Evaluate reasonableness of amounts to be disclosed
    e.  Consider simultaneous or joint audit of intercompany balances
    f.  Inspect/confirm transferability and value of collateral
    g.  Extend auditing procedures further as necessary to understand transactions
        (1)  Confirm transaction details with other party
        (2)  Inspect evidence held by other party
        (3)  Confirm information with intermediaries (e.g., banks)
        (4)  Refer to trade journals, credit agencies, etc.
        (5)  Seek assurance on material uncollected balances

## 336 Using the Work of a Specialist (SAS 73)

*Overall Objectives and Approach*—This section presents guidance on an auditor's use of the work of a specialist. For example, an auditor may engage an appraiser to help verify a client's valuation of an inventory of diamond rings. Other specialists whose work might be used by auditors include actuaries, engineers, environmental consultants, geologists, and attorneys providing services other than those related to litigation (AU 337 addresses litigation); internal auditors are **not** considered specialists for purposes of this section. The section applies to situations in which either management or the auditor engage a specialist. Note that when management has engaged the specialist the work will often have been performed prior to the audit; for example, prior to the audit a specialist may have appraised assets in support of loans issued by a bank.

    Section A of this outline summarizes the types of matters that may result in an auditor using the work of a specialist, and an auditor's consideration of specialist qualifications and work of the specialist; Section B considers the effect of the specialist's findings on the audit report.

**A.**  Types of matters, specialist qualifications, and findings
    1.  Among the **types of matters** for which an auditor may decide to use the work of a specialist are the determination of
        a.  Valuation (e.g., inventories, complex financial instruments, real estate, art)
        b.  Physical characteristics (e.g., mineral content, mineral reserves, materials stored in stockpiles)

    c.   Amounts derived by using specialized methods (e.g., actuarial determinations for employee benefits, insurance loss reserves)

    d.   Technical requirements, regulations or agreements (significance of contracts or other legal documents)

  2.  The auditor should evaluate the professional **qualifications** of the specialist by considering

    a.   Professional certification, licenses, etc.

    b.   Reputation

    c.   Experience in this type of work

  3.  The auditor should obtain an understanding of the **work** performed by the specialist including

    a.   Objectives

    b.   Specialist's relationship to client

       (1)  No relationship—work usually provides greater assurance of reliability

       (2)  A relationship—although using the work of such a specialist is acceptable under certain circumstances

          (a)  When such a relationship exists the auditor should assess the risk that the specialist's objectivity might be impaired

          (b)  If objectivity might be impaired, the auditor should perform additional procedures or engage another specialist

    c.   Methods or assumptions used

    d.   Comparison of methods or assumptions with those used in preceding period

    e.   Appropriateness of using specialist's work

    f.   Form and content of specialist's findings that will enable the auditor to

       (1)  Obtain an understanding of the methods and assumptions and their reasonableness

       (2)  Make appropriate tests of data provided to the specialist, including the auditor's assessment of control risk

       (3)  Evaluate whether the specialist's findings support the related assertions in the financial statements

*NOTE: The appropriateness and reasonableness of the methods and assumptions used are the responsibility of the specialist. However, if at any point the auditor believes the specialist's findings are unreasonable, additional procedures should be applied.*

**B.**  Effect of specialist's work on the auditor's report

  1.  If the specialist's findings support the related financial statement assertions, the auditor may conclude that sufficient competent evidential matter has been obtained, and no reference should be made to the specialist's work in the audit report

  2.  If the specialist's findings do not support the related financial statement assertions,

    a.   The auditor should (1) apply additional procedures and (2) if necessary, obtain the opinion of another specialist (unless it appears that the matter cannot be resolved)

    b.   If the difference cannot be resolved, the auditor will ordinarily qualify the opinion or disclaim an opinion because the inability to obtain sufficient competent evidential matter is a scope limitation

    c.   If the financial statements are incorrect, the auditor should express a qualified or adverse opinion due to a departure from GAAP

*NOTE: Only in b. and c. may the specialist be referred to.*

### 337 Inquiry of a Client's Lawyer Concerning Litigation, Claims, and Assessments (LCA) (SAS 12)

*Overall Objectives and Approach*—This section presents guidance on the manner in which a CPA is to obtain information from a client's lawyer concerning litigation, claims, and assessments (LCA) that affect a client. LCA may result in contingent, as well as direct liabilities. At this point, if you are unable to recall the SFAS 5 accounting standard related to contingencies, we suggest that you review that outline.

After a brief reference to SFAS 5, the section presents information on the types of evidential matter that should be gathered and the appropriate audit procedures to be followed. Next, details of the inquiry which is to be sent to the client's lawyer are provided. The section concludes by discussing how CPAs should handle various limitations in the lawyer's response to the inquiry.

**A.**  Evidential matter and appropriate audit procedures

  1.  The auditor should obtain evidential matter relating to LCA relevant to the following factors:

    a.   Conditions indicating a possible loss from LCA

      b.   The period in which the underlying cause occurred

      c.   The degree of probability of an unfavorable outcome

      d.   The amount or range of potential loss

2.   Because **management** is the primary source of information about such contingencies, the CPA's procedures for LCA should include

      a.   Inquiring as to the policies and procedures adopted for identifying, evaluating, and accounting for contingencies

      b.   Obtaining a description and evaluation of all pending contingencies at the balance sheet date and any contingencies arising after the balance sheet date

      c.   Examining relevant documents including correspondence and invoices from lawyers

      d.   Obtaining management's written assurance that all unasserted claims required to be disclosed by SFAS 5 (per client's lawyer) are disclosed

          (1)  Obtain client's permission to inform lawyer that client has given this assurance

3.   Other audit procedures which may reveal pending or possible contingencies

      a.   Reading board of directors' and other appropriate meeting minutes

      b.   Reading contracts, leases, correspondence, and other similar documents

      c.   Guarantees of indebtedness disclosed on bank confirmations

      d.   Inspecting other documents for possible client-made guarantees

**B.**  Inquiry **sent to** the client's lawyer

*NOTE: Although not explicitly stated in the section, the auditor mails this inquiry (typed on the client's letterhead) to the lawyer.*

1.   This inquiry may be sent to the client's **inside general counsel** or legal department (i.e., lawyers that are employees of the client) **and outside counsel**

      a.   Information obtained from inside counsel is **not** a substitute for information outside counsel refuses to furnish

2.   Information included in the inquiry to the lawyer

      a.   Identification of the client and the date of the audit

      b.   A list prepared by management (or a request by management that the lawyer prepare a list) describing **pending or threatened LCA** for which the lawyer has been engaged and devoted substantive attention with a request that the **lawyer indicate**

          (1)  A description of the **nature** of the matter, **progress** of the case to date, and the **action** the company intends to take (e.g., contest vigorously)

          (2)  If possible, an evaluation of the likelihood and amount of potential loss

          (3)  Identification of any omissions from list, or a statement that the list is complete with respect to LCA

      c.   A list prepared by management that describes and evaluates **unasserted claims and assessments** which management considers **probable of assertion,** and that, **if asserted,** would have a **reasonable possibility** of an unfavorable outcome and a request that the lawyer indicate any disagreements with the description or evaluation

          (1)  For unasserted claims, the lawyer **will not** inform the CPA of omissions from management's list

             (a)  The lawyer is to advise the client of the omission

             (b)  If the client does not then inform the CPA about the omission, the lawyer is generally required to resign

             *NOTE: Several exam multiple-choice questions have addressed the idea that resignation of a lawyer is to be investigated by the auditor; such resignation may indicate the existence of undisclosed unasserted claims. The auditor should inquire about reasons for changes in or resignations of lawyers.*

             (c)  A request that the lawyer specifically identify the nature of and reasons for any limitations in his/her response

3.   The client and CPA should agree on materiality limits, and then inquiry need not be made of immaterial items

4.   In some circumstances the auditor may obtain a response to the inquiry in a conference with the lawyer

      a.   The CPA should appropriately document the conference

**C.** Limitations on the lawyer's response to the inquiry

1. A lawyer may limit his/her response to material matters to which s/he has devoted substantive attention—such limitations are not considered audit scope limitations

2. **Refusal to furnish either in writing or orally information** requested in the inquiry letter is a **scope limitation sufficient to preclude an unqualified opinion**

    a. Scope limitations lead to either qualified opinions or disclaimers of opinion

3. Inherent uncertainties involving the situation may make it impossible for the lawyer to respond as to the likelihood of loss, or the amount

    a. This is an uncertainty situation which, if material, may lead to an unqualified opinion with an explanatory paragraph, or a disclaimer of opinion

    *NOTE: For more on scope limitations and uncertainties, see the outline of AU 508 and Section B of the Reporting Module.*

## 339 Audit Documentation (SAS 96)

***Overall Objectives and Approach***—Audit documentation (working papers) is the principal record of auditing procedures applied, evidence obtained, and conclusions reached by the auditor. This section discusses general information, ownership, and custody issues of documentation. It also includes an appendix with a summary of other areas of the professional standards with documentation requirements.

**A.** Audit documentation—general

1. Purposes of audit documentation

    a. Provide principal support for auditor's report

    b. Aid auditor in the conduct and supervision of the work

2. Should show that standards of fieldwork have been observed

3. Should be sufficient to

    a. Enable engagement team members with supervision and review responsibilities to understand nature, timing, extent, and results of audit procedures performed and evidence obtained

    b. Indicate who performed and reviewed work

    c. Show that accounting records agree or reconcile with financial statements (or other information being reported on)

4. Factors affecting nature and extent of needed documentation in an audit area

    a. Risk of material misstatement

    b. Extent of judgment

    c. Nature of auditing procedures

    d. Significance of evidence obtained to assertion being tested

    e. Nature and extent of exceptions identified

    f. Need to document a conclusion or basis for a conclusion not readily determinable from the documentation of the work performed

5. The following should be documented

    a. Abstracts or copies of significant contracts and agreements

    b. Tests of operating effectiveness of controls and substantive tests of details that involve inspection of documents or confirmation should include an identification of the items tested

    c. Significant findings or issues and actions taken to address them; examples

    (1) Matters that are both significant and involve complex or unusual accounting issues, estimates, and uncertainties

    (2) Results of auditing procedures indicating possible material misstatement or the need to modify audit procedures

    (3) Circumstances cause difficulty in applying auditing procedures

    (4) Other findings that could result in modification of auditor's report

**B.** Additional audit documentation issues

1. Ownership—the auditor

2. Confidentiality—auditor should adopt reasonable procedures to maintain confidentiality of information and to prevent unauthorized access to audit documentation

3. Retention—a period of time sufficient to meet the needs of the auditor's practice and to satisfy legal and regulatory requirements for records retention

4. Use by client—may sometimes be used, but should not be regarded as a part of or substitute for the client's accounting records

**C.** Requirements for written documentation in other portions of the Statements on Auditing Standards
1. AU 310—Understanding concerning the engagement with the client
2. AU 311—Written audit program (or set of written audit programs) for each audit
3. AU 312—Nature and effect of aggregated misstatements and the auditor's conclusion as to whether this amount is material
4. AU 316—Evidence of the performance of this assessment of the risk of material misstatement due to fraud and the auditor's responses thereto
5. AU 317—Oral communications to the audit committee regarding illegal acts that come to the auditor's attention
6. AU 319—Understanding of internal control and conclusion about the assessed level of control risk
7. AU 325—Oral communications with the audit committee about reportable conditions
8. AU 329—Information on analytical procedures
9. AU 330—Oral confirmations
10. AU 333—Representation letter from management
11. AU 337—In an audit inquiry letter or a separate letter to the client's attorney that the client has assured the auditor that all appropriate unasserted claims have been disclosed
12. AU 341—Conditions indicating substantial doubt, work performed in evaluating management's plans, auditor's conclusion about substantial doubt and effect on financial statements, disclosures, and audit report
13. AU 380—Oral communications about scope and results of audit
14. AU 508—Representation letter received by predecessor from a successor auditor before reissuing report of a prior period
15. AU 534—Representation regarding purposes and uses of financial statements prepared in conformity with accounting principles of another country
16. AU 801—Oral communications to management and audit committee of when required in an audit of a governmental entity or a recipient of governmental financial assistance

## 341 The Auditor's Consideration of an Entity's Ability to Continue as a Going Concern (SAS 59)

*Overall Objectives and Approach*—This section presents guidance on CPA responsibility for evaluating whether there is **substantial doubt** about a client's ability to continue as a going concern. The section suggests that continuation as a going concern is assumed in the absence of information to the contrary. The section first discusses an auditor's responsibility related to a client. Second, audit procedures which may identify conditions and events which raise a question about going concern status are presented. The third subsection, which is only appropriate after such conditions and/or events have been identified, discusses the manner in which an auditor evaluates management's plans for dealing with such adverse circumstances. The fourth and fifth subsections discuss proper financial statement and audit report reflections of such conditions and events.

**A.** The auditor's responsibility
1. The auditor must evaluate whether there is **substantial doubt about the entity's ability to continue as a going concern for a period not to exceed one year from the date of the financial statements being audited**
   a. Ordinarily, information that significantly **contradicts the going concern assumption** relates to inability to meet obligations as they become due without
   (1) Substantial disposition of assets
   (2) Restructuring debt
   (3) Externally forced revisions of operations
   (4) Similar actions
2. The evaluation is based on audit procedures planned and performed to achieve the audit objectives related to the management assertions—for more on the assertions see AU 326 outline and Section A of the Evidence Module
3. The process for evaluating whether there is substantial doubt
   a. Consider whether audit procedures identify conditions and events suggesting substantial doubt
   b. If substantial doubt from a.,
   (1) Obtain management's plans
   (2) Assess likelihood plans can be implemented
   c. If substantial doubt remains, consider

(1) Adequacy of disclosures on inability to continue and

(2) Include explanatory paragraph following opinion paragraph in audit report

*NOTE: Be familiar with this process.*

4. **Auditors are not responsible for predicting future** conditions and events

   a. The fact that an entity ceases to exist after an audit report which does not refer to substantial doubt does not in itself indicate inadequate auditor performance

   b. Absence of reference to substantial doubt in an audit report should not be viewed as providing assurance entity will continue as a going concern

**B.** Audit procedures and consideration of conditions and events

1. **It is not necessary to design audit procedures for identifying substantial doubt**

2. **Procedures for other objectives are sufficient** to identify conditions and events indicating substantial doubt. Examples of procedures

   a. Analytical procedures

   b. Review of subsequent events

   c. Compliance with terms of debt and loan agreements

   d. Reading minutes of shareholders' and board of directors' meetings

   e. Inquiry of legal counsel on litigation, claims, and assessments

   f. Confirmation of arrangements to maintain financial support

3. **Conditions** and events that may **indicate substantial doubt**

   a. Negative trends—(e.g., losses, working capital deficiencies)

   b. Other indications of financial difficulties—(e.g., defaults)

   c. Internal matters—(e.g., work stoppages, dependence on one project)

   d. External matters—(e.g., legal proceedings, loss of key franchise)

**C.** Consideration of management's plans

1. Auditor's consideration of management's plans may include the following

   a. **Plans to dispose** of assets—Consider restrictions, marketability, effects of disposal

   b. **Plans to borrow** money or restructure debt—Consider availability of financing, existing arrangements, possible effects of borrowing

   c. **Plans to reduce** or delay **expenditures**—Consider feasibility, possible effects

   d. **Plans to increase ownership equity**—Consider feasibility and existing arrangements to reduce dividend requirements, etc.

2. When prospective financial information is significant to management's plans

   a. Request such information

   b. Consider adequacy of support for assumptions

   c. If important factors are not considered, request revision

**D.** Financial statement effects

1. **When substantial doubt exists consider** the need for the following **disclosures**

   a. **Conditions** and events giving rise to substantial doubt

   b. **Possible effects** of such conditions and events

   c. **Management's evaluation** of conditions and events

   d. **Possible discontinuance** of operations

   e. **Information on recoverability and classification** of assets and liabilities

2. When, primarily because of auditor's consideration of management's plans, no substantial doubt remains, still consider need for appropriate disclosures

**E.** Effects on auditor's report

1. When substantial doubt exists, modify report to include an explanatory paragraph following opinion paragraph

   a. The report must include the phrase "substantial doubt about its ability to continue as a going concern"

2. If disclosures are inadequate, a departure from GAAP exists which may result in qualified or adverse opinion

3. When issuing comparative statements, resolution of prior substantial doubt eliminates need for modification and a standard report covering both years is appropriate

4. The auditor may also choose to disclaim an opinion when substantial doubt remains

**F.** Documentation
1. Conditions that led to belief that substantial doubt exists
2. Elements of management's plans considered important to overcoming significant doubt
3. Auditing procedures performed and evidence obtained to evaluate management's plans
4. Auditor's conclusion as to whether substantial doubt remains or is alleviated
   a. If it remains, document possible effects on the financial statements and adequacy of disclosures
   b. If it is alleviated, document conclusion as to need for disclosure of principal conditions and events that caused substantial doubt

## 342 Auditing Accounting Estimates (SAS 57)

*Overall Objectives and Approach*—This section provides guidance on auditing accounting estimates (e.g., allowance for doubtful accounts, revenues recognized on construction contracts accounted for by the percentage-of-completion method). The section discusses (a) the need for and characteristics of accounting estimates, (b) management's role in developing accounting estimates, and (c) the auditor's evaluation of accounting estimates

**A.** The need for and characteristics of accounting estimates
1. Accounting estimates are needed because
   a. Measurement or valuation of some accounts is based on future events
   b. Evidence on some accounts cannot be accumulated on a timely, cost-effective basis
2. Examples of accounting estimates: net realizable values of inventory and accounts receivable, loss reserves, percentage-of-completion revenues, pension and warranty expenses
3. Estimates are based on subjective as well as objective factors
   a. Difficult for management to establish controls over them
4. **Responsibility of the auditor** with respect to estimates
   a. Evaluate the reasonableness of accounting estimates in the context of the financial statements taken as a whole
   b. Plan and perform procedures with attitude of **professional skepticism**

**B.** Management's role in developing accounting estimates
1. Steps involved in making estimates
   a. Identify situations for which estimates are needed
   b. Identify relevant factors affecting estimate
   c. Accumulate data on which to base estimate
   d. Develop assumptions based on most likely circumstance and events
   e. Determine estimated amount
   f. Determine estimate follows GAAP and that disclosure is adequate
2. The risk of misstatement of accounting estimates is affected by
   a. Complexity and subjectivity involved in process
   b. Availability and reliability of relevant data
   c. The number and significance of assumptions made
   d. Degree of uncertainty associated with assumptions
3. An entity's internal control may reduce the likelihood of material misstatements of estimates. Relevant aspects of internal control include
   a. Communication to management need for estimate
   b. Accumulation of accurate data on which to base estimate
   c. Preparation of estimate by qualified personnel
   d. Adequate review and approval of estimates
   e. Comparison of prior estimates with subsequent results
   f. Consideration by management of whether estimate is consistent with operational plans of entity

**C.** Auditor's evaluation of accounting estimates
1. Auditor's objectives are to provide reasonable assurance that
   a. All estimates have been developed
   b. Estimates are reasonable
   c. Estimates follow GAAP and are properly disclosed

*NOTE: Know the above objectives.*

2. Procedures for determining all estimates have been developed (C.1.a. above)
   a. **Consider assertions** in financial statements to determine need for estimates
   b. **Evaluate information from other procedures** such as
      (1) Changes in entity's business or operating strategy
      (2) Change in methods of accumulating information
      (3) Information concerning litigation, claims and assessments
      (4) Minutes of stockholder, directors, and appropriate committees' meetings
      (5) Information in regulatory reports
   c. **Inquiry of management**
3. Evaluating reasonableness (C.1.b. above)
   a. Three basic approaches (of which a combination may be used)
      (1) **Review and test management's process**
         (a) Identify related controls
         (b) Identify sources of data and factors used and consider whether appropriate
         (c) Consider whether there are additional key factors or alternate assumptions about the factors
         (d) Evaluate consistency of assumptions with one another, supporting data, historical data, and industry data
         (e) Analyze historical data used
         (f) Consider changes in business or industry
         (g) Review documentation of assumptions and inquire about other plans, etc.
         (h) Consider using a specialist (see outline of AU 336)
         (i) Test management calculations
      (2) **Develop own expectation of estimate**
         (a) Auditor independently develops an expectation
      (3) **Review subsequent events** or transactions prior to completion of fieldwork

   *NOTE: Know the above three approaches.*

## 350 Audit Sampling (SAS 39)

*Overall Objectives and Approach*—This section presents guidance on the use of sampling while **planning, performing,** and **evaluating results** of an audit of financial statements. The objective is to provide the conceptual background for audit sampling. Subsequent to issuance of this section, the AICPA issued the **Audit Sampling Guide,** which provides more detailed guidance. Both this section and the **Guide** are summarized in the Audit Sampling Module, which includes detailed examples.

The various subsections of our outline are divided as follows: A. general background information; B., C., D. sampling in substantive tests of details; E., F., G. sampling in tests of controls; H. dual purpose testing and I. selecting a sampling approach.

**A.** General background information
1. Audit sampling is the application of an audit procedure to less than 100% of the items within an account balance or class of transactions (hereafter, "account")
   a. The purpose of audit sampling is to evaluate some characteristics of an account (e.g., its balance)
   b. The use of a few items to obtain an understanding of a system or operation is not covered by the guidance in this section
2. Both nonstatistical and statistical approaches to sampling are addressed in this statement, and both
   a. Are considered **acceptable**
   b. May be used to **provide sufficient competent evidential matter**
   c. Require the use of **judgment**
3. The relationship of uncertainty to audit sampling
   a. The third standard of fieldwork ("...sufficient competent evidential matter...") implies some degree of uncertainty
   b. Some items do not justify the acceptance of any uncertainty, and must be examined 100% (e.g., individually material items)
   c. This section refers to uncertainty as audit risk. Audit risk includes the risk that material misstatements will occur in the accounting process (consisting of inherent risk and control risk) and the risk that any material misstatements will not be detected by the auditor (detection risk)

    (1) The auditor relies on internal control to reduce the first risk

    (2) The auditor relies on substantive tests to reduce the second risk. Substantive tests include

        (a) Detail tests (tests of transactions)

        (b) Analytical procedures

        (c) Tests of ending balances

    (3) **Audit risk** may be expressed using the following model

$$AR = IR \times CR \times AP \times TD$$

    Where:  AR  = Audit risk

            IR   = Inherent risk

            CR  = Control risk

            AP  = Analytical procedure risk

            TD  = Substantive tests of details risk

        (a) Model is mathematical expression of formula which includes all factors affecting the determination of audit risk

        (b) Model is useful when assessing the general relationships among risk factors but should not be relied on exclusively

        (c) Model is useful when planning risk levels for audit procedures to achieve desired audit risk

    *NOTE: This formulation of the components of audit risk varies from that in AU 312. AU 312 combines AP and TD as detection risk.*

4. Audit risk includes uncertainties due to sampling, called sampling risk, and uncertainties due to factors other than sampling, called nonsampling risk

    a. Sampling risk arises from the possibility that the conclusions derived from the sample will differ from the conclusions that would be derived from the population (the sample is nonrepresentative of the population). Sampling risk varies inversely with sample size.

    b. Nonsampling risk arises from uncertainties due to factors other than sampling. For example

        (1) Inappropriate audit procedures for a given objective, and

        (2) The failure to recognize errors

    c. Nonsampling risk can be reduced through adequate planning and supervision and adherence to quality control standards.

5. In performing substantive tests, the auditor is concerned with two aspects of sampling

    a. The risk of incorrect acceptance

    b. The risk of incorrect rejection

6. In performing tests of controls, the auditor is concerned with two aspects of sampling

    a. The risk of assessing control risk too low (previously the risk of overreliance on internal control)

    b. The risk of assessing control risk too high (previously the risk of underreliance on internal control)

    *NOTE: Risks 5.a. and 6.a. relate to the effectiveness and are most important of the audit. Risks 5.b. and 6.b. relate to the efficiency of the audit.*

**B.** Sampling in substantive tests of details—planning

1. In **planning** a sample the auditor should consider

    a. The relationship of the sample to the relevant audit objective

    b. Preliminary estimates of materiality levels (the maximum error is called **tolerable misstatement** for the sample)

    c. The auditor's allowable risk of incorrect acceptance

    d. Characteristics of items comprising the account balance or class of transactions to be sampled

2. The auditor must select a **population** from which to sample and which is consistent with the specified audit objective of concern

    a. The **population** consists of items in the account balance or transaction class of interest

    b. For example, understatement due to omission could not be detected by sampling recorded items. Sampling from subsequent activities records would be preferred.

3. The extent of **substantive tests required will vary inversely with the auditor's assessment of inherent risk and control risk**

4. The greater the reliance on analytical procedures and other substantive tests of a nonsampling nature, the greater the allowable risk of incorrect acceptance and, thus, the smaller the required sample size for substantive tests

5. The auditor uses his/her judgment in determining which items should be individually tested and which items should be subject to sampling
   a. The efficiency of a sample may be improved by separating items subject to sampling into relatively homogeneous groups

**C.** Sampling in substantive tests of details—in **selecting** sample items, the auditor should ensure that
   1. The sample is representative of the population
   2. All the items have a chance of being chosen
   3. Acceptable random-based selection techniques include
      a. Random sampling
      b. Stratified random sampling
      c. Probability-proportional-to-size
      d. Systematic sampling

**D.** Sampling in substantive tests of details—in **performing** audit procedures on selected items and when **evaluating** sampling results, the auditor should
   1. Apply auditing procedures to each sample item
      a. Unexamined items should be evaluated to determine their effect on the sample results
      b. In addition, the auditor should consider the reasons for his/her inability to examine the item (e.g., a lack of supporting documentation)
   2. Project the misstatement results from the sample to the population from which the sample was selected
   3. Compare projected population misstatement results (including misstatements from the 100% examined items) to the tolerable misstatement
      a. This evaluation requires the use of judgment in both statistical and nonstatistical sampling
      b. The auditor should also consider the qualitative aspects of the misstatements
         (1) The nature and cause of the misstatement
         (2) The possible relationship of the misstatement to other phases of the audit
      c. A fraud usually requires more consideration than a misstatement
   4. The auditor should consider projected misstatement results in the aggregate from statistical and nonstatistical sources when evaluating whether the financial statements as a whole may be misstated

**E.** Sampling in tests of controls—planning
   1. In planning a sample the auditor should consider
      a. The relationship of the sample to the objective of the test
      b. The maximum rate of deviation from (tolerable rate) prescribed control procedures that would support his/her allowable risk of assessing control risk too low.
      c. The auditor's allowable risk of assessing control risk too low.
         (1) Low levels usually required because tests of controls are the primary source of evidence about whether a control procedure is being applied as prescribed
         (2) Quantitatively the auditor might consider 5% to 10% risk of assessing control risk too low as acceptable
      d. The characteristics of the population of interest
         (1) The auditor should consider the likely rate of deviation
         (2) The auditor should consider whether to test controls singly or in combination
   2. The auditor should realize that deviations from important control procedures at a given rate ordinarily result in misstatements at a lower rate

**F.** Sampling in tests of controls—sample selection should ensure that
   1. The sample is representative of the population
   2. The probability of inclusion of every item in the population is **known**

**G.** Sampling in tests of controls—performance and evaluation
   1. The auditor should apply auditing procedures to each sample item
      a. If the auditor cannot apply procedures to all sample items, s/he should consider reasons for the limitations
      b. Items to which procedures cannot be applied should be considered deviations for sample evaluation
   2. Whether statistical or nonstatistical sampling is used, if the auditor decides that s/he is not going to rely on internal control, the planned substantive tests should be adjusted

**H. Dual-purpose samples** have two purposes
1. To aid in assessing control risk (test of control)
2. **To test whether the recorded dollar amount of a transaction is correct** (substantive tests)
   a. The auditor usually assumes that there is an acceptably small planned assessed level of control risk which is greater than the tolerable level
   b. The size of the sample should be the larger of the samples otherwise designed for two separate purposes
**I.** Selecting a sampling approach
1. Statistical or nonstatistical approaches can provide sufficient evidential matter
2. Choice between statistical and nonstatistical approach depends on relative
   a. Cost
   b. Effectiveness
3. Statistical sampling helps
   a. Design efficient sampling plans
   b. Measure sufficiency of evidential matter
   c. To quantitatively evaluate sample results

## 380 Communication with Audit Committees (SAS 61)

*Overall Objectives and Approach*—This section establishes a requirement that CPAs communicate certain matters (more precisely, nine matters) related to an audit to the audit committee. The first section of our outline presents background information, while the second provides the nine matters to be communicated.

**A.** Background information
1. Applicability—the section only applies to
   a. SEC engagements or
   b. Other entities that have audit committees or equivalent oversight group
2. Form—may be **oral or written**
   a. If oral, document in working papers
   b. If written, the report should indicate that it is solely for the audit committee, board of directors, and (if appropriate) management
3. The communication is considered **incidental to the audit,** but should be communicated on a timely basis, not necessarily prior to issuance of the audit report
4. Situations in which the matters need not be communicated by the CPA
   a. When the CPA is satisfied that management has communicated them
   b. When they have been communicated in prior years, although the CPA may choose to repeat them due to changes in the audit committee or due to the passage of time
5. The CPA may also choose to communicate additional matters
**B.** Matters to be communicated
1. **Auditor responsibility** taken under GAAS audits
2. **Significant accounting policies**
   a. Management's initial selection and changes
   b. Methods used for unusual transactions
   c. Effects of accounting policies in controversial areas or areas in which there is a lack of authoritative guidance
3. **Process used in obtaining management judgments** and accounting estimates
4. **Audit adjustments**
   a. Material adjustments
   b. Uncorrected misstatements aggregated by the auditor determined by management to be immaterial, both individually and in the aggregate
5. **Auditor responsibility for other information** in documents containing audited financial statements (see AU 550)
6. Auditor **disagreements** with management
   a. Examples
      (1) Application of accounting principles
      (2) Basis for management's accounting estimates
      (3) Scope of audit

(4) Disclosures in financial statements

(5) Wording of audit report

b. Resolution of disagreements

c. Disagreements do not include differences of opinion based upon incomplete facts or preliminary information later resolved

7. **Auditor views** on auditing and accounting **matters for which other auditors were contacted** (see AU 625)

8. **Major issues** discussed with management **prior to retention**

9. **Auditor judgments** about the **quality** of the entity's **accounting principles** (only required for SEC registrants)

   a. Discuss quality of principles, not just acceptability; examples

      (1) Selection of new or changes to accounting principles

      (2) Estimates, judgments, and uncertainties

      (3) Unusual transactions

      (4) Accounting policies for significant items, including timing and period in which recorded

   b. Because objective criteria have not been developed for "quality" the discussion should be tailored to the specific circumstances (e.g., matters unique to an industry not explicitly addressed in GAAP)

10. **Difficulties** encountered in performing audit

    Examples

    a. Delays by management in allowing audit commencement

    b. Unavailability of client personnel

    c. Delays in preparation of client-prepared schedules

## 390 Consideration of Omitted Procedures after Report Date (SAS 46)

*Overall Objectives and Approach*—This brief section presents guidance on how to approach a situation in which subsequent to issuance of an audit report, an auditor determines that one or more necessary procedures may have been omitted. While the auditor has no responsibility to retroactively review his/her work, the section does address the situation in which a postissuance review (e.g., an internal inspection of a peer review) may have disclosed such an omitted procedure(s). Also, the guidance only relates to a situation in which there is no indication that the financial statements depart from GAAP—when known departures exist see the outline of AU 561 and Section C of the Evidence Module. Make certain that you are able to distinguish the omitted audit procedure responsibility described in this section from the discovery of facts relating to the financial statements in Section 561.

A. When it is determined that a procedure has been omitted, the auditor should assess its importance, considering other procedures which may have compensated for its omission

   1. This section only covers cases in which there is **no** indication that financial statements depart from GAAP. (See AU 561 when errors exist.)

   2. Although auditor has no responsibility to retroactively review his/her work, such postissuance review may occur as part of internal inspection, or peer review

   3. In all such circumstances, the auditor may be well advised to consult an attorney

B. When it is determined that a procedure has been omitted, auditor must

   1. **Assess its importance.** (Consider other procedures which may have compensated for its omission.)

      a. If omission is considered important and if auditor believes individuals are relying on financial statements, procedures (or alternate procedures) should be promptly applied

         (1) The auditor may, however, discover that the results of other procedures that **were** applied compensate for the omitted procedure

      b. If financial statement errors are detected, consult AU 561

      c. If the auditor is unable to apply procedures, consult attorney

## 410 Adherence to Generally Accepted Accounting Principles (SAS 1)

*Overall Objectives and Approach*—This very brief section states that (1) GAAP, as used in the reporting standards, includes not only accounting principles, but also the methods of applying them and (2) the auditor's report does not represent a statement of fact by the auditor, but an opinion.

**411 The Meaning of *Present Fairly in Conformity with Generally Accepted Accounting Principles* in the Auditor's Report (SAS 69)**

***Overall Objectives and Approach***—This section presents information which may be summarized as relating to (a) the meaning (in an audit report) of the terms "generally accepted accounting principles" and "present fairly" and (b) the relative authority of various sources of GAAP. This section (passed as SAS 69) replaced a section with the same codification number in December of 1991.

**A.** The meaning of "generally accepted accounting principles" and "present fairly"
1. "Generally accepted accounting principles" includes the conventions, rules, and procedures necessary to define accepted accounting practice at a particular time
   a. GAAP include not only broad guidelines of general application, but also detailed practices and procedures
   b. GAAP are the framework for judging the presentation of financial position, results of operations, and cash flows in financial statements
      (1) Fairness of overall presentation should be applied within the framework of GAAP
2. The auditor's opinion that statements "present fairly" is based on his/her judgment as to whether
   a. The accounting principles have general acceptance
   b. The accounting principles are appropriate in the circumstances
   c. The financial statements are informative of matters that may affect their use, understanding, and interpretation
   d. The information presented is classified and summarized in a reasonable manner that is neither too detailed nor too condensed
   e. The financial statements reflect transactions and events within a range of acceptable limits
3. GAAP recognize the importance of reporting transactions and events in accordance with their substance
   a. The auditor should consider whether the substance of transactions or events differs materially from their form
4. When new legislation or a new type of business transaction occurs, there are sometimes not established GAAP
   a. In such instances attempt to report on basis of substance

**B.** The sources and relative authority of established accounting principles
1. The sources of established accounting principles that are generally accepted in the US are
   a. Authoritative body pronouncements—Promulgated by a body designated by the AICPA Council to establish such principles, pursuant to Rule 203 of the Code of Professional Conduct (the FASB and the GASB)
   b. Pronouncements of bodies composed of expert accountants, exposed for public comment
   c. Pronouncements of bodies composed of expert accountants, **not** exposed for public comment
   d. Widely recognized practices and pronouncements

   *NOTE: The above is a general hierarchy; if there is a conflict between categories, the auditor should follow the higher category, or be prepared to justify a conclusion that a treatment specified in a lower category better presents the substance of the transaction in the circumstances. Also, in the absence of pronouncements covered in a. through d., the auditor may consider other accounting literature (e.g., textbooks).*

2. The following table summarizes, for nongovernmental entities, state and local governments, and the federal government, the application of the categories (presented in B.1. above)

**GAAP HIERARCHY SUMMARY**

| Category | Nongovernmental Entities | State and Local Governments | Federal Government |
|---|---|---|---|
| A. **Authoritative Body Pronouncements** | FASB *Statements* and *Interpretations* <br> APB *Opinions* <br> AICPA *Accounting Research Bulletins* | GASB *Statements* and *Interpretations* <br> FASB and AICPA pronouncements applicable by a GASB *Statement* or *Interpretation* | FASAB *Statements* and *Interpretations* <br> AICPA, FASB, and GASB pronouncements made applicable by a FASB *Statement* or *Interpretation* |
| B. **Pronouncements of Bodies Composed of Expert Accountants, Exposed for Public Comment** | FASB *Technical Bulletins* <br> AICPA *Industry Audit and Accounting Guides* and *Statements of Position* (cleared by FASB) | GASB *Technical Bulletins* <br> AICPA *Industry Audit and Accounting Guides* and *Statements of Position* (cleared by GASB) | FASB *Technical Bulletins* <br> AICPA *Industry Audit and Accounting Guides* and *Statements of Position* (cleared by FASAB) |

| | Category | Nongovernmental Entities | State and Local Governments | Federal Government |
|---|---|---|---|---|
| C. | **Pronouncements of Bodies Composed of Expert Accountants,** *Not* **Exposed for Public Comment** | *Consensus Positions of the FASB Emerging Issues Task Force* <br> AICPA *Practice Bulletins* (cleared by FASB) | *Consensus Positions of the GASB Emerging Issues Task Force* <br> AICPA *Practice Bulletins* (cleared by GASB) | *Technical Releases* of the Accounting and Auditing Policy Committee of the FASAB <br> AICPA *Practice Bulletins* (cleared by the FASAB) |
| D. | **Widely Recognized Practices and Pronouncements** | FASB staff *"Questions and Answers"* <br> AICPA *Accounting Interpretations* <br> Widely accepted industry practices | GASB staff *"Questions and Answers"* <br> Widely accepted industry practices | FASAB staff *Implementation Guides* <br> Widely accepted federal government practices |
| E. | **Other Accounting Literature** | FASB *Concepts Statements* <br> APB *Statements* <br> AICPA *Issues Papers* and *Technical Practice Aids* <br> International Accounting Standards Committee *Statements* <br> GASB *Statements, Interpretations,* and *Technical Bulletins* <br> Pronouncements of other professional associations or regulatory agencies <br> Accounting textbooks, handbooks, and articles | GASB *Concepts Statements* <br> Pronouncements in (A) through (D) of nongovernmental hierarchy not specifically made applicable <br> APB *Statements* <br> FASB *Concepts Statements* <br> AICPA *Issues Papers* and *Technical Practice Aids* <br> International Accounting Standards Committee *Statements* <br> Pronouncements of other professional associations or regulatory agencies <br> Accounting textbooks, handbooks, and articles | FASAB *Concepts Statements* <br> Pronouncements in (A) through (D) of GASB and FASB not specifically made applicable <br> FASB and GASB *Concepts Statements* AICPA *Issue Papers* and *Technical Practice Aids* <br> International Accounting Standards Committee *Statements* <br> Pronouncements of other professional associations or regulatory agencies <br> Accounting textbooks, handbooks, and articles |

## 420 Consistency of Application of GAAP (SAS 1)

*Overall Objectives and Approach*—This section presents guidance on applying the consistency reporting standard, which was revised in 1988 (it now reads, "The report shall identify those circumstances in which such principles have not been consistently observed in the current period in relation to the preceding period"). This section relates very directly to APB 20 which prescribes accounting for three types of accounting changes— change in principles, change in estimate, and change in reporting entity—and for corrections of errors in prior statements.

The general rule is that changes in accounting principles, changes in the reporting entity, and correction of error in principles require explanatory language as to consistency (i.e., an explanatory paragraph added to an unqualified report); changes in estimates do not. Yet, there are several exceptions to the rules (described below) with which you need to be familiar.

**A.** Changes that require the addition of an explanatory paragraph referring to the inconsistency

    1.  **Change in accounting principle**

        a.  As a typical example, consider changing from straight-line to the sum-of-the-years' digits method

        b.  Special cases of changes in accounting principles (which still require an explanatory paragraph)

            (1)  **Correction of an error in principle**—For example, assume that in the preceding year a client used an unacceptable method for valuing inventory; changing to a proper method (e.g., LIFO) still requires an explanatory paragraph. There is a tendency to **incorrectly** think that since the client is eliminating an error, no mention of the inconsistency is necessary.

            (2)  **Change in principle inseparable from a change in estimate**—For example, changing from deferring a cost to expensing it in the year incurred represents a change in principle from capitalization to expensing; but it also represents a change in estimate in that the life is now assessed at one year or less.

    2.  **Change in the reporting entity**

        a.  The following require an explanatory paragraph

            (1)  Presenting consolidated or combined statements in place of individual company statements

            (2)  Changing the specific subsidiaries in the group for which consolidated statements are presented

            (3)  Changing the companies included in combined statements

            (4)  Changing among the cost, equity, and consolidation methods of accounting for subsidiaries

        b.  Application of the consistency standard for a pooling of interests

*NOTE: APB 16 requires that comparative financial statements restate prior years' results to give recognition of the pooling of interests. When single-year statements are presented, the financial statement notes should adequately disclose the pooling transaction and state the revenues, extraordinary items, and net income of the constituent companies for the preceding year on a combined basis. For more information see outline of APB 16.*

(1) When prior year financial statements are presented and not restated

    (a) Add an explanatory paragraph on the inconsistency (due to the lack of application to the prior years, not due to a change in application in accounting principle in the current year)

    (b) Also, the failure to restate comparative statements to reflect the pooling is a departure from GAAP—see outline of AU 508 for proper reporting treatment (i.e., qualified or adverse opinion)

(2) When single-year statements do not properly disclose pooling transaction in notes the auditor should

    (a) Add an explanatory paragraph on the inconsistency between the current and preceding (not presented) year

    (b) Qualify the opinion due to the lack of disclosure

> *NOTE: As indicated below, when the accounting treatment of a pooling of interests has been proper, no consistency modification is necessary.*

**B.** Changes that **do not** require the addition of an explanatory paragraph referring to the inconsistency

  1. Change in estimate

    a. For example, changing either the life or salvage value of fixed assets

  2. Correction of an error **not involving a principle**

    a. For example, correction of a mathematical error in previously issued financial statements

  3. Change in classification

    a. For example, adding an additional line item expense to this year's income statement which in the preceding year was included in "miscellaneous expense"

  4. Creation, cessation, purchase, or disposition of a subsidiary or business unit

> *NOTE: Be careful here to distinguish the above circumstances from those described in A.2. above. These situations are normal business events. Those described in A.2. above may be viewed as using different accounting methods.*

  5. Properly accounted-for pooling of interest combinations

  6. Changes in principles that **do not materially** affect this year's financial statements, even when reasonably certain the change will materially affect them in later years

> *NOTE: The above exception 6. is rather unexpected, given the "conservative" nature of many of the standards. Remember it!*

  7. Accounting principles are adopted when events or transactions first become material in their effect

    a. Modification or adoption of a principle at this point does not require a paragraph referring to consistency

**C.** Miscellaneous

  1. Accounting changes may also lead to a departure from GAAP situation

    a. When a material change in principles occurs, with which the auditor does not concur, a departure from GAAP exists and a qualified opinion or an adverse opinion is appropriate—see outline of AU 508

    b. Whenever an accounting change has not been appropriately described in the financial statements, a departure from GAAP exists (in this case, inadequate disclosure) and a qualified opinion or an adverse opinion is appropriate—see outline of AU 508

  2. Periods to which the consistency standard relates

    a. When the CPA reports only on the current period, the consistency standard relates to the preceding period, regardless of whether that period is presented

    b. When the CPA reports on two or more years, the consistency standard relates to the years reported upon, and with the year prior thereto **only if** such prior year is presented

  3. For a first year audit

    a. Normally the auditor will be able to determine whether accounting principles employed are consistent with the prior year

      (1) When inadequate records make this determination impossible, when such amounts could materially affect current operating results, the auditor may be unable to express an opinion on the income statement and the statement of cash flows

### 431 Adequacy of Disclosure in Financial Statements (SAS 32)

*Overall Objectives and Approach*—This brief section interprets the third standard of reporting, which states that informative disclosures are to be regarded as reasonably adequate unless otherwise stated in the report. Omission of required information is a departure from GAAP which requires the auditor to issue either a qualified or an adverse opinion—see outline of AU 508 for details. If practicable, the auditor should provide the omitted information in his/her report; practicable means that the information is reasonably obtainable from the accounts and records and does not require the auditor to assume the position of a preparer of financial information. Thus, the auditor would **not** be expected to prepare a basic financial statement (e.g., a statement of cash flows) or segment information and include it in his/her report.

### 504 Association with Financial Statements (SAS 26)

*Overall Objectives and Approach*—This section defines what is meant by a CPA being "associated with financial statements," and discusses "unaudited statements." The issue of being "associated with financial statements" is important because the fourth standard of reporting (which requires an opinion, or a statement that an opinion cannot be expressed) requires that a CPA must make clear the character of his/her examination, and the responsibility taken, when s/he is **associated** with financial statements.

The section related to "unaudited statements" is of limited applicability since there are no "unaudited statements" for nonpublic companies—statements for such companies are compiled, reviewed, or audited. Thus, "unaudited statements" are only relevant for the occasional public company which for some reason does not require audited financial statements. In this outline we present information on (a) general association with financial information, (b) reporting on unaudited statements, and (c) reporting on comparative statements when one period is unaudited and when one period is audited.

A. General association with financial information
1. The objective of the fourth standard of reporting is **to prevent misinterpretation of the degree of responsibility** assumed by the accountant when his/her name is **associated** with financial statements

   NOTE: *Knowledge of this objective has been required on several multiple-choice questions.*

2. An accountant is **associated** with financial statements when s/he
   a. Has consented to the use of his/her name in a report, document, or written communication containing the statements or
   b. Submits to a client financial statements that s/he has prepared or assisted in preparing, even though the accountant does not append his/her name to the statements
3. Before issuing a report, **the accountant has a responsibility to read the statements for obvious material misstatements;** no other procedural requirements exist
   a. When other procedures have been performed, mention of them should **not** be made in the report issued
B. Reporting on unaudited statements
1. The following disclaimer may accompany or be on the statements:
   The accompanying balance sheet of X Company as of December 31, 20X1, and the related statement of income, retained earnings, and cash flows for the year then ended were not audited by us and accordingly, we do not express an opinion on them.
2. Each page of the statements **should be marked as "unaudited"**
3. When the client has prepared a document which includes unaudited statements, the auditor should request that
   a. His/her name not be included in the communication **or**
   b. That the financial statement be marked as unaudited and that there be a notation that s/he does not express an opinion on them
4. If the accountant is **not** independent, the disclaimer issued should indicate such nonindependence, but should **not** indicate any procedures performed or the reason for nonindependence
5. When the accountant believes that the unaudited statements do not follow GAAP
   a. S/he should request appropriate revision
   b. If unsuccessful, modify the disclaimer to refer to the departure

   NOTE: *Some CPA exam questions have suggested that a qualified or adverse opinion is appropriate when such statements do not follow GAAP. This is incorrect since an audit has not been performed. A disclaimer with the appropriate* *information **is** appropriate. If the client refuses to accept such a report, the accountant should disassociate him/herself from the statements.*

6. In no case should a report on unaudited statements include negative assurance (e.g., "nothing came to our attention"—see the outline of AU 623 for more information on negative assurance)

7. When unaudited financial statements are presented in comparative form with audited financial statements in *SEC documents*, the statements should be marked as "unaudited" but not referred to in the auditor's report
   a. In any other document, the CPA's report on the unaudited prior period financial statements should be reissued or the report on the subsequent year should include a separate paragraph describing the CPA's association with the unaudited statements

## 508 Reports on Audited Financial Statements (SAS 58 and SAS 79)

*Overall Objectives and Approach*—This section presents guidance on the nature of audit reports. The information presented constitutes the primary reporting guidance for normal GAAP GAAS audits. It is also summarized in the Reporting Module, which includes sample reports.

You should know that the objective of the fourth reporting standard (i.e., the report is to contain an opinion on the financial statements **taken as a whole** or an assertion that an opinion cannot be expressed) is to **prevent misinterpretation of the degree of responsibility** taken by the auditor. Also, the phrase "taken as a whole" applies equally to the complete set of financial statements and to the individual financial statements.

Section A of this outline summarizes information relating to the auditor's standard report. Section B deals with circumstances in which an auditor issues an unqualified report with explanatory language added. Qualified, adverse, and disclaimers of opinion are considered in Sections C through E. Sections F and G relate to comparative statements.

A. The auditor's standard report
   1. Basic elements
      a. Title that includes word "independent"
      b. Statements were audited
      c. Financial statements are management's responsibility; expressing an opinion is the auditor's responsibility
      d. Audit conducted in accordance with US GAAS
      e. Those standards require planning and performing audit to obtain reasonable assurance financial statements free of material misstatement
      f. Statement that an audit includes
         (1) Examining, on a test basis, evidence
         (2) Assessing accounting principles and estimates
         (3) Evaluating financial statement presentation
      g. Statement that auditor believes audit provides reasonable basis for opinion
      h. Opinion statements present fairly per US GAAP
      i. Manual or printed signature of firm
      j. Date of report
   2. **The report is addressed to company, board of directors, or shareholders**
      a. When an auditor is engaged by a client to report on statements of a nonclient, the report is addressed to client (e.g., a client may hire the auditor to audit statements of an acquisition candidate)
B. Explanatory language added to the auditor's standard report

   *NOTE: The report issued may still be unqualified in the following circumstances. The unqualified report includes an explanatory paragraph (or other explanatory language).*

   1. Opinion based in part on report of another auditor
      a. **Reference is made to other auditor in all three paragraphs**
   2. Departure from a promulgated accounting principle
      a. Pertains to situations in which unusual circumstances result in a situation in which following GAAP would lead to misleading results
      b. **An explanatory paragraph is added** (either preceding or following opinion paragraph)
   3. Consistency
      a. The auditor must concur with the change

             (1) **If the auditor does not concur, a departure from GAAP exists** which leads to either a qualified or adverse opinion

       b.    **Explanatory paragraph added** (following opinion paragraph)

             (1) Nonrestatement cases—as long as year of change presented and reported on

             (2) Restatements—only in year of change

       c.    See AU 420 outline

    4.    Emphasis of a matter

       a.    Pertains to situations in which **auditor wishes to draw attention** to a matter concerning financial statements (e.g., when client is component of larger entity, related-party transactions, subsequent events, matter affecting comparability)

       b.    **Explanatory paragraph** added (either preceding or following opinion paragraph)

**C.**    Qualified opinions

    1.    Scope limitation

       a.    Types—**client- and circumstance-imposed**

       b.    Type of report (unqualified, qualified, or disclaimer)

             (1) Depends upon importance of omitted procedure (consider nature, magnitude, potential effect, and number of accounts involved)

             (2) **Generally disclaim for client-imposed scope restrictions**

       c.    **Limitation described in scope, explanatory, and opinion paragraphs**

             (1) Explanatory paragraph precedes opinion paragraph

       d.    Opinion qualification pertains to possible effects on financial statements, not to scope limitation itself

       e.    A **report on only one statement** (e.g., balance sheet) **is not a scope restriction** if auditor has access to necessary information

    2.    Departure from generally accepted accounting principle

       a.    Type of report (unqualified, qualified, or adverse)

             (1) Depends on dollar magnitude, significance to operations, pervasiveness, and impact on statements as a whole

             (2) Inadequate disclosure is a departure from GAAP

       b.    **Explanatory paragraph added** (preceding opinion paragraph), and **opinion paragraph altered**

       c.    **Omission of statement of cash flows**

             (1) Auditor not required to prepare one

             (2) Ordinarily qualify report

       d.    Accounting principle changes

             (1) Auditor evaluates whether

                (a) New principle is GAAP

                (b) Method of accounting for change is GAAP

                (c) Management justification is reasonable

             (2) If any of (1) is "no," a departure from GAAP exists

             (3) Qualification (or adverse) remains as long as statements provided

**D.**    Adverse opinion

    1.    Statements taken as a whole are not fairly presented

    2.    Explanatory paragraph (preceding opinion paragraph), opinion paragraph altered

**E.**    Disclaimer

    1.    A disclaimer states that the auditor does not express an opinion on the financial statements

    2.    Disclaimer is appropriate when the auditor is unable to form an opinion or has not formed an opinion as to the fairness of presentation of the financial statements

*NOTE: Scope limitations are emphasized in the standards as a circumstance resulting in a disclaimer (or a qualified opinion). Other circumstances in which disclaimers are issued include [1] unaudited statements (AU 504), [2] a lack of auditor independence (AU 504), [3] substantial doubt about a client's ability to continue as a going concern when an auditor does not wish to issue an unqualified opinion with an explanatory paragraph (AU 341), and [4] an auditor believes that a particularly important uncertainty makes it impossible to form an opinion (AU 508).*

**F.**    Comparative financial statements

    1.    Continuing auditors should update report to cover comparative statements

    2.    Ordinarily date report as of date of completion of fieldwork of most recent audit

3. **Updating** prior-period reports may result in an opinion different from that originally issued
   a. Example—departure from GAAP in prior year statements eliminated
   b. If opinion different from previous period, explanatory paragraph should disclose
      (1) Date of previous report
      (2) Type of opinion previously expressed
      (3) Circumstances calling for changed report
      (4) State that updated opinion differs from previous opinion

G. Comparative statements—When a predecessor auditor has audited the preceding year his/her audit report may be reissued **or** summarized in the successor auditor's report
   1. Before reissuing report predecessor should
      a. **Read** the current statements
      b. **Compare** prior statements with current
      c. **Obtain letter of representations from successor** indicating any matters that might have effect on prior statements
      d. **If predecessor is aware of events** affecting previous opinion, s/he should **perform necessary audit procedures**
      e. Dating report
         (1) Not revised—use original report date
         (2) Revised—dual date
   2. Predecessor's report not presented
      a. Successor's report should indicate
         (1) **Prior statements audited by other auditors**
         (2) **Date of their report**
         (3) **Type of report** issued by predecessor
         (4) **Substantive reasons if other than unqualified**
            (a) Also, if other than standard, give reasons for explanatory paragraph

## 530 Dating the Independent Auditor's Report (SAS 1, 29)

*Overall Objectives and Approach*—This section presents guidance on dating of the auditor's report. The **general rule is that the report is dated as of the date of the completion of fieldwork**. The section discusses two exceptions—(a) events have occurred after fieldwork, but before issuance of the report, and (b) certain circumstances in which an audit report is being reissued.

A. Dating the audit report when subsequent events have occurred after fieldwork, but before issuance of the report

> *NOTE: An understanding of this section requires knowledge of AU 560 on subsequent events. That section distinguishes between the "event" (i.e., the subsequent event) which occurred after the balance sheet date, but prior to the issuance of the financial statements, and the "condition" which caused the event. The basic accounting rule developed in AU 560 is that when a subsequent event occurs the auditor must determine whether the condition which caused the event existed at the date of the balance sheet. When the condition existed at the balance sheet date, adjustment of the financial statements is appropriate. When the condition came into effect after year-end, note disclosure is appropriate. For more information on this, see the outline of AU 560.*

   1. Dating of the audit report when the **condition came into effect before year-end**
      a. When an adjustment is needed, and no note disclosure is needed, the audit report need not be changed
      b. When an adjustment **and** note disclosure is needed, the auditor must change the report date as indicated in 3. below
   2. Dating of the audit report when the condition came into existence after year-end
      a. Note disclosure is needed, and the auditor must change the report date as indicated in 3. below
   3. When the report date must be changed (from the date of completion of fieldwork), two methods are available
      a. **A dual date** in which the overall report is dated as of the last day of fieldwork, but a note such as "except for Note X, which is dated as of ___," is added following the date.

         > *EXAMPLE: A report might be dated as follows: February 17, 20X9, except for Note 1, as to which the date is February 27, 20X9.*

      b. The report date might be changed to the **date of the subsequent event**

         > *EXAMPLE: Using the above example: February 27, 20X9*

(1) When the report date is changed in this manner, the CPA's responsibility for subsequent events extends to the date of his/her report—see outline of AU 560 for these procedures

**B.** Dating the audit report when it is being reissued

*BACKGROUND: The situation here is one in which an auditor has already issued a report, and is being asked to reissue it. This may occur, for example, when the financial statements are included in a report being filed with the SEC, or, more simply, when a client asks the CPA to furnish additional copies of a previously issued report. The overall rule is that the CPA has no responsibility to make any further investigation as to events which may have occurred during the period between the original report date and the date of the release of the additional reports. The original report date is retained for the reissued report. A complicating factor arises when the CPA becomes aware of an event subsequent to the date of the original report that requires adjustment and/or disclosure.*

1. When the auditor is asked to reissue his/her report, and s/he
   a. Is **not** aware of the existence of any subsequent event, the original report date should be used
   b. Is aware of the existence of a subsequent event which requires adjustment or disclosure, the report should be dated in accordance with A.3. above
   c. Is aware of an event which requires disclosure only (i.e., no adjustment) which has occurred **between the date of the original report and the date of reissuance,** the event may be disclosed in a separate **unaudited note to the financial statements;** the audit report date is **not** changed from that used for the original report

## 532 Restricting the Use of an Auditor's Report
*Overall Objectives and Approach*—This section presents guidance on when and how auditors should restrict audit reports.

**A.** General-Use and Restricted-Use Reports
1. General-use reports are not restricted to specified parties
   a. Financial statements prepared in accordance with GAAP are ordinarily general use
2. Restricted-use reports are intended only for specified parties; an auditor should restrict the use of a report in the following circumstances:
   a. The subject matter of the auditor's report is based on measurement or disclosure criteria in contractual agreements or regulatory provisions that are not in accordance with GAAP or an other comprehensive basis of accounting
      (1) Use should be restricted to the parties to the agreement or regulatory agencies responsible for the provisions
   b. The accountant's report is based on agreed-upon procedures
      (1) Use should be restricted to the "specified parties" as per AU 622
   c. The auditor's report is issued as a "by-product" of an audit
      (1) Examples
         (a) AU 325 on internal control reportable conditions
         (b) AU 380 on communication with audit committees
         (c) AU 623 on compliance with aspects of contractual agreements or regulatory requirements
      (2) Use should be restricted to the audit committee, board of directors, management, others with the organization, specified regulatory agencies, and in compliance reports to the parties of the contract
3. An auditor's report that is restricted should contain a separate paragraph at the end of the report that includes
   a. A statement that the report is intended solely for the information and use of the specified parties
   b. An identification of the specified parties to whom use is restricted
   c. A statement that the report is not intended to be and should not be used by anyone other than the specified parties

**B.** Other issues
1. When an auditor issues a single combined report covering both subject matter that requires a restriction and subject matter that does not ordinarily require restriction, the use of such a single combined report should be restricted to the specified parties
2. Additional users may be added as "specified parties" if those parties specify, ordinarily in writing, that they understand the nature of the engagement, the measurement or disclosure criteria, and the related report

3.  While an auditor is not responsible for controlling the distribution of reports by the client, an auditor should consider informing the client that restricted-use reports are not intended for distribution to specified party
4.  Nothing this section precludes an auditor from restricting the use of any report
    a.  For example, if the auditor and client agreed, an audit report could be made "restricted use"

## 534 Reporting on Financial Statements Prepared for Use in Other Countries (SAS 51)

*Overall Objectives and Approach*—This section presents guidance for a CPA practicing **in the US** who is engaged to report on the **financial statements of a US entity** that have been prepared in conformity with the **accounting principles of another country**. For example, consider a US subsidiary of a multinational corporation with a non-US parent. Often such a subsidiary issues GAAP-based financial statements intended for use in the US, and other financial statements that are prepared in conformity with accounting principles generally accepted in another country. This section addresses the approach the CPA should use for the financial statements prepared following the principles of the other country. The guidance provided in Section A of this outline deals with the applicability of the following standards—(1) US GAAS, (2) other country accounting standards, and (3) other country auditing standards. Section B of this outline provides information on reporting requirements.

**A.**  Applicable standards and procedures other than reporting
    Overall requirements—before reporting on the statements, the auditor should have a clear understanding of, and obtain written representations from, management regarding the purpose and uses of the financial statements
    1.  Applicability of **US GAAS**
        a.  The general rule is that the CPA must perform US **general** and **fieldwork** standards
            (1) Exceptions to the rule occur when differences in the other country's accounting principles require modification of the procedures that are followed.
            Examples
                (a) When the principles of the other country do not require deferred taxes, procedures for testing deferred tax balances would not be applicable
                (b) When principles of the other country do not require or permit disclosure of related-party transactions, audit procedures related to meeting US disclosure standards would not be appropriate
    2.  Other country **accounting** standards
        a.  The auditor should understand the accounting principles of the other country; this knowledge may be obtained by considering
            (1) The professional literature of that country
            (2) Information obtained by consulting with individuals with the necessary expertise
            (3) International Accounting Standards (when the other country's principles are not well established)
    3.  Other country auditing standards
        a.  When the auditor is requested to apply the other country's auditing standards s/he may do so if
            (1) US standards are also applied
            (2) S/he has read pertinent literature, and to the extent necessary, has consulted with persons having the necessary expertise
**B.**  Reporting requirements
    1.  Report issued for the financial statements (which are to be used outside the US)—either a modified US report or the standard report of the other country **may** be appropriate
        a.  Modified US report should
            (1) Identify the financial statements that have been audited
            (2) Refer to the note in the financial statements that describes the basis of presentation (including the nationality) of the principles
            (3) State that the audit followed US auditing standards (and other country standards if appropriate)
            (4) Include a paragraph on whether the statements present fairly in conformity with the basis being followed
        b.  The standard report of the other country may be used if

      (1)  Such a report would be used by auditors in the other country in similar circumstances

      (2)  The auditor understands the attestations contained in the report

  c.  Limited distribution of the reports described above in a. and b. is acceptable (e.g., to banks, institutional investors) if the statements are to be allowed in a manner that permits such parties to discuss differences in US and other country reporting practices

2.  When the distribution in the US is more than limited, the auditor should report using the US standard form of report, modified as appropriate for departures from GAAP

  a.  The CPA may choose to include a separate report expressing an opinion on whether the financial statements are in conformity with the other country's standards **or**

  b.  May issue a US report for distribution in the US, and a report as described in B.1.a. and B.1.b. above in the other country

> NOTE: *The above section is actually requiring that when the statements following the other country's basis are being used on more than a limited basis in the US, the auditor must indicate departures from GAAP in a US style report. This will **not** normally be necessary because the statements will not in general be used in the US. Recall from our introduction of this section that more typically, when there is a US demand for such statements, dual statements will be issued— one set following US GAAP and the other set following other country's accounting principles. The auditor would then issue a standard US report on the first set of statements, and one of the reports described in "B.1." for the other country's statements.*

## 543 Part of the Examination Made by Other Independent Auditors (SAS 1)

*Overall Objectives and Approach*—This section presents guidance on reporting requirements when more than one CPA firm is involved with the audit of a particular company. As an example, consider a situation in which a parent company owns four subsidiaries. CPA firm A has audited the parent (a holding company with no operations of its own) and three of the subsidiaries; CPA firm B has audited the fourth subsidiary. This situation may occur, for example, when the parent has recently purchased the subsidiary and as a part of the purchase agreement the acquired subsidiary is allowed to keep its CPA firm for some period of time.

In such a situation a number of audit reports may be issued. First, reports might be issued for each of the four subsidiaries. The reporting for those is quite straightforward—CPA firm A would issue three reports while CPA firm B would issue one.

The situation with respect to the parent is more complicated. After consolidation, the parent will be composed of the three subsidiaries audited by CPA firm A, and one audited by CPA firm B. It is the reporting for this situation that AU 543 addresses. The section requires that a "principal" auditor be determined to report on the consolidated parent's overall financial statements and prescribes certain requirements of the CPA firm —Section A of the outline presents that material. Two basic approaches to presenting the audit report are presented—Section B discusses a decision by the principal auditor **not** to make reference to the other auditor; Section C discusses a decision **to make reference** to the other auditor. Section D of the outline provides miscellaneous related points.

**A.**  Determining the principal auditor and his/her responsibilities

1.  The following factors should be considered in determining which firm is to serve as the principal auditor

  a.  Materiality of the portion of the financial statements audited by each CPA

  b.  Each CPA's relative knowledge of the overall financial statements

  c.  The importance of the components audited by each CPA

> NOTE: *This will normally be an easy decision since in practice one CPA will normally have much more than one-half of the overall work.*

2.  The principal auditor is required to make the following types of inquiries about the other auditor

  a.  His/her **reputation***—contact

     (1)  AICPA, state society, local chapter

     (2)  Other CPAs

     (3)  Bankers and other credit grantors

     (4)  Others

  b.  Obtain representation from the other CPA that s/he is independent per AICPA requirements, and if appropriate, per the requirements of the SEC

  c.  Ascertain through communication with the other auditor that s/he

     (1)  Knows the statements and his/her report will be used by the principal CPA

     (2)  Is familiar with GAAP and GAAS*

(3) Is familiar with SEC rules (if applicable)*

(4) Knows a review of matters affecting elimination of intercompany transactions will be made by the principal CPA

* *These items are ordinarily unnecessary if the principal auditor already knows the professional reputation and standing of the other auditor and if the other auditor's primary place of business is in the US.*

NOTE: *If the CPA determines that s/he can neither assume responsibility nor rely on the work of the other CPA, s/he should qualify or disclaim an opinion, stating the reasons and the magnitude of the financial statements affected. As a practical matter, in such a situation one would expect that the principal CPA would perform the procedures necessary to eliminate the problem.*

3. The principal CPA must determine whether s/he wishes to refer to the other CPA in the audit report
   a. When no reference is made, the principal auditor is assuming responsibility for the work of the other auditor

**B.** Deciding **not** to make reference to the other CPA
1. No mention of the other CPA or of the procedures indicated in Section A.2. above are made in the report—(e.g., if a standard unqualified report is appropriate, the report would be identical to that issued if no other CPA were involved)
2. Situations in which a principal auditor might choose this course of action (not making reference)
   a. The other CPA is associated with the principal auditor in some manner
   b. The other CPA was retained by the principal auditor (e.g., the principal auditor did not have a branch, and did not wish to travel to the city in which the subsidiary was headquartered)
   c. The principal auditor is satisfied with the other auditor's work
   d. The portion of the statement examined by the other CPA is not material to the overall financial statements
3. When the principal auditor is following this course of action (not making reference), s/he should also consider whether to perform one or more of the following
   a. Visit the other CPA and discuss the audit
   b. Review the other CPA's audit programs
   c. Review the other CPA's working papers
   d. Perform additional auditing procedures

**C.** Deciding **to make reference** to the other CPA
1. The audit report will indicate the other auditor involvement in the introductory, scope, and opinion paragraphs
   a. The report should indicate the dollar amount of assets, income, and other appropriate criteria included in the other CPA's audit
   b. The other auditor may be named, but only
      (1) With his/her permission
      (2) When his/her report is presented with the principal CPA's report
   c. Absent other circumstances (e.g., a scope limitation or a departure from GAAP), the report issued is unqualified with explanatory language

NOTE: *When studying how to actually write audit reports, it is most efficient to study the various modifications of the standard report together. Section B.2. of the Reporting Module presents the necessary information.*

**D.** Miscellaneous
1. Principal auditor treatment of a situation in which the other auditor's report is **not** standard unqualified in form
   a. If the matter is material to the overall financial statements it will require modification of the principal auditor's report
   b. If the matter is **not** material to the overall financial statements, and if the other auditor's report is not presented, the principal auditor need not make reference to the matter
      (1) If the other auditor's report is presented, the principal auditor may wish to make reference to it as to its disposition
2. The advice in this section may also relate to the situation in which an investment is accounted for by use of the equity method; reference to the other auditor who is associated with the investee may be appropriate
3. Following a pooling, a CPA may express an opinion on the restated statements of prior periods; several complications may arise

a.  If the CPA cannot satisfy him/herself with respect to the restated statements
    (1) The CPA should issue the appropriate report on the current year statements (e.g., a standard unqualified one-year report), with an additional paragraph following the opinion paragraph in which the CPA expresses an opinion solely on the proper combination of the pooled companies
    (2) In these circumstances the CPA does not take responsibility for the work of the other CPAs nor for expressing an opinion on the restated statements taken as a whole; procedures should be taken to enable him/her to express an opinion as to the proper combination of the statements

## 550 Other Information in Documents Containing Audited Financial Statements (SAS 8)

*Overall Objectives and Approach*—This section presents guidance on the CPA's responsibility when audited financial statements (which include the CPA's audit report) are included in a document which includes other information. For example, consider a public company's annual report which includes audited financial statements and additional information such as a president's letter, as well as various other unaudited financial and nonfinancial information. It is important to realize that this section is dealing with the situation in which the document in which the audited statements are included is being **prepared by the client,** and not by the auditor. Also, while the section **does apply** to annual reports filed with the SEC under the 1934 Securities Exchange Act as well as to other documents to which the auditor devotes attention, it **does not apply** to SEC registration statements under the 1933 Securities Act (dealing with initial offerings).

Section A of the outline does not require the CPA to perform any audit procedures beyond reading the other information for obvious errors and inconsistencies. Section B discusses the proper action to be taken when the auditor believes that inconsistencies exist between the audited statements and the other information; Section C addresses the situation in which the auditor believes that some of the other information may be misstated, although no inconsistency with the financial statements exists.

A.  Overall auditor responsibility with respect to information in a document containing audited financial statements may be summarized as
    1.  **Audited financial statements**—the auditor assumes normal responsibility taken on an audit
    2.  **Other information**—the auditor has no obligation to perform any procedures, **beyond reading,** to corroborate the information

*NOTE: In all of the circumstances described in Sections B and C below, the CPA will first attempt to determine that the information in question is actually incorrect. When the information is determined to be incorrect, the auditor will attempt to convince the client to correct any misstated information. The following only applies when the misstatements are not eliminated by the client.*

B.  Material inconsistency between the financial statements and the other information
    1.  If the financial statements are incorrect a departure from GAAP exists which will lead to either a qualified or adverse opinion—see outline of AU 508 and Section B of Reporting Module
    2.  If the other information is incorrect the auditor should consider (depending upon the circumstances)
        a.  Insertion of an explanatory paragraph in the audit report
        b.  Withholding use of the audit report
        c.  Withdrawing from the engagement
C.  No inconsistency, but the other information seems incorrect
    1.  The appropriate action will depend upon the circumstances, but might include notification of the client in writing and consulting with legal counsel

*NOTE: Know that the circumstances described in Sections B.2. and C.1. do not result in a report which is qualified or adverse. This is because the financial statements follow GAAP—it is the other information which is incorrect.*

D.  If other information has been subjected to auditing procedures, the auditor may express an opinion on whether the information is fairly stated in all material respects in relation to the financial statements

## 551 Reporting on Information Accompanying the Basic Financial Statements in Auditor-Submitted Documents (SAS 29)

*Overall Objectives and Approach*—This section presents guidance on the CPA's responsibility when audited financial statements are included in an auditor-submitted document which also includes other information. An auditor-submitted document is one that the auditor submits to his/her client or to others. The other information covered by this statement is presented outside the basic financial statements and is not necessary for the presentation of the statements—for example, consolidating information, historical summaries, and statistical data.

The distinction between this section and the preceding section (AU 550) is that here **the auditor,** and **not the client,** is preparing the document which includes an audit report, financial statements and other information. For example, a small client may ask the CPA to prepare the report and provide it to the company. **AU 550** provides guidance for when the **client is preparing a report** in which the auditor's report is to be included.

The basic requirement for an auditor-submitted document is that the CPA must make clear his/her association with any information which is being submitted to the client (or third party). The information, depending upon the client's needs, may either be audited or unaudited. The report on the accompanying information may be added to the CPA's standard report on the basic financial statements, or may appear separately in an auditor-submitted document.

In this outline we summarize the material as follows: (a) overall responsibility, (b) details of reporting responsibility, and (c) miscellaneous points.

**A.** Overall responsibility
1. When the auditor submits a document containing audited financial statements, s/he must report on all information included in the document
2. The auditor's report on accompanying information should
   a. State that the examination was made for the purpose of forming an opinion on the basic financial statements taken as a whole
   b. Identify the accompanying information
   c. State that accompanying information is presented for purposes of additional analysis and is not a part of the basic financial statements
   d. Include an opinion on the accompanying information or a disclaimer (if audit procedures are not applied)
      (1) If an opinion is given, the report should indicate that the accompanying information is fairly stated in all material respects as it relates to the basic financial statements taken as a whole
      (2) An opinion may be expressed on portions of the accompanying information and a disclaimer on the remainder
      (3) Any accompanying information on which the auditor disclaims an opinion should be marked as "unaudited"

   *NOTE: Recall from our introduction that the above information may either be added to the standard report or may be included in a separate report.*

3. Because the materiality level for the accompanying information is the same as that used for forming an opinion on the financial statements taken as a whole, the auditor need not apply procedures as extensive as would be necessary for a separate opinion on the information taken alone
4. When a client asks for inclusion of nonaccounting information, the auditor should generally disclaim an opinion on this accompanying information unless the records supporting it were tested

**B.** Details of reporting responsibility
1. If the auditor concludes that accompanying information is materially misstated, s/he should propose revisions to the client
   a. If the revision is not accepted, the audit report should be modified or the misstated information should be omitted
   b. Since it is the accompanying information that is misstated, the audit report opinion would still be unqualified
2. The auditor must consider the effect of any modification in his/her standard report when reporting on the accompanying information
   a. If a qualified opinion is issued on the basic financial statements, the impact on the accompanying information should be indicated
   b. If an opinion on the financial statements is adverse or disclaimed, no opinion should be expressed on any accompanying information

**C.** Miscellaneous points
1. When supplementary information required by the FASB or GASB is presented outside the basic financial statements
   a. An opinion should be disclaimed unless the auditor is engaged to express an opinion on it
   b. The auditor's report should be expanded if
      (1) The information is omitted

(2) The required information departs from guidelines

(3) The auditor is unable to complete required procedures, or

(4) The auditor is unable to remove substantial doubt about whether the information conforms to guidelines

*NOTE: See the outline of AU 558 for more information on FASB and GASB required information.*

2. When consolidated financial statements and/or consolidating information is presented, the CPA should report appropriately in a manner consistent with the responsibility being taken

   a. This responsibility may range from ascertaining that the consolidating information is suitably identified to auditing individual components presented in the consolidating financial statements

3. Any comments made by the CPA describing procedures applied to specific items in the financial statements should be placed apart from the accompanying information

   a. This is done to maintain a clear distinction between management's representations and the CPA's representations

## 552 Reporting on Condensed Financial Statements and Selected Financial Data (SAS 42)

*Overall Objectives and Approach*—This section presents guidance for reporting on a client-prepared document which contains **condensed financial statements** or **selected financial data** derived from the complete audited financial statements. This section only applies when the CPA has reported on the overall financial statements from which the information is being abstracted. The section provides for separate reports on condensed financial statements and on selected financial data. Sections A and B of the outline discuss the nature of the CPA's report on condensed financial statements and selected financial data, respectively. Section C discusses miscellaneous related points.

**A.** Reporting on **condensed financial statements**

1. The report should indicate

   a. That the complete financial statements have been audited and that the auditor has expressed an opinion on them

   b. The date of the auditor's report on the complete financial statements

   c. The type of opinion expressed on the complete financial statements

   d. Whether the information in the condensed financial statements is fairly presented in all material respects in relation to the complete financial statements from which it is derived

2. Example report

> We have audited, in accordance with US generally accepted auditing standards, the consolidated balance sheet of X Company and subsidiaries as of December 3, 20X3, and the related consolidated statements of income, retained earnings, and cash flows for the year then ended (not presented herein); and in our report dated February 15, 20X4, we expressed an unqualified opinion on those consolidated financial statements. In our opinion, the information set forth in the accompanying condensed consolidated financial statements is fairly stated in all material respects in relation to the consolidated financial statements from which it has been derived.

**B.** Reporting on **selected financial data**

1. The report should be limited to data derived from the audited complete financial statements

2. The CPA's report should indicate items a., c., and d. from A.1. above

   a. The reference in d. is changed from condensed financial statements to the selected financial data

3. When comparative selected financial data are presented and some of the data were derived from financial statements audited by another CPA, the report should so state, and the auditor should not express an opinion on that data

**C.** Miscellaneous

1. When a client prepares a document with condensed financial statements or selected financial data which **names the CPA** but **does not present the complete financial statements,** the CPA should request that the client

   a. Not include the CPA's name in the document or

   b. Engage the CPA to report on the information or

   c. Include the complete financial statements in the document

## 558 Required Supplementary Information (SAS 52)

*Overall Objectives and Approach*—This section presents guidance for audits where supplementary information required by the FASB or GASB is presented. The FASB or GASB periodically require certain disclosures considered to be supplementary to the financial statements. Such information is not considered audited, although CPAs are required to perform certain limited procedures on it. The information should normally be distinct from both the audited financial statements and from other information not required by the FASB or GASB. However, when it is placed inside the audited financial statements, it should be marked "unaudited" or the CPA's report should include a disclaimer on the information.

The section also applies when a company not subject to the requirements voluntarily issues such information, unless the information indicates that the CPA did not apply any procedures or the CPA expands his/her report to include a disclaimer on the information. The section **does not** apply when a company voluntarily discloses information no longer required of any firms (e.g., the FASB rescinded the required disclosures of the effects of changing prices; such information is considered using the AU 550 requirements).

This section provides guidance on both (a) procedures to be applied by CPAs and (b) reporting considerations.

**A.** Procedures to be applied by CPAs
1. Inquire of management about the methods of preparing the information, including
    a. Whether it is measured and presented within the guidelines
    b. Whether methods of measurement or presentation have changed from those used in the prior period and the reasons for any such changes
    c. Any significant assumptions or interpretations underlying the measurement or presentation
2. Compare the information for consistency with
    a. Management's responses to the inquiries in 1. above
    b. Audited financial statements
    c. Other knowledge obtained during the audit of the financial statements
3. Consider the need to include representations on the supplementary information in the client representation letter (see outline AU 333)
4. Apply additional procedures that other guides (e.g., other SAS, interpretation, guides) prescribe for the specific type of supplementary information
5. Make additional inquiries if foregoing procedures indicate possible deviations from the appropriate guidelines

**B.** Reporting on supplementary information
1. The auditor only reports on information when the
    a. Information is omitted
    b. Information departs from guidelines
    c. Auditor is unable to perform prescribed procedures
    d. Auditor is unable to remove substantial doubts about whether information conforms to guidelines
2. The actual report modification is in the form of an explanatory paragraph, with no opinion paragraph modification

## 560 Subsequent Events (SAS 1)

*Overall Objectives and Approach*—This section presents guidance on accounting for and auditing "subsequent events." Carefully distinguish between the information presented in this section and that of AU 561. This section relates to proper accounting and auditing procedures related to events occurring subsequent to the balance sheet date, but prior to issuance of the audit report. AU 561 relates to events occurring after the date of the auditor's report, most frequently when the financial statements have been issued.

This outline first defines the relevant terms from throughout the section. Section B summarizes proper accounting for subsequent events. Section C lists normal audit procedures which should be performed to detect subsequent events.

**A.** Definitions
1. **Subsequent events**—Events or transactions having a material effect on the financial statements that occur subsequent to the balance sheet date, but prior to issuance of the financial statements
    a. **Type 1 subsequent events**—Those events that provide additional evidence about **conditions that existed** at the date of the balance sheet and affect the estimates used in preparing financial statements

   b.   **Type 2 subsequent events**—Those events that provide evidence with respect to **conditions that did not exist** at the date of the balance sheet being reported on, but arose after that date
2. **Subsequent period**—The period after the balance sheet date, extending to the date of the auditor's report

B. Proper accounting for subsequent events
   1. **Type 1**—Make an adjusting entry to adjust the financial statements
      a. Examples
         (1) Settlement of litigation for an amount different from the liability recorded in the accounts, assuming the event causing the litigation occurred before year-end
         (2) Loss on an uncollectible account receivable as a result of a customer's deteriorating financial condition that led to bankruptcy subsequent to the balance sheet date

         NOTE: *Think about the above example. Although the customer filed for bankruptcy after year-end, an adjustment is appropriate because filing for bankruptcy was simply the conclusion of the condition—deteriorating financial position—which began prior to year-end.*

   2. **Type 2—Disclose in notes** to the financial statements
      a. Examples
         (1) Sale of bond or stock issue
         (2) Purchase of a business
         (3) Litigation settlement, but only when the litigation is based on a post-balance-sheet event
            (a) Because of the time involved with litigation, this would presumably be rare
         (4) Fire or flood loss
         (5) Receivable loss, but only when the loss occurred due to a post-balance-sheet event such as a customer's major casualty arising after the balance sheet date

         NOTE: *Distinguish between this example and example 1.a.(2) above.*

   3. Several related points for Type 2 subsequent events
      a. The disclosures related to subsequent event may include pro forma statements included in the notes
      b. An auditor may wish to add an explanatory paragraph to an unqualified report to emphasize the subsequent event matter—see Emphasis of a Matter in the outline of AU 508 and Section B of the Reporting Module
      c. When statements are reissued (for example, in an SEC filing) the statements should not be adjusted for events occurring after the original issuance date

C. Subsequent period auditing procedures
   1. Certain procedures are applied to transactions after year-end
      a. To assure proper year-end cutoff
      b. To help evaluate asset and liability valuation
   2. In addition, the CPA should perform other procedures near completion of fieldwork to identify subsequent events
      a. Read latest interim statements
         (1) Make comparison with other data
      b. Discuss with management
         (1) Existence of contingent liabilities
         (2) Significant changes in shareholders' equity items
         (3) Statement items accounted for on tentative data
         (4) Unusual adjustments in the subsequent period
      c. Read minutes of Board of Directors and other committees
         (1) Make inquiries when minutes are not available
      d. Obtain lawyer's letter on
         (1) Litigation
         (2) Impending litigation, claims
         (3) Contingent liabilities
      e. Include in management representation letter representations on subsequent events

## 561 Subsequent Discovery of Facts Existing at the Date of the Auditor's Report (SAS 1)

*Overall Objectives and Approach*—This section presents guidance on procedures to be followed by the CPA who, after the date of his/her audit report, becomes aware of facts that may have existed when the audit report was issued and that might have affected that report. You might wish to study and compare this section with AU 560, which deals with events occurring subsequent to the balance sheet date, but prior to issuance of the audit report.

This outline summarizes the section's procedural guidance in a series of four steps. The outline deviates from a strict format to make obvious the sequence of audit procedures.

**A.** Appropriate procedures for events discovered subsequent to the date of the audit report

> *NOTE: The auditor has no obligation to perform additional procedures after the audit report date, **unless** s/he becomes aware of facts that may have existed at the report date. As overall advice, when any of these circumstances arise, the CPA should consult with his/her attorney.*

Step 1.  The CPA should determine if the subsequently discovered information is reliable and existed at the date of the audit report
   a.  To accomplish this, the auditor should discuss the matter with the appropriate level(s) of management, the board of directors (if deemed necessary), and should request cooperation in whatever investigation is necessary

Step 2.  When the CPA determines that the information is reliable and did exist at the date of the audit report, the following procedures are required
   a.  Determine whether the audit report would have been affected if the information had been known at the time of report issuance
   b.  Assess whether persons are likely to still be relying upon the report
      (1) The auditor will consider, among other things, the time that has elapsed since the financial statements were issued

Step 3.  When the CPA believes that the report would be affected, and that persons are relying upon the information, the CPA should insist that the client undertake appropriate disclosure, which may vary with the circumstances
   a.  If the effect on the financial statements and/or the auditor's report can be promptly determined, the statements should be revised and reissued
      (1) The reason for the revision should be described in a note to the financial statements and referred to in the auditor's report
      (2) Generally, only the most recently issued audited statements would need to be revised, even though the revision resulted from events that had happened in prior years
   b.  If issuance of statements of a subsequent period is imminent, appropriate revision can be made in those statements; disclosures should be similar to those in a. above
   c.  If the effect cannot be promptly determined and it appears that the statements will be revised after the investigation, **persons known to be relying or who are likely to rely** on the financial statements should be notified
      (1) If appropriate, the client should disclose the information to the proper regulatory bodies (e.g., SEC)

Step 4.  This step is appropriate only if the client **refuses** to cooperate with the CPA
   a.  Notify each member of the board of directors of the client's refusal to make disclosures and that the CPA will take the steps outlined in b. below
   b.  Unless the CPA's attorney recommends a different course of action, the CPA should undertake the following steps (to the extent applicable)
      (1) Notify the client that the audit report cannot be associated with the financial statements
      (2) Notify regulatory agencies that the audit report should not be relied upon
      (3) Notify each person known to be relying on the statements that the report should not be relied upon

   > *NOTE: Know that the notification is limited to the client, regulatory agencies (e.g., the SEC), and persons **known** to be relying on the statements. It will not, in general, be practicable to notify all stockholders or investors at large.*

   c.  Appropriate disclosures
      (1) If the CPA makes a satisfactory investigation and believes the information is reliable
         (a) Disclose the nature of the information and effect on the report and statements

       (b) Disclosures should be precise and factual, and should not comment on the motives of any person who is involved

    (2) If the client has not cooperated, and the auditor has been unable to conduct a satisfactory investigation, the auditor should disclose that the

       (a) Information has come to his/her attention and that

       (b) The client has not cooperated in attempting to substantiate it, and if true, the auditor believes his report should no longer be relied upon

## 623 Special Reports (SAS 63)

***Overall Objectives and Approach***—This section was passed in 1989 to update the area of "special reports" to reflect the 1988 statements (SAS 52-61). It describes five specific types of special reports issued by auditors which are based on—(a) Financial statements prepared using a **comprehensive basis of accounting other than GAAP** (hereafter, simply **a comprehensive basis**), (b) **Specified elements, accounts or items** of statements (e.g., cash, accounts receivable), (c) **Compliance** with aspects of contractual or regulatory requirements related to audited financial statements, (d) **Financial presentations** to comply with contractual or regulatory requirements, and (e) Financial information presented in **prescribed forms** or schedules that require a prescribed form of auditor's report. Be aware that the above 5 types of reports are the only types of special reports. Thus, for example, reviews of interim statements (AU 722) and forecast examinations (AT 200) are not "special reports." (A number of multiple-choice questions have presented 3 special reports, plus another type of report, and have asked "which is not a special report?")

    A confusing portion of this section relates to whether the distribution of the various reports is limited (generally to the preparer, appropriate regulatory agency and/or party to a contract), or is available to the general public. The following are the primary types of reports **not** publicly available:

1. Presentations prepared following a basis **other than GAAP or a comprehensive basis**
2. Comprehensive basis statements **prepared using a basis of accounting used to comply with requirements of a governmental regulatory agency** (A.2.a. below)
3. Incomplete GAAP or comprehensive basis presentations unless the presentation is to be filed with a regulatory agency (e.g., the SEC) **and** to be included in a document that is distributed to the general public [D.1.a.(1) below]
4. Report on compliance with contractual agreements or regulatory requirements related to audited financial statements (C. below)

    The sections of the following outline summarize proper reporting and procedural requirements for each of the five types of special reports as well as a discussion of circumstances that require explanatory language in an auditor's special report.

**A.** Reports prepared following a **comprehensive basis** of accounting
  1. GAAS apply when an auditor conducts an audit of and reports on **any financial statement**
  2. A comprehensive basis is one of the following
    a. A basis of accounting used to comply with governmental regulatory agency (e.g., rules of state insurance commission)
    b. The basis of accounting used for tax purposes
    c. The cash receipts and disbursements basis of accounting, including a method with widely accepted modifications of the method (e.g., recording depreciation, accruing income taxes)
    d. A definite set of criteria with **substantial authoritative support** applied to all material items (e.g., price level basis of accounting)

*NOTE: The effect of the above section is to limit comprehensive basis statements to regulatory basis, tax basis, cash basis, or another one with **substantial authoritative support**. Thus, a basis developed by a client or another party (e.g., a bank for use in assessing a company's compliance with debt covenants) will not in general qualify.*

  3. Reports on statements following a comprehensive basis
    a. A title that includes the word independent
    b. A paragraph stating that the financial statements
      (1) Were audited
      (2) Are the responsibility of management and that the auditor is responsible for expressing an opinion on them
    c. A paragraph stating that

      (1) The audit was conducted per GAAS

      (2) GAAS require that the auditor plan and perform the audit to obtain reasonable assurance about whether the financial statements are free of material misstatement

      (3) An audit includes

         (a) Examining on a test basis evidence supporting the amounts and disclosures in the financial statements

         (b) Assessing the accounting principles used and significant estimates and

         (c) Evaluating overall financial statement presentation

      (4) The auditor believes that the audit provides a reasonable basis for the opinion

  d.  A paragraph indicating

      (1) The basis of presentation and refers to the note in the financial statement describing the basis

      (2) That the basis is a comprehensive basis of accounting other than GAAP

  e.  A paragraph with an opinion on whether the financial statements are presented fairly, in all material respects, in conformity with the basis of accounting described

  f.  When statements are prepared in conformity with a regulatory agency's principles, a paragraph that restricts distribution of the report solely to those within the entity and for filing with the regulatory agency—see A.2.a. above

  g.  The manual or printed firm signature

  h.  The date (generally the last day of fieldwork—see AU 530 outline)

*NOTE: One might expect an occasional simulation that requires preparation of a comprehensive basis report. Notice how closely it parallels the standard audit report on whether financial statements follow GAAP. Also, an example of the report is provided in the Reporting Module, Section C.2.a.*

4.  Terms such as statement of financial position, statement of income (or operations), and statement of cash flows should not be used for comprehensive basis statements

  a.  Examples of appropriate (cash basis) titles: statements of assets and liabilities arising from cash flows, statement of revenue collected and expenses paid

*NOTE: Different titles are used so as to prevent misleading anyone into believing that the statements follow GAAP.*

5.  While comprehensive basis statement notes should include a summary of significant accounting policies and describe how the basis differs from GAAP, the differences **need not be quantified**

6.  When evaluating the adequacy of disclosures, the auditor should consider disclosure of matters such as related-party transactions, restrictions on assets and owners' equity, subsequent events, and uncertainties

**B.** Reports on **specified elements, accounts or items** of a financial statement

1.  Examples—rentals, royalties, a profit participation, provision for income tax, accounts receivable

2.  There are two basic approaches

  a.  Express an opinion on one or more elements

  b.  Provide "negative assurance" relating to the results of applying agreed-upon procedures to one or more elements

*NOTE: This section only deals with expressing an opinion (2.a.). Section AT 201 presents guidance for expressing negative assurance as a result of applying agreed-upon procedures.*

3.  In general, GAAS apply

4.  The measure of materiality must be related to the individual element, **not** the financial statements taken as a whole

5.  A special report may **only** be issued on specific elements in statements upon which an adverse opinion or a disclaimer was issued when

  a.  The element(s) are not a major part of the financial statements

  b.  The special report does not accompany the financial statements of the entity

6.  Reports on specific elements

  a.  The report issued is similar to that for comprehensive basis statements (see A.3. above); major exceptions are

      (1) The terms relating to the financial statements are replaced with a term relating to the elements, accounts or items presented

      (2) The "opinion paragraph" (A.3.e. above) should include

      (a) A description of the basis on which the elements are presented, and when applicable, any agreements specifying such basis

      (b) If considered necessary, a description and the source of significant interpretations made by management relating to the agreement

*NOTE: Review both A.3. and this section since periodically an exam will require preparation of such a report. Section C.2.a. of the Reporting Module provides a sample report.*

    7. If a specified element, account, or item is based on income or stockholders' equity, the auditor should have audited the complete financial statements to express an opinion on it

**C.** Reports on **compliance with contractual agreements** or with regulatory requirements related to **audited** financial statements

    1. The situation being considered here is one in which an audit has been performed on the financial statements, and some organization (e.g., a bank) wants assurance with respect to compliance with the conditions of an agreement

      a. Examples—loan agreements often require restriction of dividend payments and maintenance of the current ratio at a specific level

    2. The auditor provides negative assurance as to compliance with the agreement, either

      a. As a separate report, or

      b. As one or more paragraphs added to the auditor's report accompanying the financial statements

        (1) In either case indication that the negative assurance is given in connection with the audit

        (2) When a separate report is issued, it should indicate that an audit has been performed, the date of the report, and whether GAAS were followed

    3. Negative assurance should **not** be provided

      a. For covenants that relate to matters that have not been subjected to the audit procedures applied in the audit of the financial statements

      b. When the auditor has expressed an adverse opinion or disclaimed an opinion on the financial statements to which the covenants relate

    4. A separate report on compliance with contractual agreements should include

      a. A title that includes the word independent

      b. A paragraph stating that the financial statements were audited per GAAS, the date of that report, and describing any departures from standard report

      c. A paragraph that includes reference to the specific covenants, provides negative assurance relative to compliance, and specifies that the negative assurance is being given in connection with the audit

      d. A paragraph that includes a description and the source of any significant interpretations (if needed)

      e. A paragraph that restricts distribution of report solely to those within the entity and for filing with the regulatory agency

      f. The manual or printed firm signature

      g. The date

    5. When the report on compliance is included in the audit report, the auditor should include paragraphs similar to 4.c., d., and e. above (following the opinion paragraph)

*NOTE: See Section C.2.a. of the Reporting Module for a sample report.*

**D. Special-purpose financial presentations** to comply with contractual agreements or regulatory provisions

    1. In this situation the financial statements have been prepared to comply with some agreement (e.g., a loan agreement) or regulatory provision and are intended solely for the use of the parties to the agreement, regulatory bodies, or other specified parties; two types of special-purpose presentations are discussed

      a. Special-purpose financial presentations that do not constitute complete presentation of assets and liabilities, revenues and expenses, but otherwise are **presented per GAAP** or other comprehensive basis

        (1) The procedural and reporting requirements are similar to those for comprehensive basis statements (A. above), although a paragraph restricting distribution of the report is necessary unless the information is filed with a regulatory agency (e.g., the SEC) and is to be included in a publicly available report

    b.  Special-purpose financial presentations which may or may not be a complete set of financial statements that do **not follow GAAP or another comprehensive basis** of accounting

        (1)  As an example, consider an acquisition agreement that requires the borrower to prepare financial statements per GAAP, except for certain assets such as receivables, inventories, and properties for which a net realizable valuation basis is specified in the agreement

        (2)  The report, while similar to that for comprehensive basis statements (A. above) includes an opinion paragraph that explains what the presentation is intended to present and refers to the note describing that basis, and states that the presentation is not per GAAP

        (3)  A paragraph limiting distribution is included

*NOTE: See Section C.2.a. of the Reporting Module for sample reports.*

**E.**  Reports on information in prescribed forms or schedules

    1.  Printed forms or schedules (hereafter, forms) that are designed by the bodies with which they are filed often suggest a required wording for an auditor's report

*EXAMPLE: Assume that a state has a balance sheet form which companies incorporated in that state are to fill out with appropriate financial information. Also, assume that the state requires a standard unqualified report be filed with the report. The difficulty here is that the form may not provide adequate or proper disclosures. This section deals with the manner in which an auditor should report on such forms.*

    2.  When a schedule requires that an auditor make a statement that is incorrect, the auditor should respond in a manner such as the following

      a.  Revise the form so that it complies with the required statement to be made by the auditor

      b.  Attach a separate report

    3.  In no case should an auditor make an assertion that is not justified

*EXAMPLE: Continuing the above example, if the information can be made to follow GAAP an unqualified report could be issued. Otherwise, the auditor would not be able to meet the legal requirement as his/her report would include departures from the standard form.*

**F.**  Circumstances requiring explanatory language in an auditor's special report

*NOTE: Throughout the special reports, in general the circumstances which lead auditors to qualified, adverse, and disclaimers of opinions in GAAP audits generally apply. Several special considerations apply to the following circumstances which normally result in the auditor adding additional explanatory language to an unqualified report.*

    1.  Lack of consistency

      a.  An explanatory paragraph is added

      b.  When financial statements (or specified elements, accounts or items) have been prepared in conformity with GAAP in prior years, and the basis is changed to another comprehensive basis, the auditor is not required to add an explanatory paragraph on consistency (although s/he may choose to do so)

    2.  Uncertainties (including going concern uncertainties)

      a.  An explanatory paragraph is only added when the uncertainties are relevant to the presentation

        (1)  For example, an explanatory paragraph may be necessary for cash basis statements, but may **not** be necessary for a report based on compliance with loan covenants

    3.  Other auditors

      a.  When reference is made to other auditors whose report is being relied upon, the AU 508 requirements for other auditors apply (mention them in introductory, scope, and opinion paragraphs)

    4.  Comparative financial statements when a different opinion than originally issued is being issued

      a.  The auditor should disclose that the opinion is different, with all reasons therefore in a separate explanatory paragraph preceding the opinion paragraph

## 625 Reports on the Application of Accounting Principles (SAS 97)

***Overall Objectives and Approach***—This section presents guidance on a CPA's responsibilities when asked to reply as to how existing accounting principles apply to new transactions and financial products. Management and others often consult with CPAs on the application of accounting principles to such transactions. The section was developed to control "opinion shopping," the practice of going from one CPA to another until one finds an accountant who agrees with an accounting procedure which might be considered questionable.

    The guidance in the section relates to: (a) applicability, (b) performance standards, and (c) reporting standards.

**A.** Applicability
1. This section provides guidance that a reporting accountant, either in connection with a proposal to obtain a new client or otherwise, should apply when preparing a **written report** on
   a. The application of GAAP to specified completed or proposed transactions, involving facts and circumstances of a specific entity ("specific transactions")
   b. The type of opinion that may be rendered on an entity's financial statements
2. Applies to oral advice that the reporting accountant concludes is intended to be used by a principal to the transaction as an important factor considered in reaching a decision on application of GAAP to a specific transaction, or the type of opinion that may be rendered on a specific entity's financial statements
3. A reporting accountant should **not** provide a written report on the application of accounting principles to a hypothetical transaction (one not involving facts or circumstances of a specific entity)
4. Does **not** apply to regular reporting engagements, litigation assistance, expert testimony, and position papers (e.g., newsletters, articles, speeches)

**B.** Performance standards
1. Procedures
   a. **Obtain an understanding** of form and substance of transaction(s)
   b. **Review applicable GAAP**
   c. **If appropriate, consult other professionals** and experts or perform necessary research
2. If another accountant is involved, **contact** and follow AU 315 (Predecessor/Successor Auditor) procedures

**C.** Reporting standards
1. Report should include a
   a. Description of nature of engagement and statement that AICPA standards were followed
   b. Identification of the specific entity, a description of transaction(s), relevant facts, circumstances, assumptions, source(s) of information
   c. Description of appropriate accounting principles (including country of origin) to be followed
   d. Statement that responsibility for accounting treatment rests with preparers who should consult their continuing accountants
   e. Statement that any difference in facts, circumstances, or assumptions might change report
   f. A separate paragraph at the end of the report indicating report is solely for specific parties, identification of the specified parties, and a statement that report is not intended for others

## 634 Letters for Underwriters and Certain Other Requesting Parties (SAS 72)

*Overall Objectives and Approach*—This section presents guidance on letters to underwriters (also referred to as "comfort letters") which CPAs may prepare to assist underwriters who are involved with the selling of securities under the Securities Act of 1933, as well as certain other acts. Consider, for example, a company selling stock to the public. The underwriter will assist the company in meeting the various legal requirements, and may purchase and then resell the securities to the public. Under the Securities Act of 1933 the underwriter is required to perform, with "due diligence," a "reasonable investigation" of the financial and accounting data that is not audited (referred to as information "not expertized"). A comfort letter, although not specifically required by the Act, is issued by the CPA to the underwriter on certain of this information.

Because the CPA exam has only asked a few questions pertaining to letters for underwriters, less detail is provided in this outline than has been included in prior outlines. The outline is organized as follows: (a) overall issues, (b) general information, and (c) detailed information.

**A.** Overall issues
1. A comfort letter is normally for an underwriter, although it may be for a law firm or other party that has a due diligence defense
2. CPAs may only
   a. Comment on matters upon which their professional expertise is substantially relevant
   b. At the most, provide negative assurance on information that is not audited

**B.** General comfort letter information
1. Dates relevant to filings
   a. Closing date—securities delivered to underwriter (letter normally so dated)
   b. Cutoff date—last date of CPA's procedures related to comfort letter

    c.   Effective date—securities registration becomes effective

    d.   Filing date—securities first filed (recorded) with SEC

  2.   While the letter is most frequently addressed to the underwriter and the client, it may also be addressed to involved broker-dealers, financial intermediaries, buyers or sellers

  3.   In describing work, auditor should not use terms such as "general review," "check," and "test"

**C.**  Detailed information often included in a comfort letter

  1.   **Pertaining to audit**—CPAs explicitly state that they are independent and that in their opinion their audit of the financial statements complied with SEC requirements

  2.   **Other information**

    a.   The CPAs must have obtained knowledge of internal control as it relates to preparation of annual and interim financial information before providing assurance on other information

      (1)  If an audit has been performed, this knowledge will normally have been obtained

      (2)  If the CPAs have not audited the company, they should perform procedures to obtain the necessary knowledge

    b.   Types of other information

      (1)  Unaudited condensed interim financial information—provide negative assurance

      (2)  Unaudited summarized interim information (capsule financial information)—provide negative assurance

      (3)  Pro forma financial information—provide a summary of tests performed and findings

      (4)  Subsequent changes (e.g., changes in capital stock, debt, decreases in certain accounts)— provide negative assurance or a summary of tests performed and findings

        (a)  Negative assurance may only be provided within 135 days of most recent audit or review; thereafter, only a summary of tests performed and findings may be provided

        (b)  While the report may indicate changes, terms such as "adverse changes" should not be used due to lack of a clearly understood meaning

      (5)  Tables, statistics, and other financial information—provide negative assurance, but only on information obtained or derived from accounting records that is subject to the accounting system of internal control

        (a)  The term "presents fairly" should not be used

## 711 Filings under Federal Securities Statutes (SAS 37)

***Overall Objectives and Approach***—This section presents overall information on a CPA's responsibilities when s/he is associated with information included in a client's filing with the SEC. Section A of the outline presents overall responsibilities. Section B provides information on subsequent events in 1933 Act filings— this supplements the guidance in AU 560. Section C relates to the appropriate response when subsequent events have been discovered—this supplements the guidance in both AU 560 and AU 561.

**A.**  Overall responsibilities under Federal Securities Statutes

  1.   An accountant has a defense against lawsuits filed under Section 11 of the 1933 Securities Act if s/he can prove that s/he had, after a **reasonable** investigation, **reasonable** grounds to believe and did believe that the statements were true and not misleading at the effective date of the financial statements

    a.   The standard of **reasonableness** is that of a prudent person in the management of his/her own property

  2.   CPA should read the **experts section** of the prospectus under a 1933 Securities Act filing to make certain that his/her name is not used in a misleading manner

  3.   When a CPA's review report is included with interim financial information in a registration statement, a statement should be included that this is not a **report** under the meaning of Section 7 or 11 of the Securities Act of 1933

     *NOTE: The effect of the above statement is to limit CPA responsibility with respect to interim information contained in a registration statement.*

  4.   When an independent audit report is incorporated in a registration statement by reference, the CPA is described as an "expert in auditing and accounting"

**B.**  Procedures for finding subsequent events under a 1933 Securities Act Filing

  1.   A CPA should extend his/her investigation from that of his/her report to the effective date of the filing, or as close as possible; this investigation should include

    a.   Subsequent event procedures in AU 560—see outline of AU 560

    b.   Additional procedures

       (1)  Reading of the prospectus and relevant portions of the registration statement

       (2)  Obtaining written confirmation from managerial and accounting officers as to any subsequent events not mentioned in the registration statement

  2.  A predecessor accountant who has not examined the most current statements should

    a.   Read applicable portions of the prospectus and registration statement

    b.   Obtain a letter of representation from the successor CPA regarding the existence of any subsequent events

**C.**  Appropriate response when subsequent events have been discovered

  1.  Use any AU 560 or 561 guidance—see outlines of AU 560 and AU 561

  2.  Overall

    a.   Insist upon revision

    b.   Comment on the matter in the audit report

    c.   Inquire of attorney, and consider withholding opinion if client will not correct financial statements

  3.  If the unaudited financial statements are not in conformity with GAAP, insist on revision, and failing that

    a.   If CPA has issued a review report, refer to AU 561 and AU 722 for guidance

    b.   If no review has been performed, modify report on audited financial statements to describe the departure

## 722 Interim Financial Information (SAS 100)

*Overall Objectives and Approach*—The guidance in this section is primarily in response to an SEC requirement for a review of interim financial information before it is filed in a registrant's quarterly report on Form 10-Q. It is also applicable to a non-SEC registrant that makes a filing with a regulatory agency in preparation for a public offering or listing if the entity's latest annual financial statements have been or are being audited.

A review consists primarily of the performance of inquiry and analytical procedures to form a basis for reporting on whether material modifications should be made for the information to conform with GAAP. Although such a review must be conducted for SEC registrants, the accountant ordinarily only issues a review report if the registrant requests it. Otherwise, the procedures are performed with no report issuance. An exception to this rule is that if the client states in a document that the interim financial information has been reviewed, and accountant's report must be filed with the interim financial information. When a report is issued it provides limited (negative) assurance about whether material modifications should be made to the information.

**A.**  General information

  1.  The **objective of an interim review** is to provide the accountant with a basis for communicating whether he or she is aware of any material modifications that should be made to the interim financial information for it to conform with GAAP

  2.  A review does not contemplate

    a.   Tests of accounting records through inspection, observation, or confirmation

    b.   Tests of controls

    c.   Corroborating evidence in response to inquiries

    d.   Application of other procedures ordinarily performed during an audit

  3.  A CPA should obtain and document (preferably in writing) an understanding regarding

    a.   Objective of a review (A.1. above)

    b.   Management's responsibility for

       (1)  The interim financial information

       (2)  Internal control over financial reporting

       (3)  Company's compliance with laws and regulations

       (4)  Making financial records and related information available to the auditor

       (5)  Adjusting interim financial information to correct material misstatements

    c.   Accountant's responsibility for conducting the review in accordance with AICPA standards

    d.   A review includes obtaining sufficient knowledge of the business and internal control to

       (1)  Identify types of potential misstatements and their likelihood of occurrence

       (2)  Select appropriate inquiries and analytical procedures

    e.   Although a review may identify reportable conditions, it is not designed to do so; nor is it designed to provide assurance on internal control

**B.** Accountant's knowledge of entity's business and internal control
1. Accountant should have knowledge sufficient to
    a. Identify types of potential misstatements and to consider the likelihood of occurrence
    b. Select inquiries and analytical procedures to provide accountant a basis for communicating whether he or she is aware of material modifications that should be made for the information to conform with GAAP
2. The accountant should perform the following procedures to update his/her knowledge of the business and its internal control to aid in determining appropriate review procedures:
    a. Read documentation of preceding year's audit and preceding reviews
    b. Read most recent annual and comparable prior interim period financial information
    c. Consider results of any audit procedures that were performed with respect to current year's financial statements
    d. Inquire of management about changes in entity's business activities
    e. Inquire of management about significant changes in internal control as it relates to the interim financial information
3. If the accountant has not performed an audit on this client (i.e., for a new client), adequate procedures must be performed relating to internal control to allow the accountant to perform the review
    a. In an initial review make inquiries of a predecessor auditor and review predecessor accountant's documentation for preceding annual audit and any prior interim periods in the current year that have been reviewed (if the predecessor permits such access); consider
        (1) Corrected misstatements
        (2) Uncorrected misstatements
        (3) Risks of material misstatement due to fraud, including management override of controls
        (4) Significant financial and reporting matters, such as weaknesses in internal control
    b. If the accountant has not audited the most recent annual financial statements, perform procedures to obtain sufficient understanding of internal control
    c. A restriction on the scope of the review may be imposed by poor internal control and this may result in resignation because it will be impossible to complete the review
**C.** Analytical procedures, inquiries, and other review procedures
1. Analytical procedures
    a. Compare interim financial information with preceding period(s)
    b. Consider plausible relationships among financial and nonfinancial information (e.g., board of director information package)
    c. Compare amounts or ratios to expectations developed by accountant
        (1) Expectations developed by an accountant during a review are ordinarily less precise than those developed in an audit
    d. Compare disaggregated revenue data; for example, compare revenue by month and by product line with that of comparable prior periods
2. Inquiries and other review procedures
    a. Read minutes (stockholders, directors, others) and inquire about matters dealt with at meetings for which minutes are not available
    b. Obtain reports from other accountants (if any) who are reviewing components of entity
    c. Inquiries of members of management with financial and accounting responsibility
        (1) Whether information conforms with GAAP
        (2) Unusual or complex situations
        (3) Significant transactions in last several days of period
        (4) Status of uncorrected misstatements identified during previous audits and reviews
        (5) Matters about which questions have arisen during review
        (6) Events subsequent to date of interim financial information
        (7) Fraud—knowledge of, suspected, allegations
        (8) Significant journal entries and other adjustments
        (9) Communications from regulatory agencies
        (10) Significant deficiencies in internal control
3. Obtain evidence that interim financial information agrees or reconciles with accounting records (e.g., compare interim financial information to general ledger, consolidating schedule, other support)
4. Read interim financial information

5. Read other information accompanying interim financial information (e.g., Form 10-Q)
6. Although it is not ordinarily necessary to contact an entity's lawyer concerning litigation, claims, and assessments, if certain information causes the accountant to question whether GAAP is being followed arises, it may be appropriate to inquire of the lawyer
7. If matters concerning the entity's ability to continue as a going concern come to the accountant's attention, the accountant should inquire of management about plans for dealing with this matter and consider the adequacy of disclosures about such matters in the interim financial information
8. If information leads the accountant to believe quarterly financial information does not follow GAAP, the accountant should make additional inquiries or perform other procedures
   a. For example, if a sale is questioned, the accountant may discuss the transactions with appropriate personnel, read the sales contract, or both

**D.** Written representations from management should be obtained, including
1. Management acknowledges responsibility and believes that financial statements follow GAAP
2. Management acknowledges responsibility for internal control and has disclosed any known or suspected fraud to the auditor
3. Management makes available all
   a. Financial records
   b. Minutes of meetings
   c. Communications with regulatory agencies
4. Recognition, measures, and disclosure
   a. Uncorrected misstatements are immaterial
   b. Plans or intentions affecting carrying value of assets or liabilities
   c. Related-party transactions
   d. Guarantees
   e. Significant estimates
   f. Violations or possible violations of laws or regulations
   g. Unasserted claims probable of assertion
   h. Other liabilities or gain or loss contingencies required to be disclosed by SFAS 5
   i. Satisfactory title to owned assets, etc.
   j. Compliance with contracts
5. Information on subsequent events
6. When an accountant is unable to perform needed procedures, the review is incomplete, and resignation is ordinarily appropriate

**E.** Communications to management, audit committees, and others
1. If the accountant believes there is a material misstatement
   a. Inform management, and if management doesn't respond appropriately, inform the audit committee
      (1) If the audit committee doesn't respond appropriately, consider resigning; accountant may also wish to consult his/her attorney
2. If the accountant becomes aware of fraud, this information should be communicated as required in AU 316 (see point I. of that outline)
   a. It should be brought to attention of appropriate level of management (at least one above the fraud)
   b. If senior management is involved or if results in a material misstatement, it should be communicated to audit committee
   c. If illegal acts are involved, make certain audit committee is informed unless the matter is clearly inconsequential
3. If reportable conditions have been identified, report them to audit committee as per AU 325
4. If any matters requiring communication to the audit committee are identified (AU 380), report them

**F.** Accountant's report
1. Should include
   a. The title "Report of Independent Registered Public Accounting Firm"
   b. Information was reviewed
   c. Information is responsibility of management
   d. Review was conducted in accordance with standards of the Public Company Accounting Oversight Board

  e. Description of procedures

  f. Review substantially less in scope than an audit

  g. Statement on awareness of any necessary material modification to financial information

  h. Manual or printed signature of accountant's firm

  i. City and state (or country) of the office issuing the report. Date of review report (ordinarily completion of review procedures)

 2. Each page of interim financial information should be clearly marked unaudited

  a. Departures from GAAP or inadequate disclosure—state nature of departure in an explanatory paragraph

   (1) If practical, provide the effect

  b. Going concern

   (1) If prior year's audit included a going concern modification, if there is adequate disclosure, no report modification is necessary

    (a) However, a paragraph describing the matter may be added to the review report

   (2) If no prior going concern modification, but such a matter is here identified, no report modification is necessary, although an explanatory paragraph may be added to the report

 3. Subsequent discovery of facts existing at date of report—see AU 561 outline

**G.** Interim financial information accompanying audited financial statements

 1. When the interim information is presented outside the audited financial statements, each page should be marked unaudited

 2. The **audit report on the annual information** should be modified when

  a. Interim financial information included in a note is not appropriately marked as unaudited—the auditor should disclaim an opinion on the interim financial information

  b. Interim information doesn't follow GAAP—the auditor need not modify report on audited financial statement if his/her review report accompanies the information; if it does not, add explanatory paragraph to audit report

  c. Required information omitted—add explanatory paragraph

  d. Interim information not reviewed—add explanatory paragraph

**H.** Documentation

 1. Should include findings and significant issues and should allow reviewer to

  a. Understand nature, timing, extent, and results of review procedures

  b. Identify who performed and reviewed work

  c. Identify evidence accountant obtained in support of conclusion that reviewed information agreed or reconciled with accounting records

 2. Examples of documentation include

  a. Review programs

  b. Analyses

  c. Memoranda

  d. Letters of representation

**I.** Appendix A: Examples of analytical procedures include comparing interim financial information with

 1. Anticipated results (e.g., budgets, forecasts)

 2. Relevant nonfinancial information

 3. Prior periods

 4. Industry

 5. Disaggregated data

**J.** Appendix B: Describes a number of unusual or complex situations to be considered in a review (e.g., business combinations, impaired assets)

**K.** Appendix C: Provides illustrative management representation letters

## 801 Compliance Auditing Considerations in Audits of Governmental Entities and Recipient of Governmental Financial Assistance (SAS 74)

*Overall Objectives and Approach*—This section provides guidance on the auditor's responsibilities for audits performed in accordance with government auditing standards (GAS). GAS are established by the Comptroller General of the United States—the top executive within the General Accounting Office—in *Government Auditing Standards* (the "yellow book"). GAS apply to government agencies and to certain nongovernmental organizations that have received governmental financial assistance.

Everything in this section relates to what GAS refers to as "financial audits," as opposed to "performance audits." It is important to realize that, when performing an audit following GAS, the auditor must not only report on the financial statements, but also on **compliance with various laws and regulations,** and on the **entity's internal control**. Also, be aware that there are basically three levels of audits involved here: (1) GAAS, (2) GAAS + GAS, and (3) GAAS + GAS + Specific requirements (e.g., Single Audit Act, Circular A-133 on audits of institutions of higher education).

Section A of the outline summarizes how the illegal act provisions of AU 317 apply to audits of financial statements of governmental entities and other entities that receive governmental financial assistance. Section B provides guidance on financial audits in accordance with GAS. Section C addresses the scope and reporting requirement of an audit of a recipient of federal financial assistance. Section D addresses auditor communications with management if the auditor becomes aware that the entity is subject to an audit requirement that may not be encompassed in the terms of the audit engagement.

**A.** Effects of laws on financial statements
1. The GASB recognizes that governmental entities are generally subject to a variety of laws and regulations (hereafter, laws) that affect their financial statements
2. Governmental entities may provide financial assistance to other entities
   a. By accepting such assistance, both governmental and nongovernmental entities may be subject to laws that may have a direct and material effect on the financial statements
   b. The auditor's responsibility for testing and reporting on compliance with laws varies according to the terms of the engagement
3. The auditor should design the audit to provide reasonable assurance that the financial statements are free of material misstatements resulting from violations of laws that have a direct and material effect on financial statement amounts
4. The auditor should consider performing the following procedures in assessing compliance with laws:
   a. Consider knowledge obtained on laws from prior years' audits
   b. Discuss laws with the chief financial officer, legal counsel, and/or grant administrators
   c. Obtain written representation from management regarding the completeness of management's identification
   d. Review relevant portions of directly related agreements
   e. Review minutes of meetings of legislative bodies and the governing board of the entity being audited
   f. Inquire of the appropriate audit oversight organization about applicable laws
   g. Review information about compliance requirements such as *Compliance Supplement for Single Audits of State and Local Governments* (issued by the Office of Management and Budget)

**B.** Government Auditing Standards (GAS)
1. GAS contains standards for the audit of government organizations, programs, activities, etc.
   a. Those standards include designing the audit to provide reasonable assurance of detecting material misstatements with a direct and material effect on financial statement amounts
2. GAS prescribes fieldwork and reporting standards beyond those required by GAAS
3. The general standards of GAS relate to qualifications of the staff, independence, due professional care, and quality control

**C.** Federal audit requirements
1. Although requirements for the audit of a recipient of federal financial assistance vary, they generally include the following elements
   a. Audit conducted in accordance with GAAS and GAS
   b. Consideration of internal control
   c. Report on consideration of internal control
   d. Report on whether federal financial assistance has been administered in accordance with applicable laws
2. A recipient of federal financial assistance may be subject to either (1) a single (or organization-wide) audit or (b) a program-specific audit
   a. The auditor should determine which is desired (or required)
   b. Both generally require consideration of internal control beyond what is normally required by GAAS or GAS

3. The compliance requirements applicable to federal financial assistance programs are generally of two types: general or specific
   a. Specific requirements apply to a particular federal program
   b. For program-specific audits, the auditor should consult federal grantor agency audit guides to identify general requirements
   c. Generally, the auditor is required to determine whether the recipient has complied with general and specific requirements
   d. In evaluating compliance the auditor should consider the effect of identified instances of non-compliance on each program, including
      (1) The frequency of noncompliance
      (2) The adequacy of the recipient's system for monitoring subrecipients
      (3) Whether any noncompliance resulted in questioned costs
         (a) The auditor makes an estimate of the total costs questioned (referred to as "likely questioned costs")
         (b) An auditor should consider whether identified instances of noncompliance affect his/her opinion on the financial statements
**D.** Communications regarding applicable audit requirements
   1. GAAS do not require the auditor to perform procedures beyond those s/he considers necessary to obtain sufficient competent evidential matter to form an opinion on the financial statements
   2. If an auditor determines during a GAAS audit that additional audit requirements exist beyond those agreed to, s/he should communicate this fact to management and the audit committee
      a. This communication may be oral or written

## 901 Public Warehouses—Controls and Procedures for Goods Held
*Overall Objectives and Approach*—This section, from which relatively few exam questions have been asked, presents guidance on auditing a public warehouse and its internal control. Concerning the auditing of a public warehouse, a CPA should

1. Obtain an understanding of internal control relating to accountability and custody over goods and perform tests of controls to evaluate their effectiveness
2. Test the warehouseman's records for goods placed in warehouse
3. Test the warehouseman's system of receipts (a receipt is provided to entity that stores goods in the warehouse)
4. Observe physical counts of goods in the warehouse and reconcile them to the records
5. To the extent considered necessary, confirm with holders of warehouse receipts (the entities that store the goods in the warehouse)

See Section C of the internal control module for guidance on internal control over inventories; see part B of the outline of AU 331 for procedures relating to auditing inventories held in public warehouses.

## STANDARDS OF THE PUBLIC COMPANY ACCOUNTING OVERSIGHT BOARD

*Overview.* The Public Company Accounting Oversight Board issues its own series of Standards. At this point they have not been codified.

### PCAOB Auditing Standard No. 1 (and related reporting guidance)—References in Auditors' Reports to the Standards of the PCAOB
*Overall Objectives and Approach*—This very brief statement requires auditors to refer to standards of the Public Company Accounting Oversight Board (rather than to generally accepted auditing standards) in their reports on audits of public companies.

**A.** Auditors' reports for audits of public company financial statements
   1. The PCAOB adopted as interim standards, the AICPA Statements on Auditing Standards and other auditing guidance
   2. The financial statement audit report for a public client
      a. Refers to "standards of Public Company Accounting Oversight Board (United States)" rather than to generally accepted auditing standards
      b. Has a title of "Report of Independent Registered Public Accounting Firm"

      c.  Includes a paragraph referring to the auditor's report on internal control (this requirement was added subsequent to passage of Standard 1)

      d.  Includes the city and state (or country) in which the report was issued

  3.  For reports on interim financial statements

      a.  Refers to "standards of the Public Company Accounting Oversight Board (United States) rather than standards of the AICPA

      b.  Has a title of "Report of Independent Registered Public Accounting Firm"

      c.  Includes the city and state (or country in which the report was issued

**B.**  Sample audit report for financial statements

### Report of Independent Registered Public Accounting Firm

We have audited the accompanying balance sheets of X Company as of December 31, 20X3 and 20X2, and the related statements of operations, stockholders' equity, and cash flows for each of the three years in the period ended December 31, 20X3. These financial statements are the responsibility of the Company's management. Our responsibility is to express an opinion on these financial statements based on our audits.

We conducted our audits in accordance with the standards of the Public Company Accounting Oversight Board (United States). Those standards require that we plan and perform the audit to obtain reasonable assurance about whether the financial statements are free of material misstatement. An audit includes examining, on a test basis, evidence supporting the amounts and disclosures in the financial statements. An audit also includes assessing the accounting principles used and significant estimates made by management, as well as evaluating the overall financial statement presentation. We believe that our audits provide a reasonable basis for our opinion.

In our opinion, the financial statements referred to above present fairly, in all material respects, the financial position of the Company as of [at] December 31, 20X3, and 20X2, and the results of its operations and its cash flows for each of the three years in the period ended December 31, 20X3, in conformity with US generally accepted accounting principles.

We also have audited, in accordance with the standards of the Public Company Accounting Oversight Board (United States), the effectiveness of X Company's internal control over financial reporting as of December 31, 20X3, based on criteria established in Internal Control–Integrated Framework issued by the Committee of Sponsoring Organizations of the Treadway Commission and our report dated February 24, 20X4, expressed an unqualified opinion thereon.

    [Signature]
    [City and State or Country]
    [Date]

## PCAOB Auditing Standard No. 2—An Audit of Internal Control over Financial Reporting Performed in Conjunction with an Audit of Financial Statements

*Overall Objectives and Approach*—Sections 103 and 404 of the Sarbanes-Oxley Act establish requirements that (1) management must annually assess and report on the company's internal control over financial reporting, and (2) the auditor must provide an opinion both on management's assessment and on internal control itself. PCAOB Standard 2 provides guidance for auditing public companies' internal control over financial reporting (hereafter, internal control or IC) in conjunction with an audit of the financial statements (i.e., an "integrated audit"). Specifically, the standard requires the auditor to examine the design and operating effectiveness of IC to provide a sufficient basis to provide an opinion on its effectiveness in preventing or detecting material misstatements of the financial statements. We have integrated the outline of Standard. 2 into Module 2, Internal Control, as Section C.

## PCAOB Standard No. 3—Audit Documentation

*Overall Objectives and Approach*—This standard establishes general guidelines for audit documentation (working papers) that the auditor should prepare and retain in connection with engagements under the PCAOB standards—audits of financial statements, audits of internal control over financial reporting, and reviews of interim financial information.

**A.**  General

  1.  **Audit documentation**—the written record of the basis for the auditor's conclusion that provides the support for the auditor's representations, whether those representations are contained in the auditor's report or otherwise

      a.  Audit documentation also facilitates planning, performance and supervision of the engagement.

      b.  It is the basis for the review of the quality of the work because it provides the reviewer with written documentation of the evidence supporting the auditor's significant conclusions

  2.  Audit documentation should

      a.  Demonstrate that the engagement complied with PCAOB standards

      b.  Support the auditor's conclusions for every relevant financial statement assertion

      c.  Demonstrate that the underlying accounting records agree or reconcile with the financial statements

  3.  Audit documentation must contain sufficient information to enable an *experienced auditor* having no previous connection with the engagement to

      a.  Understand the nature, timing, extent, and results of the procedures performed, evidence obtained and conclusions reached

      b.  Determine who performed the work, the date such work was completed, the person who reviewed the work, and the date of such review

**B.** The Standard also contains the following specific documentation requirements:

  1.  Documentation must make it possible to identify the items examined by the auditor in areas such as the inspection of documents, confirmation, tests of details, tests of operating effectiveness of controls, and walk-throughs

  2.  Significant findings or issues must be documented, including

      a.  Significant matters involving accounting principles

      b.  Results of auditing procedures that indicate (1) the need to modify planned auditing procedures, (2) the existence of material misstatements, (3) omissions in the financial statements, or (4) the existence of significant deficiencies or material weaknesses in internal control over financial reporting

      c.  Audit adjustments

      d.  Disagreements among members of the engagement team or others consulted about final conclusions reached on significant accounting or auditing matters

      e.  Circumstances causing difficulty in applying auditing procedures

      f.  Significant changes in the assessed level of audit risk

      g.  Any matters that could result in modification of the auditor's report

      The above information should be included in an *engagement completion document*

  3.  In addition, the auditor must obtain, review, and retain information from other auditors that are involved in the audit

**C.** Retention of and subsequent changes to audit documentation

  1.  Important dates

      a.  **Report release date**—the date the auditor grants permission to use the auditor's report. On this date the auditor has

          (1)  Completed all necessary auditing procedures, including clearing review notes and providing support for all final conclusions

          (2)  Obtained sufficient evidence to support the representations in the auditor's report

      b.  **Documentation completion date**—Not more than 45 days after the report release date

  2.  Audit documentation requirements

      a.  Should be retained for 7 years from the report release date, unless a longer period of time is required by law

      b.  No deletions or discarding after the documentation completion date, but information may be added (indicating date added, name of person who prepared the additional documentation and the reason for adding it)

      c.  Audit documentation related to the work of other auditors should also be retained

      d.  If after the documentation completion date the auditor becomes aware that documentation of necessary audit procedures is lacking, the auditor should investigate whether sufficient procedures were performed

          (1)  If "yes," the auditor should consider what additional documentation is needed and add that documentation

          (2)  If the auditor is unable to determine whether sufficient procedures were performed, the auditor should comply with AU 390 (consideration of omitted procedures)

## GOVERNMENT AUDITING STANDARDS
### (Issued by the Comptroller General of the United States, General Accounting Office)

*Background*—In 1994, the Comptroller General of the United States issued a revision of *Government Auditing Standards*, also referred to as the "yellow book." These "generally accepted government auditing standards" (GAGAS) are broad statements of auditors' responsibilities. When studying this information also review the outline of AU 801 on auditing requirements in this area. In this outline we present a brief outline of the information as follows: (a) financial audits, and (b) performance audits.

**A.** Financial audits
1. Two types
   a. **Financial statement audits**—Provide reasonable assurance about whether statements follow GAAP (or other basis of accounting)
   b. **Financial related audits**—Determine whether the entity
      (1) Presented financial information in accordance with established criteria
      (2) Adhered to financial compliance requirements and
      (3) Designed and implemented suitable internal control over financial reporting and/or safeguarding assets to achieve the control objectives
      *Examples of financial related audits:* Segments of financial statements, statements of fixed assets, budget requests.
2. General requirements
   a. Staff should collectively possess adequate professional proficiency (e.g., must complete eighty hours of CPE every two years)
   b. Independence
   c. Due professional care
   d. Appropriate quality control system
3. Fieldwork standards—AICPA fieldwork standards apply (planning, internal control, evidence); plus
   a. Auditors should follow up on known material findings and recommendations from previous audits
   b. Auditors may set lower materiality levels than for audits in the private sector
   c. Auditors should design audit to provide reasonable assurance of detecting material misstatements resulting from noncompliance with provision of contracts or grant agreements that have a direct and material effect on financial statement amounts
   d. Working papers should contain sufficient information to enable an experienced auditor having no previous connection with the audit to ascertain that evidence supports the auditor's significant conclusions and judgments
4. Reporting requirements—**AICPA** reporting standards (**GODC**), plus
   a. The audit committee (or contracting party) must be informed about auditors' responsibilities to report on internal control and compliance
   b. **Audit report** should
      (1) State that audit was made in accordance with GAGAS
      (2) Describe scope of testing of compliance with laws and internal control and present results of those tests *or* refer to separate reports containing that information
   c. **Report on compliance**—Written report (unless included in b. above) on fraud and illegal acts unless they are clearly inconsequential and any other material noncompliance with contract provisions
   d. **Report on internal control**—Written report (unless included in b. above) with all "reportable conditions"
   e. Reports are available to the audited entity and the organization that required the audit; unless restricted by law or regulation, reports are available for public inspection
**B.** Performance audits
1. Two types
   a. **Economy and efficiency audits** (of an entity) include
      (1) Whether entity acquires, protects, and uses resources economically and efficiently
      (2) Causes of inefficiencies or uneconomic practices
      (3) Compliance with laws and regulations
   b. **Program audits** to determine
      (1) Whether desired benefits being achieved
      (2) Effectiveness
      (3) Compliance with laws and regulations on matters of economy and efficiency
   c. A performance audit is an objective and systematic examination of evidence for the purpose of providing an independent assessment of the performance of a governmental organization, pro-

gram, activity or function in order to provide information to improve public accountability and facilitate decision making by parties with responsibilities to oversee or initiate corrective action

2. General standards—same as for financial audits (see A.2. above)
3. Fieldwork standards
   a. Work adequately planned
   b. Work properly supervised
   c. Work planned to provide reasonable assurance on compliance with laws
   d. Auditor should obtain understanding of *management controls* that are relevant to the audit

   *NOTE: The term management controls is used for performance audits instead of internal control.*

   e. Sufficient competent and relevant evidence is to be obtained and working papers should contain information to enable an experienced auditor with no previous connection with the audit to ascertain that adequate evidence exists to support auditors' conclusions and judgments
4. Reporting standards—similar to financial audits

## STATEMENTS ON STANDARDS FOR ACCOUNTING AND REVIEW SERVICES

*Overview.* The following table summarized the various types of guidance available relating to accounting review services as well as the authority:

| *Category* | *Guidance* | *Authority* |
| --- | --- | --- |
| *Standards* | • Statement on Standards for Accounting and Review Services (SSARS) | The performance and reporting standards for compilations and reviews |
| *Interpretative publications* | • SSARS interpretations<br>• Appendixes to SSARS<br>• Review guidance in *AICPA Audit and Accounting Guides*<br>• AICPA *Statements of Position* | Recommendations on application of SSARS, but not standards |
| *Other compilation and review publications* | • AICPA annual *Compilation and Review Alert*<br>• Articles in *Journal of Accountancy* and other professional journals<br>• AICPA *CPA letter*<br>• Continuing Education programs<br>• Texts, guide books<br>• Compilation and review programs<br>• Other | No authoritative status, but may help the accountant to understand and apply the SSARS |

The following table outlines emphasize the standards as represented by the Statement on Standards for Accounting and Review Services (SSARS), since it is from the SSARS that almost all of the CPA exam questions have arisen. The SSARS have been codified as follows:

| *Section* | *Title* |
| --- | --- |
| AR 100 | Compilation and Review of Financial Statements |
| AR 200 | Reporting on Comparative Financial Statements |
| AR 300 | Compilation Reports on Financial Statements Included in Certain Prescribed Forms |
| AR 400 | Communications between Predecessor and Successor Accountants |
| AR 500 | Reporting on Compiled Financial Statements |
| AR 600 | Reporting on Personal Financial Statements Included in Written Personal Financial Plans |

### AR 100 Compilation and Review of Financial Statements (SSARS 1, 8, and 10)

*Overall Objectives and Approach*—This section presents guidance on appropriate procedures and reporting for **compilation** and **review** engagements of **nonpublic** entity financial statements. In general terms, a nonpublic entity is one whose securities are not traded in a public market; related, an entity which is in the process of registering securities for sale to the public, or is a subsidiary, joint venture, etc. of a public entity, does **not** qualify as a nonpublic entity.

Important to the section is the concept of "**submitting financial statements,**" defined as presenting to a client or third parties financial statements that the accountant has prepared either manually or through the use of computer software. A CPA should not submit unaudited financial statements of a nonpublic entity unless he or she, at a minimum, performs a compilation. While performing a compilation is the minimum service, issuance of a compilation report is only required when third-party reliance upon the compiled financial statements is reasonably expected.

Although performance of a compilation is the minimum requirement for submitting financial statements, services such as the following do **not** result in submission and accordingly may be performed without meeting the requirements included in this section:

- Simply reading or typing client-prepared financial statements,
- Preparing a working trial balance,
- Proposing adjusting or correcting entries or
- Providing a client with a financial statement format that does not include amounts.

A CPA should not consent to the use of his/her name in a document containing unaudited financial statements unless he or she has compiled or reviewed the financial statements, or the financial statements are accompanied by an indication that the accountant has not compiled or reviewed the financial statements and assumes no responsibility for them (e.g., "The accompanying [list the financial statements] were not audited, reviewed, or compiled by us and, accordingly, we do not express an opinion or any other from of assurance on them.")

The introduction to the auditing modules (immediately preceding the Engagement Planning Module) presents a discussion of the nature of the attest function and explains that compilations are an accounting service, while reviews are an attest engagement. For that reason, compilation reports provide no explicit assurance with respect to the financial statements, while reviews provide limited (negative) assurance.

The outline is organized as follows: (a) compilations, (b) reviews, (c) information relevant to both compilations and reviews.

**A.** Compilation of financial statements
1. Definition of a compilation—Presenting in the form of financial statements information that is the representation of management (owners) without undertaking to express any assurance on the statements
2. Compilation performance requirements
   a. Accountant should understand the accounting principles and practices of the industry in which the entity operates

      NOTE: *This knowledge is normally obtained through experience, AICPA guides, industry publications, financial statements of other entities in the industry, textbooks, periodicals, or individuals knowledgeable about the industry.*

   b. The accountant should understand the following relating to the entity's business
      (1) Nature of transactions
      (2) Form of accounting records
      (3) Stated qualifications of accounting personnel
      (4) Accounting basis on which financial statements are presented
      (5) Form and content of the financial statements

      NOTE: *This knowledge is normally obtained through experience with the entity or inquiry of the entity's personnel.*

   c. The accountant **is not required** to make any inquiries or perform any other verification procedures
   d. Before submitting financial statements, the accountant should read the compiled statements and consider whether such financial statements appear to be appropriate in form and free from obvious misstatements
3. A compilation report should be dated as of the date of the completion of the compilation, signed in the name of the firm, and should state that
   a. A compilation has been performed in accordance with Statements on Standards for Accounting and Review Services issued by the AICPA
   b. A compilation is limited to presenting in the form of financial statements information that is the representation of management (owners)
   c. The financial statements have not been audited or reviewed, and accordingly, the accountant does not express an opinion or any other form of assurance on them
4. Other reporting requirements for compilations
   a. Any procedures performed by the accountant should **not** be described in the accountant's report
   b. Date of report—date of completion of the compilation

    c.  Each page of statements should be marked "See Accountant's Compilation Report"

    d.  A report may be issued on one of the financial statements (e.g., submit only a balance sheet), if so requested

    e.  Assuming no intent by management to mislead users, the financial statements may omit notes to financial statements if the lack is clearly indicated in a separate paragraph added to the compilation report

> EXAMPLE PARAGRAPH:
> Management has elected to omit substantially all of the disclosures (and the statement of cash flows) required by generally accepted accounting principles. If the omitted disclosures were included in the financial statements, they might influence the user's conclusions about the company's financial position, results of operations, and cash flows. Accordingly, these financial statements are not designed for those who are not informed about such matters.

    f.  If limited note disclosures are provided, the accountant should make certain that they are labeled "Selection Information—Substantially All Disclosures Required by GAAP Are Not Included"

    g.  If the accountant is not independent, add the following paragraph to the compilation report—I am not independent with respect to XYZ Company
        (1)  Do not describe reason for lack of independence

> NOTE: Because compilations are accounting and not attestation services, independence is not required.

    h.  If compiled financial statements are not expected to be used by a third party, a written communication is required—**either** (1) a compilation report, or (2) documentation of an understanding through the use of an engagement letter, preferably signed by management, or both
        (1)  Documentation of understanding through an engagement letter
            (a)  Nature and limitations of services
            (b)  A compilation is limited to presenting in the form of financial statements information that is the representation of management
            (c)  Financial statements will not be audited or reviewed
            (d)  No opinion or any other form of assurance provided
            (e)  Management has knowledge of the nature of procedures applied and basis of accounting and assumptions used in preparation of financial statements
            (f)  Acknowledgement of management's representation and agreement that the financial statements are not to be used by third parties
            (g)  Engagement cannot be relied on to disclose errors, fraud or illegal acts

    i.  Each page of financial statements should have a restriction such as "Restricted for Management's Use Only" or "Solely for the information and use of the management of XYZ and not intended to be and should not be used by any other party"
        (1)  The accountant may rely on management's representation that the information will not be used by other parties without further inquiry, unless information contradicting management's representation comes to the accountant's attention
        (2)  If the accountant becomes aware that financial statements have been distributed to third parties, he or she should discuss the matter with client and request that client have statements returned
            (a)  If client does not comply, notify known third parties that the information is not intended for third-party use
            (b)  Consult with attorney

**B.**  Review of financial statements
    1.  Definition—a **review** involves performing **inquiry** and **analytical procedures** that provide the accountant with a reasonable basis for expressing limited assurance that there are no material modifications that should be made to the statements for them to be in conformity with GAAP, or if applicable, with another comprehensive basis of accounting
    2.  Requirements relating to performing a review
      a.  The accountant **needs sufficient knowledge of the client industry and client company** to perform inquiry and analytical procedures to provide a reasonable basis for expressing limited assurance on the statements

> NOTE: Industry knowledge may be obtained from AICPA guides, industry publications, financial statements of other entities in the industry, textbooks, periodicals, or individuals knowledgeable about the industry. The knowledge of the entity's business should include a general understanding of the entity's organization, its operating characteristics, and

*the nature of its assets, liabilities, revenues, and expenses; this knowledge is ordinarily obtained through experience with the entity or its industry and inquiry of the entity's personnel.*

3. Analytical procedures—the accountant should apply analytical procedures to the financial statements to identify and provide a basis for inquiry about the relationships and individual items that appear to be unusual and that may indicate a material misstatement
   a. Analytical procedures should include
      (1) Developing expectations by identifying plausible relationships that are expected to exist based on accountant's understanding of entity and industry
      (2) Comparing recorded amounts or ratios to expectations
         (a) Expectations developed for a review are ordinarily less encompassing than those for an audit
         (b) In a review the accountant is ordinarily not required to corroborate management's responses, although the accountant should consider those responses for reasonableness and consistency with other information
   b. Inquiries and other procedures—the accountant should consider the following:
      (1) Inquiries of management with financial/accounting responsibility
         (a) Whether financial statements prepared following GAAP
         (b) Accounting principles followed
         (c) Unusual or complex situations that might affect financial statements
         (d) Significant transactions near end of reporting period
         (e) Status of uncorrected misstatement identified during previous engagement
         (f) Questions arising in course of applying review procedures
         (g) Subsequent events
         (h) Significant journal entries and other adjustments
         (i) Communications from regulatory agencies
      (2) Inquiries concerning actions taken at meetings (shareholder, board of directors, committees of directors, or comparable meetings) that may affect financial statements
      (3) Read the financial statements to consider, on basis of information coming to accountant's attention, whether statements appear to conform to GAAP
      (4) Obtain reports from other accountants if any, which have audited or reviewed significant components of reporting entity
   c. Management representations—a representation letter is required for all financial statements and periods covered by review report (e.g., if two-year comparative statements are presented, representations should be obtained for both years); specific representations should relate to the following:
      (1) Management responsible for financial statements being in conformity with GAAP
      (2) Management believes financial statements present fairly in conformity with GAAP
      (3) Management acknowledges responsibility to prevent and detect fraud
      (4) Knowledge of any fraud or suspected fraud by management or material fraud by others
      (5) Management's full and truthful response to all inquiries
      (6) Completeness of information
      (7) Information on subsequent events

   *NOTE: The representation letter should be tailored to include additional appropriate representations from management relating the business and industry.*

   d. Details related to management's representations
      (1) Addressed to the accountant
      (2) Dated no earlier than the accountant's report
      (3) Signed by management members responsible for and knowledgeable directly or through others in the organization about the matters in the representation letter
         (a) This is the chief executive officer and chief financial officer or others with equivalent positions
         (b) If current management was not present during all periods covered by the accountant's report, the accountant still should get representations from current management for all periods

4. Documentation—the principle record of review procedures performed and conclusions reached by the accountant
   a. Other support for review report may include
      (1) Written documentation in other engagement files (e.g., compilation files)
      (2) Quality control files (e.g., consultation files)
      (3) Oral explanations, but they should be limited to those situations where the accountant finds it necessary to supplement or clarify information contained in the documentation
         (a) Oral explanations should not be the principal support for the work performed or the conclusions reached
   b. Documentation of inquiry and analytical procedures should include
      (1) Matters covered by accountant's inquiry procedures
      (2) Analytical procedures performed
      (3) Expectations formed related to analytical procedures (see B.3.a.(1) above)
      (4) Results of comparisons of expectations to recorded amounts or ratios
      (5) Any additional procedures performed in response to significant unexpected differences arising from analytical procedures and other procedures
      (6) Unusual matters considered during performance of review procedures, including disposition
      (7) Representation letter
5. A review report should be dated as of the completion of the review procedures, signed in the name of the firm, and should state that
   a. A review was performed in accordance with Statements of Standards for Accounting and Review Services issued by the AICPA
   b. All information included in the financial statements is the representation of the management (owners) of the entity
   c. A review consists principally of inquiries of company personnel and analytical procedures applied to financial data
   d. A review is substantially less in scope than an audit, the objective of which is the expression of an opinion regarding the financial statements taken as a whole and, accordingly, no such opinion is expressed
   e. The accountant is not aware of any material modifications that should be made to the financial statements in order for them to be in conformity with GAAP, other than those modifications, if any, indicated in his/her report

   NOTE: *Know the above five elements of a review report. Also know that the first two elements are in the report's first paragraph, the second two in the second paragraph; the last one is in the third paragraph.*

6. Other overall reporting requirements for reviews
   a. Any other procedures performed by the accountant should **not** be described
   b. The date of the report should be the date of completion of the procedures
   c. Each page of the statements should be marked "See Accountant's Review Report"
   d. A separate paragraph is used for modifying the standard report
C. Information relevant to both compilations and reviews
   1. Departures from GAAP should be treated as follows
      a. The client should be asked to revise the statements to comply with GAAP
      b. **If the information is not revised,** the report should be modified
         (1) Modify the final standard paragraph of the report to indicate that a misstatement has been discovered and add an additional paragraph which follows describing the departure (including its effect **if** management has calculated it)
      c. If the accountant believes that modification of the standard report is not adequate to indicate the financial statement deficiencies taken as a whole, the accountant should withdraw from the engagement and provide no further services with respect to those financial statements
         (1) The accountant may wish to consult with legal counsel in those circumstances

   NOTE: *Recall that for compilations, when note disclosures are omitted, the accountant can modify the compilation report to so cite their omission (see Sections A.4.e. and A.4.f. above). For reviews (as well as audits), such omissions are treated as departures from GAAP which will lead to reports which are other than unqualified.*

2. Subsequent discovery of facts existing at the date of the report
    a. Consult AU 561 (see outline)
    b. Consult with an attorney
3. Supplementary information
    a. The accountant should clearly indicate any responsibility being taken for the supplementary data

NOTE: *If you do not recall the nature of supplementary information (e.g., quarterly information included in the annual report) see the outline of AU 553.*

     b. When the accountant has compiled the financial statements and other data, the compilation report should also include the other data
     c. When the accountant has reviewed the financial statements, the report (or a separate report) should state that
        (1) The review has been made primarily to express limited assurance that there are no material modifications that should be made to the financial statements
        (2) The other information is presented only for supplementary analysis purposes and either
           (a) Has been subject to inquiry and analytical procedures, and the accountant did not become aware of any material misstatements, or
           (b) Has **not** been subjected to the inquiry and analytical procedures and the accountant does not express an opinion or any other form of assurance on such data

4. When an accountant has been engaged to audit financial statements, the client may request a change either to a review or compilation of financial statements due either to a misunderstanding of the nature of an audit or to a scope restriction
    a. Before agreeing to the change, the accountant should consider
       (1) The reason for the change
       (2) Additional audit effort to complete audit
       (3) Estimated additional cost to complete audit
    b. A change due to a misunderstanding of the nature of an audit is ordinarily a reasonable basis for requesting the change
    c. For scope limitations
       (1) Client imposed such as inability to communicate with legal counsel or management refusal to sign representation letter—the accountant is ordinarily precluded from issuing a review or compilation report
       (2) For all scope limitations the accountant should evaluate the possibility that the information involved is incorrect
    d. If the accountant concludes there is reasonable justification for the change s/he should issue the appropriate review or compilation report with **no reference** to the original engagement, auditing procedures performed, or the scope limitation

**AR 200 Reporting on Comparative Financial Statements (SSARS 2)***Overall Objectives and Approach—*
This section presents guidance for reporting on comparative statements of a nonpublic entity, at least a portion of which are not audited (i.e., one or more years is compiled or reviewed). The existence of compiled, reviewed, and audited financial statements, as well as financial statements with which the auditor has had no association, presents a situation in which there are numerous implementation issues related to compiled statements. For example, perhaps the first year's statements have been reviewed, and the second year's compiled.

This section presents and resolves an overwhelming number of situations which may occur in practice. In the outline we attempt to provide information on the most frequent cases which one would expect to see on the CPA exam. You should be aware that several questions on the exam have required candidates either to prepare or to critique comparative reports of this nature.

The outline provides (a) overall guidance as well as (b) enumerating important situations.

**A.** Overall guidance
1. The accountant's report should cover each period presented as a comparative statement
    a. An entity may include financial information with which the accountant is not associated (e.g., last year's statements) in a report that also includes information with which the accountant is associated (e.g., this year's compiled or reviewed statements)

(1) When the information is presented on separate pages, the information should clearly indicate that the accountant is not associated

(2) The accountant should not allow his/her name to be associated with such financial statements (i.e., the year which s/he is not associated) that are presented in columnar form with financial statements on which s/he has reported

    (a) If the entity still intends to use the accountant's name, the accountant should consult with his/her attorney

2. When compiled statements of one year omit most of the disclosures required per GAAP (e.g., do not include footnotes) they should not be presented with another year's which do have such disclosures, and the accountant should **not** issue a report on such comparative statements

3. Each page of comparative financial statements compiled or reviewed by an accountant should include a reference such as "See Accountant's Report"

4. The following is general guidance on the overall form of comparative reports

   a. When both years have been compiled or reviewed, the report uses the standard form, modified to include both years

   b. A continuing accountant who performs the same or a **higher level of service** with respect to financial statements of the current period (e.g., review this year, compilation last year) should update his/her report on the financial statements of a prior period presented with those of the current period

> *EXAMPLE: Issue a standard review report supplemented with the following paragraph:*
>
> *The accompanying 20X1 financial statements of XYZ were compiled by me. A compilation is limited to representing in the form of financial statements information that is the representation of management. I have not audited or reviewed the 20X1 financial statements and accordingly, do not express an opinion or any other form of assurance on them.*

   c. A continuing accountant who performs a **lower level of service** with respect to the financial statements of the current period (e.g., compilation this year, review last year) should either

     (1) Include a separate paragraph in his/her report with a description of the responsibility assumed for the prior period statements or

     (2) Reissue his/her report on the financial statements of the prior period

> *EXAMPLES: Approaches (1) and (2)*
> *(1) Issue a compilation report on 20X4 which includes a paragraph summarizing the responsibility assumed for the 20X3 financial statements. The description should include the original date of the review report and should state that no procedures have been performed on the review after that date.*
> *(2) Combine the compilation report on 20X4 with the reissued report on the financial statements of the prior period **or** print them separately. The combined report should state that the accountant has not performed any procedures in connection with that review engagement after the date of the review report.*

**B.** Other situations

1. **Existence of a predecessor auditor**—as is the case with audited financial statements, a decision must be made as to whether the predecessor will reissue his/her compilation or review report

> *NOTE: The situation here is one in which a choice is made as to whether two reports will be associated with the comparative information (20X3 the predecessor's, 20X4 the successor's) **or** one report in which the successor summarizes the predecessor's findings.*

   a. **Reissuance of the predecessor's report**

     (1) The predecessor must determine whether his/her report is appropriate based on

       (a) Current vs. prior period statement format

       (b) Newly discovered subsequent events

       (c) Changes in the financial statements affecting the report

     (2) The predecessor should also perform the following procedures

       (a) Read the current statements and the successor's report

       (b) Compare prior and current statements

       (c) Obtain representation letter from successor suggesting that s/he is not aware of any matters having a material effect on the prior statements

     (3) If anything comes to the predecessor's attention that affects the report, the predecessor should

       (a) Make any necessary inquiries and perform any necessary procedures

         (b) If necessary insist that the client revise the statements and revise the report as appropriate (normally add an explanatory paragraph)

             1] The report will be "dual dated"—see outline of AU 530 on dual dating

    b. No reissuance of predecessor's report (i.e., it is not presented)

      (1) The successor auditor should add a paragraph stating that the

         (a) Prior (comparative) statements were compiled (or reviewed) by another accountant

         (b) Date of the predecessor's report

         (c) Assurance, if any, provided in the predecessor's report

         (d) Reasons for any modification of the predecessor's report

2. **20X3 reviewed (or compiled) and 20X4 audited**—The situation here is similar to above with a predecessor auditor in that the prior years report may be reissued, or a summary of it included in the 20X4 report

3. When an accountant is reporting on financial statements that now omit substantially all disclosures (i.e., notes), which when originally issued did not omit such disclosures, a paragraph is added to the report indicating that the disclosures have been omitted; also, the final paragraph indicates the accountant's prior form of association with the information.

> EXAMPLE: *20X4 has been reviewed, and now, in 20X5, 20X4 statements have been compiled from the previously reviewed statements. A compilation report is issued on 20X5, with a paragraph on the omitted disclosures (see Section A.4.e. above) and with a paragraph on the 20X4 statements such as the following:*
>
> > *The accompanying 20X4 financial statements were compiled by me from financial statements that did not omit substantially all of the disclosures required by generally accepted accounting principles and that I previously reviewed as indicated in my report dated March 1, 20X5.*

4. When a company changes its status (i.e., nonpublic to public, or vice versa) the proper reporting responsibility is determined by the status at the time of reporting

## AR 300 Compilation Reports on Financial Statements Included in Certain Prescribed Forms (SSARS 3)

***Overall Objectives and Approach***—This section presents guidance on issuing compilation reports related to information presented on prescribed forms, designed by the bodies with which they filed (e.g., governmental bodies, trade associations, banks). For example, assume that a state governmental body has a balance sheet form which all companies incorporated in that state are required to fill out with appropriate financial information. Also, assume that the state requires that a compilation report be filed with the report. This section deals with the manner in which the auditor should report on such forms. This section also relates directly to the material presented in AU 623, special reports, on prescribed forms (in that section some form of association other than compilation for a nonpublic entity is assumed). The following outline provides general guidance on the report issued.

**A.** General guidance on compilation reports for prescribed forms

    1. An overall presumption is made that the form is sufficient to meet the needs of the body which has designed or adopted it

    2. Departures from GAAP

      a. **Required to appropriately complete the form**—There is **no need** to advise such bodies of this type of departure

> EXAMPLE: *If, because of the requirements of the form, inventory is included on the form at cost, rather than the lower of cost and market, no indication would be provided that this departure from GAAP existed.*

      b. **Other departures**—Indicate in second paragraph and add a final paragraph

    3. Departures from the requirements of the prescribed form—treat in the same manner as 2.b. above

    4. When a prescribed form does not conform to the guidance provided in either AR 100 or AR 300, the accountant should not sign it, but should append an appropriate report to the prescribed form

## AR 400 Communications between Predecessor and Successor Accountants (SSARS 4)

***Overall Objectives and Approach***—This section presents guidance for situations in which a successor accountant **decides to communicate** with a predecessor accountant concerning acceptance of a compilation or a review engagement of a nonpublic entity; such communication is **not** required.

The guidance provided is similar to that in AU 315, which requires such communication prior to accepting an **audit**. As is the case with that section, inquiries of a predecessor may occur: (a) in conjunction with acceptance of the engagement, and (b) other inquiries, subsequent to acceptance of the engagement. The section also provides guidance for situations in which the successor becomes aware of information indicating the need for revision of the statements with which the predecessor is associated.

**A.** Inquiries in conjunction with accepting an engagement

 1. Circumstances in which a successor might choose to communicate

  a. Information concerning client, principals, and management is limited or appears to be in need of special attention

  b. Change in accountants occurs substantially after end of period for which financial statements are to be compiled or reviewed

  c. There have been frequent changes in accountants

 2. An accountant may not disclose confidential information without consent of client

  a. Except as permitted by AICPA Code of Conduct

  b. Successor accountant should request client to

   (1) Permit him/her to make inquiries

   (2) Authorize predecessor to respond completely

  c. If client refuses to comply with request for inquiry, accountant should consider reasons for, and implications of, such denial as they relate to accepting the engagement

 3. May be oral or written and typically would include requests for information on

  a. Matters which might affect the integrity of management (owners)

  b. Disagreement about accounting principles or necessity of certain procedures

  c. If necessary, cooperation of management (owners) in providing additional or revised information

  d. Predecessor's understanding of reason for change in accountants

 4. The predecessor should respond promptly and completely to requests made in connection with engagements

  a. If, due to unusual circumstances, response must be limited, accountant should so indicate

   (1) For example, unusual circumstances include pending litigation but do not include unpaid fees

**B.** Other inquiries

 1. May be made before/after acceptance of engagement to facilitate a compilation or review

 2. Might include questions about prior periods' circumstances such as

  a. Deficiencies in underlying financial data

  b. Necessity of performing other accounting services

  c. Areas requiring inordinate amounts of time

 3. May include request for access to predecessor's working papers

  a. Successor should request client authorization

  b. Customary for predecessor to be available for consultation and provide certain of his/her workpapers

  c. Predecessor and successor should agree on which workpapers

   (1) Will be available

   (2) May be copied

  d. Generally, predecessor should provide access to workpapers relating to

   (1) Matters of continuing accounting significance

   (2) Contingencies

  e. Predecessor may refuse for valid business reasons, including but not limited to, unpaid fees

  f. If client is considering several successors

   (1) Predecessor and working papers need not be made available until client names an accountant as successor

  g. Successor should not reference report on work of predecessor in his/her report except when comparative statements are being issued—see outline of AR 200.

**C.** Predecessor accountant's financial statements

 1. If successor becomes aware of information indicating the need for revision of financial statements reported on by predecessor, the successor should

  a. Request that the client inform the predecessor accountant

 2. If the client refuses to inform the predecessor or the successor is not satisfied with the predecessor's actions, the successor should consult his/her attorney

**AR 500 Reporting on Compiled Financial Statements (SSARS 5)**
(This section amends AR 100. The amended paragraphs of SSARS 1 have been revised to reflect changes in SSARS 5.)

**AR 600 Reporting on Personal Financial Statements Included in Written Personal Financial Plans (SSARS 6)**

*Overall Objectives and Approach*—This section provides an exception to the AR 100 requirement that accountants either compile, review, or audit financial statements with which they are associated. The section allows accountant association with unaudited statements included in written personal financial plans prepared by the accountant. The outline presents related details.

**A.** Requirements relating to "unaudited" association with personal financial plans
    1. Financial statements in personal financial plans need not be compiled, reviewed, or audited if
        a. The accountant establishes an understanding (preferably in writing) with the client that statements will be used solely to assist the client and the client's advisors to develop and achieve personal financial goals and objectives
        b. Nothing came to accountant's attention to cause him/her to believe that the financial statements will be used for other purposes
    2. The accountant's report should state that the financial statements
        a. Are for the financial plan,
        b. May be incomplete or contain GAAP departures and should not be used for other purposes, and
        c. Have not been audited, reviewed, or compiled

*Because much of the IT information you need to know for auditing relates to IT systems, we have duplicated the material that appears in Module 39 of the* CPA Examination Review: Regulation *title as a supplement to this volume.*

## INFORMATION TECHNOLOGY

Computers have become the primary means used to process financial accounting information and have resulted in a situation in which auditors must be able to use and understand current information technology. Accordingly, knowledge of information technology implications is included in the Business Environment & Concepts section of the CPA exam. In addition, auditing procedures relating to information technology (IT) are included in the Auditing & Attestation portion of the CPA exam.

Ideally, to effectively reply to technology-related questions, you should have previously studied or worked in computerized business environments. However, if you do not have this background, we believe that the information in this module should prepare you to perform reasonably well on a typical exam. Keep in mind that the review of these materials cannot make you an expert, and a module such as this cannot cover all possible topics related to information technology. However, this material should help you to understand the complexities introduced by computers in sufficient detail to answer most questions.

### Study Program for IT Implications

This module is organized as follows:

A.  Information Systems within a Business

    1.   Definition
    2.   Manual vs. Computer Systems
    3.   General Types of Computer Systems

B.  Characteristics of Computer Systems—General

    1.   Types of Computers, Hardware and Software
    2.   Methods of Processing
    3.   Methods of Data Structure

C.  Characteristics of Computer Systems—Specific

    1.   Types of Networks
    2.   Local Area Networks
    3.   Microcomputers
    4.   End-User Computing
    5.   Electronic Commerce
    6.   Telecommunications
    7.   Computer Service Organizations (Bureaus, Centers)

D.  Effect of IT on Internal Control

    1.   Principles of a reliable system and examples of overall risks
    2.   Control Environment
    3.   Risk Assessment
    4.   Information and Communication
    5.   Monitoring
    6.   Control Activities—Overall
    7.   Computer General Control Activities
    8.   Computer Application Control Activities—Programmed Control Activities
    9.   Application Controls—Manual Follow-Up of Computer Exception Reports
   10.   User Control Activities
   11.   Disaster Recovery

E.  Flowcharting

    1.   Common Flowcharting Symbols
    2.   Types and Definitions
    3.   Other Documentation Charting Techniques

## A. Information Systems within a Business

1. **Definition**—An information system processes data and transactions to provide users with the information they need to plan, control and operate an organization, including

   a. Collecting transaction and other data
   b. Entering it into the information system
   c. Processing the data
   d. Providing users with the information needed
   e. Controlling the process

2. **Manual vs. Computer Systems**

   a. On an overall basis, manual accounting systems have in most circumstances been replaced by computerized accounting information systems of various types, although portions of many systems remain manual.
   b. Computer processing tends to reduce or eliminate processing time

      (1) Computational errors
      (2) Errors in processing routine transactions (when fraud is not involved)

3. **General Types of Computer Systems**

   a. **Transaction processing systems**—Involve the daily processing of transactions (e.g., airplane reservation systems, payroll recording, cash receipts, cash disbursements)
   b. **Management reporting systems**—Designed to help with the decision making process by providing access to computer data

      (1) **Management information systems**—Systems designed to provide past, present and future information for planning, organizing and controlling the operations of the organization
      (2) **Decision support systems**—Computer-based information systems that combine models and data to resolve nonstructured problems with extensive user involvement
      (3) **Expert systems**—Computer systems that apply reasoning methods to data in a specific relatively structured area to render advice or recommendations, much like a human expert
      (4) **Executive information systems**—Computerized systems that are specifically designed to support executive work

   *NOTE: It is helpful to consider these two distinct roles for systems—that is, (a) recording transactions of various types versus (b) providing support for decision making. These topics are discussed in detail under topic B.2. (Methods of Processing).*

## B. Characteristics of Computer Systems—General

1. **Types of Computers, Hardware, and Software**

   a. **Types of computers (in order of size and power)**

      (1) **Supercomputers**—Extremely powerful, high-speed computers used for extremely high-volume and/or complex processing needs
      (2) **Mainframe computers**—Large, powerful, high-speed computers. While less powerful than supercomputers, they are ordinarily more powerful than smaller computers.
      (3) **Minicomputers**—While large and powerful, they are not as large or as powerful as mainframe computers.
      (4) **Microcomputers (e.g., personal computers, laptop computers)**—Small computers, such as those in many homes and businesses
      (5) **Personal digital assistants (PDA)**—Mobile, handheld computers

   b. **Hardware—Physical equipment**

      (1) **Central processing unit (CPU)**—The principal hardware components of a computer. It contains an arithmetic/logic unit, primary memory, and a control unit. The major function of the CPU is to fetch stored instructions and data, decode the instructions, and carry out the instructions.

         (a) **Arithmetic/logic unit**—Performs mathematical operations and logical comparisons

(b) **Primary memory (storage)**—Active data and program steps that are being processed by the CPU. It may be divided into RAM (random-access memory) and ROM (read-only memory). Application programs and data are stored in the RAM at execution time.

(c) **Control unit**—Interprets program instructions and coordinates input, output, and storage devices.

(2) **Secondary storage**

   (a) **Method of access**

      1] **Random**—Accessed directly regardless of how it is physically stored. Disks are random-access devices, although they can also process data sequentially. Also referred to as direct access.

      2] **Sequential**—Data must be processed in the order in which it is physically stored. Magnetic tape is a sequential storage device.

   (b) **Storage devices**

      1] **Magnetic tape (or cartridge)**—Cheapest type of storage available. A primary medium for backing up random-access disk files.

      2] **Magnetic disks**

         a] Those for mainframe computers appear as a stack of CDs, except the space between them includes a read/write head.

         b] Those for microcomputers are referred to as "hard disks" or "hard drives."

      3] **RAID (Redundant array of independent [previously, inexpensive] disks)**—A way of storing the same data redundantly on multiple magnetic disks

         a] When originally recorded, data is written to multiple disks to decrease the likelihood of loss of data.

         b] If a disk fails, at least one of the other disks has the information and continues operation.

      4] **Compact disks**—Small, easily transportable, greater storage capacity than floppy disks

      5] **Floppy disks**—Small, easily transportable

      6] **Zip disks**—Similar to floppy diskettes, but with much greater storage capacity

      7] **Optical disks**—Use laser technology to store and read data

   (c) **Manner in which information is represented in a computer**

      1] **Digital**—A computer that represents information by numerical (binary) digits; computers that process accounting information are ordinarily digital

      2] **Analog**—A computer that represents information by variable quantities; used for research in design where many different shapes and speeds can be tried out quickly (e.g., an analog computer may be used to measure the effects of differing weights on automobile suspension)

   (d) **Related computer terms**

      1] **Online**—Equipment in direct communication with, and under the control of, the CPU

      2] **Off-line**—Equipment not in direct communication with the CPU; the operator generally must intervene to connect off-line equipment or data to the CPU (e.g., mount a magnetic tape of archival data)

      3] **Console**—A terminal used for communication between the operator and the computer (e.g., the operator of a mainframe computer)

      4] **Peripheral equipment**—All non-CPU hardware that may be placed under the control of the central processor. Classified as online or off-line, this equipment consists of input, storage, output, and communication.

      5] **Controllers**—Hardware units designed to operate specific input-output units

      6] **Buffer**—A temporary storage unit used to hold data during computer operations

7] **MIPS**—Millions of instructions per second; a unit for measuring the execution speed of computers

### (3) Input devices

(a) **Keying data**

1] **Key-to-tape** and **key-to-disk** in which data is entered on tapes and disks respectively, and then read into a computer

(b) **Online entry**

1] **Visual display terminal**—Uses keyboard to directly enter data into computer

a] **Input interface**—A program that controls the display for the user (usually on a computer monitor) and that allows the user to interact with the system

b] **Graphical user interface (GUI)** uses icons, pictures, and menus instead of text for inputs (e.g., Windows).

c] **Command line interface**—Uses text-type commands

2] **Mouse, joystick, light pens**—Familiar devices that allow data entry

3] **Touch-sensitive screen**—Allows users to enter data from a menu of items by touching the surface of the monitor

(c) **Turnaround documents**—Documents that are sent to the customer and returned as inputs (e.g., utility bills)

(d) **Automated source data input devices**

1] **Magnetic tape reader**—A device capable of sensing information recorded as magnetic spots on magnetic tape

2] **Magnetic ink character reader (MICR)**—Device that reads characters that have been encoded with a magnetic ink (e.g., bank check readers)

3] **Scanner**—A device that reads characters on printed pages

4] **Automatic teller machine (ATM)**—A machine used to execute and record transactions with financial institutions

5] **Radio frequency data communication**—Using radio waves to directly input data

6] **Point-of-sale (POS) recorders**—Devices that read price and product code data (e.g., recall purchasing groceries—items are frequently passed over a POS recorder).  POS recorders ordinarily function as both a terminal and a cash register.

a] POS processing allows one to record and track customer orders, process credit and debit cards, connect to other systems in a network, and manage inventory.  Generally, a POS terminal has as its core a personal computer, which is provided with application-specific programs and input/output devices for the particular environment in which it will serve.

b] POS terminals are used in most industries that have a point of sale such as a service desk, including restaurants, lodging, entertainment, and museums.  For example, a POS system for a restaurant is likely to have all menu items stored in a database that can be queried for information in a number of ways.

c] Increasingly, POS terminals are also Web-enabled, which makes remote training and operation possible, as well as inventory tracking across geographically dispersed locations.

7] **Voice recognition**—A system that understands spoken words and transmits them into a computer

(e) **Electronic commerce** and **electronic data interchange**—Involves one company's computer communicating with another's computer.  For example, a buyer electronically sending a purchase order to a supplier.  Discussed in further detail in section C.5. of this module.

### (4) Output devices

(a) Many automated source data input devices and electronic commerce/electronic data interchange devices [(3)(d) and (e) above] are capable of outputting data ("writing" in addition to "reading") and therefore become output devices as well as input devices.

(b) **Monitors**—Visually display output

(c) **Printers**—Produce paper output

(d) **Plotters**—Produce paper output of graphs

(e) **Computer output to microfilm or microfiche (COM)**—Makes use of photographic process to store output

c. **Software—Computer programs that control hardware**

(1) **Systems software**

(a) **Operating system**—Manages the input, output, processing and storage devices and operations of a computer (e.g., Windows, Linux, Unix)

  1] Performs scheduling, resource allocation, and data retrieval based on instructions provided in job control language

(b) **Utility programs**—Handle common file, data manipulation and "housekeeping" tasks

(c) **Communications software**—Controls and supports transmission between computers, computers and monitors, and accesses various databases

(2) **Applications software**—Programs designed for specific uses, or "applications," such as

(a) Word processing, graphics, spreadsheets, and database systems

(b) Accounting software

  1] **Low-end**—All in one package, designed for small organizations
  2] **High-end**—Ordinarily in modules (e.g., general ledger, receivables)
  3] **Enterprise Resource Planning (ERP)**—Designed as relatively complete information system "suites" for large and medium size organizations (e.g., human resources, financial applications, manufacturing, distribution). Major vendors are well known—SAP, PeopleSoft, Oracle, BAAN, and J.D. Edwards.

    a] Advantages of ERP systems—Integration of various portions of the information system, direct electronic communication with suppliers and customers
    b] Disadvantages of ERP systems—Complexity, costs, integration with supplier and customer systems may be more difficult than anticipated

(3) **Software terms**

(a) **Compiler**—Produces a machine language object program from a source program language

(b) **Multiprocessing**—Simultaneous execution of two or more tasks, usually by two or more CPUs that are part of the same system

(c) **Multitasking**—The simultaneous processing of several jobs on a computer

(d) **Object program**—The converted source program that was changed using a compiler to create a set of machine readable instructions that the CPU understands

(e) **Source program**—A program written in a language from which statements are translated into machine language; computer programming has developed in "generations"

  1] Machine language (composed of combinations of 1's and 0's that are meaningful to the computer)
  2] Assembly language (e.g., Fortran)
  3] "High-level" programming languages (e.g., C++, Java)

    a] C++ and Java are considered object-oriented programs (OOP) in that they are based on the concept of an "object" which is a data structure that uses a set of routines, called "methods," which operate on the data. The "objects" are efficient in that they often are reusable in other programs.
    b] Object-oriented programs keep together data structures and procedures (methods) through a procedure referred to as encapsulation. Basic to object-oriented pro-

grams are the concepts of a class (a set of objects with similar structures) and inheritance (the ability to create new classes from existing classes).

4] An "application specific" language usually built around database systems. These programs are ordinarily closer to human languages than the first three generations (e.g., an instruction might be *Extract all Customers where "Name" is Jones*).

5] A relatively new and developing form that includes visual or graphical interfaces used to create source language that is usually compiled with a 3rd or 4th language compiler

(f) **Virtual memory (storage)**—Online secondary memory that is used as an extension of primary memory, thus giving the appearance of larger, virtually unlimited internal memory

(g) **Protocol**—Rules determining the required format and methods for transmission of data

(4) **Programming terms**

(a) **Desk checking**—Review of a program by the programmer for errors before the program is run and debugged on the computer

(b) **Debug**—To find and eliminate errors in a computer program. Many compilers assist debugging by listing errors in the program such as invalid commands.

(c) **Edit**—To correct input data prior to processing

(d) **Loop**—A set of program instructions performed repetitively a predetermined number of times, or until all of a particular type of data has been processed

(e) **Memory dump**—A listing of the contents of storage

(f) **Patch**—A section of coding inserted into a program to correct a mistake or to alter a routine

(g) **Run**—A complete cycle of a program including input, processing and output

2. **Methods of Processing**

a. **Batch or online real-time**

(1) **Batch**

(a) Transactions flow through the system in groups of like transactions (batches). For example, all cash receipts on accounts receivable for a day may be aggregated and run as a batch.

(b) Ordinarily leaves a relatively easy-to-follow audit trail

(2) **Online real-time** (also referred to as **direct access processing**)

**General:** Transactions are processed in the order in which they occur, regardless of type. Data files and programs are stored online so that updating can take place as the edited data flows to the application. System security must be in place to restrict access to programs and data to authorized persons. Online systems are often categorized as being either online transaction processing systems or online analytical processing systems.

(a) **Online transaction processing (OLTP)**

1] Databases that support day-to-day operations

2] Examples: airline reservations systems, bank automatic teller systems, and Internet Web site sales systems

(b) **Online analytical processing (OLAP)**

1] A category of software technology that enables the user to query the system (retrieve data), and conduct an analysis, etc., ordinarily while the user is at a PC. The result is generated in seconds. OLAP systems are primarily used for analytical analysis.

> *EXAMPLE: An airline's management downloads its OLTP reservation information into another database to allow analysis of that reservation information. At a minimum, this will allow analysis without tying up the OLTP system that is used on a continuous basis; the restructuring of the data into another database is also likely to make a more detailed analysis possible.*

2] Uses statistical and graphical tools that provide users with various (often multidimensional) views of their data, and allows them to analyze the data in detail

3] These techniques are used as **decision support systems** (computer-based information systems that combine models and data in an attempt to solve relatively unstructured problems with extensive user involvement).

4] One approach to OLAP is to periodically download and combine operational databases into a **data warehouse** (a subject-oriented, integrated collection of data used to support management decision-making processes) or a **data mart** (a data warehouse that is limited in scope).

    a] **Data mining**—Using sophisticated techniques from statistics, artificial intelligence and computer graphics to explain, confirm and explore relationships among data (which is often stored in a data warehouse or data mart)

5] **Artificial intelligence (AI)**—Computer software designed to help humans make decisions. AI may be viewed as an attempt to model aspects of human thought on computers. AI ordinarily deals with decisions that may be made using a relatively structured approach. It frequently involves using a computer to quickly solve a problem that a human could ultimately solve through extremely detailed analysis.

6] **Expert system**—One form of AI. A computerized information system that guides decision processes within a well-defined area and allows decisions comparable to those of an expert. Expert knowledge is modeled into a mathematical system.

> EXAMPLE: *An expert system may be used by a credit card department to authorize credit card purchases so as to minimize fraud and credit losses.*

b. **Centralized, Decentralized, or Distributed**

(1) **Centralized**

    (a) Processing occurs at one location.

    (b) Historically, this is the model used in which a mainframe computer processes data submitted to it through terminals.

    (c) Today, centralized vs. decentralized processing is often a matter of degree—how much is processed by a centralized computer vs. how much by decentralized computers.

(2) **Decentralized**

    (a) Processing (and data) are stored on computers at multiple locations.

    (b) Ordinarily the computers involved are not interconnected by a network, so users at various sites cannot share data.

    (c) May be viewed as a collection of independent databases, rather than a single database.

    (d) End-user computing (topic D.4. below) is relatively decentralized.

(3) **Distributed**

    (a) Transactions for a single database are processed at various sites.

> EXAMPLE: *Payroll is processed for Minneapolis employees in Minneapolis, and for Santa Fe employees in Santa Fe. Yet the overall payroll information is in one database.*

    (b) Processing may be on either a batch or online real-time basis.

    (c) An overall single data base is ordinarily updated for these transactions and available at the various sites.

3. **Methods of Data Structure**

a. **Data organization for computer operations**

(1) **Bit**—A binary digit (0 or 1) which is the smallest storage unit in a computer

(2) **Byte**—A group of adjacent bits (usually 8) that is treated as a single unit by the computer. Alphabetic, special and some numeric characters can be represented by a bit. A numeric character that is used in computations may use more than one byte.

(3) **Character**—A letter, number, or other symbols; a character is ordinarily printable as a symbol (e.g., the character "a" or ";")

(4) **Alphanumeric**—Alphabetic, numeric, and special characters (special characters are pluses, minuses, dollar signs, etc.)

(5) **Field**—A group of related characters (e.g., a social security number)

(6) **Record**—An ordered set of logically related fields. For example, all payroll data (including the social security number field and others) relating to a single employee.

(7) **Array**—In a programming language, an aggregate that consists of data objects with attributes, each of which may be uniquely referenced by an index (address). For example, an array may be used to request input of various payroll information for a new employee in one step. Thus an array could include employee name, social security number, withholdings, pay rate, etc.—for example (John Jones, 470-44-5044, 2, $18.32, ...). Name would be indexed as 1 (or zero), with each succeeding attribute receiving the next higher number as an address. Also arrays may be multidimensional. They are often used with object-oriented programming such as C++ and Java.

(8) **File**—A group of related records (e.g., all the weekly pay records year-to-date) which is usually arranged in sequence

(9) **Master file**—A file containing relatively permanent information used as a source of reference and periodically updated with a detail (transaction) file (e.g., permanent payroll records)

(10) **Detail or transaction file**—A file containing current transaction information used to update the master file (e.g., hours worked by each employee during the current period used to update the payroll master file)

b. **Data file structure**

(1) **Traditional file processing systems**—These systems focus upon data processing needs of individual departments. Each application program or system is developed to meet the needs of the particular requesting department or user group. For accounting purposes these systems are often similar to traditional accounting systems, with files set up for operations such as purchasing, sales, cash receipts, cash disbursements, etc.

(a) **Advantages of traditional processing systems**

1] Currently operational for many existing (legacy) systems
2] Often cost effective for simple applications

(b) **Disadvantages of traditional processing systems**

1] Data files are dependent upon a particular application program.
2] In complex business situation there is much duplication of data between data files.
3] Each application must be developed individually.
4] Program maintenance is expensive.

(2) **Database systems**

(a) **Definitions**

1] **Database**—A collection of interrelated files, ordinarily most of which are stored online

    a] **Normalization**—The process of separating the database into logical tables to avoid certain kinds of updating difficulties (referred to as "anomalies")

2] **Database system**—Computer hardware and software that enables the database(s) to be implemented

3] **Database management system**—Software that provides a facility for communications between various applications programs (e.g., a payroll preparation program) and the database (e.g., a payroll master file containing the earnings records of the employees)

4] **Data independence**—Basic to database systems is this concept which separates the data from the related application programs

5] **Data modeling**—Identifying and organizing a database's data, both logically and physically. A data model determines what information is to be contained in a database, how the information will be used, and how the items in the database will be related to each other.

   a] **Entity-relationship modeling**—An approach to data modeling. The model divides the database in two logical parts—entities (e.g. "customer," "product") and relations ("buys," "pays for").

   b] **REA data model**—A data model designed for use in designing accounting information databases. REA is an acronym for the model's basic types of objects: **R**esources—Identifiable objects that have economic value, **E**vents—An organization's business activities, **A**gents—People or organizations about which data is collected.

6] **Data Dictionary** (also referred to as a **data repository** or **data directory** system)—A data structure that stores meta-data

   a] **Meta-data**—Definitional data that provides information about or documentation of other data managed within an application or environment. For example, data about data elements, records and data structures (length, fields, columns, etc.).

   [Structured query language (SQL)]—The most common language used for creating [and] querying relational databases (see (b)3] below), its commands may be classified [into] three types

   [Data definition language (DDL)]—Used to define a database, including creating, [a]ltering, and deleting tables and establishing various constraints

   [Data manipulation language (DML)]—Commands used to maintain and query a [d]atabase, including updating, inserting in, modifying, and querying (asking for [d]ata). For example, a frequent query involves the joining of information from [m]ore than one table.

   [Data control language (DCL)]—Commands used to control a database, including [c]ontrolling which users have various privileges (e.g., who is able to read from and [w]rite to various portions of the database)

   [Databas]e structures

   [Hier]archical—The data elements at one level "own" the data elements at the next [lowe]r level (think of an organization chart in which one manager supervises several [assis]tants, who in turn each supervise several lower level employees).

   [Netw]orked—Each data element can have several owners and can own several other [elem]ents (think of a matrix-type structure in which various relationships can be sup[porte]d.

   [Rela]tional—A database with the logical structure of a group of related spreadsheets. [Each] row represents a record, which is an accumulation of all the fields related to the [row's] identifier or key; each column represents a field common to all of the records. [Relat]ional databases have in many situations largely replaced the earlier developed hi[erarc]hical and networked databases.

   [Obje]ct-oriented—Information (attributes and methods) are included in structures [called] object classes. This is the newest database management system technology.

   [Obje]ct-relational—Includes both relational and object-oriented features

   [Distr]ibuted—A single database that is spread physically across computers in multiple locations that are connected by a data communications link. (The structure of the database is most frequently relational, object-oriented, or object-relational.)

(c) **Database controls**

1] **User department**—Because users directly input data, strict controls over who is authorized to read and/or change the database are necessary.

2] **Access controls**—In addition to the usual controls over terminals and access to the system, database processing also maintains controls within the database itself. These controls limit the user to reading and/or changing (updating) only authorized portions of the database.

    a] **Restricting privileges**—This limits the access of users to the database, as well as operations a particular user may be able to perform. For example, certain employees and customers may have only read, and not write, privileges.

    b] **Logical views**—Users may be provided with authorized *views* of only the portions of the database for which they have a valid need.

3] **Backup and recovery**—A database is updated on a continuous basis during the day. Three methods of backup and recovery are

    a] **Backup of database and logs of transactions** (sometimes referred to as "systems logs"). The approach is to backup the entire database several times per week, generally to magnetic tape. A log of all transactions is also maintained. If there is extensive damage to a major portion of the database due to catastrophic failure, such as disk crash, the recovery method is to restore the most recent past copy of the database and to reconstruct it to a more current state by reapplying or redoing transactions from the log up to the point of failure.

    b] **Database replication.** To avoid catastrophic failure, another approach is to replicate the database at one or more locations. Thus, all data may be recorded to both sets of the database.

    c] **Backup facility.** Another approach is to maintain a backup facility with a vendor who will process data in case of an emergency.

Further information on backup and recovery is included under Disaster Recovery—D.11 of this module.

4] **Database administrator (DBA)**—Individual responsible for maintaining the database and restricting access to the database to authorized personnel

5] **Audit software**—Usually used by auditors to test the database; see Auditing with Technology Module

(d) **Advantages of database systems**

1] **Data independence**—Data can be used relatively easily by differing applications.

2] **Minimal data redundancy**—The manner in which data is structured results in information being recorded in only one place, thus making updating much easier than is the case with traditional file systems.

3] **Data sharing**—The sharing of data between individuals and applications is relatively easy.

4] Reduced program maintenance

5] Commercial applications are available for modification to a company's needs.

(e) **Disadvantages of database systems**

1] Need for specialized personnel with database expertise

2] Installation of database costly

3] Conversion of traditional file systems (legacy systems) costly

4] Comprehensive backup and recovery procedures are necessary

## C. Characteristics of Computer Systems—Specific

1. **Types of Networks**

   a. **Background**

     (1) A network is a group of interconnected computers and terminals.

     (2) The development of **telecommunications**—The electronic transmission of information by radio, fiber optics, wire, microwave, laser, and other electromagnetic systems—has made possible the electronic transfer of information between networks of computers. This topic is discussed in detail later in this module.

   b. **Classified by geographical scope**

(1) **Local area networks** (LAN)—Privately owned networks within a single building or campus of up to a few miles in size.  Because this topic has been emphasized in AICPA materials, it is discussed further later in this module.

(2) **Metropolitan area network** (MAN)—A larger version of a LAN.  For example, it might include a group of nearby offices within a city.

(3) **Wide area networks** (WAN)—Networks that span a large geographical area, often a country or continent.  It is composed of a collection of computers and other hardware and software for running user programs.

c.  **Classified by ownership**

(1) **Private**—One in which network resources are usually dedicated to a small number of applications or a restricted set of users, as in a corporation's network

    (a)  A typical approach is to lease telephone lines that are dedicated to the network's use.
    (b)  Also, traditional EDI systems (discussed below) use a private network.
    (c)  Advantages:  Secure, flexible, performance often exceeds that of public
    (d)  Disadvantage:  Costly

(2) **Public**—Resources are owned by third-party companies and leased to users on a usage basis (also referred to as public-switched networks [PSN]).

    (a)  Access is typically through dial-up circuits.
    (b)  Example:  Applications using the Internet
    (c)  Advantages and disadvantage: In general, the opposite of those for private networks, but certainly a significant disadvantage is that they are less secure.

        1]  Improvements in Internet communications will decrease the disadvantages and will lead to a dramatic increase in the use of public networks (e.g., rapid increases in the use of Internet-based electronic commerce).

d.  **Classified by use of Internet**

    **General:**  The following all use the Internet.  They have in common that data communications are ordinarily through **Hypertext Markup Language (HTML)** and/or **Extensible Markup Language (XML)**—languages used to create and format documents, link documents to other Web pages, and communicate between Web browsers.  XML is increasingly replacing HTML in Internet applications due to its superior ability to tag (i.e., label) and format documents that are communicated among trading partners.

    **Extensible Business Reporting Language (XBRL)** is an XML-based language being developed specifically for the automation of business information requirements, such as the preparation, sharing, and analysis of financial reports, statements, and audit schedules.  XBRL can be used in filings with the SEC that are made available on EDGAR, the SEC's Electronic Data Gathering and Retrieval database.

(1) **Internet**—An international collection of networks made up of independently owned computers that operate as a large computing network

    (a)  Primary applications of the Internet include

        1]  E-mail
        2]  News dissemination
        3]  Remote log-in of computers
        4]  File transfer among computers
        5]  Electronic commerce

    (b)  Terminology

        1]  **Hypertext Transfer Protocol (HTTP)**—A language used to transfer documents among different types of computers and networks
        2]  **Uniform Resource Locator (URL)**—A standard for finding a document by typing in an address (e.g., www.azdiamondbacks.com).  URLs work in much the same way as addresses on mail processed by the postal department.

3] **World Wide Web (The Web or WWW)**—A framework for accessing linked documents spread out over the thousands of machines all over the Internet

4] **Web browser**—Software that provides the user with the ability to display Web site pages and locates those pages and sites on request (e.g., Internet Explorer, Netscape)

5] **Web servers**—Large computers on the Internet that are distributed around the world and contain various types of data

6] **Firewall**—A method for protecting an organization's computers and computer information from outsiders. A firewall consists of security algorithms and router communications protocols that prevent outsiders from tapping into corporate database and e-mail systems.

7] **Router**—A communications interface device that connects two networks and determines the best way for data packets to move forward to their destinations

8] **Bridge**—A device that divides a LAN into two segments, selectively forwarding traffic across the network boundary it defines; similar to a switch

9] **Switch**—A device that channels incoming data from any of multiple input ports to the specific output port that will take the data toward its intended destination

10] **Gateway**—A combination of hardware and software that links to different types of networks. For examples, gateways between e-mail systems allow users of differing e-mail systems to exchange messages.

11] **Proxy server**—A server that saves and serves copies of web pages to those who request them (e.g., potential customers). When a Web page is requested, the proxy server is able to access that page either through its cache (reserve of Web pages already sent or loaded) or by obtaining it through the original server. A proxy server can both increase efficiency of Internet operations and help assure data security.

12] **Bulletin board**—A computer system that functions as a centralized information source and message switching system for users with a particular interest. Users dial-up the bulletin board, review and leave messages for other users, as well as communicate to other users on the system at the same time.

13] **IP address**—The number that identifies a machine as unique on the Internet

14] **ISP (Internet Service Provider)**—An entity that provides access to the Internet

(c) The nature of the Internet has resulted in the spread of a series of malicious programs (often through e-mail) that may adversely affect computer operations, including

1] **Virus**—A program (or piece of code) that requests the computer operating system to perform certain activities not authorized by the computer user. Viruses can be easily transmitted through use of files that contain macros that are sent as attachment to e-mail messages.

    a] **Macro**—A single computer instruction that results in a series of instructions in machine language; macros are used to reduce the number of keystrokes needed in a variety of situations. Most macros serve valid purposes, but those associated with viruses cause problems.

    b] Unexpected changes in, or losses of, data may be an indication of the existence of a virus on one's computer.

    c] E-mail attachments and *public domain software* (generally downloadable from the Internet at no cost to users) are notorious sources of viruses.

2] **Trojan horse**—A malicious, security-breaking program that is disguised as something benign, such as a game, but actually is intended to cause IT damage

3] **Worm**—A program that propagates itself over a network, reproducing itself as it goes

**Antivirus software**—Is used to attempt to avoid the above types of problems. But the rapid development of new forms of viruses, Trojan horses, and worms results in a situation in which antivirus software developers are always behind the developers.

(2) **Intranet**—A local network, usually limited to an organization, that uses internet-based technology to communicate within the organization.

(3) **Extranet**—Similar to an intranet, but includes an organization's external customers and/or suppliers in the network.

e. **Database client-server architecture**

   **General:**  When considering networks, it is helpful to consider their architecture (design). Bear in mind that the architecture must divide the following responsibilities (1) input, (2) processing, and (3) storage.  In general the client-server model may be viewed as one in which communications ordinarily take the form of a request message from the client to the server asking for some service to be performed.  A "client" may be viewed as the computer or **workstation** of an individual user.  The server is a high-capacity computer that contains the network software and may provide a variety of services ranging from simply "serving" files to a client to performing analyses.

(1) **Overall client-server systems**—A networked computing model (usually a LAN) in which database software on a server performs database commands sent to it from client computers

**Illustration of Client/Server Architecture**

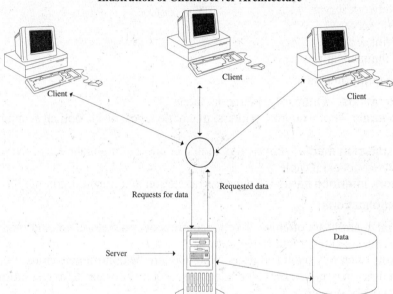

(2) **Subtypes of client/server architectures**

   (a) **File servers**—The file server manages file operations and is shared by each of the client PCs (ordinarily attached to a LAN).  The three responsibilities (input/output, processing, and storage) are divided in a manner in which most input/output, and processing occurs on client computers rather than on the server.  The file server acts simply as a shared data storage device, with all data manipulations performed by client PCs.

   (b) **Database servers**—Similar to file servers, but the server here contains the database management system and thus performs more of the processing.

   *NOTE:  The above two architectures are referred to as "two-tier" architecture—client tier and server database tier.*

   (c) **Three-tier architectures**—A client/server configuration that includes three tiers.  The change from the above systems is that this architecture includes another server layer in addition to the two tiers discussed above.  For example, application programs (e.g., a transaction processing monitor that controls the input of transactions to the database) may reside on the additional server rather than on the individual clients.  This system of adding additional servers may generalize to additional tiers and thus become **n-tier** architecture. Examples of other servers that may be added are as follows:

   1] **Print server**—Make shared printers available to various clients
   2] **Communications server**—May serve a variety of tasks, such as acting as a gateway (i.e., means of entrance) to the internet or to the corporate intranet

3]  **Fax server**—Allow clients on the network to share the hardware for incoming and outgoing fax transmissions

(3) **Distributed systems**—These systems connect all company locations to form a distributed network in which each location has its own input/output, processing, and storage capabilities. These local computers also pass data among themselves and possibly to a server (often referred to as a "host" in this context) for further processing. An illustration of this type of system is presented in the database section of this outline.

2. **Local Area Networks (LANs)**—Privately owned networks within a single building or campus of up to a few miles in size.

   a. **Software**

      (1) Software allows devices to function cooperatively and share network resources such as printers and disk storage space.

      (2) Common services

         (a)  Network server
         (b)  File server
         (c)  Print server
         (d)  Communications server

   b. **Hardware components**

      (1) **Workstations**—Ordinarily microcomputers
      (2) **Peripherals**—For example, printers, magnetic tapes, disks, optical scanners, fax board, modems
      (3) **Transmission media**—Physical path that connect components of LAN, ordinarily twisted-pair wire or coaxial cable
      (4) **Network interface cards**—Connect workstation and transmission media

   c. **Control implications**

      (1) General controls are often weak (e.g., controls over development and modification of programs, access and computer operations).
      (2) Controls often rely upon end users, who may not be control conscious.
      (3) Often users may not be provided adequate resources for problem resolution, troubleshooting and recovery support.
      (4) Controlling access and gaining accountability through logging of transactions enforces a segregation of duties.
      (5) Good management controls are essential—for example, access codes, passwords.
      (6) LAN software ordinarily does not provide security features available in larger scale environments.

      *NOTE: Tests of controls may address whether controls related to the above are effective.*

   d.  LANs generally make possible the computer audit techniques that may be performed either by internal auditors or external auditors.

3. **Microcomputers**

   a.  The proliferation of microcomputers (e.g., personal computers [PC], laptop computers) has had a profound effect on information systems. A small-business client will probably use a PC to run a commercially purchased general ledger package (off-the-shelf software). Segregation of duties becomes especially difficult in such an environment because one individual may perform all recordkeeping (processing) as well as maintain other nonrecordkeeping responsibilities.

   b.  A larger client may use a network of PCs that may or may not be linked to a large corporate mainframe computer. In all systems, management policies should be in place regarding the development and modification of programs and data files.

   c.  Regardless of the system, the control objectives remain the same. When small computers are involved, the following points need to be considered:

      (1) **Security**—Security over small computers, while still important, may not be as critical as security over the data and any in-house developed software. Most companies can easily replace

the hardware, but may suffer a severe setback if the data and/or in-house developed software is lost. Access to the software diskettes should be controlled and backup copies should be made. Access to the hard drive must be restricted since anyone turning on the power switch can read the data stored on those files. Also, a control problem may exist because the computer operator often understands the system and also has access to the diskettes. The management of the company may need to become more directly involved in supervision when a lack of segregation of duties exists in data processing.

(2) **Verification of processing**—Periodically, an independent verification of the applications being processed on the small computer system should be made to prevent the system from being used for personal projects. Also, verification helps prevent errors in internally developed software from going undetected. Controls should be in operation to assure the accuracy of in-house created spreadsheets and databases.

(3) **Personnel**—Centralized authorization to purchase hardware and software should be required to ensure that appropriate purchasing decisions are made, including decisions that minimize software and hardware compatibility difficulties. Software piracy and viruses may be controlled by prohibiting the loading of unauthorized software and data on company-owned computers.

    (a) Software is copyrighted, and violation of copyright laws may result in litigation against the company.

    (b) A company may control possible software piracy (the use of unlicensed software) by employees by procedures such as

        1] Establishing a corporate software policy
        2] Maintaining a log of all software purchase
        3] Auditing individual computers to identify installed software

4. **End-User Computing (EUC)**—The end user is responsible for the development and execution of the computer application that generates the information used by that same end user.

  a. User substantially eliminates many of the services offered by an MIS department.

  b. Risks

    (1) End-user applications are not always adequately tested before implemented.
    (2) More client personnel need to understand control concepts.
    (3) Management often does not review the results of applications appropriately.
    (4) Old or existing applications may not be updated for current applicability and accuracy.

  c. Overall physical access controls become more difficult when companies leave a controlled MIS environment and become more dependent upon individual users for controls.

  d. Control implications

    (1) Require applications to be adequately tested before used
    (2) Require adequate documentation
    (3) Physical access controls, including

      (a) Clamps or chains to prevent removal of hard disks or internal boards
      (b) Diskless workstations that require download of files
      (c) Regular backup
      (d) Security software to limit access to those who know user ID and password
      (e) Control over access from outside
      (f) Commitment to security matters written into job descriptions, employee contracts, and personnel evaluation procedures

    (4) Control access to appropriate users

      (a) Passwords and user IDs
      (b) Menus for EUC access to database
      (c) Protect system by restricting user ability to load data
      (d) When end user uploads data, require appropriate validation, authorization, and reporting control
      (e) Independent review of transactions

           (f)   Record access to company databases by EUC applications

      (5)   Control use of incorrect versions of data files

           (a)   Use control totals for batch processing of uploaded data

      (6)   Require backup of files

      (7)   Provide applications controls (e.g., edit checks, range tests, reasonableness checks)

      (8)   Support programmed or user reconciliations to provide assurance that processing is correct

        *NOTE: Since end-user computing relies upon microcomputers, the controls here required for microcomputers and EUC are similar. Also, tests of controls may address whether controls related to the above are effective.*

5. **Electronic Commerce**

    a.   **General:** Electronic commerce involves individuals and organizations engaging in a variety of electronic transactions with computers and telecommunication networks. The networks involved may be publicly available (e.g., the Internet) or private to the individuals and organizations involved (e.g., through telephone lines privately leased by the parties involved). Recent wide acceptance of the Internet (more specifically, that portion of the Internet referred to as the World Wide Web, or the Web) is currently leading to a great expansion in electronic commerce.

    b.   Five areas of risk associated with electronic commerce IT systems (as well as to varying degrees with other IT systems) are (1) security, (2) availability, (3) processing integrity, (4) online privacy, and (5) confidentiality. See section D.1 of this module for a discussion.

    c.   Use of the Web is growing rapidly as both the number and types of electronic transactions increase. However, many believe that risks such as those listed above are currently impairing its growth.

      (1)   As discussed further in the Reporting Module (Section C.2.), the AICPA and the Canadian Institute of Chartered Accountants have developed a form of assurance referred to as the "WebTrust Seal of Assurance" that tells potential customers that the firm has evaluated a Web site's business practices and controls to determine whether they are in conformity with Web-Trust principles.

      (2)   Digital certificates, also referred to as digital IDs, are a means of assuring data integrity.

           (a)   A digital certificate (signature) allows an individual to digitally sign a message so the recipient knows that it actually came from that individual and was not modified in any manner.

           (b)   Ordinarily the message is encrypted and the recipient decrypts it and is able to read the contents.

      (3)   **Encryption**—The conversion of data into a form called a cipher text, that cannot be easily understood by unauthorized people. **Decryption** is the process of converting encrypted data back into its original form so it can be understood. The conversion is performed using an algorithm and key which only the users control.

           (a)   **Algorithm**—A detailed sequence of actions to perform to accomplish some task (in this case to encrypt and/or decode data)

           (b)   **Key**—In the content of encryption, a value that must be fed into the algorithm used to decode an encrypted message in order to reproduce the original plain text

           (c)   **Private key system**—An encryption system in which both the sender and receiver have access to the electronic key, but do not allow others access. The primary disadvantage is that both parties must have the key.

           (d)   Encryption is important in a variety of contexts, including any time two or more computers are used to communicate with one another, and even to keep private information on one computer.

           (e)   The machine instructions necessary to encrypt and decrypt data constitute **system overhead;** that is, they slow down the rate of processing.

    d.   **Electronic funds transfer (EFT)**—Making cash payments between two or more organizations or individuals electronically rather than by using checks (or cash)

      (1)   Banks first became heavily involved with EFT; it is now a major part of most types of electronic commerce.

(2) EFT systems are vulnerable to the risk of unauthorized access to proprietary data and to the risk of fraudulent fund transfers; controls include

    (a) Control of physical access to network facilities

    (b) Electronic identification should be required for all network terminals authorized to use EFT.

    (c) Access should be controlled through passwords.

    (d) Encryption should be used to secure stored data and data being transmitted. See section C.5.c.(3) for more information on encryption.

e. **Electronic data interchange (EDI)**—The electronic exchange of business transactions, in a standard format, from one entity's computer to another entity's computer through an electronic communications network

    (1) Traditionally, the definition of electronic commerce has focused on EDI. Currently, Web-based commerce is replacing a portion of these EDI systems.

    (2) Risks related to EDI

        (a) EDI is commonly used for sales and purchasing, and related accounts. The speed at which transactions occur often reduces amounts receivable (payables) due to electronic processing of receipts (payments). Another effect is to make preventive controls particularly desirable, since detective controls may be too late.

        (b) In these systems, documents such as purchase orders, invoices, shipping forms, bills of lading, and checks are replaced by electronic transactions.

            1] For example, in electronic funds transfer systems, a form of EDI, electronic transactions replace checks as a means of payment. As discussed below, EDI is often conducted on private networks.

            2] To determine that transactions are properly processed, effective audit trails for both internal auditors and external auditors include activity logs, including processed and failed transactions, network and sender/recipient acknowledgment of receipt of transactions, and proper time sequence of processing.

            3] In some EDI applications, portions of the documentation of transactions are retained for only short period of time; this may require auditors to pay particular attention to controls over the transactions and to test controls on a timely basis when records remain available.

    (3) Methods of communication between trading partners

        (a) **Point-to-point**—A direct computer-to-computer private network link

            1] Automakers and governments have traditionally used this method.

            2] Advantages

                a] No reliance on third parties for computer processing

                b] Organization controls who has access to the network.

                c] Organization can enforce proprietary (its own) software standard in dealings with all trading partners.

                d] Timeliness of delivery may be improved since no third party is involved.

            3] Disadvantages

                a] Must establish connection with each trading partner

                b] High initial cost

                c] Computer scheduling issues

                d] Need for common protocols between partners

                e] Need for hardware and software compatibility

        (b) **Value-added network (VAN)**

            1] A VAN

a] Is a privately owned network that routes the EDI transactions between trading partners, and in many cases provides translation, storage, and other processing

b] Is designed and maintained by an independent company that offers specialized support to improve the transmission effectiveness of a network

c] Alleviates problems related to interorganizational communication that results from the use of differing hardware and software

2] A VAN receives data from sender, determines intended recipient, and places data in the recipient's electronic mailbox.

3] Advantages

a] Reduces communication and data protocol problems since VANs can deal with differing protocols (eliminating need for trading partners to agree on them)

b] Partners do not have to establish the numerous point-to-point connections.

c] Reduces scheduling problems since receiver can request delivery of transactions when it wishes

d] In some cases, VAN translates application to a standard format the partner does not have to reformat.

e] VAN can provide increased security.

4] Disadvantages

a] Cost of VAN

b] Dependence upon VAN's systems and controls

c] Possible loss of data confidentiality

(c) **Public networks**—For example, the Internet-based commerce solutions described earlier

1] Advantages

a] Avoids cost of proprietary lines

b] Avoids cost of VAN

c] Directly communicates transactions to trading partners

d] Software is being developed which allows communication between differing systems.

2] Disadvantages

a] Possible loss of data confidentiality on the Internet

b] Computer or transmission disruption

c] Hackers and viruses

d] Attempted electronic frauds

(d) **Proprietary networks**—In some circumstances (e.g., health care, banking) organizations have developed their own network for their own transactions. These systems are costly to develop and operate (because of proprietary lines), although they are often extremely reliable.

(4) Controls required for other network systems are required for EDI systems. In addition, disappearance of "paper transactions" and the direct interrelationship with another organization's computer makes various authentication and encryption controls particularly important for these transactions.

(a) **Authentication**—Controls must exist over the origin, proper submission, and proper delivery of EDI communications. Receiver of the message must have proof of the origin of the message, as well as its proper submission and delivery.

(b) **Packets**—A block of data that is transmitted from one computer to another. It contains data and authentication information.

(c) **Encryption**—The conversion of plain text data into cipher text data used by an algorithm and key which only the users control. See section C.5.c.(3) for more information on encryption.

(5) The AICPA Auditing Procedures Study, *Audit Implications of EDI,* lists the following benefits and exposures of EDI:

(a) Benefits

    1] Quick response and access to information
    2] Cost efficiency
    3] Reduced paperwork
    4] Accuracy and reduced errors and error-correction costs
    5] Better communications and customer service
    6] Necessary to remain competitive

(b) Exposures

    1] Total dependence upon computer system for operation
    2] Possible loss of confidentiality of sensitive information
    3] Increased opportunity for unauthorized transactions and fraud
    4] Concentration of control among a few people involved in EDI
    5] Reliance on third parties (trading partners, VAN)
    6] Data processing, application and communications errors
    7] Potential legal liability due to errors
    8] Potential loss of audit trails and information needed by management due to limited retention policies
    9] Reliance on trading partner's system

6. **Telecommunications**—The electronic transmission of information by radio, wire, fiber optic, coaxial cable, microwave, laser, or other electromagnetic system

  a. Transmitted information—Voice, data, video, fax, other
  b. Hardware involved

    (1) Computers for communications control and switching
    (2) Transmission facilities such as copper wire, fiber optic cables, microwave stations and communications satellites
    (3) Modems may be used to provide compatibility of format speed, etc.

  c. Software controls and monitors the hardware, formats information, adds appropriate control information, performs switching operations, provides security, and supports the management of communications.
  d. While telecommunications is **not** an end of itself, it enables technologies such as the following:

    (1) Electronic data interchange
    (2) Electronic funds transfer
    (3) Point of sale systems
    (4) Commercial databases
    (5) Airline reservation systems

  e. Controls needed

    (1) System integrity at remote sites
    (2) Data entry
    (3) Central computer security
    (4) Dial-in security
    (5) Transmission accuracy and completeness
    (6) Physical security over telecommunications facilities

  *NOTE: Tests of controls may address whether controls related to the above are effective.*

7. **Computer Service Organizations (Bureaus, Centers)**—Computer service organizations record and process data for companies. These organizations allow companies (users) to do away with part of the data processing function. While many computer service organizations simply record and process relatively routine transactions for a client (e.g., prepare payroll journals and payroll checks), a VAN is a

service organization that takes a broader role of providing network, storing, and forwarding (mailbox) services for the companies involved in an EDI system. Information on service organizations is presented in the Internal Control Module (Section D.4.) and in the outline of AU 324.

## D. Effect of a Computer on Internal Control

*NOTE: We have already discussed the effect of a computer on internal control of several systems under C. (microcomputers, end-user computing, and electronic commerce). In this section we discuss the effect in general terms as presented in the AICPA Audit Guide, **Consideration of Internal Control in a Financial Statement Audit**. This section presents information on controls a company may have. Information on how auditors test those controls and on audit procedures that use IT is presented in Module 6 of Auditing. We begin by discussing overall principles of a reliable system and overall risks. We then consider the effect of a computer on internal control using the five components of internal control—control environment, risk assessment, information and communication, monitoring, and control activities.*

### 1. Principles of a Reliable System and Examples of Overall Risks

a. A reliable system is one that is capable of operating without material error, fault, or failure during a specified period in a specified environment

b. One framework for analyzing a reliable system is presented by the AICPA's Trust Services. Trust Services, which provide assurance on information systems, use a framework with five principles of a reliable system—(1) security, (2) availability, (3) processing integrity, (4) online privacy, and (5) confidentiality. Accordingly, when a principle is not met a risk exists.

| *Principle* | *Examples of Risks* |
|---|---|
| **1. Security.** The system is protected against unauthorized access (both physical and logical) | Physical access—A lack of physical security allows damage or other loss (e.g., theft) to the system<br><br>• Weather<br>• Acts of war<br>• Disgruntled employees or others<br><br>Logical access—A lack of security over access to the system allows<br><br>• Malicious (or accidental) alteration of, or damage to, files and/or the system<br>• Computer based fraud<br>• Unauthorized access to confidential data |
| **2. Availability.** The system is available for operation and use as committed or agreed. The system is available for operation and use in conformity with the entity's availability policies. | System failure results in<br><br>• Interruption of business operations<br>• Loss of data |
| **3. Processing Integrity.** System processing is complete, accurate, timely, and authorized. | Invalid, incomplete, or inaccurate<br><br>• Input data<br>• Data processing<br>• Updating of master files<br>• Creation of output |
| **4. Online Privacy.** Personal information obtained as a result of e-commerce is collected, used, disclosed, and retained as committed or agreed. | Disclosure of customer information (or that of others) such as<br><br>• Social security numbers<br>• Credit card numbers<br>• Credit rating<br>• Medical conditions |
| **5. Confidentiality.** Information designated as confidential is protected as committed or agreed. | Examples of confidential data that might be disclosed<br><br>• Transaction details<br>• Engineering details of products<br>• Business plans<br>• Banking information<br>• Legal documents<br>• Inventory or other account information<br>• Customer lists<br>• Confidential details of operations |

*NOTE: Make certain that you are familiar not only with the above principles, but are familiar with the nature of the various risks relating to computer processing.*

2. **Control Environment**

   a. Recall the seven factors of the control environment

      I  -  Integrity and ethical values
      C  -  Commitment to competence
      H  -  Human resource policies and practices
      A  -  Assignment of authority and responsibility
      M  -  Management's philosophy and operating style
      B  -  Board of directors or audit committee participation
      O  -  Organizational structure

   b. Although all seven factors may be affected by computer processing, the organizational structure is modified to include an information systems department (EDP department). It is helpful to keep in mind that the information systems department is involved with two distinct functions—systems development and data processing.

   c. Organizational structure

      (1) **Segregation controls**

         (a) Segregate functions between information systems department and user departments

            1] User departments are the other departments of the company that utilize the data prepared by the information systems department.

         (b) Do not allow the information systems department to initiate or authorize transactions.

         (c) At a minimum, segregate programming, operations, and the library function within the information systems department.

         (d) A more complete segregation of key functions within the information systems department may be possible; one way to separate key functions is as follows:

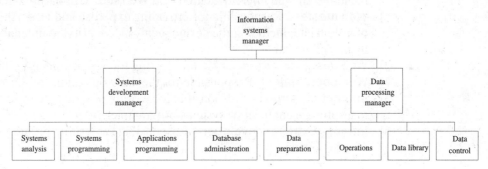

            1] **Systems analysis**—The systems analyst analyzes the present user environment and requirements and may (1) recommend specific changes, (2) recommend the purchase of a new system, or (3) design a new information system. The analyst is in constant contact with user departments and programming staff to ensure the users' actual and ongoing needs are being met. A system flowchart is a tool used by the analyst to define the systems requirements.

            2] **Systems programming**—The systems programmer is responsible for implementing, modifying, and debugging the software necessary for making the hardware work (such as the operating system, telecommunications monitor, and the database management system). For some companies the term "software engineer" is viewed as similar or identical to that of systems programmer. For others, the software engineer is involved with the creation of designs used by programmers.

            3] **Applications programming**—The applications programmer is responsible for writing, testing, and debugging the application programs from the specifications (whether general or specific) provided by the systems analyst. A program flowchart is one tool used by the applications programmer to define the program logic.

            4] **Database administration**—In a database environment, a database administrator (DBA) is responsible for maintaining the database and restricting access to the database to authorized personnel.

5] **Data preparation**—Data may be prepared by user departments and input by key to magnetic disk or magnetic tape.

6] **Operations**—The operator is responsible for the daily computer operations of both the hardware and the software. The operator mounts magnetic tapes on the tape drives, supervises operations on the operator's console, accepts any required input, and distributes any generated output. The operator should have adequate documentation available to run the program (a run manual), but should not have detailed program information.

    a] Help desks are usually a responsibility of operations because of the operational nature of their functions (for example, assisting users with systems problems and obtaining technical support/vendor assistance).

7] **Data library**—The librarian is responsible for custody of the removable media (i.e., magnetic tapes or disks) and for the maintenance of program and system documentation. In many systems, much of the library function is maintained and performed electronically by the computer.

8] **Data control**—The control group acts as liaison between users and the processing center. This group records input data in a control log, follows the progress of processing, distributes output, and ensures compliance with control totals.

Ideally, in a large system, all of the above key functions should be segregated; in a small computer environment, many of the key functions are concentrated in a small number of employees. For purposes of the CPA exam remember that, at a minimum, an attempt should be made to segregate *programming, operations,* and the *library* functions.

(e) Electronic commerce has resulted in a number of new Web-related positions, including

1] **Web administrator (Web manager)**—Responsible for overseeing the development, planning, and the implementation of a Web site. Ordinarily a managerial position.

2] **Web master**—Responsible for providing expertise and leadership in the development of a Web site, including the design, analysis, security, maintenance, content development, and updates.

3] **Web designer**—Responsible for creating the visual content of the Web site

4] **Web coordinator**—Responsible for the daily operations of the Web site

5] **Internet developer**—Responsible for writing programs for commercial use. Similar to a software engineer or systems programmer.

6] **Intranet/Extranet developer**—Responsible for writing programs based on the needs of the company

3. **Risk Assessment**

   a. Changes in computerized information systems and in operations may increase the risk of improper financial reporting.

4. **Information and Communication**

   a. The computerized accounting system is affected by whether the company uses small computers and/or a complex mainframe system.

     (1) For small computer systems, purchased commercial "off-the-shelf" software may be used.

       (a) Controls within the software may be well known.

       (b) Analysis of "exception reports" generated during processing is important to determine that exceptions are properly handled.

     (2) For complex mainframe systems a significant portion of the software is ordinarily developed within the company by information systems personnel.

       (a) Controls within the software are unknown to the auditor prior to testing.

       (b) As with small computer systems, analysis of exception reports is important, but controls over the generation of such reports must ordinarily be tested to a greater extent.

5.  **Monitoring**

    a.  Proper monitoring of a computerized system will require adequate computer skills to evaluate the propriety of processing of computerized applications.
    b.  A common method of monitoring for inappropriate access is review of system-access log.

6.  **Control Activities—Overall**

    a.  Control activities in which a computer is involved may be divided into the following categories:

        (1)  Computer **general** control activities
        (2)  Computer **application** control activities

             **Programmed** application control activities
             **Manual** follow-up of computer exception reports

        (3)  **User** control activities to test the completeness and accuracy of computer processed controls

    The following illustration, adapted from the AICPA Audit Guide, *Consideration of Internal Control in a Financial Statement Audit*, summarizes the relationships among the controls.

**COMPUTER CONTROL ACTIVITIES**

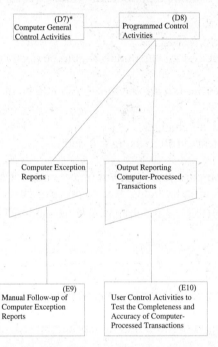

**EXPLANATION OF COMPUTER CONTROL ACTIVITIES**

**Computer General Control Activities** control program development, program changes, computer operations, and access to programs and data. These control activities increase the assurance that programmed control activities operate effectively during the period.

**Computer Application Control Activities**

**Programmed Control Activities** relate to specific computer applications and are embedded in the computer program used in the financial reporting system. The concepts presented here related to programmed control activities may also apply to other activities within the computer accounting system.

**Manual Follow-Up of Computer Exception Reports** involves employee follow-up of items listed on computer exception reports. The effectiveness of application control activities that involve manual follow-up of computer reports depends on the effectiveness of both the programmed control activities that produce the exception report and the manual follow-up activities.

**User Control Activities to Test the Completeness and Accuracy of Computer Processed Transactions** represent manual checks of computer output against source document or other input, and thus provide assurance that programmed aspects of the accounting system and control activities have operated effectively.

*  *Section below in which control discussion is presented.*

7.  **Computer General Control Activities**

    *NOTE: General control activities affect all computer applications. There are four types of general controls—(a) developing new programs and systems, (b) changing existing programs and systems, (c) controlling access to programs and data, and (d) controlling computer operations.*

    a.  **Developing new programs and systems**

        (1)  **Segregation controls**

            (a)  User departments participate in systems design.
            (b)  Both users and information systems personnel test new systems.
            (c)  Management, users, and information systems personnel approve new systems before they are placed into operation.
            (d)  All master and transaction file conversions should be controlled to prevent unauthorized changes and to verify the accuracy of the results.
            (e)  Programs and systems should be properly documented (see Section E. of outline).

(2) **Computer hardware is extremely reliable.**  This is primarily due to the chip technology. However, it is also due to the controls built into the hardware and systems software to provide for a self-diagnostic mechanism to detect and prevent equipment failures.  The following are examples of such controls:

    (a) **Parity check**—A special bit is added to each character that can detect if the hardware loses a bit during the internal movement of a character.

    (b) **Echo check**—Primarily used in telecommunications transmissions.  During the sending and receiving of characters, the receiving hardware repeats back to the sending hardware what it received and the sending hardware automatically resends any characters that were received incorrectly.

    (c) **Diagnostic routines**—Hardware or software supplied by the manufacturer to check the internal operations and devices within the computer system.  These routines are often activated when the system is booted up.

    (d) **Boundary protection**—Most CPUs have multiple jobs running simultaneously (multiprogramming environment).  To ensure that these simultaneous jobs cannot destroy or change the allocated memory of another job, the systems software contains boundary protection controls.

    (e) **Periodic maintenance**—The system should be examined periodically (often weekly) by a qualified service technician.

b. **Changing existing programs and systems**

(1) Suggestions for changes (from users and information system personnel) should be documented in a change request log.

(2) Proper *change control* procedures (also referred to as *modification controls*) should be in place.

    (a) The information systems manager should review all changes.

    (b) The modified program should be appropriately tested (often using test data).

    (c) Details of all changes should be documented.

    (d) A *code comparison program* may be used to compare source and/or object codes of a controlled copy of a program with the program currently being used to process data.

        1] This will identify any unauthorized changes (this approach may also be used by CPAs).

c. **Controlling access to programs and data**

(1) **Segregation controls**

    (a) Access to program documentation should be limited to those persons who require it in the performance of their duties.

    (b) Access to data files and programs should be limited to those individuals authorized to process data.

    (c) Access to computer hardware should be limited to authorized individuals such as computer operators and their supervisors.

(2) **Physical access to computer facility**

    (a) **Limited physical access**—The physical facility that houses the computer equipment, files, and documentation should have controls to limit access only to authorized individuals.  Possible controls include using a guard, automated key cards, and manual key locks, as well as the new access devices that permit access through fingerprints or palm prints.

    (b) **Visitor entry logs**—Used to document those who have had access to the area

(3) **Hardware and software access controls**

    (a) **Access control software** (user identification)—The most used control is a combination of a unique *identification code* and a confidential *password*.

        1] Passwords should be made up of a combination of alphabetic, numeric, and symbol elements.

        2] Passwords should be changed periodically.

3] Passwords should be disabled promptly when an employee leaves the company.

(b) **Call back**—Call back is a specialized form of user identification in which the user dials the system, identifies him/herself, and is disconnected from the system. Then either (1) an individual manually finds the authorized telephone number or (2) the system automatically finds the authorized telephone number of the individual and calls back.

(c) **Encryption**—Data is encoded when stored in computer files and/or before transmission to or from remote locations (e.g., through use of modems and telephone lines). This coding protects data, since to use the data unauthorized users must not only obtain access, but must also translate the coded form of the data. Encryption performed by physically secure hardware (often special-purpose computers) is ordinarily more secure, but more costly than that performed by software. See section 5.c.(3) for more information on encryption.

d. **Controlling computer operations**

(1) **Segregation controls**

(a) Operators should have access to an *operations manual* that contains the instructions for processing programs and solving routine operational programs, but not with detailed program documentation.

(b) The control group should monitor the operator's activities and jobs should be scheduled.

(2) **Other controls**

(a) **Backup and recovery**—Discussed in Section D.11. in this module

(b) **Contingency processing**—Detailed contingency processing plans should be developed to prepare for system failures. The plans should detail the responsibilities of individuals, as well as the alternate processing sites that should be utilized. Backup facilities with a vendor may be used to provide contingent sites in case of an emergency. This topic is discussed further in Section D.11. of this module.

(c) **File protection ring**—A file protection ring is a processing control to ensure that an operator does not use a magnetic tape as a tape to write on when it actually has critical information on it. If the ring is on the tape, data cannot be written on the tape. A file protection ring on a magnetic tape serves the same purpose as the switch on a floppy diskette that makes it "read only."

(d) **Internal and external labels**—External labels are gummed-paper labels attached to a reel of tape or other storage medium which identify the file. Internal labels perform the same function through the use of machine readable identification in the first record of a file. The use of labels allows the computer operator to determine whether the correct file has been selected for processing. Trailer labels are often used on the end of a magnetic tape file to maintain information on the number of records processed.

8. **Computer Application Control Activities—Programmed Control Activities**

*NOTE: Programmed application controls apply to a specific application rather than multiple applications. These controls operate to assure the proper input and processing of data. The input step converts human-readable data into computer-readable data. Ensuring the integrity of the data in the computer is critical during processing. The candidate should be prepared to identify the following common controls in a multiple-choice question.*

a. **Input controls**

(1) **Overall controls**

(a) Inputs should be properly authorized and approved.

(b) The system should verify all significant data fields used to record information (editing the data).

(c) Conversion of data into machine-readable form should be controlled and verified for accuracy.

(2) **Input validation (edit) controls**

(a) **Preprinted form**—Information is preassigned a place and a format on the input form.

(b) **Check digit**—An extra digit added to an identification number to detect certain types of data transmission errors. For example, a bank may add a check digit to individuals' 7-digit account numbers. The computer will calculate the correct check digit based on performing predetermined mathematical operations on the 7-digit account number and will then compare it to the check digit.

(c) **Control, batch, or proof total**—A total of one numerical field for all the records of a batch that normally would be added, (e.g., total sales dollars)

(d) **Hash total**—A control total where the total is meaningless for financial purposes (e.g., a mathematical sum of employee social security numbers)

(e) **Record count**—A control total of the total records processed

(f) **Limit (reasonableness) test**—A test of the reasonableness of a field of data, given a predetermined upper and/or lower limit (e.g., for a field that indicates auditing exam scores, a limit check would test for scores over 100)

(g) **Menu driven input**—As input is entered, the operator responds to a menu prompting the proper response (e.g., What score did you get on the Auditing part of the CPA Exam [75-100]?).

(h) **Field check**—A control that limits the types of characters accepted into a specific data field (e.g., a pay rate should include only numerical data)

(i) **Validity check**—A control that allows only "valid" transactions or data to be entered into the system (e.g., a field indicating sex of an individual where 1=female and 2=male—if the field is coded in any other manner it would not be accepted)

(j) **Missing data check**—A control that searches for blanks inappropriately existing in input data (e.g., if an employee's division number were left blank an error message would result)

(k) **Field size check**—A control of an exact number of characters to be input (e.g., if part numbers all have 6 digits, an error message would result if more or less than 6 characters were input)

(l) **Logic check**—Ensures that illogical combinations of input are not accepted (e.g., if the Tuba City branch has no company officers, an error message would result if two fields for a specified employee indicated that the employee worked as an officer in Tuba City).

(m) **Redundant data check**—Uses two identifiers in each transaction record (e.g., customer account number and the first five letters of customer's name) to confirm that the correct master file record is being updated

(n) **Closed-loop verification**—A control that allows data entry personnel to check the accuracy of input data. For example, the system might retrieve an account name of a record that is being updated, and display it on the operator's terminal. This control may be used instead of a redundant data check.

(3) **Processing controls**

**Overall:** When the input has been accepted by the computer, it usually is processed through multiple steps. Processing controls are essential to ensure the integrity of data. Essentially all of the controls listed for input may also be incorporated during processing. For example, processed information should include limit tests, record counts, and control totals. In addition, external labels should be used on floppy disks and magnetic tape files, with internal header and trailer labels used to determine that all information on a file has been read.

*NOTE: Previously, the professional standards divided application controls into three categories—input, processing, and output. The current categories of application controls (programmed and manual) and user controls have replaced that breakdown. As an aid to discussing controls we distinguish between input and processing above. User control activities include the essentials of the previous "output" controls.*

9. **Application Controls—Manual Follow-Up of Computer Exception Reports**

a. These controls involve employee (operator and/or control group) follow-up of items listed on computer exception reports. Their effectiveness depends on the effectiveness of both the programmed control activities that produce the reports and the manual follow-up activities.

10. **User Control Activities to Test the Completeness and Accuracy of Computer-Processed Controls**

a. These manual controls, previously referred to as *output controls,* include

       (1) Checks of computer output against source documents, control totals, or other input to provide assurance that programmed aspects of the financial reporting system and control activities have operated effectively

       (2) Reviewing computer processing logs to determine that all of the correct computer jobs executed properly

       (3) Maintaining proper procedures and communications specifying authorized recipients of output

  b. These procedures are often performed by both the control group and users.

  c. In some systems, user departments evaluate the reliability of output from the computer by extensive review and testing; in others, users merely test the overall reasonableness of the output.

11. **Disaster Recovery and Business Continuity**

  a. A plan should allow the firm to

       (1) Minimize the extent of disruption, damage, and loss

       (2) Establish an alternate (temporary) method for processing information

       (3) Resume normal operations as quickly as possible

       (4) Train and familiarize personnel to perform emergency operations

  b. A plan should include priorities, insurance, backup approaches, specific assignments, period testing and updating, and documentation, as described below.

       (1) **Priorities**—Which applications are most critical?

       (2) **Insurance to defer costs**

       (3) **Backup approaches**

          (a) Batch systems—The most common approach is the ***Grandfather-Father-Son*** method. A master file (e.g., accounts receivable) is updated with the day's transaction files (e.g., files of cash receipts and credit sales). After the update, the new file master file is the son. The file from which the father was developed with the transaction files of the appropriate day is the grandfather. The grandfather and son files are stored in different locations. If the son were destroyed, for example, it could be reconstructed by rerunning the father file and the related transaction files.

          (b) Online databases and master files systems

             1] **Checkpoint**—Similar to grandfather-father-son, but at certain points, "checkpoints," the system makes a copy of the database and this "checkpoint" file is stored on a separate disk or tape. If a problem occurs the system is restarted at the last checkpoint and updated with subsequent transactions.

             2] **Rollback**—As a part of recovery, to undo changes made to a database to a point at which it was functioning properly

             3] **Backup facilities**

               a] **Reciprocal agreement**—An agreement between two or more organizations (with compatible computer facilities) to aid each other with their data processing needs in the event of a disaster. This is sometimes referred to as a mutual aid pact.

               b] **Hot site**—A commercial disaster recovery service that allows a business to continue computer operations in the event of computer disaster. For example, if a company's data processing center becomes inoperable, that enterprise can move all processing to a hot site that has all the equipment needed to continue operation. This is also referred to as a recovery operations center (ROC) approach.

               c] **Cold site**—Similar to a hot site, but the customer provides and installs the equipment needed to continue operations. A cold site is less expensive, but takes longer to get in full operation after a disaster. This is sometimes referred to as an "empty shell" in that the "shell" is available and ready to receive whatever hardware the temporary user needs

    d]  **Internal site**—Large organizations with multiple data processing centers some-times rely upon their own sites for backup in the event of a disaster.

> *NOTE: Be aware that most approaches to control for catastrophic failures rely upon backup of the entire system in one form or another. Also, various combinations of the above approaches may be used.*

  (4)  **Specific assignments, including having individuals involved with**

    (a)  Arranging for new facilities
    (b)  Computer operations
    (c)  Installing software
    (d)  Establishing data communications facilities
    (e)  Recovering vital records
    (f)  Arranging for forms and supplies

  (5)  **Periodic testing and updating of plan**
  (6)  **Documentation of plan**

## E.  Flowcharting

**General:** Flowcharts analytically describe some aspect of an information system. Flowcharting is a procedure to graphically show the sequential flow of data and/or operations. The data and operations portrayed include document preparation, authorization, storage, and decision making. The more common flowcharting symbols are illustrated below. Knowledge of them would help with occasional multiple-choice questions and with problems that present a detailed flowchart that must be analyzed.

### 1.  Common Flowcharting Symbols

| Symbol | Name | Description |
| --- | --- | --- |
| | Document | This can be a manual form or a computer printout |
| | Computer Operation | Computer process which transforms input data into useful information |
| | Manual Operation | Manual (human) process to prepare documents, make entries, check output, etc. |
| | Decision | Determines which alternative path is followed (IF/THEN/ELSE Conditions) |
| | Input/Output | General input or output to a process. Often used to represent accounting journals and ledgers on document flowcharts |
| | Online Storage | Refers to direct access computer storage connected directly to the CPU. Data is available on a random access basis |
| | Disc Storage | Refers to data stored on a magnetic disk |
| | Off-Line Storage | Refers to a file or indicates the mailing of a document (i.e., invoices or statements to customers). A letter in the symbol below the line indicates the order in which the file is stored. (N-Numerical, C-Chronological, A-Alphabetical) |
| | Display | Visual display of data and/or output on a terminal screen |

| | Batch Total Tape | Manually computed total before processing (such as the number of records to be processed). This total is recomputed by the computer and compared after processing is completed |
| | Magnetic Tape | Used for reading, writing, or storage on sequential storage media |
| | Manual Data Entry | Refers to data entered through a terminal keyboard or key-to-tape or key-to-disk device |
| | Annotation | Provides additional description or information connected to symbol to which it annotates by a dotted line (not a flowline) |
| | Flowline | Shows direction of data flow, operations, and documents |
| | Communication Link | Telecommunication line linking computer system to remote locations |
| | Start/Termination | Used to begin or end a flowchart. (Not always used or shown in flowcharts on the CPA exam.) May be used to show connections to other procedures or receipt/ sending of documents to/from outsiders |
| | On Page Connector | Connects parts of flowchart on the same page |
| | Off Page Connector | Connects parts of flowchart on separate pages |

2. **Types and Definitions**

   a. **System flowchart**—A graphic representation of a data processing application that depicts the interaction of all the computer programs for a given system, rather than the logic for an individual computer program

   b. **Program flowchart**—A graphic representation of the logic (processing steps) of a computer program

   c. **Internal control (audit) flowchart** or **document flowchart**—A graphic representation of the flow of documents from one department to another, showing the source flow and final disposition of the various copies of all documents. Most flowcharts on the CPA exam have been of this type.

3. **Other Documentation Charting Techniques**

   a. **Decision table**—Decision tables use a matrix format that lists sets of conditions, and the actions that result from various combinations of these conditions. See Module 2 on internal control for an example of a decision table.

   b. **Data flow diagram (DFD)**—Presents logical flows of data and functions in a system. For example, a data flow diagram for the delivery of goods to a customer would include a symbol for the warehouse from which the goods are shipped and a symbol representing the customer. It would not emphasize details such as computer processing and paper outputs.

**SIMULATION 1**                                        (60 to 70 minutes)

**Topics—Planning, Internal Control, and Evidence**

| Situation | | | | | | | | | | |
|---|---|---|---|---|---|---|---|---|---|---|
| | Company Profile | Industry Information | Balance Sheet | Income Statement | Statement of Cash Flows | Risks | Financial Statement Analysis | Audit Procedures | Communication | Research |

   DietWeb Inc. (hereafter DietWeb) was incorporated and began business in March of 20X1, seven years ago.  You are working on the 20X8 audit—your CPA firm's fifth audit of DietWeb.

| | Company Profile | | | | | | | | | |
|---|---|---|---|---|---|---|---|---|---|---|
| Situation | | Industry Information | Balance Sheet | Income Statement | Statement of Cash Flows | Risks | Financial Statement Analysis | Audit Procedures | Communication | Research |

   The company's mission is to provide solutions that help individuals to realize their full potential through better eating habits and lifestyles.  Much of 20X1 and 20X2 was spent in developing a unique software platform that facilitates the production of individualized meal plans and shopping lists using a specific mathematical algorithm, which considers the user's physical condition, proclivity to exercise, food preferences, cooking preferences, desire to use prepackaged meals or dine out, among others. DietWeb sold its first online diet program in 20X2 and has continued to market memberships through increasing online advertising arrangements through the years.  The company has continued to develop this program throughout the years and finally became profitable in 20X6.

   DietWeb is executing a strategy to be a leading online provider of services, information and products related to nutrition, fitness and motivation. In 20X8, the company derived approximately 86% of its total revenues from the sale of approximately 203,000 personalized subscription-based online nutrition plans related to weight management, to dietary regimens such as vegetarianism and to specific medical conditions such as Type 2 diabetes. Given the personal nature of dieting, DietWeb assures customers of complete privacy of the information they provide.  To this point DietWeb's management is proud of its success in assuring the privacy of information supplied by its customers—this is a constant battle given the variety of intrusion attempts by various Internet hackers.

   DietWeb nutrition plans are paid in advance by customers and offered in increments of thirteen weeks with the customers having the ability to cancel and receive a refund of the unused portion of the subscription—this results in a significant level of "deferred revenue" each period. Although some DietWeb members are billed through use of the postal system, most DietWeb members currently purchase programs and products using credit cards, with renewals billed automatically, until cancellation. One week of a basic DietWeb membership costs less than one-half the cost of a weekly visit to the leading classroom-based diet program. The president, Mr. William Readings, suggests that in addition to its superior cost-effectiveness, the DietWeb online diet program is successful relative to classroom-based programs due to its customization, ease of use, expert support, privacy, constant availability, and breadth of choice.  The basic DietWeb membership includes

- Customized meal plans and workout schedules and related tools such as shopping lists, journals, and weight and exercise tracking.
- Interactive online support and education including approximately 100 message boards on various topics of interest to members and a library of dozens of multimedia educational segments presented by experts including psychologists, mental health counselors, dietitians, fitness trainers, a spiritual advisor and a physician.
- 24/7/365 telephone support from a staff of approximately 30 customer service representatives, nutritionists and fitness personnel.

   Throughout its nine-year history, Mr. William Readings has served as chief executive officer.  The other three founders of the company are also officers.  A fifth individual, Willingsley Williamson, also a founder, served as Chief Financial Officer until mid-20X8 when he left the company due to a difference of opinion with Mr. Readings.  The four founders purchased Mr. Williamson's stock and invested an additional approximately $1.2 million in common stock during 20X8 so as to limit the use of long-term debt.

   The company's board of directors is currently composed of the four individuals who remain active in the company; these four individuals also serve as the company's audit committee; Mr. Readings chairs both the board and the audit committee. Previously, Mr. Readings had also served on the board and the audit committee.  With Mr. Williamson's departure, Ms. Jane Jennings, another of the founders, became the company's CFO.

| | | Industry Information | | | | | | | | |
|---|---|---|---|---|---|---|---|---|---|---|
| Situation | Company Profile | | Balance Sheet | Income Statement | Statement of Cash Flows | Risks | Financial Statement Analysis | Audit Procedures | Communication | Research |

   The nutrition and diet industry in many ways thrives because individuals are becoming more aware of the negative health and financial consequences of being overweight, and consider important both weight loss and healthy weight maintenance.  A study by two respected researchers concluded that obesity was linked to higher rates of chronic illness than living in poverty, than smoking, or than drinking.  In addition, the American Cancer Society reported that as many as 14% of cancer deaths in men and 20% of cancer deaths in women could be related to being overweight.

   The financial costs of excess weight are also high.  A 20X8 study based on data from a major automobile manufacturer's health care plan showed that an overweight adult has annual health care costs that are 7.3% higher than a person in a healthy weight range, while obese individuals have annual health care costs that are 69% higher than a person of a healthy weight. With health care cost inflation running in the double digits in the United States since 20X4, supporters of the industry believe that the implementation of effective weight management tools will attract more attention from insurers, employers, consumers, and the government. As of January 20X9 five nutrition- or fitness-related bills were being considered in Congress, and several states had enacted or were considering enacting legislation relating to the sale of "junk" food in public schools. In addition, the US Food and Drug Administration, Department of Health and Human Services, and Federal Trade Commission are contemplating new labeling requirements for packaged food and restaurant food, new educational and motivational programs related to healthy eating and exercise, and increased regulation of advertising claims for food.

In response to consumers' growing demand for more healthful eating options, quick-service and full-service restaurants have introduced new offerings including salads, sandwiches, burgers, and other food items designed for the weight-conscious person. At the retail level, sales of natural and organic foods have been growing more rapidly than the overall food and over-the-counter drug market for the last several years. Nutritional supplement sales in the US, for instance, are estimated to have grown 34% between 20X4 and 20X8, while natural and organic foods are estimated to be growing at a rate of approximately 15% annually. Also, the industry has a tendency to change quickly as "dieting fads" regularly are introduced; some remain popular for years, some for only months.

Approximately 60% of the US adult population, or 120 million adults, are overweight and, of those, the Calorie Control Council estimates only about 50 million are dieting in a given year. About 15% of these dieters are using a commercial weight loss center, generating revenues of approximately $1.5 billion annually. DietWeb targets dieters who are online, which represents about two-thirds of the total universe at current Internet penetration rates, or 34 million adults, about 5 million of whom are spending approximately $1 billion at weight loss centers.

At the same time, the online dieting segment of the market is growing rapidly. The online diet industry in the US generated in excess of $100 million in 20X8, compared to revenues of approximately $75 million in 20X2. The industry includes other online nutrition and diet-oriented Web sites.

Another group of competitors to DietWeb are commercial weight loss centers, an industry that has shown marked decline in the last decade. According to Market Analysis Enterprises, the number of commercial weight loss centers in the US declined approximately 50% between 20X2 and 20X8, from over 8,600 to approximately 4,400. DietWeb competes against this segment on the basis of lower price, superior value, convenience, availability, the ability to personalize a meal plan on an ongoing basis, its extensive support capabilities, and the breadth of its meal plan options.

| Situation | Company Profile | Industry Information | Balance Sheet | Income Statement | Statement of Cash Flows | Risks | Financial Statement Analysis | Audit Procedures | Communication | Research |
|---|---|---|---|---|---|---|---|---|---|---|

**DietWeb, Inc.**
**BALANCE SHEET**
*December 31, 20X8 and 20X7*
*(in thousands)*

| | 20X8 | 20X7 |
|---|---|---|
| **Assets** | | |
| Current assets | | |
| Cash and cash equivalents | $3,032 | $1,072 |
| Trade receivables | 485 | 450 |
| Prepaid advertising expenses | 59 | 609 |
| Prepaid expenses and other current assets | 175 | 230 |
| Total current assets | 3,751 | 2,361 |
| Fixed assets, net | 3,321 | 3,926 |
| Total assets | $7,072 | $6,287 |
| | | |
| **Liabilities and shareholders' equity** | | |
| Current liabilities | | |
| Accounts payable | $1,070 | $ 909 |
| Current maturities of notes payable | 42 | 316 |
| Deferred revenue | 1,973 | 1,396 |
| Other current liabilities | 171 | 12 |
| Total current liabilities | 3,256 | 2,633 |
| Long-term debt, less current maturity | 34 | 176 |
| Accrued liabilities | 792 | 690 |
| Deferred tax liability | 15 | 145 |
| Total liabilities | 4,097 | 3,644 |
| Shareholders' equity | | |
| Common stock | 6,040 | 4,854 |
| Retained earnings | (3,065) | (2,211) |
| Total shareholders' equity | 2,975 | 2,643 |
| Total liabilities plus shareholders' equity | $7,072 | $6,287 |

| Situation | Company Profile | Industry Information | Balance Sheet | Income Statement | Statement of Cash Flows | Risks | Financial Statement Analysis | Audit Procedures | Communication | Research |
|---|---|---|---|---|---|---|---|---|---|---|

*DietWeb, Inc.*
**INCOME STATEMENT**
*Two Years Ended December 31, 20X8 and 20X7*
*(in thousands)*

|  | 20X8 | 20X7 |
|---|---|---|
| Revenue | $19,166 | $14,814 |
| Costs and expenses |  |  |
| Cost of revenue | 2,326 | 1,528 |
| Product development | 725 | 653 |
| Sales and marketing | 13,903 | 8,710 |
| General and administrative | 2,531 | 2,575 |
| Depreciation and amortization | 629 | 661 |
| Impairment of intangible assets | 35 | - |
| Total costs and expenses | 20,149 | 14,127 |
| Net income before taxes | (983) | 687 |
| Income tax benefit | 129 | 125 |
| Net income (loss) | $(854) | $812 |

| Situation | Company Profile | Industry Information | Balance Sheet | Income Statement | Statement of Cash Flows | Risks | Financial Statement Analysis | Audit Procedures | Communication | Research |
|---|---|---|---|---|---|---|---|---|---|---|

*DietWeb, Inc.*
**STATEMENT OF CASH FLOWS**
*Year Ended December 31, 20X8*

|  | 20X8 | 20X7 |
|---|---|---|
| Cash flows from operations |  |  |
| Net income (loss) | $(854) | 812 |
| Adjustments to net income |  |  |
| Depreciation | 629 | 660 |
| Increase in receivables | (35) | (47) |
| Decrease (Increase) in prepaid advertising | 550 | (650) |
| Decrease in other current assets | 55 | 74 |
| Increase (Decrease) in accounts payable | 161 | (540) |
| Increase in accrued liabilities | 102 | 43 |
| Increase (Decrease) in deferred revenue | 432 | (665) |
| Increase in common stock issued | 1,186 | - |
| Increase in other current liabilities | 159 | 43 |
| Net cash provided (used) by operations | 2,385 | (270) |
| Cash flows from investing activities |  |  |
| Purchase of property and equipment | (320) | 2,016 |
| Cash flows from financing activities |  |  |
| New debt | 613 | 40 |
| Debt payments | (718) | (918) |
| Net cash provided (used) by financing activities | (105) | (878) |
| Net increase in cash and cash equivalents | $1,960 | 868 |
| Cash and equivalents at beginning of year | $1,072 | 204 |
| Cash and equivalents at end of year | $3,032 | 1,072 |

| Situation | Company Profile | Industry Information | Balance Sheet | Income Statement | Statement of Cash Flows | Risks | Financial Statement Analysis | Audit Procedures | Communication | Research |
|-----------|-----------------|----------------------|---------------|------------------|-------------------------|-------|------------------------------|------------------|---------------|----------|

**(A) (B) (C) (D)**
○ ○ ○ ○

1. Of the following, which is likely to be one of DietWeb's major risks of doing business on the Internet in the future?

   A. Maintaining privacy of customer information.
   B. Maintaining the ability to pay Federal Communication Commission Internet use fees.
   C. Inability to provide 24/7/365 support.
   D. Inability to reach customers beyond the United States.

**(A) (B) (C) (D)**
○ ○ ○ ○

2. Which of the following is likely to be the most significant business risk for DietWeb?

   A. Internal control limitations due to the small size of the company.
   B. Inability of the Internet to provide adequate support for such a business due to its instability.
   C. Entrance of new competitors onto the Internet.
   D. Misstatements of revenues due to difficulties in determining appropriate year-end cutoffs.

| Situation | Company Profile | Industry Information | Balance Sheet | Income Statement | Statement of Cash Flows | Risks | Financial Statement Analysis | Audit Procedures | Communication | Research |
|-----------|-----------------|----------------------|---------------|------------------|-------------------------|-------|------------------------------|------------------|---------------|----------|

**(A) (B) (C) (D)**
○ ○ ○ ○

1. The most likely misstatement in the financial statements is

   A. The increase in cash in 20X8.
   B. Treatment of impaired intangible assets as an expense in 20X8.
   C. Treatment of common stock issued as an adjustment to net income.
   D. An income tax benefit on the income statement as contrasted to income tax expense.

**(A) (B) (C) (D)**
○ ○ ○ ○

2. Which of the following is the most unexpected change on the balance sheet, if one assumes the revenue increase in 20X8 is correct?

   A. Decrease in prepaid advertising expenses.
   B. Increase in accounts payable.
   C. Decrease in deferred revenues.
   D. Increase in common stock.

| Situation | Company Profile | Industry Information | Balance Sheet | Income Statement | Statement of Cash Flows | Risks | Financial Statement Analysis | Audit Procedures | Communication | Research |
|-----------|-----------------|----------------------|---------------|------------------|-------------------------|-------|------------------------------|------------------|---------------|----------|

The auditor determines that each of the following objectives will be part of DietWeb's audit. For each audit objective, select a substantive procedure that would help to achieve that objective. Each of the procedures may be used once, more than once, or not at all.

*Substantive procedure*
A. Trace opening balances in the summary schedules to the prior year's audit working papers.
B. Review the provision for deprecation expense and determine that depreciable lives and methods used in the current year are consistent with those used in the prior year.
C. Determine that responsibility for maintaining the property and equipment records is segregated from the responsibility for custody of property and equipment.
D. Examine deeds and title insurance certificates.
E. Perform cutoff test to verify that property and equipment additions are recorded in the proper period.
F. Determine that property and equipment is adequately insured.
G. Physically examine all recorded major property and equipment additions.

|   |   | (A) | (B) | (C) | (D) | (E) | (F) | (G) |
|---|---|-----|-----|-----|-----|-----|-----|-----|
| **1.** | DietWeb has legal rights to property and equipment acquired during the year. | ○ | ○ | ○ | ○ | ○ | ○ | ○ |
| **2.** | DietWeb recorded property and equipment acquired during the year that did not actually exist at the balance sheet date. | ○ | ○ | ○ | ○ | ○ | ○ | ○ |

| Situation | Company Profile | Industry Information | Balance Sheet | Income Statement | Statement of Cash Flows | Risks | Financial Statement Analysis | Audit Procedures | Communication | Research |
|---|---|---|---|---|---|---|---|---|---|---|

This is your firm's sixth audit of DietWeb. In a memorandum to the audit team (below) summarize your view of the audit committee's strengths, weaknesses, and any changes that have occurred relating to the audit committee this year.

Remember: Your response will be graded for both technical relevance and writing skills. For writing skills you should demonstrate an ability to develop your ideas, organize them, and express them clearly. Do not convey information in the form of a table, bullet point list, or other abbreviated presentation.

> To:    Audit Team
> From:  CPA Candidate
> Re:    DietWeb Audit Committee

| Situation | Company Profile | Industry Information | Balance Sheet | Income Statement | Statement of Cash Flows | Risks | Financial Statement Analysis | Audit Procedures | Communication | Research |
|---|---|---|---|---|---|---|---|---|---|---|

*NOTE: This section is only possible to work in a meaningful way if you have the professional standards available—preferably in electronic form.*

You are now working on the fieldwork for the DietWeb audit. Use the Professional Standards to identify risk factors that might indicate misstatements arising from misappropriation of assets. Do this by copying and pasting those risk factors on misappropriation of assets that are included in the Professional Standards relating to audit. You should **not** edit the list in any way.

**SOLUTION TO SIMULATION 1**

| Situation | Company Profile | Industry Information | Balance Sheet | Income Statement | Statement of Cash Flows | Risks | Financial Statement Analysis | Audit Procedures | Communication | Research |
|---|---|---|---|---|---|---|---|---|---|---|

**(A) (B) (C) (D)**

1. Of the following, which is likely to be one of DietWeb's major risks of doing business on the Internet in the future?  ● ○ ○ ○

2. Which of the following is likely to be the most significant business risk for DietWeb?  ○ ○ ● ○

**Explanation of solutions**

1. **(A)** The requirement is to identify DietWeb's major listed risk of doing business on the Internet. Answer (A) is correct because DietWeb must carefully maintain the privacy of their customers' information—both due to law and due to DietWeb's assurance provided to its customers. Answer (B) is incorrect because there are no major Federal Communications Commission Internet use fees. Answer (C) is incorrect because the case indicates no particular problem in providing 24/7/365 support. Answer (D) is incorrect because the Internet is able to reach customers beyond the United States.

2. **(C)** The requirement is to identify the most significant business risk listed for DietWeb. Answer (C) is correct because barriers to entrance on the Internet are ordinarily not high. Another organization might develop similar (or more accepted) software, and/or charge lower prices than those charged by DietWeb. Answer (A) is incorrect because internal control limitations need not necessarily be a major problem, and because internal control relates to control risk more directly than to the company's business risk. Answer (B) is incorrect because while Internet instability may cause difficulties, few would consider it as significant a problem as new competitors. Answer (D) is incorrect because determining appropriate year-end cutoffs is not likely to create major difficulties.

| Situation | Company Profile | Industry Information | Balance Sheet | Income Statement | Statement of Cash Flows | Risks | Financial Statement Analysis | Audit Procedures | Communication | Research |
|---|---|---|---|---|---|---|---|---|---|---|

**(A) (B) (C) (D)**

1. The most likely misstatement in the financial statements is  ○ ○ ● ○

2. Which of the following is the most unexpected change on the balance sheet, if one assumes the revenue increase in 20X8 is correct?  ● ○ ○ ○

**Explanation of solutions**

1. **(C)** The requirement is to identify a likely misstatement in the financial statements. Answer (C) is correct because common stock issued should be treated under financing rather than operations. Answer (A) is incorrect because an increase in cash may well occur—even during a year in which the company encounters a loss. Answer (B) is incorrect because there is no indication that the impairment expense is inappropriate. Answer (D) is incorrect because previous years' pattern of income and losses may create a situation in which a net income tax benefit occurs.

2. **(A)** The requirement is to identify, of the balance sheet changes listed, the most unexpected one. Answer (A) is unexpected in that prepaid advertising expenses decreased by more than ninety percent—at a time when the company increased its sales and marketing expenses so significantly. Answer (B) is incorrect because the relatively small increase in accounts payable may be expected given the increase in revenues. Answer (C) is incorrect because one would expect such an increase in deferred revenues as revenues increase. Answer (D) is incorrect since the company simply issued more stock—as indicated in the company profile.

| Situation | Company Profile | Industry Information | Balance Sheet | Income Statement | Statement of Cash Flows | Risks | Financial Statement Analysis | Audit Procedures | Communication | Research |
|---|---|---|---|---|---|---|---|---|---|---|

**(A) (B) (C) (D) (E) (F) (G)**

1. DietWeb has legal rights to property and equipment acquired during the year.  ○ ○ ○ ● ○ ○ ○

2. DietWeb recorded property and equipment acquired during the year that did not actually exist at the balance sheet date.  ○ ○ ○ ○ ○ ○ ●

**Explanation of solutions**

1. **(D)** The requirement is to identify the best substantive procedure to determine that DietWeb has legal rights to the property and equipment acquired during the year. Answer (D) is correct because the deeds and title insurance certificates will provide evidence that the company owns the property and equipment.

2. **(G)** The requirement is to identify the best substantive procedure to determine that DietWeb recorded property and equipment actually exists. Answer (G) is correct because physically examining the items will provide this evidence.

| | | | | | | | | | | Communication | |
|---|---|---|---|---|---|---|---|---|---|---|---|
| Situation | Company Profile | Industry Information | Balance Sheet | Income Statement | Statement of Cash Flows | | Risks | Financial Statement Analysis | Audit Procedures | | Research |

To:    Audit Team
From:  CPA Candidate
Re:    DietWeb Audit Committee

We have identified a number of concerns regarding the makeup of DietWeb's audit committee.  The audit committee membership is identical to that of the board of directors.  Accordingly, there are no independent members.  Mr. Readings, the company's CEO, serves as chairman of both the board of directors and the audit committee.  On the other hand, the committee members are competent and interested.

We will make a recommendation to the board of directors to correct this matter by bringing on independent board and audit committee members.  In addition, we should consider the implications of this weakness in control environment on our audit.

| | | | | | | | | | | | Research |
|---|---|---|---|---|---|---|---|---|---|---|---|
| Situation | Company Profile | Industry Information | Balance Sheet | Income Statement | Statement of Cash Flows | | Risks | Financial Statement Analysis | Audit Procedures | Communication | |

AU 316.85 presents the following examples of risk factors related to misstatements arising from misappropriation of assets:

**Incentives/Pressures**

   a.   Personal financial obligations may create pressure on management or employees with access to cash or other assets susceptible to theft to misappropriate those assets.

   b.   Adverse relationships between the entity and employees with access to cash or other assets susceptible to theft may motivate those employees to misappropriate those assets. For example, adverse relationships may be created by the following:

     -  Known or anticipated future employee layoffs
     -  Recent or anticipated changes to employee compensation or benefit plans
     -  Promotions, compensation, or other rewards inconsistent with expectations

**Opportunities**

   a.   Certain characteristics or circumstances may increase the susceptibility of assets to misappropriation. For example, opportunities to misappropriate assets increase when there are the following:

     -  Large amounts of cash on hand or processed
     -  Inventory items that are small in size, of high value, or in high demand
     -  Easily convertible assets, such as bearer bonds, diamonds, or computer chips
     -  Fixed assets that are small in size, marketable, or lacking observable identification of ownership

   b.   Inadequate internal control over assets may increase the susceptibility of misappropriation of those assets. For example, misappropriation of assets may occur because there is the following:

     -  Inadequate segregation of duties or independent checks
     -  Inadequate management oversight of employees responsible for assets, for example, inadequate supervision or monitoring of remote locations
     -  Inadequate job applicant screening of employees with access to assets
     -  Inadequate recordkeeping with respect to assets
     -  Inadequate system of authorization and approval of transactions (for example, in purchasing)
     -  Lack of complete and timely reconciliations of assets
     -  Lack of timely and appropriate documentation of transactions, for example, credits for merchandise returns
     -  Lack of mandatory vacations for employees performing key control functions
     -  Inadequate management understanding of information technology, which enables information technology employees to perpetrate a misappropriation
     -  Inadequate access controls over automated records, including controls over and review of computer systems event logs.

**Attitudes/Rationalizations**

Risk factors reflective of employee attitudes/rationalizations that allow them to justify misappropriations of assets, are generally not susceptible to observation by the auditor. Nevertheless, the auditor who becomes aware of the existence of such information should consider it in identifying the risks of material misstatement arising from misappropriation of assets. For example, auditors may become aware of the following attitudes or behavior of employees who have access to assets susceptible to misappropriation:

     -  Disregard for the need for monitoring or reducing risks related to misappropriations of assets
     -  Disregard for internal control over misappropriation of assets by overriding existing controls or by failing to correct known internal control deficiencies
     -  Behavior indicating displeasure or dissatisfaction with the company or its treatment of the employee
     -  Changes in behavior or lifestyle that may indicate assets have been misappropriated

**SIMULATION 2**                                        (60 to 70 minutes)

**Topics—Planning, Internal Control, Evidence, and Reporting**

| Situation | | | | | | | | | | | |
|---|---|---|---|---|---|---|---|---|---|---|---|
| | Company Profile | Industry Information | Balance Sheet | Income Statement | Statement of Cash Flows | Risks | Audit Findings | Audit Procedures | Communication | Research | |

Assume you are performing the 20X8 audit of Tommi Stone and Quarry.

| | Company Profile | | | | | | | | | | |
|---|---|---|---|---|---|---|---|---|---|---|---|
| Situation | | Industry Information | Balance Sheet | Income Statement | Statement of Cash Flows | Risks | Audit Findings | Audit Procedures | Communication | Research | |

In 20X1 Jill Tommi founded Tommi Stone and Quarry (TSQ). Within its first year of existence, the company completed initial development of the extraction pit area and constructed an aggregate processing plant which is equipped to crush, screen, and wash aggregate products. By 20X3 the sand and gravel operation was profitable and growing market conditions justified modifications and expansion. Currently, at the conclusion of 20X8, TSQ produces a wide range of sand and stone products from its pit near Albuquerque, New Mexico. The materials it develops range from various sand and stone materials for residential and commercial construction and highway projects. TSQ sells to a wide variety of residential, commercial and governmental customers, with no one customer accounting for more than 5% of its total sales.

TSQ has worked closely with stucco manufacturers and plastering contractors in the Albuquerque plastering industry to produce a plaster sand ("Plasand") that exceeds normal specifications and produces a superior ingredient which improves stucco and plastering finished products. Plasand has been increasingly widely accepted as superior to products offered by competitors, and now accounts for approximately 10% of the company's sales, and 12% of its profits. TSQ is currently working closely with sport complexes and golf course architects in conjunction with test laboratories to develop a superior sand for use in the construction and top dressing of golf courses and sport complex playing fields.

The company experienced a level of profitability in 20X8 of about the same as that of 20X7—but this is well below the net incomes of the preceding several years. Jill suggested to you that, surprisingly, intense price competition from several smaller competitors in the Albuquerque area caused the somewhat low level of profitability. But, she added, she didn't expect the problem to last for long because she doubted that those companies could continue to operate selling at these lower prices. Jill had hoped for a more profitable year in 20X8 as a significant amount of the company's long-term debt is payable in 20X9. TSQ is currently involved in discussions with the bank on refinancing.

TSQ added significant additional crushing and washing plants and equipment during 20X8 to increase production in the future by more than 100% while expanding capabilities to produce custom specification materials.

Until 20X7 and 20X8, most of earnings were distributed through dividends to TSQ's five shareholders—CEO and Chair of the Board of Directors Jill Tommi, her husband Mort Tommi, CFO Googlo Permasi and two college friends of Jill's who invested in the company, Jian Zhang and Kendra Kovano. These five individuals make up the company's Board of Directors.

This year, in reaction to pressure from a bank that provides a significant portion of the financing, TSQ established an audit committee composed of Mort Tommi, Googlo Permasi, and Jian Zhang.

You are working on your firm's fifth audit of TSQ. The previous audits have all resulted in standard unqualified audit reports.

| | | Industry Information | | | | | | | | | |
|---|---|---|---|---|---|---|---|---|---|---|---|
| Situation | Company Profile | | Balance Sheet | Income Statement | Statement of Cash Flows | Risks | Audit Findings | Audit Procedures | Communication | Research | |

The industry consists of preparation for the mining and extraction of sand and rock products. These include the activities of cleaning, separating and sorting of quarried sand and the crushing of rocks. The products are in the form of sand used in making concrete; sand used in laying bricks (contains little soil); sand used for fill (contains lots of soil, and quartz sand); and excluding the products of gravel quarrying (sandstone, gravel stone, and iron sand).

While sales within the industry are relatively unaffected by changes in technology, or obsolescence, sales rely heavily upon both the residential and commercial construction markets as well as government spending. During the past five years construction has performed well and that trend is expected to continue at least for the coming several years. Sand and gravel production has increased at approximately 3% per year during this time period, as has construction within the central Ohio area.

The sand and gravel market in central New Mexico has been particularly healthy due in large part to the growth of Albuquerque into a major metropolitan area. The most significant question facing the industry is whether the strong construction will continue as expected. During the past two years the economy of the United States has been in a recovery period, yet unemployment remains high as compared to previous periods of recovery. Thus, the questions concerning the continuing construction demand.

| Situation | Company Profile | Industry Information | Balance Sheet | Income Statement | Statement of Cash Flows | Risks | Audit Findings | Audit Procedures | Communication | Research |
|---|---|---|---|---|---|---|---|---|---|---|

*Tommi Stone and Quarry*
**BALANCE SHEET**
*December 31, 20X8 and 20X7*

|  | 20X8 | 20X7 |
|---|---|---|
| **Assets** | | |
| Current assets | | |
| Cash and cash equivalents | $    5,055 | $    3,822 |
| Trade receivables | 3,369,971 | 2,383,055 |
| Inventory | 1,713,118 | 1,810,361 |
| Other current assets | 17,140 | 10,200 |
| Total current assets | 5,105,284 | 4,207,438 |
| Fixed assets, net | 397,749 | 74,769 |
| Total assets | $5,503,033 | $4,282,207 |
| **Liabilities and shareholders' equity** | | |
| Current liabilities | | |
| Accounts payable | $ 340,995 | $ 316,164 |
| Current maturities of notes payable | 1,262,379 | 416,607 |
| Accrued expenses | 187,190 | 208,460 |
| Other current liabilities | 158,603 | 199,629 |
| Total current liabilities | 1,949,167 | 1,140,860 |
| Long-term debt, less current maturity | 3,249,934 | 2,959,200 |
| Total liabilities | 5,199,101 | 4,100,060 |
| Shareholders' equity | | |
| Common stock | 57,333 | 57,333 |
| Retained earnings | 246,599 | 124,814 |
| Total shareholders' equity | 303,932 | 182,147 |
| Total liabilities plus shareholders' equity | $5,503,033 | $4,282,207 |

| Situation | Company Profile | Industry Information | Balance Sheet | Income Statement | Statement of Cash Flows | Risks | Audit Findings | Audit Procedures | Communication | Research |
|---|---|---|---|---|---|---|---|---|---|---|

*Tommi Stone and Quarry*
**INCOME STATEMENT**
*Two Years Ended December 31, 20X8 and 20X7*
*(in thousands)*

|  | 20X8 | 20X7 |
|---|---|---|
| **Revenue** | $21,312,665 | $17,261,974 |
| Cost of goods sold | 18,029,838 | 14,397,853 |
| Gross profit on sales | 3,282,827 | 2,864,121 |
| Operating expenses | 2,707,606 | 2,185,542 |
| Repairs and maintenance | 104,168 | 132,083 |
| Depreciation | 31,673 | 30,098 |
| Interest expense | 265,398 | 314,419 |
| Total expenses | 3,108,845 | 2,662,142 |
| Net income before taxes | 173,982 | 201,979 |
| Provision for income taxes | 52,197 | 80,792 |
| Net income | $ 121,785 | $ 121,187 |

| Situation | Company Profile | Industry Information | Balance Sheet | Income Statement | Statement of Cash Flows | | Risks | Audit Findings | Audit Procedures | Communication | Research |
|---|---|---|---|---|---|---|---|---|---|---|---|

*Tommi Stone and Quarry*
### STATEMENT OF CASH FLOWS
*Year Ended December 31, 20X8*

| | |
|---|---|
| Cash flows from operations | |
| Net income (loss) | $121,785 |
| Adjustments to net income | |
| Depreciation | 31,673 |
| Increase in receivables | (986,916) |
| Decrease in inventory | 97,243 |
| Increase in other current assets | (6,940) |
| Increase in accounts payable | 24,831 |
| Decrease in accrued expenses | (21,270) |
| Decrease in other current liabilities | (41,026) |
| Net cash provided (used) by operations | (780,620) |
| Cash flows from investing activities | |
| Purchase of property and equipment | (343,270) |
| Cash flows from financing activities | |
| New debt | 1,682,666 |
| Debt payments | (557,543) |
| Net cash provided (used) by financing activities | 1,125,123 |
| Net increase in cash and cash equivalents | $1,233 |
| Cash and equivalents at beginning of year | $3,822 |
| Cash and equivalents at end of year | $5,055 |

| Situation | Company Profile | Industry Information | Balance Sheet | Income Statement | Statement of Cash Flows | Risks | Audit Findings | Audit Procedures | Communication | Research |
|---|---|---|---|---|---|---|---|---|---|---|

**(A) (B) (C) (D)**

1.  A risk factor relating to misstatements arising from fraudulent financial reporting is

    A.  Earnings this year are lower than management had hoped.
    B.  Fewer competitors exist than in the past, and this places the company in a position in which it is easier to manipulate earnings.
    C.  Sales are made to residential, commercial, and governmental purchasers.
    D.  The industry faces great technological changes in almost all of its products.

**(A) (B) (C) (D)**

2.  Which of the following correctly identifies a risk facing TSQ that might adversely affect sales during the coming years?

    A.  A general slowdown in the economy.
    B.  Sales to many different types of customers.
    C.  Increased attention to developing new products.
    D.  A board of directors dominated by management.

| Situation | Company Profile | Industry Information | Balance Sheet | Income Statement | Statement of Cash Flows | Risks | Audit Findings | Audit Procedures | Communication | Research |
|---|---|---|---|---|---|---|---|---|---|---|

| Ratio | 20X8 | 20X7 |
|---|---|---|
| Gross margin percentage | 0.154 | 0.166 |
| Current ratio | 2.619 | 3.688 |

The above table presents two ratios that were identified as significant in the current and prior years' audits of TSQ. Compare the values of each ratio. Then select an audit finding that is consistent with these metrics. The finding need not explain the entire change. But, of the replies listed, it should potentially lead to the most significant change in the direction indicated by the change in the ratio. Each of the audit findings may be used once, more than once, or not at all.

*Substantive procedure*

A.  Increases in costs of purchases were not completely passed on to customers through higher selling prices.
B.  Increases in trade receivables.
C.  Owners' equity increased due to retention of profits.
D.  A larger percentage of sales occurred during the last month of 20X8, as compared to 20X7.
E.  Interest expense decreased during 20X8.
F.  The percentage tax included in the provision for income taxes for 20X8 was less than the percentage in 20X7.
G.  A significant amount of long-term debt became current.

                                                                   (A) (B) (C) (D) (E) (F) (G)

1.  An audit finding most consistent with the change in the gross margin percentage        O   O   O   O   O   O   O

2.  An audit finding most consistent with the change in the current ratio          O   O   O   O   O   O   O

| Situation | Company Profile | Industry Information | Balance Sheet | Income Statement | Statement of Cash Flows | Risks | Audit Findings | Audit Procedures | Communication | Research |
|---|---|---|---|---|---|---|---|---|---|---|

The auditor determines that each of the following objectives will be part of TSQ's audit. For each audit objective, select a substantive procedure that would help to achieve that objective. Each of the procedures may be used once, more than once, or not at all.

*Substantive procedure*

A.  Analyze the relationship of accounts receivable and purchases and compare it with relationships for preceding periods.
B.  Analyze sales recorded in January to obtain assurance that sales transactions are recorded in the proper period.
C.  Analyze sales recorded in December to obtain assurance that sales transactions are recorded in the proper period.
D.  Review the aged trial balance for significant past due accounts.
E.  Obtain an understanding of the business purpose of transactions that resulted in accounts receivable balances.
F.  Review board of director minutes for information on sales of goods to officers.

                                                                     (A) (B) (C) (D) (E) (F)

1.  Establish the completeness of receivables transactions.      O   O   O   O   O   O

2.  Determine that the valuation of receivables is at appropriate net realizable values.      O   O   O   O   O   O

| Situation | Company Profile | Industry Information | Balance Sheet | Income Statement | Statement of Cash Flows | Risks | Financial Statement Analysis | Audit Procedures | Communication | Research |
|---|---|---|---|---|---|---|---|---|---|---|

This is your firm's fifth audit of TSQ. This year the company has formed an audit committee—composed of Mort Tommi, Jian Zhang, and Kendra Kovano. In a memorandum to the audit team (below) explain the likely effect of this change on audit risk. Mort is chairman of the audit committee.

Remember: Your response will be graded for both technical relevance and writing skills. For writing skills you should demonstrate an ability to develop your ideas, organize them and express them clearly. Do not convey information in the form of a table, bullet point list, or other abbreviated presentation.

To:      Audit Team
From: CPA Candidate
Re:      TSQ Audit Committee

| Situation | Company Profile | Industry Information | Balance Sheet | Income Statement | Statement of Cash Flows | Risks | Financial Statement Analysis | Audit Procedures | Communication | Research |
|-----------|-----------------|---------------------|---------------|------------------|-------------------------|-------|------------------------------|------------------|---------------|----------|

You have now completed the fieldwork for the TSQ audit. Using the Professional Standards, assemble model paragraphs for a standard unqualified audit report for two-year comparative statements. Do this by copying and pasting the report to a workspace. You should **not** edit the report in any way.

**SOLUTION TO SIMULATION 2**

| Situation | Company Profile | Industry Information | Balance Sheet | Income Statement | Statement of Cash Flows | Risks | Audit Findings | Audit Procedures | Communication | Research |
|---|---|---|---|---|---|---|---|---|---|---|

                                                                                                    (A)  (B)  (C)  (D)

**1.**  A risk factor relating to misstatements arising from fraudulent financial reporting is                    ●   ○   ○   ○

**2.**  Which of the following correctly identifies a risk facing TSQ that might adversely affect sales during the coming years?                    ●   ○   ○   ○

**Explanation of solutions**

**1.**  **(A)**  The requirement is to identify a risk factor relating to misstatements arising from fraudulent financial reporting.  Answer (A) is correct because historically low levels of earnings may have created pressure on management to at least exceed the previous year's net income.  Answer (B) is incorrect because there are not fewer competitors.  Answer (C) is incorrect because selling to residential, commercial, and governmental purchasers presents no particular risk. Answer (D) is incorrect because there is no indication that the company is involved with overly complex transactions (maintaining lien rights on inventory is not complex) and the industry does not face great technological changes in products.

**2.**  **(A)**  The requirement is to identify the correct statement relating to a risk that might adversely affect TSQ's sales.  Answer (A) is correct because the simulation emphasizes the fact that sales are dependent upon economic growth.  Answer (B) is incorrect because selling to different types of customers diversifies away some of the risk of declining sales.  Answer (C) is incorrect because increased attention to developing new products may help the company increase future sales.  Answer (D) is incorrect because while the board of directors may be dominated by management, it is uncertain that such lack of independence would lead to a decline in sales.

| Situation | Company Profile | Industry Information | Balance Sheet | Income Statement | Statement of Cash Flows | Risks | Audit Findings | Audit Procedures | Communication | Research |
|---|---|---|---|---|---|---|---|---|---|---|

                                                                        (A)  (B)  (C)  (D)  (E)  (F)  (G)

**1.**  An audit finding most consistent with the change in the gross margin percentage                    ●   ○   ○   ○   ○   ○   ○

**2.**  An audit finding most consistent with the change in the current ratio                    ○   ○   ○   ○   ○   ○   ●

**Explanation of solutions**

**1.**  **(A)**  The requirement is to identify an audit finding most consistent with a decrease in the gross margin percentage—gross margin/sales.  Answer (A) is correct because the inability to pass on increases in costs will decrease the gross margin because cost of goods sold as a percentage of sales will increase.

**2.**  **(G)**  The requirement is to identify an audit finding that is consistent with a decrease in the current ratio—current assets/current liabilities.  Answer (G) is correct because the long-term debt becoming current increases the denominator of the current ratio, which decreases the ratio.

| Situation | Company Profile | Industry Information | Balance Sheet | Income Statement | Statement of Cash Flows | Risks | Audit Findings | Audit Procedures | Communication | Research |
|---|---|---|---|---|---|---|---|---|---|---|

                                                                        (A)  (B)  (C)  (D)  (E)  (F)

**1.**  Establish the completeness of receivables transactions.                    ○   ●   ○   ○   ○   ○

**2.**  Determine that the valuation of receivables is at appropriate net realizable values.                    ○   ○   ○   ●   ○   ○

**Explanation of solutions**

**1.**  **(B)**  The requirement is to identify a substantive procedure to establish the completeness of receivables transactions.  Answer (B) is correct because analyzing sales recorded in January (performing cutoff tests) will reveal whether December sales were recorded in the wrong period.

**2.**  **(D)**  The requirement is to identify a procedure to determine the valuation of receivables at appropriate net realizable values.  Answer (D) is correct because a review of the aged trial balance for significant past due accounts will provide evidence on how much is expected to be realized on receivables.

| Situation | Company Profile | Industry Information | Balance Sheet | Income Statement | Statement of Cash Flows | Risks | Audit Findings | Audit Procedures | | Communication | Research |
|---|---|---|---|---|---|---|---|---|---|---|---|

To:       Audit Team
Subject:  TSQ Audit Committee

As a reaction to pressure from its bank, TSQ has recently established an audit committee of the board of directors. The committee is made up of Mort Tommi, the CEO's husband, Googlo Permasi, the CFO, and Jian Zhang, a stockholder in the company. Mort Tommi is chairman of the committee. While this results in an independence issue with respect to the committee, we should remember that this is a closely held nonpublic company. These types of entities typically do not have audit committees. We should make inquiries of Jian Zhang to obtain information about the operation of the committee.

| Situation | Company Profile | Industry Information | Balance Sheet | Income Statement | Statement of Cash Flows | Risks | Audit Findings | Audit Procedures | Communication | | Research |
|---|---|---|---|---|---|---|---|---|---|---|---|

### *Independent Auditor's Report*

We have audited the accompanying balance sheets of X Company as of December 31, 20X2 and December 31, 20X1, and the related consolidated statements of income, retained earnings, and cash flows for the years then ended. These financial statements are the responsibility of the company's management. Our responsibility is to express an opinion on these financial statements based on our audits.

We conducted our audits in accordance with auditing standards generally accepted in the United States of America. Those standards require that we plan and perform the audit to obtain reasonable assurance about whether the financial statements are free of material misstatement. An audit includes examining, on a test basis, evidence supporting the amounts and disclosures in the financial statements. An audit also includes assessing the accounting principles used and significant estimates made by management, as well as evaluating the overall financial statement presentation. We believe that our audits provide a reasonable basis for our opinion.

In our opinion, the financial statements referred to above present fairly, in all material respects, the financial position of X Company as of [at] December 31, 20X2 and 20X1, and the results of its operations and its cash flows for the years then ended in conformity with accounting principles generally accepted in the United States of America.

**SIMULATION 3**

**Topic—Audit Planning and Evidence**

| Situation | | | |
|---|---|---|---|
| | **Risk Analysis** | **Responding to Risk** | **Research and Communication** |

You are working with William Bond, CPA, and you are considering the risk of material misstatement in planning the audit of Toxic Waste Disposal (TWD) Company's financial statements for the year ended December 31, 20X0.  TWD is a privately owned entity that contracts with municipal governments to remove environmental waste.

| | **Risk Analysis** | | |
|---|---|---|---|
| **Situation** | | **Responding to Risk** | **Research and Communication** |

Based only on the information below, indicate whether each of the following factors would most likely increase (I), decrease (D), or have no effect on the risk of material misstatement (N).

|  | | (I) | (D) | (N) |
|---|---|---|---|---|
| **1.** | Because municipalities have received increased federal and state funding for environmental purposes, TWD returned to profitability for the first year following three years with losses. | O | O | O |
| **2.** | TWD's Board of Directors is controlled by Mead, the majority stockholder, who also acts as the chief executive officer. | O | O | O |
| **3.** | The internal auditor reports to the controller and the controller reports to Mead. | O | O | O |
| **4.** | The accounting department has experienced a high rate of turnover of key personnel. | O | O | O |
| **5.** | TWD's bank has a loan officer who meets regularly with TWD's CEO and controller to monitor TWD's financial performance. | O | O | O |
| **6.** | TWD's employees are paid biweekly. | O | O | O |
| **7.** | TWD has such a strong financial presence in its history so as to allow it often to dictate the terms or conditions of transactions with its suppliers. | O | O | O |
| **8.** | During 20X1, TWD changed its method of preparing its financial statements from the cash basis to generally accepted accounting principles. | O | O | O |
| **9.** | During 20X1, TWD sold one-half of its controlling interest in United Equipment Leasing (UEL) Co.  TWD retained significant influence over UEL. | O | O | O |
| **10.** | During 20X1, litigation filed against TWD from an action ten years ago that alleged that TWD discharged pollutants into state waterways was dropped by the state.  Loss contingency disclosures that TWD included in prior years' financial statements are being removed from the 20X1 financial statements. | O | O | O |
| **11.** | During December 20X1, TWD signed a contract to lease disposal equipment from an entity owned by Mead's parents.  This related-party transaction is not disclosed in TWD's notes to the 20X1 financial statements. | O | O | O |
| **12.** | During December 20X1, TWD completed a barter transaction with a municipality.  TWD removed waste from the municipally owned site and acquired title to another contaminated site at below market price.  TWD intends to service this new site in 20X2. | O | O | O |
| **13** | During December 20X1, TWD increased its casualty insurance coverage on several pieces of sophisticated machinery from historical cost to replacement cost. | O | O | O |
| **14.** | Inquiries about the substantial increase in revenue TWD recorded in the fourth quarter of 20X1 disclosed a new policy.  TWD guaranteed to several municipalities that it would refund the federal and state funding paid to TWD if any municipality fails a federal or state site clean-up inspection in 20X2. | O | O | O |
| **15.** | An initial public offering of TWD's stock is planned for late 20X2. | O | O | O |

| Situation | Risk Analysis | Responding to Risk | Research and Communication |
|-----------|---------------|--------------------|-----------------------------|

Assume that you have identified the following risks at the account level relating to TWD's property and equipment. Identify the most closely related financial statement assertion and the audit procedure that might be planned to most likely address the risk. Financial statement assertions and audit procedures may be used once, more than once, or not used at all.

*Related financial statement assertion*

A. Existence or occurrence
B. Completeness
C. Rights and obligations
D. Valuation or allocation
E. Presentation and disclosure

*Audit procedures*

F. Trace opening balances in the summary schedules to the prior year's audit working papers.
G. Review the provision for depreciation expense and determine that depreciable lives and methods used in the current year are consistent with those used in the prior year.
H. Determine that the responsibility for maintaining the property and equipment records is segregated from the responsibility for custody of property and equipment.
I. Examine deeds and title insurance certificates.
J. Perform cutoffs tests to verify that property and equipment additions are recorded in the proper period.
K. Determine that property and equipment are adequately insured.
L. Physically examine all major property and equipment additions.

| | *Risk identified* | *Related financial statement assertion* (A) (B) (C) (D) (E) | *Audit procedures* (F) (G) (H) (I) (J) (K) (L) |
|---|-------------------|-----------------------------------------------------------|-------------------------------------------------|
| **1.** | TWD may not have legal title to certain property and equipment recorded as acquired during the year. | O O O O O | O O O O O O O |
| **2.** | Recorded property and equipment acquisitions may include nonexistent assets. | O O O O O | O O O O O O O |
| **3.** | Recorded net property and equipment are for proper amounts. | O O O O O | O O O O O O O |

| Situation | Risk Analysis | Responding to Risk | Research and Communication |
|-----------|---------------|--------------------|-----------------------------|

Because controls over accounts receivable appear to operate effectively, Bond is considering performing tests of controls and using negative confirmation requests rather than positive requests. He has asked you to research the conditions under which he would be able to use negative confirmation requests for the accounts and to (1) prepare a summary, and (2) write a brief memo that provides the circumstances in which negative confirmations may appropriately be used.

*NOTE: If you do not have access to professional standards indicate the keywords or section numbers that you would use to do your search.*

**SOLUTION TO SIMULATION 3**

| Situation | Risk Analysis | Responding to Risk | Research and Communication |
|---|---|---|---|

AU 110, 312, and 316 all require that auditors consider factors influencing the risk of material misstatement and that the risk of material misstatement be considered during the planning phase of an audit engagement.

**1.** **(D)** Since TWD returned to profitable operation, its healthier financial condition leads to a decrease in the risk of material misstatement.

**2.** **(I)** The risk of material misstatement increases when management is dominated by a single person.  Since Mead controls the Board of Directors, is a majority stockholder, and is the CEO, it would appear that Mead dominates management.

**3.** **(I)** The risk of material misstatement increases when the internal auditor reports to top management rather than to the audit committee because it is less likely that the internal auditor will be able to objectively perform the function.

**4.** **(I)** The risk of material misstatement increases when the key management positions (particularly senior accounting personnel) encounter turnover.

**5.** **(D)** The loan officer's continual monitoring of TWD decreases the risk of material misstatement.

**6.** **(N)** Timing of payroll cycles would normally have no impact on the risk of material misstatement.

**7.** **(I)** A strong financial presence or ability to dominate a certain industry sector that allows a company to dictate terms or conditions to suppliers or customers may result in inappropriate or non-arm's-length transactions.

**8.** **(I)** A change to generally accepted accounting principles will increase the risk of material misstatement because the change in basis requires management to prepare a number of entries that have not been made in the past; these entries may be made improperly.  Also, difficulties in determining beginning accrual basis balances increases the risk of misstatement.

**9.** **(I)** The sale of one-half of the company's controlling interest in United Equipment Leasing is an entry that is out of the ordinary course of business, and accordingly, increases the risk of material misstatement.

**10.** **(D)** Litigation results in contentious and difficult accounting valuation issues because an accountant must attempt to determine the likelihood of loss and the amount.

**11.** **(I)** The risk of material misstatement increases when significant related-party transactions occur and management has an aggressive attitude towards reporting of the transactions.

**12.** **(I)** The risk of material misstatement increases in situations where there are unusual and difficult accounting issues present.  It would appear that the barter transaction with a below market purchase would be considered an unusual transaction.

**13.** **(N)** The amount of insurance coverage would have little impact on the risk of material misstatement.

**14.** **(I)** The risk of material misstatement increases as it appears that management has taken an aggressive attitude toward reporting this transaction.  In addition, this appears to be an unusual and difficult accounting issue involving revenue recognition.

**15.** **(I)** Experience has shown that a number of entities have intentionally misstated reported financial condition and operating results in situations in which a public (or private) placement of securities is planned.  Accordingly, an initial public offering of stock increases the risk of material misstatement.

| Situation | Risk Analysis | Responding to Risk | Research and Communication |
|---|---|---|---|

| Risk identified | Related financial statement assertion (A) (B) (C) (D) (E) | Audit procedures (F) (G) (H) (I) (J) (K) (L) |
|---|---|---|
| 1. TWD may not have legal title to certain property and equipment recorded as acquired during the year. | ○ ○ ● ○ ○ | ○ ○ ○ ● ○ ○ ○ ○ |
| 2. Recorded property and equipment acquisitions may include nonexistent assets. | ● ○ ○ ○ ○ | ○ ○ ○ ○ ○ ○ ● |
| 3. Recorded net property and equipment are for proper amounts. | ○ ○ ○ ● ○ | ○ ● ○ ○ ○ ○ ○ |

**Explanation of solutions**

**1.** **(C, I)** Legal titles relates most directly to the client having rights over the assets; an examination of deeds and title insurance certificates will provide assurance that the client has a legal right to the property and equipment acquired during the year.

**2. (A, L)** The recording of nonexistent assets relates most directly to existence of assets; physical examination of the major additions will address whether they exist.

**3. (D, G)** The proper recording of the net of property and equipment relates most directly to the valuation or allocation of the accounts; reviewing the provision for depreciation expense will address whether accumulated depreciation has been properly updated.

| Situation | Risk Analysis | Responding to Risk | Research and Communication |
|-----------|---------------|--------------------|----------------------------|

The first step is to determine the manner in which the candidate wishes to identify the pertinent research in the area. If a keyword search is to be used, words such as "negative confirmation" or "negative confirmation requests" seem appropriate. Alternatively you may be able to use the index, or you may recall that guidance on confirmations is presented in AU 330. The following is included in AU 330:

.20   The negative form requests the recipient to respond only if he or she disagrees with the information stated on the request. Negative confirmation requests may be used to reduce the risk of material misstatement to an acceptable level when (1) the combined assessed level of inherent and control risk is low, (2) a large number of small balances is involved, and (3) the auditor has no reason to believe that the recipients of the requests are unlikely to give them consideration. For example, in the examination of demand deposit accounts in a financial institution, it may be appropriate for an auditor to include negative confirmation requests with the customer's regular statements when the combined assessed level of inherent risk is low and the auditor has no reason to believe that the recipients will not consider the requests. The auditor should consider performing other substantive procedures to supplement the use of negative confirmations.

A memo such as the following is appropriate:

To:      Mr. William Bond
From:   [*Your name*]
Re:      Negative confirmation requests
Date:    [*Today's date*]

You asked that I research the conditions in which the negative confirmation form is considered appropriate for accounts receivable. AU section 330 provides information on the confirmation process and paragraph 21 of that section states that the use of negative confirmation requests is appropriate when

a.   The combined assessed level of inherent and control risk is low,
b.   A large number of small balances is involved, and
c.   The auditor has no reason to believe that the recipients of the requests are unlikely to give them consideration.

Attached are both paragraph 21 and the complete AU section 330. (*Alternatively you could choose to include paragraph 21 completely in your memo and/or simply tell Mr. Bond how AU 330 might be accessed.*)

Because TWD has receivables with large balances, it would seem that because of point b. above, the negative confirmation request is not appropriate for this client.

**SIMULATION 4**                                          (45 to 55 minutes)

**Topic—Evidence and Reporting**

| Situation | | | |
|---|---|---|---|
| | Research | Draft Report | Communication |

On September 30, 20X2, White & Co. CPAs, was engaged to audit the consolidated financial statements of National Motors Inc. for the year ended December 31, 20X2. The consolidated financial statements of National had not been audited the prior year. National's inadequate inventory records precluded White from forming an opinion as to the proper application of generally accepted accounting principles to inventory balances on January 1, 20X2. Therefore, White decided not to express an opinion on the results of operations for the year ended December 31, 20X2. National decided not to present comparative financial statements.

Rapid Parts Company, a consolidated subsidiary of National, was audited for the year ended December 31, 20X2, by Green & Co. CPAs. Green completed its fieldwork on February 28, 20X3, and submitted an unqualified opinion on Rapid's financial statements on March 7, 20X3. Rapid's statements reflect total assets and revenues constituting $700,000 and $2,000,000, respectively, of the consolidated totals of National. White decided not to assume responsibility for the work of Green. Green's report on Rapid does not accompany National's consolidated statements.

White is about to complete its fieldwork on March 28, 20X3, and planned to submit its auditor's report to National on April 4, 20X3.

| | Research | | |
|---|---|---|---|
| Situation | | Draft Report | Communication |

Before completing fieldwork, White must perform certain audit procedures with respect to the period after the balance sheet date to consider the possible occurrence of subsequent events that might require financial statement adjustment or disclosure. Research the procedures an auditor must generally perform, and paste them to your solution space.

*NOTE: If you do not have access to professional standards indicate the keywords or section numbers that you would use to do your search.*

| | | Draft Report | |
|---|---|---|---|
| Situation | Research | | Communication |

Assume that the procedures required in Research have been performed. Prepare White and Company's auditor's report on the consolidated financial statements of National Motors Inc.

| | | | Communication |
|---|---|---|---|
| Situation | Research | Draft Report | |

Draft a memo to the audit workpapers explaining the circumstances that caused the issuance of a modified audit report for National Motors.

To:     Audit Files
From: CPA Candidate

|  |
|---|
|  |

**SOLUTION TO SIMULATION 4**

| | Research | | |
|---|---|---|---|
| Situation | | Draft Report | Communication |

Because the requirement relates to subsequent events, that becomes an obvious term to search on. You might also add "auditing procedures" to the search. Paragraphs AU 560.10-.12 present the answer.

**Auditing Procedures in the Subsequent Period**

.10 There is a period after the balance sheet date with which the auditor must be concerned in completing various phases of his audit. This period is known as the "subsequent period" and is considered to extend to the date of the auditor's report. Its duration will depend upon the practical requirements of each audit and may vary from a relatively short period to one of several months. Also, all auditing procedures are not carried out as the same time and some phases of an audit will be performed during the subsequent period, whereas other phases will be substantially completed on or before the balance sheet date. As an audit approaches completion, the auditor will be concentrating on the unresolved auditing and reporting matters and he is not expected to be conducting a continuing review of those matters to which he has previously applied auditing procedures and reached satisfaction.

.11 Certain specific procedures are applied to transactions occurring after the balance sheet date such as (a) the examination of data to assure that proper cutoffs have been made and (b) the examination of data which provide information to aid the auditor in his evaluation of the assets and liabilities as of the balance sheet date.

.12 In addition, the independent auditor should perform other auditing procedures with respect to the period after the balance sheet date for the purpose of ascertaining the occurrence of subsequent events that may require adjustment or disclosure essential to a fair presentation of the financial statements in conformity with generally accepted accounting principles. These procedures should be performed at or near the completion of the fieldwork. The auditor generally should

a. Read the latest available interim financial statements; compare them with the financial statements being reported upon; and make any other comparisons considered appropriate in the circumstances. In order to make these procedures as meaningful as possible for the purpose expressed above, the auditor should inquire of officers and other executives having responsibility for financial and accounting matters as to whether the interim statements have been prepared on the same basis as that used for the statements under audit.

b. Inquire of and discuss with officers and other executives having responsibility for financial and accounting matters (limited where appropriate to major locations) as to

(i) Whether any substantial contingent liabilities or commitments existed at the date of the balance sheet being reported on or at the date of inquiry.

(ii) Whether there was any significant change in the capital stock, long-term debt, or working capital to the date of inquiry.

(iii) The current status of items, in the financial statements being reported on, that were accounted for on the basis of tentative, preliminary, or inconclusive data.

(iv) Whether any unusual adjustments had been made during the period from the balance sheet date to the date of inquiry.

c. Read the available minutes of meetings of stockholders, directors, and appropriate committees; as to meetings for which minutes are not available, inquire about matters dealt with at such meetings.

d. Inquire of client's legal counsel concerning litigation, claims, and assessments.

e. Obtain a letter of representations, dated as of the date of the auditor's report, from appropriate officials, generally the chief executive officer, chief financial officer, or others with equivalent positions in the entity, as to whether any events occurred subsequent to the date of the financial statements being reported on by the independent auditor that in the officer's opinion would require adjustment or disclosure in these statements. The auditor may elect to have the client include representations as to significant matters disclosed to the auditor in his performance of the procedures in subparagraphs (a) to (d) above and (f) below.

f. Make such additional inquiries or perform such procedures as he considers necessary and appropriate to dispose of questions that arise in carrying out the foregoing procedures, inquiries, and discussions.

| | | Draft Report | |
|---|---|---|---|
| Situation | Research | | Communication |

As we have suggested in Module 4, when preparing a report it is helpful to consider an approach of beginning with the standard short-form report and modifying it as appropriate for the circumstances presented. The following approach for preparing a report is likely to be helpful:

Step 1. Determine whether the question requires an audit report on whether the financial statements follow GAAP.

Step 2. Find the standard report and cut/paste it to your solution space.

Step 3. Determine the circumstance(s) involved and the overall type of report to be issued.

Step 4.    Research the Professional Standards to identify appropriate report modifications for the circumstances(s) and overall type of report to be issued.
Step 5.    Cut/paste the appropriate modifications to the standard report, and complete report as necessary.

*Step 1:*    Yes, the type of report is an audit report on whether the financial statements follow GAAP.
*Step 2:*    You should recall that standard audit reports are presented early in AU 508—one for a one-year report and one for comparative statements.  Since White & Co. only audited 20X2, it is most likely that the one-year report will be appropriate.  While you would probably paste the report at this point, we omit this step because, as we will see later in the problem, this is one of the few times it is not necessary to start with it since the standards provide complete examples of other audit reports.
*Step 3:*    Determining the circumstances involved requires a careful reading of the text of the simulation.

The simulation's first paragraph describes a situation in which National has inadequate inventory records which the paragraph goes on to say will result in inability to express an opinion on the results of operations (income statement).  Also, because National is not presenting comparative financial statements, we find that the single-year report is appropriate.

The second paragraph describes the fact that a consolidated subsidiary of National was audited by other auditors (Green & Co.)  Also, you find that White does not wish to take responsibility for the work of the other auditor, and that the other auditor's report is not accompanying the financial statements.  At this point you need to consider reporting responsibility when "other auditors" are involved and the principal auditor (White) is not taking responsibility for the work of the other auditor.  You might recall that all three paragraphs are modified—introductory, scope, and opinion paragraph.

*Step 4:*    The first complication involved is the statement that the auditor is disclaiming an opinion, but only on the results of operations.  AU  508 makes clear that an auditor may disclaim an opinion on one statement, and provide an opinion on others.  Yet, the only example provided disclaims an opinion on the entire set of financial statements.

.63          An example of a report disclaiming an opinion resulting from an inability to obtain sufficient competent evidential matter because of the scope limitation follows:

### *Independent Auditor's Report*

We were engaged to audit the accompanying balance sheets of X Company as of December 31, 20X2 and 20X1, and the related statements of income, retained earnings, and cash flows for the years then ended. These financial statements are the responsibility of the Company's management.  fn 21

[Second paragraph of standard report should be omitted]

The Company did not make a count of its physical inventory in 20X2 or 20X1, stated in the accompanying financial statements at $____ as of December 31, 20X2, and at $____ as of December 31, 20X1.  Further, evidence supporting the cost of property and equipment acquired prior to December 31, 20X1, is no longer available.  The Company's records do not permit the application of other auditing procedures to inventories or property and equipment.

Since the Company did not take physical inventories and we were not able to apply other auditing procedures to satisfy ourselves as to inventory quantities and the cost of property and equipment, the scope of our work was not sufficient to enable us to express, and we do not express, an opinion on these financial statements.

In researching the issue of other auditor reliance you might wish to use terms such as "other auditors" or "another auditor."  A better approach is to simply recall that most audit report modifications are included in AU 508. Indeed, early in AU 508 is a section entitled "Opinion Based in Part on Report of Another Auditor" that provides the following sample report:

### *Independent Auditor's Report*

We have audited the consolidated balance sheets of ABC Company and subsidiaries as of December 31, 20X2 and 20X1, and the related consolidated statements of income, retained earnings, and cash flows for the years then ended.  These financial statements are the responsibility of the Company's management.  Our responsibility is to express an opinion on these financial statements based on our audits.  We did not audit the financial statements of B Company, a wholly owned subsidiary, which statements reflect total assets of $____ and $____ as of December 31, 20X2 and 20X1, respectively, and total revenues $____ and $____ for the years then ended.  Those statements were audited by other auditors whose report has been furnished to us, and our opinion, insofar as it relates to the amounts included for B company, is based solely on the report of the other auditors.

We conducted our audits in accordance with auditing standards generally accepted in the United States of America.  Those standards require that we plan and perform the audit to obtain reasonable assurance about whether the financial statements are free of material misstatement.  An audit includes examining, on a test basis, evidence supporting the amounts and disclosures in the financial statements.  An audit also includes assessing the accounting principles used and significant estimates made by management, as well as evaluating the overall financial statement presentation.  We believe that our audits and the report of other auditors provide a reasonable basis for our opinion.

In our opinion, based on our audits and the report of other auditors, the consolidated financial statements referred to above present fairly, in all material respects, the financial position of ABC Company and subsidiaries as of December 31, 20X2 and 20X1, and the results of their operations and their cash flows for the years then ended in conformity with accounting principles generally accepted in the United States of America.

We find here that the above illustrations are relatively complete in that all paragraphs of the report are addressed—this frequently is not the case. But since it is the case here, we will select one of the reports to work from rather than the standard report from Step 2. Here we will select the "other auditor" report and modify it as appropriate.

*Step 5:* Beginning with the other auditor report, and tailoring it to this client.

### *Independent Auditor's Report*

**To the Board of Directors of National Motors Inc.:**

We have audited the consolidated balance sheets of ~~ABC Company~~ **National Motors Inc.,** and subsidiaries as of December 31, 20X2 ~~and 20X1,~~ and the related consolidated statements of income, retained earnings, and cash flows for the years then ended. These financial statements are the responsibility of the Company's management. Our responsibility is to express an opinion on these financial statements based on our audits. We did not audit the financial statement of ~~B~~ **Rapid Parts** Company, a wholly owned subsidiary, which statements reflect total assets of **$700,000** ~~and $~~____ as of December 31, 20X2 ~~and 20X1, respectively,~~ and total revenues of **$2,000,000** ~~and $~~____ for the year~~s~~ then ended. Those statements were audited by other auditors whose report has been furnished to us, and our opinion, insofar as it relates to the amounts included for ~~B~~ **Rapid Parts** Company, is based solely on the report of the other auditors.

We conducted our audits in accordance with auditing standards generally accepted in the United States of America. Those standards require that we plan and perform the audit to obtain reasonable assurance about whether the financial statements are free of material misstatement. An audit includes examining, on a test basis, evidence supporting the amounts and disclosures in the financial statements. An audit also includes assessing the accounting principles used and significant estimates made by management, as well as evaluating the overall financial statement presentation. We believe that our audits and the report of other auditors provide a reasonable basis for our opinion.

In our opinion, based on our audits and the report of other auditors, the consolidated financial statements referred to above present fairly, in all material respects, the financial position of ~~ABC Company~~ **National Motors Inc.** and subsidiaries as of December 31, 20X2 ~~and 20X1,~~ and the results of their operations and their cash flows for the year then ended in conformity with accounting principles generally accepted in the United States of America.

**White & Company** ~~[Signature]~~
**March 28, 20X3** ~~[Date]~~

Next, changes must be made to disclaim an opinion on the income statement. Those changes include the following:

### *Independent Auditor's Report*

**To the Board of Directors of National Motors Inc.:**

We have audited the consolidated balance sheets of ~~ABC Company~~ **National Motors Inc.,** and subsidiaries as of December 31, 20X2 ~~and 20X1,~~ and the related consolidated statements of income, retained earnings, and cash flows for the year then ended. These financial statements are the responsibility of the Company's management. Our responsibility is to express an opinion on these financial statements based on our audits. We did not audit the financial statement of ~~B~~ **Rapid Parts** Company, a wholly owned subsidiary, which statements reflect total assets of **$700,000** ~~and $~~____ as of December 31, 20X2 ~~and 20X1, respectively,~~ and total revenues of **$2,000,000** ~~and $~~____ for the year~~s~~ then ended. Those statements were audited by other auditors whose report has been furnished to us, and our opinion, insofar as it relates to the amounts included for ~~B~~ **Rapid Parts** Company, is based solely on the report of the other auditors.

**Except as explained in the following paragraph,** ~~W~~we conducted our audits in accordance with auditing standards generally accepted in the United States of America. Those standards require that we plan and perform the audit to obtain reasonable assurance about whether the financial statements are free of material misstatement. An audit includes examining, on a test basis, evidence supporting the amounts and disclosures in the financial statements. An audit also includes assessing the accounting principles used and significant estimates made by management, as well as evaluating the overall financial statement presentation. We believe that our audits and the report of other auditors provide a reasonable basis for our opinion.

**We did not observe the taking of the physical inventory as of December 31, 20X1, since that date was prior to our appointment as auditors for the company, and we were unable to satisfy ourselves regarding inventory quantities by means of other auditing procedures. Inventory amounts as of December 31, 20X1, enter into the determination of net income and cash flows for the year ended December 31, 20X1.**

**Because of the matter described in the preceding paragraph, the scope of our work was not sufficient to enable us to express, and we do not express, an opinion on the results of operations and cash flows for the year ended December 31, 20X1.**

In our opinion, based on our ~~audits~~ and the report of other auditors, the consolidated ~~financial statements~~ **balance sheet** referred to above presents fairly, in all material respects, the financial position of ~~ABC Company~~ **National Motors Inc.** and subsidiaries as of December 31, 20X2 ~~and 20X1, and the results of their operations and their cash flows for the years then ended~~ in conformity with accounting principles generally accepted in the United States of America.

**White & Company** ~~[Signature]~~
**March 28, 20X3** ~~[Date]~~

Following is the above report without the strikethroughs, which are presented only to help you follow our changes. You would not need to do this on the CPA exam.

### *Independent Auditor's Report*

**To the Board of Directors of National Motors Inc.:**

We have audited the consolidated balance sheets of National Motors Inc., and subsidiaries as of December 31, 20X2 and the related consolidated statements of income, retained earnings, and cash flows for the year then ended. These financial statements are the responsibility of the Company's management. Our responsibility is to express an opinion on these financial statements based on our audits. We did not audit the financial statement of Rapid Parts Company, a wholly owned subsidiary, which statements reflect total assets of $700,000 as of December 31, 20X2, and total revenues of $2,000,000 for the year then ended. Those statements were audited by other auditors whose report has been furnished to us, and our opinion, insofar as it relates to the amounts included for Rapid Parts Company, is based solely on the report of the other auditors.

Except as explained in the following paragraph, we conducted our audits in accordance with auditing standards generally accepted in the United States of America. Those standards require that we plan and perform the audit to obtain reasonable assurance about whether the financial statements are free of material misstatement. An audit includes examining, on a test basis, evidence supporting the amounts and disclosures in the financial statements. An audit also includes assessing the accounting principles used and significant estimates made by management, as well as evaluating the overall financial statement presentation. We believe that our audits and the report of other auditors provide a reasonable basis for our opinion.

We did not observe the taking of the physical inventory as of December 31, 20X1, since that date was prior to our appointment as auditors for the company, and we were unable to satisfy ourselves regarding inventory quantities by means of other auditing procedures. Inventory amounts as of December 31, 20X1, enter into the determination of net income and cash flows for the year ended December 31, 20X1.

Because of the matter described in the preceding paragraph, the scope of our work was not sufficient to enable us to express, and we do not express, an opinion on the results of operations and cash flows for the year ended December 31, 20X1.

In our opinion, based on our audit and the report of other auditors, the consolidated balance sheet referred to above presents fairly, in all material respects, the financial position of National Motors Inc. and subsidiaries as of December 31, 20X2, in conformity with accounting principles generally accepted in the United States of America.

White & Company
March 28, 20X3

| Situation | Research | Draft Report | **Communication** |
| --- | --- | --- | --- |

To:    Audit Files
From: CPA Candidate

We were engaged to audit the financial statements of National Motors Inc. for the year ended December 31, 20X2. The financial statements were not audited in the prior year. Due to a lack of adequate inventory records, we were unable to obtain sufficient evidence to form an opinion on the fairness of beginning inventories of the company. Accordingly, we will disclaim an opinion on the statements of income and cash flows. This disclaimer of opinion on the statement of income is necessary because the beginning inventories affect the cost of goods sold for the year. Similarly, the statement of cash flows is affected since both the beginning and ending level of inventories are used to measure the company's cash flows. The year-end balance sheet is unaffected since it reports only the ending inventory balances.

**SIMULATION 5**                    (60 to 70 minutes)

**Topic—Audit Evidence and Reporting**

| Company Profile | | | | | | | | | | |
|---|---|---|---|---|---|---|---|---|---|---|
| | Industry Profile | Balance Sheet | Income Statement/Ratios | Statement of Cash Flows | Risks | Audit Findings | Audit Procedures | Communication | | Audit Report |

You are beginning the 20X8 audit of Toastco, a nonpublic company that manufactures various kitchen products. This is your firm's sixth annual audit of Toastco.

Toastco's most profitable product is a deluxe toaster that is designed for those who want "a truly outstanding toaster." The toaster was first marketed through *Sky Mall Magazine* which offers specialty-type products to airplane passengers. Demand has grown so that at this point the company advertises the product much more broadly through a variety of media. Sales have been outstanding from the start and continue to increase. The recorded level of sales for 20X8 indicates that the company now controls approximately 5% of the toaster market, which represents 55% of company sales. In addition to the toaster, the company manufactures other products, including toaster ovens, coffee makers, food blenders, and electric can openers. Most of the manufacturing process is performed in several plants in Asia.

The highly successful toaster is the product of Bill Williams who became Toastco's chief executive officer in 20X3. Bill and several other officers invested heavily in the company at that time with the intent of ultimately selling common stock to the public. He and those individuals' lives are centered about the firm and making it a success. Consistently, Toastco is of critical importance to each of these individuals financially.

Recently you discussed the coming audit with Bill. You quickly found that he was elated that the company had earned $1.21 per share, one cent more than he had assured the bank that had provided Toastco with extensive financing during 20X8. He suggested that some had feared that Toastco wouldn't make it after somewhat weak second and third quarters, but that he knew all along that a strong fourth quarter was ahead and that it would "bring us through." He also pointed out that sales are up about 38% compared to the previous year and income by 54%. Furthermore, he indicated that an initial public offering of securities was planned for approximately eighteen months from now.

Toastco's outstanding performance for the past several years is in large part due to the highly profitable toaster, with other products gaining sales at approximately the industry's growth rate. In fact, Bill indicated that the toaster has become even more profitable this year due to reengineering of its production process and components, which brought costs of production down and decreased sales returns and allowances.

Bill also suggested to you that the $42,216,000 bank loan received during the year has been primarily used to increase inventories and fixed assets to support the rapidly rising demand for the toaster, as well as Toastco's other products. He pointed out that the company could never have achieved its projected earnings per share goal without the bank's support. This bank support has also allowed Toastco to work on developing what Bill refers to as "our next super product... an improved can opener that works well with all sizes of cans and doesn't leave a mess."

Finally, Bill said that there was some sad news. The Chairman of the Board of Directors, John Whing, an independent director, had been forced to step down for health reasons. Bill had replaced Mr. Whing as Chairman of the Board, and Toastco Vice President Sam Adamson filled the empty seat on the board of directors. The seven-member board is now composed of Bill (who will begin serving as Chairman), Sam Adamson, two others from management, and the three independent directors. The audit committee has not been affected by the change, as the three independent directors continue to serve in that role.

| | Industry Profile | | | | | | | | | |
|---|---|---|---|---|---|---|---|---|---|---|
| Company Profile | | Balance Sheet | Income Statement/Ratios | Statement of Cash Flows | Risks | Audit Findings | Audit Procedures | Communication | | Audit Report |

In the portions of the kitchen product industry in which Toastco operates, demand is influenced by economic trends such as increases or decreases in consumer disposable income, availability of credit, and housing construction. Competition is very active in all products and comes from a number of principal manufacturers and suppliers. An important factor is the degree of product differentiation achieved through innovation and new product features. Other significant factors include product quality and cost, brand recognition, customer responsiveness, and appliance service capability.

Overall, for the industry, sales have been and are expected to remain relatively stable with a slight increase—increases have approximated 3% industry-wide per year during the past five years, and are expected to continue at that rate of increase for the next five years. Much of the manufacturing of these products takes place in Asia, and to a lesser extent in South America. Increasingly, Asian companies are becoming directly involved in marketing their own household products.

| Company Profile | Industry Profile | **Balance Sheet** | Income Statement/Ratios | Statement of Cash Flows | Risks | Audit Findings | Audit Procedures | Communication | Audit Report |
|---|---|---|---|---|---|---|---|---|---|

## Toastco
## BALANCE SHEET

*Dollars (000's omitted)*

| | 12/31/X8 Unaudited | 12/31/X7 Audited |
|---|---|---|
| **Assets** | | |
| Cash | 885 | 514 |
| Accounts receivable | 51,076 | 27,801 |
| Inventories | 39,135 | 19,577 |
| Other current assets | 3,015 | 1,449 |
| Total current assets | 94,111 | 49,341 |
| **Fixed assets** | | |
| Land, property, plant, and equipment (net) | 24,029 | 15,900 |
| Total assets | 118,140 | 65,241 |
| **Liabilities and equity** | | |
| Accounts payable | 13,288 | 15,072 |
| Accrued liabilities | 4,710 | 5,468 |
| Current portion long-term debt | 1,250 | 900 |
| Income taxes payable | 3,782 | 2,619 |
| Total current liabilities | 23,030 | 24,059 |
| Bank debt | 62,057 | 19,841 |
| Deferred income taxes | 1,881 | 1,254 |
| Total liabilities | 86,968 | 45,154 |
| Common stock | 7,903 | 7,775 |
| Retained earnings | 23,269 | 12,312 |
| Total liabilities and equity | 118,140 | 65,241 |

| Company Profile | Industry Profile | Balance Sheet | **Income Statement/Ratios** | Statement of Cash Flows | Risks | Audit Findings | Audit Procedures | Communication | Audit Report |
|---|---|---|---|---|---|---|---|---|---|

## Toastco
## INCOME STATEMENT

*Dollars (000's omitted)*

| | 12/31/X8 Unaudited | 12/31/X7 Audited |
|---|---|---|
| Gross sales | 183,767 | 133,504 |
| Returns and allowances | 2,644 | 5,270 |
| Net sales | 181,123 | 128,234 |
| Cost of goods sold | 94,934 | 70,756 |
| Gross margin | 86,189 | 57,478 |
| Selling, advertising, research and development | 64,285 | 42,600 |
| Income from operations | 21,904 | 14,878 |
| Interest expense | 3,189 | 1,584 |
| Income before taxes | 18,715 | 13,294 |
| Income taxes | 7,761 | 6,189 |
| Net income | 10,954 | 7,105 |
| EPS | 1.21 | .78 |
| **Ratios*** | | |
| Current | 4.1 | 2.1 |
| Quick | 2.3 | 1.2 |
| Accounts receivable turnover | 4.7 | 6.3 |
| Days' sales in ending receivables | 76.6 | 57.1 |
| Inventory turnover | 3.2 | 4.8 |
| Days' sales in ending inventory | 112.5 | 75.0 |
| Interest expense/debt | 0.05 | 0.08 |

* Calculated using year-end data.

| Company Profile | Industry Profile | Balance Sheet | Income Statement/Ratios | Statement of Cash Flows | | Risks | Audit Findings | Audit Procedures | Communication | Audit Report |
|---|---|---|---|---|---|---|---|---|---|---|

## Toastco
## STATEMENT OF CASH FLOWS
### For the Year Ending 20X8

*Dollars (000's omitted)*

Cash flows from operation activities

| | | |
|---|---|---|
| Net income | | 10,954 |
| | | |
| Increase in accounts receivable | (23,275) | |
| Increase in inventories | (19,558) | |
| Increase in other current assets | (1,566) | |
| Decrease in accounts payable | (1,784) | |
| Increase in accrued liabilities | (758) | |
| Increase in income taxes payable | 1,166 | |
| Increase in deferred income taxes | 627 | (45,148) |
| Net cash flow from operating activities | | (34,194) |
| | | |
| Cash flows from investing activities | | |
| Increase in current long-term debt | 350 | |
| Payments for fixed assets | (8,129) | |
| Net cash flow from investing activities | | (7,779) |
| | | |
| Cash flows from financing activities | | |
| Proceeds from issuance of long-term debt | 42,216 | |
| Proceeds from issuance of stock | 128 | |
| Net cash flow from financing activities | 42,344 | |
| Net cash inflow | | 371 |

| Company Profile | Industry Profile | Balance Sheet | Income Statement/Ratios | Statement of Cash Flows | Risks | Audit Findings | Audit Procedures | Communication | Audit Report |
|---|---|---|---|---|---|---|---|---|---|

**(A) (B) (C) (D)**

1. Which of the following identifies an aspect of the company's business model, strategies, and/or business environment that is most likely to increase the risk of misstatement arising from fraudulent financial reporting?   ○ ○ ○ ○

   A. Toastco sells more than one type of product.
   B. The president's wealth is based on the success of Toastco.
   C. The audit committee is composed entirely of independent directors.
   D. Toastco continues to hire your firm for its fifth year.

| Company Profile | Industry Profile | Balance Sheet | Income Statement/Ratios | Statement of Cash Flows | Risks | Audit Findings | Audit Procedures | Communication | Audit Report |
|---|---|---|---|---|---|---|---|---|---|

Change in inventory turnover

| | 20X8 | 20X7 |
|---|---|---|
| Inventory turnover | 3.2 | 4.8 |

**(A) (B) (C) (D) (E) (F)**

1. Which of the following is most consistent with such a decrease in inventory turnover?   ○ ○ ○ ○ ○ ○

   A. A number of expense items were erroneously included in cost of goods sold (but not in ending inventory).
   B. Sales have increased and a higher percentage of customers are paying their accounts on time.
   C. Fourth quarter sales were higher than normal, thus inventory is lower than one would expect at year-end due to the increase in sales.
   D. Inventory and cost of goods sold were adjusted to the year-end inventory count, a count that overcounted a number of significant items. A periodic inventory system is in use.
   E. The new long-term debt agreement was achieved at a desirable rate of interest.
   F. A number of receivables have been affected by an employee's lapping scheme.

Change in interest expense to debt ratio

| | 20X8 | 20X7 |
|---|---|---|
| Interest expense/debt | 0.05 | 0.08 |

(A) (B) (C) (D) (E) (F)

**2.** Which of the following is most consistent with such a decrease in the ratio of interest expense to debt?

    ○   ○   ○   ○   ○   ○

   A. Short-term borrowing was refinanced on a long-term basis at the same interest rate.

   B. The company bought back shares of its common stock using proceeds from the new long-term loan.

   C. Sales increases have led to the need to expand production facilities, particularly for the popular toaster.

   D. While the significant increase in debt is at about the same interest rate as previous debt, it is at a rate well below the company's overall cost of capital.

   E. Interest expense for the year has not been accrued as of year-end.

   F. The new long-term debt was received early during 20X8, at a higher rate than existing debt.

| Company Profile | Industry Profile | Balance Sheet | Income Statement/Ratios | Statement of Cash Flows | Risks | Audit Findings | **Audit Procedures** | Communication | Audit Report |
|---|---|---|---|---|---|---|---|---|---|

For each audit objective listed below select the most appropriate audit procedure for raw materials inventory, a significant portion of Toastco's total inventories. Audit procedures may be used once, more than once, or not at all.

### *List of audit procedures*

   A. Compare standard costs of inventories with standardized market values.

   B. Determine that all direct labor and overhead has been expensed and not included in inventory valuation.

   C. Examine vendors' invoices.

   D. Perform analytical procedures comparing inventory to various industry averages.

   E. Review drafts of financial statement note disclosures.

   F. Select a sample of items during the physical count and determine that the client has included items on inventory count sheets.

   G. Select a sample of recorded items on count sheets and determine that the items are on hand.

(A) (B) (C) (D) (E) (F) (G)

**1.** Determine that company legally owns inventories   ○ ○ ○ ○ ○ ○ ○

**2.** Establish the completeness of inventories   ○ ○ ○ ○ ○ ○ ○

**3.** Determine that the cost of inventories is proper   ○ ○ ○ ○ ○ ○ ○

| Company Profile | Industry Profile | Balance Sheet | Income Statement/Ratios | Statement of Cash Flows | Risks | Audit Findings | Audit Procedures | **Communication** | Audit Report |
|---|---|---|---|---|---|---|---|---|---|

The following is one of the confirmation replies received from the confirmation process applied to accounts receivable:

**Confirmation #22**

The statement of our account showing a balance of $12,222 due Toastco, at December 31, 20X8, is correct except as noted below.

Wilson Suppliers

By <u>Kent Parry</u>

Date: 2/2/X9

Exceptions: *No way. Forget it. Toastco said we'd have these goods in 10 days on December 2. When we didn't receive them, I canceled the order on December 12th. Wilson Corp. shipped us similar goods overnight. We will never deal with Toastco again as long as I am around.*

In a memorandum to the audit team, explain any possible risks existing relating to this account and resulting additional audit procedures. Your response will be graded for both technical relevance and writing skills. For writing skills you should demonstrate an ability to develop your ideas, organize them, and express them clearly. Do not convey information in the form of a table, bullet point list, or other abbreviated presentation.

To: Audit Team
Subject: Change in Board of Directors
Re: Confirmation #22

| Company Profile | Industry Profile | Balance Sheet | Income Statement/Ratios | Statement of Cash Flows | Risks | Audit Findings | Audit Procedures | Communication | Audit Report |
|---|---|---|---|---|---|---|---|---|---|

Assume that you have completed the audit of Toastco and find that an unusually important subsequent event occurred after year-end, which Toastco has appropriately treated in the financial statements through a note disclosure. Using the research materials available to you by clicking the Standards button on the Title bar, identify any guidance available on emphasizing a matter in the audit report such as this large subsequent event. That is, while you believe that an unqualified report is appropriate, you also believe that it might be appropriate to emphasize this matter in your audit report. Provide the professional guidance on examples of circumstances in which such emphasis may be appropriate and of any phrases that might be considered inappropriate in such a report. You should not edit the guidance in any way—provide the entire paragraph.

**SOLUTION TO SIMULATION 5**

| Company Profile | Industry Profile | Balance Sheet | Income Statement/Ratios | Statement of Cash Flows | **Risks** | Audit Findings | Audit Procedures | Communication | Audit Report |
|---|---|---|---|---|---|---|---|---|---|

(A) (B) (C) (D)

1.  Which of the following identifies an aspect of the company's business model, strategies, and/or business environment that is most likely to increase the risk of misstatement arising from fraudulent financial reporting?    ○ ● ○ ○

**Explanation of solution**

1.  **(B)** The requirement is to determine an aspect of a company that is most likely to increase the risk of misstatement arising from fraudulent financial reporting. Answer (B) is correct because the president's investment in Toastco creates a situation in which losses in value of the company will profoundly affect him—particularly given his desire to take the company public. Answer (A) is incorrect because selling more than one type of product may or may not affect the risk of misstatement. Answer (C) is incorrect because it is desirable to have the audit committee composed entirely of independent directors. Answer (D) is incorrect because the fact that this is a continuing engagement has no direct tie to the risk of misstatement.

| Company Profile | Industry Profile | Balance Sheet | Income Statement/Ratios | Statement of Cash Flows | Risks | **Audit Findings** | Audit Procedures | Communication | Audit Report |
|---|---|---|---|---|---|---|---|---|---|

(A) (B) (C) (D) (E) (F)

1.  Which of the following is most consistent with such a decrease in inventory turnover?    ○ ○ ○ ● ○ ○

**Explanation of solution**

1.  **(D)** The requirement is to identify a possible cause of a decrease in the inventory turnover ratio—cost of goods sold divided by inventories. Answer (D) is correct because an overstated ending inventory count will decrease cost of goods sold and increase inventory—both of these effects decrease the inventory turnover. Answer (A) is incorrect because an increase in cost of goods sold increases the inventory turnover. Answer (B) is incorrect because there is no direct tie to a change in the relationship between cost of goods sold and inventories when sales increase and customers pay more quickly. Answer (C) is incorrect because a lower inventory will increase the inventory turnover. Answer (E) and (F) are incorrect because neither the interest rate nor a receivable lapping scheme will directly affect the inventory turnover.

(A) (B) (C) (D) (E) (F)

2.  Which of the following is most consistent with such a decrease in the ratio of interest expense to debt?    ○ ○ ○ ○ ● ○

**Explanation of solution**

2.  **(E)** The requirement is to identify a possible cause for a decrease in the ratio of interest expense to debt. Answer (E) is correct because lack of accrual of interest expense will decrease the ratio through understating interest expense. Answer (A), (B), (C), and (D) are all incorrect because refinancing at the same interest rate, buying back stock, increasing sales, and increasing the amount of debt (at a rate below the cost of capital) will not affect the ratio. Answer (F) is incorrect because the higher interest rate would increase the ratio.

| Company Profile | Industry Profile | Balance Sheet | Income Statement/Ratios | Statement of Cash Flows | Risks | Audit Findings | **Audit Procedures** | Communication | Audit Report |
|---|---|---|---|---|---|---|---|---|---|

(A) (B) (C) (D) (E) (F) (G)

1.  Determine that company legally owns inventories    ○ ○ ● ○ ○ ○ ○

2.  Establish the completeness of inventories    ○ ○ ○ ○ ○ ● ○

3.  Determine that the cost of inventories is proper    ○ ○ ● ○ ○ ○ ○

**Explanations of solutions**

1.  **(C)** Because ownership information is included on invoices, examining vendors' invoices will provide evidence that the company legally owns inventory raw material items.

2.  **(F)** Selecting a sample of items and agreeing to the physical count sheet will establish that those items have been included in the count, and this will address completeness of inventories.

3.  **(C)** Examining vendors' invoices will provide evidence as to the cost of the inventory items.

| | | | | | | | | Communication | | |
|---|---|---|---|---|---|---|---|---|---|---|
| Company Profile | Industry Profile | Balance Sheet | Income Statement/Ratios | Statement of Cash Flows | Risks | Audit Findings | Audit Procedures | | | Audit Report |

**Memorandum**

To:     Audit Team
Subject:   Change in Board of Directors
Re:      Confirmation #22

     Confirmation #22 indicates that Wilson Suppliers did not receive the goods ordered from Toastco. The sale occurred on December 2 and Kent Parry of Wilson Suppliers states on the confirmation that his company canceled the purchase on December 12 when they had not received the goods.

     Since this receivable was recorded and reflected in sales, we need to vouch it to determine whether the goods were shipped, and if so, their disposition. If we find that the goods were not shipped, it raises a questions as to whether Toastco has other receivables (and accordingly sales) for items not yet shipped. Therefore, if the item was never shipped, we must consider extending our procedures to determine whether this is a significant problem.

| | | | | | | | | | Audit Report |
|---|---|---|---|---|---|---|---|---|---|
| Company Profile | Industry Profile | Balance Sheet | Income Statement/Ratios | Statement of Cash Flows | Risks | Audit Findings | Audit Procedures | Communication | |

The guidance is provided in AU 508.19

.19   In any report on financial statements, the auditor may emphasize a matter regarding the financial statements. Such explanatory information should be presented in a separate paragraph of the auditor's report. Phrases such as "with the foregoing [following] explanation" should not be used in the opinion paragraph if an emphasis paragraph is included in the auditor's report. Emphasis paragraphs are never required; they may be added solely at the auditor's discretion. Examples of matters the auditor may wish to emphasize are

- That the entity is a component of a larger business enterprise.
- That the entity has had significant transactions with related parties.
- Unusually important subsequent events.
- Accounting matters, other than those involving a change or changes in accounting principles, affecting the comparability of the financial statements with those of the preceding period.

[Paragraph renumbered and amended, effective for reports issued or reissued on or after February 29, 1996, by the issuance of Statement on Auditing Standards 79.]

**SIMULATION 6**                              (50 to 55 minutes)

**Topic—Audit Evidence and Reporting**

| Company Profile | | | | | | | | | | |
|---|---|---|---|---|---|---|---|---|---|---|
| | Industry Profile | Balance Sheet | Income Statement/Ratios | Statement of Cash Flows | Risks | Audit Findings | Audit Procedures | Communication | Audit Report | Representation Letter |

You are beginning the 20X8 audit of Toastco, a nonpublic company that manufactures various kitchen products. This is your firm's sixth annual audit of Toastco.

Toastco's most profitable product is a deluxe toaster that is designed for those who want "a truly outstanding toaster." The toaster was first marketed through *Sky Mall Magazine* which offers specialty-type products to airplane passengers. Demand has grown so that at this point the company advertises the product much more broadly through a variety of media. Sales have been outstanding from the start and continue to increase. The recorded level of sales for 20X8 indicates that the company now controls approximately 5% of the toaster market, which represents 55% of company sales. In addition to the toaster, the company manufactures other products, including toaster ovens, coffee makers, food blenders, and electric can openers. Most of the manufacturing process is performed in several plants in Asia.

The highly successful toaster is the product of Bill Williams who became Toastco's chief executive officer in 20X3. Bill and several other officers invested heavily in the company at that time with the intent of ultimately selling common stock to the public. He and those individuals' lives are centered about the firm and making it a success. Consistently, Toastco is of critical importance to each of these individuals financially.

Recently you discussed the coming audit with Bill. You quickly found that he was elated that the company had earned $1.21 per share, one cent more than he had assured the bank that had provided Toastco with extensive financing during 20X8. He suggested that some had feared that Toastco wouldn't make it after somewhat weak second and third quarters, but that he knew all along that a strong fourth quarter was ahead and that it would "bring us through." He also pointed out that sales are up about 38% compared to the previous year and income by 54%. Furthermore, he indicated that an initial public offering of securities was planned for approximately eighteen months from now.

Toastco's outstanding performance for the past several years is in large part due to the highly profitable toaster, with other products gaining sales at approximately the industry's growth rate. In fact, Bill indicated that the toaster has become even more profitable this year due to reengineering of its production process and components, which brought costs of production down and decreased sales returns and allowances.

Bill also suggested to you that the $42,216,000 bank loan received during the year has been primarily used to increase inventories and fixed assets to support the rapidly rising demand for the toaster, as well as Toastco's other products. He pointed out that the company could never have achieved its projected earnings per share goal without the bank's support. This bank support has also allowed Toastco to work on developing what Bill refers to as "our next super product… an improved can opener that works well with all sizes of cans and doesn't leave a mess."

Finally, Bill said that there was some sad news. The Chairman of the Board of Directors, John Whing, an independent director, had been forced to step down for health reasons. Bill had replaced Mr. Whing as Chairman of the Board, and Toastco Vice President Sam Adamson filled the empty seat on the board of directors. The seven-member board is now composed of Bill (who will begin serving as Chairman), Sam Adamson, two others from management, and the three independent directors. The audit committee has not been affected by the change, as the three independent directors continue to serve in that role.

| Company Profile | Industry Profile | Balance Sheet | Income Statement/Ratios | Statement of Cash Flows | Risks | Audit Findings | Audit Procedures | Communication | Audit Report | Representation Letter |
|---|---|---|---|---|---|---|---|---|---|---|
| | | | | | | | | | | |

In the portions of the kitchen product industry in which Toastco operates, demand is influenced by economic trends such as increases or decreases in consumer disposable income, availability of credit, and housing construction. Competition is very active in all products and comes from a number of principal manufacturers and suppliers. An important factor is the degree of product differentiation achieved through innovation and new product features. Other significant factors include product quality and cost, brand recognition, customer responsiveness, and appliance service capability.

Overall, for the industry, sales have been and are expected to remain relatively stable with a slight increase—increases have approximated 3% industry-wide per year during the past five years, and are expected to continue at that rate of increase for the next five years. Much of the manufacturing of these products takes place in Asia, and to a lesser extent in South America. Increasingly, Asian companies are becoming directly involved in marketing their own household products.

| Company Profile | Industry Profile | Balance Sheet | Income Statement/Ratios | Statement of Cash Flows | Risks | Audit Findings | Audit Procedures | Communication | Audit Report | Representation Letter |
|---|---|---|---|---|---|---|---|---|---|---|

## Toastco
### BALANCE SHEET

Dollars (000's omitted)

|  | 12/31/X8 Unaudited | 12/31/X7 Audited |
|---|---|---|
| **Assets** | | |
| Cash | 885 | 514 |
| Accounts receivable | 51,076 | 27,801 |
| Inventories | 39,135 | 19,577 |
| Other current assets | 3,015 | 1,449 |
| Total current assets | 94,111 | 49,341 |
| **Fixed assets** | | |
| Land, property, plant, and equipment (net) | 24,029 | 15,900 |
| Total assets | 118,140 | 65,241 |
| **Liabilities and equity** | | |
| Accounts payable | 13,288 | 15,072 |
| Accrued liabilities | 4,710 | 5,468 |
| Current portion long-term debt | 1,250 | 900 |
| Income taxes payable | 3,782 | 2,619 |
| Total current liabilities | 23,030 | 24,059 |
| Bank debt | 62,057 | 19,841 |
| Deferred income taxes | 1,881 | 1,254 |
| Total liabilities | 86,968 | 45,154 |
| Common stock | 7,903 | 7,775 |
| Retained earnings | 23,269 | 12,312 |
| Total liabilities and equity | 118,140 | 65,241 |

| Company Profile | Industry Profile | Balance Sheet | Income Statement/Ratios | Statement of Cash Flows | Risks | Audit Findings | Audit Procedures | Communication | Audit Report | Representation Letter |
|---|---|---|---|---|---|---|---|---|---|---|

## Toastco
### INCOME STATEMENT

Dollars (000's omitted)

|  | 12/31/X8 Unaudited | 12/31/X7 Audited |
|---|---|---|
| Gross sales | 183,767 | 133,504 |
| Returns and allowances | 2,644 | 5,270 |
| Net sales | 181,123 | 128,234 |
| Cost of goods sold | 94,934 | 70,756 |
| Gross margin | 86,189 | 57,478 |
| Selling, advertising, research and development | 64,285 | 42,600 |
| Income from operations | 21,904 | 14,878 |
| Interest expense | 3,189 | 1,584 |
| Income before taxes | 18,715 | 13,294 |
| Income taxes | 7,761 | 6,189 |
| Net income | 10,954 | 7,105 |
| EPS | 1.21 | .78 |
| **Ratios*** | | |
| Current | 4.1 | 2.1 |
| Quick | 2.3 | 1.2 |
| Accounts receivable turnover | 4.7 | 6.3 |
| Days' sales in ending receivables | 76.6 | 57.1 |
| Inventory turnover | 3.2 | 4.8 |
| Days' sales in ending inventory | 112.5 | 75.0 |
| Interest expense/debt | 0.05 | 0.08 |

* Calculated using year-end data.

| Company Profile | Industry Profile | Balance Sheet | Income Statement/Ratios | Statement of Cash Flows | Risks | Audit Findings | Audit Procedures | Communication | Audit Report | Representation Letter |
|---|---|---|---|---|---|---|---|---|---|---|

*Toastco*
**STATEMENT OF CASH FLOWS**
*For the Year Ending 20X8*

*Dollars (000's omitted)*

| | | |
|---|---:|---:|
| *Cash flows from operation activities* | | |
| Net income | | 10,954 |
| Increase in accounts receivable | (23,275) | |
| Increase in inventories | (19,558) | |
| Increase in other current assets | (1,566) | |
| Decrease in accounts payable | (1,784) | |
| Increase in accrued liabilities | (758) | |
| Increase in income taxes payable | 1,166 | |
| Increase in deferred income taxes | 627 | (45,148) |
| Net cash flow from operating activities | | (34,194) |
| *Cash flows from investing activities* | | |
| Increase in current long-term debt | 350 | |
| Payments for fixed assets | (8,129) | |
| Net cash flow from investing activities | | (7,779) |
| *Cash flows from financing activities* | | |
| Proceeds from issuance of long-term debt | 42,216 | |
| Proceeds from issuance of stock | 128 | |
| Net cash flow from financing activities | | 42,344 |
| Net cash inflow | | 371 |

| Company Profile | Industry Profile | Balance Sheet | Income Statement/Ratios | Statement of Cash Flows | Risks | Audit Findings | Audit Procedures | Communication | Audit Report | Representation Letter |
|---|---|---|---|---|---|---|---|---|---|---|

**(A) (B) (C) (D)**

1. Which of the following identifies an aspect of the company's business model, strategies, and/or business environment that is most likely to increase the risk of misstatement arising from fraudulent financial reporting?   ○ ○ ○ ○

   A.  The household products industry seems stable, and is not rapidly growing.
   B.  Toastco reported a strong fourth quarter that brought it up to expectations for earnings per share.
   C.  Toastco controls approximately 5% of the market for toasters.
   D.  Toastco has one relatively profitable product, and a number of products that are not as profitable.

| Company Profile | Industry Profile | Balance Sheet | Income Statement/Ratios | Statement of Cash Flows | Risks | Audit Findings | Audit Procedures | Communication | Audit Report | Representation Letter |
|---|---|---|---|---|---|---|---|---|---|---|

Change in accounts receivable turnover

| | 20X8 | 20X7 |
|---|---|---|
| Accounts receivable turnover ratio | 4.7 | 6.3 |

**(A) (B) (C) (D)**

1. Which of the following is most consistent with a decrease in the accounts receivable turnover ratio?   ○ ○ ○ ○

   A.  A fraudulent transaction was recorded crediting sales and debiting property, plant, and equipment.
   B.  An increasing amount of the company's sales are for cash—through cash transfers.
   C.  Many items shipped on consignment during December were recorded as credit sales; no cash receipts have yet been received on those consignments.
   D.  Toastco has increased sales by selling goods for lower prices, but shortened the length of credit terms from thirty days to twenty days.

Change in current ratio

| | 20X8 | 20X7 |
|---|---|---|
| Current ratio | 4.1 | 2.1 |

**(A) (B) (C) (D)**

2. Which of the following is most consistent with an increase in the current ratio?   ○ ○ ○ ○

A. Payments for fixed assets.
B. Proceeds obtained and used relating to long-term debt.
C. Decreased accounts payable.
D. Decreased sales returns and allowances.

| Company Profile | Industry Profile | Balance Sheet | Income Statement/Ratios | Statement of Cash Flows | Risks | Audit Findings | Audit Procedures | Communication | Audit Report | Representation Letter |
|---|---|---|---|---|---|---|---|---|---|---|

For each audit objective select the most appropriate audit procedure for accounts receivable. Audit procedures may be used once, more than once, or not at all.

### *List of audit procedures*

A. Analyze relationships between accounts receivable balances and changes in the current portion of long-term debt.
B. Compare accounts receivable on the accounts receivable lead schedule with those on supporting audit schedules.
C. Compare total 20X8 annual sales with those of 20X7.
D. Examine December 20X8 sales journal and determine that sales are properly recorded in December.
E. Examine January 20X9 sales journal and determine that sales are properly recorded in January.
F. Inquire of credit manager about the collectability of various receivables.
G. Review disclosure checklist for recommended and required accounts receivable disclosures.

|  | (A) | (B) | (C) | (D) | (E) | (F) | (G) |
|---|---|---|---|---|---|---|---|
| 1. Determine that all accounts receivable are properly recorded as of year-end. | O | O | O | O | O | O | O |
| 2. Determine that accounts receivable are properly valued at net realizable value. | O | O | O | O | O | O | O |
| 3. Note disclosures related to accounts receivable are proper. | O | O | O | O | O | O | O |

| Company Profile | Industry Profile | Balance Sheet | Income Statement/Ratios | Statement of Cash Flows | Risks | Audit Findings | Audit Procedures | Communication | Audit Report | Representation Letter |
|---|---|---|---|---|---|---|---|---|---|---|

Your firm has been performing the audit of Toastco for five years. Since last year there has been a change in corporate governance in composition of the board of directors, although composition of the audit committee remains the same as in previous years. In a memorandum to the audit team, explain the impact of the change in audit risk. Your response will be graded for both technical relevance and writing skills. For writing skills you should demonstrate an ability to develop your ideas, organize them, and express them clearly. Do not convey information in the form of a table, bullet point list, or other abbreviated presentation.

To: Audit Team
From: CPA Candidate
Subject: Change in Board of Directors

| Company Profile | Industry Profile | Balance Sheet | Income Statement/Ratios | Statement of Cash Flows | Risks | Audit Findings | Audit Procedures | Communication | Audit Report | Representation Letter |
|---|---|---|---|---|---|---|---|---|---|---|

Assume that you have completed the audit of Toastco and find that you are able to issue a standard audit report on both 20X7 and 20X8, and that all the appropriate reports are presented. Using the research materials available to you by clicking the Standards button on the Title bar, assemble model paragraphs that would be used to create the audit report. You should not edit the model report in any way.

| Company Profile | Industry Profile | Balance Sheet | Income Statement/Ratios | Statement of Cash Flows | Risks | Audit Findings | Audit Procedures | Communication | Audit Report | Representation Letter |
|---|---|---|---|---|---|---|---|---|---|---|

Near the close of the review, you have been asked to begin the preparation of a representation letter for the review. Using the research materials available to you by clicking the Standards button, assemble model paragraphs that would be used to create the final representation letter. You should not edit the model paragraphs in any way.

**SOLUTION TO SIMULATION 6**

| Company Profile | Industry Profile | Balance Sheet | Income Statement/Ratios | Statement of Cash Flows | Risks | Audit Findings | Audit Procedures | Communication | Audit Report | Representation Letter |
|---|---|---|---|---|---|---|---|---|---|---|

(A) (B) (C) (D)

1. Which of the following identifies an aspect of the company's business model, strategies, and/or business environment that is most likely to increase the risk of misstatement arising from fraudulent financial reporting?  ○ ● ○ ○

**Explanation of solution**

1.  **(B)** The requirement is to determine the aspect of Toastco that is most likely to increase the risk of misstatement arising from fraudulent financial reporting. Answer (B) is correct because the president, Bill Williams, felt pressure to meet the earnings per share number he had promised the bank due to weak second and third quarters. Therefore the high earnings in the fourth quarter represents a risk. Answer (A) is incorrect because the stability of the industry presents no particular risk. Answer (C) is incorrect because Toastco's market share by itself does not seem to pose a risk of misstatement. Answer (D) is incorrect because while Toastco would certainly be in a safer position with more profitable products, this is not as significant a fraud risk as is the pressure to achieve the earnings per share target.

| Company Profile | Industry Profile | Balance Sheet | Income Statement/Ratios | Statement of Cash Flows | Risks | Audit Findings | Audit Procedures | Communication | Audit Report | Representation Letter |
|---|---|---|---|---|---|---|---|---|---|---|

(A) (B) (C) (D)

1. Which of the following is most consistent with a decrease in the accounts receivable turnover ratio?  ○ ○ ● ○

2. Which of the following is most consistent with an increase in the current ratio?  ○ ● ○ ○

**Explanation of solutions**

1.  **(C)** The requirement is to identify a possible cause of a decrease in the accounts receivable turnover—sales divided by accounts receivable. Answer (C) is correct because items on consignment, but recorded as sales, increase both the numerator and the denominator of the accounts receivable turnover ratio by the same amount (sales/accounts receivable); this will decrease the ratio. Answer (A) is incorrect because crediting sales increases the numerator of the ratio, and thereby increases the turnover ratio. Answer (B) is incorrect because sales for cash should increase sales which would increase the turnover ratio. Answer (D) is incorrect because shortening the credit terms should increase the turnover ratio.

2.  **(B)** The requirement is to identify a possible cause of an increase in the current ratio—current assets divided by current liabilities. Answer (B) is correct because the great amount of cash received from the bank loan of $42,216,000 creates a long-term debt, and a current asset of cash (most of which has already been used). Answer (A) is incorrect because payments for fixed assets decrease the current ratio through decreasing current assets. Answers (C) and (D) are incorrect because the decrease in accounts payable and in sales returns and allowances are much less than the amount of the proceeds from the loan.

| Company Profile | Industry Profile | Balance Sheet | Income Statement/Ratios | Statement of Cash Flows | Risks | Audit Findings | Audit Procedures | Communication | Audit Report | Representation Letter |
|---|---|---|---|---|---|---|---|---|---|---|

(A) (B) (C) (D) (E) (F) (G)

1. Determine that all accounts receivable are properly recorded as of year-end.  ○ ○ ○ ○ ● ○ ○

2. Determine that accounts receivable are properly valued at net realizable value.  ○ ○ ○ ○ ○ ● ○

3. Note disclosures related to accounts receivable are proper.  ○ ○ ○ ○ ○ ○ ●

**Explanations of solutions**

1.  **(E)** When examining the January 20X9 sales journal the auditor may identify sales that should have been recorded in December of 20X8.

2.  **(F)** Auditors will generally inquire of the credit manager as to his or her beliefs concerning the collectability of various receivables, and thereby obtain evidence on the net realizable value of accounts receivable. Often one would expect an answer such as "analyze aging of receivables." Since that was not present here, (F) is the best reply.

3.  **(G)** A disclosure checklist is used to determine that the disclosure requirements of generally accepted accounting principles have been met.

| Communication | | | | | | | | | | | |
|---|---|---|---|---|---|---|---|---|---|---|---|
| Company Profile | Industry Profile | Balance Sheet | Income Statement/Ratios | Statement of Cash Flows | Risks | Audit Findings | Audit Procedures | | | Audit Report | Representation Letter |

## Memorandum

To: Audit Team

Subject: Change in Board of Directors

During the past year a significant change occurred on the Toastco Board of Directors. Sam Adamson, Vice President, replaced John Whing, one of the independent directors. Mr. Williams, President, informed me that Mr. Whing resigned for health reasons. Mr. Whing had also served as Chairman of the Board, a position assumed by Mr. Williams.

The effect of this change is to decrease the independent directors to three, and increase inside directors to four. Also, the chairmanship of the board has changed from that of an independent director to that of Mr. Williams, President. This change tends to increase the power on the board of the management directors, and may adversely affect the overall independence of the board. The audit committee continues to be composed of the same three independent directors as in the past.

| | | | | | | | | | Audit Report | | |
|---|---|---|---|---|---|---|---|---|---|---|---|
| Company Profile | Industry Profile | Balance Sheet | Income Statement/Ratios | Statement of Cash Flows | Risks | Audit Findings | Audit Procedures | Communication | | | Representation Letter |

The proper guidance is provided in AU 508.08 (the report for comparative financial statements).

### Independent Auditor's Report

We have audited the accompanying balance sheets of X Company as of December 31, 20X2 and 20X1, and the related statements of income, retained earnings, and cash flows for the years then ended. These financial statements are the responsibility of the Company's management. Our responsibility is to express an opinion on these financial statements based on our audits.

We conducted our audits in accordance with auditing standards generally accepted in the United States of America. Those standards require that we plan and perform the audit to obtain reasonable assurance about whether the financial statements are free of material misstatement. An audit includes examining, on a test basis, evidence supporting the amounts and disclosures in the financial statements. An audit also includes assessing the accounting principles used and significant estimates made by management, as well as evaluating the overall financial statement presentation. We believe that our audits provide a reasonable basis for our opinion.

In our opinion, the financial statements referred to above present fairly, in all material respects, the financial position of X Company as of [at] December 31, 20X2 and 20X1, and the results of its operations and its cash flows for the years then ended in conformity with accounting principles generally accepted in the United States of America.

[Signature]

[Date]

| | | | | | | | | | | Representation Letter | |
|---|---|---|---|---|---|---|---|---|---|---|---|
| Company Profile | Industry Profile | Balance Sheet | Income Statement/Ratios | Statement of Cash Flows | Risks | Audit Findings | Audit Procedures | Communication | | Audit Report | |

[Appropriate salutation]

This letter is to confirm our understanding of the terms and objectives of our engagement and the nature and limitations of the services we will provide.

We will perform the following services:

1. We will review the balance sheet of XYZ Company as of December 31, 19XX, and the related statements of income, retained earnings, and cash flows for the year then ended, in accordance with Statements on Standards for Accounting and Review Services issued by the American Institute of Certified Public Accountants. Our review will consist primarily of inquiries of company personnel and analytical procedures applied to financial data and we will require a representation letter from management. A review does not contemplate obtaining an understanding of internal control or assessing control risk, tests of accounting records and responses to inquiries by obtaining corroborating evidential matter, and certain other procedures ordinarily performed during an audit. Thus, a review does not provide assurance that we will become aware of all significant matters that would be disclosed in an audit. Our engagement cannot be relied upon to disclose errors, fraud, or illegal acts that may exist. However, we will inform the appropriate level of management of any material errors that come to our attention and any fraud or illegal acts that come to our attention, unless they are clearly inconsequential. We will not perform an audit of such financial statements, the objective of which is the expression of an opinion regarding the financial statements taken as a whole, and, accordingly, we will not express such an opinion on them.

Our report on the financial statements is presently expected to read as follows:

We have reviewed the accompanying balance sheet of XYZ Company as of December 31, 19XX, and the related statements of income, retained earnings, and cash flows for the year then ended, in accordance with Statements on Standards for Accounting and Review Services issued by the American Institute of Certified Public Accountants.  All information included in these financial statements is the representation of the management of XYZ Company.

A review consists principally of inquiries of company personnel and analytical procedures applied to financial data.  It is substantially less in scope than an audit in accordance with generally accepted auditing standards, the objective of which is the expression of an opinion regarding the financial statements taken as a whole.  Accordingly, we do not express such an opinion.

Compilation and Review of Financial Statements

Based on our review, we are not aware of any material modification that should be made to the accompanying financial statements in order for them to be in conformity with generally accepted accounting principles.

If, for any reason we are unable to complete our review of your financial statements, we will not issue a report on such statements as a result of this engagement.

2.   We will also…(discussion of other services).

Our fees for these services…
We shall be pleased to discuss this letter with you at any time.
If the foregoing is in accordance with your understanding, please sign the copy of this letter in the space provided and return it to us.

Sincerely yours,

_____
(Signature of accountant)

Acknowledged:
XYZ Company

_____
President

_____
Date

SIMULATION 7        (60 to 70 minutes)

**Topic—Audit Evidence and Reporting**

| Company Profile | | | | | | | | |
|---|---|---|---|---|---|---|---|---|
| | Balance Sheet | Income/ Cash Flow | Industry Info | Risks | Audit Findings | Audit Procedures | Analysis and Communication | Research |

Enright Corporation is a **nonpublic** manufacturer of golf balls, golf clubs, and other golf-related equipment. The company has been in business for over fifty years and has its headquarters in San Diego, California.

Enright is divided into two divisions, which represent the major markets for the company's products. One division focuses on new golf clubs and resorts, and providing them with all of the necessary golf equipment to begin operations. The other division focuses on new product development and helps existing golf clubs and resorts to upgrade their existing equipment. Currently, each division accounts for approximately equal amounts of Enright's revenues and net income.

The company experienced its second most profitable year in 2002. However, the financial results did not meet management's expectations. Total reported revenues for the year decreased three percent compared to the prior year. Management recognizes the fact that domestic sales growth has slowed significantly in recent years. As a result, the company is now adopting a global focus for marketing its products and is looking to open up new markets in Australia and Japan.

In order to be competitive in world markets, as well as to improve their domestic market share, management believes that they must strictly control costs and make their overall operations more efficient. At the end of 2002, Enright announced it would make a series of restructuring changes as part of its overall business plan for the future.

Senior management at the company has experienced a significant turnover in recent years. The CEO has been with the company for only two years. He was hired from a major competitor after the prior CEO left to take a position with a large manufacturing company in the Northeast. In addition, the company's long-time CFO retired after twenty-five years of service. The current CFO was hired six months ago. She is a former audit manager from the office that works on Enright's annual audit.

Enright has engaged the same auditing firm for its annual audits for the past decade. There have been no disagreements over accounting issues in any of the past three years.

| | Balance Sheet | | | | | | | |
|---|---|---|---|---|---|---|---|---|
| Company Profile | | Income/ Cash Flow | Industry Info | Risks | Audit Findings | Audit Procedures | Analysis and Communication | Research |

*Enright Corporation*
**BALANCE SHEET**
*December 31, 2002 and 2001*

| | *12/31/02* | *12/31/01* |
|---|---|---|
| **Assets** | | |
| Current assets | | |
|   Cash and cash equivalents | $300,000 | $235,000 |
|   Receivables—net | 750,000 | 816,000 |
|   Investments | 600,000 | 545,000 |
|   Inventory | 1,000,000 | 1,171,000 |
|   Total current assets | 2,650,000 | 2,767,000 |
| Plant and equipment—net | 850,000 | 876,000 |
|   Total assets | $3,500,000 | $3,643,000 |
| **Liabilities and Stockholders' Equity** | | |
| Current liabilities | | |
|   Accounts payable | $390,000 | $410,000 |
|   Current portion of long-term debt | 620,000 | 620,000 |
|   Other current liabilities | 315,000 | 298,000 |
|   Total current liabilities | 1,325,000 | 1,328,000 |
| Long-term debt | 475,000 | 1,095,000 |
|   Total liabilities | 1,800,000 | 2,423,000 |
| Stockholders' equity | | |
|   Common stock | 1,000,000 | 1,000,000 |
|   Retained earnings | 700,000 | 220,000 |
|   Total stockholders' equity | 1,700,000 | 1,220,000 |
|   Total liabilities and stockholders' equity | $3,500,000 | $3,643,000 |

| Company Profile | Balance Sheet | Income/ Cash Flow | | Industry Info | Risks | Audit Findings | Audit Procedures | Analysis and Communication | Research |
|---|---|---|---|---|---|---|---|---|---|

*Enright Corporation*
## INCOME STATEMENT
*For the Years Ended December 31, 2002 and 2001*

|  | *12/31/02* | *12/31/01* |
|---|---|---|
| Sales | $5,250,000 | $5,450,000 |
| Cost of goods sold: | 2,100,000 | 2,209,000 |
| Gross profits on sales | 3,150,000 | 3,241,000 |
| Expenses |  |  |
| Selling expenses | $1,050,000 | $1,124,000 |
| General and administrative | 1,070,000 | 1,215,000 |
| Other operating expenses |  |  |
| Depreciation | 30,000 | 35,000 |
| Interest expense | 200,000 | 227,000 |
| Total expenses | $2,350,000 | $2,601,000 |
| Income before taxes | $800,000 | $640,000 |
| Provision for income taxes | 320,000 | 256,000 |
| Net income | $480,000 | $384,000 |

*Enright Corporation*
## STATEMENT OF CASH FLOWS
*For the Year Ended December 31, 2002*

| | |
|---|---|
| Cash flows from operating activities: | |
| Net income (loss) | $480,000 |
| Adjustments to reconcile net income (loss) to cash provided by (used for) operating activities | |
| Depreciation and amortization | 30,000 |
| Changes in certain assets and liabilities: | |
| Decrease (increase) in receivables | 66,000 |
| Decrease (increase) in inventory | 171,000 |
| Increase (decrease) in accounts payable | (20,000) |
| Increase (decrease) in other current liabilities | 17,000 |
| Net cash provided by (used for) operating activities | 744,000 |
| Cash flows from investing activities: | |
| Purchase of property, plant, and equipment | (4,000) |
| Change in short-term investments | (55,000) |
| Net cash provided by (used for) investing activities | (59,000) |
| Cash flows from financing activities: | |
| Principal payments on long-term debt | (620,000) |
| Net cash provided by (used for) financing activities | (620,000) |
| Net increase (decrease) in cash and cash equivalents | 65,000 |
| Cash and cash equivalents at beginning of year | 235,000 |
| Cash and cash equivalents at end of year | $300,000 |

| Company Profile | Balance Sheet | Income/ Cash Flow | Industry Info | | Risks | Audit Findings | Audit Procedures | Analysis and Communication | Research |
|---|---|---|---|---|---|---|---|---|---|

Market Forecasts
USA Sports Equipment

In 2007, the USA sports equipment market is forecast to reach $47 million, an increase of 19.3% since 2002.

The compounded annual growth rate of the global sports equipment market over the period 2002-2007 is predicted to be 3.5%.

Table 4:  USA Sports Equipment Market Value Forecasts:  $Mn (2001 Prices), 2002-2007

| *Market value* | *$Mn (2001 prices)* | *% Growth* |
|---|---|---|
| 2002 | $40,133.6 | 2.9% |
| 2003 | $41,398.3 | 3.2% |
| 2004 | $42,936.3 | 3.7% |
| 2005 | $44,389.8 | 3.4% |
| 2006 | $46,232.1 | 4.2% |
| 2007 | $46,892.1 | 3.6% |
| CAGR 2002-2007 | 3.5% | |

Golf: Play Is Steadying While Sales Struggle[1]

With 1.02 billion participants aged six and over for the year 2001, golf is ranked number 15, compared to other sports.

In what proved to be a disappointing year, sale of golf clubs, balls, bags, gloves, and shoes declined about 6% in wholesale dollars, to about $2.375 billion in 2001. Sales of irons, which enjoyed strong growth in 2000, accounted for most of the decease in 2001.

Clearly, the weak economy was the root of the problem and the continuing weakness in 2002 is expected to result in further slight sales declines as players postpone the purchase of the big-ticket items such as clubs and bags.

The total number of golfers grew by 5%, from 28.9 million to 30.4 million, between 1990 and 2000. There are as many as 40 million people who would like to play or play more often. New course development was scaled back in 2001, with 314 construction projects completed through the first nine months, compared to 408 and 379 during the same periods in 2000 and 1999, respectively.

In what might be called a "Tiger Woods" effect, some experienced golfers are trying to open the game to very young players. A small national tournament for players aged four to twelve has been created. Some manufacturers are marketing youth-sized clubs and a few facilities are developing training programs for children once considered too young to play the game.

| Company Profile | Balance Sheet | Income/ Cash Flow | Industry Info | **Risks** | Audit Findings | Audit Procedures | Analysis and Communication | Research |
|---|---|---|---|---|---|---|---|---|

(A) (B) (C) (D)

1. Which of the following correctly identifies an aspect of the company's business model, strategies, and operating environment that is most likely to increase audit risk?    ○ ○ ○ ○

   A. The lack of disagreements over accounting issues with the auditors.
   B. Difficulties in meeting management's financial results expectations for the year.
   C. The company is nonpublic.
   D. The large amount of net cash proceeds provided by operating activities.

| Company Profile | Balance Sheet | Income/ Cash Flow | Industry Info | Risks | **Audit Findings** | Audit Procedures | Analysis and Communication | Research |
|---|---|---|---|---|---|---|---|---|

The table below presents two ratios that were identified as significant in the current and prior years' audits of Enright. Compare the values of each ratio. Then select an audit finding that is consistent with these metrics.

| Ratio | 2002 | 2001 |
|---|---|---|
| Quick ratio | 1.25 | 1.20 |
| Debt to equity | 1.06 | 1.99 |

(A) (B) (C) (D)

1. Audit finding consistent with the change in the quick ratio for Enright.    ○ ○ ○ ○

   A. Although the inventory was counted and included in the year-end total, a year-end inventory purchase (for credit) was not recorded.
   B. The company made common stock acquisitions of its own stock during the year.
   C. The company accumulated excess inventories that are physically deteriorating or are becoming obsolete.
   D. The company sold many short-term investments at year-end to increase its cash position.

(A) (B) (C) (D)

2. Audit finding consistent with change in debt to equity for Enright.    ○ ○ ○ ○

   A. The company made principal payments on long-term debt.
   B. On an overall basis, the company sold short-term investments.
   C. The company recorded a significant increase in the amount of short-term debt.
   D. A dividend declared prior to the end of the year was recorded twice in the general ledger.

| Company Profile | Balance Sheet | Income/ Cash Flow | Industry Info | Risks | Audit Findings | **Audit Procedures** | Analysis and Communication | Research |
|---|---|---|---|---|---|---|---|---|

The auditor determines that each of the following objectives will be part of Enright's audit. For each audit objective, select a substantive procedure that would help to achieve the audit objectives. Each of the procedures may be used once, more than once, or not at all.

   A. Review minutes of board of directors meetings and contracts, and make inquiries of management.

---

[1] Source: *Sporting Goods Manufacturers Association*

    B.   Test inventory transactions between a preliminary physical inventory date and the balance sheet date.
    C.   Obtain confirmation of inventories pledged under loan agreement.
    D.   Review perpetual inventory records, production records, and purchasing records for indication of current activity.
    E.   Reconcile physical counts to perpetual records and general ledger balances and investigate significant fluctuation.
    F.   Examine sales after year-end and open purchase order commitments.
    G.   Examine paid vendors' invoices, consignment agreements, and contracts.
    H.   Analytically review and compare the relationship of inventory balance to recent purchasing, production, and sales activity.

|  | (A) | (B) | (C) | (D) | (E) | (F) | (G) | (H) |
|---|---|---|---|---|---|---|---|---|
| **1.**  Identify inventory transactions involving related parties. | ○ | ○ | ○ | ○ | ○ | ○ | ○ | ○ |
| **2.**  Determine that items counted are included in the inventory listing. | ○ | ○ | ○ | ○ | ○ | ○ | ○ | ○ |

| Company Profile | Balance Sheet | Income/ Cash Flow | Industry Info | Risks | Audit Findings | Audit Procedures | **Analysis and Communication** | Research |
|---|---|---|---|---|---|---|---|---|

    Use the Excel Tool to calculate "common size" income statements (vertical analysis) for the two years.  As indicated on the spreadsheet "solution," use each year's sales as "100%" and write a brief memo on whether any changes in **cost of goods sold** and **general administrative expense** seem consistent with the information provided by management in the company profile.  Discuss how changes might affect audit procedures.  Also, when considering changes, consider the fact that sales decreased by approximately 3% in 20X2.

    To:     Audit Team
    From: CPA Candidate
    Re:     Vertical Analysis—Changes in cost of goods sold and general and administrative expenses

| Company Profile | Balance Sheet | Income/ Cash Flow | Industry Info | Risks | Audit Findings | Audit Procedures | Analysis and Communication | **Research** |
|---|---|---|---|---|---|---|---|---|

    Use the research material available to you by clicking the Standards button to identify the three purposes of analytical procedures during an audit.  You should not edit the Standards in any way.

**SOLUTION TO SIMULATION 7**

| Company Profile | Balance Sheet | Income/ Cash Flow | Industry Info | Risks | Audit Findings | Audit Procedures | Analysis and Communication | Research |
|---|---|---|---|---|---|---|---|---|

(A) (B) (C) (D)

1. Which of the following correctly identifies an aspect of the company's business model, strategies, and operating environment that is most likely to increase audit risk?    ○ ● ○ ○

**Explanation of solution**

1. **(B)** The requirement is to identify the aspect of a company that is most likely to increase audit risk. Answer (B) is correct because pressure to meet or come close to management's expectations may create a pressure to commit fraud, and thereby over-state income. This will increase audit risk. Answer (A) is incorrect because disagreements, not a lack of disagreements, are likely to indicate high audit risk. Answer (C) is incorrect because being a nonpublic company does not necessarily lead to an increase in audit risk. Answer (D) is incorrect because positive cash flow from operations may simply mean that the company generated a profit and the positive cash flow accompanied it.

| Company Profile | Balance Sheet | Income/ Cash Flow | Industry Info | Risks | Audit Findings | Audit Procedures | Analysis and Communication | Research |
|---|---|---|---|---|---|---|---|---|

(A) (B) (C) (D)

1. Audit finding consistent with the change in the quick ratio for Enright.    ● ○ ○ ○
2. Audit finding consistent with change in debt to equity for Enright.    ● ○ ○ ○

**Explanation of solutions**

1. **(A)** The requirement is to identify the reply that is consistent with an increase in the quick ratio—(Cash + Short-term investments + Receivables)/ Current liabilities. Answer (A) is correct because not recording the payable portion of an inventory purchase will decrease the current liabilities, and thereby increase the quick ratio. Answer (B) is incorrect both because there does not seem to have been any common stock acquisitions, and because if there were, they would decrease the ratio, not in-crease it; the decrease would occur either due to an increase in accounts payable or a decrease in cash or accounts receivable. Answer (C) is incorrect because inventories are not included in the quick ratio and because inventory is lower at year-end rather than higher as might be suggested by obsolete inventories. Answer (D) is incorrect because the decrease in short-term invest-ments is accompanied by an increase in cash or accounts receivable—accordingly, the transaction does not affect the quick ratio.

2. **(A)** The requirement is to identify the audit finding consistent with a significant decrease in the debt to equity ratio—total debt/total equity. Answer (A) is correct because principal payments decrease the numerator of the ratio and because the financial statements reveal that such repayment of debt did occur. Answer (B) is incorrect because a sale of short-term investments does not directly affect the debt to equity ratio. Answer (C) is incorrect because an increase in short-term debt did not occur, and even if it had, it would have increased, not decreased the ratio. Answer (D) is incorrect because recording the dividend twice would increase the ratio in that total debt would increase and total equity would decrease.

| Company Profile | Balance Sheet | Income/ Cash Flow | Industry Info | Risks | Audit Findings | Audit Procedures | Analysis and Communication | Research |
|---|---|---|---|---|---|---|---|---|

(A) (B) (C) (D) (E) (F) (G) (H)

1. Identify inventory transactions involving related parties.    ● ○ ○ ○ ○ ○ ○ ○
2. Determine that items counted are included in the inventory listing.    ○ ○ ○ ○ ● ○ ○ ○

**Explanation of solutions**

1. **(A)** The requirement is to identify a procedure for identifying inventory transactions involving related parties. The best procedure listed is review minutes of Board of Directors' meeting and contracts, and to make inquiries of management; these are all procedures used to identify related-party transactions.

2. **(E)** The requirements is to identify a procedure for determining that items counted are included in the count sheet. The best procedure is to reconcile physical counts to perpetual records and general ledger balances and investigate significant fluctuations. This will allow the auditor to identify items not included.

580          APPENDIX A:  AUDITING AND ATTESTATION SIMULATIONS

| Company Profile | Balance Sheet | Income/ Cash Flow | Industry Info | Risks | Audit Findings | Audit Procedures | Analysis and Communication | Research |
|---|---|---|---|---|---|---|---|---|

**Enright Corporation**
**VERTICAL ANALYSIS**
*For Years Ended 12/31/02 and 01*

|  | 12/31/02 | 12/31/01 | 2002 | 2001 |
|---|---|---|---|---|
| Sales | 5,250,000 | 5,450,000 | 100.0% | 100.0% |
| Cost of goods sold | 2,100,000 | 2,209,000 | 40.0% | 40.5% |
| Gross profit on sales | 3,150,000 | 3,241,000 | 60.0% | 59.5% |
| Expenses |  |  |  |  |
| Selling expenses | 1,050,000 | 1,124,000 | 20.0% | 20.6% |
| General and administrative | 1,070,000 | 1,215,000 | 20.4% | 22.3% |
| Other operating expenses |  |  |  |  |
| Depreciation | 30,000 | 35,000 | 0.6% | 0.6% |
| Interest expense | 200,000 | 227,000 | 3.8% | 4.2% |
| Total expenses | 2,350,000 | 2,601,000 | 44.8% | 47.7% |
| Income before taxes | 800,000 | 2,601,000 | 15.2% | 11.8% |
| Provision of income taxes | 320,000 | 256,000 | 6.1% | 4.7% |
| Net income | 560,000 | 448,000 | 9.1% | 7.1% |

To:  Audit Team
Re: Vertical Analysis—Changes in cost of goods sold and general and administrative expenses

Sales decreased by approximately 3% in 20X2. Because of this, all things equal, one would expect expenses with fixed components to decrease by a somewhat smaller amount, while items composed largely of variable costs to retain the same percentage relationship to sales. At year-end, management announced a series of restructuring charges with the intent of making the company more profitable in the future.

The vertical analysis reveals that despite the decrease in sales, cost of goods sold as a percentage of sales decreased. This is consistent with economies due to the restructuring having been implemented, but is not consistent with a decrease in sales volume because of the fixed costs components in overhead included in cost of goods sold. Since management has indicated that the restructuring is just beginning, we should consider discussing the issue further with management.

General and administrative expenses also decreased during 20X2 as a percentage of sales. Since certain of these expenses may also be expected to have fixed components this is also not consistent with a decrease in sales, but may also indicate that Enright Corporation became more efficient during 20X2.

Our audit procedures should be aimed at determining that cost of goods sold and general and administrative expenses are properly valued. We primarily address cost of goods sold in our audit of inventories. Throughout our audit of asset accounts we must be aware of the possibility of capitalization of items that should be in expense accounts.

| Company Profile | Balance Sheet | Income/ Cash Flow | Industry Info | Risks | Audit Findings | Audit Procedures | Analysis and Communication | Research |
|---|---|---|---|---|---|---|---|---|

The guidance is provided in AU 329.04

.04  Analytical procedures are used for the following purposes:

a.  To assist the auditor in planning the nature, timing, and extent of other auditing procedures.
b.  As a substantive test to obtain evidential matter about particular assertions related to account balances or classes of transactions.
c.  As an overall review of the financial information in the final review stage of the audit.

**AUDITING AND ATTESTATION**
**TESTLET 1**

**1.** Which of the following is ordinarily considered to be a fraud risk factor?
   a. The company's financial statements include a number of last minute material adjustments.
   b. Management regularly informs investors of forecast information.
   c. The company has experienced increasing earnings over the previous five years.
   d. The company's president is included as a member of the board of directors.

**2.** Which of the following statements **best** describes the primary purpose of Statements on Auditing Standards?
   a. They are guides intended to set forth auditing procedures that are applicable to a variety of situations.
   b. They are procedural outlines that are intended to narrow the areas of inconsistency and divergence of auditor opinion.
   c. They are authoritative statements, enforced through the Code of Professional Conduct.
   d. They are interpretive guidance.

**3.** The accountant who is not independent may perform which of the following types of engagements?
   a. Audit.
   b. Agreed-upon procedures.
   c. Compilation.
   d. Review.

**4.** Which of the following should an auditor obtain from the predecessor auditor prior to accepting an audit engagement?
   a. Analysis of balance sheet accounts.
   b. Analysis of income statement accounts.
   c. All matters of continuing accounting significance.
   d. Facts that might bear on the integrity of management.

**5.** Which of the following is correct concerning allowing additions and deletions to audit documentation after the documentation completion date under requirements of the Public Company Accounting Oversight Board?

|    | Additions | Deletions |
|----|-----------|-----------|
| a. | Allowed | Allowed |
| b. | Allowed | Not allowed |
| c. | Not allowed | Allowed |
| d. | Not allowed | Not allowed |

**6.** One reason that an auditor only obtains reasonable, and not absolute, assurance that financial statements are free from material misstatement is
   a. Comprehensive basis reporting.
   b. Employee collusion.
   c. Material misstatements.
   d. Professional skepticism.

**7.** The auditors of a nonpublic company must perform a test of the operating effectiveness of a significant control
   a. In all audits.
   b. When the control relates to a significant asset.
   c. When substantive procedures alone will not provide sufficient evidence about the related assertion.

   d. When the auditors believe that the control may not be effective.

**8.** The independent auditor selects several transactions in each functional area and traces them through the entire system, paying special attention to evidence about whether or not the controls are in operation. This is an example of a(n)
   a. Application test.
   b. Tests of a control.
   c. Substantive test.
   d. Test of a function.

**9.** In obtaining an understanding of a manufacturing entity's internal control over inventory balances, an auditor most likely would
   a. Review the entity's descriptions of inventory policies and procedures.
   b. Perform test counts of inventory during the entity's physical count.
   c. Analyze inventory turnover statistics to identify slow-moving and obsolete items.
   d. Analyze monthly production reports to identify variances and unusual transactions.

**10.** Further audit procedures consist of which of the following?

|    | Risk assessment procedures | Substantive procedures | Test of controls |
|----|----------------------------|------------------------|------------------|
| a. | Yes | No | No |
| b. | Yes | Yes | No |
| c. | No | Yes | No |
| d. | No | Yes | Yes |

**11.** The risk of material misstatement increases the acceptable level of
   a. Detection risk decreases.
   b. Business risk increases.
   c. Audit risk decreases.
   d. Materiality increases.

**12.** Which is **least** likely to be a question asked of client personnel during a walk-through in an audit of the internal control of a public company?
   a. What do you do when you find an error?
   b. Who is most likely to commit fraud among your coworkers?
   c. What kind of errors have you found?
   d. Have you ever been asked to override the process or controls?

**13.** Which of the following matters is an auditor required to communicate to an entity's audit committee?

|    | Significant audit adjustments | Changes in significant accounting policies |
|----|-------------------------------|--------------------------------------------|
| a. | Yes | Yes |
| b. | Yes | No |
| c. | No | Yes |
| d. | No | No |

**14.** An abnormal fluctuation in gross profit that might suggest the need for extended audit procedures for sales and inventories would most likely be identified in the planning phase of the audit by the use of

a. Tests of transactions and balances.
b. A preliminary review of internal control.
c. Specialized audit programs.
d. Analytical procedures.

**15.** When auditing merchandise inventory at year-end, the auditor performs a purchase cutoff test to obtain evidence that

a. All goods purchased before year-end are received before the physical inventory count.
b. No goods held on consignment for customers are included in the inventory balance.
c. No goods observed during the physical count are pledged or sold.
d. All goods owned at year-end are included in the inventory balance.

**16.** An auditor who uses the work of a specialist may refer to and identify the specialist in the auditor's report if the

a. Specialist is also considered to be a related party.
b. Auditor indicates a division of responsibility related to the work of the specialist.
c. Specialist's work provides the auditor greater assurance of reliability.
d. Auditor expresses an "except for" qualified opinion or an adverse opinion related to the work of the specialist.

**17.** Which of the following statements concerning evidential matter is correct?

a. Appropriate evidence supporting management's assertions should be convincing rather than merely persuasive.
b. Effective internal control contributes little to the reliability of the evidence created within the entity.
c. The cost of obtaining evidence is **not** an important consideration to an auditor in deciding what evidence should be obtained.
d. A client's accounting data **cannot** be considered sufficient audit evidence to support the financial statements.

**18.** The auditor is **most** likely to verify accrued commissions payable in conjunction with the

a. Sales cutoff review.
b. Verification of contingent liabilities.
c. Review of post balance sheet date disbursements.
d. Examination of trade accounts payable.

**19.** A note to the financial statements of the First Security Bank indicates that all of the records relating to the bank's business operations are stored on magnetic disks, and that there are no emergency back-up systems or duplicate disks stored since the First Security Bank and their auditors consider the occurrence of a catastrophe to be remote. Based upon this, one would expect the auditor's report to express

a. An adverse opinion.
b. An "except for" opinion.
c. An unqualified opinion.
d. A qualified opinion.

**20.** A company has changed its method of inventory valuation from an unacceptable one to one in conformity with generally accepted accounting principles. The

auditor's report on the financial statements of the year of the change should include

a. No reference to consistency.
b. A reference to a prior period adjustment in the opinion paragraph.
c. An explanatory paragraph explaining the change.
d. A justification for making the change and the impact of the change on reported net income.

**21.** When an auditor reissues in 20X7 the auditor's report on the 20X5 financial statements at the request of the client without revising the 20X5 wording, the auditor should

a. Use the date of the original report.
b. Use the date of the client's request.
c. Use the date of the current period report.
d. Dual date the report.

**22.** Auditors who prefer statistical sampling to nonstatistical sampling may do so because statistical sampling helps the auditor

a. Measure the sufficiency of the evidential matter obtained.
b. Eliminate subjectivity in the evaluation of sampling results.
c. Reduce the level of tolerable misstatement (error) to a relatively low amount.
d. Minimize the failure to detect a material misstatement due to nonsampling risk.

**23.** Accounting control procedures within computer processing may leave no visible evidence indicating that the procedures were performed. In such instances, the auditor should test these accounting controls by

a. Making corroborative inquiries.
b. Observing the separation of duties of personnel.
c. Reviewing transactions submitted for processing and comparing them to related output.
d. Reviewing the run manual.

**24.** Which is **least** likely to be a response when an auditor has obtained evidence indicating a risk of material misstatement in the area of inventory?

a. Discuss questions of inventory valuation with any other auditors involved with the audit.
b. Make oral inquiries of major suppliers in addition to written confirmations.
c. Perform inventory observations on an unannounced basis.
d. Request inventory counts at the end of each month.

**25.** Confirmations of accounts receivable address which assertion most directly?

a. Completeness.
b. Existence.
c. Valuation.
d. Classification.

**26.** Which of the following is always present in an attestation engagement?

a. Assertion about the subject matter.
b. Generally accepted assurance principles.
c. Subject matter.
d. An examination report.

**27.** Which of the following is least likely to be a test of a control?

    a.   Inquiries of appropriate personnel.
    b.   Inspection of management's engagement letter.
    c.   Observation of the application of a policy.
    d.   Reperformance of the application of a policy

**28.** If information is for management's use only, which of the following forms of CPA association with financial information is most likely to result in no report being issued?
    a.   An agreed-upon procedures engagement.
    b.   An audit.
    c.   A compilation.
    d.   A review.

**29.** Which of the following examinations is most likely to result in a CPA issuing a "restricted use" report?
    a.   Financial projection.
    b.   Trust services.
    c.   Management's discussion and analysis.
    d.   Financial statements prepared following the tax basis of accounting.

**30.** Which of the following best illustrates the concept of sampling risk?
    a.   A randomly chosen sample may not be representative of the population as a whole on the characteristic of interest.
    b.   An auditor may select audit procedures that are not appropriate to achieve the specific objective.
    c.   An auditor may fail to recognize misstatements in the documents examined for the chosen sample.
    d.   The documents related to the chosen sample may not be available for inspection.

# AUDITING AND ATTESTATION

## ANSWERS TO TESTLET 1

| | | | | | | | | | | | |
|---|---|---|---|---|---|---|---|---|---|---|---|
| **1.** | a | **6.** | b | **11.** | a | **16.** | d | **21.** | a | **26.** | c |
| **2.** | c | **7.** | c | **12.** | b | **17.** | d | **22.** | a | **27.** | b |
| **3.** | c | **8.** | b | **13.** | a | **18.** | a | **23.** | c | **28.** | c |
| **4.** | d | **9.** | a | **14.** | d | **19.** | c | **24.** | d | **29.** | a |
| **5.** | b | **10.** | d | **15.** | d | **20.** | c | **25.** | b | **30.** | a |

### *Auditing and Attestation Hints*

1. Which factor deals most directly with expected intentional misstatements?

2. The SAS provide authoritative guidance.

3. Three of the services are always considered attest services

4. The auditor wants to minimize the likelihood of association with a client whose management lacks integrity.

5. Remember that audits may sometimes be affected by subsequent discovery of facts existing at the date of the audit report.

6. What real world difficulty makes detecting misstatements difficult?

7. For most assertions tests of controls are not required.

8. The auditor is trying to determine the effectiveness of internal control.

9. The auditor is not evaluating the effectiveness of internal control.

10. Which set of procedures is used to design the others?

11. Think about the audit risk components that vary inversely from one another.

12. Which question seems too aggressive?

13. The audit committee that has responsibility for the oversight of the client's financial reporting process, should be kept informed about the scope and results of the audit.

14. Which substantive test relies on the premise that plausible relationships among data may reasonably be expected to exist and continue in the absence of known conditions to the contrary?

15. The purchase cutoff test verifies that the purchasing transactions are recorded in the proper period.

16. The auditor refers to the specialist if the auditor issues a qualified, adverse, or disclaimer as a result of the specialist's work.

17. In addition to the accounting data, the auditor must obtain corroborating evidential matter.

18. The auditor wants to make sure that the liability is applied to the correct period.

19. The financial statements are presented fairly in conformity with GAAP.

20. The audit report should disclose the lack of consistency.

21. Nothing has changed with regard to the 20X5 report.

22. Statistical sampling provides the auditor with a mathematical model.

23. The auditor wants to see the effects of the controls on the transactions.

24. Think of procedures that are likely to provide additional evidence relating to the financial statements being reported upon.

25. Does a confirmation assure that the account will be collected?

26. A report may ordinarily be on two of these—but one of them is always present.

27. Which reply relates to an auditor prepared item?

28. Which situation is most likely to result in a report that only management will use?

29. Pick the reply that relies most directly upon a hypothetical assumption.

30. Sampling risk relates to not examining all of the items in the population.

## AUDITING AND ATTESTATION

### TESTLET 2

1. Which of the following statements best describes an auditor's responsibility to detect misstatements due to errors and fraud?
   a. The auditor should study and evaluate the client's internal control, and design the audit to provide reasonable assurance of detecting all errors and fraud.
   b. The auditor should assess the risk that errors and fraud may cause the financial statements to contain material misstatements, and determine whether the necessary controls are prescribed and are being followed satisfactorily.
   c. The auditor should consider the types of errors and fraud that could occur, and determine whether the necessary controls are prescribed and are being followed.
   d. The auditor should assess the risk that errors and fraud may cause the financial statements to contain material misstatements, and design the audit to provide reasonable assurance of detecting material misstatements due to errors and fraud.

2. When one auditor succeeds another, the successor auditor should request the
   a. Client to instruct its attorney to send a letter of audit inquiry concerning the status of the prior year's litigation, claims, and assessments.
   b. Predecessor auditor to submit a list of internal control weaknesses that have **not** been corrected.
   c. Client to authorize the predecessor auditor to allow a review of the predecessor auditor's working papers.
   d. Predecessor auditor to update the prior year's report to the date of the change of auditors.

3. A difference of opinion concerning accounting and auditing matters relative to a particular phase of the audit arises between an assistant auditor and the auditor responsible for the engagement. After appropriate consultation, the assistant auditor asks to be disassociated from the resolution of the matter. The working papers would probably be
   a. Silent on the matter since it is an internal matter of the auditing firm.
   b. Expanded to note that the assistant auditor is completely disassociated from responsibility for the auditor's opinion.
   c. Expanded to document the additional work required, since all disagreements of this type will require expanded substantive testing.
   d. Expanded to document the assistant auditor's position, and how the difference of opinion was resolved.

4. On the audit of a nonpublic company, the purpose of performing risk assessment procedures is to:
   a. Obtain an understanding of the entity and its environment.
   b. Reduce detection risk.
   c. Evaluate management ability.
   d. Determine the operating effectiveness of controls.

5. When an auditor becomes aware of a possible client illegal act, the auditor should obtain an understanding of the nature of the act to
   a. Increase the assessed level of control risk.
   b. Recommend remedial actions to the audit committee.
   c. Evaluate the effect on the financial statements.
   d. Determine the reliability of management's representations.

6. Which of the following controls may prevent the failure to bill customers for some shipments?
   a. Each shipment should be supported by a prenumbered sales invoice that is accounted for.
   b. Each sales order should be approved by authorized personnel.
   c. Sales journal entries should be reconciled to daily sales summaries.
   d. Each sales invoice should be supported by a shipping document.

7. Which of the following is a control weakness for a company whose inventory of supplies consists of a large number of individual items?
   a. Supplies of relatively little value are expensed when purchased.
   b. The cycle basis is used for physical counts.
   c. The storekeeper is responsible for maintenance of perpetual inventory records.
   d. Perpetual inventory records are maintained only for items of significant value.

8. The accounts payable department receives the purchase order form to accomplish all of the following **except**
   a. Compare invoice price to purchase order price.
   b. Ensure the purchase had been properly authorized.
   c. Ensure the goods had been received by the party requesting the goods.
   d. Compare quantity ordered to quantity purchased.

9. Before applying substantive tests to the details of asset and liability accounts at an interim date, the auditor should
   a. Assess the difficulty in controlling incremental audit risk.
   b. Investigate significant fluctuations that have occurred in the asset and liability accounts since the previous balance sheet date.
   c. Select only those accounts that can effectively be sampled during year-end audit work.
   d. Consider the tests of controls that must be applied at the balance-sheet date to extend the audit conclusions reached at the interim date.

10. Which of the following situations would **most** likely require special audit planning by the auditor?
    a. Some items of factory and office equipment do **not** bear identification numbers.
    b. Depreciation methods used on the client's tax return differ from those used on the books.
    c. Assets costing less than $500 are expensed even though the expected life exceeds one year.
    d. Inventory is comprised of precious stones.

**11.** After discovering that a related party transaction exists, the auditor should be aware that the
   a. Substance of the transaction could be significantly different from its form.
   b. Adequacy of disclosure of the transaction is secondary to its legal form.
   c. Transaction is assumed to be outside the ordinary course of business.
   d. Financial statements should recognize the legal form of the transaction rather than its substance.

**12.** Morgan, CPA, is the principal auditor for a multinational corporation. Another CPA has audited and reported on the financial statements of a significant subsidiary of the corporation. Morgan is satisfied with the independence and professional reputation of the other auditor, as well as the quality of the other auditor's examination. With respect to Morgan's report on the consolidated financial statements, taken as a whole, Morgan
   a. Must **not** refer to the audit of the other auditor.
   b. Must refer to the audit of the other auditor.
   c. May refer to the audit of the other auditor.
   d. May refer to the audit of the other auditor, in which case Morgan must include in the auditor's report on the consolidated financial statements a qualified opinion with respect to the examination of the other auditor.

**13.** If the objective of a test of details is to detect overstatements of sales, the auditor should trace transactions from the
   a. Cash receipts journal to the sales journal.
   b. Sales journal to the cash receipts journal.
   c. Source documents to the accounting records.
   d. Accounting records to the source documents.

**14.** The auditor's program for the examination of long-term debt should include steps that require the
   a. Verification of the existence of the bondholders.
   b. Examination of any bond trust indenture.
   c. Inspection of the accounts payable subsidiary ledger.
   d. Investigation of credits to the bond interest income account.

**15.** All corporate capital stock transactions should ultimately be traced to the
   a. Minutes of the Board of Directors.
   b. Cash receipts journal.
   c. Cash disbursements journal.
   d. Numbered stock certificates.

**16.** In testing plant and equipment balances, an auditor examines new additions listed on an analysis of plant and equipment. This procedure most likely obtains evidence concerning management's assertion of
   a. Completeness.
   b. Existence or occurrence.
   c. Presentation and disclosure.
   d. Valuation or allocation.

**17.** When the audited financial statements of the prior year are presented together with those of the current year, the continuing auditor's report should cover
   a. Both years.
   b. Only the current year.
   c. Only the current year, but the prior year's report should be presented.
   d. Only the current year, but the prior year's report should be referred to.

**18.** Information accompanying the basic financial statements in an auditor-submitted document should **not** include
   a. An analysis of inventory by location.
   b. A statement that the allowance for doubtful accounts is adequate.
   c. A statement that the depreciable life of a new asset is twenty years.
   d. An analysis of revenue by product line.

**19.** The objective of auditing procedures applied to segment information is to provide the auditor with a reasonable basis for concluding whether
   a. The information is useful for comparing a segment of one enterprise with a similar segment of another enterprise.
   b. Sufficient evidential matter has been obtained to allow the auditor to be associated with the segment information.
   c. A separate opinion on the segment information is necessary due to inconsistent application of accounting principles.
   d. The information is presented in conformity with the FASB Statement on segment information in relation to the financial statements taken as a whole.

**20.** An accountant has been asked to issue a review report on the balance sheet of a nonpublic company but not to report on the other basic financial statements. The accountant may **not** do so
   a. Because compliance with this request would result in an incomplete review.
   b. Because compliance with this request would result in a violation of the ethical standards of the profession.
   c. If the scope of the inquiry and analytical procedures has been restricted.
   d. If the review of the balance sheet discloses material departures from generally accepted accounting principles.

**21.** An auditor was unable to obtain audited financial statements or other evidence supporting an entity's investment in a foreign subsidiary. Between which of the following opinions should the entity's auditor choose?
   a. Adverse and unqualified with an explanatory paragraph added.
   b. Disclaimer and unqualified with an explanatory paragraph added.
   c. Qualified and adverse.
   d. Qualified and disclaimer.

**22.** In which of the following cases would the auditor be most likely to conclude that all of the items in an account under consideration should be examined rather than tested on a sample basis?

|  | The measure of tolerable misstatement is | Misstatement frequency is expected to be |
|---|---|---|
| a. | Large | Low |
| b. | Small | High |
| c. | Large | High |
| d. | Small | Low |

**23.** Which of the following factors is generally **not** considered in determining the sample size for a test of controls?
- a. Risk of incorrect acceptance.
- b. Tolerable rate.
- c. Risk of assessing control risk too low.
- d. Expected population deviation rate.

**24.** The most important function of generalized audit software is the capability to
- a. Access information stored on computer files.
- b. Select a sample of items for testing.
- c. Evaluate sample test results.
- d. Test the accuracy of the client's calculations.

**25.** A limitation on the scope of an auditor's procedures is likely to result in a report with a(n)

|  | Qualified opinion | Adverse opinion |
|---|---|---|
| a. | Yes | Yes |
| b. | Yes | No |
| c. | No | Yes |
| d. | No | No |

**26.** Which of the following is least likely to be considered when assessing inherent risk?
- a. Nonroutine transactions.
- b. Estimation transactions.
- c. Susceptibility to theft.
- d. Expected effectiveness of controls.

**27.** In the audit risk model, the risk of misstatement is composed of

|  | Inherent risk | Control risk | Detection risk |
|---|---|---|---|
| a. | Yes | Yes | Yes |
| b. | Yes | Yes | No |
| c. | Yes | No | Yes |
| d. | Yes | No | No |

**28.** Which of the following is most likely to result in modification of a compilation report?
- a. A departure from generally accepted accounting principles.
- b. A lack of consistency in application of generally accepted accounting principles.
- c. A question concerning an entity's ability to continue as a going concern.
- d. A major uncertainty facing the financial statements.

**29.** Analytical procedures are required

|  | Planning | Substantive tests | Final review |
|---|---|---|---|
| a. | Yes | Yes | Yes |
| b. | Yes | Yes | No |
| c. | Yes | No | Yes |
| d. | No | No | No |

**30.** Which of the following is used to obtain evidence that the client's equipment accounts are **not** understated?
- a. Analyze repairs and maintenance expense accounts.
- b. Vouching purchases of plant and equipment.
- c. Recomputing depreciation expense.
- d. Analyzing the miscellaneous revenue account.

## AUDITING AND ATTESTATION

## ANSWERS TO TESTLET 2

| | | | | | | | | | | | |
|---|---|---|---|---|---|---|---|---|---|---|---|
| 1. | d | 6. | a | 11. | a | 16. | b | 21. | d | 26. | d |
| 2. | c | 7. | c | 12. | c | 17. | a | 22. | b | 27. | b |
| 3. | d | 8. | c | 13. | d | 18. | b | 23. | a | 28. | a |
| 4. | a | 9. | a | 14. | b | 19. | d | 24. | a | 29. | c |
| 5. | c | 10. | d | 15. | a | 20. | c | 25. | b | 30. | a |

### Auditing and Attestation Hints

1. AU 316 states that the auditor should design the audit to provide reasonable assurance of detecting material misstatement due to errors and fraud.

2. AU 315 states that the successor auditor should ask the prospective client to authorize the predecessor to respond fully to the successor's inquiries.

3. Working papers document the audit procedures applied, the information obtained and the conclusions reached during the engagement.

4. Audit risk often relates to business risk.

5. The auditor wants to obtain reasonable assurance that the financial statements contain no material misstatements.

6. A control should be present which readily shows a missing sales invoice.

7. Where is it most likely that control will be lost because of information overload?

8. The accounts payable department is responsible for the recordkeeping function.

9. The auditor needs to be assured that the assessed level of control risk is the same at the balance sheet date as it is at the interim date.

10. Which situation would require the auditor to use the work of a specialist?

11. The auditor wants to determine that there is a valid business purpose for the transactions.

12. The principal auditor must decide whether or not to assume responsibility for the work of the other auditor.

13. The auditor is testing for existence.

14. The audit program should include procedures to ensure that the debt is properly presented on the balance sheet.

15. Where does authorization for these transactions originate?

16. Are the new additions valid fixed assets?

17. The auditor's opinion regarding the financial statement should apply to the financial statements as a whole.

18. Which information is the auditor required to determine when auditing the financial statements?

19. The auditor normally considers segment information when performing an audit of financial statement in accordance with generally accepted auditing standards.

20. Limited reporting objectives is not the same as limiting the available procedures.

21. How does the auditor report a scope limitation?

22. Where does the auditor have the greatest risk of a material misstatement?

23. One reply deals with variables sampling, while three deal with attributes sampling.

24. Which item is not a responsibility of the auditor?

25. A scope limitation may lead to a situation in which an auditor does not know whether the financial statements follow GAAP.

26. Remember the auditor also assesses control risk.

27. Do not get mixed up, the question is not asking about the components of audit risk.

28. Reporting of which seems most essential to the CPA's role?

29. They are not required at all stages, at one stage the auditor may decide whether to use analytical procedures.

30. Which reply is most likely to find an equipment purchase that has not been capitalized?

**AUDITING AND ATTESTATION**

**TESTLET 3**

**1.** The risk that an auditor's procedures will lead to the conclusion that a material misstatement does **not** exist in an account balance when, in fact, such misstatement does exist is referred to as
  a.  Audit risk.
  b.  Inherent risk.
  c.  Control risk.
  d.  Detection risk.

**2.** Which of the following types of fraud is an audit **least** likely to detect?
  a.  Theft of cash received from collection of accounts receivable.
  b.  Intentional omission of transactions relating to equipment purchases.
  c.  Intentional violations of occupational safety and health laws.
  d.  Misapplication of accounting principles relating to inventory.

**3.** Prior to beginning the fieldwork on a new audit engagement in which a CPA does **not** possess expertise in the industry in which the client operates, the CPA should
  a.  Reduce audit risk by lowering the preliminary levels of materiality.
  b.  Design special substantive tests to compensate for the lack of industry expertise.
  c.  Engage financial experts familiar with the nature of the industry.
  d.  Obtain a knowledge of matters that relate to the nature of the entity's business.

**4.** Which of the following is defined as a weakness in internal control that allows more than a remote likelihood of misstatement that is more than inconsequential, but less than material?
  a.  Control deficiency.
  b.  Material weakness.
  c.  An exception.
  d.  Significant deficiency.

**5.** Which of the following controls would most likely be used to maintain accurate perpetual inventory records?
  a.  Independent storeroom count of goods received.
  b.  Periodic independent reconciliation of control and subsidiary records.
  c.  Periodic independent comparison of records with goods on hand.
  d.  Independent matching of purchase orders, receiving reports, and vendors' invoices.

**6.** Evidential matter concerning proper segregation of duties ordinarily is best obtained by
  a.  Preparation of a flowchart of duties performed by available personnel.
  b.  Inquiring whether control activities operated consistently throughout the period.
  c.  Reviewing job descriptions prepared by the personnel department.
  d.  Direct personal observation of the employees who apply control activities.

**7.** In considering internal control, the auditor is basically concerned that it provides reasonable assurance that

  a.  Operational efficiency has been achieved in accordance with management plans.
  b.  Material misstatements due to errors and fraud have been prevented or detected.
  c.  Controls have **not** been circumvented by collusion.
  d.  Management **cannot** override the system.

**8.** In properly designed internal control, the same employee should **not** be permitted to
  a.  Sign checks and cancel supporting documents.
  b.  Receive merchandise and prepare a receiving report.
  c.  Prepare disbursement vouchers and sign checks.
  d.  Initiate a request to order merchandise and approve merchandise received.

**9.** Which of the following is an effective control over cash payments?
  a.  Signed checks should be mailed under the supervision of the check signer.
  b.  Spoiled checks that have been voided should be disposed of immediately.
  c.  Checks should be prepared only by persons responsible for cash receipts and cash disbursements.
  d.  A check-signing machine with two signatures should be utilized.

**10.** Inquiries of warehouse personnel concerning possible obsolete or slow-moving inventory items provide assurance about management's assertion of
  a.  Completeness.
  b.  Existence.
  c.  Presentation.
  d.  Valuation.

**11.** The primary reason an auditor requests letters of inquiry be sent to a client's attorneys is to provide the auditor with
  a.  A description and evaluation of litigation, claims, and assessments that existed at the date of the balance sheet.
  b.  An expert opinion as to whether a loss is possible, probable, or remote.
  c.  The opportunity to examine the documentation concerning litigation, claims, and assessments.
  d.  Corroboration of the information furnished by management concerning litigation, claims, and assessments.

**12.** Which of the following ratios would an engagement partner most likely calculate when reviewing the balance sheet in the overall review stage of an audit?
  a.  Quick assets/current assets.
  b.  Accounts receivable/inventory.
  c.  Interest payable/interest receivable.
  d.  Total debt/total assets.

**13.** When providing limited assurance that the financial statements of a nonpublic entity require **no** material modifications to be in accordance with generally accepted accounting principles, the accountant should

a.  Understand internal control.
b.  Test the accounting records that identify inconsistencies with the prior year's financial statements.
c.  Understand the accounting principles of the industry in which the entity operates.
d.  Develop audit programs to determine whether the entity's financial statements are fairly presented.

**14.**  A written client representation letter most likely would be an auditor's best source of corroborative information of a client's plans to
a.  Terminate an employee pension plan.
b.  Make a public offering of its common stock.
c.  Settle an outstanding lawsuit for an amount less than the accrued loss contingency.
d.  Discontinue a line of business.

**15.**  Which of the following procedures is **not** included in a review engagement of a nonpublic entity?
a.  Inquiries of management.
b.  Inquiries regarding events subsequent to the balance sheet date.
c.  Any procedures designed to identify relationships among data that appear to be unusual.
d.  Tests of internal control.

**16.**  A CPA who is associated with the financial statements of a public entity but has **not** audited or reviewed such statements, should
a.  Insist that they be audited or reviewed before publication.
b.  Read them to determine whether there are obvious material misstatements.
c.  State these facts in the accompanying notes to the financial statements.
d.  Issue a compilation report.

**17.**  Kane, CPA, concludes that there is substantial doubt about Lima Co.'s ability to continue as a going concern for a reasonable period of time.  If Lima's financial statements adequately disclose its financial difficulties, Kane's auditor's report is required to include an explanatory paragraph that specifically uses the phrase(s)

|     | "Possible discontinuance of operations" | "Reasonable period of time, **not** to exceed 1 year" |
| --- | --- | --- |
| a. | Yes | Yes |
| b. | Yes | No |
| c. | No | Yes |
| d. | No | No |

**18.**  How are management's responsibility and the auditor's responsibility represented in the standard auditor's report?

|     | Management's responsibility | Auditor's responsibility |
| --- | --- | --- |
| a. | Explicitly | Explicitly |
| b. | Implicitly | Implicitly |
| c. | Implicitly | Explicitly |
| d. | Explicitly | Implicitly |

**19.**  In estimation sampling for attributes, which one of the following must be known in order to appraise the results of the auditor's sample?
a.  Estimated dollar value of the population.
b.  Standard deviation of the values in the population.

c.  Actual occurrence rate of the attribute in the population.
d.  Sample size.

**20.**  Processing data through the use of simulated files provides an auditor with information about the reliability of controls.  One of the techniques involved in this approach makes use of
a.  Controlled reprocessing.
b.  Integrated test facility.
c.  Input validation.
d.  Program code checking

**21.**  After the audit documentation completion date, the auditor
a.  May not delete any audit documentation.
b.  May not make changes in audit documentation.
c.  May not add new information to audit documentation.
d.  May make changes or deletions to audit documentation providing that the fact that alterations were made is documented.

**22.**  Prior to or in conjunction with obtaining information to identify risks of fraud, which of the following is required?
a.  A brainstorming session among team members about where financial statements may be susceptible to fraud.
b.  A discussion with the client's legal counsel as to contingent liabilities likely to affect the financial statements.
c.  Indirect verification of significant financial statement assertions.
d.  Professional skepticism concerning indirect effect illegal acts.

**23.**  Which of the following is **not** ordinarily performed in response to the risk of management override?
a.  Evaluating the rationale for significant unusual transactions.
b.  Observe counts of inventory at all locations.
c.  Review accounting estimates for bias.
d.  Test appropriateness of journal entries and adjustments.

**24.**  When an auditor has a question concerning a client's ability to continue as a going concern, the auditor considers management's plans for dealing with the situation.  That consideration is most likely to include consideration of management's plans to
a.  Decrease ownership equity.
b.  Dispose of assets.
c.  Increase expenditures on key products.
d.  Invest in derivative securities.

**25.**  A change from one accounting principle to another with which the auditor concurs is likely to result in a report with a(n)

|     | Qualified opinion | Adverse opinion |
| --- | --- | --- |
| a. | Yes | Yes |
| b. | Yes | No |
| c. | No | Yes |
| d. | No | No |

**26.** A significant circumstance-caused scope limitation in a Sarbanes/Oxley 404 internal control audit is more likely to result in a(n)
    a. Adverse opinion.
    b. Qualified opinion.
    c. Unqualified opinion with explanatory language.
    d. Scope reduction opinion.

**27.** Which of the following statements regarding auditor documentation of the client's internal control is correct?
    a. Documentation must include flowcharts.
    b. Documentation must include procedural write-ups.
    c. No documentation is necessary, although it is desirable.
    d. No one particular form of documentation is required and the extent may vary.

**28.** Which of the following is least likely to be considered an attestation service?
    a. Agreed-upon procedures.
    b. Compilation.
    c. Examinations.
    d. Review.

**29.** Intentional misstatements of financial statements to deceive the financial statement users is considered by the AICPA to be

| | *Fraudulent financial reporting* | *Misappropriation of assets* |
|---|---|---|
| a. | Yes | Yes |
| b. | Yes | No |
| c. | No | Yes |
| d. | No | No |

**30.** Violation of which of the following is most likely to be considered a "direct effect" illegal act?
    a. Environmental protection laws.
    b. Occupational safety and health law violations.
    c. Securities trading laws.
    d. Tax law violations.

## AUDITING AND ATTESTATION
## ANSWERS TO TESTLET 3

| 1. | d | 6. | d | 11. | d | 16. | b | 21. | d | 26. | b |
|----|---|----|---|-----|---|-----|---|-----|---|-----|---|
| 2. | c | 7. | b | 12. | d | 17. | d | 22. | a | 27. | d |
| 3. | d | 8. | c | 13. | c | 18. | a | 23. | b | 28. | b |
| 4. | d | 9. | a | 14. | d | 19. | d | 24. | b | 29. | b |
| 5. | c | 10. | d | 15. | d | 20. | b | 25. | d | 30. | d |

### *Auditing and Attestation Hints*

1. The auditor performs audit procedures to detect material misstatements in the account balance.

2. Which type is least likely to misstate financial statement amounts?

3. The CPA must understand the business issues of the company and industry.

4. Remember, the amount involved is less than material.

5. Which independent check verifies the existence of the inventory?

6. Which control gives the auditor the best idea about the daily operation of the company?

7. Which area does the auditor have the most control over?

8. Segregate recordkeeping from authorization.

9. Which control helps the client maintain accountability for the cash payments?

10. Obsolete or slow moving inventory may never be sold and so the amount of inventory presented on the balance sheet may be overstated.

11. AU 337 states that a letter of audit inquiry to the client's lawyer is the auditor's primary means of obtaining corroboration of the information furnished by management concerning litigation, claims, and assessments.

12. The partner is looking at the big picture.

13. A requirement for any engagement is for the auditor to understand the environment they are working in.

14. Which situation would the client be the best source of information regarding future plans?

15. A review engagement provides only limited assurance.

16. The financial statements are the representation of management but the CPA still has a degree of responsibility.

17. Mentally "write" an explanatory paragraph and consider whether it is likely that these items would be required.

18. The standard audit report should give the reader a clear understanding about responsibilities.

19. The auditor wants to determine a deviation rate for the sample.

20. Which technique places the simulated files into the midst of live transactions?

21. Documentation should be as accurate as possible.

22. Think about SAS 99s (AU 316) requirements.

23. Which procedure may not be practical in some situations?

24. Consider a reply that will provide resources to the company.

25. Client's are able to change accounting principles.

26. Scope limitations may result in two types of opinion—only one is listed.

27. Consider the great variation in the types of entities audited.

28. Reports on one of these engagements explicitly say that no assurance is being provided.

29. Consider the differences between fraudulent financial reporting and misappropriation of assets.

30. Which is most likely to result in direct misstatement of a financial statement account balance?

**SIMULATION 1**

**Topics—Planning, Internal Control, Evidence, and Reporting**

| Situation | | | | | | | | | | |
|---|---|---|---|---|---|---|---|---|---|---|
| | Company Profile | Industry Information | Balance Sheet | Income Statement | Statement of Cash Flows | Risks | Audit Findings | Audit Procedures | Communication | Research |

Assume you are performing the 20X8 audit of Tommi Stone and Quarry.

| | Company Profile | | | | | | | | | |
|---|---|---|---|---|---|---|---|---|---|---|
| Situation | | Industry Information | Balance Sheet | Income Statement | Statement of Cash Flows | Risks | Audit Findings | Audit Procedures | Communication | Research |

In 20X1 Jill Tommi founded Tommi Stone and Quarry (TSQ).  Within its first year of existence, the company completed initial development of the extraction pit area and constructed an aggregate processing plant which is equipped to crush, screen, and wash aggregate products.  By 20X3 the sand and gravel operation was profitable and growing market conditions justified modifications and expansion.  Currently, at the conclusion of 20X8, TSQ produces a wide range of sand and stone products from its pit near Albuquerque, New Mexico. The materials it develops range from various sand and stone materials for residential and commercial construction and highway projects.  TSQ sells to a wide variety of residential, commercial and governmental customers, with no one customer accounting for more than 5% of its total sales.

TSQ has worked closely with stucco manufacturers and plastering contractors in the Albuquerque plastering industry to produce a plaster sand ("Plasand") that exceeds normal specifications and produces a superior ingredient which improves stucco and plastering finished products.  Plasand has been increasingly widely accepted as superior to products offered by competitors, and now accounts for approximately 10% of the company's sales, and 12% of its profits.  TSQ is currently working closely with sport complexes and golf course architects in conjunction with test laboratories to develop a superior sand for use in the construction and top dressing of golf courses and sport complex playing fields.

The company experienced a level of profitability in 20X8 of about the same as that of 20X7—but this is well below the net incomes of the preceding several years.  Jill suggested to you that, surprisingly, intense price competition from several smaller competitors in the Albuquerque area caused the somewhat low level of profitability.  But, she added, she didn't expect the problem to last for long because she doubted that those companies could continue to operate selling at these lower prices.  Jill had hoped for a more profitable year in 20X8 as a significant amount of the company's long-term debt is payable in 20X9.  TSQ is currently involved in discussions with the bank on refinancing.

TSQ added significant additional crushing and washing plants and equipment during 20X8 to increase production in the future by more than 100% while expanding capabilities to produce custom specification materials.

Until 20X7 and 20X8, most of earnings were distributed through dividends to TSQ's five shareholders—CEO and Chair of the Board of Directors Jill Tommi, her husband Mort Tommi, CFO Googlo Permasi and two college friends of Jill's who invested in the company, Jian Zhang and Kendra Kovano.  These five individuals make up the company's Board of Directors.

This year, in reaction to pressure from a bank that provides a significant portion of the financing, TSQ established an audit committee composed of Mort Tommi, Googlo Permasi, and Jian Zhang.

You are working on your firm's fifth audit of TSQ.  The previous audits have all resulted in standard unqualified audit reports.

| | | Industry Information | | | | | | | | |
|---|---|---|---|---|---|---|---|---|---|---|
| Situation | Company Profile | | Balance Sheet | Income Statement | Statement of Cash Flows | Risks | Audit Findings | Audit Procedures | Communication | Research |

The industry consists of preparation for the mining and extraction of sand and rock products. These include the activities of cleaning, separating and sorting of quarried sand, and the crushing of rocks. The products are in the form of sand used in making concrete; sand used in laying bricks (contains little soil); sand used for fill (contains lots of soil, and quartz sand); and excluding the products of gravel quarrying (sandstone, gravel stone, and iron sand).

While sales within the industry are relatively unaffected by changes in technology, or obsolescence, sales rely heavily upon both the residential and commercial construction markets as well as government spending.  During the past five years construction has performed well and that trend is expected to continue at least for the coming several years.  Sand and gravel production has increased at approximately 3% per year during this time period, as has construction within the central Ohio area.

The sand and gravel market in central New Mexico has been particularly healthy due in large part to the growth of Albuquerque into a major metropolitan area.  The most significant question facing the industry is whether the strong construction will continue as expected.  During the past two years the economy of the United States has been in a recovery period, yet unemployment remains high as compared to previous periods of recovery.  Thus, the questions concerning the continuing construction demand.

| Situation | Company Profile | Industry Information | Balance Sheet | Income Statement | Statement of Cash Flows | Risks | Audit Findings | Audit Procedures | Communication | Research |
|---|---|---|---|---|---|---|---|---|---|---|

### Tommi Stone and Quarry
### BALANCE SHEET
#### December 31, 20X8 and 20X7

|  | 20X8 | 20X7 |
|---|---|---|
| **Assets** |  |  |
| Current assets |  |  |
| Cash and cash equivalents | $ 5,055 | $ 3,822 |
| Trade receivables | 3,369,971 | 2,383,055 |
| Inventory | 1,713,118 | 1,810,361 |
| Other current assets | 17,140 | 10,200 |
| Total current assets | 5,105,284 | 4,207,438 |
| Fixed assets, net | 397,749 | 74,769 |
| Total assets | $5,503,033 | $4,282,207 |
| **Liabilities and shareholders' equity** |  |  |
| Current liabilities |  |  |
| Accounts payable | $ 340,995 | $ 316,164 |
| Current maturities of notes payable | 1,262,379 | 416,607 |
| Accrued expenses | 187,190 | 208,460 |
| Other current liabilities | 158,603 | 199,629 |
| Total current liabilities | 1,949,167 | 1,140,860 |
| Long-term debt, less current maturity | 3,249,934 | 2,959,200 |
| Total liabilities | 5,199,101 | 4,100,060 |
| Shareholders' equity |  |  |
| Common stock | 57,333 | 57,333 |
| Retained earnings | 246,599 | 124,814 |
| Total shareholders' equity | 303,932 | 182,147 |
| Total liabilities plus shareholders' equity | $5,503,033 | $4,282,207 |

| Situation | Company Profile | Industry Information | Balance Sheet | Income Statement | Statement of Cash Flows | Risks | Audit Findings | Audit Procedures | Communication | Research |
|---|---|---|---|---|---|---|---|---|---|---|

### Tommi Stone and Quarry
### INCOME STATEMENT
#### Two Years Ended December 31, 20X8 and 20X7
#### (in thousands)

|  | 20X8 | 20X7 |
|---|---|---|
| **Revenue** | $21,312,665 | $17,261,974 |
| Cost of goods sold | 18,029,838 | 14,397,853 |
| Gross profit on sales | 3,282,827 | 2,864,121 |
| Operating expenses | 2,707,606 | 2,185,542 |
| Repairs and maintenance | 104,168 | 132,083 |
| Depreciation | 31,673 | 30,098 |
| Interest expense | 265,398 | 314,419 |
| Total expenses | 3,108,845 | 2,662,142 |
| Net income before taxes | 173,982 | 201,979 |
| Provision for income taxes | 52,197 | 80,792 |
| Net income | $ 121,785 | $ 121,187 |

| Situation | Company Profile | Industry Information | Balance Sheet | Income Statement | Statement of Cash Flows | | Risks | Audit Findings | Audit Procedures | Communication | Research |
|---|---|---|---|---|---|---|---|---|---|---|---|

### Tommi Stone and Quarry
### STATEMENT OF CASH FLOWS
#### Year Ended December 31, 20X8

| | |
|---|---|
| Cash flows from operations | |
| Net income (loss) | $121,785 |
| Adjustments to net income | |
| Depreciation | 31,673 |
| Increase in receivables | (986,916) |
| Decrease in inventory | 97,243 |
| Increase in other current assets | (6,940) |
| Increase in accounts payable | 24,831 |
| Decrease in accrued expenses | (21,270) |
| Decrease in other current liabilities | (41,026) |
| Net cash provided (used) by operations | (780,620) |
| | |
| Cash flows from investing activities | |
| Purchase of property and equipment | (343,270) |
| | |
| Cash flows from financing activities | |
| New debt | 1,682,666 |
| Debt payments | (557,543) |
| Net cash provided (used) by financing activities | 1,125,123 |
| | |
| Net increase in cash and cash equivalents | $1,233 |
| Cash and equivalents at beginning of year | $3,822 |
| Cash and equivalents at end of year | $5,055 |

| Situation | Company Profile | Industry Information | Balance Sheet | Income Statement | Statement of Cash Flows | Risks | Audit Findings | Audit Procedures | Communication | Research |
|---|---|---|---|---|---|---|---|---|---|---|

**(A) (B) (C) (D)**

1. Which of the following correctly identifies a risk facing TSQ that might affect its ability to continue as a going concern over the long run?     ○ ○ ○ ○

   A. Competition from several competitors.
   B. Customer satisfaction with the quality of TSQ's current products.
   C. The nature of inventory items—small in size, high in value.
   D. Obsolescence of all major products due to rapid changes in technology in the industry.

**(A) (B) (C) (D)**

2. The most significant risk factor relating to the to misstatement arising from fraudulent financial reporting for TSQ is that the company     ○ ○ ○ ○

   A. Operates in the Albuquerque area.
   B. Officers serve on the board of directors.
   C. Must refinance a significant portion of its debt.
   D. Paid no dividend this year.

| Situation | Company Profile | Industry Information | Balance Sheet | Income Statement | Statement of Cash Flows | Risks | Audit Findings | Audit Procedures | Communication | Research |
|---|---|---|---|---|---|---|---|---|---|---|

| Ratio | 20X8 | 20X7 |
|---|---|---|
| Inventory turnover | 10.52 | 7.95 |
| Return on equity | 0.40 | 0.67 |

The above table presents two ratios that were identified as significant in the current and prior years' audits of TSQ. Compare the values of each ratio. Then select an audit finding that is consistent with these metrics. The finding need not explain the entire change. But, of the replies listed, it should potentially lead to the most significant change in the direction indicated by the change in the ratio. Each of the audit findings may be used once, more than once, or not at all.

*Audit findings*

A. Increases in costs of purchases were not completely passed on to customers through higher selling prices.
B. Increases in trade receivables.
C. Owners' equity increased due to retention of profits.
D. A larger percentage of sales occurred during the last month of 20X8, as compared to 20X7.
E. Interest expense decreased during 20X8.
F. The percentage tax included in the provision for income taxes for 20X8 was less than the percentage in 20X7.

|   | (A) | (B) | (C) | (D) | (E) | (F) |
|---|---|---|---|---|---|---|
| 1. An audit finding consistent with the change in inventory turnover for TSQ | ○ | ○ | ○ | ○ | ○ | ○ |
| 2. An audit finding consistent with the change in the return on equity | ○ | ○ | ○ | ○ | ○ | ○ |

| Situation | Company Profile | Industry Information | Balance Sheet | Income Statement | Statement of Cash Flows | Risks | Audit Findings | Audit Procedures | Communication | Research |
|---|---|---|---|---|---|---|---|---|---|---|

The auditor determines that each of the following objectives will be part of TSQ's audit. For each audit objective, select a substantive procedure that would help to achieve that objective. Each of the procedures may be used once, more than once, or not at all.

*Substantive procedure*

A. Examine current vendors' price lists.
B. Review drafts of the financial statements.
C. Select a sample of items during the physical inventory count and determine that they have been included on count sheets.
D. Select a sample of recorded items and examine supporting vendors' invoices and contracts.
E. Select a sample of recorded items on count sheets during the physical inventory count and determine that these items are on hand.
F. Test the reasonableness of general and administrative labor rates.

|   | (A) | (B) | (C) | (D) | (E) | (F) |
|---|---|---|---|---|---|---|
| 1. Determine that the presentation and disclosure of inventories and cost of goods sold is adequate. | ○ | ○ | ○ | ○ | ○ | ○ |
| 2. Establish that the client has rights to the recorded inventories. | ○ | ○ | ○ | ○ | ○ | ○ |

| Situation | Company Profile | Industry Information | Balance Sheet | Income Statement | Statement of Cash Flows | Risks | Audit Findings | Audit Procedures | Communication | Research |
|---|---|---|---|---|---|---|---|---|---|---|

Your firm has performed the audit of TSQ for the past five years. The preceding materials describe the company's board of directors. Recent emphasis on corporate governance has caused your firm to increasingly document its understanding of the nature of the board of directors. In a memorandum to the audit team explain your view on the likely effectiveness of the board of directors as an oversight mechanism for TSQ.

Remember: Your response will be graded for both technical relevance and writing skills. For writing skills you should demonstrate an ability to develop your ideas, organize them and express them clearly. Do not convey information in the form of a table, bullet point list, or other abbreviated presentation.

To:     Audit Team
From: CPA Candidate
Re:     TSQ Audit Committee

| Situation | Company Profile | Industry Information | Balance Sheet | Income Statement | Statement of Cash Flows | Risks | Audit Findings | Audit Procedures | Communication | Research |
|---|---|---|---|---|---|---|---|---|---|---|
| | | | | | | | | | | |

You have now completed the fieldwork for the TSQ audit and find that due to a change in accounting principle mandated by the Financial Accounting Standards Board, you will need to add an explanatory paragraph for a lack of consistency for the year 20X6. Using the Professional Standards, find an example of an appropriate explanatory paragraph for a lack of consistency. Do this by copying and pasting the report to a workspace. You should **not** edit the report in any way.

**SOLUTION TO SIMULATION 1**

| Situation | Company Profile | Industry Information | Balance Sheet | Income Statement | Statement of Cash Flows | Risks | Audit Findings | Audit Procedures | Communication | Research |
|---|---|---|---|---|---|---|---|---|---|---|

                                                               **(A) (B) (C) (D)**

**1.** Which of the following correctly identifies a risk facing TSQ that might affect its ability to continue as a going concern over the long run?      ● ○ ○ ○

**2.** The most significant risk factor relating to the to misstatement arising from fraudulent financial reporting for TSQ is that the company      ○ ○ ● ○

**Explanation of solutions**

**1.** **(A)** The requirement is to identify the risk facing TSQ that might affect its ability to continue as a going concern over the long run. Answer (A) is correct because the competition that has led to decreased sales prices may ultimately create a difficult situation for TSQ. Answer (B) is incorrect because customers are satisfied with the quality of TSQ's products. Answer (C) is incorrect because sand and gravel is not generally small in size and high in value in the quantities sold. Answer (D) is incorrect because obsolescence is not a problem.

**2.** **(C)** The requirement is to identify the most significant risk factor relating to misstatements arising from fraudulent financial reporting. Answer (C) is correct because the pressure to obtain the refinancing creates pressure on management. Answer (A) is incorrect because operating in the Albuquerque area presents no particular problem. Answer (B) is incorrect because company officers ordinarily serve on the board of directors. Answer (D) is incorrect because the lack of a dividend bears no particular relationship with fraudulent financial reporting.

| Situation | Company Profile | Industry Information | Balance Sheet | Income Statement | Statement of Cash Flows | Risks | Audit Findings | Audit Procedures | Communication | Research |
|---|---|---|---|---|---|---|---|---|---|---|

                                                              **(A) (B) (C) (D) (E) (F)**

**1.** An audit finding consistent with the change in inventory turnover for TSQ      ○ ○ ○ ● ○ ○

**2.** An audit consistent with the change in the return on equity      ○ ○ ● ○ ○ ○

**Explanation of solutions**

**1.** **(D)** The requirement is to identify the finding that is consistent with an increase in the inventory turnover ratio— cost of goods sold/inventory. Answer (D) is correct because a larger percentage of sales in the last month is likely to result in a lower ending inventory, thus increasing the inventory turnover ratio since the denominator of the fraction becomes smaller.

**2.** **(C)** The requirement is to identify the reply that is consistent with a decrease in the return on equity ratio—net income/shareholders' equity. Answer (C) is correct because retention of profits increases the shareholders' equity, thereby decreasing the ratio.

| Situation | Company Profile | Industry Information | Balance Sheet | Income Statement | Statement of Cash Flows | Risks | Audit Findings | Audit Procedures | Communication | Research |
|---|---|---|---|---|---|---|---|---|---|---|

                                                                **(A) (B) (C) (D) (E) (F)**

**1.** Determine that the presentation and disclosure of inventories and cost of goods sold is adequate.      ○ ● ○ ○ ○ ○

**2.** Establish that the client has rights to the recorded inventories.      ○ ○ ○ ● ○ ○

**Explanation of solutions**

**1.** **(B)** The requirement is to identify a substantive procedure that will help the auditor to determine that the presentation and disclosure of inventories and cost of goods sold is adequate. Answer (B) is correct because while reviewing drafts of the financial statements the auditor may discover presentation and disclosure omissions.

**2.** **(D)** The requirement is to identify a substantive procedure for establishing that the client has rights to the recorded inventories. Answer (D) is correct because examination of supporting vendors' invoices and contracts will reveal whether the transactions have been recorded properly.

| Situation | Company Profile | Industry Information | Balance Sheet | Income Statement | Statement of Cash Flows | Risks | Audit Findings | Audit Procedures | Communication | | Research |
|---|---|---|---|---|---|---|---|---|---|---|---|

To: Audit Team

Subject: TSQ Board of Directors

The makeup of the board of directors of TSQ may limit the effectiveness of this body in providing effective oversight of the organization. The board is composed of the company's CEO, Jill Tommi; her husband, Mort Tommi; the company's CFO, Googlo Permasi; and the company's other two stockholders, Jian Zhang and Kendra Kovano. Jill Tommi is chairman of the board, which brings into question the independence of the board.

This type of composition is not uncommon for small nonpublic companies. However, we should consider the implications of the lack of independence in auditing the company's financial statements. We should also get additional background information on the two outside board members, Jian Zhang and Kendra Kovano.

| Situation | Company Profile | Industry Information | Balance Sheet | Income Statement | Statement of Cash Flows | Risks | Audit Findings | Audit Procedures | Communication | Research |
|---|---|---|---|---|---|---|---|---|---|---|

The proper terminology for a lack of consistency is presented in AU 508.17.

As discussed in Note X to the financial statements, the Company changed its method of computing depreciation in 20X2.

**SIMULATION 2**

**Topic—Evidence**

| Background | | | |
|---|---|---|---|
| | Situation and Spreadsheet | Explanation for Analytical Results | Research |

Analytical procedures are evaluations of financial information made by a study of plausible relationships among financial and nonfinancial data. Understanding and evaluating such relationships are essential to the audit process.

| | Situation and Spreadsheet | | |
|---|---|---|---|
| Background | | Explanation for Analytical Results | Research |

The following spreadsheet with the financial statements were prepared by Holiday Manufacturing Co. for the year ended December 31, 20X1. Also presented are various financial statement ratios for Holiday as calculated from the prior year's financial statements. Sales represent net credit sales. The total assets and the receivables and inventory balances at December 31, 20X1, were the same as at December 31, 20X0.

| | A | B | C | D | E | F | G |
|---|---|---|---|---|---|---|---|
| 1 | Holiday Manufacturing Co. | | | | | | |
| 2 | Balance Sheet | | | | | | |
| 3 | December 31, 20X1 | | | | | | |
| 4 | | | | | | | |
| 5 | Cash | | $240,000 | | Accounts Payable | | $160,000 |
| 6 | Receivables | | 400,000 | | Notes payable | | 100,000 |
| 7 | Inventory | | 600,000 | | Other current liabilities | | 140,000 |
| 8 | Total current assets | | $1,240,000 | | Total current liabilities | | 400,000 |
| 9 | | | | | | | |
| 10 | Plant and equipment—net | | 760,000 | | Long-term debt | | 350,000 |
| 11 | | | | | Common stock | | 750,000 |
| 12 | | | | | Retained earnings | | 500,000 |
| 13 | Total assets | | $2,000,000 | | Total liabilities and capital | | $2,000,000 |
| 14 | | | | | | | |
| 15 | | | | | | | |
| 16 | Income Statement | | | | | | |
| 17 | Year ended December 31, 20X1 | | | | | | |
| 18 | | | | | | | |
| 19 | Sales | | | | $3,000,000 | | |
| 20 | Cost of goods sold | | | | | | |
| 21 | Materials | | 800,000 | | | | |
| 22 | Labor | | 700,000 | | | | |
| 23 | Overhead | | 300,000 | | 1,800,000 | | |
| 24 | Gross margin | | | | 1,200,000 | | |
| 25 | | | | | | | |
| 26 | Selling expenses | | 240,000 | | | | |
| 27 | General and admin. exp. | | 300,000 | | 540,000 | | |
| 28 | Operating income | | | | 660,000 | | |
| 29 | Less: interest expense | | | | 40,000 | | |
| 30 | Income before taxes | | | | 620,000 | | |
| 31 | Less: federal income taxes | | | | 220,000 | | |
| 32 | Net income | | | | $400,000 | | |
| 33 | | | | | | | |
| 34 | | | | | | | |
| 35 | | | | | | | |
| 36 | Ratios | | 12/31/X1 | | 12/31/X0 | | |
| 37 | Current ratio | | (1) | | 2.5 | | |
| 38 | Quick ratio | | (2) | | 1.3 | | |
| 39 | Accounts receivable turnover | | (3) | | 5.5 | | |
| 40 | Inventory turnover | | (4) | | 2.5 | | |
| 41 | Total asset turnover | | (5) | | 1.2 | | |
| 42 | Gross margin % | | (6) | | 35% | | |
| 43 | Net operating margin % | | (7) | | 25% | | |

| 44 | Times interest earned | | (8) | | 10.3 | | |
| 45 | Total debt to equity % | | (9) | | 50% | | |

Insert spreadsheet formulas into the worksheet to allow the direct calculation of each ratio (1 through 9). Use cell location rather than amounts.

| Background | Situation and Spreadsheet | Explanation for Analytical Results | Research |
| --- | --- | --- | --- |

Items 1 through 6 represent an auditor's observed changes in certain financial statement ratios or amounts from the prior year's ratios or amounts. For each observed change, select the most likely explanation or explanations from List B. Select only the number of explanations as indicated. **The observed changes are not related to the calculations in requirement a. above, and are independent of each other.** Answers on the list may be selected once, more than once, or not at all.

<u>List B—Explanations</u>

A. Items shipped on consignment during the last month of the year were recorded as sales.
B. A significant number of credit memos for returned merchandise that were issued during the last month of the year were not recorded.
C. Year-end purchases of inventory were overstated by incorrectly including items received in the first month of the subsequent year.
D. Year-end purchases of inventory were understated by incorrectly excluding items received before the year-end.
E. A larger percentage of sales occurred during the last month of the year, as compared to the prior year.
F. A smaller percentage of sales occurred during the last month of the year, as compared to the prior year.
G. The same percentage of sales occurred during the last month of the year, as compared to the prior year.
H. Sales increased at the same percentage as cost of goods sold, as compared to the prior year.
I. Sales increased at a greater percentage than cost of goods sold increased, as compared to the prior year.
J. Sales increased at a lower percentage than cost of goods sold increased, as compared to the prior year.
K. Interest expense decreased, as compared to the prior year.
L. The effective income tax rate increased, as compared to the prior year.
M. The effective income tax rate decreased, as compared to the prior year.
N. Short-term borrowing was refinanced on a long-term basis at the same interest rate.
O. Short-term borrowing was refinanced on a long-term basis at lower interest rates.
P. Short-term borrowing was refinanced on a long-term basis at higher interest rates.

<u>Auditor's observed changes</u>                                         <u>List B—Explanations</u>
(A) (B) (C) (D) (E) (F) (G) (H) (I) (J) (K) (L) (M) (N) (O) (P)

1.  Inventory turnover increased substantially from the prior year. (Select 3 explanations)
O O O O O O O O O O O O O O O O

2.  Accounts receivable turnover decreased substantially from the prior year. (Select 3 explanations)
O O O O O O O O O O O O O O O O

3.  Allowance for doubtful accounts increased from the prior year, but allowance for doubtful accounts as a percentage of accounts receivable decreased from the prior year. (Select 3 explanations)
O O O O O O O O O O O O O O O O

4.  Long-term debt increased from the prior year, but interest expense increased a larger-than-proportionate amount than long-term debt. (Select one explanation)
O O O O O O O O O O O O O O O O

5.  Operating income increased from the prior year although the entity was less profitable than in the prior year. (Select two explanations)
O O O O O O O O O O O O O O O O

6.  Gross margin percentage was unchanged from the prior year although gross margin increased from the prior year. (Select one explanation)
O O O O O O O O O O O O O O O O

| Background | Situation and Spreadsheet | Explanation for Analytical Results | Research |
| --- | --- | --- | --- |

Research the professional standards and excerpt the guidance to answer the following questions:

1.  At what stages of the audit are analytical procedures required?
2.  What is the purpose of analytical procedures performed in the planning stage of the audit?

**SOLUTION TO SIMULATION 2**

| Background | Situation and Spreadsheet | Explanation for Analytical Results | Research |
|---|---|---|---|

| | | Ratio | Spreadsheet Formula | Calculation |
|---|---|---|---|---|
| 1. | (H) | Current ratio $= \dfrac{\text{Current assets}}{\text{Current liabilities}}$ | =C8/G8 | $\dfrac{\$1,240,000}{\$400,000} = 3.1$ |
| 2. | (E) | Quick ratio $= \dfrac{\text{Quick assets*}}{\text{Current liabilities}}$<br><br>* Cash + Accounts receivable. Also marketable securities would be included if the company owned any. | =(C5+C6)/G8 | $\dfrac{\$240,000 + \$400,000}{\$400,000} = \dfrac{\$640,000}{\$400,000} = 1.6$ |
| 3. | (K) | Accounts receivable turnover $= \dfrac{\text{Sales}}{\text{Accounts receivable}}$ | =E19/C6 | $\dfrac{\$3,000,000}{\$400,000} = 7.5$ |
| 4. | (G) | Inventory turnover $= \dfrac{\text{Cost of goods sold}}{\text{Inventory}}$ | =E23/C7 | $\dfrac{\$1,800,000}{\$600,000} = 3.0$ |
| 5. | (D) | Total asset turnover $= \dfrac{\text{Sales}}{\text{Total assets}}$ | =E19/C13 | $\dfrac{\$3,000,000}{\$2,000,000} = 1.5$ |
| 6. | (T) | Gross margin percentage $= \dfrac{\text{Gross margin}}{\text{Sales}}$ | =E24/E19 | $\dfrac{\$1,200,000}{\$3,000,000} = 40\%$ |
| 7. | (P) | Net operating margin % $= \dfrac{\text{Operating income}}{\text{Sales}}$ | =E28/E19 | $\dfrac{\$660,000}{\$3,000,000} = 22\%$ |
| 8. | (N) | Times interest earned $= \dfrac{\text{Operating income}}{\text{Interest expense}}$ | =E28/E29 | $\dfrac{\$660,000}{\$40,000} = 16.5$ |
| 9. | (U) | Total debt to equity percentage $= \dfrac{\text{Total debt*}}{\text{Owners' equity**}}$<br><br>  * Total current liabilities + Long-term debt.<br>** Common stock + Retained earnings | =(G8+G10)/(G11+G12) | $\dfrac{\$400,000 + \$350,000}{\$750,000 + \$500,000} = \dfrac{\$750,000}{\$1,250,000} = 60\%$ |

| Background | Situation and Spreadsheet | Explanation for Analytical Results | Research |
|---|---|---|---|

*Auditor's observed changes*     *List B—Explanations*

(A) (B) (C) (D) (E) (F) (G) (H) (I) (J) (K) (L) (M) (N) (O) (P)

1. Inventory turnover increased substantially from the prior year. (Select 3 explanations)
 ● ● ○ ● ○ ○ ○ ○ ○ ○ ○ ○ ○ ○ ○ ○

2. Accounts receivable turnover decreased substantially from the prior year. (Select 3 explanations)
 ● ● ○ ○ ● ○ ○ ○ ○ ○ ○ ○ ○ ○ ○ ○

3. Allowance for doubtful accounts increased from the prior year, but allowance for doubtful accounts as a percentage of accounts receivable decreased from the prior year. (Select 3 explanations)
 ● ● ○ ○ ● ○ ○ ○ ○ ○ ○ ○ ○ ○ ○ ○

4. Long-term debt increased from the prior year, but interest expense increased a larger-than-proportionate amount than long-term debt. (Select one explanation)
 ○ ○ ○ ○ ○ ○ ○ ○ ○ ○ ○ ○ ○ ○ ○ ●

5. Operating income increased from the prior year although the entity was less profitable than in the prior year. (Select two explanations)
 ○ ○ ○ ○ ○ ○ ○ ○ ○ ○ ○ ○ ● ○ ○ ●

6. Gross margin percentage was unchanged from the prior year although gross margin increased from the prior year. (Select one explanation)
 ○ ○ ○ ○ ○ ○ ● ○ ○ ○ ○ ○ ○ ○ ○ ○

**Explanation of solutions**

**1.**   **(A, B, D)**   The requirement is to identify three explanations for an increase in the inventory turnover when compared to the prior year. The inventory turnover is calculated by dividing the cost of goods sold by the inventory. An increase may occur either through (1) an overstatement of the cost of goods sold (the numerator), (2) an understatement of inventory (the denominator), or (3) a combination of changes. Answer (A) is correct because the recording of the consignment shipment as a sale will overstate cost of goods sold and understate the ending inventory. Answer (B) is correct because not recording the credit memos will result in understatement of inventory. Answer (D) is correct because the understatement of purchases of inventory will understate the ending inventory.

     Answer (C) is incorrect because overstating the year-end purchases will result in overstatement of inventory, and thereby decrease the inventory turnover. Answers (E) through (J) are all incorrect because such changes in sales will not affect the inventory turnover ratio. Answers (K) through (P) are all incorrect because the interest expense, income tax rate, and the short-term borrowing do not affect the inventory turnover. Note that this question relies upon an unstated assumption that the year-end inventory is not adjusted to a year-end physical count.

**2.**   **(A, B, E)**   The requirement is to identify three explanations for a decrease in the accounts receivable turnover when compared to the prior year. The accounts receivable turnover is calculated by dividing sales by accounts receivable. A decrease may occur through (1) an understatement of sales (the numerator), (2) an overstatement of accounts receivable (the denominator), or (3) a combination of misstatements of sales and accounts receivable that decrease the ratio. Answer (A) is correct because recording the consignment as sales overstates both sales and accounts receivable by an identical amount, thus decreasing the ratio; the decrease is due to the entry debiting accounts receivable and crediting sales for the same amount. Answer (B) is correct because not recording the credit memo overstates both sales and accounts receivable by an identical amount, thus decreasing the ratio; this identical amount of decrease is due to the lack of a debit to sales returns and allowances and a credit to accounts receivable. Note that answers (A) and (B) are correct in any situation in which the ratio is greater than 1.0; when the ratio is less than 1.0 they result in an increase in the ratio. Answer (E) is correct because while the sales for the year remain at the expected level, accounts receivable at year-end will be at a higher than average level due to the year-end sales.

     Answers (C) and (D) are incorrect because the level of inventory does not affect the ratio. Answers (F) and (G) are incorrect because a larger, not a smaller or the same, percentage of sales near year-end decreases the ratio. Answers (H), (I) and (J) are incorrect because one would expect accounts receivable to increase at the same rate as the increase in sales. Answers (K) through (P) are all incorrect because interest expense, income tax rate, and the short-term borrowing do not affect the accounts receivable turnover.

**3.**   **(A, B, E)**   The requirement is to identify three explanations for an increase in the allowance for doubtful accounts, but a decrease in the allowance for doubtful accounts as a percentage of accounts receivable. The allowance for doubtful accounts as a percentage of accounts receivable is calculated by dividing the allowance for doubtful accounts by accounts receivable. The percentage may decrease due to (1) a decrease in the allowance for doubtful accounts, (2) an increase in the accounts receivable, or (3) a combination of misstatements that decrease the ratio; here, however, we are told that reason (1), a decrease in the allowance, has not occurred. Answer (A) is correct because recording the consignment as a sale results in an increase in accounts receivable which decreases the ratio. Answer (B) is correct because not recording the credit memos overstates accounts receivable, thereby decreasing the ratio. Answer (E) is correct because the larger percentage of sales occurring during the last month of the year results in accounts receivable at year-end that will be at a higher than average level due to the year-end sales.

     Answers (C) and (D) are incorrect because the level of inventory does not affect the ratio. Answers (F) and (G) are incorrect because a larger, not a smaller or the same, percentage of sales near year-end decreases the ratio. Answers (H), (I), and (J) are incorrect because one would expect accounts receivable and the allowance for doubtful accounts to increase at approximately the same rate as the increase in sales. Answers (K) through (P) are all incorrect because interest expense, income tax rate, and the short-term borrowing do not affect the accounts receivable turnover.

**4.**   **(P)**   The requirement is to identify a reason why long-term debt increased, but interest expense increased a larger-than-proportionate amount than long-term debt. Answer (P) is correct because the higher interest rates on long-term debt will result in higher interest expense. Answers (A) through (M) are all incorrect because they relate neither to long-term debt nor interest expense. Answers (N) and (O) are incorrect because refinancing at the same or a lower interest rate will result in smaller-than-proportionate amounts of interest expense.

**5.**   **(L, P)**   The requirement is to identify two reasons why operating income might increase, yet the company would be less profitable. Since operating income increased and net income decreased, the explanation must be items that are listed on the income statement between operating income and net income—interest expense and federal income taxes. The net of these two expenses must have increased to result in a situation in which the entity was less profitable. Answer (L) is correct because an increase in the effective income tax rate could decrease the profit when compared to the prior year. Answer (P) is correct because higher interest rates decrease profits. Answers (A) through (J) are all incorrect because they pertain to details of operating income. Answers (K) and (M) are incorrect because a decrease in interest expense or the income tax rate would increase net income. Answer (N) is incorrect because refinancing at the same rate will not affect net income. Answer (O) is incorrect because refinancing at a lower interest rate will increase profits.

**6.**   **(H)**   The requirement is to identify one reason why the gross margin percentage may remain unchanged, despite an increase in gross margin from the prior year. Answer (H) is correct because when sales increase at the same percentage as cost of goods sold, the gross margin percentage remains unchanged, and yet the increased sales will result in an increase in the gross margin. Answers (A) through (D) are all incorrect because they will result in a change in the gross margin percentage. Answers (E), (F), and (G) are all incorrect because no increase in sales is indicated and no information on the gross margin is provided. Answers (I) and (J) are incorrect because they suggest a decrease and an increase in the gross margin, respectively. Answers (K) through (P) are all incorrect because interest expense, income tax rate, and debt do not affect gross margin.

| Background | Situation and Spreadsheet | Explanation for Analytical Results | Research |
| --- | --- | --- | --- |

**1.** At what stages of the audit are analytical procedures required?

**AU 329.04**

.04 Analytical procedures are used for the following purposes:

    a. To assist the auditor in planning the nature, timing, and extent of other auditing procedures.

    b. As a substantive test to obtain evidential matter about particular assertions related to account balances or classes of transactions.

    c. As an overall review of the financial information in the final review stage of the audit.

Analytical procedures should be applied to some extent for the purposes referred to in (a) and (c) above for all audits of financial statements made in accordance with generally accepted auditing standards. In addition, in some cases, analytical procedures can be more effective or efficient than tests of details for achieving particular substantive testing objectives.

**2.** What is the purpose of analytical procedures performed in the planning stage of the audit?

**AU 329.06**

.06 The purpose of applying analytical procedures in planning the audit is to assist in planning the nature, timing, and extent of auditing procedures that will be used to obtain evidential matter for specific account balances or classes of transactions. To accomplish this, analytical procedures used in planning the audit should focus on (a) enhancing the auditor's understanding of the client's business and the transactions and events that have occurred since the last audit date, and (b) identifying areas that may represent specific risks relevant to the audit. Thus, the objective of the procedures is to identify such things as the existence of unusual transactions and events, and amounts, ratios and trends that might indicate matters that have financial statement and audit planning ramifications.

## AUDITING AND ATTESTATION TESTLETS RELEASED BY AICPA

**1.** Which of the following characteristics most likely would heighten an auditor's concern about the risk of material misstatements in an entity's financial statements?

    a. The entity's industry is experiencing declining customer demand.

    b. Employees who handle cash receipts are **not** bonded.

    c. Bank reconciliations usually include in-transit deposits.

    d. Equipment is often sold at a loss before being fully depreciated.

**1. (a)** The requirement is to identify the characteristic that would likely heighten an auditor's concern about the risk of material misstatements in an entity's financial statements. Answer (a) is correct because AU 316 states that a declining industry with increasing business failures and significant declines in customer demand is a risk factor relating to misstatements arising from fraudulent financial reporting. Answer (b) is incorrect because bonding will not necessarily affect the risk of material misstatements and is not included as a risk factor in AU 316. Answer (c) is incorrect because many bank reconciliations ordinarily include in-transit deposits and this does not necessarily increase the risk of material misstatement. Answer (d) is incorrect because equipment sold at a loss may often occur (as may gains) and not necessarily affect the risk of material misstatement.

**2.** Which of the following fraudulent activities most likely could be perpetrated due to the lack of effective internal controls in the revenue cycle?

    a. Fictitious transactions may be recorded that cause an understatement of revenues and an overstatement of receivables.

    b. Claims received from customers for goods returned may be intentionally recorded in other customers' accounts.

    c. Authorization of credit memos by personnel who receive cash may permit the misappropriation of cash.

    d. The failure to prepare shipping documents may cause an overstatement of inventory balances.

**2. (c)** The requirement is to identify the fraudulent activity most likely to be perpetrated due to the lack of effective internal control over the revenue cycle. Answer (c) is correct because the authorization of credit memos by personnel who receive cash presents a situation in which those individuals may issue fraudulent credit memos and misappropriate the cash. Answer (a) is incorrect because one would expect such fictitious transactions to overstate both revenues and receivables; note that the situation described in answer (a) with an understatement of revenues and an overstatement of receivables results in two debits and no credits. Answer (b) is incorrect because recording such claims in the wrong account is likely to be quickly detected when customers who have not received the credit complain. Answer (d) is incorrect because such an overstatement of inventory balances is likely to be detected through an inventory observation.

**3.** In planning an audit, the auditor's knowledge about the design of relevant controls should be used to

    a. Identify the types of potential misstatements that could occur.

    b. Assess the operational efficiency of internal control.

    c. Determine whether controls have been circumvented by collusion.

    d. Document the assessed level of control risk.

**3. (a)** The requirement is to determine how the auditor's knowledge about the design of relevant controls is used in planning an audit. Answer (a) is correct because such knowledge is used to (1) identify types of potential misstatements, (2) consider factors that affect the risk of material misstatements, and (3) design substantive tests. Answer (b) is incorrect because auditors are more concerned with identifying types of potential misstatements not detected by internal control rather than with assessing its operational efficiency. Answer (c) is incorrect because while auditors are concerned with whether controls are circumvented by collusion, this is not the primary emphasis during planning and is less complete than answer (a). Answer (d) is incorrect because documentation during planning emphasizes the auditor's understanding of the entity's internal control.

**4.** Which of the following information discovered during an audit most likely would raise a question concerning possible illegal acts?

    a. Related-party transactions, although properly disclosed, were pervasive during the year.

    b. The entity prepared several large checks payable to cash during the year.

    c. Material internal control weaknesses previously reported to management were **not** corrected.

    d. The entity was a campaign contributor to several local political candidates during the year.

**4. (b)** The requirement is to identify the information that most likely would raise a question concerning possible illegal acts. Answer (b) is correct because such large checks payable to cash raise a question as to their actual business purpose. Answer (a) is incorrect because the mere existence of **properly disclosed** related-party transactions is less likely to indicate an illegal act than are checks written to cash. Answer (c) is incorrect because management may, for valid reasons, choose to not correct material internal control weaknesses. Answer (d) is incorrect because such campaign contributions may well be legal. See AU 317 for information on illegal acts.

**5.**    During an engagement to review the financial statements of a nonpublic entity, an accountant becomes aware that several leases that should be capitalized are not capitalized.  The accountant considers these leases to be material to the financial statements.  The accountant decides to modify the standard review report because management will not capitalize the leases.  Under these circumstances, the accountant should

    a.    Issue an adverse opinion because of the departure from GAAP.

    b.    Express **no** assurance of any kind on the entity's financial statements.

    c.    Emphasize that the financial statements are for limited use only.

    d.    Disclose the departure from GAAP in a separate paragraph of the accountant's report.

**5.**    **(d)**    The requirement is to determine an accountant's reporting responsibility when associated with a nonpublic entity's **reviewed** statements which contain a material departure from generally accepted accounting principles.  Answer (d) is correct because AR 100 requires the inclusion of a separate paragraph describing the departure.  Answer (a) is incorrect because an adverse opinion may only be issued when an audit has been performed.  Answer (b) is incorrect because a review report provides negative assurance, not **no** assurance.  Answer (c) is incorrect because a review report is ordinarily available for general distribution, and need not emphasize that the financial statements are for limited use only.

**SIMULATION 1**                                    (50 to 60 minutes)

| Company Profile | Balance Sheet | Income/ Cash Flow | Industry Info | Risks | Audit Findings | Audit Procedures | Analysis and Communication | Auditors Report |
|---|---|---|---|---|---|---|---|---|

Enright Corporation is a **nonpublic** manufacturer of golf balls, golf clubs, and other golf-related equipment. The company has been in business for over fifty years and has its headquarters in San Diego, California.

Enright is divided into two divisions, which represent the major markets for the company's products. One division focuses on new golf clubs and resorts, and providing them with all of the necessary golf equipment to begin operations. The other division focuses on new product development and helps existing golf clubs and resorts to upgrade their existing equipment. Currently, each division accounts for approximately equal amounts of Enright's revenues and net income.

The company experienced its second most profitable year in 2002. However, the financial results did not meet management's expectations. Total reported revenues for the year decreased three percent compared to the prior year. Management recognizes the fact that domestic sales growth has slowed significantly in recent years. As a result, the company is now adopting a global focus for marketing its products and is looking to open up new markets in Australia and Japan.

In order to be competitive in world markets, as well as to improve their domestic market share, management believes that they must strictly control costs and make their overall operations more efficient. At the end of 2002, Enright announced it would make a series of restructuring changes as part of its overall business plan for the future.

Senior management at the company has experienced a significant turnover in recent years. The CEO has been with the company for only two years. He was hired from a major competitor after the prior CEO left to take a position with a large manufacturing company in the Northeast. In addition, the company's long-time CFO retired after twenty-five years of service. The current CFO was hired six months ago. She is a former audit manager from the office that works on Enright's annual audit.

Enright has engaged the same auditing firm for its annual audits for the past decade. There have been no disagreements over accounting issues in any of the past three years.

| Company Profile | Balance Sheet | Income/ Cash Flow | Industry Info | Risks | Audit Findings | Audit Procedures | Analysis and Communication | Auditors Report |
|---|---|---|---|---|---|---|---|---|

### Enright Corporation
### BALANCE SHEET
### December 31, 2002 and 2001

|  | 12/31/02 | 12/31/01 |
|---|---|---|
| **Assets** | | |
| Current assets | | |
| Cash and cash equivalents | $300,000 | $235,000 |
| Receivables—net | 750,000 | 816,000 |
| Investments | 600,000 | 545,000 |
| Inventory | 1,000,000 | 1,171,000 |
| Total current assets | 2,650,000 | 2,767,000 |
| Plant and equipment—net | 850,000 | 876,000 |
| Total assets | $3,500,000 | $3,643,000 |
| **Liabilities and Stockholders' Equity** | | |
| Current liabilities | | |
| Accounts payable | $390,000 | $410,000 |
| Current portion of long-term debt | 620,000 | 620,000 |
| Other current liabilities | 315,000 | 298,000 |
| Total current liabilities | 1,325,000 | 1,328,000 |
| Long-term debt | 475,000 | 1,095,000 |
| Total liabilities | 1,800,000 | 2,423,000 |
| Stockholders' equity | | |
| Common stock | 1,000,000 | 1,000,000 |
| Retained earnings | 700,000 | 220,000 |
| Total stockholders' equity | 1,700,000 | 1,220,000 |
| Total liabilities and stockholders' equity | $3,500,000 | $3,643,000 |

| Company Profile | Balance Sheet | Income/ Cash Flow | Industry Info | Risks | Audit Findings | Audit Procedures | Analysis and Communication | Auditors Report |
|---|---|---|---|---|---|---|---|---|

*Enright Corporation*
## INCOME STATEMENT
*For the Years Ended December 31, 2002 and 2001*

|  | 12/31/02 | 12/31/01 |
|---|---|---|
| Sales | $5,250,000 | $5,450,000 |
| Cost of goods sold: | 2,100,000 | 2,209,000 |
|    Gross profits on sales | 3,150,000 | 3,241,000 |
| Expenses |  |  |
|    Selling expenses | $1,050,000 | $1,124,000 |
|    General and administrative | 1,070,000 | 1,215,000 |
|    Other operating expenses |  |  |
|    Depreciation | 30,000 | 35,000 |
|    Interest expense | 200,000 | 227,000 |
|      Total expenses | $2,350,000 | $2,601,000 |
| Income before taxes | $800,000 | $640,000 |
| Provision for income taxes | 320,000 | 256,000 |
|    Net income | $480,000 | $384,000 |

*Enright Corporation*
## STATEMENT OF CASH FLOWS
*For the Year Ended December 31, 2002*

| | |
|---|---|
| Cash flows from operating activities: | |
| Net income (loss) | $480,000 |
| Adjustments to reconcile net income (loss) to cash provided by (used for) operating activities | |
|    Depreciation and amortization | 30,000 |
|    Changes in certain assets and liabilities: | |
|      Decrease (increase) in receivables | 66,000 |
|      Decrease (increase) in inventory | 171,000 |
|      Increase (decrease) in accounts payable | (20,000) |
|      Increase (decrease) in other current liabilities | 17,000 |
|      Net cash provided by (used for) operating activities | 744,000 |
| Cash flows from investing activities: | |
|    Purchase of property, plant, and equipment | (4,000) |
|    Change in short-term investments | (55,000) |
|      Net cash provided by (used for) investing activities | (59,000) |
| Cash flows from financing activities: | |
|    Principal payments on long-term debt | (620,000) |
|      Net cash provided by (used for) financing activities | (620,000) |
| Net increase (decrease) in cash and cash equivalents | 65,000 |
| Cash and cash equivalents at beginning of year | 235,000 |
| Cash and cash equivalents at end of year | $300,000 |

| Company Profile | Balance Sheet | Income/ Cash Flow | Industry Info | Risks | Audit Findings | Audit Procedures | Analysis and Communication | Auditors Report |
|---|---|---|---|---|---|---|---|---|

Market Forecasts
USA Sports Equipment

In 2007, the USA sports equipment market is forecast to reach $47 million, an increase of 19.3% since 2002.

The compounded annual growth rate of the global sports equipment market over the period 2002-2007 is predicted to be 3.5%.

Table 4: USA Sports Equipment Market Value Forecasts: $Mn (2001 Prices), 2002-2007

| Market value | $Mn (2001 prices) | % Growth |
|---|---|---|
| 2002 | $40,133.6 | 2.9% |
| 2003 | $41,398.3 | 3.2% |
| 2004 | $42,936.3 | 3.7% |
| 2005 | $44,389.8 | 3.4% |
| 2006 | $46,232.1 | 4.2% |
| 2007 | $46,892.1 | 3.6% |
| CAGR. 2002-2007 | 3.5% | |

Golf: Play Is Steadying While Sales Struggle[1]

With 1.02 billion participants aged six and over for the year 2001, golf is ranked number 15, compared to other sports.

In what proved to be a disappointing year, sale of golf clubs, balls, bags, gloves, and shoes declined about 6% in wholesale dollars, to about $2.375 billion in 2001. Sales of irons, which enjoyed strong growth in 2000, accounted for most of the decease in 2001.

Clearly, the weak economy was the root of the problem and the continuing weakness in 2002 is expected to result in further slight sales declines as players postpone the purchase of the big-ticket items such ad clubs and bags.

The total number of golfers grew by 5%, from 28.9 million to 30.4 million, between 1990 and 2000. There are as many as 40 million people who would like to play or play more often. New course development was scaled back in 2001, with 314 construction projects completed through the first nine months, compared to 408 and 379 during the same periods in 2000 and 1999, respectively.

In what might be called a "Tiger Woods" effect, some experienced golfers are trying to open the game to very young players. A small national tournament for players aged four to twelve has been created. Some manufacturers are marketing youth-sized clubs and a few facilities are developing training programs for children once considered too young to play the game.

| Company Profile | Balance Sheet | Income/ Cash Flow | Industry Info | **Risks** | Audit Findings | Audit Procedures | Analysis and Communication | Auditors Report |
|---|---|---|---|---|---|---|---|---|

                                                                            (A) (B) (C) (D)

1.  Which of the following correctly identifies an aspect of the company's business model, strategies, and operating environment that is most likely to increase audit risk?     ○ ○ ○ ○

A.  The "Tiger Woods" effect.
B.  The turnover of senior management in recent years.
C.  The company's result in the current year of its second most profitable year in over fifty years of operations.
D.  The company's organization into two divisions, which represent the major markets for the company's products.

| Company Profile | Balance Sheet | Income/ Cash Flow | Industry Info | Risks | **Audit Findings** | Audit Procedures | Analysis and Communication | Auditors Report |
|---|---|---|---|---|---|---|---|---|

The table below presents several ratios that were identified as significant in the current and prior year's audits of Enright. Compare the values for each ratio. Then double-click on each of the shaded spaces in the table and select a possible audit finding that could account for the 2002 value. For each ratio, you should select an audit finding that is consistent with these metrics. Each audit finding may be used once, more than once, or not at all. (Turnover ratios are based on year-end balances.)

*Audit findings*

A.  The company uses a periodic inventory system for determining the balance sheet amount of inventory.
B.  The company accumulated excess inventories that are physically deteriorating or are becoming obsolete.
C.  Merchandise was received, placed in the stockroom, and counted, but not included in the year-end count.
D.  A smaller percentage of sales occurred during the last month of the year, as compared to the prior year.
E.  A dividend declared prior to the end of the year was not recorded in the general ledger.
F.  A dividend declared prior to the end of the year was recorded twice in the general ledger.

| | *Ratio* | *2002* | *2001* | (A) | (B) | (C) | (D) | (E) | (F) |
|---|---|---|---|---|---|---|---|---|---|
| 1. | Inventory turnover | 2.1 | 1.9 | ○ | ○ | ○ | ○ | ○ | ○ |
| 2. | Return on equity | 28.2% | 31.5% | ○ | ○ | ○ | ○ | ○ | ○ |

| Company Profile | Balance Sheet | Income/ Cash Flow | Industry Info | Risks | Audit Findings | **Audit Procedures** | Analysis and Communication | Auditors Report |
|---|---|---|---|---|---|---|---|---|

The auditor determines that each of the following objectives will be part of Enright's audit. For each audit objective, select a substantive procedure that would help to achieve the audit objectives by double-clicking on each shaded space and selecting a procedure. Each of the procedures may be used once, more than once, or not at all.

*Substantive procedures*

A.  Review minutes of board of director's meetings and contracts, and make inquiries of management.
B.  Test inventory transactions between a preliminary physical inventory date and the balance sheet date.
C.  Obtain confirmation of inventories pledged under loan agreement.
D.  Review perpetual inventory records, production records, and purchasing records for indication of current activity.
E.  Reconcile physical counts to perpetual records and general ledger balances and investigate significant fluctuation.
F.  Examine sales after year-end and open purchase order commitments.
G.  Examine paid vendors' invoices, consignment agreements, and contracts.
H.  Analytically review and compare the relationship of inventory balance to recent purchasing, production, and sales activity.

---

[1] Source: *Sporting Goods Manufacturers Association*

|    | *Objective* | (A) | (B) | (C) | (D) | (E) | (F) | (G) | (H) |
|----|-------------|-----|-----|-----|-----|-----|-----|-----|-----|
| **1.** | Confirm that inventories represent items held for sale or use in the normal course of business. | ○ | ○ | ○ | ○ | ○ | ○ | ○ | ○ |
| **2.** | Confirm that the inventory listing is accurately completed and the totals are properly included in the inventory accounts. | ○ | ○ | ○ | ○ | ○ | ○ | ○ | ○ |

| Company Profile | Balance Sheet | Income/ Cash Flow | Industry Info | Risks | Audit Findings | Audit Procedures | Analysis and Communication | Auditors Report |
|---|---|---|---|---|---|---|---|---|

Your firm has been doing the audit of Enright Corporation for several years. Since last year, Enright changed the board of directors from family members owning stock in the company to independent executives with financial experience. In a memorandum to your audit team, explain the impact of the new board on audit risk.

*Reminder: Your response will be graded for both technical and writing skills. For writing skills, you should demonstrate an ability to develop your ideas, organize them and express them clearly. Do not convey information in the form of a table, bullet point list, or other abbreviated presentation.*

To: Audit Team
Re: New board and audit risk

| Company Profile | Balance Sheet | Income/ Cash Flow | Industry Info | Risks | Audit Findings | Audit Procedures | Analysis and Communication | Auditors Report |
|---|---|---|---|---|---|---|---|---|

During the fieldwork on Enright, the client asks that you perform a review of the financial statements for the current year only—and not a complete audit. You have now completed your fieldwork and find that you can issue a standard review report.

Using the research materials available to you by clicking the Standards button on the title bar, assemble model paragraphs that would be used to create the auditor's report that addresses this finding. In the reference, highlight and copy an appropriate paragraph. Click on the gray field below and paste the paragraph into the Auditor's Report form. Copy paragraphs as needed from the Standards, and click above, below, or in between paragraphs you have placed in the form to assemble the report. Use the controls provided to reorder or to delete paragraphs you highlight. **You should NOT edit the model paragraphs in any way.**

**SOLUTION TO SIMULATION 1**

| | | | | Risks | | | | | |
|---|---|---|---|---|---|---|---|---|---|
| Company Profile | Balance Sheet | Income/ Cash Flow | Industry Info | | Audit Findings | Audit Procedures | Analysis and Communication | Auditors Report | |

                                                                               (A) (B) (C) (D)

1. Which of the following correctly identifies an aspect of the company's business model, strategies, and operating environment that is most likely to increase audit risk?  ○ ● ○ ○

**Explanation of solution**

1. **(B)** The requirement is to identify the aspect of a company's business that is most likely to increase audit risk. Answer (B) is correct because turnover of senior management frequently signals a higher level of audit risk both because in some circumstances the reasons for turnover raise questions, and because of inexperience of new top management. Answer (A) is incorrect because the Tiger Woods effect is likely to increase sales through purchases made by young people and has no necessary tie to audit risk. Answer (C) is incorrect because simply having the second most profitable year doesn't make the information seem likely to indicate a misstatement. Answer (D) is incorrect because an organization with two divisions represents no major difficulty for the audit, and does not ordinarily increase audit risk.

| | | | | | Audit Findings | | | | |
|---|---|---|---|---|---|---|---|---|---|
| Company Profile | Balance Sheet | Income/ Cash Flow | Industry Info | Risks | | Audit Procedures | Analysis and Communication | Auditors Report | |

| | *Ratio* | *2002* | *2001* | (A) (B) (C) (D) (E) (F) |
|---|---|---|---|---|
| 1. | Inventory turnover | 2.1 | 1.9 | ○ ○ ● ○ ○ ○ |
| 2. | Return on equity | 28.2% | 31.5% | ○ ○ ○ ○ ● ○ |

**Explanation of solutions**

1. **(C)** The requirement is to identify an explanation for an increase in the inventory turnover—the ratio of cost of goods sold to inventory. Answer (C) is correct because while the inventory was received, it was not included in the final inventory count and the purchase was not recorded. Thus, the denominator of the ratio decreases, increasing the overall turnover.

2. **(E)** The requirement is to identify a possible reason for a decrease in the return on equity—net income divided by stockholders' equity. Answer (E) is correct because not recording a dividend that has been declared has the effect of overstating the denominator (owner's equity) and thereby reducing the overall return rate.

| | | | | | | Audit Procedures | | | |
|---|---|---|---|---|---|---|---|---|---|
| Company Profile | Balance Sheet | Income/ Cash Flow | Industry Info | Risks | Audit Findings | | Analysis and Communication | Auditors Report | |

| | *Objective* | (A) (B) (C) (D) (E) (F) (G) (H) |
|---|---|---|
| 1. | Confirm that inventories represent items held for sale or use in the normal course of business. | ○ ○ ○ ● ○ ○ ○ ○ |
| 2. | Confirm that the inventory listing is accurately completed and the totals are properly included in the inventory accounts. | ○ ○ ○ ○ ● ○ ○ ○ |

**Explanation of solutions**

1. **(D)** The requirement is to identify the best substantive procedure to confirm that inventories represent items held for sale or use in the normal course of business. Answer (D) is best because a review of perpetual inventory records, production records, and purchasing records for indication of current activity will reveal whether those items are being sold.

2. **(E)** The requirement is to identify the best substantive procedure to confirm that the inventory listing is accurately completed and the totals are properly included in the inventory counts. Answer (E) is correct because reconciling physical counts to perpetual records and general ledgers balances and investigating significant fluctuations will identify errors in totals.

| Company Profile | Balance Sheet | Income/ Cash Flow | Industry Info | Risks | Audit Findings | Audit Procedures | Analysis and Communication | Auditors Report |
|---|---|---|---|---|---|---|---|---|

### Memorandum

To:  Audit Team
Re: New board and audit risk

Expected responses should include

An independent board of directors should reduce the likelihood that the financial statements are materially misstated.

1.   Objectivity (lack of conflicts of interest)
2.   Competency (prior experience working with financial data)
3.   Provides a safety valve—can communicate with the audit committee rather than directly with the owners

| Company Profile | Balance Sheet | Income/ Cash Flow | Industry Info | Risks | Audit Findings | Audit Procedures | Analysis and Communication | Auditors Report |
|---|---|---|---|---|---|---|---|---|

### Auditor's Review Report

[Addressee]

Source:  AR§100.366 (SSARS)

I(we) have reviewed the accompanying balance sheet of XYZ Company as of December 31, 20X1, and the related statements of income, retained earnings, and cash flows for the year then ended, in accordance with Statements on Standards for Accounting and Review Services issued by the American Institute of Certified Public Accountants.  All information included in these financial statements is the representation of the management (owners) of XYZ Company.

A review consists principally of inquiries of company personnel and analytical procedures applied to financial data.  It is substantially less in scope than an audit in accordance with generally accepted auditing standards, the objective of which is the expression of an opinion regarding the financial statements taken as a whole.  Accordingly, I(we) do not express such an opinion.

Based on my(our) review, I am (we are) not aware of any material modifications that should be made to the accompanying financial statements in order for them to be in conformity with generally accepted accounting principles.

## AUDITING AND ATTESTATION

**1.** An auditor observes the mailing of monthly statements to a client's customers and reviews evidence of a follow-up on errors reported by the customers. This test of controls most likely is performed to support management's financial statement assertions of

|     | *Presentation and disclosure* | *Existence or occurrence* |
|-----|-------------------------------|---------------------------|
| a.  | Yes                           | Yes                       |
| b.  | Yes                           | No                        |
| c.  | No                            | Yes                       |
| d.  | No                            | No                        |

**1.** **(c)** The requirement is to determine whether (1) the presentation and disclosure assertion and (2) the existence or occurrence assertion are addressed when an auditor observes the mailing of monthly statements to a client's customers and reviews evidence of follow-up on errors reported by the customers. Reviewing evidence of follow-up on errors may identify accounts in which the customer disputes *existence* of the debt; related, when customers do not dispute the debt, evidence is obtained on *existence*. *Presentation and disclosure* is not as directly addressed since little information is obtained on whether accounts receivable are properly classified, described and disclosed. Accordingly answer (c) is correct. Answer (a) is incorrect because it suggests that presentation and disclosure is addressed. Answer (b) is incorrect because it suggests that presentation and disclosure is addressed and that existence or occurrence is not. Answer (d) is incorrect because existence or occurrence is addressed. See Module 3, Section A for information on management's assertions.

**2.** When a company's stock record books are maintained by an outside registrar or transfer agent, the auditor should obtain confirmation from the registrar or transfer agent concerning the

a. Amount of dividends paid to related parties.
b. Expected proceeds from stock subscriptions receivable.
c. Number of shares issued and outstanding.
d. Proper authorization of stock rights and warrants.

**2.** **(c)** The requirement is to identify the information that auditors should confirm with a registrar or transfer agent. Registrars verify that stock issued is properly authorized; stock transfer agents maintain detailed stockholder records and carry out transfers of stock ownership. Answer (c) is correct because registrars and transfer agents maintain records of shares issued and outstanding. Answer (a) is incorrect because neither the registrar nor the transfer agent maintains records of dividends paid to related parties. Answer (b) is incorrect because neither the registrar nor the transfer agent maintains records of expected proceeds from stock subscriptions receivable. Answer (d) is incorrect because neither the registrar nor the transfer agent ordinarily maintain records of proper authorization of stock rights and warrants.

**3.** The GAO standards of reporting for governmental financial audits incorporate the AICPA standards of reporting and prescribe supplemental standards to satisfy the unique needs of governmental audits. Which of the following is a supplemental reporting standard for governmental financial audits?

a. Auditors should report the scope of their testing of compliance with laws and regulations and of internal controls.
b. Material indications of illegal acts should be reported in a document distributed only to the entity's senior officials.
c. All changes in the audit program from the prior year should be reported to the entity's audit committee.
d. Any privileged or confidential information discovered should be reported to the organization that arranged for the audit.

**3.** **(a)** The requirement is to identify the reply which represents a supplemental reporting standard under GAO standards of reporting for governmental financial audits. Answer (a) is correct because auditors must report the scope of their testing of compliance with laws and regulations and of internal controls. Answer (b) is incorrect because material indications of illegal acts must under certain circumstances be reported to others, including funding agencies. Answer (c) is incorrect because all the changes in the audit program need not be reported to the audit committee. Answer (d) is incorrect because not all such information need be reported to the organization that arranged the audit.

**4.** Which of the following statements ordinarily is **not** included among the written client representations made by the chief executive officer and the chief financial officer?

    a.   "Sufficient evidential matter has been made available to the auditor to permit the issuance of an unqualified opinion."

    b.   "There are **no** unasserted claims or assessments that our lawyer has advised us are probable of assertion and must be disclosed."

    c.   "We have **no** plans or intentions that may materially affect the carrying value or classification of assets and liabilities."

    d.   "No events have occurred subsequent to the balance sheet date that would require adjustment to, or disclosure in, the financial statements."

**5.** When an auditor has substantial doubt about an entity's ability to continue as a going concern because of the probable discontinuance of operations, the auditor most likely would express a qualified opinion if

    a.   The effects of the adverse financial conditions likely will cause a bankruptcy filing.

    b.   Information about the entity's ability to continue as a going concern is **not** disclosed.

    c.   Management has **no** plans to reduce or delay future expenditures.

    d.   Negative trends and recurring operating losses appear to be irreversible.

**6.** To which of the following matters would materiality limits **not** apply when obtaining written client representations?

    a.   Violations of state labor regulations.

    b.   Disclosure of line-of-credit arrangements.

    c.   Information about related-party transactions.

    d.   Instances of fraud involving management.

**4.** **(a)** The requirement is to identify the statement ordinarily not included in a client representation letter. Answer (a) is correct, that is, not included, because while the chief executive officer and the chief financial officers must make information available to the auditor, they do not make a judgment on whether evidence is sufficient. Answer (b) is incorrect because management must provide a statement that there are no unasserted claims or assessments that the lawyer has advised are probable of assertion and must be disclosed of which the auditor has not been informed. Answer (c) is incorrect because management must assert that it has no plans or intentions that may materially affect the carrying value or classification of assets and liabilities. Answer (d) is incorrect because management must provide a representation related to such subsequent events. See AU 333 for information on representation letters.

**5.** **(b)** The requirement is to identify the circumstance in which a qualified opinion is most likely when an auditor has substantial doubt about an entity's ability to continue as a going concern. At first, this question is a bit surprising since substantial doubt ordinarily leads to either a report with an unqualified opinion and an explanatory paragraph or a disclaimer of opinion, not a qualified opinion. Answer (b) is correct because, when management does not disclose such information in the financial statements, a departure from GAAP exists; departures from GAAP lead to either a qualified or adverse opinion. Answers (a), (c) and (d) are all incorrect because either an unqualified opinion with explanatory language or a disclaimer of opinion is appropriate in such circumstances. See AU 341 for information on reporting on client going concern status. See AU 508 for overall information on audit reports.

**6.** **(d)** The requirement is to identify the matter for which materiality limits would **not** apply when obtaining written client representations. Answer (d) is correct because representations relating to management fraud must be obtained regardless of whether the amount involved is material or immaterial. Answer (a) is incorrect because such a violation of state labor regulations only needs to be included when material amounts are involved. Answer (b) is incorrect because a representation of such a disclosure of line-of-credit arrangements would only be necessary for material amounts and when issues related to compliance with the agreement are involved. Answer (c) is incorrect because while the materiality level may be lower for related-party transactions than for other transactions, only representations on material related-party transactions are ordinarily obtained. See AU 334 for information on related-party transactions.

**7.** Prior to commencing fieldwork, an auditor usually discusses the general audit strategy with the client's management. Which of the following details do management and the auditor usually agree upon at this time?

    a. The specific matters to be included in the communication with the audit committee.

    b. The minimum amount of misstatements that may be considered to be reportable conditions.

    c. The schedules and analyses that the client's staff should prepare.

    d. The effects that inadequate controls may have over the safeguarding of assets.

**8.** An auditor plans to apply substantive tests to the details of asset and liability accounts as of an interim date rather than as of the balance sheet date. The auditor should be aware that this practice

    a. Eliminates the use of certain statistical sampling methods that would otherwise be available.

    b. Presumes that the auditor will reperform the tests as of the balance sheet date.

    c. Should be especially considered when there are rapidly changing economic conditions.

    d. Potentially increases the risk that errors that exist at the balance sheet date will **not** be detected.

**9.** In assessing the competence of a client's internal auditor, an independent auditor most likely would consider the

    a. Internal auditor's compliance with professional internal auditing standards.

    b. Client's policies that limit the internal auditor's access to management salary data.

    c. Evidence supporting a further reduction in the assessed level of control risk.

    d. Results of ratio analysis that may identify unusual transactions and events.

**10.** Which of the following is a professional engagement that a CPA may perform to provide assurance on a system's reliability?

    a. MAS AssurAbility.

    b. CPA WebMaster.

    c. MAS AttestSure.

    d. CPA SysTrust.

**7.** **(c)** The requirement is to identify the matter on which management and the auditor would ordinarily agree while discussing the general audit strategy prior to the auditor commencing fieldwork. Answer (c) is correct because at this early point in the audit process the auditor will discuss client assistance in the audit, including schedules and analyses to be prepared by the client's staff. Answer (a) is incorrect because the information on specific matters to be included in the communication with the audit committee is beyond the scope of the general audit strategy; related, the auditor will not at this early point be aware of some of the information that will be communicated (e.g., specific deficiencies in internal control). Answer (b) is incorrect since the discussion will ordinarily not include comments on a minimum amount of misstatements that represent a reportable condition (significant deficiency). Answer (d) is incorrect because any discussion on inadequate controls ordinarily will occur later in the audit.

**8.** **(d)** The requirement is to identify a likely effect of applying substantive procedures to the details of asset and liability accounts as of an interim date rather than as of the balance sheet date. Answer (d) is correct because such interim testing increases detection risk since end-of-year balances will receive less testing. Answer (a) is incorrect because statistical sampling methods may be used for interim date testing. Answer (b) is incorrect because, while some procedures are ordinarily necessary at the balance sheet date, they will not ordinarily include a complete reperformance of the tests. Answer (c) is incorrect because interim testing is less likely to be considered in rapidly changing economic conditions due to the higher risk of misstatement that such an environment creates.

**9.** **(a)** The requirement is to identify a procedure an independent auditor would perform in assessing the competence of a client's internal auditor. Answer (a) is correct because internal auditor compliance with professional internal auditing standards will reflect positively on evaluation of the competence of the internal auditor. Answer (b) is incorrect because limitations placed by management upon the internal auditor address internal auditor independence more directly than they address competence. Answer (c) is incorrect because, while evidence supporting a further reduction in the assessed level of control risk (i.e., tests of controls) may relate to the competence of internal auditors, it is more likely that it will relate to other controls within the system. Answer (d) is incorrect because such results of ratio analysis will not ordinarily provide significant information on the competence of the client's internal auditor. See AU 322 for information on the independent auditor's consideration of the internal audit function.

**10.** **(d)** The requirement is to identify the type of CPA engagement that provides assurance on a system's reliability. Answer (d) is correct because SysTrust was developed by the AICPA to provide evidence on the reliability of electronic systems; in a SysTrust engagement the CPA is engaged to examine whether a client maintained effective controls over the system based on Trust Services criteria that have been developed by the AICPA. Answers (a), (b), and (c) are all incorrect because they do not represent currently available services relating to systems reliability.

**11.** An auditor believes that there is substantial doubt about an entity's ability to continue as a going concern for a reasonable period of time. In evaluating the entity's plans for dealing with the adverse effects of future conditions and events, the auditor most likely would consider, as a mitigating factor, the entity's plans to

    a.   Repurchase the entity's stock at a price below its book value.

    b.   Issue stock options to key executives.

    c.   Lease rather than purchase operating facilities.

    d.   Accelerate the due date of an existing mortgage.

**11.** **(c)** The requirement is to identify a mitigating factor when an auditor believes that there may be substantial doubt about an entity's ability to continue as a going concern. Answer (c) is correct because an entity's ability to lease rather than purchase operating facilities may reduce required expenditures and thereby mitigate the immediate effects of a current liquidity problem. Answer (a) is incorrect because repurchasing stock at any price results in expenditures that will not necessarily deal positively with the adverse effects of the situation. Answer (b) is incorrect because, while issuance of stock options to key executives may be appropriate and may result in those executives staying with the company, it is a weaker reply than is reply (c). Also, it might be that those executives are responsible for the condition in which the company finds itself. Answer (d) is incorrect because decelerating, rather than accelerating, the due date of an existing mortgage is more likely to be helpful in such a situation. See AU 341 for information on an auditor's consideration of an entity's ability to continue as a going concern.

**12.** An auditor is required to establish an understanding with a client regarding the services to be performed for each engagement. This understanding generally includes

    a.   The auditor's responsibility for determining the preliminary judgments about materiality and audit risk factors.

    b.   Management's responsibility for identifying mitigating factors when the auditor has doubt about the entity's ability to continue as a going concern.

    c.   The auditor's responsibility for ensuring that the audit committee is aware of any reportable conditions that come to the auditor's attention.

    d.   Management's responsibility for providing the auditor with an assessment of the risk of material misstatement due to fraud.

**12.** **(c)** The requirement is to identify the information ordinarily included in an auditor's understanding with a client regarding the services to be performed. Answer (c) is correct because the auditor must report to the audit committee reportable conditions, and accordingly, the auditor will include such information while establishing an understanding with a client. Answer (a) is incorrect because the understanding does not ordinarily involve preliminary judgments about materiality and audit risk factors. Answer (b) is incorrect because, while management may identify mitigating factors when a question concerning going concern status exists, this is not ordinarily discussed while obtaining an understanding with a client. Answer (d) is incorrect because, while management must provide auditors with certain information related to fraud, it is the auditor's, not management's, responsibility to assess the risk of material misstatement due to fraud—see AU 316.

**13.** When a client engages in transactions involving derivatives, the auditor should

    a.   Develop an understanding of the economic substance of each derivative.

    b.   Confirm with the client's broker whether the derivatives are for trading purposes.

    c.   Notify the audit committee about the risks involved in derivative transactions.

    d.   Add an explanatory paragraph to the auditor's report describing the risks associated with each derivative.

**13.** **(a)** The requirement is to identify an auditor's responsibility when that auditor knows that a client engages in transactions involving derivatives. Answer (a) is correct because an understanding of the economic substance of derivatives (as well as other transactions throughout the audit) is necessary. Answer (b) is incorrect because no such confirmation with the client's broker is ordinarily obtained. Answer (c) is incorrect because, while an auditor may discuss the accounting for derivatives with the audit committee (as well as other matters—see AU 325 and 380), a discussion of business risks relating to derivatives would ordinarily not be discussed. Answer (d) is incorrect because an explanatory paragraph to the auditor's report describing risks associated with derivatives is not included in audit reports.

**14.** A practitioner's report on agreed-upon procedures that is in the form of procedures and findings should contain
- a. Negative assurance that the procedures did **not** necessarily disclose all reportable conditions.
- b. An acknowledgment of the practitioner's responsibility for the sufficiency of the procedures.
- c. A statement of restrictions on the use of the report.
- d. A disclaimer of opinion on the entity's financial statements.

**15.** Analytical procedures performed during an audit indicate that accounts receivable doubled since the end of the prior year. However, the allowance for doubtful accounts as a percentage of accounts receivable remained about the same. Which of the following client explanations would satisfy the auditor?
- a. A greater percentage of accounts receivable are listed in the "more than 120 days overdue" category than in the prior year.
- b. Internal control activities over the recording of cash receipts have been improved since the end of the prior year.
- c. The client opened a second retail outlet during the current year and its credit sales approximately equaled the older outlet.
- d. The client tightened its credit policy during the current year and sold considerably less merchandise to customers with poor credit ratings.

**16.** Which of the following statements is correct about the sample size in statistical sampling when testing internal controls?
- a. The auditor should consider the tolerable rate of deviation from the controls being tested in determining sample size.
- b. As the likely rate of deviation decreases, the auditor should increase the planned sample size.
- c. The allowable risk of assessing control risk too low has **no** effect on the planned sample size.
- d. Of all the factors to be considered, the population size has the greatest effect on the sample size.

**17.** An auditor usually determines whether dividend income from publicly held investments is reasonable by computing the amounts that should have been received by referring to
- a. Stock ledgers maintained by independent registrars.
- b. Dividend records on file with the SEC.
- c. Records produced by investment services.
- d. Minutes of the investee's board of directors.

**14. (c)** The requirement is to determine what information is included in an agreed-upon procedures report. Answer (c) is correct because such reports must include a statement of restrictions on the use of the report because it is intended to be used solely by the specified parties (those for whom the engagement was performed). Answer (a) is incorrect because negative assurance is not included in agreed-upon procedures reports. Answer (b) is incorrect because the agreed-upon procedures report includes a statement that the sufficiency of the procedures is solely the responsibility of the specified parties, not the auditor. Answer (d) is incorrect because the report includes no disclaimer of opinion on the financial statements. See AT 201 for information on agreed-upon procedures engagements.

**15. (c)** The requirement is to identify an explanation for a situation in which accounts receivable double, while the allowance for doubtful accounts remains at about the same percentage of total accounts receivable. Answer (c) is correct because a second retail outlet of equivalent size might be expected to result in such increased sales; also, if the customer base is similar, one would expect the percentage of accounts ultimately becoming uncollectible to remain approximately the same. Answer (a) is incorrect because a greater percentage of old receivables will likely reveal the need for an increase in the allowance for doubtful accounts percentage. Answer (b) is incorrect because improvements in internal control over the recording of cash receipts is unlikely to directly address the doubling of receivables and the amount necessary in the allowance for doubtful accounts. Answer (d) is incorrect because a tightening of credit policy is likely to result in a lower percentage of doubtful accounts.

**16. (a)** The requirement is to identify the correct statement about the sample size in a statistical sampling plan that tests controls. Answer (a) is correct because the tolerable rate of deviation is an input into determination of sample size (the others include expected deviation rate, the risk of assessing control risk too low, and population size [which has only a very limited effect on sample size]). Answer (b) is incorrect because a decrease in the likely rate of deviation decreases planned sample size. Answer (c) is incorrect because the risk of assessing control risk too low has an effect on planned sample size (as it decreases, sample size increases). Answer (d) is incorrect because population size has a small effect on required sample size.

**17. (c)** The requirement is to identify how an auditor usually determines whether dividend income from publicly held investments is reasonable. Answer (c) is correct because investment services maintain records of such dividend income and auditors use such records to compare with a client's recorded dividend income. Answer (a) is incorrect because registrars will not ordinarily provide dividend income information. Answer (b) is incorrect because, while the SEC maintains information on registrants, it does not have detailed dividend records on file. Answer (d) is incorrect because the auditor of the investor will not ordinarily have access to minutes of the investee's board of directors.

**18.** Which of the following factors would most likely be considered an inherent limitation to an entity's internal control?

    a.   The complexity of the information processing system.

    b.   Human judgment in the decision-making process.

    c.   The ineffectiveness of the board of directors.

    d.   The lack of management incentives to improve the control environment.

**18.     (b)**     The requirement is to identify the factor most likely to be considered an inherent limitation of an entity's internal control.  Answer (b) is correct because faulty human judgment (1) may result in a variety of improperly recorded transactions and (2) is inherent in that it cannot be completely controlled.  Answer (a) is incorrect because complexity in and of itself is not an inherent limitation.  Answer (c) is incorrect because, while an ineffective board of directors is an internal control deficiency, an ineffective board of directors is not "inherent."  Similarly, Answer (d) is incorrect because, while a lack of management incentives to improve the control environment may be a deficiency, it is not inherent.  See Module 2 for information on internal control and its limitations.

**19.** A successor auditor is required to attempt communication with the predecessor auditor prior to

    a.   Performing test of controls.

    b.   Testing beginning balances for the current year.

    c.   Making a proposal for the audit engagement.

    d.   Accepting the engagement.

**19.     (d)**     The requirement is to determine when a successor auditor is required to attempt communication with a predecessor auditor.  Answer (d) is correct because prior to accepting an engagement the successor should attempt such communication.  Answer (a) is incorrect because no such communication is required prior to performing tests of controls.  Answer (b) is incorrect because, while the successor may communicate with the predecessor to obtain information on beginning balances, this is not required.  Answer (c) is incorrect because a proposal may be made prior to communicating with the predecessor auditor—however, final acceptance of the client is not appropriate prior to attempting such communication.  See AU 315 for information on a successor's responsibilities.

**20.** Which of the following factors would **least** likely affect the extent of the auditor's consideration of the client's internal controls?

    a.   The amount of time budgeted to complete the engagement.

    b.   The size and complexity of the client.

    c.   The nature of specific relevant controls.

    d.   The auditor's prior experience with client operations.

**20.     (a)**     The requirement is to identify the factor **least** likely to affect the extent of the auditor's consideration of a client's internal control.  Answer (a), the amount of time budgeted to complete the engagement, is least likely since an auditor should not decrease (or increase) the consideration of internal control simply due to the overall time budget.  Answer (b) is incorrect because the complexity of the client will affect the extent of the auditor's consideration of internal control.  Answer (c) is incorrect because the nature of relevant controls has a very significant effect on the extent of the auditor's consideration of internal control.  Answer (d) is incorrect because the auditor's prior experience with the client will have a large effect on the current consideration of the client's internal control.

**21.** The most reliable procedure for an auditor to use to test the existence of a client's inventory at an outside location would be to

    a.   Observe physical counts of the inventory items.

    b.   Trace the total on the inventory listing to the general ledger inventory account.

    c.   Obtain a confirmation from the client indicating inventory ownership.

    d.   Analytically compare the current year inventory balance to the prior year balance.

**21.     (a)**     The requirement is to identify the most reliable procedure for an auditor to use to test the existence of a client's inventory at an outside location.  Answer (a) is correct because observing physical counts of such inventory items provides evidence that the items exist.  Answer (b) is incorrect because tracing the total addresses item valuation (clerical accuracy), but not necessarily existence.  Answer (c) is incorrect because the confirmation from the client (an external party) is much less reliable than observation of physical counts.  Answer (d) is incorrect because such an analytical comparison is likely to provide less reliable information than observation of physical counts.  See AU 331 for information on auditing inventories, including situations in which the "outside location" is a public warehouse.

**22.** An auditor compared the current year gross margin with the prior year gross margin to determine if cost of sales is reasonable. What type of audit was performed?
- a. Test of transactions.
- b. Analytical procedures.
- c. Test of controls.
- d. Test of details.

**22. (b)** The requirement is to determine the type of audit procedure being performed when an auditor compares the current year gross margin with that of the prior year to determine whether the cost of sales is reasonable. Answer (b) is correct because this is an example of an analytical procedure (see AU 329 for information on analytical procedures). Answer (a) is incorrect because such a comparison is not a test of a transaction (e.g., examining details of a purchase transaction). Answer (c) is incorrect because such a comparison is not a test of a control (e.g., tests to determine whether a control operates effectively over the approval of sales). Answer (d) is incorrect because such a comparison is not a test of details (e.g., auditing details of a particular receivable account at year-end).

**23.** If the business environment is experiencing a recession, the auditor most likely would focus increased attention on which of the following accounts?
- a. Purchase returns and allowances.
- b. Allowance for doubtful accounts.
- c. Common stock.
- d. Noncontrolling interest of a subsidiary purchased during the year.

**23. (b)** The requirement is to identify the account an auditor would most likely focus increased attention on in a business environment that is experiencing a recession. Answer (b) is correct because during a recession one might expect customers to have difficulty paying receivables—accordingly a higher allowance for doubtful accounts might be needed. Answer (a) is incorrect because there is no particular reason to expect the client to obtain more returns and allowance during a recessionary period. Answer (c) is incorrect because, while the price of the common stock may decrease during a recession, this will have only a limited effect on the audit of the account. Answer (d) is incorrect because no increased attention need be devoted to such a noncontrolling interest of a subsidiary during a recession.

**24.** Which of the following is true regarding reportable conditions?
- a. Auditors must search for them.
- b. Auditors must communicate them to the audit committee.
- c. They must be included in the financial statements.
- d. They must be disclosed in footnotes.

**24. (b)** The requirement is to identify the correct statement relating to reportable conditions. Answer (b) is correct because they must be communicated to the audit committee. Answer (a) is incorrect because, while auditors may become aware of reportable weaknesses during an audit, they do not search for them. Answer (c) is incorrect because reportable conditions are not ordinarily included in the financial statements. Answer (d) is incorrect because reportable conditions are not ordinarily disclosed in footnotes to the financial statements. See AU 325 for information on reportable conditions.

**25.** Which of the following procedures would yield the most reliable evidence?
- a. A scanning of trial balances.
- b. An inquiry of client personnel.
- c. A comparison of beginning and ending retained earnings.
- d. A recalculation of bad debt expense.

**25. (d)** The requirement is to identify the most reliable evidence. Answer (d) is correct because recomputations of amounts represent highly reliable evidence. Answers (a), (b), and (c) are all evidence of lesser reliability.

**26.** An auditor who uses a transaction cycle approach to assessing control risk most likely would test control activities related to transactions involving the sale of goods to customers with the
- a. Collection of receivables.
- b. Purchase of merchandise inventory.
- c. Payment of accounts payable.
- d. Sale of long-term debt.

**26. (a)** The requirement is to identify the type of transactions an auditor who uses a transaction cycle approach to assessing control risk would test relating to the sale of goods to customers. Answer (a) is correct because collection of receivables relates to the valuation of accounts receivable, a part of the sales (revenue) cycle. Answer (b) is incorrect because purchase of merchandise inventory relates more directly to the conversion cycle. Answer (c) is incorrect because the payment of accounts payable relates to the purchases cycle. Answer (d) is incorrect because the sale of long-term debt relates to the financing cycle.

**27.** Tracing copies of computer-prepared sales invoices to copies of the corresponding computer-prepared shipping documents provides evidence that

    a.   Shipments to customers were properly billed.

    b.   Entries in the accounts receivable subsidiary ledger were for sales actually shipped.

    c.   Sales billed to customers were actually shipped.

    d.   No duplicate shipments to customers were made.

**28.** An auditor compares annual revenues and expenses with similar amounts from the prior year and investigates all changes exceeding 10%. This procedure most likely could indicate that

    a.   Fourth quarter payroll taxes were properly accrued and recorded, but were **not** paid until early in the subsequent year.

    b.   Unrealized gains from increases in the value of available-for-sale securities were recorded in the income account for trading securities.

    c.   The annual provision for uncollectible accounts expense was inadequate because of worsening economic conditions.

    d.   Notice of an increase in property tax rates was received by management, but was **not** recorded until early in the subsequent year.

**29.** An auditor concludes that there is a material inconsistency in the other information in an annual report to shareholders containing audited financial statements. The auditor believes that the financial statements do not require revision, but the client is unwilling to revise or eliminate the material inconsistency in the other information. Under these circumstances, what action would the auditor most likely take?

    a.   Consider the situation closed because the other information is **not** in the audited financial statements.

    b.   Issue an "except for" qualified opinion after discussing the matter with the client's audit committee.

    c.   Disclaim an opinion on the financial statements after explaining the material inconsistency in a separate explanatory paragraph.

    d.   Revise the auditor's report to include a separate explanatory paragraph describing the material inconsistency.

**27.** **(c)** The requirement is to identify the type of evidence obtained when an auditor traces sales invoices to shipping documents. Answer (c) is correct because the procedure provides evidence on whether sales billed (through sales invoices) were shipped (as per the shipping documents). Answer (a) is incorrect because to provide evidence that shipments to customers were properly billed an auditor would test in the opposite direction—from shipping documents to sales invoices. Answer (b) is incorrect because entries in the subsidiary accounts receivable ledger are not addressed by the procedure. Answer (d) is incorrect because while the procedure does provide evidence of shipment, it will not help the auditor to detect duplicate shipments.

**28.** **(b)** The requirement is to determine what might be identified when an auditor compares annual revenues and expenses with similar amounts from the prior year and investigates all changes exceeding 10%. Answer (b) is correct because the unrealized gains included in the income account for trading securities may result in that account changing by more than 10%, and accordingly being investigated. Answer (a) is incorrect because one would expect payroll taxes to be accrued and paid the subsequent year—for both of the years involved. Answer (c) is incorrect because failure to identify the worsening economic conditions is likely to result in an uncollectible accounts expense that approximates that of the prior year, and accordingly it will not be investigated since no 10% change will have occurred. Answer (d) is incorrect because property taxes for the two years would be expected to approximate one another if the increase in tax rates is not reflected. The key to understanding this question is to carefully consider the information provided and determine which account is most likely to change by 10% in the described situation.

**29.** **(d)** The requirement is to identify an auditor's responsibility when other information in annual reports to shareholders includes an inconsistency with the audited information and it is not the audited information that requires revision. Answer (d) is correct because in such a situation the auditor should consider revising the audit report to include an explanatory paragraph, withholding use of the report, or withdrawing from the engagement. Answer (a) is incorrect because auditors must consider such information. Answer (b) is incorrect because the audited information is correct, thereby making a qualified opinion inappropriate. Answer (c) is incorrect because a disclaimer of opinion is not appropriate when the auditor believes the financial statements are properly stated. See AU 550 for reporting on other information in documents containing audited financial statements.

**30.** An auditor's inquiries of management disclosed that the entity recently invested in a series of energy derivatives to hedge against the risks associated with fluctuating oil prices. Under these circumstances, the auditor should

    a.   Perform analytical procedures to determine if the derivatives are properly valued.

    b.   Examine the contracts for possible risk exposure and the need to recognize losses.

    c.   Confirm the marketablility of the derivatives with a commodity specialist.

    d.   Document the derivatives in the auditor's communication with the audit committee.

**30.** **(b)** The requirement is to identify an appropriate audit procedure for auditing a series of energy derivatives used to hedge against the risks associated with fluctuating oil prices. Answer (b) is correct because derivative risk exposure and any resulting need to recognize losses will affect the valuation of the derivatives. Answer (a) is incorrect because it is difficult to find analytical procedures aimed at the propriety of derivative valuation. Answer (c) is incorrect because marketability in and of itself will be of less concern than the need to recognize losses. Answer (d) is incorrect because while auditors may refer to the derivatives in communicating with the audit committee, they need not "document" them, and because the need to recognize losses suggested in reply (b) is ordinarily more important.

**31.** The scope of audits of recipients of federal financial assistance in accordance with federal audit regulations varies. Which of the following elements do these audits have in common?

    a.   The auditor is required to disclose all situations and transactions that could be indicative of fraud, abuse, and illegal acts to the federal inspector general.

    b.   The materiality levels are higher and are determined by the government entities that provide the federal financial assistance to the recipients.

    c.   The auditor is required to document an understanding of internal control established to ensure compliance with the applicable laws and regulations.

    d.   The accounts should be 100% verified by substantive tests because certain statistical sampling applications are **not** permitted.

**31.** **(c)** The requirement is to identify a common element of the scope of audits of recipients of federal financial assistance. Answer (c) is correct because all such audits require auditors to document an understanding of internal control established to ensure compliance with the applicable laws and regulations. Answer (a) is incorrect because all such circumstances are not reported to the federal inspector general. Answer (b) is incorrect because materiality levels are not higher. Answer (d) is incorrect because 100% of accounts need not be verified.

**32.** When an accountant compiles a financial forecast, the accountant's report should include a(n)

    a.   Explanation of the differences between a financial forecast and a financial projection.

    b.   Caveat that the prospective results of the financial forecast may **not** be achieved.

    c.   Statement that the accountant's responsibility to update the report is limited to one year.

    d.   Disclaimer of opinion on the reliability of the entity's internal controls.

**32.** **(b)** The requirement is to identify the information included in an accountant's report on a compiled financial forecast. Answer (b) is correct because a compilation report includes a caveat that the prospective results of the financial forecast may not be achieved. Answer (a) is incorrect because the report does not explain the differences between a financial forecast and a financial projection. Answer (c) is incorrect because the report states that the accountant assumes no responsibility for updating the report. Answer (d) is incorrect because no information on internal control is provided. See AT 301 for information on accountant association with forecasts and projections.

**33.** Which of the following procedures is usually the first step in reviewing the financial statements of a nonpublic entity?

    a.   Make preliminary judgments about risk and materiality to determine the scope and nature of the procedures to be performed.

    b.   Obtain a general understanding of the entity's organization, its operating characteristics, and its products or services.

    c.   Assess the risk of material misstatement arising from fraudulent financial reporting and the misappropriation of assets.

    d.   Perform a preliminary assessment of the operating efficiency of the entity's internal control activities.

**33.** **(b)** The requirement is to identify the usual first step in reviewing the financial statements of a nonpublic entity. Answer (b) is correct because accountants must obtain such a general understanding so as to allow them to design subsequent procedures. Answer (a) is incorrect because any preliminary judgments about risk and materiality occur subsequent to obtaining an understanding. Answer (c) is incorrect because no formal assessment of the risk of material misstatement arising from fraudulent financial reporting and the misappropriation of assets is required. Answer (d) is incorrect because auditors will not ordinarily assess operating efficiency of the entity's internal control activities.

**34.** In auditing a manufacturing entity, which of the following procedures would an auditor **least** likely perform to determine whether slow-moving, defective, and obsolete items included in inventory are properly identified?

   a. Test the computation of standard overhead rates.

   b. Tour the manufacturing plant or production facility.

   c. Compare inventory balances to anticipated sales volume.

   d. Review inventory experience and trends.

**35.** Which of the following procedures most likely would assist an auditor in identifying conditions and events that may indicate substantial doubt about an entity's ability to continue as a going concern?

   a. Performing cutoff tests of sales transactions with customers with long-standing receivable balances.

   b. Evaluating the entity's procedures for identifying and recording related-party transactions.

   c. Inspecting title documents to verify whether any real property is pledged as collateral.

   d. Inquiring of the entity's legal counsel about litigation, claims, and assessments.

**36.** An accountant's standard report issued after compiling the financial statements of a nonpublic entity should state that

   a. I am **not** aware of any material modifications that should be made to the accompanying financial statements.

   b. A compilation consists principally of inquiries of company personnel and analytical procedures.

   c. A compilation is limited to presenting in the form of financial statements information that is the representation of management.

   d. A compilation is substantially **less** in scope than an audit in accordance with GAAS, the objective of which is the expression of an opinion.

**37.** Which of the following circumstances would an auditor most likely consider a risk factor relating to misstatements arising from fraudulent financial reporting?

   a. Several members of management have recently purchased additional shares of the entity's stock.

   b. Several members of the board of directors have recently sold shares of the entity's stock.

   c. The entity distributes financial forecasts to financial analysts that predict conservative operating results.

   d. Management is interested in maintaining the entity's earnings trend by using aggressive accounting practices.

**34.** **(a)** The requirement is to identify the **least** likely audit procedure for determining whether slow-moving, defective, and obsolete items included in inventory are properly identified. Answer (a) is correct because the testing of standard overhead rates may provide only very limited assistance since they may be used to arrive at the cost of the item, but provide no real support relating to obsolescence. Answer (b) is incorrect because while touring the plant the auditor may identify such items. Answer (c) is incorrect because comparing inventory balances with anticipated sales will identify such items through revealing items with low expected turnover rates. Answer (d) is incorrect because a review of inventory experience and trends may reveal slow-moving items.

**35.** **(d)** The requirement is to identify the procedure most likely to assist an auditor in identifying conditions and events that may indicate substantial doubt about an entity's ability to continue as a going concern. Answer (d) is correct because the inquiry of legal counsel may reveal major litigation, claims, and assessments against the entity that raise substantial doubt about its ability to continue as a going concern. Answer (a) is incorrect because cutoff tests are used to determine that transactions have been reported in the correct period, but seldom reveal a question concerning going concern status. Answer (b) is incorrect because procedures aimed at identifying and recording related-party transactions may, but seldom do, reveal a question on going concern status. Answer (c) is incorrect because the pledging of real property is generally a disclosure issue, not an issue relating to identifying substantial doubt. However, such pledging does affect the ability of a company to recover from a situation in which going concern status is in question through limiting its financial flexibility.

**36.** **(c)** The requirement is to identify the information included in a financial statement compilation report. Answer (c) is correct because a compilation report indicates that a compilation is limited to presenting in the form of financial statements information that is the representation of management. Answer (a) is incorrect because no such negative assurance is provided. Answer (b) is incorrect because a review, not a compilation, consists primarily of inquiries of company personnel and analytical procedures. Answer (d) is incorrect because the compilation report does not refer to an audit. See AR 100 for basic information on compilation and reviews.

**37.** **(d)** The requirement is to identify the circumstance an auditor most likely would consider a risk factor relating to misstatements arising from fraudulent financial reporting. Answer (d) is correct because aggressive accounting practices used to maintain an earnings trend represent such a risk factor. Answer (a) is incorrect because management's purchase of additional shares in the entity is not ordinarily a risk factor. Answer (b) is incorrect since board of director members selling shares of stock may well be an ordinary occurrence. Answer (c) is incorrect because predicting conservative operating results is very different from fraudulent financial reporting. See AU 316 for information on the auditor's consideration of fraud in a financial statement audit. See the appendix to AU 316 for examples of fraud risk factors.

**38.** Which of the following statements extracted from a client's lawyer's letter concerning litigation, claims, and assessments most likely would cause the auditor to request clarification?

   a.  "I believe that the plaintiff will have problems establishing any liability."

   b.  "I believe that this action has only a remote chance in establishing any liability."

   c.  "I believe that the plaintiff's case against the company is without merit."

   d.  "I believe that the company will be able to defend this action successfully."

**39.** An auditor most likely would apply analytical procedures in the overall review stage of an audit to

   a.  Enhance the auditor's understanding of subsequent events.

   b.  Identify auditing procedures omitted by the staff accountants.

   c.  Determine whether additional audit evidence may be needed.

   d.  Evaluate the effectiveness of the internal control activities.

**40.** Proper segregation of duties reduces the opportunities to allow any employee to be in a position to both

   a.  Journalize cash receipts and disbursements and prepare financial statements.

   b.  Monitor internal controls and evaluate whether the controls are operating as intended.

   c.  Adopt new accounting pronouncements and authorize the recording of transactions.

   d.  Record and conceal fraudulent transactions in the normal course of assigned tasks.

**41.** Which of the following events most likely would indicate the existence of related parties?

   a.  Granting stock options to key executives at favorable prices.

   b.  High turnover of senior management and members of the board of directors.

   c.  Failure to correct internal control weaknesses on a timely basis.

   d.  Selling real estate at a price significantly different from appraised value.

**38.** **(a)** The requirement is to identify the statement extracted from a client's lawyer's letter concerning litigation, claims, and assessment that would be most likely to cause the auditor to request clarification. Answer (a) is correct because this statement is unclear and does not help the auditors to determine whether such legal matters have been properly reported. Answer (b) is incorrect because the "remote chance" is very clear. Answer (c) is incorrect because it makes clear that the lawyer does not believe the matter will cause legal difficulties. Answer (d) is incorrect because it suggests clearly the lawyer's belief that the company will be able to defend the action successfully. See AU 337 for more information on the inquiry of a client's lawyer.

**39.** **(c)** The requirement is to determine the primary objective of an auditor using analytical procedures in the overall review stage of an audit. Answer (c) is correct because the objective of analytical procedures at the overall review stage of an audit is to help the auditor in assessing the conclusions reached and in the evaluation of the overall financial statement presentation; accordingly, results of the overall review may indicate that additional evidence may be needed. Answer (a) is incorrect because those procedures ordinarily provide only limited, if any, information on subsequent events. Answer (b) is incorrect because while the procedures may lead to identification of omitted audit procedures, this is not the emphasis. Answer (d) is incorrect because while analytical procedures may reveal information on effective or ineffective internal control activities, this is not the reason they are applied.

**40.** **(d)** The requirement is to determine a purpose of the proper segregation of duties. Answer (d) is correct because a proper segregation should be designed to attempt to prevent any employee from recording and concealing fraudulent transactions. Answer (a) is incorrect since the individual recording transactions may prepare financial statements. Answer (b) is incorrect because monitoring controls will often lead to an evaluation of whether controls are operating as intended. Answer (c) is incorrect because an individual who adopts a new accounting pronouncement for an area will often be authorized to record transactions in that area; note, however, that there should be an independent review of such adoptions.

**41.** **(d)** The requirement is to identify the event most likely to indicate the existence of related parties. Answer (d) is correct because selling real estate (or, for that matter, other assets) at prices significantly different from appraised values leads one to question why the transaction occurred and whether it was truly "arm's-length." Answer (a) is incorrect because granting stock options at favorable prices is not considered a related-party transaction. Answer (b) is incorrect because while high turnover of senior management and members of the board of directors may be considered a risk factor for fraud, it is not as likely as answer (d) to indicate the existence of related parties. Answer (c) is also incorrect because, while it represents a risky situation, it is less likely to indicate a related-party situation than answer (d). See AU 334 for information on related parties.

**42.** Management's emphasis on meeting projected profit goals most likely would significantly influence an entity's control environment when

    a.  Internal auditors have direct access to the entity's board of directors.

    b.  A significant portion of management compensation is represented by stock options.

    c.  External policies established by parties outside the entity affect accounting policies.

    d.  The audit committee is active in overseeing the entity's financial reporting policies.

**42. (b)** The requirement is to identify the situation in which management's emphasis on meeting projected profit goals would be most likely to significantly influence an entity's control environment. Answer (b) is correct because when a significant portion of management's compensation is represented by stock options, risk may be involved in that management is under great pressure to report earnings that meet projected profit goals; this will ordinarily increase management compensation significantly and, under some circumstances, create a pressure to report overstated earnings to meet those projections. Answer (a) is incorrect because when internal auditors have direct access to the entity's board of directors, this may decrease the likelihood of overly aggressive accounting to meet projected profit goals and is less likely to affect the control environment. Answer (c) is incorrect because such external policies are ordinarily beyond management's control and would have a limited effect on the control environment. Answer (d) is incorrect because an active audit committee is likely to control management's aggressive reporting, and thereby is less likely to affect the entity's control environment.

**43.** Which of the following factors most likely would lead a CPA to conclude that a potential audit engagement should **not** be accepted?

    a.  There are significant related-party transactions that management claims occurred in the ordinary course of business.

    b.  Internal control activities requiring the segregation of duties are subject to management override.

    c.  Management continues to employ an inefficient system of information technology to record financial transactions.

    d.  It is unlikely that sufficient **appropriate** evidence is available to support an opinion on the financial statements.

**43. (d)** The requirement is to identify the factor that is most likely to lead a CPA to conclude that a potential audit engagement should **not** be accepted. Answer (d) is correct because the lack of sufficient appropriate evidence ordinarily negates the purpose of an audit, which is to have the CPA form an opinion on the financial statements. Answer (a) is incorrect because the simple existence of related-party transactions, while often indicating a high risk situation, is less likely to result in nonacceptance of an engagement. Answer (b) is incorrect because virtually all controls are subject to management override. Answer (c) is incorrect because inefficient information technology may still be technology that lends itself to auditing and the forming of an opinion on the company's financial statements.

**44.** Which of the following fraudulent activities most likely could be perpetrated due to the lack of effective internal controls in the revenue cycle?

    a.  Merchandise received is **not** promptly reconciled to the outstanding purchase order file.

    b.  Obsolete items included in inventory balances are rarely reduced to the lower of cost or market value.

    c.  The write-off of receivables by personnel who receive cash permits the misappropriation of cash.

    d.  Fictitious transactions are recorded that cause an understatement of revenue and an overstatement of receivables.

**44. (c)** The requirement is to identify the fraudulent activity most likely to be perpetrated due to ineffective controls in the revenue cycle. A goal under strong internal control is to segregate transaction authorization, recordkeeping and custody of assets. Answer (c) is correct because an individual who receives cash and writes off receivables has both custody of cash and recordkeeping responsibility. A possible fraudulent scheme here is for that individual to collect cash on an account, not report that payment, and then write off the receivable as uncollectible. Answer (a) is incorrect because while this lack of reconciliation represents a control deficiency, fraud is less likely here than in answer (c). Answer (b) is incorrect because while an error of inappropriate valuation of inventory may occur, it is less likely to be fraudulent than is the situation described in answer (c). Answer (d) is incorrect because one would expect a fictitious transaction to overstate both revenues and receivables; the example given results in a journal entry with no debit and two credits—revenues and receivables.

**45.** An auditor discovered that a client's accounts receivable turnover is substantially lower for the current year than for the prior year. This may indicate that

    a. Obsolete inventory has **not** yet been reduced to fair market value.

    b. There was an improper cutoff of sales at the end of the year.

    c. An unusually large receivable was written off near the end of the year.

    d. The aging of accounts receivable was improperly performed in both years.

**45.** **(b)** The requirement is to determine what may cause a decrease in a client's accounts receivable turnover ratio (credit sales/receivables). Answer (b) is correct because an improper cutoff of sales at the end of the year that overstates year-end sales and receivables will decrease the ratio since that ratio is ordinarily far greater than 1. That is, increasing the numerator and denominator of a ratio that is greater than one by the same amount will decrease the ratio (e.g., 3/2 = 1.5 → 4/3 = 1.3). Answer (a) is incorrect because any decrease in sales due to obsolete inventory should be expected to affect both credit sales and receivables in the same proportion. Answer (c) is incorrect because that write-off of the receivable will increase the ratio through decreasing its denominator. Answer (d) is incorrect because the aging of receivables does not affect the ratio.

**46.** Which of the following matters most likely would be included in a management representation letter?

    a. An assessment of the risk factors concerning the misappropriation of assets.

    b. An evaluation of the litigation that has been filed against the entity.

    c. A confirmation that the entity has complied with contractual agreements.

    d. A statement that all material internal control weaknesses have been corrected.

**46.** **(c)** The requirement is to identify the matter most likely to be included in a management representation letter. Answer (c) is correct because management representation letters ordinarily include confirmation that the entity has complied with contractual agreements. Answer (a) is incorrect because the representation letter does not include an assessment of risk factors. Answer (b) is incorrect because the lawyer's letter, not the representation letter, ordinarily includes an evaluation of litigation that has been filed against the entity. Answer (d) is incorrect because no such statement that all material internal control weaknesses have been corrected is ordinarily included in a management representation letter. See AU 333 for information on representation letters.

**47.** A CPA's standard report on audited financial statements would be inappropriate if it referred to

    a. Management's responsibility for the financial statements.

    b. An assessment of the entity's accounting principles.

    c. Significant estimates made by management.

    d. The CPA's assessment of sampling risk factors.

**47.** **(d)** The requirement is to determine what information would be **inappropriate** to include in a standard audit report. Answer (d) is correct because CPAs do not include an assessment of sampling risk factors in an audit report. Answer (a) is incorrect because the standard audit report includes an indication that management has responsibility for the financial statements. Answer (b) is incorrect because the audit report indicates that the CPA has performed an assessment of the accounting principles used. Answer (c) is incorrect because the audit report indicates that the CPA has performed an assessment of the significant estimates made by management. See AU 508 for information on audit reports.

**48.** In evaluating an entity's accounting estimates, one of the auditor's objectives is to determine whether the estimates are

    a. Prepared in a satisfactory control environment.

    b. Consistent with industry guidelines.

    c. Based on verifiable objective assumptions.

    d. Reasonable in the circumstances.

**48.** **(d)** The requirement is to identify one of an auditor's objectives when evaluating an entity's accounting estimates. Answer (d) is correct because an auditor is responsible for evaluating the reasonableness of accounting estimates made by management in the context of the financial statements taken as a whole. Answer (a) is incorrect because while it is advantageous to have accounting estimates prepared in a satisfactory control environment, this is not required. Answer (b) is incorrect because few industry guidelines exist with respect to accounting estimates. Answer (c) is incorrect because in many circumstances the assumptions may be quite subjective. See AU 342 for information on auditing accounting estimates.

**49.** When conducting fieldwork for a physical inventory, an auditor **cannot** perform which of the following steps using a generalized audit software package?
  a. Observing inventory.
  b. Selecting sample items of inventory.
  c. Analyzing data resulting from inventory.
  d. Recalculating balances in inventory reports.

**50.** Which of the following would be used on a review engagement?
  a. Examination of board minutes.
  b. Confirmation of cash and accounts receivable.
  c. Comparison of current year to prior year account balances.
  d. Recalculation of depreciation expense.

**49.** **(a)** The requirement is to identify a procedure that **cannot** ordinarily be performed using generalized audit software package when conducting fieldwork for a physical inventory. Answer (a) is correct because the software itself cannot observe the inventory. Answer (b) is incorrect because the software may be used to select a sample of items of inventory. Answer (c) is incorrect because software may be used to analyze data resulting from the inventory. Answer (d) is incorrect because software may be used to recalculate inventory balances.

**50.** **(c)** The requirement is to determine what would be included in a review engagement. Answer (c) is correct because reviews, which consist primarily of inquiries and analytical procedures, will ordinarily include a comparison of current year to prior year account balances. Answer (a) is incorrect because reviews do not ordinarily include examination of board minutes. Answer (b) is incorrect because only audits ordinarily include confirmation of cash and accounts receivable. Answer (d) is incorrect because depreciation expense is not ordinarily recalculated in a review engagement. See AR 100 for basic information on reviews.

## SIMULATION 1

| Directions | | | | | | | | | |
|---|---|---|---|---|---|---|---|---|---|
| | Company Profile | Financial Information (1) | Financial Information (2) | Risk Factors | Ratios | Analytical Results | Substantive Tests | Communication | Auditor's Report |

In the following simulation, you will be asked various questions regarding an audit engagement. You will use the content in the **Information Tabs** to complete the tasks in the **Work Tabs**. (The following pictures are for illustration only; the actual tabs in your simulation may differ from these.)

### Information Tabs:

| Directions | Situation | Standards | Resources |
|---|---|---|---|

Beginning with the Directions tab at the left side of the screen, go through each of the **Information Tabs** to familiarize yourself with the simulation content. Note that the **Resources** tab will contain useful information, including formulas and definitions, to help you complete the tasks. You may want to refer to this information while you are working.

### Work Tabs:

| ✏ Cost Method | ✏ Amt to Report | ✏ COGS | ✏ Invent Costs | ✏ Form 1065 | ✏ Communication | ✏ Review Letter |
|---|---|---|---|---|---|---|

The **Work Tabs,** on the right side of the screen, contain the tasks for you to complete.

Once you complete any part of a task, the pencil for that tab will be shaded. ✏ Note that a shaded pencil does NOT indicate that you have completed the entire task.

You must complete all of the tasks in the **Work Tabs** to receive full credit.

If you have difficulty answering a **Work Tab,** read the tab directions carefully.

*NOTE: If you believe you have encountered a software malfunction, report it to the test center staff immediately.*

| | Company Profile | | | | | | | | |
|---|---|---|---|---|---|---|---|---|---|
| Directions | | Financial Information (1) | Financial Information (2) | Risk Factors | Ratios | Analytical Results | Substantive Tests | Communication | Auditor's Report |

## Company

Pacific Gourmet, Inc. (Pacific Gourmet) is a retailer of fine food, wine and related products. The company has been in operation for fifteen years and consists of three core business operations: product sales in its retail store, product sales to food and specialty stores, and food services. The company was started as a local family business and has received additional funding over the years from several private investors.

Pacific Gourmet has a wholly owned subsidiary, which provides food services to corporate clients around the country. In addition, the company also holds investments in several private companies with whom it does business. On January 31, Year 1, Pacific Gourmet guaranteed a $15 million debt obligation of one of these investments—Vineyard Partners—for a period of five years. The company owns a 15% interest in Vineyard Partners.

## Marketing

The company experienced significant sales growth during its history and continues to expand its product offerings and market reach. Pacific Gourmet focuses its marketing efforts on demographic groups not typically affected by fluctuations in the economy and thus continues to maintain consistent revenue growth. However, Pacific Gourmet sustained a significant decline in its gross margin on product sales due to an increase in the cost of raw materials and failure to monitor compliance with budgetary guidelines.

## Management

Pacific Gourmet has a senior management team composed of seasoned business managers—many of whom have been with the company since inception. However, during the current year the CFO resigned to work for a competitor and recruited several key Pacific Gourmet financial professionals to join him at his new company. After several months of searching, a new CFO with a background in retail finance was hired.

In addition, the accounting department is currently understaffed due to staff turnover. Further, the new CFO is redesigning the accounting policies and procedures and is replacing the general ledger software to improve the effectiveness of the company's financial reporting systems.

## Engagement

Pacific Gourmet uses an independent audit firm for its annual audits, which must be provided to investors and lenders under the company's debt covenants. The company's management maintains a strong professional relationship with the audit engagement team. However, there was a disagreement between the auditors and the new CFO in the current year regarding the $15 million-debt guarantee.

| Directions | Company Profile | Financial Information (1) | Financial Information (2) | Risk Factors | Ratios | Analytical Results | Substantive Tests | Communication | Auditor's Report |
|---|---|---|---|---|---|---|---|---|---|

### Pacific Gourmet, Inc. and Subsidiary
### CONSOLIDATED BALANCE SHEETS
#### December 31, Year 2 and Year 1

|  | Year 2 | Year 1 |
|---|---|---|
| **Assets** | | |
| *Current assets:* | | |
| Cash and cash equivalents | $54,280,000 | $42,500,000 |
| Receivables—net | 12,000,000 | 10,000,000 |
| Inventory | 12,000,000 | 10,000,000 |
| Other current assets | 7,000,000 | 5,000,000 |
| Total current assets | 85,280,000 | 67,500,000 |
| Property, plant, and equipment—net | 23,000,000 | 25,000,000 |
| Other assets | 30,000,000 | 30,000,000 |
| **Total assets** | $138,280,000 | $122,500,000 |
| **Liabilities and Stockholders' Equity** | | |
| *Current liabilities:* | | |
| Accounts payable | $23,000,000 | $20,000,000 |
| Current portion of long-term debt | 1,000,000 | 1,000,000 |
| Other current liabilities | 965,000 | 1,000,000 |
| Total current liabilities | 24,965,000 | 22,000,000 |
| Long-term debt | 13,000,000 | 14,000,000 |
| **Total liabilities** | 37,965,000 | 36,000,000 |
| Stockholders' equity | | |
| Common stock | 100,000 | 100,000 |
| Additional paid-in capital | 9,900,000 | 9,900,000 |
| Retained earnings | 90,315,000 | 76,500,000 |
| **Total stockholders' equity** | 100,315,000 | 86,500,000 |
| **Total liabilities and stockholders' equity** | $138,280,000 | $122,500,000 |

| Directions | Company Profile | Financial Information (1) | Financial Information (2) | Risk Factors | Ratios | Analytical Results | Substantive Tests | Communication | Auditor's Report |
|---|---|---|---|---|---|---|---|---|---|

### Pacific Gourmet, Inc. and Subsidiary
### CONSOLIDATED INCOME STATEMENTS
#### For the years ended December 31, Year 2 and Year 1

|  | Year 2 | Year 1 |
|---|---|---|
| Sales | $100,850,000 | $ 95,600,000 |
| Cost of goods sold | 55,000,000 | 42,500 000 |
| Gross profit on sales | 45,850,000 | 53,100,000 |
| Expenses | | |
| Selling expenses | 17,600,000 | 15,000,000 |
| General and administrative | 6,015,000 | 5,000,000 |
| Interest expense | 1,120,000 | 1,200,000 |
| Total expenses | 24,735,000 | 21,200,000 |
| Income before taxes | 21,115,000 | 31,900,000 |
| Provision for income taxes | 7,300,000 | 7,500,000 |
| **Net income** | $ 13,815,000 | $ 24,400,000 |

*Pacific Gourmet, Inc. and Subsidiary*
**CONSOLIDATED STATEMENT OF CASH FLOWS**
*For the Year Ended December 31, Year 2*

| | |
|---|---:|
| Cash flows from operating activities: | |
| Net income (loss) | $13,815,000 |
| | |
| Adjustments to reconcile net income (loss) to cash provided by (used for) operating activities | |
| Depreciation | 1,500,000 |
| Changes in certain assets and liabilities: | |
| Decrease (increase) in receivables | (2,000,000) |
| Decrease (increase) in inventory | (2,000,000) |
| Decrease (increase) in other current assets | (2,000,000) |
| Increase (decrease) in accounts payable | 3,000,000 |
| Increase (decrease) in other current liabilities | (35,000) |
| Net cash provided by (used for) operating activities | 12,280,000 |
| | |
| Cash flows from investing activities: | |
| Proceeds from sales of property, plant, and equipment | 500,000 |
| Net cash provided by (used for) investing activities | 500,000 |
| | |
| Cash flows from financing activities: | |
| Principal payments on long-term debt | (1,000,000) |
| Net cash provided by (used for) investing activities | (1,000,000) |
| | |
| Net increase (decrease) in cash and cash equivalents | 11,780,000 |
| | |
| Cash and cash equivalents at beginning of year | 42,500,000 |
| | |
| Cash and cash equivalents at end of year | $54,280,000 |

| Directions | Company Profile | Financial Information (1) | Financial Information (2) | Risk Factors | | Ratios | Analytical Results | Substantive Tests | Communication | Auditor's Report |
|---|---|---|---|---|---|---|---|---|---|---|

Based on the information in Pacific Gourmet's Company Profile, which factor is most likely to increase audit risk? Select only one factor.

| | |
|---|---|
| The company was started as a local family business and has received additional funding over the years from several investors. | |
| The new CFO is redesigning the company's accounting policies and procedures. | |
| The company consists of three core business operations: product sales in its retail store, product sales to food and specialty stores, and food services. | |
| The company experienced significant sales growth during its history and continues to expand its product offerings and market reach. | |

| Directions | Company Profile | Financial Information (1) | Financial Information (2) | Risk Factors | | Ratios | Analytical Results | Substantive Tests | Communication | Auditor's Report |
|---|---|---|---|---|---|---|---|---|---|---|

Use the data in Pacific Gourmet's financial statements to calculate for Year 2 and Year 1 the analytical ratios indicated in the table below to 2 decimal places. Any formula that you use in the spreadsheet must be preceded by an equal sign (e.g. =A1 + B1). (For turnover ratios, year-end balances should be used. All calculations are based on a 365-day year).

| Ratio | Year 2 | Year 1 |
|---|---|---|
| Current ratio | | |
| Return on equity | | |

| Directions | Company Profile | Financial Information (1) | Financial Information (2) | Risk Factors | Ratios | | Analytical Results | Substantive Tests | Communication | Auditor's Report |
|---|---|---|---|---|---|---|---|---|---|---|

The table below presents several ratios that were considered significant in the current and prior years' audits of Pacific Gourmet. Compare the values for each ratio. Then double-click on each of the shaded spaces in the table and select the most likely explanation for the analytical results. An explanation may be used once, more than once, or not at all. (You should not recalculate ratios. Turnover rates are based on average balances.)

| Ratio | Year 2 | Year 1 | Explanations |
|---|---|---|---|
| Days' sales in accounts receivable | 40 | 39 | |
| Operating profit margin | 22.05% | 34.62% | |

## Explanations

1. Credit terms were restricted on several large accounts during the current year.
2. Operating expenses increased at a higher rate than sales revenue.
3. Sales revenue increased at a higher rate than operating expenses.
4. A smaller percentage of sales occurred during the last month of the year, as compared to the prior year.
5. A larger percentage of sales occurred during the last month of the year, as compared to the prior year.
6. Sales increased as compared to the prior year.

| Directions | Company Profile | Financial Information (1) | Financial Information (2) | Risk Factors | Ratios | Analytical Results | Substantive Tests | Communication | Auditor's Report |
|---|---|---|---|---|---|---|---|---|---|

The auditor determines that both of the following objectives will be part of Pacific Gourmet's audit.  For each of the following audit objectives, double-click on each shaded space and select the substantive test that would most likely provide support for the objective.  A substantive test may be used once, more than once, or not at all.

| Objective | Substantive tests |
|---|---|
| Verify existence of accounts receivable. | |
| Determine that inventory balance is accurately stated. | |

## Selection List

A. Perform tests of subsequent cash receipts after the balance sheet date.
B. Review and assess an aging schedule of accounts receivable.
C. Compare recognized revenue to related industry statistics.
D. Tour the storage facility for inventory to determine adequacy of security controls.
E. Perform shipping cutoff procedures.
F. Review payments to vendors subsequent to year-end.

| Directions | Company Profile | Financial Information (1) | Financial Information (2) | Risk Factors | Ratios | Analytical Results | Substantive Tests | Communication | Auditor's Report |
|---|---|---|---|---|---|---|---|---|---|

Pacific Gourmet has recommended your firm to Sparkle Co.  Consequently, your CPA firm has been engaged to audit the financial statements of Sparkle Co., a nonpublic entity.  During fieldwork, Sparkle's management requests that you change the engagement to a review of financial statements in accordance with *Statements on Standards for Accounting and Review Services* (SSARS).  In a memorandum to your firm's engagement partner, explain the circumstances under which such a change of engagements may be considered.

Type your communication in the response area below the horizontal line using the word processor provided.

*REMINDER:  Your response will be graded for both technical content and writing skills.  Technical content will be evaluated for information that is helpful to the intended reader and clearly relevant to the issue.  Writing skills will be evaluated for development, organization, and the appropriate expression of ideas in professional correspondence.  Use a standard business memo or letter format with a clear beginning, middle, and end.  Do not convey information in the form of a table, bullet point list, or other abbreviated presentation.*

| Directions | Company Profile | Financial Information (1) | Financial Information (2) | Risk Factors | Ratios | Analytical Results | Substantive Tests | Communication | Auditor's Report |
|---|---|---|---|---|---|---|---|---|---|

During the audit of the Pacific Gourmet financial statements, the auditor finds that Pacific Gourmet failed to present a statement of cash flows.  Pacific Gourmet's management has declined to correct this violation of generally accepted accounting principles because they believe that complying with GAAP would confuse those relying on the financial statements.

This is the only qualification that the auditor wishes to include in the standard auditor's report.

To complete this task, first split the screen and select this tab (the RESEARCH tab) in one window and the STANDARDS tab in the other.  Use the search capabilities provided by the STANDARDS tab to find the citation that addresses the issue above.  A citation may include one paragraph or more than one paragraph.  Click (highlight) each appropriate paragraph **one at a time,** and then click on the **TRANSFER TO ANSWER** button located in the upper left of the STANDARDS tab.  Your selected paragraphs will appear in the answer space below.

*NOTE:  If your cursor turns to a $\oslash$ symbol, the text or citation is not selectable as a response.  Correct responses never appear in unselectable text.*

To reorder or delete a paragraph, first select a paragraph.  Use the **Up/Down** arrows to reorder, and use the **x** button to delete.  **You must select (click on) a paragraph to activate the buttons.**

The Copy and Paste icons on the helm do **not** work with this tab.  Use the **TRANSFER TO ANSWER** button on the STANDARDS tab to complete the task.

---

***Independent Auditor's Report***

[Addressee]

**Paste report paragraphs here**


[Signature of the auditor]

[Date]

---

**SOLUTION TO SIMULATION 1**

| Directions | Company Profile | Financial Information (1) | Financial Information (2) | Risk Factors | Ratios | Analytical Results | Substantive Tests | Communication | Auditor's Report |
|---|---|---|---|---|---|---|---|---|---|

Based on the information in Pacific Gourmet's Company Profile, which factor is most likely to increase audit risk? Select only one factor.

| | |
|---|---|
| The company was started as a local family business and has received additional funding over the years from several investors. | |
| The new CFO is redesigning the company's accounting policies and procedures. | X |
| The company consists of three core business operations: product sales in its retail store, product sales to food and specialty stores, and food services. | |
| The company experienced significant sales growth during its history and continues to expand its product offerings and market reach. | |

The requirement is to identify the factor that is most likely to increase audit risk (the risk that the auditor may unknowingly fail to modify the audit report on financial statements that are materially misstated). The second reply, redesign of the company's accounting policies and procedures, is most likely to increase audit risk because, until tested thoroughly through use, the new system may produce material misstatements that are not detected. The first reply is incorrect because starting as a local family business and receiving additional funding need not necessarily increase audit risk. The third answer is incorrect because the three core business operations themselves do not seem to indicate a high level of audit risk. The fourth reply is incorrect because the sales growth, while significant, seems reasonable.

| Directions | Company Profile | Financial Information (1) | Financial Information (2) | Risk Factors | Ratios | Analytical Results | Substantive Tests | Communication | Auditor's Report |
|---|---|---|---|---|---|---|---|---|---|

Use the data in Pacific Gourmet's financial statements to calculate for year 2 and year 1 the analytical ratios indicated in the table below to 2 decimal places. Any formula that you use in the spreadsheet must be preceded by an equal sign (e.g. =A1 + B1). (For turnover ratios, year-end balances should be used. All calculations are based on a 365-day year).

| Ratio | Year 2 | Year 1 |
|---|---|---|
| Current ratio | 3.42 | 3.07 |
| Return on equity | 13.77% | 28.21% |

## Current Ratio

The current ratio is equal to current assets divided by current liabilities—$85,280,000/$24,965,000 = 3.42.

## Return on Equity

The return on equity is equal to net income divided by total owners' equity—$13,815,000/$100,315,000 = 13.77. (Notice that the question asks you to use year-end balances. That approach is very conservative for this ratio since the year-end owners' equity includes the year's net income. Accordingly, the return on equity using the beginning of the year balance, or an average of the beginning and ending balances, would be higher.)

| Directions | Company Profile | Financial Information (1) | Financial Information (2) | Risk Factors | Ratios | Analytical Results | Substantive Tests | Communication | Auditor's Report |
|---|---|---|---|---|---|---|---|---|---|

The table below presents several ratios that were considered significant in the current and prior years' audits of Pacific Gourmet. Compare the values for each ratio. Then double-click on each of the shaded spaces in the table and select the most likely explanation for the analytical results. An explanation may be used once, more than once, or not at all. (You should not recalculate ratios. Turnover rates are based on average balances.)

| Ratio | Year 2 | Year 1 | Explanations |
|---|---|---|---|
| Days' sales in accounts receivable | 40 | 39 | 5 |
| Operating profit margin | 22.05% | 34.62% | 2 |

*Explanations*
1. Credit terms were restricted on several large accounts during the current year.
2. Operating expenses increased at a higher rate than sales revenue.
3. Sales revenue increased at a higher rate than operating expenses.
4. A smaller percentage of sales occurred during the last month of the year, as compared to the prior year.
5. A larger percentage of sales occurred during the last month of the year, as compared to the prior year.
6. Sales increased as compared to the prior year.

**Days' sales in accounts receivable.**

The requirement is to identify the most likely explanation for an increase in the days' sales in accounts receivable (365/[sales/accounts receivable]). That ratio increased from 39 in year 1 to 40 in year 2. Explanation 5 is correct because an increase in uncollected sales at year-end will result in an increase in days' sales in accounts receivable. This occurs as follows:

- The denominator of the overall fraction (sales/accounts receivable) decreases since both the numerator and denominator increase by the same amount for uncollected sales. That is, increasing the numerator and denominator of a ratio that is greater than one by the same amount will decrease the ratio (e.g., picking arbitrary numbers, $3/2 = 1.5 \rightarrow 4/3 = 1.3$).
- When 365 is divided by a smaller denominator, days' sales in accounts receivable increases.

Explanation 1 is incorrect because more restricted credit terms are likely to decrease the number of days' sales in accounts receivable. Explanation 2 is incorrect because a change in the ratio of operating expenses to sales revenue does not affect days' sales in accounts receivable. Similarly explanation 3 is incorrect because an increase in sales revenue at a highter rate than operating expense does not affect days' sales in accounts receivable. Explanation 4 is incorrect because a smaller percentage of sales occurring in the last month will decrease the ratio—this is the opposite of the situation described by explanation 5. Explanation 6 is incorrect because a simple increase in sales is expected prior to result in a pro rata increase in accounts receivable.

**Operating profit margin.**

The requirement is to identify the most likely explanation for a decrease in the operating profit margin (operating income/sales). Here operating income is gross profit on sales less selling expenses and general and administrative expenses. Explanation 2 is correct because an increase in operating expenses decreases operating income, the numerator of the ratio, and therefore decreases the overall percentage. Explanation 1 is incorrect because a change in credit terms is less likely to affect the overall operating profit margin. Explanation 3 is incorrect because the increase in sales revenue compared to operating expenses will increase the ratio, not decrease it. Explanations 4 and 5 are incorrect because the timing of the sale within the year does not affect the operating profit margin. Explanation 6 is incorrect because an increase in sales will either keep the operating profit margin at its previous level or increase it somewhat (due to the existence of fixed costs which will be spread across more units of sales).

| Directions | Company Profile | Financial Information (1) | Financial Information (2) | Risk Factors | Ratios | Analytical Results | Substantive Tests | Communication | Auditor's Report |
|---|---|---|---|---|---|---|---|---|---|

The auditor determines that both of the following objectives will be part of Pacific Gourmet's audit. For each of the following audit objectives, double-click on each shaded space and select the substantive test that would most likely provide support for the objective. A substantive test may be used once, more than once, or not at all.

| Objective | Substantive tests |
|---|---|
| Verify existence of accounts receivable. | A |
| Determine that inventory balance is accurately stated. | E |

*Selection List*

A. Perform tests of subsequent cash receipts after the balance sheet date.
B. Review and assess an aging schedule of accounts receivable.
C. Compare recognized revenue to related industry statistics.
D. Tour the storage facility for inventory to determine adequacy of security controls.
E. Perform shipping cutoff procedures.
F. Review payments to vendors subsequent to year-end.

**Verify existence of accounts receivable.**

The requirement is to identify a substantive procedure that will help verify the existence of accounts receivable. Answer (a) is correct because the subsequent cash receipt will help establish both the existence of the accounts receivable and its valuation (in that it was collected). Answer (b) is incorrect because reviewing and assessing an aging schedule provides some, but less information, than answer (a); for example, it might reveal old recorded receivables that do not actually exist. Answer (c) is incorrect because comparing recognized revenue to industry statistics does not seem to address the existence of accounts receivable as directly as does answer (a). Answer (d) is incorrect because touring a storage facility will not verify the existence of accounts receivable. Answer E is incorrect because reviewing payments to vendors subsequent to year-end relates to accounts payable, not accounts receivable.

**Determine that inventory balance is accurately stated.**

The requirement is to identify a substantive procedure that will help verify that the inventory balance is accurately stated. Answer E is correct because shipping cut-off procedures will help establish that the inventory balance at year-end is correct by providing evidence that sales (and the corresponding inventory and cost of sales) around year-end are recorded in the proper period. Answer (a) is incorrect because examining cash receipts does not provide significant evidence on the inventory balance. Answer (b) is incorrect because aging of accounts receivable does not directly address the inventory balance. Answer (c) is incorrect because comparing recognized revenue to related industry statistics does not directly address the inventory balance. Answer (d) is incorrect because, while touring the storage facility and determining the accuracy of security controls addresses inventory, it provides less evidence on inventory accuracy than answer E. Answer F is incorrect because a review of only payments to vendors provides limited, if any, evidence on the inventory balance.

| Directions | Company Profile | Financial Information (1) | Financial Information (2) | Risk Factors | Ratios | Analytical Results | Substantive Tests | Communication | Auditor's Report |
|---|---|---|---|---|---|---|---|---|---|

To: Partner in charge of Sparkle Company Audit

From: Your name

Re: Changing a financial statement audit engagement to a review engagement

Sparkle Company's management requested that we change the engagement from an audit to a review of the financial statements. The appropriate standards in this situation are the *Statements on Standards for Accounting and Review Services (SSARS)*. Those standards include the following concerning such a change:

Before a CPA firm that was engaged to audit an entity's financial statements might agree to change the engagement to a review, the firm should consider the reason given for the entity's request. A change in circumstances that affects the entity's requirement for an audit or a misunderstanding concerning the nature of the audit would ordinarily be considered a reasonable basis for requesting the change. However, if the auditing procedures are substantially complete or the cost to complete such procedures is relatively insignificant, the firm should consider the propriety of accepting a change in the engagement.

Accordingly, we must consider the above requirements relating to the situation. If I may be of more assistance on this matter please contact me.

| Directions | Company Profile | Financial Information (1) | Financial Information (2) | Risk Factors | Ratios | Analytical Results | Substantive Tests | Communication | Auditor's Report |
|---|---|---|---|---|---|---|---|---|---|

### Independent Auditor's Report – 10.01

*[Addressee]*

We have audited the accompanying balance sheets of X Company as of December 31, 20X2 and 20X1, and the related statements of income and retained earnings for the years then ended. These financial statements are the responsibility of the Company's management. Our responsibility is to express an opinion on these financial statements based on our audit.

We conducted our audit in accordance with auditing standards generally accepted in the United States of America. Those standards require that we plan and perform the audit to obtain reasonable assurance about whether the financial statements are free of material misstatement. An audit includes examining, on a test basis, evidence supporting the amounts and disclosures in the financial statements. An audit also includes assessing the accounting principles used and significant estimates made by management, as well as evaluating the overall financial statement presentation. We believe that our audit provides a reasonable basis for our opinion.

The Company declined to present a statement of cash flows for the years ended December 31, 20X2 and 20X1. Presentation of such statement summarizing the Company's operating, investing, and financing activities is required by accounting principles generally accepted in the United States of America.

In our opinion, except that the omission of a statement of cash flows results in an incomplete presentation as explained in the preceding paragraph, the financial statements referred to above present fairly, in all material respects, the financial position of X Company as of December 31, 20X2 and 20X1, and the results of its operations for the years then ended in conformity with accounting principles generally accepted in the United States of America.

*[Signature of the auditor]*

*[Date]*

# A

**Access controls, 517, 532**
**Accounting changes, 272**
  Effect on consistency, 468
**Accounting estimates, auditing of**
  AU 342, 461
**Accounts payable**
  Audit procedures, 196, 205
**Accounts receivable**
  Audit procedures, 194, 200, 448
**Adverse opinion, 276, 472**
**Agreed-upon procedures, 38, 187, 400, 411**
  AT 201, 400
  Report on, 266, 284, 290, 400, 411
**AICPA Content Specification Outlines, 34**
**Alpha risk, 348, 352, 360**
**Alphanumeric characters, 516**
**Analytical procedures, 56, 190**
  AU 329, 447
**Application controls**
  Manual (user) controls, 534
  Programmed, 533
**Applications programming, 529**
**Applications software, 513**
**Assertions, 51, 98, 186, 191, 194**
  AU 326, 445
**Association with the financial statements, auditor's, 470**
**Attestation**
  Attest function, 37
  Engagements, 398
    Compliance, 294, 410
  **Examination**, 289
  Responsibilities, 57
    AU 110, 416
  Review, 281, 289
  Standards, 42, 57
    AT 101, 398
**Attorney, inquiry of client's, 209, 456**
**Audit committees, 131**
  AU 380, 465
**Audit completion, 41, 212**
**Audit defined, 38**
**Audit documentation, 458**
**Audit effectiveness and efficiency, 214, 348, 352**
**Audit evidence**
  Derivative instruments, hedging activities, and investments in securities, 451
**Audit procedures, 189, 194**
  Timing of, 57, 104
**Audit process, diagram of, 39**
**Audit programs, 56, 419**
  Substantive tests, 189
**Audit responsibilities, 57, 418**
**Audit risk, 50, 346**
  And compliance auditing, 412
  AU 312, 420
  AU 350, 462
  Risk factors, 52, 426
**Audit sampling, 344**
  Attributes sampling, 347
    Sample deviation rate, 351

    Allowance for sampling risk, 351
    Upper deviation limit, 351
  Sample selection methods
    Block sampling, 349
    Haphazard sampling, 349
    Random-number sampling, 349
    Systematic sampling, 349
  Sample size determination, 349
    Allowable risk of assessing control risk too low, 349
    Discovery sampling, 350
    Expected population deviation rate, 350
    Relationship to sample size, 350
    Sequential sampling, 350
    Tolerable deviation rate, 349
  Sampling risk, 346, 348
  AU 350, 462
  Classical variables sampling, 358, 361
  Nonsampling risk, 346
  Nonstatistical, 345
    Tests of controls, 352
  Probability-proportional-to-size sampling, 355, 357, 361
  Risk, 346, 348, 349, 352, 360, 361
  Statistical, 345
    Substantive testing, 352
    Tests of controls, 348
  Substantive tests, 347, 352, 463
  Tests of controls, 346, 347, 348, 464
  Uncertainty and, 346
  Variables sampling, 347
    Basic precision, 356
    Classical, 358
      Compared to PPS, 361
      Variations of, 358
    Probability-proportional-to-size, 355
      Compared to classical, 361
      Example, 357
    Sample size determination, 352, 355, 359, 360
      Acceptable level of risk, 353
      Allowance for sampling risk, 360
      Equation for, 355, 360
      Expansion factors, 355
      Expected amount of misstatement, 353
      Relationships to sample size, 354
      Reliability factors, 355
      Tolerable misstatement, 353, 360
    Sampling interval, 355
    Sampling risk, 346, 352, 360, 361
    Upper limit on misstatements, 356
      Allowance for sampling risk, 356
      Projected misstatement, 356, 361
**Audit software, 518**
**Audit standards, 57, 398**
  AU 150, 416
  Relationship to quality control standards, 417
**Audit strategy, 55**
**Auditor-submitted documents, 274**
  AU 551, 478
**Authentication, 526**

# B

**Backup and recovery, 518, 533**

**Bank confirmations, 198**
**Bank cutoff statements, 198**
**Bank reconciliations, 198**
**Bank transfer schedule, 198**
**Batch (control) total, 534**
**Batch processing, 514**
**Beta risk, 348, 352, 360**
**Bill and hold transactions, 208**
**Bit, 515**
**Block sampling, 349**
**Boundary protection, 532**
**Buffer memory, 511**
**Byte, 515**

# C

**Call back, 533**
**Capital stock transactions, audit considerations of, 207**
**Cartridge tape, 511**
**Cash**
  Audit procedures, 194, 197
**Cash basis financial statement reports, 284**
**Central processing unit, 510**
**Centralized processing, 515**
**Change in accounting estimate, 273, 468**
**Change in accounting principle, 272, 468**
**Change in reporting entity, 273, 468**
**Change in statement format, 273**
**Channel stuffing (trade loading), 208**
**Check digit, 534**
**Classical variables sampling, 358**
  Compared to PPS, 361
  Difference estimation, 359, 361
  Mean-per-unit, 358, 361
  Ratio estimation, 359, 361
  Regression approach, 359
**Client representation letters, 209**
  AU 333, 453
**Client's lawyer, inquiry of, 209, 456**
**Clients, acceptance and continuance of clients and engagements, 59**
**Client-server architecture, 521**
**Closed-loop verification, 534**
**Comfort letter**
  AU 634, 488
**Committee of Sponsoring Organizations (COSO), 96, 98**
**Communications between predecessor and successor auditors, 54, 56**
  AR 400, 506
  AU 315, 423
**Comparative financial statements, reports on, 273, 472**
  AR 200, 504
**Competence, 187, 439**
**Compilation of financial statements, 38, 187**
  AR 100, 499
  Procedures, 212
  Prospective financial statement compilations, 403
  Reports, 266, 279, 403
    AR 300, 506
  Responsibilities, 57